HEALTH LAW:

CASES, MATERIALS AND PROBLEMS

Abridged Seventh Edition

■ ■ ■

By

Barry R. Furrow
Professor of Law and Director, Health Law Program
Drexel University

Thomas L. Greaney
Chester A. Myers Professor of Law and
Co-Director, Center for Health Law Studies
Saint Louis University

Sandra H. Johnson
Professor Emerita of Law and Health Care Ethics
Center for Health Law Studies
Saint Louis University School of Law

Timothy Stoltzfus Jost
Robert L. Willett Family Professor of Law
Washington and Lee University

Robert L. Schwartz
Senior Visiting Professor
University of California Hastings College of the Law
Weihofen Professor of Law Emeritus,
University of New Mexico

AMERICAN CASEBOOK SERIES®

WEST®

Mat #41032920

© West, a Thomson business, 2008
© 2013 LEG, Inc. d/b/a West Academic Publishing
    610 Opperman Drive
    St. Paul, MN 55123
    1-800-313-9378

ISBN: 978–0–314–26512–8

DEDICATION

To Donna Jo, Elena, Michael, Nicholas, Eva, Robert,
Hayden, Aspen, and Grey

B.R.F.

To Nancy, T.J., and Kati

T.L.G.

To Bob, Emily, Kathleen, Colin, Nicholas, Zachary, and Abigail

S.H.J.

To Ruth, Jacob, Micah, David, Felix, and Emily

T.S.J.

To Jane, Mirra, and Elana

R.L.S.

This book is also dedicated to the memory of Nancy Rhoden and
Jay Healey, great teachers, wonderful colleagues and
warm friends.

PREFACE

This seventh edition of this casebook marks the twenty-sixth anniversary of our text, first published in 1987. Since that first edition, no part of the American landscape has changed more than the American health care system. The system has been stressed by demographic changes, buffeted by the winds of political change, and utterly transformed by social and economic developments. The formal structure of the business of health care was a small part of the subject of health law when we published our first edition; it is now the subject of entire graduate programs. The for-profit commercial sector of the health care economy sounded like a lamb twenty-five years ago; now it roars like a lion. Until a few years ago virtually no one attained elective office because of her position on issues related to health care; now health care reform is the most politically controversial issue in America. Indeed, we repeatedly delayed bringing out a seventh edition because of the uncertain fate of health care reform, threatened first by a Supreme Court case and then by the 2012 elections.

Derived from the comprehensive material contained in *Health Law: Cases, Materials, and Problems*, this abridged volume recognizes the increasingly complicated teaching environment for health law, and, in particular, the need for a concise health law casebook for law schools with curricular space for only one health law course, and for medical schools, schools of public health, and allied health schools. This abridged edition continues to use the same broad organization that has made its larger sibling so popular among health law teachers and students. We have, however, deleted some sections that appear in the unabridged edition, and we have trimmed some of the notes and problems from the remaining sections to provide for a broadly diverse health law course.

In addition to the publication of this abridged edition, portions of the full new seventh edition of *Health Law: Cases, Materials, and Problems* are being published in the form of three other casebooks. *Bioethics: Health Care Law and Ethics* presents the chapters addressing those bioethics issues that occur most commonly in the health care setting. The book contains chapters on end-of-life decision making, including medically assisted death; abortion, contraception and sterilization; human genetics; organ transplantation; distributive justice; and public health. It also includes a chapter introducing students to underlying theories and approaches to ethical analysis in the health care setting. *Law and Health Care Quality, Patient Safety, and Medical Liability* presents a comprehensive look at law and policy in the context of quality and patient safety concerns in health care. It includes extensive material introducing students to the most influential approaches to measuring and achieving quality and; the theory and practice of patient safety efforts. It also includes an introduction to the legal underpinnings of the physician-patient relationship and cases and problems on professional licensure and discipline, quality-control regulation of health care organizations, and tort liability of health care professionals and organizations. Finally, *Law of Health Care Organization and Finance* provides a sophisticated, up-to-date inquiry into the economic structure of the health care industry. It has a special focus on business forms in health care, institutional contracting, tax-exempt business structures, fraud and abuse, and antitrust law within the health care industry. The Affordable Care Act, in particular, has worked significant change in most of the areas covered in all of these texts, and every chapter in each of these volumes has been reorganized and rewritten to take account of the changes brought about by the Affordable Care Act.

We are grateful for the many comments and helpful suggestions that health law teachers across the United States (and from elsewhere, too) have made to help us improve this new edition. We attempt to present all sides of policy issues, not to evangelize for any political, economic or social agenda of our own. This task is made easier, undoubtedly, by the diverse views on virtually all policy issues that the several different authors of this casebook bring to this endeavor. A large number of very well respected health law teachers have contributed a great deal to this and previous editions by making suggestions, reviewing problems, or encouraging our more thorough investigation of a wide range of health law subjects. We are especially grateful to Charles Baron, Eugene Basanta, David Bennahum, Robert Berenson, Kathleen Boozang, Camille Carey, Don Chalmers, Ellen Wright Clayton, Judith Daar, Dena Davis, Arthur Derse, Kelly Dineen, Ileana Dominguez-Urban, Stewart Duban, Barbara Evans, Margaret Farrell, Rob Field, David Frankford, Michael Gerhart, Joan McIver Gibson, Susan Goldberg, Jesse Goldner, Andrew Grubb, Sarah Hooper, Jaime King, Art LaFrance, Diane Hoffmann, Sarah Hooper, Jill Horwitz, Amy Jaeger, Eleanor Kinney, Thomasine Kushner, Pam Lambert, Theodore LeBlang, Antoinette Sedillo Lopez, Lawrence Singer, Joan Krause, Leslie Mansfield, Thomas Mayo, Maxwell Mehlman, Alan Meisel, Vicki Michel, Frances Miller, John Munich, David Orentlicher, Elizabeth Pendo, Vernellia Randall, Ben Rich, Arnold Rosoff, Karen Rothenberg, Mark Rothstein, Sallie Sanford, Giles Scofield, Jeff Sconyers, Charity Scott, Ross Silverman, Loane Skene, George Smith, Roy Spece, Jr., Carol Suzuki, Michael Vitiello, Sidney Watson, Lois Weithorn, Ellen Wertheimer, William Winslade, and Susan M. Wolf for the benefit of their wisdom and experience.

We wish to thank those who provided support for our research and the preparation of the manuscript, including the Frances Lewis Law Center, the Robert L. Willett family, Carrie Snow, Patrick

Pedano, Yamini Laks, Erica Cohen, Laura Spencer, Melanie Rankin, Chelsea Averill, Autumn Berge, Theresa Vertucci Hacsi, Nicole Hamberger, Rebecca Kreiner, Nicole Moskowitz, Monica Smith, Vera Mencer, David Knoespel, Brittany Rainey, James Kovacs, David Fuchs, and James Bailey. We all have special appreciation for the exceptional work done by Mary Ann Jauer and Cheryl Cooper at Saint Louis University, and for the tremendous publication assistance provided by Pamela Siege Chandler, Louis Higgins, James Cahoy, Greg Olson, Pat Sparks and Jennifer Schlagel of West Academic Publishing. Finally, we wish to thank our deans, Roger Dennis, Michael Wolff, Barbara Bergman, Frank Wu, and Nora Demleitner.

It has been a splendid opportunity to work on this casebook. It has been a constant challenge to find a way to teach cutting edge issues influencing our health care system—at times before the courts or legislatures have given us much legal material for our casebook. Each time we have done a new edition, there have been developments that we find difficult to assess as to whether they will become more significant during the lifespan of the edition or are simply blips. It is always difficult to delete materials that required much labor to produce and still remain quite relevant but that have been eclipsed in importance by other developments. The length of each succeeding edition attests to our challenge, but we have removed a great deal of substantive material from our last edition. We hope that you will agree with the tough choices we have made. Finally, we do not write this casebook for our classes alone, but rather for yours as well. We enjoy teaching, and we hope that comes through to the students and teachers who use this book.

A note on editorial style: ellipses in the text of the quoted material indicate an omission of material within the quoted paragraph. Centered ellipses indicate the omission of a paragraph or more; the first line following centered ellipses may not be the first line of the next paragraph, and the last line preceding centered ellipses may not be the last line of the preceding paragraph. Brackets indicate the omission of a citation without the omission of other materials. There is no acknowledgment of omitted footnotes. To the extent it is possible, the style of this casebook is consistent with the principle that legal writing form should follow function, and the function of this text is to help students understand health law.

BARRY R. FURROW
THOMAS L. GREANEY
SANDRA H. JOHNSON
TIMOTHY S. JOST
ROBERT L. SCHWARTZ

June 2013

ACKNOWLEDGMENTS

American College of Obstetrics and Gynecology Committee on Ethics, The Limits of Conscientious Refusal in Reproductive Medicine, 110 Obstetrics Genecology 1203 (2007). Reprinted with permission.

Austin, C.R., Human Embryos: Debate on Assisted Reproduction (1989). Copyright 1989, Oxford University Press. Reprinted by permission of Oxford University Press.

Battin, Margaret, The Least Worst Death, 13 Hastings Center Report (2) 13 (April 1983). Copyright 1983, The Hastings Center. Reprinted with permission of the Hastings Center. Reprinted with permission of the Hastings Center and the author.

Bernat, James, Charles Culver and Bernard Gert, Defining Death in Theory and Practice, 12 Hastings Center Report (1) 5 (February 1982). Copyright 1982, the Hastings Center. Reprinted with permission.

Christus St. Vincent Hospital, Medical "Futility": Communicating Treatment Objectives and Potential Outcomes; Determining Medical Ineffectiveness; Resolving Conflicts (2005). Reprinted with permission.

Congregation for the Doctrine of the Faith, Responses to Certain Questions of the United States Conference of Catholic Bishops Concerning Artificial Nutrition and Hydration (2007). Reprinted with permission of the United States Conference of Catholic Bishops.

Devers, Kelly and Robert Berenson, Can Accountable Care Organizations Improve the Value of Health Care by Solving the Cost and Quality Quandries?, Copyright 2009, The Urban Institute. Reprinted with permission.

Davis, Karen, Schoen, Cathy Schoen, and Kristof Stremikis, Mirror, Mirror on the Wall: How the Performance of the U.S. Health Care System Compares Internationally 2010 Update (New York: The Commonwealth Fund, June 2010), http://www.commonwealthfund.org/Publications/Fund-Reports/2010/Jun/Mirror-Mirror-Update.aspx. Used with permission.

Donabedian, Avedis, The Definition of Quality and Approaches to its Assessment, 1st ed., 4–6, 7, 13, 14, 27, 79–84, 102, 119 (Health Administration Press, Ann Arbor, MI, 1980). Reprinted from Avedis Donabedian, The Definition of Quality and Approaches to its Assessment, in Explorations in Quality Assessment and Monitoring, Volume 1. Copyright 1980. Reprinted with permission.

Enthoven, Alain, Health Plan: The Only Practical Solution to the Soaring Costs of Health Care 1–12 (1980). Copyright 1980 Alain Enthoven. Reprinted with permission.

Ethics Committee of the American Society for Reproductive Medicine, Informing Offspring of Their Conception by Gamete Donation, 81 Fertilization and Sterilization 527 (2004). Reprinted with permission from Elsevier.

Fletcher, Joseph, Indicators of Humanhood, 2 Hastings Center Report (5) 1 (November 1972). Copyright 1972, the Hastings Center. Reprinted with permission of the Hastings Center.

Froedtert Hospital—Medical College of Wisconsin, Futility Policy. Reprinted with permission.

Gostin, Lawrence O., Public Health Law: Power, Duty, Restraint. Copyright 2000, University of California Press. Reprinted with permission of the University of California Press.

Leape, Lucian L., Error in Medicine, 272 JAMA 1851 (1994). Copyright 1994, American Medical Association. Reprinted with permission of the American Medical Association.

National Conference of Commissioners on Uniform State Laws, Uniform Anatomical Gift Act. Copyright 1977, National Conference of Commissioners on Uniform State Laws. Reprinted with permission of National Conference of Commissioners on Uniform State Laws.

National Conference of Commissioners on Uniform State Laws, Uniform Determination Death Act. Copyright 1980, National Conference of Commissioners on Uniform State Laws. Reprinted with permission of National Conference of Commissioners on Uniform State Laws.

National Conference of Commissioners of Uniform State Laws, Uniform Health-Care Decisions Act. Copyright 1994, National Conference of Commissioners on Uniform State Laws. Reprinted with permission of National Conference of Commissioners on Uniform State Laws.

National Conference of Commissioners on Uniform State Laws, Uniform Parentage Act. Copyright 1973, 2000 and 2002, National Conference of Commissions on Uniform State Laws. Reprinted with permission of National Conference of Commissioners on Uniform State Laws.

National Conference of Commissioners on Uniform State Laws, Uniform Probate Code. Copyright, National Conference of Commissioners on Uniform State Laws. Reprinted with permission of National Conference of Commissioners on Uniform State Laws.

Randall, Vernelia, Trusting the Health Care System Ain't Always Easy! An African-American Perspective on Bioethics, 15 St. Louis U. Public L. Rev. 191 (1996). Reprinted with permission of the St. Louis U. Public Law Review.

Report of the Committee of Inquiry into Human Fertilisation and Embryology (Cmnd 9314) (1984). Copyright 1984, Her Majesty's Stationery Office.

Ulrich, Lawrence P., Reproductive Rights of Genetic Disease, in J. Humber and R. Almeder, eds., Biomedical Ethics and the law. Copyright 1986. Reprinted with permission.

Veatch, Robert, Correspondence—What it Means to be Dead, 12 Hastings Center Report (5) 45 (October 1982). Copyright 1982, the Hastings Center. Reprinted with permission of the Hastings Center.

SUMMARY OF CONTENTS

TABLE OF CONTENTS

TABLE OF CASES

The principal cases are in bold type.

---

xxxi

HEALTH LAW:

CASES, MATERIALS AND PROBLEMS

Abridged Seventh Edition

CHAPTER 1

QUALITY CONTROL REGULATION: LICENSING HEALTH CARE PROFESSIONALS

■ ■ ■

I.   INTRODUCTION

Structure of the Licensure System

State law controls the licensure of health care professionals under the state's police power. State licensing statutes govern entry into the licensed professions; regulate the health care services that licensed professionals may provide; and prohibit unlicensed persons from providing services reserved for the licensed professions. The system also monitors the quality of care provided by licensees and penalizes or removes incompetent practitioners from practice.

Health professional licensure in the United States is commonly described as a system of professional self-regulation because the entities, often called "boards," which implement the applicable statutes are generally dominated by members of the licensed profession and often rely on customary practice of the profession for standards. The boards, however, operate formally as state administrative agencies; usually include lay members to represent a consumer perspective; are governed by procedures and standards set in the state's licensing statute and administrative procedures act; and are subject to judicial review in both their adjudicatory and rulemaking decisions. The concept of professional licensure and discipline as professional self-regulation has weakened over time, but the licensed professions retain significant influence over the decisions of the boards.

Although the central legal framework for licensure and discipline is a matter of state law, there is a federal overlay. Licensure is subject to federal (and state) Constitutional requirements of procedural and substantive due process and equal protection. Certain federal statutes, including antidiscrimination laws such as the Americans with Disabilities Act, apply to licensure boards as well, although there are Constitutional limits on their application.

1

Licensure is only one component of the quality control array in health care, which includes malpractice and negligence litigation, institutional licensure, private accreditation, hospital credentialing, public information disclosure requirements, and public and private payment and reimbursement standards. Each of these is covered elsewhere in this casebook.

Pressures for Change in Licensure and Discipline

Professional domination of licensure has long been a source of criticism of board performance. See, e.g., Carl F. Ameringer, State Medical Boards and the Politics of Public Protection (1999). The boards' heavy reliance on the participation of their licensees advances the public interest by bringing expertise to the evaluation of professionals' competency and behavior. In this era of more intense competition among a broader range of health care professionals, however, this reliance creates substantial opportunities for anticompetitive conduct facilitated by the authority of the board.

The traditional rationale for health care quality regulation is the lack of information available to consumers to make their own risk-benefit balance in choosing providers as well as the limited capacity of patients to evaluate the information that is available. As health care data become cheaper and more accessible, health care quality regulation will be challenged. More robust health databanks will lead to contradictory claims that greater direct consumer access to quality information reduces the need for state medical boards and that the boards should take a greater role in actively monitoring quality as data improves.

Licensure boards currently reflect the traditional way that we know what appropriate care is; i.e., the customary practice of the majority of practitioners with some reliance on a rather spotty and non-clinically relevant body of studies. The Affordable Care Act (ACA) pushes stronger reliance on scientific evidence of effectiveness and outcomes as the gold measure for quality. If the hopes for this shift toward scientific evidence are realized, it will have implications for enforcement and standard setting by the health professions boards.

The ACA also fosters expanded roles for nurses and physician assistants as the health care system is reorganized to emphasize continuity of care, accessible preventive care, and management of chronic illness at a lower cost. The activities of the licensure boards in restricting the work of these professionals are coming under increased scrutiny.

II.   DISCIPLINE

In re Williams

Supreme Court of Ohio, 1991.
60 Ohio St.3d 85, 573 N.E.2d 638.

Syllabus by the Court

* * *

* * * Between 1983 and 1986, Dr. Williams prescribed Biphetamine or Obetrol for fifty patients as part of a weight control treatment regimen. [Both drugs are controlled substances.]

On November 17, 1986, appellant, the Ohio State Medical Board ("board"), promulgated Ohio Adm.Code 4731–11–03(B), which prohibited the use of [drugs such as Biphetamine and Obetrol] for purposes of weight control. Dr. Williams ceased prescribing Biphetamine and Obetrol for weight control upon becoming aware of the rule.

By letter dated March 12, 1987, the board charged Dr. Williams with violating R.C. 4731.22(B)[2] by prescribing these stimulants without "reasonable care," and thereby failing to conform to minimal standards of medical practice. The crux of the board's charge was that Dr. Williams had departed from accepted standards of care by using these drugs as a long-term, rather than a short-term, treatment.

A hearing was held before a board examiner. The parties stipulated to the accuracy of the medical records of the patients in question, which detailed the use of Biphetamine and Obetrol for periods ranging from nearly seven months to several years. The board also introduced into evidence the Physician's Desk Reference entries for Biphetamine and Obetrol, which recommend that these drugs be used for only "a few weeks" in the treatment of obesity. The board presented no testimony or other evidence of the applicable standard of care.

Dr. Williams presented expert testimony from Dr. John P. Morgan, the director of the pharmacology program at the City University of New York Medical School, and Dr. Eljorn Don Nelson, an associate professor of

---

[2]   R.C. 4731.22(B) provides in pertinent part:

"The board, pursuant to an adjudicatory hearing. . . . shall, to the extent permitted by law,. . . . [discipline] the holder of a certificate [to practice medicine] for one or more of the following reasons:

. . . .

"(2) Failure to use reasonable care, discrimination in the administration of drugs, or failure to employ acceptable scientific methods in the selection of drugs or other modalities for treatment of disease;

"(3) Selling, prescribing, giving away, or administering drugs for other than legal and legitimate therapeutic purposes. . . .

. . . .

"(6) A departure from, or the failure to conform to, minimal standards of care. . . . [.]"

clinical pharmacology at the University of Cincinnati College of Medicine. These experts stated that there are two schools of thought in the medical community concerning the use of stimulants for weight control. The so-called "majority" view holds that stimulants should only be used for short periods, if at all, in weight control programs. The "minority" view holds that the long-term use of stimulants is proper in the context of a supervised physician-patient relationship. Both experts testified that, though they themselves supported the "majority" view, Dr. Williams's application of the "minority" protocol was not substandard medical practice.

The hearing examiner found that Dr. Williams's practices violated R.C. 4731.22(B). The examiner recommended subjecting Dr. Williams to a three-year monitored probation period. The board modified the penalty, imposing a one-year suspension of Dr. Williams's license followed by a five-year probationary period, during which he would be unable to prescribe or dispense controlled substances.

Dr. Williams appealed to the Court of Common Pleas of Franklin County pursuant to R.C. 119.12. The court found that the board's order was ". . . not supported by reliable, probative and substantial evidence and . . . [was] not in accordance with law." The court of appeals affirmed.

HERBERT R. BROWN, JUSTICE.

In an appeal from an administrative agency, a reviewing court is bound to uphold the agency's order if it is ". . . supported by reliable, probative, and substantial evidence and is in accordance with law. . . ."[ ]. In the instant case, we must determine if the common pleas court erred by finding that the board's order was not supported by sufficient evidence. For the reasons which follow, we conclude that it did not and affirm the judgment of the court below.

In its arguments to this court, the board contends that Arlen v. Ohio State Medical Bd. (1980), 61 Ohio St.2d 168, 15 O.O.3d 190, 399 N.E.2d 1251, is dispositive. In *Arlen*, the physician was disciplined because he had written prescriptions for controlled substances to a person who the physician knew was redistributing the drugs to others, a practice prohibited by R.C. 3719.06(A). The physician appealed on the ground that the board failed to present expert testimony that such prescribing practices fell below a reasonable standard of care.

We held that the board is not required in every case to present expert testimony on the acceptable standard of medical practice before it can find that a physician's conduct falls below this standard. We noted that the usual purpose of expert testimony is to assist the trier of facts in understanding "issues that require scientific or specialized knowledge or experience beyond the scope of common occurrences. . . ."[ ] The board was then made up of ten (now twelve) persons, eight of whom are licensed physicians. [ ] Thus, a majority of board members are themselves experts in the medical field who already possess the specialized knowledge needed to determine the acceptable standard of general medical practice.

While the board need not, in every case, present expert testimony to support a charge against an accused physician, the charge must be supported by some reliable, probative and substantial evidence. It is here that the case against Dr. Williams fails, as it is very different from *Arlen*.

Arlen involved a physician who dispensed controlled substances in a manner that not only fell below the acceptable standard of medical practice, but also violated the applicable statute governing prescription and dispensing of these drugs. In contrast, Dr. Williams dispensed controlled substances in what was, at the time, a legally permitted manner, albeit one which was disfavored by many in the medical community. The only evidence in the record on this issue was the testimony of Dr. Williams's expert witnesses that his use of controlled substances in weight control programs did not fall below the acceptable standard of medical practice. While the board has broad discretion to resolve evidentiary conflicts [ ] and determine the weight to be given expert testimony [ ], it cannot convert its own disagreement with an expert's opinion into affirmative evidence of a contrary proposition where the issue is one on which medical experts are divided and there is no statute or rule governing the situation.

It should be noted, however, that where the General Assembly has prohibited a particular medical practice by statute, or where the board has done so through its rulemaking authority, the existence of a body of expert opinion supporting that practice would not excuse a violation. Thus, if Dr. Williams had continued to prescribe Biphetamine or Obetrol for weight control after the promulgation of Ohio Adm.Code 4731–11–03(B), this would be a violation of R.C. 4731.22(B)(3), and the existence of the "minority" view supporting the use of these substances for weight control would provide him no defense. Under those facts, *Arlen* would be dispositive. Here, however, there is insufficient evidence, expert or otherwise, to support the charges against Dr. Williams. Were the board's decision to be affirmed on the facts in this record, it would mean that a doctor would have no access to meaningful review of the board's decision. The board, though a majority of its members have special knowledge, is not entitled to exercise such unbridled discretion.

WRIGHT, JUSTICE, dissenting.

The message we send to the medical community's regulators with today's decision is one, I daresay, we would never countenance for their counterparts in the legal community. We are telling those charged with policing the medical profession that their expertise as to what constitutes the acceptable standard of medical practice is not enough to overcome the assertion that challenged conduct does not violate a state statute. * * *

HOOVER V. THE AGENCY FOR HEALTH CARE ADMINISTRATION

District Court of Appeal of Florida, 1996.
676 So.2d 1380.

JORGENSON, JUDGE.

Dr. Katherine Anne Hoover, a board-certified physician in internal medicine, appeals a final order of the Board of Medicine penalizing her and restricting her license to practice medicine in the State of Florida. We reverse because the board has once again engaged in the uniformly rejected practice of overzealously supplanting a hearing officer's valid findings of fact regarding a doctor's prescription practices with its own opinion in a case founded on a woefully inadequate quantum of evidence.

In March 1994, the Department of Business and Professional Regulation (predecessor in these proceedings to the Agency for Health Care Administration) filed an administrative complaint alleging that Dr. Hoover (1) inappropriately and excessively prescribed various . . . controlled substances to seven of her patients and (2) provided care of those patients that fell below that level of care, skill, and treatment which is recognized by a reasonably prudent similar physician as being acceptable under similar conditions and circumstances; in violation of sections 458.331(1)(q) and (t), Florida Statutes, respectively. All seven of the patients had been treated by Dr. Hoover for intractable pain arising from various noncancerous diseases or ailments.

Dr. Hoover disputed the allegations of the administrative complaint and requested a formal hearing. * * *

The agency presented the testimony of two physicians as experts. Neither had examined any of the patients or their medical records. The sole basis for the opinions of the agency physicians was computer printouts from pharmacies in Key West where the doctor's patients had filled their prescriptions. These printouts indicated only the quantity of each drug filled for each patient, occasionally referring to a simplified diagnosis. Both of these physicians practiced internal medicine and neither specialized in the care of chronic pain. In fact, both doctors testified that they did not treat but referred their chronic pain patients to pain management clinics. The hearing officer found that this was a common practice among physicians—perhaps to avoid prosecutions like this case.[5] Both doctors "candidly testified that without being provided with copies of the medical records for those patients they could not evaluate Respondent's diagnoses or what alternative modalities were attempted or what testing was done to support the use of the medication chosen by Respondent to treat those patients." Despite this paucity of evidence, lack of famil-

---

[5] Referral to a pain management clinic was not an option for Dr. Hoover's indigent Key West resident patients.

iarity, and seeming lack of expertise, the agency's physicians testified at the hearing that the doctor had prescribed excessive, perhaps lethal amounts of narcotics, and had practiced below the standard of care.

Dr. Hoover testified in great detail concerning the condition of each of the patients, her diagnoses and courses of treatment, alternatives attempted, the patients' need for medication, the uniformly improved function of the patients with the amount of medication prescribed, and her frequency of writing prescriptions to allow her close monitoring of the patients. She presented corroborating physician testimony regarding the appropriateness of the particular medications and the amounts prescribed and her office-setting response to the patients' requests for relief from intractable pain.

Following post-hearing submissions, the hearing officer issued her recommended order finding that the agency had failed to meet its burden of proof on all charges. The hearing officer concluded, for instance, "Petitioner failed to provide its experts with adequate information to show the necessary similar conditions and circumstances upon which they could render opinions that showed clearly and convincingly that Respondent failed to meet the standard of care required of her in her treatment of the patients in question."

The agency filed exceptions to the recommended findings of fact and conclusions of law as to five of the seven patients. The board of medicine accepted all the agency's exceptions, amended the findings of fact in accordance with the agency's suggestions, and found the doctor in violation of sections 458.331(1)(q) and (t), Florida Statutes. The board imposed the penalty recommended by the agency: a reprimand, a $4,000 administrative fine, continuing medical education on prescribing abusable drugs, and two years probation. This appeal follows.

For each of the five patients, the hearing officer found the prescribing practices of Doctor Hoover to be appropriate. This was based upon (1) the doctor's testimony regarding the specific care given, (2) the corroborating testimony of her physician witness, and (3) the fact that the doctor's prescriptions did not exceed the federal guidelines for treatment of intractable pain in cancer patients, though none of the five patients were diagnosed as suffering from cancer.

The board rejected these findings as not based on competent substantial evidence. As particular reasons, the board adopted the arguments of the agency's exceptions to the recommended order that (1) the hearing officer's findings were erroneously based on irrelevant federal guidelines, and (2) the agency's physicians had testified that the doctor's prescription pattern was below the standard of care and outside the practice of medicine. * * *

First, the board mischaracterizes the hearing officer's reference to the federal guidelines. The board reasoned in its final order that "[t]he record reflects that the federal guidelines relied upon by the Hearing Officer for this finding were designed for cancer patients and [the five patients at issue were] not being treated for cancer." It is true, as the hearing officer noted,

"Respondent presented expert evidence that there is a set of guidelines which have been issued for the use of Schedule II controlled substances to treat intractable pain and that although those guidelines were established to guide physicians in treating cancer patients, those are the only guidelines available at this time. Utilizing those guidelines, because they exist, the amount of medication prescribed by Respondent to the patients in question was not excessive or inappropriate."

In so finding, however, the hearing officer did not, as the board suggests, rely solely upon the federal guidelines in its ruling that the doctor's prescribing practices were not excessive. Rather, the federal guidelines merely buttressed fact findings that were independently supported by the hearing officer's determination of the persuasiveness and credibility of the physician witnesses on each side. For example, though he admitted he had not even reviewed the federal guidelines, one of the agency physicians asserted that the amounts prescribed constituted a "tremendous number of pills" and that the doses involved would be lethal. That Dr. Hoover's prescriptions fell within the guidelines for chronic-pained cancer patients may properly be considered to refute this assertion. Such a use of the federal guidelines was relevant and reasonable.

Second, Dr. Hoover testified in great detail concerning her treatment of each patient, the patient's progress under the medication she prescribed, and that the treatment was within the standard of care and practice of medicine. The hearing officer, as arbiter of credibility, was entitled to believe what the doctor and her physician expert opined. [ ] The agency's witnesses' ultimate conclusions do not strip the hearing officer's reliance upon Dr. Hoover of its competence and substantiality. The hearing officer was entitled to give Dr. Hoover's testimony greater weight than that of the agency's witnesses, who did not examine these patients or regularly engage in the treatment of intractable pain.

[T]he hearing officer explicitly recognized that the 1994 [Florida] intractable pain law was not in effect at the time of Dr. Hoover's alleged infractions but cited it for a permissible purpose—to rebut any claim that there is a strong public policy mandate in favor of the board's draconian policy of policing pain prescription practice. [ ] * * *

Reversed.

NOTE: STATE AND FEDERAL REGULATION OF PRESCRIBING PRACTICES

Both *Williams* and *Hoover* involve disciplinary action by a state medical board based on a physician's prescribing practices. Prescribing is also regulated by the Food and Drug Administration (FDA) and the Drug Enforcement Administration (DEA).

The FDA has the authority to approve and monitor the safety of drugs and devices; and this certainly makes the FDA an important gatekeeper of access to drugs. Once a drug is approved for prescribing, however, the FDA does not have the authority to restrict physicians in their prescribing of the medication for particular purposes. Thus, once a drug is approved for a particular purpose (e.g., for the treatment of a particular sort of cancer), a physician may prescribe it for other purposes (e.g., for the treatment of another type of cancer). Prescribing for a different purpose, in a higher or lower dose, or for a different population (e.g., children) than those for which the FDA approved the medication is called "off-label" prescribing. Off-label prescribing is common and necessary in the practice of medicine and may become the standard of care in particular circumstances. Off-label prescribing also raises issues of medical judgment, evidence-based medicine, the relations between pharmaceutical firms and prescribing physicians, and standard setting by medical licensure boards, as in *Hoover* and *Williams*.

The DEA regulates prescribing through its authority under the Controlled Substances Act (CSA). 21 U.S.C. § 801. Under the CSA, the federal government governs the production and distribution of drugs that have the potential for abuse or addiction. Doctors must have a permit issued by the DEA to prescribe medications regulated under the CSA. The DEA may revoke a permit or prosecute physicians whose prescribing patterns fall outside of the DEA's view of legitimate medical practice. DEA policies have conflicted directly with state health policy on several fronts.

Several states have enacted legislation to allow physicians or patients access to marijuana for the treatment of medical conditions. See, e.g., Cal. Health & Saf. Code § 11362.5. Under the Bush administration, the federal government actively opposed such efforts by aggressively enforcing federal CSA prohibitions against prescribing marijuana. In Gonzales v. Raich, 545 U.S. 1, 125 S.Ct. 2195, 162 L.Ed.2d 1 (2005), the Supreme Court rejected the argument that the CSA in this context exceeded the federal government's authority under the Commerce Clause. The Obama administration has relied on prosecutorial discretion to reduce the level of enforcement in states legalizing marijuana for medical use, although the federal government has continued some prosecutions. The move to legalize marijuana, including beyond medical use, continues with the states taking a variety of strategies from outright legalization for personal use (by Colorado and Washington by ballot in 2012) to removing penalties for possession of small amounts.

Federal and state health policies have also been in conflict over prescribing of controlled substances for pain treatment. The Federation of State Medical Boards adopted a model policy that specifically recognizes that opioids are essential to the treatment of pain and that state medical boards should be equally concerned about the neglect of pain as they are about prescribing abuse. Nearly half of the states have enacted legislation generally referred to as "intractable pain treatment acts" which limit state agencies in taking action against physicians in certain circumstances. In contrast, the DEA continued to pursue a more aggressive stance against prescribers of controlled substances for pain management. Conflict between state and federal policy on this issue continues. There is also evidence that state prosecutions of physicians prescribing pain medication may be increasing as well. See Diane E. Hoffmann, Treating Pain v. Reducing Drug Diversion and Abuse: Recalibrating the Balance in Our Drug Control Laws and Policies, 1 St. Louis U. J. Health & Pol'y 231 (2008).

The Affordable Care Act (ACA) established the Interagency Pain Research Coordinating Committee. In response to an ACA mandate, the IOM issued a report documenting the impact of pain on public health (over 100 million persons in America are in chronic pain and costs for medical care and lost productivity exceed $560 billion annually) and making recommendations to improve pain treatment and expand research. IOM, Relieving Pain in America: A Blueprint for Transforming Prevention, Care, Education, and Research (2011).

NOTES AND QUESTIONS

1.   Should licensure boards establish standards of practice or practice guidelines that prefer one approach over another, as the Board apparently did in *Williams*; or should they simply recognize the full range of medical practices, including minority views? Would your answer depend on whether the board was acting in a rulemaking or in an adjudicatory role? Do *Williams* and *Hoover* present identical issues in that regard? Do *Williams* and *Hoover* present special challenges because the medications may have a risk of use or diversion for nontherapeutic uses? How should state boards account for the gatekeeper role of physicians in such cases?

2.   If almost all members of the medical board are physicians, what is at the heart of the dispute over expert testimony in *Williams*? On what basis did the Florida court reject the testimony of the agency's experts in *Hoover*?

3.   Rates of serious disciplinary action vary considerably among the states. In 2011, for example, South Carolina had the lowest rate of 1.33/1,000 doctors, and Wyoming had the highest at 6.79/1,000. Public Citizen's Health Research Group, Ranking of the Rate of State Medical Boards' Serious Disciplinary Actions, 2009–2011 (2012). The report notes the five-fold difference between the "best and worst state disciplinary boards." How would you measure whether the number of disciplinary actions in your state was too many, too few, or just right?

4.   Most states have programs that provide rehabilitative, non-punitive interventions for impaired nurses, doctors, and other health professionals. It

is hoped that the availability of a program of non-punitive rehabilitation encourages a higher rate of reporting and self-reporting of impaired physicians. Constitutional due process requires that discipline for behavior, including the use of drugs and alcohol, must demonstrate a nexus between the behavior and the ability to practice medicine. See, e.g., Watson v. Superior Court, 176 Cal. App.4th 1407, 98 Cal. Rptr.3d 715 (Cal. App. 2009). Should voluntary enrollment in an impaired professional program be confidential, or should the program be required to notify the board of the enrollment? Should physicians who are abusing alcohol or drugs or who are participating in a state-sanctioned rehabilitation program be required to inform their patients? Would this better protect the public? See W.Va. Code § 30–3–9, providing for confidentiality.

5. Telemedicine has become commonplace and offers increased access to medical care and potential cost reductions, for example by remote consultation on imaging by specialists. The practice has raised a host of issues. It tests the state-based structure of medical licensure, and a central issue is whether a physician must be licensed within the state where the patient is. Diane Hoffmann & Virginia Rowthorn, Legal Impediments to the Diffusion of Telemedicine (Symposium Issue on Telemedicine), 14 J. Health Care L. & Pol'y 1 (2011). State statutes have taken a variety of approaches ranging from the very restrictive to the very open.

NOTE: THE NATIONAL PRACTITIONER DATA BANK

Congress established the National Practitioner Data Bank (NPDB) in part to create an effective system for preventing doctors with disciplinary history in one state from moving to another and practicing until detected, if ever. 42 U.S.C. §§ 11101–11152. State disciplinary and licensure boards are required to report certain disciplinary actions against physicians. Hospitals and other entities engaging in peer review processes are required to report adverse actions as well. Licensure boards have access to the Data Bank to check on licensees, and hospitals must check the Data Bank for physicians applying for staff privileges and periodically for physicians who hold staff privileges. See Chapter 11. The public is not allowed access to information on individual practitioners in the Data Bank although access to deidentified information is permitted.

Most states have established publicly accessible websites where they post physician profiles. The Massachusetts site, for example, posts background information on the physician (such as education, specialties, insurance plans) as well as malpractice claims paid, hospital credentialing actions, criminal convictions, and board disciplinary actions. Mass. Bd. of Reg. in Med., On–Line Physician Profile Site. See discussion in Chapter 3 for more on public dissemination of quality data.

A review of data from the National Practitioner Data Bank revealed that only 45% of doctors with an NPDB report of adverse privileges actions or malpractice settlements also had a report of a disciplinary action by the state medical board. Alan Levine et al., State Medical Boards Fail to Discipline

Doctors with Hospital Actions Against Them, Public Citizen (2011). Should malpractice payments necessarily lead to licensure penalties? Consider the following Problem.

PROBLEM: THREE STRIKES AND YOU'RE OUT?

Some states are beginning to integrate malpractice actions into their disciplinary processes. Almost all states require that liability insurance carriers report paid claims to the board, and some states require reporting of claims filed. Some states require investigation of physicians with multiple malpractice settlements or judgments. See, e.g., Mich. Comp.Laws Ann. § 333.16231. In 2004, Florida voters approved by an overwhelming majority the following amendment to the state constitution:

> (a) No person who has been found to have committed three or more incidents of medical malpractice shall be licensed. * * *

> (b)(1) The phrase "medical malpractice" means the failure to practice medicine * * * with that level of care, skill, and treatment recognized in general law related to health care providers' licensure. * * *

> (b)(2) The phrase "found to have committed" means that the malpractice has been found in a final judgment of a court of law, final administrative agency decision, or decision of binding arbitration.

Thereafter, the Florida legislature codified the amendment in the medical licensure statute but added the following provision:

> [T]he board shall not license or continue to license a medical doctor found to have committed repeated medical malpractice [defined as three or more incidents], the finding of which was based upon clear and convincing evidence. In order to rely on an incident of medical malpractice to determine whether a license must be denied or revoked under this section, if the facts supporting the finding of the incident of medical malpractice were determined on a standard less stringent than clear and convincing evidence, the board shall review the record of the case and determine whether the finding would be supported under a standard of clear and convincing evidence.

Did the legislature significantly alter the impact of the amendment? Why might they have made this change? Two-thirds of states require the lower preponderance of the evidence rather than clear and convincing, standard for professional disciplinary actions.

Assume that your state's licensure statute provides only that disciplinary action may be taken when a physician has engaged in:

> Any conduct or practice which is or might be harmful or dangerous to the mental or physical health of a patient or the public; or incompetency, gross negligence or repeated negligence in the performance

of the functions or duties of any profession licensed or regulated by this chapter. For the purposes of this subdivision, "repeated negligence" means the failure, on more than one occasion, to use that degree of skill and learning ordinarily used under the same or similar circumstances by the member of the applicant's or licensee's profession.

Does the medical board have the authority under this provision to issue a rule or adopt a policy that it will sanction a doctor with final judgments of malpractice in three or more cases? A doctor with ten or more malpractice claims made? Should the board adopt such a rule? Or, would you argue that there should always be hearing before discipline?

III. COMPLEMENTARY AND ALTERNATIVE MEDICINE

Complementary and alternative medicine (CAM) is a broad domain of resources that encompasses health systems, modalities, and practices and their accompanying theories and beliefs, other than those intrinsic to the dominant health system of a particular society or culture in a given historical period. CAM includes such resources perceived by their users as associated with positive health outcomes. Boundaries within CAM and between the CAM domain and the domain of the dominant system are not always sharp or fixed. IOM, Complementary and Alternative Medicine in the United States (2005).

The National Institutes of Health, National Center for Complementary and Alternative Medicine (NCCAM) defines CAM as health services that "are not presently considered to be part of conventional medicine," and goes on to list four domains (whole medical systems, such as homeopathy; mind-body medicine, including music; energy medicine, including therapeutic touch; and bioelectromagnetic-based therapies, such as pulsed fields).

The IOM report notes that all proposed definitions of CAM were "imprecise, ambiguous, or otherwise subject to misinterpretation." Both the IOM and the NCCAM definitions are deficient as they use a negative to define CAM—it is unconventional. Furthermore, they define CAM in relation to allopathic medicine and do not communicate the integration and coherence of CAM systems standing alone.

Even though limited, they capture the fluid sense of what is conventional and what is alternative as well as the vastness of what might be considered complementary and alternative (or integrative) medicine. These medically oriented definitions, however, reflect the current legal framework for CAM.

State professional licensure boards become involved in CAM in at least two ways. First, licensed doctors (or nurses, dentists, and so on) may utilize CAM therapies, integrating them within conventional medicine. See IOM, Integrative Medicine and the Health of the Public: A Summary of the February 2009 Summit (2009), including discussion of integrating "evidence-based interventions or practices derived from ancient folk practices, cultural-specific sources, contemporary product development, or crafted from a blend of these" with allopathic approaches. Integrating CAM approaches, however, will attract the attention of the licensure board if the practice violates licensure standards for acceptable or appropriate treatment. That issue is addressed in this section. In addition, licensure boards may take action against unlicensed CAM practitioners for violating the state's prohibition against the unlicensed practice of a licensed health care profession, as discussed in Section IV.

IN RE GUESS

Supreme Court of North Carolina, 1990.
327 N.C. 46, 393 S.E.2d 833.

MITCHELL, JUSTICE.

*   *   *

The facts of this case are essentially uncontested. The record evidence tends to show that Dr. George Albert Guess is a licensed physician practicing family medicine in Asheville. In his practice, Guess regularly administers homeopathic medical treatments to his patients. Homeopathy has been defined as:

A system of therapy developed by Samuel Hahnermann on the theory that large doses of a certain drug given to a healthy person will produce certain conditions which, when occurring spontaneously as symptoms of a disease, are relieved by the same drug in small doses. This [is] . . . a sort of "fighting fire with fire" therapy. [ ] [Both the NCCAM and the Society of Homeopaths provide more detailed descriptions of homeopathy on their websites.]

*   *   *

[T]he Board charged Dr. Guess with unprofessional conduct [ ] specifically based upon his practice of homeopathy. * * *

Following notice, a hearing was held by the Board on the charge against Dr. Guess. The hearing evidence chiefly consisted of testimony by a number of physicians. Several physicians licensed to practice in North Carolina testified that homeopathy was not an acceptable and prevailing system of medical practice in North Carolina. In fact, there was evidence indicating that Guess is the only homeopath openly practicing in the State. Guess presented evidence that homeopathy is a recognized system of practice in at least three other states and many foreign countries. There was no evidence that Guess' homeopathic treatment had ever harmed a patient, and there was anecdotal evidence that Guess' homeopathic remedies had provided relief to several patients who were apparently unable to obtain relief through allopathic medicine.

Following its hearing, the Board revoked Dr. Guess' license to practice medicine in North Carolina, based upon findings and conclusions that Guess' practice of homeopathy "departs from and does not conform to the standards of acceptable and prevailing medical practice in this State," thus constituting unprofessional conduct as defined and prohibited by N.C.G.S. § 90–14(a)(6). The Board, however, stayed the revocation of Guess' license for so long as he refrained from practicing homeopathy.

Guess appealed the Board's decision to the Superior Court. * * * After review, the Superior Court * * * reversed and vacated the Board's decision. The Superior Court found and concluded that Guess' substantial rights had been violated because the Board's findings, conclusions and decision were "not supported by competent, material and substantial evidence and [were] arbitrary and capricious."

[T]he Court of Appeals rejected the Superior Court's reasoning to the effect that the Board's findings, conclusions and decision were not supported by competent evidence. [ ] The Court of Appeals, nonetheless, affirmed the Superior Court's order reversing the Board's decision,

> because the Board neither charged nor found that Dr. Guess' departures from approved and prevailing medical practice either endangered or harmed his patients or the public, and in our opinion the revocation of a physician's license to practice his profession in this state must be based upon conduct that is detrimental to the public; it cannot be based upon conduct that is merely different from that of other practitioners.

We granted the Board's Petition for Discretionary Review, and now reverse the Court of Appeals.

The statute central to the resolution of this case provides in relevant part:

> § 90–14. Revocation, suspension, annulment or denial of license.
>
> (a) The Board shall have the power to deny, annul, suspend, or revoke a license . . . issued by the Board to any person who has been found by the Board to have committed any of the following acts or conduct, or for any of the following reasons:
>
> . . . .
>
> (6) Unprofessional conduct, including, but not limited to, any departure from, or the failure to conform to, the standards of acceptable and prevailing medical practice, or the ethics of the

medical profession, irrespective of whether or not a patient is injured   thereby. . . .
[ ]

The Court of Appeals concluded that in exercising the police power, the legislature may properly act only to protect the public from harm. Therefore, the Court of Appeals reasoned that, in order to be a valid exercise of the police power, the statute must be construed as giving the Board authority to prohibit or punish the action of a physician only when it can be shown that the particular action in question poses a danger of harm to the patient or the public. Specifically, the Court of Appeals held that:

> Before a physician's license to practice his profession in this state can be lawfully revoked under G.S. 90–14(a)(6) for practices contrary to acceptable and prevailing medical practice that it must also appear that the deviation complained of posed some threat of harm to either the physician's patients or the public.

The Board argues, and we agree, that the Court of Appeals erred in construing the statute to add a requirement that each particular practice prohibited by the statute must pose an actual threat of harm. Our analysis begins with a basic constitutional principle: the General Assembly, in exercising the state's police power, may legislate to protect the public health, safety and general welfare. [ ] When a statute is challenged as being beyond the scope of the police power, the statute will be upheld unless it has no rational relationship to such a legitimate public purpose. [ ]

[R]egulation of the medical profession is plainly related to the legitimate public purpose of protecting the public health and safety. [ ] State regulation of the medical profession has long been recognized as a legitimate exercise of the police power. As the Supreme Court of the United States [in Dent v. West Virginia, 129 U.S. 114, 98 S.Ct. 231, 32 L.Ed. 623 (1889)] has pointed out:

> The power of the State to provide for the general welfare of its people authorizes it to prescribe all such regulations as in its judgment will secure or tend to secure them against the consequences of ignorance and incapacity as well as of deception and fraud . . . . . The nature and extent of the qualifications required must depend primarily upon the judgments of the States as to their necessity. . . .

> Few professions require more careful preparation by one who seeks to enter it than that of medicine. It has to deal with all those subtle and mysterious influences upon which health and life depend. . . . Reliance must be placed upon the assurance given by his license, issued by an authority competent to judge in that   respect,   that   he   possesses   the   requisite

tions. . . . The same reasons which control in imposing conditions, upon compliance with which the physician is allowed to practice in the first instance, may call for further conditions as new modes of treating disease are discovered, or a more thorough acquaintance is obtained of the remedial properties of vegetable and mineral substances, or a more accurate knowledge is acquired of the human system and of the agencies by which it is affected.

The provision of the statute in question here is reasonably related to the public health. We conclude that the legislature reasonably believed that a general risk of endangering the public is inherent in any practices which fail to conform to the standards of "acceptable and prevailing" medical practice in North Carolina. We further conclude that the legislative intent was to prohibit any practice departing from acceptable and prevailing medical standards without regard to whether the particular practice itself could be shown to endanger the public. * * * Therefore, the statute is a valid exercise of the police power.

* * *

Certain aspects of regulating the medical profession plainly require expertise beyond that of a layman. Our legislature recognized that need for expertise when it created a Board of Medical Examiners composed of seven licensed physicians and one additional member. * * * The statutory phrase "standards of acceptable and prevailing medical practice" is sufficiently specific to provide the Board—comprised overwhelmingly of expert physicians—with the "adequate guiding standards" necessary to support the legislature's delegation of authority.

The statute in question is a valid regulation which generally tends to secure the public health, safety, and general welfare, and the legislature has permissibly delegated certain regulatory functions connected with that valid exercise of the police power to the Board. There is no requirement, however, that every action taken by the Board specifically identify or address a particular injury or danger to any individual or to the public. It is enough that the statute is a valid exercise of the police power for the public health and general welfare, so long as the Board's action is in compliance with the statute. The Court of Appeals thus erred in requiring a showing of potential harm from the particular practices engaged in by Dr. Guess as a prerequisite to Board action, and for that reason the Court of Appeals' decision is reversed.

* * *

Findings by the Board of Medical Examiners, if supported by competent evidence, may not be disturbed by a reviewing court. * * * The Board's findings leading to its decision were based upon competent, material and substantial evidence regarding what constitutes "acceptable and prevailing" standards of medical practice in North Carolina. No more was required. Guess' evidence concerning the efficacy of homeopathy and its use outside North Carolina simply was not relevant to the issue before the Board.

Dr. Guess also contends that the Board's decision was arbitrary and capricious and, therefore, must be reversed. He argues that the Board's arbitrariness is revealed in its "selective" application of the statute against him. He seems to contend that if the Board is to take valid action against him, it must also investigate and sanction every physician who is the "first" to utilize any "new" or "rediscovered" medical procedure. We disagree. The Board properly adhered to its statutory notice and hearing requirements, and its decision was amply supported by uncontroverted competent, material and substantial evidence. We detect no evidence of arbitrariness or capriciousness.

Dr. Guess strenuously argues that many countries and at least three states recognize the legitimacy of homeopathy. While some physicians may value the homeopathic system of practice, it seems that others consider homeopathy an outmoded and ineffective system of practice. This conflict, however interesting, simply is irrelevant here in light of the uncontroverted evidence and the Board's findings and conclusion that homeopathy is not currently an "acceptable and prevailing" system of medical practice in North Carolina.

While questions as to the efficacy of homeopathy and whether its practice should be allowed in North Carolina may be open to valid debate among members of the medical profession, the courts are not the proper forum for that debate. The legislature may one day choose to recognize the homeopathic system of treatment, or homeopathy may evolve by proper experimentation and research to the point of being recognized by the medical profession as an acceptable and prevailing form of medical practice in our state; such choices, however, are not for the courts to make.

* * * The Board argues, and we agree within our admittedly limited scope of medical knowledge, that preventing the practice of homeopathy will not restrict the development and acceptance of new and beneficial medical practices. Instead, the development and acceptance of such new practices simply must be achieved by "acceptable and prevailing" methods of medical research, experimentation, testing, and approval by the appropriate regulatory or professional bodies.

* * *

REVERSED and REMANDED.

NOTES AND QUESTIONS

1. After the *Guess* decision, the North Carolina legislature amended the grounds for discipline to limit the section under which Dr. Guess was penalized:

> The Board shall not revoke the license of or deny a license to a person solely because of that person's practice of a therapy that is experimental, nontraditional, or that departs from acceptable and prevailing medical practices unless, by competent evidence, the Board can establish that the treatment has a safety risk greater than the prevailing treatment or that the treatment is generally ineffective. N.C. Gen. Stat. 90–14(a)(6).

How would the North Carolina board prove that the alternative treatment is less safe than prevailing practice where there may be little evidence that the current practice is safe? See Julie Stone & Joan Matthews, Complementary Medicine and the Law (1996), arguing that while some alternative or complementary practices have a technological base and are subject to the same type of verification as allopathic medicine, other practices are not amenable to such testing.

2. The North Carolina statute is one example of statutory approaches adopted by a good number of state legislatures to accommodate the use of CAM by licensed physicians. Other states have taken a practice-by-practice approach in statutes that specifically authorize licensed physicians to provide particular CAM interventions such as acupuncture. Some states require that licensed physicians who practice certain forms of CAM hold a separate state license or registration to do so, although this departs from the nearly universal form of medical licensure which grants physicians a general medical license and does not require separate licensure for medical specialties. See, for example, Haw. Rev. Stat. § 436–E. In a third CAM-friendly approach, some states now require that CAM practitioners be represented on the medical board. See, e.g., N.Y. Public Health Law § 230.

3. Practitioners offering solely alternative health care services without conventional medical or nursing training or licensure are a very significant arm of the CAM movement. Some argue that only alternative providers can offer such services effectively and authentically. Some states license practitioners of particular CAM therapies. See, e.g., Ariz. Rev. Stat. § 32–1521 and Alaska Stat. § 08.45.030 (licensing naturopaths); Nev. Rev. Stat. § 630A.155 (licensing homeopaths). See Section IV, below, for discussion of unlicensed health care providers.

IV.   UNLICENSED PROVIDERS

The state medical board has the primary responsibility for enforcing the prohibition against the unauthorized practice of medicine by unlicensed providers. This prohibition is enforced by criminal sanctions against the unlicensed practitioner and license revocation or criminal sanctions against any physician who aids and abets the unlicensed practitioner. The board responsible for licensure and discipline for nursing has parallel authority to pursue unlicensed practitioners charged with engaging in the unauthorized practice of nursing. The issue of the scope of practice of licensed health care professionals is taken up in Section V of this chapter.

STATE BOARD OF NURSING AND STATE BOARD OF HEALING ARTS V. RUEBKE

Supreme Court of Kansas, 1996.
259 Kan. 599, 913 P.2d 142.

LARSON, JUSTICE:

The State Board of Healing Arts (Healing Arts) and the State Board of Nursing (Nursing) appeal the trial court's denial of a temporary injunction by which the Boards had sought to stop E. Michelle Ruebke, a practicing lay midwife, from continuing her alleged practice of medicine and nursing.

*   *   *

Factual Background

*   *   *

The hearing on the temporary injunction revealed that Ruebke acts as a lay midwife comprehensively assisting pregnant women with prenatal care, delivery, and post-partum care. She is president of the Kansas Midwives Association and follows its promulgated standards, which include a risk screening assessment based upon family medical history; establishing prenatal care plans, including monthly visitations; examinations and assistance in birth; and post-partum care. She works with supervising physicians who are made aware of her mode of practice and who are available for consultation and perform many of the medical tests incident to pregnancy.

*   *   *

Dr. Debra L. Messamore, an obstetrician/gynecologist, testified she had reviewed the Kansas Midwives Association standards of care and opined those standards were similar to the assessments incident to her practice as an OB/GYN. Dr. Messamore concluded that in her judgment the prenatal assessments made by Ruebke were obstetrical diagnoses.

Dr. Messamore testified that the prescriptions Ruebke has women obtain from their physicians are used in obstetrics to produce uterine contractions. She further testified the Kansas Midwives Association standard of care relating to post-delivery conditions of the mother and baby involved obstetrical judgments. She reviewed the birth records of [one] birth and testified that obstetrical or medical judgments were reflected. [She admitted] that many procedures at issue could be performed by a nurse rather than a physician. * * * She also stated her opinion that so defined obstetrics as a branch of medicine or surgery.

Ginger Breedlove, a Kansas certified advanced registered nurse practitioner and nurse-midwife, testified on behalf of Nursing. She reviewed the records [of two births] and testified nursing functions were involved. She admitted she could not tell from the records who had engaged in certain practices and that taking notes, giving enemas, and administering oxygen is often done by people who are not nurses, although education, experience, and minimum competency are required.

* * * The court held that provisions of both acts were unconstitutionally vague, Ruebke's midwifery practices did not and were not intended to come within the healing arts act or the nursing act, and her activities fell within exceptions to the two acts even if the acts did apply and were constitutional.

The factual findings, highly summarized, were that Ruebke had not been shown to hold herself out as anything other than a lay midwife; has routinely used and consulted with supervising physicians; was not shown to administer any prescription drugs; was not shown to do any suturing or episiotomies, make cervical or vaginal lacerations, or diagnose blood type; and had engaged only in activities routinely and properly done by people who are not physicians.

Regulatory History of Midwifery

One of the specific statutory provisions we deal with, K.S.A. 65–2802(a), defines the healing arts as follows:

> The healing arts include any system, treatment, operation, diagnosis, prescription, or practice for the ascertainment, cure, relief, palliation, adjustment, or correction of any human disease, ailment, deformity, or injury, and includes specifically but not by way of limitation the practice of medicine and surgery; the practice of osteopathic medicine and surgery; and the practice of chiropractic.

K.S.A. 65–2869 specifically provides that for the purpose of the healing arts act, the following persons shall be deemed to be engaged in the practice of medicine and surgery:

> (a) Persons who publicly profess to be physicians or surgeons, or publicly profess to assume the duties incident to the practice of medicine or surgery or any of their branches.

> (b) Persons who prescribe, recommend or furnish medicine or drugs, or perform any surgical operation of whatever nature by the use of any surgical instrument, procedure, equipment or mechanical device

for the diagnosis, cure or relief of any wounds, fractures, bodily injury, infirmity, disease, physical or mental illness or psychological disorder, of human beings.

* * *

[M]idwifery belonged to women from Biblical times through the Middle Ages. However, subsequent to the Middle Ages, women healers were often barred from universities and precluded from obtaining medical training or degrees. With the rise of barber-surgeon guilds, women were banned from using surgical instruments.

When midwives immigrated to America, they occupied positions of great prestige. Some communities licensed midwives and others did not. This continued until the end of the 19th century. In the 19th and 20th centuries, medical practice became more standardized. Economically and socially well-placed doctors pressed for more restrictive licensing laws and for penalties against those who violated them. [One commentator] suggests that licensure was a market control device; midwives were depriving new obstetricians of the opportunity for training; and elimination of midwifery would allow the science of obstetrics to grow into a mature medical specialty.

There is a notable absence of anything in the history of Kansas healing arts regulation illustrating any attempt to specifically target midwives. In 1870, the Kansas Legislature adopted its first restriction on the practice of medicine. * * *

[T]here can be little doubt that in 1870 Kansas, particularly in rural areas, there were not enough educated physicians available to deliver all of the children born in the state. In fact, until 1910 approximately 50 percent of births in this country were midwife assisted. [ ]

* * *

Although obstetricians held themselves out as a medical specialty in the United States as early as 1868, midwives were not seen as engaged in the practice of obstetrics, nor was obstetrics universally viewed as being a branch of medicine. In 1901, North Carolina recognized obstetricians as engaged in the practice of medicine but women midwives, as a separate discipline, were exempted from the licensure act. [ ] * * *

Although many states in the early 1900s passed laws relating to midwifery, Kansas has never expressly addressed the legality of the practice. In 1915 [ ] this court implied that a woman with considerable midwife experience was qualified to testify as an expert witness in a malpractice case against an osteopath for allegedly negligently delivering the plaintiff's child.

* * *

The 1978 Kansas Legislature created a new classification of nurses, Advanced Registered Nurse Practitioner (ARNP). [ ] One classification of ARNP is certified nurse midwives. Although the regulations permitting the practice of certified nurse midwives might be argued to show additional legislative intent to prohibit the practice of lay midwives, this argument has been rejected elsewhere. [ ]

In 1978, Kansas Attorney General opinion No. 78–164 suggested that the practice of midwifery is a violation of the healing arts act. * * * Although potentially persuasive, such an opinion is not binding on us.

Most probably in response to the 1978 Attorney General opinion, a 1978 legislative interim committee undertook a study of a proposal to recognize and regulate the practice of lay midwifery. However, the committee reached no conclusion.

* * *

A 1986 review of the laws of every state found that lay midwifery was specifically statutorily permitted, subject to licensing or regulation, in 25 jurisdictions. Twelve states, including Kansas, had no legislation governing or prohibiting lay midwifery directly or by direct implication. Several states recognized both lay and nurse midwives. Some issued new licensing only for nurse midwives, while others regulated and recognized both, often as separate professions, subject to separate standards and restrictions. [ ]

* * *

In April 1993, the Board of Healing Arts released Policy Statement No. 93–02, in which the Board stated it reaffirmed its previous position of August 18, 1984, that

[m]idwifery is the practice of medicine and surgery and any practice thereof by individuals not regulated by the Kansas State Board of Nursing or under the supervision of or by order of or referral from a licensed medical or osteopathic doctor constitutes the unlicensed practice of medicine and surgery.

* * *

This historical background brings us to the question of whether the healing arts act is unconstitutionally vague. * * *

* * *

[A] statute "is vague and violates due process if it prohibits conduct in terms so vague that a person of common intelligence cannot understand what conduct is prohibited, and it fails to adequately guard against arbitrary and discriminatory enforcement." [ ] A statute which requires specific intent is more likely to withstand a vagueness challenge than one, like that here, which imposes strict liability. [ ]

* * *

We have held that the interpretation of a statute given by an administrative agency within its area of expertise is entitled to deference, although final construction of a statute always rests with courts. [ ] * * *

We do, of course, attempt wherever possible to construe a statute as constitutional [ ]. * * *

* * *

The definition of healing arts uses terms that have an ordinary, definite, and ascertainable meaning. The trial court's conclusion that "disease, ailment, deformity or injury" are not commonly used words with settled meanings cannot be justified.

* * *

* * * Although we hold the act not to be unconstitutionally vague, we also hold the definitional provisions do not cover midwifery. In their ordinary usage the terms in K.S.A. 65–2802(a) used to define healing arts clearly and unequivocally focus exclusively on pathologies (i.e., diseases) and abnormal human conditions (i.e., ailments, deformities, or injuries). Pregnancy and childbirth are neither pathologies nor abnormalities.

* * *

Healing Arts argues that the "practice of medicine" includes the practice of obstetrics. It reasons, in turn, that obstetrics includes the practices traditionally performed by midwives. From this, it concludes midwifery is the practice of medicine.

However, equating midwifery with obstetrics, and thus with the practice of medicine, ignores the historical reality, discussed above, that midwives and obstetricians coexisted for many years quite separately. From the time of our statehood, the relationship between obstetricians and midwives changed from that of harmonious coexistence, cooperation, and collaboration, to open market competition and hostility. [ ]

* * *

To even the most casual observer of the history of assistance to childbirth, it is clear that over the course of this century the medical profession has extended its reach so deeply into the area of birthing as to almost completely occupy the field. The introduction of medical advances to the childbirth process drew women to physicians to assist during the birth of their children. Yet, this widespread preference for physicians as birth attendants hardly mandates the conclusion that only physicians may assist with births.

* * * The fact that a person with medical training provides services in competition with someone with no medical degree does not transform the latter's practices into the practice of medicine.

* * *

Although we hold the practice of midwifery is not itself the practice of the healing arts under our statutory scheme, our conclusions should not be interpreted to mean that a midwife may engage in any activity whatsoever with regard to a pregnant woman merely by virtue of her pregnancy. * * *

* * * However, we need not decide the precise boundaries of what a midwife may do without engaging in the practice of the healing arts because, in the case before us, Ruebke was found to have worked under the supervision of physicians who were familiar with her practices and authorized her actions. Any of Ruebke's actions that were established at trial, which might otherwise have been the practice of the healing arts, were exempt from the healing arts act because she had worked under the supervision of such physicians.

K.S.A. 65–2872 exempts certain activities from the licensure requirements of the healing arts act. In relevant part it provides:

The practice of the healing arts shall not be construed to include the following persons:

(g) Persons whose professional services are performed under the supervision or by order of or referral from a practitioner who is licensed under this act.

* * *

In light of the uncontested factual findings of the trial court, which were supported by competent evidence in the record, we agree with the trial court that the exception to the healing arts act recognized by K.S.A. 65–2872(g) applies to any of Ruebke's midwifery activities which might otherwise be considered the practice of the healing arts under K.S.A. 65–2802(a) and K.S.A. 65–2869.

* * *

As we have held, the legislature has never specifically acted with the intent to restrict or regulate the traditional practice of lay midwifery. Nevertheless, Nursing argues such birth assistants must be licensed nurses before they may render aid to pregnant women. In oral argument, Nursing conceded much of its argument would be muted were we to hold, as we do above, that the practice of midwifery is not the practice of the healing arts and thus not part of a medical regimen.

* * *

The practice of nursing is defined [in the Kansas nurse practice act] by reference to the practitioner's substantial specialized knowledge in areas of the biological, physical, and behavioral sciences and educational preparation within the field of the healing arts. Ruebke claims no specialized scientific knowledge, but rather readily admits she has no formal education beyond high school. Her assistance is valued not because it is the application of a firm and rarified grasp of scientific theory, but because, like generations of midwives before, she has practical experience assisting in childbirth.

Moreover, "nursing" deals with "persons who are experiencing changes in the normal health processes." As these words are commonly understood, pregnancy and childbirth do not constitute changes in the normal health process, but the continuation of it.

* * * As we have held, the practice of lay midwifery has, throughout the history of the regulation of nursing, been separate and distinct from the practice of the healing arts, to which nursing is so closely joined. While we have no doubt of the legislature's power to place lay midwifery under the authority of the State Board of Nursing, the legislature has not done so.

We find no legislative intent manifested in the language of the nursing act clearly illustrating the purpose of including the historically separate practice of midwifery within the practice of nursing. [ ] Assistance in childbirth rendered by one whose practical experience with birthing provides comfort to the mother is not nursing under the nursing act, such that licensure is required.

Affirmed in part and reversed in part.

NOTES AND QUESTIONS

1.   Should the Kansas Supreme Court have analyzed research on the quality and safety of services provided by nurse midwives as compared to lay (also called traditional, direct-entry, or professional) midwives? If it did so, would the court have been usurping the role of the legislature or simply trying to interpret an ambiguous statute? The Kansas statute on certified nurse midwives describes substantial educational requirements for the provision of nurse midwife services. The court concluded, however, that formal education is unnecessary and that practical experience can be valued as highly. If it were to amend its statutes, should the legislature provide for minimal educational requirements for persons assisting in childbirth?

2.   Doctors, nurses, nurse-midwives, physician assistants, and lay midwives have all exerted a claim to participation in assisting in childbirth. Courts have adopted many approaches to analyzing whether services provided in assistance at childbirth constitute the unauthorized practice of medi-

cine as defined in the medical practice act. Some courts have examined individual actions that may be performed during childbirth. For example, in Leigh v. Board of Reg. in Nursing, 395 Mass. 670, 481 N.E.2d 1347 (1985), the court distinguished "ordinary assistance in the normal cases of childbirth" from that in which a lay midwife used "obstetrical instruments" and "printed prescriptions or formulas," and concluded that the former does not constitute the practice of medicine while the latter does. Statutes authorizing childbirth services by traditional midwives also set boundaries on their practice and may exclude, for example, use of any surgical instrument or assisting childbirth "by artificial or mechanical means." See, e.g., Minn. Stat. Ann. § 147D.03.

3.   *Ruebke* illustrates that professional midwifery confronts the unauthorized practice prohibitions of both nursing and medicine. In Sherman v. Cryns, 203 Ill.2d 264, 271 Ill.Dec. 881, 786 N.E.2d 139 (2003), the court, in holding that a lay midwife engaged in the unauthorized practice of nursing, distinguished its case from *Ruebke* on the basis of the broad definition of professional nursing in the Illinois statute (which was quite similar to that of the statute in *Sermchief* in the next Section, below). The Illinois statute specifically provided for licensure for certified nurse midwives but was silent on the question of lay midwifery.

4.   Most states recognize lay or direct-entry midwifery by statute. See Sarah Anne Stover, Born by the Woman, Caught by the Midwife: The Case for Legalizing Direct–Entry Midwifery in All Fifty States, 21 Health Matrix 307 (2011), reporting that 41 states permit direct-entry midwifery, most by statute, and 9 states specifically prohibit the practice by statute, regulation, or case law.   Several states have incorporated certification by the North American Registry of Midwives within their standards for recognition of lay midwives.

5.   Claims of a Constitutional right to choice of provider of health care services consistently fail even when made in the context of the woman's right to privacy in reproductive decision making and the lack of empirical evidence of better childbirth outcomes with commonly used obstetrical technology.

V.   SCOPE OF PRACTICE REGULATION

Physician-directed medical care is giving way to a team approach as a core characteristic of health care delivery and as a formal requirement for medical homes and other forms of health care delivery. See Chapter 12. A stronger emphasis on preventive care, on primary care, and on chronic disease management all point to critical and greatly expanded roles for advanced nurse practitioners (ANPs) and physician assistants (PAs). The great concern over the shortage of primary care physicians to meet these goals is also fostering a push to expand practice opportunities for these midlevel practitioners.

The Affordable Care Act provides significant support for health care workforce development directed toward advanced practice nursing and other non-physician health professionals. Perhaps even more importantly, several of the health care delivery models supported by the ACA—including the medical home, the Nurse–Managed Health Clinic, and the Independence at Home Medical Practice—mandate a team approach to care with very significant practice and leadership roles for ANPs and PAs. Still, the ACA defers to state law on the permissible scope of practice of these practitioners.

Licensed non-physician health care providers cannot legally practice medicine, but practices that fall within their own licensure (for example, as a nurse or a physician assistant) are not considered the practice of medicine. A nurse who is providing services authorized under the nurse practice act would not be practicing medicine while an unlicensed practitioner providing the same services would be guilty of the unauthorized practice of medicine or nursing. If a nurse engages in practices that exceed those authorized in the nurse practice act, however, that nurse would be guilty of exceeding the authorized scope of practice of the profession of nursing as well as violating the prohibition against the unauthorized practice of medicine.

SERMCHIEF V. GONZALES

Supreme Court of Missouri, 1983.
660 S.W.2d 683.

WELLIVER, JUDGE.

This is a petition for a declaratory judgment and injunction brought by two nurses and five physicians[1] employed by the East Missouri Action Agency (Agency) wherein the plaintiff-appellants ask the Court to declare that the practices of the Agency nurses are authorized under the nursing law of this state, § 335.016.8, RSMo 1978 and that such practices do not constitute the unauthorized practice of medicine under Chapter 334 relating to the Missouri State Board of Registration For the Healing Arts (Board). * * * The holding below was against appellants who make direct appeal to this Court alleging that the validity of the statutes is involved. []. * * *

I

The facts are simple and for the most part undisputed. The Agency is a federally tax exempt Missouri not-for-profit corporation that maintains offices in Cape Girardeau (main office), Flat River, Ironton, and Fredericktown. The Agency provides medical services to the general public in fields of family planning, obstetrics and gynecology. The services are provided to an area that includes the counties of Bollinger, Cape Girardeau, Perry, St. Francis, Ste. Genevieve, Madison, Iron and Washington. Some

---

[1]   The physicians are joined for the reason that they are charged with aiding and abetting the unauthorized practice of medicine by the nurses.

thirty-five hundred persons utilized these services during the year prior to trial. The Agency is funded from federal grants, Medicaid reimbursements and patient fees. The programs are directed toward the lower income segment of the population. Similar programs exist both statewide and nationwide.

Appellant nurses Solari and Burgess are duly licensed professional nurses in Missouri pursuant to the provisions of Chapter 335 and are employed by the Agency. Both nurses have had post-graduate special training in the field of obstetrics and gynecology. Appellant physicians are also employees of the Agency and duly licensed to practice medicine (the healing arts) pursuant to Chapter 334. Respondents are the members and the executive secretary of the Missouri State Board of Registration for the Healing Arts (Board) * * *.

The services routinely provided by the nurses and complained of by the Board included, among others, the taking of history; breast and pelvic examinations; laboratory testing of Papanicolaou (PAP) smears, gonorrhea cultures, and blood serology; the providing of and giving of information about oral contraceptives, condoms, and intrauterine devices (IUD); the dispensing of certain designated medications; and counseling services and community education. If the nurses determined the possibility of a condition designated in the standing orders or protocols that would contraindicate the use of contraceptives until further examination and evaluation, they would refer the patients to one of the Agency physicians. No act by either nurse is alleged to have caused injury or damage to any person. All acts by the nurses were done pursuant to written standing orders and protocols signed by appellant physicians. The standing orders and protocols were directed to specifically named nurses and were not identical for all nurses.

The Board threatened to order the appellant nurses and physicians to show cause why the nurses should not be found guilty of the unauthorized practice of medicine and the physicians guilty of aiding and abetting such unauthorized practice. Appellants sought Court relief in this proceeding.

*   *   *

III

The statutes involved are:

It shall be unlawful for any person not now a registered physician within the meaning of the law to practice medicine or surgery in any of its departments, or to profess to cure and attempt to treat the sick and others afflicted with bodily or mental infirmities, or engage in the practice of midwifery in this state, except as herein provided.

Section 334.010.

This Chapter does not apply . . . *to nurses licensed and lawfully practicing their profession within the provisions of chapter 335, RSMo;* . . .

Section 334.155, RSMo Supp.1982 (emphasis added).

Definitions.—As used in sections 335.011 to 335.096, unless the context clearly requires otherwise, the following words and terms shall have the meanings indicated:

* * *

(8) "Professional nursing" is the performance for compensation of any act which requires substantial specialized education, judgment and skill based on knowledge and application of principles derived from the biological, physical, social and nursing sciences, including, but not limited to:

(a) Responsibility for the teaching of health care and the prevention of illness to the patient and his family; or

(b) Assessment, nursing diagnosis, nursing care, and counsel of persons who are ill, injured or experiencing alterations in normal health processes; or

(c) The administration of medications and treatments as prescribed by a person licensed in this state to prescribe such medications and treatments; or

(d) The coordination and assistance in the delivery of a plan of health care with all members of the health team; or

(e) The teaching and supervision of other persons in the performance of any of the foregoing.

Section 335.016.8(a)–(e).

At the time of enactment of the Nursing Practice Act of 1975, the following statutes were repealed:

2.   A person practices professional nursing who for compensation or personal profit performs, *under the supervision and direction of a practitioner authorized to sign birth and death certificates,* any professional services requiring the application of principles of the biological, physical or social sciences and nursing skills in the care of the sick, in the prevention of disease or in the conservation of health.

Section 335.010.2, RSMo 1969 (emphasis added).

Nothing contained in this chapter shall be construed as conferring any authority on any person to practice medicine or osteopathy or to undertake the treatment or cure of disease.

Section 335.190, RSMo 1969.

The parties on both sides request that in construing these statutes we define and draw that thin and elusive line that separates the practice of medicine and the practice of professional nursing in modern day delivery of health services. A response to this invitation, in our opinion, would result in an avalanche of both medical and nursing malpractice suits alleging infringement of that line and would hinder rather than help with the delivery of health services to the general public. Our consideration will be limited to the narrow question of whether the acts of these nurses were permissible under § 335.016.8 or were prohibited by Chapter 334.

*   *   *

The legislature substantially revised the law affecting the nursing profession with enactment of the Nursing Practice Act of 1975. Perhaps the most significant feature of the Act was the redefinition of the term "professional nursing," which appears in § 335.016.8. Even a facile reading of that section reveals a manifest legislative desire to expand the scope of authorized nursing practices. Every witness at trial testified that the new definition of professional nursing is a broader definition than that in the former statute. A comparison with the prior definition vividly demonstrates this fact. Most apparent is the elimination of the requirement that a physician directly supervise nursing functions. Equally significant is the legislature's formulation of an open-ended definition of professional nursing. The earlier statute limited nursing practice to "services . . . in the care of the sick, in the prevention of disease or in the conservation of health." § 335.010.2, RSMo 1969. The 1975 Act not only describes a much broader spectrum of nursing functions, it qualifies this description with the phrase "including, but not limited to." We believe this phrase evidences an intent to avoid statutory constraints on the evolution of new functions for nurses delivering health services. Under § 335.016.8, a nurse may be permitted to assume responsibilities heretofore not considered to be within the field of professional nursing so long as those responsibilities are consistent with her or his "specialized education, judgment and skill based on knowledge and application of principles derived from the biological, physical, social and nursing sciences." § 335.016.8.

The acts of the nurses herein clearly fall within this legislative standard. All acts were performed pursuant to standing orders and protocols approved by physicians. Physician prepared standing orders and protocols for nurses and other paramedical personnel were so well established and accepted at the time of the adoption of the statute that the legislature could not have been unaware of the use of such practices. We see nothing in the statute purporting to limit or restrict their continued use.

Respondents made no challenge of the nurses' level of training or the degree of their skill. They challenge only the legal right of the nurses to undertake these acts. We believe the acts of the nurses are precisely the types of acts the legislature contemplated when it granted nurses the right to make assessments and nursing diagnoses. There can be no question that a nurse undertakes only a nursing diagnosis, as opposed to a medical diagnosis, when she or he finds or fails to find symptoms described by physicians in standing orders and protocols for the purpose of administering courses of treatment prescribed by the physician in such orders and protocols.

The Court believes that it is significant that while at least forty states have modernized and expanded their nursing practice laws during the past fifteen years neither counsel nor the Court have discovered any case challenging nurses' authority to act as the nurses herein acted.

* * * The hallmark of the professional is knowing the limits of one's professional knowledge. The nurse, either upon reaching the limit of her or his knowledge or upon reaching the limits prescribed for the nurse by the physician's standing orders and protocols, should refer the patient to the physician. There is no evidence that the assessments and diagnoses made by the nurses in this case exceeded such limits.

*   *   *

Having found that the nurses' acts were authorized by § 335.016.8, it follows that such acts do not constitute the unlawful practice of medicine for the reason that § 334.155 makes the provisions of Chapter 334 inapplicable "to nurses licensed and lawfully practicing their profession within the provisions of Chapter 335 RSMo."

This cause is reversed and remanded with instructions to enter judgment consistent with this opinion.

NOTES AND QUESTIONS

1.   If the board of nursing had issued regulations embracing the plaintiffs' practice within the authorized practice of nursing, under what standard would the court review such regulations if challenged? Would the regulation of the board of nursing prevent the board of medicine from proceeding against the nurses? In most such disputes, the key legal question is whether the board's rule is consistent with the state statute governing the specific practice or is otherwise arbitrary. For example, the Missouri Supreme Court reviewed a letter issued by the state medical board warning doctors that permitting CRNAs to perform a particular intervention would be a delegation to an unqualified individual and would, therefore, violate the state medical practice act. The Court relied on *Sermchief* and the state nursing practice act to hold that the state board of nursing held the authority to define the SOP of nurse anesthetists and that the state medical board lacked authority to restrict physicians in working with nurses. The nursing practice act permitted the two boards to issue joint rules, however. Mo. Assoc. of Nurse Anesthetists v. State Bd. of Registration, 343 S.W.3d 348 (Mo. 2011). See also Tex. Bd. of Chiropractic Examiners v. Tex. Med. Ass'n, 375 S.W.3d 464 (Tex.App. 2012).

2.   ANPs (including nurse midwives, nurse anesthetists, and other specialist nurse practitioners) view themselves as operating from a nursing mod-

el of health care and acting as independent practitioners who collaborate with physicians. Some advanced practice nursing statutes require a nurse practitioner, generally applicable to named nurse practitioner specialists, to practice under the supervision of a physician. See e.g., Cal. Bus. & Prof. Code § 2746.5(b) (certificate authorizes nurse midwife to practice nurse midwifery "under the supervision of a licensed physician and surgeon who has current practice or training in obstetrics"). Others recognize advanced practice nursing in collaboration with licensed physicians. See e.g., Mo. Ann. Stat. § 334.104, enacted after *Sermchief*, authorizing collaborative practice arrangements in the form of written agreements, protocols or standing orders, but describing the prescriptive authority of the nurse practitioner as delegated. Some describe the advanced nursing practice without reference to the participation of a supervisory or collaborative physician. For a review of state requirements, see Lauren E. Battaglia, Supervision and Collaboration Requirements: The Vulnerability of Nurse Practitioners and Its Implications for Retail Health, 87 Wash. U. L. Rev. 1127 (2010). See IOM, The Future of Nursing: Leading Change, Advancing Health (2011), criticizing restrictive SOP regulation, including supervision and restraining collaboration requirements, as diminishing access to care.

3.   Rather than viewing themselves as independent practitioners, PAs view themselves as working as physician delegates. General delegation exceptions in medical practice acts tend to be quite broad, as you saw in *Ruebke*. It is reasonable to assume that all general delegation statutory provisions include at least implied requirements that the physician assistant have adequate training and competency for the specific practice and that the supervising physician likewise have the competency to oversee the practice. Some states take an individualized approach and require the physician assistant or supervising physician to submit particular details about the specific position for review by an agency. See e.g., Md. Code Ann., Health Occ. § 15–302(d). Some limit the number of physician assistants a doctor may supervise. See e.g., Ohio Rev. Code Ann. § 4730.21. Other states simply define "supervision," with great variations among the states. See e.g., Mo. Ann. Stat. § 334.735(10).

4.   Authority to prescribe medication has been a major issue in debates over the appropriate scope of practice of nurses and physician assistants. Most states authorize prescribing by ANPs and many states, by PAs. Some state statutes set particular limits on prescribing. See, e.g., Cal. Bus. & Prof. Code § 2836.1(d), requiring physician supervision for the furnishing of drugs or devices by nurse practitioner; Cal. Bus. & Prof. Code § 3502.1, setting specific requirements for PAs. Some licensed health care professions, such as dentistry, commonly have prescribing authority, but others do not. Prescribing authority for licensed, doctorally trained psychologists, for example, has been particularly controversial.

5.   The Federal Trade Commission has long been active in contesting what it views as anticompetitive scope-of-practice regulation by health professions boards in establishing restrictive scope-of-practice standards. See, for

example, North Carolina Board of Dental Examiners v. FTC, 768 F.Supp.2d 818 (E.D.N.C. 2011). The FTC also issues letters of support or concern to state governments acting to expand or limit scope of practice.

PROBLEM: RETAIL CLINICS

A national pharmacy chain wants to open health clinics in several of their stores in your state. These health clinics would handle non-emergency cases, such as health screenings, vaccinations, and testing and treatment for a range of common infections, such as urinary tract infections and strep throat. Prices for services would be posted, and the clinics would be open for weekend and evening hours. The clinics would be staffed by ANPs and PAs with referral to hospitals and consultation with cooperative physicians in the area, as needed. The development of these "limited service clinics" is generating some controversy.

As the state's Attorney General, you represent both the medical board and the board of nursing, which are in conflict over these clinics. Like almost all states, your state doesn't have a statute regulating retail clinics. In the absence of a specific statute, the boards must rely on their current SOP statutes. In light of the conflict between the boards and among other stakeholders, you have decided to give negotiated rulemaking a try. This would involve gathering stakeholders to engage in assisting the boards in developing rules or regulations applicable to the clinics. Who has a stake in regulatory standards applicable to the scope of practice of nursing or physician assistants in this setting such that they would be involved in the negotiation process? What positions do you expect to be taken by the stakeholders you have identified? Where does the public interest lie?

Based on your experience with this exercise, do you believe that the ACA should have established a national standard for scope-of-practice regulation rather than relying on the states?

For more on retail clinics, see Kristin Schleiter, Retail Medical Clinics: Increasing Access to Low Cost Medical Care Amongst a Developing Legal Environment, 19 Annals Health L. 527 (2010); Lauren Battaglia, Supervision and Collaboration Requirements: The Vulnerability of Nurse Practitioners and Its Implications for Retail Health, 87 Wash. U. L. Rev. 1127 (2010).

CHAPTER 2

QUALITY CONTROL REGULATION OF HEALTH CARE INSTITUTIONS

■ ■ ■

I. INTRODUCTION

Patient safety and well-being are directly dependent on the quality of health care institutions as much as on the quality of the individual patient's doctor or nurse or therapist. The range of institutional factors that can pose a danger to patients extends from building design, maintenance, and sanitation through health information technology and management; from fiscal soundness through the selection, training, and monitoring of the individuals directly providing care; from staffing levels through food service. The patient safety movement, in fact, focuses on the quality of systems within health care organizations rather than on the behaviors of individual caregivers standing alone.

For most consumer goods and services, the market plays a significant role in setting an acceptable level of quality. State and federal governments are making efforts to strengthen the influence of the market over the quality of health care facilities. Most of these efforts have focused on collecting and posting quality data to allow consumers to select among facilities and to encourage facilities to take action to improve their performance on reportable factors.

Significant barriers to the working of the market around quality, such as a persistent lack of relevant, timely, and accurate information on quality measures; inability to evaluate available information; and decision making processes that place the choice of facility in the hands of someone other than the patient, still diminish the impact of consumer markets in health care. In the face of market failure, state and federal governments often use a "command-and-control" system of licensure or certification through which the government sets standards, monitors for compliance, and imposes sanctions for violations. The debate over whether the market or direct governmental regulation of performance is most effective in improving the quality of health care institutions has raged for decades.

State and federal governments are not the only players in the quality arena, of course. Private nonprofit organizations offer voluntary accreditation processes through which facilities can measure their compliance against standards established by their own segment of the industry. Facilities themselves also engage in internal quality assurance and quality improvement efforts, as a result of governmental mandate, accreditation standards, or risk of liability. Private tort and related litigation can create pressure for improvement. Finally, professionals working in health care facilities have ethical and legal obligations of their own to assure the quality of the organizations in which they care for patients.

These public and private mechanisms do not work the same across the wide variety of health care organizations and facilities that offer services to patients. The question of the appropriate mix of quality control mechanisms, therefore, does not produce a one-size-fits-all answer. Consider the following section.

II.   CONTEXT

The materials in this chapter focus primarily on nursing home care, a critically important and growing segment of our nation's health care sector. There are approximately 16,000 nursing homes in the United States with nearly 1.5 million people residing within them. CDC, Data Highlights from 2004 National Nursing Home Survey (2012). Nearly 3 million people receive care in a nursing home at some point during the year. CMS, 2012 Nursing Home Action Plan. In addition, the Affordable Care Act's (ACA) focus on coordination of care and payment restrictions on hospital readmissions both elevate the importance of nursing homes as an integral part of the health care system. Nursing homes are subject to a high degree of public quality control regulation by both federal and state governments, especially as compared to hospitals. The contrast between nursing homes and hospitals provides a framework for understanding the factors that determine under what circumstances particular forms of quality control efforts, whether reliant on the market or on government enforcement, are likely to be more or less effective.

A. DIFFERENCES BETWEEN HOSPITALS AND NURSING HOMES

Hospitals and nursing homes are quite distinctive organizations even though they both provide medical and nursing care for patients/residents. They differ in their patient population; their scope of services; the composition of their staffing; and other internal organizational characteristics. They are also subject to different external pressures.

Differences in Patient Population and Scope of Services

Part of what makes nursing homes unique in the health care system is their responsibility for the complete and total environment of their residents, typically over a very long time. Their involvement with the daily life of residents usually includes assistance in activities of daily living (ADLs), including bathing, dressing, toileting, and eating. Over a third of residents are totally dependent in toileting, for example, and 98% need assistance in at least one ADL. The majority of residents of a nursing home typically have resided in the facility for more than a year: approximately 20% of nursing home residents will stay for 6 months or less, but 30% stay 1–3 years and 12% stay for over 5 years. Nearly half of nursing home residents are over 85 years in age.

Nursing home residents typically bear multiple serious, chronic, and intractable medical conditions. With the increasing utilization of home care and assisted living, however, the average nursing home patient is much sicker than those of past decades. Their physical frailty often requires rigorous and sophisticated care. Younger people who are severely disabled or mentally ill also reside in nursing homes; and regulations addressing their needs are attracting more enforcement effort as well.

The choice of nursing home is unlike the choice of other consumer goods or even the selection of a doctor or a hospital. The selection of a nursing home generally is made under duress, often upon discharge from an unexpected hospitalization; with uncertainty as to the individual's prognosis which in turn influences whether the admission will be a short-stay rehabilitation admission or a longer term or permanent admission; and by an individual other than the patient/resident themselves often using persuasion or coercion to make the placement even when the patient/resident is competent. Once serious considerations (such as level of care, proximity to family due to potential lengthy stay, and whether the nursing home will accept Medicaid payments upon admission or once personal funds are exhausted) are accounted for, the remaining choice can be quite slim. Finally, the ability of a resident to transfer from a facility providing unsatisfactory services is limited as well due to the physical and mental frailty of the resident.

Differences in Organizational Structure

While hospitals developed in the United States as charitable institutions often under the direction of religious organizations, nursing homes developed originally as "mom-and-pop" enterprises, in which individuals boarded elderly persons in private homes. After the advent of Medicare and Medicaid, nursing homes attracted substantial activity from investors and were viewed primarily as real estate investments. Even today, most nursing homes are for-profit (61%), while most hospitals are not-for-profit. National for-profit chains own the majority of the for-profit nursing home industry.

Physicians are still largely absent from daily medical care in nursing homes, and professional nurses act primarily as administrators rather than direct care providers. Thus, nursing homes lack the history and embedded custom that strengthen internal professional peer review processes in hospitals. Further, hospitals have long subjected themselves to accreditation by the Joint Commission, while private accreditation of nursing homes is not as well established or influential.

In contrast to the hospital market, the demand for nursing home care exceeds available beds although demand may be ebbing somewhat in the face of more alternatives, such as assisted living facilities. Certificate of need programs in the majority of states restrict the number of nursing homes in a particular area on the theory that more beds will raise health care costs. Low supply and excess demand, however, have been associated with lower quality perhaps because of weak competition or because enforcement efforts are constrained by the lack of alternatives for continuing care of the residents.

Medicaid pays for nearly one million of the 1.5 million nursing home residents. Medicaid is generally the only source of public payment for long-term stays as Medicare covers very limited nursing home services, focusing on shorter stays for rehabilitation only. Because nursing home care consumes the bulk of the Medicaid dollar and Medicaid is the largest spending item in state budgets, Medicaid payment levels for nursing homes are contentious and many argue that they are inadequate. Research on whether increases in payment levels improve the quality of nursing home care, however, has produced mixed results.

Differences in the Impact of Private Litigation over Quality

Hospitals are subject to frequent and substantial lawsuits for injuries to patients. In contrast, the characteristics of the nursing home population generally limit their ability to bring suit themselves for harms suffered as a result of poor care or abuse. Causation may be difficult to prove. Physical injuries in very frail elderly persons may be caused either by ordinary touching or by poor care or abuse. Mental impairment makes many nursing home residents poor witnesses. Limited remaining life spans and disabilities minimize legally recognizable damages. They do not suffer lost wages, and medical costs for treatment of injuries generally will be covered by Medicaid or Medicare.

The incidence and success of private lawsuits against these facilities have increased significantly in some regions of the country, however, particularly in Florida and Texas. Some cases have produced very large verdicts, but these are rare. Even in states where private litigation has grown, the litigation is concentrated in just a few facilities. Litigation against nursing homes has raised concerns that such damage awards might divert resources for care, although this is not identified as an issue with hospital liability. Many states enacted legislation some years ago to encourage, through enhanced damages and attorney's fees, nursing home patients to pursue private remedies as a means of enforcing regulatory standards. Many states have since amended these statutes, limiting damages and attorney's fees or subjecting such claims to limitations included in general tort reform legislative packages.

Finally, nursing homes frequently include binding arbitration clauses in admission agreements. These clauses are enforceable if they meet the standards applicable to binding arbitration generally, although significant concerns regarding agreement to the clause and other issues can arise in the nursing home context. See Marmet Health Care Center, Inc. v. Brown, 132 S.Ct. 1201 (2012), relying on the Federal Arbitration Act (FAA) in reversing a decision of the West Virginia Supreme Court that binding arbitration clauses in nursing home admission agreements categorically violated public policy and were unenforceable. But see, Brown v. Genesis Healthcare Corp., 729 S.E.2d 217 (W.Va. 2012), holding the same clauses to be unenforceable under common law unconscionability applicable to all contracts and, therefore, not preempted by the FAA.

B. DEFINING QUALITY

What constitutes quality in health care? Avedis Donabedian, using the management of a specific episode of illness by a physician as the model, identifies three components on which the quality of care can be measured: the technical, the interpersonal, and amenities. He defines the technical as "the application of the science and technology of medicine, and of the other health sciences, to the management" of the patient's health issue. He defines the interpersonal as "the social and psychological interaction between client and practitioner." Finally, he categorizes as amenities "the more intimate aspects of the settings in which care is provided," although he notes that these may be integral to the care itself. The Definition of Quality and Approaches to Its Assessment (Vol. 1) (1980).

Is each of Donabedian's three factors equally important, or might one take precedence over the others? Might it depend on the context and goals of care? Would you expect that a definition of quality care might differ as between emergency room care and nursing home care?

What is the role of the patient (or "resident," in the case of nursing homes) and her values in the delivery of medical care? Donabedian concludes that quality care is that kind of care which is expected to maximize an inclusive measure of patient welfare, after one has taken account of the balance of expected gains and losses that attend the process of care in all its parts.

In what Donabedian called an "absolutist" medical view, the doctor best balances the benefits and risks of care; and other factors, including "the patient's expectations and valuations" are regarded as impeding or facilitating quality care. The alternative view, called "individualized" by Donabedian, holds that if advancing the patient's welfare is paramount, then "it is inevitable that the patient must share with the practitioner" the work of defining the goals of care and the evaluation of comparative risks and benefits.

Patient participation in weighing risks and benefits is familiar from informed consent for medical treatment. The same process is also quite relevant to measures of institutional quality. In fact, the movement for "patient-centered care," captured in parts of the Affordable Care Act, aims at shifting institutional measures of quality away from universal or patient-neutral standards toward standards that more directly account for patients' and residents' choices and values.

C. ASSESSING QUALITY

Once again, Donabedian provides a classic analysis of the work of quality assessment:

[T]here are three major approaches to quality assessment: "structure," "process," and "outcome." This three-fold approach is possible because there is a fundamental functional relationship among the three elements, which can be shown schematically as follows:

Structure→Process→Outcome

This means that structural characteristics of the settings in which care takes place have a propensity to influence the process of care so that its quality is diminished or enhanced. Similarly, changes in the process of care, including variations in its quality, will influence the effect of care on health status, broadly defined. The Definition of Quality and Approaches to Its Assessment, Vol. 1 (1980) 84.

Donabedian defines structural standards for care as "the human, physical, and financial resources that are needed to provide . . . care." Structural standards for quality perhaps are the easiest to implement, and for this reason much of quality control regulation in the past has focused on this approach. Personnel, equipment, and buildings can be counted or described; internal regulations and staff organization measured against specific criteria; and budgets critiqued. Quantifiable and concrete structural standards are particularly useful in contentious enforcement systems because there is less concern with the human factor, or variability, in the inspection process. Unfortunately, structural standards don't measure whether the care is actually any good, only that the tools required for good care are present.

Process standards relate directly to the activities that take place in the delivery of care. For example, are orders for medication written properly; are they filled and delivered to patients accurately? Are caregivers washing their hands? Is the intervention the one accepted as appropriate for that medical condition? Donabedian favored process standards because they relate directly to what happens in care. In that way, they are more direct than structural standards.

The current wave of quality control efforts, however, is quite firmly shifting the emphasis to outcomes standards. The Affordable Care Act launched several initiatives to research and implement outcomes standards for health care providers. For example, the Act established the Center for Quality Improvement and Patient Safety, which will develop research for development of standards, and the Patient–Centered Outcomes Research Institute. The ACA also required HHS to develop outcome measurements for hospitals, physicians, and other providers for the treatment of particular conditions. In addition, payment systems are increasingly orienting around performance as measured by certain outcomes.

In an important way, outcomes standards offset a critical weakness in process standards for health care; i.e., that a good deal of medical care is not grounded firmly in evidence, but rather relies on professional custom and consensus. Outcomes instead measure the actual improvement or decline in the patient's health status. Outcome measures also have their problems, however: the onset, duration, and extent of desired outcomes are often hard to specify; it is often hard to credit a good outcome to a specific intervention; and the outcome is often known too late to affect practice. At times, convenience outweighs significance, and outcomes measurements can focus on items that are easily measurable but less important to quality care. Furthermore, the measurement of outcomes must be sensitive to variations other than quality that may determine outcomes. Consider mortality rates among hospitals, which HHS gathers and releases to the public. What variables need to be controlled if this outcome measure is to reflect comparative quality among hospitals?

The maturing of health informatics provides rich opportunities for studying the outcomes of care. Data mining is potentially a powerful new addition to quality monitoring, moving beyond tracking a particular patient to a satellite view of an entire patient population over time. Using pattern recognition algorithms, data mining can be set to search databases to investigate particular problems. It can spot trends in infections using infection surveillance results, or it can be used in a broad search strategy to mine for hidden problems or patterns that are fixable.

III. REGULATORY PROCESS

A. NURSING HOMES: LICENSURE AND MEDICARE/MEDICAID CERTIFICATION

Nursing homes that wish to receive payment for services to Medicare or Medicaid beneficiaries must be licensed by the state and must meet federal standards in order to be certified to enter into a provider agreement with those programs. Medicare and Medicaid standards apply to every resident in the facility, however, and not only to beneficiaries. If a nursing facility chooses not to participate in Medicare or Medicaid, however, it will be subject only to state licensure requirements. Only approximately one-tenth of 1% of nursing homes does not participate in either Medicare or Medicaid.

Until the late 1980s, the federal agency responsible for Medicare and Medicaid certification (now the Centers for Medicare & Medicaid Services (CMS) in HHS) largely deferred to the state licensure systems to set standards and monitor quality. With federal nursing home reform in 1987 (the federal Nursing Home Reform Act), however, the federal government established standards and methods for the inspection and sanctions process to be used to enforce Medicare and Medicaid requirements, although it continues to rely substantially on the states for on-site inspections. State licensure standards and inspection processes at this point largely parallel the Medicare and Medicaid certification system, but can differ.

B. STANDARD SETTING, INSPECTION, AND SANCTIONS

The regulatory process—whether licensure or Medicare/Medicaid certification—involves three functions: standard setting; inspection (known as "survey" in nursing home regulation); and sanctions. For a comprehensive empirical and bibliographic analysis of the history and current status of federal nursing home regulation, see Philip Aka et al., Political Factors and Enforcement of the Nursing Home Regulatory Regime, 24 J. L. & Health 1 (2011).

1. Standard Setting

IN RE THE ESTATE OF MICHAEL PATRICK SMITH V. HECKLER

United States Court of Appeals, Tenth Circuit, 1984.
747 F.2d 583.

McKAY, CIRCUIT JUDGE:

Plaintiffs * * * alleged that the Secretary of Health and Human Services (Secretary) has a statutory duty under Title XIX of the Social Security Act, 42 U.S.C.A. §§ 1396–1396n * * * to develop and implement a system of nursing home review and enforcement designed to ensure that Medicaid recipients residing in Medicaid-certified nursing homes actually receive the optimal medical and psychosocial care that they are entitled to under the Act. The plaintiffs contended that the enforcement system developed by the Secretary is "facility-oriented," not "patient-oriented" and thereby fails to meet the statutory mandate. The district court found that although a patient care or "patient-oriented" management system is feasible, the Secretary does not have a duty to introduce and require the use of such a system. [ ]

The primary issue on appeal is whether the trial court erred in finding that the Secretary does not have a statutory duty to develop and implement a system of nursing home review and enforcement, which focuses on and ensures high quality patient care. * * *

Background

[P]laintiffs instituted the lawsuit in an effort to improve the deplorable conditions at many nursing homes. They presented evidence of the lack of adequate medical care and of the widespread knowledge that care is inadequate. Indeed, the district court concluded that care and life in some nursing homes is so bad that the homes "could be characterized as orphanages for the aged." [ ]

*   *   *

The Medicaid Act

An understanding of the Medicaid Act (the Act) is essential to understand plaintiffs' contentions. The purpose of the Act is to enable the federal government to assist states in providing medical assistance to "aged, blind or disabled individuals, whose income and resources are insufficient to meet the costs of necessary medical services, and . . . rehabilitation and other services to help such . . . individuals to attain or retain capabilities for independence or self care." [ ] To receive funding, a state must submit to the Secretary and have approved by the Secretary, a plan for medical assistance, which meets the requirements of [the Act].

* * * A state seeking plan approval must establish or designate a single state agency to administer or supervise administration of the state plan, [ ], and must provide reports and information as the Secretary may require. [ ] Further, the state agency is responsible for establishing and maintaining health standards for institutions where the recipients of the medical assistance under the plan receive care or services. [ ] The plan must include descriptions of the standards and methods the state will use to assure that medical or remedial care services provided to the recipients "are of high quality." [ ]

The state plan must also provide "for a regular program of medical review . . . of each patient's need for skilled nursing facility care . . . , a written plan of care, and, where applicable, a plan of rehabilitation prior to admission to a skilled nursing facility. . . ." [ ] Further, the plan must provide for periodic inspections by medical review teams of:

> (i) the care being provided in such nursing facilities . . . to persons receiving assistance under the State plan; (ii) with respect to each of the patients receiving such care, the adequacy of the services available in particular nursing facilities . . . to meet the current health needs and promote the maximum physical well-being of patients receiving care in such facilities . . . ; (iii) the necessity and desirability of continued placement of such patients in such nursing facilities . . . ; and (iv) the feasibility of meeting their health care needs through alternative institutional or non-institutional services. [ ]

The state plan must provide that any skilled nursing facility receiving payment comply with [the Act]. . . . The key requirement for purposes of this lawsuit is that a skilled nursing facility must meet "such other conditions relating to the health and safety of individuals who are furnished services in such institution or relating to the physical facilities thereof as the Secretary may find necessary. . . ." [ ]

The state plan must provide for the appropriate state agency to establish a plan, consistent with regulations prescribed by the Secretary, for professional health personnel to review the appropriateness and quality of care and services furnished to Medicaid recipients. [ ] The appropriate state agency must determine on an ongoing basis whether participating institutions meet the requirements for continued participation in the Medicaid program. [ ] While the state has the initial responsibility for determining whether institutions are meeting the conditions of participation, [the Act] gives the Secretary the authority to "look behind" the state's determination of facility compliance, and make an independent and binding determination of whether institutions meet the requirements for participation in the state Medicaid plan. Thus, the state is responsible for conducting the review of facilities to determine whether they comply with the state plan. In conducting the review, however, the states must use federal standards, forms, methods, and procedures. * * *

Implementing Regulations

* * * Congress gave the Secretary a general mandate to promulgate rules and regulations necessary to the efficient administration of the functions with which the Secretary is charged by the Act. [ ] Pursuant to this mandate the Secretary has promulgated standards for the care to be provided by skilled nursing facilities and intermediate care facilities. [ ] * * *

The Secretary has established a procedure for determining whether state plans comply with the standards set out in the regulations. This enforcement mechanism is known as the "survey/certification" inspection system. Under this system, the states conduct reviews of nursing homes pursuant to [the Act]. The Secretary then determines, on the basis of the survey results, whether the nursing home surveyed is eligible for certification and, thus, eligible for Medicaid funds. The states must use federal standards, forms, methods, and procedures in conducting the survey. [ ] At issue in this case is the form SSA–1569, [ ], which the Secretary requires the states to use to show that the nursing homes participating in Medicaid under an approved state plan meet the conditions of participation contained in the Act and the regulations. Plaintiffs contend that the form is "facility-oriented," in that it focuses on the theoretical capability of the facility to provide high quality care, rather than "patient-oriented," which would focus on the care actually provided. * * *

The Plaintiffs' Claims

* * *

The plaintiffs do not challenge the substantive medical standards, or "conditions of participation," which have been adopted by the Secretary and which states must satisfy to have their plans approved. [ ] Rather, plaintiffs challenge the enforcement mechanism the Secretary has established. The plaintiffs contend that the federal forms, form SSA–1569 in particular, which states are required to use, evaluate only the physical facilities and theoretical capability to render quality care. The surveys assess the care provided almost totally on the basis of the records, documentation, and written policies of the facility being reviewed. [ ] Further, out of the 541 questions contained in the Secretary's form SSA–1569 which must be answered by state survey and certification inspection teams, only 30 are "even marginally related to patient care or might require any patient observation. ... " [ ] Plaintiffs contend that the enforcement mechanism's focus on the facility, rather than on the care actually provided in the facility, results only in "paper compliance" with the substantive standards of the Act. Thus, plaintiffs contend, the Secretary has violated her statutory duty to assure that federal Medicaid monies are paid only to facilities, which meet the substantive standards of the Act—facilities which actually provide high quality medical, rehabilitative, and psychosocial care to resident Medicaid recipients.

The District Court's Holding

[T]he district court found the type of patient care management system advocated by plaintiffs clearly feasible and characterized the current enforcement system as "facility-oriented." [ ] However, the court concluded that the failure to implement and require the use of a "patient-oriented" system is not a violation of the Secretary's statutory duty. * * *

*   *   *

The Secretary's Duty

* * * The Secretary of Health and Human Services has a duty to establish a system to adequately inform herself as to whether the facilities receiving federal money are satisfying the requirements of the Act, including providing high quality patient care. This duty to be adequately informed is not only a duty to be informed at the time a facility is originally certified, but is a duty of continued supervision.

Nothing in the Medicaid Act indicates that Congress intended the physical facilities to be the end product. Rather, the purpose of the Act is to provide medical assistance and rehabilitative services. [ ] The Act repeatedly focuses on the care to be provided, with facilities being only part of that care. For example, the Act provides that health standards are to be developed and maintained [ ], and that states must inform the Secretary what methods they will use to assure high quality care. [ ] In addition to the "adequacy of the services available," the periodic inspections must address "the care being provided" in nursing facilities. [ ] State plans must provide review of the "appropriateness and quality of care and services furnished," [ ], and do so on an ongoing basis. [ ]

* * * The Secretary, not the states, determines which facilities are eligible for federal funds. [ ] While participation in the program is voluntary, states who choose to participate must comply with federal statutory requirements. [ ] The inspections may be conducted by the states, but the Secretary approves or disapproves the state's plan for review. Further, the inspections must be made with federal forms, procedures, and methods.

It would be anomalous to hold that the Secretary has a duty to determine whether a state plan meets the standards of the Act while holding that the Secretary can certify facilities without informing herself as to whether the facilities actually perform the functions required by the state

plan. The Secretary has a duty to ensure more than paper compliance.
* * *

* * *

* * * Congress gave the Secretary authority to promulgate regulations to achieve the functions with which she is charged. The "look-behind" provision and its legislative history clearly show that Congress intended the Secretary to be responsible for assuring that federal Medicaid money is given only to those institutions that actually comply with Medicaid requirements. The Act's requirements include providing high quality medical care and rehabilitative services. In fact, the quality of the care provided to the aged is the focus of the Act. Being charged with this function, we must conclude that a failure to promulgate regulations that allow the Secretary to remain informed, on a continuing basis, as to whether facilities receiving federal money are meeting the requirements of the Act, is an abdication of the Secretary's duty. * * *

* * * Having determined that the purpose and the focus of the Act is to provide high quality medical care, we conclude that by promulgating a facility-oriented enforcement system the Secretary has failed to follow that focus and such failure is arbitrary and capricious. [ ]

Reversed and Remanded.

NOTES AND QUESTIONS

1.   How do the plaintiffs' claims in *Smith* relate to the Donabedian triad for assessing quality, described above? Which of the three types of standards are subject to criticism for measuring only the capacity for quality care? Are those types of standards irrelevant or merely inadequate? How does the conflict over standards in *Smith* relate to the ACA's emphasis on "patient-centered care" and outcomes?

2.   After *Smith*, Congress enacted the federal Nursing Home Reform Act (NHRA), commonly also referred to as OBRA 1987, which still provides the core of federal regulation of nursing homes. The NHRA delivered a comprehensive and significant change in federal standards, surveillance methods, and enforcement. It shifted the standards toward focusing on the actual care received by residents and included in the inspection/survey process a requirement that the survey team actually interview a number of residents. The standard-setting effort continues almost thirty years later, however, and has progressed through several subsequent reforms. Why can't regulators get this right once and for all? Is there new knowledge that requires change? Does the industry have too much influence on standards? Is the nursing home population changing? Are there competing values at stake?

Prior to the mid-1980s, for example, physically restraining a nursing home resident was viewed as protecting the patient by preventing falls. It was also believed that a nursing home would be liable for injuries due to falls if it did not restrain patients. Research in the field radically changed that view. The standards on restraints in the NHRA responded to medical and legal research proving that physical restraints counterintuitively caused injuries rather than protecting patients; and that nursing homes indeed faced liability risks for falls, but that the cases did not support the use of restraints as a preventive measure. See the Problem: Residents' Rights, below.

3.   The CMS Nursing Home Quality Initiative (NHQI) identifies quality measurements (QMs) for nursing homes, using data collected in the Minimum Data Set (an instrument requiring each facility to collect and report standardized data on each resident). For long-stay residents, the QMs are the percentage of residents with infections, pain, pressure sores (with residents allocated into low-risk and high-risk groups), physical restraints, and loss of ability in basic daily tasks. Data on the QMs are posted on the publicly accessible Nursing Home Compare website (operated by CMS, which lists each nursing home certified by Medicare or Medicaid and includes quality data on a number of factors) and may eventually be used to change the reimbursement system to value-based payments. If you were an administrator of a nursing home and wanted to improve your performance on these outcome measures, you might increase or reorganize staff effort or other resources. Is it clear that the incentives produced by outcomes standards will always produce positive results? See discussion in Section II.C, above. In another quality improvement initiative, the ACA extended the Medicare Quality Assessment and Performance Improvement Program (QAPI) to nursing homes, requiring nursing homes to conduct an internal quality assurance program that is data-driven and systems-oriented. CMS is testing the program in selected facilities.

4.   The court's opinion in *Smith* describes the allocation of authority in the federal-state Medicaid quality control program. Exactly which functions are allocated to the state and which to the federal government? Is the federal-state effort duplicative and inefficient? Should Congress consider requiring that nursing facilities receiving Medicaid or Medicare dollars merely be licensed by the state? What is the justification for the federal role in this situation?

PROBLEM: RESIDENTS' RIGHTS

Assume that you are the attorney for Pine Acres Nursing Home, located in an older section of the city. The administrator has approached you regarding problems with certain patients. One patient, Francis Scott, aged 88, has been a resident of the facility for a few months. Mr. Scott's mental and physical condition has been deteriorating slowly for several years and much more rapidly in the past six months. His family placed him in the nursing home because they wanted him to be safe. They were concerned because he had often left his apartment and become totally lost on the way back. Mr. Scott's family always promptly pays the monthly fee. Mr. Scott is angry about the placement, tends to be rude to staff, and insists on walking through the hallways and around the fenced-in grounds of the facility on his own. He has always been an early riser and likes to take his shower at the crack of dawn. He refuses to be assisted in showering by a nurses' aide. In addition, his friends from the neighborhood like to visit. They like to play pinochle when they come, and they usually bring a six-pack.

Another patient, Emma Kaitz, has fallen twice, apparently while trying to get out of bed. The staff is very concerned that she will be hurt. The physician who is medical director of the facility will write an order for restraints "as needed" for any resident upon the request of the director of nursing. Mrs. Kaitz's daughter is willing to try whatever the doctor advises. The staff have begun using "soft restraints" (cloth straps on her wrists) tied to the bedrails, but Mrs. Kaitz becomes agitated and cries. She says she feels like a dog when they tie her up. Other times they just use the bedrails alone. When she becomes agitated, she is given a sedative to help her relax, but it also tends to make her appear confused. To avoid the agitation as much as possible during the day, they have been able to position her wheelchair so that she can't get out by herself. She stops trying after a while and becomes so relaxed she nods off.

The administrator wants to know what he can do. What would you advise this administrator? Can he restrict the visiting hours for Mr. Scott? Can he require Mr. Scott to be assisted in the shower? Can Mr. Scott be transferred or discharged? Is the facility providing quality care for Mrs. Kaitz? How should an inspector treat Mr. Scott's and Mrs. Kaitz's complaints? What does your nursing home client expect of you here? What role should you play in regard to quality of care standards?

The text that follows includes excerpts from the Residents' Rights section of the Medicaid statute; the regulation on the use of physical restraints; and the interpretive guidelines on physical restraints provided to surveyors for the inspection of Medicaid facilities.

42 U.S.C.A. § 1396r

(b)(1) QUALITY OF LIFE.—

(A) IN GENERAL.—A nursing facility must care for its residents in such a manner and in such an environment as will promote maintenance or enhancement of the quality of life of each resident.

* * *

(c) REQUIREMENTS RELATING TO RESIDENTS' RIGHTS—

(1) GENERAL RIGHTS.—

(A) SPECIFIED RIGHTS.—A nursing facility must protect and promote the rights of each resident, including each of the following rights:

(i) FREE CHOICE.—The right to choose a personal attending physician, to be fully informed in advance about care and treatment that may affect the resident's well-being, and (except with respect to a resident adjudged incompetent) to participate in planning care and treatment or changes in care and treatment.

(ii) FREE FROM RESTRAINTS.—The right to be free from physical or mental abuse, corporal punishment, involuntary seclusion, and any physical or chemical restraints imposed for purposes of discipline or convenience and not required to treat the resident's medical symptoms. Restraints may only be imposed—

(I) to ensure the physical safety of the resident or other residents, and

(II) only upon the written order of a physician that specifies the duration and circumstances under which the restraints are to be used (except in emergency circumstances specified by the Secretary until such an order could reasonably be obtained).

(iii) PRIVACY.—The right to privacy with regard to accommodations, medical treatment, written and telephonic communications, visits, and meetings of family and of resident groups. [Does not require private rooms.]

(v) ACCOMMODATION OF NEEDS.—The right—

(I) to reside and receive services with reasonable accommodations of individual needs and preferences, except where the health or safety of the individual or other residents would be endangered, and

(II) to receive notice before the room or roommate of the resident in the facility is changed.

*   *   *

(viii) PARTICIPATION IN OTHER ACTIVITIES.—The right of the resident to participate in social, religious, and community activities that do not interfere with the rights of other residents in the facility.

*   *   *

(D) USE OF PSYCHOPHARMACOLOGIC DRUGS.

Psychopharmacologic drugs may be administered only on the orders of a physician and only as part of a plan (included in the written plan of care * * *) designed to eliminate or modify the symptoms for which the drugs are prescribed and only if, at least annually an independent, external consultant reviews the appropriateness of the drug plan of each resident receiving such drugs.

(2) TRANSFER AND DISCHARGE RIGHTS.—

(A) IN GENERAL.—A nursing facility must permit each resident to remain in the facility and must not transfer or discharge the resident from the facility unless—

(i) the transfer or discharge is necessary to meet the resident's welfare and the resident's welfare cannot be met in the facility;

(ii) the transfer or discharge is appropriate because the resident's health has improved sufficiently so the resident no longer needs the services provided by the facility;

(iii) the safety of individuals in the facility is endangered;

(iv) the health of individuals in the facility would otherwise be endangered;

(v) the resident has failed, after reasonable and appropriate notice, to pay * * * for a stay at the facility; or

(vi) the facility ceases to operate. [The ACA added new requirements for facilities that are closing. 42 U.S.C.A. § 1320a–7j(h).]

* * *

(B) PRE–TRANSFER AND PRE–DISCHARGE NOTICE.—

(i) IN GENERAL.—Before effecting a transfer or discharge of a resident, a nursing facility must—

(I) notify the resident (and, if known, an immediate family member of the resident or legal representative) of the transfer or discharge and the reasons therefore,

(II) record the reasons in the resident's clinical record * * * and

(III) include in the notice the items described in clause (iii), [concerning appeal of transfer].

[The statute specifies the timing of the required notice. It also requires the state to establish a hearing process for transfers and discharges contested by the resident or surrogate. The ACA added required notice to the State with a plan for relocation of residents and a potential fine against a noncompliant administrator.]

(3) ACCESS AND VISITATION RIGHTS.—A nursing facility must—

(A) permit immediate access to any resident by any representative of the Secretary, by any representative of the State, by an ombudsman * * * , or by the resident's individual physician;

(B) permit immediate access to a resident, subject to the resident's right to deny or withdraw consent at any time, by immediate family or other relatives of the resident;

(C) permit immediate access to a resident, subject to reasonable restrictions and the resident's right to deny or withdraw consent at any time, by others who are visiting with the consent of the resident;

(D) permit reasonable access to a resident by any entity or individual that provides health, social, legal, or other services to the resident, subject to the resident's right to deny or withdraw consent at any time; and

(E) permit representatives of the State ombudsman * * * , with the permission of the resident (or the resident's legal representative) and consistent with State law, to examine a resident's clinical records.

(4) EQUAL ACCESS TO QUALITY CARE.—

A nursing facility must establish and maintain identical policies and practices regarding transfer, discharge and the provision of services * * * for all individuals regardless of source of payment.

42 C.F.R. § 483.13(a)

Restraints. The resident has the right to be free from any physical or chemical restraints imposed for purposes of discipline or convenience, and not required to treat the resident's medical symptoms.

GUIDANCE TO SURVEYORS—LONG TERM CARE FACILITIES

CMS State Operations Manual, Appendix PP, § 483.13(a) (Jan. 7, 2011)

* * *

"Convenience" is defined as any action taken by the facility to control a resident's behavior or manage a resident's behavior with a lesser amount of effort by the facility and not in the resident's best interest.

Restraints may not be used for staff convenience. However, if the resident needs emergency care, restraints may be used for brief periods to permit medical treatment to proceed unless the facility has a notice indicating that the resident has previously made a valid refusal of the treatment in question. If a resident's unanticipated violent or aggressive behavior places him/her or others in imminent danger, the resident does not have the right to refuse the use of restraints. In this situation, the use of restraints is a measure of last resort to protect the safety of the resident or others and must not extend beyond the immediate episode. * * *

"Physical Restraints" are defined as any manual method or physical or mechanical device, material, or equipment attached or adjacent to the resident's body that the individual cannot remove easily which restricts freedom of movement or normal access to one's body.

"Physical restraints" include, but are not limited to, leg restraints, arm restraints, hand mitts, soft ties or vests, lap cushions, and lap trays the resident cannot remove easily. Also included as restraints are facility practices that meet the definition of a restraint, such as:

- Using side rails that keep a resident from voluntarily getting out of bed;

- Tucking in or using velcro to hold a sheet, fabric, or clothing tightly so that a resident's movement is restricted;

- Using devices in conjunction with a chair, such as trays, tables, bars or belts, that the resident can not remove easily, that prevent the resident from rising;

- Placing a resident in a chair that prevents a resident from rising; and placing a chair or bed so close to a wall that the wall prevents the resident from rising out of the chair or voluntarily getting out of bed.

* * *

The same device may have the effect of restraining one individual but not another, depending on the individual resident's condition and circumstances. For example, partial rails may assist one resident to enter and exit the bed independently while acting as a restraint for another.

* * *

* * * The resident's subjective symptoms may not be used as the sole basis for using a restraint. Before a resident is restrained, the facility must determine the presence of a specific medical symptom that would require the use of restraints, and how the use of restraints would treat the medical symptom, protect the resident's safety, and assist the resident in attaining or maintaining his or her highest practicable level of physical and psychosocial well-being.

* * * While there must be a physician's order reflecting the presence of a medical symptom, CMS will hold the facility ultimately accountable for the appropriateness of that determination. The physician's order alone is not sufficient to warrant the use of the restraint. * * *

In order for the resident to be fully informed, the facility must explain, in the context of the individual resident's condition and circumstances, the potential risks and benefits of all options under consideration including using a restraint, not using a restraint, and alternatives to restraint use. * * * In addition, the facility must also explain the potential negative outcomes of restraint use which include, but are not limited to, declines in the resident's physical functioning (e.g., ability to ambulate) and muscle condition, contractures, increased incidence of infections and development of pressure sores/ulcers, delirium, agitation, and incontinence. * * * Restraints have been found in some cases to increase the incidence of falls or head trauma due to falls and other accidents (e.g., strangulation, entrapment). Finally, residents who are restrained may face a loss of autonomy, dignity and self respect, and may show symptoms of withdrawal, depression, or reduced social contact. * * *

In the case of a resident who is incapable of making a decision, the legal surrogate or representative may exercise this right based on the same information that would have been provided to the resident. [ ] However, the legal surrogate or representative cannot give permission to use restraints for the sake of discipline or staff convenience or when the restraint is not necessary to treat the resident's medical symptoms. * * *

2. Survey and Inspection

An effective quality-control regulatory system requires an effective inspection (survey) process that, with an acceptable degree of accuracy, detects and documents violations of standards. Providers tend to believe that nursing home surveyors are overly aggressive; resident advocates, that they are too lax. See Edward Miller & Vincent Mor, Balancing Regulatory Controls and Incentives: Toward Smarter and More Transparent Oversight in Long–Term Care, 33 J. Health Pol. Pol'y & L. 249 (2008).

Both providers and resident advocates agree that there is a high degree of variability among surveyors in citations for violations and among the states in terms of the average number of citations per facility. Does this variation reflect the quality of facilities or of inspection processes? What role should the courts play in the question of surveyor discretion or inconsistency? Should the survey standards be more rigid, or more flexible?

CMS requires more frequent surveys of facilities that are substantially in noncompliance with federal standards. The Affordable Care Act codifies this practice and requires surveys of "Special Focus Facilities" (SFF) at least every six months. 42 U.S.C. § 1395i–3(f)(8). The ACA also enhances the complaint filing and investigation system in long-term care. States are required to establish a complaint resolution process that tracks complaints, determines the severity of the complaint to set priority for investigation, and sets deadlines for notifying complainants of the outcome. 42 U.S.C. § 1395i–3(i) and 1320a–7j(f).

What relationship should the surveyor establish with the facility? Is the surveyor a consultant or advisor? For a critique of the enforcement-oriented survey process, see John Braithwaite et al., Regulating Aged Care: Ritualism and The New Pyramid (2007).

3. Sanctions

Intermediate sanctions were first developed in state nursing home licensure legislation and were adopted subsequently by Congress in OBRA 1987. In Vencor Nursing Ctrs. v. Shalala, 63 F. Supp.2d 1 (D.D.C. 1999), the court describes the rationale for intermediate sanctions:

> In enacting the enforcement provisions to the Medicare and Medicaid Acts [in OBRA 1987], Congress expressly wished to expand the panoply of remedies available to HHS. [ ]. Committee reports noted with concern the "yo-yo" phenomenon in which noncomplying facilities temporarily correct their deficiencies before an on-site survey and then quickly lapse into noncompliance until the next review. [ ]. [T]he new version of the statute ameliorates this problem by giving HHS a set of intermediate sanc-

tions to choose from rather than the extreme choices of termination or no sanction.

Intermediate sanctions currently available include civil fines, temporary
management, denial of payment for admissions, and so on. The financial
penalties, in particular, can be fine-tuned to match the severity of the violations. In theory, to raise the risk of violating standards, fines would be
levied whether or not the problem is corrected after inspection and citation.

The "yo-yo" problem persists, however. Some believe that recalcitrant facilities treat civil fines as a cost of doing business. In addition,
federal and state agencies still favor correction over punitive measures to
avoid closing or causing a facility to close. Closure of a nursing home puts
very sick, very frail residents at risk during transfer, and the shortage of
nursing homes in some areas makes locating alternative care a challenge.

State and federal health care fraud agencies have stepped up their
actions against nursing homes. These agencies prosecute on the basis
that deficiencies in the quality of care amount to fraud against the government because the facilities failed to deliver what the government paid
for. See Chapter 13.

IV. PRIVATE ACCREDITATION OF HEALTH CARE FACILITIES

Private accreditation is a nongovernmental, voluntary activity typically conducted by not-for-profit associations. As a voluntary process, accreditation may be viewed as a private communicative device, providing
the accredited health care entity with a seal of approval—a method for
communicating in shorthand that it meets standards established by an
external organization. In practice, however, there is a much closer marriage between some private accreditation programs and government regulation of health care facilities. This is especially true of the Joint Commission hospital accreditation program.

Both state and federal governments rely to a great extent on accreditation in their hospital licensure and Medicare/Medicaid hospital certification programs. Most states have incorporated the Commission's accreditation program into their hospital licensure standards. See e.g., Tex.
Health & Safety Code § 222.024, exempting Joint Commission accredited
hospitals from annual licensure inspection. Under the Medicare statute,
Joint Commission accredited hospitals are deemed to have met requirements for Medicare certification. Although the Secretary retains a look-
behind authority, the Joint Commission substitutes for the routine surveillance process.

Originally, the acceptance of accreditation by the Medicare program was designed to entice an adequate number of hospitals to participate in the then-new Medicare program. That original rationale has dissipated as hospitals have become much more dependent on Medicare payments. At the same time, the federal government's reliance on private accreditation as a substitute for routine government surveillance has expanded considerably beyond the original hospital setting and now extends to clinical laboratories and home health care, among others.

What might explain this extensive reliance on private organizations for public regulation? Some argue that private accreditation more effectively encourages voluntary compliance and avoids some of the prosecutorial environment of a government-conducted inspection program. Furthermore, and perhaps more pragmatically, deemed status for accreditation allows the government to shift the cost of the inspection process because facilities pay for the costs of accreditation, including the site visit. The Joint Commission must reapply periodically for deemed status. Deemed status for Medicare certification still does not extend to nursing homes.

Private accreditation programs traditionally have engaged in practices that encourage voluntary subscription to the accreditation program. Standards established by accreditation programs, which are often dominated by professionals in the industry rather than consumer groups, may differ from those set by a process that arguably fosters broader public participation. With the Joint Commission accrediting program for hospitals, in particular, governance and policymaking are dominated by physician organization members such as the AMA. The Joint Commission accreditation site visit process is explicitly consultative in nature.

The Joint Commission has had a tremendous influence on the operation of hospitals. The Joint Commission, for example, established the framework for staff privileges and credentialing in hospitals, as described in Chapter 11, and continues to be an important arena for change in those processes. The Joint Commission's embrace of the patient safety movement, described in Chapter 6, furthered diffusion of the movement's principles into hospitals. The Joint Commission's "Sentinel Event" initiative, for example, encouraged facilities to report errors and root cause analyses for the benefit of systemic change in areas such as wrong-site surgery and medication errors and has spawned a number of refinements over the years.

For a discussion of the relation between private accreditation and public regulation, see Jody Freeman, The Private Role in Public Governance, 75 N.Y.U. L.Rev. 543 (2000); Gillian Metzger, Privatization as Delegation, 103 Col. L. Rev. 1367 (2003), discussing claims of state action in relation to accreditation. On delegation of governmental functions to private organizations generally but including the Joint Commission, see Harold Krent, The Private Performing the Public: Delimiting Delegations to Private Parties, 65 U. Miami L. Rev. 507 (2011).

CHAPTER 3

THE PROFESSIONAL–PATIENT RELATIONSHIP

■ ■ ■

I.   INTRODUCTION

The focus of legal duties and ethical analysis begins with the individual physician, or other health care professional, who has primary responsibility for seeing the patient, diagnosing the problem, and prescribing the treatment. Health care today however is delivered in a variety of settings—hospitals, ambulatory care clinics, nursing homes, and doctors' offices. And the institutional framework for such care, in terms of its financing, support, and obligations, may encompass medical staffs, managed care organizations, partnerships, and institutional employers. It may also have an impact on legal obligations, especially as the duty of the physician to the patient may be extended to the organization (or not) and as organizational controls impact the capacity of the physician to meet his or her obligations to the patient.

This chapter considers the formation of the physician-patient relationship and a range of other obligations that the law imposes on physicians and other health care professionals. Professional liability, discussed in Chapter 4, focuses upon a breach of duty of care owed by the physician to a particular patient.

ESQUIVEL V. WATTERS
Court of Appeals of Kansas, 2007.
154 P.3d 1184.

Michelle and Jesse Esquivel, the parents of Jadon Esquivel, appeal the district court's entry of summary judgment in favor of Dr. Aaron T. Watters and the South Central Kansas Regional Medical Center (SCKRMC) in these survivor and wrongful death actions which arose from Jadon's death several weeks following his birth.

Upon learning she was pregnant, Michelle Esquivel obtained obstetric counseling from the Ark City Clinic. A clinic worker gave Michelle a certificate from SCKRMC for a free gender determination sonogram.

Michelle went to SCKRMC for her free sonogram on November 15, 2001. Prior to the sonogram being performed, Michelle signed a document entitled "Consent to Procedure to Determine Sex of Unborn Baby." The consent form stated in relevant part:

"2. The purpose of the procedure is to attempt to determine the sex of my unborn baby and I acknowledge there is no guarantee or assurance that an accurate determination can be made by this procedure.

"I further acknowledge that this procedure is not to determine any fetal abnormality or any other complication of pregnancy and is not considered a diagnostic examination for any medical purpose other than to attempt to determine the sex of my unborn baby.

"3. To induce Medical Center to perform this procedure the undersigned hereby waives and releases South Central Kansas Regional Medical Center, its officers, employees, agents, and affiliates from any and all claims, costs, liabilities, expenses, judgments, attorney fees, court costs, causes of action and compensation whatsoever arising out of the foregoing described procedure."

David Hazlett, an SCKRMC technician, performed the sonogram and noted that Michelle's baby's bowel was outside of his body, a condition known as gastroschisis. Hazlett did not inform Michelle of this irregularity because he is not a doctor and not qualified or licensed to make a medical diagnosis. Hazlett was unable to determine the baby's gender because of the gastroschisis. Nevertheless he took sonogram pictures which he sent to a radiologist at the Ark City Clinic. The radiologist refused to look at them because the sonogram was only for gender determination and not for diagnosis.

Hazlett also reported the irregularity to Watters, Michelle's obstetrician. Hazlett did not send any of the sonogram pictures to Watters. He sent no written report to Watters. Watters made no note of Hazlett's oral report in Michelle's medical chart. However, he directed his nurse to call Michelle. Watters' nurse made 11 attempts to contact Michelle by telephone over the next 10 days. On November 26, 2001, a man the nurse believed to be Jesse Esquivel answered the phone. The nurse told him to tell Michelle to call Watters' office. Michelle missed her prenatal appointment scheduled for that day. She next saw Watters on January 4, 2002. Since Watters had forgotten Hazlett's oral report of the abnormal sonogram and there was nothing in Michelle's chart to remind him, he failed to discuss it with her. When he saw Michelle again a month later, he again forgot to inform her of the abnormal sonogram.

On February 8, 2002, Michelle became ill and went to SCKRMC for treatment. Jadon was born by emergency caesarean section the next day. Neither Michelle nor Jesse nor the medical staff who delivered Jadon was aware that Jadon had gastroschisis until he was born.

Jadon was transferred to Wesley Medical Center (WMC) in Wichita on the day he was born. Dr. Phillip J. Knight performed surgery on Jadon that day. His examination of Jadon disclosed that almost all of Jadon's bowel had been dead for weeks prior to his birth. Since there was no hope that Jadon could survive without his bowel, Jadon was sent home with his parents on February 20, 2002, and placed on palliative care. Jadon died at home on March 3, 2002.

Michelle and Jesse commenced this action against Watters, the Ark City Clinic, and SCKRMC. The district court granted summary judgment to the Ark City Clinic, whose radiologist refused to examine Michelle's sonogram. That ruling is not a subject of this appeal.

The district court granted summary judgment in favor of Watters based upon the failure of plaintiffs to present expert testimony that Watters deviated from the applicable standard of care and the lack of proximate cause between Watters' failure to notify Michelle of the abnormal sonogram and Jadon's postnatal suffering and death. The court also granted summary judgment in favor of SCKRMC based upon its conclusions that SCKRMC did not owe Michelle and Jesse the duty upon which they based their claims, and their claims were barred by the release signed by Michelle before the sonogram.

Michelle and Jesse appeal the district court's entry of summary judgment in favor of Watters and SCKRMC.

*   *   *

[The court's discussion of the standard of care is omitted.]

1. Duty

The district court found that SCKRMC's undertaking was limited to performing a sonogram to determine the gender of Michelle's baby, which it did in a non-negligent manner. Thus, the court reasoned, having performed the sonogram in a careful manner, SCKRMC had no further duty to Michelle and was not obligated to inform her about anything other than Jadon's gender.

Our analysis of this essential element of Michelle and Jesse's causes of action is a rather disheartening exercise. As a society we expect of ourselves a certain level of looking out for the welfare of others. This is an attribute which society encourages rather than discourages. We would expect this urge to be particularly strong in the hearts of those who choose to enter the medical and health care community. However, the transition from a societal expectation to a legal duty is often determined by public policy considerations which are not within the purview of an intermediate appellate court such as ours. Consequently, we turn to the case law for guidance.

Whether a legal duty exists is a question of law over which this court exercises de novo review. [ ] In the context of a medical negligence claim, the existence of a doctor-patient relationship is crucial to the recognition of a legal duty. * * *. We recognize the distinction between a doctor-patient relationship which is fiduciary in nature, [ ] and a hospital-patient relationship which is not [ ]. Nevertheless, the doctor-patient cases are instructive.

[The Court discussed Smith v. Welch and Doss v. Manfredi. The cases involved independent medical examinations conducted as part of personal injury actions. In neither case was a traditional doctor-patient relationship recognized by the courts. [ ] Absent such a duty, the physician is under no legal obligation to discover and disclose problems in the person under examination.]

* * *

In the case now before us, no patient-healthcare provider relationship existed between Michelle and SCKRMC. Webster's II New College Dictionary 1174 (2001), defines "treatment" as "medical application of remedies so as to effect a cure." SCKRMC did not undertake to advise Michelle regarding, or to treat Michelle for, any disease, illness, or medical condition. It undertook only to determine the gender of her baby. Thus, SCKRMC only owed Michelle the duty to perform the sonogram in a non-negligent manner, and no negligence in the performance of the sonogram is alleged. Summary judgment based upon the lack of a duty was appropriate.

[The court's discussion of the release and waiver in the consent form signed by the plaintiff is omitted.].

Affirmed.

NOTES AND QUESTIONS

1.   Expert testimony in the case indicated that the standard of care would have required no different management of the pregnancy or the birth. In that case, what damage did the plaintiff suffer? How would you articulate her damage? How would early discovery of the condition have been beneficial to Michelle? Consider the time line of events—the free sonogram was performed on November 15, and the fetus was delivered by caesarean section on February 9, at 38 weeks, almost three months later.

Should the Ark City Clinic have been dismissed from the suit? Michelle went to the clinic for counseling, after all, and all their radiologist had to do was look at the sonogram to spot the problem with the fetus. And what is the relationship of the Clinic to the hospital? Is this free coupon part of a marketing strategy to bring patients to the hospital? If the coupon promises results, does this create a reliance interest in the coupon holder?

2. A physician-patient relationship is usually a prerequisite to a professional malpractice suit against a doctor, as the court in *Esquivel* observes. However, courts have disagreed about the nature of a duty to notify even in the absence of the physician-patient contract. One approach is found in Webb v. T.D., 287 Mont. 68, 951 P.2d 1008 (1997), where the court articulated a duty on physicians retained by third parties to do independent medical examinations:

> 1. to exercise ordinary care to discover those conditions which pose an imminent danger to the examinee's physical or mental well-being and take reasonable steps to communicate to the examinee the presence of any such condition;

> 2. to exercise ordinary care to assure that when he or she advises an examinee about her condition following an independent examination, the advice comports with the standard of care for the health care provider's profession.

3. The court in *Esquivel* is troubled by the failures of health care providers in the case. How should the law recognize a higher "fiduciary" duty on the part of health care providers to a person not yet a "contractual" patient, in a case such as this?

Once the physician-patient relationship is established, the law in fact imposes a higher level of duty on physicians. The language of fiduciary law is often used to describe special obligations that one person owes to another. Restatement (Third) of Agency, § 1.01 Agency defines agency as " * * * the fiduciary relationship that arises when one person (a "principal") manifests assent to another person (an "agent") that the agent shall act on the principal's behalf and subject to the principal's control, and the agent manifests assent or otherwise consents so to act."

Justice Cardozo has described the fiduciary obligation as follows: "Many forms of conduct permissible in a workaday world for those acting at arm's length, are forbidden to those bound by fiduciary ties. A trustee is held to something stricter than the morals of the market place. Not honesty alone, but the punctilio of an honor the most sensitive, is then the standard of behavior." Meinhard v. Salmon, 249 N.Y. 458, 164 N.E. 545, 546 (1928).

A fiduciary obligation in medicine means that the physician focuses exclusively on the patient's health; the patient assumes the doctor's single-minded devotion to him; and the doctor-patient relationship is expected to be free of conflict. One ethicist defines a health care fiduciary as "someone who commits to becoming and remaining scientifically and clinically competent, acts primarily to protect and promote the interests of the patient and keeps self-interest systematically secondary, and maintains and passes on medicine as a public trust for current and future physicians and patients." Laurence B. McCullough, A Primer on Bioethics (2nd Edition 2006). Is this a workable standard for physicians? Is this an appropriate standard? What about resource limitations, public health concerns about populations, and other patients. See generally Theodore W. Ruger, Can a Patient–Centered Ethics Be Other–Regarding? Should It Be? 45 Wake Forest L. Rev. 1013 (2010) (asking whether a patient-centered focus is a good model). See the discussion of the Sunshine Act and its concerns about physician financial conflicts, *infra*.

II.   THE CONTRACT BETWEEN PATIENT AND PHYSICIAN

WHITE V. HARRIS
Supreme Court of Vermont, 2011.
190 Vt. 647, 36 A.3d 203, 2011 Vt 115.

Present: REIBER, C.J., DOOLEY, JOHNSON and SKOGLUND, JJ.

ENTRY ORDER

Plaintiffs appeal from a superior court order granting summary judgment to defendant Fletcher Allen Health Care, Inc. in this wrongful death action alleging medical malpractice. This case arises from the suicide of plaintiffs' fourteen-year-old daughter. Plaintiffs sued defendant, which employed a psychiatrist who was briefly involved with decedent's case through a telepsychiatry research study. Plaintiffs argue that summary judgment was improperly granted on the issue of the duty owed to decedent by the psychiatrist. We agree, and thus reverse and remand for additional proceedings.

The record indicates the following. Decedent suffered from ongoing mental health problems. On the recommendation of her case manager, she consulted with defendant's psychiatrist through a telepsychiatry research study he was conducting. As part of the study, plaintiffs and decedent completed pre-assessment documentation, and they participated in a one-time, ninety-minute video-conference session with the psychiatrist in August 2006. Following the session, the participants completed a questionnaire about their reaction to using telemedicine. The psychiatrist later completed a consultation evaluation that described decedent and the history of her present illness; it also provided the doctor's diagnostic impression of decedent and set forth recommendations for an initial treatment plan. The evaluation specifically stated that, consistent with the telepsychiatry research protocol, no follow-up services would be provided, and no medication prescriptions would be directly provided by the doctor. The report further explained that the recommended treatment plan was to be weighed by decedent's treatment team, including her primary care physician, for possible implementation. After sending his evaluation, the psychiatrist had no further interaction with plaintiffs, decedent, or any member of her treatment team.

On June 10, 2007, decedent committed suicide. An autopsy report indicated that she died from the combined effects of ingesting Propoxyphene, opiates, and Citalopram. The psychiatrist had not prescribed or recommended any of these medications.

In June 2009, plaintiffs filed an amended complaint, alleging that defendant, among eight doctors and medical care providers, treated decedent in a manner that "fell below the standard of care required of reasonably skillful, careful, and prudent professionals," and that decedent died as a proximate result. Defendant moved for summary judgment in December 2009, asserting that its doctor had no duty to decedent when she committed suicide because there was no doctor-patient relationship. Alternatively, defendant argued that any such relationship was formally terminated in writing following their one-time interaction. Defendant acknowledged that if the trial court found that a duty existed, its motion would be premature. The trial court also recognized that the motion came at an early stage in the proceedings, but reasoned that if no duty existed, then no additional discovery to show a breach of that duty would be necessary. Ultimately, the trial court agreed that the psychiatrist's contact with decedent was "so minimal as to not establish a physician-patient relationship," and consequently found that no duty existed at the time of decedent's death. Even assuming that a doctor-patient relationship was established, the court concluded that it was terminated following the video-conference and, thus, any duty was extinguished by termination of the relationship and no duty existed at the time of decedent's death. The court thus granted defendant's summary judgment motion. This appeal followed.

Plaintiffs argue that the court erred in finding that the doctor owed no duty to decedent. They maintain that the doctor had a duty to exercise reasonable care to protect decedent from the danger she posed to herself, and that the doctor did not effectively terminate the doctor-patient relationship prior to decedent's death.

* * *

We agree that a duty applies to the service provided. The doctor had a duty of due care in his professional contact with decedent, which was not extinguished by the ministerial act of termination of their professional relationship. [ ] We have defined duty as "an expression of the sum total of those considerations of policy which lead the law to say that the plaintiff is entitled to protection." [ ] In assessing whether a duty exists, "[t]he question is whether the relationship of the parties was such that the defendant was under an obligation to use some care to avoid or prevent injury to the plaintiff." In their analysis of circumstances similar to those here, other courts have considered these factors:

> whether the doctor was in a unique position to prevent harm, the burden of preventing harm, whether the plaintiff relied upon the doctor's diagnosis or interpretation, the closeness of the connection between the defendant's conduct and the injury suffered, the degree of certainty that the plaintiff has or will suffer harm, the skill or special reputation of the actors, and public policy. [ ].

The facts here disclose a consultation of limited duration. Decedent and her mother signed an informed consent form, and the doctor stated in writing that the scope of his services was limited. At the same time, however, there is no dispute that the doctor performed a psychiatric evaluation of decedent, following which the doctor offered recommendations for decedent's treatment. And the record reveals the parties' expectation that the doctor would aid in decedent's treatment through his expertise, regardless of the mechanism of doctor-patient contact. In requesting a consultation with the doctor, decedent's treatment team specifically sought recommendations about decedent's medication, particularly given the increase in decedent's angry and aggressive behavior and self-mutilation. They also sought the doctor's diagnostic impression and recommendations about the role that Attention–Deficit Hyperactivity Disorder might play in decedent's behavior. While decedent's medical records may not have been provided to the doctor, the doctor was provided with a very recent medical evaluation of decedent performed by another doctor, which was supplemented by additional information about decedent from decedent's treatment team. This included information that decedent had a history of depressive behavior and had recently exhibited an increase in angry, aggressive behavior, along with more frequent cutting behavior. All of this information bears on the scope of the professional relationship from which defendant's duty arose and it helps to frame the applicable standard of care. We find it sufficient to support the existence of a duty here.

A professional consultation may arise in many different circumstances. Defendant's involvement here was limited, but that does not mean it was nonexistent. It may be analogized to cases in which a doctor is asked to perform an *independent medical examination* (IME) [italics supplied] of a patient as part of a legal investigation or an insurance claim. As in the current case, an IME doctor usually does not see a patient again or maintain an ongoing relationship with the patient; rather he or she performs a limited analysis of the patient's condition that is provided to a third party. [ ] Many courts addressing IME cases have concluded that an IME creates a doctor-patient relationship that "imposes fewer duties on the examining physician than does a traditional physician-patient relationship," but "still requires that the examiner conduct the examination in such a way as not to cause harm." [ ]

Here, the relationship between doctor and patient was even more direct than a third-party-retained IME doctor. The defendant became involved on referral from decedent's treatment team and reported to them his findings and recommendations after evaluation. We hold that the ninety-minute consultation performed in this case created a doctor-patient relationship. We acknowledge that the telepsychiatry research study conducted by the doctor provided no treatment component directly to decedent, other than recommendations to her treatment team. However, through this consultation, a limited doctor-patient relationship was established, and we conclude that a duty of due care applies. Through this consultation, defendant's doctor assumed a duty to act in a manner consistent with the applicable standard of care so as not to harm decedent through the consultation services provided.

Defendant argues that submission of the psychiatrist's consultation evaluation to decedent's treatment team terminated any doctor-patient relationship that ever existed, and defendant equates the ending of this relationship with the termination of any "further duty to the patient."[2] We hold, however, that even if doctor-patient contact had ended, this does not terminate the doctor's responsibility for the consequences of any lapses in his duty to provide services consistent with the applicable standard of care for the consultation. Under 12 V.S.A. § 1908(1), a doctor must exercise "the degree of care ordinarily exercised by a reasonably skillful, careful, and prudent health care professional engaged in a similar practice under the same or similar circumstances." A doctor may be liable for malpractice if "as a proximate result of . . . the failure to exercise this degree of care the plaintiff suffered injuries that would not otherwise have been incurred." [ ]. Under this statute, whether or not a doctor has ceased treating a patient is irrelevant to whether he or she may be held liable for injuries resulting from his or her failure to exercise the proper degree of care *while treating* the patient. It is the doctor's responsibility for the services provided that is significant here, and not simply the duration of the doctor-patient relationship itself.

On these facts, however, the scope of defendant's duty and the standard of care cannot yet be determined. In evaluating the standard of care,

---

[2] Defendant contends that plaintiffs failed to properly preserve their arguments pertaining to termination of the doctor-patient relationship, claiming that "[p]laintiffs here did not . . . argue that the doctor-patient relationship—if any ever existed—between [defendant] and [decedent] was not terminated in exactly the manner [defendant] contended it was." To some extent, defendant appears to conflate the issue of whether a doctor-patient relationship existed with whether defendant had a continuing responsibility for the quality of care provided to decedent. We agree that defendant had no ongoing duty to provide care for decedent after the psychiatrist's consultation ended. This does not affect, however, whether defendant can be held liable for any alleged breach of the psychiatrist's duty to meet the required standard of care during the course of the telepsychiatry research study. While plaintiffs may not have specifically addressed defendant's argument about the termination clause in the psychiatrist's consultation evaluation, whether or not the doctor-patient relationship was terminated is not dispositive.

we must not conflate the existence of a duty with the appropriate standard of care, an issue that takes us beyond the limited facts in the record before us and was not properly raised below. [ ] * * ** * * We do not yet know plaintiffs' position on the standard of care in this case, i.e., what a "reasonably skillful, careful, and prudent health care professional" would have done under similar circumstances, or how any alleged breach of this standard was the proximate cause of harm to decedent. [ ].

The issue of standard of care was not raised by defendant in its motion for summary judgment, nor decided by the trial court. It is not the role of this Court to set that standard or to evaluate whether it was breached at this stage of the proceedings. Expert testimony is required. [ ]

This is a lawsuit in its formative stages. The motion for summary judgment was filed six months after the complaint was filed and raised the sole question of the duty of care of this consulting doctor. The remaining elements of plaintiffs' claim have not yet been fully developed, and defendant did not move for summary judgment on these elements. [ ], Given our conclusion that a duty exists, we reverse and remand for additional proceedings.

Reversed and remanded.

NOTES AND QUESTIONS

1.   When a physician treating a patient consults by telephone or otherwise with another physician, some courts are reluctant to find a doctor-patient relationship created by such a conversation. The concern is that such informal conferences will be deterred by the fear of liability. See Reynolds v. Decatur Memorial Hosp., 277 Ill.App.3d 80, 214 Ill.Dec. 44, 49, 660 N.E.2d 235, 240 (1996) ("It would have a chilling effect upon practice of medicine. It would stifle communication, education and professional association, all to the detriment of the patient.") Others find a duty in such a consultation. See e.g. Diggs v. Arizona Cardiologists, Ltd., 198 Ariz. 198, 8 P.3d 386 (2000), where just being the on-call physician is not sufficient in many states to create the physician-patient relationship.

By contrast, *White* involves telepsychiatry and a real therapeutic encounter, with patient expectations. Web based psychiatry in particular has been   expanding.   See   Lucas   Mearian,   Web-Based   Counseling—Telepsychiatry—Is Taking Off, Computerworld, February 9, 2012. ("In many instances, telepsychiatry is a necessity, not just a convenience for doctors and patients. Patients are often located in regions with no private psychiatric practices or where hospitals don't employ staff psychiatrists.")

The relationship in *White* had ended, but the court noted that there was the possibility of ". . . lapses in his duty to provide services consistent with the applicable standard of care for the consultation." What does the court mean by this?

2.   The physician-patient relationship can be considered initially as a contractual one. Physicians in private practice may contract for their services as they see fit, and retain substantial control over the extent of their contact with patients. Physicians may limit their specialty, their scope of practice, their geographic area, and the hours and conditions under which they will see patients. They have no obligation to offer services that a patient may require that are outside their competence and training; or services outside the scope of the original physician-patient agreement, in which the physician has limited the contract to a type of procedure, to an office visit, or to consultation only. They may transfer responsibility by referring patients to other specialists. They may refuse to enter into a contract with a patient, or to treat patients, even under emergency conditions. When a patient goes to a doctor's office with a particular problem, he is offering to enter into a contract with the physician. When the physician engages with the patient, for example through a conversation, an examination, or perhaps through the physician's staff, she accepts the offer and an implied contract is created. The physician is free to reject the offer and send the patient away, relieving herself of any duty to that patient.

Once the physician-patient relationship has been created, physicians are subject to an obligation of "continuing attention." See Ricks v. Budge, in Chapter 8, *infra*. Refusal to continue to treat a patient is abandonment, and it also may be malpractice. See, e.g., Tierney v. University of Michigan Regents, 257 Mich.App. 681, 669 N.W.2d 575 (2003) (treating gynecologist withdrew from treating plaintiff after she filed suit against another member of the medical group). Termination of the physician-patient relationship, once created, is subject in some jurisdictions to a "continuous treatment" rule to determine when the statute of limitations is tolled. Treatment obligations cease if the physician can do nothing more for the patient. See Jewson v. Mayo Clinic, 691 F.2d 405 (8th Cir.1982).

An express written contract is rarely drafted for specific physician-patient interactions. An implied contract is usually the basis of the relationship between a physician and a patient. A physician who talks with a patient by telephone may be held to have an implied contractual obligation to that patient. Bienz v. Central Suffolk Hospital, 163 A.D.2d 269, 557 N.Y.S.2d 139 (1990). Likewise, a physician, such as a pathologist, who renders services to a patient but has not contracted with him, is nonetheless bound by certain implied contractual obligations. When the physician evaluates information provided by a nurse and makes a medical decision as to a patient's status, a doctor-patient relationship may be established. Wheeler v. Yettie Kersting Memorial Hospital, 866 S.W.2d 32 (Tex.App.1993). Merely scheduling an appointment is not by itself sufficient to create a relationship. Jackson v. Isaac, 76 S.W.3d 177 (Tex.App. 2002).

There was a written agreement in *White* in the form of the written consent that laid out limits on what the defendant physician was undertaking. Why didn't the court enforce that agreement? Is the question really a procedural one; i.e., this is a summary judgment motion, not a full examination of the facts? Or, should the courts not enforce limited agreements? The patient in *White* was participating in a research protocol.

A. PHYSICIAN CONTRACTS WITH THIRD PARTIES

Most physicians are part of managed care networks and therefore have a contractual relationship with the plan that requires them to treat subscribers. In Hand v. Tavera, 864 S.W.2d 678 (Ct.App. Texas 1993), the plaintiff went to the emergency room complaining of a headache. Dr. Tavera was the doctor responsible for authorizing admissions, and he sent Hand home and said he should be treated as an outpatient. Hand had a stroke. The court held that the contract between Humana and Southwest Medical Group (which employed Dr. Tavera) obligated Tavera to treat all Human enrollees as he would treat his other patients.

> The court concluded that the contract created a doctor-patient relationship:

> Hand paid premiums to Humana to purchase medical care in advance of need; Humana met its obligation to Hand and its other enrollees by employing Tavera's group to treat them; and Tavera's medical group agreed to treat Humana enrollees in exchange for the fees received from Humana. In effect, Hand had paid in advance for the services of the Humana plan doctor on duty that night, who happened to be Tavera, and the physician-patient relationship existed. We hold that when the health-care plan's insured shows up at a participating hospital emergency room, and the plan's doctor on call is consulted about treatment or admission, there is a physician-patient relationship between the doctor and the insured.

NOTES AND QUESTIONS

1.   Physicians who practice in organizations must provide health care within the limits of the health plan coverage or their employment contracts with the institution. In such a case, the contact between the physician and the patient is preceded by an express contract spelling out the details of the relationship. Physicians who are members of a hospital's medical staff have duties created by medical staff privilege by-laws; physicians who are part of health maintenance organizations have a duty to treat plan members as a result of their contractual obligation to the HMO. In these situations, the express contract is between the physician and the health plan, and the subscriber and the plan, with an implied contract between the subscriber and the treating physician.

2.   A physician who has staff privileges at a hospital also agrees to abide by hospital by-laws and policies, including requirements that certain physicians be on-call as needed. According to most courts that have consid-

ered the issue, the physician's agreement with the hospital extends to the patient. Physicians on call to treat emergency patients are under a duty to treat patients. See discussion of common law duties of on-call physicians in Section II of Chapter 8 and statutory obligations under EMTALA in Section III.A. of the same chapter.

B. EXCULPATORY CLAUSES

TUNKL V. REGENTS OF UNIV. OF CALIFORNIA
Supreme Court of California, 1963.
60 Cal.2d 92, 32 Cal.Rptr. 33, 383 P.2d 441.

TOBRINER, JUSTICE.

This case concerns the validity of a release from liability for future negligence imposed as a condition for admission to a charitable research hospital. For the reasons we hereinafter specify, we have concluded that an agreement between a hospital and an entering patient affects the public interest and that, in consequence, the exculpatory provision included within it must be invalid under Civil Code section 1668.

Hugo Tunkl brought this action to recover damages for personal injuries alleged to have resulted from the negligence of two physicians in the employ of the University of California Los Angeles Medical Center, a hospital operated and maintained by the Regents of the University of California as a nonprofit charitable institution. Mr. Tunkl died after suit was brought, and his surviving wife, as executrix, was substituted as plaintiff.

The University of California at Los Angeles Medical Center admitted Tunkl as a patient on June 11, 1956. The Regents maintain the hospital for the primary purpose of aiding and developing a program of research and education in the field of medicine; patients are selected and admitted if the study and treatment of their condition would tend to achieve these purposes. Upon his entry to the hospital, Tunkl signed a document setting forth certain "Conditions of Admission." The crucial condition number six reads as follows: "RELEASE: The hospital is a nonprofit, charitable institution. In consideration of the hospital and allied services to be rendered and the rates charged therefor, the patient or his legal representative agrees to and hereby releases The Regents of the University of California, and the hospital from any and all liability for the negligent or wrongful acts or omissions of its employees, if the hospital has used due care in selecting its employees."

Plaintiff stipulated that the hospital had selected its employees with due care. The trial court ordered that the issue of the validity of the exculpatory clause be first submitted to the jury and that, if the jury found that the provision did not bind plaintiff, a second jury try the issue of alleged malpractice. When, on the preliminary issue, the jury returned a verdict sustaining the validity of the executed release, the court entered judgment in favor of the Regents.[1] Plaintiff appeals from the judgment.

We shall first set out the basis for our prime ruling that the exculpatory provision of the hospital's contract fell under the proscription of Civil Code section 1668; we then dispose of two answering arguments of defendant.

We begin with the dictate of the relevant Civil Code section 1668. The section states: "All contracts which have for their object, directly or indirectly, to exempt anyone from responsibility for his own fraud, or willful injury to the person or property of another, or violation of law, whether willful or negligent, are against the policy of the law."

* * *

In one respect, as we have said, the decisions are uniform. The cases have consistently held that the exculpatory provision may stand only if it does not involve "the public interest."

* * *

If, then, the exculpatory clause which affects the public interest cannot stand, we must ascertain those factors or characteristics which constitute the public interest. * * *

* * * It concerns a business of a type generally thought suitable for public regulation. The party seeking exculpation is engaged in performing a service of great importance to the public, which is often a matter of practical necessity for some members of the public. The party holds himself out as willing to perform this service for any member of the public who seeks it, or at least for any member coming within certain established standards. As a result of the essential nature of the service, in the economic setting of the transaction, the party invoking exculpation possesses a decisive advantage of bargaining strength against any member of the public who seeks his services. In exercising a superior bargaining power the party confronts the public with a standardized adhesion contract of exculpation, and makes no provision whereby a purchaser may pay additional reasonable fees and obtain protection against negligence. Finally, as a result of the transaction, the person or property of the purchaser is placed under the control of the seller, subject to the risk of carelessness by the seller or his agents.

* * *

---

[1] Plaintiff at the time of signing the release was in great pain, under sedation, and probably unable to read. At trial plaintiff contended that the release was invalid, asserting that a release does not bind the releasor if at the time of its execution he suffered from so weak a mental condition that he was unable to comprehend the effect of his act. [ ]

In the light of the decisions, we think that the hospital-patient contract clearly falls within the category of agreements affecting the public interest. To meet that test, the agreement need only fulfill some of the characteristics above outlined; here, the relationship fulfills all of them. Thus the contract of exculpation involves an institution suitable for, and a subject of, public regulation. [ ] That the services of the hospital to those members of the public who are in special need of the particular skill of its staff and facilities constitute a practical and crucial necessity is hardly open to question.

The hospital, likewise, holds itself out as willing to perform its services for those members of the public who qualify for its research and training facilities. While it is true that the hospital is selective as to the patients it will accept, such selectivity does not negate its public aspect or the public interest in it. The hospital is selective only in the sense that it accepts from the public at large certain types of cases which qualify for the research and training in which it specializes. But the hospital does hold itself out to the public as an institution which performs such services for those members of the public who can qualify for them.

In insisting that the patient accept the provision of waiver in the contract, the hospital certainly exercises a decisive advantage in bargaining. The would-be patient is in no position to reject the proffered agreement, to bargain with the hospital, or in lieu of agreement to find another hospital. The admission room of a hospital contains no bargaining table where, as in a private business transaction, the parties can debate the terms of their contract. As a result, we cannot but conclude that the instant agreement manifested the characteristics of the so-called adhesion contract. Finally, when the patient signed the contract, he completely placed himself in the control of the hospital; he subjected himself to the risk of its carelessness.

*   *   *

We turn to a consideration of the * * * arguments urged by defendant to save the exemptive clause. Defendant contends that while the public interest may possibly invalidate the exculpatory provision as to the paying patient, it certainly cannot do so as to the charitable one. * * *

*   *   *

In substance defendant here asks us to modify our decision in *Malloy*, which removed the charitable immunity; defendant urges that otherwise the funds of the research hospital may be deflected from the real objective of the extension of medical knowledge to the payment of claims for alleged negligence. Since a research hospital necessarily entails surgery and treatment in which fixed standards of care may not yet be evolved, defendant says the hospital should in this situation be excused from such care. But the answer lies in the fact that possible plaintiffs must *prove negligence;* the standards of care will themselves reflect the research nature of the treatment; the hospital will not become an insurer or guarantor of the patient's recovery. To exempt the hospital completely from any standard of due care is to grant it immunity by the side-door method of a contractual clause exacted of the patient. We cannot reconcile that technique with the teaching of *Malloy.*

* * *

The judgment is reversed.

NOTES AND QUESTIONS

1.   Written waivers of the right to sue are typically upheld in settings other than health care, if the waiver of negligence is clearly described, the activity is a voluntary one, the waiver freely given by a party who understands what he is giving up, and there is not a serious imbalance of bargaining power. Courts view such waivers as a valid exercise of the freedom of contract. See generally Jaffe v. Pallotta Teamworks, 276 F. Supp.2d 102 (D.C.D.C. 2003) (upholding waiver by a runner in an AIDS charity event, a voluntary activity).

2.   The *Tunkl* context is a special case of a charitable teaching hospital. Why does the court view this context as special? In other health care situations other than emergencies, why shouldn't a patient be able to waive the right to sue in exchange for lower cost or free treatment? See *Esquivel,* above, and discussion of consumer-driven health care, below. Is there something special about medical care in general, or *Tunkl's* situation in particular, that makes such a choice by a patient suspect? Do the court's arguments convince you as to the reasons for invalidating such attempts by health care institutions to limit their liability? Short of a complete waiver of a right to sue, how else might hospitals or doctors protect themselves? Can a patient be asked to waive the right to sue for punitive damages? Could the parties agree on liquidated damages? Could the parties agree that an action would be brought in the local state court? Could treatment be conditioned on the patient submitting any malpractice claim to an administrative body, or to arbitration? Should the patient's source of payment determine whether an exculpatory agreement should be enforced?

California has continued to follow *Tunkl's* analysis. See, e.g Health Net of California, Inc. v. Department of Health Services (2003) 113 Cal.App.4th 224, 6 Cal.Rptr.3d 235 (2003) (exculpatory clause related to managed health care for Medi–Cal beneficiaries).

3. Partial waivers of liability have been accepted by courts under special circumstances. For example, in Shorter v. Drury, 695 P.2d 116 (Wash. 1985), Mrs. Shorter, a Jehovah's Witness, went to the hospital for a procedure.   She

had suffered a missed abortion, in which the fetus she was carrying died in her uterus. The procedure was to evacuate the uterus in order to guard against the risk of infection. Mrs. Shorter signed a waiver of her right to sue for any injuries suffered from her refusal to have blood transfusions. The procedure did not go well, she began to bleed, she refused the transfusions which would have saved her life, and she died. The court wrote:

> We find the refusal to be valid. There was sufficient evidence for the jury to find it was not signed unwittingly but rather voluntarily. * * *

> We also hold the release was not against public policy. We emphasize again the release did not exculpate Dr. Drury from his negligence in performing the surgery. Rather, it was an agreement that Mrs. Shorter should receive no blood or blood derivatives. The cases cited by defendant, [including Tunkl, above] all refer to exculpatory clauses which release a physician or hospital from all liability for negligence. The Shorters specifically accepted the risk which might flow from a refusal to accept blood. * * * We believe the procedure used here, the voluntary execution of a document protecting the physician and hospital and the patient is an appropriate alternative and not contrary to the public interest.

Shorter offers a defense of a partial waiver, under a special set of circumstances. The issue is important for two reasons. First, providers would like to limit their liability exposure in order to keep malpractice premiums under control. Second, economists and other reformers of the tort system advocate the use of contracts that allocate risk by agreement.

4.   California has a binding arbitration provision in MICRA (Medical Injury Compensation Reform Act) and it is estimated that about ten percent of medical malpractice disputes go to binding arbitration. See Michael F. Cannon, CATO Handbook for Policymakers (7th Edition), Chapter 15, Health Care Regulation.

What objections might be raised to such forms of binding arbitration imposed by contract? See discussion of enforceability of arbitration agreements, including application of the Federal Arbitration Act, in Chapter 3.

Several states have adopted contract approaches, such as elective arbitration contracts that allow the provider and the patient to change the forum for resolving the dispute. Some states do not mandate the referral of medical malpractice claims to arbitration, but instead authorize health care providers to include arbitration clauses in their contracts, so long as an agreement to arbitrate is not a condition of service. The patient must have a right to rescind within 90 days. See for example Colo. Rev. Stat. Ann. § 13–64–403. See generally Carol A. Crocca, Arbitration of Medical Malpractice Claims, 24 A.L.R.5th 1.

PROBLEM: ARBITRATING DISASTER

Rhoda Cumin went to the Gladstone Clinic in Las Vegas, Nevada to get a prescription for an oral contraceptive. Her medical history put her at a higher risk of a stroke from use of birth control pills. She did not know this, but her medical records and history would have alerted an obstetrician to the risk. She obtained a prescription for the pills, and began taking them. Six months later she suffered a cerebral incident that left her partially paralyzed. Her lifetime medical expenses, including physical therapy, lost earning capacity, and pain suffering, could be as much as $ 10 million.

Ms. Cumin has asked you to handle her suit against the clinic. Your investigation determines that the clinic was negligent in prescribing the contraceptive in light of Ms. Cumin's history. You file a negligence action. The clinic then moves to stay the lawsuit pending arbitration, and for a court order to compel arbitration. Its affidavit states that the clinic requires all patients to sign an arbitration agreement before receiving treatment. This agreement requires two things: first, it provides that all disputes must be submitted to binding arbitration and that the parties expressly waive their right to a trial. Second, it puts a cap of $250,000 on the patient's right to recover.. The clinic's standard procedure is to have the receptionist hand the patient the agreement along with two information sheets, informing her that any questions will be answered. The patient must sign the agreement before receiving treatment; the physician signs later. If the patient refuses to sign, the clinic refuses treatment. The agreement, signed by your client, is attached to the affidavit.

Ms. Cumin tells you that she does not remember either signing the agreement or having it explained to her, and you file an affidavit to that effect. Prepare a memorandum of law in support of your motion in opposition to arbitration.

III.   INFORMED CONSENT: THE PHYSICIAN'S OBLIGATION

A. ORIGINS OF THE INFORMED CONSENT DOCTRINE

Informed consent has developed out of strong judicial deference toward individual autonomy, reflecting a belief that an individual has a right to be free from nonconsensual interference with his or her person, and a basic moral principle that it is wrong to force another to act against his or her will. This principle was articulated in the medical context by Justice Cardozo in Schloendorff v. Society of New York Hospital, 211 N.Y. 125, 105 N.E. 92 (1914): "Every human being of adult years and sound mind has a right to determine what shall be done with his own body . . . ".

Informed consent doctrine has guided medical decision making by setting boundaries for the doctor-patient relationship and is one of the forces altering the attitudes of a new generation of doctors toward their patients. Informed consent is a foundation for federal regulations on human experimentation (See Chapter 20), and the touchstone for end-of-life decision making (See Chapters 18 and 19). The consent forms that health care institutions require all patients to sign upon admission and before various procedures are performed are the most concrete manifestations of the doctrine.

Professor Alexander Capron has argued that the doctrine can serve six salutary functions. Informed consent can:

1) protect individual autonomy;

2) protect the patient's status as a human being;

3) avoid fraud or duress;

4) encourage doctors to carefully consider their decisions;

5) foster rational decision-making by the patient; and

6) involve the public generally in medicine.

Alexander Capron, Informed Consent in Catastrophic Disease Research and Treatment, 123 U.Penn.L.Rev. 340, 365–76 (1974).

Current research suggests that patient health outcomes may in fact improve if patients are fully involved in understanding their treatments and their illness, and in managing their own treatments to a greater extent. We are moving beyond informed consent to a more robust model of "patient engagement" and "activation." As one study argues, "[t]he assumption is that if individual patients made more informed health care choices, were better able to manage their own conditions, and adopted healthier lifestyles, their health care costs would be lessened." The quality of care is also expected to improve when patients are engaged in their own care. See generally Judith H. Hibbard, Jessica Greene, and Valerie Overton, Patients With Lower Activation Associated With Higher Costs: Delivery Systems Should Know Their Patients' 'Scores', 32 Health Affairs 216 (2013).

This is not just a policy debate. Patient engagement and shared decisionmaking are two central components of both Stage 2 meaningful use requirements and the Medicare Shared Savings Program. Medical Homes discussions also emphasize patient engagement as crucial to quality, and the Accountable Care Organization regulations spend a great deal of time on the importance of patient engagement. See Centers for Medicare & Medicaid Services, Medicare Program; Medicare Shared Savings Program: Accountable Care Organizations, 425.106, Shared governance (discussing the promotion of patient engagement.) For a discussion of "meaningful use", Medical Homes, and the Medicare Shared Savings program, see Chapters 10 and 12 *infra*.

As you read the cases in this section, ask how far the courts have gone toward permitting patients to control treatment decisions that affect them. Consider also what a plaintiff must show to make out an informed consent case in various jurisdictions. Finally, ask if any other processes are likely to serve the purposes of informed consent more efficiently, and with less adverse effect on the doctor-patient relationship. Has the law improved the doctor-patient relationship?

B. THE LEGAL FRAMEWORK OF INFORMED CONSENT

1. Negligence as a Basis for Recovery

CANTERBURY V. SPENCE

United States Court of Appeals, District of Columbia Circuit, 1972.
464 F.2d 772.

SPOTTSWOOD W. ROBINSON, III, CIRCUIT JUDGE:

This appeal is from a judgment entered in the District Court on verdicts directed for the two appellees at the conclusion of plaintiff-appellant Canterbury's case in chief. His action sought damages for personal injuries allegedly sustained as a result of an operation negligently performed by appellee Spence, a negligent failure by Dr. Spence to disclose a risk of serious disability inherent in the operation, and negligent post-operative care by appellee Washington Hospital Center. On close examination of the record, we find evidence which required submission of these issues to the jury. We accordingly reverse the judgment as to each appellee and remand the case to the District Court for a new trial.

I

The record we review tells a depressing tale. A youth troubled only by back pain submitted to an operation without being informed of a risk of paralysis incidental thereto. A day after the operation he fell from his hospital bed after having been left without assistance while voiding. A few hours after the fall, the lower half of his body was paralyzed, and he had to be operated on again. Despite extensive medical care, he has never been what he was before. Instead of the back pain, even years later, he hobbled about on crutches, a victim of paralysis of the bowels and urinary incontinence. In a very real sense this lawsuit is an understandable search for reasons.

At the time of the events which gave rise to this litigation, appellant was nineteen years of age, a clerk-typist employed by the Federal Bureau of Investigation. In December, 1958, he began to experience severe pain between his shoulder blades. He consulted two general practitioners, but the medications they prescribed failed to eliminate the pain. Thereafter, appellant secured an appointment with Dr. Spence, who is a neurosurgeon.

Dr. Spence examined appellant in his office at some length but found nothing amiss. On Dr. Spence's advice appellant was x-rayed, but the films did not identify any abnormality. Dr. Spence then recommended that appellant undergo a myelogram—a procedure in which dye is injected into the spinal column and traced to find evidence of disease or other disorder—at the Washington Hospital Center.

Appellant entered the hospital on February 4, 1959. The myelogram revealed a "filling defect" in the region of the fourth thoracic vertebra. Since a myelogram often does no more than pinpoint the location of an aberration, surgery may be necessary to discover the cause. Dr. Spence told appellant that he would have to undergo a laminectomy—the excision of the posterior arch of the vertebra—to correct what he suspected was a ruptured disc. Appellant did not raise any objection to the proposed operation nor did he probe into its exact nature.

Appellant explained to Dr. Spence that his mother was a widow of slender financial means living in Cyclone, West Virginia, and that she could be reached through a neighbor's telephone. Appellant called his mother the day after the myelogram was performed and, failing to contact her, left Dr. Spence's telephone number with the neighbor. When Mrs. Canterbury returned the call, Dr. Spence told her that the surgery was occasioned by a suspected ruptured disc. Mrs. Canterbury then asked if the recommended operation was serious and Dr. Spence replied "not any more than any other operation." He added that he knew Mrs. Canterbury was not well off and that her presence in Washington would not be necessary. The testimony is contradictory as to whether during the course of the conversation Mrs. Canterbury expressed her consent to the operation. Appellant himself apparently did not converse again with Dr. Spence prior to the operation.

Dr. Spence performed the laminectomy on February 11 at the Washington Hospital Center. Mrs. Canterbury traveled to Washington, arriving on that date but after the operation was over, and signed a consent form at the hospital. The laminectomy revealed several anomalies: a spinal cord that was swollen and unable to pulsate, an accumulation of large tortuous and dilated veins, and a complete absence of epidural fat which normally surrounds the spine. A thin hypodermic needle was inserted into the spinal cord to aspirate any cysts which might have been present, but no fluid emerged. In suturing the wound, Dr. Spence attempted to relieve the pressure on the spinal cord by enlarging the dura—the outer protective wall of the spinal cord—at the area of swelling.

For approximately the first day after the operation appellant recuperated normally, but then suffered a fall and an almost immediate setback. Since there is some conflict as to precisely when or why appellant fell, we reconstruct the events from the evidence most favorable to him. Dr. Spence left orders that appellant was to remain in bed during the process of voiding. These orders were changed to direct that voiding be done out of bed, and the jury could find that the change was made by hospital personnel. Just prior to the fall, appellant summoned a nurse and was given a receptacle for use in voiding, but was then left unattended. Appellant testified that during the course of the endeavor he slipped off the side of the bed, and that there was no one to assist him, or side rail to prevent the fall.

Several hours later, appellant began to complain that he could not move his legs and that he was having trouble breathing; paralysis seems to have been virtually total from the waist down. Dr. Spence was notified on the night of February 12, and he rushed to the hospital. Mrs. Canterbury signed another consent form and appellant was again taken into the operating room. The surgical wound was reopened and Dr. Spence created a gusset to allow the spinal cord greater room in which to pulsate.

Appellant's control over his muscles improved somewhat after the second operation but he was unable to void properly. As a result of this condition, he came under the care of a urologist while still in the hospital. In April, following a cystoscopic examination, appellant was operated on for removal of bladder stones, and in May was released from the hospital. He reentered the hospital the following August for a 10–day period, apparently because of his urologic problems. For several years after his discharge he was under the care of several specialists, and at all times was under the care of a urologist. At the time of the trial in April, 1968, appellant required crutches to walk, still suffered from urinal incontinence and paralysis of the bowels, and wore a penile clamp.

In November, 1959 on Dr. Spence's recommendation, appellant was transferred by the F.B.I. to Miami where he could get more swimming and exercise. Appellant worked three years for the F.B.I. in Miami, Los Angeles and Houston, resigning finally in June, 1962. From then until the time of the trial, he held a number of jobs, but had constant trouble finding work because he needed to remain seated and close to a bathroom. The damages appellant claims include extensive pain and suffering, medical expenses, and loss of earnings.

II

*   *   *

At the close of appellant's case in chief, each defendant moved for a directed verdict and the trial judge granted both motions. The basis of the ruling, he explained, was that appellant had failed to produce any medical evidence indicating negligence on Dr. Spence's part in diagnosing appellant's malady or in performing the laminectomy; that there was no proof that Dr. Spence's treatment was responsible for appellant's disabilities; and that notwithstanding some evidence to show negligent postoperative care, an absence of medical testimony to show causality precluded submission of the case against the hospital to the jury. The judge did not allude specifically to the alleged breach of duty by Dr. Spence to divulge the possible consequences of the laminectomy.

We reverse. The testimony of appellant and his mother that Dr. Spence did not reveal the risk of paralysis from the laminectomy made out a prima facie case of violation of the physician's duty to disclose which Dr. Spence's explanation did not negate as a matter of law. * * *

III

*   *   *

* * * True consent to what happens to one's self is the informed exercise of a choice, and that entails an opportunity to evaluate knowledgeably the options available and the risks attendant upon each. The average patient has little or no understanding of the medical arts, and ordinarily has only his physician to whom he can look for enlightenment with which to reach an intelligent decision. From these almost axiomatic considerations springs the need, and in turn the requirement, of a reasonable divulgence by physician to patient to make such a decision possible.

A physician is under a duty to treat his patient skillfully but proficiency in diagnosis and therapy is not the full measure of his responsibility. The cases demonstrate that the physician is under an obligation to communicate specific information to the patient when the exigencies of reasonable care call for it. Due care may require a physician perceiving symptoms of bodily abnormality to alert the patient to the condition. It may call upon the physician confronting an ailment which does not respond to his ministrations to inform the patient thereof. It may command the physician to instruct the patient as to any limitations to be presently observed for his own welfare, and as to any precautionary therapy he should seek in the future. It may oblige the physician to advise the patient of the need for or desirability of any alternative treatment promising greater benefit than that being pursued. Just as plainly, due care normally demands that the physician warn the patient of any risks to his well-being which contemplated therapy may involve.

The context in which the duty of risk-disclosure arises is invariably the occasion for decision as to whether a particular treatment procedure is to be undertaken. To the physician, whose training enables a self-satisfying evaluation, the answer may seem clear, but it is the prerogative of the patient, not the physician, to determine for himself the direction in which his interests seem to lie. To enable the patient to chart his course understandably, some familiarity with the therapeutic alternatives and their hazards becomes essential.

A reasonable revelation in these respects is not only a necessity but, as we see it, is as much a matter of the physician's duty. It is a duty to warn of the dangers lurking in the proposed treatment, and that is surely a facet of due care. It is, too, a duty to impart information which the patient has every right to expect. The patient's reliance upon the physician is a trust of the kind which traditionally has exacted obligations beyond those associated with arms-length transactions. His dependence upon the physician for information affecting his well-being, in terms of contemplated treatment, is well-nigh abject. As earlier noted, long before the instant litigation arose, courts had recognized that the physician had the responsibility of satisfying the vital informational needs of the patient. More recently, we ourselves have found "in the fiducial qualities of [the physician-patient] relationship the physician's duty to reveal to the patient that which in his best interests it is important that he should know." We now find, as a part of the physician's overall obligation to the patient, a similar duty of reasonable disclosure of the choices with respect to proposed therapy and the dangers inherently and potentially involved.

* * *

IV

Duty to disclose has gained recognition in a large number of American jurisdictions, but more largely on a different rationale. The majority of courts dealing with the problem have made the duty depend on whether it was the custom of physicians practicing in the community to make the particular disclosure to the patient. If so, the physician may be held liable for an unreasonable and injurious failure to divulge, but there can be no recovery unless the omission forsakes a practice prevalent in the profession. We agree that the physician's noncompliance with a professional custom to reveal, like any other departure from prevailing medical practice, may give rise to liability to the patient. We do not agree that the patient's cause of action is dependent upon the existence and nonperformance of a relevant professional tradition.

There are, in our view, formidable obstacles to acceptance of the notion that the physician's obligation to disclose is either germinated or limited by medical practice. To begin with, the reality of any discernible custom reflecting a professional concensus [sic] on communication of option and risk information to patients is open to serious doubt. We sense the danger that what in fact is no custom at all may be taken as an affirmative custom to maintain silence, and that physician-witnesses to the so-called custom may state merely their personal opinions as to what they or others would do under given conditions. We cannot gloss over the inconsistency between reliance on a general practice respecting divulgence and,

on the other hand, realization that the myriad of variables among patients makes each case so different that its omission can rationally be justified only by the effect of its individual circumstances. Nor can we ignore
the fact that to bind the disclosure obligation to medical usage is to arro-
gate the decision on revelation to the physician alone. Respect for the patient's right of self-determination on particular therapy demands a standard set by law for physicians rather than one which physicians may or
may not impose upon themselves.

* * * The caliber of the performance exacted by the reasonable-care
standard varies between the professional and non-professional worlds,
and so also the role of professional custom. * * *

* * *

The majority rule, moreover, is at war with our prior holdings that a
showing of medical practice, however probative, does not fix the standard
governing recovery for medical malpractice. Prevailing medical practice,
we have maintained, has evidentiary value in determinations as to what
the specific criteria measuring challenged professional conduct are and
whether they have been met, but does not itself define the standard. That
has been our position in treatment cases, where the physician's performance is ordinarily to be adjudicated by the special medical standard of
due care. We see no logic in a different rule for nondisclosure cases, where
the governing standard is much more largely divorced from professional
considerations. And surely in nondisclosure cases the factfinder is not invariably functioning in an area of such technical complexity that it must
be bound to medical custom as an inexorable application of the community standard of reasonable care.

Thus we distinguished, for purposes of duty to disclose, the special-
and general-standard aspects of the physician-patient relationship. When
medical judgment enters the picture and for that reason the special
standard controls, prevailing medical practice must be given its just due.
In all other instances, however, the general standard exacting ordinary
care applies, and that standard is set by law. In sum, the physician's duty
to disclose is governed by the same legal principles applicable to others in
comparable situations, with modifications only to the extent that medical
judgment enters the picture. We hold that the standard measuring performance of that duty by physicians, as by others, is conduct which is reasonable under the circumstances.

V

Once the circumstances give rise to a duty on the physician's part to
inform his patient, the next inquiry is the scope of the disclosure the physician is legally obliged to make. * * *The larger number of courts, as
might be expected, have applied tests framed with reference to prevailing

fashion within the medical profession. * * * We have explored this rather considerable body of law but are unprepared to follow it. The duty to disclose, we have reasoned, arises from phenomena apart from medical custom and practice. The latter, we think, should no more establish the scope of the duty than its existence. Any definition of scope in terms purely of a professional standard is at odds with the patient's prerogative to decide on projected therapy himself. That prerogative, we have said, is at the very foundation of the duty to disclose, and both the patient's right to know and the physician's correlative obligation to tell him are diluted to the extent that its compass is dictated by the medical profession.

In our view, the patient's right of self-decision shapes the boundaries of the duty to reveal. That right can be effectively exercised only if the patient possesses enough information to enable an intelligent choice. The scope of the physician's communications to the patient, then, must be measured by the patient's need, and that need is the information material to the decision. Thus the test for determining whether a particular peril must be divulged is its materiality to the patient's decision: all risks potentially affecting the decision must be unmasked. And to safeguard the patient's interest in achieving his own determination on treatment, the law must itself set the standard for adequate disclosure.

Optimally for the patient, exposure of a risk would be mandatory whenever the patient would deem it significant to his decision, either singly or in combination with other risks. Such a requirement, however, would summon the physician to second-guess the patient, whose ideas on materiality could hardly be known to the physician. That would make an undue demand upon medical practitioners, whose conduct, like that of others, is to be measured in terms of reasonableness. Consonantly with orthodox negligence doctrine, the physician's liability for nondisclosure is to be determined on the basis of foresight, not hindsight; no less than any other aspect of negligence, the issue on nondisclosure must be approached from the viewpoint of the reasonableness of the physician's divulgence in terms of what he knows or should know to be the patient's informational needs. If, but only if, the fact-finder can say that the physician's communication was unreasonably inadequate is an imposition of liability legally or morally justified.

Of necessity, the content of the disclosure rests in the first instance with the physician. Ordinarily it is only he who is in position to identify particular dangers; always he must make a judgment, in terms of materiality, as to whether and to what extent revelation to the patient is called for. He cannot know with complete exactitude what the patient would consider important to his decision, but on the basis of his medical training and experience he can sense how the average, reasonable patient expectably would react. Indeed, with knowledge of, or ability to learn, his patient's background and current condition, he is in a position superior to that of most others—attorneys, for example—who are called upon to make judgments on pain of liability in damages for unreasonable miscalculation.

From these considerations we derive the breadth of the disclosure of risks legally to be required. The scope of the standard is not subjective as to either the physician or the patient; it remains objective with due regard for the patient's informational needs and with suitable leeway for the physician's situation. In broad outline, we agree that "[a] risk is thus material when a reasonable person, in what the physician knows or should know to be the patient's position, would be likely to attach significance to the risk or cluster of risks in deciding whether or not to forego the proposed therapy."

The topics importantly demanding a communication of information are the inherent and potential hazards of the proposed treatment, the alternatives to that treatment, if any, and the results likely if the patient remains untreated. The factors contributing significance to the dangerousness of a medical technique are, of course, the incidence of injury and the degree of the harm threatened. A very small chance of death or serious disablement may well be significant; a potential disability which dramatically outweighs the potential benefit of the therapy or the detriments of the existing malady may summon discussion with the patient.

There is no bright line separating the significant from the insignificant; the answer in any case must abide a rule of reason. Some dangers—infection, for example—are inherent in any operation; there is no obligation to communicate those of which persons of average sophistication are aware. Even more clearly, the physician bears no responsibility for discussion of hazards the patient has already discovered, or those having no apparent materiality to patients' decision on therapy. The disclosure doctrine, like others marking lines between permissible and impermissible behavior in medical practice, is in essence a requirement of conduct prudent under the circumstances. Whenever nondisclosure of particular risk information is open to debate by reasonable-minded men, the issue is for the finder of the facts.

NOTES AND QUESTIONS

1.   Imagine you are a trial judge in the District Court of the District of Columbia circuit. What will you extract from *Canterbury* as a clear and precise statement of the law of informed consent? How will you craft jury instructions on the evaluation of a physician's disclosure? Can you criticize Judge Robinson's logic? His statement of the standard? For the backstory on this case, see Alan Meisel, Canterbury v. Spence: The Inadvertent Landmark Case in Health Law & Bioethics Cases in Context, Sandra H. Johnson, et al. (eds.) (2009).

2.   A slight majority of courts has adopted the professional disclosure standard, measuring the duty to disclose by the standard of the reasonable medical practitioner similarly situated. Expert testimony is required to establish the content of a reasonable disclosure. The *Canterbury* rule, using the "reasonable patient" as the measure of the scope of disclosure, has won over several states in the last few years. Some states have adopted tort reform legislation that imposes the professional disclosure standard. See Eady v. Lansford, 351 Ark. 249, 92 S.W.3d 57 (2002); Walls v. Shreck, 265 Neb. 683, 658 N.W.2d 686 (2003). King and Moulton conclude that twenty five states have the physician-based standard, two a hybrid standard, and the rest a patient-based standard. Jaime Staples King and Benjamin Moulton, Rethinking Informed Consent: The Case for Shared Medical Decisionmaking, 32 Am. J. Law & Med. 429, 493–501 (2006) (Appendix).

What justifies the professional standard? Jurisdictions that follow the professional standard ordinarily require the plaintiff to offer medical testimony to establish 1) that a reasonable medical practitioner in the same or similar community would make this disclosure, and 2) that the defendant did not comply with this community standard. Fuller v. Starnes, 268 Ark. 476, 597 S.W.2d 88 (1980). Expert testimony is essential, since determination of what information needs to be disclosed is viewed as a medical question.

3.   Judge Robinson suggests that the *Canterbury* standard is nothing more than the uniform application of the negligence principle to medical practice. However, the negligence principle normally evaluates the conduct of a reasonable actor—not the expectations of a reasonable victim. The values served by the doctrine—patient autonomy and dignity—are unrelated to the values served by the doctrine of negligence. Informed consent really serves the values we otherwise identify with the doctrine of battery. It is ironic that a doctrine developed to foster and recognize individual choice should be measured by an objective standard.

4.   The effect of a patient-oriented disclosure standard is to ease the plaintiff's burden of proof, because the trier of fact could find that a doctor acted unreasonably in failing to disclose, in spite of unrebutted expert medical testimony to the contrary. The question of whether a physician disclosed risks that a reasonable person would find material is for the trier of fact, and technical expertise is not required. Pedersen v. Vahidy, 209 Conn. 510, 552 A.2d 419 (1989). Expert testimony is still needed, however, to clarify the treatments and their probabilities of risks. Cross v. Trapp, 170 W.Va. 459, 294 S.E.2d 446, 455 (1982).

5.   The doctor must consider disclosure of a variety of factors:

a.   Diagnosis. This includes the medical steps preceding diagnosis, including tests and their alternatives.

b.   Nature and purpose of the proposed treatment.

c.   Risks of the treatment. The threshold of disclosure, as the *Canterbury* court suggests, varies with the product of the probability and the severity of the risk. Thus a five percent risk of lengthened recuperation might be ignored, while a one percent risk of paralysis, as in *Canterbury* or an even smaller risk of death, should be disclosed. Cobbs v. Grant, 8 Cal.3d 229, 104 Cal.Rptr. 505, 502 P.2d 1 (1972). The risk, even if small, may be significant to the particular plaintiff because of unique health considerations. Hartke v. McKelway, 707 F.2d 1544, 1549 (D.C.Cir.1983).

The difference between a temporary and permanent risk can be critical: even the mention in a consent form of the general risk, characterized as temporary when it could be permanent, will be insufficient to constitute full disclosure. See, e.g., Johnson v. Brandy, 1995 WL 29230 (Ohio App.1995) (risk of scalp numbness after scalp-reduction surgery for baldness not described as permanent risk, but only temporary; consent form held to be inadequate disclosure).

Where a drug or injectable substance is part of treatment, a patient is entitled to know whether that drug or substance has been tested or approved by Federal authorities such as the Food and Drug Administration. Gaston v. Hunter, 121 Ariz. 33, 588 P.2d 326 (App.1978) (investigational procedure must be disclosed).

One area of controversy has been the disclosure of physician experience with a surgical procedure where his or her experience and skill affects patient risks in a significant way. In Johnson v. Kokemoor, 545 N.W.2d 495 (Wisconsin1996), the plaintiff suffered from a posterior brain aneurysm. The defendant surgeon clipped the aneurysm, a "technical success", but the plaintiff was rendered an incomplete quadriplegic, unable to walk or control bowel and bladder; , her vision, speech and upper body coordination were partially impaired. The court held admissible the defendant's failure to reveal his relative lack of experience in performing posterior aneurysms; to compare the morbidity and mortality rates for this type of surgery between experienced surgeons and inexperienced surgeons like himself; and to refer the plaintiff to a tertiary care center with more experience brain surgeons. The plaintiff had questioned the defendant about his experience, and the defendant had responded to her questioning with inaccurate information.

Another similar case is Willis v. Bender, 596 F.3d 1244 (10th Circuit 2010), in which the defendant, a general surgeon, perforated the plaintiff small bowel while performing a laparoscopic surgery to remove her gallbladder. The plaintiff had asked the defendant several questions before deciding to proceed, including whether he had ever been sued, had had problems with his medical license, and the extent of his experience and track record with the laparoscopic procedure. The court observed that "Bender had in fact been sued several times, including by a family of a patient who had died after undergoing [the same procedure] performed by Bender in 2001." The court framed the issue as "not whether Bender had a duty under Wyoming's informed consent law to voluntarily disclose physician-specific information but rather whether he had a duty to truthfully answer Willis' physician-specific questions." The court concluded that the Wyoming Supreme Court would allows an informed consent in a case like this where the patient sought *concrete verifiable facts.*" See section 3 infra for a discussion of the Physician Compare website.

     d.   Treatment alternatives. Doctors should disclose those alternatives that are generally acknowledged within the medical community as feasible, Martin v. Richards, 192 Wis.2d 156, 531 N.W.2d 70, 78 (1995), their risks and consequences, and their probability of success. Even if the alternative is more hazardous, some courts have held that it should be disclosed. Logan v. Greenwich Hospital Association, 191 Conn. 282, 465 A.2d 294 (1983).

     A physician must disclose medical information even if the procedure is noninvasive, because forgoing aggressive treatments in order to wait and observe a patient may entail significant risks. Martin v. Richards, 192 Wis.2d 156, 531 N.W.2d 70, 79 (1995) (physician failed to disclose to parents the risks of intracranial bleeding and the need for a CT scan or transfer to another facility in that case).

     If the alternative is not a legitimate treatment option, it need not be disclosed to the patient. See Morris v. Ferriss, 669 So.2d 1316 (La.App. 4 Cir.1996) (physician did not have to advise patient that psychiatric treatment was an alternative treatment for epileptic partial complex seizures because it was not accepted as feasible).

     e.   Consequences of patient refusal of tests or treatments. How about offering a patient a test that may prevent a life-threatening outcome, and having the patient refuse the test? Must the doctor explain the consequences of such refusal? The California Supreme Court has held that "[i]f the physician knows or should know of a patient's unique concerns or lack of familiarity with medical procedures, this may expand the scope of required disclosure". Truman v. Thomas, 27 Cal.3d 285, 165 Cal.Rptr. 308, 611 P.2d 902 (1980).

     f.   Disclosing the tradeoffs of treatment versus watchful waiting. In a health care environment of cost-effective care, conservative practice is the goal—doing nothing and "watchful waiting" are desirable clinical approaches to patient care. A physician may have a duty to advise a patient of the option of choosing no treatment at all. Wecker v. Amend, 22 Kan.App.2d 498, 918 P.2d 658 (1996).

     6.   More than half of the states have enacted legislation dealing with informed consent, largely in response to various "malpractice crises" in their states. The statutes take a variety of forms, from specific to general, but they all share the common thread of moving the informed consent standard toward greater deference to medical judgment. Given the current state and national mood of legislative limitations on common law tort remedies, it may be expected that the common law of informed consent will continue to be affected by legislative action. A consent form, or other written documentation of the patient's verbal consent, is treated in many states as presumptively valid

consent to the treatment at issue, with the burden on the patient to rebut the presumption. See Jaime Staples King & Benjamin W. Moulton, *supra*, note 2, for a fifty-state review of the law of informed consent.

2. Decision Aids and Informed Consent

John Wennberg and others have long argued for the use of decision aids to help patients decide whether or not to have procedures that Wennberg calls "preference-based"—such as prostate surgery or treatments for heart disease. John E. Wennberg & Philip G. Peters, Unwanted Variations in the Quality of Health Care: Can the Law Help Medicine Provide a Remedy/Remedies?, 37 Wake Forest L. Rev. 925,925–941 (2002). Decision aids (DAs) are decision support tools that provide patients with detailed and specific information on options and outcomes, help them clarify their values, and guide them through the decision making process. See, e.g., Elie A. Akl, et al., A Decision Aid for COPD Patients Considering Inhaled Steroid Therapy: Development and Before and After Pilot Testing, 15 BMC Med. Inform. Dec. Mak. 7 (2007).

The process by which such decision aids are used by the provider and the patient has come to be called "shared medical decision-making." Shared decision making is defined by King and Moulton as "a process in which the physician shares with the patient all relevant risk and benefit information on all treatment alternatives and the patient shares with the physician all relevant personal information that might make one treatment or side effect more or less tolerable than others. Then, both parties use this information to come to a mutual medical decision." Jaime Staples King and Benjamin Moulton, Rethinking Informed Consent: The Case for Shared Medical Decisionmaking, 32 Am. J. Law & Med. 429, 431 (2006). Numerous studies indicate that when decision aids (such as brochures, DVDs, or online tools) are available to patients and they have the opportunity to participate in medical decision-making with their physician, the patient-physician dialogue and patient well-being both improves. See generally the website of the Foundation for Informed Medical Decisionmaking; Michael J. Barry, Health Decision Aids To Facilitate Shared Decision Making in Office Practice, 136 Annals Internal Med. 127, 127 (2002); website of the Center for Informed Patient Shared Decision Making, Decision Aid Library, Dartmouth–Hitchcock.

The Affordable Care Act adopts the use of decision aids for preference-sensitive care in section 3506. Preference-sensitive care is defined as follows:

> medical care for which the clinical evidence does not clearly support one treatment option such that the appropriate course of treatment depends on the values of the patient or the preferences of the patient, caregivers or authorized representatives re-

garding the benefits, harms and scientific evidence for each treatment option, the use of such care should depend on the informed patient choice among clinically appropriate treatment options.

Section 3501 of the ACA adopts the patient decision aid concept, as described above, and develops a regulatory approach for implementing shared decision aids. The stated purpose is to facilitate collaboration between patients and caregivers in decisionmaking, provide information on trade-offs among treatment options, and incorporate ". . . patient preferences and values into the medical plan."

Section 3506 requires the Secretary of HHS to contract with an independent entity to develop consensus-based standards for such aids and to develop a certification process for such patient decision aids for use in federal health programs and by other interested parties. This entity will, under (2)(A), ". . . synthesize evidence and convene a broad range of experts and key stakeholders to develop and identify consensus-based standards to evaluate patient decision aids for preference sensitive care." Subsection (B) then requires that such aids be endorsed by the entity through a certification process. The Secretary will, in collaboration with other federal agencies, disseminate these aids and develop information and training for providers in their use.

Shared Decisionmaking Resource Centers will be created under the ACA, funded "to provide technical assistance to providers and to develop and disseminate best practices and other information to support and accelerate adoption, implementation, and effective use of patient decision aids and shared decisionmaking by providers." The idea is to present current clinical evidence about the risks and benefits of treatment options in an age-appropriate way, with sensitivity to different cultural and educational backgrounds.

The certification process for approving decision aids under the ACA has not yet been funded. However, some states are adopting them, and health care organizations have also been disseminating such aids.

NOTES AND QUESTIONS

1.   Section 3501 of the ACA appears to federalize the informed consent process for a certain category of medical problems, so-called "preference sensitive care," without saying so. It proposes a federal requirement for certain procedures on top of the common law of informed consent. Why did Congress think that this particular type of care was sufficiently important to require the development of federal decision aids? Take a look at the list of decision aids described in the Dartmouth website above and consider what treatments might be eligible for such aids.

Nothing in Section 3501 really "mandates" the use of such decision aids. There are no sanctions mentioned. However, given the size of the Medicare program and its role in setting practice standards in many cases by default, it would appear that decision aids will gradually start to be adopted with or without an explicit mandate. See for example the use of decision aids by Group Health Cooperative in Seattle, Washington. Group Health introduced the aids for patients with hip and knee arthritis who faced elective surgeries. See David Arterburn, et al., Introducing Decision Aids at Group Health was Linked to Sharply Lower Hip and Knee Surgery Rates and Cost, 31 Health Affairs 2094 (2012) (The authors concluded that ". . . our findings provide further evidence to support the view that the implementation of patient decision aids for some preference sensitive health conditions may both reduce the rates of elective surgery and lower costs in a setting that integrates health care and coverage.")

2.   Why does section 3501 offer such decision aids only for a certain category of care? Will not all treatment decisions benefit from an evidence-based set of tools to help patients decide at a minimum between treatment and no treatment?

3.   Section 3501 requires certification of decision aids. The certification process is found in many areas of the law, for example employment certification, such as for perioperative nursing; or LEED certification for "green" buildings. Certification validates a status or a product as meeting an understood standard of performance or reliability. Why did section 3501 choose this approach? Are there other approaches you might suggest for validating a model of informed disclosure, such as accrediting organizations like the Foundation for Informed Medical Decision Making, or the Center for Informed Choice at Dartmouth as approved issuers of decision aids? (See discussion of accreditation in Chapter 2.) Or allowing a group to "grade" the aids, much as the ECRI Institute now "grades" practice guidelines under contract with HHS? See National Guideline Clearinghouse. Are the endorsements of the National Quality Forum (a non-profit organization) more or less trustworthy than a certification? Or is the issue simply whether or not the organization itself is seen as reliable in its development and testing of standards?

4.   Washington State already has amended its informed consent statute to fund demonstration projects and to incorporate decision aids into state informed consent law. The provisions of the ACA do not describe how the burden of proof might be altered, if at all, by requirements that such aids be used. Washington State requires that such aids be used, once developed and certified. Rev. Code Wash § 7.70.060 creates a presumption of informed consent if a practitioner uses decision aids, and the presumption can only be rebutted by clear and convincing evidence.

5.   For a critical perspective on mandated disclosures in health care and other domains, see generally Omri Ben Shahar and Carl E. Schneider, The Failure of Mandated Disclosure, 159 U.Pa.L.Rev. 647 (2011), noting that

doctors fail to disclose full information, forms are poorly written, and patients fail to understand or remember even clearly described choices. Their bottom line: "Patients prefer not to make medical decisions, and the sicker and older they are, the less they wish to do so." Is their criticism equally applicable to decision aids and the procedures they explain? If you can distinguish among treatments, explain your distinctions.

PROBLEM: STATE LEGISLATION

Your state legislature is considering legislation that would provide that any physician that uses a patient decision aid, certified through the process described in the ACA, will be immune from suit under state informed consent law. You are counsel to the Governor, and she has asked you to brief her on what she should expect should the bill reach her desk. What stakeholders or interests do you expect will be contacting the Governor, and what positions will they be taking? Would you advocate that she veto the bill? What amendments might you propose to improve the legislation?

Should Congress instead choose to preempt state informed consent law and provide the same immunity? Does it have the constitutional authority to do so? Does it make any difference to you in your role as counsel whether the immunity proceeds from federal or state law?

3.   Disclosure of Physician–Specific Risk Information

Section 10331 of the ACA adopts a model of disclosure of provider performance information to consumers, creating a *Physician Compare* Internet website based on the model of the *Hospital Compare* site now in operation. This website will contain information on physician performance that will allow the public to compare physician performance on quality and patient experience measures with respect to physicians enrolled in the Medicare program.

Such information under ACA will include:

(A) measures collected under the Physician Quality Reporting Initiative;

(B) an assessment of patient health outcomes and the functional status of patients;

(C) an assessment of the continuity and coordination of care and care transitions, including episodes of care and risk-adjusted resource use;

(D) an assessment of efficiency;

(E) an assessment of patient experience and patient, caregiver, and family engagement;

(F) an assessment of the safety, effectiveness, and timeliness of care; and

(G) other information as determined appropriate by the Secretary [of HHS].

Physicians will be able to review their results before they are publicly reported, and the Secretary of HHS is admonished to ensure that the data is statistically valid and reliable, including risk adjustment mechanisms; that it provides "a robust and accurate portrayal of a physician's performance"; that appropriate attribution of care can be done when multiple physicians and other providers are involved in care; that "timely statistical performance feedback" is provided; and that Centers for Medicare & Medicaid Services (CMS) has computer and data systems capable of supporting "valid, reliable, and accurate public reporting activities authorized under this section."

Such an Internet comparison site assumes that consumers will access the site and use it to make choices among providers. Section 10331 goes one step further by providing financial incentives to patients to choose high quality providers. Subsection (h) provides that the Secretary may establish a demonstration program, not later than January 1, 2019, to provide financial incentives to Medicare beneficiaries who are furnished services by high quality physicians, as determined by the Secretary based on factors in subparagraphs (A) through (G) of subsection (a)(2).

These provisions of the ACA reinforce a consumerist movement in health, giving patients information about health care risks and costs to maximize their choice. Kristen Madison defines consumerism as "individual choice within a health care marketplace characterized by the exchange of money for health care services for health care good or services." See Kristin Madison, Patients as Regulators? Patients' Evolving Influence over Health Care Delivery, 31 J. Legal Med. 9, 15 (2010).

Consumers rely on information from many different sources, particularly websites. This consumerist approach moves the patient from a passive recipient of medical advice to an aggressive shopper seeking information to satisfy her preferences for treatments, risks, and costs. Sources of information include existing web-based sites such as WebMD®, health care report cards issued by private and public organizations, and a range of government-run websites including *Physician Compare*, *Hospital Compare*, and *Home Health Compare*. See discussion of Nursing Home Compare *infra*.

CMS has added infection rate comparisons among hospitals to the consumer shopping list. Medicare is now reporting three sets of patient safety measures on the *Hospital Compare* website:

- The Serious Complications and Deaths measures, developed by the Agency for Healthcare Research and Quality (AHRQ), provide information about how likely it is that patients will suffer from preventable complications and deaths while in the hospital.

- The Hospital Acquired Conditions measures show how often patients got certain serious conditions while in the hospital that might have been prevented if the hospital followed procedures based on best practices and scientific evidence.

- The Healthcare Associated Infection measures are developed by Centers for Disease Control and Prevention (CDC) and collected through the National Healthcare Safety Network. They provide information on infections, many of which are preventable, that occur while the patient is in the hospital. These infections can be related to devices, such as central lines and urinary catheters, or spread from patient to patient after contact with an infected person or surface.

PROBLEM: CONTENT FOR PHYSICIAN COMPARE

The Secretary has discretion to add information to the *Physician Compare* site beyond what is required in the ACA. Should the Secretary include disciplinary information provided by the state medical boards? If so, should it include complaints and investigations as well as final disciplinary actions? Should the Secretary include information on denial, limitation, or revocation of staff privileges? Should the *Physician Compare* website include malpractice filings, settlements, or judgments? In other words, should the Secretary incorporate the information that is now collected in the National Practitioner Data Bank (NPDB) which is not open to the public? (See discussion of the NPDB in Chapter 11, *infra*.) Was the failure to mention the NPDB simply a legislative oversight? Or is the ACA quietly deemphasizing the NPDB?

Note: Physician Payment Sunshine Act

The Affordable Care Act included two provisions regarding the disclosure of physician financial interests related to treatment of patients. The first creates a publicly accessible data base on industry payments made to physicians. The second requires that physicians disclose certain ownership interests to patients.

The ACA included the Physician Payment Sunshine Act (PPSA), codified at 42 U.S.C.A. § 1320a–7h (2010). The PPSA requires that manufacturers of drugs, devices, biologics, medical supplies or other items covered by Medicare or Medicaid must submit to the Secretary of HHS a list of physicians and teaching hospitals ("covered entities") to whom they have made payments or financial transfers. Reportable transfers include consulting fees, entertainment, travel (including the destination), food, honoraria, education, research, speaking or service as a faculty member, royalties, grants, or "any other" payment. The statute includes a list of exempt items, such as educational materials supplied for patients. See Chapter 20 for discussion of the PPSA and research.

Any benefit or transfer that is valued at more than $10 must be reported. Exceptions include items provided for use in charity care, educational materials intended for the benefit of the patient, distributions or dividends paid on stock held in a publicly traded company, or devices loaned to the provider for a trial period not to exceed 90 days, among a few others. Manufacturers must also disclose if they have made a payment or contribution to any other party at the request of a covered entity. If a reportable transfer is made in connection with a specific product, the name or other identifier of the item must be disclosed as well.

The reporting obligation is enforced through civil monetary penalties. The data included in the reports will be available to the public, including physicians' patients, in a searchable web site, listed by name of the manufacturer and the covered entity. The Act also includes reporting requirements for distribution of drug samples by manufacturers.

HHS issued proposed rules under the Act. 76 Fed. Reg. 78742 (Dec. 19, 2011). See also Igor Gorlach, The Shaping of the Physician Payment Sunshine Rule, 40 J.L. Med. & Ethics 700 (2012); David Sclar and Gary Keilty, Sunshine and Strategy: Managing and Monitoring Compliance with PPACA's Sunshine Provisions—Evolving Legal Requirements and Operational Considerations, 24 The Health Lawyer 5, 14 (2012) (including discussion of state sunshine statutes).

The ACA also requires that certain doctors who are referring patients for certain radiology tests, including MRIs, in which the doctors have an ownership interests (self-referrals) disclose those interests to the patients. The disclosure must be in writing and must inform the patients that they may choose a different provider for that service.

C. CAUSATION COMPLEXITIES

CANTERBURY V. SPENCE

United States Court of Appeals, District of Columbia Circuit, 1972.
464 F.2d 772.

VII.

*   *   *

Better it is, we believe, to resolve the causality issue on an objective basis: in terms of what a prudent person in the patient's position would have decided if suitably informed of all perils bearing significance. If adequate disclosure could reasonably be expected to have caused that person to decline the treatment because of the revelation of the kind of risk or danger that resulted in harm, causation is shown, but otherwise not. The patient's testimony is relevant on that score of course but it would not threaten to dominate the findings. And since that testimony would probably be appraised congruently with the factfinder's belief in its reasonableness, the case for a wholly objective standard for passing on causation is strengthened. Such a standard would in any event ease the fact-finding process and better assure the truth as its product.

NOTES AND QUESTIONS

Causation can only be established if there is a link between the failure of a doctor to disclose and the patient's injury. Two tests of causation have emerged: the objective reasonable patient test and the subjective particular patient test. The former asks what a reasonable patient would have done. The latter asks what the particular patient would have done. *Canterbury* adopted the objective test, after a good deal of vacillation. The court was concerned with patient hindsight testimony that he or she would have foregone the treatment, testimony which the court feared would be "hardly * * * more than a guess, perhaps tinged by the circumstance that the uncommunicated hazard has in fact materialized." The fear is of self-serving testimony.

The risk must be "material" to a reasonable patient in the shoes of the plaintiff. Under this standard, a patient's testimony is not needed to get the issue of causation to the jury. The testimony may be admissible and relevant on causation, but not dispositive. The jury can decide without it "what a reasonable person in that position would have done." Hartke v. McKelway, 707 F.2d 1544 (D.C.Cir.1983).

Even if the plaintiff can establish that a reasonable patient would not have consented if properly informed, evidence that the plaintiff would have consented if fully informed may be presented to the jury. Bourgeois v. McDonald, 622 So.2d 684 (La.App. 4 Cir.1993).

For a critique of the objective test of causation, see Evelyn M. Tenenbaum, Revitalizing Informed Consent and Protecting Patient Autonomy: An Appeal to Abandon Objective Causation, 64 Okla. L. Rev. 697 (2012).

IV.   CONFIDENTIALITY AND DISCLOSURE IN THE PHYSICIAN–PATIENT RELATIONSHIP

A.   BREACHES OF CONFIDENTIALITY

One of the most important obligations owed by a professional to a patient is the protection of confidences revealed by the patient to the professional. State courts have developed common law rules to protect these confidences, and most states have adopted either a comprehensive medical confidentiality statute or several statutes addressing specific types of medical information. The Federal Medical Privacy Rules under HIPAA and the amendments provided by HITECH offer an elaborate protective framework for patient information. These state and federal obligations are discussed in this section.

HUMPHERS V. FIRST INTERSTATE BANK OF OREGON

Supreme Court of Oregon, In Banc, 1985.
298 Or. 706, 696 P.2d 527.

LINDE, JUSTICE.

We are called upon to decide whether plaintiff has stated a claim for damages in alleging that her former physician revealed her identity to a daughter whom she had given up for adoption.

In 1959, according to the complaint, plaintiff, then known as Ramona Elwess or by her maiden name, Ramona Jean Peek, gave birth to a daughter in St. Charles Medical Center in Bend, Oregon. She was unmarried at the time, and her physician, Dr. Harry E. Mackey, registered her in the hospital as "Mrs. Jean Smith." The next day, Ramona consented to the child's adoption by Leslie and Shirley Swarens of Bend, who named her Leslie Dawn. The hospital's medical records concerning the birth were sealed and marked to show that they were not public. Ramona subsequently remarried and raised a family. Only Ramona's mother and husband and Dr. Mackey knew about the daughter she had given up for adoption.

Twenty-one years later the daughter, now known as Dawn Kastning, wished to establish contact with her biological mother. Unable to gain access to the confidential court file of her adoption (though apparently able to locate the attending physician), Dawn sought out Dr. Mackey, and he agreed to assist in her quest. Dr. Mackey gave Dawn a letter which stated that he had registered Ramona Jean Peek at the hospital, that although he could not locate his medical records, he remembered administering diethylstilbestrol to her, and that the possible consequences of this medication made it important for Dawn to find her biological mother. The latter statements were untrue and made only to help Dawn to breach the confidentiality of the records concerning her birth and adoption. In 1982, hospital personnel, relying on Dr. Mackey's letter, allowed Dawn to make copies of plaintiff's medical records, which enabled her to locate plaintiff, now Ramona Humphers.

Ramona Humphers was not pleased. The unexpected development upset her and caused her emotional distress, worry, sleeplessness, humiliation, embarrassment, and inability to function normally. She sought damages from the estate of Dr. Mackey, who had died, by this action against defendant as the personal representative. After alleging the facts recounted above, her complaint pleads for relief on five different theories: First, that Dr. Mackey incurred liability for "outrageous conduct"; second, that his disclosure of a professional secret fell short of the care, skill and diligence employed by other physicians in the community and commanded by statute; third, that his disclosure wrongfully breached a confidential or privileged relationship; fourth, that his disclosure of confidential information was an "invasion of privacy" in the form of an "unauthorized intrusion upon plaintiff's seclusion, solitude, and private affairs;" and fifth, that his disclosures to Dawn Kastning breached a contractual obligation of secrecy. The circuit court granted defendant's motion to dismiss the complaint on the grounds that the facts fell short of each theory of relief and ordered entry of judgment for defendant. On appeal, the Court of Appeals affirmed the dismissal of the first, second, and fifth counts but reversed on the third, breach of a confidential relationship, and the fourth, invasion of privacy. [ ] We allowed review. We hold that if plaintiff has a claim, it arose from a breach by Dr. Mackey of a professional duty to keep plaintiff's secret rather than from a violation of plaintiff's privacy.

A physician's liability for disclosing confidential information about a patient is not a new problem. In common law jurisdictions it has been more discussed than litigated throughout much of this century. There are precedents for damage actions for unauthorized disclosure of facts conveyed in confidence, although we know of none involving the disclosure of an adoption. Because such claims are made against a variety of defendants besides physicians or other professional counselors, for instance against banks [ ], and because plaintiffs understandably plead alternative theories of recovery, the decisions do not always rest on a single theory.

Sometimes, defendant may have promised confidentiality expressly or by factual implication, in this case perhaps implied by registering a patient in the hospital under an assumed name. * * * [ ] A contract claim may be adequate where the breach of confidence causes financial loss, and it may gain a longer period of limitations; but contract law may deny damages for psychic or emotional injury not within the contemplation of the contracting parties, [ ] though perhaps this is no barrier when emotional security is the very object of the promised confidentiality. A contract claim is unavailable if the defendant physician was engaged by someone other than the plaintiff [ ] and it would be an awkward fiction at best if age, mental condition, or other circumstances prevent the patient from contracting; yet such a claim might be available to someone less interested than the patient, for instance her husband [ ].

Malpractice claims, based on negligence or statute, in contrast, may offer a plaintiff professional standards of conduct independent of the defendant's assent. * * * Finally, actions for intentional infliction of severe emotional distress fail when the defendant had no such intention or * * * when a defendant was not reckless or did not behave in a manner that a factfinder could find to transcend "the farthest reaches of socially tolerable behavior." [ ] Among these diverse precedents, we need only consider the counts of breach of confidential relationship and invasion of privacy on which the Court of Appeals allowed plaintiff to proceed. Plaintiff did not pursue her other theories * * * and we express no view whether the dismissal of those counts was correct.

Privacy

Although claims of a breach of privacy and of wrongful disclosure of confidential information may seem very similar in a case like the present, which involves the disclosure of an intimate personal secret, the two claims depend on different premises and cover different ground. Their common denominator is that both assert a right to control information, but they differ in important respects. Not every secret concerns personal or private information; commercial secrets are not personal, and governmental secrets are neither personal nor private. Secrecy involves intentional concealment. * * *

For our immediate purpose, the most important distinction is that only one who holds information in confidence can be charged with a breach of confidence. If an act qualifies as a tortious invasion of privacy, it theoretically could be committed by anyone. In the present case, Dr. Mackey's professional role is relevant to a claim that he breached a duty of confidentiality, but he could be charged with an invasion of plaintiff's privacy only if anyone else who told Dawn Kastning the facts of her birth without a special privilege to do so would be liable in tort for invading the privacy of her mother.

Whether "privacy" is a usable legal category has been much debated in other English-speaking jurisdictions as well as in this country, especially since its use in tort law, to claim the protection of government against intrusions by others, became entangled with its use in constitutional law, to claim protection against rather different intrusions by government. No concept in modern law has unleashed a comparable flood of commentary, its defenders arguing that "privacy" encompasses related interests of personality and autonomy, while its critics say that these interests are properly identified, evaluated, and protected below that exalted philosophical level. Indeed, at that level, a daughter's interest in her personal identity here confronts a mother's interest in guarding her own present identity by concealing their joint past. But recognition of an interest or value deserving protection states only half a case. Tort liability depends on the defendant's wrong as well as on the plaintiff's interest, or "right," unless some rule imposes strict liability. One's preferred seclusion or anonymity may be lost in many ways; the question remains who is legally bound to protect those interests at the risk of liability.

* * *

In this country, Dean William L. Prosser and his successors, noting that early debate was more "preoccupied with the question whether the right of privacy existed" than "what it would amount to if it did," concluded that invasion of privacy "is not one tort but a complex of four" * * * Prosser and Keeton, Torts 851, § 117 (5th ed. 1984). They identify the four kinds of claims grouped under the "privacy" tort as, first, appropriation of the plaintiff's name or likeness; second, unreasonable and offensive intrusion upon the seclusion of another; third, public disclosure of private facts; and fourth, publicity which places the plaintiff in a false light in the public eye. *Id.* at 851–66. [ ]

This court has not adopted all forms of the tort wholesale. * * *

* * *

* * * The Court of Appeals concluded that the complaint alleges a case of tortious intrusion upon plaintiff's seclusion, not by physical means such as uninvited entry, wiretapping, photography, or the like, but in the sense of an offensive prying into personal matters that plaintiff reasonably has sought to keep private. [ ] We do not believe that the theory fits this case.

Doubtless plaintiff's interest qualifies as a "privacy" interest. That does not require the judgment of a court or a jury; it is established by the statutes that close adoption records to inspection without a court order. [ ]. * * * But as already stated, to identify an interest deserving protection does not suffice to collect damages from anyone who causes injury to that interest. Dr. Mackey helped Dawn Kastning find her biological mother, but we are not prepared to assume that Ms. Kastning became liable for invasion of privacy in seeking her out. Nor, we think, would anyone who knew the facts without an obligation of secrecy commit a tort simply by telling them to Ms. Kastning.

Dr. Mackey himself did not approach plaintiff or pry into any personal facts that he did not know; indeed, if he had written or spoken to his former patient to tell her that her daughter was eager to find her, it would be hard to describe such a communication alone as an invasion of privacy. The point of the claim against Dr. Mackey is not that he pried into a confidence but that he failed to keep one. If Dr. Mackey incurred liability for that, it must result from an obligation of confidentiality beyond any general duty of people at large not to invade one another's privacy. We therefore turn to plaintiff's claim that Dr. Mackey was liable for a breach of confidence, the third count of the complaint.

Breach of Confidence

It takes less judicial innovation to recognize this claim than the Court of Appeals thought. A number of decisions have held that unauthorized and unprivileged disclosure of confidential information obtained in a confidential relationship can give rise to tort damages. [ ] * * *.

* * *

In the case of the medical profession, courts in fact have found sources of a nonconsensual duty of confidentiality. Some have thought such a duty toward the patient implicit in the patient's statutory privilege to exclude the doctor's testimony in litigation[ ]. More directly in point are legal duties imposed as a condition of engaging in the professional practice of medicine or other occupations.

[The court noted that medical licensing statutes and professional regulations have been used as sources of a duty.]

This strikes us as the right approach to a claim of liability outside obligations undertaken expressly or implied in fact in entering a contractual relationship. [ ] The contours of the asserted duty of confidentiality are determined by a legal source external to the tort claim itself.

* * *

Because the duty of confidentiality is determined by standards outside the tort claim for its breach, so are the defenses of privilege or justification. Physicians, like members of many ordinary confidential professions and occupations, also may be legally obliged to report medical information to others for the protection of the patient, of other individuals, or of the public. *See, e.g.,* ORS 418.750 (physician's duty to report child abuse); ORS 433.003, 434.020 (duty to report certain diseases). * * * Even without such a legal obligation, there may be a privilege to disclose information for the safety of individuals or important to the public in matters of public interest. [ ] Some cases have found a physician privileged in disclosing information to a patient's spouse, [ ] or perhaps an intended spouse, [ ] In any event, defenses to a duty of confidentiality are determined in the same manner as the existence and scope of the duty itself. They necessarily will differ from one occupation to another and from time to time. A physician or other member of a regulated occupation is not to be held to a noncontractual duty of secrecy in a tort action when disclosure would not be a breach or would be privileged in direct enforcement of the underlying duty.

A physician's duty to keep medical and related information about a patient in confidence is beyond question. It is imposed by statute. ORS 677.190(5) provides for disqualifying or otherwise disciplining a physician for "wilfully or negligently divulging a professional secret." * * *

It is less obvious whether Dr. Mackey violated ORS 677.190(5) when he told Dawn Kastning what he knew of her birth. She was not, after all, a stranger to that proceeding. * * * If Ms. Kastning needed information about her natural mother for medical reasons, as Dr. Mackey pretended, the State Board of Medical Examiners likely would find the disclosure privileged against a charge under ORS 677.190(5); but the statement is alleged to have been a pretext designed to give her access to the hospital records. If only ORS 677.190(5) were involved, we do not know how the Board would judge a physician who assists at the birth of a child and decades later reveals to that person his or her parentage. But as already noted, other statutes specifically mandate the secrecy of adoption records. * * * Given these clear legal constraints, there is no privilege to disregard the professional duty imposed by ORS 677.190(5) solely in order to satisfy the curiosity of the person who was given up for adoption.

For these reasons, we agree with the Court of Appeals that plaintiff may proceed under her claim of breach of confidentiality in a confidential relationship. The decision of the Court of Appeals is reversed with respect to plaintiff's claim of invasion of privacy and affirmed with respect to her claim of breach of confidence in a confidential relationship, and the case is remanded to the circuit court for further proceedings on that claim.

NOTES AND QUESTIONS

1.   What harm was the plaintiff exposed to by the disclosure of her relationship to the plaintiff? Was the doctor's action a breach of medical ethics? Should he have been sanctioned by the state medical licensing board? See discussion of interaction of ethics and licensure in Chapter 2.

2.   Who uses medical information? Professional and non-professional medical staff must have access to records of patients in medical institutions for treatment purposes. Consent to such access is commonly presumed. Third party payers are the most common requestors of medical records outside the treatment setting. Access to records also is sought routinely for a variety of medical evaluation and support purposes. For example, in-house quality assurance committees, Joint Commission accreditation inspection teams, and state institutional licensure reviewers all must review medical records to assess the quality of hospital care. State public health laws require medical professionals and institutions to report a variety of medical conditions and incidents: venereal disease, contagious diseases, wounds inflicted by violence, poisonings, industrial accidents, abortions, and child abuse.

3.   Access to medical records is also sought for secondary, nonmedical purposes. Law enforcement agencies, for example, often seek access to medical information. A moderate-size Chicago hospital reported that the FBI requested information about patients as often as twice a month. Attorneys seek medical records to establish disability, personal injury, or medical malpractice claims for their clients. Though they most commonly will ask for records of their own clients, they may also want to review records of other patients to establish a pattern of knowing medical abuse by a physician or the culpability of a hospital for failing to supervise a negligent practitioner. Life, health, disability, and liability insurers often seek medical information, as do employers and credit investigators. Disclosure of information from medical records may occur without a formal request. Though secondary users of medical information commonly receive information pursuant to patient record releases, they have been known to seek and compile information surreptitiously. These secondary disclosures of medical information are of great import to patients, as disclosure can result in loss of employment or denial of insurance or

credit, or, at least, severe embarrassment. See generally the Preamble to the Medical Privacy Rules, *infra*.

4.   What legal devices have traditionally protected the confidentiality of medical information? The physician-patient privilege comes first to mind, but in fact it plays a very limited role. First, and most important, it is only a testimonial privilege, not a general obligation to maintain confidentiality: though it may permit a doctor to refuse to disclose medical information in court, it does not require the doctor to keep information from employers or insurers. Second, it is a statutory privilege or one created through judicial rulemaking and does not exist in all jurisdictions. Third, as a privilege created by state statute, it does not apply in non-diversity federal court proceedings. Fourth, the privilege in most states is subject to many exceptions. Finally, the privilege applies only to confidential disclosures made to a physician in the course of treatment and is easily waived.

5.   Several federal and state statutes protect the confidentiality of medical information. Most notable among these are amendments to the Drug Abuse and Treatment Acts and Comprehensive Alcohol Abuse and Alcoholism Prevention, Treatment, and Rehabilitation Act, 42 U.S.C.A. §§ 290dd–3, 390ee–3 (West 1982 & Supp.1986), and implementing regulations, 42 C.F.R. Part 2 (1985), which impose rigorous requirements on the disclosure of information from alcohol and drug abuse treatment programs. Some state statutes provide civil penalties for disclosure of confidential information. See Ill.Rev.Stat. ch. 91, § 815; West's Fla.Stat.Ann. § 395.018.

6.   State courts have imposed liability on doctors for violating a duty of confidentiality expressed or implied in state licensure or privilege statutes. Several common law theories have also been advanced to impose liability on professionals who disclose medical information. Two of these, invasion of privacy and breach of confidential relationship, are discussed in *Humphers*.

7.   Medical records often play a pivotal role in medical malpractice cases. By the time a malpractice action comes to trial memories may have dimmed as to what actually occurred at the time negligence is alleged to have taken place, leaving the medical record as the most telling evidence. Medical records, if properly authenticated, will usually be admitted under the business records exception to the hearsay rule. Because either documentation of inadequate care or inadequate documentation of care may result in liability, physicians are sometimes tempted to destroy records or to alter them to reflect the care they wish in retrospect they had rendered. There is nothing wrong with correcting records, so long as corrections are made in such a way as to leave the previous entry clearly readable and the new entry clearly identified as a corrected entry. Conscious concealment, fabrication, or falsification of records may result in an inference of awareness of guilt, Pisel v. Stamford Hospital, 180 Conn. 314, 340, 430 A.2d 1, 15 (1980), or punitive damages. It may also toll the statute of limitations. Finally, premature disposition of records could result in negligence liability, Fox v. Cohen, 84 Ill.App.3d 744, 40 Ill.Dec. 477, 406 N.E.2d 178 (1980).

PROBLEM: THE HUNT FOR PATIENT RECORDS

Two partners of a law firm, Findem and Howe, got the idea of working with a hospital to determine whether unpaid medical bills could be submitted to the Social Security Administration for payment as reimbursable disability treatment. They proposed the idea to the President of the law firm, who was also a trustee of the Warner General Hospital Health System.

The hospital agreed to search patient records and provide four pieces of patient information: name, telephone number, age, and medical condition. The patient registration forms were then furnished to the firm. The hospital agreed to pay a contingency fee to the firm for claims paid by Social Security. Patients who were possible candidates were called by the firm, on behalf of the hospital, telling them that they might be entitled to Social Security benefits that would help them pay their hospital bills. Some of the patients came in to talk with firm lawyers. A total of twelve thousand patient records were examined as part of this enterprise.

A group of angry former patients of Warner General have come to you to see what rights they have for what they feel is a violation of their privacy rights. How will you proceed? What arguments can you make on their behalf?

B. FEDERAL MEDICAL PRIVACY STANDARDS

Concerns about the privacy of patient medical information have intensified with the growth of both electronic recordkeeping and the Internet. The federal government studied this problem for several years before developing a highly detailed set of standards for health care providers. The HIPAA standards were effective in 2003, were amended in 2009 by the American Recovery and Reinvestment Act of 2009 (ARRA) (the Stimulus or The Recovery Act) and were amended again in 2013 by the final HIPAA Amendments.

STANDARDS FOR PRIVACY OF INDIVIDUALLY IDENTIFIABLE HEALTH INFORMATION

Department of Health and Human Services Office of the Secretary.
45 CFR Parts 160 and 164.

This regulation has three major purposes: (1) To protect and enhance the rights of consumers by providing them access to their health information and controlling the inappropriate use of that information; (2) to improve the quality of health care in the U.S. by restoring trust in the health care system among consumers, health care professionals, and the multitude of organizations and individuals committed to the delivery of care; and (3) to improve the efficiency and effectiveness of health care delivery by creating a national framework for health privacy protection that builds on efforts by states, health systems, and individual organizations and individuals.

*   *   *

In enacting HIPAA, Congress recognized the fact that administrative simplification cannot succeed if we do not also protect the privacy and confidentiality of personal health information. The provision of high-quality health care requires the exchange of personal, often-sensitive information between an individual and a skilled practitioner. Vital to that interaction is the patient's ability to trust that the information shared will be protected and kept confidential. Yet many patients are concerned that their information is not protected. Among the factors adding to this concern are the growth of the number of organizations involved in the provision of care and the processing of claims, the growing use of electronic information technology, increased efforts to market health care and other products to consumers, and the increasing ability to collect highly sensitive information about a person's current and future health status as a result of advances in scientific research.

Rules requiring the protection of health privacy in the United States have been enacted primarily by the states. While virtually every state has enacted one or more laws to safeguard privacy, these laws vary significantly from state to state and typically apply to only part of the health care system. Many states have adopted laws that protect the health information relating to certain health conditions such as mental illness, communicable diseases, cancer, HIV/AIDS, and other stigmatized conditions. An examination of state health privacy laws and regulations, however, found that "state laws, with a few notable exceptions, do not extend comprehensive protections to people's medical records." Many state rules fail to provide such basic protections as ensuring a patient's legal right to see a copy of his or her medical record. See Health Privacy Project, "The State of Health Privacy: An Uneven Terrain," Institute for Health Care Research and Policy, Georgetown University (July 1999) [] (the "Georgetown Study").

Until now, virtually no federal rules existed to protect the privacy of health information and guarantee patient access to such information. This final rule establishes, for the first time, a set of basic national privacy standards and fair information practices that provides all Americans with a basic level of protection and peace of mind that is essential to their full participation in their care. The rule sets a floor of ground rules for health care providers, health plans, and health care clearinghouses to follow, in order to protect patients and encourage them to seek needed care. The rule seeks to balance the needs of the individual with the needs of the society. It creates a framework of protection that can be strengthened by both the federal government and by states as health information systems continue to evolve.

The Office of Civil Rights, which enforces the HIPAA Privacy Rule, summarized its key provisions as promulgated in 2003.

OFFICE OF CIVIL RIGHTS, SUMMARY OF THE HIPAA PRIVACY RULE

* * *

Who Is Covered By the Privacy Rule?

The Privacy Rule, as well as all the Administrative Simplification rules, apply to health plans, health care clearinghouses, and to any health care provider who transmits health information in electronic form in connection with transactions for which the Secretary of HHS has adopted standards under HIPAA (the "covered entities"). * * * Individual and group plans that provide or pay the cost of medical care are covered entities.

* * *

Health Care Providers. Every health care provider, regardless of size, who electronically transmits health information in connection with certain transactions, is a covered entity. These transactions include claims, benefit eligibility inquiries, referral authorization requests, or other transactions for which HHS has established standards under the HIPAA Transactions Rule. Using electronic technology, such as email, does not mean a health care provider is a covered entity; the transmission must be in connection with a standard transaction. The Privacy Rule covers a health care provider whether it electronically transmits these transactions directly or uses a billing service or other third party to do so on its behalf. Health care providers include all "providers of services" (e.g., institutional providers such as hospitals) and "providers of medical or health services" (e.g., non-institutional providers such as physicians, dentists and other practitioners) as defined by Medicare, and any other person or organization that furnishes, bills, or is paid for health care.

* * *

Business Associates

Business Associate Defined. In general, a business associate is a person or organization, other than a member of a covered entity's workforce, that performs certain functions or activities on behalf of, or provides certain services to, a covered entity that involve the use or disclosure of individually identifiable health information. Business associate functions or activities on behalf of a covered entity include claims processing, data analysis, utilization review, and billing.

Business associate services to a covered entity are limited to legal, actuarial, accounting, consulting, data aggregation, management, administrative, accreditation, or financial services. However, persons or organizations are not considered business associates if their functions or services do not involve the use or disclosure of protected health information, and where any access to protected health information by such persons would be incidental, if at all. A covered entity can be the business associate of another covered entity. [Note: The definition of "business associate" is substantially expanded by the 2013 Amendments. See below.]

What Information is Protected.

Protected Health Information. The Privacy Rule protects all "individually identifiable health information" held or transmitted by a covered entity or its business associate, in any form or media, whether electronic, paper, or oral. The Privacy Rule calls this information "protected health information (PHI)."

"Individually identifiable health information" is information, including demographic data, that relates to:

- the individual's past, present or future physical or mental health or condition,
- the provision of health care to the individual, or
- the past, present, or future payment for the provision of health care to the individual,

and that identifies the individual or for which there is a reasonable basis to believe can be used to identify the individual. Individually identifiable health information includes many common identifiers (e.g., name, address, birth date, Social Security Number).

* * *

De–Identified Health Information. There are no restrictions on the use or disclosure of de-identified health information. [See discussion of de-identified information in Chapter 20.]

General Principle for Uses and Disclosures

Basic Principle. A major purpose of the Privacy Rule is to define and limit the circumstances in which an individual's protected heath information may be used or disclosed by covered entities. A covered entity may not use or disclose protected health information, except either: (1) as the Privacy Rule permits or requires; or (2) as the individual who is the subject of the information (or the individual's personal representative) authorizes in writing.

Required Disclosures. A covered entity must disclose protected health information in only two situations: (a) to individuals (or their personal representatives) specifically when they request access to, or an accounting of disclosures of, their protected health information; and (b) to HHS when it is undertaking a compliance investigation or review or enforcement action.

Permitted Uses and Disclosures.

Permitted Uses and Disclosures. A covered entity is permitted, but not required, to use and disclose protected health information, without an individual's authorization, for the following purposes or situations: (1) To the Individual [who is the subject of the information] (unless required for access or accounting of disclosures); (2) Treatment, Payment, and Health Care Operations; (3) Opportunity to Agree or Object; (4) Incident to an otherwise permitted use and disclosure; (5) Public Interest and Benefit Activities; and (6) Limited Data Set for the purposes of research, public health or health care operations. Covered entities may rely on professional ethics and best judgments in deciding which of these permissive uses and disclosures to make.

* * *

(2) **Treatment, Payment, Health Care Operations**. A covered entity may use and disclose protected health information for its own treatment, payment, and health care operations activities.

A covered entity also may disclose protected health information for the treatment activities of any health care provider, the payment activities of another covered entity and of any health care provider, or the health care operations of another covered entity involving either quality or competency assurance activities or fraud and abuse detection and compliance activities, if both covered entities have or had a relationship with the individual and the protected health information pertains to the relationship. [ ]

> **Treatment** is the provision, coordination, or management of health care and related services for an individual by one or more health care providers, including consultation between providers regarding a patient and referral of a patient by one provider to another.

> **Payment** encompasses activities of a health plan to obtain premiums, determine or fulfill responsibilities for coverage and provision of benefits, and furnish or obtain reimbursement for health care delivered to an individual and activities of a health care provider to obtain payment or be reimbursed for the provision of health care to an individual.

> **Health care operations** are any of the following activities: (a) quality assessment and improvement activities, including case management and care coordination; (b) competency assurance activities, including provider or health plan performance evalua-

tion, credentialing, and accreditation; (c) conducting or arranging for medical reviews, audits, or legal services, including fraud and abuse detection and compliance programs; (d) specified insurance functions, such as underwriting, risk rating, and reinsuring risk; (e) business planning, development, management, and administration; and (f) business management and general administrative activities of the entity, including but not limited to: de-identifying protected health information, creating a limited data set, and certain fundraising for the benefit of the covered entity.

Most uses and disclosures of psychotherapy notes for treatment, payment, and health care operations purposes require an authorization as described below.

Obtaining "consent" (written permission from individuals to use and disclose their protected health information for treatment, payment, and health care operations) is optional under the Privacy Rule for all covered entities. The content of a consent form, and the process for obtaining consent, are at the discretion of the covered entity electing to seek consent.

(3) **Uses and Disclosures with Opportunity to Agree or Object**. Informal permission may be obtained by asking the individual outright, or by circumstances that clearly give the individual the opportunity to agree, acquiesce, or object. Where the individual is incapacitated, in an emergency situation, or not available, covered entities generally may make such uses and disclosures, if in the exercise of their professional judgment, the use or disclosure is determined to be in the best interests of the individual.

(4) **Incidental Use and Disclosure**. The Privacy Rule does not require that every risk of an incidental use or disclosure of protected health information be eliminated. A use or disclosure of this information that occurs as a result of, or as "incident to," an otherwise permitted use or disclosure is permitted as long as the covered entity has adopted reasonable safeguards as required by the Privacy Rule, and the information being shared was limited to the "minimum necessary," as required by the Privacy Rule.[ ]

(5) **Public Interest and Benefit Activities**. The Privacy Rule permits use and disclosure of protected health information, without an individual's authorization or permission, for 12 national priority purposes. These disclosures are permitted, although not required, by the Rule in recognition of the important uses made of health information outside of the health care context. Specific conditions or limitations apply to each public interest purpose, striking the balance between the individual privacy interest and the public interest need for this information.

Required by Law. Covered entities may use and disclose protected health information without individual authorization as required by law (including by statute, regulation, or court orders).

Public Health Activities. Covered entities may disclose protected health information to: (1) public health authorities authorized by law to collect or receive such information for preventing or controlling disease, injury, or disability and to public health or other government authorities authorized to receive reports of child abuse and neglect; (2) entities subject to FDA regulation regarding FDA regulated products or activities for purposes such as adverse event reporting, tracking of products, product recalls, and postmarketing surveillance; (3) individuals who may have contracted or been exposed to a communicable disease when notification is authorized by law; and (4) employers, regarding employees, when requested by employers, for information concerning a work-related illness or injury or workplace related medical surveillance, because such information is needed by the employer to comply with the Occupational Safety and Health Administration (OSHA), the Mine Safety and Health Administration (MSHA), or similar state law.

[Other permissive disclosures may be made for example regarding victims of abuse, health oversight activities, judicial and administrative proceedings, law enforcement, research, serious threats to public safety, Workers' Compensation, and essential government functions.]

*   *   *

Authorized Uses and Disclosures

Authorization. A covered entity must obtain the individual's written authorization for any use or disclosure of protected health information that is not for treatment, payment or health care operations or otherwise permitted or required by the Privacy Rule. A covered entity may not condition treatment, payment, enrollment, or benefits eligibility on an individual granting an authorization, except in limited circumstances.

An authorization must be written in specific terms. It may allow use and disclosure of protected health information by the covered entity seeking the authorization, or by a third party. Examples of disclosures that would require an individual's authorization include disclosures to a life insurer for coverage purposes, disclosures to an employer of the results of a pre-employment physical or lab test, or disclosures to a pharmaceutical firm for their own marketing purposes.

All authorizations must be in plain language, and contain specific information regarding the information to be disclosed or used, the person(s) disclosing and receiving the information, expiration, right to revoke in writing, and other data. * * *

Psychotherapy Notes. A covered entity must obtain an individual's authorization to use or disclose psychotherapy notes * * *.

Marketing. Marketing is any communication about a product or service that encourages recipients to purchase or use the product or service. The Privacy Rule carves out the following health-related activities from this definition of marketing:

- Communications to describe health-related products or services, or payment for them, provided by or included in a benefit plan of the covered entity making the communication;

- Communications about participating providers in a provider or health plan network, replacement of or enhancements to a health plan, and health-related products or services available only to a health plan's enrollees that add value to, but are not part of, the benefits plan;

- Communications for treatment of the individual; and

- Communications for case management or care coordination for the individual, or to direct or recommend alternative treatments, therapies, health care providers, or care settings to the individual.

Marketing also is an arrangement between a covered entity and any other entity whereby the covered entity discloses protected health information, in exchange for direct or indirect remuneration, for the other entity to communicate about its own products or services encouraging the use or purchase of those products or services. A covered entity must obtain an authorization to use or disclose protected health information for marketing, except for face-to-face marketing communications between a covered entity and an individual, and for a covered entity's provision of promotional gifts of nominal value. No authorization is needed, however, to make a communication that falls within one of the exceptions to the marketing definition. An authorization for marketing that involves the covered entity's receipt of direct or indirect remuneration from a third party must reveal that fact.[ ]

Limiting Uses and Disclosures to the Minimum Necessary

Minimum Necessary. A central aspect of the Privacy Rule is the principle of "minimum necessary" use and disclosure. A covered entity must make reasonable efforts to use, disclose, and request only the minimum amount of protected health information needed to accomplish the intended purpose of the use, disclosure, or request. A covered entity must develop and implement policies and procedures to reasonably limit uses and disclosures to the minimum necessary. When the minimum necessary standard applies to a use or disclosure, a covered entity may not use, disclose, or request the entire medical record for a particular purpose, unless it can specifically justify the whole record as the amount reasonably needed for the purpose. [ ]

The minimum necessary requirement is not imposed in any of the following circumstances: (a) disclosure to or a request by a health care provider for treatment; (b) disclosure to an individual who is the subject of the information, or the individual's personal representative; (c) use or disclosure made pursuant to an authorization; (d) disclosure to HHS for complaint investigation, compliance review or enforcement; (e) use or disclosure that is required by law; or (f) use or disclosure required for compliance with the HIPAA Transactions Rule or other HIPAA Administrative Simplification Rules.

Access and Uses. For internal uses, a covered entity must develop and implement policies and procedures that restrict access and uses of protected health information based on the specific roles of the members of their workforce. * * *

Disclosures and Requests for Disclosures. Covered entities must establish and implement policies and procedures (which may be standard protocols) for routine, recurring disclosures, or requests for disclosures, that limits the protected health information disclosed to that which is the minimum amount reasonably necessary to achieve the purpose of the disclosure. Individual review of each disclosure is not required. For nonroutine, non-recurring disclosures, or requests for disclosures that it makes, covered entities must develop criteria designed to limit disclosures to the information reasonably necessary to accomplish the purpose of the disclosure and review each of these requests individually in accordance with the established criteria.

* * *

Notice and Other Individual Rights

Privacy Practices Notice. Each covered entity, with certain exceptions, must provide a notice of its privacy practices. The Privacy Rule requires that the notice contain certain elements. The notice must describe the ways in which the covered entity may use and disclose protected health information. The notice must state the covered entity's duties to protect privacy, provide a notice of privacy practices, and abide by the terms of the current notice. The notice must describe individuals' rights including the right to complain to HHS and to the covered entity if they believe their privacy rights have been violated. The notice must include a point of contact for further information and for making complaints to the covered entity. Covered entities must act in accordance with their notices. The Rule also contains specific distribution requirements for direct treatment providers, all other health care providers, and health plans. [ ]

* * *

[The Privacy rules specify when and how the notice of privacy practices is presented to patients. It requires that a patient give a written acknowledgement of the receipt of the privacy practices notice, without specifying any particular form for the acknowledgment.]

Access. Except in certain circumstances, individuals have the right to review and obtain a copy of their protected health information in a covered entity's designated record set. The "designated record set" is that group of records maintained by or for a covered entity that is used, in whole or part, to make decisions about individuals, or that is a provider's medical and billing records about individuals or a health plan's enrollment, payment, claims adjudication, and case or medical management record systems. [Cost-based fees may be charged for copying and postage.]

* * *

Administrative Requirements

* * *

Privacy Policies and Procedures. A covered entity must develop and implement written privacy policies and procedures that are consistent with the Privacy Rule.

Privacy Personnel. A covered entity must designate a privacy official responsible for developing and implementing its privacy policies and procedures, and a contact person or contact office responsible for receiving complaints and providing individuals with information on the covered entity's privacy practices.

Workforce Training and Management. * * * A covered entity must train all workforce members on its privacy policies and procedures, as necessary and appropriate for them to carry out their functions. A covered entity must have and apply appropriate sanctions against workforce members who violate its privacy policies or the Privacy Rule.

Mitigation. A covered entity must mitigate, to the extent practicable, any harmful effect it learns was caused by use or disclosure of protected health information by its workforce or its business associates in violation of its privacy policies and procedures or the Privacy Rule.

Data Safeguards. A covered entity must maintain reasonable and appropriate administrative, technical, and physical safeguards to prevent intentional or unintentional use or disclosure of protected health information in violation of the Privacy Rule and to limit its incidental use and disclosure pursuant to otherwise permitted or required use or disclosure. * * *

* * *

Enforcement and Penalties for Noncompliance

* * *

Civil Money Penalties. [See Note on HITECH, below.]

Criminal Penalties. A person who knowingly obtains or discloses individually identifiable health information in violation of HIPAA faces a fine of $50,000 and up to one-year imprisonment. The criminal penalties increase to $100,000 and up to five years imprisonment if the wrongful conduct involves false pretenses, and to $250,000 and up to ten years imprisonment if the wrongful conduct involves the intent to sell, transfer, or use individually identifiable health information for commercial advantage, personal gain, or malicious harm. Criminal sanctions will be enforced by the Department of Justice.

* * *

NOTES AND QUESTIONS

1.   The obvious benefits of computerized record-keeping have propelled medical records to a central position in health care delivery. A standardized database of patient information has the potential to promote efficiency, further competition, and allow providers to better track patient outcomes. Only a computerized record, in spite of its confidentiality dimensions, can further such goals. The Medical Privacy Standards offer considerable protection to patients; they also require substantial expenditures by providers to achieve compliance with the complex requirements.

2.   Who is covered by the Medical Privacy Rules? What are "covered entities?"

3.   HIPAA penalties have been substantially increased by subsequent legislation. See *Note: 2013 Amendments to HIPAA Privacy, Security, Breach Notification, and Enforcement Rules, infra.* Hospital medical staff are worried that they will be jailed if they inadvertently release health care information to an unauthorized person. The Office of Civil Rights (OCR) has reassured providers that they can discuss a patient's treatment among themselves. "Disclosures for treatment purposes (including requests for disclosures) between health care providers are explicitly exempted from the minimum necessary requirements."

Incidental uses and disclosures of individual identifiable health information are generally allowed when the covered entity has in place reasonable safeguards and "minimum necessary" policies and procedures to protect an individual's privacy. OCR confirmed that providers may have confidential conversations with other providers and patients even when there is a chance that they might be overheard. Nurses can speak over the phone with a patient or family member about the patient's condition. Providers may also discuss a patient's condition during training rounds at an academic medical institution.

4.   Notice the substantial compliance obligations imposed on health care providers. Critics note that HIPAA standards create little more than a federal confidentiality code based around a regulatory compliance model rather than one that creates patient rights. Nicolas P. Terry and Leslie P. Francis, Ensuring the Privacy and Confidentiality of Electronic Health Records, 2007 Univ. Ill. Law. Rev. 681, 714 (2007). Terry and Francis note that the HIPAA standards focus on the process of patient consent to disclosure, not on limits to collection of data; lack any consent-to-disclosure restrictions; lack a true national standard, given the interplay between state and federal law; apply overbroad exceptions to consent such as public health; are too lax as to secondary uses of patient information; and fail to cover all medical data or users of data.

However, the creation of privacy compliance officers in hospitals, and the requirement of staff education, is surely a good thing in terms of protection of patient's medical privacy.

5.   The Medical Privacy Standards quoted above in an abbreviated form give some sense of the scope and detail of the rules as originally promulgated. They have several laudatory goals. First and foremost, they aim to give consumers some control over their own health information. Health providers must inform patients about how their information is being used and to whom it is disclosed. The rules create a "disclosure history" for individuals. Most important, the release of private health information is limited by a requirement of authorization under some circumstances. Some nonroutine disclosure requires specific patient authorization. Patients may access their own health files and request correction of potentially harmful errors.

Second, the rules set boundaries on medical record use and release. The amount of information to be disclosed is restricted to the "minimum necessary" in contrast to prevailing practice of releasing a patient's entire health record even if an entity needs very specific information.

Third, the rules attempt to ensure the security of personal health information. The rules are very specific in their mandates on providers and others who might access health information. They require privacy-conscious business practices, with internal procedures and privacy officers to protect the privacy of medical records. The rules create a whole new category of compliance officer within health care institutions as a result of the mandates in the rules.

Fourth, the rules create accountability for medical record use and release, with new criminal and civil penalties for improper use or disclosure.

Fifth, the rules attempt to balance public responsibility with privacy protections, requiring that information be disclosed only limited public purposes such as public health and research. They attempt to limit disclosure of information without sacrificing public safety.

The Office of Civil Rights website provides useful information on HIPAA and its interpretation. In addition, the Health Privacy Project produces materials that critically address all aspects of HIPAA.

6.   HIPAA does not preempt state medical privacy statutes, according to recent court decisions. See, e.g., Yath v. Fairview Clinics, N.P., 767 N.W. 2d 34 (C.A. Minn. 2009). The plaintiff sued for invasion-of-privacy, among other theories, in a case involving the Internet posting of embarrassing personal information taken surreptitiously from her patient medical file. A clinic employee saw the plaintiff at the clinic and read her medical file, learning that she had a sexually transmitted disease and a new sex partner other than her husband. The employee disclosed this information to another employee, who then disclosed it to others, including the patient's estranged husband. Then someone created a MySpace.com webpage posting the information on the Internet. The defendants argued that Minnesota law created an obstacle to HIPAA and should be preempted. The court disagreed, concluding that the state law supported one of HIPAA's goals by establishing a disincentive to wrongful disclosure of a patient's health care record, and held that the Minnesota statute was not preempted by HIPAA.

See also R.K. v. St. Mary's Medical Center, Inc., 735 S.E.2d 715, 2012 WL 5834577 (West Virginia Supreme Court of Appeal, 2012) (quoting *Yath* case at length, the court found that " * * * such state-law claims compliment HIPAA by enhancing the penalties for its violation and thereby encouraging HIPAA compliance.") Variation among state laws regarding health information privacy presents a significant hurdle for the establishment of health information exchanges (HIEs) or even the interstate exchange of patient information. See discussion of HIEs, below.

7.   HIPAA creates a standard of care for the handling of confidential patient information, but does not create a private right of action for individuals, only criminal remedies. A person must file a written complaint with the Secretary of Health and Human Services via the Office for Civil Rights. It is then within the Secretary's discretion to investigate the complaint. HHS may impose civil penalties ranging from $100 to $25,000. Criminal sanctions range from $50,000 to $250,000, with corresponding prison terms, enforced by the Department of Justice. However, according to the 2013 Amendments, HHS "intends to seek and promote voluntary compliance" and "will seek to resolve matters by informal means whenever possible." Therefore enforcement "will be primarily complaint driven," and civil penalties will only be imposed if the violation was willful. Such penalties will not be imposed if the failure to comply was due to reasonable cause and is corrected within 30 days from when the covered entity knew or should have known of the failure to

comply. The standard is even higher for imposing criminal penalties. §§ 160.306, 160.312 (a)(1), 160.304(b), 42 U.S.C § 1320 et seq.

8.   *HIPAA Standards and Private Actions.* HIPAA has been held by the federal courts not to create a private right of action, which was not altered by the 2013 Amendments. See e.g. Acara v. Banks, 470 F.3d 569, 571 (5th Cir. 2006), in which the Fifth Circuit held: "HIPAA does not contain any express language conferring private rights upon a specific class of individuals. * * * Because HIPAA specifically delegates enforcement, there is a strong indication that Congress intended to preclude private enforcement."

One state court has allowed a plaintiff to use HIPAA standards as some evidence of a standard of care for medical records privacy. In Acosta v. Byrum, 638 S.E.2d 246 (N.C. Ct. App. 2006), *Acosta* recognized HIPAA as a basis for determining the appropriate level of care in relation to the privacy of medical information.

One court has allowed a plaintiff's tort complaint to proceed on a negligence per se theory. See I.S. v. The Washington University, Case No. 4:11CV235SNLJ (U.S. District Court, Missouri 2011), where the federal court held that the plaintiff's claim for negligence per se was valid; HIPAA was clearly implicated in the claim, which falls within the broad class of state claims based on federal regulations brought in the state court.

9.   One major liability risk created by reliance on computer record-keeping is the failure to protect such computerized patient records. Computer storage raises issues of security, privacy, and integrity of computer records. Breaches of security and unauthorized access to patient information can lead to a range of tort suits, from invasion of privacy to negligence in record maintenance. As patient records are computerized, it becomes easier to gain access to a full patient history. Patient records can be easily stored on flash drives, laptops or iPads or other media, so that access is virtually instantaneous. Computers can be hacked, and records extracted and used for a variety of criminal purposes. And they can be misplaced or stolen, a surprisingly common way in which large numbers of patient records are exposed. See generally Office of Civil Rights, Health Information Privacy, Breaches Affecting 500 or More Individuals, (listing unsecured breaches of health information; a large percentage of the breaches involve laptops or other electronic devices that were lost or stolen).10. The use of electronic health records has worried physicians. Will they reduce the risk of malpractice suits or create new risks? One study found that EHRs had substantial advantages, reducing the rate of claims to about one-sixth the rate when EHRs were not used. " * * * The results of this study support the hypothesis that EHR adoption and use lead to improved quality of care and patient safety, resulting in fewer adverse events and fewer paid malpractice claims." See Anunta Virapongse et al., Electronic Health Records and Malpractice Claims in Office Practice, 168 Arch. Intern. Med. 2362 (2008).

NOTE: 2013 AMENDMENTS TO HIPAA PRIVACY, SECURITY, BREACH NOTIFICATION, AND ENFORCEMENT RULES

The 2013 Amendments to HIPAA include a number of sweeping changes to the HIPAA Rules, finalizing the 2009 changes under the ARRA. Below is a summary of some of the amendments and their effect on the Medical Privacy rule, as first amended in 2009.

Breach. The 2013 Amendments modify the definition of "breach", originally defined as an inappropriate use or disclosure of PHI involving a *significant risk* of financial, reputational or other harm. The 2013 Amendments now provide that an impermissible use or disclosure of PHI is *presumed* to be a breach, unless it can be demonstrated that there is a *low probability* that PHI has been compromised based upon a four-part risk assessment that considers: (1) the nature and extent of the PHI involved in the breach; (2) the unauthorized person who used the PHI or to whom the disclosure was made; (3) whether the PHI was actually acquired or viewed; and (4) the extent to which the risk to PHI has been mitigated. If the risk assessment evaluation fails to demonstrate there is a low probability that any PHI has been compromised, breach notification is required. Certain exceptions to the definition of a breach continue to apply.

Notification of a Breach. Covered entities must now notify each affected individual whose unsecured PHI has been compromised. Even if such breach is caused by a business associate, the covered entity is ultimately responsible for providing the notification (although the covered entity is free to delegate the breach response function to the business associate). Moreover, a business associate's knowledge of a breach will be imputed to a covered entity. If the breach involves more than 500 persons, the Office of Civil Rights (OCR) must be notified in accordance with instructions posted on its website. The HIPAA-covered entity bears the ultimate burden of proof to demonstrate that all notifications were given or that the impermissible use or disclosure of PHI did not constitute a breach. The covered entity must maintain supporting documentation, including documentation pertaining to the risk assessment.

Marketing Rules. The 2013 Amendments substantially modify the definition of marketing to require an authorization from an individual for the receipt of certain marketing materials for treatment or operations purposes. Patients must first approve the use of their data for marketing communications if the maker of the product or service pays for that sales pitch. This change is aimed at patient concerns about the use of their personal health information for marketing without their consent. Marketing broadly applies to any communications about a product or service that encourages a recipient to purchase or use the product or service. The definition also includes communications issued by a covered entity or business associate regarding a treatment- or operations-related product or service offered by a third party *and* the third party has compensated the covered entity or business associate for the communication.

In these situations, an individual's authorization that covers subsidized communications is required.

Exceptions to the definition of marketing communications include any communication that is made: (1) to provide refill reminders or information regarding a drug that is currently being prescribed, as long as any financial remuneration received by the covered entity is "reasonably related" to the cost related to the marketing; (2) regarding the product or service of a third party for certain treatment or operations purposes, *except* *where financial remuneration is involved.*

The kinds of communications covered include (1) those offered to an individual as part of treatment, or to a larger population as part of operations, regarding case management, care coordination, or alternative treatment modalities; or (2) to describe a health-related product or service, or payment for the product or service, provided by the covered entity or included in a plan of benefits—examples would be communications about network-participating providers or value-added products or services not offered by a plan such as vision plan enhancements.

When the covered entity makes the communication face-to-face or the communication consists of a promotional gift of nominal value, patient authorization is not required.

Business Associates. The *Business Associates* definition was expanded by HITECH, and the 2013 regulations continue that expansion. Individuals handling patient health information in order to perform services for an entity covered by HIPAA (doctors, hospitals, health plans) are now accountable for complying with the HIPAA Privacy and Security Rules—and this accountability extends to any subcontractors that access data to help perform those services. Business associates—and their subcontractors—are now directly liable both for violations of the Security Rule and for uses and disclosures of PHI in violation of the Privacy Rule.

Business associates also have the following responsibilities:

1.   To keep records and submit compliance reports to HHS, when HHS requires such disclosure in order to investigate the business associate's compliance with HIPAA, and to cooperate with complaint investigations and compliance reviews;

2.   To disclose PHI as needed by a covered entity to respond to an individual's request for an electronic copy of his/her medical record;

3.   To notify the covered entity of a breach of unsecured PHI;

4.   To make reasonable efforts to limit use and disclosure of PHI, and requests for PHI, to the minimum necessary;

5.   To provide an accounting of disclosures; and

6.   To enter into agreements with subcontractors that comply with the Privacy and Security Rules.

Copies of Patient Health Data. Patients now have the right to receive an electronic copy of their health data and to have that copy sent at their request somewhere else, for example, to a doctor, a caregiver, or a personal health record or mobile health app. Electronic copies can be received by insecure email. The final rule still allows for a sixty day turnaround on records requested, but encourages a faster response when feasible.

Payment in Cash to Avoid PHI Sharing with Health Plans. HHS responded to concerns about sharing of certain health information that might lead to economic or other negative effects on patients. "When individuals pay by cash they can instruct their provider not to share information about their treatment with their health plan." HHS News Release, January 17, 2013.

This allows patients worried about the harms they might suffer if their personal health information got back to their employers or others can now avoid any sharing of such information by paying in cash. Physicians worry however that this may mean, in the case of diseases like HIV/AIDS, that specialists will not have access to essential patient information, defeating the purpose of the electronic health record, and putting the patient at risk of inadequate care.

Civil Monetary Liability. The 2013 Amendments substantially increase the potential civil monetary fines for violations for covered entities and business associates, and establish tiers of escalating penalty amounts based on increasing degrees of culpability of violators and other responsible parties. The 2013 Amendments also reduce OCR's discretion in assessing these fines. Fines range from $100 to $50,000 per each violation, with the minimum increasing with the degree of culpability and with an annual maximum of $1,500,000.

In circumstances where discretion is available, the Secretary, in determining the amount of penalty, is required to take into account the nature of the claims and the circumstances under which they were presented, the degree of culpability, history of prior offenses, financial condition of the person presenting the claims and other matters. OCR also intends to consider factors, such as the time period during which the violations occurred; reputational harm; and the number of individuals affected.

Breaches of Health Information, or the "Wall of Shame". The Secretary must post a list of breaches of unsecured protected health information affecting 500 or more individuals. These breaches are now posted in a new, more accessible format that allows users to search and sort the posted breaches. See Breaches Affecting More Than 500 Individuals, on the HHS Health Privacy web site.

PROBLEM: LEAKING PATIENT INFORMATION

1.   Dr. Jasmine is a dentist in solo practice. He submits his bills only by mail, not electronically; and he does not email his patients or use electronic media in any part of his business. He therefore does not give patients a Notice of Privacy Practices nor in any way indicate to patients what their rights are as to their dental history information. Jasmine sells his patient lists to various dental supply companies for their use in marketing. Has he violated HIPAA?

2.   Goldberg goes to the medical office laboratory for a series of tests, and her physician gives her a form indicating which tests have been ordered and tells her to take the form to the lab. When she arrives at the lab, she sees a sign-in sheet and a notice advising patients to deposit the form in the open basket that sits next to the sign-in sheet. The forms lie face-up in the basket, and they show a patient's name, address, birth date, social security number, and other demographic information, as well as the tests ordered. Is this a violation of HIPAA? If so, how can it be corrected?

3.   Dr. Newman, a psychiatrist, is having dinner out with colleagues when she is paged by her answering service with an urgent message to call one of her patients. She left her cell phone at home, so she borrows the phone of one of her dinner companions to return the patient's call. The borrowed cell phone automatically maintains a log of the outgoing phone number. Can a patient whose identity is thereby revealed file a complaint against Dr. Newman?

4.   During a routine blood test, Frent chats with the lab technician, Gosford, about a new football game. Gosford responds by telling an amusing story about a well known sports figure who happened to have his blood test done on the previous day by Gosford. The technician mentions the high level of steroids that the test revealed. Can the athlete sue Gosford? The laboratory? What are his options?

5.   Gosford obtains her prescriptions for genital herpes treatment from XYZ pharmacies in her area. One day she receives a mailing from a pharmaceutical company advertising their herpes treatment product. The mail has piled up with other pieces on the lobby of her apartment building, and her fellow tenants can easily see the description of the product and her name on the flyer. What recourse does Gosford have?

6.   Reconsider *Doe v. Medlantic Health Care Group, Inc., supra,* in light of HIPAA requirements and penalties. What if anything do the Medical Privacy Rules add to Doe's rights?

7.   Reconsider **Problem: The Hunt for Patient Records** in light of HIPAA requirements and penalties. Did the hospital violate HIPAA? Did the law firm?

PROBLEM: HITECH AND HIPAA

The HITECH Act both limits access to patient information beyond that required by HIPAA and also substantially improves the enforcement mechanisms available to medical consumers. If you are general counsel to a large hospital chain, what steps will you recommend in a memorandum to all system hospitals? What are the issues you will red flag? Will you propose a redesign of the compliance mechanisms to place a stronger emphasis on patient privacy issues?

Now suppose that you are the Physician Director of a large multipractice physician group. What are your worries now? Do you see different risks with a group practice, compared to a hospital chain?

C. PRIVACY, CONFIDENTIALITY, AND SECURITY IN HEALTH INFORMATION EXCHANGES

The Health Information Technology for Economic and Clinical Health Act (HITECH), which was part of the American Recovery and Reinvestment Act of 2009 (ARRA), provided federal grants to the states to establish statewide health information exchanges (HIEs). The goal of these health information exchanges is to magnify the gains in quality and efficiency that are expected generally from electronic medical records.

In its most basic form an HIE allows clinicians treating a patient to access necessary patient records—including lab test results, allergies, diagnoses made by others treating the patient, and so on—through a one-stop portal rather than by contacting each of the patient's health care providers individually. With a master patient index that gives each patient and each provider a unique identifier, the HIE consolidates patient health information from the patient's many health care providers into one virtual record. Of course, system-wide electronic medical records (EMRs)—for example, an EMR system adopted by a multi-hospital system and provided to affiliated health care professionals—are HIEs of a sort (sometimes called "enterprise HIEs"). HIEs also have the capacity to aggregate the data from EMRs to create very large data sets for research, monitoring, and performance-based payment.

Under the HITECH amendments to HIPAA, discussed in the previous section, the HIE itself is obliged to protect patient privacy by assuring that disclosure of and access to patient health information meets, at a minimum, HIPAA standards. As you saw in the discussion of HIPAA, HIPAA permits disclosure of personal health information without patient consent for treatment and payment purposes and, in itself, does not form an obstacle to HIEs. The aggregation of personal data and the broader access to that data that is part of the purpose of an HIE, however, both work to raise concerns about confidentiality and privacy that are more pointed than are currently attached to paper medical record systems.

State law may impose higher standards than does HIPAA for privacy and confidentiality and more restrictive standards for disclosure of personal health information. Variation among the states in this regard is extreme. Most states still have a variety of statutes that address specific types of information, such as genetic information and information relating to HIV, or specific disclosures, such as disclosure to parents of minors or to litigants or to government agencies. These statutes are quite specific in some respects and entirely ambiguous in others. Some of these statutes in some states fall within the authority of specific state agencies, so that there is an option of clarifying their application to HIE through agency rulemaking or policy guidance. Many of these statutes, however, simply establish a duty on the part of the provider and a legal claim on the part of the patient, with ambiguities to be resolved through litigation. Finally, most states have recognized a common law duty of confidentiality for medical information. The common law duty tends to be rather broadly stated in one or two state court cases but applied in very few specific circumstances.

Some states have enacted privacy or confidentiality statutes that replace this more episodic statutory pattern with a more coherent framework. Some states are hoping to propose and enact a statute specifically to govern the confidentiality and privacy issues for an HIE. Most states, however, are planning to work with their state law as it is and to use consent and contracts to assure that disclosures through the HIE comply with state law.

One of the major goals of a statewide HIE must be to assure providers that their mere participation will not subject them to legal risk for violation of their duties under these laws. Of course, the state variation could be leveled if Congress would preempt state law entirely or would pay states to voluntarily submit to federal standards for privacy of personal health information.

An HIE's consent, privacy, and confidentiality standards must inspire trust on the part of patients that the information will not be misused or distributed inappropriately. That concern extends to providers as well.

Patient trust is viewed as a significant factor in encouraging participation and has led most developing HIEs to adopt some form of consent for the exchange of clinical information for treatment purposes even though this is not required in HIPAA. State law may also require consent for the exchange of clinical information even if HIPAA doesn't. Providers currently are not required to participate in a regional or statewide HIE.

A counterweight to trust-building through individualized consent requirements, however, is the important goal of assuring a high participation rate among providers and patients. Burdensome consent policies may encumber broad participation.

For discussion of these issues, see Consumer Consent Options for Electronic Health Information Exchange: Policy Considerations and Analysis, Privacy and White Paper Series, ONC (March 2010); Tiger Team Recommendations Concerning Privacy and Security Policies and Practices (September 2010), both available on the website of the Office of the National Coordinator.

PROBLEM: CONSENT TO DISCLOSURE WITHIN AN HIE

Your state's HITECH project is developing a structure for a statewide HIE, including rules for privacy and confidentiality. The consent policies are not the only protection for patients, of course. The HIE will have policies concerning security, authorization of individuals to have access to information, authentication of the identity of persons disclosing and accessing information, an audit process for compliance, and so on. There are federal standards for authentication, authorization, and audit, which your HIE intends to adopt. The stickier question is how the HIE should handle the issue of patient consent for disclosure of personal health information for treatment purposes.

Three options have been identified. First, the HIE could adopt HIPAA standards and allow the exchange of information for treatment and payment purposes without consent. Second, the HIE could presume that patients consent to disclosure and allow patients to opt out of the HIE. The opt-out model usually requires that providers give their patients notice of the HIE and the opportunity to refuse to participate. Opting out could be made easier or more difficult as the HIE chooses. Third, the HIE could require that patients opt in to the HIE by recording their affirmative consent. The opt in model could make the consent durable (i.e., not requiring a refresh and having no expiration date); it is likely to provide that the consent is easily revocable; and it might require only a global consent to both disclosure and access given at one point of service or on the web or, alternatively, could require consent for each provider to disclose or access information. Most states are choosing among different forms of the opt-out and opt-in models.

HITECH requires that the state use an open and transparent process to develop its HIE policies. Who are the stakeholders who should participate in making the decision concerning consent? What positions would you expect them to take? How would you expect the choice to affect the participation rate, trust in the exchange, workflow for providers, and so on? Which model do you think should be chosen?

The issue of consent is linked directly to the type of information that is included in the EMRs in the HIE. Assume that your state has several statutes that govern the confidentiality and disclosure of information relating to particularly sensitive types of health information. Statutes in your state specifically require patient "authorization" or "permission" or "written authorization" for the disclosure of genetic information, HIV status, and mental health treatment information. How would this influence your choice of the no-consent-needed, opt-out, or opt-in model? How easy would it be to exclude the restricted information, if you choose the no-consent-needed or opt-out model? Assuming that you will have the technical capacity to block particular discrete information bits, would you be able to exclude lab results of a genetic or HIV test? If your statute concerning genetic information defines that information more broadly than a DNA test, as many such statutes do, how easy will it be to exclude that information? Your statute prohibits disclosing HIV status, with certain exceptions that are quite narrow and ambiguous. What clinical information is likely to disclose HIV status? What kind of clinical information concerns mental health treatment?

So far, your HITECH project is examining only the use of personal health information for treatment purposes. Do you anticipate that you will use a uniform consent model for all the uses you may permit for the data in the exchange? Or, will you use different models for different uses? Will you require consent for access to de-identified data for research purposes, for example? (See discussion in Chapter 19.) For quality monitoring or quality improvement efforts? For access by insurers, or would that depend on the purpose for which they are accessing the information? Should employers have access to the HIE? Should courts be permitted to issue subpoenas requiring the HIE to open the information to plaintiffs and defendants in litigation in which a party's health is at issue? Will your HIE adopt a policy concerning whether payers—private, Medicaid, or Medicare—can require patients to consent to the payer's access to their information in the HIE as a condition of coverage?

CHAPTER 4

LIABILITY OF HEALTH CARE PROFESSIONALS

■ ■ ■

This chapter will examine the framework for a malpractice suit against health care professionals and the doctrinal and evidentiary dimensions of such litigation. As you read the chapter, think about the cases and materials on three levels. First, how is the plaintiff's case proved and how does the defendant counter it? Second, how does tort doctrine respond to medical error? And third, how does malpractice litigation affect medical practice and the cost and quality of medical care?

I. THE STANDARD OF CARE

A. ESTABLISHING THE STANDARD OF CARE

HALL V. HILBUN
Supreme Court of Mississippi, 1985.
466 So.2d 856.

ROBERTSON, JUSTICE, for the Court:

I.

This matter is before the Court on Petition for Rehearing presenting primarily the question whether we should, as a necessary incident to a just adjudication of the case at bar, refine and elaborate upon our law regarding (a) the standard of care applicable to physicians in medical malpractice cases and (b) the matter of how expert witnesses may be qualified in such litigation.

*   *   *

When this matter was before the Court on direct appeal, we determined that the judgment below in favor of the surgeon, Dr. Glyn R. Hilbun, rendered following the granting of a motion for a directed verdict, had been correctly entered. * * *

For the reasons set forth below, we now regard that our original decision was incorrect. * * *

II.

Terry O. Hall was admitted to the Singing River Hospital in Jackson County, Mississippi, in the early morning hours of May 18, 1978, complaining of abdominal discomfort. Because he was of the opinion his patient had a surgical problem, Dr. R.D. Ward, her physician, requested Dr. Glyn R. Hilbun, a general surgeon, to enter the case for consultation. Examination suggested that the discomfort and illness were probably caused by an obstruction of the small bowel. Dr. Hilbun recommended an exploratory laparotomy [sic]. Consent being given, Dr. Hilbun performed the surgery about noon on May 20, 1978, with apparent success.

Following surgery Mrs. Hall was moved to a recovery room at 1:35 p.m., where Dr. Hilbun remained in attendance with her until about 2:50 p.m. At that time Mrs. Hall was alert and communicating with him. All vital signs were stable. Mrs. Hall was then moved to a private room where she expired some 14 hours later.

On May 19, 1980, Glenn Hall commenced this wrongful death action by the filing of his complaint * * *.

* * *

At trial Glenn Hall, plaintiff below and appellant here, described the fact of the surgery. He then testified that he remained with his wife in her hospital room from the time of her arrival from the recovery room at approximately 3:00 p.m. on May 20, 1978, until she ultimately expired at approximately 5:00 a.m. on the morning of May 21. Hall stated that his wife complained of pain at about 9:00 p.m. and was given morphine for relief, after which she fell asleep. Thereafter, Hall observed that his wife had difficulty in breathing which he reported to the nurses. He inquired if something was wrong and was told his wife was all right and that such breathing was not unusual following surgery. The labored breathing then subsided for an hour or more. Later, Mrs. Hall awakened and again complained of pain in her abdomen and requested a sedative, which was administered following which she fell asleep. Mrs. Hall experienced further difficulty in breathing, and her husband reported this, too. Again, a nurse told Hall that such was normal, that patients sometimes make a lot of noise after surgery.

After the nurse left the following occurred, according to Hall.

[A]t this time I followed her [the nurse] into the hall and walked in the hall a minute. Then I walked back into the room, and walked back out in the hall. Then I walked into the room again and I walked over to my wife and put my hand on her arm because she had stopped making that noise. Then I bent over and flipped the light on and got closer to her where I could see her, and it looked like she was having a real hard problem breathing

and she was turning pale or a bluish color. And I went to scream-
ing.

Dr. Hilbun was called and came to the hospital immediately only to
find his patient had expired. The cause of the death of Terry O. Hall was
subsequently determined to be adult respiratory distress syndrome (car-
dio-respiratory failure).

Dr. Hilbun was called as an adverse witness and gave testimony
largely in accord with that above. * * *.

Dr. Hilbun stated the surgery was performed on a Saturday. Following the patient's removal to her room, he "went home and was on call that
weekend for anything that might come up." Dr. Hilbun made no follow-up
contacts with his patient, nor did he make any inquiry that evening regarding Mrs. Hall's post-operative progress. Moreover, he was *not* contacted by the nursing staff or others concerning Mrs. Hall's condition during the afternoon or evening of May 20 following surgery, or the early
morning hours of May 21, although the exhibits introduced at trial disclose fluctuations in the vital signs late in the evening of May 20 and
more so, in the early morning hours of May 21. Dr. Hilbun's next contact
with his patient came when he was called by Glenn Hall about 4:55 or
5:00 that morning. By then it was too late.

*   *   *

The autopsy performed upon Mrs. Hall's body revealed the cause of
death and, additionally, disclosed that a laparotomy [sic] sponge had been
left in the patient's abdominal cavity. The evidence, however, without
contradiction establishes that the sponge did not contribute to Mrs. Hall's
death. Although the sponge may ultimately have caused illness, this possibility was foreclosed by the patient's untimely death.

Plaintiff's theory of the case centered around the post-operative care
provided by Dr. Hilbun. Two areas of fault suggested were Dr. Hilbun's
failure to make inquiry regarding his patient's post-operative course prior
to his retiring on the night of May 20 and his alleged failure to give appropriate post-operative instructions to the hospital nursing staff.

When questioned at trial, Dr. Hilbun first stated that he had practiced for 16 years in the Singing River Hospital and was familiar with the
routine of making surgical notes, i.e., a history of the surgery. He explained that the post-operative orders were noted on the record out of
courtesy by Dr. Judy Fabian, the anesthesiologist on the case. He stated
such orders were customarily approved by his signature or he would add
or subtract from the record to reflect the exact situation.

[Dr. Hilbun testified as to the post-operative orders noted in the medical records as of May 20, 1978. Mrs. Hall had a nasogastric tube, an i.v.,
a catheter; she was receiving medications for pain, nausea, and infections.

He testified that he checked on Mrs. Hall in the recovery room and stayed with her, took her vital signs, and discharged her to the floor. He confirmed on cross examination that he customarily followed his patient postoperatively, Until the patient left the hospital.]

* * *

Insofar as the record reflects, Dr. Hilbun gave the nursing staff no instructions regarding the post-operative monitoring and care of Mrs. Hall beyond those [summarized above]. Dr. Hilbun had no contact with Mrs. Hall after 3:00 p.m. on May 20. Fourteen hours later she was dead.

The plaintiff called Dr. S.O. Hoerr, a retired surgeon of Cleveland, Ohio, as an expert witness. The record reflects that Dr. Hoerr is a *cum laude* graduate of the Harvard Medical School, enjoys the respect of his peers, and has had many years of surgical practice. Through him the plaintiff sought to establish that there is a national standard of surgical practice and surgical care of patients in the United States to which all surgeons, including Dr. Hilbun, are obligated to adhere. Dr. Hoerr conceded that he did not know for a fact the standard of professional skill, including surgical skills and post-operative care, practiced by general surgeons in Pascagoula, Mississippi, but that he did know what the standard should have been.

* * * [T]he trial court ruled that Dr. Hoerr was not qualified to give an opinion as to whether Dr. Hilbun's post-operative regimen departed from the obligatory standard of care. * * *.

* * *

Parts of Dr. Hoerr's testimony excluded under the trial judge's ruling follow:

A. My opinion is that she [Mrs. Hall] did not receive the type of care that she should have received from the general surgical specialist and that he [Dr. Hilbun] was negligent in not following this patient; contacting, checking on the condition of his patient sometime in the evening of May 20th. *It is important in the post-operative care of patients to remember that very serious complications can follow abdominal operations, in particular in the first few hours after a surgical procedure.* And this can be inward bleeding; it can be an explosive development in an infection; or *it can be the development of a serious pulmonary complication, as it was in this patient. As a result of her condition, it is my opinion that he lost the opportunity to diagnose a condition, which in all probability could have been diagnosed at the time by an experienced general surgeon, one with expertise in thoracic surgery. And then appropriate treatment could have been undertaken to abort the complications and save her life.*

There are different ways that a surgeon can keep track of his patient—"follow her" as the expression goes—besides a bedside visit, which is the best way and which need not be very long at all, in which the vital signs are checked over. The surgeon gets a general impression of what's going on. He can delegate this responsibility to a competent physician, who need not be a surgeon but could be a knowledgeable family practitioner. He could call in and ask to speak to the registered nurse in charge of the patient and determine through her what the vital signs are, and if she is an experienced Registered Nurse what her evaluation of the patient is. *From my review of the record, none of these things took place, and there is no effort as far as I can see that Dr. Hilbun made any effort to find out what was going on with this patient during that period of time.* I might say or add an additional belief that I felt that the nursing responsibility which should have been exercised was not exercised, particularly at the 4:00 a.m. level when the pulse rate was recorded at 140 per minute without any effort as far as I can see to have any physician see the patient or to get in touch with the operating surgeon and so on.

There is an additional thing that Dr. Hilbun could have done if he felt that the nursing services might be spotty—sometimes good, sometimes bad. This is commonly done in Columbus, Ohio, in Ashtabula, Pascagoula, etcetera. *He could put limits on the degree in which the vital signs can vary, expressing the order that he should be called if they exceeded that.* Examples would be: Call me if the pulse rate goes over 110; call me if the temperature exceeds 101; call me if the blood pressure drops below 100. There is a simple way of spelling out for the nursing services what the limits of discretion belong to them and the point at which the doctor should be called.

*   *   *

Dr. Hilbun did not place any orders on the chart for the nurses to call him in the event of a change in the vital signs of Mrs. Hall. He normally made afternoon rounds between 4:00 and 5:00 p.m. but didn't recall whether he went by to see her before going home. Dr. Hilbun was on call at the hospital that weekend for anything which might come up. Subsequent to the operation and previous to Mrs. Hall's death, he was called about one other person on the same ward, one door down, twice during the night. He made no inquiry concerning Mrs. Hall, nor did he see or communicate with her.

Dr. Donald Dohn, of expertise unquestioned by plaintiff and with years of practical experience, gave testimony for the defendant. He had practiced on the staff at the Cleveland Clinic Foundation in Cleveland, Ohio, beginning in 1958. Fortuitously, he had moved to Pascagoula, Mississippi, about one month before the trial. Dr. Dohn stated he had practiced in the Singing River Hospital for a short time and there was a great difference in the standard of care in medical procedures in Cleveland, Ohio, and those in Pascagoula, Mississippi. Although he had practiced three weeks in Pascagoula, he was still in the process of acquainting himself with the local conditions. He explained the differences as follows:

> Well, there are personnel differences. There are equipment differences. There are diagnostic differences. There are differences in staff responsibility and so on. For example, at the Cleveland Clinic on our service we had ten residents that we were training. They worked with us as our right hands. Here we have no staff. So it is up to us to do the things that our residents would have done there. There we had a team of five or six nurses and other personnel in the operating room to help us. Here we have nurses in the operating room, but there is no assigned team. You get the luck of the draw that day. I am finding out these things myself. Up there it is a big center; a thousand beds, and it is a regional center. We have tremendous advantages with technical systems, various types of x-ray equipment that is [sic] sophisticated. Also in terms of the intensive care unit, we had a Neurosurgical Intensive Care with people who were specially trained as a team to work there. From my standpoint personally, I seldom had to do much paperwork there as compared to what I have to do now. I have to dictate everything and take all my notes. So, as you can see, there is a difference.

Finally, he again stated the standard of care in Ohio and the standard of care in the Singing River Hospital are very different, although it is obvious to the careful reader of Dr. Dohn's testimony that in so doing he had reference to the differences in equipment, personnel and resources and not differences in the standards of skill, medical knowledge and general medical competence a physician could be expected to bring to bear upon the treatment of a patient.

At the conclusion of the plaintiff's case, defendant moved for a directed verdict on the obvious grounds that, the testimony of Drs. Hoerr and Sachs having been excluded, the Plaintiff had failed to present a legally sufficient quantum of evidence to establish a prima facie case. The Circuit Court granted the motion. * * *

III.

A. *General Considerations*

Medical malpractice is legal fault by a physician or surgeon. It arises from the failure of a physician to provide the quality of care required by law. When a physician undertakes to treat a patient, he takes on an obligation enforceable at law to use minimally sound medical judgment and render minimally competent care in the course of the services he provides. A physician does not guarantee recovery. If a patient sustains injury because of the physician's failure to perform the duty he has assumed under our law, the physician may be liable in damages. A competent physician is not liable *per se* for a mere error of judgment, mistaken diagnosis or the occurrence of an undesirable result.

The twin principles undergirding our stewardship of the law regulating professional liability of physicians have always been reason and fairness. For years in medical malpractice litigation we regarded as reasonable and fair what came to be known as the "locality rule" (but which has always consisted of at least two separate rules, one a rule of substantive law, the other a rule of evidence).

*   *   *

C.   *The Physician's Duty of Care: A primary rule of substantive law*

1.   *The Backdrop*

*   *   *

2.   *The Inevitable Ascendency of National Standards*

*   *   *

We would have to put our heads in the sand to ignore the "nationalization" of medical education and training. Medical school admission standards are similar across the country. Curricula are substantially the same. Internship and residency programs for those entering medical specialties have substantially common components. Nationally uniform standards are enforced in the case of certification of specialists. Differences and changes in these areas occur temporally, not geographically.

Physicians are far more mobile than they once were. They frequently attend medical school in one state, do a residency in another, establish a practice in a third and after a period of time relocate to a fourth. All the while, they have ready access to professional and scientific journals and seminars for continuing medical education from across the country. Common sense and experience inform us that the laws of medicine do not vary from state to state in anything like the manner our public law does.

Medicine is a science, though its practice be an art (as distinguished from a business). Regarding the basic matter of the learning, skill and competence a physician may bring to bear in the treatment of a given patient, state lines are largely irrelevant. That a patient's temperature is 105 degrees means the same in New York as in Mississippi. Bones break and heal in Washington the same as in Florida, in Minnesota the same as in Texas. * * *

*   *   *

3.   The Competence–Based National Standard of Care: Herein of the Limited Role of Local Custom

All of the above informs our understanding and articulation of the competence-based duty of care. Each physician may with reason and fairness be expected to possess or have reasonable access to such medical knowledge as is commonly possessed or reasonably available to minimally competent physicians in the same specialty or general field of practice throughout the United States, to have a realistic understanding of the limitations on his or her knowledge or competence, and, in general, to exercise minimally adequate medical judgment. Beyond that, each physician has a duty to have a practical working knowledge of the facilities, equipment, resources (including personnel in health related fields and their general level of knowledge and competence), and options (including what specialized services or facilities may be available in larger communities, e.g., Memphis, Birmingham, Jackson, New Orleans, etc.) reasonably available to him or her as well as the practical limitations on same.

In the care and treatment of each patient, each physician has a nondelegable duty to render professional services consistent with that objectively ascertained minimally acceptable level of competence he may be expected to apply given the qualifications and level of expertise he holds himself out as possessing and given the circumstances of the particular case. The professional services contemplated within this duty concern the entire caring process, including but not limited to examination, history, testing, diagnosis, course of treatment, medication, surgery, follow-up, after-care and the like.

*   *   *

Mention should be made in this context of the role of good medical judgment which, because medicine is not an exact science, must be brought to bear in diagnostic and treatment decisions daily. Some physicians are more reluctant to recommend radical surgery than are other equally competent physicians. There exist legitimate differences of opinion regarding medications to be employed in particular contexts. "Waiting periods" and their duration are the subject of bona fide medical controversy. * * *We repeat: a physician may incur civil liability only when the quality of care he renders (including his judgment calls) falls below minimally acceptable levels.

Different medical judgments are made by physicians whose offices are across the street from one another. Comparable differences in medical judgment or opinion exist among physicians geographically separated by much greater distances, and in this sense local custom does and must continue to play a role within our law, albeit a limited one.

We recognize that customs vary within given medical communities and from one medical community to another. Conformity with established medical custom practiced by minimally competent physicians in a given area, while evidence of performance of the duty of care, may never be conclusive of such compliance. [ ] The content of the duty of care must be objectively determined by reference to the availability of medical and practical knowledge which would be brought to bear in the treatment of like or similar patients under like or similar circumstances by minimally competent physicians in the same field, given the facilities, resources and options available. The content of the duty of care may be informed by local medical custom but never subsumed by it.

* · *   *

4.   The Resources–Based Caveat to the National Standard of Care

The duty of care, as it thus emerges from considerations of reason and fairness, when applied to the facts of the world of medical science and practice, takes two forms: (a) a duty to render a quality of care consonant with the level of medical and practical knowledge the physician may reasonably be expected to possess and the medical judgment he may be expected to exercise, and (b) a duty based upon the adept use of such medical facilities, services, equipment and options as are reasonably available. With respect to this second form of the duty, we regard that there remains a core of validity to the premises of the old locality rule.

*   *   *

A physician practicing in Noxubee County, for example, may hardly be faulted for failure to perform a CAT scan when the necessary facilities and equipment are not reasonably available. In contradistinction, objectively reasonable expectations regarding the physician's knowledge, skill, capacity for sound medical judgment and general competence are, consistent with his field of practice and the facts and circumstances in which the patient may be found, *the same everywhere.*

*   *   *

As a result of its resources-based component, the physician's nondelegable duty of care is this: given the circumstances of each patient, each physician has a duty to use his or her knowledge and therewith treat through maximum reasonable medical recovery, each patient, with such reasonable diligence, skill, competence, and prudence as are practiced by minimally competent physicians in the same specialty or general field of practice throughout the United States, who have available to them the same general facilities, services, equipment and options.

* * *

As we deal with general principles, gray areas necessarily exist. One involves the case where needed specialized facilities and equipment are not available locally but are reasonably accessible in major medical centers—New Orleans, Jackson, Memphis. Here as elsewhere the local physician is held to minimally acceptable standards. In determining whether the physician's actions comport with his duty of care, consideration must always be given to the time factor—is the physician confronted with what reasonably appears to be a medical emergency, or does it appear likely that the patient may be transferred to an appropriate medical center without substantial risk to the health or life of the patient? Consideration must also be given to the economic factors—are the proposed transferee facilities sufficiently superior to justify the trouble and expense of transfer? Further discussion of these factors should await proper cases.

D.   Who May Qualify As Expert Medical Witness In Malpractice Case: A rule of evidence

As a general rule, if scientific, technical or other specialized knowledge will assist the trier of fact to understand the evidence or to determine a fact in issue, a witness qualified as an expert by knowledge, skill, experience, training or education (or a combination thereof), coupled with independence and lack of bias, may testify thereto in the form of an opinion or otherwise. Medical malpractice cases generally require expert witnesses to assist the trier of fact to understand the evidence.[ ]

Generally, where the expert lives or where he or she practices his or her profession has no relevance per se with respect to whether a person may be qualified and accepted by the court as an expert witness. There is no reason on principle why these factors should have per se relevance in medical malpractice cases.

* * *

In view of the refinements in the physician's duty of care * * * we hold that a qualified medical expert witness may without more express an opinion regarding the meaning and import of the duty of care * * *, given the peculiar circumstances of the case. Based on the information reasonably available to the physician, i.e., symptoms, history, test results, results of the doctor's own physical examination, x-rays, vital signs, etc., a qualified medical expert may express an opinion regarding the conclusions (possible diagnoses or areas for further examination and testing) minimally knowledgeable and competent physicians in the same specialty or general field of practice would draw, or actions (not tied to the availability of specialized facilities or equipment not generally available) they would take.

Before the witness may go further, he must be familiarized with the facilities, resources, services and options available. This may be done in any number of ways. The witness may prior to trial have visited the facilities, etc. He may have sat in the courtroom and listened as other witnesses described the facilities. He may have known and over the years interacted with physicians in the area. There are no doubt many other ways in which this could be done, but, significantly, we should allow the witness to be made familiar with the facilities (and customs) of the medical community in question via a properly predicated and phrased hypothetical question.

Once he has become informed of the facilities, etc. available to the defendant physician, the qualified medical expert witness may express an opinion what the care duty of the defendant physician was and whether the acts or omissions of the defendant physician were in compliance with, or fell substantially short of compliance with, that duty.

* * *

V.   Disposition of the Case at Bar

[The court reversed and remanded for a new trial, on the grounds that the testimony of Drs. Hoerr and Sachs was improperly excluded, and with their testimony, the plaintiff might have survived the defense motion for a directed verdict.]

NOTES AND QUESTIONS

1.   How does the court in Hall v. Hilbun view the customary practice of the defendant's medical specialty? Why does it adopt this position? How much of a burden is it for a defendant to rebut the plaintiff's evidence on customary practice? Could a plaintiff use the studies cited in Chapter 1 to support a position that the efficacy of a standard practice is not proven? How would a court react to such studies?

2.   The medical profession sets standards of practice and the courts have historically enforced these standards in tort suits. Defendants trying to prove a standard of care normally present expert testimony describing the actual pattern of medical practice, without any reference to the effectiveness of that practice. Courts have traditionally given professional medical standards conclusive weight, so that the trier of fact is not allowed to reject the practice as improper. See, e.g., Doe v. American Red Cross Blood Serv., 297 S.C. 430, 435, 377 S.E.2d 323, 326 (1989) (involving issue of blood bank failing to screening for HIV/AIDS at time when customary practice was not to screen).

3.   The evidence of medical practice variation, described in Chapter 6, *infra*, certainly supports the argument that customary practices are often little more than habitual practices lacking evidence of efficacy. In tort litigation not involving professionals, courts are willing to reject customary prac-

tice if they find the practice dangerous or out of date. See Joseph King, In Search of a Standard of Care for the Medical Profession—the "Accepted Practice" Formula, 28 Vand.L.Rev. 1213, 1236 (1975). Critics such as King worry that standard practice may at times be little more than a routine into which physicians have drifted by default.

4.   The customary or accepted practice standard measures physicians against the standard of their profession, not merely the standard of a reasonable and prudent person. Medical practices are always evolving as new developments and scientific studies alter the customary practice. Such evolution in medical practices often creates tensions for the physician who believes that the customary practice is dangerous but the new standard has not yet been generally accepted. See, e.g., Burton v. Brooklyn Doctors Hospital, 88 A.D.2d 217, 452 N.Y.S.2d 875 (1982), where the plaintiff was exposed while in the hospital as a newborn to a prolonged liberal application of oxygen and developed retrolental fibroplasia (RFL) as a result. The court allowed a jury instruction to the effect that adherence to acceptable practice is not a defense if the physician fails to use his best judgment. See also Toth v. Community Hospital at Glen Cove, 22 N.Y.2d 255, 292 N.Y.S.2d 440, 239 N.E.2d 368 (1968).

5.   Physicians who hold themselves out as having specialized knowledge will be held to the standard of specialists with those enhanced qualifications. See Zaverl v. Hanley, 64 P.3d 809 (Alaska 2003) (affirmative steps to present himself or herself to public as specialist is sufficient to elevate the standard).

6.   *Hall* provides an excellent discussion of the locality rule. Most states have moved from the locality rule to a similar locality or a national standard, in part due to worries about a "conspiracy of silence" that unfairly limits the pool of available experts. Doctors do not like to testify against one another. As the court noted in Mulder v. Parke Davis & Co., 288 Minn. 332, 181 N.W.2d 882 (1970), "All too frequently, and perhaps understandably, practicing physicians are reluctant to testify against one another. Unfortunately, the medical profession has been slow to fashion machinery for making impartial and objective assessments of the performance of their fellow practitioners."

Legislatures enacting malpractice reform statutes on the other hand have often imposed modified locality rule tests in order to protect physicians from out-of-state witnesses testifying for plaintiffs. See e.g. Henry v. Southeastern Ob–Gyn Associates, 142 N.C.App. 561, 543 S.E.2d 911 (2001) ("similar locality" test of N.C.Gen.Stat. S. 90–21.12 was intended to avoid the adoption of a national standard for health care providers).

NOTE: EXPERT TESTIMONY IN PROFESSIONAL LIABILITY CASES

The standard of practice in the defendant doctor's specialty or area of practice is normally established through the testimony of medical experts.

Hall illustrates the burden that the plaintiff bears. In any jurisdiction, plaintiffs, to withstand a motion for a directed verdict, must 1) qualify their medical witnesses as experts; 2) satisfy the court that the expert's testimony will assist the trier of fact; and 3) have the witnesses testify based upon facts that support their expert opinions. The requirement that the expert be of the same specialty as the defendant typically governs the qualifying of the expert for testifying at trial. The standard of care may be based upon the expert's own practice and education. See Wallbank v. Rothenberg, M.D., 74 P.3d 413 (Colo.App. 2003) (personal practices of medical experts may be relevant to the standard of care).

The abolition of the locality rule has been one way to ease the plaintiff's burden of proof, broadening the plaintiff's choices of available experts. Many states still require that the expert at least be familiar with the standard of practice in a similar locality, and some testimony is required as to the similarities between the two localities. See, e.g., First Commercial Trust Company v. Rank, 323 Ark. 390, 915 S.W.2d 262 (1996) (family practitioner was sued for medical negligence and failure to report suspected child abuse; held that Florida emergency room physician should have been allowed to testify on the standard of care for diagnosing child abuse).

Plaintiff's experts normally must be in the same specialty as the defendant. Under some circumstances, however, courts have allowed physicians in other specialties to testify, so long as the alleged negligence involved matters within the knowledge of every physician. A general surgeon can testify as to the standard of care of a plastic surgeon performing elective surgery, as to general surgical issues as to whether nerves in the forehead should have been protected, Hauser v. Bhatnager, 537 A.2d 599 (Me.1988); a cardiologist can testify in a case involving a family practice physician, Fiedler v. Spoelhof, 483 N.W.2d 486 (Minn.App.1992); and a psychiatrist has been allowed to testify as to the standard of post-operative care for a breast implant procedure, Miller v. Silver, 181 Cal.App.3d 652, 226 Cal.Rptr. 479 (1986).

An expert need not be board certified in the subject of the suit, so long as he has the appropriate education and experience. Hanson v. Baker, 534 A.2d 665 (Me.1987). Some jurisdictions adopt a narrower view, requiring that the expert have practiced in the same area as the defendant. See Bell v. Hart, 516 So.2d 562 (Ala.1987) (pharmacist and toxicologist testimony disallowed).

Expert testimony is often based upon clinical literature, FDA statements, and other evidence of the standard of practice and of side-effects of treatments and drugs. Several sources of reliable and authoritative statements may be used by experts in professional liability cases, or relied upon by the trial judge as definitive.

   a.   *Practice guidelines or parameters.* Statements by medical societies as to good practice will provide a ready-made particularized standard that an expert can use as a benchmark against which to test a defendant's conduct. See section B. *infra.*

b.   *Pharmaceutical package insert instructions and warnings.* Package inserts may be used to establish the standard of care for use of the particular drug. In Thompson v. Carter, 518 So.2d 609 (Miss.1987), the physician used Bactrim, a sulfonamide antibiotic, to treat the plaintiff's kidney infection. She developed Stevens Johnson Syndrome, a severe allergic reaction associated with use of Bactrim. The court allowed the admission of the package insert, holding that the package insert was prima facie proof of the proper method of use of Bactrim, an "authoritative published compilation by a pharmaceutical manufacturer."

c.   *Physicians Desk Reference (PDR).* The PDR is allowed by most courts as some evidence of the standard of care, if an expert witness relies on it. See, e.g., Morlino v. Medical Center, 152 N.J. 563, 706 A.2d 721 (1998). Other courts allow the PDR as prima facie evidence of the standard of the standard of care under some circumstances. See Garvey v. O'Donoghue, 530 A.2d 1141 (D.C. 1987) (holding that " * * * in a medical malpractice case alleging improper administration, dosage, and monitoring of the drug, they are admissible as both *prima facie* evidence of the standard of care and physicians' notice of their contents.")

d.   *Judicial notice.* When the defendant physician's clinical decisions violate a clearly articulated practice within the specialty, courts are sometimes even willing in rare cases to make a finding of per se negligence. See Deutsch v. Shein, 597 S.W.2d 141 (Ky.1980), where the defendant was negligent per se in ordering radiology and other tests on the pregnant plaintiff, injuring the fetus.

e.   *Substantive use of a learned treatise.* At the common law, a treatise could be used only to impeach the opponent's experts during cross-examination. It could only undercut the expert's testimony, not build the plaintiff's case. The concern was hearsay, because the author of the treatise was not available for cross-examination as to statements contained in the treatise. Federal Rule of Evidence (FRE) 803(18) creates an exception to the hearsay rule so that the learned treatise can be used for substantive purposes, so long as the treatise is accepted as reliable. Jacober v. St. Peter's Med. Ctr., 128 N.J. 475, 608 A.2d 304 (1992). An expert must be on the stand to explain and assist in the application of the treatise. Tart v. McGann, 697 F.2d 75 (2d Cir.1982). The treatise must be declared reliable by the trial court after a motion by the moving lawyer to use the treatise substantively under FRE 803(18) or its state equivalent. Maggipinto v. Reichman, 481 F.Supp. 547 (E.D.Pa.1979).

f.   *Expert reliance on research findings.* Experts in malpractice cases base their testimony on their knowledge, education, and experience. They may also rely on outside studies in the research literature. On rare occasions, courts have allowed such research material into evidence in a malpractice suit. In Young v. Horton, 259 Mont. 34, 855 P.2d 502 (1993), the court allowed into evidence four medical journal articles that had concluded that a majority of patients forget that they gave informed consent to their doctors prior to surgery. The medical expert then testified based both on his experience with informed consent and on the articles' conclusions.

The admissibility of "novel" scientific evidence is often a thorny issue in environmental and toxic tort cases, although rarely in malpractice cases. The standard for evaluating such evidence was established by the Court in Frye v. United States, 54 App.D.C. 46, 293 F. 1013 (1923), a case in which Supreme Court considered the polygraph test and its limitations. The Court held that expert opinion based on a scientific technique is inadmissible unless the technique is "generally accepted" as reliable in the relevant scientific community.

In Daubert v. Merrell Dow Pharmaceuticals, Inc., 509 U.S. 579, 113 S.Ct. 2786, 125 L.Ed.2d 469 (1993), the Court again considered the admissibility of scientific evidence, in this case epidemiological and other evidence of birth defects caused by mothers' ingestion of Bendectin. The Court rejected the *Frye* test of "general acceptability" as a threshold test of admissibility of novel scientific evidence, holding that the Federal Rules of Evidence, particularly Rule 702, make the trial judge the gatekeeper of such evidence, with the responsibility to assess the reliability of an expert's testimony, its relevance, and the underlying reasoning or methodology. Expert testimony must have a valid scientific connection to the issues in the case, and be based on "scientifically valid principles". The scientific evidence must pertain to scientific knowledge defined as falsifiable scientific theories capable of empirical testing.

The Supreme Court has extended the *Daubert* factors to all expert testimony, not just scientific testimony. In Kumho Tire v. Carmichael, 526 U.S. 137, 119 S.Ct. 1167, 143 L.Ed.2d 238 (1999), the Court held that *Daubert's* gatekeeping role for federal courts, requiring an inquiry into both relevance and reliability, applies not only to scientific testimony but to all expert testimony. The Court noted that this was a flexible test, not a checklist, and it is tied to the particular facts of the case. But "some of these factors may be helpful in evaluating the reliability even of experience-based expert testimony . . . " Id. At 1176. The use of the *Daubert* test is to "make certain that an expert, whether basing testimony upon professional studies or personal experience, employs in the courtroom the same level of intellectual rigor that characterizes the practice of an expert in the relevant field." Id. This would seem to impose a higher level of scrutiny on the typical malpractice expert, particularly in cases involving institutional liability, where the expert may testify about a system design in a hospital or a salary incentive system in a managed care system.

Courts have usually found that a qualified expert is reliable without going into the underlying scientific qualities of the opinion. See, e.g. Potter ex rel. Potter v. Bowman, 2006 WL 3760267 (D.Colo.2006) ("the touchstone of reliability is 'whether the reasoning or methodology underlying the testimony is scientifically valid'". * * *; [t]he party proffering the expert opinion must demonstrate both that the expert has employed a method that is scientifically sound and that the opinion is "based on facts which enable [the expert] to express a reasonably accurate conclusion as opposed to conjecture or speculation." The court allowed all three of plaintiff's witnesses to testify). But see Carlen v. Minnesota Comprehensive Epilepsy Program, 2001 WL 1078633 (D. Minn. 2001) (rejecting expert testimony for failing to satisfy *Daubert* factors.). The court concluded that the expert's opinion on causation was not based on a proper differential diagnosis; while he reviewed several studies, there was no evidence as to the known or potential rate of error for his methodology of evaluating causation, or whether it was generally accepted within the medical community.

B. PRACTICE GUIDELINES AS STANDARDS OF CARE

The Institute of Medicine has defined clinical guidelines as "systematically developed statements to assist practitioner and patient decisions about appropriate health care for specific clinical circumstances." They are standardized specifications for using a procedure or managing a particular clinical problem. Such guidelines may be quality-oriented, reducing variations in practice with improving patient care; they may also be cost-reducing, promoting a lower cost approach to care. The Agency for Health Care Policy and Research (AHCPR) within the Public Health Service, a subdivision of the Department of Health and Human Services (DHHS), has the responsibility for the Department's Medical Treatment Effectiveness Program. This program supports research, data development, and other activities to develop and review clinically relevant guidelines, standards of quality, performance measures, and medical review criteria, in order to improve the quality and effectiveness of health care services.

Courts have been cautious about the use of clinical practice guidelines as evidence of the standard of care. In Conn v. United States, 880 F. Supp 2d 741 (U.S.Dis.Ct, So.Dist. Miss. 2012), the federal court sitting in diversity looked at Mississippi caselaw and concluded that the Mississippi courts are open to allowing expert witnesses to rely on clinical practice guidelines when articulating the standard of care. The court wrote:

> Therefore, were this Court to hazard an *Erie* guess on the subject, it would follow Judge Koch's suggestions and find that Mississippi law permits expert witnesses to rely on clinical practice guidelines if the conduct prescribed by those guidelines does indeed describe the specific actions that would be taken by a minimally competent physician." The court however found that the plaintiff's expert neither pointed to a specific guidelines nor testifically specifically as to what a minimally competent physician would have relied on in his treatment of the plaintiff.

The court in *Conn* refers to Frakes v. Cardiology Consultants, P.C., 1997 WL 536949 (Tenn.Ct.App. 1997), a case in which the issue was the effect of a Table, "Exercise Test Parameters Associated With Poor Prognosis and/or Increased Severity of CAD" (CAD=coronary heart disease), contained in a brochure produced by the American College of Cardiology and the American Heart Association as a consensus statement on the interpretation of exercise treadmill tests. The court held that "all the experts had adopted the document as a correct statement of the standard of care, and that it would serve as a useful tool for the jury." By contrast, in Liberatore v. Kaufman et al., 835 So.2d 404 (C.A. Fla. 2003), the Court of Appeals held that the trial court had abused its discretion in allowing defendants to use a bulletin published by the American College of Obstetricians and Gynecologists (ACOG) to bolster the testimony of their expert witnesses.

NOTE: OUTCOMES, PRACTICE GUIDELINES, BEST PRACTICES, AND THE AFFORDABLE CARE ACT

The ACA has several sections that affect the potential tort liability of physicians, even though nothing in the Act deals explicitly with tort issues except the tort demonstration project section, Section 10607, *State Demonstration Programs to Evaluate Alternatives to Current Medical Tort Litigation.* What the ACA does, however, is to create four streams of pressure that converge toward measurable and specific standards of care in practice. (See generally the discussion in Chapter 1 for a fuller treatment of the quality and safety features of the ACA.)

First, outcome measures will be researched, developed, and disseminated. Section 10303 of the ACA instructs the Secretary of HHS to develop provider-level outcome measures for both hospitals and physicians, as well as other providers, in Section 10303. Such measures will include at least ten outcome measurements for acute and chronic diseases.

Second, best practices will be researched and disseminated. Section 10303 inserts a new Subpart II—Health Care Quality Improvement Programs. It mandates the Director to "identify, develop, evaluate, disseminate, and provide training in innovative methodologies and strategies for quality improvement practices in the delivery of health care services that represent best practices in health care quality, safety, and value" in collaboration with other Federal agencies.

Third, clinical practice guidelines will be developed in light of the research on outcome measures and best practice. Section 10303 (c) requires the Secretary of HHS to identify existing and new clinical practice guidelines.

Fourth, outcomes, best practices and guidelines will be disseminated rapidly to practice settings. The Center for Quality Improvement and Patient Safety will support research on system improvements and the development of tools "to facilitate adoption of best practices that improve the quality, safety, and efficiency of health care delivery services. Such support may include establishing a *Quality Improvement Network Research Program* for the purpose of testing, scaling, and disseminating of interventions to improve quality and efficiency in health care." Findings will be disseminated through multiple media and linked with the Office of the National Coordinator of Health Information Technology and used to "inform the activities of the health information technology extension program under Section 3012, as well as any relevant standards, certification criteria, or implementation specifications."

A Patient–Centered Outcomes Research Institute (PCORI) is created by Section 6301, Patient–Centered Outcomes Research. This institute is to " * * * assist patients, clinicians, purchasers, and policy-makers in making informed health decisions by advancing the quality and relevance of evidence concerning the manner in which diseases, disorders, and other health conditions can effectively and appropriately be prevented, diagnosed, treated, monitored, and managed through research and evidence synthesis." The PCORI must release its findings within 90 days of receipt and make them available to clinicians, patients, and the general public.

NOTES AND QUESTIONS

1.   Judges and academics have written about the diffusion of new medical technologies and standards of practice through social and cultural forces aided by medical specialty societies—a slow evolutionary process. The effect of the cumulative ACA requirements—with money allocated for research on practice guidelines, best practices and outcome measures—will be to accelerate the diffusion of these new standards for best practice. First, federal research dollars under the American Recovery and Reinvestment Act of 2009 are supporting research to analyze what the practice-outcome linkage and what best practices should be.

Second, the ACA mandates dissemination in a variety of ways, including websites, pay-for-performance reforms, and models of integrated practice. New payment reforms in particular will tie physician performance to these measures, particularly in ACOs, medical homes, and other new integrated modes of practice. Best practices, grounded in research and made accessible and transparent to providers, patients, and payers, will start to squeeze out medical practice variation in clinical practice. The tort effect of such narrowing of practice is clear: defenses under liability rules (e.g., respectable minority defenses, variations in practice, and proximate causation) will rapidly narrow as practice choices also narrow. The physician who doesn't keep up with new research will not only suffer income loss; she will also suffer a higher risk of liability for failing to conform to what becomes the new standard of care.

2.   How will such practice guidelines and best practices be used in a malpractice suit? The section of the ACA that creates the *Patient–Centered Outcomes Research Institute* specifies that its findings must be rapidly disseminated to clinicians, presumably so that they can adopt them. However, Section 1181 (8)(A)(iv) specifies that such research findings shall ". . . not be construed as mandates for practice guidelines, coverage recommendations, payment, or policy recommendations . . . "

How do you interpret this language? Does it mean only that dissemination is not a command to clinicians? Or that plaintiff lawyers cannot use the findings as evidence of a standard of care? Surely they can be some evidence of such a standard, and very powerful evidence at that. As a constitutional matter, could Congress limit the way state courts use the guidelines and data developed as a result of the ACA in state tort actions?

PROBLEM: THE BATTLE OF STANDARDS II

Robert Guido is recovering from a myocardial infarction (a heart attack, when blood vessels that supply blood to the heart are blocked, preventing enough oxygen from getting to the heart, so that the heart muscle dies or becomes permanently damaged.) The current practice guidelines for implantable cardioverterdefibrillator (ICD) therapy do not recommend use of an implantable cardioverterdefibrillator (ICD) for primary prevention in patients recovering from a myocardial infarction or coronary artery bypass graft surgery and those with severe heart failure symptoms or a recent diagnosis of heart failure.

Dr. Perry, Robert's cardiologist, recommends the implantation of an ICD and the procedure goes well for Robert without any immediate complications. Within six months of the angiogram, Robert suffers stent thrombosis (the stent closes off the blood vessel completely) and he suffers a major heart attack and dies. The risk of a stent thrombosis is 1% after a cardiac catheterization, carrying a 60% risk of death (with the risk of such thrombosis rising to 2.4% three years after the intervention).

You are retained by Robert's family to bring a malpractice suit against Dr. Guido. How will you develop evidence as to the standard of care and the defendant's failure to comply with it? What kinds of claims will you make in the complaint, based on what you know of the treatment choices and best practices? Can you use any of the provisions of the ACA to your advantage in this case?

See Epstein AE, DiMarco JP, Ellenbogen KA, et al., ACC/AHA/HRS 2008 Guidelines for Device–Based Therapy of Cardiac Rhythm Abnormalities: a Report of the American College of Cardiology/American Heart Association Task Force on Practice Guidelines (Writing Committee to Revise the ACC/AHA/NASPE 2002 Guideline Update for Implantation of Cardiac Pacemakers and Antiarrhythmia Devices): developed in collaboration with the American Association for Thoracic Surgery and Society of Thoracic Surgeons, 117 Circulation e350 (2008) (Guidelines emphasize limits on ICD therapy, specifying that ICDs apply only to patients whose left ventricular ejection fraction is low (30% or 35%) despite receiving optimal medical therapy.)

For a discussion of unnecessary implantations, see Sana M. Al–Khatib et al, Non–Evidence–Based ICD Implantations in the United States, 305 JAMA 43 (2011) (more than 40 percent of the total number of implanted ICDs are not based on evidence); Senate Finance Committee Staff Report on Cardiac Stent Usage at St. Joseph Medical Center(2010 (describing the overuse of stenting at one hospital and the cost to Medicare of such unnecessary procedures).

The Reasonable Practice Standard. Many jurisdictions may be moving to a *reasonable practice standard* that allows the jury to consider evidence that a custom is no longer reasonable or acceptable. The Court in Nowatske v. Osterloh, 198 Wis.2d 419, 543 N.W.2d 265 (1996) stated:

> " * * *in most situations there will be no significant difference between customary and reasonable practices. In most situations physicians, like other professionals, will revise their customary practices so that the care they offer reflects a due regard for advances in the profession. An emphasis on reasonable rather than customary practices, however, insures that custom will not shelter physicians who fail to adopt advances in their respective fields and who consequently fail to conform to the standard of care which both the profession and its patients have a right to expect.".

See generally Philip G. Peters, Jr., The Role of the Jury in Modern Malpractice Law, 87 Iowa L. Rev. 909 (2002). Peters concludes that many state courts are reconsidering deference to medical custom in malpractice cases.

C. AFFIRMATIVE DEFENSES

An affirmative defense is one that a defendant can raise by the pleadings, and may lead to a dismissal of the lawsuit after a judicial hearing on a defendant's motion to dismiss or summary judgment motion. Some affirmative defenses are ruled on by the trial court judge, and thus can resolve a case without letting the jury ever hear the plaintiff's case, while others may require factual determinations by the jury. A defendant asserting an affirmative defense may not contest negligence, but instead argue that other factors excuse his conduct as a matter of law or prevent the plaintiff from suing him at all. Consider a defense of conflicting legal duty. A doctor who releases information about a patient's medical condition normally violates the patient's right to confidentiality, but in some situations he is legally required to inform others of a patient's medical condition. If a patient suffers from a gunshot wound, the doctor treating him or her must inform the police; if he has a contagious disease the doctor must inform the department of health in the state; if child abuse is suspected, the authorities must be notified.

Consent is perhaps the most frequently asserted affirmative defense in medical malpractice cases. Doctors and hospitals have tried to protect themselves from malpractice suits by having patients sign consent forms before patients receive treatment. See discussion of informed consent in Chapter 3 *supra*.

Other less commonly asserted affirmative defenses are available under the right circumstances, such as the bar of statute of limitations and Good Samaritan laws.

1. Statute of Limitations

Malpractice litigation is subject in most states to its own statute of limitation, often shorter than other civil litigation. The complication in medical cases is often how and when the plaintiff becomes aware that her injury was caused by her physician.

The usual rule in most state jurisdictions is based on statutes of repose, so called "discovery" rules: the statute begins to run once the plaintiff: (1) has some knowledge of the injury, (2) its cause in fact, and (3) some evidence of wrongdoing on the part of the person responsible. See Hardi v. Mezzanotte, 818 A.2d 974 (D.C. Court of Appeals, 2003). The federal rule, exemplified in *Arroy,* does not require evidence of negligence by the provider but only a suspected causal connection before the statute begins to run.

2. Good Samaritan Acts

Forty-nine states and the District of Columbia have adopted Good Samaritan legislation to protect health care professionals who render emergency aid from civil liability for damages for any injury they cause or enhance. The statutes take a variety of forms. West's Ann.Cal.Bus. & Prof.Code § 2395, for example, states, in relevant part:

> No licensee, who in good faith renders emergency care at the scene of an emergency, shall be liable for any civil damages as a result of any acts or omissions by such person in rendering the emergency care.

> "The scene of an emergency" as used in this section shall include, but not be limited to, the emergency rooms of hospitals in the event of a medical disaster. * * *

Some statutes protect health care professionals, while others protect all Good Samaritans, without regard to their profession. Some states grant statutory immunity from suit to emergency medical personnel unless gross negligence is shown. Mallory v. City of Detroit, 181 Mich.App. 121, 449 N.W.2d 115 (1989). Physicians working in state institutions often are granted immunity. Verhoff v. Ohio State Univ. Medical Center, 125 Ohio Misc.2d 30, 797 N.E.2d 592 (Ct.Cl. 2003). See generally Anno., Construction of "Good Samaritan" Statutes Excusing from Civil Liability One Rendering Care in Emergency, 39 A.L.R.3d 222.

D. CONTRIBUTORY FAULT OF THE PATIENT

Patients through their own mistakes or lifestyle often enhance, or even cause, their injuries. People don't take their doctor's advice; they fall off their diets, stop exercising, start smoking, or act in a variety of ways counterproductive to their health. Very few tort cases have raised a patient's lifestyle choice as a defense to a malpractice claim. Consider the following case.

OSTROWSKI V. AZZARA

Supreme Court of New Jersey, 1988.
111 N.J. 429, 545 A.2d 148.

O'HERN, J.

This case primarily concerns the legal significance of a medical malpractice claimant's pre-treatment health habits. Although the parties agreed that such habits should not be regarded as evidencing comparative fault for the medical injury at issue, we find that the instructions to the jury failed to draw the line clearly between the normal mitigation of damages expected of any claimant and the concepts of comparative fault that can preclude recovery in a fault-based system of tort reparation. Accordingly, we reverse the judgment below that disallowed any recovery to the diabetic plaintiff who had bypass surgery to correct a loss of circulation in a leg. The need for this bypass was found by the jury to have been proximately caused by the physician's neglect in performing an improper surgical procedure on the already weakened plaintiff.

I

As noted, the parties do not dispute that a physician must exercise the degree of care commensurate with the needs of the patient as she presents herself. This is but another way of saying that a defendant takes the plaintiff as she finds her. The question here, however, is much more subtle and complex. The complication arose from the plaintiff's seemingly routine need for care of an irritated toe. The plaintiff had long suffered from diabetes attributable, in unfortunate part perhaps, to her smoking and to her failure to adhere closely to her diet. Diabetic patients often have circulatory problems. For purposes of this appeal, we shall accept the general version of the events that led up to the operation as they are set forth in defendant-physician's brief.

On May 17, 1983, plaintiff, a heavy smoker and an insulin-dependent diabetic for twenty years, first consulted with defendant, Lynn Azzara, a doctor of podiatric medicine, a specialist in the care of feet. Plaintiff had been referred to Dr. Azzara by her internist whom she had last seen in November 1982. Dr. Azzara's notes indicated that plaintiff presented a sore left big toe, which had troubled her for approximately one month, and calluses. She told Dr. Azzara that she often suffered leg cramps that caused a tightening of the leg muscles or burning in her feet and legs after walking and while lying in bed. She had had hypertension (abnormally high blood pressure) for three years and was taking a diuretic for this condition.

Physical examination revealed redness in the plaintiff's big toe and elongated and incurvated toenails. Incurvated toenails are not ingrown; rather, they press against the skin. Diminished pulses on her foot indicated decreased blood supply to that area, as well as decreased circulation and impaired vascular status. Dr. Azzara made a diagnosis of onychomycosis (a fungous disease of the nails) and formulated a plan of treatment to debride (trim) the incurvated nail. Since plaintiff had informed her of a high blood sugar level, Dr. Azzara ordered a fasting blood sugar test and a urinalysis; she also noted that a vascular examination should be considered for the following week if plaintiff showed no improvement.

Plaintiff next saw Dr. Azzara three days later, on May 20, 1983. The results of the fasting blood sugar test indicated plaintiff's blood sugar was high, with a reading of 306. The urinalysis results also indicated plaintiff's blood sugar was above normal. At this second visit, Dr. Azzara concluded that plaintiff had peripheral vascular disease, poor circulation, and diabetes with a very high sugar elevation. She discussed these conclusions with plaintiff and explained the importance of better sugar maintenance. She also explained that a complication of peripheral vascular disease and diabetes is an increased risk of losing a limb if the diabetes is not controlled. The lack of blood flow can lead to decaying tissue. The parties disagree on whether Dr. Azzara told plaintiff she had to return to her internist to treat her blood sugar and circulation problems, or whether, as plaintiff indicates, Dr. Azzara merely suggested to plaintiff that she see her internist.

In any event, plaintiff came back to Dr. Azzara on May 31, 1983, and, according to the doctor, reported that she had seen her internist and that the internist had increased her insulin and told her to return to Dr. Azzara for further treatment because of her continuing complaints of discomfort about her toe. However, plaintiff had not seen the internist. Dr. Azzara contends that she believed plaintiff's representations. A finger-stick glucose test administered to measure plaintiff's non-fasting blood sugar yielded a reading of 175. A physical examination of the toe revealed redness and drainage from the distal medial (outside front) border of the nail, and the toenail was painful to the touch. Dr. Azzara's proposed course of treatment was to avulse, or remove, all or a portion of the toenail to facilitate drainage.

Dr. Azzara says that prior to performing the removal procedure she reviewed with Mrs. Ostrowski both the risks and complications of the procedure, including nonhealing and loss of limb, as well as the risks involved with not treating the toe. Plaintiff executed a consent form authorizing Dr. Azzara to perform a total removal of her left big toenail. The nail was cut out. (Defendant testified that she cut out only a portion of the nail, although her records showed a total removal.)

Two days later, plaintiff saw her internist. He saw her four additional times in order to check the progress of the toe. As of June 30, 1983, the internist felt the toe was much improved. While plaintiff was seeing the internist, she continued to see Dr. Azzara, or her associate, Dr. Bergman. During this period the toe was healing slowly, as Dr. Azzara said one would expect with a diabetic patient.

During the time plaintiff was being treated by her internist and by Dr. Azzara, she continued to smoke despite advice to the contrary. Her internist testified at the trial that smoking accelerates and aggravates peripheral vascular disease and that a diabetic patient with vascular disease can by smoking accelerate the severity of the vascular disease by as much as fifty percent. By mid-July, plaintiff's toe had become more painful and discolored.

At this point, all accord ceases. Plaintiff claims that it was the podiatrist's failure to consult with the patient's internist and defendant's failure to establish by vascular tests that the blood flow was sufficient to heal the wound, and to take less radical care, that left her with a non-healing, pre-gangrenous wound, that is, with decaying tissue. As a result, plaintiff had to undergo immediate bypass surgery to prevent the loss of the extremity. If left untreated, the pre-gangrenous toe condition resulting from the defendant's nail removal procedure would have spread, causing loss of the leg. The plaintiff's first bypass surgery did not arrest the condition, and she underwent two additional bypass surgeries which, in the opinion of her treating vascular surgeon, directly and proximately resulted from the unnecessary toenail removal procedure on May 31, 1983. In the third operation a vein from her right leg was transplanted to her left leg to increase the flow of blood to the toe.

At trial, defense counsel was permitted to show that during the pre-treatment period before May 17, 1983, the plaintiff had smoked cigarettes and had failed to maintain her weight, diet, and blood sugar at acceptable levels. The trial court allowed this evidence of the plaintiff's pre-treatment health habits to go to the jury on the issue of proximate cause. Defense counsel elicited admissions from plaintiff's internist and vascular surgeon that some doctors believe there is a relationship between poor self-care habits and increased vascular disease, perhaps by as much as fifty percent. But no medical expert for either side testified that the plaintiff's post-treatment health habits could have caused her need for bypass surgery six weeks after defendant's toenail removal. Nevertheless, plaintiff argues that defense counsel was permitted to interrogate the plaintiff extensively on her post-avulsion and post-bypass health habits, and that the court allowed such evidence of plaintiff's health habits during the six weeks after the operation to be considered as acts of comparative negligence that could bar recovery rather than reduce her damages. The jury found that the doctor had acted negligently in cutting out the plaintiff's toenail without adequate consideration of her condition, but found plaintiff's fault (fifty-one percent) to exceed that of the physician (forty-nine percent). She was therefore disallowed any recovery. On appeal the Appellate Division affirmed in an unreported decision. We granted certification to review plaintiff's claims.[ ] We are told that since the trial, the plaintiff's left leg has been amputated above the knee. This was foreseen, but not to a reasonable degree of medical probability at the time of trial.

II

Several strands of doctrine are interwoven in the resolution of this matter. The concepts of avoidable consequences, the particularly susceptible victim, aggravation of preexisting condition, comparative negligence, and proximate cause each play a part. It may be useful to unravel those strands of doctrine for separate consideration before considering them in the composite.

Comparative negligence is a legislative amelioration of the perceived harshness of the common-law doctrine of contributory negligence. * * *

Comparative negligence was intended to ameliorate the harshness of contributory negligence but should not blur its clarity. It was designed only to leave the door open to those plaintiffs whose fault was not greater than the defendant's, not to create an independent gate-keeping function. Comparative negligence, then, will qualify the doctrine of contributory negligence when that doctrine would otherwise be applicable as a limitation on recovery. * * *

* * * The doctrine [of avoidable consequences] proceeds on the theory that a plaintiff who has suffered an injury as the proximate result of a tort cannot recover for any portion of the harm that by the exercise of ordinary care he could have avoided.[ ] * * * Avoidable consequences, then, normally comes into action when the injured party's carelessness occurs *after* the defendant's legal wrong has been committed. Contributory negligence, however, comes into action when the injured party's carelessness occurs *before* defendant's wrong has been committed or concurrently with it.[ ]

A counterweight to the doctrine of avoidable consequences is the doctrine of the particularly susceptible victim. This doctrine is familiarly expressed in the maxim that "defendant 'must take plaintiff as he finds him.' "[ ] * * * It is ameliorated by the doctrine of aggravation of a preexisting condition. While it is not entirely possible to separate the doctrines of avoidable consequence and preexisting condition, perhaps the simplest way to distinguish them is to understand that the injured person's conduct is irrelevant to the consideration of the doctrine of aggravation of a preexisting condition. Negligence law generally calls for an apportionment of damages when a plaintiff's antecedent negligence is "found not to contribute in any way to the original accident or injury, but to be a substantial contributing factor in increasing the harm which ensues." *Restatement (Second) of Torts*, § 465 at 510–11, comment c. Courts recognize that a defendant whose acts aggravate a plaintiff's preexisting condition is liable only for the amount of harm actually caused by the negligence.[ ] * * *

Finally, underpinning all of this is that most fundamental of risk allocators in the tort reparation system, the doctrine of proximate cause. * * *

We have sometimes melded proximate cause with foreseeability of unreasonable risk. * * *

We have been candid in New Jersey to see this doctrine, not so much as an expression of the mechanics of causation, but as an expression of line-drawing by courts and juries, an instrument of "overall fairness and sound public policy."[ ] * * * [ ]

III

Each of these principles, then, has some application to this case.[3] Plaintiff obviously had a preexisting condition. It is alleged that she failed to minimize the damages that she might otherwise have sustained due to mistreatment. Such mistreatment may or may not have been the proximate cause of her ultimate condition.

But we must be careful in reassembling these strands of tort doctrine that none does double duty or obscures underlying threads. In particular, we must avoid the indiscriminate application of the doctrine of comparative negligence (with its fifty percent qualifier for recovery) when the doctrines of avoidable consequences or preexisting condition apply.

The doctrine of contributory negligence bars any recovery to the claimant whose negligent action or inaction *before* the defendant's wrongdoing has been completed has contributed to cause actual invasion of plaintiff's person or property. By contrast,

> "[t]he doctrine of avoidable consequences comes into play at a later stage. Where the defendant has already committed an actionable wrong, whether tort or breach of contract, then this doctrine [avoidable consequences] limits the plaintiff's recovery by disallowing only those items of damages which could reasonably

---

[3] Each principle, however, has limitations based on other policy considerations. For example, the doctrine of avoidable consequences, although of logical application to some instances of professional malpractice, is neutralized by countervailing policy. Thus, a physician who performed a faulty tubal litigation cannot suggest that the eventual consequences of an unwanted pregnancy could have been avoided by termination of the fetus.[ ]

have been averted * * * [.]" "[C]ontributory negligence is to be asserted as a complete defense, whereas the doctrine of avoidable consequences is not considered a defense at all, but merely a rule of damages by which certain particular items of loss may be excluded from consideration * * *."

Hence, it would be the bitterest irony if the rule of comparative negligence, designed to ameliorate the harshness of contributory negligence, should serve to shut out any recovery to one who would otherwise have recovered under the law of contributory negligence. Put the other way, absent a comparative negligence act, it would have never been thought that "avoidable consequences" or "mitigation of damages" attributable to post-accident conduct of any claimant would have included a shutout of apportionable damages proximately caused by another's negligence. * * *

* * *

In this context of post-injury conduct by a claimant, given the understandable complexity of concurrent causation, expressing mitigation of damages as a percentage of fault which reduces plaintiff's damages may aid juries in their just apportionment of damages, provided that the jury understands that neither mitigation of damages nor avoidable consequences will bar the plaintiff from recovery if the defendant's conduct was a substantial factor without which the ultimate condition would not have arisen.

* * * In the field of professional health care, given the difficulty of apportionment, sound public policy requires that the professional bear the burden of demonstrating the proper segregation of damages in the aggravation context.[ ] The same policy should apply to mitigation of damages.[ ] Hence, overall fairness requires that juries evaluating apportionment of damages attributable in substantial part to a faulty medical procedure be given understandable guidance about the use of evidence of post-treatment patient fault that will assist them in making a just apportionment of damages and the burden of persuasion on the issues. This is consistent with our general view that a defendant bear the burden of proving the causal link between a plaintiff's unreasonable conduct and the extent of damages.[ ] Once that is established, it should be the "defendant who also has the burden of carving out that portion of the damages which is to be attributed to the plaintiff."[ ]

IV

As noted, in this case the parties agree on certain fundamentals. The pre-treatment health habits of a patient are not to be considered as evidence of fault that would have otherwise been pled in bar to a claim of injury due to the professional misconduct of a health professional. This conclusion bespeaks the doctrine of the particularly susceptible victim or recognition that whatever the wisdom or folly of our life-styles, society, through its laws, has not yet imposed a normative life-style on its members; and, finally, it may reflect in part an aspect of that policy judgment that health care professionals have a special responsibility with respect to diseased patients.[ ]

This does not mean, however, that the patient's poor health is irrelevant to the analysis of a claim for reparation. While the doctor may well take the patient as she found her, she cannot reverse the frames to make it appear that she was presented with a robust vascular condition; likewise, the physician cannot be expected to provide a guarantee against a cardiovascular incident. All that the law expects is that she not mistreat such a patient so as to become a proximate contributing cause to the ultimate vascular injury.

However, once the patient comes under the physician's care, the law can justly expect the patient to cooperate with the health care provider in their mutual interests. Thus, it is not unfair to expect a patient to help avoid the consequences of the condition for which the physician is treating her. * * *

Hence, we approve in this context of post-treatment conduct submission to the jury of the question whether the just mitigation or apportionment of damages may be expressed in terms of the patient's fault. If used, the numerical allocation of fault should be explained to the jury as a method of achieving the just apportionment of the damages based on their relative evaluation of each actor's contribution to the end result— that the allocation is but an aspect of the doctrine of avoidable consequences or of mitigation of damages. In this context, plaintiff should not recover more than she could have reasonably avoided, but the patient's fault will not be a bar to recovery except to the extent that her fault caused the damages.

An important caveat to that statement would be the qualification that implicitly flows from the fact that health care professionals bear the burden of proving that their mistreatment did not aggravate a preexisting condition: that the health care professional bear the burden of proving the damages that were avoidable.

Finally, before submitting the issue to the jury, a court should carefully scrutinize the evidence to see if there is a sound basis in the proofs for the assertion that the post-treatment conduct of the patient was indeed a significant cause of the increased damages. Given the short onset between the contraindicated surgery and the vascular incident here, plaintiff asserts that defendant did not present proof, to a reasonable degree of medical probability, that the plaintiff's post-treatment conduct was a proximate cause of the resultant condition. Plaintiff asserts that the only evidence given to support the defense's theory of proximate cause between plaintiff's post-treatment health habits and her damages was her internist's testimony regarding generalized studies showing that smoking increases vascular disease by fifty percent, and her vascular surgeon's testimony that some physicians believe there is a relationship among diabetes, smoking, and vascular impairment. Such testimony did not address with any degree of medical probability a relationship between her smoking or not between May 17, 1983, and the plaintiff's need for bypass surgery in July 1983. Defendant points to plaintiff's failure to consult with her internist as a cause of her injury, but the instruction to the jury gave no guidance on whether this was to be considered as conduct that concurrently or subsequently caused her injuries.[ ]

V

We acknowledge that it is difficult to parse through these principles and policies in the course of an extended appeal. We can well imagine that in the ebb and flow of trial the lines are not easily drawn. There are regrettably no easy answers to these questions.

* * *

[The court noted the factual complexities of the case, and concluded that "the instructions to the jury in this case did not adequately separate or define the concepts that were relevant to the disposition of the plaintiff's case." The case was remanded for a new trial.]

NOTES AND QUESTIONS

1.   Do you advocate applying contributory negligence, or comparative negligence (depending upon the jurisdiction), to situations such as that of *Ostrowski*? Such cases raise fundamental questions about the limits of medicine and the role of patients in their own illnesses. Can a smoker easily stop? Is it fair to bar his recovery when his smoking is not a simple, easily abandoned, choice? See Sawka v. Prokopowycz, 104 Mich.App. 829, 306 N.W.2d 354 (1981), where the plaintiff sued the defendant for his failure to diagnose lung cancer. The court rejected the claim that the plaintiff's continued smoking and failure to return for further examination as instructed were contributory negligence.

2.   Should a doctor be able to argue that a patient's negligent pre-treatment conduct as contributory negligence? See for example Cavnes v. Zabrerdac, 849 N.E.2d 526 (Indiana 2006), where a patient being treated for severe asthma had an attack. She took several doses of her medication in the course of the morning before going to the hospital emergency room, where she went into cardiac arrest and died. Defendant argued that Peggy "improperly used her medications in excess of their prescribed doses, which probably aggravated her condition, and that Peggy unreasonably delayed seeking medical treatment and emergency room care, which decreased her chances of surviving." The Court rejected the defendant's arguments:

It is people who are sick or injured that most often seek medical attention. Many of these infirmities result, at least in part, from the patients' own carelessness (e.g. negligent driving or other activities, failure to regularly exercise, unhealthy diet, smoking, etc.). To permit healthcare providers to assert their patients' pre-treatment negligent conduct to support a contributory negligence defense would absolve such providers from tort responsibility in the event of medical negligence and thus operate to undermine substantially such providers' duty of reasonable care.

3.   If a patient continues to refuse to take steps to reduce his health care risks, over a period of time, he may be held liable in comparative negligence. In Striff v. Luke Medical Practitioners, 2010 WL 5296941 (Ohio App. 3 Dist. 2010), the plaintiff Striff had a fatal heart attack. He suffered from coronary artery disease, and the defendants claimed that they followed the standard of care, but that "Striff was completely responsible for his medical condition due to his life-style choices and, more importantly, his failure to follow through with the recommendations and follow-up treatments ordered by Appellees. Mr. Striff was overweight, smoked a pack of cigarettes a day, and drank several alcoholic beverages every day. Mr. Striff also failed to obtain a lipid profile to measure his cholesterol and did not see a cardiologist, as he was instructed to do on many occasions." The jury found that 100% of the negligence that caused Striff's death was attributable to him, and the verdict was upheld on appeal.

4.   See the reporters' note on Restatement Torts, 3d, Apportionment of Liability, § 7, comment m, p. 83:

. . . the best explanation of pre-presentment negligence is that the consequences of the plaintiff's negligence—the medical condition requiring medical treatment—caused the very condition the defendant doctor undertook to treat so it would be unfair to allow the doctor to complain about that negligence.

5.   Would you treat an overzealous jogger who had cardiac arrest while running in the same way as a chain smoking or obese sedentary patient? How much of your decision is based on your desire to punish the smoker or glutton for immoral or irresponsible behavior which may be virtually impossible to control? Blaming the victim, or scapegoating, is a frequent argument used by employers, insurers and the government to reduce obligations to insure, pay benefits, or, as in Ostrowski, to pay damages for patient injury. See Robert Schwartz, Life Style, Health Status, and Distributive Justice, 3 Health Matrix 195, 198 (1993)("If all of those whose life style choices have health consequences were required to bear the full burden of those consequences, there would be few of us (and few diseases or injuries) that would not be implicated.")

6.   Providers are expected to consider the needs and limitations of their patients. Bryant v. Calantone, 286 N.J.Super. 362, 669 A.2d 286 (A.D.1996). In Windisch v. Weiman, 161 A.D.2d 433, 555 N.Y.S.2d 731 (1990), the court

held that the failure of a physician to properly follow-up a patient, resulting in a missed diagnosis of lung cancer, may provide the basis for imposing liability even when the patient is partially responsible for the delay in diagnosis.

7.   Contributory fault is typically invoked when a patient failed to follow a physician's instructions after a procedure was performed, or while in the hospital. Musachia v. Rosman, 190 So.2d 47 (Fla.App.1966) (decedent left the hospital over the objections of, and contrary to the advice of, the defendants; and drank liquor and ignored instructions to eat only baby food. He then died from fecal peritonitis due to small perforations in the bowel, and his recovery was barred)

8.   Almost all American jurisdictions have adopted comparative fault, simplifying the issue by eliminating the harsh all-or-nothing effect of contributory negligence. Courts in comparative fault jurisdictions are likely to be more willing to allow evidence of plaintiffs' contributions to their injuries. See generally Victor Schwartz, Comparative Negligence (5th ed. 2010).

9.   Assumption of the risk. The doctrine of assumption of the risk is a viable defense even in many comparative fault jurisdictions. In Schneider v. Revici, 817 F.2d 987, 995 (2d Cir.1987), the Second Circuit considered whether a patient undergoing unconventional treatment for breast cancer after signing a consent form had waived all her rights to sue or assumed the risk of injury from the treatment. The court held that the consent form was not clear and unequivocal as a covenant not to sue, but that the doctrine of assumption of risk was available:

> * * * we see no reason why a patient should not be allowed to make an informed decision to go outside currently approved medical methods in search of an unconventional treatment. While a patient should be encouraged to exercise care for his own safety, we believe that an informed decision to avoid surgery and conventional chemotherapy is within the patient's right to "determine what shall be done with his own body,"[ ]

The court held that the jury could consider assumption of the risk as a total bar to recovery, based on the language of the signed consent form and the patient's general awareness of the risks of treatment.

PROBLEM: THE DIFFICULT PATIENT

Alice Frost is profoundly obese. She is a smoker and drinks a bottle of gin a day. She works for the State as a disability counselor and her state health insurance coverage is excellent. She sees Dr. Wilson regularly. He has admonished her to stop smoking and cut down on her drinking, and to begin a program of exercise. He has also set up a series of monthly appointments with her to monitor her health. She fails to obtain a lipid profile to measure her cholesterol and never sees a cardiologist, even though Dr. Wilson has instructed her to do so on many occasions. She continues to smoke and drink.

She also begins to miss her monthly appointments. Dr. Wilson has his nurse call her to remind her several times, but Alice never calls back. After six months of missed appointments, Alice has a heart attack and dies.

Can her estate sue Dr. Wilson?

II.   DAMAGE INNOVATIONS

In the typical malpractice case, the available damages are the standard tort list: medical expenses, past and future; loss wages; diminished future earning capacity; loss of consortium; and noneconomic losses such as pain and suffering. In many health care settings, however, the alleged malpractice of the provider occurs to a patient who has a preexisting illness, such as a cancer patient. If the patient's chances of recovery are less than fifty percent, the old rule would deny recovery. The problem is one both of causation—did a provider's inaction increase the risk to the patient—and damage—exactly how should harm be quantified in such a situation.

THE "LOSS OF A CHANCE" DOCTRINE

HERSKOVITS V. GROUP HEALTH COOPERATIVE OF PUGET SOUND
Supreme Court of Washington, 1983.
99 Wash.2d 609, 664 P.2d 474.

DORE, JUSTICE.

This appeal raises the issue of whether an estate can maintain an action for professional negligence as a result of failure to timely diagnose lung cancer, where the estate can show probable reduction in statistical chance for survival but cannot show and/or prove that with timely diagnosis and treatment, decedent probably would have lived to normal life expectancy.

Both counsel advised that for the purpose of this appeal we are to *assume* that the respondent Group Health Cooperative of Puget Sound and Dr. William Spencer negligently failed to diagnose Herskovits' cancer on his first visit to the hospital and *proximately* caused a 14 percent reduction in his chances of survival. It is undisputed that Herskovits had less than a 50 percent chance of survival at all times herein.

The main issue we will address in this opinion is whether a patient, with less than a 50 percent chance of survival, has a cause of action against the hospital and its employees if they are negligent in diagnosing a lung cancer which reduces his chances of survival by 14 percent.

* * *

I

The complaint alleged that Herskovits came to Group Health Hospital in 1974 with complaints of pain and coughing. In early 1974, chest x-rays revealed infiltrate in the left lung. Rales and coughing were present. In mid–1974, there were chest pains and coughing, which became persistent and chronic by fall of 1974. A December 5, 1974 entry in the medical records confirms the cough problem. Plaintiff contends that Herskovits was treated thereafter only with cough medicine. No further effort or inquiry was made by Group Health concerning his symptoms, other than an occasional chest x-ray. In the early spring of 1975, Mr. and Mrs. Herskovits went south in the hope that the warm weather would help. Upon his return to the Seattle area with no improvement in his health, Herskovits visited Dr. Jonathan Ostrow on a private basis for another medical opinion. Within 3 weeks, Dr. Ostrow's evaluation and direction to Group Health led to the diagnosis of cancer. In July of 1975, Herskovits' lung was removed, but no radiation or chemotherapy treatments were instituted. Herskovits died 20 months later, on March 22, 1977, at the age of 60.

At hearing on the motion for summary judgment, plaintiff was unable to produce expert testimony that the delay in diagnosis "probably" or "more likely than not" caused her husband's death. The affidavit and deposition of plaintiff's expert witness, Dr. Jonathan Ostrow, construed in the most favorable light possible to plaintiff, indicated that had the diagnosis of lung cancer been made in December 1974, the patient's possibility of 5–year survival was 39 percent. At the time of initial diagnosis of cancer 6 months later, the possibility of a 5–year survival was reduced to 25 percent. Dr. Ostrow testified he felt a diagnosis perhaps could have been made as early as December 1974, or January 1975, about 6 months before the surgery to remove Mr. Herskovits' lung in June 1975.

Dr. Ostrow testified that if the tumor was a "stage 1" tumor in December 1974, Herskovits' chance of a 5–year survival would have been 39 percent. In June 1975, his chances of survival were 25 percent assuming the tumor had progressed to "stage 2". Thus, the delay in diagnosis may have reduced the chance of a 5–year survival by 14 percent.

Dr. William Spencer, the physician from Group Health Hospital who cared for the deceased Herskovits, testified that in his opinion, based upon a reasonable medical probability, earlier diagnosis of the lung cancer that afflicted Herskovits would not have prevented his death, nor would it have lengthened his life. He testified that nothing the doctors at Group Health could have done would have prevented Herskovits' death, as death within several years is a virtual certainty with this type of lung cancer regardless of how early the diagnosis is made.

Plaintiff contends that medical testimony of a reduction of chance of survival from 39 percent to 25 percent is sufficient evidence to allow the proximate cause issue to go to the jury. Defendant Group Health argues conversely that Washington law does not permit such testimony on the issue of medical causation and requires that medical testimony must be at least sufficiently definite to establish that the act complained of "probably" or "more likely than not" caused the subsequent disability. It is Group Health's contention that plaintiff must prove that Herskovits "probably" would have survived had the defendant not been allegedly negligent; that is, the plaintiff must prove there was at least a 51 percent chance of survival.

II

*   *   *

This court heretofore has not faced the issue of whether, under § 323(a), [of the Restatement (Second) of Torts (1965)] proof that the defendant's conduct increased the risk of death by decreasing the chances of survival is sufficient to take the issue of proximate cause to the jury. Some courts in other jurisdictions have allowed the proximate cause issue to go to the jury on this type of proof.[ ] These courts emphasized the fact that defendants' conduct deprived the decedents of a "significant" chance to survive or recover, rather than requiring proof that with absolute certainty the defendants' conduct caused the physical injury. The underlying reason is that it is not for the wrongdoer, who put the possibility of recovery beyond realization, to say afterward that the result was inevitable.[ ]

Other jurisdictions have rejected this approach, generally holding that unless the plaintiff is able to show that it was *more likely than not* that the harm was caused by the defendant's negligence, proof of a decreased chance of survival is not enough to take the proximate cause question to the jury.[ ] These courts have concluded that the defendant should not be liable where the decedent more than likely would have died anyway.

The ultimate question raised here is whether the relationship between the increased risk of harm and Herskovits' death is sufficient to hold Group Health responsible. Is a 36 percent (from 39 percent to 25 percent) reduction in the decedent's chance for survival sufficient evidence of causation to allow the jury to consider the possibility that the physician's failure to timely diagnose the illness was the proximate cause of his death? We answer in the affirmative. To decide otherwise would be a blanket release from liability for doctors and hospitals any time there was less than a 50 percent chance of survival, regardless of how flagrant the negligence.

III

[The court then discusses at length the case of *Hamil v. Bashline*, [ ], where the plaintiff's decedent, suffering from severe chest pains, was negligently treated in the emergency unit of the hospital. The wife, because of the lack of help, took her husband to a private physician's office, where he died. If the hospital had employed proper treatment, the decedent would have had a substantial chance of surviving the attack, stated by plaintiff's medical expert as a 75 percent chance of survival. The defendant's expert witness testified that the patient would have died regardless of any treatment provided by the defendant hospital.]

*   *   *

* * * In *Hamil* and the instant case, however, the defendant's act or omission failed in a *duty* to protect against harm from *another source*. Thus, as the *Hamil* court noted, the fact finder is put in the position of having to consider not only what *did* occur, but also what *might have* occurred.

*   *   *

The *Hamil* court held that once a plaintiff has demonstrated that the defendant's acts or omissions have increased the risk of harm to another, such evidence furnishes a basis for the jury to make a determination as to whether such increased risk was in turn a substantial factor in bringing about the resultant harm.

*   *   *

Under the *Hamil* decision, once a plaintiff has demonstrated that defendant's acts or omissions in a situation to which § 323(a) applies have increased the risk of harm to another, such evidence furnishes a basis for the fact finder to go further and find that such increased risk was in turn a substantial factor in bringing about the resultant harm. The necessary proximate cause will be established if the jury finds such cause. It is not necessary for a plaintiff to introduce evidence to establish that the negligence resulted in the injury or death, but simply that the negligence increased the *risk* of injury or death. The step from the increased risk to causation is one for the jury to make.

*   *   *

Where percentage probabilities and decreased probabilities are submitted into evidence, there is simply no danger of speculation on the part of the jury. More speculation is involved in requiring the medical expert to testify as to what would have happened had the defendant not been negligent.

Conclusion

* * * We reject Group Health's argument that plaintiffs *must show* that Herskovits "probably" would have had a 51 percent chance of survival if the hospital had not been negligent. We hold that medical testimony of a reduction of chance of survival from 39 percent to 25 percent is sufficient evidence to allow the proximate cause issue to go to the jury.

Causing reduction of the opportunity to recover (loss of chance) by one's negligence, however, does not necessitate a total recovery against the negligent party for all damages caused by the victim's death. Damages should be awarded to the injured party or his family based only on damages caused directly by premature death, such as lost earnings and additional medical expenses, etc.

We reverse the trial court and reinstate the cause of action.

PEARSON, J., concurring.

*   *   *

* * * I am persuaded * * * by the thoughtful discussion of a recent commentator. King, *Causation, Valuation, and Chance in Personal Injury Torts Involving Preexisting Conditions and Future Consequences,* 90 Yale L.J. 1353 (1981).

*   *   *

Under the all or nothing approach, typified by *Cooper v. Sisters of Charity of Cincinnati, Inc.,* 27 Ohio St.2d 242, 272 N.E.2d 97 (1971), a plaintiff who establishes that but for the defendant's negligence the decedent had a 51 percent chance of survival may maintain an action for that death. The defendant will be liable for all damages arising from the death, even though there was a 49 percent chance it would have occurred despite his negligence. On the other hand, a plaintiff who establishes that but for the defendant's negligence the decedent had a 49 percent chance of survival recovers nothing.

This all or nothing approach to recovery is criticized by King on several grounds, 90 Yale L.J. at 1376–78. First, the all or nothing approach is arbitrary. Second, it

> subverts the deterrence objectives of tort law by denying recovery for the effects of conduct that causes statistically demonstrable losses * * *. A failure to allocate the cost of these losses to their tortious sources * * * strikes at the integrity of the torts system of loss allocation.

90 Yale L.J. at 1377. Third, the all or nothing approach creates pressure to manipulate and distort other rules affecting causation and damages in an attempt to mitigate perceived injustices.[ ] Fourth, the all or nothing

approach gives certain defendants the benefit of an uncertainty which, were it not for their tortious conduct, would not exist. * * * Finally, King argues that the loss of a less than even chance is a loss worthy of redress.

These reasons persuade me that the best resolution of the issue before us is to recognize the loss of a less than even chance as an actionable injury. Therefore, I would hold that plaintiff has established a prima facie issue of proximate cause by producing testimony that defendant probably caused a substantial reduction in Mr. Herskovits' chance of survival. * * *

Finally, it is necessary to consider the amount of damages recoverable in the event that a loss of a chance of recovery is established. Once again, King's discussion provides a useful illustration of the principles which should be applied.

> To illustrate, consider a patient who suffers a heart attack and dies as a result. Assume that the defendant-physician negligently misdiagnosed the patient's condition, but that the patient would have had only a 40% chance of survival even with a timely diagnosis and proper care. Regardless of whether it could be said that the defendant caused the decedent's death, he caused the loss of a chance, and that chance-interest should be completely redressed in its own right. Under the proposed rule, the plaintiff's compensation for the loss of the victim's chance of surviving the heart attack would be 40% of the compensable value of the victim's life had he survived (including what his earning capacity would otherwise have been in the years following death). The value placed on the patient's life would reflect such factors as his age, health, and earning potential, including the fact that he had suffered the heart attack and the assumption that he had survived it. The 40% computation would be applied to that base figure.

(Footnote omitted.) 90 Yale L.J. at 1382.

I would remand to the trial court for proceedings consistent with this opinion.

BRACHTENBACH, JUSTICE (dissenting).

I dissent because I find plaintiff did not meet her burden of proving proximate cause. While the statistical evidence introduced by the expert was relevant and admissible, it was not alone sufficient to maintain a cause of action.

Neither the majority nor Justice Dolliver's dissent focus on the key issue. Both opinions focus on the significance of the 14 percent differentiation in the patient's chance to survive for 5 years and question whether this statistical data is sufficient to sustain a malpractice action. The issue is not so limited. The question should be framed as whether all the evidence amounts to sufficient proof, rising above speculation, that the doctor's conduct was a proximate cause of the patient's death. While the relevancy and the significance of the statistical evidence is a subissue bearing on the sufficiency of the proof, such evidence alone neither proves nor disproves plaintiff's case.

II

Furthermore, the instant case does not present evidence of proximate cause that rises above speculation and conjecture. The majority asserts that evidence of a statistical reduction of the chance to survive for 5 years is sufficient to create a jury question on whether the doctor's conduct was a proximate cause of the death. I disagree that this statistical data can be interpreted in such a manner.

Use of statistical data in judicial proceedings is a hotly debated issue.[ ] Many fear that members of the jury will place too much emphasis on statistical evidence and the statistics will be misused and manipulated by expert witnesses and attorneys.[ ]

Such fears do not support a blanket exclusion of statistical data, however. Our court system is premised on confidence in the jury to understand complex concepts and confidence in the right of cross examination as protection against the misuse of evidence. Attorneys ought to be able to explain the true significance of statistical data to keep it in its proper perspective.

Statistical data should be admissible as evidence if they are relevant, that is, if they have

> any tendency to make the existence of any fact that is of consequence to * * * the action more probable or less probable than it would be without the evidence.

ER 401. The statistics here met that test; they have some tendency to show that those diagnosed at stage one of the disease may have a greater chance to survive 5 years than those diagnosed at stage two.

The problem is, however, that while this statistical fact is relevant, it is not sufficient to prove causation. There is an enormous difference between the "any tendency to prove" standard of ER 401 and the "more likely than not" standard for proximate cause.

* * *

Thus, I would not resolve the instant case simply by focusing on the 14 percent differentiation in the chance to survive 5 years for the different stages of cancer. Instead, I would accept this as an admissible fact, but not as proof of proximate cause. To meet the proximate cause burden, the record would need to reveal other facts about the patient that tended to show that he would have been a member of the 14 percent group whose chance of 5 years' survival could be increased by early diagnosis.

Such evidence is not in the record. Instead, the record reveals that Mr. Herskovits' cancer was located such that corrective surgery "would be more formidable". This would tend to show that his chance of survival may have been less than the statistical average. Moreover, the statistics relied on did not take into consideration the location of the tumor, therefore their relevance to Mr. Herskovits' case must be questioned. Clerk's Papers, at 41.

In addition, as the tumor was relatively small in size when removed (2 to 3 centimeters), the likelihood that it would have been detected in 1974, even if the proper test were performed, was less than average. This uncertainty further reduces the probability that the doctor's failure to perform the tests was a proximate cause of a reduced chance of survival.

Other statistics admitted into evidence also tend to show the inconclusiveness of the statistics relied on by the majority. One study showed the *two*-year survival rate for this type of cancer to be 46.6 percent for stage one and 39.8 percent for stage two. Mr. Herskovits lived for 20 months after surgery, which was 26 months after defendant allegedly should have discovered the cancer. Therefore, regardless of the stage of the cancer at the time Mr. Herskovits was examined by defendant, it cannot be concluded that he survived significantly less than the average survival time. Hence, it is pure speculation to suppose that the doctor's negligence "caused" Mr. Herskovits to die sooner than he would have otherwise. Such speculation does not rise to the level of a jury question on the issue of proximate cause. Therefore, the trial court correctly dismissed the case.[ ]

The apparent harshness of this conclusion cannot be overlooked. The combination of the loss of a loved one to cancer and a doctor's negligence in diagnosis seems to compel a finding of liability. Nonetheless, justice must be dealt with an even hand. To hold a defendant liable without proof that his actions *caused* plaintiff harm would open up untold abuses of the litigation system.

Cases alleging misdiagnosis of cancer are increasing in number, perhaps because of the increased awareness of the importance of early detection. These cases, however, illustrate no more than an inconsistency among courts in their treatment of the problems of proof. [ ]. Perhaps as medical science becomes more knowledgeable about this disease and more sophisticated in its detection and treatment of it, the balance may tip in favor of imposing liability on doctors who negligently fail to promptly diagnose the disease. But, until a formula is found that will protect doctors against liability imposed through speculation as well as afford truly aggrieved plaintiffs their just compensation, I cannot favor the wholesale abandonment of the principle of proximate cause. For these reasons, I dissent.

NOTES AND QUESTIONS

1.   How would damages be figured under the majority's approach? Under the Pearson/King theory? What is the relationship between causation and damages in these cases? The majority and Pearson opinions would effectively permit recovery but reduce damages as the causation link weakens. Is this a reasonable approach?

2.   A judicial illustration of the calculation process for loss of a chance is found in McKellips v. St. Francis Hospital, Inc., 741 P.2d 467 (Okl.1987):

> "To illustrate the method in a case where the jury determines from the statistical findings combined with the specific facts relevant to the patient, the patient originally had a 40% chance of cure and the physician's negligence reduced the chance of cure to 25%, (40%— 25%) 15% represents the patient's loss of survival. If the total amount of damages proved by the evidence is $500,000, the damages caused by defendant is 15% × $500,000 or $75,000 * * *."

This has come to be called the "proportional damages" approach. See Matsuyama v. Birnbaum, 452 Mass. 1, 890 N.E.2d 819 (Supreme Judicial Court, Massachusetts 2008). The court must measure the monetary value of the patient's full life expectancy and, if relevant, work life expectancy as it would in any wrongful death case. The defendant must then be held liable only for the portion of that value that the defendant's negligence destroyed.

PROBLEM: MISSING THE DIAGNOSIS

Jane Rogers was a fair complected woman in her early thirties. She had worked every summer during high school and college as a lifeguard at the beach. While she was in graduate school, one of her sisters was diagnosed as having melanoma, a deadly cancer that is often fatal if not detected and treated early. Melanoma is more prevalent in people who have fair complexions, and prolonged exposure to the sun over time, particularly severe sun burns, are a risk factor for the cancer.

Ms. Roger's sister died. The family physician, Dr. James, told the family members that they should all get a thorough physical to check for signs of skin tumors that might be precancerous. Ms. Rogers went to the University Student Clinic and requested a physical examination. She explained why she was worried. Dr. Gillespie, an older physician who had retired from active practice and now helped out part-time at the Clinic, examined her. He observed a nodule on her upper back, but incorrectly diagnosed it as a birthmark. He told her not to worry. She continued her lifeguarding and water safety instruction activities during the summer to pay for her graduate education.

At a party one Friday night, Ms. Rogers met a young physician who was a resident at the University hospital. She was wearing a strapless dress, and the resident, Dr. Wunch, noted a mole on her shoulder. He recognized it as a melanoma. He pointed it out to her, and told her that she really ought to get it checked. He gave her his card, with his phone number, and said he would be glad to set her up with an appointment with a good cancer specialist at the hospital. Ms. Rogers called, made an appointment, and filled out the forms required by the University Hospital, but then missed her appointment. She never went back.

A year later, during a routine physical as part of an employment application, the examining physician found several large growths on Ms. Roger's back. She was diagnosed as having melanoma, which had spread into her blood and had metastasized into her lymph nodes. She was dead within a year.

What problems do you see with the suit by her estate against the available defendants?

CHAPTER 5

LIABILITY OF HEALTH CARE INSTITUTIONS

■ ■ ■

I. INTRODUCTION

The hospital is the classic health care "institution". The U.S. has over 5,700 hospitals—almost 3,000 are nonprofit, 1,000 for-profit, and 1,200 are local, state and federal government owned. The remainder are psychiatric and long term care hospitals. See American Hospital Association, Fast Facts on U.S. Hospitals (2013).

Hospitals are major providers of emergency care and highly complicated surgical and other procedures. They are therefore the largest sources of patient harms in the U.S. system. Hospitals provide acute care in severe health crises and, given the possibility of errors and serious adverse events, we also think of institutional liability for those injuries.

The Affordable Care Act has created pressure on hospitals to coordinate care and move patients safely from acute care situations to other institutions—assisted living, long term care, or home. Hospitals have also been acquiring physician practices in response to the incentives of the Affordable Care Act and the pressures for a better coordinated health care system.

Faced with the high cost of the HITECH Act's mandate for electronic health records and other regulatory mandates, many free standing hospitals are joining systems; and these systems are merging to achieve market share and necessary economies of scale in an increasingly competitive environment. As a result, 3,000 of these hospitals are now in systems, defined as either a multihospital or a diversified single hospital system. A multihospital system is two or more hospitals owned, leased, sponsored, or contract managed by a central organization. Single, freestanding hospitals may be categorized as a system by bringing into membership three or more, and at least 25 percent, of their owned or leased non-hospital preacute or postacute health care organizations. Hospitals in systems are likely to have more resources to devote to patient safety, and system pressures are likely to push hospitals toward the adoption of safety-based standards more rapidly.

Health care delivery also includes institutional forms such as managed care organizations that finance health care and contract with physicians and hospitals to provide care, as well as ambulatory care facilities such as surgicenters and physician offices. As more and more medicine is moved out of the hospital into less expensive settings, the liability of these institutional arrangements emerges as a new concern. Most caselaw has originated with hospitals as the predominant form of delivery of high technology high risk care—where the most severe patient harms can occur—and the courts are now adapting to changes in the delivery system.

II.   AGENCY LAW AND THE TEST OF "CONTROL"

A. DEFINING "EMPLOYEE" IN THE HOSPITAL SETTING

Hospitals employ nurses, technicians, clerks, custodians, cooks, and others who are clearly employees of the hospital under agency principles. Their terms and conditions of employment are controlled by the hospital, which sets their hours, wages and working conditions. When employees are negligent, the hospital is vicariously liable for their acts as a result of the master-servant relationship of agency law. It is the relationship of physicians to the hospital that raises more complicated agency problems.

The hospital-physician relationship is an unusual one by corporate standards. A typical hospital may have several categories of practicing physicians, but the largest group is comprised of private physicians with staff privileges. Staff privileges include the right of the physicians to admit and discharge their private patients to and from the hospital and the right to use the hospital's facilities. These physicians have typically been independent contractors rather than employees of the hospital. This legal status means that the hospital is therefore not easily targeted as a defendant in a malpractice suit. Only if the doctor whose negligence injured a patient is an employee could the hospital be reached through the doctrine of vicarious liability. The hospital is independently liable only if it is negligent in its administrative or housekeeping functions, for example causing a patient to slip and fall on a wet floor. Otherwise, the hospital has been immune in the past from liability. This has changed as the courts have confronted the evolution of the modern hospital and expanded vicarious liability doctrine in the health care setting.

Hospitals employ approximately 212,000 physicians. Hospitals have a range of relationships with privileged physicians: 55.1 percent of physicians are not employed or under contract, while 20.3 percent are covered by a group contract; 17.3 percent are directly employed and 7.2 percent have individual contracts. See the 2012 edition of *AHA Hospital Statistics*. From 2003 to 2010, the proportion of hospitals with hospitalists on staff grew from 29.6 percent to 59.8 percent. From 2007–10, the proportion of hospitals employing intensivists grew from 20.7 percent to 29.7 percent. Many physicians are moving from practicing in small groups to some form of employee in a changing delivery system.

The test of whether a physician is an employee is based on "control". The general definition of the term "servant" in the Restatement (Second) of Agency § 2(2) (1957) refers to a person whose work is "controlled or is subject to the right to control by the master." The Restatement's more specific definition of the term "servant" lists factors to be considered when distinguishing between servants and independent contractors, the first of which is "the extent of control" that one may exercise over the details of the work of the other. Id. The relevant factor for analyzing the hospital-physician relationship by agency tests is § 220(2)(a), which looks to "the extent of control which, by the agreement, the master may exercise over the details of the work." This becomes a fact-intensive analysis for the trier of fact.

Physicians need considerable autonomy in practice, given the complexity of their decisions and their relationship to particular patients. As a result, determining the degree of control necessary to create an employment relationship in a medical malpractice claim poses a unique set of difficulties. As the court writes in Lilly v. Fieldstone, 876 F.2d 857 (C.A. 10 Kan.),1989. " * * * [i]t is uncontroverted that a physician must have discretion to care for a patient and may not surrender control over certain medical details. Therefore, the 'control' test is subject to a doctor's medical and ethical obligations.... What we must do in the case of professionals is determine whether other evidence manifests an intent to make the professional an employee subject to other forms of control which are permissible. A myriad of doctors become employees by agreement without surrendering their professional responsibilities."

B. THE MEDICAL STAFF: VICARIOUS LIABILITY

Absent evidence of indicia of control sufficient to make a physician the employee of a hospital, courts have turned to traditional agency tests that evaluate whether the health care institution is vicariously liable for the negligence of its independent contractors.

BURLESS V. WEST VIRGINIA UNIVERSITY HOSPITALS, INC.

Supreme Court of West Virginia, 2004.
215 W.Va. 765, 601 S.E.2d 85.

DAVIS, JUSTICE:

* * *

I.   Factual Procedural History

Each of the two cases consolidated for purposes of this opinion involve a woman who gave birth to her child at WVUH under circumstances that she alleges resulted in severe birth defects to her child. The relevant facts of each case, as developed in the pleadings, depositions, affidavits, and exhibits, follow.

A.   Jaclyn Burless

In July of 1998 Jaclyn Burless learned she was pregnant and sought prenatal care at the Cornerstone Care Clinic (hereinafter referred to as "the Cornerstone Clinic" or simply "the clinic") located in Greensboro, Pennsylvania. The Cornerstone Clinic was where Ms. Burless had routinely sought her primary medical care. Similarly, Ms. Burless elected to receive her prenatal care at the clinic. She received her prenatal care from Dr. Douglas Glover for approximately seven months.

In November, 1998, Dr. Glover sent Ms. Burless to WVUH for an ultrasound. At that time, Ms. Burless signed a WVUH consent form that stated: "I understand that the faculty physicians and resident physicians who provide treatment in the hospital are not employees of the hospital." Thereafter, in February of 1999 when she was at approximately 37 weeks of gestation, Ms. Burless experienced an elevated blood pressure and edema. On February 15, 1999, Dr. Glover advised Ms. Burless to report to the WVU Emergency Department for an evaluation. On February 17, 1999, Ms. Burless presented herself at the WVUH Emergency Department as instructed and, after an evaluation, was instructed to return to the High Risk Clinic, which is located on the WVUH premises, in two days with a urine sample for testing. Ms. Burless was also advised that she would receive the remainder of her prenatal care at the High Risk Clinic. She followed the instructions to return to the High Risk Clinic in two days. She was then instructed to return in one week for further evaluation. When she returned, on February 26, 1999, she was induced into labor at 7:50 p.m. Her labor was permitted to continue throughout the remainder of February 26 and until 4:00 p.m. on February 27. She alleges that during this time, doctors, residents, and nurses at WVUH noted variable decelerations in the fetal heart rate of her unborn daughter, Alexis Price. At 4:00 p.m. on February 27 the decision was made to deliver the baby via cesarean section, and such delivery was accomplished at 4:16 p.m. The child was born with an APGAR[2] score of two at one minute and six at five minutes. Soon after birth the child began to experience seizures

---

[2]   An APGAR Score is a newborn's first evaluation and serves as a predictive indicator of any potential problems. The infant is examined at one and five minutes after birth and ranked on a scale of zero to two on five characteristics: 1) skin color; 2) heart rate; 3) response to stimuli of inserting a catheter in the nose; 4) muscle tone; and 5) respiratory effort. Thus, the maximum score is 10 with most healthy newborns scoring an eight or nine. The five APGAR factors can be mnemonically summarized as *A*-ppearance, *P*-ulse, *G*-rimace, *A*-ctivity, *R*-espiration.[ ].

and suffered a stroke. Ms. Burless has alleged that the doctors and hospital were negligent, *inter alia,* in failing to monitor her labor and delivery, which negligence caused severe and permanent mental, neurological, and psychological injuries to the infant, Alexis Price.

[Ms. Burless later sued, in part claiming vicarious liability on the part of WVUH based upon a theory of apparent agency between WVUH and the physicians who provided the allegedly negligent care. The circuit court granted the defendant's summary judgment motion, concluding that there was no evidence of an apparent agency relationship between Ms. Burless and WVUH.]

B.   *Melony Pritt*

[Plaintiff Melony Pritt had an ovarian cyst, and scheduled a laparotomy and left ovarian cystectomy. She signed several consent forms, all of which contained the statement " "I understand that the faculty physicians and resident physicians who provide treatment in the hospital are not employees of the hospital." The surgery did not go well, and she suffered a massive abdominal infection, which infection caused premature labor. Her son was alleged therefore to have suffered severe permanent mental, neurological, and psychological injuries]

II.

[The court's discussion of the standard of review is omitted.]

III.

Discussion

Ms. Burless and Ms. Pritt assert that the circuit courts erred both in finding no actual agency relationship between the doctors who treated them and WVUH, and in finding no apparent agency relationship. We address each of these assignments of error in turn.

A.   *Actual Agency*

[The court found no actual agency, since the hospital did not have "power of control" over the physicians who provided treatment to Ms. Burless and Ms. Pritt.]

B.   *Apparent Agency*

Although we have addressed using a theory of apparent agency to overcome the physician/independent contractor rule in the context of emergency room treatment, we have never expressly defined such a rule for use outside of the emergency room setting. We do so now.

1.   Hospital/Physician Apparent Agency Outside the Emergency Room Setting. The public's confidence in the modern hospital's portrayal of itself as a full service provider of health care appears to be at the foundation of the national trend toward adopting a rule of apparent agency to find hospitals liable, under the appropriate circumstances, for the negligence of physicians providing services within its walls.

* * *

[ ] * * * [W]e now hold that for a hospital to be held liable for a physician's negligence under an apparent agency theory, a plaintiff must establish that: (1) the hospital either committed an act that would cause a reasonable person to believe that the physician in question was an agent of the hospital, or, by failing to take an action, created a circumstance that would allow a reasonable person to hold such a belief, and (2) the plaintiff relied on the apparent agency relationship.

   2. Hospital's Actions or Inactions. The first element of our test requires evidence that the hospital either committed an act that would cause a reasonable person to believe that the physician in question was an agent of the hospital, or, by failing to take an action, created a circumstance that would allow a reasonable person to hold such a belief. This portion of the test focuses on the acts of the hospital and is generally satisfied when "the hospital 'holds itself out' to the public as a provider of care."[* * *It has been said that "[l]iability under apparent agency . . . will not attach against a hospital where the patient knows, or reasonably should have known, that the treating physician was an independent contractor."[ ] Thus, a hospital's failure to provide a meaningful written notice may constitute "failing to take an action" and thereby allowing a reasonable person to believe that a particular doctor is an agent of the hospital. Conversely, absent other overt acts by the hospital indicating an employer/employee relationship, an unambiguous disclaimer by a hospital explaining the independent contractor status of physicians will generally suffice to immunize the hospital from being vicariously liable for physician conduct.

   Turning to the cases before us, the circuit courts in both cases relied on the disclaimers signed by Ms. Pritt & Ms. Burless in granting summary judgment in favor of WVUH. In addition, the circuit court considering Ms. Pritt's case summarily concluded that WVUH had not "held the physicians out to be its employees." We disagree with these conclusions.

   The disclaimer that WVUH required both Ms. Pritt and Ms. Burless to sign stated: "I understand that the faculty physicians and resident physicians who provide treatment in the hospital are not employees of the hospital." WVUH contends that this "disclaimer" was sufficient to unequivocally inform Ms. Pritt and Ms. Burless that the physicians treating them were not employees of the hospital. We disagree.

   We do not find the disclaimer language used by WVUH, which indicated that "faculty physicians and resident physicians who provide treatment in the hospital" are independent contractors, was sufficient to support a grant of summary judgment in their favor. The WVUH disclaimer provision presupposes that all patients can distinguish between "faculty physicians," "resident physicians" and any other type of physician having privileges at the hospital. In other words, for this disclaimer to be meaningful, a patient would literally have to inquire into the employment status of everyone treating him or her. Obviously, "[i]t would be absurd to require . . . a patient . . . to inquire of each person who treated him whether he is an employee of the hospital or an independent contractor."

Consequently, it was improper for the circuit court to grant summary judgment in favor of WVUH. Ms. Burless and Ms. Pritt have established a genuine question of material fact as to whether WVUH has either committed an act that would cause a reasonable person to believe that the physician in question was an agent of the hospital, or, by failing to take an action, created a circumstance that would allow a reasonable person to hold such a belief.

3.   Reliance. The reliance prong of the apparent agency test is a subjective molehill. "Reliance . . . is established when the plaintiff 'looks to' the hospital for services, rather than to an individual physician."[ ] It is "sometimes characterized as an inquiry as to whether 'the plaintiff acted in reliance upon the conduct of the hospital or its agent, consistent with ordinary care and prudence.'[ ] This factor 'simply focuses on the "patient's belief that the hospital or its employees were rendering health care." ' " "[ ] However, this portion of the test also requires consideration of the 'reasonableness of the patient's [subjective] belief that the hospital or its employees were rendering health care.' " "This . . . determination is made by considering the totality of the circumstances, including . . . any special knowledge the patient[/plaintiff] may have about the hospital's arrangements with its physicians."[ ]

Mrs. Pritt and Ms. Burless provided evidence indicating that they believed that the physicians treating them were employees of WVUH.

In the deposition testimony of Ms. Burless she stated her belief that the people treating her at the hospital were employees, as follows: "Q. Did anyone do anything to make you believe that they were employees of WVU Hospital? A. They were all wearing their coats and name tags and in the building, so, you know, you know they're—they work there, they're employees." In the affidavit submitted by Ms. Pritt in opposition to WVUH's motion for summary judgment, the following was stated:

2.   At the West Virginia University Hospitals, I was assigned doctors who treated me and consulted me through my prenatal care, surgery and delivery of my son Adam.

3.   Throughout all of my treatment and consultations, I believed that the doctors and nurses who treated me and spoke to me were employees of the West Virginia University Hospitals.

Ms. Burless and Ms. Pritt have also established a genuine question of material fact on the issue of their reliance on the apparent agency relationship between WVUH and their treating physicians. Consequently, on the issue of apparent agency, it is clear that summary judgment should not have been granted in favor of WVUH.

NOTES AND QUESTIONS

1.   *The Medical Staff.* The medical staff is a self-governing body charged with overseeing the quality of care, treatment, and services delivered by practitioners who are credentialed and privileged through the medical staff process. The medical staff must credential and privilege all licensed independent practitioners. The self-governing organized medical staff creates and maintains a set of bylaws that defines its role within the context of a hospital setting and clearly delineates its responsibilities in the oversight of care, treatment, and services. It elects its own officers, and appoints its own committees. See Chapter 11, *infra.*

The organized medical staff is intimately involved in carrying out, and in providing leadership in, all patient care functions conducted by practitioners privileged through the medical staff process. The medical staff oversees the quality of patient care, treatment, and services provided by practitioners privileged through the medical staff process. It recommends practitioners for privileges to perform medical histories and physical examinations. The hospital governing body approves such privileges.

The organized medical staff is not simply another administrative component of the hospital, and it has typically been subject to only limited authority of the governing board of the hospital. While the hospital board must approve the staff's bylaws and can approve or disapprove particular staff actions, it cannot usually discipline individual physicians directly or appoint administrative officers to exercise direct authority. A hospital's medical staff is therefore a powerful body within the larger organization.

2.   What can a hospital do to avoid liability under the *Burless* court's analysis? Will explicit notice to the plaintiff at the time of admission be sufficient? How about a large sign in the admitting area of the hospital? A brochure handed to each patient? If the hospital advertises aggressively, will the reliance created by such advertising overwhelm all of the hospital's targeted attempts to inform patients about the intricacies of the physicians' employment relationships with the hospital?

Explicit language in a patient consent form is in theory the most effective way to put a patient on notice of the physician's legal status. A few states allow a clear statement in a consent form—that physicians in the hospital are independent contractors and not agents—to put a patient on notice. See

Pendley v. Southern Regional Health System, Inc., 307 Ga.App. 82, 704 S.E.2d 198 (2010) (hospital had bolded the independent contractor disclaimers in both the General Consent for Treatment and the Routine Consent, and the Routine Consent also cautioned readers in bold: **"Important: Do not sign this form without reading and understanding its contents."** The court also noted that the defendant physician had made no representations to the plaintiff as to his employment status.)

PROBLEM: CREATING A SHIELD

You represent Bowsman Hospital, a small rural hospital in Iowa. The hospital has until now relied on Dr. Headley for radiology services. It provides him with space, equipment, and personnel for the radiology department, sends and collects bills on his behalf, and provides him with an office. It also pays him $300 a day in exchange for which Dr. Headley agrees to be at the hospital one day a week. Bowsman is one of several small hospitals in this part of Iowa that use Dr. Headley's services. Bowsman advertises in the local papers of several nearby communities. Its advertisements stress its ability to handle trauma injuries, common in farming areas. The ads say in part:

"Bowsman treats patient problems with big league medical talent. Our physicians and nurses have been trained for the special demands of farming accidents and injuries."

What advice can you give as to methods of shielding Bowsman from liability for the negligent acts of Dr. Headley? Must it insist that Dr. Headley operate his own outside laboratory? Or furnish his own equipment? Pay his own bills? Should the hospital hire its own radiologist?

The Chief Executive Officer asks you to develop guidelines to protect the hospital from liability for medical errors of the radiologist. Your research has uncovered the following cases.

III.   HOSPITAL LIABILITY

Patients may suffer injury in hospitals in many ways: they may fall out of bed, they may slip on the way to the bathroom, they may be given the wrong drug or the wrong dosage in their IV, the MRI machine may not be working, etc.. If expert testimony is not needed, that is, if an ordinary person could evaluate the failure, then the case may not be considered malpractice but rather ordinary negligence. Negligence may have a different statute of limitations and may not be subject to restrictive legislative restrictions on malpractice recovery such as certificates of merit, caps on noneconomic loss, or other restrictions.

Most hospital cases that involve treatment or diagnosis will require expert testimony of some sort. If the case involves the standard of care applicable to a hospital rather than one of the medical staff physicians, then the courts will look at the standard applicable to hospitals of that type, and inquire into the professional judgment of providers or decisions of a hospital governing body or the administration of the hospital. Such breaches of duty are considered malpractice, are subject to the rules pertaining to such cases, and require expert testimony.

A. NEGLIGENCE

WASHINGTON V. WASHINGTON HOSPITAL CENTER
District of Columbia Court of Appeals, 1990.
579 A.2d 177.

[The Court considered two issues: whether the testimony of the plaintiff's expert was sufficient to create a issue for the jury; and whether the hospital's failure to request a finding of liability of the settling defendants or to file a cross claim for contribution against any of the defendants defeated the hospital's claim for a pro rata reduction in the jury verdict. The discussion of the first issue follows.]

FARRELL, ASSOCIATE JUDGE:

This appeal and cross-appeal arise from a jury verdict in a medical malpractice action against the Washington Hospital Center (WHC or the hospital) in favor of LaVerne Alice Thompson, a woman who suffered permanent catastrophic brain injury from oxygen deprivation in the course of general anesthesia for elective surgery * * *

*   *   *

I.   The Facts

On the morning of November 7, 1987, LaVerne Alice Thompson, a healthy 36–year–old woman, underwent elective surgery at the Washington Hospital Center for an abortion and tubal ligation, procedures requiring general anesthesia. At about 10:45 a.m., nurse-anesthetist Elizabeth Adland, under the supervision of Dr. Sheryl Walker, the physician anesthesiologist, inserted an endotracheal tube into Ms. Thompson's throat for the purpose of conveying oxygen to, and removing carbon dioxide from, the anesthetized patient. The tube, properly inserted, goes into the patient's trachea just above the lungs. Plaintiffs alleged that instead Nurse Adland inserted the tube into Thompson's esophagus, above the stomach. After inserting the tube, Nurse Adland "ventilated" or pumped air into the patient while Dr. Walker, by observing physical reactions—including watching the rise and fall of the patient's chest and listening for breath sounds equally on the patient's right and left sides—sought to determine if the tube had been properly inserted.

At about 10:50 a.m., while the surgery was underway, surgeon Nathan Bobrow noticed that Thompson's blood was abnormally dark, which indicated that her tissues were not receiving sufficient oxygen, and reported the condition to Nurse Adland, who checked Thompson's vital signs and found them stable. As Dr. Bobrow began the tubal ligation part of the operation, Thompson's heart rate dropped. She suffered a cardiac arrest and was resuscitated, but eventually the lack of oxygen caused catastrophic brain injuries. Plaintiffs' expert testified that Ms. Thompson remains in a persistent vegetative state and is totally incapacitated; her cardiac, respiratory and digestive functions are normal and she is not "brain dead," but, according to the expert, she is "essentially awake but unaware" of her surroundings. Her condition is unlikely to improve, though she is expected to live from ten to twenty years.

* * *

The plaintiffs alleged that Adland and Walker had placed the tube in Thompson's esophagus rather than her trachea, and that they and Dr. Bobrow had failed to detect the improper intubation in time to prevent the oxygen deprivation that caused Thompson's catastrophic brain injury. WHC, they alleged, was negligent in failing to provide the anesthesiologists with a device known variously as a capnograph or end-tidal carbon dioxide monitor which allows early detection of insufficient oxygen in time to prevent brain injury.

* * *

II.   Washington Hospital Center's Claims on Cross–Appeal

A.   *Standard of Care*

On its cross-appeal, WHC first asserts that the plaintiffs failed to carry their burden of establishing the standard of care and that the trial court therefore erred in refusing to grant its motion for judgment notwithstanding the verdict.

* * *

In a negligence action predicated on medical malpractice, the plaintiff must carry a tripartite burden, and establish: (1) the applicable standard of care; (2) a deviation from that standard by the defendant; and (3) a causal relationship between that deviation and the plaintiff's injury. [ ] * * *

Generally, the "standard of care" is "the course of action that a reasonably prudent [professional] with the defendant's specialty would have taken under the same or similar circumstances." [ ] With respect to institutions such as hospitals, this court has rejected the "locality" rule, which refers to the standard of conduct expected of other similarly situated members of the profession in the same locality or community, [ ] in favor of a national standard. [ ] Thus, the question for decision is whether the evidence as a whole, and reasonable inferences therefrom, would allow a reasonable juror to find that a reasonably prudent tertiary care hospital,[3] at the time of Ms. Thompson's injury in November 1987, and according to national standards, would have supplied a carbon dioxide monitor to a patient undergoing general anesthesia for elective surgery.

* * *

* * * [WHC] asserts that * * * Steen gave no testimony on the number of hospitals having end-tidal carbon dioxide monitors in place in 1987, and that he never referred to any written standards or authorities as the basis of his opinion. We conclude that Steen's opinion * * * was sufficient to create an issue for the jury.

Dr. Steen testified that by 1985, the carbon dioxide monitors were available in his hospital (Los Angeles County—University of Southern California Medical Center (USC)), and "in many other hospitals." In response to a question whether, by 1986, "standards of care" required carbon dioxide monitors in operating rooms, he replied, "I would think that by that time, they would be [required]." As plaintiffs concede, this opinion was based in part on his own personal experience at USC, which * * * cannot itself provide an adequate foundation for an expert opinion on a national standard of care. But Steen also drew support from "what I've read where [the monitors were] available in other hospitals." He referred to two such publications: The American Association of Anesthesiology (AAA) Standards for Basic Intra–Operative Monitoring, approved by the AAA House of Delegates on October 21, 1986, which "encouraged" the use of monitors, and an article entitled *Standards for Patient Monitoring During Anesthesia at Harvard Medical School,* published in August 1986 in the Journal of American Medical Association, which stated that as of July 1985 the monitors were in use at Harvard, and that "monitoring end-tidal carbon dioxide is an emerging standard and is strongly preferred."

WHC makes much of Steen's concession on cross-examination that the AAA Standards were recommendations, strongly encouraged but not mandatory, and that the Harvard publication spoke of an "emerging" standard. In its brief WHC asserts, without citation, that "[p]alpable indicia of widespread *mandated* practices are necessary to establish a standard of care" (emphasis added), and that at most the evidence spoke of "recommended" or "encouraged" practices, and "emerging" or "developing" standards as of 1986–87. A standard of due care, however, necessarily embodies what a *reasonably prudent* hospital would do, [ ] and hence care and foresight exceeding the minimum required by law or mandatory professional regulation may be necessary to meet that standard. It certainly cannot be said that the 1986 recommendations of a professional association (which had no power to issue or enforce mandatory requirements), or

---

[3]   Plaintiffs' expert defined a tertiary care hospital as "a hospital which has the facilities to conduct clinical care management of patients in nearly all aspects of medicine and surgery."

an article speaking of an "emerging" standard in 1986, have no bearing on an expert opinion as to what the standard of patient monitoring equipment was fully one year later when Ms. Thompson's surgery took place.

Nevertheless, we need not decide whether Dr. Steen's testimony was sufficiently grounded in fact or adequate data to establish the standard of care. The record contains other evidence from which, in combination with Dr. Steen's testimony, a reasonable juror could fairly conclude that monitors were required of prudent hospitals similar to WHC in late 1987. The evidence showed that at least four other teaching hospitals in the United States used the monitors by that time. In addition to Dr. Steen's testimony that USC supplied them and the article reflecting that Harvard University had them, plaintiffs introduced into evidence an article entitled *Anesthesia at Penn,* from a 1986 alumni newsletter of the Department of Anesthesia at the University of Pennsylvania, indicating that the monitors were then in use at that institution's hospital, and that they allowed "instant recognition of esophageal intubation and other airway problems. * * * " Moreover, WHC's expert anesthesiologist, Dr. John Tinker of the University of Iowa, testified that his hospital had installed carbon dioxide monitors in every operating room by early 1986, and that "by 1987, it is certainly true that many hospitals were in the process of converting" to carbon dioxide monitors.

Perhaps most probative was the testimony of WHC's own Chairman of the Department of Anesthesiology, Dr. Dermot A. Murray, and documentary evidence associated with his procurement request for carbon dioxide monitors. In December 1986 or January 1987, Dr. Murray submitted a requisition form to the hospital for end-tidal carbon dioxide units to monitor the administration of anesthesia in each of the hospital's operating rooms, stating that if the monitors were not provided, the hospital would "fail to meet the national standard of care." The monitors were to be "fully operational" in July of 1987. Attempting to meet this evidence, WHC points out that at trial

> Dr. Murray was *never asked to opine,* with a reasonable degree of medical certainty, that the applicable standard of care at the relevant time *required* the presence of CO_2 monitors. Indeed, his testimony was directly to the contrary. Moreover, the procurement process which he had initiated envisioned obtaining the equipment * * * over time, not even beginning until fiscal year 1988, a period ending June 30, 1988. [Emphasis by WHC.]

Dr. Murray opined that in November 1987 there was *no* standard of care relating to monitoring equipment. The jury heard this testimony and Dr. Murray's explanation of the procurement process, but apparently did not credit it, perhaps because the requisition form itself indicated that the equipment ordered was to be operational in July 1987, four months before

Ms. Thompson's surgery, and not at some unspecified time in fiscal year 1988 as Dr. Murray testified at trial.

On the evidence recited above, a reasonable juror could find that the standard of care required WHC to supply monitors as of November 1987. The trial judge therefore did not err in denying the motion for judgment notwithstanding the verdict.

NOTES AND QUESTIONS

1.   Does the plaintiff present sufficient evidence that the carbon dioxide monitor is now standard equipment for tertiary care hospitals? The court seems to say that expert testimony is not critical, that the evidence of use by other institutions is something a lay juror could evaluate even if expert testimony is deficient?

2.   A companion device to the carbon dioxide monitor is the blood-monitoring pulse oximeter, which has become a mandatory device in hospital operating rooms. In 1984 no hospital had them; by 1990 all hospitals used oximeters in their operating rooms. The device beeps when a patient's blood oxygen drops due to breathing problems or overuse of anesthesia. That warning can give a vital three or four minute warning to physicians, allowing them to correct the problem before the patient suffers brain damage. These devices have so improved patient safety that malpractice insurers have lowered premiums for anesthesiologists. The Joint Commission requires hospitals to develop protocols for anesthesia care that mandate pulse oximetry equipment for measuring oxygen saturation. See Revisions to Anesthesia Care Standards Comprehensive Accreditation Manual for Hospitals Effective January 1, 2001 (Standards and Intents for Sedation and Anesthesia Care).

3.   Joint Commission standards often provide the basis for jury instructions in hospital negligence cases. See for example Tavares v. Evergreen Hospital Medical Center, 2010 WL 1541475 (Wash.App.Div.1, Unpublished, 2010). The plaintiff had sought prenatal care, and was a high risk pregnancy, having had an emergency cesarean section with her first child. The couple debated the risks of a vaginal birth after cesarean delivery (VBAC) or another cesarean section. They wanted to try a VBAC, if possible, despite contrary medical advice. The plaintiff began to experience contractions, and went to the hospital. She was put on a fetal monitor, decelerations were noted, and the baby was delivered by emergency cesarean section. The baby had significant brain damage including cerebral palsy. The parents sued for medical and corporate negligence. Claims against the doctors were settled, and the jury found Evergreen liable to the plaintiff.

The jury instructions were at issue. Instruction 14 was taken from a Joint Commission standard: "The hospital is required to provide an adequate number of staff members whose qualifications are consistent with job responsibilities." The court held, following *Pedroza v. Bryant,* [ ] "that because hospitals are members of national organizations and subject to accreditation, the

JCAHO standards are particularly relevant to defining the proper standard of care."

4.   A health care institution, whether hospital, nursing home, or clinic, is liable for negligence in maintaining its facilities; providing and maintaining medical equipment; hiring, supervising and retaining nurses and other staff; and failing to have in place procedures to protect patients. Basic negligence principles govern hospital liability for injuries caused by other sources than negligent acts of the medical staff. As *Washington* holds, hospitals are generally held to a national standard of care for hospitals in their treatment category. Reed v. Granbury Hospital Corporation, 117 S.W.3d 404 (2003). They must provide a safe environment for diagnosis, treatment, and recovery of patients. Bellamy v. Appellate Department, 50 Cal.App.4th 797, 57 Cal.Rptr.2d 894 (5 Dist.1996).

a.   Hospitals must have minimum facility and support systems to treat the range of problems and side effects that accompany procedures they offer. In Hernandez v. Smith, 552 F.2d 142 (5th Cir.1977), for example, an obstetrical clinic that lacked surgical facilities for cesarean sections was found liable for " * * * the failure to provide proper and safe instrumentalities for the treatment of ailments it undertakes to treat * * *."

b.   Staffing must be adequate. Staff shortages can be negligence. See Merritt v. Karcioglu, 668 So.2d 469 (La.App. 4th Cir.1996) (hospital ward understaffed in having only three critical care nurses for six patients). If, however, existing staff can be juggled to cover a difficult patient, short staffing is no defense. See Horton v. Niagara Falls Memorial Medical Center, 51 A.D.2d 152, 380 N.Y.S.2d 116 (1976).

c.   Equipment must be adequate for the services offered, although it need not be the state of the art. See Emory University v. Porter, 103 Ga.App. 752, 120 S.E.2d 668, 670 (1961); Lauro v. Travelers Ins. Co., 261 So.2d 261 (La.App.1972).

d.   A hospital and its contracting physicians may be liable for damages caused by inadequate or defective systems they develop and implement, particularly where emergency care is involved. On-call systems in smaller hospitals are a recurring issue in the caselaw. Delays in contacting physicians may be negligent, without the need for expert testimony. In Partin v. North Mississippi Medical Center, Inc., 929 So.2d 924 (Miss.Ct.App.2005), the plaintiff became septic while in the hospital recovering from surgery; the nurses failed to notify the on-call physician for more than twenty hours, and the patient died.

5.   An institution's own internal rules and safety regulations for medical procedures must be followed, and a failure to follow them may be offered as evidence of a breach of a standard of care for the trier of fact to consider. They are material and relevant on the issue of quality of care, but are usually not sufficient by themselves to establish the degree of care owed. Jackson v. Oklahoma Memorial Hospital, 909 P.2d 765 (Okl.1995).

B. DUTIES TO TREAT PATIENTS

The relationship of the medical staff to the hospital insulates the hospital from liability, while giving physicians substantial autonomy in their treating decisions. What happens when the patient's insurance or other resources are exhausted but the staff physician believes that the standard of care requires continued hospitalization? Must the hospital accede to the doctor's request?

MUSE V. CHARTER HOSPITAL OF WINSTON–SALEM, INC.
Court of Appeals of North Carolina, 1995.
117 N.C.App. 468, 452 S.E.2d 589.

LEWIS, JUDGE.

* * *

The facts on which this case arose may be summarized as follows. On 12 June 1986, Joe, who was sixteen years old at the time, was admitted to Charter Hospital for treatment related to his depression and suicidal thoughts. Joe's treatment team consisted of Dr. Barnhill, as treating physician, Fernando Garzon, as nursing therapist, and Betsey Willard, as social worker. During his hospitalization, Joe experienced auditory hallucinations, suicidal and homicidal thoughts, and major depression. Joe's insurance coverage was set to expire on 12 July 1986. As that date neared, Dr. Barnhill decided that a blood test was needed to determine the proper dosage of a drug he was administering to Joe. The blood test was scheduled for 13 July, the day after Joe's insurance was to expire. Dr. Barnhill requested that the hospital administrator allow Joe to stay at Charter Hospital two more days, until 14 July, with Mr. and Mrs. Muse signing a promissory note to pay for the two extra days. The test results did not come back from the lab until 15 July. Nevertheless, Joe was discharged on 14 July and was referred by Dr. Barnhill to the Guilford County Area Mental Health, Mental Retardation and Substance Abuse Authority (hereinafter "Mental Health Authority") for outpatient treatment. Plaintiffs' evidence tended to show that Joe's condition upon discharge was worse than when he entered the hospital. Defendants' evidence, however, tended to show that while his prognosis remained guarded, Joe's condition at discharge was improved. Upon his discharge, Joe went on a one-week family vacation. On 22 July he began outpatient treatment at the Mental Health Authority, where he was seen by Dr. David Slonaker, a clinical psychologist. Two days later, Joe again met with Dr. Slonaker. Joe failed to show up at his 30 July appointment, and the next day he took a fatal overdose of Desipramine, one of his prescribed drugs.

On appeal, defendants present numerous assignments of error. We find merit in one of defendants' arguments.

II.

* * *

Our Supreme Court has recognized that hospitals in this state owe a duty of care to their patients. Id.In Burns v. Forsyth County Hospital Authority, Inc. [ ] this Court held that a hospital has a duty to the patient to obey the instructions of a doctor, absent the instructions being obviously negligent or dangerous. Another recognized duty is the duty to make a reasonable effort to monitor and oversee the treatment prescribed and administered by doctors practicing at the hospital. [ ] In light of these holdings, it seems axiomatic that the hospital has the duty not to institute policies or practices which interfere with the doctor's medical judgment. We hold that pursuant to the reasonable person standard, Charter Hospital had a duty not to institute a policy or practice which required that patients be discharged when their insurance expired and which interfered with the medical judgment of Dr. Barnhill.

III.

Defendants next argue that even if the theory of negligence submitted to the jury was proper, the jury's finding that Charter Hospital had such a practice was not supported by sufficient evidence. * * * We conclude that in the case at hand, the evidence was sufficient to go to the jury.

Plaintiffs' evidence included the testimony of Charter Hospital employees and outside experts. Fernando Garzon, Joe's nursing therapist at Charter Hospital, testified that the hospital had a policy of discharging patients when their insurance expired. Specifically, when the issue of insurance came up in treatment team meetings, plans were made to discharge the patient. When Dr. Barnhill and the other psychiatrists and therapists spoke of insurance, they seemed to lack autonomy. For example, Garzon testified, they would state, "So and so is to be discharged. We must do this." Finally, Garzon testified that when he returned from a vacation, and Joe was no longer at the hospital, he asked several employees why Joe had been discharged and they all responded that he was discharged because his insurance had expired. Jane Sims, a former staff member at the hospital, testified that several employees expressed alarm about Joe's impending discharge, and that a therapist explained that Joe could no longer stay at the hospital because his insurance had expired. Sims also testified that Dr. Barnhill had misgivings about discharging Joe, and that Dr. Barnhill's frustration was apparent to everyone. One of plaintiffs' experts testified that based on a study regarding the length of patient stays at Charter Hospital, it was his opinion that patients were discharged based on insurance, regardless of their medical condition. Other experts testified that based on Joe's serious condition on the date of discharge, the expiration of insurance coverage must have caused Dr.

Barnhill to discharge Joe. The experts further testified as to the relevant standard of care, and concluded that Charter Hospital's practices were below the standard of care and caused Joe's death. We hold that this evidence was sufficient to go to the jury.

* * * We conclude that the jury could have reasonably found from the above-stated evidence that Charter Hospital acted knowingly and of set purpose, and with reckless indifference to the rights of others. Therefore, we hold that the finding of willful or wanton conduct on the part of Charter Hospital was supported by sufficient evidence.

* * *

For the reasons stated, we find no error in the judgment of the trial court, except for that part of the judgment awarding punitive damages, which is reversed and remanded for proceedings consistent with this opinion.

No error in part, reversed in part and remanded.

NOTES AND QUESTIONS

1.   Should the *Muse* duty extend to all situations in which the physician and the hospital administration are in conflict? If the physician always prevails, then how does a hospital control its costs and its bad debts? Why does the court treat health care as special in this case? Surely a grocery store does not have to give us free groceries if we are short of cash as the checkout counter, nor does our landlord have to allow us to stay for free if we cannot cover our next month's rent. Is it simply the advantage of hindsight here that impels the court's imposition of such a duty on hospitals?

A provision in many hospital admissions forms states:

The patient is under the care and supervision of his attending physician and it is the responsibility of the hospital and its nursing staff to carry out the instructions of such physician.

Could the *Muse* case have been brought as a breach of contract case by the plaintiff as third party beneficiary under the contract?

2.   Does such a duty extend as well to managed care organizations, whose very design is premised on mechanisms for containing health care costs? What would happen to the underlying premises of cost control in managed care organizations if the *Muse* doctrine were held to apply?

C. CORPORATE NEGLIGENCE

The stretching of vicarious liability doctrine to sweep in doctors as conduits to hospital liability led inevitably to the imposition of corporate negligence liability on the hospital. Courts had often been willing to hold hospitals liable for institutional failures, such as not using modern technologies (see *Washington, infra*), but had not examined the broader range of functions that a hospital engaged in as part of managing the safety of its patients. It wasn't until the *Darling* case was decided in 1965 that hospital liability began to expand to encompass the problem of physician errors and medical system failures, and the hospital's responsibility for such failures. The focus on the functions of a modern hospital corporation moved the law from discussions of ordinary institutional negligence to a broader focus on corporate duties to manage a complex institution safely.

1. The Elements of Corporate Negligence

The next step was to hold the hospital directly liable for the failure of administrators and staff to properly monitor and supervise the delivery of health care within the hospital.

THOMPSON V. NASON HOSP.
Supreme Court of Pennsylvania, 1991.
527 Pa. 330, 591 A.2d 703.

ZAPPALA, JUSTICE.

Allocatur was granted to examine the novel issue of whether a theory of corporate liability with respect to hospitals should be recognized in this Commonwealth. For the reasons set forth below, we adopt today the theory of corporate liability as it relates to hospitals. * * *

* * *

Considering this predicate to our analysis, we now turn to the record which contains the facts underlying this personal injury action. At approximately 7 a.m. on March 16, 1978, Appellee, Linda A. Thompson, was involved in an automobile accident with a school bus. Mrs. Thompson was transported by ambulance from the accident scene to Nason Hospital's emergency room where she was admitted with head and leg injuries. The hospital's emergency room personnel were advised by Appellee, Donald A. Thompson, that his wife was taking the drug Coumadin, that she had a permanent pacemaker, and that she took other heart medications.

Subsequent to Mrs. Thompson's admission to Nason Hospital, Dr. Edward D. Schultz, a general practitioner who enjoyed staff privileges at Nason Hospital, entered the hospital via the emergency room to make his rounds. Although Dr. Schultz was not assigned duty in the emergency room, an on-duty hospital nurse asked him to attend Mrs. Thompson due to a prior physician-patient relationship. Dr. Schultz examined Mrs. Thompson and diagnosed her as suffering from multiple injuries including extensive lacerations over her left eye and the back of her scalp, constricted pupils, enlarged heart with a Grade III micro-systolic murmur, a brain concussion and amnesia. X-rays that were taken revealed fractures of the right tibia and right heel.

Following Dr. Schultz's examination and diagnosis, Dr. Larry Jones, an ophthalmologist, sutured the lacerations over Mrs. Thompson's left eye. It was during that time that Dr. Schultz consulted with Dr. Rao concerning orthopedic repairs. Dr. Rao advised conservative therapy until her critical medical condition improved.

Dr. Schultz knew Mrs. Thompson was suffering from rheumatic heart and mitral valve disease and was on anticoagulant therapy. Because he had no specific training in establishing dosages for such therapy, Dr. Schultz called Dr. Marvin H. Meisner, a cardiologist who was treating Mrs. Thompson with an anticoagulant therapy. Although Dr. Meisner was unavailable, Dr. Schultz did speak with Dr. Meisner's associate Dr. Steven P. Draskoczy.

Mrs. Thompson had remained in the emergency room during this time. Her condition, however, showed no sign of improvement. Due to both the multiple trauma received in the accident and her pre-existing heart disease, Dr. Schultz, as attending physician, admitted her to Nason Hospital's intensive care unit at 11:20 a.m.

The next morning at 8:30 a.m., Dr. Mark Paris, a general surgeon on staff at Nason Hospital, examined Mrs. Thompson. He found that she was unable to move her left foot and toes. It was also noted by Dr. Paris that the patient had a positive Babinski—a neurological sign of an intracerebral problem. Twelve hours later, Dr. Schultz examined Mrs. Thompson and found more bleeding in her eye. He also indicated in the progress notes that the problem with her left leg was that it was neurological.

On March 18, 1978, the third day of her hospitalization, Dr. Larry Jones, the ophthalmologist who treated her in the emergency room, examined her in the intensive care unit. He indicated in the progress notes an "increased hematuria secondary to anticoagulation. Right eye now involved". Dr. Schultz also examined Mrs. Thompson that day and noted the decreased movement of her left leg was neurologic. Dr. Paris's progress note that date approved the withholding of Coumadin and the continued use of Heparin.

The following day, Mrs. Thompson had complete paralysis of the left side. Upon examination by Dr. Schultz he questioned whether she needed to be under the care of a neurologist or needed to be watched there. At 10:30 a.m. that day, Dr. Schultz transferred her to the Hershey Medical Center because of her progressive neurological problem.

Linda Thompson underwent tests at the Hershey Medical Center. The results of the tests revealed that she had a large intracerebral hematoma in the right frontal temporal and parietal lobes of the brain. She was subsequently discharged on April 1, 1978, without regaining the motor function of her left side.

* * * The complaint alleged inter alia that Mrs. Thompson's injuries were the direct and proximate result of the negligence of Nason Hospital acting through its agents, servants and employees in failing to adequately examine and treat her, in failing to follow its rules relative to consultations and in failing to monitor her conditions during treatment. * * *

* * *

The first issue Nason Hospital raised is whether the Superior Court erred in adopting a theory of corporate liability with respect to a hospital. This issue had not heretofore been determined by the Court. Nason Hospital contends that it had no duty to observe, supervise or control the actual treatment of Linda Thompson.

Hospitals in the past enjoyed absolute immunity from tort liability. [ ] The basis of that immunity was the perception that hospitals functioned as charitable organizations. [ ] However, hospitals have evolved into highly sophisticated corporations operating primarily on a fee-for-service basis. The corporate hospital of today has assumed the role of a comprehensive health center with responsibility for arranging and coordinating the total health care of its patients. As a result of this metamorphosis, hospital immunity was eliminated. [ ]

Not surprisingly, the by-product of eliminating hospital immunity has been the filing of malpractice actions against hospitals. Courts have recognized several bases on which hospitals may be subject to liability including respondeat superior, ostensible agency and corporate negligence. [ ]

The development of hospital liability in this Commonwealth mirrored that which occurred in other jurisdictions. * * * We now turn our attention to the theory of corporate liability with respect to the hospital, which was first recognized in this Commonwealth by the court below.

Corporate negligence is a doctrine under which the hospital is liable if it fails to uphold the proper standard of care owed the patient, which is to ensure the patient's safety and well-being while at the hospital. This theory of liability creates a nondelegable duty which the hospital owes directly to a patient. Therefore, an injured party does not have to rely on and establish the negligence of a third party.

The hospital's duties have been classified into four general areas: (1) a duty to use reasonable care in the maintenance of safe and adequate facilities and equipment—Candler General Hospital Inc. v. Purvis, 123 Ga.App. 334, 181 S.E.2d 77 (1971); (2) a duty to select and retain only competent physicians—Johnson v. Misericordia Community Hospital, 99 Wis.2d 708, 301 N.W.2d 156 (1981); (3) a duty to oversee all persons who practice medicine within its walls as to patient care—Darling v. Charleston Community Memorial Hospital, *supra.*; and (4) a duty to formulate, adopt and enforce adequate rules and policies to ensure quality care for the patients—Wood v. Samaritan Institution, 26 Cal.2d 847, 161 P.2d 556 (Cal. Ct. App.1945). [ ]

Other jurisdictions have embraced this doctrine of corporate negligence or corporate liability such as to warrant it being called an "emerging trend". [ ]

*   *   *

Today, we take a step beyond the hospital's duty of care delineated in Riddle in full recognition of the corporate hospital's role in the total health care of its patients. In so doing, we adopt as a theory of hospital liability the doctrine of corporate negligence or corporate liability under which the hospital is liable if it fails to uphold the proper standard of care owed its patient. In addition, we fully embrace the aforementioned four categories of the hospital's duties. It is important to note that for a hospital to be charged with negligence, it is necessary to show that the hospital had actual or constructive knowledge of the defect or procedures which created the harm. [ ] Furthermore, the hospital's negligence must have been a substantial factor in bringing about the harm to the injured party. [ ].

*   *   *

It is well established that a hospital staff member or employee has a duty to recognize and report abnormalities in the treatment and condition of its patients. [ ] If the attending physician fails to act after being informed of such abnormalities, it is then incumbent upon the hospital staff member or employee to so advise the hospital authorities so that appropriate action might be taken. [ ] When there is a failure to report changes in a patient's condition and/or to question a physician's order which is not in accord with standard medical practice and the patient is injured as a result, the hospital will be liable for such negligence. [ ]

A thorough review of the record of this case convinces us that there is a sufficient question of material fact presented as to whether Nason Hospital was negligent in supervising the quality of the medical care Mrs. Thompson received, such that the trial court could not have properly granted summary judgment on the issue of corporate liability.

The order of Superior Court is affirmed. Jurisdiction is relinquished.

NOTES AND QUESTIONS

1.   Hospitals create their own medical errors, and courts have shifted some liability to hospitals as a result. One early case is Darling v. Charleston Community Memorial Hospital, 211 N.E. 2d 253 (Illiois 1965), which held the

hospital responsible for not monitoring the competence of a physican on the medical staff, as well as the treating nurses for not reporting the physician to the administration.

The proportion of errors with interactive or administrative causes in the hospital has been found to be as high as 25 percent. *See* Lori B. Andrews et al., *An Alternative Strategy for Studying Adverse Events in Medical Care*, 349 Lancet 309, 312 (1997). As you think about the typical hospital's complexity in both its administrative and operational structure, where do you think liability should best be focused? On its physicians? On the hospital? Joint liability? Or something different? Some states have adopted corporate negligence for institutional providers. Florida, for example, has incorporated "institutional liability" or "corporate negligence" in its regulation of hospitals. Hospitals and other providers will be liable for injuries caused by inadequacies in the internal programs that are mandated by the statute. West's Fla.Stat.Ann. § 768.60.

2. Expert testimony is required to establish a corporate negligence claim, unless it involves simple issues such as structural defects within the common knowledge and experience of the jury. See generally Neff v. Johnson Memorial Hospital, 93 Conn.App. 534, 889 A.2d 921 (Conn.App. 2006) (noting the complexity of the staff credentialing process, and holding that plaintiff needed an expert to determine what the standard of care was for a hospital in allowing a physician with three malpractice cases in his history to be recredentialed).

2. Negligent Credentialing

CARTER V. HUCKS–FOLLISS
North Carolina Court of Appeals, 1998.
131 N.C.App. 145, 505 S.E.2d 177.

GREENE, JUDGE.

Tommy and Tracy Carter (collectively, Plaintiffs) appeal from the granting of Moore Regional Hospital's (Defendant) motion for summary judgment entered 26 June 1997.

On 20 August 1993, Dr. Anthony Hucks–Folliss (Dr. Hucks–Folliss) performed neck surgery on plaintiff Tommy Carter at Defendant. Dr. Hucks–Folliss is a neurosurgeon on the medical staff of Defendant. He first was granted surgical privileges by Defendant in 1975, and has been reviewed every two years hence to renew those privileges. Though he has been on Defendant's staff for over twenty years, Dr. Hucks–Folliss never has been certified by the American Board of Neurological Surgery. Presently, Dr. Hucks–Folliss is ineligible for board certification because he has taken and failed the certification examination on three different occasions.

The credentialing and re-credentialing of physicians at Defendant is designed to comply with standards promulgated by the Joint Commission on Accreditation of Healthcare Organizations (JCAHO). In 1992, the time when Dr. Hucks–Folliss was last re-credentialed by Defendant prior to the neck surgery performed on Tommy Carter, the JCAHO provided that board certification "is an excellent benchmark and is [to be] considered when delineating clinical privileges."

On the application filed by Dr. Hucks–Folliss, seeking to renew his surgical privileges with Defendant, he specifically stated, in response to a question on the application, that he was not board certified. Dr. James Barnes (Dr. Barnes), one of Plaintiffs' experts, presented an affidavit wherein he states that Defendant "does not appear [to have] ever considered the fact that Dr. Hucks–Folliss was not board certified, or that he had failed board exams three times," when renewing Dr. Hucks–Folliss's surgical privileges. Jean Hill (Ms. Hill), the manager of Medical Staff Services for Defendant, stated in her deposition that board certification was not an issue in the re-credentialing of active staff physicians. There is no dispute that Dr. Hucks–Folliss was on active staff in 1992. Additionally, this record does not reveal any further inquiry by Defendant into Dr. Hucks–Folliss's board certification status (beyond the question on the application).

In the complaint, it is alleged that Defendant was negligent: (1) in granting clinical privileges to Dr. Hucks–Folliss; (2) in failing to ascertain whether Dr. Hucks–Folliss was qualified to perform neurological surgery; and (3) in failing to enforce the standards of the JCAHO. It is further alleged that as a proximate result of Defendant's negligence, Tommy Carter agreed to allow Dr. Hucks–Folliss to perform surgery on him in Defendant. As a consequence of that surgery, Tommy Carter sustained "serious, permanent and painful injuries to his person including quadraparesis, scarring and other disfigurement."

The issue is whether a genuine issue of fact is presented on this record as to the negligence of Defendant in re-credentialing Dr. Hucks–Folliss.

Hospitals owe a duty of care to its patients to ascertain that a physician is qualified to perform surgery before granting that physician the privilege of conducting surgery in that hospital.[ ] In determining whether a hospital, accredited by the JCAHO, has breached its duty of care in ascertaining the qualifications of the physician to practice in the hospital, it is appropriate to consider whether the hospital has complied with standards promulgated by the JCAHO. Failure to comply with these standards "is some evidence of negligence."[ ]

In this case, Defendant has agreed to be bound by the standards promulgated by JCAHO and those standards provided in part that board certification was a factor to be "considered" when determining hospital privileges. Defendant argues that the evidence reveals unequivocally that it "considered," in re-credentialing Dr. Hucks–Folliss, the fact that he was not board certified. It points to the application submitted by Dr. Hucks–Folliss, specifically stating that he was not board certified, to support this argument. We disagree. Although this evidence does reveal that Defendant was aware of Dr. Hucks–Folliss's lack of certification, it does not follow that his lack of certification was considered as a factor in the re-credentialing decision. In any event, there is evidence from Dr. Barnes and Ms. Hill that supports a finding that Defendant did not consider Dr. Hucks–Folliss's lack of certification, or his failure to pass the certification test on three occasions, in assessing his qualifications to practice medicine in the hospital. This evidence presents a genuine issue of material fact and thus precludes the issuance of a summary judgment.[ ]

We also reject the alternative argument of Defendant that summary judgment is proper because there is no evidence that any breach of duty (in failing to consider Dr. Hucks–Folliss's lack of board certification prior to re-credentialing) by it was a proximate cause of the injuries sustained by Tommy Carter. Genuine issues of material fact are raised on this point as well. [ ].

Reversed and remanded.

NOTES AND QUESTIONS

1.   Does Dr. Hucks–Follis's lack of certification speak to his skill and qualifications? How should a doctor's experience be weighed against his testing abilities? The court considers Joint Commission (formerly JCAHO) standards as an important source of duties with regard to hospital credentialing, and failure to comply "some evidence of negligence." Would it be sufficient if the hospital had noted the deficiencies and made a finding that the doctor's experience and references were enough to outweigh any negative implications of lack of certification?

2.   The core function of a hospital is to select high quality physicians for its medical staff. The hospital's governing board retains the ultimate responsibility for the quality of care provided, but their responsibility is normally delegated to the hospital staff, and discharged in practice by medical staff review committees. The organization and function of these committees in accredited hospitals are described in publications of the Joint Commission.

3.   The requirement of staff self-governance under Joint Commission standards maintains and reinforces this physician authority within hospitals. Courts have found, however, that the chief executive officer of a hospital and the governing board have the "inherent authority to summarily suspend clinical privileges to prevent an imminent danger to patients". See Lo v. Provena Covenant Medical Center, 342 Ill.App.3d 975, 277 Ill.Dec. 521, 796 N.E.2d 607, 614 (4 Dist. 2003).

4. *Joint Commission Prospective Monitoring of Quality.* The Joint Commission issued new standards on medical staff governance in 2010 that prescribe the relationship between the medical staff, the medical staff's Executive Committee, and the hospital's Board. Joint Commission standards have intensified the institutional focus on prospective monitoring of physician quality. One of the Standards, for example, specifically provides that the hospital must establish a system for collecting, recording, and addressing individual reports of concerns about individual physicians. See Joint Commission, Focused Professional Practice Evaluation, October 13, 2008.

The Joint Commission now requires a period of focused review for all new privileges and all new privileges for existing practitioners, without any exemption for board certification, documented experience, or reputation. Professional practice evaluation includes several elements: periodic chart review; direct observation; monitoring of diagnostic and treatment techniques; and discussion with other individuals involved in the care of each patient including consulting physicians, assistants at surgery, nursing, and administrative personnel.

The duration of the period of review however can be varied for different levels of documented training and experience, e.g. practitioners coming directly from an outside residency program; practitioners coming directly from the organization's residency program; practitioners coming with a documented record of performance of the privilege and its associated outcomes; and practitioners coming with no record of performance of the privilege and its associated outcomes.

The standard requires the organized medical staff to develop criteria to be used for evaluating the performance of practitioners when issues affecting the provision of safe, high quality patient care are identified. Criteria for performance issues, according to the Joint Commission, might include several triggering events:

- small number of admissions or procedures over an extended period of time that raise the concern of continued competence

- a growing number of longer lengths of stay than other practitioners

- returns to surgery

- frequent or repeat readmission suggesting possibly poor or inadequate initial management/treatment

- patterns of unnecessary diagnostic testing/treatments

- failure to follow approved clinical practice guidelines—may or may not indicate care problems but why the variance

- frequent or repeat readmission suggesting possibly poor or inadequate initial management/treatment

- patterns of unnecessary diagnostic testing/treatments

- failure to follow approved clinical practice guidelines—may or may not indicate care problems but why the variance

5. *Medicare Conditions of Participation.* Federal law requires among other things that hospital bylaws reflect the hospital governing board's responsibility to ensure that ". . . the medical staff is accountable to the governing body for the quality of care provided to patients." 42 C.F.R. § 482.12(a)(5)(2001). The federal government is also involved in credentialing issues through the 2008 *Medicare Improvement for Providers and Patients Act*, which removed permanent deemed status from the Joint Commission for hospitals and required it to periodically reapply for deemed status. This mandate has allowed CMS to engage the Joint Commission on its standards for hospitals. 20 BNA Health Law Rptr. 886 (June 9, 2011). See discussion of accreditation generally in Chapter 2, *supra.*

6. Under the Health Care Quality Improvement Act of 1986 (HCQIA), hospitals must check a national database maintained under contract with the Department of Health and Human Services, before a new staff appointment is made. This National Practitioner Data Bank (NPDB) contains information on individual physicians who have been disciplined, had malpractice claims filed against them, or had privileges revoked or limited. If the hospital fails to check the registry, it is held constructively to have knowledge of any information it might have gotten from the inquiry. See discussion of staff privileges in Chapter 11, *infra.*

PROBLEM: CASCADING ERRORS

Carolyn Gadner was driving her car on the highway when another car driven by Bob Sneed passed her, sideswiped her, ran her off the road, and drove off. Gadner caught up with Sneed and forced him to stop. She got out of her vehicle and started to walk to his car when he drove away. While Gadner was walking back to her car, Charles Otis struck her with his vehicle. Gadner was transported to Bay Hospital, a small rural hospital, where Dr. Dick Samson, a second-year pediatric resident, was the attending emergency room physician. Upon arriving at Bay, Gadner's skin was cool and clammy and her blood pressure was 95/55, indicative of shock. Gadner received 200 ccs per hour of fluid and was x-rayed. She actively requested a transfer because of vaginal bleeding. Nurse Gilbert voiced her own concerns about the need for a transfer to the other nurses in the emergency room. Dr. Samson did not order one.

Bay is a rural hospital and is not equipped to handle multiple trauma patients like Gadner. Bay had no protocol or procedure for making transfers to larger hospitals. Bay breached its own credentialing procedures in hiring a physician who lacked the necessary training, expertise, or demonstrated competence to work the ER. Dr. Bay, the hospital's chief of staff, had screened Samson, who was not properly evaluated before he was hired. A second-year pediatric resident is not normally assigned to an ER setting, give his lack of experience.

The nurses failed to notice that Gadner was in shock and that this failure was substandard. After they initially noted that she arrived with cool and clammy skin and a blood pressure of 95/55, they did not advise Dr. Samson that the patient was likely in shock; they failed to place her on IV fluids, elevate her feet above her head, and give oxygen as needed. Dr. Samson ordered the administration of 500 cc's of fluid per hour, but Gadner received only about 200 cc's per hour because the IV infiltrated, delivering the fluid to the surrounding tissue instead of the vein. The nursing staff normally would discover infiltration and correct it. Scanty nurses' notes revealed that vital signs were not taken regularly, depriving Dr. Samson of critical and ongoing information about Gadner's condition. Nurse Gilbert administered Valium and morphine to Gadner, following Dr. Samson's orders, a mixture of drugs counter-indicated for a patient with symptoms of shock. Nurse Gilbert did not notice or protest.

Three hours after arriving at Bay, Gadner "coded" and Dr. Samson tried unsuccessfully to revive her. After she coded, Dr. Samson attempted to use the laryngoscope, following standard practice, but the one provided was broken. He then ordered epinephrine, but there was none in the ER. An autopsy was performed, and Gadner died of treatable shock according to the coroner.

Consider the various theories of liability available to the plaintiff. Then develop a plan to improve the hospital from a patient safety perspective so that this kind of disaster will not happen again.

3. Peer Review Immunity and Corporate Negligence

Credentialing decisions may be the central feature of corporate negligence claims, but such decisions are often the most difficult to prove. Virtually all American jurisdictions have peer review immunity statutes that limit access to hospital decisionmaking about physician problems that have been discovered.

LARSON V. WASEMILLER

Supreme Court of Minnesota, 2007.
738 N.W.2d 300.

Opinion

HANSON, JUSTICE.

Appellants Mary and Michael Larson commenced this medical malpractice claim against respondent Dr. James Wasemiller, Dr. Paul Wasemiller and the Dakota Clinic for negligence in connection with the performance of gastric bypass surgery on Mary Larson. The Larsons also joined respondent St. Francis Medical Center as a defendant, claiming, among other things, that St. Francis was negligent in granting surgery privileges to Dr. James Wasemiller. St. Francis then moved to dismiss for failure to state a claim. The district court denied the motion to dismiss, holding that Minnesota does recognize a claim for negligent credentialing, but certified two questions to the court of appeals. The court of appeals reversed the district court's denial of the motion to dismiss, holding that Minnesota does not recognize a common-law cause of action for negligent credentialing. [ ] We reverse and remand to the district court for further proceedings.

In April 2002, Dr. James Wasemiller, with the assistance of his brother, Dr. Paul Wasemiller, performed gastric bypass surgery on Mary Larson at St. Francis Medical Center in Breckenridge, Minnesota. Larson experienced complications following the surgery, and Dr. Paul Wasemiller performed a second surgery on April 12, 2002 to address the complications. On April 22, 2002, after being moved to a long-term care facility, Larson was transferred to MeritCare Hospital for emergency surgery. Larson remained hospitalized until June 28, 2002.

The Larsons claim that St. Francis was negligent in credentialing Dr. James P. Wasemiller. Credentialing decisions determine which physicians are granted hospital privileges and what specific procedures they can perform in the hospital. *See* Craig W. Dallon, Understanding Judicial Review of Hospitals' Physician Credentialing and Peer Review Decisions, 73 Temp. L.Rev. 597, 598 (2000). The granting of hospital privileges normally does not create an employment relationship with the hospital, but it allows physicians access to the hospital's facilities and imposes certain professional standards. [ ]. The decision to grant hospital privileges to a physician is made by the hospital's governing body based on the recommendations of the credentials committee. A credentials committee is a type of peer review committee. Minnesota, like most other states, has a peer review statute that provides for the confidentiality of peer review proceedings and grants some immunity to those involved in the credentialing process. [ ].

* * *

After denying St. Francis' motion to dismiss, the district court certified the following two questions to the court of appeals:

A.   Does the state of Minnesota recognize a common law cause of action of privileging of a physician against a hospital or other review organization?

B.   Does Minn.Stat. §§ 145.63–145.64 grant immunity from or otherwise limit liability of a hospital or other review organization for a claim of negligent credentialing/privileging of a physician?

*   *   *

A.   Does Minnesota's peer review statute create a cause of action for negligent credentialing?

[The court concludes that " * * * the tort of negligent credentialing is inherent in and the natural extension of well-established common law rights." It further noted that more than half of the state courts have adopted the tort, and it has support in Restatement (Second) Tort sections such as section 320 and 411.]

     3.   Would the tort of negligent credentialing conflict with Minnesota's peer review statute?

St. Francis argues that the fact that a majority of other jurisdictions have recognized a negligent-credentialing claim is not dispositive because such a claim would conflict with Minnesota's peer review statute. Minnesota's peer review statute contains both confidentiality and limited liability provisions. [ ].

The Confidentiality Provision

The confidentiality provision of the peer review statute provides in part that

> [D]ata and information acquired by a review organization, in the exercise of its duties and functions, or by an individual or other entity acting at the direction of a review organization, shall be held in confidence, shall not be disclosed to anyone except to the extent necessary to carry out one or more of the purposes of the review organization, and shall not be subject to subpoena or discovery. No person described in section 145.63 shall disclose what transpired at a meeting of a review organization except to the extent necessary to carry out one or more of the purposes of a review organization. The proceedings and records of a review organization shall not be subject to discovery or introduction into evidence in any civil action against a professional arising out of the matter or matters which are the subject of consideration by the review organization.

[ ]. Credentialing committees are "review organizations" under the statutory definition. [ ]. Any unauthorized disclosure of the above information is a misdemeanor.[ ].

> [The court notes that under Minnesota's confidentiality provision, information otherwise available from original sources are not immune from discovery or use, and anyone who testified before a review organization can testify in a civil case about any matters within that witness' knowledge.]

Thus, although section 145.64, subdivision 1 would prevent hospitals from disclosing the fact that certain information was considered by the credentials committee, it would not prevent hospitals from introducing the same information, as long as it could be obtained from original sources. **

* * *

Although the confidentiality provision of Minnesota's peer review statute may make the proof of a common law negligent-credentialing claim more complicated, we conclude that it does not preclude such a claim.

The Limited Liability Provision

[The court finds that the limited liability provision in Minnesota law provides some immunity from liability both for individual credentials committee members and hospitals, for claims brought by either a physician or a patient.]

* * *

We conclude that the liability provisions of section 145.63 do not materially alter the common law standard of care and that, although the confidentiality provisions of section 145.64 present some obstacles in both proving and defending a claim of negligent credentialing, they do not preclude such a claim.

      4.   Do the policy considerations in favor of the tort of negligent credentialing outweigh any tension caused by conflict with the peer review statute?

The function of peer review is to provide critical analysis of the competence and performance of physicians and other health care providers in order to decrease incidents of malpractice and to improve quality of patient care. [ ] This court has held that the purpose of Minnesota's peer review statute is to promote the strong public interest in improving health care by granting certain protections to medical review organizations,[ ] and to encourage the medical profession to police its own activities with minimal judicial interference,[ ]. This court has also recognized that "the quality of patient care could be compromised if fellow professionals are reluctant to participate fully in peer review activities."[ ].

* * *

We recognize that a claim of negligent credentialing raises questions about the necessity of a bifurcated trial and the scope of the confidentiality and immunity provisions of the peer review statute. We likewise recognize that there is an issue about whether a patient must first prove negligence on the part of a physician before a hospital can be liable for negligently credentialing the physician. But, in part, these are questions of trial management that are best left to the trial judge. [ ] Further, they cannot be effectively addressed in the context of this Rule 12 motion.

We conclude that the policy considerations underlying the tort of negligent credentialing outweigh the policy considerations reflected in the peer review statute because the latter policy considerations are adequately addressed by the preclusion of access to the confidential peer review materials. We therefore hold that a claim of negligent credentialing does exist in Minnesota, and is not precluded by Minnesota's peer review statute. We reverse the answer of the court of appeals to the first certified question, answer that question in the affirmative, and remand to the district court for further proceedings consistent with this opinion.

Reversed and remanded.

NOTES AND QUESTIONS

1. *Hospital Committee Proceedings.* Plaintiffs in malpractice actions frequently seek discovery of the proceedings of hospital quality assurance committees, as the problem above illustrates. If the suit is against the hospital on a theory of corporate liability (i.e., claiming that the hospital itself was negligent in appointing or failing to supervise a professional), evidence of committee proceedings may prove vital to establishing the hospital's liability.

These discovery requests are usually met with a claim that information generated within or by hospital committees is not discoverable. In Coburn v. Seda, 101 Wash.2d 270, 677 P.2d 173 (1984), the court considered the policy justifications for the discovery protection. The court pointed out that the protection "prevents the opposing party from taking advantage of a hospital's careful self-assessment", and promotes open and conscientious evaluate of clinical practices under the shelter of a confidentiality protection.

2. A number of statutes immunizing committee proceedings from discovery do not explicitly render information from those committees privileged from admission into evidence if the plaintiff can obtain it otherwise. But would such information be otherwise admissible? Would it be hearsay? If so, would it be subject to the business records exception? See Fed.R.Evid. 803(6). Might committee records indicating that a hospital was concerned about the performance of a physician be admissible as an admission in a subsequent corporate negligence action against the hospital? See Fed.R.Evid. 801(d)(2)(D). Might a plaintiff's expert be permitted to testify on the basis of information gleaned from committee records, even though those records were themselves hearsay? See Fed.R.Evid. 703. In a suit brought by one particular patient, would committee records documenting errors made by a physician in the treatment of other patients be relevant? Might opinions concerning a physician's negligence found in committee records or reports invade the province of the jury? See, addressing these questions, Robert F. Holbrook & Lee J. Dunn, Medical Malpractice Litigation: The Discoverability and Use of Hospitals' Quality Assurance Records, 16 Washburn L.J. 54, 68–70 (1976).

3. *Hospital Incident Reports.* When a plaintiff seeks discovery of incident reports rather than committee proceedings, policy considerations are somewhat different. Hospitals have greater incentives to investigate untoward events than they have to carry on continuing quality review, and are less dependent on voluntary participation. The incident report would usually be more directly relevant to a single claim for malpractice than would general committee investigations. Possibly for these reasons, immunity statutes that protect committee proceedings less often protect incident reports, and courts have been less willing to immunize incident reports from discovery. On the other hand, since incident reports are more directly related to litigation of specific mishaps, two privileges can be asserted to protect them that would seldom apply to committee proceedings: the work product immunity and attorney client privilege.

4. *Hospital Sentinel Event Investigations.* Root cause investigations in compliance with Joint Commission guidelines have been denied discovery and confidentiality protections. In Reyes v. Meadowlands Hospital Medical Center, 809 A.2d 875 (N.J.Super. 2001), the defendant hospital argued that its root cause analysis of a sentinel event under Joint Commission guidelines should be protected from discovery. The court rejected the defendant's arguments, concluding that " * * * the Sentinel Event Policy invoked by defendant Meadowlands Hospital does not create a self-critical analysis privilege, insulating any and all discussions and statements made and conclusions reached by the participants therein and actions taken by the Hospital pursuant thereto not subject to the Civil Rules of Discovery."

5. The work product immunity protects materials prepared in anticipation of litigation. See Federal Rules of Civil Procedure 56. Courts look to the nature and purpose of incident reports. If they are regularly prepared and distributed for future loss prevention, they are not considered to be documents prepared in anticipation of litigation so as to invoke application of the work product exception to discovery. See St. Louis Little Rock Hospital, Inc. v. Gaertner, 682 S.W.2d 146, 150–51 (Mo.App.1984).

This attorney-client privilege protects communications, even if the attorney is not yet representing a client, provided that the communication was made between the client as an insured to his liability insurer during the course of an existing insured-insurer relationship. To be privileged, a communication between a client and his attorney, or between an insured and his insurer, must be within the context of the attorney-client relationship, with a purpose of securing legal advice from the client's attorney. See The St. Luke Hospitals, Inc. v. Kopowski, 160 S.W.3d 771 (Kentucky 2005) (Two nurses communicated about the post-delivery care of an infant who died at the hospital to the officer in charge of risk management, who had conducted the interviews of the nurses at the direction of the hospital's attorney. The court held that the communications were protected by the privilege.)

PROBLEM: PROCTORING PEERS

You have been asked by Hilldale Adventist Hospital to advise it on the implications of its use of proctors for assessing candidates for medical staff privileges. The hospital has used Dr. Hook, a surgeon certified by the American Board of Orthopedic Surgery, as a proctor during two different operations on the plaintiff at two different hospitals during the process of evaluation of Dr. Frank DiBianco for staff privileges. Dr. Hook had been asked to observe ten surgeries by Dr. DiBianco and then file a report. He observed an operation on the plaintiff during one of these observations. Two months later, he was again asked to proctor Dr. DiBianco at another hospital, and he again observed a procedure on the plaintiff. Prior to each procedure, Dr. Hook had reviewed the x-rays and discussed the operative plan, but he otherwise had taken no part in the care and treatment of the plaintiff. He did not participate in the operations, did not scrub in, and always observed from outside the "sterile field." He got no payment for his proctoring efforts, and he had never met the plaintiff nor had any other contact with her.

Can Hilldale be liable for its use of Dr. Hook as a proctor? Can Dr. Hook be directly liable for failing to stop negligent work by Dr. DiBianco?

What if the process by which a hospital evaluates the credentials of a physician for staff privileges fails?

KADLEC MEDICAL CENTER V. LAKEVIEW ANESTHESIA ASSOCIATES

Fifth Circuit Court of Appeals, 2008.
527 F.3d 412.

REAVLEY, CIRCUIT JUDGE:

Kadlec Medical Center and its insurer, Western Professional Insurance Company, filed this diversity action in Louisiana district court against Louisiana Anesthesia Associates (LAA), its shareholders, and Lakeview Regional Medical Center (Lakeview Medical). The LAA shareholders worked with Dr. Robert Berry-an anesthesiologist and former LAA shareholder-at Lakeview Medical, where the defendants discovered his on-duty use of narcotics. In referral letters written by the defendants and relied on by Kadlec, his future employer, the defendants did not disclose Dr. Berry's drug use.

While under the influence of Demerol at Kadlec, Dr. Berry's negligent performance led to the near-death of a patient, resulting in a lawsuit against Kadlec. Plaintiffs claim here that the defendants' misleading referral letters were a legal cause of plaintiffs' financial injury, i.e., having to pay over $8 million to defend and settle the lawsuit. The jury found in favor of the plaintiffs and judgment followed. We reverse the judgment against Lakeview Medical, vacate the remainder of the judgment, and remand.

I.   Factual Background

Dr. Berry was a licensed anesthesiologist in Louisiana and practiced with Drs. William Preau, Mark Dennis, David Baldone, and Allan Parr at LAA. From November 2000 until his termination on March 13, 2001, Dr. Berry was a shareholder of LAA, the exclusive provider of anesthesia services to Lakeview Medical (a Louisiana hospital).

In November 2000, a small management team at Lakeview Medical investigated Dr. Berry after nurses expressed concern about his undocumented and suspicious withdrawals of Demerol. The investigative team found excessive Demerol withdrawals by Dr. Berry and a lack of documentation for the withdrawals.

Lakeview Medical CEO Max Lauderdale discussed the team's findings with Dr. Berry and Dr. Dennis. Dr. Dennis then discussed Dr. Berry's situation with his partners. They all agreed that Dr. Berry's use of Demerol had to be controlled and monitored. But Dr. Berry did not follow the agreement or account for his continued Demerol withdrawals. Three months later, Dr. Berry failed to answer a page while on-duty at Lakeview Medical. He was discovered in the call-room, asleep, groggy, and unfit to work. Personnel immediately called Dr. Dennis, who found Dr. Berry not communicating well and unable to work. Dr. Dennis had Dr. Berry taken away after Dr. Berry said that he had taken prescription medications.

Lauderdale, Lakeview Medical's CEO, decided that it was in the best interest of patient safety that Dr. Berry not practice at the hospital. Dr. Dennis and his three partners at LAA fired Dr. Berry and signed his termination letter on March 27, 2001, which explained that he was fired "for cause":

> [You have been fired for cause because] you have reported to work in an impaired physical, mental, and emotional state. Your impaired condition has prevented you from properly performing your duties and puts our patients at significant risk. . . . [P]lease consider your termination effective March 13, 2001.

At Lakeview Medical, Lauderdale ordered the Chief Nursing Officer to notify the administration if Dr. Berry returned.

Despite recognizing Dr. Berry's drug problem and the danger he posed to patients, neither Dr. Dennis nor Lauderdale reported Dr. Berry's impairment to the hospital's Medical Executive Committee, eventually noting only that Dr. Berry was "no longer employed by LAA." Neither one reported Dr. Berry's impairment to Lakeview Medical's Board of Trustees, and no one on behalf of Lakeview Medical reported Dr. Berry's impairment or discipline to the Louisiana Board of Medical Examiners or to the National Practitioner's Data Bank. In fact, at some point Lauderdale took the unusual step of locking away in his office all files, audits, plans, and notes concerning Dr. Berry and the investigation.

After leaving LAA and Lakeview Medical, Dr. Berry briefly obtained work as a *locum tenens* (traveling physician) at a hospital in Shreveport, Louisiana. In October 2001, he applied through Staff Care, a leading *locum tenens* staffing firm, for *locum tenens* privileges at Kadlec Medical Center in Washington State. After receiving his application, Kadlec began its credentialing process. Kadlec examined a variety of materials, including referral letters from LAA and Lakeview Medical.

LAA's Dr. Preau and Dr. Dennis, two months after firing Dr. Berry for his on-the-job drug use, submitted referral letters for Dr. Berry to Staff Care, with the intention that they be provided to future employers. The letter from Dr. Dennis stated that he had worked with Dr. Berry for four years, that he was an excellent clinician, and that he would be an asset to any anesthesia service. Dr. Preau's letter said that he worked with Berry at Lakeview Medical and that he recommended him highly as an anesthesiologist. Dr. Preau's and Dr. Dennis's letters were submitted on June 3, 2001, only sixty-eight days after they fired him for using narcotics while on-duty and stating in his termination letter that Dr. Berry's behavior put "patients at significant risk."

On October 17, 2001, Kadlec sent Lakeview Medical a request for credentialing information about Berry. The request included a detailed confidential questionnaire, a delineation of privileges, and a signed consent for release of information. The interrogatories on the questionnaire asked whether "[Dr. Berry] has been subject to any disciplinary action," if "[Dr. Berry has] the ability (health status) to perform the privileges requested," whether "[Dr. Berry has] shown any signs of behavior/personality problems or impairments," and whether Dr. Berry has satisfactory "judgement."

Nine days later, Lakeview Medical responded to the requests for credentialing information about fourteen different physicians. In thirteen cases, it responded fully and completely to the request, filling out forms with all the information asked for by the requesting health care provider. The fourteenth request, from Kadlec concerning Berry, was handled differently. Instead of completing the multi-part forms, Lakeview Medical staff drafted a short letter. In its entirety, it read:

This letter is written in response to your inquiry regarding [Dr. Berry]. Due to the large volume of inquiries received in this office, the following information is provided.

Our records indicate that Dr. Robert L. Berry was on the Active Medical Staff of Lakeview Regional Medical Center in the field of Anesthesiology from March 04, 1997 through September 04, 2001.

If I can be of further assistance, you may contact me at (504) 867–4076.

The letter did not disclose LAA's termination of Dr. Berry; his on-duty drug use; the investigation into Dr. Berry's undocumented and suspicious withdrawals of Demerol that "violated the standard of care"; or any other negative information. The employee who drafted the letter said at trial that she just followed a form letter, which is one of many that Lakeview Medical used.

Kadlec then credentialed Dr. Berry, and he began working there. After working at Kadlec without incident for a number of months, he moved temporarily to Montana where he worked at Benefis Hospital. During his stay in Montana, he was in a car accident and suffered a back injury. Kadlec's head of anesthesiology and the credentialing department all knew of Dr. Berry's accident and back injury, but they did not investigate whether it would impair his work.

After Dr. Berry returned to Kadlec, some nurses thought that he appeared sick and exhibited mood swings. One nurse thought that Dr. Berry's entire demeanor had changed and that he should be watched closely. In mid-September 2002, Dr. Berry gave a patient too much morphine during surgery, and she had to be revived using Narcan. The neurosurgeon was irate about the incident.

On November 12, 2002, Dr. Berry was assigned to the operating room beginning at 6:30 a.m. He worked with three different surgeons and multiple nurses well into the afternoon. According to one nurse, Dr. Berry was "screwing up all day" and several of his patients suffered adverse affects from not being properly anesthetized. He had a hacking cough and multiple nurses thought he looked sick. During one procedure, he apparently almost passed out.

Kimberley Jones was Dr. Berry's fifth patient that morning. She was in for what should have been a routine, fifteen minute tubal ligation. When they moved her into the recovery room, one nurse noticed that her fingernails were blue, and she was not breathing. Dr. Berry failed to resuscitate her, and she is now in a permanent vegetative state.

Dr. Berry's nurse went directly to her supervisor the next morning and expressed concern that Dr. Berry had a narcotics problem. Dr. Berry later admitted to Kadlec staff that he had been diverting and using Demerol since his June car accident in Montana and that he had become addicted to Demerol. Dr. Berry wrote a confession, and he immediately admitted himself into a drug rehabilitation program.

Jones's family sued Dr. Berry and Kadlec in Washington. Dr. Berry's insurer settled the claim against him. After the Washington court ruled that Kadlec would be responsible for Dr. Berry's conduct under *respondeat superior,* Western, Kadlec's insurer, settled the claim against Kadlec.

II. Procedural History

[The procedural history is omitted.]

III. Discussion

A. The Intentional and Negligent Misrepresentation Claims

The plaintiffs allege that the defendants committed two torts: intentional misrepresentation and negligent misrepresentation. The elements of a claim for *intentional* misrepresentation in Louisiana are: (1) a misrepresentation of a material fact; (2) made with intent to deceive; and (3) causing justifiable reliance with resultant injury. To establish a claim for intentional misrepresentation when it is by silence or inaction, plaintiffs also must show that the defendant owed a duty to the plaintiff to disclose the information. To make out a *negligent* misrepresentation claim in Louisiana: (1) there must be a legal duty on the part of the defendant to supply correct information; (2) there must be a breach of that duty, which can occur by omission as well as by affirmative misrepresentation; and (3) the breach must have caused damages to the plaintiff based on the plaintiff's reasonable reliance on the misrepresentation.

* * *

1. The Affirmative Misrepresentations

The defendants owed a duty to Kadlec to avoid affirmative misrepresentations in the referral letters. In Louisiana, "[a]lthough a party may keep absolute silence and violate no rule of law or equity, . . . if he volunteers to speak and to convey information which may influence the conduct of the other party, he is bound to [disclose] the whole truth." In negligent misrepresentation cases, Louisiana courts have held that even when there is no initial duty to disclose information, "once [a party] volunteer[s] information, it assume[s] a duty to insure that the information volunteered [is] correct.".

Consistent with these cases, the defendants had a legal duty not to make affirmative misrepresentations in their referral letters. A party does not incur liability every time it casually makes an incorrect statement. But if an employer makes a misleading statement in a referral letter about the performance of its former employee, the former employer may be liable for its statements if the facts and circumstances warrant. Here, defendants were recommending an anesthesiologist, who held the lives of patients in his hands every day. Policy considerations dictate that the defendants had a duty to avoid misrepresentations in their referral letters if they misled plaintiffs into thinking that Dr. Berry was an "excellent" anesthesiologist, when they had information that he was a drug addict. Indeed, if defendants' statements created a misapprehension about Dr. Berry's suitability to work as an anesthesiologist, then by "volunteer[ing] to speak and to convey information which ... influence[d] the conduct of [Kadlec], [they were] bound to [disclose] the whole truth." In other words, if they created a misapprehension about Dr. Berry due to their own statements, they incurred a duty to disclose information about his drug use and for-cause firing to complete the whole picture.

We now review whether there is evidence that the defendants' letters were misleading. [The court found that the LAA defendants' letters were "false on their face and materially misleading." Furthermore, because of the misleading statements in the letters, Dr. Dennis and Dr. Preau incurred a duty to cure these misleading statements by disclosing to Kadlec that Dr. Berry had been fired for on-the-job drug use.]

The question as to whether Lakeview Medical's letter was misleading is more difficult. The letter does not comment on Dr. Berry's proficiency as an anesthesiologist, and it does not recommend him to Kadlec. Kadlec says that the letter is misleading because Lakeview Medical stated that it could not reply to Kadlec's detailed inquiry in full "[d]ue to the large volume of inquiries received." But whatever the real reason that Lakeview Medical did not respond in full to Kadlec's inquiry, Kadlec did not present evidence that this could have affirmatively misled it into thinking that Dr. Berry had an uncheckered history at Lakeview Medical.

Kadlec also says that the letter was misleading because it erroneously reported that Dr. Berry was on Lakeview Medical's active medical staff until September 4, 2001. Kadlec presented testimony that had it known that Dr. Berry never returned to Lakeview Medical after March 13, 2001, it would have been suspicious about the apparently large gap in his employment. While it is true that Dr. Berry did not return to Lakeview Medical after March 13, this did not terminate his privileges at the hospital, or mean that he was not on "active medical staff." In fact, it appears that Dr. Berry submitted a formal resignation letter on October 1, 2001, weeks *after* September 4. Therefore, while the September 4 date does not accurately reflect when Dr. Berry was no longer on Lakeview Medical's active medical staff, it did not mislead Kadlec into thinking that he had less of a gap in employment than he actually had.

In sum, we hold that the letters from the LAA defendants were affirmatively misleading, but the letter from Lakeview Medical was not. Therefore, Lakeview Medical cannot be held liable based on its alleged affirmative misrepresentations. It can only be liable if it had an affirmative duty to disclose information about Dr. Berry. We now examine the theory that, even assuming that there were no misleading statements in the referral letters, the defendants had an affirmative duty to disclose. We discuss this theory with regard to both defendants for reasons that will be clear by the end of the opinion.

2.   The Duty to Disclose

In Louisiana, a duty to disclose does not exist absent special circumstances, such as a fiduciary or confidential relationship between the parties, which, under the circumstances, justifies the imposition of the duty. Louisiana cases suggest that before a duty to disclose is imposed the defendant must have had a pecuniary interest in the transaction. In Louisiana, the existence of a duty is a question of law, and we review the duty issue here *de novo*.

*   *   *

Despite these compelling policy arguments, we do not predict that courts in Louisiana-absent misleading statements such as those made by the LAA defendants-would impose an affirmative duty to disclose. The defendants did not have a fiduciary or contractual duty to disclose what it knew to Kadlec. And although the defendants might have had an ethical obligation to disclose their knowledge of Dr. Berry's drug problems, they were also rightly concerned about a possible defamation claim if they communicated negative information about Dr. Berry. As a general policy matter, even if an employer believes that its disclosure is protected because of the truth of the matter communicated, it would be burdensome to impose a duty on employers, upon receipt of a employment referral request, to investigate whether the negative information it has about an employee fits within the courts' description of *which* negative information must be disclosed to the future employer. Finally, concerns about protecting employee privacy weigh in favor of not mandating a potentially broad duty to disclose.

The Louisiana court in *Louviere* recognized that no court in Louisiana has imposed on an employer a duty to disclose information about a former employee to a future employer. [The court examined caselaw outside Louisiana, concluding that mere nondisclosure was never sufficient.] * * * These cases reinforce our conclusion that the defendants had a duty to avoid misleading statements in their referral letters, but they do not support plaintiffs' duty to disclose theory. * * *

*   *   *

D.   Negligent Monitoring and Investigation

[The Court upheld the district court's holding that any duties under the HCQIA and Louisiana regulations do not reach these plaintiffs.]

E. Summary and Remand Instructions

The district court properly instructed the jury to find for the plaintiffs on their intentional and negligent misrepresentation claims if the jury concluded that the defendants' letters to Kadlec were intentionally and negligently misleading in a manner that caused injury to the plaintiffs. * * * The letters from Dr. Dennis and Dr. Preau were false on their face and patently misleading. There is no question about the purpose or effect of the letters. Because no reasonable juror could find otherwise, we uphold the finding of liability against Dr. Dennis and Dr. Preau. But because Lakeview Medical's letter was not materially misleading, and because the hospital did not have a legal duty to disclose its investigation of Dr. Berry and its knowledge of his drug problems, the judgment against Lakeview Medical must be reversed.

*   *   *

The judgment of the district court is REVERSED in part, VACATED in part, and REMANDED for proceedings consistent with this opinion.

NOTES AND QUESTIONS

1. The Fifth Circuit treated the case as just another employment case, applying a simple "materially misleading" test to the letter sent by Lakeview Medical, and finding it did not meet the test. As to a duty to disclose, the court found that ". . . . [t]he defendants did not have a fiduciary or contractual duty to disclose what it knew to Kadlec."

Why didn't the court consider the special fiduciary nature of health care, and the harm that a substance-abusing anesthesiologist can cause his patients? Can you make a strong argument for a special rule for a wide range of severe health care risks that transcend normal employment risks?

For a criticism of the case, see Sallie Thieme Sanford, Candor After Kadlec: Why, Despite the Firth Circuit's Decision, Hospitals Should Anticipate an Expanded Obligation to Disclose Risky Physician Behavior, 1 Drexel L. Rev. 383 (2009).

2. In Douglass v. Salem Community Hospital, 153 Ohio App.3d 350, 794 N.E.2d 107 (2003), the hospital hired Wagner, a pedophile, as the assistant director of social services. It appears that in 1987, the police informed Western Reserve, his earlier hospital employer, that Wagner had been accused of exposing himself and molesting children and those accusations were being investigated at that time. Wagner resigned his employment on the condition that Western Reserve would state to those conducting reference checks in the future that he had voluntarily resigned. He then later resigned from Salem Hospital. A boy who had received counseling was invited to spend the weekend with Wagner, and his mother checked with an employee of Salem whom she knew, Williams; Williams told her that Wagner "would be good".

Wagner sexually assaulted the boy and his cousin at his house over the weekend.

The court accepted the plaintiff's argument that Restatement (Second) of Torts (1965), § 323, negligent performance of an undertaking to render service, would apply in this situation of a failure to warn:

> One who undertakes, gratuitously or for consideration, to render services to another which he should recognize as necessary for the protection of the other's person or things, is subject to liability to the other for physical harm resulting from his failure to exercise reasonable care to perform his undertaking, if * * * (b) the harm is suffered because of the other's reliance upon the undertaking.

The theory of recovery under § 323(b) is that "when one undertakes a duty voluntarily, and another reasonably relies on that undertaking, the volunteer is required to exercise ordinary care in completing the duty." [ ] In other words, "[a] voluntary act, gratuitously undertaken, must be * * * performed with the exercise of due care under the circumstances." [ ] This theory of negligence does not require proof of a special relationship between the plaintiff and the defendant, or proof of somewhat overwhelming circumstances. This type of negligence follows the general rules for finding negligence, with the addition of one extra element of proof, that of reasonable reliance by the plaintiff on the actions of the defendant.

Why were the various institutions so hypercautious, when the harm threatened was criminal in nature? Is this level of defensiveness something the law should tolerate?

3.   Can you make an argument that a hospital should be responsible, under some circumstances, for the negligent acts of physicians in their private practice, so long as they have staff privileges? What if the hospital is on notice of a long history of malpractice claims against one of its staff, resulting from negligence in that physician's private practice? If the physician has performed adequately while treating patients within the hospital, should the hospital have any further responsibility?

IV.   LIABILITY AND THE AFFORDABLE CARE ACT

The rules governing hospital liability are largely based on the role of physicians and physician groups as independent contractors, and the hospital medical staff as an independent decision making body. The previous material has indicated that the courts have been increasingly willing to reject agency defenses for independent contractors in the health care setting. The ACA has no provisions that directly address agency relationships or corporate negligence, nor does it explicitly alter the existing common law rules relating to vicarious liability and independent contractors. What the ACA does do, however, is create strong pressures—

through centers, demonstration projects, and Medicare reimbursement incentives—for providers to integrate and coordinate their delivery of health care for Medicare recipients. (See Chapters 10 and 11 for further discussion of some of these approaches.)

A. ACA COORDINATION REFORMS

The ACA offers coordination models to reduce fee-for-service medicine and decrease fragmentation in the U.S. health care system. Some of these are listed below.

1.   *Centers.* Centers can fund research, disseminate findings, and create a powerful force for the diffusion of effective models. A *Center for Medicare and Medicaid Innovation* (CMI) will research, develop, test, and expand innovative payment and delivery arrangements to improve the quality and reduce the cost of care provided to patients in each program. Centers such as the CMI can channel millions of dollars toward research and expansion of payment and delivery reforms and are likely to be influential on the future of medical practice.

2.   *Healthcare Innovation Zones.* Section 3210 (xviii) aims to create such zones, comprised of groups of providers that include a teaching hospital, physicians, and other clinical entities that can deliver a full spectrum of integrated and comprehensive health care services to applicable individuals.

3.   *Accountable Care Organizations.* Section 3022, the *Medicare Shared Savings Program,* creates a program that "promotes accountability for a patient population and coordinates items and services under parts A and B, and encourages investment in infrastructure and redesigned care processes for high quality and efficient service delivery. These Accountable Care organizations will offer a much more integrated model of care, including providers and institution within a coordinated legal structure. See the full description of ACOs in Chapter 12 *supra.*

4.   *Performance-based Care Coordination.* Other coordination innovations include, among others, patient-centered medical homes, direct contracting with groups of providers to promote new delivery models "through risk-based comprehensive payment or salary-based payment", and coordinated care models.

5.   *Payment Bundling.* Similar services are grouped together and are compensated using a single or global payment. Services could be grouped according to the care provided by a single doctor or multiple doctors.

6.   *Patient-centered medical homes.* Primary care physicians receive additional monthly payments for effectively using health information technology and other innovations to monitor, coordinate and manage care.

B. THE EFFECT OF COORDINATION REFORMS ON INSTITUTIONAL LIABLITY

Assume that within a few years ACOs and Medical Homes are successfully formed, comprehensive patient bundling is implemented in many hospitals, and salary-based payment systems proliferate. These reforms do several things at once: they move physicians from solo or small group practice into a salaried position in a group model or a hospital; they shift power toward enterprises that can buy and coordinate the technologies—from EHRs to case management strategies—to meet the demands of the federal government; and they therefore turn more providers into agents of institutional providers.

The liability result is clear if these various reforms, incentives and forces converge. First, institutional providers will become liable for patient injury, as well as the physicians causing patient injury directly, because agency law will carry liability upstream from agent to principal. Physicians will be much more integrated into the system, whether or not they are salaried, and any argument of independent contractor status will evaporate.

Second, even if ACOs and other entities operate without a hospital as part of the organization, they have become institutional health care providers, subject to liability just as a hospital or managed care organization is, on both vicarious liability and direct negligence principles.

Third, corporate negligence principles will likely apply to integrated organizations that manage care, whether a patient medical home, an ACO, or some other delivery form that the ACA creates. The courts are willing to look beyond the hospital form in deciding whether a health care entity might be liable for corporate negligence. For example, in Gianquitti v. Atwood Medical Associates, LTD., 973 A.2d 580 (R.I. 2009), the court held that a professional medical-group practice that provides on-call medical care to its patients if and when they are hospitalized could be liable for corporate negligence if it lacked a formal backup system. In another case, Davis v. Gish, 2007 WL 5007253 (Pa.Com. Pl. 2007), the court noted the kinds of activities that would turn a professional group or a physicians' practice group into an entity subject to corporate negligence. The entity would, like an HMO, "involve themselves daily in decisions affecting their subscriber's medical care. These decisions may, among others, limit the length of hospital stays, restrict the use of specialists, prohibit or limit post-hospital care, restrict access to therapy, or prevent rendering of emergency room care." *Id.* at 835. The entity must have general responsibility for "for arranging and coordinating the total health care of its patients" It must take "an active role in patients' care".

Today most physician groups or physician office-based practices would not be said to possess such responsibility. But the entities fostered by the ACA and its millions of dollars in demonstration grants and Medicare mandates are far more likely to coordinate care, taking on new responsibilities that will make them appropriate defendants in tort litigation.

PROBLEM: THE BIRTHING CENTER

You have been approached by Rosa Hernandez to handle a tort suit for damages for the death of her infant during delivery at the Hastings Birthing Center. Discovery reveals the following facts.

The death of the infant is attributable to the negligence of Dr. Jones, the physician who attended Ms. Hernandez at the Center during delivery. The death was caused in part by the infant's aspiration of meconium into the lungs. Although the Center is equipped to suction meconium and other material from a newborn's throat, it is not equipped to perform an intubation and attach the infant to a ventilator. To intubate the infant, it would have to be transferred to the hospital. Even if the infant had been transferred, it would probably have suffered brain damage due to oxygen deprivation before the procedure could have been undertaken.

Dr. Jones has a spotless record, but over the two weeks preceding the incident he had appeared at the hospital smelling of alcohol and evidencing other signs of intoxication. He was apparently having marital problems at the time. Nurses at the hospital had reported this behavior to their supervisor and had watched the physician's work very carefully, calling his attention to things he missed. The nurse supervisor had reported the situation to the head of OB/GYN, who said he would "look into it". Ms. Hernandez noticed the smell of liquor on Dr. Jones' breath during her labor, and was upset by his apparent intoxication. Dr. Jones has also dropped his malpractice insurance coverage, a fact of which the hospital is aware.

Further discovery has revealed that the nurse-midwife had observed that Dr. Jones' acts were questionable, but she had not intervened because she knew of his excellent reputation. She knew that doctors were resentful of the independence of nurse-midwives at the Center, and she believed she could "compensate" for his mistakes during the delivery. By the time she realized the extent of Dr. Jones' intoxication and took over the delivery, it was too late.

Your discovery reveals that there is a complicated relationship between the Birthing Center and the nearby Columbia Hospital. The hospital found that it had needed to increase its patient census, and that neonatology was one of its most profitable services. To increase its census in this area and to better serve the community, Columbia established the Hastings Birthing Center last year. The hospital receives a percentage of the profits of the Center.

The Center is located in a former convent one block from the hospital. The hospital owns the building and rents it to the Center. This particular birthing center, according to its promotional literature, offers "both a home-like setting for the delivery of your child and the security of the availability of back-up physicians and hospital care." The Center is separately incorporated and has its own Board of Directors. It is totally self-governing and is solely responsible for staff, provision of equipment, and policy.

The phone listing in the Yellow Pages describes the Hospital as a "cooperating hospital that will provide hospital care for mother and child if needed." Columbia has a contract with the Center requiring the Center to establish a screening program that will exclude high-risk patients and require that doctors attending patients at the Center have privileges at Columbia Hospital. The hospital allows the employees of the Center to participate in the hospital's group health and pension plans. Nurses from the hospital moonlight at the Center. When they do so, they receive a separate paycheck from the Center.

Although the Center's by-laws provide for a committee to review the qualifications of physicians who attend at the Center, it has in fact relied on the hospital's review of qualifications, since the hospital has a better opportunity to review credentials and performance. It is not clear that the hospital is aware of this; while it does notify the Center of the suspension, denial or revocation of privileges, it does not provide the Center with information used in investigations.

If you decide to litigate, should you sue both the Center and the hospital as well as Dr. Jones? Describe your theories, based on the information you have discovered to date, and consider what other facts you would like to know.

PROBLEM: SYSTEM REFORMS AND LIABILITY

Axis University Hospital (*Axis*) has decided that it needs to better coordinate its patient care from the moment patients enter the hospital until they leave and return to the care of their own physicians or specialists. Its CEO and CFO have scoured the ACA and have decided to adopt the following steps.

First, they have developed their own model of direct contracting with local physician groups, particularly cardiologists and oncologists, designed to promote risk-based comprehensive payments.

Second, for elderly patients with comorbidities, who often seem to move between home or nursing home and the hospital, they propose a coordinated care model in which gerontologists will be paid by salary rather than fee-for-service.

Third, for primary care physicians in their community catchment area, they propose patient-centered medical homes that entail the use of medical technologies of monitoring, along with extensive electronic medical record-keeping. Physicians who agree to participate in such medical homes will receive bonus payments based on their adoption of a range of treatment measures.

You are the general counsel of *Axis*, and have been asked to make a presentation to the Board of Directors on any negatives that such new payment models might create for *Axis*. Consider in particular the liability consequences of each of the three approaches. Are traditional tort concepts undermined by moving to these delivery forms? Who is more at risk for liability with these reforms—physicians, hospitals and systems, other providers?

V.   TORT LIABILITY OF MANAGED CARE

Managed care rapidly supplanted fee-for-service medicine during the 1990s and after. By 2012 employment-based insurance covered 155 million members. Fewer than 1 percent of the employees in all firms are enrolled in fee-for-service indemnity plans. Preferred Provider Plans (PPOs) now cover 56 percent of insured workers, and HMO plans cover 16 perent, Point Of Service (POS) plans 9 percent, and High Deductible Plans cover 19 percnt, having risen from just 8 percent in 2009. The shift away from the more intensively cost managed HMO model is apparent, as the tools of managed care—preapproval of specialists, capitation, and other features—managed to alienate both providers and subscribers during those decades. See Kaiser Family Foundation et al., Employer Benefits: 2012 Annual Survey (2012) particularly Exhibit E, page 4.

"Managed care" is a phrase often used to describe organizational groupings that attempt to control the utilization of health care services through a variety of techniques, including limiting enrollees to contracted provider networks, reviewing the utilization of various services, or using incentives such as per capita payments to encourage providers to limit the provision of services. The groups cover a wide variety of plans—from plans that require little more than preauthorization of patient hospitalization, to staff model HMOs—that focus on utilization and price of services. The goal is reduction of health care costs and maximization of value to both patient and payer. A Managed Care Organization (MCO) is a reimbursement framework combined with a health care delivery system, an approach to the delivery of health care services that contrasts with "fee-for-service" medicine. Managed care is usually distinguished from traditional indemnity plans by the existence of a single entity responsible for integrating and coordinating the financing and delivery of services that were once scattered between providers and payers. See Chapter 9, *infra*, for a fuller discussion of managed care features and definitions.

Managed care plans can avoid liability for state law claims— including tort claims—if they are "qualified" ERISA plans. The Employee Retirement Income Security Act of 1974 (ERISA) preempts either explicitly, or by U.S. Supreme Court interpretation the vast majority of managed care plans that are employment based and ERISA-qualified. ERISA does not cover insurance plans that are not employment-based, including individual, Medicaid, workers' compensation, or auto medical plans. The following discussion is therefore applicable to managed care plans that fall in the category of non-ERISA qualified plans for which federal preemption is not a defense to the defendant, or to the increasingly limited range of theories that the Supreme Court has left open to plaintiffs in state courts. Individual coverage will become much more widespread under the Affordable Care Act, thus this body of law is likely to become more important as the ACA is implemented. Moerover, the liability principles discussed below will apply to the new delivery models promoted by the ACA, such as Accountable Care Organizations and Medical Homes, among others, that are not protected by ERISA preemption from being sued. See generally Chapter 9, *infra*.

A. VICARIOUS LIABILITY

Health maintenance organizations (HMOs) and Independent Practice Associations (IPAs) in theory face the same vicarious and corporate liability questions as hospitals because they provide services through physicians, whether the physicians are salaried employees or independent contractors. These medical services can injure patients/subscribers, leading to a malpractice suit for such injuries.

PETROVICH V. SHARE HEATH PLAN OF ILLINOIS, INC.
Supreme Court of Illinois, 1999.
188 Ill.2d 17, 241 Ill.Dec. 627, 719 N.E.2d 756.

JUSTICE BILANDIC delivered the opinion of the court:

The plaintiff brought this medical malpractice action against a physician and others for their alleged negligence in failing to diagnose her oral cancer in a timely manner. The plaintiff also named her health maintenance organization (HMO) as a defendant. The central issue here is whether the plaintiff's HMO may be held vicariously liable for the negligence of its independent-contractor physicians under agency law. The plaintiff contends that the HMO is vicariously liable under both the doctrines of apparent authority and implied authority.

* * *

Facts

In 1989, plaintiff's employer, the Chicago Federation of Musicians, provided health care coverage to all of its employees by selecting Share and enrolling its employees therein. Share is an HMO and pays only for medical care that is obtained within its network of physicians. In order to qualify for benefits, a Share member must select from the network a primary care physician who will provide that member's overall care and authorize referrals when necessary. Share gives its members a list of participating physicians from which to choose. Share has about 500 primary care physicians covering Share's service area, which includes the counties of Cook, Du Page, Lake, McHenry and Will. Plaintiff selected Dr. Marie Kowalski from Share's list, and began seeing Dr. Kowalski as her primary care physician in August of 1989. Dr. Kowalski was employed at a satellite facility of Illinois Masonic Medical Center (Illinois Masonic), which had a contract with Share to provide medical services to Share members.

In September of 1990, plaintiff saw Dr. Kowalski because she was experiencing persistent pain in the right sides of her mouth, tongue, throat and face. Plaintiff also complained of a foul mucus in her mouth. Dr. Kowalski referred plaintiff to two other physicians who had contracts with Share: Dr. Slavick, a neurologist, and Dr. Friedman, an ear, nose and throat specialist.

Plaintiff informed Dr. Friedman of her pain. Dr. Friedman observed redness or marked erythema alongside plaintiff's gums on the right side of her mouth. He recommended that plaintiff have a magnetic resonance imaging (MRI) test or a computed tomography (CT) scan performed on the base of her skull. According to plaintiff's testimony at her evidence deposition, Dr. Kowalski informed her that Share would not allow new tests as recommended by Dr. Friedman. Plaintiff did not consult with Share about the test refusals because she was not aware of Share's grievance procedure. Dr. Kowalski gave Dr. Friedman a copy of an old MRI test result at that time. The record offers no further information about this old MRI test.

Nonetheless, Dr. Kowalski later ordered an updated MRI of plaintiff's brain, which was performed on October 31, 1990. Inconsistent with Dr. Friedman's directions, however, this MRI failed to image the right base of the tongue area where redness existed. Plaintiff and Dr. Kowalski discussed the results of this MRI test on November 19, 1990, during a follow-up visit. Plaintiff testified that Dr. Kowalski told her that the MRI revealed no abnormality.

Plaintiff's pain persisted. In April or May of 1991, Dr. Kowalski again referred plaintiff to Dr. Friedman. This was plaintiff's third visit to Dr. Friedman. Dr. Friedman examined plaintiff and observed that plaintiff's tongue was tender. Also, plaintiff reported that she had a foul odor in her mouth and was experiencing discomfort. On June 7, 1991, Dr. Friedman performed multiple biopsies on the right side of the base of plaintiff's tongue and surrounding tissues. The biopsy results revealed squamous cell carcinoma, a cancer, in the base of plaintiff's tongue and the surrounding tissues of the pharynx. Later that month, Dr. Friedman operated on plaintiff to remove the cancer. He removed part of the base of plaintiff's tongue, and portions of her palate, pharynx and jaw bone. After the surgery, plaintiff underwent radiation treatments and rehabilitation.

Plaintiff subsequently brought this medical malpractice action against Share, Dr. Kowalski and others. Dr. Friedman was not named a party defendant. Plaintiff's complaint, though, alleges that both Drs. Kowalski and Friedman were negligent in failing to diagnose plaintiff's cancer in a timely manner, and that Share is vicariously liable for their negligence under agency principles. Share filed a motion for summary judgment, arguing that it cannot be held liable for the negligence of Dr. Kowalski or Friedman because they were acting as independent contractors in their treatment of plaintiff, not as Share's agents. Plaintiff countered that Share is not entitled to summary judgment because Drs. Kowalski and Friedman were Share's agents. The parties submitted various depositions, affidavits and exhibits in support of their respective positions.

Share is a for-profit corporation. At all relevant times, Share was organized as an "independent practice association-model" HMO under the Illinois Health Maintenance Organization Act (Ill.Rev.Stat.1991, ch. 111 ½, par. 1401et seq.). This means that Share is a financing entity that arranges and pays for health care by contracting with independent medical groups and practitioners. [ ] Share does not employ physicians directly, nor does it own, operate, maintain or supervise the offices where medical care is provided to its members. Rather, Share contracts with independent medical groups and physicians that have the facilities, equipment and professional skills necessary to render medical care. Physicians desiring to join Share'snetwork are required to complete an application procedure and meet with Share's approval.

Share utilizes a method of compensation called "capitation" to pay its medical groups. Share also maintains a "quality assurance program." Share's capitation method of compensation and "quality assurance program" are more fully described later in this opinion.

Share provides a member handbook to each of its members, including plaintiff. The handbook states to its members that Share will provide "all your healthcare needs" and "comprehensive high quality services." The handbook also states that the primary care physician is "your health care manager" and "makes the decisions" about the member's care. The handbook further states that Share is a "good partner in sickness and in health." Unlike the master agreements and benefits contract discussed below, the member handbook which plaintiff received does not contain any provision that identifies Share physicians as independent contractors or nonemployees of Share. Rather, the handbook describes the physicians as "your Share physician," "Share physicians" and "our staff." Furthermore, Share refers to the physicians' offices as "Your Share physician's office" and states: "All of the Share staff and Medical Offices look forward to serving you * * *."

Plaintiff confirmed that she received the member handbook. Plaintiff did not read the handbook in its entirety, but read portions of it as she needed the information. She relied on the information contained in the handbook while Drs. Kowalski and Friedman treated her.

The record also contains a "Health Care Services Master Agreement," entered into by Share and Illinois Masonic. Dr. Kowalski is a signatory of this agreement. The agreement states, "It is understood and agreed that [Illinois Masonic] and [primary care physicians] are independent contractors and not employees or agents of SHARE." A separate agreement between Share and Dr. Friedman contains similar language. Plaintiff did not receive these agreements.

Share's primary care physicians, under their agreements with Share, are required to approve patients' medical requests and make referrals to specialists. These physicians use Share's standard referral forms to indicate their approval of the referral. Dr. Kowalski testified at an evidence deposition that she did not feel constrained by Share in making medical decisions regarding her patients, including whether to order tests or make referrals to specialists.

Another document in the record is Share's benefits contract. The benefits contract contains a subscriber certificate. The subscriber certificate sets forth a member's rights and obligations with respect to Share. Additionally, the subscriber certificate states that Share's physicians are independent contractors and that "SHARE Plan Providers and Enrolling Groups are not agents or employees of SHARE nor is SHARE or any employee of SHARE an agent or employee of SHARE Plan Providers or Enrolling Groups." The certificate elaborates: "The relationship between a SHARE Plan Provider and any Member is that of provider and patient. The SHARE Plan Physician is solely responsible for the medical services provided to any Member. The SHARE Plan Hospital is solely responsible for the Hospital services provided to any Member."

Plaintiff testified that she did not recall receiving the subscriber certificate. In response, Share stated that Share customarily provides members with this information. Share does not claim to know whether Share actually provided plaintiff with this information. Plaintiff acknowledged that she received a "whole stack" of information from Share upon her enrollment.

Plaintiff was not aware of the type of relationship that her physicians had with Share. At the time she received treatment, plaintiff believed that her physicians were employees of Share.

* * *

Analysis

This appeal comes before us amidst great changes to the relationships among physicians, patients and those entities paying for medical
care. Traditionally, physicians treated patients on demand, while insurers merely paid the physicians their fee for the services provided. Today,
managed care organizations (MCOs) have stepped into the insurer's
shoes, and often attempt to reduce the price and quantity of health care
services provided to patients through a system of health care cost containment. MCOs may, for example, use prearranged fee structures for
compensating physicians. MCOs may also use utilization-review procedures, which are procedures designed to determine whether the use and
volume of particular health care services are appropriate. MCOs have developed in response to rapid increases in health care costs.

HMOs, i.e., health maintenance organizations, are a type of MCO.
HMOs are subject to both state and federal laws. [ ] Under Illinois law, an
HMO is defined as "any organization formed under the laws of this or another state to provide or arrange for one or more health care plans under
a system which causes any part of the risk of health care delivery to be
borne by the organization or its providers." [ ]. Because HMOs may differ
in their structures and the cost-containment practices that they employ, a
court must discern the nature of the organization before it, where relevant to the issues. As earlier noted, Share is organized as an independent
practice association (IPA)-model HMO. IPA-model HMOs are financing
entities that arrange and pay for health care by contracting with independent medical groups and practitioners. [ ]

This court has never addressed a question of whether an HMO may
be held liable for medical malpractice. Share asserts that holding HMOs
liable for medical malpractice will cause health care costs to increase and
make health care inaccessible to large numbers of people. Share suggests
that, with this consideration in mind, this court should impose only narrow, or limited, forms of liability on HMOs. We disagree with Share that
the cost-containment role of HMOs entitles them to special consideration.
The principle that organizations are accountable for their tortious actions
and those of their agents is fundamental to our justice system. There is no
exception to this principle for HMOs. Moreover, HMO accountability is
essential to counterbalance the HMO goal of cost-containment. To the extent that HMOs are profit-making entities, accountability is also needed
to counterbalance the inherent drive to achieve a large and ever-
increasing profit margin. Market forces alone "are insufficient to cure the
deleterious [e]ffects of managed care on the health care industry." [ ]
Courts, therefore, should not be hesitant to apply well-settled legal theo-

ries of liability to HMOs where the facts so warrant and where justice so requires.

Indeed, the national trend of courts is to hold HMOs accountable for medical malpractice under a variety of legal theories, including vicarious liability on the basis of apparent authority, vicarious liability on the basis of respondeat superior, direct corporate negligence, breach of contract and breach of warranty. [ ] * * * Share concedes that HMOs may be held liable for medical malpractice under these five theories.

This appeal concerns whether Share may be held vicariously liable under agency law for the negligence of its independent-contractor physicians. We must determine whether Share was properly awarded summary judgment on the ground that Drs. Kowalski and Friedman were not acting as Share's agents in their treatment of plaintiff. Plaintiff argues that Share is not entitled to summary judgment on this record. Plaintiff asserts that genuine issues of material fact exist as to whether Drs. Kowalski and Friedman were acting within Share'sapparent authority, implied authority or both.

* * *

As a general rule, no vicarious liability exists for the actions of independent contractors. Vicarious liability may nevertheless be imposed for the actions of independent contractors where an agency relationship is established under either the doctrine of apparent authority [ ] or the doctrine of implied authority [ ].

I.   Apparent Authority

Apparent authority, also known as ostensible authority, has been a part of Illinois jurisprudence for more than 140 years. [ ] Under the doctrine, a principal will be bound not only by the authority that it actually gives to another, but also by the authority that it appears to give. [ ]. The doctrine functions like an estoppel. [ ]. Where the principal creates the appearance of authority, a court will not hear the principal's denials of agency to the prejudice of an innocent third party, who has been led to reasonably rely upon the agency and is harmed as a result.[ ]

* * *

We now hold that the apparent authority doctrine may also be used to impose vicarious liability on HMOs. * * * [ ]

To establish apparent authority against an HMO for physician malpractice, the patient must prove (1) that the HMO held itself out as the provider of health care, without informing the patient that the care is given by independent contractors, and (2) that the patient justifiably relied upon the conduct of the HMO by looking to the HMO to provide health care services, rather than to a specific physician. Apparent agency is a question of fact. [ ]

A. Holding Out

The element of "holding out" means that the HMO, or its agent, acted in a manner that would lead a reasonable person to conclude that the physician who was alleged to be negligent was an agent or employee of the HMO. [ ] Where the acts of the agent create the appearance of authority, a plaintiff must also prove that the HMO had knowledge of and acquiesced in those acts. [ ] The holding-out element does not require the HMO to make an express representation that the physician alleged to be negligent is its agent or employee. Rather, this element is met where the HMO holds itself out as the provider of health care without informing the patient that the care is given by independent contractors. [ ] Vicarious liability under the apparent authority doctrine will not attach, however, if the patient knew or should have known that the physician providing treatment is an independent contractor. [ ]

Here, Share contends that the independent-contractor provisions in the two master agreements and the benefits contract conclusively establish, as a matter of law, that Share did not hold out Drs. Kowalski and Friedman to be Share's agents. Although all three of these contracts clearly express that the physicians are independent contractors and not agents of Share, we disagree with Share's contention for the reasons explained below.

First, the two master agreements at issue are private contractual agreements between Share and Illinois Masonic, with Dr. Kowalski as a signatory, and between Share and Dr. Friedman. The record contains no indication that plaintiff knew or should have known of these private contractual agreements between Share and its physicians. Gilbert expressly rejected the notion that such private contractual agreements can control a claim of apparent agency. [ ] * * * We hold that this same rationale applies to private contractual agreements between physicians and an HMO. [ ] Because there is no dispute that the master agreements at bar were unknown to plaintiff, they cannot be used to defeat her apparent agency claim.

Share also relies on the benefits contract. Plaintiff was not a party or a signatory to this contract. The benefits contract contains a subscriber certificate, which states that Share physicians are independent contractors. Share claims that this language alone conclusively overcomes plaintiff's apparent agency claim. We do not agree.

Whether a person has notice of a physician's status as an independent contractor, or is put on notice by the circumstances, is a question of fact. [ ] In this case, plaintiff testified at her evidence deposition that she did not recall receiving the subscriber certificate. Share responded only that it customarily provides members with this information. Share has never claimed to know whether Share actually provided plaintiff with this information. Thus, a question of fact exists as to whether Share gave this information to plaintiff. If this information was not provided to plaintiff, it cannot be used to defeat her apparent agency claim.

*   *   *

Evidence in the record supports plaintiff's contentions that Share held itself out to its members as the provider of health care, and that plaintiff was not aware that her physicians were independent contractors. Notably, plaintiff stated that, at the time that she received treatment, plaintiff believed that Drs. Kowalski and Friedman were Share employees. Plaintiff was not aware of the type of relationship that her physicians had with Share.

Moreover, Share's member handbook contains evidence that Share held itself out to plaintiff as the provider of her health care. The handbook stated to Share members that Share will provide "all your healthcare needs" and "comprehensive high quality services." The handbook did not contain any provision that identified Share physicians as independent contractors or nonemployees of Share. Instead, the handbook referred to the physicians as "your Share physician," "Share physicians" and "our staff." Share also referred to the physicians' offices as "Your Share physician's office." The record shows that Share provided this handbook to each of its enrolled members, including plaintiff. Representations made in the handbook are thus directly attributable to Share and were intended by Share to be communicated to its members.

*   *   *

We hold that the above testimony by plaintiff and Share's member handbook support the conclusion that Share held itself out to plaintiff as the provider of her health care, without informing her that the care was actually provided by independent contractors. Therefore, a triable issue of fact exists as to the holding-out element. We need not resolve whether any other evidence in the record also supports plaintiff's claim. Our task here is to review whether Share is entitled to summary judgment on this element. We hold that Share is not.

B.   Justifiable Reliance

A plaintiff must also prove the element of "justifiable reliance" to establish apparent authority against an HMO for physician malpractice. This means that the plaintiff acted in reliance upon the conduct of the HMO or its agent, consistent with ordinary care and prudence. [ ]

The element of justifiable reliance is met where the plaintiff relies upon the HMO to provide health care services, and does not rely upon a specific physician. This element is not met if the plaintiff selects his or her own personal physician and merely looks to the HMO as a conduit through which the plaintiff receives medical care. [ ]

Concerning the element of justifiable reliance in the hospital context, Gilbert explained that the critical distinction is whether the plaintiff sought care from the hospital itself or from a personal physician. * * *

This rationale applies even more forcefully in the context of an HMO that restricts its members to the HMO's chosen physicians. Accordingly, unless a person seeks care from a personal physician, that person is seeking care from the HMO itself. A person who seeks care from the HMO itself accepts that care in reliance upon the HMO's holding itself out as the provider of care.

Share maintains that plaintiff cannot establish the justifiable reliance element because she did not select Share. * * *

* * * We reject Share's argument. It is true that, where a person selects the HMO and does not rely upon a specific physician, then that person is relying upon the HMO to provide health care. This principle, derived directly from Gilbert, is set forth above. Equally true, however, is that where a person has no choice but to enroll with a single HMO and does not rely upon a specific physician, then that person is likewise relying upon the HMO to provide health care.

In the present case, the record discloses that plaintiff did not select Share. Plaintiff's employer selected Share for her. Plaintiff had no choice of health plans whatsoever. Once Share became plaintiff's health plan, Share required plaintiff to obtain her primary medical care from one of its primary care physicians. If plaintiff did not do so, Share did not cover plaintiff's medical costs. In accordance with Share's requirement, plaintiff selected Dr. Kowalski from a list of physicians that Share provided to her. Plaintiff had no prior relationship with Dr. Kowalski. As to Dr. Kowalski's selection of Dr. Friedman for plaintiff, Share required Dr. Kowalski to make referrals only to physicians approved by Share. Plaintiff had no prior relationship with Dr. Friedman. We hold that these facts are sufficient to raise the reasonable inference that plaintiff relied upon Share to provide her health care services.

Were we to conclude that plaintiff was not relying upon Share for health care, we would be denying the true nature of the relationship among plaintiff, her HMO and the physicians. Share, like many HMOs, contracted with plaintiff's employer to become plaintiff's sole provider of health care, to the exclusion of all other providers. Share then restricted plaintiff to its chosen physicians. Under these facts, plaintiff's reliance on Shareas the provider of her health care is shown not only to be compelling, but literally compelled. Plaintiff's reliance upon Share was inherent in Share's method of operation.

* * *

In conclusion, as set forth above, plaintiff has presented sufficient evidence to support justifiable reliance, as well as a holding out by Share. Share, therefore, is not entitled to summary judgment against plaintiff's claim of apparent authority.

* * *

II.   Implied Authority

Implied authority is actual authority, circumstantially proved. [ ] One context in which implied authority arises is where the facts and circumstances show that the defendant exerted sufficient control over the alleged agent so as to negate that person's status as an independent contractor, at least with respect to third parties. [ ] The cardinal consideration for determining the existence of implied authority is whether the alleged agent retains the right to control the manner of doing the work. [ ] Where a person's status as an independent contractor is negated, liability may result under the doctrine of respondeat superior.

Plaintiff contends that the facts and circumstances of this case show that Share exerted sufficient control over Drs. Kowalski and Friedman so as to negate their status as independent contractors. Share responds that the act of providing medical care is peculiarly within a physician's domain because it requires the exercise of independent medical judgment. Share thus maintains that, because it cannot control a physician's exercise of medical judgment, it cannot be subject to vicarious liability under the doctrine of implied authority.

* * *

We now address whether the implied authority doctrine may be used against HMOs to negate a physician's status as an independent contractor. Our appellate court in Raglin suggested that it can. [ ] Case law from other jurisdictions lends support to this view as well. [ ]

* * *

We do not find the above decisions rendered in the hospital context to be dispositive of whether an HMO may exert such control over its physicians so as to negate their status as independent contractors. We can readily discern that the relationships between physicians and HMOs are often much different than the traditional relationships between physicians and hospitals. * * *

Physicians, of course, should not allow the exercise of their medical judgment to be corrupted or controlled. Physicians have professional ethical, moral and legal obligations to provide appropriate medical care to their patients. These obligations on physicians, however, will not act to relieve an HMO of its own legal responsibilities. Where an HMO effectively controls a physician's exercise of medical judgment, and that judgment is exercised negligently, the HMO cannot be allowed to claim that the physician is solely responsible for the harm that results. In such a circumstance, both the physician and the HMO are liable for the harm that results. We therefore hold that the implied authority doctrine may be used against an HMO to negate a physician's status as an independent contractor. An implied agency exists where the facts and circumstances show that an HMO exerted such sufficient control over a participating physician so as to negate that physician's status as an independent contractor, at least with respect to third parties. [ ] No precise formula exists for deciding when a person's status as an independent contractor is negated. Rather, the determination of whether a person is an agent or an independent contractor rests upon the facts and circumstances of each case. [ ] As noted, the cardinal consideration is whether that person retains the right to control the manner of doing the work. [ ] * * *

With these established principles in mind, we turn to the present case. Plaintiff contends that her physicians' status as independent contractors should be negated. Plaintiff asserts that Share actively interfered with her physicians' medical decisionmaking by designing and executing its capitation method of compensation and "quality assurance" programs. Plaintiff also points to Share's referral system as evidence of control.

Plaintiff submits that Share's capitation method of compensating its medical groups is a form of control because it financially punishes physicians for ordering certain medical treatment. The record discloses that Share utilizes a method of compensation called "capitation."[ ]. Under capitation, Share prepays contracting medical groups a fixed amount of money for each member who enrolls with that group. In exchange, the medical groups agree to render health care to their enrolled Share members in accordance with the Share plan. Each medical group contracting with Share has its own capitation account. Deducted from that capitation account are the costs of any services provided by the primary care physician, the costs of medical procedures and tests, and the fees of all consulting physicians. The medical group then retains the surplus left in the capitation account. The costs for hospitalizations and other services are charged against a separate account. Reinsurance is provided for the capitation account and the separate account for certain high cost claims. Share pays Illinois Masonic in accordance with its capitation method of compensation. Dr. Kowalski testified that Illinois Masonic pays her the same salary every month. Plaintiff maintains that a reasonable inference to be drawn from Share's capitation method of compensation is that Share provides financial disincentives to its primary care physicians in order to discourage them from ordering the medical care that they deem appropriate. Plaintiff argues that this is an example of Share's influence and control over the medical judgment of its physicians.

Share counters that its capitation method of compensation cannot be used as evidence of control here because Dr. Kowalski is paid the same salary every month. We disagree with Share that this fact makes Share's capitation system irrelevant to our inquiry. Whether control was actually exercised is not dispositive in this context. Rather, the right to control the alleged agent is the proper query, even where that right is not exercised. [ ]

[The court rejects Share's "quality assurance program" as evidence of control, since it is done primarily to comply with state regulations of the Department of Public Health. The court however allows as evidence of control chart review by Share; control over referral to specialists; and use of primary care physicians as gatekeepers.]

We conclude that plaintiff has presented adequate evidence to entitle her to a trial on the issue of implied authority. All the facts and circumstances before us, if proven at trial, raise the reasonable inference that Share exerted such sufficient control over Drs. Kowalski and Friedman so as to negate their status as independent contractors. As discussed above, plaintiff presents relevant evidence of Share's capitation method of compensation, Share's "quality assurance review," Share's referral system and Share's requirement that its primary care physicians act as gatekeepers for Share. These facts support plaintiff's argument that Share subjected its physicians to control over the manner in which they did their work. The facts surrounding treatment also support plaintiff's argument. According to plaintiff's evidence, Dr. Kowalski referred plaintiff to Dr. Friedman. Dr. Friedman evaluated plaintiff and recommended that plaintiff have either an MRI test or a CT scan performed on the base of her skull. Dr. Friedman, however, did not order the test that he recommended for plaintiff. Rather, he reported this information back to Dr. Kowalski in her role as plaintiff's primary care physician. Dr. Kowalski initially sent Dr. Friedman a copy of an old MRI test. Dr. Kowalski later ordered that an updated MRI be taken. In doing so, she directed that the MRI be taken of plaintiff's "brain." Hence, that MRI failed to image the base of plaintiff's skull as recommended by Dr. Friedman. Dr. Kowalski then reviewed the MRI test results herself and informed plaintiff that the results revealed no abnormality. From all the above facts and circumstances, a trier of fact could reasonably infer that Share promulgated such a system of control over its physicians that Share effectively negated the exercise of their independent medical judgment, to plaintiff's detriment.

We note that Dr. Kowalski testified at an evidence deposition that she did not feel constrained by Share in making medical decisions regarding her patients, including whether to order tests or make referrals to specialists. This testimony is not controlling at the summary judgment stage. The trier of fact is entitled to weigh all the conflicting evidence above against Dr. Kowalski's testimony.

In conclusion, plaintiff has presented adequate evidence to support a finding that Share exerted such sufficient control over its participating physicians so as to negate their status as independent contractors. Share, therefore, is not entitled to summary judgment against plaintiff's claim of implied authority.

* * *

Conclusion

An HMO may be held vicariously liable for the negligence of its independent-contractor physicians under both the doctrines of apparent authority and implied authority. Plaintiff here is entitled to a trial on both doctrines. The circuit court therefore erred in awarding summary judgment to Share. The appellate court's judgment, which reversed the circuit court's judgment and remanded the cause to the circuit court for further proceedings, is affirmed.

Affirmed.

NOTES AND QUESTIONS

1.   Does a subscriber to an IPA-style managed care organization look to it for care rather than solely to the individual physicians? In an IPA, there is no central office, staffed by salaried physicians; the subscriber instead goes to the individual offices of the primary care physicians or the specialists. What justifies extending ostensible agency doctrine to this arrangement?

Managed care advertising often holds out the plan in words such as "total care program," or "an entire health care system." A reliance by the subscriber on the managed care organization (MCO) for his or her choice of physicians, and any holding out by the MCO as a provider, is sufficient. See McClellan v. Health Maintenance Organization of Pennsylvania, 413 Pa.Super. 128, 604 A.2d 1053 (1992) (ostensible agency based on advertisements by HMO claiming that it carefully screened in primary care physicians).

2.   IPA-model HMOs that become "the institution," that "hold out" the independent contractor as an employee, and also restrict provider selection are vulnerable to ostensible agency arguments. Where the HMO exercises substantial control over the independent physicians by controlling the patients they must see and by paying on a per capita basis, an agency relationship has been found. See Dunn v. Praiss, 256 N.J.Super. 180, 606 A.2d 862 (App.Div.1992); Boyd v. Albert Einstein Medical Center, 377 Pa.Super. 609, 547 A.2d 1229 (1988).

3.   A breach of contract suit can be brought against an MCO on the theory of a "contract" to provide quality health care. *Williams v. HealthAmerica*, 41 Ohio App.3d 245, 535 N.E.2d 717 (1987) (MCO contracts and literature may also contain provisions to the effect that "quality" health care will be provided or that the organization will promote or enhance subscriber health). The *Share* literature contained such language. Where such assurances are made in master contracts of HMO-physician agreements, subscribers may be able to bring a contract action under a third party beneficiary theory. In *Williams*, for example, the court suggested that the subscriber could be a third-party beneficiary of the HMO-physician contract that required the physician to "promote of the rights of enrollees as patients."

A claim for breach of an express contract or an implied contract may also be argued based on representations by an HMO as to quality of care. Express promises, if proven, can give rise to a separate claim.

MCOs also typically market themselves by describing the quality of the providers on the panel. An assertion of quality furnishes courts another reason to impose on the organization the duty to investigate the competency of participating physicians. Such assertions might even be viewed as a warranty that all panel members maintain a certain minimum competence.

4.   MCOs can be held liable for contracting with substandard providers or imposing overly constraining contracts on those providers. See Pagarigan v. Aetna U.S. Healthcare of California, Inc., 2005 WL 2742807 (California Court of Appeal, 2005.) (holding that "the HMO owes a duty to avoid contracting with deficient providers or negotiating contract terms which require or unduly encourage denials of service or below-standard performance by its providers.").

B. CORPORATE NEGLIGENCE

SHANNON V. MCNULTY
Superior Court of Pennsylvania, 1998.
718 A.2d 828.

[The Shannons sued Dr. McNulty for his failure to timely diagnose and treat signs of pre-term labor. They sued HealthAmerica on a vicarious liability theory for the negligence of its nursing staff in failing to refer Mrs. Shannon in a timely manner to an appropriate physician or hospital for diagnosis and treatment of her pre-term labor; and also that HealthAmerica was corporately liable for its negligent supervision of Dr. McNulty's care and its lack of appropriate procedures and protocols when dispensing telephonic medical advice to subscribers. The court invoked the four duties of *Thompson, supra.*]

Where the HMO is providing health care services rather than merely providing money to pay for services their conduct should be subject to scrutiny. We see no reason why the duties applicable to hospitals should not be equally applied to an HMO when that HMO is performing the same or similar functions as a hospital. When a benefits provider, be it an insurer or a managed care organization, interjects itself into the rendering of medical decisions affecting a subscriber's care it must do so in a medically reasonable manner. Here, HealthAmerica provided a phone service for emergent care staffed by triage nurses. Hence, it was under a duty to oversee that the dispensing of advice by those nurses would be performed in a medically reasonable manner. Accordingly, we now make explicit that which was implicit in McClellanand find that HMOs may, under the right circumstances, be held corporately liable for a breach of any of the Thompson duties which causes harm to its subscribers.

[The court also held that HealthAmerican was vicariously liable for the negligent rendering of services by its triage nurses, under Section 323 of the Restatement (Second) of Torts.]

NOTES AND QUESTIONS

1.   Consider the underlying failures of the system in *Shannon*. The treating physician was impatient and inattentive to warning signs, but it was the triage nurses staffing the phone lines who failed to properly direct Shannon to a physician or hospital. How should the system have been designed to avoid such an error? What would you suggest to avoid a repetition of this kind of disaster?

2.   *Poor Plan Design*. Many of the ERISA preemption cases involve claims of negligent design of the managed care plan, including telephone call-in services staffed by nurses, as in *Shannon*. Other claims of negligent design and administration of the delivery of health care services have been allowed. See McDonald v. Damian, 56 F.Supp.2d 574 (E.D.Pa.1999) (claim for inadequacies in the delivery of medical services).

3.   *Negligent Selection of Providers*. The MCO, like the hospital, has been held to owe its subscribers a duty to properly select its panel members. Harrell v. Total Health Care, Inc., 1989 WL 153066 (Mo.App.1989), affirmed, 781 S.W.2d 58 (Mo.1989).

The logic of a direct duty imposed on MCOs to properly select providers is even stronger for an MCO than for a hospital. In the hospital setting, the patient has often selected the physician. He is then admitted to the hospital because his physician has admitting privileges at that hospital. By contrast, in a managed care program, the patient has chosen the particular program, but not the physicians who are provided. The patient must use the physicians on the panel. The patient thus explicitly relies on the MCO for its selection of health care providers. A duty of proper selection will expose a managed care organization to liability both for failing to properly screen its physicians' competence, and also for failing to evaluate physicians for other problems. If the MCO selects a panel physician or dentist who has evidenced incompetence in her practice, it may risk liability.

4. *Failures to supervise and control staff.* Just as hospitals have duties to supervise and control staff, MCOs are likely to face similar duties to supervise. MCO liability for negligent control of its panel physicians derives from the same common law duty that underlies the negligent selection basis of liability as well as federal and state quality assurance regulations. As courts continue to characterize MCOs as health care providers, suits are likely to increase. Only PPOs with their reduced level of physician control might have an argument that liability should not be imposed for negligent supervision. However, statutes in some states require PPOs to implement quality assurance programs and others contemplate the use of such programs by PPOs. See e.g., Iowa Code Ann. § 514.21.

C. PHYSICIAN INCENTIVE SYSTEMS

Most managed care programs have three relevant features from a liability perspective. First, such programs select a restricted group of health care professionals who provide services to the program's participants. Second, such programs accept a fixed payment per subscriber, in exchange for provision of necessary care. This capitation system, discussed in *Petrovich, supra,* pressures MCOs to search for ways to minimize costs. Third, following from number two, MCOs use a variety of strategies to ensure cost effective care. Altering physician incentives is central to managed care, since physicians influence 70 percent of total health spending, while receiving only about 20 percent of each health care dollar. Such plans use utilization review techniques, incentives systems, and gatekeepers to control costs. The subscriber typically pays a fee to the MCO rather than the provider, relinquishing control over treatment and choice of treating physician. The payer in turn shifts some of its financial risk to its approved providers, who must also accept certain controls over their practice. See Chapter 9, *infra.*

The argument that physician judgment might be "corrupted" by cost-conserving payment systems in managed care systems has been litigated over the years without much success. See, e.g., Sweede v. Cigna Healthplan of Delaware, Inc., 1989 WL 12608 (Del.Super.1989) (claim that doctor withheld necessary care because of financial incentives rejected on facts of case).

Is it hard to prove what motivates physician decisionmaking? How would you establish that a particular HMO payment structure motivated physicians to forego needed care for their patients?

VI.   REFORMING THE TORT SYSTEM FOR MEDICAL INJURIES

Malpractice crises come and go in the United States, driven by an apparent insurance cycle of competitive entry in the market, followed by rapid premium increases as the insurers' returns dropped. A new malpractice crisis resurfaced in 1999, precipitated by a rapid escalation in malpractice insurance premiums for most physicians and limited availability of coverage in some states—as carriers went bankrupt or left the malpractice line of insurance. A new round of legislative reform efforts, spearheaded by angry physician groups, emerged from this latest "crisis," as physicians faced increases in their insurance premiums and pockets of unavailability in some areas and for some specialties. The "crisis," following the cyclical pattern common to malpractice insurance, has abated, but the outpouring of research and writing on the topic continues.

The explanations for the current crises are as varied as their proponents

A. MEDICAL PROGRESS AND OTHER CHANGES IN THE HEALTH CARE ENVIRONMENT

The hazards of health care are substantial. Error rates in medicine are surprisingly high. As the Harvard Medical Practice study discovered in surveying medical iatrogenesis in New York hospitals, as many as 4 percent of hospitalized patients suffer an adverse medical event that results in disability or death. The Harvard Study projected that approximately one percent of all hospital patients suffer injury due to negligently provided care. Harvard Medical Practice Study, Patients, Doctors, and Lawyers: Medical Injury, Malpractice Litigation, and Patient Compensation in New York, Exec.Summ. 3–4 (1990). See Chapter 6, *infra*.

Medical progress has been one of the drivers of expanded tort liability; medicine has increased its power to treat and diagnose, and this power has created increased risks to patients along with it. Second, industrialization in the health care industry has brought expanded liability. Health care is delivered in institutions and group practices. As a result, hospital actions are subject to increasingly intense scrutiny; long term care has become a new and growing target for malpractice litigation; managed care companies are less protected by ERISA preemption than a decade ago; even pharmacists are now exposed to substantial new risks. While malpractice crises historically have been driven by perceived litigation risks to physicians, this crisis includes increased exposure to malpractice suits by all the institutional players in the health care system.

Third, managed care and its cost containment mechanisms have had a strong effect on the system. Physicians are no longer able to pass increased malpractice premiums on to their patients or insurers, the result of tightened reimbursement by both private and public payers. At the same time, physicians have less time to talk to their patients, leaving an injured patient disgruntled and angry at the loss of personal relationship. Angry and injured patients are more likely to sue in such a situation.

Fourth, as a result of the above forces and others, the malpractice insurance market has become less profitable and less stable. See section B below.

Fifth, complexity in medicine—the combination of medical progress and industrialization—is producing more medical adverse events and errors. Lori Andrews conducted a study in a large Chicago area hospital, looking at the actual incidence of negligent events in hospital wards. She discovered that many injuries were not recorded on the records as required, especially when the main person responsible for the error was a senior physician. 17.7 percent of patients in her study experienced errors with a significant impact, many more than the 3.7 percent found in the Harvard Study. See Lori Andrews, Studying Medical Error In Situ: Implications for Malpractice Law and Policy, 54 DePaul L. Rev. 357 (2005).

See Robert I. Field, The Malpractice Crisis Turns 175: What Lessons Does History Hold for Reform? 4 Drexel L. Rev. 7 (2011); Medical Malpractice and the U.S. Health Care System (William M. Sage and Rogan Kersh, eds.2006); William M. Sage, Understanding the First Malpractice Crisis of the 21st Century, in The Health Law Handbook, 2003 Edition, Alice Gosfield, Editor.

For a review of the claims for and against the existence of a medical malpractice crisis, see Tom Baker, The Medical Malpractice Myth (2005); Barry R. Furrow, Reforming Medical Malpractice Liability, in Debates on U.S. Health Care 189 (Jennie Jacobs Kronenfeld, Wendy E. Parmet, and Mar A. Zezza, eds. 2012).

B. INCENTIVE EFFECTS OF MALPRACTICE LITIGATION ON PROVIDER BEHAVIOR

Are tort suits likely to change potentially dangerous patterns of medical practice? Malpractice litigation in theory operates as a quality control mechanism. From the economist's perspective, tort doctrine should be designed to achieve an optimal prevention policy, reducing the sum total of the costs of medical accidents and the costs of preventing them. In theory, the tort system deters accident producing behavior. How? The existence of a liability rule and the resulting threat of a lawsuit and judgment encourage health care providers to reduce error and patient injury in circumstances where patients themselves lack the information (and ability) to monitor the quality of care they receive. Potential defendants will take precautions to avoid error and will buy insurance to cover any errors that injure patients. By finding fault and assessing damages against a defendant, a court sends a signal to health care providers that if they wish to avoid similar damages in the future they may need to change their behavior.

Malpractice claims have proved to provide useful evidence for discovering problematic physicians. Multiple malpractice claims are predictive of medical discipline, confirming the validity of such claims as predictors. One study of problems with state medical licensing boards concluded that "physicians with high numbers of medical malpractice reports in the NPDB [National Practitioner Data Bank] tend to have at least some adverse actions reports (e.g. hospital disciplinary report, medical board report) and Medicare/Medicaid exclusion reports and vice versa." Alan Levine et al., State Medical Boards Fail to Discipline Doctors With Hospital Actions Against Them, Pub. Citizen 9 (March. 2011). Ten or more payouts predict adverse action reports, and almost 9 percent of those were excluded from the Medicare and Medicaid programs. The NPBD data reveals that a few physicians account for most of the malpractice dollars paid: "[e]leven percent . . . of physicians [in the NPDB] with at least one malpractice payment were responsible for half of all malpractice dollars paid from September 1, 1990 through December 31, 2006." Health Resources & Servs. Admin. Bureau of Health Professions Div. of Prac. Data Banks, U.S. Dep't of Health & Hum. Servs., National Practitioner Data Bank 2006 Ann. Rep. 42.

Does the existence of malpractice insurance weaken deterrence? If the insurer does not employ experience rating to distinguish the litigation-prone providers from their colleagues, it is in effect causing an inaccurate signal to be sent, since all physicians in a practice area pay the same premiums regardless of their level of malpractice claims. This may dilute or eliminate the financial incentives for these physicians to change their behavior.

Liability insurers however use several mechanisms to assess physician insurance risks, and physicians are in fact likely to feel the effects of increased malpractice litigation in terms of insurance availability and pricing. Private insurance operates as a mode of regulation in liability insurance as well as other lines of insurance. See generally Omri Ben–Shahar and Kyle D. Logue, Outsourcing Regulation: How Insurance Reduces Moral Hazard, 111 Mich. L. Rev. 197 (2012); Tom Baker, Liability Insurance as Tort Regulation: Six Ways that Liability Insurance Shapes Tort Law in Action, 12 Conn. Ins. L.J. 1, 3–4 (2005).

Malpractice litigation does affect medical practice, making anxious providers either overestimate the risks of a suit or at least adjust their practice to a new assessment of the risk of suit, regardless of the incentive effects of judgments and premium increases. Physicians perceive a threat from the system, judging their risk of being sued as much higher than it actually is. See David M. Studdert et al., Defensive Medicine Among High–Risk Specialist Physicians in a Volatile Malpractice Environment, 293 JAMA 2609 (2005). Studies conclude that physicians who have been malpractice defendants often alter their practice as a reaction, even if they win the litigation. They also suffer chronic stress until the trial is over. See, for example, Charles, Wilbert, and Kennedy, Physicians' Self–Reports of Reactions to Malpractice Litigation, 141 Am. J. Psychiatry 563, 565 (1984) ("A malpractice suit was considered a serious and often a devastating event in the personal and professional lives of the respondent physicians").

Physician stress is compounded by the length of time that it takes a malpractice case to either settle or reach a verdict. See Seth A. Seabury et al., On Average, Physicians Spend Nearly 11 Percent Of Their 40–Year Careers With An Open, Unresolved Malpractice Claim, 32 Health Affairs, 111 (2013).

The Harvard New York Study, surveying New York physicians, found that physicians who had been sued were more likely to explain risks to patients, to restrict their scope of practice, and to order more tests and procedures. Patients, Doctors, and Lawyers: Medical Injury, Malpractice Litigation, and Patient Compensation in New York 9–29 (1990). Physicians surveyed in the New York study also felt that the malpractice threat was important in maintaining standards of care. Id. at 9–24.

What other forces and incentives affect the quality of health care delivery by physicians, other professionals, and institutions? A technological innovation for example may reduce both the level of medical injury for a procedure and the risks of being sued. Consider the pulse oximeter, discussed in Washington v. Washington Medical Center, *infra.* In 1984, no hospital operating room had such a device, but by 1990 all operating rooms did, and the incidence of patient injuries due to anesthesia errors has dropped precipitiously.

As Professors Hyman and Silver put it, "The main problem with the legal system is that it exerts too little pressure on health care providers to improve the quality of the services they deliver. * * * Safe health care is expensive, and the tort system forces providers to pay only pennies on the dollar for the injuries they inflict." David A. Hyman and Charles Silver, Medical Malpractice Litigation and Tort Reform: It's the Incentives, Stupid, 59 Vand. L. Rev. 1085, 1130 (2006).

C. THE NATURE OF THE INSURANCE INDUSTRY

Any serious analysis of the malpractice "crisis" begins (and some say it ends) with the insurance industry. Health care providers buy medical malpractice insurance to protect themselves from medical malpractice claims. Under the insurance contract, the insurance company agrees to accept financial responsibility for payment of any claims up to a specific level of coverage during a fixed period in return for a fee. The insurer investigates the claim and defends the health care provider. This insurance is sold by commercial insurance companies, health care provider-owned companies, and joint underwriting associations. Some large hospitals also self-insure for medical malpractice losses rather than purchasing insurance, and a few physicians practice without insurance. Joint underwriting associations are nonprofit pooling arrangements created by state legislatures to provide medical malpractice insurance to health care providers in the states in which they are established.

Insurance rate setting uses actuarial techniques to set rates, to generate funds to cover (1) losses occurring during the period, (2) the administrative costs of running the company, and (3) an amount for unknown contingencies, which may become a profit if not used. The profit may be retained as capital surplus or returned to stockholders as dividends.

See generally U.S.General Accounting Office, Medical Malpractice: No Agreement on the Problems or Solutions 66–72 (1986), from which the above discussion was taken, describing the crises of the 1970s and mid–1980s.

NOTES AND QUESTIONS

1. *The Flaws in the Malpractice Insurance Market.* The market for malpractice insurance fails to satisfy many of the economist's conditions for an ideal insurance market. The ideal market consists of a pooling by the insurer of a large number of homogeneous but independent random events. The auto accident insurance market is perhaps closest to fulfilling this condition. The large numbers of events involved make outcomes for the insurance pool actuarially predictable. Malpractice lacks these desirable qualities of "... large numbers, independence, and risk beyond the control of the insured." Patricia Danzon, Medical Malpractice: Theory, Evidence, and Public Policy 90 (1985) The pool of potential policyholders is small, as is the pool of claims, and a few states have most of the claims. The awards vary tremendously, with 50 percent of the dollars paid out on 3 percent of the claims. In small insurance programs, a single multimillion dollar claim can have a tremendous effect on total losses and therefore average loss per insured doctor.

Second, losses are not independent, since neither claims against an individual doctor nor against doctors as a group are independent; multiple claims against a doctor relate usually to some characteristic of his practice or his technique, and a lawyer can use knowledge gained in one suit in another. Claims and verdicts against doctors generally reflect social forces—shifts in jury attitudes and legal doctrine. Given the long tail, or time from medical intervention to the filing of a claim, the impact of these shifts is increased.

Finally, the problems of moral hazard and adverse selection distort the market. Moral hazard characterizes the effect of insurance in reducing an insured's incentives to prevent losses, since he is not financially responsible for losses. Adverse selection occurs when an insurer attracts policy holders of above-average risk, ending up with higher claim costs and lower profits as a result.

2. *Premium Increases and the Medical Rate of Inflation.* Studies in
some states have confirmed that all increases in award sizes are accounted
for by medical inflation, wage inflation (for lost earnings) and the increase in
severity of the injury to the patient. Missouri Department of Insurance, Medical Malpractice Insurance in Missouri: The Current Difficulties in Perspective 6 (February 2003).

3. *The Underwriting Cycle.* The malpractice crisis is more a product of
the way the insurance industry does business than of changes in the frequency of medical malpractice litigation or the severity of judgments. The malpractice market is a "lumpy" market, prone to cycles of underpricing and
catchup. What doctors and hospitals see as "sudden" price increases are actually deferred costs passed on when premiums no longer cover payments plus
profit. Once premiums reach actuarially sound levels, profits rise, new insurers enter the market with lower rates, competitive pressures return, and the
cycle starts all over again.

The cyclical nature of interest rates, as a measure of return on investments, plays a central role in insurers' pricing decisions. The insurance industry engages in cash-flow underwriting, in which insurers invest the premiums they collect in the bond market and to a lesser extent in the stock
market. When interest rates and investment returns are high, insurance
companies accept riskier exposures to acquire more investable premium and
loss reserves. If underwriting and investment results are combined during
these periods, investment gains more than offset losses. Malpractice insurance premiums charged by insurance companies do not relate to payouts, but
rather rise and fall in concert with the state of the economy, reflecting gains
and losses of invested reserves and the insurance industry's calculation of
their rate of return on the investment "float" (the time between collecting
premium dollars and paying out losses) provided by the physician premiums.
See generally Mimi Marchev, The Medical Malpractice Insurance Crisis: Opportunity for State Action (National Academy for State Health Policy, July
2002).

4. *Limitations on State Insurance Regulation.* Many states grant their
insurance regulators only limited authority to regulation medical malpractice
insurance rates unless they are either excessive and the market is not competitive. States tend to rely on the marketplace to adjust rates instead of
granting broader regulatory powers to their insurance commissioners. Some
states are considering allowing their insurance departments to reject malpractice rate filings that do not meet acceptable standards. See, e.g., Missouri
Department of Insurance, Medical Malpractice Insurance in Missouri: The
Current Difficulties in Perspective 4 (February 2003).

D. APPROACHES TO REFORMING THE MEDICAL MALPRACTICE SYSTEM

1. Improving Insurance Availability

The response to the perceived "crisis" in malpractice litigation and insurance availability over the past thirty years has been twofold. First, the availability of insurance has been enhanced by a variety of changes in the structure of the insurance industry. Second, physicians have lobbied with substantial success at the state level for legislation to impede the ability of plaintiffs to bring tort suits and to restrict the size of awards.

a. *New Sources of Insurance.* New sources of insurance were created in response to earlier crises, either by the states or by providers. Joint underwriting associations, reinsurance exchanges, hospital self-insurance programs, state funds, and provider owned insurance companies have sprung into being.

b. *Claims–Made Policies.* Medical malpractice insurers changed in the late seventies to writing policies on a claims-made rather than an occurrence basis. Most insurers have shifted to a claims-made policy, allowing them to use more recent claims experience to set premium prices and reserve requirements. The claims-made policy covers claims made during the year of the policy coverage, avoiding the predictability problem of the occurrence policy. Such policies arguably have allowed companies to continue to carry malpractice insurance lines, serving the goal of availability by keeping premium costs lower than they would otherwise have been.

c. *Selective Insurance Marketing.* Physician mutual companies, with physician-investors, have often ridden out the underwriting cycle with less distress than the commercial carriers. Other companies have begun to adopt aggressive risk management practices to control rate increases. One example is *Healthcare Providers Insurance Exchange* (HPIX), formed in 2002.

d. *Hospital Complaint Profiling.* For hospitals, complaint profiling has been proposed, spotting litigation-prone staff physicians and intervening to retrain them to avoid risks. The Hickson study took six years worth of hospital patient advocacy files and concluded that unsolicited patient complaints about physicians are a highly reliable predictor of litigation-prone physicians. The study found that 9 percent of the physicians produced 50 percent of the complaints, and the study showed an 86 percent success rate in predicting physicians with multiple claims. See Gerald B. Hickson et al., Patient Complaints and Malpractice Risk, 287 J.A.M.A. 2951 (2002).

2. Altering the Litigation Process

Starting in the 1970s, states enacted tort reform legislation. Tort reform measures were intended by their proponents to reduce either the frequency of malpractice litigation or the size of the settlement or judgment. The goal was not to improve the lot of the injured patient, but instead to satisfy both the medical profession and the insurance industry.

These measures were designed to restrict the operation of the tort system in several: (1) affecting the filing of malpractice claims; (2) limiting the award recoverable by the plaintiff; (3) altering the plaintiff's burden of proof through changes in evidence rules and legal doctrine; (4) reducing the plaintiff lawyer's contingency fee recovery; and (5) changing the role of the courts by substituting an alternative forum. These are characterized by Eleanor Kinney as "first generation" reforms. See generally Eleanor D. Kinney, Learning from Experience, Malpractice Reforms in the 1990s: Past Disappointments, Future Success?, 20 J. Health Pol. Pol'y & L. 99 (1995).

The most powerful reform in actually reducing the size of malpractice awards has been a dollar limit, or cap, on awards. Caps may take the form of a limit on the amount of recovery of general damages, typically pain and suffering; or a maximum recoverable per case, including all damages. See David A. Hyman, Bernard Black, Charles Silver, and William M. Sage, Estimating the Effect of Damage Caps in Medical Malpractice Cases: Evidence From Texas, 1 J. Legal Analysis 355 (2009).

E. ALTERNATIVE APPROACHES TO COMPENSATION OF PATIENT INJURY

Second-generation reform proposals aimed to eliminate or reduce some of these perceived flaws of the current system, without impairing consumer access to compensation. Such proposals can be categorized in light of several central attributes. They involve combining different reforms, choosing variables from a series of categories into a single package. The categories that are available include: (1) the compensable event, (2) the measure of compensation, (3) the payment mechanism, (4) the forum used to resolve disputes, and (5) the method of implementing the new rights and responsibilities. See generally Kenneth Abraham, Medical Liability Reform: A Conceptual Framework, 260 Journal of the American Medical Association 68–72 (1988).

Abraham summarizes the categories and reform choices in the following table:

Compensable Event	Measure of Compensation	Payment Mechanism	Forum for Resolution of Disputes	Method of Implementation

Fault
Cause
Loss
	Full tort damages
	Full out-of-pocket losses
	Partial out-of- pocket losses
	Scheduled damages
	Lump-sum payment
	Periodic payment
		First-party insurance
		Third-party insurance
		Taxation
		Hybrid Funding
			Jury trial
			Expert review panels
			Bench trial
			Binding arbitration
			Administrative boards
			Insurance company decision
				Legislation
				  Mandatory reform
				  Elective options
				Private contract

1. Alternative Dispute Resolution (ADR)

Arbitration is often proposed as a way to solve the problems of the tort system. It is pervasive in all consumer contracts, from brokerage agreements to telephone contracts. The expected advantages of arbitration include diminished complexity in fact-finding, lower cost, fairer results, greater access for smaller claims, and a reduced burden on the courts. No state requires compulsory arbitration. Like screening panels, the arbitration process uses a panel to resolve the dispute after an informal presentation of evidence. The panel typically consists of a doctor, a lawyer and a layperson or retired judge. The arbitration panel, however, uses members trained in dispute resolution and has the authority to make a final ruling as to both provider liability and damages. The process is initiated only when there is an agreement between the patient and the health care provider to arbitrate any claims.

Arbitration has distinct disadvantages from a consumer perspective. Lawyers can drive up the costs and length of arbitration to match litigation. Evidence is also emerging that the "repeat player" phenomenon means a much higher victory rate for employers and other institutional players who regularly engage in arbitration in contrast to one-shot players such as employees or consumers. In employment arbitration cases, one study found that the odds are 5–to–1 against the employee in a repeat-player case. Much of this imbalance may be due to the ability and incentive of repeat players to track the predisposition of arbitrators and bias the selection process in their favor. See generally Ann H. Nevers, Medical Malpractice Arbitration in the New Millennium: Much Ado About Nothing?, 1 Pepperdine Dispute Resolution Law Journal 45 (2001); Thomas Metzloff, Alternative Dispute Resolution Strategies in Medical Malpractice, 9 Alaska L. Rev. 429 (1992).

Mediation has also been proposed as an attractive alternative to litigation. See generally Edward A. Dauer, Leonard J. Marcus, and Susan M. C. Payne, Prometheus and the Litigators: A Mediation Odyssey, 21 J. Leg. Med. 159 (2000).

2. No–Fault Systems

(1) Provider–Based Early Payment

Under this approach providers would voluntarily agree to identify and promptly compensate patients for avoidable injuries. Damages would be limited under most proposals. This approach was first proposed by Clark Havighurst and Lawrence Tancredi, and has been recommended in Institute of Medicine, Fostering Rapid Advances in Health Care: Learning from System Demonstrations 82 (2002). One example of such a model has been pioneered by the University of Michigan Health System, a self-insured system. Michigan limits compensation to cases where the institution determines that the care was inappropriate, tendering an offer to the injured patient. The offer may include compensation for all elements of loss that are compensable in tort cases, including medical expenses, lost income, other economic losses, and "pain and suffering." A patient can only accept the tendered money after agreeing that it is a final settlement, foreclosing a lawsuit. See generally Richard C. Boothman et al., A Better Approach to Medical Malpractice Claims? The University of Michigan Experience, 2 J. Health & Life Sci. L. 125, 135 (2009) (summarizing the approach); Michelle M. Mello and Thomas H. Gallagher, Malpractice Reform—Opportunities for Leadership by Health Care Institutions and Liability Insurers (March 31, 2010 at NEJM.org.

(2) Administrative Systems

The most recent administrative idea is the health court, a hybrid model based on earlier "early-settlement" models around since the seventies. See *Problem: Health Courts as a Solution? infra* for a description of such courts. Another proposal offered by the Institute of Medicine has been to create by legislation a state system loosely based on the Workers' Compensation model. Under this approach, providers would receive immunity from tort in exchange for "mandatory participation in a state-sponsored, administrative system established to provide compensation to patients who have suffered avoidable injuries." See Institute of Medicine, Fostering Rapid Advances in Health Care: Learning from System Demonstrations 82 (2002). The AMA also developed an elaborate proposal in the late 1980s, but to date such state-administered systems have been limited to special categories of injuries, such as brain-damaged infants.

NOTES AND QUESTIONS

1.   If you represent a hospital, what problems would you see in a system like that of the University of Michigan, tendering an offer of settlement to a plaintiff? Why should a provider come forward to inform a patient that he has suffered a compensable injury? What is in it for the provider in an uncertain case? Is the doctor in charge of the case likely to admit error, so that

the hospital can present its offer to the patient? How can the hospital encourage staff doctors to come forward? How might legal rules improve the possibilities of disclosure of errors?

2.   One of the primary goals in a no-fault system is to reduce the cost of insurance to providers. The California study in the 1970s estimated that a no-fault system in California could increase malpractice premiums 300 percent higher than the tort system's insurance costs. California Medical and Hospital Associations, Report on the Medical Insurance Feasibility Study (1977).

If a compensation system rewards many more claimants, particularly small ones, in an evenhanded and more rapid fashion than does the current tort system, it may well be an improvement. But it is unlikely to be a cheaper system. And if it ends up offering plaintiffs considerably smaller awards that they would receive in a trial system, such a compensation system may trade speed and smaller payouts for defendants for inadequate compensation for plaintiffs. In considering tort reform, one always must ask who is proposing the reforms and what do they stand to gain from them.

3.   Disclosure, Apology, and Resolution Systems

Disclosure-and-resolution programs are described in Chapter 6, particularly the program implemented by the Veteran's Administration. Such programs have become more common in hospitals, as risk managers search for ways to control their liability costs. For a detailed description of how to design such systems, see ECRI Institute, Disclosure of Unanticipated Outcomes (January 2008) (outlining the disclosure steps developed by the American Society for Healthcare Risk Management (ASHRM)).

A hospital using this approach typically adopts several steps. First, a representative discloses adverse events to affected patients and their families. Second, she apologizes on behalf of the institution for causing the adverse event and harms suffered by the patient. Third, she offers compensation where appropriate. The approach combines the "early offer" ideas described above with the strategy of full disclosure and apology. The Michigan approach, above, uses elements of these ideas. The idea is to induce settlements more quickly by co-opting plaintiff lawyers with the promise of much quicker, less adversarial settlements that bring the injured plaintiffs into the conversation earlier.

Apology strategies have a real downside. From a defendant's perspective, such proposals offer a strategic tool to buy off plaintiffs by showing them how sorry the provider is, and to rush settlement by getting plaintiffs (and their lawyers) to buy into early settlement by the offer of money up front. The problem is that the provider and its insurer control the screening for potential adverse event claims, using the process as a filter for payouts. Strategic apologies may improve claims resolution, but at the cost of lower payments because conciliation has discounted the level of compensation that a plaintiff may really need. See Erin Ann O'Hara & Douglas Yarn, On Apology and Consilience, 77 Wash. L. Rev. 1121, 1186 (2002).

F. THE AFFORDABLE CARE ACT AND TORT REFORM

The Affordable Care Act makes big changes to the Medicaid and Medicare programs and private insurance regulation. Its impact on medical liability reform is much more modest, promoting state demonstration programs that are limited in their scope by the terms of grants to the states. Tort reform was never seriously considered as a central part of health care reform, in part because cost savings from reform were not expected to be substantial, and because it is a Democratic bill. The Congressional Budget Office, in a letter to Senator Orrin Hatch (October 9, 2009), responded to his request for an updated analysis of the effects of proposals to limit costs related to medical malpractice ("tort reform"). The CBO began with the assumption that "[t]ort reform could affect costs for health care both directly and indirectly: directly, by lowering premiums for medical liability insurance; and indirectly, by reducing the use of diagnostic tests and other health care services when providers recommend those services principally to reduce their potential exposure to lawsuits."

The CBO estimated that such reforms would reduce medical malpractice premiums by about 10 percent. The CBO estimated that the direct costs to providers for liability, including premiums, awards, and settlements, and administrative costs, would in 2009 be around $35 billion, or about 2 percent of total health care expenditures. A savings of 10 percent in premium plus costs would therefore, in the CBO's words, ". . . reduce total national health care expenditures by about 0.2 percent." This is hardly a significant savings.

The CBO also noted that there remains a large area of uncertainty about the possible negative effect on health outcomes of limiting the rights of injured patients to sue for injuries form medical errors. They noted that the studies are in conflict, ranging from an estimate that a 10 percent reduction in costs would increase the overall mortality rate by 0.2 percent, to an estimate of no serious adverse outcomes for patient health. The hope of tort reformers that extensive reforms could be sold as cost reduction, as part of the the ACA package, was limited by this CBO analysis.

The primary liability reform provision in the ACA is Section 10607, *State Demonstration Programs to Evaluate Alternatives to Current Medical Tort Litigation*. The Secretary of the Department of Health and Human Services may award demonstration grants for a period not to exceed five years to the States "for the development, implementation, and evaluation of alternatives to current tort litigation for resolving disputes over injuries allegedly caused by health care providers or health care organizations."

The ACA in (1) A specifies that the models should resolve disputes over patient injuries and promote a reduction in medical errors "by encouraging the collection and analysis of patient safety data related to disputes resolved under subparagraph (A) by organizations that engage in efforts to improve patient safety and the quality of health care."

Subsection (2) requires the State grant seeker to demonstrate how their model:

(A) makes the medical liability system more reliable by increasing the availability of prompt and fair resolution of disputes;

(B) encourages the efficient resolution of disputes;

(C) encourages the disclosure of health care errors;

(D) enhances patient safety by detecting, analyzing, and helping to reduce medical errors and adverse events;

(E) improves access to liability insurance;

(F) fully informs patients about the differences in the alternative and current tort litigation;

(G) provides patients the ability to opt out of or voluntarily withdraw from participating in the alternative at any time and to pursue other options, including litigation, outside the alternative;

(H) would not conflict with State law at the time of the application in a way that would prohibit the adoption of an alternative to current tort litigation; and

(I) would not limit or curtail a patient's existing legal rights, ability to file a claim in or a access a State's legal system, or otherwise abrogate a patient's ability to file a medical malpractice claim.

* * *

(B) NOTIFICATION OF PATIENTS.—A State shall demonstrate how patients would be notified that they are receiving health care services that fall within such scope, and the process by which they may opt out of or voluntarily withdraw from participating in the alternative. The decision of the patient whether to participate or continue participating in the alternative process shall be made at any time and shall not be limited in any way.

NOTES AND QUESTIONS

What kinds of alternative dispute resolution models will be eligible for one of these demonstration grants? How about mandatory arbitration of the sort in every brokerage agreement, telephone contract, or publishing contract? Why does the Act so constrain the kinds of models that can be considered? Whose interests are represented?

G. CONCLUSION

First-generation reforms are now in place in most states. Second-generation reforms, ranging from enterprise liability to contractual arbitration models, are far less likely to be adopted by either Congress or the states. The American Medical Association and state medical societies continue to advocate for statutory caps on pain and suffering awards, using the California model of a $250,000 cap on noneconomic losses as the solution to the problem. It remains to be seen whether broader innovations in malpractice compensation systems will be tried at either the federal or state levels. The vested interests are entrenched at this point, and serious system reform seems unlikely, particularly as the latest malpractice crisis abates as insurance costs drop for providers.

PROBLEM: HEALTH COURTS AS A SOLUTION?

A *health court* is a system of administrative compensation for medical injuries. It has five core features. First, injury compensation decisions are made outside the regular court system by specially trained judges. Second, compensation decisions are based on a standard of care that is broader than the negligence standard (but does not approach strict liability). "Avoidability" or "preventability" of the injury is the touchstone. To obtain compensation, claimants must show that the injury would not have occurred if best practices had been followed or an optimal system of care had been in place, but they need not show that care fell below the standard expected of a reasonable practitioner. Third, compensation criteria are based on evidence; that is, they are grounded in experts' interpretations of the leading scientific literature. To the maximum extent feasible, compensation decisions are guided by *ex ante* determinations about the preventability of common medical adverse events. Fourth, this knowledge, coupled with precedent, is converted to decision aids that allow fast-track compensation decisions for certain types of injury. Fifth and finally, *ex ante* guidelines also inform decisions about how much for economic and noneconomic damages should be paid.

Patients are informed, at the time an injury is disclosed by the provider, that they can file a compensation claim with the provider or its insurer. A panel of experts, aided by decision guidelines, determines whether the injury was avoidable—would the injury ordinarily have occurred if the care had been provided by the best specialist or an optimal health care system? For avoidable injuries, the institution offers full compensation for economic losses plus a scheduled amount for pain and suffering based on injury severity.

A voluntary model would allow patients to reject the compensation offer and file a lawsuit, unless they had waived this right as a condition of receiving care.

The health courts proposal is presented in Michelle M. Mello, David M. Studdert, Allen B. Kachalia, and Troyen A. Brennan, "Health Courts" and Accountability for Patient Safety, 84 The Milbank Quarterly 459, 460–461 (2006).

What problems do you see with this proposal? Given what you know of the current liability system, what advantages does the health court offer to defendants? Plaintiffs? Insurers? Will this model be promising even if plaintiffs choose to litigate at any time?

CHAPTER 6

REGULATING PATIENT SAFETY

■ ■ ■

I. FROM DEFINING QUALITY TO REGULATING PATIENT SAFETY

Lawyers are involved with quality of health care issues through a variety of routes. They file, or defend against, malpractice suits when a patient is injured during the course of medical treatment. They handle medical staff privileges cases that frequently turn on the quality of the staff doctor's performance. They represent the government in administering programs that aim to cut the cost of health care and improve its quality as well as providers who must adjust to these programs. They contest insurer refusals to pay claims, or represent insurers who don't want to pay for poor quality or unproven treatments.

A. THE NATURE OF QUALITY IN MEDICINE

The Institute of Medicine has developed a definition that is a useful starting point:

> * * * quality of care is the degree to which health services for individuals and populations increase the likelihood of desired health outcomes and are consistent with current professional knowledge. Institute of Medicine, Medicare: A Strategy for Quality Assurance, Vol. I, 20 (K. Lohr, Ed.1990).

1. Medical Practice Variation

The phenomenon of medical practice variation highlights the role of uncertainty in the setting of medical standards. John Wennberg, whose studies in this area are often cited, has analyzed states and regions within states for variation in surgical and other practices:

> [I]n Maine by the time women reach seventy years of age in one hospital market the likelihood they have undergone a hysterectomy is 20 percent while in another market it is 70 percent. In Iowa, the chances that male residents who reach age eighty-five have undergone prostatectomy range from a low of 15 percent to

a high of more than 60 percent in different hospital markets. In Vermont the probability that resident children will undergo a tonsillectomy has ranged from a low of 8 percent in one hospital market to a high of nearly 70 percent in another.

John E. Wennberg, Dealing with Medical Practice Variations: A Proposal for Action, 3 Health Affairs 6, 9 (1984).

Wennberg's studies of medical practice variation are based on studies of three categories of care: effective care, preference-sensitive care, and supply-sensitive care.

(1) "Effective Care": interventions that are viewed as medically necessary on the basis of clinical outcomes evidence and for which the benefits so outweigh the risks that virtually all patients with medical need should receive them.

(2) "Preference-sensitive Care": treatments, such as discretionary surgery, for which there are two or more valid treatment alternatives, and the choice of treatment involves tradeoffs that should be based on patients' preferences. Variation in such care is typified by elective surgeries, such as hip fracture, knee replacement, or back surgery. Surgeons in adjoining counties in Florida, for example, may operate at very different levels for the same condition and patient.

(3) "Supply-sensitive Care": services such as physician visits, referrals to specialists, hospitalizations, and stays in intensive care units involved in the medical (non-surgical) management of disease. In Medicare, the large majority of these services are for patients with chronic illness.

See generally John E. Wennberg, Variation in Use of Medicare Services Among Regions and Selected Academic Medical Centers: Is More Better?, Commonwealth Fund Pub. No. 874, at 4 (Dec. 2005).

The attitudes of individual doctors influence the range of variation where consensus is lacking. Wennberg has termed this the "practice style factor." This style can exert its influence in the absence of scientific information on outcomes; in other cases it may be unrelated to controversies. See John E. Wennberg, The Paradox of Appropriate Care, 258 J.A.M.A. 2568 (1987). See generally John Eisenberg, Doctors' Decisions and the Cost of Medical Care (1986).

2. Quality and the Patient Protection and Affordable Care Act of 2010

The ACA has an astonishing variety of provisions aimed at improving the quality of the U.S. health care system, reducing errors, and generally promoting patient safety. These provisions include new centers, demonstration projects, and funding awards for a wide range of quality improvement projects.

The ACA has a variety of quality definitions and measurements. Quality is defined in Section 3013 of the ACA as "a standard for measuring the performance and improvement of population health or of health plans, providers of services, and other clinicians in the delivery of health care services."

Section 3013 contains a range of useful benchmarks for defining quality. Good quality care is care that improves patient health outcomes and their functional status. It provides management and coordination of care across episodes of care and care transitions across providers, settings, and plans. It makes patients part of the decision making process through a variety of tools. It uses health information technology effectively. The care provided must be safe, effective, patient-centered, patient satisfying, appropriate, timely, efficient, and innovative. The ACA also has a strong focus on population health, and one of its quality tests is whether care given promotes "the equity of health services and health disparities across health disparity populations [ ] and geographic areas." ACA, section 3013, subsections A through J.

Quality improvement is central to the ACA. Section 3501 mandates the Director of the Center for Quality Improvement Programs to "identify, develop, evaluate, disseminate, and provide training in innovative methodologies and strategies for quality improvement practices in the delivery of health care services that represent best practices in health care quality, safety, and value" in collaboration with other Federal agencies. The Center for Quality Improvement and Patient Safety of the Agency for Healthcare Research and Quality sets quality priorities.

Excess readmissions are presumed to indicate lower quality care by hospitals. The ACA creates the Hospital Readmission Reduction Program. Section 3025 ties excess readmissions (however defined) to a reduction in Medicare payments that would otherwise be made to that hospital. Information on all patient readmission rates shall be made available on the CMS Hospital Compare website in a form and manner determined appropriate by the Secretary.

Section 3021 establishes a new Center for Medicare and Medicaid Innovation (CMI) within the Centers for Medicare & Medicaid Services (CMS). The purpose of the Center will be to research, develop, test, and expand innovative payment and delivery arrangements to improve the quality and reduce the cost of care provided to patients in each program.

Dedicated funding is provided to allow for testing of models that require benefits not currently covered by Medicare. The expectation is that successful models would then be expanded nationally.

The goals of the models to be researched and tested include promoting payment and practice reform, including patient-centered medical homes and models that move toward comprehensive payment or salary payment; direct contracting with groups of providers, through risk-based or salary-based payments; care coordination; patient decision making support tools; hospital care using specialists linked by electronic monitoring at integrated systems; and payments to Healthcare Innovation Zones. The Medicare Shared Savings Program (Section 3022) creates Accountable Care Organizations (ACOs).

PROBLEM: BATTLING STANDARDS I

As the CEO of the large integrated health system described in the previous problem, you are well aware that cardiac care is an important and profitable component of patient care. You have recently begun a study of cardiac care in your system, with particular attention to the treatment of heart patients with clogged arteries. Cardiologists routinely use stents for stable coronary artery disease (CAD). In angioplasties, doctors guide a narrow tube through a blood vessel near the groin up toward the heart, inflate a tiny balloon to flatten blockages, and insert a stent to keep arteries propped open. The procedure costs about $20,000, based on average Medicare reimbursement for doctor and hospital fees, and generally requires an overnight hospital stay. You are aware of the COURAGE study, a major research study in 2007 that concluded that intensive drug treatment in non-emergency patients with chest pain (aspirin, beta blockers, and statins) worked as well as angioplasty in preventing heart attacks, improving survival and relieving discomfort in the long run. In a seven-year follow-up, the study found that the outcomes were the same for stents and drug therapies.

The use of stents by cardiologists in your system hospitals has continued at about the same level in 2011 as in 2007, in spite of their much higher costs and identical outcomes. You would like to change the practice patterns of the cardiologists in your system. How should you proceed? What kind of approach do you advise to deal with the problem of variation in practice approaches in cardiology? What ideas do you have to reduce such conflicts and to guide providers into the best practices? Given the structure of most hospitals, how will you orchestrate a unified approach to cardiology practice? Are you likely to be conflicted about this choice, given the likelihood of substantial hospital revenue from interventions like angioplasty?

What mechanisms might be used to resolve such possible conflicts among best practices, comparative effectiveness research findings, practice guidelines, and other standards of ACA? To what extent do variations inherent in medical practice styles confound such research? And what about the confounding effects of variations in patients, physician and support teams, and available resources? See William B. Borden et al., Patterns and Intensity of Medical Therapy in Patients Undergoing Percutaneous Coronary Intervention, 305 J.A.M.A. 1882 (2010), reporting that fewer than half of patients undergoing percutaneous coronary intervention (PCI) are receiving optimal medical therapy (OMT), despite the guideline-based recommendations to maximize OMT and the clinical logic of doing so before PCI.

B. EVIDENCE–BASED MEDICINE (EBM) AND COMPARATIVE EFFECTIVENESS RESEARCH (CER)

Evidence-based medicine (EBM) has been defined as "the conscientious, explicit, and judicious use of current best evidence in making decisions about the care of individual patients." David L. Sackett et al., Evidence–Based Medicine: What It Is and What It Isn't, 312 Brit. Med. J. 71, 71 (1996). EBM incorporates clinical expertise and patient values as well, but the emphasis is on the use of current best evidence. EBM assumes that the physician will keep up with and incorporate the best evidence into his practice in advance of the development of clinical practice guideline..

Comparative effectiveness research (CER) is a natural outgrowth of EBM. It is a major component of current federal health policy. This "effectiveness initiative" in modern medicine is based on three premises. First, many current medical practices either are ineffective or could be replaced with less expensive substitutes. Wennberg's medical practice variation studies support this premise to a large extent.

Second, physicians often select more expensive treatments because of bias, fear of litigation, or financial incentives. Physician defensive medical practices like unnecessary tests, motivated by fear of litigation, supports this premise. So do payment incentives like fee-for-service medicine, where the more a physician does, the more she gets paid.

Third, patients would often choose different options from those recommended by their physicians if they had better information about treatment risks, benefits, and costs. The burgeoning literature on shared decision making and the use of decision aids supports this idea that patient choices might often lead to conservative treatment or no treatment at all. See Chapter 3, supra.

The goal of evidence-based medicine and comparative effectiveness research is to narrow variation in medical practice by developing guidelines and best practices for clinicians. *See* M.C. Weinstein & J.A. Skinner, Comparative Effectiveness and Health Care Spending: Implications for Reform, 326 NEJM 460 (2010).

The ACA continues the strong emphasis in federal health policy on comparative effectiveness research. Section 6301 of the ACA defines "comparative clinical effectiveness research" to mean research evaluating and comparing health outcomes and the clinical effectiveness, risks, and benefits of two or more medical treatments, services, and items. These include "health care interventions, protocols for treatment, care management, and delivery, procedures, medical devices, diagnostic tools, pharmaceuticals (including drugs and biologics), integrative health practices, and any other strategies or items being used in the treatment, management, and diagnosis of, or prevention of illness or injury in, individuals."

The ACA created several entities to further CER. The primary new entity is a nonprofit corporation, the Patient–Centered Outcomes Research Institute (PCORI). The Institute's purpose is:

> * * * to assist patients, clinicians, purchasers, and policymakers in making informed health decisions by advancing the quality and relevance of evidence concerning the manner in which diseases, disorders, and other health conditions can effectively and appropriately be prevented, diagnosed, treated, monitored, and managed through research and evidence synthesis that considers variations in patient subpopulations, and the dissemination of research findings with respect to the relative health outcomes, clinical effectiveness, and appropriateness of the medical treatments, services, and other items.

For a full list of federal programs, see National Information Center on Health Services Research and Health Technology (NICHSR), Comparative Effectiveness Research.

C. THE PROBLEM OF MEDICAL ERROR

1. Adverse Events: Definition and Scope

Injury caused by doctors and health care institutions, or iatrogenesis, is the inverse of quality medicine. The literature on adverse events is growing rapidly as the patient safety movement begins to permeate federal health policies. What is an adverse event?

The U.S. Agency for Healthcare Research and Quality (AHRQ) defines an adverse event as "Any negative or unwanted effect from any drug, device, or medical test." AHRQ cites the following examples of adverse events: "pneumothorax from central venous catheter placement," "anaphylaxis to penicillin," "postoperative wound infection," and "hospital-acquired delirium (or 'sundowning') in elderly patients."

The law has historically focused on physician "error." Until recently, malpractice cases were brought against the treating physician and not his institution because of a variety of legal rules that shielded the hospital. State licensing boards brought disciplinary actions against the individual errant doctor. Staff privileges cases involved the individual doctor's qualifications. The narrow focus on individual error facilitated a clear definition of "bad medicine." Bad medicine was what bad doctors did. The "bad apples" were doctors whose incompetence was obvious.

The larger problem of quality in medical care must also address systemic failures, poor administrative design for review of health care, inadequacies in training of physicians, and the nature of practice incentives. The concept of "error" often misses the point of quality improvement, which requires a look at many other facets of health care delivery.

2. The Extent of Medical Misadventures

PATIENTS, DOCTORS, AND LAWYERS: MEDICAL INJURY, MALPRACTICE LITIGATION, AND PATIENT COMPENSATION IN NEW YORK

The Report of the Harvard Medical Practice.
Study to the State of New York (1990).

[The Harvard Medical Practice Study in New York looked at the incidence of injuries resulting from medical interventions (adverse events) beginning with a sample of more than 31,000 New York hospital records drawn from the study year 1984. The review was conducted by medical record administrators and nurses in the screening phase, and by board certified physicians for the physician-review phase.]

*   *   *

We analyzed 30,121 (96%) of the 31,429 records selected for the study sample. After preliminary screening, physicians reviewed 7,743 records from which a total of 1,133 adverse events were identified that occurred as a result of medical management in the hospital or required hospitalization for treatment. Of this group, 280 were judged to result from negligent care. Weighting these figures according to the sample plan, we estimated the incidence of adverse events for hospitalizations in New York in 1984 to be 3.7%, or a total of 98,609. Of these, 27.6%, 27,179 cases, or 1.0% of all hospital discharges, were due to negligence.

*   *   *

The Nature of Adverse Events

Nearly half (47%) of all adverse events occurred in patients undergoing surgery, but the percent caused by negligence was lower than for non-surgical adverse events (17% vs 37%). Adverse events resulting from errors in diagnosis and in non-invasive treatment were judged to be due to negligence in over three-fourths of patients. Falls were considered due to negligence in 45% of instances.

The high rate of adverse events in patients over 65 years occurred in three categories: non-technical postoperative complications, complications of non-invasive therapy, and falls. A larger proportion of adverse events in younger patients was due to surgical failures. The operating room was the site of management for the highest fraction of adverse events, but relatively few of these were negligent. On the other hand, most (70%) adverse events in the emergency room resulted from negligence.

The most common type of error resulting in an adverse event was that involved in performing a procedure, but diagnostic errors and prevention errors were more likely to be judged negligent, and to result in serious disability.

The more severe the degree of negligence the greater the likelihood of resultant serious disability (moderate impairment with recovery taking more than six months), permanent disability, or death).

Litigation data

We estimated that the incidence of malpractice claims filed by patients for the study year was between 2,967 and 3,888. Using these figures, together with the projected statewide number of injuries from medical negligence during the same period, we estimated that eight times as many patients suffered an injury from negligence as filed a malpractice claim in New York State. About 16 times as many patients suffered an injury from negligence as received compensation from the tort liability system.

*   *   *

NOTES AND QUESTIONS

1.   The Harvard Study was designed to produce empirical data to better inform the debate about reform of the tort system, including no-fault reforms. Do the findings of the study, as to level of patient injury attributable to medical error, surprise you? The Study is generally acknowledged as one of

the first to take an epidemiological approach to medical errors. It has also been criticized on a number of grounds. See generally Tom Baker, Reconsidering the Harvard Medical Practice Study Conclusions about the Validity of Medical Malpractice Claims, 33 J. L., Med. & Ethics 501 (2005). The IOM Report extrapolated from the Harvard Study to predict almost 100,000 patient deaths annually due to medical errors. IOM Report 26–27.

2.   More recent studies have confirmed that adverse events occur at even higher levels than previously thought. The Office of the Inspector General found that 13.5% of Medicare hospital admissions suffered an adverse event, with an equal percentage experiencing temporary harm. U.S. Dep't of Health & Human Servs., Office of Inspector Gen., Adverse Events in Hospitals: National Incidence Among Medicare Beneficiaries, at i-ii (2010). Another study, using newer methodologies for discovering adverse events, concluded that patients suffer adverse events in one-third of all admissions. David C. Classen et al., 'Global Trigger Tool' Shows that Adverse Events in Hospitals May Be Ten Times Greater than Previously Measured, 30 Health Affairs 581, 581 (2011).

3.   While the Harvard data were based on hospital records, studies analyzing the actual incidence of negligent events in hospital wards found that many injuries were not reported in hospital records as required—especially when the main person responsible for the error was a senior physician. Lori Andrews, Studying Medical Error In Situ: Implications for Malpractice Law and Policy, 54 DePaul L. Rev. 357 (2005).

4.   Most malpractice claims do involve medical errors, and those claims that lack evidence of error are usually denied compensation. David M. Studdert et al., Claims, Errors, and Compensation Payments in Medical Malpractice Litigation, 354 N.E.J.M. 2024 (2006).

5.   Errors in office-based surgery are a significant problem, as surgical procedures have migrated from hospitals to surgicenters and physician offices. One study of surgical procedures performed in doctors' offices and ambulatory surgery centers in Florida found that there was a 10–fold increased risk of adverse events and death in the office setting. See Hector Vila, et al., Comparative Outcomes Analysis of Procedures Performed in Physician Offices and Ambulatory Surgery Centers, 138 Arch.Surg. 991 (2003).

D. THE PATIENT SAFETY MOVEMENT

LUCIAN L. LEAPE, ERROR IN MEDICINE
272 JAMA 1851 (1994).

* * *

Why Is the Error Rate in the Practice of Medicine So High?

Physicians, nurses, and pharmacists are trained to be careful and to function at a high level of proficiency. Indeed, they probably are among the most careful professionals in our society. It is curious, therefore, that high error rates have not stimulated more concern and efforts at error prevention. One reason may be a lack of awareness of the severity of the problem. Hospital-acquired injuries are not reported in the newspapers like jumbo-jet crashes, for the simple reason that they occur one at a time in 5000 different locations across the country. Although error rates are substantial, serious injuries due to errors are not part of the everyday experience of physicians or nurses, but are perceived as isolated and unusual events—"outliers." Second, most errors do no harm. Either they are intercepted or the patient's defenses prevent injury. (Few children die from a single misdiagnosed or mistreated urinary infection, for example.)

But the most important reason physicians and nurses have not developed more effective methods of error prevention is that they have a great deal of difficulty in dealing with human error when it does occur. The reasons are to be found in the culture of medical practice.

Physicians are socialized in medical school and residency to strive for error-free practice. There is a powerful emphasis on perfection, both in diagnosis and treatment. In everyday hospital practice, the message is equally clear: mistakes are unacceptable. Physicians are expected to function without error, an expectation that physicians translate into the need to be infallible. One result is that physicians, not unlike test pilots, come to view an error as a failure of character—you weren't careful enough, you didn't try hard enough. This kind of thinking lies behind a common reaction by physicians: "How can there be an error without negligence?"

* * *

Role models in medical education reinforce the concept of infallibility. The young physician's teachers are largely specialists, experts in their fields, and authorities. Authorities are not supposed to err. It has been suggested that this need to be infallible creates a strong pressure to intellectual dishonesty, to cover up mistakes rather than to admit them. The organization of medical practice, particularly in the hospital, perpetuates these norms. Errors are rarely admitted or discussed among physicians in private practice. Physicians typically feel, not without reason, that admission of error will lead to censure or increased surveillance or, worse, that their colleagues will regard them as incompetent or careless. Far better to conceal a mistake or, if that is impossible, to try to shift the blame to another, even the patient.

Yet physicians are emotionally devastated by serious mistakes that harm or kill patients. Almost every physician who cares for patients has had that experience, usually more than once. The emotional impact is often profound, typically a mixture of fear, guilt, anger, embarrassment, and humiliation. Thus, although the individual may learn from a mistake and change practice patterns accordingly, the adjustment often takes place in a vacuum. Lessons learned are shared privately, if at all, and external objective evaluation of what went wrong often does not occur. * * * Finally, the realities of the malpractice threat provide strong incentives against disclosure or investigation of mistakes. Even a minor error can place the physician's entire career in jeopardy if it results in a serious bad outcome. It is hardly surprising that a physician might hesitate to reveal an error to either the patient or hospital authorities or to expose a colleague to similar devastation for a single mistake.

The paradox is that although the standard of medical practice is perfection—error-free patient care—all physicians recognize that mistakes are inevitable. Most would like to examine their mistakes and learn from them. From an emotional standpoint, they need the support and understanding of their colleagues and patients when they make mistakes. Yet, they are denied both insight and support by misguided concepts of infallibility and by fear: fear of embarrassment by colleagues, fear of patient reaction, and fear of litigation. Although the notion of infallibility fails the reality test, the fears are well grounded.

The Medical Approach to Error Prevention

Efforts at error prevention in medicine have characteristically followed what might be called the perfectibility model: if physicians and nurses could be properly trained and motivated, then they would make no mistakes. The methods used to achieve this goal are training and punishment. Training is directed toward teaching people to do the right thing. In nursing, rigid adherence to protocols is emphasized. In medicine, the emphasis is less on rules and more on knowledge.

Punishment is through social opprobrium or peer disapproval. The professional cultures of medicine and nursing typically use blame to encourage proper performance. Errors are regarded as someone's fault, caused by a lack of sufficient attention or, worse, lack of caring enough to make sure you are correct. Punishment for egregious (negligent) errors is primarily (and capriciously) meted out through the malpractice tort litigation system.

Students of error and human performance reject this formulation. While the proximal error leading to an accident is, in fact, usually a 'human error,' the causes of that error are often well beyond the individual's control. All humans err frequently. Systems that rely on error-free performance are doomed to fail.

The medical approach to error prevention is also reactive. Errors are usually discovered only when there is an incident—an untoward effect or injury to the patient. Corrective measures are then directed toward preventing a recurrence of a similar error, often by attempting to prevent that individual from making a repeat error. Seldom are underlying causes explored.

* * *

It seems clear, and it is the thesis of this article, that if physicians, nurses, pharmacists, and administrators are to succeed in reducing errors in hospital care, they will need to fundamentally change the way they think about errors and why they occur. Fortunately, a great deal has been learned about error prevention in other disciplines, information that is relevant to the hospital practice of medicine.

* * *

Prevention of Accidents

* * *

The primary objective of system design for safety is to make it difficult for individuals to err. But it is also important to recognize that errors will inevitably occur and plan for their recovery. Ideally, the system will automatically correct errors when they occur. If that is impossible, mechanisms should be in place to at least detect errors in time for corrective action. Therefore, in addition to designing the work environment to minimize psychological precursors, designers should provide feedback through instruments that provide monitoring functions and build in buffers and redundancy. Buffers are design features that automatically correct for human or mechanical errors. Redundancy is duplication (sometimes triplication or quadruplication) of critical mechanisms and instruments, so that a failure does not result in loss of the function.

Another important system design feature is designing tasks to minimize errors. Norman has recommended a set of principles that have general applicability. Tasks should be simplified to minimize the load on the weakest aspects of cognition: short-term memory, planning, and problem solving. The power of constraints should be exploited. One way to do this is with "forcing functions," which make it impossible to act without meeting a precondition (such as the inability to release the parking gear of a car unless the brake pedal is depressed). Standardization of procedures, displays, and layouts reduces error by reinforcing the pattern recognition that humans do well. Finally, where possible, operations should be easily reversible or difficult to perform when they are not reversible.

Training must include, in addition to the usual emphasis on application of knowledge and following procedures, a consideration of safety issues. These issues include understanding the rationale for procedures as well as how errors can occur at various stages, their possible consequences, and instruction in methods for avoidance of errors. Finally, it must be acknowledged that injuries can result from behavioral problems that may be seen in impaired physicians or incompetent physicians despite well-designed systems; methods for identifying and correcting egregious behaviors are also needed.

The Aviation Model

The practice of hospital medicine has been compared, usually unfavorably, to the aviation industry, also a highly complicated and risky enterprise but one that seems far safer. Indeed, there seem to be many similarities. As Allnutt observed,

> Both pilots and doctors are carefully selected, highly trained professionals who are usually determined to maintain high standards, both externally and internally imposed, whilst performing difficult tasks in life-threatening environments. Both use high technology equipment and function as key members of a team of specialists . . . both exercise high level cognitive skills in a most complex domain about which much is known, but where much remains to be discovered.

While the comparison is apt, there are also important differences between aviation and medicine, not the least of which is a substantial measure of uncertainty due to the number and variety of disease states, as well as the unpredictability of the human organism. Nonetheless, there is much physicians and nurses could learn from aviation.

*　*　*

There are strong incentives for making flying safe. Pilots, of course, are highly motivated. Unlike physicians, their lives are on the line as well as those of their passengers. But, airlines and airplane manufacturers also have strong incentives to provide safe flight. Business decreases after a large crash, and if a certain model of aircraft crashes repeatedly, the manufacturer will be discredited. The lawsuits that inevitably follow a crash can harm both reputation and profitability.

Designing for safety has led to a number of unique characteristics of aviation that could, with suitable modification, prove useful in improving hospital safety.

First, in terms of system design, aircraft designers assume that errors and failures are inevitable and design systems to "absorb" them, building in multiple buffers, automation, and redundancy. * * *

Second, procedures are standardized to the maximum extent possible. Specific protocols must be followed for trip planning, operations, and maintenance. Pilots go through a checklist before each takeoff. Required maintenance is specified in detail and must be performed on a regular (by flight hours) basis.

Third, the training, examination, and certification process is highly developed and rigidly, as well as frequently, enforced. Airline pilots take proficiency examinations every 6 months. Much of the content of examinations is directly concerned with procedures to enhance safety.

Pilots function well within this rigorously controlled system, although not flawlessly. For example, one study of cockpit crews observed that human errors or instrument malfunctions occurred on the average of one every 4 minutes during an overseas flight. Each event was promptly recognized and corrected with no untoward effects. Pilots also willingly submit to an external authority, the air traffic controller, when within the constrained air and ground space at a busy airport.

Finally, safety in aviation has been institutionalized. * * *. The FAA recognized long ago that pilots seldom reported an error if it led to disciplinary action. Accordingly, in 1975 the FAA established a confidential reporting system for safety infractions, the Air Safety Reporting System (ASRS). If pilots, controllers, or others promptly report a dangerous situation, such as a near-miss midair collision, they will not be penalized. This program dramatically increased reporting, so that unsafe conditions at airports, communication problems, and traffic control inadequacies are now promptly communicated. Analysis of these reports and subsequent investigations appear as a regular feature in several pilots' magazines. The ASRS receives more than 5000 notifications each year.

The Medical Model

By contrast, accident prevention has not been a primary focus of the practice of hospital medicine. It is not that errors are ignored. Mortality and morbidity conferences, incident reports, risk management activities, and quality assurance committees abound. But, as noted previously, these activities focus on incidents and individuals. When errors are examined, a problem-solving approach is usually used: the cause of the error is identified and corrected. Root causes, the underlying systems failures, are rarely sought. System designers do not assume that errors and failures are inevitable and design systems to prevent or absorb them. There are, of course, exceptions. Implementation of unit dosing, for example, markedly reduced medication dosing errors by eliminating the need for the nurse to measure out each dose. * * *.

Second, standardization and task design vary widely. In the operating room, it has been refined to a high art. In patient care units, much more could be done, particularly to minimize reliance on short-term memory, o ne of the weakest aspects of cognition. On-time and correct delivery of medications, for example, is often contingent on a busy nurse remembering to do so, a nurse who is responsible for four or five patients at once and is repeatedly interrupted, a classic set up for a "loss-of-activation" error.

On the other hand, education and training in medicine and nursing far exceed that in aviation, both in breadth of content and in duration, and few professions compare with medicine in terms of the extent of continuing education. Although certification is essentially universal, including the recent introduction of periodic recertification, the idea of periodically testing performance has never been accepted. Thus, we place great emphasis on education and training, but shy away from demonstrating that it makes a difference.

Finally, unlike aviation, safety in medicine has never been institutionalized, in the sense of being a major focus of hospital medical activities. Investigation of accidents is often superficial, unless a malpractice action is likely; noninjurious error (a "near miss") is rarely examined at all. Incident reports are frequently perceived as punitive instruments. As a result, they are often not filed, and when they are, they almost invariably focus on the individual's misconduct.

One medical model is an exception and has proved quite successful in reducing accidents due to errors: anesthesia. Perhaps in part because the effects of serious anesthetic errors are potentially so dramatic—death or brain damage—and perhaps in part because the errors are frequently transparently clear and knowable to all, anesthesiologists have greatly emphasized safety. The success of these efforts has been dramatic. Whereas mortality from anesthesia was one in 10,000 to 20,000 just a decade or so ago, it is now estimated at less than one in 200,000. Anesthesiologists have led the medical profession in recognizing system factors as causes of errors, in designing fail-safe systems, and in training to avoid errors.

Systems Changes to Reduce Hospital Injuries

Can the lessons from cognitive psychology and human factors research that have been successful in accident prevention in aviation and other industries be applied to the practice of hospital medicine? There is every reason to think they could be. Hospitals, physicians, nurses, and pharmacists who wish to reduce errors could start by considering how cognition and error mechanisms apply to the practice of hospital medicine. Specifically, they can examine their care delivery systems in terms of the systems' ability to discover, prevent, and absorb errors and for the presence of psychological precursors.

Discovery of Errors

The first step in error prevention is to define the problem. Efficient, routine identification of errors needs to be part of hospital practice, as does routine investigation of all errors that cause injuries. The emphasis is on "routine." Only when errors are accepted as an inevitable, although manageable, part of everyday practice will it be possible for hospital personnel to shift from a punitive to a creative frame of mind that seeks out and identifies the underlying system failures.

Data collecting and investigatory activities are expensive, but so are the consequences of errors. Evidence from industry indicates that the savings from reduction of errors and accidents more than make up for the costs of data collection and investigation. * * *.

Prevention of Errors

Many health care delivery systems could be redesigned to significantly reduce the likelihood of error. Some obvious mechanisms that can be used are as follows:

Reduced Reliance on Memory.—Work should be designed to minimize the requirements for human functions that are known to be particularly fallible, such as short-term memory and vigilance (prolonged attention). * * * Checklists, protocols, and computerized decision aids could be used more widely. * * *.

Improved Information Access.—Creative ways need to be developed for making information more readily available: displaying it where it is needed, when it is needed, and in a form that permits easy access. Computerization of the medical record, for example, would greatly facilitate bedside display of patient information, including tests and medications.

Error Proofing.—Where possible, critical tasks should be structured so that errors cannot be made. The use of "forcing functions" is helpful. For example, if a computerized system is used for medication orders, it can be designed so that a physician cannot enter an order for a lethal overdose of a drug or prescribe a medication to which a patient is known to be allergic.

Standardization.—One of the most effective means of reducing error is standardizing processes wherever possible. The advantages, in efficiency as well as in error reduction, of standardizing drug doses and times of administration are obvious. * * * Training.—Instruction of physicians, nurses, and pharmacists in procedures or problem solving should include greater emphasis on possible errors and how to prevent them. * * *.

Absorption of Errors

Because it is impossible to prevent all error, buffers should be built into each system so that errors are absorbed before they can cause harm to patients. At minimum, systems should be designed so that errors can be identified in time to be intercepted. The drug delivery systems in most hospitals do this to some degree already. Nurses and pharmacists often identify errors in physician drug orders and prevent improper administration to the patient. As hospitals move to computerized records and ordering systems, more of these types of interceptions can be incorporated into the computer programs. * * *.

Psychological Precursors

Finally, explicit attention should be given to work schedules, division of responsibilities, task descriptions, and other details of working arrangements where improper managerial decisions can produce psychological precursors such as time pressures and fatigue that create an unsafe environment. While the influence of the stresses of everyday life on human behavior cannot be eliminated, stresses caused by a faulty work environment can be. Elimination of fear and the creation of a supportive working environment are other potent means of preventing errors.

Institutionalization of Safety

Although the idea of a national hospital safety board that would investigate every accident is neither practical nor necessary, at the hospital level such activities should occur. Existing hospital risk management activities could be broadened to include all potentially injurious errors and deepened to seek out underlying system failures. Providing immunity, as in the FAA ASRS system, might be a good first step. At the national level, the Joint Commission on Accreditation of Healthcare Organizations should be involved in discussions regarding the institutionalization of safety. Other specialty societies might well follow the lead of the anesthesiologists in developing safety standards and require their instruction to be part of residency training.

Leape's analysis laid the foundation for a new federal focus on patient safety, which was launched in 1999 by the first in a series of Institute of Medicine publications dealing with medical errors.

To Err Is Human: Building a Safer Health System
Institute of Medicine, 2000.

Executive Summary

* * *

When extrapolated to the over 33.6 million admissions to U.S. hospitals in 1997, the results of the study in Colorado and Utah imply that at least 44,000 Americans die each year as a result of medical errors. The results of the New York Study suggest the number may be as high as 98,000. Even when using the lower estimate, deaths due to medical errors exceed the number attributable to the 8th leading cause of death. More people die in a given year as result of medical errors than from motor vehicle accidents (43,458), breast cancer (42,297), or AIDS (16,516).

Total national costs (lost income, lost household production, disability and health care costs) of preventable adverse events (medical errors resulting in injury) are estimated to be between $17 billion and $29 billion, of which health care costs represent over one half.

In terms of lives lost, patient safety is as important an issue as worker safety. Every year, over 6,000 Americans die from workplace injuries. Medication errors alone, occurring either in or out of the hospital, are estimated to account for over 7,000 deaths annually.

Medication-related errors occur frequently in hospitals and although not all result in actual harm, those that do, are costly. One recent study conducted at two prestigious teaching hospitals, found that about two out of every 100 admissions experienced a preventable adverse drug event, resulting in average increased hospital costs of $4,700 per admission or about $2.8 million annually for a 700 bed teach hospital. If these findings are generalizable, the increased hospital costs alone of preventable adverse drug events affecting inpatients are about $2 billion for the nation as a whole.

* * *

Errors are also costly in terms of opportunity costs. Dollars spent on having to repeat diagnostic tests or counteract adverse drug events are dollars unavailable for other purposes. Purchasers and patients pay for errors when insurance costs and copayments are inflated by services that would not have been necessary had proper care been provided. It is impossible for the nation to achieve the greatest value possible from the hundreds of millions of dollars spent on medical care if the care contains errors.

But not all the costs can be directly measured. Errors are also costly in terms of loss of trust in the system by patients and diminished satisfaction by both patients and health professionals. Patients who experienced a longer hospital stay or disability as a result of errors pay with physical and psychological discomfort. Health care professionals pay with loss of morale and frustration at not being able to provide the best care possible. Employers and society, in general, pay in terms of lost worker productivity, reduced school attendance by children, and lower levels of population health status.

* * *

In this report, safety is defined as freedom from accidental injury. This definition recognizes that this is the primary safety goal from the patient's perspective. Error is defined as the failure of a planned action to be completed as intended or the use of a wrong plan to achieve an aim. According to noted expert James Reason, errors depend on two kinds of failures: either the correct action does not proceed as intended (an error of execution) or the original intended action is not correct (an error of planning). Errors can happen in all stages in the process of care, from diagnosis, to treatment, to preventive care.

Not all errors result in harm. Errors that do result in injury are sometimes called preventable adverse events. An adverse event is an injury resulting from a medical intervention, or in other words, it is not due to the underlying condition of the patient. While all adverse events result from medical management, not all are preventable (i.e., not all are attributable to errors). For example, if a patient has surgery and dies from pneumonia he or she got postoperatively, it is an adverse event. If analysis of the case reveals that the patient got pneumonia because of poor hand washing or instrument cleaning techniques by staff, the adverse event was preventable (attributable to an error of execution). But the analysis may conclude that no error occurred and the patient would be presumed to have had a difficult surgery and recovery (not a preventable adverse event).

* * *

Recommendations

* * *

The recommendations contained in this report lay out a four-tiered approach:

- establishing a national focus to create leadership, research, tools and protocols to enhance the knowledge base about safety;
- identifying and learning from errors through immediate and strong mandatory reporting efforts, as well as the encouragement of voluntary efforts, both with the aim of making sure the system continues to be made safer for patients;
- raising standards and expectations for improvements in safety through the actions of oversight organizations, group purchasers, and professional groups; and
- creating safety systems inside health care organizations through the implementation of safe practices at the delivery level. This level is the ultimate target of all the recommendations.

NOTES AND QUESTIONS

1.   The IOM Report on error in medicine caused an upheaval in health care. It was, in the words of one commentator, " * * * the single most important spur to the development of patient safety, catapulting it into public and political awareness and galvanizing political and professional will at the highest levels in the United States." Charles Vincent, Patient Safety 25 (Wiley–Blackwell, 2d ed. 2010) (2006). See Lucian L. Leape and Donald M. Berwick, Five Years After To Err Is Human: What Have We Learned? 293 JAMA 2384 (2005).

2.   The Report turned a critical eye on health care systems as a primary source of many adverse events. What are the implications of a focus on system errors? Does the physician as a virtuoso disappear from the model of the health care system as we move toward a model of organizations that that deliver care, rather than physicians that treat patients? Do we care if we reduce the level of patient injuries from adverse events to a significantly lower level?

PROBLEM: WHY OPERATE?

Bonnie Bowser, eighty-two years old, fell and severely injured her elbow. She was examined at the Emergency Department of the Miraculous Regional Health System and diagnosed with a fractured olecranon process, and referred to an orthopedic surgeon. The surgeon who examined Mrs. Bowser scheduled her for corrective surgery the next day. He noted in his examination that she had a past medical history of hypertension, diabetes mellitus, two myocardial infarctions with quadruple bypass surgery, and a cerebrovascular accident affecting her left side. She was taking several medications including Lasix (a diuretic), Vasotec (for treatment of hypertension and symptomatic congestive heart failure), Klotrix (potassium supplement), and Glyburide (for the treatment of hyperglycemia related to diabetes). He noted that she smoked an average of one pack of cigarettes per day; that she had abnormal chest x-rays, suggesting congestive heart failure; an EKG that indicated ischemic heart disease; and signs of edema, indicating congestive heart failure. She was a high risk candidate for any kind of surgery. After the anesthesia was administered, she deteriorated rapidly, had cardiopulmonary failure and stroke, and died a few days later from complications of the stroke. The anesthesia was the cause of her death, as she was severely "medically compromised" and an elbow operation did not justify the obvious risks. Bonnie had consented to the operation. Her health insurance paid for the procedure. The hospital allowed the operation to proceed.

What do you propose to reduce this kind of risk to patients, as Vice–President and General Counsel of the System?

What system-wide rules will you propose to avoid a repetition of such cases, as the head of your state's Department of Health?

As a congressman from your state, what legislation might you propose?

For a general overview of the patient safety provisions of the ACA, and programs that now operate in tandem with the Act, see generally Barry R. Furrow, Regulating Patient Safety: The Patient Protection and Affordable Care Act, 159 U. Pa. L. Rev. 101 (2011).

E. REGULATING TO REDUCE MEDICAL ADVERSE EVENTS

1. Patient Safety and the Affordable Care Act

The ACA has a variety of provisions aimed at improving the quality of the U.S. health care system, reducing errors, and generally promoting patient safety. These provisions include new centers, demonstration projects, and funding awards for a wide range of quality improvement projects.

Patient safety strategies can be summed up in six major regulatory categories:

(1) *Standardizing Good Medical Practices.* The ACA aims to reduce medical practice variation by promoting best practices, practice guidelines, and research on what works, as noted above.

(2) *Tracking Adverse Events in Hospitals.* Policies mandating adverse event data as to infections, readmissions, and other adverse events are coming online, since both health care providers and regulators need data in order to select the most serious problem areas for repair.

(3) *Disclosing Provider Performance.* Disclosure of adverse events can occur at three levels: (a) induced disclosure of hospital adverse events and "near misses" to state regulators and quasi-regulators like the Joint Commission; (b) disclosure by the provider of adverse events to patients; and (c) publication of performance data about relative risks by private/public agents, designed for purchaser use.

(4) *Reforming Payment Systems.* These strategies include creating a range of financial incentives for providers to promote safety, through "pay for performance" initiatives, including bonuses and docking reimbursement for failures to meet minimum standards as well as using insurance exchanges to promote quality and safety improvements. (b) disclosure by the provider of adverse events to patients; and (c) publication of performance data about relative risks by private/public agents, designed for purchaser use.

(5*) Coordinating and Integrating Care.* This strategy is the largest and most innovative category of federal health care reform, which promotes several new models for integrating health care delivery in the fragmented U.S. system.

6) *Expanding Provider Responsibility.* This strategy includes implementing legislative requirements for disclosure, such as the requirement of "decision aids" in the ACA, changing tort liability rules through new doctrines, expanding damage remedies, and developing alternative dispute resolution approaches that focus on health care organizations as systems.

2.   Error Tracking and System Improvements

The Institute of Medicine reports, beginning with To Err Is Human, focused attention on medical systems and the level of errors they produced. Hospitals and other providers were asked to respond by developing error tracking systems and strategies for improvement including disclosure of both errors and so-called "near misses," events that could have resulted in patient injury but were detected in time.

a. Sentinel Events and the Joint Commission

The Joint Commission is a private accreditor, granted authority by federal and state governments to accredit hospitals. See Chapter 2, *supra*. The Joint Commission Sentinel Event Policy has adopted the view of medical errors of the Institute of Medicine report To Err is Human.

SENTINEL EVENT POLICY AND PROCEDURES
December 6, 2012.

In support of its mission to continuously improve the safety and quality of health care provided to the public, the Joint Commission reviews organizations' activities in response to sentinel events in its accreditation process, including all full accreditation surveys and random unannounced surveys and, as appropriate, for-cause surveys.

- A sentinel event is an unexpected occurrence involving death or serious physical or psychological injury, or the risk thereof. Serious injury specifically includes loss of limb or function. The phrase "or the risk thereof" includes any process variation for which a recurrence would carry a significant chance of a serious adverse outcome.

- Such events are called "sentinel" because they signal the need for immediate investigation and response.

- The terms "sentinel event" and "medical error" are not synonymous; not all sentinel events occur because of an error and not all errors result in sentinel events.

NOTES AND QUESTIONS

1.   Hospitals may report serious events to the Joint Commission, and if they do not and the Joint Commission learns of the events from a third party, the hospital must conduct an analysis of the root cause or risk loss of accreditation. Loss of accreditation is rarely exercised, however.

2.   The Joint Commission is a private accreditation organization, and its primary weapon for hospital improvement is the threat that accreditation will be revoked, or the hospital placed on the "Accreditation Watch List". Given the infrequency of revocation of hospital accreditation, how does the Joint Commission have a significant effect on hospital behavior? It does not mandate the reporting of its serious adverse events to the Joint Commission, although it does mandate a "root cause analysis" and will check during accreditation inspections to make sure that such analyses have been done.

b. Reporting Hospital Adverse Events: Hospital Acquired Conditions and "Never Events"

The regulatory response to the 1999 Institute of Medicine study—identifying medical errors as a leading cause of illness and death in the United States—branched in several directions. Given the complexity of our state-federal system, and the mix of private accreditation and standard-setting bodies, as well as the rapid maturation of the Center for Medicare & Medicaid Services (CMS) as a quality regulator, adverse event regulation took several steps.

First, the National Quality Forum ("NQF"), a not-for-profit organization "created to develop and implement a national strategy for health care quality measurement and reporting," identified 28 serious preventable conditions, including events such as wrong-site and wrong-patient surgeries, foreign object retention post surgery, and discharge of an infant to the wrong person. These were initially termed "never events," and later renamed "serious reportable events".

Second, state regulators saw the value of the list of adverse events, given the recognized impartiality of the NQF and the obvious nature of the harms described by "never events." Twenty odd states created their own reporting systems based on the events. This was a major regulatory step forward, forcing hospitals to disclose adverse outcomes on the list to the state department responsible, with the goal of improving their operations. Such reporting allows for systematic recording and tracking of errors, for purpose of analysis of patterns of adverse events, feedback to hospitals, and in some states, information for consumers as to the relative performance of hospitals and other providers.

Minnesota was the first state to adopt the approach in 2003, now calling these conditions "serious adverse health events", requiring hospitals and now ambulatory surgical centers, to report whenever a serious adverse health event occurs and to conduct a thorough analysis of the reasons for the event. See Adverse Health Events in Minnesota, Ninth Annual Public Report, January 2013.

Third, large businesses wanted quality metrics to use in reducing the costs of employee health care plans and in improving the quality of that care. The Leapfrog Group, a group of private companies that purchased health care for their employees, saw the Never Events list as a first step toward specific quality improvement based on clear adverse events. The Leapfrog Group was created for the purpose of focusing on health care quality improvement and affordability, and many private insurers have used this list in an attempt to improve quality and health care affordability. By late 2006, The Leapfrog Group developed a policy for hospitals to handle Never Events that some hospitals have adopted. The Leapfrog policy required issuing an apology to the patient and family involved in the event, reporting the event to an accrediting agency such as the Joint Commission, performing a root cause analysis per the accrediting agency's instruction, and waiving all costs directly related to the event.

NOTES AND QUESTIONS

Consider the nature of the regulatory incentives described above. Does a reporting obligation change hospital corporate behavior? There are no sanctions involved—no penalties, either civil or criminal; no obvious financial impact. Why would a hospital report honestly its full range of adverse events when there is little risk in not doing so? What about the Leapfrog approach? If corporate purchasers adopt the adverse event approach, what can they do to get health care providers that serve their employees to do? What incentives can such parties offer and what penalties can they impose?

3. Federal Reimbursement Strategies

The federal government began to rethink its approach to reimbursing adverse events under the federal Medicare program, with the Deficit Reduction Act of 2005 (DRA) the first step in a new regulatory approach. The DRA requires the Secretary of the U.S. Department of Health and Human Services (DHHS) to identify at least two reasonably preventable high-cost conditions that result in higher payment when they occur in a patient as a secondary diagnosis. The Act anticipated that identifying such conditions would promote both efficiency and quality in patient care.

When the Centers for Medicare & Medicaid Services (CMS) issued a Final Rule in 2007, it excluded payment for several hospital-acquired conditions (HACs) if these conditions occurred during a Medicare beneficiary's inpatient stay. The CMS Final Rule for the 2009 Inpatient Prospective Payment System (IPPS) then expanded the exclusions for HACs. These actions clearly reflected the earlier initiatives of both NQF and Leapfrog. This regulatory approach used Medicare reimbursement to force these hospitals to internalize the costs of certain Never Events or hospital-acquired conditions (HACs)—conditions that were high volume, involved higher payment, and could be easily prevented. This was a significant change in regulatory incentives for hospitals receiving Medicare payments. These hospital-acquired conditions are no longer reimbursed at the normal rate for the costs of treatment, as they are presumptively preventable patient charges.

For a useful history of the origins of the federal policy involving hospital-acquired conditions, see CMS Rules for Hospital–Acquired Conditions Pose Challenges and Opportunities, The Q. J. for Health Care Practice & Risk Man. 13 (Fall 2010).

Another example of a regulatory reimbursement strategy has been the Hospital Readmission Reduction Program, created by section 3025 of the ACA. This program ties excess readmissions to a reduction in Medicare payments that would otherwise be made to that hospital. Information on all patient readmission rates are made available on the CMS Hospital Compare website.

4. Disclosure of Errors to Patients

Adverse event reporting is often coupled with disclosure of bad outcomes to patients and their families. This disclosure idea developed as the result of a program begun by a Veterans Administration hospital, and has been adopted by the VA system.

DISCLOSURE OF ADVERSE EVENTS TO PATIENTS
October 2, 2012 VHA HANDBOOK 1004.08.

*   *   *

3. Definitions.

*   *   *

d. Disclosure of Adverse Events * * * refers to the forthright and empathetic discussion of clinically-significant facts between providers or other VHA personnel and patients or their personal representatives about the occurrence of a harmful adverse event, or an adverse event that could result in harm in the foreseeable future. VA recognizes three types of adverse event disclosure. * * *

(1) Clinical Disclosure of Adverse Events. Clinical disclosure of adverse events is a process by which the patient's clinician informs the patient or the patient's personal representative, as part of routine clinical care, that a harmful or potentially harmful adverse event has occurred during the patient's care. * * *.

(2) Institutional Disclosure of Adverse Events. Institutional disclosure of adverse events (sometimes referred to as "administrative disclosure") is a formal process by which facility leader(s) together with clinicians and others, as appropriate, inform the patient or the patient's personal representative that an adverse event has occurred during the pa-

tient's care that resulted in, or is reasonably expected to result in, death or serious injury, and provide specific information about the patient's rights and recourse.

*   *   *

5.   Adverse Events That Warrant Disclosure

a.   Disclosure is warranted for harmful or potentially-harmful adverse events, defined broadly to include:

(1) Adverse events that cause death or disability, lead to prolonged hospitalization, require life-sustaining intervention or intervention to prevent impairment or damage (or that are reasonably expected to result in death or serious and/or permanent disability), or that are "sentinel events" as defined by [the Joint Commission].

(2) Adverse events that have had, or are reasonably expected to have, an effect on the patient that is perceptible to either the patient or the health care team. For example, if a patient is mistakenly given a dose of a diuretic (a medication that dramatically increases urine output), disclosure is required because a perceptible effect has, or is anticipated to occur.

(3) Adverse events that precipitate a change in the patient's care. For example, a medication error that necessitates extra blood tests, extra hospital days, or follow-up visits that would otherwise not be required, or a surgical procedure that necessitates further (corrective) surgery.

(4) Adverse events with a clinically-significant risk of serious future health consequences to patients, even if the likelihood of that risk is small. For example, a known, accidental exposure of a patient to "ionizing radiation," "a toxin," "an organism," or "infectious entity" associated with a rare, but recognized serious short-term or long-term effect (e.g., blood borne pathogen infection or increased incidence of cancer). * * *

(5) Any event that requires an unexpected treatment or procedure to be initiated without the patient's consent (e.g., if an event occurs while a patient is under anesthesia, necessitating a deviation from the procedure the patient expected). Patients have a fundamental right to be informed about what is done to them and why.

b.   Where adverse events occur that have a potential to affect, or may have already affected multiple patients at one or more VHA facilities, the process for large-scale disclosure must be followed * * *.

*   *   *

6.   Communicating Adverse Events

a.   The process for disclosing an adverse event depends on the nature and circumstances of the event. VA recognizes three types of adverse event disclosure: clinical disclosure of adverse events, institutional disclosure of adverse events, and large-scale disclosure of adverse events.

b.   The process of adverse event disclosure is not necessarily a singular event but may involve a series of conversations. For example, as more information is learned in a particular case, a clinical disclosure may need to be followed by an institutional disclosure, which itself may involve multiple conversations. In some cases, the disclosure process may ultimately involve all three types of disclosure.

*   *   *

8.   Institutional Disclosure of Adverse Events

a.   Institutional disclosure of adverse events [as defined above]. Serious injury may include significant or permanent disability, injury that leads to prolonged hospitalization, injury requiring life-sustaining intervention, or intervention to prevent impairment or damage, including, for example "sentinel events" as defined by [the Joint Commission]. Such adverse events require institutional disclosure regardless of whether they resulted from an error.

(1) When an adverse event has resulted in or is reasonably expected to result in death or serious injury, an institutional disclosure must be performed regardless of when the event is discovered. This disclosure is required even if clinical disclosure has already occurred. If an initial clinical disclosure has been made, it is important to determine what role, if any, the treating clinician(s) will play in the institutional disclosure process, as well as in the ongoing care of the patient.

(2) Institutional disclosure must be initiated as soon as reasonably possible and generally within 72 hours. This timeframe does not apply to adverse events that are only recognized after the associated episode of care (e.g., through investigation of a sentinel event, a routine quality review, or a look-back). Under such circumstances, if the adverse event has resulted in or is reasonably expected to result in death or serious injury, institutional disclosure is required, but disclosure may be delayed to allow for a thorough investigation of the facts provided.

b.   Institutional disclosure of adverse events needs to take place after organizational leaders (e.g., the Facility Director, Chief of Staff, Associate Director for Patient Care Services, members of the treatment team, and/or others as appropriate), have conferred with Regional Counsel and have determined what is to be communicated, by whom, and how.

c.   When initiating an institutional disclosure, institutional leaders invite the patient or personal representative to meet. * * *.

d.   Institutional disclosure ideally needs to be made face-to-face with the patient or the patient's personal representative, unless it is neither possible nor practical. * * *.

e.   If the patient is not capable of understanding either the situation or the information provided in a disclosure, and does not have a personal representative * * *, the facility must make the institutional disclosure to a family member involved in the patient's care, if available. * * *

f.   A request made in advance of the discussion by a patient or personal representative to bring an attorney must be honored, but may influence the choice of participants on behalf of the institution.

g.   Institutional disclosure of adverse events must include:

(1) An expression of concern and an apology, including an explanation of the facts to the extent that they are known.

(2) An outline of treatment options, if appropriate.

(3) Arrangements for a second opinion, additional monitoring, expediting clinical consultations, bereavement support, or whatever might be appropriate depending on the circumstances and within the constraints of VA's statutory and regulatory authority.

(4) Contact information regarding designated staff who are to respond to questions regarding the disclosed information or clinical sequelae associated with the adverse event.

(5) Notification that the patient or personal representative has the option of obtaining outside medical or legal advice for further guidance.

(6) Offering information about potential compensation under 38 U.S.C. § 1151 and the Federal Tort Claims Act where the patient is a Veteran or under the Federal Tort Claims Act where the patient is a non-Veteran. * * *

NOTES AND QUESTIONS

1.   What do you think motivated the development of such a remarkable policy? What problems if any do you see with the VA policy?

2.   Pennsylvania created a Patient Safety Authority that mandates reports to the Authority by hospitals of all "serious events". Fines may be levied

for failures to report, and the statute provides for whistleblower protections among other things. Pennsylvania also adopted a patient notification requirement if a patient is affected by a serious event. The statute provides:

> A medical facility through an appropriate designee shall provide written notification to a patient affected by a serious event or, with the consent of the patient, to an available family member or designee, within seven days of the occurrence or discovery of a serious event. * * *

Section 308(b) of the Medical Care Availability and Reduction of Error (Mcare) Act.3.   The patient notification requirements of Pennsylvania and the Veterans Administration raise the risk that patients will become aware of adverse events that they might not otherwise have discovered. Will the incidence of malpractice claims increase? Or will disclosure and an apology reduce litigation?

Patient disclosure requirements have the potential to not only reduce medical errors but also the frequency of malpractice litigation, if done well. There is evidence that disclosure and apology is desired by patients, and it may even serve to reduce patient inclinations to sue for malpractice when they have experience a bad outcome. See Thomas H. Gallagher, et al., Disclosing Harmful Medical Errors to Patients, 356 N. Eng. J. Med. 2713 (2007) (discusses the movement by regulators, hospitals and accreditors to develop standards for communication with patients after harmful errors have occurred).

PROBLEM: DISCLOSING ERRORS

You represent St. Jude Hospital in Pennsylvania, which has implemented a new error management policy in light of the new Joint Commission, CMS, and Pennsylvania rules. How should the hospital handle the following medical misadventures?

1.   Joseph Banes entered the hospital for surgery on a cervical disk to relieve his chronic back pain. During the surgery a nerve was severed at the base of his spine, causing severe pain and limitations in mobility in his left leg and foot. The injury is likely to be permanent. This is a rare risk of lower back surgery generally, but in this case the surgeon made a slip of the scalpel and cut the nerve. Your investigation reveals that the surgeon and the nurses in the operating room were aware of the surgical error. What steps should the hospital take to comply with Joint Commission sentinel event requirements? The VA rules? The Pennsylvania state requirements?

2.   Sally Thomas, a 45–year–old woman with a history of abdominal pain, was found lying on the floor of her home in severe pain. She was taken to the emergency room of St. Jude, admitted for diagnosis, and tested to de-

termine the source of the problem. After several days of diagnostic uncertainty, the physicians considered an exploratory laparoscopy, suspecting an abnormality in her small intestine. Before surgery an anesthesiologist inserted a central venous catheter (central line) in Sally. She then underwent surgery, and her right fallopian tube and ovary were removed because of infection. She was taken to the Post Anesthesia Care Unit (PACU) with the central line still in place. A surgical resident who had assisted during the surgery wrote out post-operative orders. These orders included a portable chest x-ray to be taken in the PACU. The purpose of the chest x-ray was to check the placement of the central line. The x-ray was completed by approximately 1:45 p.m. Sally continued to have pain, and was given pain medications. Finally the x-ray, taken four hours earlier, was checked and it revealed that the central line was inserted incorrectly, and the tip went into the pericardial sac of Thomas' heart. The doctors successfully resuscitated her. She recovered after a week in the hospital, narrowly escaping a cardiac tamponade, in which her heart would have been crushed by fluid pressure, leading to cardiac arrest. What steps do you advise the hospital to take?

    3.   Wilhelm Gross entered St. Jude to have surgery on his left leg to repair an artery. The surgical team prepped Wilhelm, preparing his right leg for the procedure. Minutes before the surgeon was to make the first incision, nurse Jost noticed on the chart that the procedure was to be done on his left leg. The team then prepped the correct leg and the operation went smoothly. What reporting obligations does the hospital have?

5. Shopping for Quality: Information for Consumers

Section 3015 of the ACA provides for performance websites. Performance websites shall make available to the public "performance information summarizing data on quality measures." The ACA provides for a range of information to facilitate shopping for health care providers. Comparison websites existed prior to the ACA, most notably *Hospital Compare* and *Nursing Home Compare*. The *Hospital Compare* website now includes data on the rate of hospital-based infections, as required by the ACA.

The ACA institutes several new sites to complement these. The ACA creates a *Physician Compare* website based on the model of the *Hospital Compare*. This new website will contain information on physician performance that allowing the public to compare physicians on performance measures, including measures collected under the Physician Quality Reporting Initiative; assessments of patient health outcomes and the functional status of patients; continuity and coordination of care and care transitions, including episodes of care and risk-adjusted resource use; efficiency; patient experience and patient, caregiver, and family engagement; safety, effectiveness, and timeliness of care.

CHAPTER 7

HEALTH CARE COST AND ACCESS: THE AFFORDABLE CARE ACT

■ ■ ■

I.   INTRODUCTION

Approaches to expanding access to and controlling the cost of health care can basically be divided between those that rely on direct public action and those that rely more on private initiatives and markets. All nations, including the United States, have adopted a mixed strategy for addressing cost control issues. All have public programs for providing health insurance or health care to a portion of their population. Even in the United States, the bastion of private enterprise, almost half of health care expenditures are borne by the government (more if one adds tax expenditures and the cost of insurance for government employees), even though government programs cover less than one third of the population. All nations also have private insurance markets. Even in England, whose National Health Service is the quintessential example of socialized medicine, about one ninth of the population has private insurance.

This chapter focuses on the approach the United States has taken to expanding access through the Affordable Care Act, adopted in 2010. This includes both public and private sector approaches to expanding access, and includes many of the strategies that other nations have followed as well. The primary strategy of the ACA for expanding access to health insurance for middle-income Americans is the use of means-tested tax credits to subsidize the purchase of private health insurance. This is historically a Republican strategy for expanding access, but was from the beginning the strategy adopted by all of the Democratic House and Senate versions of the reform legislation. A "single-payer" system, which would have provided direct government payment for health care and which is the way many other nations provide access to health care (as does the United States for certain populations like veterans or the elderly and disabled), was never seriously considered. Until quite late in the deliberations, Congress debated permitting the choice of a "public option," a public insurance company that would compete with private insurers, but the idea was unable to garner the sixty votes needed in the Senate to overcome a filibuster. Even though the public option consistently received strong public support, the public option eventually was dropped from the legislation.

The second prong of the ACA's strategy to expand access was a dramatic expansion in Medicaid, a means-tested public insurance program. Under the legislation, all American adults under age 65 and children with household modified gross adjusted income below 133 percent of the poverty level (actually 138 percent, as income is disregarded sufficient to raise the eligibility level five percentage points) would have been eligible for Medicaid coverage. In 2013, 133 percent of the poverty level is $15,282 for an individual and $31,322 for a family of four. As is discussed in Chapter 10, Medicaid has historically been available only to those who qualified as the "worthy poor," such as children, the elderly, or the disabled. The reform statute expanded Medicaid coverage to able-bodied adults. It also eliminated the asset test for the newly eligible adults. On the other hand, it also discontinued a number of income disregards that have allowed applicants to deduct expenses such as child care from their income, thus tightening up financial eligibility for some even as it opens Medicaid to new categories of individuals. As is explained in chapter 10, the Supreme Court's 2012 Affordable Care Act decision made the adult Medicaid expansion a state option. As of this writing, it appears that a number of states will not expand Medicaid for 2014.

The legislation also seeks to ensure nearly universal coverage by including a minimum coverage requirement (individual mandate) and an employer mandate of sorts. In general, individuals who can afford health insurance and who are not otherwise insured will need to purchase insurance or pay a penalty. Employers are not required to offer health insurance to their employees, but are required to enroll their employees in offered coverage automatically unless the individual employee affirmatively opts out. Employers will also be required to pay a penalty if they fail to offer their employees coverage or offer inadequate or unaffordable coverage and their employees end up purchasing insurance through the exchanges funded by public subsidies. The exchanges and other insurance market reforms are examined in Chapter 9.

Finally, between 2010 and 2013, the ACA provided temporary assistance through the Preexisting Condition High Risk Pool Program, which offered coverage to uninsured individuals with preexisting conditions, and the early-retiree reinsurance program which offered reinsurance to cover the costs of high-cost enrollees in early retirement program. These programs end in 2013 and will not be discussed here.

II.   PREMIUM ASSISTANCE TAX CREDITS: SECTION 1401

The ACA's primary strategy for expanding coverage is the premium assistance tax credit. Beginning in 2014, Americans earning up to 400% of the poverty level ($45,960 for a family of one and $94,200 for a family of four in 2010) who purchase nongroup (individual) health insurance through an exchange will be eligible for a tax credit. The amount of the individual's tax credit will be calculated on a monthly basis and will be the lesser of (i) the monthly premium cost for the plan that an individual or family is enrolled in or (ii) the monthly premium for the second lowest cost "silver" plan (a plan in which the insurance pays for 70% of the expected medical costs covered by the plan, discussed further in Chapter 9) that would cover the taxpayer or his family minus 1/12 of the product of the applicable percentage and the taxpayer's household income for the taxable year. The applicable percentage will increase on a sliding scale from the initial to the final premium percentage within an income tier as follows:

In the case of household income (expressed as a percent of poverty line) within the following income tier:	The initial premium percentage is:	The final premium percentage is:
Up to 133%	2.0%	2.0%
133% up to 150%	3.0%	4.0%
150% up to 200%	4.0%	6.3%
200% up to 250%	6.3%	8.05%
250% up to 300%	8.05%	9.5%
300% up to 400%	9.5%	9.5%

The percentages will increase over time to reflect the growth in health insurance premiums relative to income, so that the share of premiums paid by individuals will remain more or less constant. That is to say, if premiums increase significantly more rapidly than income, as they have in the past, the percentage of income that individuals will have to spend on premiums will increase so that the individual and the government will continue to pay roughly the same proportion of the premium.

The premium tax credit will be adjusted for age as permitted under the law but not for any premium discount attributable to a wellness program or for a premium surcharge based on tobacco use. The cost of any benefits covered by an insurance policy in addition to the essential benefits will not be considered in setting the adjusted monthly premium, although states must cover the cost of additional benefits that they require qualified health plans to provide to individuals, whether or not the insurance is subsidized by a tax credit or provided through an exchange. Aliens legally present in the United States who are not eligible for Medicaid (generally, those present in the country for fewer than 5 years) but who have incomes below 100 percent of the poverty level are also eligible. But United States citizens with incomes below 100 percent of the poverty level in states that reject the Medicaid expansion will not be eligible for premium tax credits.

Most persons who have employer coverage will not be eligible for premium credits. An employee may be eligible to purchase individual coverage through the exchange with assistance from a premium tax credit, however, if the employee is eligible for an employer-sponsored plan but the employee's required contribution for the plan exceeds 9.5 percent of household income (indexed for inflation). Under current regulations, this calculation would be based on the cost of self-only coverage, so a family may be refused a premium tax credit if coverage of the individual employee is affordable even though the premium for family coverage exceeds 9.5 percent. An employee may also be eligible if the employment-related "plan's share of total allowed costs of benefits provided under the plan is less than 60% of such costs." These provisions only apply if the employee or family is in fact not covered by the employment-related plan. As discussed further below, if an employee of a large employer in fact takes advantage of these provisions and seeks premium subsidies, the employer will face a "free loader" penalty. What explains these particular provisions? What is their effect likely to be?

III.   COST–SHARING REDUCTION PAYMENTS: SECTION 1402

The reform legislation provides not only for tax credits to reduce the cost of health insurance premiums, but also for direct payments to qualified health plans to reduce the cost-sharing (including deductibles, coinsurance, and copayments) of eligible individuals beginning in 2014. As will be explained further in Chapter 9, cost sharing is limited for plans available through the exchange in two different ways. First, the legislation imposes a maximum out-of-pocket expenditure limit, basically equal to the limit imposed on high-deductible policies that accompany health savings accounts ($6250 for an individual and $12,500 for a family in 2013). Second, qualified health plans in the individual and small group market must offer coverage of a specific actuarial value fitting into one of four "precious metal" tiers (bronze, silver, gold, and platinum), ranging from 60% to 90% actuarial value. Although "actuarial value" is determined by the overall structure of a plan and does not dictate the out-of-pocket expenses a particular individual or family will incur in a particular year, higher actuarial value plans offer lower cost-sharing and more affordable health care, but will charge higher premiums.

"Cost-sharing reduction payments" are payments made by the federal government directly to an insurer on behalf of an "eligible individual" to lower that individual's cost-sharing obligations. An eligible individual is a person who enrolls in a silver tier plan in the individual market through the exchange and whose household income is above 100% and does not exceed 400% of the poverty level. They are not available to persons with employment-based coverage. Cost-sharing reduction payments will reduce the statutory out-of-pocket limit for persons with household income not exceeding 250% of poverty. These reductions in the out-of-pocket limit cannot increase the actuarial value of the plan above levels specified in the statute. In addition, however, to the reduction of the out-of-pocket maximums, cost-sharing subsidies must also increase the actuarial value of plans for lower-income enrollees. Cost-sharing reduction subsidies must assure that persons with incomes above 100% and not exceeding 150% of poverty have coverage with an actuarial value of at least 94%; persons with household incomes of above 150% and not exceeding 200% of poverty have coverage with at least 87% actuarial value; and persons with household income above 200% and not exceeding 250% of poverty, 73%. Native Americans with household incomes not exceeding 300% of poverty are not responsible for cost-sharing. Cost-sharing reductions apply only for essential benefits.

NOTE AND QUESTIONS

Actuarial analyses performed for the Kaiser Family Foundation by three actuarial firms estimated bronze level plans as having deductibles of $6350 with no coinsurance, $4350 with 20 percent coinsurance and $2750 with 30 percent coinsurance. Unsubsidized silver plans would have deductibles of $4200 with no coinsurance, $1850 to $2050 with 20 percent coinsurance. Silver plans with the highest level of cost-sharing reduction payments (below 150 percent of poverty), could have deductibles as low as $200 with 5 percent coinsurance or $0 with 8 percent coinsurance. In sum, plans without subsidized cost-sharing are likely to have high deductibles and coinsurance. Kaiser Family Foundation, What the Actuarial Values in the Affordable Care Act Mean (2011).

What factors explain the complexity of the ACA approach to providing access to health insurance? How will it affect consumers, insurers, providers, and employers? How could this have been done more simply?

IV.   APPLICATION PROCESS: SECTIONS 1411 TO 1415

Once the ACA is fully in place in 2014, individuals and families will apply for premium assistance tax credits and cost-sharing reduction subsidies through their exchange. The exchange will collect information and send it to a federal data hub at the Department of Health and Human Services, which will verify income information with the Internal Revenue Service and citizenship with Homeland Security. The final eligibility determination will be made by the exchange. Financial eligibility determinations will generally be made on the basis of the individual's household income for the most recent taxable year for which information is available. If, as will often be the case, an applicant has had substantial changes in income, family size or other household circumstances, or in filing status, or has filed for unemployment benefits since last filing taxes, the advance determination can be made on the basis of household income for a later period or on the basis of an individual's estimate of income for the taxable year. The exchange can also determine or assess eligibility, where appropriate, for Medicaid, the Children's Health Insurance Program, or other relevant public programs. Individuals will have an opportunity to appeal adverse decisions.

Information provided for the eligibility determination process is confidential and cannot be used for other purposes. Failure to provide correct information for eligibility determination can result in a fine, and willful and knowing provision of false information can result in stiffer fines.

Premium tax credits and cost-sharing reduction payments will be paid directly to the insurer. If individuals fail to pay their share of the premiums, the insurer must notify HHS and may discontinue coverage after a 3–month grace period. After the first month of non-payment, the insurer can suspend payments to providers. If the individual pays up the premium during the three month grace period, the insurer will reinstate coverage. Otherwise, the individual will be responsible for provider payments. States may make payments on behalf of an individual in addition to the federal premium tax credits and cost-sharing reduction payments.

Each household that claims a tax credit will face a reconciliation process at the end of the year when it files a tax return. If there has been an overpayment, the individual will be responsible for repayment. Overpayments will in fact be common, as it will be difficult for lower-income workers to accurately project their income (or household composition) a year in advance. Moreover, if a recipient loses or gets a job half-way through the year, his or her total income for the year may be very different than the income at the time he or she applied for a tax credit. Under the original ACA, liability for repayment was capped at $250 for an individual, $400 for a family, but full repayment was required if final income exceeded 400 percent of the poverty level. Congress has subsequently amended the provision twice making it less forgiving. Currently households with incomes up to 200% of poverty can be required to pay back up to $600, households with incomes above 200% and not exceeding 300%, $1500, and households with incomes above 300% and not exceeding 400% may have to pay back up to $2500. If household income at the time of reconciliation exceeds 400% of poverty, for example because a wage earner received a year-end bonus boosting his or her income over that amount, the entire tax credit must be returned.

PROBLEM: HELP FROM HEALTH CARE REFORM

Assume for the following problems the following facts: the health care reform provisions that go into effect in 2014 are already in place the "second lowest cost silver plan" in the exchange costs $4000 for individual coverage, $12,000 for family (including couple) coverage; the federal poverty level is $12,000 for a single individual, $16,000 for a couple, and $25,000 for a family of four; none of the people in the problem are Native Americans; and only essential benefits are covered by the insurance premiums. Disregard age rating.

John is currently unemployed and his wife Naomi is employed at a job that does not offer health insurance. Their modified adjusted gross household income is $32,000. How large a premium assistance credit are they eligible for? How much are they eligible for in cost-sharing reduction payments?

Bill's employer offers health insurance, but the employee must pay half of the premium, or $2,500 a year. Bill, who is unmarried and has no children, has a modified adjusted gross income of $18,000 per year. Is he eligible for a premium-assistance tax credit? For cost-sharing reduction payments?

Rosa, also unmarried and without children, is self-employed and has a modified adjusted gross income of $60,000 a year. Her insurance policy costs her $8000 per year. Is she eligible for premium assistance tax credits or cost-sharing reduction payments?

Martha and Carlos have two children. Between them they have a modified adjusted gross income of $75,000 per year. They are not offered health insurance by their employers. Are they eligible for premium assistance tax credits? For cost-sharing reduction payments?

At the beginning of 2014, Kalim and Fozia are both employed with a combined income in excess of 400% of the poverty level. Nine months into the year, Fozia loses her job and Kalim's job is reduced to part-time status, leaving them with an income of $2,667 per month. Kalim's employer does not offer health insurance to part time employees. Kalim and Fozia apply immediately for a tax credit and are granted a premium tax credit based on a projected annual income of below 400 percent of poverty. When they file their taxes, however, they discover that their total income for the year was still above 400 percent of the poverty level. How much was their tax credit? How much will they need to pay back?

V.   SMALL EMPLOYER TAX CREDIT: SECTION 1421

The ACA also provides a small employer health insurance tax credit that covers a portion of the lesser of (i) the aggregate amount of contributions by a small employer on behalf of its employees for premiums for qualified health plans or (ii) the aggregate amount the employer would have contributed if each employee had enrolled in a qualified health plan with the average premium for the small group market in which the enrollee enrolls for coverage. Until 2014 the program will cover 35% for for-profit employers, 25% for nonprofits. Beginning in 2014, the portion that it will cover will be 50% for for-profit businesses and 35% for nonprofits. The tax credit will only be available for policies purchased through the exchange.

Employers are eligible for the program if they have fewer than 25 employees, pay an average annual wage per full-time equivalent employee that does not exceed $50,000, and pay for at least half of the cost of their employee's health insurance premiums through the exchange. The amount of the credit phases out as the total number of full time employees of the employer rises from 10 to 25 and as the average annual wages of the employer rises from $25,000 to $50,000 (for 2010 to 2013, with the amount thereafter adjusted for inflation).

The credit is available until the end of 2013, and then for the first two years during which a small employer offers its employees coverage through an exchange. Tax-exempt organizations can write off the credit against their payroll tax liability, while taxable businesses can write off the credit against taxes they would otherwise owe.

PROBLEM: HELP FOR SMALL BUSINESSES

Luigi's Landscaping employs 10 full time employees with an average annual wage of $25,000. Luigi purchases insurance for his employees that costs an average of $8000 per employee and pays 75 percent of the cost. He applies for a small business tax credit. How much is his business eligible for prior to 2014? How much will it be eligible for after 2013 if he purchases insurance through the exchange?

VI.   THE MINIMUM COVERAGE REQUIREMENT: SECTIONS 1501 AND 1502

Individuals whose income exceeds the income tax filing limit (the sum of the standard deduction plus the exemptions to which the individual is entitled, which amounts to $9,750 for a single individual, $20,650 for a married couple filing jointly for 2012) and who do not have insurance coverage through their employment or under some public program are required to purchase health insurance if it is affordable. Insurance coverage is affordable if the lowest cost bronze level plan purchasable through the exchange costs less than 8 percent of household income, after the application of premium affordability tax credits. (A bronze plan has an actuarial value of 60 percent, basically a high-deductible plan). A number of categories of individuals are exempt from this requirement, including members of religious groups that object to insurance coverage (such as the Amish) and who hold to the tenets of those groups, members of established religious sharing ministries, incarcerated individuals, Native Americans, people uninsured for less than a three-month period, expatriates, and individuals not legally present in the United States. Finally, the statute provides for hardship exemptions, which the IRS has interpreted quite broadly. Several categories of individuals will be eligible for these, including individuals in states that do not expand Medicaid with incomes below the poverty level.

Individuals subject to the requirement who fail to purchase insurance are subject to a penalty, which will, in 2016 when fully phased in, be the greater of $695 for each adult and half that amount for each child in the household, up to $2085 total for a family (updated for inflation) or 2.5 percent of household income above the filing limit, but not more than the cost of a bronze-level (basic, high cost-sharing) insurance policy.

The statute prohibits the use of liens or levies on property or of criminal sanctions for enforcing the requirement. The IRS will likely offset penalties against refunds owed to taxpayers. But compliance will be largely voluntary. The penalty will fall primarily on families with incomes below 250 percent of the poverty level (who will be able to afford health insurance for less than 8 percent of their household income once premium tax credits are applied) and on higher-income families (who will be able to afford health insurance unassisted). Middle-income families will not be subject to the penalties, because they will be unable to find health insurance policies costing less than 8 percent of their income without tax credits. Amy Monahan, On Subsidies and Mandates: A Regulatory Critique of the ACA, 36 J.Corp. L. 781 (2011). Of course, the vast majority of Americans receive health insurance through their jobs or public programs and will also not be subject to the requirement. Many of those affected by the requirement will be self-employed individuals with incomes well above the median. These persons are likely to have complicated taxes and will be unlikely to want to provoke the curiosity or the ire of the IRS. Further, most people would probably prefer to be insured if they can afford it.

The minimum coverage requirement is a key to the coverage expansions in the ACA. For reasons just described, it will encourage eligible persons to sign up for Medicaid and for the premium assistance tax credits. It will also drive employees to demand insurance from their employ-ers, supporting our employer-based insurance system. Finally, it will en-courage higher-income uninsured individuals who do not have access to public or employer-based coverage to buy insurance. A Rand study con-cluded that removing the requirement would expand the number of unin-sured by 13 million. Christine Eibner, et al., Establishing State Health Insurance Exchanges (2011)

Compliance with the Massachusetts mandate has been very high, and compliance with the federal requirement is likely to be high as well. Nevertheless, there will be some people who simply cannot afford health insurance, even with the tax credits, and others who object to being re-quired by law to purchase a private product. The CBO has estimated that about 6 million Americans a year will pay the penalty once it is in force.

PROBLEM: INDIVIDUAL RESPONSIBILITY

Assume that John and Naomi, Bill, Rosa, and Martha and Carlos in the Help from Health Care Reform Problem above each fail to purchase health insurance. Assume that none of the individuals are incarcerated, Amish (or members of another religious group that objects to insurance coverage and meets statutory requirements), undocumented aliens, expatriates, or mem-bers of a health care sharing ministry, and that all have been uninsured for at least three months. Assume that the penalty amounts are those that will apply once the penalties are fully in place in 2016. The total penalty is capped at three times the individual penalty for families, and at the cost of a bronze plan for all households subject to the penalty.

Assume that the lowest cost bronze level plan available through the ex-change costs $3000 for individuals, $9000 for families (including couples), that the assistance available to them to purchase a silver plan will also be available for a bronze plan, and that the individual responsibility provisions of the legislation are already in effect. Also assume the tax filing threshold is $10,000 for an individual, $20,000 for a couple filing jointly. Which, if any, of them will owe penalties, and how much?

VII.   MINIMUM COVERAGE REQUIREMENT LITIGATION

Even before the health reform legislation was adopted into law, legis-latures in many States were considering legislation in opposition to the federal reforms. Early versions of this legislation seems to have been aimed at provisions that would have limited access to private health in-surance or providers, but later iterations were more narrowly aimed at the minimum coverage requirement. The Virginia statute, for example, provides:

§ 38.23430.1:1. Health insurance coverage not required.

No resident of this Commonwealth, regardless of whether he has or is eligible for health insurance coverage under any policy or program provided by or through his employer, or a plan sponsored by the Commonwealth or the federal government, shall be required to obtain or maintain a policy of individual insurance coverage except as required by a court or the Department of Social Services where an individual is named a party in a judicial or administrative proceeding. * * *

No sooner was the ink of the President's signature dry on the health care reform legislation than the attorneys general from Florida and a dozen other states filed a lawsuit challenging the constitutionality of the legislation. The State of Virginia filed a separate action specifically defending its statute against the federal law. After the lawsuits were filed, several other attorneys general joined in the Florida lawsuit, which eventually included 26 state plaintiffs, as well as the National Federation of Independent Business and two individual plaintiffs. About two dozen other lawsuits were brought by various individuals or groups across the country, with most of them challenging the minimum coverage requirement, but some raising other issues as well.

The Florida case focused on the constitutionality of the minimum coverage requirement (commonly referred to as the individual mandate). The basic argument of the case was that the federal government lacks the authority to require individuals to purchase health insurance. That question was decided by the Supreme Court, which upheld the minimum coverage requirement in June of 2012.

NATIONAL FEDERATION OF INDEPENDENT BUSINESS ET AL., PETITIONERS V. SEBELIUS

Supreme Court of the United States, Decided June 28, 2012.
132 S.Ct. 2566.

CHIEF JUSTICE ROBERTS announced the judgment of the Court and delivered the opinion of the Court.

Today we resolve constitutional challenges to two provisions of the Patient Protection and Affordable Care Act of 2010: the individual mandate, which requires individuals to purchase a health insurance policy providing a minimum level of coverage; and the Medicaid expansion, which gives funds to the States on the condition that they provide specified health care to all citizens whose income falls below a certain threshold. We do not consider whether the Act embodies sound policies. That judgment is entrusted to the Nation's elected leaders. We ask only whether Congress has the power under the Constitution to enact the challenged provisions.

In our federal system, the National Government possesses only limited powers; the States and the people retain the remainder. * * * In this case we must again determine whether the Constitution grants Congress powers it now asserts, but which many States and individuals believe it does not possess. * * *

* * *

This case concerns two powers that the Constitution does grant the Federal Government, but which must be read carefully to avoid creating a general federal authority akin to the police power. The Constitution authorizes Congress to "regulate Commerce with foreign Nations, and among the several States, and with the Indian Tribes." [ ] Our precedents read that to mean that Congress may regulate "the channels of interstate commerce," "persons or things in interstate commerce," and "those activities that substantially affect interstate commerce." [ ] The power over activities that substantially affect interstate commerce can be expansive. That power has been held to authorize federal regulation of such seemingly local matters as a farmer's decision to grow wheat for himself and his livestock, and a loan shark's extortionate collections from a neighborhood butcher shop. [ ]

Congress may also "lay and collect Taxes, Duties, Imposts and Excises, to pay the Debts and provide for the common Defence and general Welfare of the United States." U.S. Const., Art. I, § 8, cl. 1. Put simply, Congress may tax and spend. This grant gives the Federal Government considerable influence even in areas where it cannot directly regulate. The Federal Government may enact a tax on an activity that it cannot authorize, forbid, or otherwise control. [ ]

The reach of the Federal Government's enumerated powers is broader still because the Constitution authorizes Congress to "make all Laws which shall be necessary and proper for carrying into Execution the foregoing Powers." Art. I, § 8, cl. 18. * * *

Our permissive reading of these powers is explained in part by a general reticence to invalidate the acts of the Nation's elected leaders. "Proper respect for a coordinate branch of the government" requires that we strike down an Act of Congress only if "the lack of constitutional authority to pass [the] act in question is clearly demonstrated." [ ] Members of this Court are vested with the authority to interpret the law; we possess neither the expertise nor the prerogative to make policy judgments. Those decisions are entrusted to our Nation's elected leaders, who can be thrown out of office if the people disagree with them. It is not our job to protect the people from the consequences of their political choices.

Our deference in matters of policy cannot, however, become abdication in matters of law. "The powers of the legislature are defined and limited; and that those limits may not be mistaken, or forgotten, the constitution is written."[ ] Our respect for Congress's policy judgments thus can never extend so far as to disavow restraints on federal power that the Constitution carefully constructed. * * * And there can be no question that it is the responsibility of this Court to enforce the limits on federal power by striking down acts of Congress that transgress those limits. [ ]

* * *

The Government's first argument is that the individual mandate is a valid exercise of Congress's power under the Commerce Clause and the Necessary and Proper Clause. According to the Government, the health care market is characterized by a significant cost-shifting problem. Everyone will eventually need health care at a time and to an extent they cannot predict, but if they do not have insurance, they often will not be able to pay for it. Because state and federal laws nonetheless require hospitals to provide a certain degree of care to individuals without regard to their ability to pay, [ ] hospitals end up receiving compensation for only a portion of the services they provide. To recoup the losses, hospitals pass on the cost to insurers through higher rates, and insurers, in turn, pass on the cost to policy holders in the form of higher premiums. Congress estimated that the cost of uncompensated care raises family health insurance premiums, on average, by over $1,000 per year. [ ]

In the Affordable Care Act, Congress addressed the problem of those who cannot obtain insurance coverage because of preexisting conditions or other health issues. It did so through the Act's "guaranteed-issue" and "community rating" provisions. These provisions together prohibit insurance companies from denying coverage to those with such conditions or charging unhealthy individuals higher premiums than healthy individuals. [ ]

The guaranteed-issue and community-rating reforms do not, however, address the issue of healthy individuals who choose not to purchase insurance to cover potential health care needs. In fact, the reforms sharply exacerbate that problem, by providing an incentive for individuals to delay purchasing health insurance until they become sick, relying on the promise of guaranteed and affordable coverage. The reforms also threaten to impose massive new costs on insurers, who are required to accept unhealthy individuals but prohibited from charging them rates necessary to pay for their coverage. This will lead insurers to significantly increase premiums on everyone.[ ]

The individual mandate was Congress's solution to these problems. By requiring that individuals purchase health insurance, the mandate prevents cost-shifting by those who would otherwise go without it. In addition, the mandate forces into the insurance risk pool more healthy individuals, whose premiums on average will be higher than their health care expenses. This allows insurers to subsidize the costs of covering the unhealthy individuals the reforms require them to accept. * * *

The Government contends that the individual mandate is within Congress's power because the failure to purchase insurance "has a substantial and deleterious effect on interstate commerce" by creating the cost-shifting problem. [ ] The path of our Commerce Clause decisions has not always run smooth, [ ] but it is now well established that Congress has broad authority under the Clause. We have recognized, for example, that "[t]he power of Congress over interstate commerce is not confined to the regulation of commerce among the states," but extends to activities that "have a substantial effect on interstate commerce." [ ] Congress's power, moreover, is not limited to regulation of an activity that by itself substantially affects interstate commerce, but also extends to activities that do so only when aggregated with similar activities of others. [ ]

Given its expansive scope, it is no surprise that Congress has employed the commerce power in a wide variety of ways to address the pressing needs of the time. But Congress has never attempted to rely on that power to compel individuals not engaged in commerce to purchase an unwanted product. Legislative novelty is not necessarily fatal; there is a first time for everything. But sometimes "the most telling indication of [a] severe constitutional problem . . . is the lack of historical precedent" for Congress's action. [ ]

The Constitution grants Congress the power to "*regulate* Commerce." Art. I, § 8, cl. 3 The power to *regulate* commerce presupposes the existence of commercial activity to be regulated. * * * The language of the Constitution reflects the natural understanding that the power to regulate assumes there is already something to be regulated. [ ]

Our precedent also reflects this understanding. As expansive as our cases construing the scope of the commerce power have been, they all have one thing in common: They uniformly describe the power as reaching "activity." It is nearly impossible to avoid the word when quoting them. [ ]

The individual mandate, however, does not regulate existing commercial activity. It instead compels individuals to *become* active in commerce by purchasing a product, on the ground that their failure to do so affects interstate commerce. Construing the Commerce Clause to permit Congress to regulate individuals precisely *because* they are doing nothing would open a new and potentially vast domain to congressional authority. Every day individuals do not do an infinite number of things. In some cases they decide not to do something; in others they simply fail to do it. Allowing Congress to justify federal regulation by pointing to the effect of inaction on commerce would bring countless decisions an individual could *potentially* make within the scope of federal regulation, and—under the

Government's theory—empower Congress to make those decisions for him.

*   *   *

Applying the Government's logic to the familiar case of *Wickard v. Filburn* shows how far that logic would carry us from the notion of a government of limited powers. In *Wickard,* the Court famously upheld a federal penalty imposed on a farmer for growing wheat for consumption on his own farm. [ ] That amount of wheat caused the farmer to exceed his quota under a program designed to support the price of wheat by limiting supply. The Court rejected the farmer's argument that growing wheat for home consumption was beyond the reach of the commerce power. It did so on the ground that the farmer's decision to grow wheat for his own use allowed him to avoid purchasing wheat in the market. That decision, when considered in the aggregate along with similar decisions of others, would have had a substantial effect on the interstate market for wheat. [ ]

Wickard has long been regarded as "perhaps the most far reaching example of Commerce Clause authority over intrastate activity," but the Government's theory in this case would go much further. Under *Wickard* it is within Congress's power to regulate the market for wheat by supporting its price. But price can be supported by increasing demand as well as by decreasing supply. The aggregated decisions of some consumers not to purchase wheat have a substantial effect on the price of wheat, just as decisions not to purchase health insurance have on the price of insurance. Congress can therefore command that those not buying wheat do so, just as it argues here that it may command that those not buying health insurance do so. The farmer in *Wickard* was at least actively engaged in the production of wheat, and the Government could regulate that activity because of its effect on commerce. The Government's theory here would effectively override that limitation, by establishing that individuals may be regulated under the Commerce Clause whenever enough of them are not doing something the Government would have them do.

Indeed, the Government's logic would justify a mandatory purchase to solve almost any problem. [ ] To consider a different example in the health care market, many Americans do not eat a balanced diet. That group makes up a larger percentage of the total population than those without health insurance. [ ] The failure of that group to have a healthy diet increases health care costs, to a greater extent than the failure of the uninsured to purchase insurance. [ ] Those increased costs are borne in part by other Americans who must pay more, just as the uninsured shift costs to the insured. [ ] Congress addressed the insurance problem by ordering everyone to buy insurance. Under the Government's theory, Congress could address the diet problem by ordering everyone to buy vegetables. [ ]

People, for reasons of their own, often fail to do things that would be good for them or good for society. Those failures—joined with the similar failures of others—can readily have a substantial effect on interstate commerce. Under the Government's logic, that authorizes Congress to use its commerce power to compel citizens to act as the Government would have them act.

That is not the country the Framers of our Constitution envisioned. * * * While Congress's authority under the Commerce Clause has of course expanded with the growth of the national economy, our cases have "always recognized that the power to regulate commerce, though broad indeed, has limits." [ ] The Government's theory would erode those limits, permitting Congress to reach beyond the natural extent of its authority, "everywhere extending the sphere of its activity and drawing all power into its impetuous vortex." [ ] Congress already enjoys vast power to regulate much of what we do. Accepting the Government's theory would give Congress the same license to regulate what we do not do, fundamentally changing the relation between the citizen and the Federal Government.

To an economist, perhaps, there is no difference between activity and inactivity; both have measurable economic effects on commerce. But the distinction between doing something and doing nothing would not have been lost on the Framers, who were "practical statesmen," not metaphysical philosophers. * * * The Framers gave Congress the power to *regulate* commerce, not to *compel* it, and for over 200 years both our decisions and Congress's actions have reflected this understanding. * * *

The Government sees things differently. It argues that because sickness and injury are unpredictable but unavoidable, "the uninsured as a class are active in the market for health care, which they regularly seek and obtain." [ ] The individual mandate "merely regulates how individuals finance and pay for that active participation—requiring that they do so through insurance, rather than through attempted self-insurance with the back-stop of shifting costs to others."[ ]

The Government repeats the phrase "active in the market for health care" throughout its brief, [ ] but that concept has no constitutional significance. An individual who bought a car two years ago and may buy another in the future is not "active in the car market" in any pertinent sense. The phrase "active in the market" cannot obscure the fact that most of those regulated by the individual mandate are not currently engaged in any commercial activity involving health care, and that fact is fatal to the Government's effort to "regulate the uninsured as a class." [ ] Our precedents recognize Congress's power to regulate "class[es] of *activities*,"[ ], not classes of *individuals,* apart from any activity in which they are engaged [ ].

The individual mandate's regulation of the uninsured as a class is, in fact, particularly divorced from any link to existing commercial activity. The mandate primarily affects healthy, often young adults who are less likely to need significant health care and have other priorities for spending their money. It is precisely because these individuals, as an actuarial class, incur relatively low health care costs that the mandate helps counter the effect of forcing insurance companies to cover others who impose greater costs than their premiums are allowed to reflect. [ ] If the individual mandate is targeted at a class, it is a class whose commercial inactivity rather than activity is its defining feature.

The Government, however, claims that this does not matter. The Government regards it as sufficient to trigger Congress's authority that almost all those who are uninsured will, at some unknown point in the future, engage in a health care transaction. * * *

The proposition that Congress may dictate the conduct of an individual today because of prophesied future activity finds no support in our precedent. We have said that Congress can anticipate the *effects* on commerce of an economic activity. [ ] But we have never permitted Congress to anticipate that activity itself in order to regulate individuals not currently engaged in commerce. * * *

Everyone will likely participate in the markets for food, clothing, transportation, shelter, or energy; that does not authorize Congress to direct them to purchase particular products in those or other markets today. The Commerce Clause is not a general license to regulate an individual from cradle to grave, simply because he will predictably engage in particular transactions. Any police power to regulate individuals as such, as opposed to their activities, remains vested in the States.

The Government argues that the individual mandate can be sustained as a sort of exception to this rule, because health insurance is a unique product. According to the Government, upholding the individual mandate would not justify mandatory purchases of items such as cars or broccoli because, as the Government puts it, "[h]ealth insurance is not purchased for its own sake like a car or broccoli; it is a means of financing health-care consumption and covering universal risks." [ ] But cars and broccoli are no more purchased for their "own sake" than health insurance. They are purchased to cover the need for transportation and food.

The Government says that health insurance and health care financing are "inherently integrated." [ ] But that does not mean the compelled purchase of the first is properly regarded as a regulation of the second. No matter how "inherently integrated" health insurance and health care consumption may be, they are not the same thing: They involve different transactions, entered into at different times, with different providers. And for most of those targeted by the mandate, significant health care needs will be years, or even decades, away. The proximity and degree of connection between the mandate and the subsequent commercial activity is too lacking to justify an exception of the sort urged by the Government. * * *

The Government next contends that Congress has the power under the Necessary and Proper Clause to enact the individual mandate because the mandate is an "integral part of a comprehensive scheme of economic regulation"—the guaranteed-issue and community-rating insurance reforms. [ ] Under this argument, it is not necessary to consider the effect that an individual's inactivity may have on interstate commerce; it is enough that Congress regulate commercial activity in a way that requires regulation of inactivity to be effective.

The power to "make all Laws which shall be necessary and proper for carrying into Execution" the powers enumerated in the Constitution, Art. I, § 8, cl. 18, vests Congress with authority to enact provisions "incidental to the [enumerated] power, and conducive to its beneficial exercise," [ ] Although the Clause gives Congress authority to "legislate on that vast mass of incidental powers which must be involved in the constitution," it does not license the exercise of any "great substantive and independent power[s]" beyond those specifically enumerated. [ ] Instead, the Clause is " 'merely a declaration, for the removal of all uncertainty, that the means of carrying into execution those [powers] otherwise granted are included in the grant.' " [ ]

As our jurisprudence under the Necessary and Proper Clause has developed, we have been very deferential to Congress's determination that a regulation is "necessary." We have thus upheld laws that are " 'convenient, or useful' or 'conducive' to the authority's 'beneficial exercise.' " [ ] But we have also carried out our responsibility to declare unconstitutional those laws that undermine the structure of government established by the Constitution. Such laws, which are not "consist[ent] with the letter and spirit of the constitution," [ ] are not *proper* [means] for carrying into Execution" Congress's enumerated powers. Rather, they are, "in the words of The Federalist, 'merely acts of usurpation' which 'deserve to be treated as such.' " [ ]

Applying these principles, the individual mandate cannot be sustained under the Necessary and Proper Clause as an essential component of the insurance reforms. Each of our prior cases upholding laws under that Clause involved exercises of authority derivative of, and in service to, a granted power. * * * The individual mandate, by contrast, vests Congress with the extraordinary ability to create the necessary predicate to the exercise of an enumerated power.

This is in no way an authority that is "narrow in scope," [ ] or "incidental" to the exercise of the commerce power [ ]. Rather, such a conception of the Necessary and Proper Clause would work a substantial expansion of federal authority. No longer would Congress be limited to regulating under the Commerce Clause those who by some preexisting activity bring themselves within the sphere of federal regulation. Instead, Congress could reach beyond the natural limit of its authority and draw within its regulatory scope those who otherwise would be outside of it. Even if the individual mandate is "necessary" to the Act's insurance reforms, such an expansion of federal power is not a "proper" means for making those reforms effective.

*   *   *

Just as the individual mandate cannot be sustained as a law regulating the substantial effects of the failure to purchase health insurance, neither can it be upheld as a "necessary and proper" component of the insurance reforms. The commerce power thus does not authorize the mandate. [ ]

That is not the end of the matter. Because the Commerce Clause does not support the individual mandate, it is necessary to turn to the Government's second argument: that the mandate may be upheld as within Congress's enumerated power to "lay and collect Taxes." Art. I, § 8, cl. 1.

The Government's tax power argument asks us to view the statute differently than we did in considering its commerce power theory. In making its Commerce Clause argument, the Government defended the mandate as a regulation requiring individuals to purchase health insurance. The Government does not claim that the taxing power allows Congress to issue such a command. Instead, the Government asks us to read the mandate not as ordering individuals to buy insurance, but rather as imposing a tax on those who do not buy that product.

Under the mandate, if an individual does not maintain health insurance, the only consequence is that he must make an additional payment to the IRS when he pays his taxes. See § 5000A(b). That, according to the Government, means the mandate can be regarded as establishing a condition—not owning health insurance—that triggers a tax—the required payment to the IRS. Under that theory, the mandate is not a legal command to buy insurance. Rather, it makes going without insurance just another thing the Government taxes, like buying gasoline or earning income. And if the mandate is in effect just a tax hike on certain taxpayers who do not have health insurance, it may be within Congress's constitutional power to tax.

*   *   *

The exaction the Affordable Care Act imposes on those without health insurance looks like a tax in many respects. The "[s]hared responsibility payment," as the statute entitles it, is paid into the Treasury by "taxpayer[s]" when they file their tax returns. [ ] It does not apply to individuals who do not pay federal income taxes because their household income is less than the filing threshold in the Internal Revenue Code. [ ] For taxpayers who do owe the payment, its amount is determined by such familiar factors as taxable income, number of dependents, and joint filing status. [ ]. The requirement to pay is found in the Internal Revenue Code and enforced by the IRS, which—as we previously explained—must assess and collect it "in the same manner as taxes." [ ] This process yields the essential feature of any tax: it produces at least some revenue for the Government.* * *

It is of course true that the Act describes the payment as a "penalty," not a "tax." * * *

We have similarly held that exactions not labeled taxes nonetheless were authorized by Congress's power to tax. * * * ("[M]agic words or labels" should not "disable an otherwise constitutional levy" [ ]

Our cases confirm this functional approach. For example, in *Drexel Furniture,* we focused on three practical characteristics of the so-called tax on employing child laborers that convinced us the "tax" was actually a penalty. First, the tax imposed an exceedingly heavy burden—10 percent of a company's net income—on those who employed children, no matter how small their infraction. Second, it imposed that exaction only on those who knowingly employed underage laborers. Such scienter requirements are typical of punitive statutes, because Congress often wishes to punish only those who intentionally break the law. Third, this "tax" was enforced in part by the Department of Labor, an agency responsible for punishing violations of labor laws, not collecting revenue. [ ]

The same analysis here suggests that the shared responsibility payment may for constitutional purposes be considered a tax, not a penalty: First, for most Americans the amount due will be far less than the price of insurance, and, by statute, it can never be more. * * * Second, the individual mandate contains no scienter requirement. Third, the payment is collected solely by the IRS through the normal means of taxation—except that the Service is *not* allowed to use those means most suggestive of a punitive sanction, such as criminal prosecution. [ ] * * *

None of this is to say that the payment is not intended to affect individual conduct. Although the payment will raise considerable revenue, it is plainly designed to expand health insurance coverage. But taxes that seek to influence conduct are nothing new. * * * Today, federal and state taxes can compose more than half the retail price of cigarettes, not just to raise more money, but to encourage people to quit smoking. And we have upheld such obviously regulatory measures as taxes on selling marijuana and sawed-off shotguns. * * *

In distinguishing penalties from taxes, this Court has explained that "if the concept of penalty means anything, it means punishment for an unlawful act or omission." [ ] While the individual mandate clearly aims to induce the purchase of health insurance, it need not be read to declare that failing to do so is unlawful. Neither the Act nor any other law attaches negative legal consequences to not buying health insurance, beyond requiring a payment to the IRS. The Government agrees with that reading, confirming that if someone chooses to pay rather than obtain health insurance, they have fully complied with the law. [ ]

* * *

The plaintiffs contend that Congress's choice of language—stating that individuals "shall" obtain insurance or pay a "penalty"—requires reading § 5000A as punishing unlawful conduct, even if that interpretation would render the law unconstitutional. We have rejected a similar argument before. * * *

The joint dissenters argue that we cannot uphold § 5000A as a tax because Congress did not "frame" it as such. [ ] In effect, they contend that even if the Constitution permits Congress to do exactly what we interpret this statute to do, the law must be struck down because Congress used the wrong labels. An example may help illustrate why labels should not control here. Suppose Congress enacted a statute providing that every taxpayer who owns a house without energy efficient windows must pay $50 to the IRS. * * * No one would doubt that this law imposed a tax, and was within Congress's power to tax. That conclusion should not change simply because Congress used the word "penalty" to describe the payment. * * *

* * *

The Affordable Care Act's requirement that certain individuals pay a financial penalty for not obtaining health insurance may reasonably be characterized as a tax. Because the Constitution permits such a tax, it is not our role to forbid it, or to pass upon its wisdom or fairness.

The Federal Government does not have the power to order people to buy health insurance. Section 5000A would therefore be unconstitutional if read as a command. The Federal Government does have the power to impose a tax on those without health insurance. Section 5000A is therefore constitutional, because it can reasonably be read as a tax.

[Justice Ginsburg in an opinion joined by Justices Breyer, Sotomayor, and Kagan dissented from the Chief Justice's opinion on the Commerce Clause issue but concurred in the holding that the law was a constitutional tax. Justices Scalia, Kennedy, Alito, and Thomas dissented jointly against the Chief Justice's conclusion that the mandate was constitutional. They would have held the mandate and the Medicaid expansions to be unconstitutional and the entire ACA to be nonseverable and thus nullified. The Medicaid portion of the decision is reproduced in chapter 10 below).

* * *

NOTE AND QUESTIONS

Are uninsured individuals who can afford insurance less likely to buy insurance if they are not required to purchase it by law, but rather only subject to a tax for failing to do so? Does the NFIB decision limit the ability of Congress to further address problems of access, cost, and quality in health care? What types of solutions is it most likely to discourage? Did opponents of the ACA win the battle but lose the war, or could this be said of health reform supporters?

The Affordable Care Act litigation has generated an unprecedented outpouring of legal scholarship. Over 100 articles on the litigation were published on the Social Science Research Network before the case was even decided. Many more are sure to follow. And many, many more articles, blog posts, and opinion columns have been published by nonlegal sources. The reader is referred to Westlaw and the SSRN for current scholarship.

VIII. EMPLOYER RESPONSIBILITY: SECTIONS 1511 THROUGH 1515

The ACA does not include an employer mandate as such. Employers with more than 50 employees who do not provide health insurance for their employees (including coverage of children for employees with families), however, will owe a penalty of $2000 for every full-time employee after the first 30 employees if any full-time employee ends up getting insurance through the exchange and collecting premium tax credits. Under proposed regulations, employers will only owe this penalty if more than 5 percent of their eligible employees (or 5 employees, if greater) are not covered. Employers who offer insurance coverage but who require their employees to pay more than 9.5% of their income for individual coverage premiums or who offer insurance that does not cover 60% of allowable plan expenses and whose employees purchase coverage through the exchange and receive a tax credit will also face a penalty of $3000 for every full-time employee who fits into this category up to a total of $2000 times the total number of full-time employees (after the first 30 employees).

Solely for determining whether an employer is a large employer, the ACA requires that there be added to the number of actual full-time employees a number equal to the number of hours worked by all other employees in a month divided by 120. But only full-time employees are counted in determining the amount of the penalty, not part-time or seasonal workers, and the first 30 full-time employees are not counted for penalty purposes. Full-time employee means an employee who is employed at least 30 hours per week. Employers with more than 200 employees that offer health insurance to their employees must also automatically enroll new employees in a health insurance plan unless an employee opts out.

Virtually all large employers now offer health benefits, as do many small employers. Health insurance is an important benefit for most employees who do not have insurance available through a spouse or otherwise, and the cost of health insurance is taxable neither to the employer nor employee. Employers will have all of the reasons they now have for covering their employees, plus the potential penalties. But how will the mandate affect employer behavior? Will it cause employers to hire fewer employees or more seasonal or part-time employees? Will it encourage employers to contract out lower wage jobs, like janitorial work or catering, to small firms not subject to the mandate? Will employers choose to pay the penalty rather than purchase insurance, which in 2012 cost $15,745 for an average family policy? Might employers find a way to dump their high cost employees into the exchange while continuing to cover their healthy employees? What other incentives do employers have to offer health insurance to their employees?

Predictions of employer behavior vary dramatically, ranging at the extremes from a McKinsey and Company study that reported that nine percent of employers would definitely and 21 percent would probably drop coverage, to a study by the Rand Corporation, which predicted that employer-sponsored insurance would grow by 8.7 percent. Most studies, however, including studies by Booz, Lewin, Urban, and Mercer, predict that coverage will remain largely unchanged. See Avalere Health, The Affordable Care Act's Impact on Employer Sponsored Insurance (2011); McKinsey Quarterly, How Health Care Reform will Affect Employee Benefits (2011). The Congressional Budget Office, which Congress entrusts with analyzing the effects of legislation, projected that the number of Americans covered by employment-related insurance would grow from 157 million in 2013 to 158 million in 2022, 3 million fewer than would have been covered had the ACA not been adopted. CBO, Analysis of ACA (March 20, 2010). See also Amy Monahan and Daniel Schwarcz, Will Employers Undermine Health Care Reform by Dumping Sick Employees?, 97 Va. L. Rev. 125 (2011), and, in response, David Hyman, PPACA in Theory and Practice: The Perils of Parallelism, 97 Va. L. Rev. in Brief 83 (2011).

An additional complication is an excise tax imposed by the statute on high-cost employer-sponsored health plans. Beginning in 2018, insurers will be required to pay a 40 percent excise tax on employment-related health coverage that costs more than $10,200 for individual or $27,500 for family coverage. These thresholds will be increased to $11,850 for individuals or $30,950 for families for retirees over age 55, electrical or telecommunications repairmen, law enforcement or fire protection workers, out-of-hospital emergency medical providers, and persons engaged in the construction, mining, agriculture, forestry, and fishing industries. Thresholds will be subject to adjustment for unexpected increases in medical costs between now and 2018, and will be indexed for inflation by the consumer price index plus 1 percent after that date, with additional adjustments based on age and gender profiles of covered employees. While the tax is levied on insurers, it will likely be passed on to employers and then to employees, and most likely result in reduction in the generosity of insurance coverage for plans that exceed the threshold.

The Excise tax on high-cost plans has received enthusiastic support from many health economists, who argue that excessively generous employment-based health plans, heavily subsidized by tax exclusions and deductions, are one of the primary explanations for high health care costs in the United States. They contend that lower cost, higher-cost sharing plans, will lead to a reduction in unnecessary use of services, and thus to lower health care costs. They also believe that reductions in health benefit costs would lead to higher wages. See David Leonhardt, How a Tax Can Cut Health Costs. New York Times, Sept. 29, 2009; Paul van de Water, Excise Tax on Very High Cost Plans is a Sound Element of Health Reform, Center of Budget and Policy Priorities (2009).

Opponents of the high cost plan tax, on the other hand, argue that high cost plans are usually the result of insuring sicker and older employees in risky occupations in regions with high medical costs rather than unreasonable plan generosity. Moreover, the money that employers save by reducing health insurance coverage is unlikely to be passed on to employees. Finally, reduction in insurance driven by the "Cadillac plan tax" will likely result in diminished use of medically necessary as well as unnecessary services. See Timothy Jost and Joe White, What is the Cost of an Excise Tax that Keeps People from Going to the Doctor? (2010).

PROBLEMS: EMPLOYER RESPONSIBILITY

Would the employer of Bill in the Help from Health Care Reform problem above owe a penalty? If so, how much? Would Luigi in the Help for Small Businesses problem owe a penalty if he terminated his employee's health insurance?

Jack's Supermarket employs 45 full-time employees and 20 part-time, each of whom works 20 hours a week. Jack's does not provide any health insurance for its employees. Ten of them apply for and receive premium assistance credits. How much is the penalty Jack's owes? What would the penalty by if Jack offered health insurance to its employees, but the plan covered only 50 percent of allowable plan expenses?

CHAPTER 8

DUTIES TO TREAT

∎ ∎ ∎

I. INTRODUCTION

The traditional legal principle of freedom of contract governs the physician-patient relationship, which the physician may choose to enter or not. Legal obligations on the part of health care professionals to provide treatment, whether as a matter of common law doctrine or statute, operate as exceptions to this general rule. The resulting legal fabric is a patchwork rather than a universal right to care, however. As you review the materials in this chapter, consider whether this approach responds to the systemic challenges described here.

Ability to Pay

Projections anticipate that the Affordable Care Act will reduce the number of uninsured in the United States from 54 million to 23 million—not immediately, but over the next ten years. See Chapter 7. The remaining 23 million people will be seeking care directly from health care professionals and hospitals, especially when the need is extreme.

Among the 23 million are approximately 11 million undocumented immigrants. The ACA excludes all U.S. residents not "lawfully present" in the United States from access to the health insurance exchanges and subsidies for insurance. See Chapter 9. Moreover, the Act continues Medicaid's exclusion of undocumented immigrants, although limited federal funds to hospitals for emergency care will probably continue. These exclusions leave the problem of caring for millions of people at the door of physicians and hospitals.

Legally documented immigrants in the United States legally are eligible for the Medicaid program, but state Medicaid rules typically bar them from the program until they have resided in the United States for five years. Once eligible for Medicaid, state rules often exclude this group specifically from particular medical treatments and services. Although the ACA provides for federal insurance subsidies for legal immigrants purchasing insurance through an exchange, it is likely that a good proportion of legal immigrants will be relegated to Medicaid.

Even with the ACA's subsidies, elimination of lifetime caps, and no-co-pay preventive care, individuals relying on private health insurance will still be faced with significant out-of-pocket costs. For some persons and families, and not only the poor, these costs may place needed medical care out of their reach. Data on consumer bankruptcies, for example, demonstrated that study participants with private health insurance faced higher out-of-pocket costs for health care on average ($13,460) than those who were uninsured when they or a family member became ill ($10,893). These studies, which played a role in advocacy for the ACA, also revealed that nearly half of all consumer bankruptcies were the result of costs related to illness. Melissa Jacoby & Mirya Holman, Managing Medical Bills on the Brink of Bankruptcy, 10 Yale J. Health Pol'y, L. & Ethics 239 (2010).

Source of payment operates independently as a barrier to access to care. For example, Medicaid beneficiaries have significant problems in finding physicians who accept Medicaid payment. Advocates for access to care argue that Medicaid payment levels are an access issue, and the ACA includes funding to reduce the gap between Medicaid and Medicare payment rates for primary care physicians. Some, however, have expressed concern that expected reductions in Medicare physician payment levels will drive physicians away from accepting Medicare as well.

Race–Based Barriers

The legacy of racial segregation is still engraved on the U.S. health care system. Hospitals and nursing homes, formally and openly racially segregated through the 1960s, to this day avoid predominantly African–American neighborhoods; only one-quarter of pharmacies in these neighborhoods carry necessary prescription medications; and health insurers market different and more limited health plans, if they market at all, than they do in predominantly Caucasion neighborhoods. Sidney Watson, Section 1557 of the Affordable Care Act: Civil Rights, Health Reform, Race, and Equity, 55 How. L. J. 855 (2012); David Barton Smith, Healthcare's Hidden Civil Rights Legacy, 48 St. Louis U. L.J. 37 (2003). Race-based residential patterns originally established as a matter of *de jure* segregation in housing produce continuing *de facto* segregation in health care facilities. Ruqaiijah Yearby, African Americans Can't Win, Break Even, or Get Out of the System: The Persistence of "Unequal Treatment" in Nursing Home Care, 82 Temple L. Rev. (2010). Racially segregated neighborhoods also produce higher incidences of chronic illness and shorter lifespan due to a number of environmental factors, including exposure to environmental hazards, unsafe housing, and lack of health care services. Thomas LaVeist, Segregated Spaces, Risky Places: The Effects of Racial Segregation on Health Inequalities (2011).

The story of persistent racial disparities in access to quality health care is not captured entirely in the story of geographic segregation. Nor does socioeconomic status explain these distinctions in access to care. Disparities in treatment decisions appear in a great variety of medical conditions. See also Rene Bowser, The Affordable Care Act and Beyond: Opportunities for Advancing Health Equity and Social Justice, 10 Hastings Race & Poverty L. J. 69 (2013), citing studies documenting that African–American and Latino patients are categorized as needing less urgent care by ER personnel than whites with the same cardiac symptoms; are less likely to receive aspirin upon discharge after heart attack; and are less likely to receive pain medication in the ER for long-bone fractures. An Institute of Medicine report, reviewing all available empirical data, found serious "racial or ethnic differences in the quality of healthcare that are not due to access-related factors or clinical needs, preferences and appropriateness of intervention." IOM, Unequal Treatment: Confronting Racial and Ethnic Disparities in Health Care (2002).

Inequality in access to needed medical care is influenced by institutional issues, including decisions of health care organizations in determining their location, service area, and programs, and by interpersonal issues, including individual physician treatment decisions. Inequality also can be supported by structural design of public health payment programs and civil rights enforcement policy. Ruqaiijah Yearby, Breaking the Cycle of "Unequal Treatment" with Health Care Reform: Acknowledging and Addressing the Continuation of Racial Bias, 44 Conn. L. Rev. 1281 (2012).

Access Barriers by Medical Condition

Persons with particular medical or physical conditions face a variety of condition-related barriers to accessing care. Men and women with mobility disabilities, for example, may not be able to get the care they need because of a hospital's or physician office's lack of accessible medical equipment. Persons with chronic pain, obesity, addiction, mental illness, HIV/AIDS, or other conditions may find their access to medical care and the quality of care they receive impeded by the stigma attached to their condition. See Jeffrey Friedman, Modern Science versus the Stigma of Obesity, 10 Nature Medicine 563 (2004); Julie Greenberg, Health Care Issues Affecting People with an Intersex Condition or DSD: Sex or Disability Discrimination, 45 Loy. L.A. L. Rev. 849 (2012); Richard Boldt, Introduction: Obstacles to the Development and Use of Pharmacotherapies for Addiction, 13 J. Health Care L. & Pol'y 1 (2010); Pamela Das & Richard Horton, The Cultural Challenge of HIV/AIDS, 380 The Lancet 309 (2012).

Other factors intersect with medical condition and can exacerbate lack of care. For example, lack of accessible medical equipment for mobility-impaired women reflects stereotypes about sexuality. Elizabeth Pendo, Disability, Equipment Barriers, and Women's Health: Using the ADA to Provide Meaningful Access, 2 St. Louis U. J. Health L. & Pol'y 15 (2008). Denial of adequate treatment for pain intersects directly with race and gender. Vence Bonham, Race, Ethnicity, and The Disparities in Pain Treatment: Striving to Understand the Causes and Solutions to the Disparities in Pain Treatment, 29 J. L. Med. & Ethics 52 (2001); Diane E. Hoffmann & Anita J. Tarzian, The Girl Who Cried Pain: A Bias Against Women in the Treatment of Pain, 29 J. L. Med. & Ethics 13 (2001).

II.   COMMON LAW APPROACHES

RICKS V. BUDGE
Supreme Court of Utah, 1937.
91 Utah 307, 64 P.2d 208.

EPHRAIM HANSON, JUSTICE.

This is an action for malpractice against the defendants who are physicians and surgeons at Logan, Utah, and are copartners doing business under the name and style of the "Budge Clinic." * * * [P]laintiff alleges that he was suffering from an infected right hand and was in immediate need of medical and surgical care and treatment, and there was danger of his dying unless he received such treatment; that defendants for the purpose of treating plaintiff sent him to the Budge Memorial Hospital [BMH] at Logan, Utah; that while at the hospital and while he was in need of medical and surgical treatment, defendants refused to treat or care for plaintiff and abandoned his case. * * *

*   *   *

[T]he evidence shows that when plaintiff left the hospital on March 15th, Dr. [S.M.] Budge advised him to continue the same treatment that had been given him at the hospital, and that if the finger showed any signs of getting worse at any time, plaintiff was to return at once to Dr. Budge for further treatment; that on the morning of March 17th, plaintiff telephoned Dr. Budge, and explained the condition of his hand; that he was told by the doctor to come to his office, and in pursuance of the doctor's request, plaintiff reported to the doctor's office at 2 p.m. of that day. Dr. Budge again examined the hand, and told plaintiff the hand was worse; he called in Dr. D.C. Budge, another of the defendants, who examined the hand, scraped it some, and indicated thereon where the hand should be opened. Dr. S.M. Budge said to plaintiff: "You have got to go back to the hospital." * * * Within a short time after the arrival of plaintiff, Dr. S.M. Budge arrived at the hospital. Plaintiff testified: "He [meaning Dr. S.M. Budge] came into my room and said, 'You are owing us. I am not going to touch you until that account is taken care of.' " (The account referred to was, according to plaintiff, of some years' standing and did not relate to any charge for services being then rendered.) Plaintiff testified that he did not know what to say to the doctor, but that he finally asked the doctor if he was going to take care of him, and the doctor replied: "No, I am not going to take care of you. I would not take you to the operating table and operate on you and keep you here thirty days, and then there is another $30.00 at the office, until your account is taken care of." Plaintiff replied: "If that is the idea, if you will furnish me a little help, I will try to move."

[A]fter being dressed, he left [BMH] to seek other treatment. At that time it was raining. He walked to the Cache Valley Hospital [CVH], a few blocks away, and there met Dr. Randall, who examined the hand. Dr. Randall testified that when the plaintiff arrived at [CVH], the hand was swollen with considerable fluid oozing from it; that the lower two-thirds of the forearm was red and swollen from the infection which extended up in the arm, and that there was some fluid also oozing from the back of the hand, and that plaintiff required immediate surgical attention; that immediately after the arrival of plaintiff at the hospital he made an incision through the fingers and through the palm of the hand along the tendons that led from the palm, followed those tendons as far as there was any bulging, opened it up thoroughly all the way to the base of the hand, and put drain tubes in. * * * About two weeks after the plaintiff entered [CVH], it became necessary to amputate the middle finger and remove about an inch of the metacarpal bone.

*   *   *

Defendants contend: (1) That there was no contract of employment between plaintiff and defendants and that defendants in the absence of a valid contract were not obligated to proceed with any treatment; and (2) that if there was such a contract, there was no evidence that the refusal of Dr. S.M. Budge to operate or take care of plaintiff resulted in any damage to plaintiff.

*   *   *

Under this evidence, it cannot be said that the relation of physician and patient did not exist on March 17th. It had not been terminated after its commencement on March 11th. When the plaintiff left the hospital on March 15th, he understood that he was to report to Dr. S.M. Budge if the occasion required and was so requested by the doctor. Plaintiff's return to the doctor's office was on the advice of the doctor. While at the doctor's office, both Dr. S.M. Budge and Dr. D.C. Budge examined plaintiff's hand and they ordered that he go at once to the hospital for further medical attention. That plaintiff was told by the doctor to come to the doctor's office and was there examined by him and directed to go to the hospital for further treatment would create the relationship of physician and patient.

That the relationship existed at the time the plaintiff was sent to the hospital on March 17th cannot be seriously questioned.

We believe the law is well settled that a physician or surgeon, upon undertaking an operation or other case, is under the duty, in the absence of an agreement limiting the service, of continuing his attention, after the first operation or first treatment, so long as the case requires attention. The obligation of continuing attention can be terminated only by the cessation of the necessity which gave rise to the relationship, or by the discharge of the physician by the patient, or by the withdrawal from the case by the physician after giving the patient reasonable notice so as to enable the patient to secure other medical attention. A physician has the right to withdraw from a case, but if the case is such as to still require further medical or surgical attention, he must, before withdrawing from the case, give the patient sufficient notice so the patient can procure other medical attention if he desires.[ ]

*   *   *

We cannot say as a matter of law that plaintiff suffered no damages by reason of the refusal of Dr. S.M. Budge to further treat him. The evidence shows that from the time plaintiff left the office of the defendants up until the time that he arrived at [CVH] his hand continued to swell; that it was very painful; that when he left [BMH] he was in such condition that he did not know whether he was going to live or die. That both his mental and physical suffering must have been most acute cannot be questioned. While the law cannot measure with exactness such suffering and cannot determine with absolute certainty what damages, if any, plaintiff may be entitled to, still those are questions which a jury under proper instructions from the court must determine.

*   *   *

FOLLAND, JUSTICE (concurring in part, dissenting in part).

*   *   *

* * * The theory of plaintiff as evidenced in his complaint is that there was no continued relationship from the first employment but that a new relationship was entered into. He visited the clinic on March 17th; the Doctors Budge examined his hand and told him an immediate operation was necessary and for him to go to the hospital. I do not think a new contract was entered into at that time. There was no consideration for any implied promise that Dr. Budge or the Budge Clinic would assume the responsibility of another operation and the costs and expenses incident thereto. As soon as Dr. Budge reached the hospital he opened negotiations with the plaintiff which might have resulted in a contract, but before any contract arrangement was made the plaintiff decided to leave the hospital and seek attention elsewhere. As soon as he could dress himself he walked away. There is conflict in the evidence as to the conversation. Plaintiff testified in effect that Dr. Budge asked for something to be done about an old account. The doctor's testimony in effect was that he asked that some arrangement be made to take care of the doctor's bill and expenses for the ensuing operation and treatment at the hospital. The result, however, was negative. No arrangement was made. The plaintiff made no attempt whatsoever to suggest to the doctor any way by which either the old account might be taken care of or the expenses of the ensuing operation provided for. * * * Dr. Budge had a right to refuse to incur the obligation and responsibility incident to one or more operations and the treatment and attention which would be necessary. If it be assumed that the contract relationship of physician and patient existed prior to this conversation, either as resulting from the first employment or that there was an implied contract entered into at the clinic, yet Dr. Budge had the right with proper notice to discontinue the relationship. While plaintiff's condition was acute and needed immediate attention, he received such immediate attention at [CVH]. There was only a delay of an hour or two, and part of that delay is accounted for by reason of the fact that the doctor at [CVH] would not operate until some paper, which plaintiff says he did not read, was signed. Plaintiff said he could not sign it but that it was signed by his brother before the operation was performed. We are justified in believing that by means of this written obligation, provision was made for the expenses and fees about to be incurred. I am satisfied from my reading of the record that no injury or damage resulted from the delay occasioned by plaintiff leaving the Budge Hospital and going to [CVH]. He was not in such desperate condition but that he was able to walk the three or four blocks between the two hospitals. * * *

CHILDS V. WEIS

Court of Civil Appeals of Texas, 1969.
440 S.W.2d 104.

WILLIAMS, J.

On or about November 27, 1966 Daisy Childs, wife of J.C. Childs, a resident of Dallas County, was approximately seven months pregnant. On that date she was visiting in Lone Oak, Texas, and about two o'clock A.M. she presented herself to the Greenville Hospital emergency room. At that time she stated she was bleeding and had labor pains. She was examined by a nurse who identified herself as H. Beckham. According to Mrs. Childs, Nurse Beckham stated that she would call the doctor. She said the nurse returned and stated "that the Dr. said that I would have to go to my doctor in Dallas. I stated to Beckham that I'm not going to make it to Dallas. Beckham replied that yes, I would make it. She stated that I was just starting into labor and that I would make it. The weather was cold that night. About an hour after leaving the Greenville Hospital Authority I had the baby while in a car on the way to medical facilities in Sulphur Springs. The baby lived about 12 hours."

[Dr. Weis] said that he had never examined or treated Daisy Childs and in fact had never seen or spoken to either Daisy Childs or her husband, J.C. Childs, at any time in his life. He further stated that he had never at any time agreed or consented to the examination or treatment of either Daisy Childs or her husband. He said that on a day in November 1966 he recalled a telephone call received by him from a nurse in the emergency room at the Greenville Surgical Hospital; that the nurse told him that there was a negro girl in the emergency room having a "bloody show" and some "labor pains." He said the nurse advised him that this woman had been visiting in Lone Oak, and that her OB doctor lived in Garland, Texas, and that she also resided in Garland. The doctor said, "I told the nurse over the telephone to have the girl call her doctor in Garland and see what he wanted her to do. I knew nothing more about this incident until I was served with the citation and a copy of the petition in this lawsuit."

*   *   *

Since it is unquestionably the law that the relationship of physician and patient is dependent upon contract, either express or implied, a physician is not to be held liable for arbitrarily refusing to respond to a call of a person even urgently in need of medical or surgical assistance provided that the relation of physician and patient does not exist at the time the call is made or at the time the person presents himself for treatment.

*   *   *

Applying these principles of law to the factual situation here presented we find an entire absence of evidence of a contract, either express or implied, which would create the relationship of patient and physician as between Dr. Weis and Mrs. Childs. Dr. Weis, under these circumstances, was under no duty whatsoever to examine or treat Mrs. Childs. When advised by telephone that the lady was in the emergency room he did what seems to be a reasonable thing and inquired as to the identity of her doctor who had been treating her. Upon being told that the doctor was in Garland he stated that the patient should call the doctor and find out what should be done. This action on the part of Dr. Weis seems to be not only reasonable but within the bounds of professional ethics.

We cannot agree with appellant that Dr. Weis' statement to the nurse over the telephone amounted to an acceptance of the case and affirmative instructions which she was bound to follow. Rather than give instructions which could be construed to be in the nature of treatment, Dr. Weis told the nurse to have the woman call her physician in Garland and secure instructions from him.

The affidavit of Mrs. Childs would indicate that Nurse Beckham may not have relayed the exact words of Dr. Weis to Mrs. Childs. Instead, it would seem that Nurse Beckham told Mrs. Childs that the doctor said that she would "have to go" to her doctor in Dallas. Assuming this statement was made by Nurse Beckham, and further assuming that it contained the meaning as placed upon it by appellant, yet it is undisputed that such words were uttered by Nurse Beckham, and not by Dr. Weis.
* * *

[The court affirmed summary judgment in favor of the defendant.]

NOTES AND QUESTIONS

1.   Why did the doctor refuse to treat Mr. Ricks? Ms. Childs? Should the courts distinguish among such cases on the basis of the reason for the refusal? If the court were willing to make a distinction, how would you go about proving the basis for the refusal in each of these cases? See, Section III.B, below. What establishes a physician-patient relationship under *Ricks*?

2.   Physicians often commit by contract to treat a certain group of patients, for example in contracts with health plans or in employment contracts with health care facilities or employers. Physician specialists often have a contractual relationship with the hospital to be on-call for essential services, either for compensation or as required in the medical staff by-laws as a condition of staff privileges. See also Section III.A, below. These commitments to an organization may be sufficient to create a physician-patient relationship and trigger a duty to provide treatment. See, e.g., Millard v. Carrado, 14 S.W.3d 42 (Mo. Ct. App. 1999).

III.   STATUTORY EXCEPTIONS TO THE COMMON LAW

A.   EMTALA

The federal Emergency Medical Treatment and Labor Act, 42 U.S.C. § 1395dd (EMTALA), was enacted in response to "patient dumping," a practice in which patients are transferred from one hospital's emergency room to another's for other than therapeutic reasons. Several empirical studies documented patient dumping as a widespread practice.

EMTALA applies only to hospitals that accept payment from Medicare *and* operate an emergency department; however, EMTALA applies to all patients of such a hospital and not just to Medicare beneficiaries. While EMTALA does not require a hospital to offer emergency room services, some state hospital licensure statutes do; federal tax law encourages tax-exempt hospitals to do so; and Medicare Conditions of Participation require that all hospitals be capable of providing initial treatment in emergency situations as well as arrange for referral or transfer to more comprehensive facilities.

EMTALA specifically empowers patients to bring civil suits for damages against participating hospitals, but does not provide a private right of action against a treating physician. The Office of the Inspector General (OIG) of HHS enforces EMTALA against both hospitals and physicians. Private EMTALA litigation has burgeoned, while government enforcement has been much less active. Administrative enforcement actions under EMTALA are few; monetary penalties are quite small; and exclusion from Medicare is almost unheard of. Despite the passage of EMTALA, and perhaps because of its lax enforcement by the agency, patient dumping continues. Sara Rosenbaum et al., Case Studies at Denver Health: "Patient Dumping" in the Emergency Department Despite EMTALA, the Law that Banned It, 31 Health Affairs 1749 (2012).

EMERGENCY MEDICAL TREATMENT AND LABOR ACT
42 U.S.C. § 1395dd.

(a) Medical screening requirement. In the case of a hospital that has a hospital emergency department, if any individual * * * comes to the emergency department and a request is made on the individual's behalf for examination or treatment for a medical condition, the hospital must provide for an appropriate medical screening examination within the capability of the hospital's emergency department, including ancillary services routinely available to the emergency department, to determine whether or not an emergency medical condition * * * exists.

(b) Necessary stabilizing treatment for emergency medical conditions and labor.

(1) In general. If any individual * * * comes to a hospital and the hospital determines that the individual has an emergency medical condition, the hospital must provide either—

(A) within the staff and facilities available at the hospital, for such further medical examination and such treatment as may be required to stabilize the medical condition, or

(B) for transfer of the individual to another medical facility in accordance with subsection (c).

* * *

(c) Restricting transfers until individual stabilized.

(1) Rule. If an individual at a hospital has an emergency medical condition which has not been stabilized * * *, the hospital may not transfer the individual unless—

(A)(i) the individual (or a legally responsible person acting on the individual's behalf) after being informed of the hospital's obligations under this section and of the risk of transfer, in writing requests transfer to another medical facility, [or]

(ii) a physician * * * has signed a certification that[,] based upon the information available at the time of transfer, the medical benefits reasonably expected from the provision of appropriate medical treatment at another medical facility outweigh the increased risks to the individual and, in the case of labor, to the unborn child from effecting the transfer.

* * *

(B) [and] the transfer is an appropriate transfer * * * to that facility * * *.

* * *

(2) Appropriate transfer. An appropriate transfer to a medical facility is a transfer—

(A) in which the transferring hospital provides the medical treatment within its capacity which minimizes the risks to the individual's health and, in the case of a woman in labor, the health of the unborn child;

(B) in which the receiving facility—

(i) has available space and qualified personnel for the treatment of the individual, and

(ii) has agreed to accept transfer of the individual and to provide appropriate medical treatment;

(C) in which the transferring hospital sends to the receiving facility all medical records * * * related to the emergency condition for which the individual has presented, available at the time of the transfer * * *; [and]

(D) in which the transfer is effected through qualified personnel and transportation equipment. . . .

(d) Enforcement.

(1) Civil monetary penalties.

(A) A participating hospital that negligently violates a requirement of this section is subject to a civil money penalty of not more than $50,000 for each such violation* * *.

(B) [A]ny physician who is responsible for the examination, treatment, or transfer of an individual in a participating hospital

* * * and who negligently violates a requirement of this section, including a physician on-call for the care of such individual, is subject to a civil money penalty of not more than $50,000 for each such violation and, if the violation is gross and flagrant or is repeated, to exclusion from participation in [Medicare and Medicaid]* * *.

(2) Civil enforcement.

(A) Personal harm. Any individual who suffers personal harm as a direct result of a participating hospital's violation of a requirement of this section may, in a civil action against the participating hospital, obtain those damages available for personal injury under the law of the State in which the hospital is located, and such equitable relief as is appropriate.

(B) Financial loss to other medical facility. Any medical facility that suffers a financial loss as a direct result of a participating hospital's violation of a requirement of this section may, in a civil action against the participating hospital, obtain those damages available for financial loss, under the law of the State in which the hospital is located, and such equitable relief as is appropriate.* * *

(e) Definitions. In this section:

(1) The term "emergency medical condition" means—

(A) a medical condition manifesting itself by acute symptoms of sufficient severity (including severe pain) such that the absence of immediate medical attention could reasonably be expected to result in—

(i) placing the health of the individual (or, with respect to a pregnant woman, the health of the woman or her unborn child) in serious jeopardy,

(ii) serious impairment to bodily functions, or

(iii) serious dysfunction of any bodily organ or part; or

(B) with respect to a pregnant woman who is having contractions—

(i) that there is inadequate time to effect a safe transfer to another hospital before delivery, or

(ii) that transfer may pose a threat to the health or safety of the woman or the unborn child * * *.

*   *   *

(3)(A) The term "to stabilize" means * * * to provide such medical treatment of the condition as may be necessary to assure, within reasonable medical probability, that no material deterioration of the condition is likely to result from or occur during the transfer of the individual from a facility.* * *

(B) The term "stabilized" means * * * that no material deterioration of the condition is likely, within reasonable medical probability, to result from or occur during the transfer of the individual from a facility, or, with respect to an emergency medical condition described in paragraph (1)(B), that the woman has delivered (including the placenta) * * *.

BABER V. HOSPITAL CORPORATION OF AMERICA

United States Court of Appeals, Fourth Circuit, 1992.
977 F.2d 872.

WILLIAMS, CIRCUIT JUDGE:

Barry Baber, Administrator of the Estate of Brenda Baber, instituted this suit against * * * Raleigh General Hospital (RGH), Beckley Appalachian Regional Hospital (BARH), and the parent corporations of both hospitals. Mr. Baber alleged that the Defendants violated the Emergency Medical Treatment and Active Labor Act (EMTALA)[ ]. The Defendants moved to dismiss the EMTALA claim under Rule 12(b)(6) of the Federal Rules of Civil Procedure. Because the parties submitted affidavits and depositions, the district court treated the motion as one for summary judgment. See Fed.R.Civ.P. 12(b).

* * *

Mr. Baber's complaint charged the various defendants with violating EMTALA in several ways. Specifically, Mr. Baber contends that Dr. Kline, RGH, and its parent corporation violated EMTALA by:

(a) failing to provide his sister with an "appropriate medical screening examination;"

(b) failing to stabilize his sister's "emergency medical condition;" and

(c) transferring his sister to BARH without first providing stabilizing treatment.

* * *

After reviewing the parties' submissions, the district court granted summary judgment for the Defendants. * * * Finding no error, we affirm.

* * *

* * * Brenda Baber, accompanied by her brother, Barry, sought treatment at RGH's emergency department at 10:40 p.m. on August 5, 1987. When she entered the hospital, Ms. Baber was nauseated, agitated, and thought she might be pregnant. She was also tremulous and did not appear to have orderly thought patterns. She had stopped taking her anti-psychosis medications, * * * and had been drinking heavily. Dr. Kline, the attending physician, described her behavior and condition in the RGH Encounter Record as follows: Patient refuses to remain on stretcher and cannot be restrained verbally despite repeated requests by staff and by me. Brother has not assisted either verbally or physically in keeping patient from pacing throughout the Emergency Room. Restraints would place patient and staff at risk by increasing her agitation.

In response to Ms. Baber's initial complaints, Dr. Kline examined her central nervous system, lungs, cardiovascular system, and abdomen. He also ordered several laboratory tests, including a pregnancy test.

While awaiting the results of her laboratory tests, Ms. Baber began pacing about the emergency department. In an effort to calm Ms. Baber, Dr. Kline gave her [several medications]. The medication did not immediately control her agitation. Mr. Baber described his sister as becoming restless, "worse and more disoriented after she was given the medication," and wandering around the emergency department.

While roaming in the emergency department around midnight, Ms. Baber * * * convulsed and fell, striking her head upon a table and lacerating her scalp. [S]he quickly regained consciousness and emergency department personnel carried her by stretcher to the suturing room, [where] Dr. Kline examined her again. He obtained a blood gas study, which did not reveal any oxygen deprivation or acidosis. Ms. Baber was verbal and could move her head, eyes, and limbs without discomfort. * * * Dr. Kline closed the one-inch laceration with a couple of sutures. Although she became calmer and drowsy after the wound was sutured, Ms. Baber was easily arousable and easily disturbed. Ms. Baber experienced some anxiety, disorientation, restlessness, and some speech problems, which Dr. Kline concluded were caused by her pre-existing psychiatric problems of psychosis with paranoia and alcohol withdrawal.

Dr. Kline discussed Ms. Baber's condition with Dr. Whelan, the psychiatrist who had treated Ms. Baber for two years. * * * Dr. Whelan concluded that Ms. Baber's hyperactive and uncontrollable behavior during her evening at RGH was compatible with her behavior during a relapse of her serious psychotic and chronic mental illness. Both Dr. Whelan and Dr. Kline were concerned about the seizure she had while at RGH's emergency department because it was the first one she had experienced. * * * They also agreed Ms. Baber needed further treatment * * * and decided to transfer her to the psychiatric unit at BARH because RGH did not have a psychiatric ward, and both doctors believed it would be beneficial for her to be treated in a familiar setting. The decision to transfer Ms. Baber was further supported by the doctors' belief that any tests to diagnose the cause of her initial seizure, such as a computerized tomography scan (CT scan), could be performed at BARH once her psychiatric condition was under control. The transfer to BARH was discussed with Mr. Baber who neither expressly consented nor objected. His only request was that his sister be x-rayed because of the blow to her head when she fell.

* * *

Because Dr. Kline did not conclude Ms. Baber had a serious head injury, he believed that she could be transferred safely to BARH where she would be under the observation of the BARH psychiatric staff personnel. At 1:35 a.m. on August 6, Ms. Baber was admitted directly to the psychiatric department of BARH upon Dr. Whelan's orders. She was not processed through BARH's emergency department. Although Ms. Baber was restrained and regularly checked every fifteen minutes by the nursing staff while at BARH, no physician gave her an extensive neurological examination upon her arrival. Mr. Baber unsuccessfully repeated his request for an x-ray.

At the 3:45 a.m. check, the nurse found Ms. Baber having a grand mal seizure. At Dr. Whelan's direction, the psychiatric unit staff transported her to BARH's emergency department. Upon arrival in the emergency department, her pupils were unresponsive, and hospital personnel began CPR. The emergency department physician ordered a CT scan, which was performed around 6:30 a.m. The CT report revealed a fractured skull and a right subdural hematoma. BARH personnel immediately transferred Ms. Baber back to RGH because that hospital had a neurosurgeon on staff, and BARH did not have the facility or staff to treat serious neurological problems. When RGH received Ms. Baber for treatment around 7 a.m., she was comatose. She died later that day, apparently as a result of an intracerebrovascular rupture.

* * *

Mr. Baber * * * alleges that RGH, acting through its agent, Dr. Kline, violated several provisions of EMTALA. These allegations can be summarized into two general complaints: (1) RGH failed to provide an appropriate medical screening to discover that Ms. Baber had an emergency medical condition as required by 42 U.S.C.A. § 1395dd(a); and (2) RGH transferred Ms. Baber before her emergency medical condition had been stabilized, and the appropriate paperwork was not completed to transfer a non-stable patient as required by 42 U.S.C.A. § 1395dd(b) & (c). Because we find that RGH did not violate any of these EMTALA provisions, we affirm the district court's grant of summary judgment to RGH.

Mr. Baber first claims that RGH failed to provide his sister with an "appropriate medical screening". He makes two arguments. First, he contends that a medical screening is only "appropriate" if it satisfies a national standard of care. In other words, Mr. Baber urges that we construe EMTALA as a national medical malpractice statute, albeit limited to whether the medical screening was appropriate to identify an emergency medical condition. We conclude instead that EMTALA only requires hospitals to apply their standard screening procedure for identification of an emergency medical condition uniformly to all patients and that Mr. Baber has failed to proffer sufficient evidence showing that RGH did not do so. Second, Mr. Baber contends that EMTALA requires hospitals to provide some medical screening. We agree, but conclude that he has failed to show no screening was provided to his sister.

* * *

While [the Act] requires a hospital's emergency department to provide an "appropriate medical screening examination," it does not define that term other than to state its purpose is to identify an "emergency medical condition."

* * *

[T]he goal of "an appropriate medical screening examination" is to determine whether a patient with acute or severe symptoms has a life threatening or serious medical condition. The plain language of the statute requires a hospital to develop a screening procedure[6] designed to identify such critical conditions that exist in symptomatic patients and to apply that screening procedure uniformly to all patients with similar complaints.

[W]hile EMTALA requires a hospital emergency department to apply its standard screening examination uniformly, it does not guarantee that the emergency personnel will correctly diagnose a patient's condition as a result of this screening.[7] The statutory language clearly indicates that

---

[6] While a hospital emergency room may develop one general procedure for screening all patients, it may also tailor its screening procedure to the patient's complaints or exhibited symptoms. For example, it may have one screening procedure for a patient with a heart attack and another for women in labor. Under our interpretation of EMTALA, such varying screening procedures would not pose liability under EMTALA as long as all patients complaining of the same problem or exhibiting the same symptoms receive identical screening procedures. We also recognize that the hospital's screening procedure is not limited to personal observation and assessment but may include available ancillary services through departments such as radiology and laboratory.

[7] Some commentators have criticized defining "appropriate" in terms of the hospital's medical screening standard because hospitals could theoretically avoid liability by providing very cursory and substandard screenings to all patients, which might enable the doctor to ignore a medical condition. [ ] Even though we do not believe it is likely that a hospital would endanger all of its patients by establishing such a cursory standard, theoretically it is possible. Our holding, however, does not foreclose the possibility that a future court faced with such a situation may decide that the hospital's standard was so low that it amounted to no "appropriate medical

EMTALA does not impose on hospitals a national standard of care in screening patients. The screening requirement only requires a hospital to provide a screening examination that is "appropriate" and "within the capability of the hospital's emergency department," including "routinely available" ancillary services. 42 U.S.C.A. § 1395dd(a). This section establishes a standard, which will of necessity be individualized for each hospital, since hospital emergency departments have varying capabilities. Had Congress intended to require hospitals to provide a screening examination which comported with generally-accepted medical standards, it could have clearly specified a national standard. Nor do we believe Congress intended to create a negligence standard based on each hospital's capability. * * * EMTALA is no substitute for state law medical malpractice actions.

*   *   *

The Sixth Circuit has also held that an appropriate medical screening means "a screening that the hospital would have offered to any paying patient" or at least "not known by the provider to be insufficient or below their own standards."

*   *   *

Applying our interpretation of section (a) of EMTALA, we must next determine whether there is any genuine issue of material fact regarding whether RGH gave Ms. Baber a medical screening examination that differed from its standard screening procedure. Because Mr. Baber has offered no evidence of disparate treatment, we find that the district court did not err in granting summary judgment.

*   *   *

Mr. Baber does not allege that RGH's emergency department personnel treated Ms. Baber differently from its other patients. Instead, he merely claims Dr. Kline did not do enough accurately to diagnose her condition or treat her injury.[ ] The critical element of an EMTALA cause of action is not the adequacy of the screening examination but whether the screening examination that was performed deviated from the hospital's evaluation procedures that would have been performed on any patient in a similar condition.

*   *   *

Dr. Kline testified that he performed a medical screening on Ms. Baber in accordance with standard procedures for examining patients with head injuries. He explained that generally, a patient is not scheduled for

---

screening." We do not decide that question in this case because Ms. Baber's screening was not so substandard as to amount to no screening at all.

advanced tests such as a CT scan or x-rays unless the patient's signs and symptoms so warrant. While Ms. Baber did exhibit some of the signs and symptoms of patients who have severe head injuries, in Dr. Kline's medical judgment these signs were the result of her pre-existing psychiatric condition, not the result of her fall. He, therefore, determined that Ms. Baber's head injury was not serious and did not indicate the need at that time for a CT scan or x-rays. In his medical judgment, Ms. Baber's condition would be monitored adequately by the usual nursing checks performed every fifteen minutes by the psychiatric unit staff at BARH. Although Dr. Kline's assessment and judgment may have been erroneous and not within acceptable standards of medical care in West Virginia, he did perform a screening examination that was not so substandard as to amount to no examination. No testimony indicated that his procedure deviated from that which RGH would have provided to any other patient in Ms. Baber's condition.

* * *

The essence of Mr. Baber's argument is that the extent of the examination and treatment his sister received while at RGH was deficient. While Mr. Baber's testimony might be sufficient to survive a summary judgment motion in a medical malpractice case, it is clearly insufficient to survive a motion for summary judgment in an EMTALA case because at no point does Mr. Baber present any evidence that RGH deviated from its standard screening procedure in evaluating Ms. Baber's head injury. Therefore, the district court properly granted RGH summary judgment on the medical screening issue.

Mr. Baber also asserts that RGH inappropriately transferred his sister to BARH. EMTALA's transfer requirements do not apply unless the hospital actually determines that the patient suffers from an emergency medical condition. Accordingly, to recover for violations of EMTALA's transfer provisions, the plaintiff must present evidence that (1) the patient had an emergency medical condition; (2) the hospital actually knew of that condition; (3) the patient was not stabilized before being transferred; and (4) prior to transfer of an unstable patient, the transferring hospital did not obtain the proper consent or follow the appropriate certification and transfer procedures.

* * *

Mr. Baber argues that requiring a plaintiff to prove the hospital had actual knowledge of the patient's emergency medical condition would allow hospitals to circumvent the purpose of EMTALA by simply requiring their personnel to state in all hospital records that the patient did not suffer from an emergency medical condition. Because of this concern, Mr. Baber urges us to adopt a standard that would impose liability upon a hospital if it failed to provide stabilizing treatment prior to a transfer when the hospital knew or should have known that the patient suffered from an emergency medical condition.

The statute itself implicitly rejects this proposed standard. Section 1395dd(b)(1) states the stabilization requirement exists if "any individual . . . comes to a hospital and the hospital determines that the individual has an emergency medical condition." Thus, the plain language of the statute dictates a standard requiring actual knowledge of the emergency medical condition by the hospital staff.

Mr. Baber failed to present any evidence that RGH had actual knowledge that Ms. Baber suffered from an emergency medical condition. Dr. Kline stated in his affidavit that Ms. Baber's condition was stable prior to transfer and that he did not believe she was suffering from an emergency medical condition. While Mr. Baber testified that he believed his sister suffered from an emergency medical condition at transfer, he did not present any evidence beyond his own belief that she actually had an emergency medical condition or that anyone at RGH knew that she suffered from an emergency medical condition. In addition, we note that Mr. Baber's testimony is not competent to prove his sister actually had an emergency medical condition since he is not qualified to diagnose a serious internal brain injury.

* * * [W]e hold that the district court correctly granted RGH summary judgment on Mr. Baber's claim that it transferred Ms. Baber in violation of EMTALA.

*　*　*

Therefore, the district court's judgment is affirmed.

NOTES AND QUESTIONS

1. In contrast to the standard for medical screening, the standard applied to the question of whether the patient was unstable when discharged or transferred is an objective professional standard and not defined by the specific hospital's policy. How should plaintiff structure discovery to meet each of these two standards? What is the role for expert testimony, if any, in an "unstable transfer or discharge" claim? In an "inappropriate screening" claim?

2. Improper motive is not required for a violation of the EMTALA requirement that the patient be stabilized. Roberts v. Galen of Va., Inc., 525 U.S. 249, 119 S.Ct. 685, 142 L.Ed.2d 648 (1999). The Court expressed no opinion, however, as to whether proof of improper motive is essential for a claim of failure to provide an appropriate screening. The Circuits, except for the Sixth Circuit in *Cleland*, have held that proof of bad motive is not required for either a screening or a stabilization claim.

3.   One of the sticky issues in EMTALA is whether a patient has "come to" the hospital's emergency room. After years of court opinions with conflicting results, HHS promulgated regulations in 2003 delineating under what circumstances a patient being transported by ambulance or a patient otherwise on hospital property is considered to have "come to" the emergency room. 42 C.F.R. § 489.24(b)

4.   Emergency treatment in the ED often requires the services of an on-call specialist. Hospitals generally don't employ on-call specialists, but may contract with individual physicians to provide on-call services or may require on-call coverage by physicians as a condition of receiving admitting privileges. The division of labor inherent in the ED/on-call relationship can be contentious and raise EMTALA risks. Consider the Problem below.

PROBLEM: *EMTALA* AND *HHS* REGULATIONS

On May 21, Ms. Nancy Miller, who was eight months pregnant, called her obstetrician, Dr. Jennifer Gibson, at 2:00 a.m. because she was experiencing severe pain which appeared to her to be labor contractions. Dr. Gibson advised Ms. Miller to go to the emergency department of the local hospital and promised to meet her there shortly. Ms. Miller was admitted to the emergency department of General Hospital at 2:30 a.m., and Dr. Gibson joined her there at 3:14 a.m. After examining Ms. Miller, Dr. Gibson concluded that Ms. Miller had begun labor and that, despite the fact that the pregnancy had not reached full-term, the labor should be continued to delivery. At that time, Dr. Gibson asked that the on-call anesthesiologist, Dr. Martig, see Ms. Miller to discuss anesthesia during the delivery. At the same time, the procedure to admit Ms. Miller to the hospital's maternity floor was begun. The nurse informed Ms. Miller that there would be a short wait because there was no space available at that point.

Dr. Martig saw Ms. Miller at 4:00 a.m. When asked, Dr. Martig informed Ms. Miller that he was not qualified to and would not be able to perform an epidural (a spinal nerve-block anesthesia, often used in childbirth). Instead, he gave her Demerol and left the emergency department.

At 4:30 a.m., Ms. Miller was admitted to the labor and delivery floor. At 4:45 a.m., the obstetrical nurse observed fetal distress and called Dr. Gibson. At 4:50 a.m., Dr. Gibson concluded that Ms. Miller had a prolapsed umbilical cord and ordered an emergency caesarean section. The OB nurse paged Dr. Martig, but he could not be located. (Dr. Martig later stated that his pager had malfunctioned.) Because Dr. Martig could not be located, Dr. Gibson and a resident performed the C-section without an anesthetic and delivered the child healthy and alive. (These facts are based on Miller v. Martig, 754 N.E.2d 41 (Ind. Ct. App. 2001).)

Assume that Ms. Miller has brought suit against the hospital and Dr. Martig. What federal and state claims might Ms. Miller make? Assume that

Dr. Martig and the hospital have filed a motion for summary judgment on all claims. What result? What result if the hospital had transferred Ms. Miller? Include the applicable regulations, below, in your discussion.

42 C.F.R. § 489.24(D)(2)

* * * Application [of screening, stabilization, and transfer obligations] to inpatients

(i) If a hospital has screened an individual * * * and found the individual to have an emergency medical condition, and admits that individual as an inpatient in good faith in order to stabilize the emergency medical condition, the hospital has satisfied its special responsibilities under this section with respect to that individual.

(ii) This section is not applicable to an inpatient who was admitted for elective (nonemergency) diagnosis or treatment.

[Note: The original proposed language for this regulation provided: "If a hospital admits an individual with an unstable emergency medical condition for stabilizing treatment, as an inpatient, and stabilizes that individual's emergency medical condition, the period of stability would be required to be documented by relevant clinical data in the individual's medical record, before the hospital has satisfied its special responsibilities under this section with respect to that individual. * * *" 67 Fed.Reg. 314045, 31496 (Dec. 32, 2002).]

42 C.F.R. § 489.24(j)

[A] hospital must have written policies and procedures in place—

(1) To respond to situations in which a particular specialty is not available or the on-call physician cannot respond because of circumstances beyond the physician's control; * * *

42 C.F.R. § 489.20(r)(2)

[The hospital must maintain an] on-call list of physicians who are on the hospital's medical staff or who have privileges at the hospital, or who are on the staff or have privileges at another hospital participating in a formal community call plan * * * available to provide treatment necessary after the initial examination to stabilize individuals with emergency medical conditions who are receiving [emergency care] in accordance with the resources available to the hospital * * *.

B. OBLIGATIONS UNDER FEDERAL ANTIDISCRIMINATION STATUTES

1. The Americans with Disabilities Act and Section 504 of the Rehabilitation Act

The Americans with Disabilities Act (ADA) and Section 504 of the Rehabilitation Act of 1973 (29 U.S.C. § 749) prohibit discrimination against the disabled. The ADA and § 504 are quite similar in most respects, and courts have used cases under the Rehabilitation Act to assist in interpreting the later ADA. There are some significant differences, however. For example, Section § 504, in contrast to the ADA, applies only to programs and services receiving federal funding. The Affordable Care Act, however, broadens the reach of § 504 significantly. See Section III.B.2, below.

BRAGDON V. ABBOTT
Supreme Court of the United States, 1998.
524 U.S. 624, 118 S.Ct. 2196, 141 L.Ed.2d 540.

KENNEDY, J., delivered the opinion of the Court, in which STEVENS, SOUTER, GINSBERG, and BREYER, JJ., joined. STEVENS, J., filed a concurring opinion. REHNQUIST, C.J., filed an opinion concurring in the judgment in part and dissenting in part, in which SCALIA and THOMAS, JJ., joined, and in Part II of which O'CONNOR, J., joined. O'CONNOR, J., filed an opinion concurring in the judgment in part and dissenting in part.

* * * We granted certiorari to review * * * whether the Court of Appeals, in affirming a grant of summary judgment, cited sufficient material in the record to determine, as a matter of law, that respondent's infection with HIV posed no direct threat to the health and safety of her treating dentist.

I

Respondent Sidney Abbott has been infected with HIV since 1986. When the incidents we recite occurred, her infection had not manifested its most serious symptoms. On September 16, 1994, she went to the office of petitioner Randon Bragdon in Bangor, Maine, for a dental appointment. She disclosed her HIV infection on the patient registration form. Petitioner completed a dental examination, discovered a cavity, and informed respondent of his policy against filling cavities of HIV-infected patients. He offered to perform the work at a hospital with no added fee for his services, though respondent would be responsible for the cost of using the hospital's facilities. Respondent declined.

* * *

* * * Notwithstanding the protection given respondent by the ADA's definition of disability, petitioner could have refused to treat her if her infectious condition "posed a direct threat to the health or safety of others."[ ] The ADA defines a direct threat to be "a significant risk to the health or safety of others that cannot be eliminated by a modification of policies, practices, procedures, or by the provision of auxiliary aids or services."[ ] * * *

The ADA's direct threat provision stems from the recognition in School Bd. of Nassau Cty. v. Arline[ ] of the importance of prohibiting discrimination against individuals with disabilities while protecting others from significant health and safety risks, resulting, for instance, from a contagious disease. In *Arline,* the Court reconciled these objectives by construing the Rehabilitation Act not to require the hiring of a person who posed "a significant risk of communicating an infectious disease to others."[ ] * * * [The ADA's] direct threat provision codifies *Arline.* Because few, if any, activities in life are risk free, *Arline* and the ADA do not ask whether a risk exists, but whether it is significant.[ ]

The existence, or nonexistence, of a significant risk must be determined from the standpoint of the person who refuses the treatment or accommodation, and the risk assessment must be based on medical or other objective evidence.[ ] As a health care professional, petitioner had the duty to assess the risk of infection based on the objective, scientific information available to him and others in his profession. His belief that a significant risk existed, even if maintained in good faith, would not relieve him from liability. To use the words of the question presented, petitioner receives no special deference simply because he is a health care professional. It is true that *Arline* reserved "the question whether courts should also defer to the reasonable medical judgments of private physicians on which an employer has relied."[ ] At most, this statement reserved the possibility that employers could consult with individual physicians as objective third-party experts. It did not suggest that an individual physician's state of mind could excuse discrimination without regard to the objective reasonableness of his actions.

* * * In assessing the reasonableness of petitioner's actions, the views of public health authorities, such as the U.S. Public Health Service, CDC, and the National Institutes of Health, are of special weight and authority.[ ] The views of these organizations are not conclusive, however. A health care professional who disagrees with the prevailing medical consensus may refute it by citing a credible scientific basis for deviating from the accepted norm.[ ]

[An] illustration of a correct application of the objective standard is the Court of Appeals' refusal to give weight to the petitioner's offer to treat respondent in a hospital.[ ] Petitioner testified that he believed hospitals had safety measures, such as air filtration, ultraviolet lights, and respirators, which would reduce the risk of HIV transmission.[ ] Petitioner made no showing, however, that any area hospital had these safeguards or even that he had hospital privileges.[ ] His expert also admitted the lack of any scientific basis for the conclusion that these measures would lower the risk of transmission.[ ] Petitioner failed to present any objective, medical evidence showing that treating respondent in a hospital would be safer or more efficient in preventing HIV transmission than treatment in a well-equipped dental office.

We are concerned, however, that the Court of Appeals might have placed mistaken reliance upon two other sources. In ruling no triable issue of fact existed on this point, the Court of Appeals relied on the CDC Dentistry Guidelines and the 1991 American Dental Association Policy on HIV.[ ] This evidence is not definitive. * * * [T]he CDC Guidelines recommended certain universal precautions which, in CDC's view, "should reduce the risk of disease transmission in the dental environment."[ ] The Court of Appeals determined that, "[w]hile the guidelines do not state explicitly that no further risk-reduction measures are desirable or that routine dental care for HIV-positive individuals is safe, those two conclusions seem to be implicit in the guidelines' detailed delineation of procedures for office treatment of HIV-positive patients."[ ] In our view, the Guidelines do not necessarily contain implicit assumptions conclusive of the point to be decided. The Guidelines set out CDC's recommendation that the universal precautions are the best way to combat the risk of HIV transmission. They do not assess the level of risk.

Nor can we be certain, on this record, whether the 1991 American Dental Association Policy on HIV carries the weight the Court of Appeals attributed to it. The Policy does provide some evidence of the medical community's objective assessment of the risks posed by treating people infected with HIV in dental offices. It indicates:

> "Current scientific and epidemiologic evidence indicates that there is little risk of transmission of infectious diseases through dental treatment if recommended infection control procedures are routinely followed. Patients with HIV infection may be safely treated in private dental offices when appropriate infection control procedures are employed. Such infection control procedures provide protection both for patients and dental personnel."[ ]

We note, however, that the Association is a professional organization, which, although a respected source of information on the dental profession, is not a public health authority. It is not clear the extent to which the Policy was based on the Association's assessment of dentists' ethical and professional duties in addition to its scientific assessment of the risk to which the ADA refers. Efforts to clarify dentists' ethical obligations and to encourage dentists to treat patients with HIV infection with compassion may be commendable, but the question under the statute is one of statistical likelihood, not professional responsibility. Without more information on the manner in which the American Dental Association formulated this Policy, we are unable to determine the Policy's value in evaluating whether petitioner's assessment of the risks was reasonable as a matter of law.

* * *

There are reasons to doubt whether petitioner advanced evidence sufficient to raise a triable issue of fact on the significance of the risk. Petitioner relied on two principal points: First, he asserted that the use of high-speed drills and surface cooling with water created a risk of airborne HIV transmission. The study on which petitioner relied was inconclusive, however, determining only that "further work is required to determine whether such a risk exists."[ ] Petitioner's expert witness conceded, moreover, that no evidence suggested the spray could transmit HIV. His opinion on airborne risk was based on the absence of contrary evidence, not on positive data. Scientific evidence and expert testimony must have a traceable, analytical basis in objective fact before it may be considered on summary judgment.[ ]

[P]etitioner argues that, as of September 1994, CDC had identified seven dental workers with possible occupational transmission of HIV.[ ] These dental workers were exposed to HIV in the course of their employment, but CDC could not determine whether HIV infection had resulted.[ ] It is now known that CDC could not ascertain whether the seven dental workers contracted the disease because they did not present themselves for HIV testing at an appropriate time after their initial exposure.[ ] It is not clear on this record, however, whether this information was available to petitioner in September 1994. If not, the seven cases might have provided some, albeit not necessarily sufficient, support for petitioner's position. Standing alone, we doubt it would meet the objective, scientific basis for finding a significant risk to the petitioner.

* * *

We conclude the proper course is to give the Court of Appeals the opportunity to determine whether our analysis of some of the studies cited by the parties would change its conclusion that petitioner presented neither objective evidence nor a triable issue of fact on the question of risk.

CHIEF JUSTICE REHNQUIST, with whom JUSTICE SCALIA and JUSTICE THOMAS join, and with whom JUSTICE O'CONNOR joins as to Part II, concurring in the judgment in part and dissenting in part.

* * *

II

I agree with the Court that "the existence, or nonexistence, of a significant risk must be determined from the standpoint of the person who refuses the treatment or accommodation," as of the time that the decision refusing treatment is made.[ ] I disagree with the Court, however, that "in assessing the reasonableness of petitioner's actions, the views of public health authorities . . . are of special weight and authority."[ ] Those views are, of course, entitled to a presumption of validity when the actions of those authorities themselves are challenged in court, and even in disputes between private parties where Congress has committed that dispute to adjudication by a public health authority. But in litigation between private parties originating in the federal courts, I am aware of no provision of law or judicial practice that would require or permit courts to give some scientific views more credence than others simply because they have been endorsed by a politically appointed public health authority (such as the Surgeon General). In litigation of this latter sort, which is what we face here, the credentials of the scientists employed by the public health authority, and the soundness of their studies, must stand on their own. * * *

Applying these principles here, it is clear to me that petitioner has presented more than enough evidence to avoid summary judgment on the "direct threat" question * * *. Given the "severity of the risk" involved here, i.e., near certain death, and the fact that no public health authority had outlined a protocol for *eliminating* this risk in the context of routine dental treatment, it seems likely that petitioner can establish that it was objectively reasonable for him to conclude that treating respondent in his office posed a "direct threat" to his safety.

*   *   *

NOTES AND QUESTIONS

1.   On remand, the Ninth Circuit upheld the District Court's grant of summary judgment in favor of the plaintiff, emphasizing that the American Dental Association's policy at issue was promulgated by its Council on Scientific Affairs (and not its Council on Ethics) and rested on a firm scientific foundation. Abbott v. Bragdon, 163 F.3d 87 (1st Cir. 1998), cert. denied, 526 U.S. 1131, 119 S.Ct. 1805, 143 L.Ed.2d 1009 (1999).

2.   The CDC reports that there have been no confirmed cases of occupational transmission of HIV to health care workers since 1991. CDC, Occupational HIV Transmission and Prevention Among Health Care Workers (2011). The CDC recommends "universal precautions" (using barriers such as gloves; handwashing; and design and use of sharps to reduce accidental needle sticks) against transmission of infectious diseases (including hepatitis, which is much more prevalent than HIV) be taken. The risk of transmission

of disease from needle stick is 0.3% for needles contaminated with HIV; up to 7%, for hepatitis C; and up to 40%, for hepatitis B. See the Note on Employment Discrimination in Chapter 11.

3.   A significant number of health care professionals refuse to provide care for persons with HIV/AIDS. See Brad Sears et al., HIV Discrimination in Dental Care: Results of a Testing Study in Los Angeles County, 45 Loy. L.A.L.Rev. 909 (2012), including results of studies from 2003–2008 demonstrating that 46% of skilled nursing facilities, 55% of OB/GYNs, and 26% of plastic surgeons in Los Angeles County refused to treat persons with HIV.

.   4.   Much current ADA and § 504 private litigation concerning access to care involves the provision of sign language interpreters for deaf patients. The Department of Justice also has brought a number of suits against providers for failing to provide sign language interpreters leading to settlements with payment of damages and injunctive relief. Settlement agreements are available on the DOJ website. The Office of Civil Rights has also brought suit against health care facilities for violation of the ADA and § 504 for failure to provide services for deaf persons.

5.   The Affordable Care Act establishes the Patient–Centered Outcomes Research Institute (PCORI) to focus on comparative clinical effectiveness and other outcomes research. PCORI's research findings may be used in coverage determinations by the Secretary of HHS, but with some limitations, including one related directly to disability status. It provides that HHS may not use the Institute's findings

> in a manner that treats extending the life of an elderly, disabled, or terminally ill individual as of lower value than extending the life of an individual who is younger, nondisabled, or not terminally ill.

Comparative effectiveness findings can be used, however, in coverage determinations that compare "the difference in the effectiveness of alternative treatments in extending an individual's life due to the individual's age, disability, or terminal illness." The statute also prohibits the Institute from developing and the Secretary from using a "dollars-per-quality adjusted life year (or similar measure that discounts the value of a life because of an individual's disability)" in determining cost effectiveness. 42 U.S.C. § 1320e–1.

2.   Title VI of the Civil Rights Act of 1964

Title VI of the Civil Rights Act of 1964 (42 U.S.C.A. § 2000d) prohibits discrimination on the basis of race, color, or national origin by any program receiving federal financial assistance. The advent of Medicare and Medicaid in 1965, providing federal payments to physicians, hospitals, nursing homes, and other health care organizations, presented an opportunity for the enforcement of the nondiscrimination requirement of Title VI to reach into most parts of the then-segregated health care system. The precursor agency to HHS, however, declared that Title VI did not apply to physicians who received payment under Part B of Medicare, interpreting that program as a "contract of insurance" rather than payment of public funds. The Affordable Care Act displaces this narrow interpretation and extends the reach of Title VI (and other federal nondiscrimination statutes, including Section 504 of the Rehabilitation Act, discussed in the previous section):

§ 42 U.S.C. 18116

(a) * * * [A]n individual shall not, on the ground prohibited under title VI of the Civil Rights Act of 1964 (42 U.S.C. 2000d et seq.), title IX of the Education Amendments of 1972 (20 U.S.C. 1681 et seq.), the Age Discrimination Act of 1975 (42 U.S.C. 6101 et seq.), or section 504 of the Rehabilitation Act of 1973 (29 U.S.C. 794), * * * be excluded from participation in, be denied the benefits of, or be subjected to discrimination under, any health program or activity, any part of which is receiving Federal financial assistance, including credits, subsidies, or contracts of insurance, or under any program or activity that is administered by an Executive Agency or any entity established under this title (or amendments). The enforcement mechanisms provided for and available under title VI * * * shall apply for purposes of violations of this subsection.

There are many questions of interpretation and implementation under this section but it is likely to increase scrutiny of practices that result in race and national origin discrimination in previously undisturbed corners of the health care system. For example, the section appears in Title I of the ACA which governs the health insurance exchanges and private health plans; and it would seem to definitively resolve the issue of whether Title VI applies to physician practices. See Sidney Watson, Section 1557 of the Affordable Care Act: Civil Rights, Health Reform, Race and Equity, 55 How. L.J. 855 (2012).

Current regulations under Title VI prohibit both intentional discrimination and discrimination through facially neutral activities that have a disparate impact. Individuals, however, may bring suit for violations under Title VI only in cases of intentional discrimination. Alexander v. Sandoval, 532 U.S. 275, 121 S.Ct. 1511, 149 L.Ed.2d 517 (2001). The ACA leaves the *Sandoval* limitation on private litigation intact. The federal Office of Civil Rights (OCR), however, can pursue both intentional and disparate impact cases under Title VI.

Prior to *Sandoval*, the most successful of Title VI private litigation efforts relied on disparate impact to challenge Tennessee's Medicaid plan. Linton v. Commissioner of Health and Environment, 779 F.Supp. 925 (M.D. Tenn. 1990), aff'd, 65 F.3d 508 (6th Cir. 1995), cert. denied, 517

U.S. 1155, 116 S.Ct. 1542, 134 L.Ed.2d 646 (1996). The case illustrates the impact of payment programs and institutional organization upon access to health care.

Plaintiffs in *Linton* challenged state law that allowed nursing homes to limit the number of the facility's beds that would be certified for Medicaid and to decertify individual beds (i.e., accepting only private pay and excluding Medicaid beneficiaries) rather than foregoing Medicaid payments entirely. The trial court in *Linton* concluded:

> [T]he limited bed certification policy * * * leads to disruption of care and displacement of Medicaid patients after they have been admitted to a nursing home. Such displacement often occurs when a patient exhausts his or her financial resources and attempts transition from private pay to Medicaid. In this situation, a patient who already occupies a bed in a nursing home is told that his or her bed is no longer available to the patient because he or she is dependent upon Medicaid. * * *

> * * * Because of the higher incidence of poverty in the black population, and the concomitant increased dependence on Medicaid, a policy limiting the amount of nursing home beds available to Medicaid patients will disproportionately affect blacks.

> Indeed, while blacks comprise 39.4 percent of the Medicaid population, they account for only 15.4 percent of those Medicaid patients who have been able to gain access to Medicaid-covered nursing home services. In addition, testimony indicates that the health status of blacks is generally poorer than that of whites, and their need for nursing home services is correspondingly greater. Finally, such discrimination has caused a "dual system" of long term care for the frail elderly: a statewide system of licensed nursing homes, 70 percent funded by the Medicaid program, serves whites; while blacks are relegated to substandard boarding homes which receive no Medicaid subsidies. * * *

How might OCR use its authority under Title VI to challenge institutional decisions such as the decision to require pre-admission deposits; to place childbirth services at a suburban rather than urban hospital within an integrated delivery system; to acquire physician practices only in high income areas; or to limit a home-care agency's services to a particular geographic area? If a nursing home requires the resident or family to prove that they have resources adequate to support one or two years of care upon admission in order to be eligible for a Medicaid bed in the facility when it is needed later, is that nursing home acting in a racially discriminatory way if its Medicaid patient population is, in fact, 95% white in an area where the population is 40% minorities? Ruqaiijah Yearby, African Americans Can't Win, Break Even, or Get Out of the System: The Persistence of "Unequal Treatment" in Nursing Home Care in Post–Racial America, 82 Temp. L. Rev. 1177 (2010). On hospital closures, see Ruqaiijah Yearby, Breaking the Cycle of "Unequal Treatment" with Health Care Reform: Acknowledging and Addressing the Continuation of Racial Bias, 44 Conn. L. Rev. 1281 (2012).

CHAPTER REVIEW PROBLEM: THE HEALTH FAIR

Elaine Osborne lives in Springfield. She works in a minimum-wage job that provides no health insurance, but she does not qualify for Medicaid. There is no public hospital in Springfield.

Ms. Osborne attended a free public health fair, and an evaluation by a volunteer medical student revealed a site suspicious for melanoma (cancer) on her face and some swelling of her lymph nodes. The student recommended that Ms. Osborne have a dermatologist do a biopsy as a follow up to the screening. She called several doctors' offices but was told that they required insurance or payment in advance. Ms. Osborne then went to the emergency department of each of the three local hospitals but was told that she was not in need of emergency care. Does Ms. Osborne have a claim against the hospitals or the medical student or the public health fair?

Eight months later, Ms. Osborne went to Westhaven Hospital complaining of pain and shortness of breath. Physicians in the ED first suspected that she was having a heart attack. They eventually concluded, however, that her pain and shortness of breath were due to the spread of the cancer. Ms. Osborne was discharged from the hospital with a prescription for pain medication. Does she have a claim against Westhaven or the emergency physicians? In your own community, where could Ms. Osborne go for treatment of the cancer?

CHAPTER 9

PRIVATE HEALTH INSURANCE AND MANAGED CARE REGULATION

■ ■ ■

I.   INSURANCE REGULATION UNDER THE AFFORDABLE CARE ACT

The regulation of health insurance is revolutionized by the Affordable Care Act. This does not mean that pre-existing state and federal law is entirely repealed or replaced. Much of the state law that regulated insurance and managed care will remain unchanged. Aggrieved members of health insurance plans that are not protected by ERISA can still sue their insurers in contract and tort. Much of pre-existing federal law remains unchanged as well. The ACA neither expands nor contracts the scope of ERISA preemption of state law. Under 29 U.S.C. § 1144, state law that "relates to" employee benefit plans will still be preempted except insofar as it "regulates insurance," and self-insured plans will continue to be completely exempt from state regulation. ERISA remedies provided under 29 U.S.C. § 1132 will continue to be available to ERISA participants and beneficiaries and will continue to preempt all state remedies and permit removal of litigation by ERISA plans to federal court. The ADA and other antidiscrimination laws will continue to apply to health insurance to the extent they do now.

Nevertheless, the ACA dramatically changes the scope of federal insurance regulation. The ACA extends federal regulation over the nongroup (individual) market to an unprecedented extent. Previously, the nongroup market was largely untouched by federal law. The ACA also applies a much larger body of federal requirements to group health insurance plans, including self-insured plans. Section 1563(e) and (f) of the statute create a new section 715 of ERISA and 9815 of the Internal Revenue Code purporting to apply all but two of the insurance regulation provisions of Title A of title XXVII of the Public Health Services Act (PHSA), as amended by the ACA, to ERISA plans. In fact, however, each of the insurance reform provisions in the statute has its own scope. Some extend to all nongroup and group plans, some only to insured plans, and some only to nongroup and small group insured plans. In the end, however, federal regulation of health insurance will be much more extensive after the legislation is fully implemented than before.

Title I of the health reform legislation adopts a comprehensive strategy to expand health insurance coverage. Chapter 7 examines the three major elements of this strategy: 1) premium and cost-sharing subsidies, 2) a minimum coverage requirement that requires individuals to purchase health insurance, and 3) taxes imposed on employers who fail to provide adequate coverage for their employees and whose employees end up benefiting from public subsidies, as well as interim assistance programs. Title I of the ACA also, however, dramatically expands insurance regulation as part of this comprehensive strategy.

The regulatory provisions of Title I have several objectives. These include:

1) Ending insurance underwriting and premiums based on health status,

2) Requiring plans to cover essential health benefits in the nongroup (individual) and small group market,

3) Eliminating unreasonable or unfair restriction on coverage and coverage exclusions,

4) Requiring insurers to spend a minimum proportion of premiums on medical claims and on programs to enhance quality of care and limiting "unreasonable" increases in premiums,

5) Expanding and making more accessible the information available to consumers on health insurance options, and

6) Enhancing competition among insurers through the creation of "exchanges" in the nongroup and small group markets.

A few of the reforms took effect upon enactment or for the first plan year beginning more than six months after enactment. Most, however, do not go into effect until 2014. This delay was necessary for several reasons. The primary reason is that implementation of the reforms takes time. Time had to be allowed for the federal government to draft implementing regulations (and final regulations are still not out on many of the reforms), for state legislatures to adopt implementing legislation (and most have not yet done so as of 2013), and for the states to actually implement the reforms. Four years is not, therefore, overly generous, and as we go to press in 2013, it seems like too little time. Moreover, the reforms are highly interdependent; insurers cannot be expected to forego health status underwriting or pre-existing condition exclusions in the nongroup and small group market until they are assured of a substantial pool of healthy enrollees, and thus underwriting reforms must await the implementation of the mandates. The mandates cannot be implemented, however, until the premium affordability subsidies are available to ensure that those who are required to purchase insurance can afford it. But the availability of the premium subsidies must await the implementation of the exchanges, through which they will be offered. And the exchanges are to be established by the states, and again must await federal regulatory and state legislative action (still in progress in 2013 as we go to press). Finally, the premium subsidies will cost the federal government $88 billion a year when fully implemented and delayed implementation was necessary to meet ten year budget targets. Both immediate and 2014 reforms are discussed below by category.

The exchanges will play a key role in organizing, regulating, and financing insurance once they are in place in 2014. Briefly, exchanges are organized markets for nongroup and small group health insurance plans. They will market qualified health plans (QHPs) and administer the premium affordability tax credits and cost-sharing reduction subsidies, but will also play a regulatory role. Because they will not become operational until 2014, when many of the other provisions of the legislation are already in force, they are not discussed until later. Keep in mind, however, that once they come online, exchanges will play a key role in administering the other health care reforms.

As you work through the materials that follow, keep in mind that the ACA recognizes a number of categories of private health plans, and to some extent regulates them differently. The main categories are individual QHPs within the exchange, individual plans outside of the exchange, small group QHPs within the exchange, small group health plans outside of the exchange, large group plans, self-insured plans, grandfathered plans, and plans not subject to the ACA (such as early retiree plans, fixed-dollar indemnity plans, or Medicare Supplement plans). While some requirements apply to all categories of plans regulated under the ACA, some requirements only apply to a subset of regulated plans. See, Timothy Stoltzfus Jost, Loopholes in the Affordable Care Act: Regulatory Gaps and Border Crossing Techniques and How to Address Them, 5 St. Louis U. J. Health L. & Pol'y 27 (2011).

A. UNDERWRITING REFORMS

A fundamental characteristic of modern health care is that a very high percent of health care costs are incurred in any given year by a very small proportion of the population, while the vast majority of the population accounts for a very small proportion of health care costs. The most rational strategy for an insurer, therefore, is to match premiums as closely as possible to the predicted costs of any particular enrollee (or group of enrollees) based on health status, to refuse to cover pre-existing conditions, and to reject applicants who can be predicted to present essentially uninsurable risks because of their health status. This strategy, however, means that those most in need of health care will not be well served by a normally functioning health private health insurance market. This is one of the reasons why most developed countries have instituted social insurance systems or public health care delivery systems to assure universal access to health care.

The Health Insurance Portability and Accountability Act of 1986 prohibited group health insurance plans from taking into account health status in determining eligibility or premium rates for group coverage and limited the use of pre-existing conditions exclusions by group plans. The ACA goes further and, effective January 1, 2014, outlaws all health status underwriting in the nongroup market and prohibits all pre-existing conditions clauses.

Section 2701 of the PHSA, added by Section 1201 of the ACA, provides:

SECTION 2701. FAIR HEALTH INSURANCE PREMIUMS.

(a) Prohibiting Discriminatory Premium Rates—

(1) With respect to the premium rate charged by a health insurance issuer for health insurance coverage offered in the individual or small group market—

(A) such rate shall vary with respect to the particular plan or coverage involved only by—

(i) whether such plan or coverage covers an individual or family;

(ii) rating area, * * *

(iii) age, except that such rate shall not vary by more than 3 to 1 for adults * * *; and

(iv) tobacco use, except that such rate shall not vary by more than 1.5 to 1; and

(B) such rate shall not vary with respect to the particular plan or coverage involved by any other factor not described in subparagraph (A).

Section 2705 of the statute provides:

PROHIBITING DISCRIMINATION AGAINST INDIVIDUAL PARTICI-
PANTS AND BENEFICIARIES BASED ON HEALTH STATUS.

(a) In General—A group health plan and a health insurance issuer offering group or individual health insurance coverage may not establish rules for eligibility (including continued eligibility) of any individual to enroll under the terms of the plan or coverage based on any of the following health status-related factors in relation to the individual or a dependent of the individual:

(1) Health status.

(2) Medical condition (including both physical and mental illnesses).

(3) Claims experience.

(4) Receipt of health care.

(5) Medical history.

(6) Genetic information.

(7) Evidence of insurability (including conditions arising out of acts of domestic violence).

(8) Disability.

(9) Any other health status-related factor determined appropriate by the Secretary.

* * *

Section 2705, however, contains a general exception allowing plans to permit premium discounts or rebates, or reduced cost sharing, for participation in "Programs of Health Promotion or Disease Prevention," also called "wellness programs." The ACA provides:

(j) Programs of Health Promotion or Disease Prevention.—

(1) GENERAL PROVISIONS.—

(A) GENERAL RULE.—* * * a program of health promotion or disease prevention * * * shall be a program offered by an employer that is designed to promote health or prevent disease that meets the applicable requirements of this subsection.

(B) NO CONDITIONS BASED ON HEALTH STATUS FACTOR.—If none of the conditions for obtaining a premium discount or rebate or other reward for participation in a wellness program is based on an individual satisfying a standard that is related to a health status factor, such wellness program shall not violate this section if participation in the program is made available to all similarly situated individuals and the requirements of paragraph (2) are complied with.

(C) CONDITIONS BASED ON HEALTH STATUS FACTOR.—If any of the conditions for obtaining a premium discount or rebate or other reward for participation in a wellness program is based on an individual satisfying a standard that is related to a health status factor, such wellness program shall not violate this section if the requirements of paragraph (3) are complied with.

(2) WELLNESS PROGRAMS NOT SUBJECT TO REQUIREMENTS.—If none of the conditions for obtaining a premium discount or rebate or other reward under a wellness program as described in paragraph (1)(B) are based on an individual satisfying a standard that is related to a health status factor (or if such a wellness program does not provide such a reward), the wellness program shall not violate this section if participation in the pro-

gram is made available to all similarly situated individuals. The following programs shall not have to comply with the requirements of paragraph (3) if participation in the program is made available to all similarly situated individuals:

(A) A program that reimburses all or part of the cost for memberships in a fitness center.

(B) A diagnostic testing program that provides a reward for participation and does not base any part of the reward on outcomes.

(C) A program that encourages preventive care related to a health condition through the waiver of the copayment or deductible requirement under group health plan for the costs of certain items or services related to a health condition (such as prenatal care or well-baby visits).

(D) A program that reimburses individuals for the costs of smoking cessation programs without regard to whether the individual quits smoking.

(E) A program that provides a reward to individuals for attending a periodic health education seminar.

(3) WELLNESS PROGRAMS SUBJECT TO REQUIRE-MENTS.—If any of the conditions for obtaining a premium discount, rebate, or reward under a wellness program as described in paragraph (1)(C) is based on an individual satisfying a standard that is related to a health status factor, the wellness program shall not violate this section if the following requirements are complied with:

(A) The reward for the wellness program, together with the reward for other wellness programs with respect to the plan that requires satisfaction of a standard related to a health status factor, shall not exceed 30 percent of the cost of employee-only coverage under the plan. * * * A reward may be in the form of a discount or rebate of a premium or contribution, a waiver of all or part of a cost-sharing mechanism (such as deductibles, copayments, or coinsurance), the absence of a surcharge, or the value of a benefit that would otherwise not be provided under the plan. The Secretaries of Labor, Health and Human Services, and the Treasury may increase the reward available under this subparagraph to up to 50 percent of the cost of coverage if the Secretaries determine that such an increase is appropriate.

(B) The wellness program shall be reasonably designed to promote health or prevent disease. A program complies with the preceding sentence if the program has a reasonable chance of improving the health of, or preventing disease in, participating individuals and it is not overly burdensome, is not a subterfuge for discriminating based on a health status factor, and is not highly suspect in the method chosen to promote health or prevent disease.

(C) The plan shall give individuals eligible for the program the opportunity to qualify for the reward under the program at least once each year.

(D) The full reward under the wellness program shall be made available to all similarly situated individuals. For such purpose, among other things:

(i) The reward is not available to all similarly situated individuals for a period unless the wellness program allows—

(I) for a reasonable alternative standard (or waiver of the otherwise applicable standard) for obtaining the reward for any individual for whom, for that period, it is unreasonably difficult due to a medical condition to satisfy the otherwise applicable standard; and

(II) for a reasonable alternative standard (or waiver of the otherwise applicable standard) for obtaining the reward for any individual for whom, for that period, it is medically inadvisable to attempt to satisfy the otherwise applicable standard.

(ii) If reasonable under the circumstances, the plan or issuer may seek verification, such as a statement from an individual's physician, that a health status factor makes it unreasonably difficult or medically inadvisable for the individual to satisfy or attempt to satisfy the otherwise applicable standard.

(E) The plan or issuer involved shall disclose in all plan materials describing the terms of the wellness program the availability of a reasonable alternative standard (or the possibility of waiver of the otherwise applicable standard) required under subparagraph (D). If plan materials disclose that such a program is available, without describing its terms, the disclosure under this subparagraph shall not be required.

* * *

The ACA also requires insurers to guarantee issue and renewability of coverage to all applicants, prohibits all pre-existing condition exclusions, and bans waiting periods for coverage in excess of 90 days.

Finally, the ACA introduces risk adjustment programs to ensure that insurers who are successful in gaming the system and disproportionately attracting good risks and repelling bad risks are not rewarded for it. Indeed, the ACA institutes three risk accommodation programs, two interim for the three years following the 2014 implementation date and one permanent.

First, Section 1341 creates a reinsurance program for the years 2014, 2015, and 2016 that will collect about $25 million from health insurers and third party administrators of self-insured health plans and distribute these funds equitably to reinsure insurers who insure high risk individuals in the individual market. Second, Section 1342 establishes a risk corridor program for the same time period to move funds from insurers in the exchange whose claims costs come in under a "target amount" to those whose claims costs come in over that amount. Third, Section 1343 establishes a permanent program under which states assess a charge against health plans and health insurers in the individual and small group market (other than self-insured group health plans or grandfathered plans) whose enrollees' average actuarial risk is below average and make payments to plans and insurers (other than self-insured group health plans or grandfathered plans) whose enrollees' average actuarial risk is above average. See Mark A. Hall, Risk Adjustment Under the Affordable Care Act: Issues and Options, 20 Kan. J. L. & Pub. Pol'y 222 (2011); Mark Hall, The Three Types of Reinsurance Created by Federal Health Reform, 29 Health Aff. 1168 (2010); Tom Baker, Health Insurance, Risk, and Responsibility after the Patient Protection and Affordable Care Act, U of Penn, Inst for Law & Econ Research Paper No. 11–03. Final regulations implementing this program are found at 77 Fed. Reg. 17220 (2012).

Only one ACA underwriting reform went into effect before 2014. The ACA banned the application of pre-existing conditions exclusions to minors effective for plan years beginning six months after the effective date of the law. HHS interpreted the legislation to ban not only pre-existing condition clauses, but also the exclusion of minors with pre-existing conditions. The enforcement of this provision caused serious disruption in the availability of child-only insurance coverage as insurers dropped or limited child-only coverage or raised premiums to avoid adverse selection by families with sick children. The states and administration responded by expanding child coverage in the pre-existing conditions high risk pool, authorizing open enrollment periods, or requiring insurers to sell child-only policies, but the child-only market remains problematic in many states. The experience dramatically demonstrates why a mandate is necessary to preserve insurance markets once pre-existing conditions exclusions are eliminated.

NOTES AND QUESTIONS

1.   Is the 3 to 1 ratio in rate variation based on age in fact a surrogate for health status underwriting, as health status tends to deteriorate with age? Is it otherwise justified? Is the fact that the ACA also eliminates gender discrimination in the individual and small group market. In fact, 60 year old males have claims costs about 5 times those of 25 year old males, while 60 year old females have claims costs twice those of 25 year old females. See William F. Bluhm, Individual Health Insurance (2007) at 121.

2.   Wellness programs are touted as improving the health of individuals who participate in them while saving employers money. They are very popular with those who believe that ill health (and accompanying health care

costs) are largely the fault of individuals with poor health habits and that individuals who do not take care of themselves should bear their own health care's costs rather than be allowed to impose them on society. Much was made during the health care reform debate of the success of the Safeway Company in particular in saving money through employee wellness programs. An investigation of these claims, however, found them largely unfounded. David Hilzenrath, Misleading Claims About Safeway Wellness Incentives Shape Health Care Bill, Washington Post, Jan. 17, 2010.

Although it would seem to be intuitive that enrollees would respond to financial incentives by improving health habits, the extent to which these programs really improve health or save money is not clearly established, except perhaps for smoking cessation programs. A recent meta-analysis of the literature on workplace wellness programs claimed that they save about $3.27 in medical costs and $2.73 in reduced absenteeism for every dollars spent. Katherine Baicker, David Cutler, & Zirui Song, Workplace Wellness Programs Can Generate Savings, 29 Health Aff. 304 (February 2010). It is not at all clear, however, that published reports are representative of experience generally or that they could be reproduced more broadly. See also Kevin Volpp et al., P4P4P: An Agenda for Research on Pay-for-Performance for Patients, 28 Health Aff. 206 (Jan./Feb. 2009); Jill Horwitz, Brenna Kelly, John DiNardo, Wellness Incentives in the Workplace: Cost Savings by Cost Shifting to Unhealthy Workers, 32 Health Aff. 468 (2013).

Consumer groups are particularly concerned that wellness programs based on biometric measurements (blood glucose or cholesterol levels or body mass index (BMI) measurements) will penalize enrollees who have health conditions about which they can do little, and that provisions for reasonable alternative standards may be burdensome and inadequate, particularly if they are based on premium surcharges rather than discounts. Programs based on biometric measurements are permissible under the current federal regulations if certain safeguards are observed. 29 C.F.R. § 2590.702(f). How are wellness premium surcharges based on biometric measures different from premiums based on health status?

Under regulations proposed late in 2012, health-contingent wellness programs, which condition the receipt of a reward on meeting a health status standard, such as a BMI or blood pressure measure or not smoking, must meet five requirements to fall within the exception to the health status underwriting prohibition. First, all persons eligible for the program must be given an opportunity at least once a year to qualify. Second, the size of the reward cannot exceed 30 percent of the total cost of coverage, including both the employer and employee's contribution. The proposed rule would allow a 20 percent additional reward (for a 50 percent of cost of coverage total) for smoking cessation to counterbalance the permissible 1.5 to 1 tobacco use surcharge in the individual and small group market.

A third critical standard that health-contingent wellness programs must meet is that they must provide a "reasonable alternative standard" or waiver of the health-contingent standard for individuals who find it unreasonably difficult to meet the otherwise applicable standard because of their medical condition, or for whom it is medically inadvisable to attempt to satisfy the standard. Such an alternative must be provided on request and cannot be refused simply because the individual has not been successful in prior attempts to address an issue. A reasonable alternative standard cannot be one that requires the participant to pay for the cost of the program or for a membership or participation fee. If an alternative is proposed by a medical professional who is an employee or agent of the plan, but the individual's personal physician states that the proposal is not medically appropriate, the treating physician's judgment must prevail. A plan or insurer can require verification of a claim that it is unreasonably difficult for an individual to comply with a health standard, but only if such a request is reasonable under the circumstances. A request would be unreasonable if the plan or insurer is already aware of the individual's medical condition.

Fourth, health-contingent wellness programs must also be reasonably designed to promote health or prevent disease, not be overly burdensome, not be a subterfuge for health status discrimination, and not use a highly suspect approach. Fifth, the program must require plans and insurers to disclose the availability of other means of qualifying for a reward or the possibility of waiver of a standard.

To what extent will the wellness incentive provisions of the legislation continue to in fact allow health status underwriting? Are the protections built into the legislation and regulations to keep wellness programs from becoming a substitute for health status underwriting likely to be effective? Are they realistic? See, discussing these issues, Scott D. Halpern, Kristin M. Madison, & Kevin G. Volpp, Patients as Mercenaries? 2 Circulation: Cardiovascular Quality & Outcomes 514 (2009). See also, on the appropriateness of using health insurance to encourage wellness, Wendy Mariner, The Affordable Care Act and Health Promotion: The Role of Insurance in Defining Responsibility for Health Risks and Costs, 50 Duq.L.Rev. 271 (2012).

3.   Wellness programs must also comply with the Americans with Disabilities Act. Although health conditions are not necessarily disabilities under the ADA, some may be, particularly given the broader definition of disability that became law in 2009 under the ADA Amendments Act and that was meant to reverse Supreme Court decisions limiting the definition of disability. The ADA prohibits mandatory medical examinations or workplace health inquiries unless the examination or inquiry is job-related and consistent with business necessity. 42 U.S.C. § 12112(d)(4). Employers may conduct voluntary medical examinations or inquiries as part of an employee health program. An employer that does so must keep the wellness program records confidential and separate from personnel records. Equal Employment Opportunity Commission Guidance also provides that "a wellness program is 'voluntary' as long as an employer neither requires participation nor penalizes employees who do not participate." The EEOC has offered the opinion that a

wellness program could be considered voluntary if inducements to participate did not exceed 20 percent of program cost, which was all that was allowed by HIPAA before the ACA was adopted, but has not offered an opinion with respect to whether larger incentives are allowable.

Wellness incentives may have other legal consequences as well. The Genetic Information Nondiscrimination Act includes a provision allowing employers to permit wellness programs that provide health or genetic services to ask employees to voluntarily provide genetic information, as long as the information is not disclosed in identifiable form to the employer. 42 U.S.C. § 2000ff–1(b)(2). The Age Discrimination in Employment Act and Title VII would also prohibit wellness programs that had a disparate effect based on age or race. Wellness incentives provided to employees that are not health benefits (such as gym memberships) may be taxable income. Finally, state laws—such as those prohibiting employers from discriminating against smokers or obese persons—might further limit wellness programs.

See Nancy Lee Jones, et al., Wellness Programs: Selected Legal Issues (Congressional Research Service 2010); Anita K. Chancey, Getting Healthy: Issues to Consider before Implementing a Wellness Program, 2 J. Health & Life Sci. L. 73 (2009); Lucinda Jesson, Weighing the Wellness Programs: The Legal Implications of Imposing Personal Responsibility Obligations, 15 Va. J. Soc. Pol'y & L. 217 (2008).

4.   In one of the more bizarre twists of the often bizarre health care reform debate, the claim was spread among gun rights advocates that the wellness provisions of the legislation were a veiled attempt to attack gun ownership. In response, the manager's amendment added a lengthy provision prohibiting wellness and health promotion programs from requiring disclosure of information about the lawful use, possession, or storage of firearms or ammunition and barring insurers from basing premium rates or health insurance eligibility on the lawful, use, ownership or storage of ammunition or possession of firearms or ammunition and from collecting data regarding firearms or ammunition. The implementing agencies have clarified that this provision does not prohibit physicians from discussing firearm issues with their patients.

5.   Might ACA regulation of insurance underwriting raise constitutional questions? Might rate regulation result in a taking, prohibited by the Fifth Amendment? See Richard Epstein and Paula Stannard, Constitutional Ratemaking and the Affordable Care Act: A New Source of Vulnerability, 38 Am. J. L. & Med. 243 (2012).

B. MINIMUM ESSENTIAL BENEFIT AND COST–SHARING REQUIRMENTS

1. Requirements Effective in 2014: Section 1302

Never before has federal law attempted to specify the benefits that private insurance plans must cover, beyond a handful of specific mandates. Indeed, although many states require insurers to cover specific services, providers, or insureds, states do not generally specify comprehensively the bundle of items and services that health insurance must cover.

The ACA requires that, effective January 1, 2014, insurers that offer coverage in the individual and small group market (groups of 100 or fewer employees except that, for 2014 and 2015, a state can defined "small group" as 50 or fewer) must cover an "essential benefits package" specified by the law. The requirement does not apply to large group or self-insured plans, nor does it apply to "grandfathered" plans, that is plans that existed as of the date of enactment of the ACA. It does apply, however, to all nongrandfathered nongroup and small group plans. It applies whether or not plans are sold through the exchange.

Section 1302 requires HHS to define "essential health benefits." The statute lists categories of benefits that must be included in this category, including:

- ambulatory patient services,
- emergency services,
- hospitalization,
- maternity and newborn care,
- mental health and substance use disorder services,
- prescription drugs,
- rehabilitation and habilitation services,
- laboratory services,
- preventive and wellness services including chronic disease management, and
- pediatric services, including oral and vision care.

The ACA-defined essential benefits must be equal in scope to those offered under a typical employer plan. HHS must, as it defines essential health benefits, also make sure that benefits:

- are "not unduly weighted toward any category;"
- do not discriminate based on age, disability, or expected length of life;

- do take into account the needs of diverse segments of the population;
- ensure that essential benefits are not denied individuals against their wishes based on age, expected length of life, present or predicted disability, dependency, or quality of life;
- provide access to emergency care without prior approval, limitation to in-network providers, or higher cost-sharing for using out-of-network providers; and
- are periodically reviewed and updated.

HHS has decided to implement this provision initially by asking each state to designate a "benchmark" plan, the benefits of which will become the standard against whose benefits other plans will be measured. The state may either choose the largest plan of one of the three largest small group products in the state, one of the three largest state employee plans in the state, any of the largest three national Federal Employee Health Benefits plans, or the state's largest commercial non-Medicaid HMO plan. If the plan chosen does not cover any of the ten required benefit categories, the state must add benefits from another plan. Under HHS rules, plans must offer the greater of one drug in every United States Pharmacopeia (USP) category or class or the number of drugs in each category and class as the EHB-benchmark plans. Plans need not cover the same drugs as are covered by the benchmark plan as long as they cover the minimum number of drugs. Insurers will have some flexibility in substituting benefits within categories as long as they are equivalent in value and none of the other requirements are violated.

The ACA also itself contains a few additional explicit benefit mandates. Beginning in 2014, group health plans and health insurance issuers must cover the routine patient costs of enrollees participating in approved clinical trials for cancer or other life-threatening conditions. If in-network providers are participating in the trial, the plan can require an enrollee to participate through the in-network provider, but if the trial is conducted out of the state in which the individual resides, the care can be provided by an out-of-network provider if out-of-network benefits are otherwise provided under the plan. Additional mandates that take effect immediately are discussed below.

Plans may offer benefits in excess of the essential benefits. States may also require benefits in addition to the essential benefits mandated by federal law, but states must pay the additional cost of those benefits for individuals and families enrolled in QHPs. Current small group plans are likely to cover state-mandated benefits (unless state mandates apply only in the nongroup market) and so by choosing a small group plan as its benchmark a state can probably ensure that it will not have to pay for mandated benefits, at least until 2016, when HHS has indicated it might change the essential health benefit rules. If a state does have to pay, it is unclear how exactly the costs of state mandates will be calculated, as some mandates arguably save money by helping to prevent costly future care and others are for services almost universally covered in any event. This requirement is unlikely to lead to the immediate repeal of existing state benefit mandates, which are numerous in some states, but will discourage the adoption of mandates in the future.

Although all exchange plans must offer all essential benefits, most will probably not offer significant additional benefits since additional benefits will not be eligible for federal subsidies. Plans will vary significantly in the amount of cost-sharing that they require. The statute does set some cost-sharing limits. For 2014, cost-sharing may not exceed the limits imposed on high-deductible insurance plans that are coupled with health savings accounts (set at $6,250 for an individual and $12,500 for a family for 2013). Health plan deductibles in the small group market may not exceed $2,000 for an individual or $4,000 for a family (except in situations where this deductible limit would make it impossible for insurers to offer plans that comply with metal level actuarial value requirements). After 2014, the out-of-pocket limit and small group plan deductible limits will be adjusted upward annually based on the amount that the average per capita premium for health coverage exceeds the average per capita premium in 2013. Cost-sharing is defined to include deductibles, coinsurance, and copayments, but does not include premiums, balance billing amounts for out-of-network providers, or spending for non-covered services.

The ACA further requires that health plans offered in the individual and small group markets cover specific percentages of actuarial value specified in the statute. As noted in Chapter 7, these are arrayed in "precious metal" categories. "Bronze" plans must cover 60 percent of actuarial value; silver, 70 percent of actuarial value; gold, 80 percent of actuarial value; and platinum, 90 percent of actuarial value. The actuarial value of services is to be determined on the basis of the cost of providing the essential benefits to a standard population, not the actual population of the plan. Employer contributions to a health reimbursement or health savings account are taken into account in determining actuarial value. Insurers may also offer a catastrophic plan, with a deductible equal to the out-of-pocket limit for high deductible plans plus coverage for at least three primary care visits, but the catastrophic plan can only be offered to individuals in the individual market who are under age 30 or who are exempted from the individual mandate because they cannot afford coverage or because of hardship.

Actuarial value is a concept that is unfamiliar to most Americans, who typically think about coverage and cost-sharing in terms of deductibles ($500 which must be paid by the enrollee before insurance coverage begins), copayments ($20 per doctors visit, $10 for each generic drug prescription, $30 for each name-brand prescription), coinsurance (20% of the hospital bill), or out-of-pocket limits ($5,000 per year). Because medical costs vary dramatically from insured to insured while actuarial value is defined in terms of average costs, the actual cost-sharing experienced by individuals will vary significantly regardless of the actuarial value of a plan. For purposes of comparison, the average actuarial value of employment-based plans is estimated to be about 80 percent, the Federal Employee Health Benefits Program Blue Cross Blue Shield standard option has an actuarial value of about 84 percent to 87 percent, while Medicare Parts A and B alone have an actuarial value of about 64 percent and Medicare Parts A, B and D with a Medigap policy would have a value of about 90 percent. The concept of actuarial value is explored further in the discussion of cost-sharing reduction payments in Chapter 7.

2.   Benefit Requirements in Effect Prior to 2014: Section 1001

Although the essential benefit and cost-sharing requirements do not go into effect until 2014, several benefit mandates have already gone into effect for plan years beginning after September of 2010. First, non-grandfathered (see below) group health plans and health insurers must cover preventive services without cost-sharing. These services include at least the evidence-based items and services rated A or B by the United States Preventive Services Task Force, immunizations recommended by the Advisory Committee on Immunization of the CDC, and preventive care and screening for women and children recommended by the guidelines of the Health Resources and Services Administration (including the pre–2009 breast cancer recommendations). Plans may alternatively use value-based insurance designs permitted by guidelines provided by HHS. See John Aloysius Cogan, The Affordable Care Act's Preventive Services Mandate: Breaking Down the Barriers to Nationwide Access to Preventive Services, 39 J. L. Med. & Ethics 355 (2011).

Second, the ACA requires group health plans and insurers that cover children as dependents to offer such coverage for adult children until the child turns 26 (but not to the children's children), regardless of whether the adult child is in fact a dependent or even lives with the parent. This Section also covers grandfathered plans, but prior to 2014 group plans need not cover adult dependents if they can be covered under any other employment-related group plan that is not grandfathered coverage. Plans may not charge more for adult dependents than they would charge for other family members. This has been one of the most popular provisions of the legislation, and was implemented by many insurers and group plans even before its actual effective date. As of 2012, 2.5 million young adults have been covered under this provision. See Joel Cantor, et al.,

Expanding Dependent Coverage for Young Adults: Lessons from State Initiatives, 37 J. Health Pol., Pol'y & L. 99 (2012).

Third, the ACA requires group health plans or health insurers that obligate enrollees to designate a primary care provider to permit enrollees to designate any available participating primary care provider. Group health plans or health insurers that cover emergency department services must cover emergency medical conditions without prior authorization and whether or not an emergency care provider is in-network. Plans are also prohibited from charging higher cost sharing for out-of-network than for in-network emergency services. The HHS regulation implementing this Section interprets it to mean that plans must pay out-of-network emergency care providers the greater of the amount they pay in-network providers, out-of-network emergency care providers without regard to out-of-network cost sharing, or the Medicare rate. Group health plans and health insurers that require designation of a primary care provider must permit designation of a pediatric specialist for children. Group health plans and health insurers must also provide direct access without authorization or referral of women to gynecologists or obstetricians for obstetrical or gynecological care.

NOTES AND QUESTIONS

1. Many of the requirements of the ACA do not apply to "grandfathered" plans. One of the promises made by President Obama was that "if you like the insurance you have, you can keep it." Group and nongroup insurance plans that existed on the effective date of the statute can continue in force indefinitely and be renewed without having to comply with many of the requirements of the statute. New family members and employees can be added to these plans. At some point, however, plans may change sufficiently that they lose their grandfathered status. Regulations implementing this provision stipulate that a plan loses its grandfathered status if any of the following changes take place:

- Elimination of all or substantially all of any benefit necessary to diagnose or treat a particular condition;

- Any increase in coinsurance percentages;

- An increase in a deductible, out-of-pocket limit, or other fixed dollar cost-sharing requirement or limit other than a copayment by more than the increase in the medical component of the CPI since March 2010 plus a total of 15 percentage points;

- An increase in a copayment in excess of the greater of 1) medical inflation plus $5.00 or 2) medical inflation plus a total of 15 percentage points;

- A decrease of the employer contribution, whether based on the cost of coverage or on a formula, by more than 5 percentage points below the contribution rate in place on March 23, 2010; and

- A reduction in the dollar value of existing annual limits, the imposition of an annual limit on coverage by plans that did not impose any limits before, or the adoption of annual limits less than any lifetime limits a plan imposed before if it only imposed lifetime limits before the effective date.

Even grandfathered plans must comply with a number of the requirements of the ACA, including:

- Coverage disclosure and transparency provisions;

- The minimum medical loss ratio provision requiring plans to pay out a minimum of 80 or 85 percent of their premiums to cover health care claims or quality improvement activities;

- The prohibition against waiting periods in excess of 90 days;

- The provision prohibiting lifetime limits;

- The ban on rescissions except in the case of fraud; and

- The requirement that plans cover adult children up to age 26.

In addition, the provisions relating to annual limits and prohibiting exclusion of pre-existing conditions (initially only for children) apply to grandfathered group plans, although grandfathered group plans need not cover adult children if other non-grandfathered coverage is available. Elizabeth Weeks Leonard, Can you Really Keep Your Health Plan? The Limits of Grandfathering Under the Affordable Care Act, 36 J. Corp. L. 753 (2011).

2.   Section 1303 of the ACA prohibits the use of federal subsidies to finance abortion coverage beyond coverage for rape, incest, or to protect the mother from physical life endangerment. The pre-existing condition, high-risk pool is also prohibited from paying for abortions. Several cases have been brought challenging the preventive service regulation's requirement that group health plans and insurers cover post-intercourse contraceptives, thought by some to be abortifacients

3.   HHS has defined contraception as a preventive service for women that insurers must cover without cost-sharing. This ruling was met with strong resistance from Catholic organizations. HHS exempted religious employers from covering contraception, and gave nonprofit organizations sponsored by religious organizations (such as universities, hospitals, and charities) until August of 2013 to comply. HHS has further proposed a compromise under which religious organizations do not need to cover contraception, but their insurers or self-insured plan administrators must offer contracep-

tion coverage to employees of the religious organizations. The agencies have not proposed any accommodation for for-profit employers with objections to contraceptive coverage. This issue is currently being litigated in dozens of cases, which are being brought under the First Amendment and Religious Freedom Restoration Act.

C. INSURANCE REFORMS: SECTIONS 1001, 1003, 10101

Several provisions of the ACA respond to insurance industry practices that have been regarded as unfair or unreasonable. Other provisions require plans to offer procedural protections to their members. Most of these provisions are already in effect, having become effective for the first plan year following the six-month anniversary of enactment.

Lifetime and Annual Limits. The ACA prohibits group health plans and health insurers, including grandfathered plans, from imposing lifetime limits on the dollar value of benefits. The ACA also prohibits annual limits on the dollar value of benefits after 2014. Prior to 2014, group health plans and insurers were only allowed to impose "restricted annual limits" on essential health services that would make needed services available while having only "a minimal impact on premiums," as determined by HHS guidance. HHS regulations prohibited annual limits below $750,000 for 2010, $1.25 million for 2011, and $2 million for 2012 and 2013. HHS also, however, set up a waiver process in 2010 for group health plans and insurers that could not meet these requirements, so-called "limited benefit" or "mini-med" plans. Over 1200 waiver requests were granted, covering almost 3.4 million enrollees before HHS ceased accepting waiver applications in 2011. Special rules also applied to annual limits found in university student health plans. But as of 2014, the vast majority of Americans will be covered by plans meeting the annual limit requirements. Group health plans and insurers may also impose limits on benefits that are not essential benefits as permitted by federal and state law. The prohibition against annual limits does not apply to grandfathered individual plans, but does apply to grandfathered group plans that do not qualify for a waiver.

Rescissions. The ACA prohibits rescission of coverage except for fraud or intentional misrepresentation of material fact. This provision also applies to grandfathered plans. It addresses the problem of "post-claims underwriting," under which insurers have insured individuals with minimal investigation and then gone back carefully over their application forms once expensive medical problems have developed to find grounds for rescission for "misrepresentation."

Medical Loss Ratios. Section 10101 adds Section 2718 of the Public Health Service Act, which requires insurers to spend a minimum proportion of their premium revenues on health care services and activities that improve health care quality, the so-called "minimum medical loss ratio" requirement. Since 2011, health insurers (including grandfathered plans but not self-insured plans) have been required to report to HHS the ratio that their loss adjustment expenses bear to earned premiums. An insurer must also report the percentage of premium revenue that it spends on clinical services, activities that improve health care quality, and on all other non-claim (administrative) costs. Premium revenues are adjusted for payments to or collections for risk adjustment, risk corridor, and reinsurance programs (see below) and reduced by taxes, licensing, or regulatory fees.

Since January 1, 2011, health insurers have had to provide annual rebates to their enrollees if their medical loss ratios (the ratio of amounts incurred for claims and paid for activities that improve health care quality to adjusted premium revenue) are less than 85 percent of premium revenue in the large group market or 80 percent in the small group or individual market. The rebates must equal the product of the percentage by which a company's MLR falls short of the allowed percentage for its state and market and the total amount of premium revenue (excluding federal and state taxes and licensing or regulatory fees and payments or receipts for risk adjustment, risk corridor, and reinsurance costs). In other words, if an insurer in the nongroup market pays 75 percent of its adjusted premiums for clinical services and 2 percent for health care quality improvement activities (such as disease management or patient education programs), it would owe a rebate of 3 percent for the year. These rebates will be paid on August 1 of the following year, usually through reductions in premiums. After January 1, 2014, the rebate must be based on the average MLRs of the preceding three years and will not be paid until the end of September HHS and the states must consider insurance market conditions in setting and adjusting the required MLRs.

As directed by the statute, the National Association of Insurance Commissioners developed definitions and methodologies for implementing this provision during an exhaustive months-long process. HHS in turn adopted a regulation based on these recommendations. The regulation allows insurers to apply the costs of a wide range of quality improvement activities against the MLR, including activities that reduce medical errors and protect patient safety, improve outcomes of care, encourage prevention and wellness, and prevent rehospitalizations, as well as a range of health IT costs. All but the largest insurers receive "credibility adjustments" to account for the fact that they do not have enough enrollees in the state to produce a statistically credible medical loss ratio in any one year, given the fluctuation of claims from year to year. Some types of plans, including mini-med plans, international and expatriate plans, student health plans, and new plans are also given special treatment because of their unusual characteristics. Finally, states that believed that immediate application of the federal minimum MLRs would destabilize their markets were allowed to apply for an "adjustment." Seventeen states applied for such adjustments, but only seven were granted. In 2012, insurers returned $1.1 billion to their enrollees under the MLR requirement.

Unreasonable Premium Increases. Section 1003 of the bill adds Section 2794 to the Public Health Services Act, establishing immediately a process for annual review by HHS and the states of "unreasonable" increases in health insurance premiums. Health insurers must submit to HHS and to all relevant states justifications for unreasonable premium increases and prominently post this information on their websites. Under regulations adopted by HHS, insurers had to justify any annual increases in excess of 10 percent during 2011 and in excess of 10 percent or a state-specific standard thereafter. If a state has an "effective" rate review program, premium increases above this level are evaluated by the state. If the state does not have such a program, HHS reviews the rate increase. HHS does not have authority, however, to disapprove proposed rate increases.

Beginning in 2014, HHS and the states must monitor premium increases inside and outside of the exchanges. A state must "take into account" excess premium growth outside of the exchange in determining whether to open the exchange to larger groups. The ACA authorizes $250 million for the five-year period between 2010 and 2014 to assist the states in conducing premium reviews and for funding medical reimbursement data centers at academic and other nonprofit institutions to collect, analyze, and make available information to the public on provider fee schedules and costs. It does not, however, give the states authority to actually deny unreasonable premium increases. Some states have this authority under state law, others do not, but the ACA does not expand their authority. The ACA does, however, require exchanges to consider whether there is a pattern or practice of excessive or unjustified premium increases in determining whether or not to make a particular health plan available.

Discrimination. A new section 2706 of the PHSA prohibits group health plans and insurers from discriminating against providers acting within the scope of their license or certification under state law. This section also prohibits group health plans and insurers from discriminating against an individual who benefits from a premium tax credit or cost-sharing reduction payment. Section 2716 prohibits employers from discriminating in favor of highly-compensated employees in insured coverage. A similar non-discrimination provision already applies to self-insured and cafeteria plans.

Internal and External Reviews. The ACA requires group health plans and insurers to offer plan members both internal and external review procedures for coverage and claims determinations. Plans and insurers must provide notices to enrollees in a culturally and linguistically appropriate manner of available internal and external appeal procedures and of the availability of a state office of health insurance consumer assistance or ombudsman for assistance with appeals. They must allow enrollees to review their files and to present evidence and testimony. Group health plan internal appeals processes must comply with the ERISA regulations discussed below and individual insurance internal review procedures must comply with state law and with standards promulgated by HHS.

The internal appeals rule issued by HHS and the Departments of Labor and Treasury require all plans and insurers to comply with the Department of Labor ERISA claims and appeals regulations, and imposes several additional requirements on group plans. The additional requirements are that plans must:

- Allow appeals of rescissions as well as adverse benefit determinations;
- Notify members of determinations in urgent care claims within 72 hours;
- Provide claimants, without charge, with any new or additional information relied upon or generated by the plan as soon as possible and far enough in advance of a determination to allow an opportunity to respond;
- Ensure that internal reviewers do not have a conflict of interest;
- Provide culturally and linguistically appropriate notices.

If plans or insurers fail to adhere to the requirements of the process, the claimant may proceed to an external appeal or judicial review. Individual plans, which are often offered by insurers, must comply with the same rules.

Group health plans and insurers must comply with either their state or the federal external review requirements. If a state has in place an external review process offering at least as much protection as the NAIC Model Act, an insurer must comply with the state law. Plans and insurers not subject to state law (self-insured employee benefit plans) or located in states without external review laws as protective as the NAIC Model Act, must comply with a federal external review process.

State external review processes must comply with a number of requirements. Specifically they must:

- Provide external review of adverse determinations based on medical necessity, appropriateness, health care setting, level of care, or effectiveness requirements, as well as of determinations involving coverage of experimental or investigational treatments;

- Ensure that it is unnecessary to pursue an internal review first if the insurer fails to comply with regulatory requirements or if the claimant is pursuing internal and external review at the same time for urgent claims;

- Require the insurer to pay the cost of external review, although the claimant can be charged $25 for an appeal (up to $75 per plan year) if it would not impose a hardship and if the fee is refunded if the claimant wins;

- Not impose a minimum dollar amount requirement for appeals;

- Assign claims to independent review organizations (IROs) that are accredited and qualified to review the type of claim involved on a random basis;

- Use only Independent Review Organizations (IROs) that have no conflicts of interest;

- Provide that the decision of the IRO is binding on the insurer;

- Require an external review decision to be made within 45 days; and

- Provide for an expedited process in urgent circumstances.

Existing state external review requirements that do not contain these essential elements but that meet lower standards contained in the rule will govern plans and insurers for a transitional period through 2015. The Department has established an external review process similar to the state process to govern self-insured plans and insured plans not governed by state law. See, discussing IROs, Marc A. Rodwin, New Standards for Medical Review Organizations: Holding Them and Health Plans Accountable for their Decisions, 30:3 Health Aff. 519 (2011); Dustin Berger, The Management of Health Care Costs: Independent Medical Review After "Obamacare," 42 U. Mem. L. Rev. 255 (2011).

PROBLEMS: INSURANCE REFORMS

1.   Joan Hart purchased a nongroup health insurance policy early in 2012. She filled out a detailed questionnaire asking about her health history. She neglected to mention that she had received medication for depression a year earlier following the death of her brother, even though the form asked for all medications she had taken in the past two years. Late in 2012, she was diagnosed with cancer. Her health insurer reviewed her medical history, discovered the earlier medication, and rescinded her policy under a contract provision that permits rescission for material misrepresentations retroactive to the date the policy was issued. Was the rescission legal? What are Joan's remedies? If the same thing had happened in 2014, would it be legal?

2.   George McNamara purchased an insurance policy in 2014. The policy covers pharmaceuticals but does not cover a particular drug that he is taking for his asthma. Must the plan do so? It also does not cover physical thera-

py, which he has been prescribed because of a recent injury. Must the plan cover physical therapy, and can it limit the number of visits to which George is entitled?

3.   Valley Products has covered all of its employees with health insurance since the year 2000. Since 2010 it has increased its deductibles three times, but each time the increase did not exceed the percentage in growth in the medical care component of the Consumer Price Index since the last increase. Must the plan comply with the ACA's internal and external review requirements?

NOTES

1.   Whether and to what extent external review will be subject to judicial review is an open question. Section 2719(b)(1) provides that the external review must be binding on the health plan. The federal guidance further provides, "Upon receipt of a notice of a final external review decision reversing the adverse benefit determination or final internal adverse benefit determination, the plan immediately must provide coverage or payment (including immediately authorizing or immediately paying benefits) for the claim." It would seem, therefore, that the external review decision is effectively a final decision. The federal regulation implementing the provision, however, states that the decision of an external reviewer "is binding on the plan or issuer, as well as the claimant, except to the extent other remedies are available under State or Federal law." Moreover, the ACA does not amend Section 502 of ERISA (29 U.S.C. § 1332), which allows ERISA plan beneficiaries a federal cause of action for benefits due to them under an ERISA plan. The scope of review of federal courts reviewing decisions of health plans (or of external reviewers) is not, therefore, wholly clear.

A number of states have adopted external review laws that make the decisions of an external reviewer binding on the insurer or both the insurer and enrollee. See William Pitsenberger, "SezWho?" State Constitutional Concerns with External Review Laws and the Resulting Conundrum Posed by Ruth Prudential HMO v. Moran, 15 Conn. Ins. L. J. 85, 94–99 (2008). There are few reported cases addressing the question of whether "binding" external review decisions are reviewable. A series of New York cases, interpreting the New York statute, which provides that the external review decision shall "be binding on the plan and the insured," but also provides that the decision "shall be admissible in any court proceeding," have held this to mean that the external review is the final step of the administrative process but is also reviewable by a court. Schulman v. Group Health Inc., 833 N.Y.S.2d 62 (N.Y. App. Div. 2007); Vellios v. IPRO, 765 N.Y.S.2d 222 (N.Y. Sup. Ct. 2003).

No reported case has simply held an external review decision to be final, binding, and unreviewable. In *Rush Prudential HMO v. Moran*, 536 U.S. 355 (2002), (see below) the Supreme Court characterized external review as a "second opinion." In his dissent, however, Justice Thomas correctly characterized external review as essentially compulsory arbitration. The ACA does not set out the parameters of judicial review of external review decisions, unlike other laws that require or permit arbitration. Judicial review of statutory-based arbitration is usually limited to very narrow grounds, such as whether the award was in "manifest disregard of the law" or "exceeded the power of the arbitrator." See Peter Hoffman & Lindsee Gendro, Judicial Review of Arbitration Awards after Cable Connection: Towards a Due Process Model, 17 UCLA Ent. L. Rev. 1, 16 (2010). This could be the approach courts will take in reviewing ACA administrative decisions, but they may review decisions more broadly. Serious constitutional questions would be raised, however, if an external review decision were in fact totally unreviewable. See Pitsenberger, *supra*, at 103–112; Jean R. Sternlight, Rethinking the Constitutionality of the Supreme Court's Preference for Binding Arbitration: A Fresh Assessment of Jury Trial, Separation of Powers, and Due Process Concerns, 72 Tul. L. Rev. 1 (1997). It seems most likely that courts will review external review decisions applying the deferential "arbitrary and capricious" standard commonly applied currently in ERISA cases (see below). Federal courts will review ERISA plan decisions under 29 U.S.C. § 1132, state courts will review non-ERISA plan decisions under special state statutes, state administrative procedure laws, or possibly the common law. In the vast majority of cases, however, the external review decisions will not be appealed and will, as a practical matter, have the final say; external review will in fact be binding.

2.   In early 2011, HHS issued a regulation recognizing a new category of health insurance plans: student health plans. Student health plans are health insurance plans that are only available to college and university students. They are regulated like individual insurance coverage except that they are not subject to some of the regulatory provisions of the ACA. Student health plans, for example, do not need to admit all applicants, only students. They also can have annual limits as low as $500,000 for policy years beginning before 2014, can charge an administrative fee for the use of the student health services, and are only subject to a medical loss ratio of 70% for 2013. Finally, student health plans at religious universities are subject to the same rules regarding contraception coverage that apply to employees at those institutions. See Final Rule on Student Health Insurance Coverage. Otherwise, however, they must comply with the ACA.

D. DISCLOSURE REQUIREMENTS: SECTIONS 1001, 1002, 1311

The ACA imposes a number of requirements on health plans to increase the information available to plan enrollees or prospective enrollees. Disclosure enhances consumer control by allowing consumers to identify and choose plans with the features that they desire and avoid plans with characteristics they wish to avoid. Disclosure increases competition—reducing price and improving quality—by identifying differences in price and quality and focusing consumer choice on these differences. It also can improve performance by making poor performance more visible and thus more costly.

The ACA provides both for channels through which information must be made available and for specific types of information that must be disclosed. HHS has established a website, healthcare.gov, through which the residents of any state can identify health insurance coverage options that are available to them, including private insurance, Medicaid, CHIP, a state high-risk pool, or the pre-existing condition risk pool established by the statute. The website also identifies sources of employer coverage, including the reinsurance for early retiree and small business tax credit programs. HHS has developed a standard format for presenting information on this website, including information on eligibility, availability, premium rates, cost-sharing, and medical loss ratios.

HHS has also, pursuant to Section 2715 of the PHSA, added by Section 1001 of the ACA, developed standards for disclosure of benefits and coverage to applicants, enrollees, and policy or certificate-holders by insurers and self-insured plans. These were developed in conjunction with a stakeholder committee appointed by the NAIC. The HHS standards preempt state laws that allow plans to provide less information. The HHS standards provide a uniform format for plans to use that is no longer than 4 pages (double-sided, in fact 8 pages) and with type no smaller than 12–point. The form is intended to use culturally and linguistically appropriate, readily understandable language. HHS has also developed uniform definitions of insurance and medical terms to use in the forms. All plans must use these forms for plan years beginning after September 23, 2012.

The forms include a description of coverage for all categories of health benefits, including a description of exceptions, reductions and limitations on coverage; cost-sharing provisions; and renewability provisions. The coverage descriptions also must include "coverage facts labels" which illustrate coverage and cost sharing requirements for common benefits scenarios, including initially a normal delivery and type II diabetes. For example, a coverage fact label could say that if you have diabetes, you can expect coverage for the following listed products and services with cost-sharing obligations as described. The form also sets forth an amount the insurer is likely to pay and an amount the patient is likely to pay. Plans are required to disclose whether they cover at least 60 percent of allowed costs. This is important because if any employer plan fails to do so, the employee may be able to get a premium tax credit and purchase insurance through the exchange. Finally, a plan must provide a contact number for consumers to call with additional questions and a web address where a copy of the actual policy or certificate can be found. Notice of any modifications in benefits must be provided 60 days prior to the effective date.

The exchange provisions of the Act, described in the next section, require QHPs to disclose in plain language information on claims payment policies, financial data, enrollment and disenrollment data, data on claims denials and rating practices, information on cost-sharing relevant to out-of-network coverage, and information on enrollee and participant rights. QHPs must also provide information on cost-sharing for specific services in a timely manner on request through an internet website and otherwise for individuals without internet access. Non-exchange plans, including self-insured plans, must provide this same information to HHS and to state insurance commissioners, who shall in turn disclose the information to the public. Plans must also, as noted above, provide to insurance commissioners and to the public justification for unreasonable premium increases.

HHS is required to develop reporting requirements for use by group health plans and health insurers to report information related to improving health outcomes, preventing hospital readmissions, improving patient safety, and promoting wellness but has not yet done so. Group health plans and health insurance issuers must report annually information regarding their conformity with these requirements to HHS, their enrollees, and the public.

Section 1002 authorizes federal grants to the states to establish and support independent offices of health insurance consumer assistance or health insurance ombudsman programs. These offices are supposed to assist consumers in filing complaints and appeals; collect, track, and quantify information on consumer problems and inquiries; educate insurance consumers on their rights and responsibilities; assist consumers in enrolling in health plans; and resolve problems with obtaining premium tax credits. The consumer assistance offices are supposed to collect and report data on consumer problems to HHS. Thirty-five states received the first round of grants in 2010, totaling $30 million..

Finally, although most of the disclosure provisions of the ACA apply to health plans, Section 2718 requires hospitals to establish, update, and publish their standard charges for items and services. To a considerable degree, insurers merely pass on costs that they incur to health care providers, so if transparency is to play a role in bringing down costs, we will need provider cost transparency as well.

NOTES AND QUESTIONS

1.   What is the legal effect of the disclosure document created by Section 2715? The document is supposed to use language that "accurately describes the benefits and coverage under the applicable plan or coverage" but also must also include "a statement that the outline is a summary of the policy or certificate and that the coverage document itself should be consulted to

determine the governing contractual provisions." The disclosure document is intended for comparison-shopping and it would be of little value for this purpose if it has no binding legal effect. On the other hand, it is likely that there will be provisions found in insurance contracts that are not in the four-page disclosure document.

2.   Another question that has arisen with respect to the Section 2715 document is who is entitled to see it. Section 2715 provides that the information should be provided to "applicants, enrollees, and policyholders or certificate holders," but the document will be useless for comparison-shopping purposes unless it is also available to prospective applicants as well. The HHS rule requires insurers to provide the 2715 information to "shoppers," but they may do so through the healthcare.gov website rather than mailing individual copies. Insurers are permitted to disclose the 2715 document electronically as long as consumers have notice that this is how it is being provided.

E. CONSUMER CHOICES AND INSURANCE COMPETITION THROUGH HEALTH BENEFIT EXCHANGES: SECTIONS 1301, 1311, 1312, 1313, 1321

At the heart of the health care reforms is the concept of the health insurance exchange. An exchange is a consumer-friendly market for health insurance, resembling a farmer's market, stock market, or online travel service. It will be a place where consumers can go, browse through the range of available insurance options, and choose the insurance plan that is best for themselves and their families. Small business health options (SHOP) exchanges will offer the same opportunities to small businesses. Given the range of understandable and transparent information that consumers will have available under the provisions just examined, they should be able to make intelligent choices.

But exchanges will also play a regulatory role, as described below. The extent to which exchanges become, on the one hand, passive markets for displaying the wares of insurers, or, on the other, take responsibility for ensuring that their customers actually receive quality health insurance products, remains to be seen.

Under Section 1311, states are responsible for establishing an exchange for the nongroup market and a SHOP exchange by January 1, 2014. A state can choose to combine the two exchanges. Exchanges may operate regionally if all participating states and HHS approve of a regional approach. States may also operate subsidiary exchanges that serve geographically distinct areas. Exchanges may be governmental or non-profit entities. One of the most contentious issues that has arisen as states establish exchanges is who should have a seat on the exchange governing board, and in particular whether insurers or agents and brokers or others with a conflict of interest can serve on the governing board.

HHS has determined that boards must contain at least one consumer representative and a majority of members must not have a conflict of interest, but insurers, agents and brokers, and others with conflicted interests are allowed to serve on the board and participate in board business where they are not conflicted.

Exchanges may contract with the state Medicaid agency or with "eligible entities" that have relevant experience but are not health insurers to carry out certain exchange functions. The federal government is providing the states with grants and technical assistance between 2011 and 2015 to establish the exchanges. After January 1, 2015, exchanges must be self-sustaining through charging assessments or user fees to health insurers or consumers, or though raising revenue in some other way.

The exchanges may only offer QHPs (and dental plans that offer pediatric benefits). Exchanges are responsible for:

- certifying, recertifying, and decertifying health plans;
- operating a toll-free consumer hotline;
- maintaining an internet website providing standardized comparative information on QHPs;
- providing for annual open enrollment periods and for special enrolment periods under certain circumstances;
- rating plans, using a standardized format for providing health benefit information;
- assisting individuals in applying for Medicaid, CHIP, or other government programs;
- making available a calculator to assist individuals to determine the cost of coverage after the application of premium and cost-sharing subsidies;
- certifying individuals as exempt from the individual mandate;
- providing the IRS with a list of persons who are exempt from the mandate and of employers whose employees are receiving premium tax credits and of employers who have failed to provide affordable minimum essential coverage; and
- establishing a Navigator program.

Navigators will be trade, industry, professional, consumer, employer, or labor organizations with which exchanges contract to conduct public education, distribute information, and help individuals to enroll in QHPs and to apply for premium credits and cost-sharing reduction payments. They can also refer enrollees to resources for the processing of grievances, complaints, and inquires. Navigators cannot be insurers or receive consideration from insurers for enrollment.

The extent to which navigators must or should be licensed brokers or agents has become one of the most contentious issues at the state level, as agents and brokers have tried to protect their traditional role in selling insurance while consumer advocacy groups have pushed for the creation of navigator programs that would reach out to currently underserved groups to provide education and information about insurance and public programs. It is likely that agents and brokers will serve as navigators in many states, but the exchange final rules provide that exchanges must provide at least two kinds of navigators, and one must be a consumer organization. States cannot require navigators to have agent or broker licenses.

Under Section 1321, HHS has issued regulations establishing standards for the establishment and operation of exchanges, including SHOP exchanges, and for the offering of QHPs through the exchanges. As noted above, each state that chooses to set up an exchange itself and apply these standards must have in place not later than January 1, 2014 either the federal standards or a state law that HHS determines will implement the federal standards. If a state elects not to implement the standards or HHS determines, on or before January 1, 2013, that an electing state will not have an operating exchange in place by January 1, 2014 or will not implement the ACA and standards promulgated under it, then HHS must on its own establish an exchange within that state or do so through a nonprofit organization. As of this writing, it appears that no more than 17 states and the District of Columbia could be ready to run an exchange by 2014. The federal government is planning, therefore, to establish "federally facilitated" exchanges in all other states. The federal government is planning to partner with states that wish to work with it, with the federal government performing some functions and the state government others in "partnership exchanges."

The exchanges may only offer QHPs. The standards that QHPs must meet are established in the exchange final rule. QHPs will not be permitted to employ marketing practices or benefit designs that discourage enrollment by persons with significant health needs. They will be required to:

- ensure network adequacy and information;
- include essential community providers, where available, to serve low income, medically underserved individuals;
- be accredited by an entity recognized by HHS;
- implement a quality improvement strategy;
- utilize a uniform enrollment form and the standard format developed for presenting health benefits options;

- provide information on cost-sharing for specific services in a timely manner on request through an internet website and otherwise for individuals without internet access;
- provide information in plain language; and
- provide information on health plan quality performance.

Quality improvement strategies include activities to improve health outcomes and prevent hospital readmissions, patient safety and error reduction activities, prevention and wellness activities, and activities to reduce health and health care disparities. After January 1, 2015, QHPs may only contract with 1) hospitals with more than 50 beds if those hospitals have patient safety evaluation programs and mechanisms to assure appropriate discharge planning, and 2) with providers that have implemented required quality improvement programs.

The ACA requires HHS to develop a system for rating plans based on quality and price. Exchanges must rate plans using this system. HHS is also required to develop an enrollee satisfaction survey system. The exchanges must post information that will allow enrollees to compare satisfaction levels among plans. The mental health parity law applies to QHPs.

One of the major debates surrounding exchanges involves whether they should become "active purchasers," trying to influence the insurance market through selective purchasing or negotiating with insurers, or whether they should simply accept any insurer willing to meet minimum standards. An exchange may only certify a qualified health plan (QHP) for participation in the exchange if the QHP meets certification requirements and if "the Exchange determines that making available such health plan through such Exchange is in the interests of qualified individuals and qualified employers in the State or States in which such Exchange operates," so to that extent they cannot be completely passive. On the other hand, an exchange may not exclude a QHP because it is a fee-for-service plan or because the plan provides treatments for preventing patients' deaths that the exchange deems too costly. HHS has announced that the federally facilitated exchange will not be an active purchaser, at least not for the first year.

Exchanges are prohibited from imposing premium price controls. The exchange must require plans to justify premium increases before implementing them and must take information regarding premium increases into account before certifying a plan. Health plans seeking certification must disclose information on claims payment policies, financial data, enrollment and disenrollment data, data on claim denials and rating practices, information on cost-sharing relevant to out-of-network coverage, and information on enrollee and participant rights.

One potentially valuable role of an exchange is to standardize the plans available in the exchange to simplify consumer choice. See, on standardization, Troy Oechsner and Magda Schaler–Haynes, Keeping it Simple: Health Plan Benefit Standardization and Regulatory Choice Under the Affordable Care Act, 74 Albany L. Rev. 241 (2010–2011). See on how exchanges can assist people without web access, Brendan S. Maher, Some Thoughts on Health Care Exchanges: Choice, Defaults, and the Unconnected, 44 Conn. L. Rev. 1099 (2012).

F. CONSUMER CHOICE: SECTIONS 1312, 1322, 1334

Section 1312 specifies that qualified individuals may enroll through the exchange in any QHP. A qualified individual is a resident of a state who is not otherwise insured through employment or a public program and who is neither incarcerated (other than pending the disposition of charges) nor an alien who is illegally in the United States. Qualified employers may offer their employees insurance through the exchange and may specify the level of coverage to be made available to their employees. A qualified employer is a small employer that covers all of its full-time employees through the exchange, or, beginning in 2017 at a state's option, larger employers. Although the ACA defines small employer as having 100 or fewer employees, states can elect to limit small employers to those with 50 or fewer employees until 2016, and most probably will.

Under the statute, employees may choose any QHP offered through the exchange within the tier specified by their employer. The final rules also allow employers to pick a particular plan for their employees or to allow employees wider choice, among plans in multiple tiers for example. Exchanges must aggregate premiums for employers and present the employer with a single bill, so that employers will not have to pay multiple bills to multiple insurers. For 2014, federally facilitated exchanges will not provide employee choice or premium aggregation. Employers will only be able to pick a single plan for their employees. The FFE is expected to offer employee choice in future years.

One strategy that employers who purchase insurance for their employees through the SHOP exchange are likely to pursue is a "defined contribution" approach—the employer will pay an amount sufficient to cover a share of the cost of a lower-cost plan and the employee must pay extra if the employee wants a higher cost plan. How this will work legally depends on how premiums are set for health plans in a SHOP exchange. The Age Discrimination in Employment Act regulations prohibit employers with 20 or more employees from paying a lower proportion of the cost of health benefits for older employees (aged 40 or older) than for younger employees. 29 C.F.R. § 1625.10(d)(4)(ii). An employer subject to the ADEA could not, therefore, pay a flat dollar amount if it meant older employees would need to pay a higher proportion of their premiums. An employer could, however, pay a fixed percentage of premiums, or pick a particular plan and require employees to pay the additional cost of a more expensive plan.

Insurers can offer policies outside of the exchange and individuals and employers may purchase insurance policies outside of the exchange. The only people in the United States who must enroll in QHPs through the exchange are members of Congress and their staffs. QHPs may not penalize enrollees who cancel their enrollment because they have become eligible for coverage through their employer or a public program. States must allow agents and brokers to assist individuals and employers to enroll in plans and apply for premium tax credits and cost-sharing reductions. The exchange final rules specify that web-based brokers can assist in the exchange enrollment process, although they are not permitted to determine eligibility for premium tax credits or actually enroll exchange participants in plans.

Although insurers may sell policies both through the exchange and outside of the exchange, they must consider all enrollees in all health plans (except grandfathered plans) in the individual market, in and outside of the exchange, to be a single risk pool. The same is true with respect to the small group market. A state may require the merger of the individual and small group risk pools. Policies sold outside of the exchange to individuals and small groups must offer the essential benefits package. They also must charge the same premium for QHPs purchased in and outside of the exchange. State benefit requirements continue to apply outside of the exchange. Insurers will undoubtedly find ways to steer good risks outside of the exchange, but the legislation is intended to minimize this. One way in which insurers may risk select is through offering stop-loss insurance to self-insured plans outside of the exchange. Many of the requirements of the ACA, including the essential health benefits package, metal tiers, the risk pooling and risk adjustment programs, medical loss ratio requirements, unreasonable premium increase justification requirement, and premium tax do not apply to self-insured plans. Self-insured plans are now common in the large group market, but are becoming more common in the small group market. Small employers can rarely bear the risk of catastrophic medical costs, but insurers are increasingly selling "stop-loss" insurance to small employers, effectively insuring them for significant medical costs but allowing the employer to claim to be self-insured. This strategy could destabilize the small group market both in and outside of the exchange. Mark A. Hall, Regulating Stop–Loss Coverage May be Needed to Deter Self–Insuring Small Employers from Undermining Market Reforms, 31 Health Aff. 316 (2012); Timothy Stoltzfus Jost, Loopholes in the Affordable Care Act: Regulatory Gaps and Border Crossing Techniques and How to Address Them, 5 St. Louis U. J. Health L. & Pol'y 27 (2011). See, also on self-insured plan,

Robert W. Miller, The Effects of the Health Reform of Self–Insured Employer Plans, 4 J. Health & Life Sci L. 59 (2010).

The ACA provides several other options to increase consumer choice and competition, although most of the insurance plans sold within the exchange are expected to be offered by private insurers that otherwise operate within the state of the exchange. First, Section 1322 provides federal grants and loans to encourage the creation of nonprofit, member-owned consumer insurance cooperatives governed by majority vote. These entities cannot be government entities or pre-existing insurance companies. They will be tax-exempt, but are also subject to a number of requirements to make sure that they do not compete unfairly with private insurers. A number of cooperative plans have received federal funding and are now in the planning stage. Second, states may, under Section 1333, after January 1, 2016, enter into interstate compacts under which insurance plans may be offered in one state subject to the laws and regulations of another. Although the interstate insurer will basically be regulated by its home state, it will remain subject to the market conduct, unfair trade practices, network adequacy, consumer protection, and dispute resolution standards of any state in which the insurance was sold. It will also have to be licensed in each state, and notify consumers that it was not otherwise subject to the laws of the selling state. HHS will have to approve interstate insurance compacts.

Finally, Section 1334 of the law authorizes the Office of Personnel Management to enter into contracts with multi-state insurance plans for insurers to offer individual or small group coverage through the exchanges. Plans that have contracts with OPM will be deemed to be certified to participate in the exchanges. At least two plans must be available in each state, at least one of which must be a non-profit. OPM may negotiate with the plans a medical loss ratio, profit margin, premium levels, and other terms and conditions that are in the interests of the enrollees. Multi-state plans must be licensed and comply with the requirements of each state in which they do business and with all standards that apply to the Federal Employees Health Benefit Plan that are not inconsistent with the reform law. Although multi-state plans are administered by the OPM, which also administers the FEHBP, FEHBP plans are not required to participate in the multi-state insurance program and the two programs will be administered separately. See, on multi-state plans, Sidney Watson, Yolanda Campbell, Timothy McBride, Creating Multi–State Qualified Health Plans in Health Insurance Exchanges: Lessons for Rural and Urban America From the Federal Employees Health Benefit Program, 6 St. Louis U. J. Health L. and Pol'y 103 (2011).

II.   THE EMPLOYEE RETIREMENT
INCOME SECURITY ACT OF 1974: ERISA

Although regulation of health insurance has traditionally been the responsibility of the states, the ACA is not the first foray of Congress into regulating private health insurance. Since the 1970s, a series of federal laws have been enacted regulating private health insurance. The most important of these is the Employee Retirement Income Security Act of 1974, ERISA. ERISA's primary role throughout the 1980s and 1990s was deregulatory, as its preemptive provisions repeatedly blocked state common law actions against health plans as well as state attempts at plan regulation. The Supreme Court seemed to relax its interpretation of ERISA preemption in the late 1990s, however, giving the states somewhat more flexibility for regulating insured health plans, although it has become clear that there are limits to this flexibility. Finally, ERISA itself provides employee health plan beneficiaries with a positive right to sue to recover denied benefits, while also imposing fiduciary obligations on plan fiduciaries.

ERISA is not the only pre-ACA federal statute to regulate health plans. The Americans with Disabilities Act places at least minimal constraints on the ability of employers and insurers to discriminate against the disabled in the provision of health insurance. The Health Insurance Portability and Accountability Act of 1996 (which amended ERISA, as well as other federal statutes) limited the use of pre-existing condition clauses while prohibiting discrimination in coverage and rates within employee groups. It also offered certain protections in the small group and individual insurance markets. Until the ACA becomes fully effective in 2014, HIPAA will continue to be the primary federal law governing health insurance underwriting. The Consolidated Omnibus Budget Reconciliation Act of 1985 provides some protection for some who lose employee coverage. Finally, Congress has adopted in the past few years a handful of coverage mandates, which will continue to be in effect until overtaken by the essential benefits requirements in 2014.

A.   ERISA PREEMPTION OF STATE HEALTH
INSURANCE REGULATION

Section 514 of ERISA (codified as 29 U.S.C.A. § 1144) expressly preempts state statutes and common law claims that "relate to" employee benefit plans. Section 514, however, also explicitly exempts state regulation of insurance from preemption, while also prohibiting state regulation of self-insured plans. Section 502 of ERISA (codified as 29 U.S.C.A. § 1132) has been interpreted by the Supreme Court as providing for exclusive federal court jurisdiction over and an exclusive federal cause of action for cases that could be brought as ERISA claims. The text of these provisions follows:

29 U.S.C.A. § 1132 (Section 502)

A civil action may be brought—

(1) by a participant or beneficiary—

*   *   *

(B) to recover benefits due to him under the terms of his plan, to enforce his rights under the terms of the plan, or to clarify his rights to future benefits under the terms of the plan;

(2) by the Secretary, or by a participant, beneficiary or fiduciary for appropriate relief under section 1109 of this title [which imposes on plan fiduciaries the obligation to "make good" to a plan any losses resulting from a breach of fiduciary duties, and authorizes "other equitable or remedial relief" for breaches of fiduciary obligations];

(3) by a participant, beneficiary, or fiduciary (A) to enjoin any act or practice which violates any provision of this subchapter or the terms of the plan, or (B) to obtain other appropriate equitable relief (i) to redress such violations or (ii) to enforce any provisions of this subchapter or the terms of the plan;

*   *   *

29 U.S.C.A. § 1144 (Section 514)

(a) Except as provided in subsection (b) of this section, the provisions of this subchapter and subchapter III of this chapter shall supersede any and all State laws insofar as they may now or hereafter relate to any employee benefit plan * * *

(b) Construction and application

*   *   *

(2)(A) Except as provided in subparagraph (B), nothing in this subchapter shall be construed to exempt or relieve any person from any law of any State which regulates insurance, banking, or securities.

(B) Neither an employee benefit plan * * * nor any trust established under such a plan, shall be deemed to be an insurance company * * * or to be engaged in the business of insurance or banking for purposes of any law of any State purporting to regulate insurance companies, insurance contracts, banks, trust companies, or investment companies.

The task of sorting out ERISA's complex preemption scheme has resulted in a tremendous volume of litigation, including, to date, over twenty Supreme Court decisions and hundreds of state and federal lower court decisions. In this subsection we will examine the effect of Section 502 and 514 preemption on state laws "relating to" health insurance. In this context we will also consider the effect of Section 514's "savings clause," (§ 514(b)(2)(A)), which saves from preemption state laws "which regulate insurance," as well as § 514's "deemer" clause (§ 514(b)(2)(B)), which exempts self-insured ERISA plans from state insurance regulation. In the second subsection of this section, we will consider the effect of ERISA preemption on state common law tort causes of action against managed care plans and insurers. We begin with one of the more recent Supreme Court cases, which sets out the basic framework of ERISA preemption and debates the policies that ground it.

RUSH PRUDENTIAL, INC. V. DEBRA C. MORAN, ET. AL.

Supreme Court of the United States, 2002.
536 U.S. 355, 122 S.Ct. 2151, 153 L.Ed.2d 375.

JUSTICE SOUTER delivered the opinion of the Court.

*   *   *

Petitioner, Rush Prudential HMO, Inc., is a health maintenance organization (HMO) that contracts to provide medical services for employee welfare benefit plans covered by ERISA. Respondent Debra Moran is a beneficiary under one such plan, sponsored by her husband's employer. Rush's "Certificate of Group Coverage," issued to employees who participate in employer-sponsored plans, promises that Rush will provide them with "medically necessary" services. The terms of the certificate give Rush the "broadest possible discretion" to determine whether a medical service claimed by a beneficiary is covered under the certificate. * * *

As the certificate explains, Rush contracts with physicians "to arrange for or provide services and supplies for medical care and treatment" of covered persons. Each covered person selects a primary care physician from those under contract to Rush, while Rush will pay for medical services by an unaffiliated physician only if the services have been "authorized" both by the primary care physician and Rush's medical director.[ ]

In 1996, when Moran began to have pain and numbness in her right shoulder, Dr. Arthur LaMarre, her primary care physician, unsuccessfully administered "conservative" treatments such as physiotherapy. In October 1997, Dr. LaMarre recommended that Rush approve surgery by an unaffiliated specialist, Dr. Julia Terzis, who had developed an unconventional treatment for Moran's condition. Although Dr. LaMarre said that Moran would be "best served" by that procedure, Rush denied the request and, after Moran's internal appeals, affirmed the denial on the ground that the procedure was not "medically necessary."[ ] Rush instead proposed that Moran undergo standard surgery, performed by a physician affiliated with Rush.

In January 1998, Moran made a written demand for an independent medical review of her claim, as guaranteed by § 4–10 of Illinois's HMO Act,[ ] which provides:

> Each Health Maintenance Organization shall provide a mechanism for the timely review by a physician * * * who is unaffiliated with the Health Maintenance Organization, jointly selected by the patient . . . , primary care physician and the Health Maintenance Organization in the event of a dispute between the primary care physician and the Health Maintenance Organization regarding the medical necessity of a covered service proposed by a primary care physician. In the event that the reviewing physician determines the covered service to be medically necessary, the Health Maintenance Organization shall provide the covered service. * * *

*   *   *

When Rush failed to provide the independent review, Moran sued in an Illinois state court to compel compliance with the state Act. Rush removed the suit to Federal District Court, arguing that the cause of action was "completely preempted" under ERISA.[ ]

While the suit was pending, Moran had surgery by Dr. Terzis at her own expense and submitted a $94,841.27 reimbursement claim to Rush. Rush treated the claim as a renewed request for benefits and began a new inquiry to determine coverage. The three doctors consulted by Rush said the surgery had been medically unnecessary.

Meanwhile, the federal court remanded the case back to state court on Moran's motion, concluding that because Moran's request for independent review under § 4–10 would not require interpretation of the terms of an ERISA plan, the claim was not "completely preempted" so as to permit removal * * * The state court enforced the state statute and ordered Rush to submit to review by an independent physician. * * * [The reviewer] decided that Dr. Terzis's treatment had been medically necessary, based on the definition of medical necessity in Rush's Certificate of Group Coverage, as well as his own medical judgment. Rush's medical director, however, refused to concede that the surgery had been medically necessary, and denied Moran's claim in January 1999.

Moran amended her complaint in state court to seek reimbursement for the surgery as "medically necessary" under Illinois's HMO Act, and Rush again removed to federal court, arguing that Moran's amended complaint stated a claim for ERISA benefits and was thus completely preempted by ERISA's civil enforcement provisions, 29 U.S.C. § 1132(a) [§ 502], * * * The District Court treated Moran's claim as a suit under ERISA, and denied the claim on the ground that ERISA preempted Illinois's independent review statute.

The Court of Appeals for the Seventh Circuit reversed. * * *

* * *

To "safeguar[d] . . . the establishment, operation, and administration" of employee benefit plans, ERISA sets "minimum standards . . . assuring the equitable character of such plans and their financial soundness,"[ ] and contains an express preemption provision that ERISA "shall supersede any and all State laws insofar as they may now or hereafter relate to any employee benefit plan. . . ." § 1144(a)[§ 514(a)]. A saving clause then reclaims a substantial amount of ground with its provision that "nothing in this subchapter shall be construed to exempt or relieve any person from any law of any State which regulates insurance, banking, or securities." § 1144(b)(2)(A) [§ 514(b)(2)(A)]. The "unhelpful" drafting of these antiphonal clauses * * * occupies a substantial share of this Court's time. In trying to extrapolate congressional intent in a case like this, when congressional language seems simultaneously to preempt everything and hardly anything, we "have no choice" but to temper the assumption that " 'the ordinary meaning . . . accurately expresses the legislative purpose,' "[ ] with the qualification " 'that the historic police powers of the States were not [meant] to be superseded by the Federal Act unless that was the clear and manifest purpose of Congress.' "[ ]

It is beyond serious dispute that under existing precedent § 4–10 of the Illinois HMO Act "relates to" employee benefit plans within the meaning of § 1144(a). * * * As a law that "relates to" ERISA plans under § 1144(a), § 4–10 is saved from preemption only if it also "regulates insurance" under § 1144(b)(2)(A). * * *

[The Court then proceeded to apply the savings clause analysis method that it had developed in earlier cases, concluding that the Illinois external review law was saved from preemption. As this analysis was superseded by the Court's decision in *Kentucky Association of Health Plans v. Miller*, described below, this discussion is omitted here. Ed.]

* * *

Given that § 4–10 regulates insurance, ERISA's mandate that "nothing in this subchapter shall be construed to exempt or relieve any person from any law of any State which regulates insurance," 29 U.S.C. § 1144(b)(2)(A), ostensibly forecloses preemption. [ ] Rush, however, does not give up. It argues for preemption anyway, emphasizing that the question is ultimately one of congressional intent, which sometimes is so clear that it overrides a statutory provision designed to save state law from being preempted. * * *

In ERISA law, we have recognized one example of this sort of overpowering federal policy in the civil enforcement provisions, 29 U.S.C. § 1132(a), * * * In *Massachusetts Mut. Life Ins. Co. v. Russell,*[ ] we said those provisions amounted to an "interlocking, interrelated, and interdependent remedial scheme,"[ ] which *Pilot Life* described as "represent[ing] a careful balancing of the need for prompt and fair claims settlement procedures against the public interest in encouraging the formation of employee benefit plans"[ ]. So, we have held, the civil enforcement provisions are of such extraordinarily preemptive power that they override even the "well-pleaded complaint" rule for establishing the conditions under which a cause of action may be removed to a federal forum. *Metropolitan Life Ins. Co. v. Taylor*[ ].

Although we have yet to encounter a forced choice between the congressional policies of exclusively federal remedies and the "reservation of the business of insurance to the States,"[ ] we have anticipated such a conflict, with the state insurance regulation losing out if it allows plan participants "to obtain remedies . . . that Congress rejected in ERISA."

In *Pilot Life*, an ERISA plan participant who had been denied benefits sued in a state court on state tort and contract claims. He sought not merely damages for breach of contract, but also damages for emotional distress and punitive damages, both of which we had held unavailable under relevant ERISA provisions.[ ] We not only rejected the notion that these common-law contract claims "regulat[ed] insurance,"[ ] but went on to say that, regardless, Congress intended a "federal common law of rights and obligations" to develop under ERISA,[ ] without embellishment by independent state remedies.

Rush says that the day has come to turn dictum into holding by declaring that the state insurance regulation, § 4–10, is preempted for creating just the kind of "alternative remedy" we disparaged in *Pilot Life*. As Rush sees it, the independent review procedure is a form of binding arbitration that allows an ERISA beneficiary to submit claims to a new decisionmaker to examine Rush's determination *de novo,* supplanting judicial review under the "arbitrary and capricious" standard ordinarily applied when discretionary plan interpretations are challenged[ ]. * * *

We think, however, that Rush overstates the rule expressed in *Pilot Life*. * * *

*   *   *

[T]his case addresses a state regulatory scheme that provides no new cause of action under state law and authorizes no new form of ultimate relief. While independent review under § 4–10 may well settle the fate of a benefit claim under a particular contract, the state statute does not enlarge the claim beyond the benefits available in any action brought under § 1132(a). And although the reviewer's determination would presumably replace that of the HMO as to what is "medically necessary" under this contract, the relief ultimately available would still be what ERISA authorizes in a suit for benefits under § 1132(a). * * *

Rush still argues for going beyond *Pilot Life,* making the preemption issue here one of degree, whether the state procedural imposition interferes unreasonably with Congress's intention to provide a uniform federal regime of "rights and obligations" under ERISA. However, "[s]uch disuniformities . . . are the inevitable result of the congressional decision to 'save' local insurance regulation."[ ][11] Although we have recognized a limited exception from the saving clause for alternative causes of action and alternative remedies in the sense described above, we have never indicated that there might be additional justifications for qualifying the clause's application. * * *

To be sure, a State might provide for a type of "review" that would so resemble an adjudication as to fall within *Pilot Life's* categorical bar. Rush, and the dissent,[ ] contend that § 4–10 fills that bill by imposing an alternative scheme of arbitral adjudication at odds with the manifest congressional purpose to confine adjudication of disputes to the courts. * * *

In the classic sense, arbitration occurs when "parties in dispute choose a judge to render a final and binding decision on the merits of the controversy and on the basis of proofs presented by the parties."[ ] Arbitrators typically hold hearings at which parties may submit evidence and conduct cross-examinations.[ ]

Section 4–10 does resemble an arbitration provision, then, to the extent that the independent reviewer considers disputes about the meaning of the HMO contract and receives "evidence" in the form of medical records, statements from physicians, and the like. But this is as far as the resemblance to arbitration goes, for the other features of review under § 4–10 give the proceeding a different character, one not at all at odds with the policy behind § 1132(a). The Act does not give the independent

---

11 Thus, we do not believe that the mere fact that state independent review laws are likely to entail different procedures will impose burdens on plan administration that would threaten the object of 29 U.S.C. § 1132(a); it is the HMO contracting with a plan, and not the plan itself, that will be subject to these regulations, and every HMO will have to establish procedures for conforming with the local laws, regardless of what this Court may think ERISA forbids. This means that there will be no special burden of compliance upon an ERISA plan beyond what the HMO has already provided for. And although the added compliance cost to the HMO may ultimately be passed on to the ERISA plan, we have said that such " "indirect economic effect[s],"[ ], are not enough to preempt state regulation even outside of the insurance context. We recognize, of course, that a State might enact an independent review requirement with procedures so elaborate, and burdens so onerous, that they might undermine § 1132(a). No such system is before us.

reviewer a free-ranging power to construe contract terms, but instead, confines review to a single term: the phrase "medical necessity," used to define the services covered under the contract.[ ] This limitation, in turn, implicates a feature of HMO benefit determinations that we described in *Pegram v. Herdrich,*[ ] We explained that when an HMO guarantees medically necessary care, determinations of coverage "cannot be untangled from physicians' judgments about reasonable medical treatment."[ ] This is just how the Illinois Act operates; the independent examiner must be a physician with credentials similar to those of the primary care physician,[ ] and is expected to exercise independent medical judgment in deciding what medical necessity requires. * * *

Once this process is set in motion, it does not resemble either contract interpretation or evidentiary litigation before a neutral arbiter, as much as it looks like a practice (having nothing to do with arbitration) of obtaining another medical opinion. * * *

The practice of obtaining a second opinion, however, is far removed from any notion of an enforcement scheme, and once § 4–10 is seen as something akin to a mandate for second-opinion practice in order to ensure sound medical judgments, the preemption argument that arbitration under § 4–10 supplants judicial enforcement runs out of steam.

Next, Rush argues that § 4–10 clashes with a substantive rule intended to be preserved by the system of uniform enforcement, stressing a feature of judicial review highly prized by benefit plans: a deferential standard for reviewing benefit denials. Whereas *Firestone Tire & Rubber Co. v. Bruch,*[ ] recognized that an ERISA plan could be designed to grant "discretion" to a plan fiduciary, deserving deference from a court reviewing a discretionary judgment, § 4–10 provides that when a plan purchases medical services and insurance from an HMO, benefit denials are subject to apparently *de novo* review. If a plan should continue to balk at providing a service the reviewer has found medically necessary, the reviewer's determination could carry great weight in a subsequent suit for benefits under § 1132(a), depriving the plan of the judicial deference a fiduciary's medical judgment might have obtained if judicial review of the plan's decision had been immediate.

Again, however, the significance of § 4–10 is not wholly captured by Rush's argument, which requires some perspective for evaluation. First, in determining whether state procedural requirements deprive plan administrators of any right to a uniform standard of review, it is worth recalling that ERISA itself provides nothing about the standard. It simply requires plans to afford a beneficiary some mechanism for internal review of a benefit denial, * * *.

Not only is there no ERISA provision directly providing a lenient standard for judicial review of benefit denials, but there is no requirement necessarily entailing such an effect even indirectly. When this Court dealt with the review standards on which the statute was silent, we held that a general or default rule of *de novo* review could be replaced by deferential review if the ERISA plan itself provided that the plan's benefit determinations were matters of high or unfettered discretion[ ]. Nothing in ERISA, however, requires that these kinds of decisions be so "discretionary" in the first place; whether they are is simply a matter of plan design or the drafting of an HMO contract. In this respect, then, § 4–10 prohibits designing an insurance contract so as to accord unfettered discretion to the insurer to interpret the contract's terms. As such, it does not implicate ERISA's enforcement scheme at all, and is no different from the types of substantive state regulation of insurance contracts we have in the past permitted to survive preemption, such as mandated-benefit statutes and statutes prohibiting the denial of claims solely on the ground of untimeliness.[ ] * * *

* * *

In deciding what to make of these facts and conclusions, it helps to go back to where we started and recall the ways States regulate insurance in looking out for the welfare of their citizens. Illinois has chosen to regulate insurance as one way to regulate the practice of medicine, which we have previously held to be permissible under ERISA[ ]. While the statute designed to do this undeniably eliminates whatever may have remained of a plan sponsor's option to minimize scrutiny of benefit denials, this effect of eliminating an insurer's autonomy to guarantee terms congenial to its own interests is the stuff of garden variety insurance regulation through the imposition of standard policy terms. * * * And any lingering doubt about the reasonableness of § 4–10 in affecting the application of § 1132(a) may be put to rest by recalling that regulating insurance tied to what is medically necessary is probably inseparable from enforcing the quintessentially state-law standards of reasonable medical care. See *Pegram v. Herdrich* [ ]. To the extent that benefits litigation in some federal courts may have to account for the effects of § 4–10, it would be an exaggeration to hold that the objectives of § 1132(a) are undermined. The savings clause is entitled to prevail here, and we affirm the judgment.

JUSTICE THOMAS, with whom THE CHIEF JUSTICE, JUSTICE SCALIA, and JUSTICE KENNEDY join, dissenting.

This Court has repeatedly recognized that ERISA's civil enforcement provision, § 502 of the Employee Retirement Income Security Act of 1974 (ERISA), 29 U.S.C. § 1132, provides the exclusive vehicle for actions asserting a claim for benefits under health plans governed by ERISA, and therefore that state laws that create additional remedies are pre-empted.[ ] Such exclusivity of remedies is necessary to further Congress' interest in establishing a uniform federal law of employee benefits so that employers are encouraged to provide benefits to their employees.[ ]

* * * Therefore, as the Court concedes,[ ] even a state law that "regulates insurance" may be pre-empted if it supplements the remedies provided by ERISA, despite ERISA's saving clause,[ ]. Today, however, the Court takes the unprecedented step of allowing respondent Debra Moran to short circuit ERISA's remedial scheme by allowing her claim for benefits to be determined in the first instance through an arbitral-like procedure provided under Illinois law, and by a decisionmaker other than a court.[ ] * * *

From the facts of this case one can readily understand why Moran sought recourse under § 4–10. * * *

In the course of its review, petitioner informed Moran that "there is no prevailing opinion within the appropriate specialty of the United States medical profession that the procedure proposed [by Moran] is safe and effective for its intended use and that the omission of the procedure would adversely affect [her] medical condition."[ ] Petitioner did agree to cover the standard treatment for Moran's ailment,[ ] concluding that peer-reviewed literature "demonstrates that [the standard surgery] is effective therapy in the treatment of [Moran's condition]."[ ]

Moran, however, was not satisfied with this option. * * * She invoked § 4–10 of the Illinois HMO Act, which requires HMOs to provide a mechanism for review by an independent physician when the patient's primary care physician and HMO disagree about the medical necessity of a treatment proposed by the primary care physician. * * *

Dr. A. Lee Dellon, an unaffiliated physician who served as the independent medical reviewer, concluded that the surgery for which petitioner denied coverage "was appropriate," that it was "the same type of surgery" he would have done, and that Moran "had all of the indications and therefore the medical necessity to carry out" the nonstandard surgery. * * * Under § 4–10, Dr. Dellon's determination conclusively established Moran's right to benefits under Illinois law.

*   *   *

Section 514(a)'s broad language provides that ERISA "shall supersede any and all State laws insofar as they . . . relate to any employee benefit plan," except as provided in § 514(b). 29 U.S.C. § 1144(a). This language demonstrates "Congress's intent to establish the regulation of employee welfare benefit plans 'as exclusively a federal concern.' "[ ] It was intended to "ensure that plans and plan sponsors would be subject to a uniform body of benefits law" so as to "minimize the administrative and financial burden of complying with conflicting directives among States or between States and the Federal Government" and to prevent "the potential for conflict in substantive law . . . requiring the tailoring of plans and employer conduct to the peculiarities of the law of each jurisdiction."[ ]

* * * [T]he Court until today had consistently held that state laws that seek to supplant or add to the exclusive remedies in § 502(a) of ERISA, 29 U.S.C. § 1132(a), are pre-empted because they conflict with Congress' objective that rights under ERISA plans are to be enforced under a uniform national system.[ ] The Court has explained that § 502(a) creates an "interlocking, interrelated, and interdependent remedial scheme," and that a beneficiary who claims that he was wrongfully denied benefits has "a panoply of remedial devices" at his disposal. * * *

* * *

Section 4–10 cannot be characterized as anything other than an alternative state-law remedy or vehicle for seeking benefits. In the first place, § 4–10 comes into play only if the HMO and the claimant dispute the claimant's entitlement to benefits; the purpose of the review is to determine whether a claimant is entitled to benefits. * * *

There is no question that arbitration constitutes an alternative remedy to litigation.[ ] Consequently, although a contractual agreement to arbitrate—which does not constitute a "State law" relating to "any employee benefit plan"—is outside § 514(a) of ERISA's pre-emptive scope, States may not circumvent ERISA preemption by mandating an alternative arbitral-like remedy as a plan term enforceable through an ERISA action.

To be sure, the majority is correct that § 4–10 does not mirror all procedural and evidentiary aspects of "common arbitration."[ ] But as a binding decision on the merits of the controversy the § 4–10 review resembles nothing so closely as arbitration. * * *

* * *

[I]t is troubling that the Court views the review under § 4–10 as nothing more than a practice "of obtaining a second [medical] opinion." * * * [W]hile a second medical opinion is nothing more than that—an opinion—a determination under § 4–10 is a conclusive determination with respect to the award of benefits. * * *

Section 4–10 constitutes an arbitral-like state remedy through which plan members may seek to resolve conclusively a disputed right to benefits. Some 40 other States have similar laws, though these vary as to applicability, procedures, standards, deadlines, and consequences of independent review. * * *

For the reasons noted by the Court, independent review provisions may sound very appealing. Efforts to expand the variety of remedies available to aggrieved beneficiaries beyond those set forth in ERISA are obviously designed to increase the chances that patients will be able to receive treatments they desire, and most of us are naturally sympathetic to those suffering from illness who seek further options. Nevertheless, the Court would do well to remember that no employer is required to provide any health benefit plan under ERISA and that the entire advent of managed care, and the genesis of HMOs, stemmed from spiraling health costs. To the extent that independent review provisions such as § 4–10 make it more likely that HMOs will have to subsidize beneficiaries' treatments of choice, they undermine the ability of HMOs to control costs, which, in turn, undermines the ability of employers to provide health care coverage for employees.

As a consequence, independent review provisions could create a disincentive to the formation of employee health benefit plans, a problem that Congress addressed by making ERISA's remedial scheme exclusive and uniform. While it may well be the case that the advantages of allowing States to implement independent review requirements as a supplement to the remedies currently provided under ERISA outweigh this drawback, this is a judgment that, pursuant to ERISA, must be made by Congress. I respectfully dissent.

NOTES AND QUESTIONS

1.   ERISA only governs employee benefit plans, i.e. benefit plans established and maintained by employers to provide benefits to their employees. It does not reach health insurance purchased by individuals as individuals (including self-employed individuals) or health benefits not provided through employment-related group plans, such as uninsured motorist insurance policies or workers' compensation. Certain church and government-sponsored plans are also not covered. See Macro v. Independent Health Ass'n, Inc., 180 F. Supp.2d 427 (W.D.N.Y.2001). Finally, ERISA does not regulate group insurance offered by insurers to the employees of particular businesses without employer contributions or administrative involvement. See 29 C.F.R. § 2510.3–1(j); Taggart Corp. v. Life & Health Benefits Admin., Inc., 617 F.2d 1208 (5th Cir.1980), cert. denied, 450 U.S. 1030, 101 S.Ct. 1739, 68 L.Ed.2d 225 (1981). Despite these exceptions, ERISA govern the vast majority of private health insurance in America, which is provided through employment-related group plans.

2.   Part of the confusion inherent in ERISA preemption decisions is attributable to the fact that there are three distinct forms of ERISA preemption. One of these is express preemption based on § 514(a) (29 U.S.C. § 1144(a)). Section 514(a), reproduced above, provides that ERISA "supersedes" any state law that "relates to" an employee benefits plan. Express 514(a) preemption, however, is subject to the "savings" clause, § 514(b)(2)(A), and thus does not reach state insurance regulation.

Just because a law is saved from 514(a) preemption, however, does not mean that it is not preempted, as the controversy in *Rush* illustrates. ERISA preemption can also be based on § 502(a) of ERISA (29 U.S.C. § 1132(a)) which provides for federal court jurisdiction over specified types of claims against ERISA plans. The Supreme Court has long held that ERISA plans may remove into federal court claims that were brought in state courts but that could have been brought under § 502(a) in federal court. Removal is permitted under the "complete preemption" exception to the well-pleaded complaint rule. The well-pleaded complaint rule normally limits removal of cases from state into federal court on the basis of federal question jurisdiction (under 28 U.S.C.A. § 1331) to cases in which federal claims are explicitly raised in the plaintiff's complaint. However, under the "complete preemption" exception to this rule (sometimes called "superpreemption"), federal jurisdiction is permitted when Congress has so completely preempted an area of law that any claim within it is brought under federal law, and thus is removable to federal court. "Complete preemption" is, in reality, not a preemption doctrine, but rather a rule of federal jurisdiction.

Third, Section 502(a) also plays another role in ERISA jurisprudence, ousting state claims and remedies that would take the place of § 502 claims. The federal courts have interpreted § 502 to indicate a Congressional intent to preempt comprehensively the "field" of judicial oversight of employee benefits plans. Thus state tort, contract, and even statutory claims that could have been brought as claims for benefits or for breach of fiduciary duty under § 502(a) have been held to be preempted by § 502(a). As *Moran* demonstrates, § 502(a) preemption, like § 514(a) explicit preemption, is not comprehensive. In particular, ERISA does not necessarily preempt state court malpractice cases brought against managed care plans that provide as well as pay for health care, as we will see in subsection D. Also claims brought by persons who are not proper plaintiffs under § 502(a) or against persons who are not ERISA fiduciaries are not preempted by ERISA § 502(a) preemption. *Moran* also holds that external review procedures imposed by the states prior to the onset of litigation also may be exempt from § 502 preemption.

Section 502(a) and § 514(a) preemption are not, however, coextensive. Just because a lawsuit invokes a law that might be preempted as relating to an employee benefits claim does not mean that the claim could be brought under § 502(a), and is thus subject to "complete preemption." Not infrequently federal courts remand cases that are not § 502(a) claims to state court for resolution of § 514(a) preemption issues. As we see below in *Aetna Health Insurance v. Davila*, moreover, laws that are saved from preemption by an exception to § 514(a), may still be preempted as inconsistent with § 502(a) field preemption.

3. Early cases interpreting § 514(a) read it very broadly. The Supreme Court's first consideration of § 514(a), Shaw v. Delta Air Lines, Inc., 463 U.S. 85, 103 S.Ct. 2890, 77 L.Ed.2d 490 (1983), adopted a very literal and liberal reading of "relates to" as including any provisions having a "connection with

or reference to" a benefits plan. The Court rejected narrower readings of ERISA preemption that would have limited its reach to state laws that explicitly attempted to regulate ERISA plans or that dealt with subjects explicitly addressed by ERISA. For over a decade following *Shaw*, the Court applied the § 514(a) tests developed in *Shaw* expansively in a variety of contexts, almost always finding preemption when it found an ERISA plan to exist. The Court repeatedly expressed allegiance to the opinion that ERISA § 514(a) preemption had a "broad scope," Metropolitan Life v. Massachusetts, 471 U.S. 724, 739, 105 S.Ct. 2380, 85 L.Ed.2d 728 (1985), and "an expansive sweep," Pilot Life Ins. Co. v. Dedeaux, 481 U.S. 41, 47, 107 S.Ct. 1549, 95 L.Ed.2d 39 (1987), and that it was "conspicuous for its breadth," FMC Corp. v. Holliday, 498 U.S. 52, 58, 111 S.Ct. 403, 112 L.Ed.2d 356 (1990).

Attending to these Supreme Court pronouncements, lower courts in the 1980s and 1990s held a wide range of state regulatory programs and common law claims that arguably "related to" the administration of an ERISA plan or imposed costs upon plans to be preempted. As the *Fiedler* case discussed below demonstrates, the "connection with or reference to" test continues to sweep broadly. The Supreme Court finally recognized the limits of ERISA preemption, however, in New York State Conference of Blue Cross and Blue Shield Plans v. Travelers Ins. Co., 514 U.S. 645, 115 S.Ct. 1671, 131 L.Ed.2d 695 (1995). *Travelers* held that a New York law that required hospitals to charge different rates to insured, HMO, and self-insured plans was not preempted by § 514(a). Retreating from earlier expansive readings of ERISA preemption, the Court reaffirmed the principle applied in other areas of the law that Congress is generally presumed not to intend to preempt state law. 514 U.S. at 654. The Court proceeded to note that in cases involving traditional areas of state regulation, such as health care, congressional intent to preempt state law should not be presumed unless it was "clear and manifest." Id. at 655. Recognizing that the term "relate to" was not self-limiting, the Court turned for assistance in defining the term to the purpose of ERISA, which it defined as freeing benefit plans from conflicting state and local regulation. Id. at 656–57. Preemption was intended, the Court held, to affect state laws that operated directly on the structure or administration of ERISA plans, id. at 657–58, not laws that only indirectly raised the cost of various benefit options, id. at 658–64. Accordingly, the Court held that the challenged rate-setting law was not "related to" an ERISA plan, and thus not preempted.

The Court's post-*Travelers* preemption cases suggest that the Court in fact turned a corner in *Travelers*. It has rejected ERISA 514 preemption in a number of cases, though it had almost never done so before *Travelers*. Post–*Travelers* lower court cases on the whole continued to apply ERISA preemption broadly, generally finding that state programs aimed at regulating insurance and managed care "relate to" an ERISA plan. Some, however, have limited ERISA preemption. See, for example, Louisiana Health Service & Indemnity Co. v. Rapides Healthcare System, 461 F.3d 529 (5th Cir.2006), holding that a Louisiana statute that required insurance companies to honor all assignments of benefits by patients to hospitals did not have an impermissible connection with ERISA. See, reviewing comprehensively federal and state court cases applying ERISA to managed care regulation, Robert F. Rich, Christopher T. Erb, and Louis J. Gale, Judicial Interpretation of Managed Care Policy, 13 Elder L.J. 85 (2005).

4.   As *Moran* notes, a state law that is otherwise preempted under § 514(a) is saved from preemption if it regulates insurance under the "savings clause" found in § 514(b)(2)(A) (29 U.S.C.A. § 1144(b)(2)(A)). In its early cases interpreting this clause, the Court read the savings clause conservatively, applying both a "common sense" test as well as the three part test developed in antitrust cases applying the McCarran–Ferguson Act for determining whether a law regulated "the business of insurance" to determine whether the savings clause applied. Metropolitan Life Ins. Co. v. Massachusetts, 471 U.S. 724, 740–44, 105 S.Ct. 2380, 85 L.Ed.2d 728 (1985), Pilot Life Ins. Co. v. Dedeaux, 481 U.S. 41, 107 S.Ct. 1549, 95 L.Ed.2d 39 (1987).

In Kentucky Association of Health Plans, Inc. v. Miller, 538 U.S. 329, 123 S.Ct. 1471, 155 L.Ed.2d 468 (2003) the court abandoned its earlier precedents and crafted a new approach to interpreting the savings clause. This case involved the claim of an association of managed care plans that Kentucky's "any willing provider" law was preempted by ERISA. The Sixth Circuit had held that the regulatory provision was saved from preemption under ERISA's savings clause. In a brief and unanimous opinion written by Justice Scalia (who had dissented in *Moran*), the Court held that the law was saved from preemption, abandoning its previous savings clause jurisprudence. The Court acknowledged that use of the McCarran–Ferguson test had "misdirected attention, failed to provide clear guidance to lower federal courts, and * * * added little to relevant analysis." The Court also admitted that the McCarran–Ferguson tests had been developed for different purposes and interpreted different statutory language.

The Court concluded:

> Today we make a clean break from the McCarran–Ferguson factors and hold that for a state law to be deemed a 'law . . . which regulates insurance' under § 1144(b)(2)(A), it must satisfy two requirements. First, the state law must be specifically directed toward entities engaged in insurance.[ ] Second, * * * the state law must substantially affect the risk pooling arrangement between the insurer and the insured. Kentucky's law satisfies each of these requirements. 123 S.Ct. at 1479.

Earlier in the opinion it had interpreted the "risk pooling" requirement as follows:

> We have never held that state laws must alter or control the actual terms of insurance policies to be deemed 'laws . . . which regulat[e] insurance' under § 1144(b)(2)(A); it suffices that they substantially affect the risk pooling arrangement between insurer and insured. By expanding the number of providers from whom an insured may

receive health services, AWP laws alter the scope of permissible bargains between insurers and insureds * * *. No longer may Kentucky insureds seek insurance from a closed network of health-care providers in exchange for a lower premium. The AWP prohibition substantially affects the type of risk pooling arrangements that insurers may offer. 123 S.Ct. at 1477–78.

Kentucky Association significantly clarifies, and expands, the coverage of ERISA's savings clause. Virtually any state law that requires insurers to provide particular benefits would seem to be covered. See Matthew O. Gatewood, The New Map: The Supreme Court's New Guide to Curing Thirty Years of Confusion in ERISA Savings Clause Analysis, 62 Wash. & Lee U. L. Rev. 643 (2005). What effect is this green light to state regulation of managed care and health insurance likely to have on the willingness of employers to offer health insurance plans to their workers, or to offer insured rather than self-insured plans? Might Justice Thomas' prediction on this matter prove true? See Haavi Morreim, ERISA Takes a Drubbing: Rush Prudential and Its Implications for Health Care, 38 Tort Trial and Ins. Practice J. 933 (2003). Does the adoption of the ACA change the calculus, as it addresses many of the regulatory issues formerly addressed by state law?

5.   As *Moran* acknowledges, even a statute saved from § 514(a) preemption by the savings clause may nevertheless, under *Pilot Life*, be preempted by § 502(a) if it provides a state remedy that takes the place of § 502(a). Aetna Health Inc. v. Davila, 542 U.S. 200, 124 S.Ct. 2488, 159 L.Ed.2d 312 (2004), reproduced below, applied this exception, holding that the Texas Health Care Liability Act, which allowed lawsuits against managed care companies for failing to exercise ordinary care in making coverage decisions, was preempted. Section 502 preemption is not limited to tort cases, however, it also extends to state statutes that provide private actions for civil penalties to the extent that these cases could have been brought under § 502. See, for example, Prudential Insurance Co. v. National Park Medical Center, Inc., 413 F.3d 897 (8th Cir.2005), holding that the provisions of the Arkansas Patient Protection Act allowing private suits for injunctive relief, damages of at least $1,000, and attorney's fees were preempted by ERISA § 502 to the extent that the lawsuits could have been brought under § 502. Thus an action to recover payment denied by a plan for the services of a provider who should have been qualified for payment under a state's "any willing provider" law would be preempted. In Hawaii Management Alliance Assoc. v. Insurance Comm'r, 100 P.3d 952 (Hawai'i 2004), the Hawaiian Supreme Court held that Hawaii's external review statute was preempted by ERISA because it provided a remedy alternative to § 502.

6.   ERISA's § 514(b)(2)(A) savings clause is subject to its own exception, the § 514(b)(2)(B) "deemer" clause. This subsection, reproduced above, provides that "neither an employee benefit * * * nor any trust established under such a plan, shall be deemed to be an insurance company or other insurer, * * * or to be engaged in the business of insurance * * * for purposes of any

law of any State purporting to regulate insurance companies, [or] insurance contracts, * * *." 29 U.S.C.A. § 1144(b)(2)(B). In FMC Corporation v. Holliday, 498 U.S. 52, 111 S.Ct. 403, 112 L.Ed.2d 356 (1990), the Supreme Court interpreted this clause broadly to exempt self-funded ERISA plans entirely from state regulation and state law claims.

The deemer clause offers a significant incentive for employers to become self-insured, as a self-insured plan can totally escape state regulation, and in particular, benefit mandates. Self-insurance, however, also has disadvantages—it imposes upon the employer the burden of administering the plan as well as open-ended liability for employee benefit claims made under the plan. To mitigate these problems, self-insured employers often contract with third-party administrators to administer claims and with stop-loss insurers to limit their claims exposure. The courts have overwhelmingly held that employer plans remain self-insured even though they are reinsured through stop-loss plans, and have prohibited states from attempting to impose requirements on self-insured plans through regulation of stop-loss coverage. See, e.g., Bill Gray Enterprises, Inc. Employee Health and Welfare Plan v. Gourley, 248 F.3d 206 (3rd Cir.2001) and Lincoln Mutual Casualty v. Lectron Products, Inc. 970 F.2d 206 (6th Cir.1992). Third-party administrators that administer self-insured plans are also protected from state insurance regulation. NGS American, Inc. v. Barnes, 805 F.Supp. 462, 473 (W.D.Texas 1992). Thus an employer who is willing to bear some risk can escape state regulation under the "deemer" clause, even though most of the risk of insuring the plan is borne by a stop-loss insurer and the burden of administering the plan is assumed by a third-party administrator.

States may, however, regulate stop-loss coverage itself as a form of insurance. Some states ban stop loss coverage for small group plans, while others prohibit stop-loss policies that cover losses below a certain level. See, e.g. N.Y. Ins. Law § 3231(h); 4317(a). See also Edstom Indus. v. Companion Life Ins. 516 U.S. 546, 551 (7th Cir. 2008).

The calculus that an employer faces in deciding whether or not to self-insure changes under the ACA. A number of the ACA requirements that apply to small group plans—including the essential benefits package and single risk pool requirements, the risk adjustment program, the medical loss ratio and unreasonable premium increase justification requirement—do not apply to self-insured plans. It is likely, therefore, that a significant number of small employers that currently cover their employees through insured plans will switch to self-insured plans. Under the regulations governing the SHOP exchanges, however, a self-insured small employer may shift to exchange coverage at any time. This creates a serious potential adverse selection problem because healthy small groups can be self-insured, but then move to the exchange with a community rate if a member incurs high health care expenses. See, Timothy Stoltzfus Jost, Loopholes in the Affordable Care Act: Regulatory Gaps and Border Crossing Techniques and How to Address Them, 5 St. Louis J. Health L. & Pol'y 27 (2011).

7.   One issue that arose occasionally in pre-*Moran* savings clause litigation is whether health maintenance organizations are in the business of insurance and thus subject to state regulation. Early cases tended to say no, often on very formalistic grounds, see, e.g., O'Reilly v. Ceuleers, 912 F.2d 1383 (11th Cir.1990). *Moran* seems to have settled this issue once and for all. The defendant, Rush, argued that an HMO was a health care provider rather than an insurer, and thus regulations affecting it would not be protected by the savings clause. The Court responded:

> The answer to Rush is, of course, that an HMO is both: it provides health care, and it does so as an insurer. Nothing in the saving clause requires an either-or choice between health care and insurance in deciding a preemption question, and as long as providing insurance fairly accounts for the application of state law, the saving clause may apply. * * *

> The defining feature of an HMO is receipt of a fixed fee for each patient enrolled under the terms of a contract to provide specified health care if needed. *Pegram v. Herdrich,*[ ]. "The HMO thus assumes the financial risk of providing the benefits promised: if a participant never gets sick, the HMO keeps the money regardless, and if a participant becomes expensively ill, the HMO is responsible for the treatment. . . . " *Id.,* * * *. 536 U.S. at 367.

8.   Among the most litigated ERISA issues in the past decade has been the effect ERISA has on the rights of health plans to recover amounts they paid for health care when a beneficiary subsequently recovers a tort judgment for the injuries that necessitated the care. These cases are either brought by a plan trying to recover from the beneficiary or by a beneficiary trying to block recovery by the plan or to get money back that a plan has already obtained by exercising its rights of subrogation. Some cases involve state statutes limiting a plan's right of subrogation. The Supreme Court has decided thru recent cases involving the rights of plans to recover benefits under ERISA, U.S. Airways v. McCutchen, ___ S.Ct. ___ (2013), Sereboff v. Mid Atlantic Medical Services, Inc., 547 U.S. 356, 126 S.Ct. 1869, 164 L.Ed.2d 612 (2006) and Great–West Life & Annuity Ins. Co. v. Knudson, 534 U.S. 204, 122 S.Ct. 708, 151 L.Ed.2d 635 (2002). These decisions interpret provisions of ERISA authorizing equitable relief and turn on arcane interpretations of the historical distinction between law and equity. They are beyond the scope of this chapter.

NOTE: ERISA PREEMPTION AND THE AFFORDABLE CARE ACT

The ACA does not explicitly change ERISA's preemption provisions. Inevitably, however, it will change the nature of ERISA plan regulation in two important respects.

First, the ACA applies a whole new group of federal requirements to group health insurance plans through amendments to the Public Health Services Act and through section 1563, which adopts a new section 715 to ERISA and section 9815 to the Internal Revenue Code that apply most of the new ACA insurance regulation requirements to ERISA plans, including self-insured plans. As already noted, not all of the protections of the law apply to self-insured plans, however, and neither large group nor self-insured group plans have to provide the essential benefits. Also, the exchanges will, at least initially, not cover large group plans, so large group plans will not be required to meet the QHP requirements. But most of the ACA insurance reforms will apply to all non-grandfathered ERISA plans, and some of these requirements, such as the provisions relating to rescissions, dependent coverage, pre-existing condition exclusions, excessive waiting periods, uniform benefits, and coverage disclosure, medical loss ratios, and lifetime and annual limits will even apply to grandfathered ERISA plans. ERISA has until now imposed only minimal requirements on employment-related plans. That will change dramatically with this legislation. Federal regulation will look much more like state regulation.

Second, because of this, some of the issues that have caused conflict with respect to state regulation of insured ERISA plans will probably be less salient under the ACA. The ACA has its own preemption provision, mentioned earlier in this chapter: "Nothing in this title shall be construed to preempt any State law that does not prevent the application of the provisions of this title." Section 1321(d). The implication, of course, is that where the ACA and state law are incompatible, the ACA will govern. Thus, section 2712 prohibiting rescissions except in cases of intentional misrepresentation will apply to group health plans even though state law would otherwise have permitted rescission for unintentional misrepresentations.

But the ACA also applies state law to group plans. As noted above, for example, Section 2719, which requires plans to offer external review of coverage and claims denials, generally requires insured group health plans to comply with state external review requirements, which in turn must at a minimum comply with the NAIC External Review Model Act, as described above. The precise issue raised by *Rush Prudential*, that is, would not come up today, as the ACA would determine whether or not a state external review law applied to a group health plan. Where the ACA does not address a particular issue, however, the preemption rules of ERISA section 514 still apply. Moreover, the ACA does nothing to change the jurisdictional or remedial preemption rules of ERISA section 502. See, Mallory Jensen, Is ERISA Preemption Superfluous in the New Age of Health Care Reform, 2011 Colum. Bus.L. Rev. 464 (2011).

B. ERISA PREEMPTION OF STATE TORT LITIGATION

Courts have struggled to determine the nature and extent of ERISA preemption in medical negligence cases. Managed care plans as defendants are subject to the same theories of liability as hospitals—vicarious liability, corporate negligence, ordinary negligence. Vicarious liability against managed care organizations has been allowed by most courts that have considered the question. The Supreme Court, however, has severely limited the reach of state tort actions against ERISA-qualified health plans.

AETNA HEALTH INC. V. DAVILA

Supreme Court of the United States, 2004.
542 U.S. 200, 124 S.Ct. 2488, 159 L.Ed.2d 312.

JUSTICE THOMAS delivered the opinion of the Court.

In these consolidated cases, two individuals sued their respective health maintenance organizations (HMOs) for alleged failures to exercise ordinary care in the handling of coverage decisions, in violation of a duty imposed by the Texas Health Care Liability Act (THCLA)[ ]. We granted certiorari to decide whether the individuals' causes of action are completely pre-empted by the "interlocking, interrelated, and interdependent remedial scheme,"[ ] found at § 502(a) of the Employee Retirement Income Security Act of 1974 (ERISA)[ ]. We hold that the causes of action are completely pre-empted and hence removable from state to federal court. The Court of Appeals, having reached a contrary conclusion, is reversed.

Respondent Juan Davila is a participant, and respondent Ruby Calad is a beneficiary, in ERISA-regulated employee benefit plans. Their respective plan sponsors had entered into agreements with petitioners, Aetna Health Inc. and CIGNA HealthCare of Texas, Inc., to administer the plans. Under Davila's plan, for instance, Aetna reviews requests for coverage and pays providers, such as doctors, hospitals, and nursing homes, which perform covered services for members; under Calad's plan sponsor's agreement, CIGNA is responsible for plan benefits and coverage decisions.

Respondents both suffered injuries allegedly arising from Aetna's and CIGNA's decisions not to provide coverage for certain treatment and services recommended by respondents' treating physicians. Davila's treating physician prescribed Vioxx to remedy Davila's arthritis pain, but Aetna refused to pay for it. Davila did not appeal or contest this decision, nor did he purchase Vioxx with his own resources and seek reimbursement. Instead, Davila began taking Naprosyn, from which he allegedly suffered a severe reaction that required extensive treatment and hospitalization. Calad underwent surgery, and although her treating physician recommended an extended hospital stay, a CIGNA discharge nurse determined that Calad did not meet the plan's criteria for a continued hospital stay. CIGNA consequently denied coverage for the extended hospital stay. Calad experienced postsurgery complications forcing her to return to the hospital. She alleges that these complications would not have occurred had CIGNA approved coverage for a longer hospital stay.

Respondents brought separate suits in Texas state court against petitioners. Invoking THCLA § 88.002(a), respondents argued that petitioners' refusal to cover the requested services violated their "duty to exercise ordinary care when making health care treatment decisions," and that these refusals "proximately caused" their injuries. Ibid. Petitioners removed the cases to Federal District Courts, arguing that respondents' causes of action fit within the scope of, and were therefore completely pre-empted by, ERISA § 502(a). The respective District Courts agreed, and declined to remand the cases to state court. Because respondents refused to amend their complaints to bring explicit ERISA claims, the District Courts dismissed the complaints with prejudice.

Both Davila and Calad appealed the refusals to remand to state court. The United States Court of Appeals for the Fifth Circuit consolidated their cases with several others raising similar issues. The Court of Appeals recognized that state causes of action that "duplicat[e] or fal[l] within the scope of an ERISA § 502(a) remedy" are completely pre-empted and hence removable to federal court.[ ]. After examining the causes of action available under § 502(a), the Court of Appeals determined that respondents' claims could possibly fall under only two: § 502(a)(1)(B), which provides a cause of action for the recovery of wrongfully denied benefits, and § 502(a)(2), which allows suit against a plan fiduciary for breaches of fiduciary duty to the plan.

Analyzing § 502(a)(2) first, the Court of Appeals concluded that, under *Pegram v. Herdrich*,[ ], the decisions for which petitioners were being sued were "mixed eligibility and treatment decisions" and hence were not fiduciary in nature.[3] The Court of Appeals next determined that respondents' claims did not fall within § 502(a)(1)(B)'s scope. It found significant that respondents "assert tort claims," while § 502(a)(1)(B) "creates a cause of action for breach of contract,"[ ], and also that respondents "are not seeking reimbursement for benefits denied them," but rather request "tort damages" arising from "an external, statutorily imposed duty of 'ordinary care,' "[ ]. From *Rush Prudential HMO, Inc. v. Moran*,[ ], the Court of Appeals derived the principle that complete pre-emption is limited to situations in which "States . . . duplicate the causes of action listed in ERISA § 502(a)," and concluded that "[b]ecause the THCLA does not provide an action for collecting benefits," it fell outside the scope of § 502(a)(1)(B). 307 F.3d, at 310–311.

Under the removal statute, "any civil action brought in a State court of which the district courts of the United States have original jurisdiction, may be removed by the defendant" to federal court.[ ] One category of cas-

---

[3] In this Court, petitioners do not claim or argue that respondents' causes of action fall under ERISA § 502(a)(2). Because petitioners do not argue this point, and since we can resolve these cases entirely by reference to ERISA § 502(a)(1)(B), we do not address ERISA § 502(a)(2).

es of which district courts have original jurisdiction is "[f]ederal question" cases: cases "arising under the Constitution, laws, or treaties of the United States." § 1331. We face in these cases the issue whether respondents' causes of action arise under federal law.

Ordinarily, determining whether a particular case arises under federal law turns on the " 'well-pleaded complaint' " rule.[ ] The Court has explained that

> "whether a case is one arising under the Constitution or a law or treaty of the United States, in the sense of the jurisdictional statute[,] . . . must be determined from what necessarily appears in the plaintiff's statement of his own claim in the bill or declaration, unaided by anything alleged in anticipation of avoidance of defenses which it is thought the defendant may interpose."[ ].

In particular, the existence of a federal defense normally does not create statutory "arising under" jurisdiction,[ ], and "a defendant may not [generally] remove a case to federal court unless the *plaintiff's* complaint establishes that the case 'arises under' federal law,"[ ]. There is an exception, however, to the well-pleaded complaint rule. "[W]hen a federal statute wholly displaces the state-law cause of action through complete pre-emption," the state claim can be removed.[ ] This is so because "[w]hen the federal statute completely pre-empts the state-law cause of action, a claim which comes within the scope of that cause of action, even if pleaded in terms of state law, is in reality based on federal law."[ ] ERISA is one of these statutes.

Congress enacted ERISA to "protect . . . the interests of participants in employee benefit plans and their beneficiaries" by setting out substantive regulatory requirements for employee benefit plans and to "provid[e] for appropriate remedies, sanctions, and ready access to the Federal courts."[ ]. The purpose of ERISA is to provide a uniform regulatory regime over employee benefit plans. To this end, ERISA includes expansive pre-emption provisions, see ERISA § 514,[ ], which are intended to ensure that employee benefit plan regulation would be "exclusively a federal concern."[ ]

ERISA's "comprehensive legislative scheme" includes "an integrated system of procedures for enforcement."[ ] This integrated enforcement mechanism, ERISA § 502(a),[ ] is a distinctive feature of ERISA, and essential to accomplish Congress' purpose of creating a comprehensive statute for the regulation of employee benefit plans. As the Court said in *Pilot Life Ins. Co. v. Dedeaux,*[ ]:

> "[T]he detailed provisions of § 502(a) set forth a comprehensive civil enforcement scheme that represents a careful balancing of the need for prompt and fair claims settlement procedures

against the public interest in encouraging the formation of employee benefit plans. The policy choices reflected in the inclusion of certain remedies and the exclusion of others under the federal scheme would be completely undermined if ERISA-plan participants and beneficiaries were free to obtain remedies under state law that Congress rejected in ERISA. 'The six carefully integrated civil enforcement provisions found in § 502(a) of the statute as finally enacted ... provide strong evidence that Congress did *not* intend to authorize other remedies that it simply forgot to incorporate expressly.' "[ ]

Therefore, any state-law cause of action that duplicates, supplements, or supplants the ERISA civil enforcement remedy conflicts with the clear congressional intent to make the ERISA remedy exclusive and is therefore pre-empted.[ ]

The pre-emptive force of ERISA § 502(a) is still stronger. In *Metropolitan Life Ins. Co. v. Taylor,*[ ] the Court determined that the similarity of the language used in the Labor Management Relations Act, 1947 (LMRA), and ERISA, combined with the "clear intention" of Congress "to make § 502(a)(1)(B) suits brought by participants or beneficiaries federal questions for the purposes of federal court jurisdiction in like manner as § 301 of the LMRA," established that ERISA § 502(a)(1)(B)'s pre-emptive force mirrored the pre-emptive force of LMRA § 301. Since LMRA § 301 converts state causes of action into federal ones for purposes of determining the propriety of removal,[ ] so too does ERISA § 502(a)(1)(B). Thus, the ERISA civil enforcement mechanism is one of those provisions with such "extraordinary pre-emptive power" that it "converts an ordinary state common law complaint into one stating a federal claim for purposes of the well-pleaded complaint rule."[ ] Hence, "causes of action within the scope of the civil enforcement provisions of § 502(a) [are] removable to federal court."[ ]

ERISA § 502(a)(1)(B) provides:

"A civil action may be brought—(1) by a participant or beneficiary—. . . (B) to recover benefits due to him under the terms of his plan, to enforce his rights under the terms of the plan, or to clarify his rights to future benefits under the terms of the plan."
[ ]

This provision is relatively straightforward. If a participant or beneficiary believes that benefits promised to him under the terms of the plan are not provided, he can bring suit seeking provision of those benefits. A participant or beneficiary can also bring suit generically to "enforce his rights" under the plan, or to clarify any of his rights to future benefits. Any dispute over the precise terms of the plan is resolved by a court under a *de novo* review standard, unless the terms of the plan "giv[e] the administrator or fiduciary discretionary authority to determine eligibility for benefits or to construe the terms of the plan."[ ]

It follows that if an individual brings suit complaining of a denial of coverage for medical care, where the individual is entitled to such coverage only because of the terms of an ERISA-regulated employee benefit plan, and where no legal duty (state or federal) independent of ERISA or the plan terms is violated, then the suit falls "within the scope of" ERISA § 502(a)(1)(B)[ ]. In other words, if an individual, at some point in time, could have brought his claim under ERISA § 502(a)(1)(B), and where there is no other independent legal duty that is implicated by a defendant's actions, then the individual's cause of action is completely preempted by ERISA § 502(a)(1)(B).

To determine whether respondents' causes of action fall "within the scope" of ERISA § 502(a)(1)(B), we must examine respondents' complaints, the statute on which their claims are based (the THCLA), and the various plan documents. Davila alleges that Aetna provides health coverage under his employer's health benefits plan.[ ]. Davila also alleges that after his primary care physician prescribed Vioxx, Aetna refused to pay for it.[ ]. The only action complained of was Aetna's refusal to approve payment for Davila's Vioxx prescription. Further, the only relationship Aetna had with Davila was its partial administration of Davila's employer's benefit plan.[ ].

Similarly, Calad alleges that she receives, as her husband's beneficiary under an ERISA-regulated benefit plan, health coverage from CIGNA.[ ]. She alleges that she was informed by CIGNA, upon admittance into a hospital for major surgery, that she would be authorized to stay for only one day.[ ] She also alleges that CIGNA, acting through a discharge nurse, refused to authorize more than a single day despite the advice and recommendation of her treating physician.[ ] Calad contests only CIGNA's decision to refuse coverage for her hospital stay.[ ] And, as in Davila's case, the only connection between Calad and CIGNA is CIGNA's administration of portions of Calad's ERISA-regulated benefit plan.[ ].

It is clear, then, that respondents complain only about denials of coverage promised under the terms of ERISA-regulated employee benefit plans. Upon the denial of benefits, respondents could have paid for the treatment themselves and then sought reimbursement through a § 502(a)(1)(B) action, or sought a preliminary injunction,[ ].

Respondents contend, however, that the complained-of actions violate legal duties that arise independently of ERISA or the terms of the employee benefit plans at issue in these cases. Both respondents brought suit specifically under the THCLA, alleging that petitioners "controlled, influenced, participated in and made decisions which affected the quality of the diagnosis, care, and treatment provided" in a manner that violated "the duty of ordinary care set forth in §§ 88.001 and 88.002."[ ] Respondents contend that this duty of ordinary care is an independent legal duty. They analogize to this Court's decisions interpreting LMRA § 301,[ ] with particular focus on *Caterpillar Inc. v. Williams,* (suit for breach of individual employment contract, even if defendant's action also constituted a breach of an entirely separate collective-bargaining agreement, not preempted by LMRA § 301). Because this duty of ordinary care arises independently of any duty imposed by ERISA or the plan terms, the argument goes, any civil action to enforce this duty is not within the scope of the ERISA civil enforcement mechanism.

The duties imposed by the THCLA in the context of these cases, however, do not arise independently of ERISA or the plan terms. The THCLA does impose a duty on managed care entities to "exercise ordinary care when making health care treatment decisions," and makes them liable for damages proximately caused by failures to abide by that duty.[ ] However, if a managed care entity correctly concluded that, under the terms of the relevant plan, a particular treatment was not covered, the managed care entity's denial of coverage would not be a proximate cause of any injuries arising from the denial. Rather, the failure of the plan itself to cover the requested treatment would be the proximate cause.[3] More significantly, the THCLA clearly states that "[t]he standards in Subsections (a) and (b) create no obligation on the part of the health insurance carrier, health maintenance organization, or other managed care entity to provide to an insured or enrollee treatment which is not covered by the health care plan of the entity."[ ] Hence, a managed care entity could not be subject to liability under the THCLA if it denied coverage for any treatment not covered by the health care plan that it was administering.

Thus, interpretation of the terms of respondents' benefit plans forms an essential part of their THCLA claim, and THCLA liability would exist here only because of petitioners' administration of ERISA-regulated benefit plans. Petitioners' potential liability under the THCLA in these cases, then, derives entirely from the particular rights and obligations established by the benefit plans. So, unlike the state-law claims in *Caterpillar, supra,* respondents' THCLA causes of action are not entirely independent of the federally regulated contract itself.[ ].

Hence, respondents bring suit only to rectify a wrongful denial of benefits promised under ERISA-regulated plans, and do not attempt to remedy any violation of a legal duty independent of ERISA. We hold that respondents' state causes of action fall "within the scope of" ERISA

---

[3]   To take a clear example, if the terms of the health care plan specifically exclude from coverage the cost of an appendectomy, then any injuries caused by the refusal to cover the appendectomy are properly attributed to the terms of the plan itself, not the managed care entity that applied those terms.

§ 502(a)(1)(B),[ ] and are therefore completely pre-empted by ERISA § 502 and removable to federal district court.[4]

The Court of Appeals came to a contrary conclusion for several reasons, all of them erroneous. First, the Court of Appeals found significant that respondents "assert a tort claim for tort damages" rather than "a contract claim for contract damages," and that respondents "are not seeking reimbursement for benefits denied them."[ ] But, distinguishing between pre-empted and non-pre-empted claims based on the particular label affixed to them would "elevate form over substance and allow parties to evade" the pre-emptive scope of ERISA simply "by relabeling their contract claims as claims for tortious breach of contract." * * *[ ]. Nor can the mere fact that the state cause of action attempts to authorize remedies beyond those authorized by ERISA § 502(a) put the cause of action outside the scope of the ERISA civil enforcement mechanism. In *Pilot Life, Metropolitan Life,* and *Ingersoll–Rand,* the plaintiffs all brought state claims that were labeled either tort or tort-like.[ ] And, the plaintiffs in these three cases all sought remedies beyond those authorized under ERISA.[ ] And, in all these cases, the plaintiffs' claims were pre-empted. The limited remedies available under ERISA are an inherent part of the "careful balancing" between ensuring fair and prompt enforcement of rights under a plan and the encouragement of the creation of such plans. [ ].

Second, the Court of Appeals believed that "the wording of [respondents'] plans is immaterial" to their claims, as "they invoke an external, statutorily imposed duty of 'ordinary care.' "[ ] But as we have already discussed, the wording of the plans is certainly material to their state causes of action, and the duty of "ordinary care" that the THCLA creates is not external to their rights under their respective plans.

Ultimately, the Court of Appeals rested its decision on one line from *Rush Prudential.* * * * Nowhere in *Rush Prudential* did we suggest that the pre-emptive force of ERISA § 502(a) is limited to the situation in which a state cause of action precisely duplicates a cause of action under ERISA § 502(a).

Nor would it be consistent with our precedent to conclude that only strictly duplicative state causes of action are pre-empted. Frequently, in order to receive exemplary damages on a state claim, a plaintiff must prove facts beyond the bare minimum necessary to establish entitlement to an award.[ ]. In order to recover for mental anguish, for instance, the plaintiffs in *Ingersoll–Rand* and *Metropolitan Life* would presumably

---

[4] Respondents also argue that ERISA § 502(a) completely pre-empts a state cause of action only if the cause of action would be pre-empted under ERISA § 514(a); respondents then argue that their causes of action do not fall under the terms of § 514(a). But a state cause of action that provides an alternative remedy to those provided by the ERISA civil enforcement mechanism conflicts with Congress' clear intent to make the ERISA mechanism exclusive.[ ].

have had to prove the existence of mental anguish; there is no such element in an ordinary suit brought under ERISA § 502(a)(1)(B).[ ] This did not save these state causes of action from pre-emption. Congress' intent to make the ERISA civil enforcement mechanism exclusive would be undermined if state causes of action that supplement the ERISA § 502(a) remedies were permitted, even if the elements of the state cause of action did not precisely duplicate the elements of an ERISA claim.

Respondents also argue—for the first time in their brief to this Court—that the THCLA is a law that regulates insurance, and hence that ERISA § 514(b)(2)(A) saves their causes of action from pre-emption (and thereby from complete pre-emption).[5] This argument is unavailing. The existence of a comprehensive remedial scheme can demonstrate an "over-powering federal policy" that determines the interpretation of a statutory provision designed to save state law from being pre-empted.[ ] ERISA's civil enforcement provision is one such example.[ ]

As this Court stated in *Pilot Life,* "our understanding of [§ 514(b)(2)(A)] must be informed by the legislative intent concerning the civil enforcement provisions provided by ERISA § 502(a).[ ]" The Court concluded that "[t]he policy choices reflected in the inclusion of certain remedies and the exclusion of others under the federal scheme would be completely undermined if ERISA-plan participants and beneficiaries were free to obtain remedies under state law that Congress rejected in ERISA."[ ] The Court then held, based on

> "the common-sense understanding of the saving clause, the McCarran–Ferguson Act factors defining the business of insurance, and, *most importantly,* the clear expression of congressional intent that ERISA's civil enforcement scheme be exclusive, . . . that [the plaintiffs] state law suit asserting improper processing of a claim for benefits under an ERISA-regulated plan is not saved by § 514(b)(2)(A)."[ ]

Pilot Life's reasoning applies here with full force. Allowing respondents to proceed with their state-law suits would "pose an obstacle to the purposes and objectives of Congress."[ ] As this Court has recognized in both *Rush Prudential* and *Pilot Life,* ERISA § 514(b)(2)(A) must be interpreted in light of the congressional intent to create an exclusive federal remedy in ERISA § 502(a). Under ordinary principles of conflict pre-emption, then, even a state law that can arguably be characterized as "regulating insurance" will be pre-empted if it provides a separate vehicle to assert a claim for benefits outside of, or in addition to, ERISA's remedial scheme.

---

[5]   ERISA § 514(b)(2)(A)[ ] reads, as relevant: "['[N]othing in this subchapter shall be construed to exempt or relieve any person from any law of any State which regulates insurance, banking, or securities.'."

Respondents, their *amici,* and some Courts of Appeals have relied heavily upon *Pegram v. Herdrich,*[ ], in arguing that ERISA does not pre-empt or completely pre-empt state suits such as respondents'. They contend that *Pegram* makes it clear that causes of action such as respondents' do not "relate to [an] employee benefit plan," ERISA § 514(a),[ ] and hence are not pre-empted.[ ]

Pegram cannot be read so broadly. In *Pegram,* the plaintiff sued her physician-owned-and-operated HMO (which provided medical coverage through plaintiff's employer pursuant to an ERISA-regulated benefit plan) and her treating physician, both for medical malpractice and for a breach of an ERISA fiduciary duty.[ ] The plaintiff's treating physician was also the person charged with administering plaintiff's benefits; it was she who decided whether certain treatments were covered.[ ] We reasoned that the physician's "eligibility decision and the treatment decision were inextricably mixed."[ ] We concluded that "Congress did not intend [the defendant HMO] or any other HMO to be treated as a fiduciary to the extent that it makes mixed eligibility decisions acting through its physicians."[ ]

A benefit determination under ERISA, though, is generally a fiduciary act.[ ] "At common law, fiduciary duties characteristically attach to decisions about managing assets and distributing property to beneficiaries."[ ] Hence, a benefit determination is part and parcel of the ordinary fiduciary responsibilities connected to the administration of a plan.[ ] The fact that a benefits determination is infused with medical judgments does not alter this result.

Pegram itself recognized this principle. *Pegram,* in highlighting its conclusion that "mixed eligibility decisions" were not fiduciary in nature, contrasted the operation of "[t]raditional trustees administer[ing] a medical trust" and "physicians through whom HMOs act."[ ] A traditional medical trust is administered by "paying out money to buy medical care, whereas physicians making mixed eligibility decisions consume the money as well."[ ] And, significantly, the Court stated that "[p]rivate trustees do not make treatment judgments."[ ] But a trustee managing a medical trust undoubtedly must make administrative decisions that require the exercise of medical judgment. Petitioners are not the employers of respondents' treating physicians and are therefore in a somewhat analogous position to that of a trustee for a traditional medical trust.

ERISA itself and its implementing regulations confirm this interpretation. ERISA defines a fiduciary as any person "to the extent . . . he has any discretionary authority or discretionary responsibility in the administration of [an employee benefit] plan.[ ]. When administering employee benefit plans, HMOs must make discretionary decisions regarding eligibility for plan benefits, and, in this regard, must be treated as plan fiduciaries.[ ]" Also, ERISA § 503, which specifies minimum requirements for a plan's claim procedure, requires plans to "afford a reasonable opportunity to any participant whose claim for benefits has been denied for a full and fair review by the appropriate named fiduciary of the decision denying the claim."[ ] This strongly suggests that the ultimate decisionmaker in a plan regarding an award of benefits must be a fiduciary and must be acting as a fiduciary when determining a participant's or beneficiary's claim. The relevant regulations also establish extensive requirements to ensure full and fair review of benefit denials.[ ] These regulations, on their face, apply equally to health benefit plans and other plans, and do not draw distinctions between medical and nonmedical benefits determinations. Indeed, the regulations strongly imply that benefits determinations involving medical judgments are, just as much as any other benefits determinations, actions by plan fiduciaries.[ ] Classifying any entity with discretionary authority over benefits determinations as anything but a plan fiduciary would thus conflict with ERISA's statutory and regulatory scheme.

Since administrators making benefits determinations, even determinations based extensively on medical judgments, are ordinarily acting as plan fiduciaries, it was essential to *Pegram*'s conclusion that the decisions challenged there were truly "mixed eligibility and treatment decisions,"[ ], i.e., medical necessity decisions made by the plaintiff's treating physician *qua* treating physician and *qua* benefits administrator. Put another way, the reasoning of *Pegram* "only make[s] sense where the underlying negligence also plausibly constitutes medical maltreatment by a party who can be deemed to be a treating physician or such a physician's employer."[ ] Here, however, petitioners are neither respondents' treating physicians nor the employers of respondents' treating physicians. Petitioners' coverage decisions, then, are pure eligibility decisions, and *Pegram* is not implicated.

We hold that respondents' causes of action, brought to remedy only the denial of benefits under ERISA-regulated benefit plans, fall within the scope of, and are completely pre-empted by, ERISA § 502(a)(1)(B), and thus removable to federal district court. The judgment of the Court of Appeals is reversed, and the cases are remanded for further proceedings consistent with this opinion.[7]

It is so ordered.

---

[7] The United States, as *amicus,* suggests that some individuals in respondents' positions could possibly receive some form of "make-whole" " relief under ERISA § 502(a)(3).[ ] However, after their respective District Courts denied their motions for remand, respondents had the opportunity to amend their complaints to bring expressly a claim under ERISA § 502(a). Respondents declined to do so; the District Courts therefore dismissed their complaints with prejudice.[ ] Respondents have thus chosen not to pursue any ERISA claim, including any claim arising under ERISA § 502(a)(3). The scope of this provision, then, is not before us, and we do not address it.

NOTES AND QUESTIONS

1.   What state law claims are left to plaintiff employee benefit plan subscribers after *Davila*? In general, *Davila* leaves a "regulatory vacuum" in which consumer have no remedies if they are injured as the result of health care provided through ERISA plans. It would seem to allow tort actions for direct or vicarious liability only for physician-owned and operated managed care plans. And these are not the norm. The typical health plan today is an insurance vehicle that imposes coverage constraints on providers in its network, and would not be subject to tort liability. *Davila* does state that ERISA plan administrators are fiduciaries as to coverage decisions. But it does not explicitly recognize a cause of action for damages for breach of fiduciary duty, which earlier cases would seem to have foreclosed.

See, on ERISA preemption of managed care liability after *Davila*, Timothy S. Jost, The Supreme Court Limits Lawsuits Against Managed Care Organizations, Health Affairs Web Exclusive 4–417 (11 August 2004). See also Theodore W. Ruger, The Supreme Court Federalizes Managed Care Liability, 32 J.L. Med. & Ethics 528, 529 (2004) (criticizing the current ERISA enforcement scheme as crabbed and penurious, failing to serve remedial goals of either tort or contract.) For a full discussion of litigation leading up to *Davila*, see generally Margaret Cyr–Provost, Aetna v. Davila: From Patient–Centered Care to Plan–Centered Care, A Signpost or the End of the Road? 6 Hous. J. Health L. & Pol'y 171 (2005); M.Gregg Bloche and David Studdert, A Quiet Revolution: Law as an Agent of Health System Change, 23 Health Affairs 2942 (2004). See also Peter Jacobson, Strangers in the Night (New York: Oxford, 2002).

2.   Tort cases against managed care plans are not entirely dead after *Davila*, however. Consider Smelik v. Mann, Texas Dist. Ct. (224th Jud. Dist., Bexar Co. No. 03–CI–06936 2006), where a Texas jury awarded $7.4 million in actual damages to the family of an HMO participant who died from complications of acute renal failure. The jury found Humana liable for 35 percent of the $7.4 million in actual damages for negligence, but found no evidence that Humana committed fraud. The jury also determined that Humana's behavior was consistent with gross negligence, and the company stipulated to $1.6 million in punitive damages pursuant to an out-of-court agreement. Humana was found to be responsible for a total of $4.2 million.

The plaintiff in *Smelik* argued that Humana was liable for "mismanaged managed care," or negligence in the coordination of medical care, rather than for a denial of medical care, as in *Davila*, and thus ERISA did not apply. Plaintiffs convinced the jury that Humana failed to follow its own utilization management policies, failing to refer Smelik to a kidney specialist or to its disease management program. Plaintiffs also established that Humana negligently approved payment for a combination of drugs considered dangerous for patients with kidney problems.

Vicarious liability also remains a viable theory post *Davila*. In Badal v. Hinsdale Memorial Hospital, 2007 WL 1424205 (N.D.Ill.2007), plaintiff's injured ankle was misdiagnosed by a plan physician as only a "sprain," causing serious injury. The court analyzed ERISA preemption arguments in light of *Davila*. The court noted that the plaintiff's claims under *Davila* were brought under THCLA, the Texas Health Care Liability Act, and asserted duties that did not arise independently of ERISA or the plan terms. *Davila* was about wrongful denial of benefits. In *Badal,* by contrast, the plaintiff alleged that "[w]hile committing the above acts and omissions, Dr. Lofthouse failed to apply, use or exercise the standard of care ordinarily exercised by reasonably well qualified or competent medical doctors." The court noted that the plaintiff was not complaining of the wrongful denial of benefits, quoting the plaintiff: "Plaintiff is asking for damages for the injuries caused, and does not give one iota if it was covered under the plan, or whether it should in the future be covered under some plan[ ]. In short, whether or not it was a violation of ERISA is of no concern to plaintiff."

It may also be possible to sue insurance brokers and agents for negligent misrepresentation or insurers for simple clerical errors where the misrepresentation or error results in loss of coverage. In McMurtry v. Wiseman, 445 F. Supp.2d 756 (2006), the U.S. District Court for the Western District of Kentucky held that negligent misrepresentations by an insurance broker that induced the plaintiff to buy disability insurance coverage were not ERISA preempted. The plaintiff claimed that agent Botts' duty was independent of any duty related to ERISA, and that he, like any insurance agent, had a duty not to negligently misrepresent the terms of the policy and/or fraudulently induce the Plaintiff to purchase the coverage. The court quoted with approval the language of Morstein v. National Ins. Services, Inc., 93 F.3d 715, 723 (11th Cir.1996), "[a]llowing preemption of a fraud claim against an individual insurance agent will not serve Congress's purpose for ERISA. As we have discussed, Congress enacted ERISA to protect the interests of employees and other beneficiaries of employee benefit plans. To immunize insurance agents from personal liability for fraudulent misrepresentation regarding ERISA plans would not promote this objective." The court held that the plaintiff's claims for "fraud and negligent misrepresentation did not arise directly from the plan, but rather from Botts' inducement to have the Plaintiff join the plan. The legal duty not to misrepresent the plan did not arise from the plan itself, but from an independent source of law; state tort law within Tennessee."

In Duchesne–Baker v. Extendicare Health Services, Inc., 2004 WL 2414070 (E.D. La. Oct. 28, 2004), the district court concluded that, while Aetna was a defendant in both this action and in *Davila,* and each case was removed to federal court, there was no other similarity between these two cases. The court noted that *Davila* fell within the scope of ERISA Section 502(a)(1)(B) because an essential part of the plaintiffs' state law claim in *Davila* required an examination and interpretation of the relevant plan documents. By contrast, the allegation in *Duchesne–Baker* was that the insurance coverage was wrongly terminated due to a clerical error and Aetna failed to exercise due care to correct this error. Thus, the court concluded that, because the allegation did not involve improper processing of a benefit claim and did not otherwise seek enforcement of the plaintiff's rights under the plan or to clarify future right under the plan, the claim in *Duchesne–Baker* was distinguishable from *Davila* and, therefore, required remand back to the state court.

3.   ERISA was interpreted by the federal courts in the first wave of litigation as totally preempting common law tort claims. See, e.g., Ricci v. Gooberman, 840 F.Supp. 316 (D.N.J.1993). It appeared from this caselaw that any managed care plan that was ERISA-qualified would receive virtually complete tort immunity.

In the 1990s, however, the federal courts began to split as to the limits of such preemption. The result was a litigation explosion against managed care as theories were imported from hospital liability case law, fiduciary law, and contract law to use against managed care organizations. See, e.g., Prihoda v. Shpritz, 914 F.Supp. 113 (D.Md.1996) (ERISA does not preempt an action against physicians and an HMO for physicians' failure to diagnose a cancerous tumor, allowing a vicarious liability action to proceed). See also Independence HMO, Inc. v. Smith, 733 F.Supp. 983 (E.D.Pa.1990) (ERISA does not preempt medical malpractice-type claims brought against HMOs under a vicarious liability theory); Elsesser v. Hospital of the Philadelphia College of Osteopathic Medicine, 802 F.Supp. 1286 (E.D.Pa.1992) (ERISA does not preeempt a claim against an HMO for the HMO's negligence in selecting, retaining, and evaluating plaintiff's primary-care physician); Kearney v. U.S. Healthcare, Inc., 859 F.Supp. 182 (E.D.Pa.1994) (ERISA preempts plaintiff's direct negligence claim, but not vicarious liability claim). See generally Barry Furrow, Managed Care Organizations and Patient Injury: Rethinking Liability, 31 Ga. L. Rev. 419 (1997).

Dukes v. U.S. Healthcare, Inc., 57 F.3d 350 (3d Cir.1995) was the watershed case that opened up a major crack in ERISA preemption of common law tort claims. In *Dukes*, the Third Circuit found that Congress intended in passing ERISA to insure that promised benefits would be available to plan participants, and that section 502 was "intended to provide each individual participant with a remedy in the event that promises made by the plan were not kept." The court was unwilling, however, to stretch the remedies of 502 to "control the quality of the benefits received by plan participants." The court concluded that " * * * [q]uality control of benefits, such as the health care benefits provided here, is a field traditionally occupied by state regulation and we interpret the silence of Congress as reflecting an intent that it remain such." The court developed the distinction between a right to benefits under a plan and a right to good quality care, holding that " * * * patients enjoy the right to be free from medical malpractice regardless of whether or not their medical care is provided through an ERISA plan." Quality of care could be so poor that it is essentially a denial of benefits. Or the plan could describe a benefit in terms that are quality-based, such as a commitment that all x-rays will be analyzed by radiologists with a certain level of training. But absent either of these extremes, poor medical care—malpractice—is not a benefits issue under ERISA.

Theories of liability based on the organizational structure of health plans were used by most courts to determine what is preempted and what is allowed under ERISA. While some meaningful functional distinctions can be made on this basis, the courts have not been consistent, and liability was often variable, depending on the court's attitude toward managed care. See Peter J. Hammer, Pegram v. Herdrich: On Peritonitis, Preemption, and the Elusive Goal of Managed Care Accountability, 26 J. Health Pol. Pol'y & L. 767, 768 n.2 (2001). The federal courts were often hostile to managed care plans, and struggled mightily to work around ERISA preemption and allow a common law tort action to go forward.

For an excellent overview of the interaction of ERISA preemption and MCO malpractice liability, see Gail B. Agrawal and Mark A. Hall, What If You Could Sue Your HMO? Managed Care Liability Beyond the ERISA Shield, 47 St. Louis U. L.J. 235 (2003). See also Wendy K. Mariner, Slouching Toward Managed Care Liability: Reflections on Doctrinal Boundaries, Paradigm Shifts, and Incremental Reform, 29 J.L. Med. & Ethics 253 (2001) (favoring enhanced liability); David Orentlicher, The Rise and Fall of Managed Care: A Predictable "Tragic Choices" Phenomenon, 47 St. Louis U. L.J. 411 (2003) (analyzing managed care as a device for concealing and avoiding tragic choices in a public forum).

4.   The Affordable Care Act does not address the issue of health plan negligence liability. It does not, therefore, change ERISA preemption law with respect to health plan negligence.

CHAPTER 10

PUBLIC HEALTH CARE FINANCING PROGRAMS: MEDICARE AND MEDICAID

▪ ▪ ▪

I.   INTRODUCTION

Government provision or financing of health care has a long history in the United States. The first federal medical program was established in 1798 to provide care for sick seamen in the coastal trade. State hospitals for the mentally ill and local public hospitals were well established by the mid-nineteenth century.

Today, government at all levels finances a plethora of health care institutions and programs. In 2011, direct government health care financing programs accounted for $1,215 billion, 45 percent, of total national health expenditures. The federal government provides health care to 5.5 million veterans each year in 1100 veterans' hospitals, clinics, and nursing facilities; 9.5 million active and retired members of the military and their dependents through the TRICARE program; 1.9 million Native Americans in over 600 Indian Health Service and tribal facilities; disabled coal miners through the Black Lung program; and a variety of special groups through block grants to the states for maternal and child health, alcohol and drug abuse treatment, mental health, preventive health, and primary care. States provide health care both through traditional programs like state mental hospitals, state university hospitals, and workers' compensation, but also increasingly through a variety of newer programs intended to shore up the tattered safety net, including insurance pools for the high-risk uninsured, pharmaceutical benefit programs for the elderly, and programs to provide health insurance for the poor uninsured. County and local governments operate local hospitals. Federal, state, and local governments provide comparatively generous health insurance programs for their own employees and less generous health care programs for their prisoners (the only Americans constitutionally entitled to government-funded health care). Even a decade ago, if one added to the cost of direct government health care programs, the cost of government employee health benefits and tax subsidies that support private health benefits, tax-financed health care spending in the United States amounted to sixty percent of total health care spending. See Steffie

Woolhandler and David Himmelstein, Paying For National Health Insurance—And Not Getting It, Health Affairs, July/Aug. 2002, at 88, 91, 93.

By far the largest public health care programs, however, are the federal Medicare program and the state and federal Medicaid program, which respectively spent about $554 and $403 billion in 2011. This chapter focuses on these two programs, although it also briefly discusses the State Children's Health Insurance Program, established in 1997 to provide health insurance for poor children.

For the past decade and a half, the future of Medicare and Medicaid has been a key target of the federal debate on health care reform. Although public attention has focused on the ACA's private insurance reforms, the ACA also makes substantial changes in the Medicare program, and even greater changes in Medicaid. Medicare, and to a lesser extent, Medicaid, became focal issues in the 2012 presidential campaign. Going forward these programs promise to be at the center of the national health care debate.

There are several reasons why these programs remain to center on our national debate on health policy, and on why this debate has been so passionate and contentious. First, Medicare and Medicaid policy have been driven by federal budget policy. Together the two programs consume over 21 percent of the federal budget. Moreover, if one excludes from consideration the costs of defense, Social Security, and the national debt—all of which are more or less protected from budget cuts at this time—Medicare and Medicaid consume 39 percent of what remains of the federal budget. Medicaid is also one of the largest, and fastest growing, items in state budgets. Congress is very aware of the cost of these programs.

Second, growth in the Medicare program threatens not only to continue to claim a large slice of the federal budget, but also ultimately to overwhelm the financing mechanisms that currently support it. The Part A trust fund (which funds the hospital insurance part of Medicare and is in turn funded by payroll taxes) is currently projected to go into deficit status in 2024. Part B expenditures (which cover the services of physicians and other professionals, as well as other non-institutional care), three quarters of which are covered by federal general revenue funds are growing even faster than Part A expenditures. The financing of the program is projected to become even more problematic as a huge group of baby-boomers becomes eligible for Medicare in the first half the 21st century. By 2037, Medicare will be responsible for the health care of eighty million Americans, compared to 48 million today. By 2030, moreover, there will be 2.3 workers for every Medicare beneficiary compared to 2010's 3.4 to one ratio.

Third, debates about how to reform the programs touch repeatedly upon issues that divide policy makers sharply along ideological lines. Can costs be most effectively controlled through regulatory or market strategies? Should Medicare remain available to all beneficiaries equally, or should it be means tested in some way? Should Medicare continue to provide direct financing for provider services for most of its beneficiaries, or should it move to a premium support program, where the federal government provides vouchers to beneficiaries, who in turn purchase managed care plans from private insurers. Should the financing of health care services for the poor be a federal or state responsibility? Should poor persons have an entitlement to health care coverage, or should states have discretion to limit access? Or should the states simply receive block grants from the federal government for health care?

Finally, Medicare insures 16 and Medicaid 20 percent of the population (although some Americans participate in both programs.) Medicare covers one of the most politically active segments of the American populace (the elderly). These programs also affect immediately the fortunes of most health care providers, who are invariably contributors to political campaigns. Politicians are acutely aware, therefore, of the existence and the exigencies of these programs.

To understand the debates raging around these programs, we must first understand how the programs work. Anyone designing or seeking to understand a public health care financing program must consider several basic questions.

First, who receives the program's benefits? Are the targeted recipients characterized by economic need, a particular disease, advanced age, disability, residence in a particular geographic jurisdiction, employment in a certain industry, or status as an enrollee and contributor to a social insurance fund? From these questions others follow: Who in fact receives most of the program's benefits? Whom does the program leave out? Why are some groups included and others excluded? Also, should beneficiaries receive an entitlement or should coverage otherwise be subject to governmental discretion or programs have capped enrollments?

Second, what benefits will be provided? Should the program stress institutional services such as hospitalization or nursing home care or non-institutional alternatives such as home health care, or should it encourage preventive care? Should the program be limited to services commonly covered by private insurance like hospital and physician care, or should it also cover services such as dental care and eyeglasses that private insurance covers less often because their use is more predictable and middle class insureds can afford to pay for them out of pocket? These services may be inaccessible to the poor unless the program covers them. Should the program cover medically controversial services, such as care provided by chiropractors or midwives? Should a public program cover socially controversial services such as abortion or treatment for erectile dysfunction?

Should it cover services that provide relatively small marginal benefits at a very high cost, such as some organ transplants or some last ditch cancer therapies? Finally, how can the benefits package be kept up to date? In particular, how should it evaluate new technologies as they become available?

Third, how should the program provide or pay for benefits? Should it pay private professionals and institutions to deliver the services, as do Medicare and Medicaid, or should it deliver services itself directly, as does the Veterans' Administration through its hospitals? To what extent should a government program use provider payment systems to encourage changes in the health care delivery system or to improve the quality of care? Should it purchase services through "vendor payments" based on cost or charge, as Medicare used to, or through an administered price system, as Medicare does now for most services, or on a capitated basis through managed care plans, as Medicare does through parts C and D and most state Medicaid plans do for many recipients? Alternatively, should beneficiaries simply be given vouchers and be expected to purchase their own insurance in the private market? Should public health insurance programs be defined-contribution or defined-benefit programs? Should recipients be expected to share in the costs through coinsurance or deductibles?

Who should play what role in administering the program? Should the program be run by the federal, state, or local government? Should policy be set by the legislature or by an administrative agency (or by the courts)? Should payments to providers be administered by the government or by private contractors? Should program beneficiaries (or providers) have rights enforceable in court, or should the government retain unreviewable discretion in running the program? If rights are recognized, should these rights be enforceable in state or federal court, or perhaps only through administrative proceedings?

How should the program be financed? Through payroll taxes, income taxes, consumption taxes, or premiums? By state or federal taxes? Should taxes be earmarked (hypothecated) for health care, or should it be funded through general revenue funds? If premiums play a role, should they be means tested?

This chapter will explore each of these issues with respect first to the Medicare and then to the Medicaid and CHIP programs.

As you consider these major questions, keep in mind several other themes. First, notice the fragmentation and disconnectedness of our public health care financing programs. Unlike some other nations, we do not have a single public system creating a safety net for all of society, but rather a patchwork of programs, creating a variety of safety nets, some higher and some lower, many fairly tattered, and none catching everyone.

Whom do the safety nets miss? What problems does this fragmented system create? What opportunities does it offer?

Second, notice who, other than covered populations of patients, benefits from federal and state programs. Consider which providers benefit most from public programs. Note the role Medicare and Medicaid have played in financing medical education or in subsidizing care for safety net providers, such as inner city hospitals. Consider how providers position their operations to maximize their benefits from public programs, and how the mix of health care services in this country reflects the policies of these programs.

Third, pay special attention to how the Affordable Care Act changes the Medicare, Medicaid, and CHIP programs. Both the Medicare and Medicaid programs were changed extensively by the ACA. Medicare changes affecting provider payments, covered benefits, graduate medical education, quality assurance, managed care, and the delivery of care are found in seven separate titles of the new law. A number of considerations drove these changes. First was widespread dissatisfaction with the effects of fee-for-service (FFS) provider payment under Medicare. The need to add financial incentives to provide high quality care and reduce errors was an aspect of reform that enjoyed strong bipartisan support. Second, Congress sought to use Medicare as a vehicle for changing the way care was delivered, especially by encouraging development of new models for delivering health care and making adjustments in the FFS payment system to reward deserving services (in particular, primary care). Third, many members of Congress believed that the changes made under the Medicare Modernization Act of 2004 went too far by paying overly generous subsidies to encourage the growth of Medicare Advantage plans and wanted to bring these payments in line with those of traditional Medicare. Finally, an overarching concern was the effect of Medicare (and Medicaid) on the deficit, or to use the phrase adopted by the drafters of the ACA, the law dealt with the "long term sustainability" of the Medicare program. Medicaid too was extensively changed under the ACA, which expanded eligibility to all Americans with incomes below 133 percent of the poverty level and changed benefits and federal funding of the program in significant respects. The Medicaid program was changed further by the Supreme Court's ACA decision. All of these changes are discussed below.

II.   MEDICARE

A.   ELIGIBILITY

In 2011 Medicare covered nearly 48.7 million elderly and disabled beneficiaries, nearly one in six Americans. 8.3 million Medicare beneficiaries were disabled, 40.4 million elderly. Medicare eligibility is generally linked to that of the Social Security program, the other major social insurance program of the United States. Persons who are eligible for retirement benefits under Social Security are automatically eligible for Medicare upon reaching age 65. Spouses or former spouses who qualify for Social Security as dependents may also begin receiving Medicare at 65, as may former federal employees eligible for Civil Service Retirement and Railroad Retirement beneficiaries, 42 U.S.C.A. § 426(a).

Disabled persons who are eligible for Social Security or Railroad Retirement benefits may also receive Medicare, but only after they have been eligible for cash benefits for at least two years, 42 U.S.C.A. § 426(b). The number of disabled persons covered by Medicare is growing rapidly. Benefits are also available to persons eligible for Social Security, although not necessarily receiving it, who have end-stage renal (kidney) disease, who may receive Medicare benefits after a three-month waiting period, 42 U.S.C.A. § 426–1. About 442,000 Medicare beneficiaries are eligible for this reason. Persons disabled with ALS get Medicare Parts A and B the month their disability benefits begin.

CRITICAL THINKING ABOUT MEDICARE: EXERCISE 1

Consider what alternative approaches might be taken for defining the scope of Medicare eligibility. First, why is Medicare, a social insurance program, only available to the elderly and disabled? Why is it available to all members of these groups, regardless of their income or wealth? Historically, Medicare beneficiaries all paid the same premiums and cost-sharing regardless of wealth, but in recent years higher income beneficiaries have faced higher premiums for the Part B (professional services) and Part D (prescription drug) programs, while since 1989, low-income beneficiaries have received help with their premiums and cost-sharing through Medicaid and since 2006 through the Medicare prescription drug low-income subsidy program.

Next consider the relationship between benefits and financing. Is it a good idea to charge more for program benefits to those who have higher incomes, as does the recent legislation? What effect does Medicare have on the workers who support it through their payroll taxes? What effect does it have on the children of Medicare recipients? What effect might it have on the children of Medicare recipients at the death of the recipient? The idea surfaces from time to time of extending Medicare to cover all of the uninsured. Why has this idea not been adopted?

Medicare has been generally successful in assuring broad and equitable access to health care for many who would probably otherwise be uninsured. Fifty-four percent of Medicare beneficiaries have incomes of 200 percent of the federal poverty level or less, and eighty percent of elderly Medicare beneficiaries receive at least half of their income from Social

Security. When the program began only fifty-six percent of the elderly had hospital insurance and the poor and nonwhite elderly received substantially less medical care than did the wealthier or white elderly. While these disparities have been substantially reduced, disparities still remain. In particular, there is a great deal of evidence that racial and ethnic minority Medicare beneficiaries have poorer health status than white beneficiaries, as well as evidence that they receive fewer common medical procedures. See Marian E. Gornick, Effects of Race and Income on Mortality and Use of Services Among Medicare Beneficiaries, 335 New Eng. J. Med. 791 (1996); A. Marshall McBean and Marian Gornick, Difference by Race of Procedures Performed in Hospitals for Medicare Beneficiaries, Health Care Fin. Rev., Summer 1994 at 77 (1994); Bruce C. Vladeck, Paul N. Van de Water, and June Eichner, eds., Strengthening Medicare's Role in Reducing Racial and Ethnic Health Disparities (2006); Timothy Stoltzfus Jost, Racial and Ethnic Disparities in Medicare: What the Department of Health and Human Services and the Center for Medicare and Medicaid Services Can, and Should, Do, 1 DePaul J. Health Care L. 667 (2005).

B. BENEFITS

1. Coverage

The Medicare Hospital Insurance (HI) program, Part A, pays for hospital, nursing home, home health and hospice services. The Medicare Supplemental Medical Insurance (SMI) program, Part B, covers physicians' services and a variety of other items and services including outpatient hospital services, home health care, physical and occupational therapy, prosthetic devices, durable medical equipment, and ambulance services. As described below, Medicare beneficiaries can alternatively enroll in a Medicare Advantage plan and receive Part A and B services through the plan with cost-sharing determined by the plan. Medicare covers only 90 days of hospital services in a single benefit period ("spell of illness"*). Each beneficiary also has an extra 60 "lifetime reserve" days of hospital coverage. A one-time deductible, set at $1,156 in 2012, must be paid each year before hospital coverage begins, and a daily copayment of $289 (in 2012) must be paid after the sixtieth day of hospital care, 42 U.S.C.A. § 1395e. Although the Medicare statute provides for coverage of up to 100 days of skilled nursing care, 42 U.S.C.A. § 1395d(a)(2), the nursing home benefit is intended to cover those recovering from an acute illness or injury and not to cover long term chronic care. Hospice benefits are provided on a limited basis, 42 U.S.C.A. § 1395d(a)(4). Physician services are provided subject to an annual deductible ($140 in 2012) and a twenty percent coinsurance amount. In recent years, Medicare has added many preven-

---

* A spell of illness begins when a patient is hospitalized, and continues until the patient has been out of a hospital or nursing home for at least 60 days. 42 U.S.C.A. § 1345x(a). Thus, a chronically ill person could remain indefinitely in a single spell of illness.

tive services, including prostate cancer screening; bone mass density measurement; diabetes self-management; mammography screening; glaucoma screening; pap smears; an initial physical examination; cardiovascular screening blood tests; diabetes screening tests; and hepatitis B, pneumococcal, and flu shots. See, Michael DeBoer, Medicare Coverage Policy and Decision Making, Preventive Services, and Comparative Effectiveness Research Before and After the Affordable Care Act, 7 J. Health & Biomedical L. 493 (2012).

The ACA contains a number of Medicare benefit enhancements. For the first time, traditional Medicare will cover, with no co-payment or deductible, an annual wellness visit and personalized prevention plan services, including a comprehensive health risk assessment. In addition, the ACA eliminates beneficiary coinsurance requirements for most preventive services. Furthermore, the Secretary of HHS is authorized to modify the coverage of any currently covered preventive service in the Medicare program to the extent that the modification is consistent with recommendations of the U.S. Preventive Services Task Force. The Act also establishes new programs that expand coverage while also aiming to reduce long term costs. For example, the Act establishes a program for pre-Medicare eligibles aimed at controlling chronic illnesses. It funds hospitals and community-based entities that furnish evidence-based care transition services to beneficiaries at high risk for readmission into hospitals.

Leaving aside preventive services and prescription drug coverage, added since 2000, the traditional Medicare benefits package still closely resembles the standard federal employee or Blue Cross/Blue Shield benefits package available in the mid–1960s when Medicare was established and is thus quite antiquated. It is very different, therefore, from standard benefit packages available today, which are likely to be managed care rather than fee-for-service based, have relatively low fixed-dollar copayments rather than percentage coinsurance requirements, have variable cost-sharing between in- and out-of-plan providers, and have higher catastrophic coverage limits. Medicare's lack of out-of-pocket limits for beneficiary cost-sharing for Part B services and caps on the number of covered days of hospitalization are particularly problematic.

Medicare pays for about 48 percent of the health care received by the elderly in this country, while private insurance pays for 14 percent, and Medicaid 8 percent. Beneficiaries pay for 25 percent of their costs out-of-pocket. Many Medicare recipients purchase, or more commonly receive as a retirement benefit, Medicare Supplement (Medigap) insurance, which covers their cost-sharing obligations and some services not covered by Medicare. The average Medicare beneficiary spends 16 percent of household income on medical expenses not covered by Medicare. Medicare accounts for 30 percent of the nation's expenditures for hospital care, 24 percent of prescription drug cost, 20 percent of physician expenditures, and 40 percent of home health expenditures.

CRITICAL THINKING ABOUT MEDICARE: EXERCISE 2

What categories of services should Medicare cover? Should its coverage be identical to employment-related benefit packages, or should it vary in some respects? What items might be more, or less, important to its beneficiary population than to working-age Americans? Should Medicare cover nursing home care—a benefit of obvious interest to the elderly—to a greater extent? Should Medicare take cost into account in setting coverage policy for new technologies? If so, what role should cost play in coverage determinations? Though "added value" is among the criteria that CMS proposed in 2000 for evaluating technologies, CMS asserts that it does not consider cost explicitly. Is the public interest served by having private "contractors" make many coverage decisions with limited opportunities for appeal?

2.   Prescription Drugs

At the time Medicare was created in 1965, private insurance policies did not generally cover outpatient prescription drugs. Prescription drugs were still relatively affordable and were not as an important part of the management of medical problems as they are today. Not surprisingly, therefore, Medicare did not include a drug benefit. Medicare was expanded briefly to cover prescription drugs by the 1988 Medicare Catastrophic Coverage Act, but the legislation proved intensely unpopular with higher-income beneficiaries who were charged higher premiums. It was repealed in 1989 before it could even be implemented. By the late 1990s, however, sharply escalating drug costs brought a Medicare prescription drug benefit back to the top of the political agenda. Pressure built on Congress to do something.

The national political leadership that took on the challenge of providing a Medicare drug benefit in the early 2000s, however, was very different from that which led the country in 1965 when the Medicare program was established. Whereas the presidency and both houses of Congress were held by Democrats in 1965, the presidency and both houses of Congress were held by Republicans in 2003. Whereas the inspiration for the Medicare program in 1965 had been the Social Security program and social insurance programs like it in other developed countries, the conservative leadership of the Republican Congress in 2003 was enamored with market approaches to providing health care coverage. The 2003 Congress had benefitted heavily from political contributions from drug manufacturers and from insurance and managed care companies, and thus was oriented toward a solution that would help rather than harm these interests. Any drug legislation adopted by Congress, therefore, had to meet several requirements.

First, the program had to be a voluntary program that beneficiaries could choose to join or not to join, like Part B. To encourage voluntary membership, however, the program would have to appeal to beneficiaries who had relatively low drug costs as well as to those with higher costs. Second, it had to be administered by private "prescription drug plans," rather than directly by the government. In particular, administered prices set by the Medicare program, which have been used in other parts of the Medicare program to hold down costs, were not acceptable to the drug companies and not acceptable to congressional leadership. Third, the cost of the program could not exceed $400 billion over ten years. This meant that Medicare beneficiaries would have to continue to bear a considerable share of total Medicare drug costs through cost-sharing obligations and premiums. Finally, the legislation had to provide some relief for the poor from these cost-sharing obligations and premiums. Medicare could not continue to be a social insurance program available to all on equal terms, but would become partially means tested.

As negotiations continued through the fall of 2003 between the House and Senate, other decisions were made. Medicare rather than Medicaid would cover the drug costs of beneficiaries eligible for both programs and employers who continued to provide drug benefits for their retirees would receive subsidies for doing so. In November of 2003, Congress, after an all-night session and by the narrowest of margins, adopted a Medicare drug benefit, signed into law by President Bush as Public Law 108–173.

This legislation created a voluntary Prescription Drug Benefit Program, establishing a new Part D of Medicare, which went into effect on January 1, 2006. All Medicare beneficiaries are eligible for the program. Beneficiaries who enroll in Part D pay a premium, the amount of which is basically set at twenty-six percent of the cost of the benefits provided (as calculated using a complex formula). The premiums vary from plan to plan relative to each plan's bid amount, and are increased if the beneficiary receives supplemental benefits and for higher-income beneficiaries. Those who chose not to join the program initially (or at the time when they later became eligible for Medicare or lost drug coverage from some other source) are penalized by having to pay higher premiums. Beneficiaries can also receive coverage through Medicare Advantage plans, which usually offer drug coverage at much lower premiums than free-standing PDPs. In any event, the vast majority of the cost of the program is borne by government, which pays not only three quarters of the premium cost, but also most of the cost of catastrophic coverage (and heavily subsidizes Medicare Advantage plans).

Drug benefits are provided by private Prescription Drug Plans (PDPs), by Medicare Advantage Medicare managed care plans, and by employers who offer drug coverage to employed or retired beneficiaries. The U.S. is divided up into thirty-four PDP regions, and PDPs submit bids to cover these regions. Plans are paid their bid price, adjusted to reflect the risk profile of their members. Each beneficiary must have a choice of at least two PDPs or of one PDP and one Medicare Advantage plan.

Free-standing risk-bearing drug plans did not exist at the time the legislation was adopted. To encourage the creation of such plans and to lure them into the Medicare market, the legislation transferred much of the risk for providing drug benefits to the Medicare program. Even "full-risk" plans in fact only bear risk within "risk corridors." Medicare also provides "reinsurance" at a level of eighty percent to plans for allowable costs of enrollees whose costs exceed the out-of-pocket threshold, described below.

The benefits offered by PDPs vary from plan to plan. "Standard prescription drug coverage" under the legislation is defined largely in terms of cost-sharing obligations. For 2013, "standard" coverage includes a $325 deductible and a twenty-five percent enrollee coinsurance obligation for the next $2605 in drug costs. This relatively generous coverage at the low end is intended to attract relatively healthy beneficiaries to the program. Once total drug expenditures reach $2930, however, the beneficiary hits the "doughnut hole." Under the original 2003 law, the beneficiary would receive no further coverage from the program until reaching the catastrophic level, set for 2013 at $6733.75 in total costs. At this "out-of-pocket threshold" amount, stop-loss coverage kicks in, and the beneficiary is thereafter responsible for only five percent of further costs (or for a co-payment of $2.65 for generics or $6.60 for brand name drugs if this is higher).

The ACA will, over time, plug the doughnut hole. Drug manufacturers must provide a 50 percent discount to Part D beneficiaries for brand-name drugs and biologics purchased during the coverage gap. The Act also gradually reduces the coinsurance amount paid by beneficiaries until 2020, when it reaches the 25 percent level applicable for expenditures below the doughnut hole. As of 2013, enrollees paid for 47.5 percent of brand name drug costs and 79 percent of generic drug costs in the doughnut hole.. An estimated 3.6 million Part D enrollees reached the coverage gap in 2011.

Although this is "standard coverage," only a small share of PDPs nationwide offer the standard drug benefit. Most offer "actuarially equivalent" coverage instead. The majority of PDPs (55 percent) charge a deductible, with 46 percent charging the full $325. After the deductible is met, most plans charge tiered copayments for covered drugs rather than a flat 25 percent coinsurance amount. A substantial majority of PDPs use specialty tiers for high-cost medications. Most PDPs (67 percent) will not offer additional doughnut hole coverage in 2013 beyond what is required under the standard benefit. Additional gap coverage, when offered, is generally limited to generic drugs only. In any event, plans must make available to the beneficiary the actual prices that they negotiate for drugs, including any discounts, concessions, rebates, or other remuneration, even in situations where no benefits are payable because of cost-sharing obligations.

Medicare provides PDP beneficiaries with a number of protections. PDP sponsors are required to permit the participation of any pharmacy that accepts a plan's terms and conditions, although PDPs may reduce cost-sharing obligations to encourage the use of in-network pharmacies. Plans must secure participation of enough pharmacies in their networks to meet "convenient access" requirements, and may not charge more for using community rather than mail-order pharmacies. PDPs may use formularies (lists of drugs covered by the plan), but a formulary must be based on scientific standards, and must include each therapeutic category and class of covered Part D drugs. Benefits may not be designed so as to discourage enrollment by particular categories of beneficiaries. PDPs must offer grievance and appeal procedures like those available in the Medicare Advantage program, including independent review. A beneficiary may gain access to drugs not included in the formulary or avoid increased cost-sharing for non-preferred drugs only if the prescribing physician determines that formulary or preferred drugs are not as effective for the beneficiary, cause adverse effects, or both. PDP sponsors must be licensed by their state or meet federal solvency requirements. See Geraldine Dallek, Consumer Protection Issues Raised by the Medicare Prescription Drug, Improvement, and Modernization Act of 2003 (2004); Vicki Gottlich, Beneficiary Challenges in Using the Medicare Part D Appeals Process to Obtain Medically Necessary Drugs (2006); Vicki Gottlich, The Exceptions and Appeals Process: Issues and Concerns in Obtaining Coverage Under the Medicare Part D Prescription Drug Benefit (2005).

Because the high cost-sharing obligations imposed by the legislation would limit its value to low-income beneficiaries, the Act provides additional assistance for low-income beneficiaries. Persons who are eligible for Medicaid, or whose incomes fall below 135 percent of the poverty level and have resources in 2013 below $6,940 for an individual or $10,410 for a couple receive a subsidy that covers their premium, relieves them from any deductible, and limits their cost-sharing obligations up to the out-of-pocket threshold to $2.65 for generic or preferred multiple source drugs or $6.60 for other drugs. Dual eligibles (persons eligible for both Medicare and Medicaid) with incomes up to 100 percent of poverty level only have to pay $1.15 for generic or multiple source drugs and $3.50 for other drugs, and nursing home residents on Medicaid have no cost-sharing obligations. Persons with incomes between 135 percent and 150 percent of the poverty level and with up to $10,411 in resources for an individual or

$23,120 for a couple benefit from a sliding scale premium subsidy, a $66 deductible, and cost-sharing up to the out-of-pocket threshold of $2.65 for generic or preferred multiple source drugs, and $6.60 for other drugs.

The states are required to pay over to the Medicare program a "clawback" amount initially equal to ninety percent of what they would have spent to cover the dual eligibles under the Medicaid program. That amount will be reduced gradually to seventy-five percent after 2015. States may face marginally lower expenses than they would have faced had Medicaid continued to be responsible for these costs, but will have less control over spending.

CRITICAL THINKING ABOUT MEDICARE: EXERCISE 3

What effect is this program likely to have on drug prices? PDPs negotiate with drug manufacturers over drug prices, but HHS is prohibited from interfering in these negotiations. Why did Congress choose this approach rather than an administrative price approach, as Medicare uses elsewhere? Who has more bargaining power, the federal government or prescription drug plans? Why might PDPs have considerable bargaining power, even though their market share is much less than that of the federal government? What can they do that the federal government cannot? Which approach is in the end more likely to lead to lower drug costs? What other effects might either approach have? What interest groups other than drug companies will benefit from the approach Congress initially chose? Who in particular among Medicare beneficiaries is most likely to benefit from this legislation; who will be least helped by it?

Early results of the prescription drug program were in many respects impressive. Part D premiums have risen slowly and for 2013 were $30 a month. At least 25 plans are available in every region of the country. In 2012, about 31.5 million Medicare beneficiaries were enrolled in Medicare drug plans, including 19.7 million in PDPs and 11.7 million in Medicare Advantage prescription drug plans. Nearly 11 million enrollees were enrolled in the Part C Low Income Subsidy program. See, describing the drug legislation, Richard L. Kaplan, The Medicare Drug Benefit: A Prescription for Confusion, 1 NAELA J. 165 (2005).

PROBLEM: THE MEDICARE PRESCRIPTION DRUG BENEFIT

Mary Belmont has just become eligible for Medicare and is trying to decide in which Medicare pharmacy benefit plan to enroll. Three options are available in her area. One PDP costs twenty-five dollars a month and offers the benefits of the standard benefit package, though its formulary does not cover two of the drugs she is currently using, and she would have to switch to drugs that the plan designates as therapeutically equivalent. The second PDP costs only thirty dollars a month, and covers all of the drugs that she is currently using, but imposes an actuarially equivalent tiered copayment plan (i.e. it charges higher copays for brand name than generic drugs and even higher copays for non-preferred brand-name drugs) and would require her to pay fifty dollars each for a thirty day supply of two of her drugs. Her third option is a Medicare Advantage plan that covers drugs, and that also has a limited formulary, but that has only a 200 dollar deductible for drugs and a tiered copayment formula with a maximum of forty dollars per prescription. To join the Medicare Advantage plan, however, she would have to leave her current primary care doctor, whom she has seen for ten years, because he is not part of the plan's network. The Medicare Advantage plan would only charge twenty dollars a month premium for drug benefits. The first PDP plan also offers a supplementary drug plan at an additional thirty dollars a month that would reduce her cost-sharing obligations from twenty-five percent to twenty percent for the first $2,000 of coverage, and also cover certain over-the-counter drugs. Which plan should she choose? Should she be grateful for all of these choices?

C. PAYMENT FOR SERVICES

1. Introduction

Over Medicare's history, the program has relied primarily on three payment strategies: cost-or charge-based reimbursement, prospective payment, and managed competition. At the outset, it followed the then current practice of health insurers by paying institutions on the basis of their reported costs and professionals on the basis of their charges. This proved, not surprisingly, to be wildly inflationary, and over time Medicare increasingly imposed restrictions on cost- and charge-based payment. In the end, Medicare abandoned cost- and charge-based payment in favor of administered payment systems, under which Medicare itself sets the price it will pay for services. It began by implementing prospective payment for hospitals in the early 1980s. The next major step toward prospective payment was the resource-based relative value scale (RBRVS) for paying physicians, implemented in the early 1990s. Under the Balanced Budget Act of 1997, Medicare implemented prospective payment systems for home health, skilled nursing facilities, outpatient hospital care, and inpatient rehabilitation hospitals. Paying for almost one-third of the nation's hospital care and one-fifth of physician care, Medicare has been able to offer payment rates to many professionals and providers on a take-it-or-leave-it basis, and to hold rates to levels that are below those paid generally in the private market. It has been less successful, however, at controlling the volume of services it pays for, leading to continuing increases in overall costs.

The following subsections describe two of the major administered price programs under Medicare, the diagnosis-related group prospective payment system for hospitals under Part A and the resource-based relative value scale for physicians under Part B. The next subsection examines the managed care option under Part C of Medicare, Medicare Advantage. The final section describes some of the significant changes made by Affordable Care Act to revise administered payment methodologies and to encourage new delivery methods.

2. Medicare Prospective Payment Under Diagnosis–Related Groups

Congress established the diagnosis-related group (DRG) prospective payment system for hospitals in 1982. A DRG is a means of categorizing patients to reflect relative intensity of use of services. DRG-based payment treats hospitals as coordinating services to produce particular products, such as the diagnosis and treatment of heart attacks, ulcers, or tumors. The DRG system groups patients primarily by principal (admitting) diagnoses, which, together with other factors, are used to categorize patients. The purpose of this analysis is to yield groups of hospital patients, each covered by a distinct DRG, that more or less require the same quantity of medical resources. Once DRGs were defined, Medicare arrayed DRGs by relative intensity of resource consumption, with average resource use defined as a single unit. In 2008, CMS refined DRG classification to take into account comorbidities and complications, resequenced groups, and consolidated many codes into new groups. The number of these new "MS–DRGs" (Medicare Severity DRGs) is now 751. In addition, where there was previously only one code for each procedure there are now three codes distinguished by levels of severity: 1) MCC—Major Complication / Comorbidity, reflecting the highest level of severity; 2) CC—Complication / Comorbidity, reflecting the next level of severity; and 3) Non–CC—Non–Complication / Comorbidity, reflecting no severity. For example, for 2013, the MS–DRG code series 163/164/165, associated with "surgery, major chest procedures", is weighted at 5.1193/2.6191/1.7922 for the MCC, CC and non-CC procedures respectively. Thus, the MCC level is weighted at over five times the average admission cost, while the non-CC level is only 1.8 times greater. For comparison, the MS–DRG code series 88/89/90, associated with "concussion", is weighted much lower at 1.5687/0.9791/0.7218 for the three severity levels. See Fed. Reg., Vol. 77, No. 170, Table 5, Friday, August 31, 2012; Table 5; HHS, Acute Care Hospital Inpatient Prospective Payment System: Payment System Fact Sheet Series (February 2012)).

To determine a hospital's actual payment for caring for a Medicare patient, the relative DRG weight assigned to that patient is first multiplied by standardized amounts for labor, non-labor, and capital costs. The standardized amounts in theory represent the cost of an efficient hospital for an average case. For FY 2013, the standardized amounts for hospitals that complied with performance disclosure requirements was $3,679.95 for labor costs, $1,668.81 for non-labor costs, and $425.49 for capital costs. These amounts are multiplied by the DRG weight (e.g., .7218 for non-CC concussion) to achieve the basic DRG reimbursement amount per case. See Fed. Reg., Vol. 77, No. 170, Table 1a, Friday, August 31, 2012.

This basic amount, however, is only the starting point for determining PPS hospital reimbursement. The sum of the product of the DRG weight and standardized amounts (or rather the sum of the products of the total DRG weights of all Medicare cases treated in the hospital during the payment period and the standardized amounts) is adjusted in several respects to determine a hospital's actual PPS payment. Because labor costs vary greatly throughout the country, the labor-related portion of the PPS payment is adjusted by an area wage index factor. PPS payments are further adjusted to recognize the cost of extraordinarily expensive cases, or "outliers." PPS payments are also enhanced to compensate teaching hospitals for the indirect costs of operating educational programs. Finally, PPS payments are increased or otherwise adjusted to benefit special categories of hospitals, such as disproportionate share hospitals (which serve large numbers of low-income patients, who presumably cost more to treat) or sole-community hospitals (which serve communities distant from other hospitals and are protected by federal policy). These adjustments can be very important for hospitals in particular situations. While major urban teaching hospitals have in the past received about 32 percent of their PPS payments from disproportionate share and indirect medical education cost adjustments (compared to 9 percent for nonteaching hospitals), changes under the ACA will reduce those payments significantly.

A few categories of hospital costs continue to be reimbursed on a cost basis. The direct costs of medical education programs are reimbursed on a pass-through cost basis, as are hospital bad debts related to uncollectible Medicare deductible and coinsurance amounts and a few other miscellaneous expenses.

Any evaluation of DRG–PPS must certainly be mixed. PPS succeeded at its principal goal, limiting the escalation of Medicare expenditures for inpatient care. PPS also resulted in (or at least was accompanied by) a massive shift of care within hospitals from inpatient to outpatient settings or to long-term care units, often located within or owned by the same hospitals that had previously provided inpatient care. A great deal of surgery that used to be done on an inpatient basis, such as cataract surgery, is now done outpatient. PPS payment also encouraged hospitals to find ways to align their interests with those of their doctors, who in the end are responsible for admitting and discharging patients and ordering the tests and procedures that increase hospital costs. Although prospective payment mimics the incentives of the marketplace to the extent it encourages cost-economizing, in other ways it is quite distinct. For example, quality and outcomes are not rewarded: the best and worst hospitals receive the same base payment. (As the Chairman of the Mayo Clinic put it: "It doesn't pay to be good.")

In addition, the system has led to efforts to skirt the law or game the system. For example, there is considerable evidence that there has been "DRG creep" over the years, as hospitals have moved to coding cases as more complicated, and thus earned higher payment. CMS has responded by including a rate reduction as a "behavioral offset" to acknowledge the likelihood that hospitals will inflate coding of case severity as CMS moves to severity-adjusted DRGs. As discussed in Chapter 13, the government has devoted enormous resources to prosecute knowing violations of the coding system as illegal false claims.

Insofar as PPS generates work for lawyers, it is primarily in the area of advising clients how to take advantage of PPS. Consider the following problem:

PROBLEM: PPS

You are the in-house counsel for a large urban hospital that has a high percentage of Medicare patients. In recent years your hospital has either lost money or barely broken even. At the request of the hospital's CEO, you are serving on a committee considering how to improve the financial situation of the hospital, focusing particularly on your situation with respect to Medicare.

What strategies might be available for increasing your hospital's PPS revenues? Would changing your case-mix help? How might you achieve that? What opportunities might be available in terms of how discharges are coded? (Reconsider this question after you study Medicare fraud and abuse in Chapter 13). What possibilities are available under Medicare prospective payment for increasing your Medicare payments that are not strictly tied to your case-mix? How does the teaching mission of your hospital affect your Medicare reimbursement? How might you go about increasing your Medicare reimbursement for non-inpatient services?

Alternatively, how might you go about lowering the cost of treating Medicare patients? In particular, what strategies can you use to create incentives for your doctors to reduce costs? (See Chapters 12 and 13 for further discussion of these strategies.) Will cost reductions be accompanied by Medicare payment reductions?

3. Medicare Payment of Physicians (Part B)

Medicare Part B payment for most services (including physician services) was based initially, at least in theory, on reimbursement of actual charges (minus deductibles and coinsurance). A number of concerns, however, including the rapid rise in the cost of physician services, increasing "balance-billing" to beneficiaries, and inequities in payments among medical specialties, led to consensus that payment reform was needed. In 1989, a political consensus came together around a package of reforms that were enacted by the Omnibus Budget Reconciliation Act of 1989 and codified at 42 U.S.C.A. 1395w–4(a) to (j).

At the heart of the payment reform was the creation of a physician fee schedule. As with Part A prospective payment, fees are determined by multiplying a weighted value (in this case representing a medical procedure rather than a diagnosis) times a conversion factor, which is adjusted to consider geographic variations in cost. Relative value units (RVUs) are assigned to procedures based on the CMS Common Procedure Coding System (HCPCS) and AMA Common Procedural Terminology (CPT) codes. The Relative Value Scale consists of three components: a physician work component, a practice expense component, and a malpractice component. Thus, for example, for CPT 45378, "diagnostic colonoscopy," the work RVU is 3.69; the practice expense RVU is 7.79 if the procedure is done in a physician's office; and the malpractice RVU is .59 for 2013. See Fed. Reg., Vol. 77, No. 222, Addendum B, Friday, November 16, 2012.

The physician work component is based on estimates of the relative time and intensity of physician work involved in delivering specified services. The practice expense component accounts for physician overhead, including rent and office expenses. The practice expense is based on resource use. Different practice expense RVUs are applied depending on whether the services are furnished in a facility (hospital, SNF or ASC) or in a physician's office. Malpractice expenses for particular services are separated out from other practice expenses, and are based on the malpractice expense resources required to furnish the service.

The RVUs are adjusted by a geographic practice cost index (GPCI) to recognize differences in cost in various parts of the country and then multiplied by a conversion factor to reach a final fee payment amount (of which Medicare pays eighty percent, the other twenty percent representing the beneficiary coinsurance obligation). While most practice expenses are fully adjusted for geographic variation, physician work is only adjusted for one quarter of the variation, which offers some incentive for physicians to work in rural areas. The RBRVS system also provides special bonuses for physicians working in health practitioner shortage areas and for physicians working in rural areas. While the resource-based prices set by RBRVS addressed the problem of price inflation in physician payment, previous attempts to control prices through fee freezes had been defeated by providers simply increasing the volume of their services. To address this problem, the 1989 legislation established an astonishingly naïve mechanism, the Volume Performance Standard (VPS), to control the volume or intensity of services provided. As originally designed, the VPS sought to discourage physicians from overusing services by reducing per service payment levels if overall volume increases exceeded a specified threshold. This approach ignored the patent collective action problem: there was simply no reason for an individual physician to reduce the volume of services based on a net reduction in per service payment levels nationally or even regionally.

A few years later in 1997, CMS upped the ante, adopting the Sustainable Growth Rate (SGR) formula which imposes *cumulative* forced reductions in physician payments when total physician spending exceeds a fixed spending. 42 U.S.C. § 1395w–4(f). That is, if the total spending on physician services in a given year exceeds an aggregate target based on the GDP and other factors, the formula requires recouping that excess spending by reducing fee levels the next year. What more effective mechanism can you recommend that would create incentives for doctors to restrain volume increases? Bear in mind that antitrust laws discussed in Chapter 14 prohibit collective action by competitors to fix prices or limit output.

Besides ignoring the collective action problem, the SGR process was doubly naïve in its failure to anticipate Congress's response to proposed reductions in physician incomes resulting from the process. Each year since 2001 except one, Congress has passed legislation that overrode fee reductions. Medicare Payment Advisory Comm'n, Report to Congress: Assessing Alternatives to the Sustainable Growth Rate System 7 (June 2011). With the passage of the fiscal cliff resolution package, the American Taxpayer Relief Act of 2012, Congress delayed the projected cuts of 26.5 percent in doctors' fees through the end of 2013. The law pays for the one-year postponement by lowering in-patient hospital payments for in-patient care and reducing Medicaid payments to disproportionate share hospitals. Finding a permanent solution to the problems inherent in the so-called "doc fix" has been stymied by the sheer magnitude of the accumulated deficit incurred.

Another critical flaw of Medicare physician payment has been its failure to satisfy the central goal of the RBRVS experiment: rationalizing payment to reward cognitive services and reducing overpayments to procedure-oriented practices. Owing to its reliance on the American Medical Association's Relative Value Update Committee (RUC), which is dominated by specialists, CMS has tended to over-weight specialty procedures and undervalue primary care. See Thomas Bodenheimer et al., The Primary Care–Specialty Income Gap: Why It Matters, 146 Ann. Internal Med. 301 (2007); Miriam J. Laugesen, Roy Wada & Eric M. Chen, In Setting Doctors' Medicare Fees, CMS Almost Always Accepts the Relative Value Update Panel's Advice on Work Values, 31 Health Affairs 965, 968 (2012).

PROBLEM: RESOURCE–BASED PAYMENT FOR LAWYERS

It has recently become apparent to Congress that the high cost of legal services is having a substantial negative effect on the American economy and on our international competitive position. Congress also becomes concerned that there are gross and irrational disparities among the payments lawyers receive for legal services. Congress, therefore, proposes the adoption of a resource-based relative value schedule, limiting lawyers to the charges allowed by such a schedule (plus 15 percent where the client agrees). Adherence to the charges is enforced by criminal laws plus civil penalties ($5500 per infraction).

Legal services for representing corporations in corporate takeovers and tax and securities work and for representing individuals in estate planning, domestic relations, real estate transactions or criminal defense matters, will all be evaluated considering the (1) time, (2) mental effort and judgment, and (3) psychological stress involved in delivering each service.* Geographic variations in practice overhead will also be recognized in fee-setting, though historic geographical variations in payments for the work of lawyers will be recognized only to a very limited extent (i.e., a lawyer will be paid for his or her own work—as opposed to overhead—the same payment for similar work whether it is performed in Manhattan or in Peoria). No explicit recognition will be given in the fee schedule for experience, skill, or law school class standing of individual practitioners.

How might such a fee schedule affect access to legal services? The volume of legal services provided? The geographic and specialty distribution of lawyers? The quality of legal services? Innovation in developing new legal theories? Your plans after law school? How hard you study for the final in this class?

Where does the analogy between this problem and RBRVS break down? How, that is, does the market for physician services differ from the market for legal services?.

4.   Medicare Managed Care (Medicare Advantage or Part C)

The Turbulent History of Medicare HMOs. Although Medicare began as a fee-for-service program, it has offered managed care options since the early 1980s.. Managed care enrollment grew slowly at first, but growth was rapid in the mid–1990s: between 1995 and 1997 enrollment doubled from three to six million. Prior to the Balanced Budget Act of 1997, Medicare health maintenance organizations (HMOs) were paid ninety-five percent of the cost of Medicare fee-for-service costs in the same county (with crude risk adjustment). Because of biased selection (i.e., HMOs got healthier beneficiaries), HMOs did very well, particularly in counties with high fee-for-service costs. Because they were required to share their excess income with beneficiaries, Medicare managed care plans generally offered attractive benefit packages-in particular prescription drug coverage—which in turn led to rapid growth. The Balanced Budget Act of 1997 created the Medicare+Choice program, attempting to encourage contin-

---

* These factors plus technical skill and physical effort are all considered in setting the physician RBRVS, see William Hsaio, et al., Estimating Physicians' Work for a Resource–Based Relative–Value Scale, 319 New Eng. J. Med. 835 (1988). Unless the additional physical exertion on the golf course consumed in soliciting corporate clients is considered, this latter factor does not seem relevant to legal services.

ued growth in Medicare managed care, while at the same time dealing with some of the problems of the prior program. The hope was that Medicare+Choice would give beneficiaries a choice of health plans, benefits, and cost-sharing options, and that managed competition among health plans would hold down the cost of the Medicare program. The BBA changes, however, were a disaster for Medicare managed care, leading to a rapid decline in plan participation and enrollment. This, in turn, led to the Medicare Prescription Drug, Improvement and Modernization Act, enacted in 2003, which renamed the program "Medicare Advantage," added regional PPOs and private fee-for-service plans to expand the availability of plans to previously unserved or underserved areas, and adopted new bidding and risk sharing regulations.

Underlying the MMA changes was a straightforward purpose: promote MA enrollment by overpaying private plans. The changes achieved that goal: by 2009, MA plans were receiving payments in excess of 114 percent of fee for service (FFS) and some of the newly designed MA plans (the so-called "private fee-for-service plans") were not even designed to provide integrated care. The roller coaster for Medicare managed care continued under the Affordable Care Act which instituted another series of bidding reforms, discussed below, which are designed to "level the playing field" between MA plans and traditional fee-for-service Medicare by reducing payments to plans to 101 percent of FFS payment by 2017. As of the end of 2012, 27 percent of all Medicare beneficiaries are enrolled in Medicare Advantage. With HMOs constituting 65 percent of MA enrollment, many MA plans have proven successful at actively managing provider networks to deliver Part A and B services while avoiding excess utilization.

The turbulent history of Medicare Advantage carries an important lesson. Key aspects of the methodology for setting payments to plans have been subject to Congressional decisions that are directed at achieving specific policy goals and not based on competitive market principles. For example the MMA's changes resulting in overpayments were transparently political:

> [MMA reforms to Medicare Advantage] was wrong for the self-evident reason that overpayments to HMOs do not accomplish the goal of saving money. But in addition, overpayments suffer from a dynamic flaw: they undermine incentives to innovate provide care more efficiently. The only rationale that can be ascribed to Congress is the desire to turbo-charge HMO enrollments, or perhaps more accurately to undermine traditional Medicare. After all, it was Newt Gingrich who acknowledged that a central aim of his voucher plan was to make traditional Medicare unattractive so that it would "wither on the vine." Another lesson that can be gleaned from understanding the histori-

cal context: Medicare Advantage plans are not inherently more expensive than FFS Medicare but are the inexorable product of administratively set, high benchmarks. As one commentary aptly put it, "We pay these plans more because we choose to do so"[ ]

Thomas L. Greaney, Controlling Medicare Costs: Moving Beyond Inept Administered Pricing and Ersatz Competition? 6 Saint Louis J. Health L. & Pol'y ___ (2013).

Plan Bidding under Medicare Advantage. Medicare Advantage reimbursement to private plans is based on a bidding system. Although superficially designed to emulate competition in the private sector, the process falls short of replicating a competitive market even after important amendments made by the ACA. Payments to MA plans are determined by comparing each plan's bid (which must reflect the plan's estimated costs) to a benchmark. Plans bidding below the benchmark receive their bid plus a "rebate" equal to 75 percent of the difference between the bid and the benchmark. Those bidding above the benchmark—a rare occurrence—receive the benchmark but must require that each of their enrollees pay a premium equal to the difference between the bid and the benchmark. The ACA adjusted the bidding framework by gradually lowering plan benchmarks to levels closer to the cost of enrollees in traditional Medicare in each county, setting relatively lower benchmarks in counties with high fee-for-service Medicare costs, and relatively higher benchmarks in counties with lower fee-for-service costs. Note however that the process differs significantly from a competitive bidding process in that benchmarks continue to be based in part on historic private plan payment rates and are subject to annual increases based on the growth in Medicare spending. By retaining bidding against a preset benchmark, the process does not fully encourage plans to compete as strongly as one in which payments are based on the average of plans' bids.

Beneficiary Protections in Medicare Managed Care. Medicare beneficiaries receiving care from managed care organizations may be subject to the abuses previously discussed in Chapter 9, which may be even more harmful because of the greater needs and lesser capacities of some beneficiaries. MA organizations are, therefore, subject to a host of regulatory requirements including obligations to provide their members with detailed descriptions of plan provisions, including disclosure of any coverage limitations or regulations; provide adequate access to providers and have mechanisms for quality review. In addition, MA organizations may not discriminate against professionals on the basis of their licensure or certification, and must provide notice and hearing to physicians whose participation rights are terminatedand may not interfere with provider advice to enrollees regarding care and treatment. Other provisions seek to assure that plans provide medically necessary services, refrain from interfering with practitioners' advice to enrollees.

Can Medicare Advantage and Traditional Medicare Compete on a Level Playing Field? Should They? A recurring issue is whether the managed care sector should in some sense compete against the traditional fee for service sector. The meaning of "competition" here is somewhat obscure. Various proposals including premium support plans have insisted that fee-for-service payments should be adjusted downward if total reimbursements to Medicare managed care plans are lower than paid under traditional Medicare. There is obviously no way in which the diffused providers delivering services under traditional Medicare can collectively "compete"; so the notion is that loss of patients to MA plans will encourage providers to accept lower administered prices without abandoning Medicare patients.

However, several regulatory issues complicate this picture. First, as noted above, traditional Medicare is required to make some payments that are not directly linked to the cost of caring for Medicare beneficiaries, such as payments for direct and indirect medical education costs and disproportionate share hospital payments, or special payments to rural providers. MA rates are reduced to exclude direct medical education costs, but otherwise are not modified to reflect payments made by traditional Medicare for non-Medicare purposes, even though MA plans do not have to cover these costs when they make payments to providers. Second, although payments to MA plans are supposed to be risk-adjusted to take into account the fact that Medicare managed care beneficiaries are usually younger, healthier, and less expensive than beneficiaries who stay with traditional Medicare, risk adjustment is less than an exact science. In the past, MA plans have received payments substantially in excess of the cost of traditional Medicare because they draw a healthier population. However, recent evidence based on disenrollment data suggests that improved risk adjustment methodologies have mitigated the extent of favorable selection for Medicare Advantage plans. See J. Michael McWilliams et al, New Risk–Adjustment System Was Associated with Reduced Favorable Selection in Medicare Advantage, Health Aff. (Dec. 2012). As you read the following section concerning how the ACA has begun to establish new methods of payment under traditional Medicare and has created incentives for creation of integrated delivery systems, consider whether the factors underlying managed care and administered pricing are converging.

5. Improving Traditional Medicare: Affordable Care Act Payment Reforms

After private insurance, the Medicare program received the most attention from the ACA. Among the most important factors driving reform was widespread dissatisfaction with the effects of fee-for-service (FFS) provider payment under Medicare. The need to add financial incentives to provide high quality care and reduce errors was an aspect of reform that enjoyed strong bipartisan support. A second driver was the perceived need to deal with fragmentation in care delivery and encourage development of integrated delivery systems. The following summarizes some of the key reforms.

Value-Based Purchasing. While not eliminating or even radically restructuring provider payments under Parts A and B, the ACA moves traditional Medicare away from its historic focus on payment for services. Section 3001 of the ACA creates a new "value-based purchasing program" (VBP), which ties a percentage of hospital payments to performance on high-cost conditions, including acute myocardial infarction, surgical and healthcare infections, and pneumonia. In its Final Rule implementing the VBP program, CMS set out three domains within which the program will measure performance: Process of Care, Experience of Care, and Outcomes. 76 Fed. Reg. 26489 (May 6, 2011). Process of Care regulation includes twelve clinical measures and four quality measures that will be used to determine the FY 2013 incentive payments. For example, among the measures will be assessments as to whether hospitals: ensure that patients who might have had a heart attack receive care within 90 minutes; provide care within a 24–hour window to surgery patients to prevent blood clots; and communicate discharge instructions to heart-failure patients; and ensure hospital facilities are clean and well-maintained.

The ACA requires CMS to evaluate each hospital's performance using the higher of either an achievement score or an improvement score, and also requires CMS to establish an appeals procedure limited to the review of the calculation of a hospital's performance assessment with respect to the performance standards. Because the ACA imposes a budget neutrality requirement, funding for the VBP program requires across-the-board reductions to Medicare DRG payments (increasing from a one percent reduction for discharges beginning in 2012 to a two percent reduction in FY 2017). The domains and measures will change from year to year to incentivize hospitals to continually improve their quality of care. CMS anticipates developing a VBP program for skilled nursing facilities in the future.

Bundled Payments. As discussed above, with a few exceptions Medicare's fee-for-service payment system reimburses providers one at a time for individual items or services provided to patients even when those services are provided for a single acute episode. With many Medicare beneficiaries having complex health conditions and multiple co-morbidities, most observers agree this system has significant cost and quality implications: it provides no incentives for coordination of care and it tolerates duplicative and costly provision of services. Following the recommendation of MedPAC and others, the ACA requires the Secretary of HHS to establish, test, and evaluate a five-year pilot program "for integrated care during an episode of care . . . around a hospitalization in order to improve the coordination, quality, and efficiency of health care services." Under bundled payment, a single payment is made for an "episode of care"—i.e., a defined set of services delivered by designated providers in specified health care settings, usually delivered within a certain period of time, related to treating a patient's medical condition or performing a major surgical procedure.

Readmissions. With almost 18 percent of hospitalizations resulting in readmission within 30 days (accounting for $15 billion in Medicare spending), the ACA directed HHS to establish a hospital readmissions reduction program for certain conditions involving potentially preventable Medicare inpatient hospital readmissions. In the FY 2012 Inpatient Prospective Payment Final Rule, CMS finalized regulations that included measures for rates of readmissions for three conditions—acute myocardial infarction (AMI), heart failure (HF), and pneumonia (PN). 76 Fed. Reg. 51,476. CMS defined readmission as an admission to an applicable hospital within 30 days of a discharge from the same or another applicable hospital. CMS also finalized the calculation of a hospital's excess readmission ratio for the three conditions. This ratio is a measure of a hospital's readmission performance compared to the national average for the hospital's set of patients with that applicable condition. Finally, the rule established a policy using the risk adjustment methodology endorsed by the National Quality Forum for the readmissions measures for AMI, HF and PN to calculate the excess readmission ratios.

Concerns have been expressed about the impact of this program, especially on safety net hospitals. Public interest groups have suggested that if risk adjustment mechanisms prove inadequate, the policy could disadvantage vulnerable populations and punish those hospitals that have a more socioeconomically complex mix of patients whose lack of community support systems are difficult to account for in risk adjustment models. Payments for Inpatient Hospitals Would Decrease $498 Million Under Proposal, Medicare Report (BNA) (April 22, 2011). Would factors such as the incidence of chronic conditions or family support increase the likelihood of readmissions? Are more nuanced measures needed? Consider for example, Karen E. Joynt & Ashish K. Jha, Thirty Day Readmissions—Truth and Consequences, 366 N. Eng. J. Med. 1366 (2012) (hospitals with high readmission rates arguably provide higher quality of care because they have lower mortality rates).

Payment Adjustments. The ACA seeks to correct many of the flaws in FFS payment methodology. Under the title "Improving Payment Accuracy," the Act directs the Secretary of HHS to "regularly review fee schedule rates," focusing especially on those with the fastest growth. The Act strengthens the Secretary's ability to adjust rates found to be misvalued or inaccurate. It also tackles some of the payment rules that have contributed to explosive growth in certain sectors, such as the equipment utilization factor applied to advanced imaging services as well as various rules affecting the base payments and adjustments for the prospective payment system applicable to home health agencies. Among other provisions adding sticks to the carrots in HHS's toolbox, is a new penalty for hospitals ranking in the top 25th percentile for rates of hospital infections.

An important change for hospitals under the ACA was a sharp reduction in the Medicare Disproportionate Share Hospital (DSH) payments. Beginning in 2014, the Act reduces DSH payments to equal 25 percent of what they otherwise would be. DSH payments had originally been included as an add-on to PPS payments in 1986 because low income patients were more costly to treat, and hospitals treating large numbers of such patients were therefore likely to have higher costs. Over time, however, the justification for DSH payments changed, with the payments being seen as a way to ensure access to hospital care. In its 2007 Report to Congress, MedPAC concluded that approximately 75 percent of DSH payments were not justified under the "higher program cost" rationale. Hospitals had predicted dire consequences would result from Medicare and Medicaid DSH reductions particularly for hospitals that served large numbers of undocumented immigrants, who will continue to lack health insurance. The ACA softened the blow somewhat by allowing add-on payments to certain hospitals based on the percentage of uncompensated care provided by the hospital (relative to all acute care hospitals) for a selected period.

The Independent Payment Advisory Board. One of the most intriguing and controversial provisions of the ACA is the establishment of the Independent Payment Advisory Board ("IPAB" or "the Board"). The Board's principal mission is to develop and submit detailed proposals to Congress and the President to reduce Medicare spending and improve the quality of care. At bottom, proponents sought to delegate to an expert, independent group the power to make hard and controversial decisions on program costs, thereby maximizing their ability to insulate IPAB's decisions from the possibility of Congressional overrides. Whether the final compromise achieves that goal is unclear. However, the Congressional delegation of authority is significant, and its potential power is immense. In the opinion of Peter Orszag, the Administration's Director of the Office of Management and Budget, IPAB represents "the largest yielding of sovereignty from the Congress since the creation of the Federal Reserve." Ezra Klein, Can We Control Costs Without Congress?, The Washington Post (March 26, 2010, 2:46 PM).

The Board will consist of 15 members appointed by the President with the advice and consent of the Senate plus the Secretary of HHS and the administrators of CMS and the Health Resources and Services Administration. Members will serve six-year terms and must include physicians and other health providers who have expertise in health finance, payment or other areas. The Board is given remarkable powers to initiate cost cutting in Medicare (which some have likened to the "Doomsday Device" in the movie Dr. Strangelove). In years when 5–year Medicare costs two years later are projected by the CMS Chief Actuary to exceed a specified benchmark, the Board must make a proposal that will reduce Medicare spending by a specified amount (e.g., 5 percent in 2015, 1 percent in 2016). These proposals will take effect unless Congress passes (under expedited consideration) an alternative measure that achieves the same level of savings on a fast-track basis. Even in the event of Congressional override, a Presidential veto of the Congressional alternative that was not overridden would allow the IPAB proposal to go into effect. However, the ACA places some significant restrictions on the recommendations that IPAB may put forward. It is prohibited from making proposals that ration care, raise taxes or Part B premiums, or change Medicare benefit, eligibility, or cost-sharing standards. In addition, for years prior to 2020, the Board may not propose payment cuts to hospitals and perhaps for hospice services; physician payment however remains fair game for the Board.

Will it work? IPAB's success will largely depend on the kinds of changes it recommends, particularly whether its recommendations go beyond payment rates to include proposals to change the methods of payment and beneficiary responsibilities. IPAB's successful implementation also depends on whether Congress acquiesces in or resists cost-cutting as it has done repeatedly with respect to physician payment under the SGR. See Timothy Stoltzfus Jost, The Independent Payment Advisory Board, New Eng. J. Med. (May 26, 2010). IPAB will also have responsibility for monitoring and making recommendations and proposals to Congress and the President every two years beginning in 2015 regarding how to slow the growth of private expenditures on health care in the private sector.

Will it be implemented? In March, 2012, the House of Representatives voted to repeal the IPAB but no action was taken by the Senate. Notably seven House Democrats supported repeal based on concerns the panel could usurp the power of Congress to set Medicare policy. Repeal legislation has garnered support from a variety of provider groups. With hospitals exempt from the board's recommendations for the first five years, trade groups representing doctors, drug companies, and device manufacturers contend they will be unfairly targeted for any Medicare cuts the Board implements. Moreover, noting that IPAB has "limited tools at its disposal to make fundamental and necessary changes to the Medicare program," they contend that IPAB is likely to focus on reducing provider payment rates rather than new methods of payment. Finally, opponents contend that if reimbursement rates become inadequate, costs will shift to private payers and consumers.

NOTES AND QUESTIONS

1.   Is IPAB a realistic way of "depoliticizing" difficult spending decisions? Is it realistic to assume that Congress will not intervene either to override IPAB's proposals or to legislatively restrict IPAB's powers?

2.   On its face, pay for performance (P4P), which includes value-based purchasing and other reforms under the ACA, seem like a good idea. It hardly makes sense to reward nonperformance or poor performance. High-quality care is something that Medicare should be prepared to pay for. Despite the obviousness of the potential benefits of P4P, it has not been greeted universally with open arms. The main objections to P4P group into two general categories—technical objections on the one hand, and philosophical or policy objections on the other. Technical objections include disagreements over what should be measured; recall the structure-conduct-performance typology developed by Avedis Donabedian discussed in Chapter 1. Issues of finding an appropriate sample size and accounting for variations in risk and other factors complicate the matter considerably.

6.   Fixing the Delivery System: ACOs, Pilots, Demonstrations, and Other New Things

As discussed below, the ACA establishes at least 35 pilots programs and demonstrations—same of which experiment with moving medicine away from fee-for-service payment altogether. Generally focused on incentivizing clinicians to work together to control costs and improve care, these plans range from offering new bonuses and penalties, to permitting gainsharing among providers, to establishing entirely new payment methodologies, and even to funding new organizations to take responsibility for the full range of patient care.

a.   Center for Medicare and Medicaid Innovation

The ACA empowered the Secretary of HHS with broad authority to establish within CMS a new Center for Medicare & Medicaid Innovation to research, develop, test, and expand innovative payment and delivery arrangements that improve quality of care and reduce costs. While instructing that models chosen must address a defined population with poor clinical outcomes or avoidable expenditures, Congress provided a wide-ranging mandate and vested considerable powers in this center. First, it enables HHS to initiate demonstration models that involve medical homes, coordinated care, alternative payment mechanisms, health information technology (HIT), medication management, patient education, integrated care for dual-eligibles, care for cancer patients, post-acute care, chronic care management, and collaboration among mixed provider types, rural telehealth and various payment reform models. Second, it empowers the Secretary to waive the requirements of Titles XI and XVIII of the Social Security Act, which include prohibitions on self-referrals (the Stark law) as well as kickbacks (the anti-kickback law) and the Gainsharing Civil Monetary Penalty (all of which are covered in Chapter 13). The ACA also prohibits administrative or judicial review of selection of models or participants, the duration or design of models and determinations regarding budget neutrality under the program.

b. Accountable Care Organizations (The Medicare Shared Savings Program)

Undoubtedly, the most widely discussed (and in the opinion of some, most promising) systemic reform contained in the ACA is the "Medicare Shared Savings Program" (MSSP), which is designed to test and spur the development of Accountable Care Organizations (ACOs). In many respects, the ACO is the latest in a long line of efforts to develop integrated delivery systems that bear financial responsibility for treatment decisions. In addition, a number of experiments involving bundled payments to ACOs and to other innovative organizations (as in Medicare's Physician Group Practice demonstration) have been underway for some time.

Although the program implicates only the provision of Part A and B services under Medicare, its goals extend much further. As summarized in the preamble to Section 3022 of the ACA, the program seeks to:

- promote accountability;

- encourage investment in infrastructure;

- coordinate provision of services under Parts A and B of Medicare; and

- redesign care processes for high quality and efficient service delivery.

The objectives of the program encompass fostering health systems capable of controlling costs and improving the quality of care. See Donald M. Berwick, Launching Accountable Care Organizations—The Proposed Rule for the Medicare Shared Savings Program, New Eng. J. Med. (April 21, 2011) (purpose of ACOs is to achieve a "triple aim": "better care for individuals, better health for populations, and slower growth in costs through improvements in care"). At bottom, the aspiration is to transform the delivery system by incentivizing diverse and fragmented providers to abandon their silos and instead offer services jointly. Proponents tout ACOs as vehicles for coordinating, developing, and using evidence-based medicine which would in turn foster quality improvement and cost control.

The MSSP makes groups of providers who voluntarily meet certain quality criteria eligible to share in the cost savings they achieve for the Medicare program. To qualify, an ACO must agree to be accountable for the overall care of a defined group of Medicare beneficiaries, have sufficient participation of primary care physicians, have processes that promote evidence-based medicine, report on quality and costs, and be capable of coordinating care. Additionally, an ACO must be comprised of a group of providers and suppliers who have an established mechanism for joint decision making, and may include practitioners (physicians, regardless of specialty; nurse practitioners; physician assistants; and clinical nurse specialists) in group practice arrangements; networks of practices; as well as partnerships or joint venture arrangements between hospitals and practitioners.

ACOs will qualify for an annual incentive bonus if they achieve a threshold level of savings for total per beneficiary spending under Medicare parts A and B for those beneficiaries assigned to the ACO. ACOs receive a percentage of the difference between the benchmark and the savings. The ACA empowers the Secretary to employ other payment models including a "partial capitation model" in which an ACO is at financial risk for some, but not all, of the items and services covered under parts A and B, such as at risk for some or all physicians' services or all items and services under part B. CMS has established the Pioneer Program for advanced ACOs able to assume capitated risk.

ACO Regulation. In November 2011, the Centers for Medicare & Medicaid Services (CMS) issued its Final Rule implementing the Shared Savings Program. 76 Fed. Reg. 67,802 (November 2, 2011). This lengthy regulation covers many issues including eligibility, governance, payment, and quality standards for entities applying for certification as ACOs under the program. It substantially amended the agency's proposed rule which generated over 1300 comments, many of which were highly critical. Provider groups were especially concerned with the extensive quality requirements CMS proposed to employ to review ACO performance; the imposition of downside risk in the third year of operation; identification of assigned beneficiaries for whom the ACO would be held accountable for at the end of the year, after care had been delivered, instead of the beginning; and the requirement that at least 50 percent of an ACO's primary care physicians be meaningful users of electronic health records. As discussed below, CMS relaxed its regulations on these and other issues.

Contemporaneously with the Final Rule, several other agencies also provided guidance: CMS and the Office of Inspector General (OIG) jointly issued an Interim Final Rule describing the waiver of application of various fraud and abuse laws with respect to ACOs (discussed in Chapter 13); the Federal Trade Commission (FTC) and the Department of Justice (DOJ) jointly issued a Final Policy Statement concerning the application of antitrust laws to ACOs (discussed in Chapter 14); and the Internal Revenue Service (IRS) issued a Notice and Fact Sheet concerning tax-exempt entity participation in the MSSP (discussed in Chapter 12). The following sections summarize some of the key provisions of the CMS Final Rule.

Definitions and Eligibility. The Final Rule defines an Accountable Care Organization as a legal entity that is recognized and authorized under applicable state law and comprised of an eligible group of ACO participants that work together to manage and coordinate care for Medicare FFS beneficiaries and have established a mechanism for shared governance that provides all ACO participants with an appropriate proportionate control over the ACO's decision making process. "ACO participants" are Medicare-enrolled providers of services and/or a supplier that alone or together with other participants "comprise" the ACO. Each ACO must be constituted as a legal entity appropriately recognized and authorized under applicable State law; however, existing legal entities recognized under State law do not need to form a separate new entity. ACOs must apply to CMS for approval. Those selected will enter into a contract that will last for not less than three years after the application has been approved. Performance will be measured every 12 months.

Beneficiary Assignment. Medicare beneficiaries will be "attributed" under the MSSP to the primary care doctor (and assigned to that doctor's ACO) from whom they receive a plurality of their primary care services. Beneficiaries who have not recently had primary care services provided by a primary care physician will be assigned to an ACO on the basis of the specialist physician or certain non-physician providers including clinical nurse specialists and physician assistants from whom the beneficiary has received a plurality of primary care services. CMS will create a list of beneficiaries likely to receive care from the ACO based on primary care utilization during the most recent period and will update the list periodically to allow the ACO to adjust to likely changes in its assigned population. At the end of each performance year, CMS will reconcile the list to reflect beneficiaries who actually meet the criteria for assignment to the ACO during the performance year.Most importantly, assignment to an ACO does not restrict the right of the beneficiaries assigned to an ACO to opt to receive health benefits from providers outside the ACO to which they are assigned.

Payment: Benchmarks, Tracks, and Performance Standards. CMS will develop a benchmark for each ACO against which the ACO's performance is measured to assess whether it qualifies to receive shared savings or, for some ACOs, will be held accountable for losses. The benchmark is an estimate of what the total Medicare FFS Parts A and B expenditures for ACO beneficiaries otherwise would have been in the absence of the ACO. The benchmark takes into account beneficiary characteristics and other factors that may affect the need for health care services, and it will be updated for each performance year within the three-year performance period. The Final Rule also establishes a minimum savings rate (MSR), which is a percentage of the benchmark that ACO expenditure savings must exceed in order for an ACO to qualify for shared savings in any given year. In a relaxation of its proposed rule, CMS will allow "first dollar savings" for all ACOs that meet their MSR requirement.

ACOs that meet quality performance thresholds will be eligible to receive shared savings in each year of their three year contracts if their Part A and Part B expenditures fall below established benchmarks. ACOs may choose one of two risk models. Under the "Track 1" (or "one-sided risk") model, an ACO is eligible to receive 50 percent of total shared savings (or up to 52.5 percent if the ACO includes a Federally Qualified Health Center or Rural Health Center) in all three years of the agreement. In an important change from its proposed rule, CMS removed the requirement that Track 1 ACOs must share risk for losses in their third year. ACOs electing "Track 2" (or the "two-sided risk") model will be at risk for shared losses in all three years but would be eligible to receive a higher percentage of shared savings than Track 1 ACOs (up to 60 percent of shared savings or up to 65 percent if the ACO includes a Federally Qualified Health Center or Rural Health Center). There is also a maximum sharing cap that distinguishes the two tracks: Track 1 ACOs may not share savings exceeding 10 percent of benchmark, while Track 2 ACOs may share savings up to 15 percent of benchmark. Track 1 ACOs will be required to transition to Track 2 after their first three-year agreement period.

Quality. Reversing its proposed rule, which had set forth quality standards that included 65 separate measures, CMS reduced the number to 33 measures grouped into four domains: Patient/Caregiver Experience; Care Coordination and Patient Safety; Preventive Health; and At–Risk Population/Frail Elderly Health. CMS will assign a performance score on each domain and will reduce shared savings for ACOs falling below a performance benchmark.

A physician-directed committee must be responsible for overseeing ACOs' quality assurance and improvement program. This program must establish internal performance standards for quality of care, cost-effectiveness, and process and outcome improvements. The committee is charged with developing processes and procedures to hold providers accountable and to identify and correct poor compliance.

Governance. The Final Rule removed a proposed requirement that each ACO participant have a representative on the ACO governing body in favor of requirement that ACOs provide for meaningful participation by participants in the composition and control of the governing body. However, at least 75 percent of the governing body must consist of ACO participants, although as discussed in Chapter 13, the Rule allows for variation in some of these rules.

Provider participation. Each ACO must have at least 5,000 Medicare beneficiaries assigned to it and must also have a sufficient number of primary care physicians to treat its ACO beneficiary population. Responding again to criticisms, CMS dropped a proposed requirement that at least 50 percent of an ACO's primary care physicians must be meaningful electronic health record (EHR) users. It also removed a requirement that primary care providers (defined to include internal medicine, general practice, family practice and geriatric medicine specialists) may only participate in one ACO. A primary care physician may participate of multiple ACOs if he/she has not been billing under an individual taxpayer identification number; however, for beneficiary assignment purposes, the primary care physician can only be associated with one ACO.

Potential Savings The Centers for Medicare & Medicaid Services estimated that the new ACOs could serve five million beneficiaries and save Medicare between $170 million and $960 million over three years. Compared to total spending of $1.8 trillion during this period, the savings may seem insignificant.

c.   *Patient-Centered Medical Homes*

The Patient–Centered Medical Home (PCMH) is not far removed in principle from the ACO. The PCMH model envisions a primary care practice that provides comprehensive and timely care and that builds on a combination of "teamwork by a group of health professionals and more active engagement by those receiving care." Proponents link the PCMH concept with the acceptance of accountability for the quality and cost of providing care to their patients. The underlying concept was the subject of the HHS Physician Group Practice Demonstration which successfully tested a system of rewards to selected physician groups for improving patient outcomes by coordinating their patients' total health care needs, especially for beneficiaries with chronic illness, multiple co-morbidities, and transitioning care settings. See Center for Medicare and Medicaid Services (CMS), Medicare Physician Group Practice Demonstration (Aug. 2009) (reporting success of ten groups under study in improving performance); but cf. Devers and Berenson *supra* (noting that given their large size (500 doctors) and sophistication, the ten groups in the PGP demonstration had exceptional capacity to take joint actions to change care protocols, improve quality metrics, and constrain capacity growth). The ACA directed the Secretary to establish a program to provide grants to enter into contracts to establish community-based interdisciplinary, interprofessional "health teams" to support primary care practices (including obstetrics and gynecology practices) in establishing medical homes.

NOTES AND QUESTIONS

1.   What influence did the nation's experience with managed care have on the nature and scope of ACO regulations proposed by CMS? In what respects do ACOs differ from HMOs?What problems do you foresee ACOs encountering as a result of the patient attribution process and rules allowing beneficiaries to choose to receive care from any provider? What considerations might be relevant in choosing primary care providers to participate in an ACO? As of the beginning of 2013, CMS had approved 250 ACOs serving over 4 million beneficiaries and almost half of the approved ACOs are physician-driven organizations. CMS, Press Release, More Doctors, Hospitals Partner to Coordinate Care for People with Medicare: Providers Form 106 New Accountable Care Organizations (January 10, 2013).

2.   *The Pioneer ACO model.* Responding in part to the initial reluctance of many of the nation's leading integrated systems to participate in the MSSP, CMS inaugurated its Pioneer ACO model, a program administered by the Center for Medicare and Medicaid Innovation. The models being tested in the first two years of the program are a shared savings payment policy with generally higher levels of shared savings and risk for Pioneer ACOs than those applicable in the MSSP. In year three of the program, participating ACOs that have shown a specified level of savings over the first two years will be eligible to move a substantial portion of their payments to a population-based, capitation model. Designed primarily for organizations that are already highly integrated and experienced in coordinating care for patients across care settings, the program began in 2012 with 32 selected participants. The program requires that Pioneer ACOs "commit to entering outcomes-based contracts" with other purchasers (private health plans, state Medicaid agencies, and/or self-insured employers) such that the majority of the ACO's total revenues (including revenues from Medicare) will be derived from such arrangements by the end of the second performance period in December 2013.

III.   MEDICAID

Medicare is a social insurance program whose benefits are available to the elderly and disabled without regard for their means. It is popular and enjoys broad-based support. The debate surrounding Medicare concerns its enormous cost and how best to control it. There has been little discussion about cutting eligibility or benefits, or about devolving responsibility for Medicare from the federal to the state governments.

Medicaid, on the other hand, is a welfare program for the poor. It was created almost as an afterthought during the Medicare debate in the 1960s and has always been controversial, always vulnerable. All aspects of the program, eligibility, benefits, payment mechanisms, federal and state responsibility for the program—even whether Medicaid should continue to exist at all as an entitlement program—have been hotly contested over the past two decades. Despite this, Medicaid is the nation's largest and most expensive health insurance program, covering more Americans than Medicare. The Affordable Care Act, as written, would expand Medicaid to cover millions more, effectively turning the program into a public insurance program that covers all poor Americans. The Supreme Court's Affordable Care Act decision (see below) limits the extent of this change by turning the expansion into a state option, but how much the change will be limited remains to be seen.

This section will examine Medicaid as it has developed over nearly four decades and as it exists in the winter of 2013. When you read this book, Medicaid may again be radically changed. It is indeed possible that it will no longer exist as an entitlement program. The poor, however, will always be with us, and they will always need health care. Any governmental program intended to help them obtain health care will need to consider the issues of eligibility, benefits, payment structure, administration, and financing addressed in this section.

DEPARTMENT OF HEALTH AND HUMAN SERVICES, ET. AL. V. FLORIDA, ET AL., PETITIONERS

Supreme Court of the United States, 2012.
132 S.Ct. 2566.

CHIEF JUSTICE ROBERTS, JUSTICES BREYER and KAGAN

(The first part of the decision, upholding the individual mandate as a tax, is reproduced in chapter 7).

The States also contend that the Medicaid expansion exceeds Congress's authority under the Spending Clause. They claim that Congress is coercing the States to adopt the changes it wants by threatening to withhold all of a State's Medicaid grants, unless the State accepts the new expanded funding and complies with the conditions that come with it. This, they argue, violates the basic principle that the "Federal Government may not compel the States to enact or administer a federal regulatory program." [ ]

There is no doubt that the Act dramatically increases state obligations under Medicaid. The current Medicaid program requires States to cover only certain discrete categories of needy individuals—pregnant women, children, needy families, the blind, the elderly, and the disabled. [ ] There is no mandatory coverage for most childless adults, and the States typically do not offer any such coverage. The States also enjoy considerable flexibility with respect to the coverage levels for parents of needy families. [ ] On average States cover only those unemployed parents who make less than 37 percent of the federal poverty level, and only those employed parents who make less than 63 percent of the poverty line. [ ]

The Medicaid provisions of the Affordable Care Act, in contrast, re-quire States to expand their Medicaid programs by 2014 to cover *all* indi-viduals under the age of 65 with incomes below 133 percent of the federal poverty line. [ ] The Act also establishes a new "[e]ssential health bene-fits" package, which States must provide to all new Medicaid recipients—a level sufficient to satisfy a recipient's obligations under the individual mandate. [ ] The Affordable Care Act provides that the Federal Govern-ment will pay 100 percent of the costs of covering these newly eligible in-dividuals through 2016. [ ] In the following years, the federal payment level gradually decreases, to a minimum of 90 percent. * * *

The Spending Clause grants Congress the power "to pay the Debts and provide for the . . . general Welfare of the United States." [ ]. We have long recognized that Congress may use this power to grant federal funds to the States, and may condition such a grant upon the States' "tak-ing certain actions that Congress could not require them to take." [ ] Such measures "encourage a State to regulate in a particular way, [and] influ-enc[e] a State's policy choices." [ ] The conditions imposed by Congress ensure that the funds are used by the States to "provide for the . . . gen-eral Welfare" in the manner Congress intended.

At the same time, our cases have recognized limits on Congress's power under the Spending Clause to secure state compliance with federal objectives. "We have repeatedly characterized . . . Spending Clause legis-lation as 'much in the nature of a *contract*.' " [ ] The legitimacy of Con-gress's exercise of the spending power "thus rests on whether the State voluntarily and knowingly accepts the terms of the 'contract.' " [ ] Re-specting this limitation is critical to ensuring that Spending Clause legis-lation does not undermine the status of the States as independent sover-eigns in our federal system. * * * For this reason, "the Constitution has never been understood to confer upon Congress the ability to require the States to govern according to Congress' instructions." [ ] Otherwise the two-government system established by the Framers would give way to a system that vests power in one central government, and individual liberty would suffer.

That insight has led this Court to strike down federal legislation that commandeers a State's legislative or administrative apparatus for federal purposes. [ ] It has also led us to scrutinize Spending Clause legislation to ensure that Congress is not using financial inducements to exert a "power akin to undue influence." [ ] Congress may use its spending power to cre-ate incentives for States to act in accordance with federal policies. But when "pressure turns into compulsion," [ ] the legislation runs contrary to our system of federalism. * * * That is true whether Congress directly commands a State to regulate or indirectly coerces a State to adopt a fed-eral regulatory system as its own.

Permitting the Federal Government to force the States to implement a federal program would threaten the political accountability key to our federal system. "[W]here the Federal Government directs the States to regulate, it may be state officials who will bear the brunt of public disapproval, while the federal officials who devised the regulatory program may remain insulated from the electoral ramifications of their decision." [ ] Spending Clause programs do not pose this danger when a State has a legitimate choice whether to accept the federal conditions in exchange for federal funds. In such a situation, state officials can fairly be held politically accountable for choosing to accept or refuse the federal offer. But when the State has no choice, the Federal Government can achieve its objectives without accountability * * * Indeed, this danger is heightened when Congress acts under the Spending Clause, because Congress can use that power to implement federal policy it could not impose directly under its enumerated powers.

*   *   *

* * * Congress may attach appropriate conditions to federal taxing and spending programs to preserve its control over the use of federal funds. In the typical case we look to the States to defend their prerogatives by adopting "the simple expedient of not yielding" to federal blandishments when they do not want to embrace the federal policies as their own. [ ] The States are separate and independent sovereigns. Sometimes they have to act like it.

The States, however, argue that the Medicaid expansion is far from the typical case. They object that Congress has "crossed the line distinguishing encouragement from coercion," [ ] in the way it has structured the funding: Instead of simply refusing to grant the new funds to States that will not accept the new conditions, Congress has also threatened to withhold those States' existing Medicaid funds. The States claim that this threat serves no purpose other than to force unwilling States to sign up for the dramatic expansion in health care coverage effected by the Act.

Given the nature of the threat and the programs at issue here, we must agree. We have upheld Congress's authority to condition the receipt of funds on the States' complying with restrictions on the use of those funds, because that is the means by which Congress ensures that the funds are spent according to its view of the "general Welfare." Conditions that do not here govern the use of the funds, however, cannot be justified on that basis. When, for example, such conditions take the form of threats to terminate other significant independent grants, the conditions are properly viewed as a means of pressuring the States to accept policy changes.

*   *   *

In this case, the financial "inducement" Congress has chosen is much more than "relatively mild encouragement"—it is a gun to the head. Section 1396c of the Medicaid Act provides that if a State's Medicaid plan does not comply with the Act's requirements, the Secretary of Health and Human Services may declare that "further payments will not be made to the State." [ ] A State that opts out of the Affordable Care Act's expansion in health care coverage thus stands to lose not merely "a relatively small percentage" of its existing Medicaid funding, but *all* of it. [ ] Medicaid spending accounts for over 20 percent of the average State's total budget, with federal funds covering 50 to 83 percent of those costs. * * * In addition, the States have developed intricate statutory and administrative regimes over the course of many decades to implement their objectives under existing Medicaid. * * * The threatened loss of over 10 percent of a State's overall budget, in contrast, is economic dragooning that leaves the States with no real option but to acquiesce in the Medicaid expansion.[12]

* * * The States contend that the expansion is in reality a new program and that Congress is forcing them to accept it by threatening the funds for the existing Medicaid program. We cannot agree that existing Medicaid and the expansion dictated by the Affordable Care Act are all one program simply because "Congress styled" them as such. [ ] If the expansion is not properly viewed as a modification of the existing Medicaid program, Congress's decision to so title it is irrelevant.

Here, the Government claims that the Medicaid expansion is properly viewed merely as a modification of the existing program because the States agreed that Congress could change the terms of Medicaid when they signed on in the first place. The Government observes that the Social Security Act, which includes the original Medicaid provisions, contains a clause expressly reserving "[t]he right to alter, amend, or repeal any provision" of that statute. 42 U.S.C. § 1304. So it does. But "if Congress intends to impose a condition on the grant of federal moneys, it must do so unambiguously." A State confronted with statutory language reserving the right to "alter" or "amend" the pertinent provisions of the Social Security Act might reasonably assume that Congress was entitled to make adjustments to the Medicaid program as it developed. Congress has in fact done so, sometimes conditioning only the new funding, other times both old and new. [ ]

---

[12] JUSTICE GINSBURG observes that state Medicaid spending will increase by only 0.8 percent after the expansion. [ ] That not only ignores increased state administrative expenses, but also assumes that the Federal Government will continue to fund the expansion at the current statutorily specified levels. It is not unheard of, however, for the Federal Government to increase requirements in such a manner as to impose unfunded mandates on the States. More importantly, the size of the new financial burden imposed on a State is irrelevant in analyzing whether the State has been coerced into accepting that burden. "Your money or your life" is a coercive proposition, whether you have a single dollar in your pocket or $500.

The Medicaid expansion, however, accomplishes a shift in kind, not merely degree. The original program was designed to cover medical services for four particular categories of the needy: the disabled, the blind, the elderly, and needy families with dependent children. [ ] Previous amendments to Medicaid eligibility merely altered and expanded the boundaries of these categories. Under the Affordable Care Act, Medicaid is transformed into a program to meet the health care needs of the entire nonelderly population with income below 133 percent of the poverty level. It is no longer a program to care for the neediest among us, but rather an element of a comprehensive national plan to provide universal health insurance coverage.

Indeed, the manner in which the expansion is structured indicates that while Congress may have styled the expansion a mere alteration of existing Medicaid, it recognized it was enlisting the States in a new health care program. Congress created a separate funding provision to cover the costs of providing services to any person made newly eligible by the expansion. * * * The conditions on use of the different funds are also distinct. Congress mandated that newly eligible persons receive a level of coverage that is less comprehensive than the traditional Medicaid benefit package. [ ]

As we have explained, "[t]hough Congress' power to legislate under the spending power is broad, it does not include surprising participating States with postacceptance or 'retroactive' conditions." [ ]

JUSTICE GINSBURG claims that in fact this expansion is no different from the previous changes to Medicaid, such that "a State would be hard put to complain that it lacked fair notice." [ ] But the prior change she discusses—presumably the most dramatic alteration she could find—does not come close to working the transformation the expansion accomplishes. She highlights an amendment requiring States to cover pregnant women and increasing the number of eligible children.[ ] But this modification can hardly be described as a major change in a program that—from its inception—provided health care for "families with dependent children." Previous Medicaid amendments simply do not fall into the same category as the one at stake here.

The Court in *Steward Machine* [an earlier Supreme Court case that had mentioned the coercion doctrine in dicta] did not attempt to "fix the outermost line" where persuasion gives way to coercion. [ ]. The Court found it "[e]nough for present purposes that wherever the line may be, this statute is within it." [ ] We have no need to fix a line either. It is enough for today that wherever that line may be, this statute is surely beyond it. Congress may not simply "conscript state [agencies] into the national bureaucratic army," [ ]

Nothing in our opinion precludes Congress from offering funds under the Affordable Care Act to expand the availability of health care, and requiring that States accepting such funds comply with the conditions on their use. What Congress is not free to do is to penalize States that choose not to participate in that new program by taking away their existing Medicaid funding. * * * In light of the Court's holding, the Secretary cannot apply § 1396c to withdraw existing Medicaid funds for failure to comply with the requirements set out in the expansion.

That fully remedies the constitutional violation we have identified. The chapter of the United States Code that contains § 1396c includes a severability clause confirming that we need go no further. That clause specifies that "[i]f any provision of this chapter, or the application thereof to any person or circumstance, is held invalid, the remainder of the chapter, and the application of such provision to other persons or circumstances shall not be affected thereby." [ ] Today's holding does not affect the continued application of § 1396c to the existing Medicaid program. Nor does it affect the Secretary's ability to withdraw funds provided under the Affordable Care Act if a State that has chosen to participate in the expansion fails to comply with the requirements of that Act.

*   *   *

The question remains whether today's holding affects other provisions of the Affordable Care Act. * * * The question here is whether Congress would have wanted the rest of the Act to stand, had it known that States would have a genuine choice whether to participate in the new Medicaid expansion. Unless it is "evident" that the answer is no, we must leave the rest of the Act intact. [ ]

We are confident that Congress would have wanted to preserve the rest of the Act. It is fair to say that Congress assumed that every State would participate in the Medicaid expansion, given that States had no real choice but to do so. The States contend that Congress enacted the rest of the Act with such full participation in mind; they point out that Congress made Medicaid a means for satisfying the mandate, [ ] and enacted no other plan for providing coverage to many low-income individuals. According to the States, this means that the entire Act must fall.

We disagree. The Court today limits the financial pressure the Secretary may apply to induce States to accept the terms of the Medicaid expansion. As a practical matter, that means States may now choose to reject the expansion; that is the whole point. But that does not mean all or even any will. Some States may indeed decline to participate, either because they are unsure they will be able to afford their share of the new funding obligations, or because they are unwilling to commit the administrative resources necessary to support the expansion. Other States, however, may voluntarily sign up, finding the idea of expanding Medicaid coverage attractive, particularly given the level of federal funding the Act offers at the outset.

We have no way of knowing how many States will accept the terms of the expansion, but we do not believe Congress would have wanted the whole Act to fall, simply because some may choose not to participate. The other reforms Congress enacted, after all, will remain "fully operative as a law," [ ] and will still function in a way "consistent with Congress' basic objectives in enacting the statute," [ ] Confident that Congress would not have intended anything different, we conclude that the rest of the Act need not fall in light of our constitutional holding.

*   *   *

NOTES AND QUESTIONS

As you read the material that follows, consider the following questions. Did Chief Justice Roberts understand the history and nature of the Medicaid program? Does he describe accurately the relationship between the federal and state governments that has traditionally characterized the program? How does the Court's opinion change that relationship? Does the opinion accurately characterize the changes brought about in Medicaid by the ACA? Does it affect any of the changes made in the program by the ACA other than the adult expansion (described below)? How does this decision limit the power of Congress to change the program in the future?

A. ELIGIBILITY

PROBLEM: MEDICAID ELIGIBILITY

Four generations of the Sawatsky family live together in two neighboring apartments. Stanislaus Sawatsky immigrated from Poland in the 1970s. He became a U.S. citizen ten years later and has worked for thirty years in construction. Work has been intermittent, however, and he has never been able to build up a nest egg. For the past year Stanislaus, now in his late 50s, has been unable to work because of his heart condition. He was recently awarded federal supplemental security assistance (SSI) because of his disability. His son, Peter, is married to Maria and lives next door to Stanislaus with his three children, aged 1, 5, and 7. Peter was recently laid off from his job in a trailer factory. He is working in a fast food restaurant, but his income is only a fraction of what it used to be. Maria is currently pregnant and not employed outside the home. Finally, Stanislaus' mother, Elzbieta, aged 83, has been living with Peter for a year now. She came to the U.S. from Poland last year on a tourist visa, and has not returned (even though the visa has expired). She fell yesterday and is in the hospital with a broken hip. No one in the family can afford to help pay her medical bills, and the hospital is saying she will need to be discharged to a nursing home. Who in this group, if anyone, is eligible for Medicaid? What sources of law would you consult to answer this question? What additional facts would you have to know to determine eligibility?

1. Traditional Medicaid Eligibility

Medicaid eligibility has traditionally been very complex. Medicaid is a federally and state-funded, state-administered program, and each state has historically established its own eligibility requirements, subject to the basic constraints of federal laws and regulations. The federal Medicaid law contains mandatory and optional provisions for eligibility, benefits, and program administration. As will be described later, states can also request waivers to shape their Medicaid programs in ways not otherwise authorized by federal law. Each state must file with HHS a "state plan" setting out the provisions of its own Medicaid program.

Because Medicaid is a welfare program, eligibility has almost always been tied to both economic need and to being in a category of people who are deemed to be worthy of receiving aid. This means that in almost all states, prior to the ACA, most poor persons were not eligible for Medicaid. Rather Medicaid has traditionally assisted only certain favored groups of the needy considered to be the "deserving" poor, although in recent decades utilitarian considerations such as providing prenatal care or care for infants to avoid more expensive conditions later have arguably become as important as moral judgments in determining who should receive Medicaid.

The Affordable Care Act greatly simplifies Medicaid eligibility, but builds on the platform of the prior law and retains many of its categories and distinctions. We will first describe traditional Medicaid eligibility; then turn to the Affordable Care Act's Medicaid eligibility rules, and conclude by examining how the Supreme Court's Decision changes eligibility.

Who are the categories of "deserving" poor traditionally covered by Medicaid? Historically the categories of mandatory eligibiles that states had to cover included the aged, blind, and permanently and totally disabled, who were either eligible for assistance under the Federal Supplemental Security Income Program (SSI) or, if a state elected the "209(b)" option, persons who would have been eligible for state assistance under the eligibility requirements in effect in 1972 for the earlier state Aid to the Aged, Blind and Disabled program. They were also dependent children and their caretaker relatives who were eligible for assistance under the former federal/state Aid to Families with Dependent Children Program (AFDC). These groups were known as the "categorically needy" and states that participate in the Medicaid program have historically been required to cover these groups. In the 1980s, poor children and pregnant women were added as mandatory coverage categories.

The deserving poor also include a whole host of "optional categorically needy," a variety of groups that states can choose to cover, but who then must be provided the full scope of benefits offered the categorically needy. 42 C.F.R. § 435.201. These groups are typically other children, parents, aged, and disabled who have too much income to fit in the mandatory eligibility groups that states have to cover. Such groups also include persons who would be eligible for Medicaid if institutionalized, but who are instead receiving services in the community. 42 C.F.R. §§ 436.217.

States have also from the beginning been permitted to cover a third group, the "medically needy" if they choose to do so. The medically needy are categorically-related (aged, disabled, blind, or families with dependent children) persons whose income exceeds the financial eligibility levels established by the states, but who incur regular medical expenses that, when deducted from their income, bring their net disposable income below the eligibility level for financial assistance. The medically needy are generally persons in need of expensive nursing home or hospital care. The medically needy program is effectively a catastrophic health insurance program that covers many Americans who were comfortably middle-class until their need for long-term care consumed their life savings.

Traditionally, Medicaid eligibility was conditioned not just on income but also on assets—Medicaid recipients could only possess nominal assets, other than their home. This continues to be true for some categories of Medicaid recipients, but not for the Medicaid expansion population, as is described below.

Over time the link between cash assistance and Medicaid eligibility has further frayed, particularly after the abolition of the Aid to Families with Dependent Children program in 1996. Nevertheless, except in states operating under waiver programs, eligibility has continued to require membership in some category of the "deserving poor." Absent a waiver, federal Medicaid law has prohibited states from covering non-disabled adults who are not parents.

2.   The ACA Medicaid Expansions

The Patient Protection and Affordable Care Act represents the biggest change in the Medicaid program in its history, leading Justice Roberts to opine that the change was "a shift in kind, not merely in degree." Sections 2001 and 2002 of the ACA create a new category of Medicaid eligibility that includes adults age 19–64 with household incomes that do not exceed 133 percent of the federal poverty level and who are not pregnant, covered by Medicare, or otherwise entitled to Medicaid. (In 2013,

133 percent of the poverty level is $15, 282 for an individual and $31,322 for a family of four.) In fact, although the statute sets the eligibility level at 133 percent of poverty, to this is added a 5 percent income disregard, raising the effective eligibility level to 138 percent. This "newly-eligible" category of Medicaid provides Medicaid coverage for many adults who did not fit within any of the previous eligibility categories but are in fact poor. Medicaid eligibility for this "newly-eligible" category will be based solely on income, with no asset test. Of course, under the *Florida* decision, states can now decide whether to participate in the expansion or stick with traditional Medicaid. If states choose to expand Medicaid, however, they must cover the entire expansion population up to 138 percent of the poverty level if they want to take advantage of the enhanced federal match for this population (see below).

Even in states that participate in the expansion, however, categories of eligibility are still important. First, different income counting rules apply for different categories of Medicaid eligibility. Eligibility for the "newly-eligible" adult category, as well as pregnant women and children will be based on "modified adjusted gross income,, the same approach as that is used for the new private insurance subsidies. "Modified adjusted gross income" (MAGI) takes into account virtually all income, although, as already noted, the ACA excludes five percentage points of income from consideration. By contrast, many adults who currently qualify for Medicaid are subject to much lower eligibility levels in many states, but are often eligible for a variety of income disregards, including some of their earned income, child care and child support, which will no longer be recognized after 2013. Current income and asset eligibility rules will continue to apply to some individuals who are not part of the expansion group, including individuals who are eligible for Medicaid because of their eligibility for Supplemental Security Income or other benefits, persons who are 65 or older, the medically needy, or persons dually-eligible for Medicaid and Medicare. Different income computation rules also apply to individuals and families who qualify based upon age or disability and those receiving nursing facility services or home-and community-based care services.

States that participate in the Medicaid expansion under the terms of the ACA will receive an enhanced Federal Medical Assistance Percentage for the "newly-eligible" category: 100 percent for 2014, 2015 and 2016, 95 percent for 2017, 94 percent for 2018, 93 percent for 2019, and 90 percent for 2020 and thereafter. States currently receive FMAP ranging from 50 to around 74 percent, and will continue to receive this level of funding for the traditional Medicaid population. States that already cover the expansion population will receive federal assistance for the expansion population at lower percentage levels initially, but federal funding will gradually increase until it reaches the levels received by expansion states. The Congressional Budget Office has estimated that the Medicaid (and CHIP) expansions, if fully implemented in all states would cost the federal government $642 billion between 2012 and 2022, while they will cost the states about $41 billion. The states have argued, however, that the reforms will increase their Medicaid expenditures substantially more than this amount, in part because it will increase enrollment in traditional Medicaid. The reconciliation bill also increased Medicaid funding for the territories.

If implemented nationwide, this "newly-eligible" category of adults in Medicaid would increase Medicaid coverage by 11 million recipients by 2019 over the 32 million Americans who already receive Medicaid, accounting for almost a third of those newly insured under the Affordable Care Act. Most Americans with a full-time minimum-wage job (at current minimum wage levels) would be eligible for Medicaid under the Medicaid expansions. In 39 states, parents would become eligible for Medicaid who are not eligible under current standards if those states decide to expand; all but five of the states could provide broader coverage for childless adults than they do now. See The Henry J. Kaiser Family Foundation, Medicaid and Children's Health Insurance Program Provisions in the New Health Reform Law (2010).

Medicaid coverage is limited to U.S. citizens and qualified aliens (except in emergency situations). Until 2006, an applicant could attest citizenship under penalty of perjury. Under the 2006 Deficit Reduction Act, however, a Medicaid applicant needed to prove citizenship, using a U.S. passport, certificate of citizenship or of naturalization, a valid driver's license in states that require proof of citizenship to get a license, or a combination of two specified documents (such as a birth certificate and voter registration card). The ACA makes establishing citizenship somewhat easier. Under the ACA, citizenship will be verified either through documentation supplied by the applicant or through data matches with the Social Security Administration or Homeland Security.

The cost of the Medicaid expansions to the states has become a major bone of contention as implementation is moving forward. Opponents of the ACA have argued that the ACA Medicaid expansions will impose a crushing burden on the states. Supporters, on the other hand, contend that the ACA will actually save money for the states. As noted above, the ACA does provide enhanced federal funding for the expansion population. On the other hand, maintenance-of-effort provisions limit the ability of states to cut Medicaid spending prior to 2014.. Streamlined eligibility determinations, the ability of hospitals to make presumptive eligibility requirements, and, for a few higher-income Medicaid eligibles, the minimum coverage requirement (discussed in Chapter 7), will likely increase participation in traditional Medicaid, and thus state spending. See, for contrasting perspectives, January Angeles, Jagadeesh Gokale, How Medicaid's Expansion will Impact State Budgets (Center on Budget and Policy

Priorities, 2012); Michael Tanner, Medicaid Expansion Would Lead to Unsustainable Growth (Cato, 2012).

Even if the Medicaid expansion imposes some additional costs on the states, there are many reasons for states to participate in the expansion. First, the ACA offers no other form of assistance to individuals not otherwise eligible for Medicaid whose household incomes fall below 100 percent of the poverty level. Premium tax credits will be available to individuals with household incomes below 100 and 133 percent of poverty, although they will have to pay premiums for coverage and will face higher cost-sharing than they would under Medicaid. This population will presumably continue to receive uncompensated care, thus hospitals and other providers will face serious financial consequences in states that refuse to expand. The pressure on hospitals will be particularly strong because the ACA also makes significant cuts to Medicaid disproportionate share hospital payments (payments to hospitals that treat a disproportionate number of poor patients) on the assumption that such payments will no longer by as needed once Medicaid is expanded. Presumably most of the expansion population would receive Medicaid through managed care plans, so managed care companies also will lose big in states that do not expand. Individuals with incomes between 100 and 133 percent of poverty who live in states that choose not to expand Medicaid will have to purchase insurance using premium tax credits or pay the individual responsibility penalty. Employers in non-expansion states who fail to offer affordable and adequate insurance whose employees with incomes below 133 percent of poverty will owe employer responsibility penalties, which they would not face if their employees received Medicaid. States that expand Medicaid are likely to save state funds that would have been spent for the uninsured and for their mental health programs. Finally, citizens of states that refuse the expansion will still have to pay federal taxes to finance the expansion in states that do expand. In sum, there is every reason for states to expand, few reasons other than politics not to expand.

In spite of this, the Medicaid expansion has proved very controversial. As many as half of the states may not proceed with the Medicaid expansion on January 1, 2014, although more are likely to do so later.

B. BENEFITS

PROBLEM: MEDICAID BENEFITS

Each member of the Sawatsky family needs medical services. Elzbieta is in the hospital and needs a hip replacement and a nursing home placement. Stanislaus needs to take regularly an expensive medication for his heart, and worries that he may need another bypass operation like the one he had last year. Peter badly needs some dental work. Maria, of course, needs prenatal care and will soon need maternity care. The teacher of the seven-year-old boy claims that he has attention deficit disorder, while the five year-old needs glasses and the one-year old has recurrent earaches. If the Sawatsky's are entitled to Medicaid, to what services are they entitled? What problems might they encounter in receiving covered services?

1. Traditional Medicaid Benefits

As with eligibility, the benefits provided by Medicaid programs have historically varied significantly from state to state. This variation will continue after the ACA is implemented, although coverage of the expansion population should become more uniform. This section first describes the benefits covered by traditional Medicaid law, which continues to apply to the non-expansion population. It then describes an option created by the Deficit Reduction Act of 2005 that allows states to provide certain Medicaid beneficiaries with "benchmark" or "benchmark equivalent" coverage. It next discusses provisions in the ACA that require benchmark coverage to comply with essential health benefits requirements in the ACA and require states to provide benchmark coverage to newly eligible adults (although, with approval from HHS, states can offer their traditional Medicaid package to the expansion population if it covers essential health benefit services.) This section concludes with information about new services made available under the ACA.

The Medicaid statute lists several categories of mandatory services that States are required to provide the traditional categorically needy: inpatient hospital services; outpatient hospital services and rural health clinic services; other laboratory and X-ray services; nursing facility services; rural health clinic (RHC) and federally-qualified health center (FQHC) services; early and periodic screening, diagnostic and treatment (EPSDT) services for children; family planning services and supplies; physicians' services; and nurse-midwife and other certified nurse practitioner services. 42 U.S.C.A. § 1396a(a)(10)(A). State must also provide transportation to and from medically necessary care. The Medicaid statute also identifies about three dozen categories of optional services that states may cover for traditional Medicaid recipients, but also permits coverage under a final category coverage of "any other medical care, and any other type of remedial care recognized under State law, specified by the Secretary." 42 U.S.C.A. § 1396d(a)(28). At least one state has covered acupuncture under this category. Every state covered some optional services, most notably prescription drugs.

States have had considerably more discretion in the benefits that they provide to the medically needy. There have been some limits to this discretion, however. States that provide institutional services for any group   must   also   cover   ambulatory   services,   42   U.S.C.A.

§ 1396a(a)(10)(C)(iii)(I). Moreover, if a state covers institutional care for the mentally ill or retarded, it must also provide them with either the services it provides to the categorically needy or any seven services offered generally to Medicaid recipient. If a state covers nursing facility services, it must also pay for home health services, 42 U.S.C.A. § 1396a(a)(10)(C)(iv). What policy considerations explain these requirements?

Some Medicaid services are aimed at specific population groups. The most prominent example of these is the EPSDT program, which requires not only that states provide screening to diagnose physical or mental conditions in children, but also obligates states to provide treatment for identified conditions, whether or not the services required are otherwise included in its Medicaid plan. Medicaid must continue to cover EPSDT services for children even after the 2014 expansions. Much of the litigation challenging state Medicaid programs has involved the EPSTD program. See, e.g., Frew v. Hawkins, 540 U.S.431, 124 S.Ct. 899, 157 L.Ed.2d 855 (2004); Oklahoma Chapter of the American Academy of Pediatrics v. Fogarty, 472 F.3d 1208 (10th Cir. 2007); Westside Mothers v. Olszewski, 454 F.3d. 532 (6th Cir. 2006); Pediatric Specialty Care, Inc. v. Arkansas Department of Human Serv's, 293 F.3d 472 (8th Cir. 2002); Antrican v. Odom, 290 F.3d 178 (4th Cir. 2002).

Under traditional Medicaid law, a state's Medicaid plan is required to specify the "amount, duration, and scope" for each category of service that it provided for the categorically needy and each group of the medically needy. 42 C.F.R. § 440.230(a). Each service must be of sufficient amount, duration, and scope to achieve its purpose reasonably. 42 C.F.R. § 440.230(b). The Medicaid agency is not allowed arbitrarily to deny or reduce the amount, duration, or scope of a required service solely because of the diagnosis, type of illness, or condition. 42 C.F.R. § 440.230(c). States can refuse to cover specified optional categories of services (such as eyeglasses or dental care), but if they cover a service, they could not simply decide to cover it for some medical diagnoses or conditions and not for others. Thus a state's provision covering eyeglasses for individuals suffering from eye disease, but not for individuals with refractive error, was invalidated, White v. Beal, 555 F.2d 1146 (3d Cir.1977), as was a $50,000 cap on payment for hospital services which precluded coverage of $200,000 liver transplants, Montoya v. Johnston, 654 F.Supp. 511 (W.D.Tex.1987), and a state's refusal to cover sex reassignment surgery (which would fall within the general mandatory categories of hospital and physician services), Smith v. Rasmussen, 57 F.Supp.2d 736 (N.D.Iowa 1999). Although some courts have held that the benefits of a state Medicaid program are sufficient if they meet the needs of the Medicaid population of the state as a whole, (Desario v. Thomas, 139 F.3d 80, 95 (2d Cir. 1998) cert. granted, judgment vacated on other grds, sub nom. Slekis v.

Thomas, 525 U.S. 1098, 119 S.Ct. 864, 142 L.Ed.2d 767 (1999); Charleston Mem. Hosp. v. Conrad, 693 F.2d 324 (4th Cir. 1982)) most circuits have held that Medicaid must fund all medically necessary services (see Hern v. Beye, 57 F.3d 906, 911 (10th Cir. 1995); Dexter v. Kirschner, 984 F.2d 979, 983 (9th Cir. 1992)), which seems also to be the position of CMS (Koenning v. Suehs, 2012 WL 4127956 (S.D. Tex. 2012); T.L. v. Colo. Dept. of Health Care Pol'y and Fin., 42 P.3d 63, 66 (2002)).

2. Benchmark and Benchmark–Equivalent Coverage

The Deficit Reduction Act of 2005 (actually adopted in 2006), created a new benchmark or benchmark-equivalent coverage option allowing state Medicaid plans to ignore requirements regarding mandatory and optional service coverage, state-wideness, freedom of choice, and comparability with respect to most children and parents and to pregnant women with incomes above 133 percent of poverty. A number of groups remain subject to the preexisting laws governing benefits, however, including aged, blind, and disabled SSI recipients; dually-eligible Medicare beneficiaries; most institutionalized recipients; the medically frail; pregnant women with incomes not exceeding 133 percent of poverty; and the medically needy. The ACA specifically requires benchmark or benchmark-equivalent coverage for the adult expansion population.

Benchmark coverage is coverage that is pegged to private insurance available in the state or, with HHS approval, to the traditional Medicaid package offered to other Medicaid-eligibles. A state may choose a benchmark plan from several options, including the standard Blue Cross/Blue Shield PPO option under the Federal Employees Health Benefit Plan, the HMO plan with the largest commercial enrollment in state, any generally-available state employees plan (regardless of whether anyone actually enrolls in it), or any plan approved by HHS. Alternatively, states my choose a plan that covers a list of services and is the actuarial equivalent of a benchmark plan. Benchmark equivalent coverage can also cover the traditional Medicaid services.

Under section 2001 of the ACA, "benchmark" or "benchmark-equivalent" coverage, must, as of 2014, cover at least the categories of essential health benefits that must be offered by qualified health plans under Title I of the ACA and, with limited exceptions, meet mental health parity requirements. Prior to 2014, they must cover physician, hospital, laboratory and X-ray, well-baby and well-child, and preventive services and prescription drugs. Benchmark and benchmark-equivalent coverage must also cover EPSDT services for children and rural health clinic and federally qualified health center services.

The ACA also requires states to make available premium subsidies for Medicaid-eligible individuals covered by employer coverage rather than cover them under Medicaid directly if it is cost effective to do so.

States cannot, however, require Medicaid recipients to enroll in employer coverage.

Because many individuals and families will frequently move back and forth between Medicaid and premium tax credit coverage as their income fluctuates, and because many families will have children covered by Medicaid or CHIP and parents covered by premium tax credits, it is very important that plans be available through the exchange that serve both Medicaid recipients and premium tax credit beneficiaries. The fact that Medicaid plans must offer the essential benefits package will facilitate this. HHS Guidance, however, indicates that the essential health benefits plan provided under Medicaid need not be the same as that provided by nongroup and small group private insurance plans. It is important, nonetheless, that states align these packages as much as possible. It is also vital that plans offer the same provider networks to both Medicaid recipients and tax-credit beneficiaries so that families will not need to change providers as they move back and forth between programs.

Several provisions of the ACA offer Medicaid recipients additional benefits. Section 2301 requires the states to offer coverage for freestanding (non-hospital) birth centers and for the providers—such as nurse midwives and birth attendants recognized under state law—who staff them. Section 2302 permits children in hospice care to receive concurrently Medicaid payment for services for medical treatment of the terminal illness. Section 4106 offers a 1 percent increase in federal funding to states that offer the preventive services that are recommended by the U.S. Preventive Services Task Force with an A or B grade and recommended immunizations without cost-sharing for the cost of those services, while Section 4107 requires Medicaid coverage of smoking cessation programs for pregnant women.

The ACA also includes a number of provisions intended to encourage the states to provide long-term care for Medicaid recipients in the community rather than in nursing homes. States can already cover community-based personal care services through three avenues: by covering personal care in their state plan, through the home-and community-based-services state plan option, or via home-and community-based waiver services. Section 2401 of the ACA gives states yet a fourth option, offering states an enhanced federal match that is 6 percent higher than the other alternatives.

The ACA requires HHS to promulgate regulations to ensure that states develop coordinated and effective, non-institutionally-based, long-term care services and supports. The law gives states a great deal of flexibility in determining eligibility and scope of services for home-and community-based care. States may, for example, use need-based criteria for individuals with family income up to 300 percent of the poverty level and offer home-and community-based care services that are different in type, amount, duration, and scope to individuals who have higher levels of need as demonstrated by specific need-based criteria. The ACA also includes additional financial incentives for states that have an imbalance toward nursing facility care to increase home-and community-based care. For a five-year period beginning in 2014, the ACA extends to the spouses of individuals receiving home-and community-based care the same protections against impoverishment that are available to the spouses of institutionalized persons.

Finally, the ACA includes a number of state options and demonstration projects intended to improve the quality and coordination of care offered Medicaid recipients. These include provisions for improving the coordination of care for persons eligible for both Medicare and Medicaid ("dual-eligibles"); demonstration projects for pediatric accountable care organizations, global payment systems, integrated care around a hospitalization, and state options for providing health homes to enrollees with chronic conditions. The law also provides for payment adjustments to states for health care acquired conditions, such as hospital-acquired infections, to penalize hospitals that permit such conditions to develop. Finally, section 10211 adds a new program to provide support for pregnant and parenting teens and women, funded at $25 million a year for 10 years.

NOTES AND QUESTIONS

1.   Who should make coverage decisions under the Medicaid program: the personal physicians of beneficiaries, low level state bureaucrats, national professional consensus groups, grass roots consensus panels? What should be the relationship between the federal and state governments in making coverage decisions? In particular, what role should the federal courts play?

2.   The additional flexibility provided the states by the DRA for benefit coverage merely supplements the flexibility already provided under § 1115 of the Social Security Act which authorizes demonstration projects. Since the beginning of the Medicaid program, the federal government has under this provision permitted the states to deviate from federal Medicaid requirements to conduct "demonstration" projects (42 U.S.C. § 1315). Section 1115 is discussed further below.

C. PAYMENT FOR SERVICES

1. Fee-for-Service Medicaid

The original vision of the Medicaid program was that it would provide mainstream care for its recipients. In line with this dream, the Medicaid statute guaranteed recipients free choice of participating providers. 42 U.S.C.A. § 1396a(a)(23). With respect to access to physician services, however, this goal has always been more a dream than a reality. Physicians also have freedom of choice as to whether or not to participate in Medicaid. Medicaid physician fee schedules have been largely driven by state budget constraints, and low Medicaid fees have discouraged physician participation in the program. On average, Medicaid only pays physicians about 72 percent of what Medicare pays (which is less than commercial rates), but some states only pay 40 percent of Medicare rates, or less. Low payment levels, along with paperwork and billing hassles and possibly the characteristics of Medicaid recipients, have contributed to low physician participation in Medicaid. Nationally, about three quarters of physicians participate in Medicaid and CHIP, although fewer than half of these accept all new children covered by these programs and nine percent are not accepting any new Medicaid patients. Over 80 percent, moreover, report difficulty in referring Medicaid and CHIP patients to specialists, compared to about a quarter of doctors referring privately insured patients. GAO, Most Physicians Serve Covered Children but have Difficulty Referring them for Specialty Care (2011).

Fee-for-service Medicaid recipients have also received a distinctive sort of physician care. One study of pediatricians who treated a high volume of Medicaid patients in New York City, for example, found that ninety-one percent had attended medical schools outside the United States, only forty-two percent were board certified (compared to eighty-nine percent statewide), and only 49 percent had hospital admitting privileges. Gerry Fairbrother, et al., New York City Physicians Serving High Volumes of Medicaid Children, 32 Inquiry 345 (Fall 1995). When physicians are not readily available, Medicaid recipients have often had to rely on hospital outpatient clinics and emergency rooms for primary care.

Hospitals and nursing homes are more limited in their ability to refuse Medicaid patients. Many hospitals are obligated to serve Medicaid patients because of their tax-exempt status or because of lingering obligations under the Hill–Burton program. Many nursing homes also are not able to count on enough private pay business to permit them to decline Medicaid participation.

Prior to 1997 federal law required that the states pay hospitals and nursing homes "reasonable" rates, and many lawsuits were brought by providers challenging low state rates. The 1997 Balanced Budget Act repealed these provisions, but did not end litigation over Medicaid rates. Current federal Medicaid law requires payment rates to be "consistent with efficiency, economy, and quality of care and * * * sufficient to enlist enough providers so that care and services are available under the plan at least to the extent that such care and services are available to the general population in the geographic area." 42 U.S.C.A. § 1396a(a)(30). The federal appellate courts have generally in recent years held that this provision does not create a federal right in providers, enforceable under § 1983. (See below) See Sanchez v. Johnson, 416 F.3d. 1051 (9th Cir. 2005); Long

Term Care Pharmacy Alliance v. Ferguson, 362 F.3d 50 (1st Cir.2004) Pennsylvania Pharmacists Ass'n v. Houstoun, 283 F.3d 531 (3rd Cir.2002). See also Evergreen Presbyterian Ministries v. Hood, 235 F.3d 908 (5th Cir.2000) (beneficiaries have right to sue under equal access provision, but not providers). See Abigail Moncrieff, Payments to Medicaid Doctors: Interpreting the Equal Access Provisions, 73 U. Chi. L. Rev. 673 (2006). Douglas v. Independent Living Center, set out below, addresses the question of whether this provision is enforceable under the Supremacy Clause.

HHS has proposed a regulatory approach to the problem of inadequate Medicaid provider participation. In May of 2011, HHS published a proposed rule that would require the states to review their Medicaid rates at least once every five years (and any time they reduced or restructured rates) to ensure that recipients have sufficient access to care, considering the extent to which enrollee needs are met, availability of care and providers, and changes in beneficiary utilization of services. Under the proposal, states must also provide opportunities for beneficiary input on access to care issues. If the survey identifies access issues, states must submit a corrective action plan and take steps to solve the problem within 12 months.

PROBLEM: REPRESENTING PROVIDERS IN MEDICAID LITIGATION

You represent a hospital association in a state that has just cut Medicaid hospital payments by five percent to address a state budget crisis. Do you challenge the cut through litigation, or do you rather try lobbying or grass-roots organizing? Do you sue in federal or state court if you litigate? What evidence would you present if you litigate under § 1396a(a)(30) (and if the court lets your proceed under this section) arguing that the rates do not meet the standards set forth in that section? What arguments and evidence would you expect the state to present? Would your strategy be different if you represented a group of physicians and physician payments were at issue?

2. Medicaid Cost Sharing

One strategy for controlling health care utilization and cost favored by conservative advocates is increased cost-sharing by consumers. Whatever merits this strategy may offer in the private sector, it has very limited possibilities in the Medicaid program because of the limited financial abilities of Medicaid recipients. Until 2006, the law permitted only very nominal cost-sharing for Medicaid recipients, and prohibited cost sharing altogether for children, pregnant women with respect to pregnancy-related services, terminally ill individuals in hospice, and institutionalized recipients. Perhaps most importantly, the law prohibited Medicaid providers from denying services to recipients who could not afford a co-payment.

The 2006 Deficit Reduction Act dramatically changed this. The DRA allowed cost-sharing for most services of up to ten percent of service cost for recipients with income of 100 to 150 percent of the poverty level, and up to twenty percent of the service cost for recipients with incomes above 150 percent of the poverty level, capped at five percent of total income. The DRA also allowed states to charge premiums for recipients with incomes above 150 percent of the poverty level. Cost-sharing is still prohibited for the recipient groups listed above, as well as for emergency and family planning services. Updated rules provide for copayments of up to $4 for outpatient visits for persons with incomes up to 100 percent of poverty and for $8 for nonemergency use of emergency rooms, $4 for preferred prescription drugs and $8 for non-preferred drugs for recipients with incomes up to 150 percent of poverty. States may allow participating providers to refuse services to recipients with household incomes above 100 percent of poverty who do not pay required cost-sharing amounts. What reasons can be given for imposing additional cost-sharing obligations on recipients? What effect might this have on access to services for recipients? See Bill J. Wright, et al., The Impact of Increased Cost Sharing on Medicaid Enrollees, 24 Health Aff. (4) 1106 (2005); Leighton Ku & Victoria Wachino, The Effect of Increased Cost–Sharing in Medicaid: A Summary of Research Findings (2005).

3. Medicaid Managed Care

Although the original vision of Medicaid was that recipients would have the same free choice of providers then enjoyed by the general population, Medicaid has in recent years, like private health insurance, moved dramatically in the direction of managed care. By 2011, 42 million Medicaid beneficiaries (74.2 percent) were enrolled in managed care, compared to 2.7 million in 1991. In twenty-eight states, over 75 percent of Medicaid recipients were enrolled in managed care, and in three states, 100 percent were enrolled. While most families and children are covered by managed care, the big push in the recent past has been to move disabled recipients to managed care as well. Medicaid managed care refers to both HMOs that receive capitated payments and Primary Care Case Management (PCCM) programs in which primary care providers received additional payments to serve as the primary care home for Medicaid enrollees who continue to receive services on a fee for service basis.

This move to managed care has been driven by several factors. The most important, perhaps, has been the hope of saving money. Managed care seemed to have cut costs in the private sector, and it was hoped that it would work for Medicaid as well. Managed care advocates claimed that it might not only reduce the price of services, but that it would also reduce inappropriate use of expensive services like emergency room care. The move to managed care was also driven by the hope, however, that it would increase access by Medicaid recipients to providers and improve quality and coordination of care. A number of states, including Tennessee and Oregon, also hoped that savings from managed care might enable them to expand coverage to low income uninsured not otherwise eligible for Medicaid.

Attempts to move Medicaid recipients to managed care were thwarted for a time by federal requirements that guaranteed Medicaid recipients free choice of providers. In the late 1980s and 1990s, however, it became increasingly common for states to seek waivers under §§ 1915(b) of the Social Security Act (42 U.S.C.A. § 1396n(b)) which permitted CMS to waive the freedom of choice requirement, or under § 1115 (42 U.S.C.A. § 1315), which permits CMS to waive virtually all statutory requirements in the context of approved research and demonstration projects.

The 1997 Balanced Budget Act amended the Medicaid statute to permit states to require recipients to enroll with Medicaid Managed Care (MMC) organizations or a primary care case manager. 42 U.S.C. § 1396u–2. States are not permitted, however, to require dual-eligible Medicare beneficiaries, Native Americans, or special needs children to enroll in managed care plans without federal permission. States must generally permit recipients a choice of two or more MMC plans, but this requirement is loosened in rural areas. 42 U.S.C.A. § 1396u–2(a)(3). Medicaid recipients who do not exercise their choice may be assigned by the State through a default enrollment process, and states may establish enrollment priorities for plans that are oversubscribed. 42 U.S.C.A. § 1396u–2(a)(4)(c) & (D). Recipients may terminate (or change) enrollment in an MMC organization for cause at any time, but may only do so without cause during the ninety day period following enrollment and once a year thereafter. 42 U.S.C.A. § 1396u–2(a)(4)(A). MMC plans are not permitted to discriminate on the basis of health status or need for health service in enrollment, reenrollment, or disenrollment of recipients. 42 U.S.C.A. § 1396b(m)(2)(A)(v).

Medicaid managed care has, not surprisingly, a mixed record. Medicaid managed care is often very different from their normal lines of business. Medicaid recipients are needy and often plagued by chronic and expensive problems. Medicaid pays parsimoniously, but imposes demanding program requirements. In particular, it requires services that many commercial plans do not cover and coverage of populations that live in places where commercial plans do not have providers. Some providers that contract with commercial plans, moreover, are often not eager to have Medicaid recipients in their waiting rooms. Nonprofit plans tend to have lower administrative costs and offer better quality than commercial plans. Michael McCue and Michael Balit, Assessing the Financial Health of Medicaid Managed Care Plans and the Quality of Patient Care They Provide (Commonwealth Fund, 2011).

Medicaid managed care does, however, offer states the opportunity to shift the cost risk of covering Medicaid recipients to private insurers, and states have increasingly embraced this opportunity. There is some evidence that managed care saves the state and federal government money, and this is a powerful motivator for the states. See John Iglehart, Desperately Seeking Savings: States Shift More Medicaid Enrollees to Managed Care, 20 Health Aff. 1627 (2011). The ACA contains provisions for improving coordination of care for Medicare/Medicaid dual eligibles, including demonstration projects using managed care to coordinate Medicare and Medicaid services.

In the end, managed care has arguably proved more successful in Medicaid than in Medicare. In most states managed care has not saved Medicaid programs a great deal of money, but neither has it added to program cost. Several studies show that it has decreased dependence of Medicaid recipients on emergency rooms, but most studies show that access to care has otherwise been unaffected. In some states, however, money has been saved and access and quality improved. The bottom line seems to be that in some states Medicaid had so many problems before managed care that improvement was not difficult and was sometimes achieved. See Robert Hurley and Stephen Zuckerman, Medicaid Managed Care: State Flexibility in Action (2002). See also, discussing Medicaid managed care, Jane McCahill & Joseph T. Van Leer, The Challenges of Reform for Medicaid Managed Care, 21 Annals Health L. 541 (2012).

4. Medicaid Payment Under Health Care Reform

The ACA contains provisions increasing payments for some Medicaid providers, cutting payments for others. The legislation increases Medicaid payments for family and general practitioners and for pediatricians providing primary care services, to 100 percent of Medicare payment levels for 2013 and 2014 with a 100 percent federal match of increased state expenditures attributable to the requirement. Medicaid eligibility expansions will mean little if there are no practitioners to care for Medicaid recipients, so this provision will play a vital role in making Medicaid work. Unfortunately, this provision is limited to two years. The law also increases to $11 billion new appropriations for community health centers, which will also serve the new Medicaid recipients (as well as the immigrants excluded from the exchanges).

On the other hand, some ACA provisions reduce provider payments. Section 2501 increases the rebates that must be paid by drug manufacturers for pharmaceuticals covered by Medicaid, and claims all of the additional rebates for the federal government. Section 2551 reduces Medicaid disproportionate share hospital payments for the states, in part in recognition that the uncompensated care burden of hospitals should diminish as a higher proportion of the population is insured.

Section 2304 of the ACA provides that "medical assistance" includes provision of care and services as well as of payment of the cost of care and services. This provision was intended to clarify a misinterpretation of the Medicaid law found in some recent cases that had held that the states had only an obligation to pay for Medicaid services, not actually to make certain that services were actually available. See Equal Access for El Paso v. Hawkins, 562 F.3d 724, 728 (5th Cir. 2009) (finding reasonable promptness provision only required state to make reasonably prompt payments for services received and did not require state to take steps to ensure that recipients actually receive prompt medical care and services); Okla. Chap. of the Am. Acad. of Pediatrics v. Fogerty, 472 F.3d 1208, 1215 (10th Cir. 2007), cert. denied, 552 U.S. 813, (2007); and Mandy R. v. Owens, 464 F.3d 1139 (10th Cir. 2006), cert. denied, 549 U.S. 1305(2007).

Finally, Section 3021 of the Act creates a new Center for Medicare and Medicaid Innovation with broad authority to create new approaches to paying Medicare and Medicaid providers to improve quality and control cost. This Center is discussed further in the Medicare section of this chapter.

D. PROGRAM ADMINISTRATION AND FINANCING: FEDERAL/STATE RELATIONSHIPS

Perhaps the most contentious of all of the controversial issues surrounding the Medicaid program has been the nature of the relationship between the federal and state governments in setting policy and administering the program. This is the primary issue addressed by the Florida case, with which we began this section. Particularly controversial has been the role of the federal courts in enforcing the rights that the program affords recipients and providers.

As of this writing in late 2012, Medicaid is still a federal entitlement program administered and partially funded by the states. It is an entitlement program in the sense that the federal Medicaid statute and regulations create at least some rights under federal law enforceable against the states. The federal government also contributes a share of the Medicaid program's cost, known as Federal Financial Participation or FFP, which currently ranges from 50 percent to 74 percent.

The Medicaid program is also in a very real sense a state program. As should be clear by now, state legislatures and Medicaid agencies have significant discretion in deciding what groups to cover (reinforced by the Florida decision), which benefits to provide, how much to pay for benefits, and how to provide benefits. Nevertheless, states often consider the federal role in the Medicaid program as intrusive and oppressive.

Medicaid state programs are subject to federal oversight at several levels. States must submit a Medicaid state plan to CMS demonstrating that their programs conform with the federal statutes and regulations. If a state Medicaid program ceases to be in substantial compliance with federal requirements, CMS may, after a hearing, terminate federal funding to the state. Because this remedy is so drastic, CMS has rarely convened a hearing and has never terminated a state program. Additional statutory provisions permit HHS to disallow reimbursement claimed by the state where the services covered by the state (such as elective abortions) are not eligible for reimbursement, 42 C.F.R. §§ 457.204, 457.212. These provisions are used more frequently, and occasionally result in litigation between the federal government and the states. For an excellent review of the range of administrative law issues involved in the governance of the Medicaid Program, see Eleanor Kinney, Rule and Policy Making for the Medicaid Program: A Challenge to Federalism, 51 Ohio St.L.J. 855 (1990).

Perhaps most objectionable to the states, however, is the fact that the courts have for decades permitted both recipients and providers a federal cause of action under 42 U.S.C.A. § 1983 to sue for violations of rights guaranteed by the Medicaid statute. See, e.g., Wilder v. Virginia Hosp. Ass'n, 496 U.S. 498, 110 S.Ct. 2510, 110 L.Ed.2d 455 (1990); Doe v. Chiles, 136 F.3d 709 (11th Cir.1998). The courts have also held that Medicaid recipients and providers can obtain injunctive relief against the states to compel compliance with the Medicaid statute, even though the Eleventh Amendment bars damage actions against the states for past violations of the Act. Edelman v. Jordan, 415 U.S. 651, 94 S.Ct. 1347, 39 L.Ed.2d 662 (1974).

The 2001 lower court decision in Westside Mothers v. Haveman, 133 F.Supp.2d 549 (E.D. Mich. 2001), sent shockwaves through the Medicaid advocacy community. It effectively held that Medicaid was no longer a federal entitlement (i.e. the rights of Medicaid recipients and, by extension, providers, were no longer enforceable in federal court under § 1983, and actions to enforce them prospectively were barred by the Eleventh Amendment). In 2002, the district court decision was reversed, in a Sixth Circuit opinion that thoroughly explores the legal nature of the Medicaid entitlement:

WESTSIDE MOTHERS V. HAVEMAN

United States Court of Appeals, Sixth Circuit, 2002.
289 F.3d 852.

MERRITT, CIRCUIT JUDGE.

This suit filed under 42 U.S.C. § 1983 alleges that the state of Michigan has failed to provide services required by the Medicaid program. Plaintiffs, Westside Mothers, * * * allege that defendants James Haveman, director of the Michigan Department of Community Health,* * * did not provide the early and periodic screening, diagnosis, and treatment services mandated by the Medicaid Act and related laws.

*   *   *

At issue here is the federal requirement that participating states provide "early and periodic screening, diagnostic, and treatment services . . . for individuals who are eligible under the plan and are under the age of 21." *Id.* § 1396d(a)(4)(B)[ ]. The required services include periodic physical examinations, immunizations, laboratory tests, health education, *see* 42 U.S.C. § 1396d(r)(1), eye examinations, eyeglasses, *see id.* § 1396d(r)(2), teeth maintenance, *see id.* § 1396d(r)(3), diagnosis and treatment of hearing disorders, and hearing aids, *see id.* § 1396d(r)(4).

In 1999, plaintiffs sued the named defendants under § 1983, which creates a cause of action against any person who under color of state law deprives an individual of "any right, privileges, or immunities secured by the Constitution and laws" of the United States. 42 U.S.C. § 1983. They alleged that the defendants had refused or failed to implement the Medicaid Act, its enabling regulations and its policy requirements, by (1) refusing to provide, and not requiring * * * HMOs [participating in the Medicaid program] to provide, the comprehensive examinations required by §§ 1396a(a)(43) and 1396d(r)(1) and 42 C.F.R. § 441.57; (2) not requiring participating HMOs to provide the necessary health care, diagnostic services, and treatment required by § 1396d(r)(5); (3) not effectively informing plaintiffs of the existence of the screening and treatment services, as required by § 1396a(a)(43); (4) failing to provide plaintiffs the transportation and scheduling help needed to take advantage of the screening and treatment services, as required by § 1396a(a)(43)(B) and 42 C.F.R. § 441.62; and (5) developing a Medicaid program which lacks the capacity to deliver to eligible children the care required by §§ 1396(a)(8), 1396a(a)(30)(A), and 1396u–2(b)(5).[ ]

Defendants moved to dismiss the plaintiffs and for dismissal of the suit. * * *

In March 2001 the district court granted defendants' motion to dismiss all remaining claims. *See Westside Mothers v. Haveman,* 133 F.Supp.2d 549, 553 (E.D.Mich.2001). In a detailed and far-reaching opinion, the district court held that Medicaid was only a contract between a state and the federal government, that spending-power programs such as Medicaid were not supreme law of the land, that the court lacked jurisdiction over the case because Michigan was the "real defendant and therefore possess[ed] sovereign immunity against suit," *id.,* that in this case *Ex parte Young* was unavailable to circumvent the state's sovereign immunity, and that even if it were available §§ 1983 does not create a cause of action available to plaintiffs to enforce the provisions in question.

This appeal followed. We reverse on all issues presented.

Analysis

A.   Medicaid Contracts and the Spending Power

Much of the district court's decision rests on its initial determinations that the Medicaid program is only a contract between the state and federal government and that laws passed by Congress pursuant to its power under the Spending Clause are not "supreme law of the land." We address these in turn.

1.   Whether Medicaid is only a contract.—The district court held that "the Medicaid program is a contract between Michigan and the Federal government." [ ] The program, it points out, is not mandatory; states choose whether to participate. [ ] If a state does choose to participate, Congress may then "condition receipt of federal moneys upon compliance by the recipient with federal statutory and administrative directives." [ ]

To characterize precisely the legal relationship formed between a state and the federal government when such a program is implemented, the district court turned to two Supreme Court opinions on related subjects. In *Pennhurst State School and Hosp. v. Halderman* ("*Pennhurst I*"), the Court described the Medicaid program as "much in the nature of a contract," and spoke of the " 'contract' " formed between the state and the federal government. [ ] * * *

Justice Scalia expanded on this contract analogy in his concurrence in *Blessing v. Freestone.* He maintained that the relationship was "in the nature of a contract" because:

> The state promises to provide certain services to private individuals, in exchange for which the Federal government promises to give the State funds. In contract law, when such an arrangement is made (A promises to pay B money, in exchange for which B promises to provide services to C), the person who receives the benefit of the exchange of promises between two others C is called a third-party beneficiary.

520 U.S. 329, 349, 117 S.Ct. 1353, 137 L.Ed.2d 569 (1997) (Scalia, J., concurring).

Drawing on above language, the district judge then concluded that the "Medicaid program is a contract between Michigan and the Federal government," [ ] * * * The only significant difference between Medicaid and an ordinary contract, he asserted, is "the sovereign status of the parties," which limits the available remedies each can seek against the other. [ ]

Contrary to this narrow characterization, the Court in *Pennhurst I* makes clear that it is using the term "contract" metaphorically, to illuminate certain aspects of the relationship formed between a state and the federal government in a program such as Medicaid. It does not say that Medicaid is *only* a contract. It describes the program as "much in the nature of" a contract, and places the term "contract" in quotation marks when using it alone. [ ] It did not limit the remedies to common law contract remedies or suggested that normal federal question doctrines do not apply. * * *

Binding precedent has put the issue to rest. The Supreme Court has held that the conditions imposed by the federal government pursuant to statute upon states participating in Medicaid and similar programs are not merely contract provisions; they are federal laws. In Bennett v. Kentucky Department of Education, Kentucky argued that a federal-state grant agreement "should be viewed in the same manner as a bilateral contract." 470 U.S. 656, 669, 105 S.Ct. 1544, 84 L.Ed.2d 590 (1985). The Court rejected this approach, holding that, "[u]nlike normal contractual undertakings, federal grant programs originate in and remain governed by statutory provisions expressing the judgment of Congress concerning desirable public policy." * * *

2.   *Whether acts passed under the Spending Power are Supreme Law of the Land.*—After holding that Medicaid is only a contract to pay money enacted under the spending power, the district court then held that programs enacted pursuant to the Constitution's spending power are not the "supreme law of the land" and do not give rise to remedies invoked for the violation of federal statutes.[ ] Relying on its determination that Medicaid and similar programs are "contracts consensually entered into by the States with the Federal Government . . . ," the district court then reasons that they are "not statutory enactments by which States must automatically submit to federal prerogatives." [ ]. There are two ways to understand this passage. One is that the district court is merely following the logic of its previous finding, and holding that federal-state programs are not supreme law because they are only contracts. We have already rejected the line of reasoning that begins with the assumption that Medicaid is only a contract.

The district court may also be claiming that acts passed under the spending power are not supreme law because the spending power only gives Congress the power to set up these programs, not to force states to participate in them.* * * *South Dakota* [v. Dole] upholds the power of Congress to place conditions on a state's receipt of federal funds. 483 U.S. at 211–12, 107 S.Ct. 2793. *Pennhurst I* holds that if Congress wishes to impose obligations on states that choose to participate in volitional spending power programs, it must make the obligations explicit. 451 U.S. at 25, 101 S.Ct. 1531.

* * *

The district court acknowledges that "the Supreme Court has in the past held that federal-state cooperative programs enacted under the Spending Power fall within the ambit of the Supremacy Clause." [ ] It then states that in "recent years . . . the Supreme Court has conducted a more searching analysis of the nature and extent of the Supremacy Clause," suggesting erroneously that its departure from precedent is dictated by recent Supreme Court jurisprudence. [ ] * * * The well-established principle that acts passed under Congress's spending power are supreme law has not been abandoned in recent decisions.

* * *

B.   Whether the Suit is Barred Under Sovereign Immunity

The district court next held that the plaintiffs' suit is foreclosed by doctrines of sovereign immunity because Michigan is the "real party at interest" in the suit and plaintiffs cannot invoke any of the exceptions to sovereign immunity that would allow their suit. [ ]

> As explained by the Supreme Court in many cases, sovereign
> immunity, though partially codified in the Eleventh Amendment,
> is a basic feature of our federal system. [ ] * * *

Under the doctrine developed in *Ex parte Young* and its progeny, a suit that claims that a state official's actions violate the constitution or federal law is not deemed a suit against the state, and so barred by sovereign immunity, so long as the state official is the named defendant and the relief sought is only equitable and prospective. [ ]

Of course, *Ex parte Young* is a "fiction" to the extent it sharply distinguishes between a state and an officer acting on behalf of the state, but it is a necessary fiction, required to maintain the balance of power between state and federal governments. "The availability of prospective relief of the sort awarded in *Ex parte Young* gives life to the Supremacy Clause."[ ] * * * On its surface this case fits squarely within *Ex parte Young*. Plaintiffs allege an ongoing violation of federal law, the Medicaid Act, and seek prospective equitable relief, an injunction ordering the named state officials henceforth to comply with the law.

The district court nonetheless held that *Ex parte Young* was inapplicable for four separate reasons. Two can be quickly dismissed. First, it held that plaintiffs could not invoke *Ex parte Young* because that doctrine can only be invoked to enforce federal laws that are supreme law of the land. [ ] Since we held above that spending clause enactments are supreme law of the land, they may be the basis for an *Ex parte Young* action. Second, the district court held *Ex parte Young* is unavailable because under this doctrine a court lacks "authority to compel state officers performing discretionary functions." [ ] This correctly states the holding in *Young,* but misunderstands what it means by "discretion." "An injunction to prevent [a state official] from doing that which he has no legal right to do is not an interference with the discretion of an officer." *Ex parte Young,* 209 U.S. at 159, 28 S.Ct. 441. Since the plaintiffs here claim that the defendants are acting unlawfully in refusing to implement mandatory elements of Medicaid's screening and treatment program, they seek only to prevent the defendants from doing "what [they] have no legal right to do," and their suit is permitted under *Ex parte Young.*

Third, the district court asserts that *Ex parte Young* is unavailable because the state "is the real party in interest when its officers act within their lawful authority." [ ] It has two reasons for finding Michigan the real party in interest. Its first reason follows from its finding that Medicaid is a contract. If Medicaid were only a contract, then this would be a suit seeking to compel a state to specific performance of a contract. Such suits are barred under a nineteenth century Supreme Court case, *In re Ayers*, 123 U.S. 443, 8 S.Ct. 164, 31 L.Ed. 216 (1887), which held that a "claim for injunctive relief against state officials under the Contracts Clause is barred by state sovereign immunity because the state [is] the real party at interest." [ ] We have already held that Medicaid is not merely a contract, but a federal statute. This suit seeks only to compel state officials to follow federal law, and thus is not barred by *Ayers.*

The district court also says erroneously that Michigan is the real party in interest because "[t]here is no personal, unlawful behavior attributed" to the defendants that plaintiffs seek to enjoin [ ]. In their initial complaint, plaintiffs make clear that they are suing the named defendants because of "their failure to provide children in Michigan . . . with essential medical, dental, and mental health services *as required by federal law.*" [ ]

Finally, the district court refused to allow plaintiffs to proceed under *Young* because of the Supreme Court's holding in *Seminole Tribe* that "[w]here Congress has prescribed a detailed remedial scheme for the enforcement against a State of a statutorily created right, a court should hesitate before casting aside those limitations and permitting an action against a state officer based upon *Ex parte Young.*" [ ] The Medicaid Act allows the Secretary of Health and Human Services to reduce or cut off funding to states that do not comply with the program's requirements.[ ] This one provision, the district court held, was a detailed remedial scheme sufficient to make *Ex parte Young* unavailable. [ ]

We disagree. In *Seminole Tribe,* the Supreme Court found *Ex parte Young* was unavailable because Congress had established a *"carefully crafted and intricate* remedial scheme. . . . for the enforcement of a *particular* federal right." [ ] The scheme here, in contrast, simply allows the Secretary to reduce or cut off funds if a state's program does not meet federal requirements. *See* 42 U.S.C. § 1396c. This is not a detailed "remedial" scheme sufficient to show Congress's intent to preempt an action under *Ex parte Young.* [ ]

Plaintiffs seek only prospective injunctive relief from a federal court against state officials for those officials' alleged violations of federal law, and they may proceed under *Ex parte Young.*

C.   Whether There is a Private Right of Action Under § 1983

Section 1983 imposes liability on anyone who under color of state law deprives a person of "rights, privileges, or immunities" secured by the laws or the constitution of the United States 42 U.S.C. § 1983. The Supreme Court and this court have held that in some circumstances a provision of the Medicaid scheme can create a right privately enforceable against state officers through § 1983. *See Wilder* [ ].

In *Blessing,* the Supreme Court set down the framework for evaluating a claim that a statute creates a right privately enforceable against state officers through § 1983. [ ] A statute will be found to create an enforceable right if, after a particularized inquiry, the court concludes (1) the statutory section was intended to benefit the putative plaintiff, (2) it sets a binding obligation on a government unit, rather than merely expressing a congressional preference, and (3) the interests the plaintiff asserts are not so " 'vague and amorphous' that [their] enforcement would strain judicial competence." [ ] If these conditions are met, we presume the statute creates an enforceable right unless Congress has explicitly or implicitly foreclosed this.[ ] The district court erred when it did not apply this test to evaluate plaintiffs' claims.

We now apply this test. First, the provisions were clearly intended to benefit the putative plaintiffs, children who are eligible for the screening and treatment services. [ ] We have found no federal appellate cases to the contrary. Second, the provisions set a binding obligation on Michigan. They are couched in mandatory rather than precatory language, stating that Medicaid services *"shall* be furnished" to eligible children, 42 U.S.C. § 1396a(a)(8) (emphasis added), and that the screening and treatment provisions *"must* be provided," *id.* § 1396a(a)(10)(A). Third, the provisions are not so vague and amorphous as to defeat judicial enforcement, as the statute and regulations carefully detail the specific services to be provided. *See* 42 U.S.C. § 1396d(r). Finally, Congress did not explicitly foreclose recourse to § 1983 in this instance, nor has it established any remedial scheme sufficiently comprehensive to supplant § 1983. [ ]

Plaintiffs have a cause of action under § 1983 for alleged noncompliance with the screening and treatment provisions of the Medicaid Act.

*   *   *

NOTE

The debate over the nature of the Medicaid entitlement has focused since *Westside Mothers* on the enforceability of Medicaid rights under 42 U.S.C. § 1983, particularly after the Supreme Court again tightened the screws on § 1983 claims in Gonzaga University v. Doe, 536 U.S. 273, 122 S.Ct. 2268, 153 L.Ed.2d 309 (2002). In recent cases, the courts are examining the Medicaid statute section by section, holding that some provisions grant enforceable rights to recipients (or perhaps to providers), while other sections are only statements of policy and do not create rights enforceable under § 1983. All circuit court of appeals that have considered the issue, for example, have held that Medicaid recipients can enforce 42 U.S.C. § 1396a(a)(8) (which requires the states to provide Medicaid with "reasonable promptness") and 42 U.S.C. § 1396a(a)(10)(A) (which requires states to provide Medicaid to all mandatory categories) under 42 U.S.C. § 1983. On the other hand, all courts of appeal have held that providers cannot enforce 42 U.S.C. § 1396a(a)(30)(A) (the provider payment provision at issue in the Douglas case below) under § 1983. Thirty-seven federal appellate court cases decided between the Gonzaga decision in 2002 and 2012 held thirteen provisions of the Medicaid statute enforceable under § 1983 and seven provisions unenforceable. Jane Perkins, Update on Private Enforcement of the Medicaid Act Pursuant to 42 U.S.C. § 1983,

Even if provisions of the Medicaid statute are not enforceable as federal laws under § 1983, however, they may be enforceable under the Supremacy Clause. The question of whether Medicaid rights are enforceable under the Supremacy Clause reached the Supreme Court in *Douglas v. Independent Living Center* in 2012:

DOUGLAS V. INDEPENDENT LIVING CENTER OF SOUTHERN CALIFORNIA, INC., ET AL.

Supreme Court of the United States, 2012.
132 S.Ct. 1204.

JUSTICE BREYER delivered the opinion of the Court.

We granted certiorari in these cases to decide whether Medicaid providers and recipients may maintain a cause of action under the Supremacy Clause to enforce a federal Medicaid law-a federal law that, in their view, conflicts with (and pre-empts) state Medicaid statutes that reduce payments to providers. Since we granted certiorari, however, the relevant circumstances have changed. The federal agency in charge of administering Medicaid, the Centers for Medicare & Medicaid Services (CMS), has now approved the state statutes as consistent with the federal law. In light of the changed circumstances, we believe that the question before us now is whether, once the agency has approved the state statutes, groups of Medicaid providers and beneficiaries may still maintain a Supremacy Clause action asserting that the state statutes are inconsistent with the federal Medicaid law. For the reasons set forth below, we vacate the Ninth Circuit's judgments and remand these cases for proceedings consistent with this opinion.

Medicaid is a cooperative federal-state program that provides medical care to needy individuals. To qualify for federal funds, States must submit to a federal agency (CMS, a division of the Department of Health and Human Services) a state Medicaid plan that details the nature and scope of the State's Medicaid program. It must also submit any amendments to the plan that it may make from time to time. And it must receive the agency's approval of the plan and any amendments. Before granting approval, the agency reviews the State's plan and amendments to determine whether they comply with the statutory and regulatory requirements governing the Medicaid program. * * *

The federal statutory provision relevant here says that a State's Medicaid plan and amendments must:

> provide such methods and procedures relating to the utilization of, and the payment for, care and services available under the plan . . . as may be necessary to safeguard against unnecessary utilization of such care and services and to assure that payments are consistent with efficiency, economy, and quality of care and are sufficient to enlist enough providers so that care and services are available under the plan at least to the extent that such care and services are available to the general population in the geographic area. 42 U.S.C. § 1396a(a)(30)(A)

In 2008 and 2009, the California Legislature passed three statutes changing that State's Medicaid plan [reducing payments to providers] * * *

In September and December 2008, the State submitted to the federal agency a series of plan amendments designed to implement most of the reductions contained in these bills. Before the agency finished reviewing the amendments, however, groups of Medicaid providers and beneficiaries filed a series of lawsuits seeking to enjoin the rate reductions on the ground that they conflicted with, and therefore were pre-empted by, federal Medicaid law, in particular the statutory provision that we have just set forth. * * *

The consolidated cases before us encompass five lawsuits brought by Medicaid providers and beneficiaries against state officials. * * * The decisions ultimately affirmed or ordered preliminary injunctions that prevented the State from implementing its statutes. They (1) held that the Medicaid providers and beneficiaries could directly bring an action based on the Supremacy Clause; (2) essentially accepted the claim that the State had not demonstrated that its Medicaid plan, as amended, would provide sufficient services; (3) held that the amendments consequently conflicted with the statutory provision we have quoted; and (4) held that, given the Constitution's Supremacy Clause, the federal statute must prevail. That is to say, the federal statute pre-empted the State's new laws.

In the meantime, the federal agency was also reviewing the same state statutes to determine whether they satisfied the same federal statutory conditions. In November 2010, agency officials concluded that they did not satisfy those conditions, and the officials disapproved the amendments. California then exercised its right to further administrative review within the agency. The cases were in this posture when we granted certiorari to decide whether respondents could mount a Supremacy Clause challenge to the state statutes and obtain a court injunction preventing California from implementing its statutes.

About a month after we heard oral argument, the federal agency reversed course and approved several of California's statutory amendments to its plan. * * * The State, in turn, withdrew its requests for approval of the remaining amendments, * * *

All parties agree that the agency's approval of the enjoined rate reductions does not make these cases moot. * * *

While the cases are not moot, they are now in a different posture. The federal agency charged with administering the Medicaid program has determined that the challenged rate reductions comply with federal law. That agency decision does not change the underlying substantive question, namely whether California's statutes are consistent with a specific federal statutory provision (requiring that reimbursement rates be "sufficient to enlist enough providers"). But it may change the answer. And it may require respondents now to proceed by seeking review of the agency determination under the Administrative Procedure Act (APA), [ ] rather than in an action against California under the Supremacy Clause.

For one thing, the APA would likely permit respondents to obtain an authoritative judicial determination of the merits of their legal claim. The Act provides for judicial review of final agency action. [ ] It permits any person adversely affected or aggrieved by agency action to obtain judicial review of the lawfulness of that action. [ ] And it requires a reviewing court to set aside agency action found to be "arbitrary, capricious, an abuse of discretion, or otherwise not in accordance with law." [ ]

For another thing, respondents' basic challenge now presents the kind of legal question that ordinarily calls for APA review. The Medicaid Act commits to the federal agency the power to administer a federal program. And here the agency has acted under this grant of authority. That decision carries weight. * * *

Finally, to allow a Supremacy Clause action to proceed once the agency has reached a decision threatens potential inconsistency or confusion. * * *

But ordinarily review of agency action requires courts to apply certain standards of deference to agency decisionmaking. [ ] And the parties have not suggested reasons why courts should not now (in the changed posture of these cases) apply those ordinary standards of deference.

Nor have the parties suggested reasons why, once the agency has taken final action, a court should reach a different result in a case like this one, depending upon whether the case proceeds in a Supremacy Clause action rather than under the APA for review of an agency decision. * * * If the two kinds of actions should reach the same result, the Supremacy Clause challenge is at best redundant. And to permit the continuation of the action in that form would seem to be inefficient, for the agency is not a participant in the pending litigation below, litigation that will decide whether the agency-approved state rates violate the federal statute.

In the present posture of these cases, we do not address whether the Ninth Circuit properly recognized a Supremacy Clause action to enforce this federal statute before the agency took final action. To decide whether these cases may proceed directly under the Supremacy Clause now that the agency has acted, it will be necessary to take account, in light of the proceedings that have already taken place, of at least the matters we have set forth above. * * * Given the complexity of these cases, rather than ordering reargument, we vacate the Ninth Circuit's judgments and remand the cases, thereby permitting the parties to argue the matter before that Circuit in the first instance.

CHIEF JUSTICE ROBERTS, with whom JUSTICE SCALIA, JUSTICE THOMAS, and JUSTICE ALITO join, dissenting.

The Medicaid Act established a collaborative federal-state program to assist the poor, elderly, and disabled in obtaining medical care. The Act is Spending Clause legislation; in exchange for federal funds a State agrees to abide by specified rules in implementing the program. One of those rules is set forth in s 30(A) of the Act, * * * In 2008 and 2009, California enacted legislation reducing the rates at which it would compensate some providers. Certain providers and individuals receiving Medicaid benefits thought the new reimbursement rates did not comply with the criteria set forth in § 30(A). They sued the State to prevent the new rates from going into effect.

But those plaintiffs faced a significant problem: Nothing in the Medicaid Act allows providers or beneficiaries (or anyone else, for that matter) to sue to enforce § 30(A). The Act instead vests responsibility for enforcement with a federal agency, the Centers for Medicare & Medicaid Services * * * Thus, as this case comes to us, the federal rule is that Medicaid reimbursement rates must meet certain criteria, but private parties have no statutory right to sue to enforce those requirements in court.

The providers and beneficiaries sought to overcome that difficulty by arguing that they could proceed against the State directly under the Supremacy Clause of the Constitution, even if they could not do so under the Act. They contended that the new state reimbursement rates were inconsistent with the requirements of § 30(A). The Supremacy Clause provides that a federal statute such as § 30(A) preempts contrary state law. Therefore, the providers and beneficiaries claimed, they could sue to enforce the Supremacy Clause, which requires striking down the state law and giving effect to § 30(A). The Ninth Circuit agreed with this argument and blocked the new state reimbursement rates.

* * * The question presented in the certiorari petitions is narrow: "Whether Medicaid recipients and providers may maintain a cause of action under the Supremacy Clause to enforce [§ 30(A)] by asserting that the provision preempts a state law reducing reimbursement rates." To decide this case, it is enough to conclude that the Supremacy Clause does not provide a cause of action to enforce the requirements of § 30(A) when Congress, in establishing those requirements, elected not to provide such a cause of action in the statute itself.

* * * The Supremacy Clause, on the other hand, is "not a source of any federal rights." [ ] The purpose of the Supremacy Clause is instead to ensure that, in a conflict with state law, whatever Congress says goes. [ ]

Thus, if Congress does not intend for a statute to supply a cause of action for its enforcement, it makes no sense to claim that the Supremacy Clause itself must provide one. Saying that there is a private right of action under the Supremacy Clause would substantively change the federal rule established by Congress in the Medicaid Act. That is not a proper role for the Supremacy Clause, which simply ensures that the rule established by Congress controls.

Indeed, to say that there is a federal statutory right enforceable under the Supremacy Clause, when there is no such right under the pertinent statute itself, would effect a complete end-run around this Court's implied right of action and 42 U.S.C. § 1983 jurisprudence. We have emphasized that "where the text and structure of a statute provide no indication that Congress intends to create new individual rights, there is no basis for a private suit, whether under s 1983 or under an implied right of action.[ ] This body of law would serve no purpose if a plaintiff could overcome the absence of a statutory right of action simply by invoking a right of action under the Supremacy Clause to the exact same effect. [ ]

The providers and beneficiaries argue, however, that the traditional exercise of equity jurisdiction supports finding a direct cause of action in the Supremacy Clause. This contention fails for the same reason. * * * Here the law established by Congress is that there is no remedy available to private parties to enforce the federal rules against the State. For a court to reach a contrary conclusion under its general equitable powers would raise the most serious concerns regarding both the separation of powers (Congress, not the Judiciary, decides whether there is a private right of action to enforce a federal statute) and federalism (the States under the Spending Clause agree only to conditions clearly specified by Congress, not any implied on an ad hoc basis by the courts).

This is not to say that federal courts lack equitable powers to enforce the supremacy of federal law when such action gives effect to the federal rule, rather than contravening it. The providers and beneficiaries rely heavily on cases of this kind, * * * Those cases, however, present quite different questions involving "the pre-emptive assertion in equity of a defense that would otherwise have been available in the State's enforcement proceedings at law." [ ] Nothing of that sort is at issue here; the respondents are not subject to or threatened with any enforcement proceeding * * *. They simply seek a private cause of action Congress chose not to provide.

The Court decides not to decide the question on which we granted certiorari but instead to send the cases back to the Court of Appeals, because of the recent action by CMS approving California's new reimbursement rates. But the CMS approvals have no impact on the question before this Court. * * *

* * *

So what is the Court of Appeals to do on remand? It could change its view and decide that there is no cause of action directly under the Supremacy Clause to enforce § 30(A). * * *

The majority acknowledges * * * that the Supremacy Clause challenge appears "at best redundant," and that "continuation of the action in that form would seem to be inefficient." [ ] Still, according to the majority, the Court of Appeals on remand could determine that the Supremacy Clause action may be brought but then must abate "now that the agency has acted," * * * Such a scenario would also create a bizarre rush to the courthouse, as litigants seek to file and have their Supremacy Clause causes of action decided before the agency has time to arrive at final agency action reviewable in court.

Or perhaps the suits should continue in a different "form," by which I understand the Court to suggest that they should morph into APA actions. The APA judicial review provisions, however, seem to stand in the way of such a transformation. * * * Given that APA actions also feature-among other things-different standards of review, different records, and different potential remedies, it is difficult to see what would be left of the original Supremacy Clause suit. Or, again, why one should have been permitted in the first place, when agency review was provided by statute, and the parties were able to and did participate fully in that process.

I would dispel all these difficulties by simply holding what the logic of the majority's own opinion suggests: When Congress did not intend to provide a private right of action to enforce a statute enacted under the Spending Clause, the Supremacy Clause does not supply one of its own force. * * *

NOTES

1.   What is the status of Supremacy Clause challenges by recipients and providers to state payment rates or to coverage requirements after *Douglas*? It is clear that four members of the Court believe that there is no cause of action under the Supremacy Clause. But what do the other five think? For commentary on *Douglas*, see Brietta Clark, Medicaid Access, Rate Setting, and Payment Suits: How the Obama Administration is Undermining its own Health Reform Goals, 55 Howard L.J. (2012); Sara Rosenbaum, Suing States over Threatened Access to Care: The Douglas Decision, 366 N. Eng. J. Med. 22(1) (Mar. 28, 2012); Rochelle Bobroff, Medicaid Preemption Claims in Douglas Avert the Astra Abyss, 122 Yale. J. Online 19 (2012); Nicole Huberfeld, Post–Reform Medicaid Before the Court: Discordant Advocacy Reflects Conflicting Attitudes, 21 Annals. Health L. 513 (2012).

2.   In the Supreme Court's most recent Medicaid case, Wos v. E.M.A, S.Ct.   (2013), the Court struck down a state Medicaid lien statute in a 6 to 3 decision written by Justice Kennedy. Although most of the decision focused on the validity of the North Carolina lien statute, which permitted the state to sieze up to one third of a tort settlement obtained by a Medicaid recipient where the state had paid for medical care related to the tortious injury, the Court did hold that the state statute violated the Supremacy Clause and accepted without comment the fact that the case was brought under 42 U.S.C. § 1983.

IV.   THE STATE CHILDREN'S HEALTH INSURANCE PROGRAM (CHIP)

Though one of the primary functions of Medicaid in recent years has been to provide health insurance for children, many children have remained uninsured. Even after Medicaid eligibility expansions in the late 1980s and early 1990s, over 10 million children, many of them in low-income families, were still without health insurance. In response to this continuing problem, Congress created, as part of the 1997 Balanced Budget Act, the Children's Health Insurance Program (CHIP), title XXI of the Social Security Act. 42 U.S.C.A. §§ 1397aa–1397jj.

The CHIP program, however, was created in a very different political climate than that which saw the birth of the Medicaid program. It was, therefore, not created as an entitlement for recipients, but rather as a grant-in-aid program to the states, established for ten years and affording the states considerable flexibility in program administration within broad federal guidelines.

States that wish to participate in the CHIP program may use CHIP funds either to expand Medicaid coverage for children or to establish a new CHIP program to cover children who are neither eligible for Medicaid nor covered by private health insurance, or use a combination of these approaches. As of 2011, 16 states had separate CHIP programs, 11 states plus the District of Columbia had expanded Medicaid, and 23 states used a combined approach. Although CHIP is intended to provide health insurance for children, a number of states have obtained § 1115 waiver authority to use it to cover adults as well. Through waivers, eight states (as of 2007) were using CHIP to cover parents, four to cover childless adults, and 11 to cover pregnant women (by considering fetuses to be unborn children). The 2006 Deficit Reduction Act prohibited new waivers for covering childless adults.

CHIP programs are supposed to target children in families with incomes of at or below 200 percent of the federal poverty level or 150 percent of the state's Medicaid income level, whichever is greater. 42 U.S.C.A. §§ 1397bb(b)(1); 1397jj(b), (c)(4). States may set eligibility standards that take into account geographic location, age, income and resources, residency, disability status, access to other health coverage, and duration of eligibility. They cannot discriminate on the basis of diagnosis or exclude children on the basis of preexisting condition.

CHIP explicitly does not create an entitlement for any particular child to receive coverage. 42 U.S.C.A. § 1396bb(b)(4). Children who are eligible for Medicaid coverage, however, must be enrolled under Medicaid, and CHIP coverage is not to substitute for coverage under group health plans. States are also not supposed to cover children with higher family incomes unless children from poorer families are covered, nor may they cover children in state institutions. States may subsidize premiums for employment-related insurance to use this route for expanding coverage. States are to establish outreach programs to identify children eligible for SCHIP coverage or other public programs, including Medicaid.

States that choose to establish separately-administered CHIP programs must provide health care benefit packages equivalent to coverage provided by benchmark or benchmark equivalent plans, as discussed earlier. 42 U.S.C.A. § 1397cc(a)–(c).

States may impose cost-sharing obligations on CHIP beneficiaries, including premiums and copayments, subject to statutory limits. Thirty-one states require premium payments and twenty-six states require co-payments for services, in part to reduce program costs, but also to make the program look less like a welfare program and to discourage "crowd out" (i.e., families dropping employment-related insurance for CHIP coverage). Though cost sharing might achieve these results, it also discourages participation and increases administrative complexity. See Mary Jo O'Brien, et al., State Experiences with Cost–Sharing Mechanisms in Children's Health Insurance Expansions (Commonwealth Fund, 2000). Further, although early studies seemed to show high levels of crowd-out, the most recent work demonstrates that a very small proportion of CHIP enrollees—fewer than 10 percent—in fact had affordable private coverage that they gave up in favor of CHIP. Anna Sommers, et al., Substitution of CHIP for Private Coverage: Results from a 2002 Evaluation in Ten States, 26 Health Aff. 529 (2007).

States that participate in CHIP must match federal funds in accordance with a formula that provides more generous federal participation than is afforded under Medicaid. This invites gaming on the part of the states to move children from Medicaid to CHIP, even though this is prohibited under the statute. Federal funds are allotted according to a formula that takes into account the number of low income children in the states and geographic variations in health care costs.

The CHIP program was reauthorized and its funding extended by the Children's Health Insurance Program Reauthorization Act of 2009 or CHIPRA. CHIPRA increased CHIP funding and modified funding formulas to reward states that used their allocations; reduced shortfalls; and adopted outreach, enrollment, and retention best practices. CHIPRA made it easier for the states to cover pregnant women and legal immigrants but limited the use of CHIP funds to cover adults. The legislation extended CHIP dental benefits and applied the mental health parity law to CHIP.

The ACA authorizes CHIP through 2019 and requires states to maintain current eligibility standards through that date. It extends CHIP funding to 2015. Federal CHIP match rates are increased by 23 percentage points (up to a maximum of 100) percent beginning in 2015, but this increased funding may simply exhaust federal funding faster if allotments are not increased. Children who cannot be included in the CHIP program because of allotment caps are supposed to be covered through the exchanges. See, examining the role of CHIP at the boundary of social class, Janet L. Dolgin, Class Competition and American Health Care: Debating the State Children's Health Insurance Program, 70 La. L. Rev. 683 (2010).

In summary, CHIP is a remarkably different program than Medicaid, evidencing a very different philosophy of federal responsibility for health care financing. CHIP affords maximum flexibility to the states in the apparent hope that they will generously and responsibly provide for poor children if given an incentive to do so. On the other hand, it provides minimal protection to beneficiaries, who are wholly dependent on state generosity and responsibility.

What explains the differences between the CHIP program and Medicaid? Why was a separate program created instead of Medicaid expanded? Why was Medicaid coverage of indigent children continued when CHIP was created? What barriers does CHIP erect to participation that are not present with Medicaid? Why might CHIP reach some children who whose families might refuse Medicaid coverage? An excellent analysis of the CHIP program is found in Sara Rosenbaum, et al., Public Health Insurance Design for Children: The Evolution from Medicaid to SCHIP, 1 J. Health & Biomedical L. 1 (2004).

CHAPTER 11

PROFESSIONAL RELATIONSHIPS IN HEALTH CARE ENTERPRISES

■ ■ ■

I.   INTRODUCTION

Privileges

A physician, or other independent health care professional, may treat his or her patients in a particular hospital only if the practitioner has "privileges" at that hospital. Hospital privileges include several distinct parts. Privileges may include admitting privileges for the authority to admit patients to the hospital and clinical privileges for the authority to use hospital facilities to treat patients, among other subsets of authority. The scope of an individual provider's clinical privileges must be delineated specifically by the hospital. The process through which privileges are awarded is called credentialing. A provider who is awarded privileges by the hospital is usually also a member of the hospital's medical staff and so is said to hold staff privileges. The hospital does not pay a fee or salary to a health care professional who only holds privileges and who has no other relationship (such as employment, a contract for services, or a joint business venture) with the hospital.

In the context of the customary hospital staff privileges system, physicians exercised considerable control over the conditions under which they practiced; the resources that the hospital would provide them; the selection of other physicians permitted to practice in the hospital; and the oversight exercised over physician decision making. Individual doctors generally no longer have this degree of control over their work environment at the hospital. Hospitals generally have driven toward more management control of medical care in the hospital as changes in the payment system put the hospital at risk for excessive intensity of care or poor quality. In addition, the emerging data banks maintained by health care organizations as a result of electronic medical records are stimulating significant expectations for increased organizational vigilance around quality. Greater consumer access to outcomes data in the form of report cards, which often include patient satisfaction data, also produces a market pressure toward more management control. Finally, the Affordable Care Act links some payment to outcomes and establishes accountability for population health. Both of these forces push health care systems to take more control of the continuum of care. This means that health systems will be concerned about the quality of care that the patient receives in the primary care office, in the hospital, in the various step-down facilities (rehabilitation centers, nursing homes), and so on.

At the same time, doctors have adopted the entrepreneurial lessons of the new payment and delivery forms. Physicians often are direct competitors of the hospitals in which they practice.

The Medical Staff

The hospital medical staff historically has functioned as a relatively independent association within the hospital organization, subject to the hospital's corporate by-laws but under its own medical staff by-laws as well. The medical staff as an entity has substantial authority over the hospital's internal quality assurance system including the credentialing process through which physicians receive and maintain privileges. Only the hospital's governing board has legal authority to grant, deny, limit, or revoke privileges; but it is the hospital's medical staff that generally controls the credentialing process up to the point of the final decision. Medical staff committees review physicians applying for and holding privileges; may set substantive standards for privileges for particular services; and make a decision, reviewable by the hospital board, as to denial or granting of privileges. The hospital medical staff by-laws may require the hospital's board to yield some deference to medical staff decision making in some circumstances. A side-by-side comparison of a hospital's by-laws and its medical staff by-laws, however, often reveals substantial ambiguities or conflicts in authority between the two bodies.

There is an inherent tension built into the common governance structure of a hospital. This tension periodically erupts into spectacular conflicts over the allocation of authority among the so-called "three legged stool"—the administration, the board of directors or trustees, and the medical staff. These battles usually are fought on issues relating to medical staff authority in credentialing and often in the context of conflict between the economic interests of the doctors and those of the hospital.

The Shift to Contract and Employment

Approximately a third of physicians caring for patients in hospitals are working under a formal contract (but as independent contractors), and another nearly 20% work as formal employees of the hospital. AHA Hospital Statistics (2012 edition). Contracts for medical services are especially prevalent among the hospital-based practice areas, such as radiology, anesthesiology, pathology, emergency medicine, and hospitalists (who oversee or manage the in-hospital care of patients admitted to the hospital by private physicians), and for some essential surgical specialties. In addition, joint ventures between hospitals and physicians often will involve formal contracts requiring the physicians to provide particular services. Physicians working under a hospital contract are still required to have privileges to care for patients, but the contract can substantially alter physician rights and expand management control by limiting the applicability of the procedural protections of the medical staff by-laws. In addition, the terms of contracts for physician services—whether with a hospital or another organization such as a group practice or health plan—may raise particular concerns because of the patient care context.

Most nurses, and many other health care professionals, customarily have worked as employees of health care organizations, and it has become increasingly common for physicians to work as employees as well. Employment law issues are critically important, then, in professional relationships in the health care setting. In addition, federal labor law has become quite significant as unionization among health care workers has increased considerably, and federal labor law applies, even in the absence of formal unions, when two or more employees join together to respond to workplace concerns.

II.   STAFF PRIVILEGES AND HOSPITAL–
PHYSICIAN CONTRACTS

SOKOL V. AKRON GENERAL MEDICAL CENTER
United States Court of Appeals for the Sixth Circuit, 1999.
173 F.3d 1026.

NORRIS, CIRCUIT JUDGE.

Plaintiff is a cardiac surgeon on staff at Akron General. The Medical Council at Akron General received information in the mid–1990's indicating that plaintiff's patients had an excessively high mortality rate. Concerned about plaintiff's performance of coronary artery bypass surgery ("CABG"), the Medical Council created the CABG Surgery Quality Task Force in 1994 to conduct a review of the entire cardiac surgery program at Akron General. The Task Force hired Michael Pine, M.D., a former practicing cardiologist who performs statistical risk assessments for evaluating the performance of hospitals. At a presentation in 1994 attended by plaintiff, Dr. Pine identified plaintiff as having a mortality rate of 12.09%, a "high risk-adjusted rate." Risk adjustment analyzes the likelihood that a particular patient or group of patients will die, as compared to another patient or group of patients. Dr. Pine stated in a summary of his findings that the predicted mortality rate for plaintiff's CABG patients was 3.65%, and plaintiff's "high mortality rate was of great concern and warrants immediate action."

James Hodsden, M.D., Chief of Staff at Akron General, requested that the Medical Council consider plaintiff for possible corrective action. Pursuant to the Medical Staff Bylaws, the Medical Council forwarded the complaint to the chairman of plaintiff's department, who appointed an Ad Hoc Investigatory Committee to review plaintiff's CABG surgery performance. The Medical Staff Bylaws require the Investigatory Committee to interview the staff member being reviewed and provide the Medical Council with a record of the interview and a report. The Investigatory Committee met with plaintiff three times. At the first meeting, the Investigatory Committee identified the issues before it to include addressing questions raised by plaintiff about the Pine study and determining the cause of plaintiff's excessive mortality rate. At the second meeting, the Investigatory Committee examined the mortality rate of plaintiff's patients using the Society of Thoracic Surgeons ("STS") methodology. Under STS methodology, the Investigatory Committee, like Dr. Pine, determined that plaintiff's CABG risk-adjusted mortality rate was roughly three times higher than the predicted mortality rate. The Investigatory Committee discussed the results of this analysis with plaintiff at the meeting.

At the third meeting, the Investigatory Committee reviewed with plaintiff various records of his twenty-six CABG patients who died either during or around the time of surgery. The Investigatory Committee determined that one factor leading to the deaths of these patients was poor case selection, meaning plaintiff did not adequately screen out those patients for whom CABG surgery was too risky. The Investigatory Committee also found that the excessive number of deaths may have been due to insufficient myocardial protection, which led to heart attacks.

The Investigatory Committee ultimately reported to the Medical Council that plaintiff's mortality rate was excessively high and that the two principal causes for this high mortality rate were poor case selection and "improper myocardial protection." The Investigatory Committee recommended that all cases referred to plaintiff for CABG surgery undergo a separate evaluation by another cardiologist who could cancel surgery felt to be too risky. It also recommended that plaintiff not be permitted to do emergency surgery or serve on "cathlab standby" and that there be an ongoing review of his CABG patients by a committee reporting to the Medical Council. Finally, it recommended that a standardized myocardial protection protocol be developed, and that all cardiac surgeons should be required to comply with the protocol.

Plaintiff appeared before the Medical Council on November 21, 1996, and the Medical Council voted to implement the recommendations. Under the Akron General Medical Staff Bylaws, when the Medical Council makes a decision adverse to the clinical privileges of a staff member, the staff member must be given notice of the decision of the Medical Council, and the notice shall specify "what action was taken or proposed to be taken and the reasons for it." This notice allows the staff member to prepare for a hearing to review the Medical Council's decision. * * *

Plaintiff and representatives from the Medical Council appeared before an Ad Hoc Hearing Committee on March 27, 1997. Plaintiff was represented by legal counsel, submitted exhibits, and testified on his own behalf. Dr. Gardner, a member of the Investigatory Committee, testified that although the Pine study and the STS methodology tended to underestimate the actual risk in some of plaintiff's cases, the Investigatory Committee concluded that the STS risk stratification tended to corroborate the Pine analysis. When asked about the Medical Council's determination that plaintiff engaged in poor case selection, Dr. Gardner had difficulty identifying specific cases that should not have had CABG surgery, yet he stated that "in the aggregate" there was poor case selection.

The Hearing Committee recommended that the Medical Council restore all plaintiff's CABG privileges. The Medical Council rejected the recommendation of the Hearing Committee and reaffirmed its original decision. In accordance with the Bylaws, plaintiff appealed the Medical Council's determination to the Executive Committee of the Board of Trustees of Akron General. This Committee affirmed the Medical Council's decision. Plaintiff then asked the district court for injunctive relief against Akron General.

*   *   *

Under Ohio law, private hospitals are accorded broad discretion in determining who will enjoy medical staff privileges at their facilities, and courts should not interfere with this discretion "unless the hospital has acted in an arbitrary, capricious or unreasonable manner or, in other words, has abused its discretion." [ ] However, hospitals must provide "procedural due process . . . in adopting and applying" "reasonable, nondiscriminatory criteria for the privilege of practicing" surgery in the hospital. [ ]

A.   Insufficient notice

This appeal requires us to examine the extent of the procedural protections afforded plaintiff under Ohio law. In addition to an appeals process, "[f]air procedure requires meaningful notice of adverse actions and the grounds or reasons for such actions" when a hospital makes an adverse decision regarding medical staff privileges. [ ] Akron General's Medical Staff Bylaws require that notice of an adverse decision by the Medical Council state "what action was taken or proposed to be taken and the reasons for it" and thus do not contractually provide for a quality of notice exceeding that required by Ohio law.

The President of Akron General sent plaintiff a letter notifying him of the Medical Council's initial decision. The letter refers plaintiff to the minutes of the Medical Council's meeting which set out the reasons for the Council's decision. These minutes, provided to plaintiff, indicate that the findings and recommendations of the Investigatory Committee were presented. The Investigatory Committee found that "[t]he number and percentage of deaths in Dr. Sokol's population was excessively high compared to the published national statistics and other local surgeons." Two reasons for this high percentage were offered—poor case selection and problems with protecting against myocardial infarctions. * * *

According to the magistrate judge, the notice provided plaintiff was insufficient because [it failed] to provide Dr. Sokol with specific cases where he engaged in poor case selection and where he failed to provide appropriate myocardial protection.

The sort of notice demanded by the magistrate judge was not required by the circumstances of this case. Had Akron General restricted plaintiff's rights because the Medical Council determined that he had poor case selection or provided insufficient protections against myocardial infarctions, then perhaps specific patient charts should have been indicated, along with specific problems with each of those charts. However, Akron General had a more fundamental concern with plaintiff's performance: too many of his patients, in the aggregate, were dying, even after accounting for risk adjustment. Poor case selection and problems in preventing myocardial infarction were just two reasons suggested by the Investigatory Committee for the high mortality rate.

Plaintiff takes issue with the Pine study and the STS algorithm, claiming that they do not present an accurate picture of his performance as a surgeon because he is the "surgeon of last resort." In other words, so many of his patients die because so many of his patients are already at death's door. Perhaps plaintiff is correct about that. However, it is not for us to decide whether he has been inaccurately judged by the Investigatory Committee and the Medical Council. Instead, we are to determine whether plaintiff had sufficient notice of the charges against him to adequately present a defense before the Hearing Committee. He knew that the Medical Council's decision was based upon the results of the Pine study and the STS analysis, knew the identity of his patients and which ones had died, and had access to the autopsy reports and medical records of these patients. * * * Manifestly, he had notice and materials sufficient to demonstrate to the Hearing Committee's satisfaction that limiting his privileges was inappropriate.

It was well within Akron General's broad discretion to base its decision upon a statistical overview of a surgeon's cases. We are in no position to say that one sort of evidence of a surgeon's performance—a statistical overview—is medically or scientifically less accurate than another sort of evidence—the case-by-case study plaintiff suggests we require of Akron General.

B.   Arbitrary decision

The magistrate judge also ruled that the Medical Council's decision was arbitrary. She reasoned that because Akron General did not have a fixed mortality rate by which to judge its surgeons before it limited plaintiff's privileges, it was arbitrary to take action against him based upon his mortality rate. We cannot agree. Surely, if plaintiff's mortality rate were 100%, the Medical Council would not be arbitrary in limiting his medical staff privileges, despite not having an established mortality rate. The magistrate judge's reasoning would prevent the Medical Council from instituting corrective action unless there were a preexisting standard by which to judge its staff. It is true that surgeons must be judged by "non-discriminatory criteria." [ ]. However, in this context, that means, for example, that if it came to the attention of the Medical Council that another surgeon had a mortality rate as high as plaintiff's, the latter surgeon's medical privileges would be similarly limited. * * *

On appeal, plaintiff argues that the Medical Council's decision was so wrong that it was arbitrary, capricious, or unreasonable. He points to evidence tending to show that the Medical Council's case against him was assailable. Indeed, the Hearing Committee recommended that plaintiff's full privileges be restored. But as the Ohio Supreme Court has recognized, "[t]he board of trustees of a private hospital has broad discretion in determining who shall be permitted to have staff privileges." [ ] The board of trustees will not have abused its discretion so long as its decision is supported by any evidence. Here, the Medical Council had both the Pine Study and the STS analysis. While it is conceivable that these are inaccurate measurements of plaintiff's performance, they are evidence that the hospital was entitled to rely upon, and accordingly, we are unable to say that Akron General abused its discretion in limiting plaintiff's privileges.

MERRITT, CIRCUIT JUDGE, dissenting.

* * *

The heart surgeon has been treated unfairly by his hospital. The Hearing Committee was the only group composed of experts independent of the hospital administration. * * * The Committee completely exonerated Dr. Sokol. No one has cited a single operation or a single instance in which Dr. Sokol has made a mistake, not one.

*   *   *

NOTES AND QUESTIONS

1.   The court in *Sokol* examines the fairness of the procedures used by the hospital using the common law doctrine of "fundamental fairness" as applied to private associations generally. The requirements of fundamental fairness have been established on a case-by-case basis, and so its minimum requirements are not always clear. The majority of states supplement common law requirements by imposing specific substantive and procedural requirements by statute. See, e.g., N.Y. Public Health Law § 2801–b. The federal Health Care Quality Improvement Act, discussed below, also establishes minimum procedures for hospitals desiring HCQIA immunity. The procedures for credentialing in public hospitals must meet constitutional due process requirements. See, e.g., Osuagwu v. Gila Reg. Med. Ctr. 850 F.Supp. 1216 (D.N.M. 2012).

2.   In contrast to *Sokol*, the law in most states does not allow the courts to review the merits of privileges decisions at all. Instead, most states restrict judicial review to the question of whether the hospital followed its own by-laws; and for most of these states, the question is limited to compliance with the by-laws' procedural requirements only. What policy and practical considerations support broader and narrower judicial review? Why is the staff privileges system generally considered protective of physicians if judicial review is so limited in the majority of states?

3.   The Joint Commission (described in Chapter 2) has had extraordinary influence on credentialing procedures through its hospital accreditation standards. Joint Commission standards for the credentialing and privileges process set the following core expectations: that privileging and re-privileging assess physician performance against several competencies including patient care, medical/clinical knowledge, interpersonal and communication skills, and professionalism, among others; that there be continuous evaluation of practitioners rather than annual or biennial reviews alone; and that a separate standardized process be established to flag practitioners when there are competency concerns, including a process for newly credentialed physicians. Joint Commission standards on credentialing are increasing the focus on the prospective monitoring of physician quality. These standards are intended to accelerate the use of data such as that relied upon in *Sokol*.

4.   In 2009, the Joint Commission adopted a standard that requires hospitals to establish a code of conduct that specifically defines what constitutes disruptive behavior and how that behavior will be addressed. Courts have been supportive of hospitals in these circumstances. See, e.g., Poirier v. Our Lady of Bellefonte Hosp. 2006 W: 358241 (Ky. App.), holding that by-laws provision requiring doctors to "use a generally recognized level of quali-

ty" would reach a doctor engaging in a "recurring pattern of unacceptable and unprofessional behavior." But see the discussion of the National Labor Relations Act in the Note on Unionization in Health Care Organizations in Section III, below.

NOTE: THE HEALTH CARE QUALITY IMPROVEMENT ACT (HCQIA)

The federal Health Care Quality Improvement Act, 42 U.S.C. § 11101, affords hospitals immunity from damages actions, except for civil rights claims. (See the Note on Employment Discrimination in Section III, below.) The HCQIA provides immunity to hospitals (and other entities) only if their credentialing decisions meet substantive and procedural statutory standards. Several states have also enacted local variations on the HCQIA, as the Act does not override or preempt state laws which provide "incentives, immunities, or protection for those engaged in a professional review action that is in addition or greater than that provided" in the federal statute.

The HCQIA creates a presumption that the credentialing decision (termed a "professional review action" in the Act) complies with the standards of the Act. To rebut this presumption, the plaintiff must prove by a preponderance of the evidence that the health care entity: (1) did not act in the reasonable belief that the action was in furtherance of quality health care; (2) did not make a reasonable effort to obtain the facts of the matter; (3) did not afford the physician adequate notice and hearing procedures and such other procedures required by fairness under the circumstances; or (4) did not act in the reasonable belief that the action was warranted by the facts known after such reasonable effort to determine the facts and after meeting the Act's procedural requirements. In testing these "four reasonables," courts use an objective standard of reasonableness. Neither the ultimate accuracy of the hospital's conclusions nor direct evidence of improper motive or bad faith is considered relevant to the objective reasonableness of the hospital's actions. Although evidence of improper motive or bad faith is not relevant under the HCQIA, such evidence may be used to prove violation of civil rights or discrimination laws.

The courts have been generous with HCQIA immunity, ordinarily resolving cases through summary judgment in favor of the hospital. In fact, physicians only rarely succeed in overturning the rebuttable presumption of immunity; but when they do, the damage awards have been very significant.

Hospitals generally have been successful in claiming HCQIA immunity for actions based on disruptive conduct (see note 4, above) without evidence of substandard medical treatment or specific harm to patients. See, e.g., Sternberg v. Nanticoke Mem. Hosp., 15 A.3d 1225 (Del. 2011); Guier v. Teton County Hosp. Dist., 248 P.3d 623 (Wyo. 2011).

To earn HCQIA immunity, hospitals must report certain adverse credentialing decisions to the National Practitioner Data Bank (NPDB, see the Note on the National Practitioner Daba Bank in Chapter 1) and must check Data Bank records on the individual physician when considering an application for privileges and every two years for physicians who hold privileges. The HCQIA also provides hospitals limited immunity for their reports to the Data Bank, with the physician bearing the burden of proving that the hospital did not meet statutory standards in its reporting.

The hospital's obligation to report to the NPDB extends to situations where the physician has resigned once an investigation into quality of care issues has begun but before an adverse action has been taken. This has created a small window where a physician may resign prior to the beginning of an "investigation." Some argue that this allows hospitals and doctors too great an opportunity to bypass reporting, and that hospitals use this for leverage in pushing physicians out "voluntarily" with the result that there is no evidence in the Data Bank that the doctor has had problems. In any case, it is not entirely clear when the opportunity to resign without report has passed.

MATEO–WOODBURN V. FRESNO COMMUNITY HOSPITAL
Court of Appeal, Fifth District, 1990.
221 Cal.App.3d 1169, 270 Cal.Rptr. 894

BROWN, J.

* * *

Prior to August 1, 1985, and as early as 1970, the FCH department of anesthesiology operated as an open staff. The department was composed of anesthesiologists who were independently competing entrepreneurs with medical staff privileges in anesthesiology. Collectively, the anesthesiologists were responsible for scheduling themselves for the coverage of regularly scheduled, urgent and emergency surgeries.

[E]ach anesthesiologist was rotated, on a daily basis, through a first-pick, second-pick, etc., sequence whereby each anesthesiologist chose a particular operating room for that particular date. Usually no work was available for one or more anesthesiologists at the end of the rotation schedule. Once an anesthesiologist rotated through first-pick, he or she went to the end of the line. In scheduling themselves, the anesthesiologists established a system that permitted each anesthesiologist on a rotating basis to have the "pick" of the cases. This usually resulted in the "first-pick" physician taking what appeared to be the most lucrative cases available for that day.

The rotation system encouraged many inherent and chronic vices. For example, even though members of the department varied in their individual abilities, interests, skills, qualifications and experience, often "first-picks" were more consistent with economic advantage than with the individual abilities of the physician exercising his or her "first-pick" option. At times, anesthesiologists refused to provide care for government subsidized patients, allegedly due to economic motivations.

The department chairman had the authority to suggest to fellow physicians that they only take cases for which they were well qualified. However, the chairman was powerless to override the rotation system in order to enforce these recommendations.

Under the open-staff rotation system, anesthesiologists rotated into an "on call" position and handled emergencies arising during off hours. This led to situations where the "on-call" anesthesiologist was not qualified to handle a particular emergency and no formal mechanism was in place to ensure that alternative qualified anesthesiologists would become promptly available when needed. * * *

* * *

These chronic defects in the system led to delays in scheduling urgent cases because the first call anesthesiologists in charge of such scheduling at times refused to speak to each other. Often, anesthesiologists, without informing the nursing staff, left the hospital or made rounds while one or more of their patients were in post-anesthesia recovery. This situation caused delays as the nurses searched for the missing anesthesiologist.

The trial court found these conditions resulted in breaches of professional efficiency, severely affected the morale of the department and support staff, and impaired the safety and health of the patients. As a result of these conditions, the medical staff (not the board of trustees) initiated action resulting ultimately in the change from an "open" to a "closed" system. We recite the highlights of the processes through which this change took place.

* * *

[Mr.] Helzer, President and Chief Executive Officer of FCH, established an "Anesthesia Task Force" to study the proposed closure. In a subsequent memo to Helzer, dated April 6, 1984, the task force indicated it had considered four alternative methods of dealing with problems in the department of anesthesiology: (1) continuation of the status quo, i.e., independent practitioners with elected department chairman, (2) competitive groups of anesthesiologists with an elected department chairman, (3) an appointed director of anesthesia with independent practitioners and (4) an appointed director with subcontracted anesthesiologists, i.e., a closed staff.

The memo noted that under the third alternative—a director with independent practitioners—the director would have no power to determine who would work in the department of anesthesiology. "Any restriction or disciplinary action recommended by the director would need to go through the usual hospital staff procedure, which can be protracted." It was also noted in the memo that a director with subcontracted practitioners "would have the ability to direct their activities without following usual hospital staff procedures." The committee recommended a director with subcontracted practitioners.

[The board accepted the committee's recommendation and formed a search committee to recruit a director for the department.]

* * *

Mateo–Woodburn was offered the position of interim director on June 13, 1984, which position she accepted. Mateo–Woodburn was interviewed for the position of director on September 25, 1984. Hass was interviewed for the position on March 7, 1985.

At a special meeting of the board of trustees held on April 10, 1985, the anesthesia search committee recommended to the board that Hass be hired as director of the department of anesthesiology, and the recommendation was accepted by the board.

At the same April 10 meeting, the board authorized its executive committee to close the department of anesthesiology. On the same day, the executive committee met and ordered the department closed.

* * *

An agreement between FCH and the Hass corporation was entered into on June 7, 1985. On June 18, 1985, Helzer sent a letter to all members of the department of anesthesiology which states in relevant part:

* * *

"The Board of Trustees has now entered into an agreement with William H. Hass, M.D., a professional corporation, to provide anesthesiology services for all hospital patients effective July 1, 1985. The corporation will operate the Department of Anesthesia under the direction of a Medical Director who will schedule and assign all medical personnel. The corporation has appointed Dr. Hass as Medical Director, and the hospital has concurred with the appointment. The agreement grants to the corporation the exclusive right to provide anesthesia services to all hospital patients at all times."

"To provide the services called for by the agreement, it is contemplated that the Hass Corporation will enter into contractual arrangements with individual physician associates who must obtain Medical Staff membership and privileges as required by the staff bylaws. The negotiations with such associates are presently ongoing, and the hospital does not participate in them."

"Effective August 1, 1985, if you have not entered into an approved contractual agreement, with the Hass Corporation, you will not be permitted to engage in direct patient anesthesia care in this hospital. However, at your option, you may retain your staff membership and may render professional evaluation and assessment of a patient's medical condition at the express request of the attending physician."

The contract between the Hass corporation and FCH provided that the corporation was the exclusive provider of clinical anesthesiology services at the hospital; the corporation was required to provide an adequate number of qualified physicians for this purpose; physicians were to meet specific qualifications of licensure, medical staff membership and clinical privileges at FCH, and to have obtained at least board eligibility in anesthesiology; and the hospital had the right to review and approve the form of any contract between the corporation and any physician-associate prior to its execution.

Subject to the terms of the master contract between the Hass corporation and FCH, the corporation had the authority to select physicians with whom it would contract on terms chosen by the corporation subject to the approval of FCH. The contract offered to the anesthesiologists, among many other details, required that a contracting physician be a member of the hospital staff and be board certified or board eligible. The Hass corporation was contractually responsible for all scheduling, billing and collections. Under the contract, the corporation was to pay the contracting physician in accordance with a standard fee arrangement. The contracting physician was required to limit his or her professional practice to FCH except as otherwise approved by the FCH board of trustees.

[The contract also provided:] ". . . Provider shall not be entitled to any of the hearing rights provided in the Medical Staff Bylaws of the Hospital and Provider hereby waives any such hearing rights that Provider may have. However, the termination of this Agreement shall not affect Provider's Medical Staff membership or clinical privileges at the Hospital other than the privilege to provide anesthesiology services at the Hospital."

Seven of the thirteen anesthesiologists on rotation during July 1985 signed the contract. Of the six plaintiffs in this case, five refused to sign the contract offered to them. The sixth plaintiff, Dr. Woodburn, was not offered a contract but testified that he would not have signed it, had one been offered.

*　*　*

Some of the reasons given for refusal to sign the contract were: (1) the contract required the plaintiffs to give up their vested and fundamental rights to practice at FCH; (2) the 60–day termination clause contained no provisions for due process review; (3) the contract failed to specify amounts to be taken out of pooled income for administrative costs; (4) the contract required plaintiffs to change medical malpractice carriers; (5) the contract required plaintiffs to obtain permission to practice any place other than FCH; (6) the contract imposed an unreasonable control over plaintiffs' financial and professional lives; (7) the contract failed to provide tenure of employment. The Hass corporation refused to negotiate any of the terms of the contract with plaintiffs.

*   *   *

* * * Numerous cases recognize that the governing body of a hospital, private or public, may make a rational policy decision or adopt a rule of general application to the effect that a department under its jurisdiction shall be operated by the hospital itself through a contractual arrangement with one or more doctors to the exclusion of all other members of the medical staff except those who may be hired by the contracting doctor or doctors. * * *

*   *   *

[The position] of a staff doctor in an adjudicatory one-on-one setting, wherein the doctor's professional or ethical qualifications for staff privileges is in question, take[s] on a different quality and character when considered in light of a rational, justified policy decision by a hospital to reorganize the method of delivery of certain medical services, even though the structural change results in the exclusion of certain doctors from the operating rooms. If the justification is sufficient, the doctor's vested rights must give way to public and patient interest in improving the quality of medical services.

It is also noted, where a doctor loses or does not attain staff privileges because of professional inadequacy or misconduct, the professional reputation of that doctor is at stake. In that circumstance, his or her ability to become a member of the staff at other hospitals is severely impaired. On the other hand, a doctor's elimination by reason of a departmental reorganization and his failure to sign a contract does not reflect upon the doctor's professional qualifications and should not affect his opportunities to obtain other employment. The trial court correctly found the decision to close the department of anesthesiology and contract with Hass did not reflect upon the character, competency or qualifications of any particular anesthesiologist.

*   *   *

[I]f the hospital's policy decision to make the change is lawful, and we hold it is, then the terms of the contracts offered to the doctors was part of the administrative decision and will not be interfered with by this court unless those terms bear no rational relationship to the objects to be accomplished, i.e., if they are substantially irrational or they illegally discriminate among the various doctors.

Given the conditions existing under the open rotation method of delivering anesthesia services, including among others the lack of control of scheduling and the absence of proper discipline, we cannot say the terms of the contract were irrational, unreasonable or failed to bear a proper relationship to the object of correcting those conditions. Considered in this light, the terms are not arbitrary, capricious or irrational.

*   *   *

As to the contract provision which required waiver of hearing rights set forth in the staff bylaws, * * * those rights do not exist under the circumstances of a quasi-legislative reorganization of a department by the board of trustees. This quasi-legislative situation is to be distinguished from a quasi-judicial proceeding against an individual doctor grounded on unethical or unprofessional conduct or incompetency. Accordingly, the waiver did not further detract from or diminish plaintiffs' rights.

*   *   *

Plaintiffs contend the department of anesthesiology could not be reorganized without amending the bylaws of the medical staff in accordance with the procedure for amendment set forth therein. Closely allied to this argument is the assertion the hospital unlawfully delegated to Hass the medical staff's authority to make staff appointments.

* * * The hospital's action did not change the manner or procedure by which the medical staff passes upon the qualifications, competency or skills of particular doctors in accordance with medical staff bylaws. * * * In fact, plaintiffs remain members of the staff and the contract requires contracting anesthesiologists to be members of the staff. Moreover, it is clear the medical staff does not appoint medical staff members—it makes recommendations to the board of trustees who then makes the final medical staff membership decision. Hass was never given authority to appoint physicians to medical staff and never did so. Hass was merely hired to provide anesthesiology services to the hospital. His decision to contract with various anesthesiologists in order to provide those services was irrelevant to medical staff appointments except that all persons contracting with Hass were required to qualify as members of the medical staff.

We conclude the trial court's determination that the defendants' "actions were proper under the circumstance and that plaintiffs' Medical Staff privileges were not unlawfully terminated, modified or curtailed" is fully supported by the evidence and is legally correct.

NOTES AND QUESTIONS

1.   *Mateo–Woodburn* considers two issues related to exclusive contracting. In addition to resolving the question of the procedural rights of the physician who held privileges prior to the institution of the exclusive contract, it reviews the termination provision in the exclusive contract itself. What contractual provision is made for termination of the contract and termination of staff privileges between Hass, P.C., and the anesthesiologists at Fresno Community Hospital? Some court opinions have separated "staff" privileges from "clinical" privileges with the result that hospitals are not required to use procedures required for revocation of staff privileges when they have revoked or significantly limited only the physician's clinical privileges, which allow the physician to admit or treat patients. See, e.g., Ripley v. Wyoming Med. Ctr., Inc., 2008 WL 5875551 (D.Wyo. 2008). Would a contract clause that provides that termination of the contract will result automatically in termination of staff privileges without benefit of the by-laws' procedures (known as a "clean sweep" clause) be enforceable? See, for example, Madsen v. Audrain Health Care, 297 F.3d 694 (8th Cir. 2002) which, like most cases, upholds clean sweep agreements.

2.   Financial factors are often a central issue in relations between a hospital and physicians with staff privileges. "Economic credentialing," a term that that the AMA coined, occurs when a hospital makes privileges decisions based on financial factors unrelated to quality. How would HCQIA immunity apply in such a case? Is it clear that utilization—for example, in terms of surgery, scans, biopsies—relates only to cost? Many states have enacted legislation relevant to economic credentialing, some restrictive and some permissive. "Conflicts credentialing" refers to the apparent conflict of interest of a physician who is both a member of a hospital's medical staff and the owner of an entity that competes directly with the hospital. Conflicts credentialing, however, also may reflect a conflict between the hospital's economic interests and that of individual physicians seeking privileges. For example, in Mahan v. Avera St. Luke's, 621 N.W.2d 150 (N.D. 2001), the court upheld a hospital's denial of privileges to doctors who admitted patients to a competing physician-owned hospital. In contrast to *Mahan*, the Arkansas Supreme Court affirmed a preliminary injunction against the exclusion of competing doctor-owners holding, in part, that the doctors were likely to succeed in their claims that the hospital intended that the exclusion of the doctor-owners interfere with their relationships with their patients and that the hospital's action violated the state deceptive trade practices statute (as an "unconscionable" act) thus making the principle of nonreview of privileges decisions in state law inapplicable. Baptist Health v. Murphy, 365 Ark. 115, 226 S.W.3d 800 (2006). See also Pacific Radiation Oncology, LLC v. Queen's Medical Center, 861 F.Supp. 2d 1170 (D. Hawai'i 2012), granting preliminary injunction (limited to a specified list of procedures that could be performed only in the defendant hospital) in favor of radiation oncologist claiming that hospital closed staff of unit and offered privileges only if the plaintiff physi-

cian would agree to admit all patients to the hospital rather than to a competing facility.

3. Conflicts over privileges can pit the hospital's governing board against the hospital's medical staff. For example, the administration at Lawnwood Medical Center in Florida decided to limit privileges for its new cardiovascular surgery unit to a single physician. The executive committee of the medical staff disagreed with the corporate decision and awarded privileges to another physician, following the procedures in the medical staff by-laws. The board of Trustees promptly denied privileges to that physician. Thereafter, the board asked that the physician leaders of the medical staff be investigated by the hospital for failure to meet their fiduciary duty to the corporation. The board ultimately removed the medical staff's elected officers, whereupon the officers sued. The board also amended the hospital's corporate by-laws to give the board unilateral authority to amend the medical staff by-laws, even though the latter by-laws required approval of the medical staff for amendment. The court upheld the authority of the medical staff as against the board. See Lawnwood Med. Ctr. v. Seeger, 990 So.2d 503 (Fla. 2008); Lawnwood Med. Ctr. Inc. v. Sadow, 43 So.3d 710 (Fla. App. 2010), refusing to set aside a jury verdict in favor of the physician applicant. But see, *Mahan*, discussed in note 2, upholding the authority of the board as against the medical staff. See also, John D. Blum, The Quagmire of Hospital Governance, 31 J. Legal Med. 35 (2010).

REVIEW PROBLEM: DR. BENNETT AND HOLY GRAIL HOSPITAL

Holy Grail Hospital (HGH) is a 500–bed hospital in Metropolis, a major city with six other hospitals. Several health insurance plans and major employers have negotiated substantial discounts with Metropolis hospitals for hospital services. The insurers and employers asking for the discounts control the choice of hospital for thousands of insured individuals in Metropolis. What each hospital might lose in the discount, it hopes it will gain in having a relatively stable stream of patients.

HGH has been constrained in its negotiations for a number of reasons, however. It has exclusive contracts for physician services in anesthesiology and radiology that are comparatively costly. The contracts are near the end of their terms, and HGH wants to renegotiate the terms of the contracts or replace the current physician groups with others more compatible with a cost-conscious and outcomes-oriented style of practice. The anesthesiology group, Physicians' Practice Group (PPG), has been responsive to the needs of the hospital relating to coverage and quality of anesthesia services; but a new group, General Anesthesiology Services (GAS), has approached HGH with much more favorable financial terms. Although the surgeons have been very happy with PPG, HGH believes that they will become equally satisfied with GAS. HGH has agreed to enter into an exclusive contract with GAS and has given PPG notice that their exclusive contract will not be renewed. The HGH–PPG contract provides for termination of the contract without cause.

Two of the three PPG anesthesiologists have already joined GAS, though at lower salaries than they enjoyed with PPG. GAS has refused to consider hiring Dr. Charles Bennett, however. Dr. Bennett is considered somewhat difficult. He does not work well with the nurse anesthetists because he limits the procedures they can perform, and he sometimes has conflicts with the surgeons when he thinks they are taking too long. He has had two malpractice suits filed against him in the last five years; but both were dropped by the plaintiffs, one after the payment of a settlement and one without any payment. Other than these problems, his work has been of good quality, although he often tells patients that they should "just get tough" when they complain of post-operative pain.

Dr. Bennett's contract with PPG provides that PPG may terminate him "without cause with 60 days' notice," but is silent on the question of his privileges at HGH. The PPG contract with HGH, however, states that the contract is exclusive and "only physician members of PPG may provide anesthesiology services at HGH." The original letter from HGH awarding Dr. Bennett staff privileges, including clinical privileges in anesthesiology, states: "Because you will be providing services at HGH under an exclusive contract, your clinical privileges will be automatically terminated upon termination of that contract." Each of the subsequent renewal letters contained the same statement.

The medical staff was quite concerned a few years ago about automatic termination of privileges of physician administrators dismissed from their administrative positions and amended its by-laws to provide: "A physician member of the medical staff providing services to the hospital under contract will retain privileges even if that contract is terminated." The Board of Directors never approved this amendment and has essentially ignored it. The governing by-laws provide that the governing body must approve amendments to the medical staff by-laws, but they also require the Board to give some deference to the medical staff on individual credentialing decisions.

What should HGH do? Should it simply terminate Bennett's privileges without procedural review and for no cause? Or, should it follow the procedures in the medical staff by-laws? Should HGH proceed against Dr. Bennett on the basis of the quality of his work? If the medical staff by-laws provide that the hospital may revoke privileges of "any physician whose inability to work well with others jeopardizes patient care," would you recommend that they proceed under that clause? Are there any other alternatives? How might a court handle the case under each of these alternatives should Bennett sue?

HGH is facing another problem as well. Several of the surgeons with privileges at HGH are developing and will be co-owners of SportsMed Center, Inc., a joint venture with a competing hospital. SportsMed will limit its services to diagnostic imaging, certain orthopedic surgeries, and post-operative physical therapy. Originally, HGH had approached the SportsMed developers with a proposal that it enter into a joint venture with HGH. During those discussions, HGH let it be known that it may decide not to grant privileges to doctors recruited by SportsMed or to renew privileges for SportsMed doctors who already had privileges at HGH. SportsMed declined the offer, and HGH has since informed its medical staff that privileges at HGH would not be granted or renewed for doctors who practiced at SportsMed.

HGH has called you for legal advice. What do you tell them?

III.   LABOR AND EMPLOYMENT

A. EMPLOYMENT–AT–WILL

Doctors, nurses, administrators, and in-house counsel working without an employment contract or under a contract that does not provide for a specific term of employment are subject to the doctrine of employment-at-will. By contrast, employees working under a collective bargaining agreement or under a contract with express provisions concerning length of employment or termination for just cause alone are not employees-at-will.

The common law at-will doctrine varies widely among the states, but generally provides that the employment relationship can be terminated without cause at the will of either the employer or the employee. The at-will doctrine allows a few exceptions, which in most states are relatively narrow.

TURNER v. MEMORIAL MEDICAL CENTER
Illinois Supreme Court, 2009.
233 Ill. 2d 494, 911 N.E.2d 369.

JUSTICE FREEMAN delivered the judgment of the court, with opinion.

Plaintiff, Mark Turner, brought a retaliatory discharge action * * * against defendant, Memorial Medical Center (Memorial). The circuit court dismissed plaintiff's * * * complaint. A divided panel of the appellate court upheld the dismissal. We * * * affirm the judgment of the appellate court.

* * * Plaintiff is a trained and licensed respiratory therapist. Beginning in 1983, plaintiff was employed by Memorial, which is a community hospital. During his employment, plaintiff had consistently met legitimate employment expectations, and his employment evaluations consistently indicated excellent work performance.

In September 2006, the Joint Commission * * * performed an on-site survey at Memorial. The Joint Commission is an independent, not-for-profit organization that establishes various health-care standards and evaluates an organization's compliance with those standards and other accreditation requirements. The purpose of the on-site survey was to determine whether Memorial would continue to receive Joint Commission accreditation. Memorial's failure to receive this accreditation would result in the loss of federal Medicare/Medicaid funding.

Memorial uses a computer charting program that allows medical professionals to electronically chart a patient's file. The Joint Commission standard is that such electronic charting be performed immediately after care is provided to a patient. However, Memorial's respiratory therapy department did not require immediate charting. Rather, Memorial required a respiratory therapist to chart patient care merely at some point during his or her shift.

On September 28, 2006, plaintiff was asked to speak with a Joint Commission surveyor. Also present at this meeting was Memorial's vice-president of patient care services. During this meeting, plaintiff truthfully advised the surveyor of the discrepancy between the Joint Commission standard of immediate charting and Memorial's requirement of charting at some point during the shift. Plaintiff further advised the surveyor that Memorial's deviation from the Joint Commission standard was jeopardizing patient safety. Plaintiff alleged that as a result of his truthful statements to the Joint Commission surveyor, Memorial discharged plaintiff on October 4, 2006.

* * *

In Illinois, "a noncontracted employee is one who serves at the employer's will, and the employer may discharge such an employee for any reason or no reason." [ ] * * * However, an exception to this general rule of at-will employment arises where there has been a retaliatory discharge of the employee. This court has recognized a limited and narrow cause of action for the tort of retaliatory discharge. [ ] To state a valid retaliatory discharge cause of action, an employee must allege that (1) the employer discharged the employee, (2) in retaliation for the employee's activities, and (3) that the discharge violates a clear mandate of public policy. [ ] Surveying many cases from across the country, this court [in an earlier case has noted]:

> "There is no precise definition of the term [clear mandate of public policy]. In general, it can be said that public policy concerns what is right and just and what affects the citizens of the State collectively. It is to be found in the State's constitution and statutes and, when they are silent, in its judicial decisions. Although there is no precise line of demarcation dividing matters that are the subject of public policies from matters purely personal, a survey of cases in other States involving retaliatory discharges shows that a matter must strike at the heart of a citizen's social rights, duties, and responsibilities before tort will be allowed." [ ]

* * *

At the outset, we reject plaintiff's contention that whether the failure to perform immediate charting jeopardizes the public policy of "patient safety" is a question of fact that precludes dismissal of his complaint. * * * It is widely recognized that the existence of a public policy, as well as the issue whether that policy is undermined by the employee's discharge, presents questions of law for the court to resolve. * * * Accordingly, the questions of whether "patient safety" is a clearly mandated public policy and, if so, whether plaintiff's discharge violated that policy are questions of law for the court.

Turning to the merits, plaintiff contends that Memorial, by discharging him in retaliation for reporting the alleged patient charting discrepancy, violated the clearly mandated public policy of "patient safety." Indeed, plaintiff asks us to "definitively declare that patient safety is a matter of public policy in the state of Illinois and that terminating an employee who speaks out in favor of patient safety violates that public policy." Plaintiff overlooks a basic substantive requirement of a common law retaliatory discharge action.

The tort of retaliatory discharge "seeks to achieve 'a proper balance * * * among the employer's interest in operating a business efficiently and profitably, the employee's interest in earning a livelihood, and society's interest in seeing its public policies carried out.'" * * * A broad, general statement of policy is inadequate to justify finding an exception to the general rule of at-will employment. [ ] Indeed: "Any effort to evaluate the public policy exception with generalized concepts of fairness and justice will result in an elimination of the at-will doctrine itself. [ ]

Further, generalized expressions of public policy fail to provide essential notice to employers. * * * "An employer should not be exposed to liability where a public policy standard is too general to provide any specific guidance or is so vague that it is subject to different interpretations." [ ]

[U]nless an employee at will identifies a "specific" expression of public policy, the employee may be discharged with or without cause. [ ] * * *

* * *

The [plaintiff's] complaint contains the following specific allegations concerning the Joint Commission standards. * * * Plaintiff alleged that the Joint Commission's "role is recognized by the federal government as an important component in assuring patient safety." Plaintiff then alleged that the Joint Commission "has certain standards and criteria" pertaining to electronic patient charting. "One of the standards requires that [electronic] charting be done immediately after care is provided to a patient." Plaintiff further alleged: "The rationale behind immediate [electronic] charting is to enhance patient care and safety."

The circuit court found that plaintiff "failed to establish the existence of a public policy clearly mandated by a provision of law which is violated when a concern is voiced to a [Joint Commission] surveyor about the time during a given work shift when patient care is charted. No Illinois law or administrative regulation directly requires immediate bedside charting of patient care." However, the circuit court further found that Joint Commission "standards are not Illinois law and thus cannot be said to be representative of the public policy of the State of Illinois." * * * Regardless of whether * * * the Joint Commission "is the functional equivalent of [a] government regulator," plaintiff's complaint fails to recite or even refer to a specific Joint Commission standard in support of his allegation. This allegation fails to set forth a specific public policy.

Plaintiff did identify an additional, specific source of his alleged clearly mandated public policy of "patient safety." The complaint alleged that section 3 of the Medical Patient Rights Act "recognizes Illinois public policy establishing '[t]he right of each patient to care consistent with sound nursing and medical practices.' "[ ] * * *

We do not read section 3 of the Medical Patients Rights Act to establish a clearly mandated public policy of patient safety that was violated by plaintiff's discharge. Section 3(a) of the Act establishes the following rights:

> (a) The right of each patient to care consistent with sound nursing and medical practices, to be informed of the name of the physician responsible for coordinating his or her care, to receive information concerning his or her condition and proposed treatment, to refuse any treatment to the extent permitted by law, and to privacy and confidentiality of records except as otherwise provided. * * *

It is apparent that, as far as this section addresses medical record preparation at all, it is only concerned with record confidentiality, rather than record timeliness. This is understandable since the Hospital Licensing Act requires hospitals licensed in Illinois to develop a medical record for each of its patients as required by Department of Public Health rules. [ ] In turn, Department of Public Health rules require that patient medical records be "accurate, *timely* and complete." [ ]

*   *   *

We agree with the appellate court's view of this case. * * * The appellate court * * * reasoned that plaintiff simply told the Joint Commission surveyor that Memorial's practice was to update patients' charts before the end of the employee's shift, instead of immediately updating patients' charts as the Joint Commission allegedly recommended. The court concluded: "Such action falls short of the supreme court's public-policy threshold * * *."

[Court of Appeals] Presiding Justice Appleton wrote separately to state that "the limitations on the determination of what is 'public policy' are not only cumbersome but also so restrictive as to emasculate any common understanding of what we, as a society, expect." He further opined that it should be "the public policy of the State of Illinois for professional health-care providers to speak truthfully to State regulatory agencies concerning hospital practices involving—even tangentially—patient safety."

We agree with the appellate court special concurrence to the extent that the provision of good medical care by hospitals is in the public interest. "It does not follow, however, that all health care employees should be immune from the general at-will employment rule simply because they claim to be reporting on issues that they feel are detrimental to health care." [ ] * * * Adherence to a narrow definition of public policy, as an element of a retaliatory discharge action, maintains the balance among the recognized interests. Employees will be secure in knowing that their jobs are safe if they exercise their rights according to a clear mandate of public policy. Employers will know that they may discharge their at-will employees for any or no reason unless they act contrary to public policy. Finally, the public interest in the furtherance of its public policies, the stability of employment, and the elimination of frivolous lawsuits is maintained. [ ]

* * *

Affirmed. [By a unanimous court.]

NOTES AND QUESTIONS

1.   Most courts employ a narrow concept of public policy and exclude, for example, professional codes of conduct as a legitimate basis for an exception to at-will employment. See, e.g., Lurie v. Mid–Atlantic Permanente Medical Group, P.C., 729 F.Supp.2d 304 (D.D.C. 2010), holding that physician's reliance on professional standards for public policy fails both Maryland and D.C. public policy exceptions; Tanay v. Encore Healthcare, LLC, 810 F.Supp 2d 734 (E.D. Pa. 2011), detailing Pennsylvania case law with narrow public policy exception but holding that plaintiff met the exception.

2.   Many states have whistleblower statutes that protect employees who report wrongdoing to government agencies. See, e.g., Stewart–Dore v. Webber Hosp. Assn, 13 A.3d 733 (Me. 2011), interpreting Maine's general whistleblower statute. Several states have statutes that provide protection specifically for health care professionals. See e.g., Colo. Rev. St. § 8–2–123; Lark v. Montgomery Hospice, Inc., 994 A.2d 968 (Md. 2010), extending state health care whistleblower statute to cover internal as well as external reports

of quality concerns. A great number of statutes include specific protections for reports of their violation, including for example, the federal False Claims Act and the Emergency Medical Treatment and Labor Act. Health care professionals working in public hospitals also have some very limited protection under the First Amendment for their expressed opposition to hospital policies. Finally, some professionals who are within the protection of the National Labor Relations Act may be protected from adverse employment actions for complaints about workplace issues, as described below.

3.   While the employment-at-will doctrine does not admit a general conscience claim, state and federal legislation may protect health care professionals, including at-will employees, in refusing to participate in otherwise lawful treatment that they object to as a matter of conscience. These statutes tend to be quite specific, however; and most such statutes apply only to particular interventions, including abortion or end-of-life care. These statutes balance a number of competing interests and moral claims, including the autonomy and well-being of the patient; the autonomy of the health care professional; and the objectives of the health care organization, among others. See discussion in Chapter 15.

NOTE: UNIONIZATION IN HEALTH CARE ORGANIZATIONS

The 21st century has seen a surge in unionization in the health care field, including unionization of doctors and nurses. Health care workplace issues driving unionization include compensation levels, benefits, mandatory overtime, and workplace safety, just as in other settings, but staffing levels for professionals has been a key issue for health care unions. Union organizing among nurses, for example, has provided a platform for advocacy on staffing issues in hospitals and nursing homes. Physicians have sometimes pursued unionization to gain its exemption from antitrust law prohibitions against anticompetitive conduct. See Chapter 14.

The National Labor Relations Act governs the relationships between unions and employers. Its protection for collective action among employees is not confined, however, to those who are members of a formal union. Instead, the NLRA provides protection against adverse job actions (such as termination, demotion, or reduction in salary) to employees who join together, even informally, to engage in "concerted activity" related to terms and conditions of employment. The scope of "terms and conditions" of employment has been held to include concerns relating to staffing, quality of care, and even hospital billing. Thus, the NLRA can provide protection for actions that employment-at-will does not. See, e.g., Gaylord Hospital and Jeanine Connelly, 2012 WL 3878931 (2012).

For an individual worker to be covered by the NLRA, a worker must be an employee, and not an independent contractor. The NLRA relies on the traditional common law distinction between independent contractors and employees, rather than the formal title of the worker's position, and thus focuses on the degree of control exercised over the work of the health care professional. The NLRB has certified physician unions in HMOs that employ rather than contract with doctors as well as in hospitals with physician-employees. See generally Micah Prieb Stoltzfus Jost, Independent Contractors, Employees, and Entrepreneurialism under the National Labor Relations Act: A Worker-by-Worker Approach, 68 Wash. & Lee L.Rev. 311 (2011).

While an employee need not be a member of a formal union to be protected by the NLRA, an employee who is a "supervisor," as defined by the Act, is not covered. Prior to 2006, the National Labor Relations Board interpreted the statutory definition of supervisor narrowly. After a serial battle with the Supreme Court, in which the Court twice demanded that the Board adopt a broader interpretation, the Board issued a trilogy of decisions that appeared to broaden the reach of the supervisor exclusion. See, NLRB v. Health Care & Retirement Corp. of America, 511 U.S. 571, 114 S.Ct. 1778, 128 L.Ed.2d 586 (1994); NLRB v. Kentucky River Community Care, 532 U.S. 706, 121 S.Ct. 1861, 149 L.Ed.2d 939 (2001); Oakwood Healthcare, Inc., 348 NLRB No. 37 (2006). In practice, however, it is not clear that *Oakwood* and its companion cases have had that effect.

NOTE: EMPLOYMENT DISCRIMINATION

Discrimination cases arise in the health care setting as they do in any workplace, but there appears to be an increase in such litigation by health care professionals and especially by physicians. One factor that might explain the increased activity includes the movement toward formal employment relationships or significant control of practice rather than independent contractor arrangements, which may bring more physicians within the scope of the nondiscrimination statutes. In addition, the HCQIA (described in Section I, above) does not provide immunity for civil rights violations so it may be funneling litigation concerning staff privileges toward discrimination claims.

For most issues, the health care workplace does not present unique issues for the application of state and federal law protecting individuals against employment discrimination on account of age (the Age Discrimination in Employment Act, 29 U.S.C. § 621) and gender, national origin, religion, or race (Title VII of the Civil Rights Act of 1964, 42 U.S.C. § 2000e). Disability discrimination claims (under the Americans with Disabilities Act, 42 U.S.C. § 12101 or the Rehabilitation Act, 29 U.S.C. § 701), however, can intersect with concerns over patient safety in the health care setting.

An employee claiming under one of the federal disability statutes must be able to perform the essential functions of the job either with or without reasonable accommodation for his or her disability. Much of the litigation in disability discrimination cases addresses whether accommodations, in the form of job assignment, assignment of duties, or provision of protective or assistive equipment, were reasonable or, alternatively, were themselves discriminatory. See Robert R. Niccolini & Nina Basu, Disability and Accommodation in the Healthcare Workplace, 2 J. Health & Life Sci. L. 93 (2009).

If the employee poses a "direct threat" to health and safety (either the employee's or others'), which cannot be eliminated through a reasonable accommodation, the employee is not qualified for the job and has no claim. The question of patient safety arises in nearly every disability case involving a health care worker. Much of the case law concerning direct threat, however, has arisen in the context of HIV. Estate of Mauro v. Borgess Medical Center, 137 F.3d 398 (1998) is one example:

> The "direct threat" standard applied in the Americans with Disabilities Act is based on the same standard as "significant risk" applied by the Rehabilitation Act. [ ]. Our analysis under both Acts thus merges into one question: Did Mauro's activities as a surgical technician at Borgess pose a direct threat or significant risk to the health or safety of others?
>
> [F]our factors [are to be considered] in this analysis: (a) the nature of the risk (how the disease is transmitted), (b) the duration of the risk (how long is the carrier infectious), (c) the severity of the risk (what is the potential harm to third parties) and (d) the probabilities the disease will be transmitted and will cause varying degrees of harm. [ ]
>
> * * * [A] person with an infectious disease "who poses a significant risk of communicating an infectious disease to others in the workplace," is not otherwise qualified to perform his or her job. [ ] If the risk is not significant, however, the person is qualified to perform the job. * * *
>
> * * *
>
> The parties agree that the first three factors * * *: the nature, duration, and severity of the risk, all indicate that Mauro posed a significant risk to others. Mauro argues, however, that because the probability of transmission * * * was so slight, it overwhelmed the first three factors and created a genuine issue of material fact.
>
> In determining whether Mauro posed a significant risk or a direct threat in the performance of the essential functions of his job as a surgical technician, * * * courts should defer to the "reasonable medical judgments of public health officials." [ ] The Centers for Disease Control is such a body of public health officials. [ ] * * *
>
> * * *

The majority in *Mauro* conclude that Mauro's work as a surgical technician involved him in activities that the CDC would consider "exposure prone," and hold that his work posed a direct threat to the health and safety of others. The dissent, however, notes:

> The CDC "has estimated that the risk to a single patient from an HIV-positive surgeon ranges from .0024% (1 in 42,000) to .00024% (1 in 417,000)." [ ] This estimate, of course, is for surgeons, who by the very nature of their work enter surgical wounds with sharp instruments during virtually every procedure they perform. Common sense—and, of course, the court's obligation to interpret the evidence in the light most

favorable to the nonmovant—requires us to suppose, in the absence of contrary information, that the activities of a surgical technician such as Mauro who touched only the margin of the wound, and that only very rarely, would pose an even smaller risk. So, may the resulting coefficients of risk—numbers somewhat smaller than .0024% to .00024%— still be deemed "significant?"

* * * To assess whether Mauro posed a significant risk, the decision-maker should know more about any particular hazards (physical or moral) that might have affected the likelihood that this individual would transmit HIV to others. If surgeons whom the surgical technician assisted were to testify, for instance, that the assistant had a record of impeccable reliability, technical skills, and professionalism, and that they themselves were not concerned about risks they incurred by performing surgery with him, then a fact-finder could easily conclude that an employee with a contagious blood-borne disease did not pose a significant risk. On the other hand, if the testimony showed that the employee's co-workers found him to be inattentive, careless, and physically clumsy, then the jury might well conclude that, however small the theoretical risk of transmission, it would not be a safe bet for this particular person to continue working in surgery, and that he was not, therefore, "otherwise qualified."

* * * One can imagine many other important facts that could be developed at trial and influence a jury's conclusions—for instance, the employees' viral load (and therefore his degree of contagiousness) at the time of his termination, and whether the person reliably took prescribed antiviral medications, and the effectiveness thereof.

* * *

* * *The court appears to have misunderstood the [CDC] Guidelines, which clearly contemplate that, in the ordinary case, "surgical entry into tissues, cavities, or organs or repair of major traumatic injuries" should be regarded only as "invasive" procedures, not "exposure-prone" ones.

* * *

There have been no cases of provider-to-patient transmission of HIV worldwide since 2003. David Henderson et al., Society for Healthcare Epidemiology of America (SHEA) Guidelines for Management of Healthcare Workers Who Are Infected with Hepatitis B Virus, Hepatitis C Virus, and/or Human Immunodeficiency Virus, 31 Inf. Control & Hospital Epidemiology 203 (2010). There have been only six patients with HIV transmitted by a health care worker in the United States, and these are all reported from a single dentist before 1990. Studies conducted on 22,000 patients treated by 63 HIV-positive health care providers found no evidence of transmission from the providers. CDC, Are Patients in a Health Care Setting at Risk of Getting HIV?

Current guidelines for health care workers with HIV are much more granular than in years past and relate the specific viral load of the individual healthcare worker to the categories of work they are able to perform in light of risks to patients. In fact, workers with the lowest viral load can safely work in "exposure-prone" activities (now called Category III activities). See SHEA Guidelines, *supra*. See discussion of discrimination claims by HIV-positive patients in the Note on Employment Discrimination in Chapter 11.

Health care workers with a wide variety of disabilities have brought claims under § 504 and the ADA. These cases raise similar issues of reasonable accommodation and patient risk as do the HIV cases. See, e.g., Grosso v. UPMC, 857 F.Supp.2d 517 (W.D.Pa. 2012), diabetic perfusionist with repeated episodes of low blood sugar posed a direct threat to surgical patients; Jakubowski v. The Christ Hospital, Inc., 627 F.3d 195 (6th Cir. 2010), physician with mental disability producing patterns of confusion and errors in patient care not qualified to perform the essential functions of the position.

Only employees are covered by the ADA, Title VII, and the ADEA. A formal employment relationship is not required, however. If the plaintiff can prove that he or she is dependent upon the defendant for opportunities to practice or that the defendant exercises sufficient control over the plaintiff's work, the plaintiff generally will meet the requirement of an employment relationship under the statutes. Health care professionals whose only relationship with a hospital is traditional staff privileges, however, would not meet the statutory standard for employment. See e.g., Shah v. Deaconess Hosp., 355 F.3d 496 (6th Cir. 2004).

CHAPTER 12

THE STRUCTURE OF THE HEALTH CARE ENTERPRISE

∎ ∎ ∎

I. INTRODUCTION

Where's Waldo—Part I

In 1981, Waldo, a 25–year–old graphic artist, visited his family physician, Doctor Goodscalpel, complaining of gas, bloating and irregularity. Doctor Goodscalpel, a solo practitioner, took a brief history and ordered blood tests, urinalysis and various chemistry tests, all of which were performed at Llama Labs. Llama Labs was an outpatient facility organized as a corporation, the shares of which were owned by Dr. Goodscalpel and two other physicians. On a subsequent office visit several weeks later, Dr. Goodscalpel performed a rigid sigmoidoscopy and ordered x-rays for an upper GI, which were done at the Midstate Hospital. Midstate was a small community hospital from which Dr. Goodscalpel leased his office and at which he maintained staff privileges.

The results of these tests led Dr. Goodscalpel to recommend that Waldo consult a specialist, Dr. Jones, a gastroenterologist, who was a member of Practice Group, a professional corporation located in an adjacent town. Dr. Jones admitted Waldo as an inpatient and performed a colonoscopy at Mt. St. Hilda Hospital, a not-for-profit teaching hospital controlled by the Order of Caramel Fellowship, a religious denomination that operates 20 hospitals nationwide. Unfortunately, during this procedure Waldo suffered a perforated colon and required additional surgery which was performed by Dr. Smith, whom Waldo met the night before the surgery, and Dr. Mack, a resident studying at Mt. St. Hilda.

The bill for these services ran four pages and included over 150 separate services, items and supplies. Waldo's not-for-profit health insurance company, Red Flag, paid each provider separately for their services, although Waldo was responsible for nominal co-payments and, in some cases, for the "balance billing" where the billed charges of the provider exceeded Red Flag's "maximum allowable charges."

Waldo's encounter with the health care system brought him into contact with a number of different kinds of health care providers doing business in a variety of organizational structures. Arrangements of this kind were not unusual a few years ago and persist even today in many communities. What kinds of problems and inefficiencies do you see arising from this "system" of delivery of services? What are its advantages? As a "consumer" of health services, was Waldo well-served in this episode? For example, how were choices made and on what basis?

This chapter will explore the legal issues posed by many of these business and institutional arrangements. It will also analyze the current trend toward integration that has created many new organizational structures designed to unite the various providers of care. These arrangements, spurred most recently by the health reform legislation, entail a host of legal issues for the modern health law practitioner. Health care lawyers encounter providers, payers, and insurers spanning the full range of business organization forms: for-profit corporations, not-for-profit corporations, partnerships, professional corporations, limited liability corporations, partnerships, and more. Lawyers advising clients need to be aware of the opportunities and limitations of each business form across a wide variety of issues, including liability, governance, tax, and government regulation. A large majority of American hospitals are incorporated under state law as not-for-profit corporations and qualify for tax exemption under state and federal tax law.

II.   FORMS OF BUSINESS ENTERPRISES AND THEIR LEGAL CONSEQUENCES

A.   GOVERNANCE AND FIDUCIARY DUTIES IN BUSINESS ASSOCIATIONS

The governance of corporations is shared by three groups: shareholders (or members in the case of some not-for-profits), the board of directors, and officers. In practice, particularly in large corporations, the officers have almost complete control over the business affairs of the corporation. This separation of ownership and control in the for-profit corporate setting may give rise to the exploitation of shareholders. It also poses problems in not-for-profit corporations as boards may not faithfully or diligently pursue the entity's charitable purposes. To deal with this problem, the common law imposes fiduciary duties on those who govern the corporation, essentially obligating directors and officers to act in its best interests.

STERN V. LUCY WEBB HAYES NATIONAL TRAINING SCHOOL FOR DEACONESSES AND MISSIONARIES

United States District Court, District of Columbia, 1974.
381 F.Supp. 1003.

GESELL, DISTRICT JUDGE.

This is a class action which was tried to the Court without a jury. Plaintiffs were certified as a class under Rule 23(b)(2) of the Federal Rules of Civil Procedure and represent patients of Sibley Memorial Hospital, a District of Columbia non-profit charitable corporation organized under D.C.Code s 29–1001 et seq. They challenge various aspects of the Hospital's fiscal management. The amended complaint named as defendants nine members of the Hospital's Board of Trustees, six financial institutions, and the Hospital itself. Four trustees and one financial institution were dropped by plaintiffs prior to trial, and the Court dismissed the complaint as to the remaining financial institutions at the close of plaintiffs' case.

* * *

The two principal contentions in the complaint are that the defendant trustees conspired to enrich themselves and certain financial institutions with which they were affiliated by favoring those institutions in financial dealings with the Hospital, and that they breached their fiduciary duties of care and loyalty in the management of Sibley's funds. The defendant financial institutions are said to have joined in the alleged conspiracy and to have knowingly benefited from the alleged breaches of duty. The Hospital is named as a nominal defendant for the purpose of facilitating relief.

I.   Corporate History

The Lucy Webb Hayes National Training School for Deaconesses and Missionaries was established in 1891 by the Methodist Women's Home Missionary Society for the purpose, in part, of providing health care services to the poor of the Washington area. The School was incorporated under the laws of the District of Columbia as a charitable, benevolent and educational institution by instrument dated August 8, 1894. During the following year, the School built the Sibley Memorial Hospital on North Capitol Street to facilitate its charitable work. Over the years, operation of the Hospital has become the School's principal concern, so that the two institutions have been referred to synonymously by all parties and will be so treated in this Opinion.

* * *

Under the ... by-laws, the Board was to consist of from 25 to 35 trustees, who were to meet at least twice each year. Between such meetings, an Executive Committee was to represent the Board, and was authorized, inter alia, to open checking and savings accounts, approve the Hospital budget, renew mortgages, and enter into contracts. A Finance Committee was created to review the budget and to report regularly on the amount of cash available for investment. Management of those investments was to be supervised by an Investment Committee, which was to work closely with the Finance Committee in such matters.

In fact, management of the Hospital from the early 1950's until 1968 was handled almost exclusively by two trustee officers: Dr. Orem, the Hospital Administrator, and Mr. Ernst, the Treasurer. Unlike most of their fellow trustees, to whom membership on the Sibley Board was a charitable service incidental to their principal vocations, Orem and Ernst were continuously involved on almost a daily basis in the affairs of Sibley. They dominated the Board and its Executive Committee, which routinely accepted their recommendations and ratified their actions. Even more significantly, neither the Finance Committee nor the Investment Committee ever met or conducted business from the date of their creation until 1971, three years after the death of Dr. Orem. As a result, budgetary and investment decisions during this period, like most other management decisions affecting the Hospital's finances, were handled by Orem and Ernst, receiving only cursory supervision from the Executive Committee and the full Board.

Dr. Orem's death on April 5, 1968, obliged some of the other trustees to play a more active role in running the Hospital. The Executive Committee, and particularly defendant Stacy Reed (as Chairman of the Board, President of the Hospital, and ex officio member of the Executive (Committee), became more deeply involved in the day-to-day management of the Hospital while efforts were made to find a new Administrator. The man who was eventually selected for that office, Dr. Jarvis, had little managerial experience and his performance was not entirely satisfactory. Mr. Ernst still made most of the financial and investment decisions for Sibley, but his actions and failures to act came slowly under increasing scrutiny by several of the other trustees, particularly after a series of disagreements between Ernst and the Hospital Comptroller which led to the discharge of the latter early in 1971.

Prompted by these difficulties, Mr. Reed decided to activate the Finance and Investment Committee in the Fall of 1971. However, as Chairman of the Finance Committee and member of the Investment Committee as well as Treasurer, Mr. Ernst continued to exercise dominant control over investment decisions and, on several occasions, discouraged and flatly refused to respond to inquiries by other trustees into such matters. It has only been since the death of Mr. Ernst on October 30, 1972, that the other trustees appear to have assumed an identifiable supervisory role over investment policy and Hospital fiscal management in general.

Against this background, the basic claims will be examined.

II. Conspiracy

Plaintiffs first contend that the five defendant trustees and the five defendant financial institutions were involved in a conspiracy to enrich themselves at the expense of the Hospital. They point to the fact that each named trustee held positions of responsibility with one or more of the defendant institutions as evidence that the trustees had both motive and opportunity to carry out such a conspiracy.

* * *

Plaintiffs further contend that the defendants accomplished the alleged conspiracy by arranging to have Sibley maintain unnecessarily large amounts of money on deposit with the defendant banks and savings and loan associations, drawing inadequate or no interest . . . [T]he Hospital in fact maintained much of its liquid assets in savings and checking accounts rather than in Treasury bonds or investment securities, at least until the investment review instituted by Mr. Reed late in 1971. In that year, for example, more than one-third of the nearly four million dollars available for investment was deposited in checking accounts, as compared to only about $135,000 in securities and $311,000 in Treasury bills.

* * *

It is also undisputed that most of these funds were deposited in the defendant financial institutions. A single checking account, drawing no interest whatever and maintained alternately at Riggs National Bank and Security National Bank, usually contained more than $250,000 and on one occasion grew to nearly $1,000,000.

Defendants were able to offer no adequate justification for this utilization of the Hospital's liquid assets. By the same token, however, plaintiffs failed to establish that it was [the] result of a conscious direction on the part of the named defendants.

* * *

[The court concluded that plaintiffs failed to establish a conspiracy between the trustees and the financial institutions or among the members of each group.]

III. Breach of Duty

Plaintiffs' second contention is that, even if the facts do not establish a conspiracy, they do reveal serious breaches of duty on the part of the defendant trustees and the knowing acceptance of benefits from those breaches by the defendant banks and savings and loan associations.

A.   The Trustees

Basically, the trustees are charged with mismanagement, nonmanagement and self-dealing . . . [T]he modern trend is to apply corporate rather than trust principles in determining the liability of the directors of charitable corporations, because their functions are virtually indistinguishable from those of their "pure" corporate counterparts.

1.   Mismanagement

Both trustees and corporate directors are liable for losses occasioned by their negligent mismanagement of investments. However, the degree of care required appears to differ in many jurisdictions. A trustee is uniformly held to a high standard of care and will be held liable for simple negligence, while a director must often have committed "gross negligence" or otherwise be guilty of more than mere mistakes of judgment. [ ]

This distinction may amount to little more than a recognition of the fact that corporate directors have many areas of responsibility, while the traditional trustee is often charged only with the management of the trust funds and can therefore be expected to devote more time and expertise to that task. Since the board members of most large charitable corporations fall within the corporate rather than the trust model, being charged with the operation of ongoing businesses, it has been said that they should only be held to the less stringent corporate standard of care. Beard v. Achenbach Mem. Hosp. Ass'n, 170 F.2d 859, 862 (10th Cir.1948). [ ] More specifically, directors of charitable corporations are required to exercise ordinary and reasonable care in the performance of their duties, exhibiting honesty and good faith. Beard v. Achenbach Mem. Hosp. Ass'n, *supra*, at 862.

2.   Nonmanagement

Plaintiffs allege that the individual defendants failed to supervise the management of Hospital investments or even to attend meetings of the committees charged with such supervision. Trustees are particularly vulnerable to such a charge, because they not only have an affirmative duty to "maximize the trust income by prudent investment," Blankenship v. Boyle, 329 F.Supp. 1089, 1096 (D.D.C. 1971), but they may not delegate that duty, even to a committee of their fellow trustees. Restatement (Second) of Trusts § 171, at 375 (1959). A corporate director, on the other hand, may delegate his investment responsibility to fellow directors, corporate officers, or even outsiders, but he must continue to exercise general supervision over the activities of his delegates. [ ] Once again, the rule for charitable corporations is closer to the traditional corporate rule: directors should at least be permitted to delegate investment decisions to a committee of board members, so long as all directors assume the responsibility for supervising such committees by periodically scrutinizing their work.[ ]

Total abdication of the supervisory role, however, is improper even under traditional corporate principles. A director who fails to acquire the information necessary to supervise investment policy or consistently fails even to attend the meetings at which such policies are considered has violated his fiduciary duty to the corporation. While a director is, of course, permitted to rely upon the expertise of those to whom he has delegated investment responsibility, such reliance is a tool for interpreting the delegate's reports, not an excuse for dispensing with or ignoring such reports. [ ] A director whose failure to supervise permits negligent mismanagement by others to go unchecked has committed an independent wrong against the corporation; he is not merely an accessory under an attenuated theory of respondent [sic] superior or constructive notice. [ ]

3. Self-dealing

Under District of Columbia Law, neither trustees nor corporate directors are absolutely barred from placing funds under their control into a bank having an interlocking directorship with their own institution. In both cases, however, such transactions will be subjected to the closest scrutiny to determine whether or not the duty of loyalty has been violated. [ ] A deliberate conspiracy among trustees or Board members to enrich the interlocking bank at the expense of the trust or corporation would, for example, constitute such a breach and render the conspirators liable for any losses. [ ] In the absence of clear evidence of wrongdoing, however, the courts appear to have used different standards to determine whether or not relief is appropriate, depending again on the legal relationship involved. Trustees may be found guilty of a breach of trust even for mere negligence in the maintenance of accounts in banks with which they are associated [ ], while corporate directors are generally only required to show "entire fairness" to the corporation and "full disclosure" of the potential conflict of interest to the Board. [ ]

Most courts apply the less stringent corporate rule to charitable corporations in this area as well. [ ] It is, however, occasionally added that a director should not only disclose his interlocking responsibilities but also refrain from voting on or otherwise influencing a corporate decision to transact business with a company in which he has a significant interest or control. [ ]

Although defendants have argued against the imposition of even these limitations on self-dealing by the Sibley trustees, the Hospital Board recently adopted a new by-law, based upon guidelines issued by the American Hospital Association, which essentially imposes the modified corporate rule.

*   *   *

Having surveyed the authorities as outlined above and weighed the briefs, arguments and evidence submitted by counsel, the Court holds that a director or so-called trustee of a charitable hospital organized under the Non–Profit Corporation Act of the District of Columbia . . . is in default of his fiduciary duty to manage the fiscal and investment affairs of the hospital if it has been shown by a preponderance of the evidence that:

> (1) while assigned to a particular committee of the Board having general financial or investment responsibility under the by-laws of the corporation, he has failed to use due diligence in supervising the actions of those officers, employees or outside experts to whom the responsibility for making day-to-day financial or investment decisions has been delegated; or

> (2) he knowingly permitted the hospital to enter into a business transaction with himself or with any corporation, partnership or association in which he then had a substantial interest or held a position as trustee, director, general manager or principal officer without having previously informed the persons charged with approving that transaction of his interest or position and of any significant reasons, unknown to or not fully appreciated by such persons, why the transaction might not be in the best interests of the hospital; or

> (3) except as required by the preceding paragraph, he actively participated in or voted in favor of a decision by the Board or any committee or subcommittee thereof to transact business with himself or with any corporation, partnership or association in which he then had a substantial interest or held a position as trustee, director, general manager or principal officer; or

> (4) he otherwise failed to perform his duties honestly, in good faith, and with a reasonable amount of diligence and care.

Applying these standards to the facts in the record, the Court finds that each of the defendant trustees has breached his fiduciary duty to supervise the management of Sibley's investments. All except Mr. Jones were duly and repeatedly elected to the Investment Committee without ever bothering to object when no meetings were called for more than ten years. Mr. Jones was a member of the equally inactive Finance Committee, the failure of which to report on the existence of investable funds was cited by several other defendants as a reason for not convening the Investment Committee. In addition, Reed, Jones and Smith were, for varying periods of time, also members of the Executive Committee, which was charged with acquiring at least enough information to vote intelligently on the opening of new bank accounts. By their own testimony, it is clear that they failed to do so. And all of the individual defendants ignored the investment sections of the yearly audits which were made available to them as members of the Board. In short, these men have in the past failed to exercise even the most cursory supervision over the handling of Hospital funds and failed to establish and carry out a defined policy.

The record is unclear on the degree to which full disclosure preceded the frequent self-dealing which occurred during the period under consideration. It is reasonable to assume that the Board was generally aware of the various bank affiliations of the defendant trustees, but there is no indication that these conflicting interests were brought home to the relevant committees when they voted to approve particular transactions. Similarly, while plaintiffs have shown no active misrepresentation on defendants' part, they have established instances in which an interested trustee failed to alert the responsible officials to better terms known to be available elsewhere.

It is clear that all of the defendant trustees have, at one time or another, affirmatively approved self-dealing transactions. Most of these incidents were of relatively minor significance.

*   *   *

That the Hospital has suffered no measurable injury from many of these transactions—including the mortgage and the investment contract—and that the excessive deposits which were the real source of harm were caused primarily by the uniform failure to supervise rather than the occasional self-dealing vote are both facts that the Court must take into account in fashioning relief, but they do not alter the principle that the trustee of a charitable hospital should always avoid active participation in a transaction in which he or a corporation with which he is associated has a significant interest.

*   *   *

IV. Relief

*   *   *

[The Court ordered by injunction (1) that the appropriate committees and officers of the Hospital present to the full Board a written policy statement governing investments and the use of idle cash in the Hospital's bank accounts and other funds, (2) the establishment of a procedure for the periodic reexamination of existing investments and other financial arrangements to insure compliance with Board policies, and (3) that each trustee fully disclose his affiliation with financial institutions doing business with the Hospital. Declining to remove defendant trustees from the

Board or to impose personal liability on directors, Judge Gesell offered the following guidance.]

The management of a non-profit charitable hospital imposes a severe obligation upon its trustees. A hospital such as Sibley is not closely regulated by any public authority, it has no responsibility to file financial reports, and its Board is self-perpetuating. The interests of its patients are funneled primarily through large group insurers who pay the patients' bills, and the patients lack meaningful participation in the Hospital's affairs. It is obvious that, in due course, new trustees must come to the Board of this Hospital, some of whom will be affiliated with banks, savings and loan associations and other financial institutions. The tendency of representatives of such institutions is often to seek business in return for advice and assistance rendered as trustees. It must be made absolutely clear that Board membership carries no right to preferential treatment in the placement or handling of the Hospital's investments and business accounts. The Hospital would be well advised to restrict membership on its Board to the representatives of financial institutions which have no substantial business relationship with the Hospital. The best way to avoid potential conflicts of interest and to be assured of objective advice is to avoid the possibility of such conflicts at the time new trustees are selected.

As an additional safeguard, the Court will require that each newly-elected trustee read this Opinion and the attached Order. [The Court also required public disclosure of all business dealings between the hospital and any financial institution with which any officer or trustee of the hospital is affiliated and that the hospital make summaries of all such dealings available on request to all patients.]

IN RE CAREMARK INTERNATIONAL INC. DERIVATIVE LITIGATION

Court of Chancery of Delaware, 1996.
698 A.2d 959.

ALLEN, CHANCELLOR.

Pending is a motion . . . to approve as fair and reasonable a proposed settlement of a consolidated derivative action on behalf of Caremark International, Inc. ("Caremark"). The suit involves claims that the members of Caremark's board of directors (the "Board") breached their fiduciary duty of care to Caremark in connection with alleged violations by Caremark employees of federal and state laws and regulations applicable to health care providers. As a result of the alleged violations, Caremark was subject to an extensive four year investigation by the United States Department of Health and Human Services and the Department of Justice. In 1994 Caremark was charged in an indictment with multiple felonies. It thereafter entered into a number of agreements with the Department of Justice and others. Those agreements included a plea agreement in which Caremark pleaded guilty to a single felony of mail fraud and agreed to pay civil and criminal fines. Subsequently, Caremark agreed to make reimbursements to various private and public parties. In all, the payments that Caremark has been required to make total approximately $250 million.

This suit was filed in 1994, purporting to seek on behalf of the company recovery of these losses from the individual defendants who constitute the board of directors of Caremark. The parties now propose that it be settled.

*   *   *

The ultimate issue then is whether the proposed settlement appears to be fair to the corporation and its absent shareholders.

*   *   *

Legally, evaluation of the central claim made entails consideration of the legal standard governing a board of directors' obligation to supervise or monitor corporate performance. For the reasons set forth below I conclude, in light of the discovery record, that there is a very low probability that it would be determined that the directors of Caremark breached any duty to appropriately monitor and supervise the enterprise. Indeed the record tends to show an active consideration by Caremark management and its Board of the Caremark structures and programs that ultimately led to the company's indictment and to the large financial losses incurred in the settlement of those claims. It does not tend to show knowing or intentional violation of law. Neither the fact that the Board, although advised by lawyers and accountants, did not accurately predict the severe consequences to the company that would ultimately follow from the deployment by the company of the strategies and practices that ultimately led to this liability, nor the scale of the liability, gives rise to an inference of breach of any duty imposed by corporation law upon the directors of Caremark.

[As part of its patient care business, which accounted for the majority of its revenues, Caremark provided alternative site health care services, including infusion therapy, growth hormone therapy, HIV/AIDS-related treatments and hemophilia therapy. Caremark's managed care services included prescription drug programs and the operation of multi-specialty group practices and it employed over 7,000 employees in ninety branch operations. It had a decentralized management structure but began to centralize operations in 1991 to increase supervision over branch operations. Caremark had taken a number of steps to assure compliance with the anti-kickback provisions of the Medicare fraud and abuse law discussed in Chapter 13. As early as 1989, Caremark's predecessor issued an internal "Guide to Contractual Relationships" ("Guide"), which was reviewed and updated, annually, to govern its employees in entering into contracts with physicians and hospitals. Caremark claimed there was uncertainty concerning the interpretation of federal anti-kickback laws because of the scarcity of court decisions and the "limited guidance" afforded by HHS "safe harbor" regulations. After the federal government had commenced its investigation, Caremark announced that it would no longer pay management fees to physicians for services to Medicare and Medicaid patients and required its regional officers to approve each contractual relationship it entered into with a physician. Caremark also established an internal audit plan designed to assure compliance with its business and ethics policies. Although a report by Price Waterhouse, its outside auditor, concluded that there were no material weaknesses in Caremark's control structure, the Board's ethics committee adopted a new internal audit charter, and took various other steps throughout to assure compliance with its policies.

In August and September, 1994, two federal grand juries indicted Caremark and individuals for violations of the anti-kickback laws, charging among other things that Caremark had made payments to a physician under "the guise of research grants . . . and consulting agreements" so he would prescribe Protropin, a Caremark-manufactured drug. Plaintiff shareholders filed this derivative suit claiming Caremark directors breached their duty of care by failing adequately to supervise Caremark employees or institute corrective measures thereby exposing the company to liability. In September, 1994, Caremark publicly announced that as of January 1, 1995, it would terminate all remaining financial relationships with physicians in its home infusion, hemophilia, and growth hormone lines of business.]

B.   Directors' Duties To Monitor Corporate Operations

The complaint charges the director defendants with breach of their duty of attention or care in connection with the on-going operation of the corporation's business. The claim is that the directors allowed a situation to develop and continue which exposed the corporation to enormous legal liability and that in so doing they violated a duty to be active monitors of corporate performance. The complaint thus does not charge either director self-dealing or the more difficult loyalty-type problems arising from cases of suspect director motivation, such as entrenchment or sale of control contexts. The theory here advanced is possibly the most difficult theory in corporation law upon which a plaintiff might hope to win a judgment.

*   *   *

1. *Potential liability for directorial decisions*: Director liability for a breach of the duty to exercise appropriate attention may, in theory, arise in two distinct contexts. First, such liability may be said to follow *from a board decision* that results in a loss because that decision was ill advised or "negligent". Second, liability to the corporation for a loss may be said to arise from an *unconsidered failure of the board to act* in circumstances in which due attention would, arguably, have prevented the loss. [ ] The first class of cases will typically be subject to review under the director-protective business judgment rule, assuming the decision made was the product of a process that was *either* deliberately considered in good faith or was otherwise rational. [ ] What should be understood, but may not widely be understood by courts or commentators who are not often required to face such questions, is that compliance with a director's duty of care can never appropriately be judicially determined by reference to *the content of the board decision* that leads to a corporate loss, apart from consideration of the good faith or rationality of the process employed. That is, whether a judge or jury considering the matter after the fact, believes a decision substantively wrong, or degrees of wrong extending through "stupid" to "egregious" or "irrational", provides no ground for director liability, so long as the court determines that the process employed was either rational or employed in *a good faith* effort to advance corporate interests. To employ a different rule—one that permitted an "objective" evaluation of the decision—would expose directors to substantive second guessing by ill-equipped judges or juries, which would, in the long-run, be injurious to investor interests.[16] Thus, the business judgment rule is process oriented and informed by a deep respect for all *good faith* board decisions.

* * *

2. *Liability for failure to monitor*: The second class of cases in which director liability for inattention is theoretically possible entail circumstances in which a loss eventuates not from a decision but, from unconsidered inaction. Most of the decisions that a corporation, acting through its human agents, makes are, of course, not the subject of director attention. Legally, the board itself will be required only to authorize the most significant corporate acts or transactions: mergers, changes in capital structure, fundamental changes in business, appointment and

---

[16] The vocabulary of negligence while often employed, is not well-suited to judicial review of board attentiveness, especially if one attempts to look to the substance of the decision as any evidence of possible "negligence." . . . It is doubtful that we want business men and women to be encouraged to make decisions as hypothetical persons of ordinary judgment and prudence might. The corporate form gets its utility in large part from its ability to allow diversified investors to accept greater investment risk. If those in charge of the corporation are to be adjudged personally liable for losses on the basis of a substantive judgment based upon what persons of ordinary or average judgment and average risk assessment talent regard as "prudent," "sensible" or even "rational", such persons will have a strong incentive at the margin to authorize less risky investment projects.

compensation of the CEO, etc. As the facts of this case graphically demonstrate, ordinary business decisions that are made by officers and employees deeper in the interior of the organization can, however, vitally affect the welfare of the corporation and its ability to achieve its various strategic and financial goals.

* * *

Modernly this question has been given special importance by an increasing tendency, especially under federal law, to employ the criminal law to assure corporate compliance with external legal requirements, including environmental, financial, employee and product safety as well as assorted other health and safety regulations. In 1991, pursuant to the Sentencing Reform Act of 1984, the United States Sentencing Commission adopted Organizational Sentencing Guidelines which impact importantly on the prospective effect these criminal sanctions might have on business corporations. The Guidelines set forth a uniform sentencing structure for organizations to be sentenced for violation of federal criminal statutes and provide for penalties that equal or often massively exceed those previously imposed on corporations. The Guidelines offer powerful incentives for corporations today to have in place compliance programs to detect violations of law, promptly to report violations to appropriate public officials when discovered, and to take prompt, voluntary remedial efforts.

* * *

[I]t would, in my opinion, be a mistake to conclude that our Supreme Court's [prior statements regarding directors' duty to monitor] means that corporate boards may satisfy their obligation to be reasonably informed concerning the corporation, without assuring themselves that information and reporting systems exist in the organization that are reasonably designed to provide to senior management and to the board itself timely, accurate information sufficient to allow management and the board, each within its scope, to reach informed judgments concerning both the corporation's compliance with law and its business performance.

Obviously the level of detail that is appropriate for such an information system is a question of business judgment. And obviously too, no rationally designed information and reporting system will remove the possibility that the corporation will violate laws or regulations, or that senior officers or directors may nevertheless sometimes be misled or otherwise fail reasonably to detect acts material to the corporation's compliance with the law. But it is important that the board exercise a good faith judgment that the corporation's information and reporting system is in concept and design adequate to assure the board that appropriate information will come to its attention in a timely manner as a matter of ordinary operations, so that it may satisfy its responsibility.

Thus, I am of the view that a director's obligation includes a duty to attempt in good faith to assure that a corporate information and reporting system, which the board concludes is adequate, exists, and that failure to do so under some circumstances may, in theory at least, render a director liable for losses caused by non-compliance with applicable legal standards.

*   *   *

[The Court went on to find that the Caremark directors had not breached their duty of care because, first, there was no evidence they knew of the violations of the law and they reasonably relied on expert reports that their company's practices, although "contestable," were lawful. Second, applying a test of whether there was a "sustained or systematic failure . . . to exercise reasonable oversight," it found no actionable failure to monitor. The court concluded that the corporate oversight systems described above constituted a "good faith effort to be informed of relevant facts."]

NOTES AND QUESTIONS

1.   Almost all states adopt the corporate standard for the members of the board ("trustees") of not-for-profits. What arguments support a stricter standard for not-for-profit corporations? For one case applying a trust standard, see Lynch v. John M. Redfield Foundation, 9 Cal.App.3d 293, 88 Cal. Rptr. 86 (1970). See generally Daniel L. Kurtz, Board Liability: Guide for Nonprofit Directors 22 (1988). Might a shifting standard of care apply, depending on the nature of the decision and how important that decision is to the organization's core functions or the community benefits it was designed to supply? See James J. Fishman & Stephen Schwarz, Nonprofit Organizations, 225–6 (2d. ed. 2000).

2.   In the case of for-profit corporations, the business judgment rule has come to pose an almost impermeable shield protecting directors and officers charged with breaches of the duty of care in connection with business decisions that prove to be unwise or imprudent. As long as the director has made a business judgment that is informed, in good faith, and free of conflicts of interest, that judgment will not be subject to attack, even if the decision would not meet the simple negligence standard applicable to the "ordinarily prudent person." Should the business judgment rule apply with equal force to not-for-profit corporations? See Beard v. Achenbach Mem. Hosp. Association, 170 F.2d 859, 862 (10th Cir. 1948) (business judgment rationale used to uphold hospital's payment of questionable retroactive "incentive bonuses"). Under certain circumstances a parent may owe fiduciary duties to its nonprofit subsidiary. In an important recent case, a district court found that Lifespan Corporation, which became the sole voting member of a financially troubled teaching hospital, had violated its fiduciary duties of care and loyalty to the hospital. Lifespan Corp. v. New England Medical Center, 2011 WL 2134286

(May 24, 2011). The fiduciary breaches included Lifespan's failure to help the hospital improve its contracts with health insurers and an undisclosed conflict of interest by Lifespan's Chief Financial Officer involving the hospital's participation in a risky interest rate swap. However, fiduciary duties do not arise from customer-seller relationships. Crosse v. BCBSD, Inc., 836 A. 2d 492 (Del. 2003) (nonprofit insurance company's relation to its plan participants is purely contractual and therefore it owes no fiduciary duty).

3.   Does the standard established by the Chancellor in approving the settlement of the Caremark litigation give directors and senior officers of large, far-flung corporate enterprises sufficient incentives to ensure that their employees comply with the law? What factors militate against imposing a simple negligence standard with regard to the duty to monitor? Are the interests of the Caremark shareholders advanced by this holding? What role, if any, should the public interest in compliance with the anti-kickback laws play?

4.   The duty of loyalty applies to a variety of transactions in which directors or officers acting in their corporate capacity serve their own interests at the expense of those of the corporation. Self-dealing, taking of corporate opportunities, and acting in competition with the corporation may violate this duty. However, directors owe fiduciary duties only to their corporations, not to individual shareholders. Hence a professional corporation's termination of the contract of a physician shareholder-employee will not implicate the duty of loyalty. Berman v. Physical Medicine Associates, 225 F.3d 429 (4th Cir. 2000). State attorneys general have frequently advanced claims based on breaches of the duty of loyalty in cases involving conflicts of interest such as a hospital entering into an emergency room contract with a physician group owned by the chairman of its board; loans from a hospital to a physician serving on the board; and the hiring of architectural firms and employment agencies in which trustees have an interest. See Michael W. Peregrine, The Nonprofit Board's Duty of Loyalty in an "Integrated" World, 29 J. Health L. 211 (1996). See also Lifespan Corp. v. New England Medical Center, 2011 WL 2134286 (May 24, 2011) (finding conflict of interest in the desire of a parent corporation's advisor to join a banker's wine club which motivated him to adopt the banker's risky financial strategy for a subsidiary hospital).

Most state statutes governing nonprofit and for-profit corporations make it relatively easy to resolve such conflicts of interest. Can you explain the policy underlying this? For example, most allow a majority of disinterested directors, shareholders, or members (in the case of not-for-profit corporations) to validate in advance interested transactions provided there is full disclosure of all material facts about the transaction, and that the approving directors reasonably believe the transaction is fair to the corporation. See, e.g., Revised Model Business Corp. Act. §§ 8.60 et seq.; Model Nonprofit Corporations Act (MNCA) § 8.60. Conflicting interests involving not-for-profit corporations may also be resolved if the transaction was "fair" at the time it was entered into (i.e., it "carries the earmarks of an arms-length transaction"). MNCA § 8.60 (a)(3).

5. *Conversions and the "Duty of Obedience"*. Over the past two decades, a large number of not-for-profit health insurance companies, HMOs and hospitals have chosen to convert to for-profit status or to merge with, be acquired by, or joint venture with for-profit entities. Many Blue Cross organizations have undertaken steps to do so and hundreds of hospitals have been acquired by or entered into some form of joint venture with proprietary entities. In the typical conversion, the assets of the not-for-profit organization are sold to a for-profit entity (often controlled by management of the not-for-profit). The proceeds must be distributed to organizations eligible under § 501(c)(3) of the Internal Revenue Code or pursuant to applicable state law. Once the assets are distributed, the not-for-profit entity dissolves. Often the for-profit entity later makes a public sale of its stock, which may occur at a substantial premium over the price paid by the investors. See generally John D. Colombo, A Proposal for An Exit Tax on Nonprofit Conversion Transactions, 23 J. Corp. L. 779 (1998).

Board and executive actions involving conversions have raised fiduciary duty issues, particularly where conflicts of interest were evident and assets of the converting hospital were grossly undervalued. See Eleanor Hamburger et al., The Pot of Gold: Monitoring Health Care Conversions Can Yield Billions of Dollars for Health Care, 29 Clearinghouse Rev. 473 (1995); Lawton R. Burns et al., The Fall of the House of AHERF: The Allegheny Bankruptcy, 19 Health Aff. 7 (Jan/Feb 2000). In addition some courts have invoked the "duty of obedience" to judge whether directors were giving adequate attention to their corporation's nonprofit mission in deciding to convert or sell assets. Manhattan Eye, Ear and Throat Hospital v. Spitzer, 715 N.Y.S. 575 (1999). This duty, which is similar to the duty of trustees to administer trusts in a manner faithful to the wishes of the creator of the trust, obligates directors to adhere to the dictates of the corporation's "mission" or other statement of charitable or public interest purpose. Any substantial deviation from such purpose may subject directors to personal liability. Even when the duty of obedience is explicitly recognized, does it help solve the central problem that directors of nonprofits face; i.e., how to balance "mission and margin"? One proposal would establish a principle of "mission primacy" to guide directors and courts in situations in which business interests and charitable purposes conflict:

> As a general guiding principle, we suggest that "mission primacy" should be recognized as a central objective of the nonprofit enterprise with the corollary that directors enjoy presumptive deference in defining and, within limits, amending that mission. This focus would incorporate mission-centered values into interpretations of the traditional fiduciary duties of care and loyalty [while] preserving managerial discretion to balance the various constituents of the nonprofit firm including donors, consumers and the community. . . . [M]ission primacy would allow legitimate mission-centered factors to override corporate fiduciary standards in some cases while

imposing a more exacting standard of care and loyalty where mission issues predominate.

Thomas L. Greaney & Kathleen Boozang, Mission, Margin and Trust in the Nonprofit Health Care Enterprise, 5 Yale J. Health Pol. L. & Ethics 1 (2005).

PROBLEM: THE CATCH–22 OF DIVIDED LOYALTY

As a result of changes in federal reimbursement policies and anti-kickback laws and because of persistently high maintenance costs, Corsica Medical Group, LLC (CMG) has concluded that it is impractical for it to continue to own the lithotripter it uses in its outpatient clinic. As part of negotiations with Pianosa Community Hospital regarding a joint venture to operate outpatient facilities, CMG has offered to sell its lithotripter to the hospital. Dr. Daneka is a member of CMG and also serves on the board of directors of Pianosa Community Hospital. What advice would you give to CMG regarding its proposed transaction? What information should the Pianosa Community Hospital board review before making its decision?

NOTE: CERTIFICATE OF NEED REGULATION

Many states require that local facilities obtain a certificate of need (CON) prior to undertaking construction or renovation of facilities, purchasing major equipment, or offering new health services. Operating under the mandates of state statutory schemes, health planning agencies require that health care facilities demonstrate the "need" for such improvements and meet other financial and regulatory requirements. CON regulation is often criticized for inhibiting competition and innovation by requiring that providers satisfy regulatory requirements that are often vague, subjective, and conflicting. Moreover, the process of demonstrating need, financial feasibility, and quality of service may entail lengthy and costly administrative proceedings. At the same time CON laws provide the states one of the few mechanisms by which they can control the supply and location of health care resources.

Most commentary is highly critical of CON regulation, arguing that it imposes obstacles to efficient reorganization of healthcare markets, invites obstructionist behavior, and is incompatible with the evolution of competitive health care markets. See, e.g., Patrick J. McGinley, Beyond Health Care Reform: Reconsidering Certificate of Need Laws in a "Managed Competition" System, 23 Fla., St. U. L. Rev. 141, 167–68 (1995) ("Certificate of need laws shelter health care providers from the price-cutting demands of health care alliances"); Lauretta H. Wolfson, State Regulation of Health Facility Planning: The Economic Theory and Political Realities of Certificate of Need, 4 DePaul J. Health Care L. 261, 310 (1997) ("The process of obtaining a CON has become an enterprise in itself, becoming so lucrative that it attracts many politicians and former politicians who successfully use their influence to weight the process for those who employ their services."). A number of studies question whether CON achieved its purposes of lowering costs and allocating services more equitably. See, e.g., Morrissey and Shafeldt, J. Reg. Econ. 187 (1991). CON regulation has also invited abuse. For example, Richard Scrushy, CEO of HealthSouth Corporation, was convicted in 2006 of bribery and other counts and sentenced to seven years in federal prison for paying then-governor of Alabama Don Siegelman $500,000 for a seat on Alabama's Certificate of Need Review Board, which Scrushy then used to promote HealthSouth's interests. See Press Release, U.S. Dep't of Justice, Former Alabama Governor Don Siegelman, Former HealthSouth CEO Richard Scrushy Convicted of Bribery, Conspiracy and Fraud (June 29, 2006).

Another difficulty with CON statutes lies in their drafting. In many cases, the approach is to set forth a "laundry list" of numerous factors, many of which are vague and thus invite subjective determinations. For example, West Virginia's statute contains twenty-two criteria for assessing need; a twenty-third allows the regulators to utilize any additional criteria they see fit in determining need. W. Va. Code Ann. § 16–2D–6 (West 2008).

As noted, CON laws were widely regarded as out of step with the development of competitive health care markets. Can you make a case for maintaining or strengthening CON laws as a backstop for health reform? We will revisit the role of CON regulation in several contexts such as its effect on the development of specialty hospitals and its importance in planning joint ventures and integrated systems.

NOTE: LIMITED LIABILITY FOR INVESTORS

An important objective for many investors is limited liability, i.e., the guarantee that they will not be personally liable for the acts or debts of the business except to the extent of their investment. Limited liability is a key characteristic of corporations, limited partnerships, limited liability companies, and limited liability partnerships. Although it is not a common occurrence, courts have been willing to disregard the corporate form, or "pierce the corporate veil," and hold shareholders personally liable in certain circumstances. The jurisprudence on piercing is somewhat incoherent, with courts remarkably prone to rely on labels or characterizations of relationships (like "alter ego," "instrumentality" or "sham") or mechanically recite piercing factors (such as the failure to follow corporate formalities, the absence of adequate capitalization, or the commingling of personal and corporate assets) without explaining why it is appropriate to upset the parties' expectation of limited liability. Although piercing is rarely allowed, egregious facts, coupled with severe undercapitalization bordering on fraud, may occasionally justify disregard of the corporate entity. See, e.g., Autrey v. 22 Texas Services Inc., 79 F.Supp.2d 735 (S.D. Tex. 2000) (triable issues found in wrongful death action against severely undercapitalized corporation that owned forty nine nursing homes).In cases involving hospital systems with multiple corporate entities, courts are usually reluctant to pierce the corporate veil even where the parent exercises extensive control over the subsidiary and its name is prominently displayed in the advertising, signs and literature of the subsidiary hospital. See, e.g., Humana, Inc. v. Kissun, 221 Ga. App. 64, 471 S.E.2d 514 (1996); see also Ritter v. BJC Barnes Jewish Christian Health Systems, 987 S.W.2d 377 (Mo. Ct. App. 1999) (refusing to hold parent entity liable on agency, veil-piercing, vicarious liability or apparent authority theories despite extensive control over subsidiary hospital's operations). However, where regulatory evasion is possible, piercing might be available. In United States v. Pisani, 646 F.2d 83 (3d Cir. 1981), the government sought to recover Medicare overpayments made to a corporation owned by a single physician/shareholder.

Many professional corporations statutes expressly limit professionals' liability, providing for example: (1) limited liability for shareholders as to the ordinary business obligations of the corporation (e.g., business debts, negligence unassociated with professional services, bankruptcy); (2) unlimited liability as to the shareholder's own professional negligence and the negligence of those under her direct supervision and control; and (3) limited liability (or capped joint and several liability) for the negligent acts of other shareholders or other employees not under their supervision or control. See, e.g., Kan. Stat. Ann. § 17–2715; Me. Rev. Stat. 13–C, § 1107. What policies justify these differences? Are they still valid in an era of greater integration among practitioners operating in business entities? What arrangements might you advise for a professional corporation that anticipates purchasing expensive assets like an MRI or valuable interests in real estate? Are there arrangements that might also help allocate capital expenditures in a multi-specialty practice where not every physician will be using the MRI?

III.   INTEGRATION AND NEW ORGANIZATIONAL STRUCTURES

Where's Waldo—Part II

The year is 1999 and Waldo, now 43 years old, visits Dr. Goodscalpel for a routine check-up. Doctor Goodscalpel, who has joined a 10–doctor partnership called Medical Associates, recommends a PSA screening test. He sends Waldo down the hall to MedServices, an outpatient for-profit corporation owned by a subsidiary of the Llama Hilda Foundation. Llama Hilda is a not-for-profit corporation that now controls Mt. St. Hilda Hospital and numerous other entities providing health and administrative services. Unfortunately, the lab tests come back positive and Dr. Goodscalpel refers Waldo to a surgeon, Dr. Mack, who has joined Doctors Inc., a large (50–doctor) multi-specialist group organized as a professional corporation. Doctors Inc. and Medical Associates both are co-owners, along with Mt. St. Hilda Hospital, of a physician-hospital organization (PHO), an entity that negotiates contracts with insurance companies and supplies billing and other services to the medical groups.

After receiving prior approval from the PHO utilization manager, Dr. Mack sends Waldo to the Radiology Center for an MRI. The Radiology Center, an outpatient facility on Mt. St. Hilda's campus, is a joint venture organized as a corporation. Fifty percent of its stock is owned by Llama Hilda Foundation, and the other 50 percent is owned by a partnership comprised of 5 radiologists. After getting the MRI report back from the consulting radiologists, Dr. Mack recommends surgery to be performed at Mt. St. Hilda.

Waldo has joined BlueStaff's new managed care plan, CarePlan, which provides coverage only if he visits participating providers. Although Waldo had wanted Dr. Immel, an internationally known anesthesiologist who teaches at a local medical school, to assist in the operation, Dr. Immel was not a CarePlan participating provider and did not have staff privileges at Mt. St. Hilda hospital. Instead, Mt. St. Hilda has an exclusive contract with GasAssociates, a professional group organized as a limited liability company controlled by its anesthesiologist-owners. The anesthesia was furnished by a CRNA under the supervision of an anesthesiologist.

Most of the providers furnishing services to Waldo were paid on a pre-paid capitated basis. Waldo was responsible for a small co-payment on certain services.

Comparing Waldo's recent episode of care to his experience in 1981 (set forth at the beginning of this chapter), what changes have occurred in terms of provider coordination and control of their activities? How do the organizational structures to which the physicians and hospitals belong accommodate the changed environment? How have the economic incentives facing the providers changed? Is Waldo, the "consumer," better off under managed care?

A. THE STRUCTURE OF THE MODERN HEALTH CARE ENTERPRISE

Organizational arrangements for the delivery of health services have undergone dramatic changes over the last forty years. As depicted in Where's Waldo–Part I, for many years health care services were delivered primarily by doctors working in solo practice or as members of small groups usually practicing the same specialty, and by non-profit hospitals operating independently or as part of relatively simple systems that shared a few administrative or operational services. This began to change with the advent of managed care in the 1980's as hospitals adopted more complex organizational structures and entered into joint ventures and alliances with other hospitals and with their physicians. Prompted by developments in health care financing and the possibility of health care reform, physicians, hospitals and other providers began to reorganize their business enterprises and contractual relationships. In particular, some developed so-called "integrated delivery systems" via physician practice acquisitions and mergers, and establishing physician hospital organizations, joint ventures and other organizations that enhanced inter-provider linkages in order to meet the demands of capitated payments and the requirements of managed care. However, a consumer "backlash" against managed care occurred at the end of the 1990's as increasing concerns about patient safety, limitations on choice of providers, and quality of care arose, and a new era began and organizational structures began to change once again. Physicians and hospitals "dis-integrated," with many organizations disbanding and hospitals selling back to physicians their practices. Looser networks of physicians and alliances became more prominent, while administrators focused on means of improving the flow of information both internally and to consumers. See Cara S. Lesser et al., The End of an Era: What Became of the "Managed Care Revolution?" 38 Health Serv. Research 337 (2003).

The adoption of the Affordable Care Act reinvigorated interest in integration. As discussed in Chapter 14 *infra*, there has been a "merger wave" as hospitals have acquired other hospitals, physicians have consolidated practices, and hospitals have gone on a buying spree acquiring physician practices. Further, in response to incentives created by the ACA's reforms to Medicare and private insurance, providers have undertaken joint ventures specifically geared to providing integrated care though accountable care organizations, medical homes, and other arrangements.

The health care organizations discussed in this section are business entities (e.g., corporations, LLCs, partnerships or contractual joint ventures) that link providers "horizontally," "vertically," or on both levels. That is, physicians may combine horizontally with other physicians to form group practices, IPAs, PPOs, or other networks. Likewise, hospitals may merge or establish joint ventures and alliances with other hospitals. Hospitals and physicians have also integrated vertically by creating various kinds of integrated delivery systems, which bring together complementary provider services at several levels. Some of these organizations only loosely link hospitals and physicians and are primarily devices to facilitate joint contracting with payers. Other forms of vertical integration more fully bind hospitals and physicians by having them share both financial risk and control. Many kinds of arrangements are available: physicians and hospitals may co-own and co-manage services or enterprises; the hospital may undertake administrative or management services for physicians; the hospital may purchase the physician practices, with the physicians either becoming employees or independent contractors for the organization; or the physicians may control the enterprise with hospitals assuming a contracting relationship. Vertical integration may also include the insurance component, as provider systems may integrate into insurance or insurers may integrate into delivery through HMOs or joint ventures with providers. The following excerpt from the Physician Payment Review Commission [predecessor to Medicare Payment Advisory Commission (MEDPAC)] describes many of the organizational models, and how they enhance integration.

PHYSICIAN PAYMENT REVIEW COMMISSION, ANNUAL REPORT TO CONGRESS
(1995).

* * *

Integrating Organizations

* * *

Independent Practice Association

The independent practice association (IPA) is typically a physician-organized entity that contracts with payers on behalf of its member physicians. The typical IPA negotiates contracts with insurers and pays physicians on a fee-for-service basis with a withhold. Physicians may maintain significant business outside the IPA, join multiple IPAs, retain ownership of their own practices, and typically continue in their traditional style of practice. Physicians usually invest a modest fee (a few thousand dollars) to join the IPA. IPAs may also undertake a variety of additional roles, including utilization review, and practice management functions such as billing and group purchasing, resulting in greater centralization and standardization of medical practice.

* * *

Physician–Hospital Organization

The physician-hospital organization [PHO] contracts with payers on behalf of the hospital and its affiliated physicians. The organization is responsible for negotiating health plan contracts, and in some cases, conducting utilization review, credentialing, and quality assurance. The PHO may centralize some aspects of administrative services or encourage use of shared facilities for coordination of clinical care.

The typical PHO is a hospital-sponsored organization that centers around a single hospital and its medical staff. PHOs may also form as joint ventures between hospitals and existing physician organizations such as a large multispecialty medical group or an IPA. PHOs are further divided into open PHOs, which are open to all members of the hospital's staff, and closed PHOs, where the PHO chooses some physicians and excludes others.

As with the IPA, the typical PHO accounts for only a modest share of the physician's (or the hospital's) business. Physicians retain their own practices, and their relationship to payers other than those with whom the PHO negotiates is unchanged. As with IPAs, the PHO can move toward greater centralized control over practice management and medical practice.

* * *

Group Practice

A medical group practice is defined as "the provision of health care services by three or more physicians who are formally organized as a legal entity in which business and clinical facilities, records, and personnel are shared. Income from medical services provided by the group are treated as receipts of the group and are distributed according to some prearranged plan."

* * *

Group Practice Without Walls

A group practice without walls (GPWW) refers to physicians in physically independent facilities who form a single legal entity to centralize the business aspects of their organization. In the typical case, the GPWW is organized by a strong, centralized clinic that adds individual physicians or small groups in satellite offices. In some cases, the GPWW is financially identical to a traditional group practice: It owns the assets of the individual practices and physicians share ownership of the GPWW, making it a unified business organization for the decentralized delivery of care. In other cases, physicians retain ownership of their own practices but enter into agreements for administrative and marketing functions. The GPWW may itself own certain ancillary services such as laboratory services.

Management Services Organization

The management services organization provides administrative and practice management services to physicians. An MSO may typically be owned by a hospital, hospitals, or investors. Large group practices may also establish MSOs as a way of capitalizing on their organizational skill by selling management services to otherwise unorganized physician groups.

MSOs can provide a very wide variety of services. Smaller and not-for-profit MSOs may limit operations to selling to physicians various administrative support services, such as billing, group purchasing, and various aspects of office administration. In other cases, hospital-owned MSOs are the vehicle through which hospitals purchase physician practices outright, leaving the physician either as an employee of the hospital or as an independent contractor with the physical assets of the practice owned by the hospital. Large, for-profit MSOs typically purchase the assets of physician practices outright, install office managers and other personnel, hire the physician through a professional services contract, and negotiate contracts with managed-care plans, all in exchange for a share of gross receipts typically based on the physicians' current practice expenses.

* * *

Hospital–Owned Medical Practice

In addition to the purchase of a medical practice through an MSO, hospitals can directly purchase medical practices, typically as part of their outpatient department.

* * *

Integrated Delivery System

Finally, a number of functionally similar organizations are built around hospitals and physicians linked in exclusive arrangements. In these integrated delivery systems (IDSs), a hospital or hospitals and large multispecialty group practices form an organization for the delivery of care, with all physician revenues coming through the organization.[7] These include foundation model, staff model, and equity model IDSs.

The main difference among these organizations is in the legal formalities of who works for whom and in the professional autonomy of the affiliated physicians. In a typical foundation model system, the hospital establishes a not-for-profit foundation that purchases the assets of an existing physician group, signing an exclusive professional services contract with the physician corporation. Payers pay the foundation, which then pays the physicians' professional corporation.[8] In a staff model system, physicians work directly for the system without the intervening not-for-profit foundation and professional corporation. In an equity model system, physicians own a part of the system and share significantly in its financial success or failure.

NOTES AND QUESTIONS

1. *Integration: Objectives.* The integrating organizations described above bring together physicians, hospitals and other providers that had previously operated independently. Medicare payment reforms contained in the ACA, such as bundled payments and value-based reimbursement, and organizational innovations, such as accountable care organizations (all described in

---

[7] While some researchers would call these integrated delivery systems a form of PHO, most reserve the term PHO for those organizations where only a small fraction of the physicians' revenues come through the organization.

[8] The presence of the foundation model system is due in part to state laws prohibiting the corporate practice of medicine, and the need for arms-length financial agreements between for-profit and not-for-profit entities.

Chapter 10) have signaled that payers will reward coordinated, efficient, and seamless delivery systems in the future. Moreover many of these new arrangements shift risk to providers. Therefore, integrating organizations must take up the challenge of promoting high quality, cost-effective care while also assuring that providers with somewhat divergent economic interests cooperate.

In counseling in this area, it is critical to have a firm understanding of the different objectives of the various parties. For example, physicians typically are looking for a structure that will assist them in the contracting process by providing capital, information systems, administrative support, patient referrals, and access to a competitively strong network. At the same time, physicians want some assurance that their incomes will not erode and that they will have a substantial voice in the governance of the new organization. Hospitals are eager to assure themselves of an adequate flow of patients to fill their beds and outpatient facilities and a cadre of physicians committed to their organization. At the same time, hospitals are reluctant to give up control of the organizational structure of the enterprise (after all, they usually supply the lion's share of the financial investment), although shared control is sometimes attempted.

2.   *Organizational Structures for Physician Integration*. Physicians face a choice of a number of structural and contractual organizations in which to conduct their practices. The most complete form of organization is the formation of a Fully Integrated Medical Group (FIMGs), which usually takes the form of professional corporations or unincorporated entities such as LLCs and typically entails considerable operational integration. A tightly integrated FIMG, for example, might entail: centralized governance that controls all aspects of the group's business; formal quality control and utilization management programs; FIMG taking responsibility for entering into managed care contracts; and income allocation systems that rely on achievement of the group rather than individual performance. These groups may be formed among members of a single specialty or kind of practice (single-specialty groups) or among practitioners of multiple specialties (multi-specialty group practices, MSGPs). Less complete integration is available through several kinds of physician organizations. Partially Integrated Medical Groups (PIMGs) or "Group Practices Without Walls" entail physicians operating as a single legal entity (e.g. a professional corporation) with common management, staff, and administrative services. However, physicians in PIMGs may maintain their practice locations and employment relationships with certain staff; they also retain autonomy in many respects, such as participation in managed care contracts and purchasing and other business decisions. Costs and profits are frequently allocated on an individualized or "cost center" basis.

Finally, physicians may join organizations which are essentially contracting entities that enable them to offer a single network to payers, with perhaps some integration through common utilization controls. The Preferred Provider Organization (PPO), for example, usually entails contractual agreements to deliver care to a defined group of patients at discounted fee-for-service rates and to submit to certain controls on utilization or membership restrictions based on quality and utilization criteria. Similarly, physicians may join Independent Practice Associations (IPAs), which also involve only limited operational integration of physician practices through billing services and utilization review. Although IPA members sometimes agree to accept distributions of capitated revenues, which create incentives to alter practice styles, neither IPAs nor PPOs typically have strong controls over physician behavior and the percentage of each physician's revenues from the IPA is often not sufficient to cause significant changes in the way he or she provides care.

3. *Organizational Structures for Physician–Hospital Integration.* As described by the Physician Payment Review Commission above, physicians and hospitals desiring to achieve some degree of integration can choose from several organizational models: e.g., the MSO, the PHO or the staff, equity, or foundation model (fully integrated) IDS. The PHO is in most respects the least structurally integrated and least complex form. Its primary purpose is to negotiate and administer managed care contracts for its providers; it may even do so on a capitated basis, in which case the PHO is regarded as a provider of care. However, PHOs typically provide fewer services for physician practices than do the other forms and do not significantly alter the clinical practice patterns of providers. MSOs also provide contracting services as well as many of the "back-room" functions necessary to operate physician offices, including billing, claims processing, ancillary services and many of the credentialing and utilization control services needed for contracting. In the more comprehensive form, MSOs may acquire physician practices outright or supply "turnkey" operations by purchasing and leasing equipment and office space and hiring staff for physicians. Finally, fully integrated systems, including the foundation model IDS, are entities that bring together ownership of an organization that supplies all types of health services and coordinates case management and the flow of information. This may be done through foundations or clinics that acquire physician practices or through "equity models" that enable physicians to acquire an ownership interest in the system.

B. THE NEW LANDSCAPE FOR HEATH CARE ORGANIZATIONS

1. Health Financing and Organizational Arrangements

Managing Risk. Recall from earlier chapters that public and private payers have moved decisively to shift risk to providers. However payment methodologies differ in the amount and nature of risk that is shifted. As organizations take on greater risk they may require more complete integration of providers. Moreover, it is also generally true that greater risk produces greater potential rewards. The following chart illustrates this relationship for several forms of physician integration.

Organizational Structure and Ability to Manage Risk

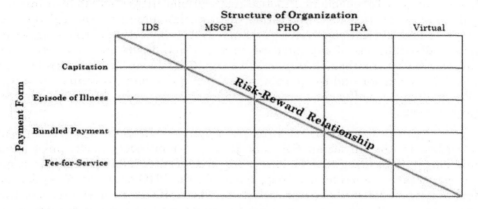

Notice also that differences between risk sharing and other forms of payment may influence physicians' choice of practice arrangements. While capitation encourages the formation of multi-specialty groups and integrated delivery systems to enable providers to make cost-benefit tradeoffs, fee-for-service reimbursement creates very different incentives. Under FFS payment, physicians have incentives to provide the most profitable procedures and ancillary services, with procedure- and service-intensive specialties benefiting more than other specialists and primary care physicians. In the 90s and early 2000s, physicians in such specialties found they could form large single-specialty practices that could aggregate capital to invest in equipment and facilities to provide their services without having to redistribute income to primary care physicians—as is traditionally the case in multispecialty groups. See Allison Liebhaber & Joy M. Grossman, Physicians Moving to Mid–Sized, Single Specialty Practice, Center for Studying Health System Change, Tracking Report No. 18 (August, 2007). Today, however, as payment moves away from fee-for-service (upward on the chart), organizational arrangements may be moving toward greater integration (leftward on the chart).

2. Accountable Care Organizations

Review the material in Chapter 10 discussing ACOs under the Medicare Shared Savings Program. Recall that the ACA permits ACOs to form under a wide variety of arrangements, ranging from fully integrated delivery systems to organizations that link providers or entities such as PHOs and IPAs by contractual agreements. Private entities are also rapidly developing ACOs to serve commercial insurance markets and are doing so in diverse organizational forms. As of 2012, hospitals were the dominant sponsor of commercial ACOs (53%), with physician groups second (32%), and insurers third (13%). David Muhlestein et al., Leavitt Partners, Dispersion of Accountable Care Organizations: June 2012 Update. Health insurers typically participate in ACOs either in partnership with providers or by offering new PPO products that encourage enrollees to select an ACO and obtain their care from physicians and hospitals associated within that organization. Typically these products offer low consumer cost sharing when the patient obtains services from a physician who is part of the patient's chosen ACO, "intermediate" cost sharing when the patient obtains services from a physician who is not part of the ACO but still part of the PPO contractual network, and "high" cost sharing when services are obtained from a physician who is outside the PPO contractual provider network. See James C. Robinson, Accountable Care Organizations for PPO Patients: Challenges and Opportunities in California (2011). An important caveat: ACOs are in a very early stage of development and the wide diversity of forms make categorizations misleading. Although most Medicare ACOs plan to serve commercial markets there are some significant differences with private ACOs. See Levitt Partners, *supra* (private ACOs are "more flexible and are experimenting with more varied payment and risk-bearing models" and are likely to influence the direction of Medicare ACOs).

3. Patient-Centered Medical Homes

The patient-centered medical home (PCMH) is a model for primary care delivery typically led by a physicians, physician assistants or nurse practitioners that provides comprehensive medical care and relies heavily on care coordination among team of providers that may include nurses, pharmacists, nutritionists, social workers and care coordinators. Originally developed for use in pediatric care, the medical home concept has been expanded under a variety of programs created by the ACA. (See discussion of medical homes in Chapter 10). Although some medical home practices may bring together large teams of care providers to meet the needs of their patients, others, including smaller practices may build virtual teams linking themselves and their patients to providers and services in their communities. The model contemplates expanded use of integrated data systems and reporting of performance to improve quality and assure better access to care. See Elliot Fisher, Building a Medical Neighborhood for the Medical Home, 359 New Eng. J. Med. 1202 (2008). The PCMH structure may stand alone in some cases or be part of an ACO in others. Developing a well-functioning PCMH is dependent on assembling a collection of primary care providers of sufficient size and scope and adopting management, communication and coordination policies that support the multiple goals of the organization. See Robert Berenson, A House is Not a Home: Keeping Patients at the Center of Practice Redesign, 27 Health Aff. 1219 (2008).

NOTE: THE SPECIALTY HOSPITAL PHENOMENON

An important, but perhaps short-lived, development in health care organization was the emergence of physician-owned "specialty hospitals" in the mid 2000's. These facilities (also referred to as "carve-out" or "boutique" hospitals) are hospitals that provide care for a limited range of conditions or perform only specified procedures. See United States General Accounting Office ("GAO") Specialty Hospitals: Geographic Location, Services Provided, and Financial Performance, GAO–04–167 (Washington D.C., Oct. 2003). Typically these hospitals concentrate their service in one of several profitable areas of medicine or illness such as heart care, surgery and orthopedics. A number of factors contributed to the rapid growth of these facilities: generous reimbursement rates for certain hospital and facility-based services, such as cardiology; stagnant physician incomes for specialist physicians practicing in these fields; declining effectiveness of certificate of need laws in limiting development of new facilities; and increased convenience for patients and doctors able to obtain care in different geographic location than older community hospitals.

For physicians owning or investing in such hospitals, these hospitals were a dream come true. Physicians could exercise greater control over the quality and conditions of practice in the facility and with increased specialization and familiarity with staff, outcomes may improve and medical error can be reduced. Further, physician investors in specialty hospitals share in the facility fee paid by insurers for their services, thus enhancing their incomes considerably. With patients usually willing to "follow their doctor," the financial risk of the doctors' investment is often minimal. However, for hospitals, the picture was rather less rosy. Community hospitals argued that specialty hospitals threaten their viability and do not compete on a level playing field. Not only are the most profitable services pulled out of the general purpose hospital, but it is left with EMTALA obligations to provide uncompensated care and must bear regulatory costs that the specialty hospital does not. Ultimately, as discussed in Chapter 13, the ACA came down against specialty hospitals, eliminating the "whole hospital" exception to the Stark law that allowed physicians to refer to hospitals in which they had ownership interest.

PROBLEM: ORGANIZING FOR INTEGRATION

Magna Hospital is a not-for-profit, tax-exempt hospital located in East Timbuktu, New Jersey. It operates 200 licensed acute care beds and an ambulatory surgery center (ASC) located two miles from its main campus. Magna employs 40 physicians and its medical staff also includes 140 independent physicians. It has recently contracted to erect on its campus a new doctors' office building with an adjoining site for high-technology ancillary services.

East Timbuktu is a mid-sized community with a substantial and growing elderly, retired population. Two other hospitals operate in the area. Tenacious Hospital, a for-profit hospital owned by a large, publically traded hospital corporation, operates two hospitals in the area: a 300-bed teaching hospital in East Timbuktu and a 100-bed facility in LaDont, an affluent nearby suburb. Tenacious is planning to organize an ACO for participation in the Medicare Shared Savings Program and to provide services to commercial insurers. One other hospital, Merciful Hospital, a Catholic, non-profit tax-exempt hospital, operates a 120-bed facility in West Timbuktu, an area with a large number of indigent residents. A large proportion of Merciful's patients are uninsured or covered by Medicaid which provides very low hospital reimbursement in New Jersey.

Approximately 70 percent of the physicians practicing in the area are in solo or small group practices (5 for fewer physicians). Doctors Group, LLP (DG), a large multispecialty practice comprised of primary care physicians, surgeons, cardiologists, and oncologists is the most highly respected and expensive practice in the community. Most DG doctors have staff privileges at both Tenacious Hospital and at Magna; none practice to any significant extent at Merciful. Another independent multispecialty physician group, Physicians for Seniors (PFS), is comprised of primary care physicians and physicians specializing in cardiology, geriatrics and oncology and focusing on serving senior citizens. Although PFS physicians primarily admit their patients to one of the Tenacious hospitals, they have a substantial number of low-income, dual eligible patients living in West Timbuktu whom they admit at Merciful. Finally, there is an ambulatory surgical center in the area, Sport-Fixers (SX) owned by Acme Orthopedics, an orthopedic surgery group located in LaDont that specializes in surgeries involving sports injuries and serving a high-income patient base.

Magna is anxious to take advantage of the new opportunities under the Affordable Care Act and its leadership is quite concerned about Tenacious Hospital's aggressive courting of doctors. The Magna's Board of Directors, which includes two doctors who are members of DG, has asked Magna's CEO, Wilma Worrisome, for an analysis of all possible mergers, affiliations, or new organizational structures that would serve the hospital's long-term interests. Ms. Worrisome is aware that the Affordable Care Act has wrought big changes and that the Timbuktu hospital market is becoming quite competitive. She says she is prepared to get the board to spend "whatever is necessary" and to "aggressively use our new buildings to attract physicians" in order to secure Magna's position. Your law firm has been retained to provide strategic advice on any opportunities to partner with other providers and to assess any legal obstacles that are likely to arise.

IV.   TAX–EXEMPT HEALTH CARE ORGANIZATIONS

A. CHARITABLE PURPOSES: HOSPITALS

1. Exemption Under State Law

UTAH COUNTY v. INTERMOUNTAIN HEALTH CARE, INC.
Supreme Court of Utah, 1985.
709 P.2d 265.

DURHAM, JUSTICE:

Utah County seeks review of a decision of the Utah State Tax Commission reversing a ruling of the Utah County Board of Equalization. The Tax Commission exempted Utah Valley Hospital, owned and operated by Intermountain Health Care (IHC), and American Fork Hospital, leased and operated by IHC, from *ad valorem* property taxes. At issue is whether such a tax exemption is constitutionally permissible. We hold that, on the facts in this record, it is not, and we reverse.

* * *

IHC is a nonprofit corporation that owns and operates or leases and operates twenty-one hospitals throughout the intermountain area, including Utah Valley Hospital and American Fork Hospital. IHC also owns other subsidiaries, including at least one for-profit entity. It is supervised by a board of trustees who serve without pay. It has no stock, and no dividends or pecuniary profits are paid to its trustees or incorporators. Upon dissolution of the corporation, no part of its assets can inure to the benefit of any private person.

* * *

* * * These [tax] exemptions confer an indirect subsidy and are usually justified as the *quid pro quo* for charitable entities undertaking functions and services that the state would otherwise be required to perform. A concurrent rationale, used by some courts, is the assertion that the exemptions are granted not only because charitable entities relieve government of a burden, but also because their activities enhance beneficial community values or goals. Under this theory, the benefits received by the community are believed to offset the revenue lost by reason of the exemption.

* * *

An entity may be granted a charitable tax exemption for its property under the Utah Constitution only if it meets the definition of a "charity" or if its property is used exclusively for "charitable" purposes. Essential to this definition is the element of gift to the community.

* * * A gift to the community can be identified either by a substantial imbalance in the exchange between the charity and the recipient of its services or in the lessening of a government burden through the charity's operation.

* * *

Given the complexities of institutional organization, financing, and impact on modern community life, there are a number of factors which must be weighed in determining whether a particular institution is in fact using its property "exclusively for . . . charitable purposes." Utah Const. art. XIII, § 2 (1895, amended 1982). These factors are: (1) whether the stated purpose of the entity is to provide a significant service to others without immediate expectation of material reward; (2) whether the entity is supported, and to what extent, by donations and gifts; (3) whether the recipients of the "charity" are required to pay for the assistance received, in whole or in part; (4) whether the income received from all sources (gifts, donations, and payment from recipients) produces a "profit" to the entity in the sense that the income exceeds operating and long-term maintenance expenses; (5) whether the beneficiaries of the "charity" are restricted or unrestricted and, if restricted, whether the restriction bears a reasonable relationship to the entity's charitable objectives; and (6) whether dividends or some other form of financial benefit, or assets upon dissolution, are available to private interests, and whether the entity is organized and operated so that any commercial activities are subordinate or incidental to charitable ones. * * *

Because the "care of the sick" has traditionally been an activity regarded as charitable in American law, and because the dissenting opinions rely upon decisions from other jurisdictions that in turn incorporate unexamined assumptions about the fundamental nature of hospital-based medical care, we deem it important to scrutinize the contemporary social and economic context of such care. We are convinced that traditional assumptions bear little relationship to the economics of the medical-industrial complex of the 1980's. Nonprofit hospitals were traditionally treated as tax-exempt charitable institutions because, until late in the 19th century, they were true charities providing custodial care for those who were both sick and poor. The hospitals' income was derived largely or entirely from voluntary charitable donations, not government subsidies, taxes, or patient fees.[7] The function and status of hospitals began to

---

7 Paul Starr, *The Social Transformation of American Medicine* at 150 (1982). "Voluntary" hospitals, like public hospitals (which evolved from almshouses for the dependent poor), performed a "welfare" function rather than a medical or curing function: the poor were housed in large wards, largely cared for themselves, and often were not expected to recover. *See id.* at 145, 149, 160. Early voluntary hospitals had paternalistic, communal social structures in which pa-

change in the late 19th century; the transformation was substantially completed by the 1920's. "From charities, dependent on voluntary gifts, [hospitals] developed into market institutions financed increasingly out of payments from patients." The transformation was multidimensional: hospitals were redefined from social welfare to medical treatment institutions; their charitable foundation was replaced by a business basis; and their orientation shifted to "professionals and their patients," away from "patrons and the poor."

*   *   *

Also of considerable significance to our review is the increasing irrelevance of the distinction between nonprofit and for-profit hospitals for purposes of discovering the element of charity in their operations. The literature indicates that two models, described below, appear to describe a large number of nonprofit hospitals as they function today.

(1) The "physicians' cooperative" model describes nonprofit hospitals that operate primarily for the benefit of the participating physicians. Physicians, pursuant to this model, enjoy power and high income through their direct or indirect control over the nonprofit hospitals to which they bring their patients. . . . A minor variation of the above theory is the argument that many nonprofit hospitals operate as "shelters" within which physicians operate profitable businesses, such as laboratories. [ ]

(2) The "polycorporate enterprise" model describes the increasing number of nonprofit hospital chains. Here, power is largely in the hands of administrators, not physicians. Through the creation of holding companies, nonprofit hospitals have grown into large groups of medical enterprises, containing both for-profit and nonprofit corporate entities. Nonprofit corporations can own for-profit corporations without losing their federal nonprofit tax status as long as the profits of the for-profit corporations are used to further the nonprofit purposes of the parent organization. [ ]

*   *   *

* * * Dramatic advances in medical knowledge and technology have resulted in an equally dramatic rise in the cost of medical services. At the same time, elaborate and comprehensive organizations of third-party payers have evolved. Most recently, perhaps as a further evolutionary response to the unceasing rise in the cost of medical services, the provision of such services has become a highly competitive business.

*   *   *

tients entered at the sufferance of their benefactors, "had the moral status of children," and received more moralistic and religious help than medical treatment. *Id.* at 149, 158. * * *

[Ed. note: The opinion relies on Starr's book extensively. Further citations have been omitted.]

The stated purpose of IHC regarding the operation of both hospitals clearly meets at least part of the first criterion we have articulated for determining the existence of a charitable use. Its articles of incorporation identify as "corporate purposes," among other things, the provision of "care and treatment of the sick, afflicted, infirm, aged or injured within and/or without the State of Utah." The same section prevents any "part of the net earnings of this Corporation" to inure to the private benefit of any individual. Furthermore, under another section, the assets of the corporation upon dissolution likewise may not be distributed to benefit any private interest.

The second factor we examine is whether the hospitals are supported, and to what extent, by donations and gifts. * * * [W]e have examined the testimony and exhibits in evidence on this question. The latter demonstrate that current operating expenses for both hospitals are covered almost entirely by revenue from patient charges. * * * The evidence was that both hospitals charge rates for their services comparable to rates being charged by other similar entities, and no showing was made that the donations identified resulted in charges to patients below prevailing market rates.

*   *   *

One of the most significant of the factors to be considered in review of a claimed exemption is the third we identified: whether the recipients of the services of an entity are required to pay for that assistance, in whole or in part. The Tax Commission in this case found as follows:

> The policy of [IHC's hospitals] is to collect hospital charges from patients whenever it is reasonable and possible to do so; however, no person in need of medical attention is denied care solely on the basis of a lack of funds.

The record also shows that neither of the hospitals in this case demonstrated any substantial imbalance between the value of the services it provides and the payments it receives apart from any gifts, donations, or endowments. The record shows that the vast majority of the services provided by these two hospitals are paid for by government programs, private insurance companies, or the individuals receiving care.

*   *   *

Between 1978 and 1980, the value of the services given away as charity by these two hospitals constituted less than one percent of their gross revenues. Furthermore, the record also shows that such free service as did exist was deliberately not advertised out of fear of a "deluge of people" trying to take advantage of it. Instead, every effort was made to recover payment for services rendered. * * *

The defendants argue that the great expense of modern hospital care and the universal availability of insurance and government health care subsidies make the idea of a hospital solely supported by philanthropy an anachronism. We believe this argument itself exposes the weakness in the defendants' position. It is precisely because such a vast system of third-party payers has developed to meet the expense of modern hospital care that the historical distinction between for-profit and nonprofit hospitals has eroded. * * *

The fourth question we consider is whether the income received from all sources by these IHC hospitals is in excess of their operating and maintenance expenses. Because the vast majority of their services are paid for, the nonprofit hospitals in this case accumulate capital as do their profit-seeking counterparts.

* * *

A large portion of the profits of most for-profit entities is used for capital improvements and new, updated equipment, and the defendant hospitals here similarly expend their revenues in excess of operational expenses. There can be no doubt, in reviewing the references in the record by members of IHC's administrative staff, that the IHC system, as well as the two hospitals in question, has consistently generated sufficient funds in excess of operating costs to contribute to rapid and extensive growth, building, competitive employee and professional salaries and benefits, and a very sophisticated management structure. While it is true that no financial benefits or profits are available to private interests in the form of stockholder distributions or ownership advantages, the user *entity* in this case clearly generates substantial "profits" in the sense of income that exceeds expenses.

* * *

On the question of benefits to private interests, certainly it appears that no individuals who are employed by or administer the defendants receive any distribution of assets or income, and some, such as IHC's board of trustees members, volunteer their services. We have noted, however, that IHC owns a for-profit entity, as well as nonprofit subsidiaries, and there is in addition the consideration that numerous forms of private commercial enterprise, such as pharmacies, laboratories, and contracts for medical services, are conducted as a necessary part of the defendants' hospital operations. The burden being on the taxpayer to demonstrate eligibility for the exemption, the inadequacies in the record on these questions cannot be remedied by speculation in the defendants' favor. * * *

Neither can we find on this record that the burdens of government are substantially lessened as a result of the defendants' provision of services. The record indicates that Utah County budgets approximately

$50,000 annually for the payment of hospital care for indigents. Further-more, the evidence described two instances within a three-month period where, after a Utah County official had declined to authorize payment for a person in the emergency room, Utah Valley Hospital refused to admit the injured person on the basis of that person's inability to pay. The coun-ty official was told in these instances to either authorize payment or to "come and get" the person. Such behavior on the hospital's part is incon-sistent with its argument that it functions to relieve government of a bur-den. Likewise, as we have pointed out, there has been no showing that the tax exemption is a significant factor in permitting these defendants to operate, thereby arguably relieving government of the burden of estab-lishing its own medical care providers. In fact, government is already car-rying a substantial share of the operating expenses of defendants, in the form of third-party payments pursuant to "entitlement" programs such as Medicare and Medicaid.

* * *

We reverse the Tax Commission's grant of an *ad valorem* property tax exemption to defendants as being unconstitutional. * * *

* * *

STEWART, JUSTICE (dissenting):

* * *

III. Definition of Charity

* * *

The legal concept of charity does not require, as the majority appar-ently requires, that a hospital incur a deficit to qualify as a charitable in-stitution. Charitable hospitals need not be self-liquidating. [ ]

* * *

It is true that the hospitals in this case receive substantial revenues from third-party payors and patients, but there is not a shred of evidence in this record, much less a finding by the Tax Commission, that one cent of the revenues is used for any purpose other than furthering the charita-ble purposes of providing hospital services to the sick and infirm. On the contrary, the Tax Commission's findings affirmatively establish that no person has profited from the revenues produced at either Utah Valley or American Fork Hospitals other than patients. Under time-honored legal principles, both hospitals qualify as charitable institutions.

IV. Utah Valley Hospital's and American Fork Hospital's Gifts to the Community

* * *

A. Direct Patient Subsidies

* * * During the years 1978–80, Utah Valley Hospital rendered wholly free services to indigents in the amount of $200,000, and in each of those years the amount increased substantially over the preceding year. During the same period, the hospital subsidized services rendered to Medicare, Medicaid, and worker's compensation patients in the amount of $3,174,024. The corresponding figures for American Fork Hospital were $39,906 in indigent care and $421,306 for subsidization of Medicare, Medicaid, and worker's compensation benefits.

However, the value of the charity extended to indigents is in fact greater than the amounts stated. The cost of the charity extended to patients who are first identified as charity patients *after* admission rather than *at* admission is charged to the "bad debts" account, along with traditional uncollectible accounts or bad debts, instead of being charged to charity. * * *

In sum, the *direct* cost of patient charity given away by Utah Valley Hospital for the period in question is in excess of $3,374,024, but less than $4,942,779 (which includes bad debts). The *direct* cost of the charity given away by American Fork Hospital is in excess of $461,212, but less than $639,024 (which includes bad debts).

* * * Unlike for-profit hospitals, Utah Valley and American Fork have a policy against turning away indigent patients. Therefore, that portion of the hospitals' bad debts which is attributable to indigency is bona fide charity since the charges would have been initially made to the charity account had the patient's indigency been discovered at admission. Those charges are not just ordinary business bad debts experienced by all commercial enterprises, as the majority would have it.

* * *

B. Capital Subsidies and Gifts

The most glaring lapse in the majority opinion, in my view, is its flat-out refusal to recognize that there would be no Utah Valley Hospital—at all—if it had not been given lock, stock, and barrel to IHC by the Church of Jesus Christ of Latter–Day Saints, which initially built the hospital. American Fork Hospital apparently was initially erected by taxpayers' money. At the City's request, IHC took over the operation of the hospital as a lessee of American Fork City to relieve the City of a governmental burden. It follows that all patients at both hospitals, whether indigent, part-paying, or fully paying patients, are direct beneficiaries of large monetary investments in land, buildings, and medical equipment. * * *

In addition to the "gift to the community" of the actual physical facilities, each and every patient benefits from the fact that IHC is a nonprofit corporation whose hospitals make no profit on the value of the assets dedicated to hospital care. The majority's effort to portray IHC hospitals as if they were operated as for-profit entities has no substance in the record whatsoever. A for-profit hospital, unlike a nonprofit hospital, must necessarily price its services to make a profit on its investment if it is to stay in business. The surplus that Utah Valley and American Fork budget for is not by any means the equivalent of profit, as the majority wrongly suggests.

*   *   *

Furthermore, the majority inaccurately asserts that Utah Valley charges rates comparable to other similar entities. The evidence is to the contrary. Utah Valley Hospital, with its 385 beds and expensive, sophisticated acute care equipment, charges rates comparable to the rates charged by Payson Hospital, a small for-profit hospital that renders inexpensive types of services. *   *   *

*   *   * In addition, there are no "prevailing market rates" for tertiary care hospitals, if by that term the majority means prevailing rates of competitive for-profit hospitals. There is no for-profit tertiary care hospital in the entire state of Utah; all tertiary care hospitals are non-profit institutions. In fact, there is no other tertiary care hospital, whether non-profit or for-profit, in the immense, sparsely populated area served by the Utah Valley Hospital, which extends from Utah County to the Nevada–Arizona border. Indeed, the facts strongly suggest that a for-profit tertiary care hospital could not survive in the geographical market area served by Utah Valley.

*   *   *

V.   Tax Exempt Status of Non–Profit Hospitals Under the
Majority Opinion

*   *   *

The record also demonstrates that the primary care hospital and the tertiary care hospital involved in this case relieve a significant governmental burden, one of the two alternative tests for determining whether a nonprofit hospital qualifies to be treated as a charitable institution. *   *   * In the wide-open spaces of the West, where small communities are widely separated, the profit motive has not been sufficient to provide the needed impetus for the building of community hospitals (except in rare instances). Nor has it resulted in the construction of tertiary care hospitals in the more populous parts of the state.

The majority's argument is that no government burden is relieved by providing hospital service to those who can pay for it on a for-profit basis. The argument misses the mark for two reasons. First, the alternatives are not for-profit or nonprofit hospitals. The alternatives are nonprofit hospital care or no hospital care at all, at least within the relevant geographical markets. Second, the charitable status of a hospital does not turn on whether it provides care for patients who can pay. The basic policy is not to tax the sick and infirm irrespective of ability to pay. A county provides many services to rich and poor alike without charging the rich for those services. Parks and playgrounds are but examples. Providing medical services may not be mandatory for counties or cities, but if they do, they most certainly promote the public health, safety, morals, and welfare in a most fundamental way. Surely cities and counties would, as a practical matter, be compelled to provide hospital services if the nonprofit hospitals in this state did not exist. * * *

* * *

VI. Differences Between For–Profit and Nonprofit Hospitals

* * *

* * * [A] for-profit hospital's investment decisions as to what markets or communities to enter and what kinds of equipment to invest in are made from a basically different motive than a nonprofit hospital's. The decisions of a for-profit hospital corporation must be based upon careful calculations as to the rate of return that may be expected on invested capital. If the rate of return is not sufficient, the investment is not made. Whether the surplus is reinvested in part or paid out to investors in dividends in whole or in part, the investor receives personal monetary benefit either in the increased value of his stock or in dividends.

* * *

Nonprofit hospitals must, of course, be concerned with generating sufficient revenue to maintain themselves, but they are not concerned with earning a return on their investment for the benefit of stockholders. Their purposes are altruistic. Any surplus must be used in a manner that aggrandizes no one, such as for the lowering of rates, the acquisition of new equipment, or the improvement of facilities. * * *

* * *

* * * IHC's Board of Trustees considers itself a trustee of the health care facilities for the public. "[W]e see ourselves as owned by the community since the corporation owns itself and in effect the church gave the hospitals to the communities, and we're entrusted with the running of the hospitals. We see them as in effect owned by the communities." * * *

* * *

PROVENA COVENANT MEDICAL CENTER V. THE DEPARTMENT OF REVENUE

Supreme Court of Illinois, 2010.
236 Ill.2d 368, 925 N.E.2d 1131.

JUSTICE KARMEIER

The central issue in this case is whether Provena Hospitals established that it was entitled to a charitable exemption under section 15–65 of the Property Tax [ ] for the 2002 tax year for various parcels of real estate it owns in Urbana. The Director of Revenue determined that it had not and denied the exemption. . . . For the reasons that follow, we now affirm the judgment of the appellate court upholding the decision by the Department of Revenue to deny the exemption.

The appellant property owner and taxpayer in this case is Provena Hospitals. Provena Hospitals is one of four subsidiaries of Provena Health, a corporation created when the Servants of the Holy Heart and two other groups affiliated with the Roman Catholic Church merged their health-care operations. . . . Provena Hospitals owns and operates six hospitals, including Provena Covenant Medical Center (PCMC), a full-service hospital located in the City of Urbana.

* * *

Provena Hospitals is exempt from federal income tax under section 501(c)(3) of the Internal Revenue Code (26 U.S.C. § 501(c)(3) (1988)). The Illinois Department of Revenue has also determined that the corporation is exempt from this state's retailers' occupation tax [ ], service occupation tax [ ], use tax [ ], and service use tax. [ ]

* * *

PCMC was not required to participate in the Medicare and Medicaid programs, but did so because it believed participation was "consistent with its mission." Participation was also necessary in order for Provena Hospitals to qualify for tax exemption under federal law. In addition, it provided the institution with a steady revenue stream.

* * *

During 2002, the amount of aid provided by Provena Hospitals to PCMC patients under the facility's charity care program was modest. The hospital waived $1,758,940 in charges, representing an actual cost to it of only $831,724. This was equivalent to only 0.723% of PCMC's revenues for that year and was $268,276 less than the $1.1 million in tax benefits which Provena stood to receive if its claim for a property tax exemption were granted.

* * *

Under Illinois law, taxation is the rule. Tax exemption is the exception. All property is subject to taxation, unless exempt by statute, in conformity with the constitutional provisions relating thereto. * * *

The burden of establishing entitlement to a tax exemption rests upon the person seeking it. [ ]. The burden is a very heavy one. The party claiming an exemption must prove by clear and convincing evidence that the property in question falls within both the constitutional authorization and the terms of the statute under which the exemption is claimed. [ ] * * *

* * * Provena Hospitals has been granted a tax exemption by the federal government. There is no dispute, however, that tax exemption under federal law is not dispositive of whether real property is exempt from property tax under Illinois law. [ ] * * *

* * *

In Methodist Old Peoples Home v. Korzen, 39 Ill.2d 149, 156–57, 233 N.E.2d 537 (1968), we identified the distinctive characteristics of a charitable institution as follows: (1) it has no capital, capital stock, or shareholders; (2) it earns no profits or dividends but rather derives its funds mainly from private and public charity and holds them in trust for the purposes expressed in the charter; (3) it dispenses charity to all who need it an d apply for it; (4) it does not provide gain or profit in a private sense to any person connected with it; and (5) it does not appear to place any obstacles in the way of those who need and would avail themselves of the charitable benefits it dispenses. [ ]For purposes of applying these criteria, we defined charity as "a gift to be applied * * * for the benefit of an indefinite number of persons, persuading them to an educational or religious conviction, for their general welfare-or in some way reducing the burdens of government."[ ].

* * *

Provena Hospitals clearly satisfies the first of the factors identified by this court *Methodist Old Peoples Home v. Korzen* for determining whether an organization can be considered a charitable institution: it has no capital, capital stock, or shareholders. Provena Hospitals also meets the fourth *Korzen* factor. It does not provide gain or profit in a private sense to any person connected with it. While the record focused on PCMC rather than Provena Hospitals, it was assumed by all parties during the administrative proceedings that Provena Hospitals' policies in this regard were the same as those of PCMC, and it was stipulated that PCMC diverted no profits or funds to individuals or entities for their own interests or private benefit.

* * *

While *Korzen* factors one and four thus tilt in favor of characterizing Provena Hospitals as a charitable institution, application of the remaining factors demonstrates that the characterization will not hold. Provena Hospitals plainly fails to meet the second criterion: its funds are not derived mainly from private and public charity and held in trust for the purposes expressed in the charter. They are generated, overwhelmingly, by providing medical services for a fee. While the corporation's consolidated statement of operations for 2002 ascribes $25,282,000 of Provena Hospitals' $739,293,000 in total revenue to "other revenue," that sum represents a mere 3.4% of Provena's income, and no showing was made as to how much, if any, of it was derived from charitable contributions. The only charitable donations documented in this case were those made to PCMC, one of Provena Hospitals' subsidiary institutions, and they were so small, a mere $6,938, that they barely warrant mention.

Provena Hospitals likewise failed to show by clear and convincing evidence that it satisfied factors three or five, namely, that it dispensed charity to all who needed it and applied for it and did not appear to place any obstacles in the way of those who needed and would have availed themselves of the charitable benefits it dispenses. * * *

* * * [E]ligibility for a charitable exemption under section 15–65 of the Property Tax Code (35 ILCS 200/ 15–65 (West 2002)) requires not only charitable ownership, but charitable use. Specifically, an organization seeking an exemption under section 15–65 must establish that the subject property is "actually and exclusively used for charitable or beneficent purposes, and not leased or otherwise used with a view to profit." 35 ILCS 200/15–65 (West 2002). When the law says that property must be "exclusively used" for charitable or beneficent purposes, it means that charitable or beneficent purposes are the primary ones for which the property is utilized. Secondary or incidental charitable benefits will not suffice, nor will it be enough that the institution professes a charitable purpose or aspires to using its property to confer charity on others. * * *

In rejecting Provena Hospitals' claim for exemption, the Department determined that the corporation also failed to satisfy this charitable use requirement. As with the issue of charitable ownership, the appellate court concluded that this aspect of the Department's decision was not clearly erroneous. Again we agree.

In explaining what constitutes charity, *Methodist Old Peoples Home v. Korzen*, applied the definition adopted by our court more than a century ago [ ]. We held there that

> " 'charity, in a legal sense, may be more fully defined as a gift, to be applied consistently with existing laws, for the benefit of an indefinite number of persons, either by bringing their hearts under the influence of education or religion,

by relieving their bodies from disease, suffering or constraint, by assisting them to establish themselves for life, or by erecting or maintaining public buildings or works, or otherwise lessening the burdens of government.' " [ ].

* * *

Conditioning charitable status on whether an activity helps relieve the burdens on government is appropriate. After all, each tax dollar lost to a charitable exemption is one less dollar affected governmental bodies will have to meet their obligations directly. If a charitable institution wishes to avail itself of funds which would otherwise flow into a public treasury, it is only fitting that the institution provide some compensatory benefit in exchange. While Illinois law has never required that there be a direct, dollar-for-dollar correlation between the value of the tax exemption and the value of the goods or services provided by the charity, it is a *sine qua non* of charitable status that those seeking a charitable exemption be able to demonstrate that their activities will help alleviate some financial burden incurred by the affected taxing bodies in performing their governmental functions.

* * *

NOTES AND QUESTIONS

1.   *Intermountain Health Care* provides a useful history of the nonprofit hospital in America. How have changing practices, technologies, and payment systems affected those institutions? How do those factors influence the obligation to provide charity care? Should uncompensated care be provided this way or through direct governmental expenditures? How does the approach of the *Provena* decision compare to the *Intermountain Health Care* case? What aspects of the decision suggest that courts are becoming more concerned with evaluating the affirmative efforts of exempt organizations to provide charitable care to those most in need?

2.   A few states have adopted a "prescriptive" approach, requiring hospitals to make specified minimum expenditures on community benefits. State quantitative standards vary widely however. See, e.g. Pa. Cons. Stat. Ann. Sec. 371–85 (setting forth five statutory standards including providing uncompensated goods or services equal to at least 5% of costs or maintaining an open admissions policy and providing uncompensated goods or services equal to at least 75% of net operating income, but not less than 3% of total operating expenses; also allowing payments in lieu of taxes); Nevada Revised Statutes § 439B.320 (requiring that hospitals with at least 100 beds provide 0.6 percent of their net revenue in free care to indigent patients each year); Tx Code Ann. § 11.1801 (a)(4) (charity care and community benefits combined must equal at least five percent of the hospital's or hospital system's net patient revenues). Following the *Provena* decision, the Illinois legislature

passed a law governing hospitals' property and sales tax exemptions requiring that the value of uncompensated care equal or exceed the estimated value of its property tax liability based on the fair market value of its property. Notably, the new Illinois statute also provides an income tax credit for *investor-owned* hospitals in the amount of the lesser of property tax paid or charity care provided. What policy rationale would justify giving tax credits to for-profit entities? Looking at the bigger picture, should state legislatures or taxing authorities reconsider their laws requiring minimum levels of charity care in view of the changing magnitude and characteristics of the uninsured population?

3.   Whether the amount of charity care provided by tax-exempt hospitals justifies the benefit of the tax exemption is hotly disputed. Studies comparing the value of tax exemptions for hospitals to the amount of charity care (measured in terms of costs, not charges) find that most hospitals could not justify their exemption on the basis of charity care alone. See Cong. Budget Office, Nonprofit Hospitals and the Provision of Community Benefits (Dec. 2006); David Walker, Nonprofit, For–Profit, and Government Hospitals: Uncompensated Care and Other Community Benefits, U.S. Government Accountability Office (2006) (little difference in uncompensated care burden shouldered by nonprofit and investor-owned hospitals; government hospitals provide much greater proportion than either). These and other studies questioning the extent to which nonprofits contribute additive charitable care have spawned an intense debate over the proper legal standard under tax exemption laws. Some commentators dispute the normative assumptions underlying the critique, raising the issue of the meaning of "charity" and pointing to various unrecognized benefits supplied by nonprofit hospitals. For example, extensive empirical research conducted by Professor Jill Horwitz shows that nonprofit hospitals are more likely than for-profits to offer unprofitable services needed by poor and uninsured patients, though less so than government-controlled hospitals. Jill R. Horwitz, Why We Need the Independent Sector: The Behavior, Law and Ethics of Not–For–Profit Hospitals, 50 UCLA L. Rev. 1345 (2003);

2.   Federal Tax Exemption: Charitable Purpose Under Section 501(c)(3)

Exemption from federal taxation plays a more prominent role in the affairs of tax-exempt hospitals than does state tax exemption. This is not necessarily because more money is at stake—the loss of state and local property tax exemptions may be more costly to a nonprofit hospital that has small or no earnings subject to income taxation—but because federal tax law reaches into many aspects of hospitals operations, including governance, relationships with other providers, and charity care policies. Of course, federal tax-exempt status carries with it significant benefits. Besides exemption from the corporate income tax, it permits the organization to enjoy exemption from federal unemployment taxes, preferred postal rates and various other benefits respecting pensions and special treatment under various regulatory laws. Second, only donations to charitable organizations exempt under 501(c)(3) are deductible to donors under IRC Section 170. Third, only charitable organizations can issue tax-exempt bonds, an important source of financing for nonprofit hospitals. IRC § 145.

Section 501(c)(3) of the Internal Revenue Code exempts from federal income tax entities "organized and operated exclusively for religious, charitable, scientific, testing for public safety, literary, or educational purposes, or to foster . . . amateur sports competition . . . or for the prevention of cruelty to animals." An organization must meet three important requirements to qualify for tax-exempt status:

(1) no part of its net earnings may inure to the benefit of any private shareholder or individual;

(2) no substantial part of its activities may consist of certain activities aimed at influencing legislation; and

(3) it may not participate or intervene in any political campaign on behalf of any candidate for public office. 26 U.S.C.A. § 501(c)(3).

Is there an internal logic to these requirements? Does the view that foregoing taxes on charitable and other organizations amounts to a "subsidy" help explain these provisions?

To qualify for § 501(c)(3) status, a health care facility must meet both an "organizational test," which requires that the hospital's constitutive documents, such as the corporate articles of incorporation, limit its activities to exempt purposes, and an "operational test," which requires that the hospital be operated primarily for exempt purposes, including "charitable," "educational," or "religious" purposes. Most hospitals must qualify as charities as healthcare is not specifically listed among exempt purposes. The definition of charitable purposes under the Code has been quite controversial, with the Internal Revenue Service attempting to adjust the definition to meet changes in the modern health care sector while the statute remained unchanged. Unfortunately, the federal tax authorities have not been clear or consistent in explaining when provisions of health care services are charitable. As a practical matter, few hospitals have failed to satisfy the flexible—some say overly flexible—standard that has evolved. However, as you read subsequent sections in this chapter, notice that the IRS and courts have, especially in recent years, been far less lenient with other kinds of health care entities.

The confused trail of the exemption standard for hospitals begins with a 1956 Revenue Ruling that required a tax-exempt hospital to be operated "to the extent of its financial ability for those not able to pay for the services rendered." Rev. Ruling 56–185. In 1958, the Tax Court upheld the denial of exempt status for a hospital that devoted between 2% and 5% of its revenue to care for the indigent (Lorain Avenue Clinic v. Commissioner, 31 T.C. 141). Thus one can identify in the early history of IRS analysis of the issue a direct link between exempt status and the provision of a specified quantum of free care for the poor. A pivotal turning point, however, occurred in 1969 when an IRS Revenue Ruling adopted a "community benefit" standard, under which the provision of charity care was no longer the sine qua non for charitable status as long as the hospital "promot[ed] health for the general benefit of the community." The Ruling went on to suggest that the existence of a community board, an open emergency room treating indigent patients free of charge, an open medical staff and treatment of government-insured patients would provide adequate evidence the entity was serving charitable purposes.

The Service illustrated its position by describing a hospital that operated an emergency room that was open to all regardless of ability to pay and whose care for the indigent was not otherwise described, which it stated met the Revenue Ruling's standards for exemption. This remarkable shift was not the product of an informed analysis of the benefits of nonprofit health care, nor did it involve legislative action. Instead it appears it was the result of the erroneous assumption of IRS staff attorneys that the recently-enacted Medicaid statute would obviate the need for charity care and that a new justification was therefore needed to preserve the dominant nonprofit hospital sector. See generally, Daniel M. Fox & Daniel C. Schaffer, Tax Administration as Health Policy: Hospitals, The Internal Revenue Service and the Courts, 16 J. Health Pol. Pol'y & L. 251 (1991).

The link to the provision of charity care under federal law was further diluted by a 1983 Revenue Ruling in which a hospital that did not even operate an emergency room and usually referred indigent patients to another hospital was described as qualifying for tax-exempt status. The illustrative hospital did not operate an ER because the state health planning agency had concluded that the emergency room was not needed in the area as other nearby hospitals had adequate emergency services. Rev. Rul. 83–157. Thus, for almost forty years federal tax-exempt status has not been strictly tied to the provision of charity care, or for that matter to doing anything terribly differently than for-profit hospitals. For academic criticism of the standard and a thoughtful proposal to shift the IRS's focus to the question of whether an exempt hospital increases access to health services, see John D. Colombo, The Role of Access in Charitable Tax Exemption, 82 Washington U. L.Q. 343 (2004).

Growing dissatisfaction with the community benefit standard led to increasing scrutiny at the federal level in the 2000s.See e.g., Senate Finance Committee Minority Staff, Tax–Exempt Hospitals: Discussion

Draft (July, 2007)(proposing restrictions on conversions and joint ventures between nonprofit and for-profit hospitals and limiting charges billed to the uninsured).See also U.S. Gov't Accountability Office, GAO–08–880, Nonprofit Hospitals: Variation in Standards and Guidance Limits Comparison of How Hospitals Meet Community Benefit Requirements (2008); and Catholic Health Ass'n, A Guide for Planning and Reporting Community Benefit (2012).One of the most important outcomes of this flurry of activity has been the issuance by the IRS of a redesigned Form 990—the annual information return that most exempt hospitals must file annually. Modeled to some extent on SEC disclosure forms, the new Form 990 radically changed the reporting requirements for nonprofit entities, requiring under a new Schedule H that each exempt organization to submit a Community Benefit Report that includes reporting for seven categories of charity care and community benefit, a description of its charity care policy, a statement of how it assesses community needs, and detailed information about billing and debt collection practices. Following the passage of the ACA, the IRS amended Schedule H again to account for changes imposed by the ACA, including the new requirements for exempt status discussed in the following section.

3. New Standards for Tax-Exempt Charitable Hospitals: IRC Section 501(r)

The Affordable Care Act addressed the issue of community benefit, incorporating some ideas from previous reform proposals dealing with the issue, but stopping short of mandating specific levels of charity care as advocated by some in Congress. The law adds new Section 501(r) to the Code, which imposes a series of specific statutory requirements that hospitals must satisfy in order to qualify for exemption under Code Section 501(c)(3). These provisions apply to any "hospital organization," defined as an organization that operates a facility that is required to be licensed or registered as a hospital under state law, as well as any organization that the Secretary of the Treasury determines provides hospital care as the principal basis for its tax exemption. Significantly, hospital organizations operating more than one hospital must meet the new requirements separately for each facility. The statute leaves it unclear whether an entity operating multiple hospitals will lose its overall Section 501(c)(3) status where only one of its hospitals fails to meet the requirements of 501(r) or whether that facility will only be treated as unrelated trade or business of the organization.

501(r) includes the following requirements:

1. Community health needs assessment

Tax-exempt hospitals must conduct a community health needs assessment (CHNA) at least once during any three-year period and must make that assessment widely available to the public. The ACA mandates that hospitals then adopt an implementation strategy to meet the needs identified in the assessment. In so doing, hospitals must obtain input from a broad cross-section of the community they serve. Any hospital that fails to conduct the CHNA will be subject to an excise tax of $50,000.

The Treasury Department and the Internal Revenue Service (IRS) have published a Notice and Request for comment concerning the Community Health Needs Assessment (CHNA) requirements for exempt hospitals. IRS Notice 2011–52 (July 8, 2011). The Notice proposed that hospitals' written CHNA report must describe the following: the community served and how the community was determined; the process and methods used to conduct the assessment; how the organization took into account input from persons representing the broad interests of the community served by the hospital facility, including a description of when and how the hospital consulted with these persons or the organizations they represent; the prioritized community health needs identified through the CHNA as well as a description of the process and criteria used in prioritizing such needs; and the existing health care facilities and other resources within the community and available to meet community health needs. On the question of what community is served by a hospital, the Notice stated, "[g]enerally Treasury and the IRS expect that a hospital facility's community will be defined by geographic location," but also state that a hospital's community may take into account target populations served. The Notice cautions, however, that "[n]otwithstanding the foregoing, a community may not be defined in a manner that circumvents the requirement to assess the health needs of (or consult with persons who represent the broad interests of) the community served by a hospital facility by excluding, for example, medically underserved populations, low-income persons, minority groups, or those with chronic disease needs."

2. *Financial assistance and emergency medical care policies*

The Act requires tax-exempt hospitals to have written policies that address financial assistance and emergency medical care. The financial assistance policy (FAP) must address eligibility criteria for financial assistance and the type of assistance (i.e., free or discounted care), the application process, the basis for calculating the amount charged to patients, and measures undertaken to publicize the policy widely within the community that the hospital serves. The hospital's emergency care policy must require it to provide, without discrimination, care for emergency medical conditions regardless of the patient's eligibility under the financial assistance policy. Exempt hospitals must also have a billing and collections policy, or alternatively include in their financial assistance policies the actions the hospital may take if bills are not paid. The IRS has issued proposed rules for FAPs. 77 Fed. Reg. 38,148 (June 26, 2012).

3. Limitations on charges

For individuals who are eligible to receive financial assistance under the hospital's policy, a hospital cannot charge more than the "amounts generally billed" to insured individuals for emergency and other medically necessary care. Hospitals are prohibited from the use of "gross charges." Although that term is not defined in the legislation, it likely signifies charges that do not reflect discounts received by third party payors.

4. Billing and collection

A hospital must make reasonable efforts to determine whether a patient is eligible for assistance under its financial assistance policy before taking any "extraordinary actions" to collect unpaid bills. Extraordinary collection actions generally include lawsuits, arrests, liens on residences, and similar collection methods. While the Act requires the Treasury Department to issue regulations defining "reasonable efforts," that term is understood to include notifying the patient of the hospital's financial assistance policy at the time of admission, submitting invoices, and providing written and oral communications before taking collection actions or reporting to credit rating agencies.

5. Audited Financial Statements

Exempt hospitals will be required to provide along with their IRS Form 990 filing (and hence publicly disclose) copies of audited financial statements for the organization or consolidated financial statements for organizations that prepare financials on a consolidated basis.

NOTES AND QUESTIONS

1.   The ACA mandates new reports and studies by the Secretary of the Treasury regarding charity care that may provide the basis for further regulation. Given that the aggregate amount of charity care needed in the United States will be a "moving target" as subsidies assist in the purchase of private insurance and Medicaid eligibility is expanded, how should Congress assess the need for charity care? Consider also which populations are likely to slip through the new safety net. Will the burden of charity care be borne disproportionately by certain hospitals? Can the charity standard be enforced in a way that accounts for differences in the amount of uninsured residents in their area?

2.   What factors might have prompted policymakers' newfound interest in the standard for tax-exempt status applicable to hospitals? Is the approach of §501(r) requiring greater disclosure and transparency enough? Are there pitfalls in attempting to define, quantify, and prescribe the obligations of charitable institutions? In answering these questions, return to the underlying issue of why the law prefers (and subsidizes) a nonprofit sector. See Gloria J. Bazzoli et al., Community Benefit Activities of Private, Nonprofit Hospitals, 35 J. Health Pol. Pol'y and L. 999 (2010); Jack E. Karns, Justifying the

Nonprofit Hospital Tax Exemption in a Competitive Market Environment, 13 Widener L.J. 383 (2004).

PROBLEM: IMPLEMENTING SECTION 501(R)

Congress left much to the IRS to determine in implementing Section 501(r). Assuming you represent the hospital industry, what action would you advocate the IRS take with respect to the following issues and how would you justify your position if you represented the tax-exempt hospital sector?

- The ACA does not mandate that a hospital's financial assistance plan (FAP) contain any particular eligibility criteria that an individual must meet to receive a discount. Should the IRS impose some minimum requirements?

- In implementing the requirement that hospitals not charge more than the "amount generally billed to individuals with insurance" (AGB) for emergency services or other medically necessary medical care. Should the AGB calculation include Medicare fee for service rates as well as private insurance rates?

- Hospitals frequently sell or refer debts to third parties. Should hospitals be held accountable for "extraordinary collection actions"(ECAs) taken by third parties before "reasonable efforts" were undertaken to ascertain eligibility for an FAP? Alternatively, should a hospital be required to contract with third parties not to undertake ECAs until it has satisfied the reasonable efforts requirement?

- Hospitals must undertake "reasonable efforts" to ascertain an individual's eligibility under its FAP. Should obtaining a written waiver from the individual suffice?

Now change sides and represent an advocacy group for low-income citizens.

B. CHARITABLE PURPOSES: HEALTH MAINTENANCE ORGANIZATIONS AND INTEGRATED DELIVERY SYSTEMS

As discussed in previous chapters, health maintenance organizations typically deliver both office-based primary care and hospital-based acute care to their subscribers who prepay a premium to the HMO to cover needed services regardless of the amount or cost of medical services actually used. In this way, HMOs combine the functions of insurance and health care delivery. In their provision of office-based primary care, HMOs resemble doctors' medical practices, which traditionally have not been organized on a not-for-profit basis and have not received tax exemption. The following cases discuss exempt status for stand-alone HMOs and those that are part of an integrated delivery system.

IHC HEALTH PLANS, INC. V. COMMISSIONER OF INTERNAL REVENUE

United States Court of Appeals, Tenth Circuit, 2003.
325 F.3d 1188.

Before TACHA, CHIEF CIRCUIT JUDGE, HOLLOWAY, and EBEL, CIRCUIT JUDGES.

TACHA, CHIEF CIRCUIT JUDGE.

I.   Background

IHC Health Plans, Inc. ("Health Plans"), on its own behalf and as successor in interest to IHC Care, Inc. ("Care") and IHC Group, Inc. ("Group") (collectively "petitioners"), appeals the Tax Court's decision denying petitioners' request for tax exemption under 26 U.S.C. § 501(c)(3). The sole issue presented in this appeal is whether petitioners qualify for tax-exempt status under 26 U.S.C. § 501(c)(3) as organizations operated exclusively for charitable purposes.

A.   *The IHC Integrated Delivery System*

* * *

[Intermountain Health Care Inc. ("IHC") formed IHC Health Services ("Health Services") in 1982 as a Utah nonprofit corporation to operate twenty-two hospitals located in Utah and Idaho, employing approximately 300 primary care physicians and 100 specialist physicians in its Physician Division and separately employing approximately 120 physicians in its Hospital Division.] * * * Between 1997 and 1999, Health Services provided nearly $1.2 billion in health care services, without reimbursement to patients covered by Medicare, Medicaid, and other governmental programs. During the same period, Health Services furnished more than $91 million in free health-care services to indigent patients.

The Commissioner has recognized Health Services as a tax-exempt organization under section 501(c)(3).

* * *

3.   *Health Plans, Care, and Group*

In order to further integrate its provision of health-care services, IHC formed Health Plans, Care, and Group to operate as health maintenance organizations ("HMOs") within the IHC Integrated Delivery System. * * *

* * *

E.   *The Commissioner's Decision*

In 1999, the Commissioner concluded that neither Health Plans, Care, nor Group operated exclusively for exempt purposes under section 501(c)(3). . . . Accordingly, the Commissioner revoked Health Plans' tax-exempt status, retroactive to January 1, 1987, and denied exemptions to Care and Group.

Health Plans, Care, and Group brought suit in the United States Tax Court, seeking a declaratory judgment reversing the Commissioner's adverse determinations. On September 25, 2001, the Tax Court affirmed the Commissioner's conclusions in three separate opinions. [ ] This appeal followed.

II.   Discussion

A.   Standard of Review

* * * The appropriate legal standard for determining whether an organization operates for a "charitable" purpose is a legal question, which we review de novo. Whether an organization in fact operates exclusively for a charitable purpose, however, is a question of fact, which we review for clear error. [ ] As the taxpayer claiming entitlement to exemption, petitioners bear the burden of proof. [ ]

B.   Overview of Applicable Law

*   *   *

* * * In this case, the sole question we must consider is whether Health Plans, Care, and Group operated exclusively for exempt purposes within the meaning of section 501(c)(3).

C.   Whether Health Plans, Care, and Group Operated for a Charitable Purpose

This inquiry requires us to address two basic questions. First, we must consider whether the purpose proffered by petitioners qualifies as a "charitable" purpose under section 501(c)(3). "The term 'charitable' is used in section 501(c)(3) in its generally accepted legal sense and is . . . not to be construed as limited by the separate enumeration in section 501(c)(3)." 26 C.F.R. § 1.501(c)(3)–1(d)(2). An organization will not be considered charitable, however, "unless it serves a *public rather than a private interest.*" 26 C.F.R. § 1.501(c)(3)–1(d)(1)(ii) (emphasis added).[11]

Second, we must determine whether petitioners in fact operated *primarily* for this purpose. [ ] Under the "operational test" set forth in the IRS regulations, "[a]n organization will be regarded as 'operated exclusively' for one or more exempt purposes only if it engages primarily in activities which accomplish one or more of such exempt purposes specified in section 501(c)(3). An organization will not be so regarded if more than

---

[11] Although we are not bound by IRS regulations or revenue rulings, we do accord them deference. [ ]

an insubstantial part of its activities is not in furtherance of an exempt purpose."[12] 26 C.F.R. § 1.501(c)(3)–1(c)(1).

In this case, the Tax Court concluded that "the promotion of health for the benefit of the community is a charitable purpose," [ ] but found that neither Health Plans, Care, nor Group operated primarily to benefit the community. [ ] For the reasons set forth below, we agree.

1.   *The promotion of health as a charitable purpose*

In defining "charitable," our analysis must focus on whether petitioners' activities conferred a *public* benefit.[ ] The public-benefit requirement highlights the *quid pro quo* nature of tax exemptions: the public is willing to relieve an organization from the burden of taxation in exchange for the public benefit it provides. [ ] As the Supreme Court has recognized, "[c]haritable exemptions are justified on the basis that the exempt entity confers a *public benefit*—a benefit which the society or the community may not itself choose or be able to provide, or which supplements and advances the work of public institutions already supported by tax revenues." *Bob Jones Univ. v. United States,* 461 U.S. 574, 591, 103 S.Ct. 2017, 76 L.Ed.2d 157 (1983) (emphasis added).

* * *

[The Court reviews the IRS and judicial interpretations of the community benefit standard]. Thus, under the IRS's interpretation of section 501(c)(3), in the context of health-care providers, we must determine whether the taxpayer operates *primarily for the benefit of the community.*[16] And while the concept of "community benefit" is somewhat amorphous, we agree with the IRS, the Tax Court, and the Third Circuit that it provides a workable standard for determining tax exemption under section 501(c)(3).

b.   Defining "community benefit"

In giving form to the community-benefit standard, we stress that "not every activity that promotes health supports tax exemption under § 501(c)(3). For example, selling prescription pharmaceuticals certainly promotes health, but pharmacies cannot qualify for . . . exemption under § 501(c)(3) on that basis alone." [ ] In other words, engaging in an activity

---

[12] The Supreme Court construed a similar provision under the Social Security Act in *Better Business Bureau v. United States,* concluding that "a single non-[exempt] purpose, if substantial in nature, will destroy the exemption regardless of the number or importance of truly [exempt] purposes." 326 U.S. 279, 283, 66 S. Ct. 112, 90 L. Ed. 67 (1945).

[16] [C]ourt decisions have highlighted several factors relevant under the "community benefit" analysis. These factors include:

(1) size of the class eligible to benefit; (2) free or below-cost products or services; (3) treatment of persons participating in governmental programs such as Medicare or Medicaid; (4) use of surplus funds for research or educational programs; and (5) composition of the board of trustees. [ ] Douglas M. Mancino, Income Tax Exemption of the Contemporary Nonprofit Hospital, 32 ST. LOUIS U. L.J. 1015, 1037–70 (1988).

that promotes health, *standing alone,* offers an insufficient indicium of an organization's purpose. Numerous for-profit enterprises offer products or services that promote health.

Similarly, the IRS rulings in 69–545 and 83–157 demonstrate that an organization cannot satisfy the community-benefit requirement based solely on the fact that it offers health-care services to all in the community[17] in exchange for a fee.[18] Although providing health-care products or services to all in the community is necessary under those rulings, it is insufficient, standing alone, to qualify for tax exemption under section 501(c)(3). Rather, the organization must provide some additional "plus."

This plus is perhaps best characterized as "a benefit which the society or the community may not itself choose or be able to provide, or which supplements and advances the work of public institutions already supported by tax revenues." [ ] Concerning the former, the IRS rulings provide a number of examples: providing free or below-cost services, *see* Rev. Rul. 56–185; maintaining an emergency room open to all, regardless of ability to pay, *see* Rev. Rul. 69–545; and devoting surpluses to research, education, and medical training, *see* Rev. Rul. 83–157. These services fall under the general umbrella of "positive externalities" or "public goods."[19] Concerning the latter, the primary way in which health-care providers advance government-funded endeavors is the servicing of the Medicaid and Medicare populations.

c.   Quantifying "community benefit"

Difficulties will inevitably arise in quantifying the required community benefit. The governing statutory language, however, provides some guidance. Under section 501(c)(3), an organization is not entitled to tax exemption unless it operates for a charitable *purpose.* Thus, the existence of some incidental community benefit is insufficient. Rather, the magnitude of the community benefit conferred must be sufficient to give rise to

---

[17] We recognize that certain health-care entities provide specialized services, which are not required by "all" in the community, and we do not mean to foreclose the possibility that such entities may qualify as "charitable" under section 501(c)(3). As the IRS recognized in Rev. Rul. 83–157:

Certain specialized hospitals, such as eye hospitals and cancer hospitals, offer medical care limited to special conditions unlikely to necessitate emergency care and do not, as a practical matter, maintain emergency rooms. These organizations may also qualify under section 501(c)(3) if there are present similar, significant factors that demonstrate that the hospitals operate exclusively to benefit the community.

[18] At least where the fee is above cost. We express no opinion on whether an enterprise that sold health-promoting products or services entirely at or below cost would qualify for tax exemption under 501(c)(3).

[19] Under the Treasury Department's view, for-profit enterprises are unlikely to provide such services since " 'market prices . . . do not reflect the benefit [these services] confer on the community as a whole.' "[ ] Thus, the provision of such "public goods"—at least when conducted on a sufficiently large scale—arguably supports an inference that the enterprise is responding to some inducement that is not market-based. *Cf. id.*

a strong inference that the organization operates *primarily for the purpose of benefitting the community.* [ ]

Thus, our inquiry turns "not [on] the nature of the activity, but [on] the *purpose* accomplished thereby." [ ] Of course, because of the inherent difficulty in determining a corporate entity's subjective purpose, we necessarily rely on objective indicia in conducting our analysis. [ ] In determining an organization's purpose, we primarily consider the manner in which the entity carries on its activities. [ ]

d.   The resulting test

In summary, under section 501(c)(3), a health-care provider must make its services available to all in the community *plus* provide additional community or public benefits. The benefit must either further the function of government-funded institutions or provide a service that would not likely be provided within the community but for the subsidy. Further, the additional public benefit conferred must be sufficient to give rise to a strong inference that the public benefit is the *primary purpose* for which the organization operates. In conducting this inquiry, we consider the totality of the circumstances. With these principles in mind, we proceed to review the Tax Court's decision in the present case.

*   *   *

3.   *The Tax Court correctly concluded that petitioners do not operate primarily to promote health for the benefit of the community.*

Petitioners . . . argue that the Tax Court erred in concluding that petitioners did not operate primarily for the benefit of the community. We disagree.

a.   Nature of the product or service and the character of the transaction

In this case, we deal with organizations that do not provide health-care services directly. Rather, petitioners furnish group insurance entitling enrollees to services of participating hospitals and physicians. Petitioners determine premiums using two methods: (1) an adjusted community rating for individuals and small employers; and (2) past-claims experience for large employers. Thus, [ ] petitioners "sell [ ] insurance coverage . . . extend[ing] benefits in return for a premium based generally on the risk assumed." [ ] In other words, petitioners primarily perform a "risk-bearing function." In *Church of the Brethren,* as in the instant case, the commercial nature of this activity inspired doubt as to the entity's charitable purpose. 759 F.2d at 795; *cf. Federation Pharmacy Servs., Inc. v. C.I.R.,* 72 T.C. 687, 691–92, 1979 WL 3712 (1979), *aff'd* 625 F.2d 804 (8th Cir.1980) (noting that selling pharmaceuticals is "an activity that is normally carried on by a commercial profit making enterprise[ ]"). Where, as here, "[i]t is difficult to distinguish the plaintiff corporation from a mutual insurance company," we must carefully scrutinize the organization's operation.[23] [ ]

b.   Free or below-cost products or services

The fact that an activity is normally undertaken by commercial for-profit entities does not necessarily preclude tax exemption, particularly where the entity offers its services at or below-cost. [ ]. But petitioners provide virtually no free or below-cost health-care services.[ ] All enrollees must pay a premium in order to receive benefits.[25] As the Eighth Circuit has recognized, "[a]n organization which does not extend some of its benefits to individuals financially unable to make the required payments [generally] reflects a commercial activity rather than a charitable one." *Federation Pharmacy Servs., Inc. v. C.I.R.*, 625 F.2d 804, 807 (8th Cir.1980). Further, the fact that petitioners in no way subsidize dues for those who cannot afford subscribership distinguishes this case from the HMOs in *Sound Health Ass'n v. C.I.R.*, 71 T.C. 158, 1978 WL 3393 (1979), and *Geisinger I*, 985 F.2d at 1219.

We acknowledge, as did the Tax Court, that petitioners' "adjusted community rating system[ ] likely allowed its enrollees to obtain medical care at a lower cost than might otherwise have been available." [ ] Again, however, selling services at a discount tells us little about the petitioners' *purpose*. "Many profit making organizations sell at a discount." [ ] In considering price as it relates to an organization's purpose, there is a qualitative difference between selling at a discount and selling below cost.[26]

In sum, petitioners['] sole activity is arranging for health-care services in exchange for a fee. To elevate the attendant health benefit over the character of the transaction would pervert Congress' intent in providing for charitable tax exemptions under section 501(c)(3). Contrary to petitioners' insinuation, the Tax Court did not accord dispositive weight to the absence of free care. Neither do we. Rather, it is yet another factor that belies petitioners' professions of a charitable purpose.[27]

---

[23] We are primarily concerned with this characteristic as it bears on our determination of petitioners' purpose. However, we also note that petitioners not only resemble commercial insurance providers, petitioners in fact compete with commercial insurance providers. Thus, "granting a tax exemption to [petitioners] would necessarily disadvantage other for-profit [entities] with which [petitioners] compete[ ]."

[25] Petitioners note that Care and Group offered "risk" and "cost" Medicare health plans, and contend that Care and Group went forward with these plans "with the full knowledge that those plans might lose money." Care and Group discontinued these plans, however, based on concerns of "financial feasibility."

[26] Further, as the Tax Court noted, "the benefit associated with these cost savings is more appropriately characterized as a benefit to petitioner[s]' enrollees as opposed to the community at large."

[27] As the Eighth Circuit has noted, "a 'charitable' hospital may impose charges or fees for services rendered, and indeed its charity record may be comparatively low depending upon all the facts . . . but a serious question is raised where its charitable operation is virtually inconse-

[The court also found that nothing in the record indicates that petitioners conducted research or offered free educational programs to the public, noting that petitioners' "Core Wellness Program" was offered exclusively to enrollees.]

d.   The class eligible to benefit

(1) Health Plans

As the Tax Court noted, "[Health Plans] offered its [coverage] to a broad cross-section of the community including individuals, the employees of both large and small employers, and individuals eligible for Medicaid benefits." In fact, in 1999, Health Plans' enrollees represented twenty percent of Utah's total population and fifty percent of Utah residents eligible for Medicaid benefits.[29]

Nevertheless, even though almost all Utahans were potentially eligible to enroll for Health Plans coverage, the self-imposed requirement of membership tells us something about Health Plans' operation. As the Third Circuit noted in *Geisinger I:*

> The community benefited is, in fact, limited to those who belong to [the HMO] since the requirement of subscribership remains a condition precedent to any service. Absent any additional indicia of a charitable purpose, this self-imposed precondition suggests that [the HMO] is primarily benefitting itself (and, perhaps, secondarily benefiting the community) by promoting subscribership throughout the areas it serves.

985 F.2d at 1219. Further, while the absence of a large class of potential beneficiaries may preclude tax-exempt status, its presence standing alone provides little insight into the organization's purpose. Offering products and services to a broad segment of the population is as consistent with self promotion and profit maximization as it is with any "charitable" purpose.

(2) Care and Group

Neither Care nor Group offered their health plans to the general public. Rather, both Care and Group limited their enrollment to employees of large employers (employers with 100 or more employees). Thus, as the Tax Court found, "[Care and Group] operate[d] in a manner that substantially limit[ed] [the] universe of potential enrollees." [ ] Based on this find-

---

quential." *Federation Pharmacy*, 625 F.2d at 807 (8th Cir.1980) (quoting *Sonora Cmty. Hosp. v. C.I.R.*, 46 T.C. 519, 526, 1966 WL 1319 (1966)) (internal quotation marks omitted).

[29] We acknowledge that Health Plans' service to Utah's Medicaid community provides some community benefit. The relevant inquiry, however, is not "whether [petitioner] benefited the community at all . . . [but] whether it primarily benefited the community, as an entity must in order to qualify for tax-exempt status." [ ]

ing, the Tax Court correctly concluded that neither Care nor Group promoted health for the benefit of the community.

e.   Community board of trustees

Finally, we consider petitioners' board composition. Prior to 1996, Health Plans' bylaws provided that "[a] plurality of Board members shall represent the buyer-employer community and an approximately equal number of physicians and hospitals representatives shall be appointed." As the IRS noted, Health Plans' pre–1996 bylaws skewed control towards subscribers, rather than the community at large. In 1996, however, Health Plans amended its bylaws to require that a majority of board members be disinterested and broadly representative of the community.

It makes little difference whether we consider petitioners' board prior to 1996 or following the amendments. Even if we were to conclude petitioners' board broadly represents the community, the dearth of any actual community benefit in this case rebuts any inference we might otherwise draw.

4.   *Conclusion*

For the above reasons, we agree with the Tax Court's conclusion that petitioners, standing alone, do not qualify for tax exemption under section 501(c)(3).

* * *

[The Court next discussed the integral part doctrine, which follows in the next section of this casebook.]

NOTES AND QUESTIONS

1.   What factors short of operating a free emergency service will enable an HMO to obtain 501(c)(3) status? Does the court's "plus" standard mean that the provision of health services is not a sufficient community benefit to carry the day? See also Geisinger Health Plan v. Commissioner, 985 F.2d 1210 (3d Cir. 1993) ("Geisinger I") (applying similar analysis of qualitative factors and also finding that providing subsidy to only 35 people constituted quantitatively an insufficient community benefit).

2.   How do the requirements for § 501(c)(3) status for HMOs compare to those the IRS applies for hospitals? Should subsidized memberships, which satisfy an unmet need for primary care, be considered the equivalent of charity care? Should the provision of primary care in medically underserved areas be counted favorably as a charitable purpose? Or, does the fact that the subsidized or free enrollees become "members" of the HMO simply make it definitionally impossible for the subsidization to be counted as a "community" benefit?

3.   What factors might influence whether other entities such as nursing homes, clinics and physician practice organizations can obtain exempt status? See Rev. Rul. 72–124 which states that 501(c)(3) exemption is conditioned on relieving financial distress by providing care and housing on a gratuitous or below cost basis and meets the "three primary needs of aged persons . . . for housing, . . . health care . . . and financial security." With regard to the need for financial security, it stated "the organization must be committed to an established policy, whether in writing or in actual practice, of maintaining in residence any persons who become unable to pay their regular charges." It can readily be seen that most physician practice associations, including physician corporations, provide private benefit and lack charitable purpose to qualify for exemption, although some may qualify based on their relationship to research and teaching hospitals or as an integral part of an integrated delivery system as discussed in the following case. See Kenneth L. Levine, Obtaining 501(c)(3) Status for Professional Medical Corporations, 2 DePaul J. Health Care L. 231 (1998). In other instances, such as operation of a pharmacy, the business is regarded as "inherently commercial" and not eligible for exempt status. See Federal Pharmacy Services v. Commissioner, 625 F.2d 804 (8th Cir. 1980).

4. *Integrated Delivery Systems.* The IRS has issued a number of favorable rulings to integrated delivery systems. See, e.g., Friendly Hills Healthcare Network Exemption Ruling, 93 Tax Notes Today 31–8 (Feb. 9, 1993); Facey Medical Foundation Exemption Ruling, 93 Tax Notes Today 83–116 (Apr. 15, 1993). Although the IRS originally seemed to require that physicians represent no more than 20 percent of an exempt IDS's board, it subsequently adopted a flexible policy, stating that a board with a disinterested majority of board members that adopted a conflict of interest policy and routinely monitored compliance with the entity's charitable mission would satisfy its requirements. Model Conflicts of Interest Policy, 1997 CPE Text reprinted in 97 Tax Notes Today 198–80. However, it has denied exemption to HMOs seeking exemption under §501(c)(3) as an "integral part" of an IDS. See IHC Health Plans, Inc. v. Comm'r of Internal Revenue, 325 F. 2d 1188 (10th Cir. 2003); see also Geisinger Health Plan v. Commissioner, 30 F.3d 494 (3d Cir. 1994). Somewhat paradoxically HMOs that are placed in an integrated delivery system the issue for exemption purposes turns on whether the system considered as a whole satisfies the community benefit standard, which appears likely based on the cases just discussed. See John D. Colombo, Health Care Reform and Federal Tax Exemption: Rethinking the Issues, 29 Wake Forest L. Rev. 215, 249 ("had the Geisinger Clinic operated the HMO, little doubt exists that it could have done so on an exempt basis"). So, if not based on organizational form, on what basis should the law draw distinctions for analyzing charitable purpose? Drawing on IRC standards distinguishing "public charities" from "private foundations," Professor John Colombo offers a test that would inquire into the extent of common ownership, supervision, control, or in some cases, the responsiveness of the organizations.

5.   *Physician-hospital organizations (PHOs).* PHOs, described earlier in this chapter, are often used to more closely bind hospitals and physicians. and negotiate health plan contracts that cover both physician and hospital services. Some also take on utilization review, credentialing and quality management activities, and some may foster shared administrative services. Outside of a fully integrated system, however, PHOs standing alone typically do not qualify as tax-exempt. Because most PHOs do not themselves provide care and merely negotiate contracts on behalf of providers, it is difficult to make a case that a charitable purpose is served; even more difficult is compliance with the requirement that no more than incidental private benefits are provided. However, at least one PHO has run the gauntlet, although its approval may be attributable to its base in an academic medical center and other unique factors. See Hyatt & Hopkins, *supra*, § 23.2(b). Of course, a tax-exempt entity may establish or participate in a for-profit PHO if the tax-exempt entity abides by the restrictions of its tax-exempt status.

6..   *Accountable Care Organizations.* Will ACOs be able to claim exempt status? Given the IRS unwillingness to accord exempt status to PHOs and IPAs, ACOs serving commercial business either exclusively or in addition to participating in the Medicare Shared Savings Program may be expected to encounter skepticism. A recent Private Letter Ruling suggests that ACOs will have to clearly articulate how they are benefitting their communities and/or lessening the burdens of government if they are to obtain exemptions. Internal Revenue Service, Private L. Rul. 2011–45025 (Aug. 18, 2011) (proposal to "establish and participate in a health care network," negotiating and entering into payor agreements and agreements with participating physicians). In its advisory on ACOs, however, the IRS demonstrated flexibility and indicated that ACOs participating in the MSSP may qualify for exempt status under certain circumstances. IRS, Fact Sheet on Exempt Organizations Participating in Medicare Shared Savings Program through Accountable Care Organizations (October 20, 2011).

C. JOINT VENTURES BETWEEN TAX–EXEMPT AND FOR–PROFIT ORGANIZATIONS

Tax-exempt organizations may engage in some non-tax-exempt activities. Section 501(c)(3) requires that the exempt entity be organized and operated "exclusively" for exempt purposes, but the Internal Revenue Code regulations interpret that standard as requiring that exempt organizations engage "primarily in activities that accomplish one or more . . . exempt purposes" and further state that the exempt organization violates this standard only if "more than an insubstantial" amount of its activities are not in furtherance of exempt purposes. 26 C.F.R. § 1.501(c)(3)–1(c)(1). Thus, § 501(c)(3) organizations may engage in trade or business unrelated to their exempt purposes, although income from such unrelated business is taxable and the activity must be "insubstantial" as compared to the organization's exempt activities.

An exempt organization also may engage in business activities jointly with for-profit organizations and may own for-profit organizations. Its participation in a joint venture with a for-profit entity will not affect its tax-exempt status provided the purpose of its involvement in the venture is in furtherance of its exempt purpose. Activities of a joint venture that is itself tax-exempt results in nontaxable, exempt income to the tax-exempt member of the venture. If the joint venture's activities are not tax-exempt, the income will be taxable as "unrelated business taxable income" to the exempt organization; and, if not insubstantial, may jeopardize the organization's exempt status. In evaluating the permissibility of joint ventures between for-profit and exempt entities, the IRS has long used a two-prong "close scrutiny" test. That test requires (1) that the exempt organization's participation in the venture furthers a charitable purpose, and (2) that the structure of the venture permits the exempt organization to act exclusively in furtherance of its charitable purpose and does not allow private inurement or private benefit to be conferred on private investors or other for-profit persons. IRS, GCM 39005 (Dec. 17, 1982). The following material takes us through the several strands of law that apply to a wide variety of joint ventures between for-profit and tax exempt entities in health care.

GENERAL COUNSEL MEMORANDUM
39862.
(Dec. 2, 1991).

[The Service reviews a physician-hospital agreement in which the hospital sold its future net income from certain departments to entities that were owned by physicians who admitted and treated patients at the hospital. For example, obstetricians who treated patients at the hospital could invest in the hospital's OB department with the return on investment being a proportionate share of the net income of that department. Thus, the physician practicing in the department would experience financial gain or loss depending on the department's financial performance.]

The [net income stream] joint venture arrangements . . . are just one variety of an increasingly common type of competitive behavior engaged in by hospitals in response to significant changes in their operating environment. Many medical and surgical procedures once requiring inpatient care, still the exclusive province of hospitals, now are performed on an outpatient basis, where every private physician is a potential competitor. The marked shift in governmental policy from regulatory cost controls to competition has fundamentally changed the way all hospitals, for-profit and not, do business.

A driving force behind the new hospital operating environment was the federal Medicare Program's 1983 shift from cost-based reimbursement for covered inpatient hospital services to fixed, per-case, prospective payments. This change to a diagnosis-related prospective payment system ("PPS") dramatically altered hospital financial incentives. PPS severed the link between longer hospital stays with more services provided each patient and higher reimbursement. It substituted strong incentives to control the costs of each individual inpatient's care while attracting a greater number of admissions. Medicare policies are highly influential; the program accounts for nearly 40% of the average hospital's revenues.

The need to increase admission volume was accompanied by a perceived need to influence physician treatment decisions which, by and large, were unaffected by the change to PPS. Hospitals realized that, in addition to attracting more patients, they needed to control utilization of ancillary hospital services, discharge Medicare beneficiaries as quickly as is medically appropriate, and operate more efficiently. Traditionally, physicians treating their private patients at a hospital had enjoyed nearly complete independence of professional judgment. Since they are paid separately by Medicare and other third party payers on the basis of billed charges, they still have an incentive to render more services to each patient over a longer period in order to enhance their own earnings. Once hospital and physician economic incentives diverged, hospitals began seeking ways to stimulate loyalty among members of their medical staffs and to encourage or reward physician behaviors deemed desirable.

*   *   *

* * * Here, there appears to be little accomplished that directly furthers the hospitals' charitable purposes of promoting health. No expansion of health care resources results; no new provider is created. No improvement in treatment modalities or reduction in cost is foreseeable. We have to look very carefully for any reason why a hospital would want to engage in this sort of arrangement.

*   *   *

Assuming, arguendo, that [a hospital engaged in the transaction because it had] a pressing need for an advance of cash, we could examine this type of transaction strictly as a financing mechanism. . . . [W]e do not believe it would be proper under most circumstances for a charitable organization to borrow funds under an agreement, even with an outside commercial lender, where the organization would pay as interest a stated percentage of its earnings. . . . In any event, we do not believe these transactions were undertaken to raise needed cash.

Whether admitted or not, we believe the hospitals engaged in these ventures largely as a means to retain and reward members of their medical staffs; to attract their admissions and referrals; and to pre-empt the physicians from investing in or creating a competing provider [of outpatient services].

* * *

* * * In our view, there are a fixed number of individuals in a community legitimately needing hospital services at any one time. Paying doctors to steer patients to one particular hospital merely to improve its efficiency seems distant from a mission of providing needed care. We question whether the Service should ever recognize enhancing a hospital's market share vis-a-vis other providers, in and of itself, as furthering a charitable purpose. In many cases, doing so might hamper another charitable hospital's ability to promote the health of the same community.

* * *

NOTES AND QUESTIONS

1.   Evaluate the economic incentives created by the proposed arrangement. How would a physician gain by making such an investment? Why would a hospital sell a share of its income? Isn't the potential improvement in the hospital's competitive position in the community or enhancement of its efficiency a community benefit? Compare these arrangements to "gainsharing" arrangements discussed in the next chapter which allow staff physicians to share in the savings arising from process improvement initiatives or other cost-effective methods which are attributable in part to the physician's efforts. What distinguishes gainsharing arrangements from the sale of revenue stream at issue in GCM 39862? See Stacey L. Murphy & Edward J. Buchholz, Internal Revenue Service Approval of Two Gainsharing Programs—The Rulings and Their Implications, 32 J. Health L. 381 (1999).

2.   Unrelated trade or business is that which an exempt organization regularly carries on "the conduct of which is not substantially related (aside from the need of such organization for income or funds or the use it makes of the profits derived)" to its exempt purpose and is taxable as "unrelated business taxable income" (UBTI). 26 CFR § 1.513–1(a). Services that contribute to patient recovery and convenience are "related" to the exempt purposes of the health care organization and income from these activities is not taxable. Generally, services provided to non-hospital patients are taxable unless they fall within certain narrow exceptions relating to (1) whether the services to non-patients are otherwise available in the community or (2) whether the services to non-patients contribute to the achievement of other exempt purposes, such as medical education. Thus sales of pharmaceuticals to individuals who are not hospital patients are taxable, with limited exceptions made for situations in which there are no local alternatives. See Hi–Plains Hosp. v. U.S., 670 F.2d 528 (5th Cir. 1982). See also Private Letter Ruling 8125007 (undated), in which the Service decided that sophisticated lab services, not otherwise available and provided by an exempt hospital to industry for employee examinations, did not produce UBTI. The PLR concluded, however, that the provision of ordinary lab services performed for non-hospital patients of private physicians may do so. This may lead to rather confusing results. A

hospital's revenues from providing MRI services to patients of another hospital or to outpatients served by its staff physicians might well produce UBTI, though the revenues from the same services to admitted patients would not. Likewise income from management or administrative services sold by a tax-exempt hospital to physicians in private practices could certainly be considered UBTI. If the hospital purchased the physician practices, would the provision of these services to the hospital-owned practices produce taxable income? On the issue of gift shops, parking facilities and cafeterias on hospital campuses, the law carves out an exception to taxable income by excluding business "carried on by the organization primarily for the convenience of its . . . members, patients or employees." I.R.C. § 513(a) (2006).

REVENUE RULING 98–15

1998–12 I.R.B. 6.

[In this Revenue Ruling, the IRS provides the following examples to illustrate whether an organization that operates an acute care hospital constitutes an organization whose principal purpose is providing charitable hospital care when it forms a limited liability company (LLC) with a for-profit corporation and then contributes its hospital and all of its related operating assets to the LLC, which then operates the hospital.]

Situation 1

A is a nonprofit corporation that owns and operates an acute care hospital. A has been recognized as exempt from federal income tax * * * as an organization described in § 501(c)(3). * * * B is a for-profit corporation that owns and operates a number of hospitals.

A concludes that it could better serve its community if it obtained additional funding. B is interested in providing financing for A's hospital, provided it earns a reasonable rate of return. A and B form a limited liability company, C. A contributes all of its operating assets, including its hospital to C. B also contributes assets to C. In return, A and B receive ownership interests in C proportional and equal in value to their respective contributions.

C's Articles of Organization and Operating Agreement ("governing documents") provide that C is to be managed by a governing board consisting of three individuals chosen by A and two individuals chosen by B. A intends to appoint community leaders who have experience with hospital matters, but who are not on the hospital staff and do not otherwise engage in business transactions with the hospital.

The governing documents further provide that they may only be amended with the approval of both owners and that a majority of three board members must approve certain major decisions relating to C's operation including decisions relating to any of the following topics:

    A.   C's annual capital and operating budgets;

    B.   Distributions of C's earnings;

    C.   Selection of key executives;

    D.   Acquisition or disposition of health care facilities;

    E.   Contracts in excess of $x per year;

    F.   Changes to the types of services offered by the hospital; and

    G.   Renewal or termination of management agreements.

The governing documents require that C operate any hospital it owns in a manner that furthers charitable purposes by promoting health for a broad cross section of its community. The governing documents explicitly provide that the duty of the members of the governing board to operate C in a manner that furthers charitable purposes by promoting health for a broad cross section of the community overrides any duty they may have to operate C for the financial benefit of its owners. Accordingly, in the event of a conflict between operation in accordance with the community benefit standard and any duty to maximize profits, the members of the governing board are to satisfy the community benefit standard without regard to the consequences for maximizing profitability.

The governing documents further provide that all returns of capital and distributions of earnings made to owners of C shall be proportional to their ownership interests in C. The terms of the governing documents are legal, binding, and enforceable under applicable state law.

C enters into a management agreement with a management company that is unrelated to A or B to provide day-to-day management services to C. The management agreement is for a five-year period, and the agreement is renewable for additional five-year periods by mutual consent. The management company will be paid a management fee for its services based on C's gross revenues. The terms and conditions of the management agreement, including the fee structure and the contract term, are reasonable and comparable to what other management firms receive for similar services at similarly situated hospitals. C may terminate the agreement for cause.

None of the officers, directors, or key employees of A who were involved in making the decision to form C were promised employment or any other inducement by C or B and their related entities if the transaction were approved. None of A's officers, directors, or key employees have any interest * * * in B or any of its related entities.

    * * * C will be treated as a partnership for federal income tax purposes.

A intends to use any distributions it receives from C to fund grants to support activities that promote the health of A's community and to help the indigent obtain health care. Substantially all of A's grantmaking will be funded by distributions from C. A's projected grant making program and its participation as an owner of C will constitute A's only activities.

Situation 2

D is a nonprofit corporation that owns and operates an acute care hospital. D has been recognized as exempt from federal income tax . . . as an organization described in § 501(c)(3). . . . E is a for-profit hospital corporation that owns and operates a number of hospitals and provides management services to several hospitals that it does not own.

D concludes that it could better serve its community if it obtained additional funding. E is interested in providing financing for D's hospital, provided it earns a reasonable rate of return. D and E form a limited liability company, F. D contributes all of its operating assets, including its hospital to F. E also contributes assets to F. In return, D and E receive ownership interests proportional and equal in value to their respective contributions.

F's Articles of Organization and Operating Agreement ("governing documents") provide that F is to be managed by a governing board consisting of three individuals chosen by D and three individuals chosen by E. D intends to appoint community leaders who have experience with hospital matters, but who are not on the hospital staff and do not otherwise engage in business transactions with the hospital.

The governing documents further provide that they may only be amended with the approval of both owners and that a majority of board members must approve certain major decisions relating to F's operation, including decisions relating to any of the following topics:

A. F's annual capital and operating budgets;

B. Distributions of F's earnings over a required minimum level of distributions set forth in the Operating Agreement;

C. Unusually large contracts; and

D. Selection of key executives.

F's governing documents provide that F's purpose is to construct, develop, own, manage, operate, and take other action in connection with operating the health care facilities it owns and engage in other health care-related activities. The governing documents further provide that all returns of capital and distributions of earnings made to owners of F shall be proportional to their ownership interests in F.

F enters into a management agreement with a wholly-owned subsidiary of E to provide day-to-day management services to F. The management agreement is for a five-year period, and the agreement is renewable for additional five-year periods at the discretion of E's subsidiary. F may terminate the agreement only for cause. E's subsidiary will be paid a management fee for its services based on gross revenues. The terms and conditions of the management agreement, including the fee structure and the contract term other than the renewal terms, are reasonable and comparable to what other management firms receive for similar services at similarly situated hospitals.

As part of the agreement to form F, D agrees to approve the selection of two individuals to serve as F's chief executive officer and chief financial officer. These individuals have previously worked for E in hospital management and have business expertise. They will work with the management company to oversee F's day-to-day management. Their compensation is comparable to what comparable executives are paid at similarly situated hospitals.

* * * F will be treated as a partnership for federal income tax purposes.

D intends to use any distributions it receives from F to fund grants to support activities that promote the health of D's community and to help the indigent obtain health care. Substantially all of D's grant making will be funded by distributions from F. D's projected grant making program and its participation as an owner of F will constitute D's only activities.

ANALYSIS

A § 501(c)(3) organization may form and participate in a partnership, including an LLC treated as a partnership for federal income tax purposes, and meet the operational test if participation in the partnership furthers a charitable purpose, and the partnership arrangement permits the exempt organization to act exclusively in furtherance of its exempt purpose and only incidentally for the benefit of the for-profit partners. Similarly, a § 501(c)(3) organization may enter into a management contract with a private party giving that party authority to conduct activities on behalf of the organization and direct the use of the organization's assets provided that the organization retains ultimate authority over the assets and activities being managed and the terms and conditions of the contract are reasonable, including reasonable compensation and a reasonable term. However, if a private party is allowed to control or use the nonprofit organization's activities or assets for the benefit of the private party, and the benefit is not incidental to the accomplishment of exempt purposes, the organization will fail to be organized and operated exclusively for exempt purposes.

Situation 1

After A and B form C, and A contributes all of its operating assets to C, A's activities will consist of the health care services it provides through C and any grantmaking activities it can conduct using income distributed to C. A will receive an interest in C equal in value to the assets it contributes to C, and A's and B's returns from C will be proportional to their respective investments in C. The governing documents of C commit C to providing health care services for the benefit of the community as a whole and to give charitable purposes priority over maximizing profits for C's owners. Furthermore, through A's appointment of members of the community familiar with the hospital to C's board, the board's structure, which gives A's appointees voting control, and the specifically enumerated powers of the board over changes in activities, disposition of assets, and renewal of the management agreement. A can ensure that the assets it owns through C and the activities it conducts through C are used primarily to further exempt purposes. Thus, A can ensure that the benefit to B and other private parties, like the management company, will be incidental to the accomplishment of charitable purposes. Additionally, the terms and conditions of the management contract, including the terms for renewal and termination are reasonable. Finally, A's grants are intended to support education and research and give resources to help provide health care to the indigent. All of these facts and circumstances establish that, when A participates in forming C and contributes all of its operating assets to C, and C operates in accordance with its governing documents, A will be furthering charitable purposes and continue to be operated exclusively for exempt purposes.

* * *

Situation 2

When D and E form F, and D contributes its assets to F, D will be engaged in activities that consist of the health care services it provides through F and any grantmaking activities it can conduct using income distributed by F. However, unlike A, D will not be engaging primarily in activities that further an exempt purpose. * * * In the absence of a binding obligation in F's governing documents for F to serve charitable purposes or otherwise provide its services to the community as a whole, F will be able to deny care to segments of the community, such as the indigent. Because D will share control of F with E, D will not be able to initiate programs within F to serve new health needs within the community without the agreement of at least one governing board member appointed by E. As a business enterprise, E will not necessarily give priority to the health needs of the community over the consequences for F's profits. The primary source of information for board members appointed by D will be the chief executives, who have a prior relationship with E and the management company, which is a subsidiary of E. The management company itself will have broad discretion over F's activities and assets that may not always be under the board's supervision. For example, the management company is permitted to enter into all but "unusually large" contracts without board approval. The management company may also unilaterally renew the management agreement. Based on all these facts and circumstances, D cannot establish that the activities it conducts through F further exempt purposes. "[I]n order for an organization to qualify for exemption under § 501(c)(3) the organization must 'establish' that it is neither organized nor operated for the 'benefit of private interests.' "[ ] Consequently, the benefit to E resulting from the activities D conducts through F will not be incidental to the furtherance of an exempt purpose. Thus, D will fail the operational test when it forms F, contributes its operating assets to F, and then serves as an owner to F.

NOTES AND QUESTIONS

1.   While Situation 1 effectively carves out a safe harbor for structuring who may form and participate in hospital joint ventures, what lessons can be drawn about the required degree of control the exempt organization must possess? For example, consider whether the following changes for the hospital in Situation 2 would enable it to retain its § 501(c)(3) status: shortening the management term to five years, requiring a 24–hour emergency room at one or more of the LLC hospitals, and adopting a list of reserved powers similar to those in Situation 1. See Gerald M. Griffith, Revenue Ruling 98–15: Dimming the Future of All Nonprofit Joint Ventures?, 31 J. Health L. 71, 88 (1998).

2..   Two notable cases affirm the analytic framework of Rev. Ruling 98–15 stressing the centrality of control in evaluating hospital joint ventures with for-profit partners. In St. David's Health Care System v. United States, 349 F.3d 232 (5th Cir. 2003). the Court of Appeals for the Fifth Circuit examined a limited partnership between St. David's Health Care System, a tax-exempt entity operating an acute care hospital, and HCA Inc. pursuant to which HCA would operate and manage the hospital in a whole hospital joint venture arrangement. The court concluded that St. David's was no longer engaged in activities that primarily furthered its charitable purpose, rejecting the hospital's contention, which the district court had endorsed, that the pivotal question was one of function, not control. The Court found that where private parties or for-profit entities have either "formal or effective control," a presumption attaches "that the organization furthers the profit seeking motivations of those private individuals or entities." While remanding the case to the district court to determine whether control was effectively ceded to HCA, the court was openly skeptical of the claim that various protective measures were sufficient to save the day for St. David's. It questioned, for example, whether St. David's ability to appoint half the members of the board, its right to unilaterally remove the venture's CEO, assurances in the management services agreement that St. David's exempt status would not be endangered, and its right to compel dissolution, sufficed to establish control. Although on remand a jury held that St. David's should retain its exempt status, the IRS adheres to the view that the Fifth Circuit opinion "provided the proper framework for judging joint ventures between non-profits and for-profits . . . [i.e.] a non-profit must have effective control in the joint venture." Fred Sokeld, IRS Official Unfazed by Jury Decision in Joint Venture Case, 2004 Tax Notes Today 50 (May 12, 2004).

In a second case, Redlands Surgical Services v. Comm'r of Internal Revnue, 113 T.C. 47 (1999), the Tax Court examined a complex joint venture involving a tax exempt hospital sytem, its exempt subsidiaries and a for-profit entity to own and operate an ambulatory surgical center. In upholding the denial of exempt status, the court stressed both the absence voting control in the partnership (evidenced by a 2-2 split in managing directors of the general partner) and the absence of "any binding commitments establishing an obligation that charitable purposes be put ahead of economic objectives." Notably the court also found wanting any indicia of "informal control" by the exempt entity such as the ability to effectively monitor performance or "command allegiance or loyalty" of those managing the joint venture.

2. The succinct verdict of the commentators after Revenue Ruling 98–15 and the decisions in *Redlands* and *St. David's* was that "control is king." Why should that be so? Can you make an argument based on the language and history of the tax code that control should not be the ultimate touchstone for exemption? Can you imagine a compelling set of circumstances in which exemption is warranted even though the exempt organization lacked control over a partnership with a for-profit entity?

3. The implications of *Redlands* and *St. David's* for "ancillary joint ventures" are somewhat uncertain. The IRS has approved dozens of such joint ventures involving medical office buildings, imaging centers, ambulatory surgical centers, treatment centers, physical therapy centers, hospital home care services, and nursing homes. See e.g., Private Letter Ruling (PLR) 200206058 (Nov. 16, 2001) (L.L.C. formed by hospital and physicians to provide new medical service); PLR 9517029 (Jan. 27, 1995) (acute care hospital and psychiatric hospital L.L.C. joint venture between an exempt university subsidiary and a for-profit company). Note an important distinction between ancillary joint ventures and the whole hospital ventures involved in Revenue Ruling 98–15: in the former, the exempt hospital retains its separate existence, is subject to the community benefit standard, and often is contributing only a fraction of its assets. See Nicholas A. Mirkay, Relinquish Control! Why the IRS Should Change its Stance on Exempt Organizations in Ancillary Joint Ventures, 6 Nev. L. J. 21, 50 (2005).

Whether the IRS is ready to move off the control standard for such ventures remains unclear. However, in a notable ruling the IRS approved an LLC joint venture between a tax-exempt university offering seminars to teachers to improve their skills and a for-profit entity that conducted interactive video training programs. Rev. Rul. 2004–51. Membership in the LLC was divided equally between the for-profit and the university, but the latter retained "exclusive right to approve curriculum, training materials and instructors and determine standards" for the seminars. Noting that the venture did not constitute a substantial part of the University's activities, the IRS ruled that its participation in the venture would not jeopardize its exempt status. The fact that the ruling cited *St. David's* and Rev. Ruling 98–15, but did not explicitly apply those precedents or invoke the "control" standard and permitted a 50–50 venture to go forward has been interpreted by some to suggest that the test may be loosened in the future. See Mirkay, *supra*, but also quoting. an IRS official reminding tax lawyers that Revenue Ruling 98–15 is "still on the books."

What alternative approaches might be applied to ancillary joint ventures? Professor John Colombo has proposed a framework that would employ the principles of UBIT to analyze distinct scenarios under which exempt organizations may engage in joint undertakings that involve businesses not in furtherance of their charitable purpose without losing their exempt status. See John D. Colombo, Commercial Activity and Charitable Tax Exemption, 44 Wm. & Mary L. Rev. 487 (2002). Others have proposed a bright-line quantitative rule that would also employ a UBIT analysis, but would impose a quantitative safe harbor (e.g., use of less than fifteen percent of the exempt organization's assets in the ancillary joint venture)..

D. INUREMENT, PRIVATE BENEFIT, AND EXCESS BENEFIT TRANSACTIONS: RELATIONSHIPS BETWEEN PHYSICIANS AND TAX–EXEMPT HEALTH CARE ORGANIZATIONS

Physicians and hospitals are highly interdependent both clinically and financially. In the language of economics, they jointly produce the end services provided to patients. As you have seen in the previous sections of this chapter, hospitals may establish joint ventures with physicians for ancillary services both inside and outside the hospital or to provide care through free standing entities. Hospitals are motivated by both the desire to more efficiently use these resources and to cement their relationships with the physicians and thus assure themselves a steady flow of patients. For similar reasons, hospitals and integrated delivery system also have frequently purchased physician practices or recruited physicians to establish a private practice in their geographic area, usually supplying some form of financial support provided to entice the doctor to relocate or open a practice.

These relationships between physicians and tax-exempt organizations raise issues for the tax-exempt provider. Several of these have been explored in the earlier sections of this chapter: IRS limitations on control in joint ventures; standards for unrelated trade or business income; and the achievement and protection of its charitable purposes. In addition, the exempt organization must comply with three other major legal constraints on relationships between non-exempt (which includes physicians) and tax-exempt health care organizations. These are the proscriptions against private benefit and against private inurement (both of which flow from the language of Section 501(c)(3)) and the statutory sanctions against excess benefit transactions (codified in IRC Section 4958). It appears that the excess benefit statute, which is discussed at the end of this section, will be the predominant tool for future enforcement by the IRS.

GENERAL COUNSEL MEMORANDUM
39862 (Dec. 2, 1991).

[The Service reviews a physician-hospital agreement in which the hospital sold its future net income from certain departments to entities owned by physicians who admitted and treated patients at the hospital. Other excerpts from the GCM are included in the previous section on joint ventures.]

I.   Sale of the Revenue Stream From a Hospital Activity Allows
      Net Profits To Inure to the Benefit of Physician–Investors

*   *   *

[Editors' Note: At the time of this GCM, the IRS took the position that all physician members of the medical staffs of hospitals—including those not employed by the hospital—have a such a close working relationship with and a private interest in the exempt hospital so as to be subject to the prohibition against inurement, which applies only to "insiders." The GCM stressed physicians' close professional working relationship with the hospitals, that "they largely control the flow of patients to and from the hospital and patients' utilization of hospital services while there," the binding effect of the medical staff bylaws, and the fact that some may serve other roles at the hospital, such as that of part-time employee, department head, Board member, etc. As we will see later in this chapter, the Service does not take the position that staff physician are "disqualified persons" with regard to application of the Excess Benefit statute, which will govern most inurement-type questions in the future. It is therefore unlikely that it would adhere to the position taken in this GCM that staff member physicians are categorically considered "insiders" for purposes of inurement analysis.]

Even though medical staff physicians are subject to the inurement proscription, that does not mean there can be no economic dealings between them and the hospitals. The inurement proscription does not prevent the payment of reasonable compensation for goods or services. It is aimed at preventing dividend-like distributions of charitable assets or expenditures to benefit a private interest. This Office has stated "inurement is likely to arise where the financial benefit represents a transfer of the organization's financial resources to an individual solely by virtue of the individual's relationship with the organization, and without regard to the accomplishment of exempt purposes." [ ]* * *

* * *

Whether admitted or not, we believe the hospitals engaged in these ventures largely as a means to retain and reward members of their medical staffs; to attract their admissions and referrals; and to pre-empt the physicians from investing in or creating a competing provider. . . . Giving (or selling) medical staff physicians a proprietary interest in the net profits of a hospital under these circumstances creates a result that is indistinguishable from paying dividends on stock. Profit distributions are made to persons having a personal and private interest in the activities of the organization and are made out of the net earnings of the organization. Thus, the arrangements confer a benefit which violates the inurement proscription of section 501(c)(3).

* * *

II.   Sale of the Revenue Stream From a Hospital Activity Benefits Private Interests More Than Incidentally

[A] key principle in the law of tax exempt organizations is that an entity is not organized and operated exclusively for exempt purposes unless it serves a public rather than a private interest. Thus, in order to be exempt, an organization must establish that it is not organized or operated for the benefit of private interests such as designated individuals, the creator or his family, shareholders of the organization, or persons controlled, directly or indirectly, by such private interests. [ ] However, this private benefit prohibition applies to all kinds of persons and groups, not just to those "insiders" subject to the more strict inurement proscription.

* * *

In our view, some private benefit is present in all typical hospital-physician relationships. Physicians generally use hospital facilities at no cost to themselves to provide services to private patients for which they earn a fee. The private benefit accruing to the physicians generally can be considered incidental to the overwhelming public benefit resulting from having the combined resources of the hospital and its professional staff available to serve the public. Though the private benefit is compounded in the case of certain specialists, such as heart transplant surgeons, who depend heavily on highly specialized hospital facilities, that fact alone will not make the private benefit more than incidental.

In contrast, the private benefits conferred on the physician-investors by the instant revenue stream joint ventures are direct and substantial, not incidental. If for any reason these benefits should be found not to constitute inurement, they nonetheless exceed the bounds of prohibited private benefit. Whether viewed as giving the physicians a substantial share in the profits of the hospital or simply as allowing them an extremely profitable investment, the arrangements confer a significant benefit on them. Against this, we must balance the public benefit achieved by the hospitals in entering into the arrangements. The public benefit expected to result from these transactions—enhanced hospital financial health or greater efficiency achieved through improved utilization of their facilities—bears only the most tenuous relationship to the hospitals' charitable purposes of promoting the health of their communities. Obtaining referrals or avoiding new competition may improve the competitive position of an individual hospital, but that is not necessarily the same as benefiting its community.

*   *   *

NOTES AND QUESTIONS

1.   Note the key differences between private inurement and private benefit. The former is akin to a per se rule, requiring revocation or denial of exempt status, with no *de minimis* exception. Moreover, it applies only to "insiders," defined as private shareholders or individuals having a personal and private interest in or opportunity to influence the activities of the organization from the inside. Treas. Reg. § 1.50(a)–1(c). The private benefit limitation applies to transactions with "outsiders" to the exempt organization and entails a broader inquiry, weighing private benefits against community benefits. What goals of the two proscriptions explain the different approaches? What factors did the Service take into account in evaluating each of the scenarios in Rev. Ruling 97–21? Why did the balance tip against the hospital in GCM 39862?

2.   The core of the analysis of private benefit and private inurement is the relationship between what the exempt organization pays and the value of what it receives. Might not-for-profit entities behave differently than for-profits in acquiring physician practices, recruiting physicians or structuring physician compensation and investment? Do a tax-exempt hospital's relationships with physicians require more careful scrutiny than its contracts with third party vendors? The IRS's view that staff physicians were in a position to influence administrators of tax-exempt hospitals led to treating them as "insiders" for inurement purposes, a position that it no longer adheres to as seen in the discussion of the Excess Benefits Transactions law in the next section of this chapter.

3.   Inurement and private benefit issues frequently arise in a variety of other contexts, such as joint ventures involving hospitals and physicians. See

e.g., Anclote Psychiatric Ctr., Inc. v. Commissioner, T.C. Memo 1998–273, aff'd 190 F.3d 541 (11th Cir. 1999) (upholding IRS' revocation of converting hospital's exemption based on inurement where the sale of its assets to for profit entity owned by its former board members was for consideration less than fair market value).

E. EXCESS BENEFIT TRANSACTIONS: PROTECTING HOSPITALS AND OTHER TAX-EXEMPT ORGANIZATIONS FROM EXPLOITATION BY INSIDERS

In 1996 Congress adopted the Taxpayer Bill of Rights II (26 U.S.C.A. § 4958), an important law designed to clarify the obligations of insiders in exempt organizations and to provide an alternative sanction for violations. The basic concept of the law is straightforward: it imposes an excise tax on insiders ("disqualified persons") engaged in "excess benefit transactions" and on organizational mangers who approve them. But, as we've seen, nothing in tax law is simple. In January 2002, following four years of comment and revision, the Department of the Treasury issued final regulations which supply guidance concerning the numerous new concepts contained in § 4958. 26 C.F.R. § 53.4958–1—53.4958–8. Some key terminology and concepts must be mastered to apply the supposedly simple, "bright line" approach of the statute. The following material outlines the key elements of the law.

Scope. Congress intended § 4958 to be the exclusive sanction unless the conduct arises to such an extreme level (evidenced by the size and scope of the excess benefit and the organization's efforts to prevent the conduct) that the tax-exempt organization can no longer be regarded as "charitable" and hence revocation is the appropriate sanction.

Excess Benefit Transactions. The statute defines an "excess benefit transaction" (EBT) as any transaction in which an economic benefit is provided by a tax-exempt organization directly or indirectly to or for the use of a "disqualified person" where the value of the economic benefit provided by the organization exceeds the value of the consideration (including the performance of services) received for providing the benefit. 26 U.S.C.A. § 4958(c)(1). The core prohibited transactions are those in which the disqualified person engages in *non-fair market transactions*, such as a bargain sale or loan; *unreasonable compensation arrangements*; or proscribed *revenue sharing arrangements*. The regulations give some additional guidance, such as indicating that compensation is reasonable only if it is an amount that ordinarily would be paid for like services by like enterprises under like circumstances existing at the time the contract was made. Treas. Reg. 534958–4(b)(3). Further, compensation includes all forms of deferred income if earned and vested and fringe benefits (even if not taxable); however, payments must be intended as compensation by the tax-exempt entity. Treas. Reg. 534958–4(c).

Disqualified Persons. "Disqualified persons" (DQPs) include "any person who was, at any time during the 5–year period ending on the date of such transaction, in a position to exercise substantial influence over the affairs of the organization, a member of the family of [such] an individual, or a 35–percent controlled entity [an entity in which such persons own more than 35% of the combined voting power if a corporation or of the profits interest if a partnership or of the beneficial interest of a trust or estate]." I.R.C. 4958(f)(1)(A).

Among those included in the category of DQPs are: officers, directors, and their close relatives. However, the detailed regulations make clear that persons with such titles are not to be so regarded if their position is honorary or they have no powers or ability to exercise substantial influence. Treas. Reg. 534958–3(c). Conversely, those with "substantial influence" can be DQPs regardless of whether they hold a formal position with the exempt organization.

An important issue for hospitals has been whether staff physicians will automatically be considered to have substantial influence. Although the IRS had previously indicated that they would be considered "insiders" for inurement purposes, it has reversed its position for excess benefit analysis, as the following excerpts from the regulations indicate. What generalizable principles emerge from these examples that can be applied in other factual settings?

TREAS. REG. 534958–3(G)

* * *

Example 10. U is a large acute-care hospital that is an applicable tax-exempt organization for purposes of section 4958. U employs X as a radiologist. X gives instructions to staff with respect to the radiology work X conducts, but X does not supervise other U employees or manage any substantial part of U's operations. X's compensation is primarily in the form of a fixed salary. In addition, X is eligible to receive an incentive award based on revenues of the radiology department. X's compensation is greater than the amount referenced for a highly compensated employee in section 414(q)(1)(B)(i) in the year benefits are provided. X is not related to any other disqualified person of U. X does not serve on U's governing body or as an officer of U. Although U participates in a provider-sponsored organization [ ] X does not have a material financial interest in that organization. X does not receive compensation primarily based on revenues derived from activities of U that X controls. X does not participate in any management decisions affecting either U as a whole or a discrete segment of U that represents a substantial portion of its activities, assets, income, or expenses. Under these facts and circumstances, X does not have substantial influence over the affairs of U, and therefore X is not a disqualified person with respect to U.

Example 11. W is a cardiologist and head of the cardiology department of the same hospital U described in Example 10. The cardiology department is a major source of patients admitted to U and consequently represents a substantial portion of U's income, as compared to U as a whole. W does not serve on U's governing board or as an officer of U. W does not have a material financial interest in the provider-sponsored organization (as defined in section 1855(e) of the Social Security Act) in which U participates. W receives a salary and retirement and welfare benefits fixed by a three-year renewable employment contract with U. W's compensation is greater than the amount referenced for a highly compensated employee in section 414(q)(1)(B)(i) in the year benefits are provided. As department head, W manages the cardiology department and has authority to allocate the budget for that department, which includes authority to distribute incentive bonuses among cardiologists according to criteria that W has authority to set. W's management of a discrete segment of U that represents a substantial portion of its income and activities (as compared to U as a whole) places W in a position to exercise substantial influence over the affairs of U. Under these facts and circumstances, W is a disqualified person with respect to U.

Organization Managers. Besides imposing penalties on the individuals receiving the benefits (see below), the act also levies a separate excise tax of 10 per cent on "organization managers," whose participation in the transaction was "knowing, willful and not due to reasonable cause." The regulations define organization managers to include directors, trustees or officers and administrators with delegated or regularly exercised administrative powers, but not independent contractors such as lawyers and accountants, investment advisors or middle managers with power to make recommendations but not to implement decisions. See Treas. Reg. 534958–3(d)(2)(i). Where the organizational manager makes full disclosure of all facts to a professional advisor and relies on that advisor's reasoned, written legal opinion, no penalty will be imposed; the advisor may be a lawyer, accountant or independent valuation firm with expertise. Treas. Reg. 534958–1(d)(4)(iii).

Rebuttable Presumption of Reasonableness. A key element of the intermediate sanctions statutory scheme is a rebuttable presumption of reasonableness applicable to compensation arrangements and transfers of property with a disqualified person where specified procedural steps are followed. To qualify for the presumption, the terms of the transaction must be approved by a board of directors or committee thereof composed entirely of individuals who (1) have no conflicts of interest with respect to the transaction and (2) have obtained and relied upon appropriate comparability data prior to making their determination and have adequately documented the basis for the determination. See Treas. Reg. 534958–6. The IRS may rebut the presumption with evidence that the compensation was not reasonable or the transfer was not at fair market value, such as by contesting the validity of comparables. The regulations give detailed instructions on standards for comparability determinations and give some relief for small organizations as to the data that must be used. Id. In an advisory on compensation, the IRS found reliance by an independent board on a five-year old consultant report and the board's failure to separately evaluate compensation to comparable CEOs rendered the record inadequate to establish the rebuttable presumption under Section 4958. Internal Revenue Service, Technical Advice Memorandum 200244028 (June 21, 2002).

Penalties and "Correction." Sanctions, in the form of an initial tax of 25 percent of the excess benefit, are imposed on individuals who benefited from the transaction; the excess benefit is calculated as the amount by which a transaction differs from fair market value. Disqualified persons are subject to an additional tax of 200 percent of the excess benefit unless the transaction is "corrected" promptly (generally meaning that the disqualified person must undo the transaction and compensate the exempt organization for any losses caused by the transaction). Notably, no sanctions are imposed on the exempt organization (however, as described above, organizational managers who knowingly and willfully participate are subject to a 10 percent tax). Abatement of penalties is possible where the violation is due to reasonable cause and not willful neglect. In the notorious Bishop Estate case, one of the first cases brought under § 4958, the IRS imposed sanctions against the trustees of an estate in Hawaii who paid themselves exorbitant salaries for its management. See Carolyn D. Wright, IRS Assesses Intermediate Sanctions Against Bishop Estate Incumbent Trustees, 2001 Tax Notes Today 405 (January 5, 2001).

PROBLEMS: EXCESS BENEFIT TRANSACTIONS

1.   Analyze whether the excess benefit law would apply in the following situations:

- Expenditures by a tax-exempt hospital to recruit an obstetrician, currently practicing at a nearby hospital, to relocate his office nearby and obtain staff privileges. The expenditures (free rent, moving allowances, and malpractice insurance subsidies) exceed payments customarily made and there is no documentation of a community shortage of obstetricians.

- Payment by a tax-exempt hospital to certain Department Chairs, a fixed percentage of all revenues of the department.

- C, a tax-exempt hospital, contracts with Y, a management company, which will provide a wide range of services for a management fee of 7% of C's adjusted gross revenues, as specifically defined in the contract. Y will also receive payments for any expenses it incurs including legal, consulting or accounting throughout the term of the contract.

2. Larry Levy, CEO of Exempt Hospital (EH) has received an offer from a for-profit system in another state that will pay him $2.2 million per year; provide him with a loan of $1 million; and give a performance bonus of $500,000 per year if he meets revenue targets. This package amounts to 50 percent more than EH currently pays him. It is believed to be in line with compensation at for-profit systems but is about 20 percent more than comparable nonprofit hospital systems pay. What should the Board of EH do and why?

3. EH currently pays Dr. Brady, an independent staff physician who serves as its Department Chair of Oncology (with responsibility for hiring staff, supervising credentialing, and handling administrative duties of hospital but no role in budgetary matters), a sum of $1000 per month. Dr. Brady has requested a new compensation arrangement pursuant to which EH would pay him an additional $1000 for each new patient he or any member of the staff admits to EH who incurs total bills greater than $10,000. The EH Board approved this arrangement after a short briefing from its CEO who stressed that EH would have to shut down its oncology department if they didn't accede to Dr. Brady's demand. What excess benefit tax liability and for whom? What steps should the parties take?

CHAPTER REVIEW PROBLEM

Revisit the Organizing for Integration problem on page 528. How would your recommendations for Magna Hospital change based on what you have learned about tax exemption issues?

CHAPTER 13

FRAUD AND ABUSE

■ ■ ■

Health care providers are subject to a large body of law governing their financial arrangements with each other and with payors. These state and federal laws cover many practices that amount to fraud, bribery, or stealing. In addition, they prohibit many contractual relationships, investments, and marketing and recruitment practices that are perfectly legal in other businesses. As will be seen, these laws are well-intentioned: they seek to rectify a number of serious flaws in the health care financing system, save the government money, and prevent conflicts of interest that taint the physician-patient relationship. Indeed, they have been used to bring to justice a large number of providers, including some major corporate entities, that have engaged in systematic fraud. Unfortunately, the fraud and abuse statutes (and the regulations, cases, and interpretative rulings and guidelines they have spawned) are also bewilderingly complicated and have generated confusion and cynicism in the health care industry. Further, some aspects of these laws may prove anachronistic under evolving payment systems. Nevertheless, they continue to have a profound impact on the health care industry and generate an enormous amount of work for health care lawyers designing organizational structures that must comply with their strictures.

I.   FALSE CLAIMS

According to some estimates, Medicare and Medicaid fraud and abuse costs federal and state governments tens of billions of dollars per year. By one estimate, fraud and abuse added as much as $98 billion to federal spending on Medicare and Medicaid in 2011. Donald M. Berwick & Andrew D. Hackbarth, Eliminating Waste in US Health Care, 307 JAMA 1513 (2012). When one adds the costs of "waste"—defined as overtreatment, failures of coordination and execution, administrative complexity and pricing failures—the lowest published estimates find that 20% of total health expenditures are misspent. Id. 1514. Much of this problem undoubtedly can be traced to the structure and complexities of Medicare and Medicaid payment systems which give incentives and opportunities to engage in fraud or to "game the system" to maximize reimbursement and to laws requiring rapid payment to providers that allows perpetrators of fraud to avoid prosecution. See Health Affairs, Health Policy Brief, Eliminating Fraud and Abuse (July 31, 2012).

The term "fraud and abuse" is a broad one, covering a large number of activities ranging from negligent or careless practices that result in overbilling, to "self-referral arrangements" that are seen as improperly enriching providers and encouraging overutilization, to outright fraudulent schemes to bill for services never rendered. Indeed, the "fraud" aspects of "fraud and abuse" prosecutions have involved overtly criminal schemes, sometimes with elements of racketeering and the involvement of organized crime. Federal prosecutors have also sought to expand the reach of the anti-fraud laws to reach deficiencies in quality of care or products and the provision of misleading information by providers. This section deals with the law of false claims, which is designed to protect the government from paying for goods or services that have not been provided or were not provided in accordance with government regulations. Specific problems addressed by the law include: provider charges or claims for unreasonable costs, services not rendered, services provided by unlicensed or unapproved personnel or for claims not in compliance with CMS regulations, excessive or unnecessary care, and fraudulent cost reports.

A. GOVERNMENTAL ENFORCEMENT

UNITED STATES V. KRIZEK

United States District Court, District of Columbia, 1994.
859 F.Supp. 5.

SPORKIN, DISTRICT JUDGE.

Memorandum Opinion and Order

On January 11, 1993, the United States filed this civil suit against George O. Krizek, M.D. and Blanka H. Krizek under the False Claims Act, 31 U.S.C. §§ 3729–3731, and at common law. The government brought the action against the Krizeks alleging false billing for Medicare and Medicaid patients. The five counts include claims for (1) "Knowingly Presenting a False or Fraudulent Claim", 31 U.S.C. § 3729(a)(1); (2) "Knowingly Presenting a False or Fraudulent Record", 31 U.S.C. § 3729(a)(2); (3) "Conspiracy to Defraud the Government"; (4) "Payment under Mistake of Fact"; and (5) "Unjust Enrichment". In its claim for relief, the government asks for triple the alleged actual damages of $245,392 and civil penalties of $10,000 for each of the 8,002 allegedly false reimbursement claims pursuant to 31 U.S.C. § 3729.

The government alleges two types of misconduct related to the submission of bills to Medicare and Medicaid. The first category of misconduct relates to the use of billing codes found in the American Medical Association's "Current Procedural Terminology" ("CPT"), a manual that lists terms and codes for reporting procedures performed by physicians. The government alleges that Dr. Krizek "up-coded" the bills for a large percentage of his patients by submitting bills coded for a service with a higher level of reimbursement than that which Dr. Krizek provided. As a second type of misconduct, the government alleges Dr. Krizek "performed services that should not have been performed at all in that they were not medically necessary." [ ]

Given the large number of claims, and the acknowledged difficulty of determining the "medical necessity" of 8,002 reimbursement claims, it was decided that this case should initially be tried on the basis of seven patients and two hundred claims that the government believed to be representative of Dr. Krizek's improper coding and treatment practices. [ ] It was agreed by the parties that a determination of liability on Dr. Krizek's coding practices would be equally applicable to all 8,002 claims in the complaint. A three week bench trial ensued.

Findings of Fact

Dr. Krizek is a psychiatrist. Dr. Krizek's wife, Blanka Krizek was responsible for overseeing Dr. Krizek's billing operation for a part of the period in question. Dr. Krizek's Washington, D.C. psychiatric practice consists in large part in the treatment of Medicare and Medicaid patients. Much of Doctor Krizek's work involves the provision of psychotherapy and other psychiatric care to patients at the Washington Hospital Center.

Under the Medicare and Medicaid systems, claims for reimbursement are submitted on documents known as Health Care Financing Administration ("HCFA") 1500 Forms. These forms are supposed to contain the patient's identifying information, the provider's Medicaid or Medicare identification number, and a description of the provided procedures for which reimbursement is sought. These procedures are identified by a standard, uniform code number as set out in the American Medical Association's "Current Procedural Terminology" ("CPT") manual, a book that lists the terms and codes for reporting procedures performed by physicians.

* * *

The government in its complaint alleges both improper billing for services provided and the provision of medically unnecessary services. The latter of these two claims will be addressed first.

Medical Necessity

The record discloses that Dr. Krizek is a capable and competent physician. * * * The trial testimony of Dr. Krizek, his colleagues at the Washington Hospital Center, as well as the testimony of a former patient, established that Dr. Krizek was providing valuable medical and psychiatric care during the period covered by the complaint. The testimony was undisputed that Dr. Krizek worked long hours on behalf of his patients, most of whom were elderly and poor.

Many of Dr. Krizek's patients were afflicted with horribly severe psychiatric disorders and often suffered simultaneously from other serious medical conditions.* * *

The government takes issue with Dr. Krizek's method of treatment of his patients, arguing that some patients should have been discharged from the hospital sooner, and that others suffered from conditions which could not be ameliorated through psychotherapy sessions, or that the length of the psychotherapy sessions should have been abbreviated. The government's expert witness's opinions on this subject came from a cold review of Dr. Krizek's notes for each patient. The government witness did not examine or interview any of the patients, or speak with any other doctors or nurses who had actually served these patients to learn whether the course of treatment prescribed by Dr. Krizek exceeded that which was medically necessary.

Dr. Krizek testified credibly and persuasively as to the basis for the course of treatment for each of the representative patients. The medical necessity of treating Dr. Krizek's patients through psychotherapy and hospitalization was confirmed via the testimony of other defense witnesses. The Court credits Dr. Krizek's testimony on this question as well as his interpretation of his own notes regarding the seriousness of each patients' condition and the medical necessity for the procedures and length of hospital stay required. The Court finds that the government was unable to prove that Dr. Krizek rendered services that were medically unnecessary.

Improper Billing

On the question of improper billing or "up-coding," the government contends that for approximately 24 percent of the bills submitted, Dr. Krizek used the CPT Code for a 45–50 minute psychotherapy session (CPT Code 90844) when he should have billed for a 20–30 minute session (CPT Code 90843). The government also contends that for at least 33 percent of his patients, Dr. Krizek billed for a full 45–50 minute psychotherapy session, again by using CPT code 90844, when he should have billed for a "minimal psychotherapy" session (CPT 90862). These two latter procedures are reimbursed at a lower level than 90844, the 45–50 minute psychotherapy session, which the government has referred to as "the Cadillac" of psychiatric reimbursement codes.

The primary thrust of the government's case revolves around the question whether Dr. Krizek's use of the 90844 CPT code was appropriate. For the most part, the government does not allege that Dr. Krizek did not see the patients for whom he submitted bills. Instead, the government posits that the services provided during his visits either did not fall within the accepted definition of "individual medical psychotherapy" *or*, if the services provided *did* fit within this definition, the reimbursable service provided was not as extensive as that which was billed for. In sum, the government claims that whenever Dr. Krizek would see a patient, regardless of whether he simply checked a chart, spoke with nurses, or merely prescribed additional medication, his wife or his employee, a Mrs. Anderson, would, on the vast majority of occasions, submit a bill for CPT code 90844—45–50 minutes of individual psychotherapy.

[Documents sent to providers by Pennsylvania Blue Shield, the Medicare carrier for Dr. Krizek's area, explained the services in the 90800 series of codes as involving "[i]ndividual medical psychotherapy by a physician, with continuing medical diagnostic evaluation, and drug management when indicated, including insight oriented, behavior modifying or supportive psychotherapy" for specified periods of time.]

* * *

The government's witnesses testified that as initially conceived, the definition of the CPT codes is designed to incorporate the extra time spent in its level of reimbursement. It was expected by the authors of the codes that for a 45–50 minute 90844 session a doctor would spend additional time away from the patient reviewing or dictating records, speaking with nurses, or prescribing medication. The government's witnesses testified that the reimbursement rate for 90844 took into account the fact that on a 45–50 minute session the doctor would likely spend twenty additional minutes away from the patient. As such, the doctor is limited to billing for time actually spent "face-to-face" with the patient.

Dr. and Mrs. Krizek freely admit that when a 90844 code bill was submitted on the doctor's behalf, it did not always reflect 45–50 minutes of face-to-face psychotherapy with the patient. Instead, the 45–50 minutes billed captured generally the total amount of time spent on the patient's case, including the "face-to-face" psychotherapy session, discussions with medical staff about the patient's treatment/progress, medication management, and other related services. Dr. Krizek referred to this as "bundling" of services, all of which, Dr. and Mrs. Krizek testified, they reasonably believed were reimbursable under the 90844 "individual medical psychotherapy" code.

Defendant's witnesses testified that it was a common and proper practice among psychiatrists nationally, and in the Washington, D.C. area, to "bundle" a variety of services, including prescription management, review of the patient file, consultations with nurses or the patients' relatives into a bill for individual psychotherapy, whether or not these services took place literally in view of the patient. Under the defense theory, if a doctor spent 20 minutes in a session with a patient and ten minutes before that in a different room discussing the patient's symptoms with a nurse, and fifteen minutes afterwards outlining a course of treatment to the medical staff, it would be entirely appropriate, under their reading and interpretation of the CPT, to bill the 45 minutes spent on that patients' care by using CPT code 90844.

The testimony of the defense witnesses on this point was credible and persuasive. * * * The CPT codes which the government insists require face-to-face rendition of services never used the term "face-to-face" in its code description during the time period covered by this litigation. The relevant language describing the code is ambiguous.

The Court finds that the government's position on this issue is not rational and has been applied in an unfair manner to the medical community, which for the most part is made up of honorable and dedicated professionals. One government witness testified that a 15 minute telephone call made to a consulting physician in the patient's presence would be reimbursable, while if the doctor needed to go outside the patient's room to use the telephone—in order to make the *same* telephone call—the time would not be reimbursable. * * *

The Court will not impose False Claims Act liability based on such a strained interpretation of the CPT codes. The government's theory of liability is plainly unfair and unjustified. Medical doctors should be appropriately reimbursed for services legitimately provided. They should be given clear guidance as to what services are reimbursable. The system should be fair. The system cannot be so arbitrary, so perverse, as to subject a doctor whose annual income during the relevant period averaged between $100,000 and $120,000, to potential liability in excess of 80 million dollars[3] because telephone calls were made in one room rather than another.

The Court finds that Doctor Krizek did not submit false claims when he submitted a bill under CPT Code 90844 after spending 45–50 minutes working on a patient's case, even though not all of that time was spent in direct face-to-face contact with the patient. * * * The Court finds that the defendants' "bundled" services interpretation of the CPT code 90844 is not inconsistent with the plain, common-sense reading of the "description of services" listed by Pennsylvania Blue Shield in its published Procedure Terminology Manual.

---

[3]   The government alleges in the complaint that overbills amounted to $245,392 during the six-year period covered by the lawsuit. Trebling this damage amount, and adding the $10,000 statutory maximum penalty requested by the government for each of the 8,002 alleged false claims, results in a total potential liability under the complaint of more than $80,750,000. Dr. Krizek is not public enemy number one. He is at worst, a psychiatrist with a small practice who keeps poor records. For the government to sue for more than eighty million dollars in damages against an elderly doctor and his wife is unseemly and not justified. During this period, a psychiatrist in most instances would be reimbursed between $48 and $60 for a 45–50 minute session and $40 or less for a 20–30 minute session. This is hardly enough for any professional to get rich.

Billing Irregularities

While Dr. Krizek was a dedicated and competent doctor and cannot be faulted for his interpretation of the 90844 code, his billing practices, or at a minimum his oversight of his wife's and Mrs. Anderson's billing system, was seriously deficient. Dr. Krizek knew little or nothing of the details of how the bills were submitted by his wife and Mrs. Anderson. * * *

The basic method of billing by Mrs. Krizek and Mrs. Anderson was to determine which patients Dr. Krizek had seen, and then to assume what had taken place was a 50–minute psychotherapy session, unless told specifically by Dr. Krizek that the visit was for a shorter duration. Mrs. Krizek frequently made this assumption without any input from her husband. Mrs. Krizek acknowledged at trial that she never made any specific effort to determine exactly how much time was spent with each patient. Mrs. Krizek felt it was fair and appropriate to use the 90844 code as a rough approximation of the time spent, because on some days, an examination would last up to two hours and Mrs. Krizek would still bill 90844.

Mrs. Anderson also would prepare and submit claims to Medicare/Medicaid with no input from Dr. Krizek. Routinely, Mrs. Anderson would simply contact the hospital to determine what patients were admitted to various psychiatrists' services, and would then prepare and submit claims to Medicare/Medicaid without communicating with Dr. or Mrs. Krizek about the claims she was submitting and certifying on Dr. Krizek's behalf. * * *

The net result of this system, or more accurately "nonsystem," of billing was that on a number of occasions, Mrs. Krizek and Mrs. Anderson submitted bills for 45–50 minute psychotherapy sessions on Dr. Krizek's behalf when Dr. Krizek could not have spent the requisite time providing services, face-to-face, or otherwise. * * * The defendants do not deny that these unsubstantiated reimbursement claims occurred or that billing practices which led to such inaccurate billings continued through March of 1992.

While the Court does not find that Dr. Krizek submitted bills for patients he did not see, the Court does find that because of Mrs. Krizek's and Mrs. Anderson's presumption that whenever Dr. Krizek saw a patient he worked at least 45 minutes on the matter, bills were improperly submitted for time that was not spent providing patient services. Again, the defendants admit this occurred. [ ]

At the conclusion of the trial, both parties agreed that an appropriate bench-mark for excessive billing would be the equivalent of twelve 90844 submissions (or nine patient-service hours) in a single service day. [ ] Considering the difficulty of reviewing all Dr. Krizek's patient records over a seven-year period, Dr. Wilson's testimony as to having submitted as many as twelve 90844 submissions in a single day, and giving full credence to unrefuted testimony that Dr. Krizek worked very long hours, the Court believes this to be a fair and reasonably accurate assessment of the time Dr. Krizek actually spent providing patient services. *See Bigelow v. RKO Radio Pictures, Inc.*, 327 U.S. 251, 264, 66 S.Ct. 574, 579, 90 L. Ed. 652 (1946) (permitting factfinder to make "just and reasonable estimate of damage based on relevant data" where more precise computation is not possible). Dr. and Mrs. Krizek will therefore be presumed liable for bills submitted in excess of the equivalent of twelve 90844 submissions in a single day.

Nature of Liability

While the parties have agreed as to the presumptive number of excess submissions for which Dr. and Mrs. Krizek may be found liable, they do not agree on the character of the liability. The government submits that the Krizeks should be held liable under the False Claims Act, 31 U.S.C. § 3729, *et seq.* By contrast, defendants posit that while the United States may be entitled to reimbursement for any unjust enrichment attributable to the excess billings, the Krizeks' conduct with regard to submission of excess bills to Medicare/Medicaid was at most negligent, and not "knowing" within the definition of the statute. In their defense, defendants emphasize the "Ma and Pa" nature of Dr. Krizek's medical practice, the fact that Mrs. Krizek did attend some Medicare billing seminars in an effort to educate herself, and the fact that Mrs. Krizek consulted hospital records and relied on information provided by her husband in preparing bills.

By its terms, the False Claims Act provides, *inter alia*, that: Any person who—

(1) knowingly presents, or causes to be presented, to [the Government] . . . a false or fraudulent claim for payment or approval;

(2) knowingly makes, uses, or causes to be made or used, a false record or statement to get a false or fraudulent claim paid or approved by the Government;

(3) conspires to defraud the Government by getting a false or fraudulent claim allowed or paid;

* * *

is liable to the United States Government for a civil penalty of not less than $5,000.00 and not more than $10,000.00, plus three times the amount of damages which the Government sustains because of the act of that person. * * *

31 U.S.C. § 3729(a). The mental state required to find liability under the False Claims Act is also defined by the statute:

For the purposes of this section, the terms "knowing" and "knowingly" mean that a person, with respect to information—

(1) has actual knowledge of the information;

(2) acts in deliberate ignorance of the truth or falsity of the information; or

(3) acts in reckless disregard of the truth or falsity of the information, and no proof of specific intent is required.

31 U.S.C. § 3729(b). The provision allowing for a finding of liability without proof of specific intent to defraud was a feature of the 1986 amendments to the Act.

*   *   *

The Court finds that, at times, Dr. Krizek was submitting claims for 90844 when he did not provide patient services for the requisite 45 minutes. The testimony makes clear that these submissions were made by Mrs. Krizek or Mrs. Anderson with little, if any, factual basis. Mrs. Krizek made no effort to establish how much time Dr. Krizek spent on a particular matter. Mrs. Krizek and Mrs. Anderson simply presumed that 45–50 minutes had been spent. There was no justification for making that assumption. In addition, Dr. Krizek failed utterly in supervising these agents in their submissions of claims on his behalf. As a result of his failure to supervise, Dr. Krizek received reimbursement for services which he did not provide.

These were not "mistakes" nor merely negligent conduct. Under the statutory definition of "knowing" conduct, the Court is compelled to conclude that the defendants acted with reckless disregard as to the truth or falsity of the submissions. As such, they will be deemed to have violated the False Claims Act.

Conclusion

Dr. Krizek must be held accountable for his billing system along with those who carried it out. Dr. Krizek was not justified in seeing patients and later not verifying the claims submitted for the services provided to these patients. Doctors must be held strictly accountable for requests filed for insurance reimbursement.

The Court believes that the Krizeks' billing practices must be corrected before they are permitted to further participate in the Medicare or Medicaid programs. Therefore an injunction will issue, enjoining the defendants from participating in these systems until such time as they can show the Court that they can abide by the relevant rules.

***

Other Observations

While the Court does not discount the seriousness of the Krizeks' conduct here, this case demonstrates several flaws in this country's government health insurance program. The government was right in bringing this action, because it could not countenance the reckless nature of the reimbursement systems in this case. While we are in an age of computers, this does not mean that we can blindly allow coding systems to determine the amount of reimbursement without the physician being accountable for honestly and correctly submitting proper information, whether by code or otherwise.

Nonetheless, the Court found rather troubling some of the government's procedures that control reimbursements paid to providers of services. Here are some of these practices:

1) The government makes no distinction in reimbursement as to the status or professional attainment or education of the provider. Thus, a non-technical person rendering a coded service will be reimbursed the same amount as a board-certified physician.

2) The sums that the Medicare and Medicaid systems reimburse physicians for services rendered seem to be so far below the norm for charges reimbursed by non-governmental insurance carriers. Indeed, the amount could hardly support a medical practice. As the evidence shows in this case, Board certified physicians in most instances were paid at a rate less than $60 per hour and less than $35 per 1/2 hour. The government must certainly review these charges because if providers are not adequately compensated, they may not provide the level of care that our elderly and underprivileged citizens require. What is more, the best physicians will simply not come into the system or will refuse to take on senior citizens or the poor as patients.

3) The unrealistic billing concept of requiring doctors to bill only for face-to-face time is not consistent with effective use of a doctor's time or with the provision of good medical services. Doctors must be able to study, research, and discuss a patient's case and be reimbursed for such time.

4) When Medicare dictates that a physician must report each service rendered as a separate code item, the physician is entitled to believe that he will be reimbursed for each of the services rendered. In actuality, the system pays for only one of the multitude of services provided. If this were done by a private sector entity, it would be considered deceitful. Because the government engages in such a deceitful practice does not make it right.

These are the lessons learned by this Court during this case. Hopefully, HCFA will reexamine its reimbursement practices to see what, if any, changes should be made.

UNITED STATES V. KRIZEK

United States Court of Appeals, District of Columbia Circuit, 1997.
111 F.3d 934.

SENTELLE, CIRCUIT JUDGE.

This appeal arises from a civil suit brought by the government against a psychiatrist and his wife under the civil False Claims Act ("FCA"), 31 U.S.C. §§ 3729–3731, and under the common law. The District Court found defendants liable for knowingly submitting false claims and entered judgment against defendants for $168,105.39. The government appealed, and the defendants filed a cross-appeal. We hold that the District Court erred and remand for further proceedings.

[The Court held that the district court erred in changing its benchmark for a presumptively false claim from 9 hours billed in any given day to 24 hours because it did not afford the government the opportunity to introduce additional evidence. It also agreed with the Krizeks cross-appeal that the District Court erroneously treated each CPT code as a separate "claim" for purposes of computing civil penalties instead of treating the government form 1500 which contained multiple codes as the "claim."

The court questioned the fairness of the government's definition of claim because it "permitted it to seek an astronomical $81 million worth of damages for alleged actual damages of $245,392."

* * *

[W]e turn now to the question whether, in considering the sample, the District Court applied the appropriate level of scienter. The FCA imposes liability on an individual who "knowingly presents" a "false or fraudulent claim." 31 U.S.C. § 3729(a). A person acts "knowingly" if he:

(1) has actual knowledge of the information;

(2) acts in deliberate ignorance of the truth or falsity of the information; or

(3) acts in reckless disregard of the truth or falsity of the information,

and no proof of specific intent to defraud is required.

31 U.S.C. § 3729(b). The Krizeks assert that the District Court impermissibly applied the FCA by permitting an aggravated form of gross negligence, "gross negligence-plus," to satisfy the Act's scienter requirement.

In Saba v. Compagnie Nationale Air France, 78 F.3d 664 (D.C. Cir. 1996), we considered whether reckless disregard was the equivalent of willful misconduct for purposes of the Warsaw Convention. We noted that reckless disregard lies on a continuum between gross negligence and intentional harm. In some cases, recklessness serves as a proxy for forbidden intent. [ ] Such cases require a showing that the defendant engaged in an act known to cause or likely to cause the injury. [ ] Use of reckless disregard as a substitute for the forbidden intent prevents the defendant from "deliberately blind[ing] himself to the consequences of his tortuous action." Id. at 668. In another category of cases, we noted, reckless disregard is "simply a linear extension of gross negligence, a palpable failure to meet the appropriate standard of care." Id. In *Saba*, we determined that in the context of the Warsaw Convention, a showing of willful misconduct might be made by establishing reckless disregard such that the subjective intent of the defendant could be inferred. [ ]

The question, therefore, is whether "reckless disregard" in this context is properly equated with willful misconduct or with aggravated gross negligence. In determining that gross negligence-plus was sufficient, the District Court cited legislative history equating reckless disregard with gross negligence. A sponsor of the 1986 amendments to the FCA stated,

> Subsection 3 of Section 3729(c) uses the term "reckless disregard of the truth or falsity of the information" which is no different than and has the same meaning as a gross negligence standard that has been applied in other cases. While the Act was not intended to apply to mere negligence, it is intended to apply in situations that could be considered gross negligence where the submitted claims to the Government are prepared in such a sloppy or unsupervised fashion that resulted in overcharges to the Government. The Act is also intended not to permit artful defense counsel to require some form of intent as an essential ingredient of proof. This section is intended to reach the "ostrich-with-his-head-in-the-sand" problem where government contractors hide behind the fact they were not personally aware that such overcharges may have occurred. This is not a new standard but clarifies what has always been the standard of knowledge required.

132 Cong. Rec. H9382–03 (daily ed. Oct. 7, 1986) (statement of Rep. Berman).While we are not inclined to view isolated statements in the legislative history as dispositive, we agree with the thrust of this statement that the best reading of the Act defines reckless disregard as an extension of gross negligence. Section 3729(b)(2) of the Act provides liability for false statements made with deliberate ignorance. If the reckless disregard standard of section 3729(b)(3) served merely as a substitute for willful misconduct—to prevent the defendant from "deliberately blind[ing] himself to the consequences of his tortuous action"—section (b)(3) would be redundant since section (b)(2) already covers such struthious conduct. [ ] Moreover, as the statute explicitly states that specific intent is not required, it is logical to conclude that reckless disregard in this context is

not a "lesser form of intent," [ ] but an extreme version of ordinary negligence.

**

We are also unpersuaded by the Krizeks' argument that their conduct did not rise to the level of reckless disregard. The District Court cited a number of factors supporting its conclusion: Mrs. Krizek completed the submissions with little or no factual basis; she made no effort to establish how much time Dr. Krizek spent with any particular patient; and Dr. Krizek "failed utterly" to review bills submitted on his behalf. [ ] Most tellingly, there were a number of days within the seven-patient sample when even the shoddiest record keeping would have revealed that false submissions were being made—those days on which the Krizeks' billing approached twenty-four hours in a single day. On August 31, 1985, for instance, the Krizeks requested reimbursement for patient treatment using the 90844 code thirty times and the 90843 code once, indicating patient treatment of over 22 hours. Outside the seven-patient sample the Krizeks billed for more than twenty-four hours in a single day on three separate occasions. [ ] These factors amply support the District Court's determination that the Krizeks acted with reckless disregard.

Finally, we note that Dr. Krizek is no less liable than his wife for these false submissions. As noted, an FCA violation may be established without reference to the subjective intent of the defendant. Dr. Krizek delegated to his wife authority to submit claims on his behalf. In failing "utterly" to review the false submissions, he acted with reckless disregard.

*   *   *

NOTES AND QUESTIONS

1.   Exactly what conduct by Dr. Krizek did the government charge violated the False Claims Act? For what conduct and on what basis was he exonerated by the district court? Did the court's liability finding rest on the actions of Dr. Krizek or those of his subordinates?

2.   The United States introduced expert evidence that the CPT codes 90843 and 90844 (individual psychotherapy) envisioned face-to-face therapy with the patient for the entire time for which the service was billed (either 25 or 50 minutes). The Krizeks admitted they received reimbursement for time spent other than in face-to-face therapy, and introduced evidence from other physicians that "bundling" was common practice in obtaining reimbursement for private payors. What was the legal basis for absolving Dr. Krizek of liability for "upcoding"? For an account of the colorful back story of this case, see Thomas L. Greaney & Joan H. Krause, U.S. v. Krizek: Rough Justice Under the False Claims Act in Cases In Context: Healthlaw and Bioethics (2009).

3.   *Materiality.* A number of cases have held that plaintiffs should be required to establish materiality, i.e., prove that a false statement contained in a Medicare cost report would have affected the likelihood of payment. See Luckey v. Baxter Healthcare Corporation, 183 F.3d 730 (7th Cir. 1999) (failure to perform tests on blood plasma does not give rise to false certification claims in the absence of evidence that the tests were material to the government's decision to purchase plasma). However, the Fraud Enforcement and Recovery Act of 2009 (FERA) resolved an important question regarding the specific application of the materiality requirement. It adopted the approach of most courts by requiring that under the FCA a false record or statement must be "material to a false or fraudulent claim," with "materiality" defined as "having a natural tendency to influence, or be capable of influencing, the payment or receipt of money or property."

The Affordable Care Act also expanded the reach of the FCA in several respects. Section 1313 provides that "payments made by, through, or in connection with an Exchange are subject to the False Claims Act if those payments include any Federal funds." The law also stipulates that compliance with the ACA's requirements concerning health insurance issuers' eligibility to participate in the Exchange "shall be a material condition of an issuer's entitlement to receive payments, including payments of premium tax credits and cost-sharing reductions through the Exchange." In addition, as discussed *infra*, the ACA codifies the holding of several courts finding that anti-kickback violations are material for purposes of the FCA.

4.   *False Certification.* Courts frequently find falsity based on express or implied certifications of compliance with federal regulations made by providers in submitting claims to the government. An especially thorny issue has been whether the act of submitting a claim implies certification of compliance with the many applicable regulations that one finds in the Code of Federal Regulations. See e.g., U.S. ex rel. Mikes v. Straus, 274 F.3d 687 (2d Cir. 2001)(no implied certification where regulation was not a condition of payment).

5.   Especially controversial has been the use of the implied certification theory to support False Claims Act challenges to quality deficiencies in rendering care. The spectrum of fact situations includes those in which providers provide no care or "worthless services," see United States ex rel. Lee v. SmithKline Beecham, Inc., 245 F.3d 1048 (9th Cir. 2001), and United States v. NHC Healthcare Corp., 115 F. Supp. 2d 1149, 1153 (W.D. Mo. 2000) (government claim allowed to proceed where defendants' nursing home "was so severely understaffed that it could not possibly have administered all of the care it was obligated to perform" under government program standards and could amount to claims for services not actually performed), as well as scenarios in which severe quality deficiencies lead to the conclusion that the care provided does not amount to the kind of care for which the government was billed. See United States ex rel. Aranda v. Community Psychiatric Ctrs., 945 F.Supp. 1485, 1487 (W.D. Okla. 1996) (denying motion to dismiss False Claims Act case involving a psychiatric hospital that allegedly failed to com-

ply with Medicaid regulations requiring that facilities afford patients a "reasonably safe environment"); cf. United States ex rel. Bailey v. Ector County Hosp., 386 F.Supp.2d 759, 766 (W.D. Tex. 2004) (FCA "should not be used to call into question a health care provider's judgment regarding a specific course of treatment").What problems do you anticipate might be associated with extending the False Claims Act to reach quality of care concerns? Do such cases offer benefits that regulation and malpractice law cannot achieve? See Joan Krause, Medical Error As False Claim, 27 Am. J.L. & Med. 181 (2001) (quoting federal prosecutor explaining "what I want to show [in quality of care cases] is the entire idea that the [defendant] is providing care to these people is a fraud . . . ").

6. *Reverse False Claims.* Reverse false claims actions bring the knowing retention of funds erroneously paid by the government within the scope of the FCA. In an important change from prior law, FERA amended the statute to make it unlawful to "knowingly conceal [ ] or knowingly and improperly avoid [ ] or decrease [ ] an obligation to pay." By making illegality turn on concealing or avoiding an obligation to pay (rather than requiring the submission of a false record or statement), Congress extended the reach of the FCA to cover the situation in which a provider receives an overpayment and elects to hold on to those funds rather than promptly repay them. However, in defining "obligation" broadly to include an "established duty, whether or not fixed," Congress added an additional measure of uncertainty as to when the "obligation" attaches. The ACA subsequently gave some guidance by specifying that unless overpayments are returned no later than 60 days after the date on which it is "identified" (a term not defined by the statute or regulation) or the date any corresponding cost report is due, whichever is later, the False Claims Act will apply. ACA § 1128J(d)(2).

B. QUI TAM ACTIONS

31 U.S.C. § 3730. Civil actions for false claims

*   *   *

(b) Actions by private persons.—(1) A person may bring a civil action for a violation of [the False Claims Act] for the person and for the United States Government. The action shall be brought in the name of the Government. The action may be dismissed only if the court and the Attorney General give written consent to the dismissal and their reasons for consenting.

(2) A copy of the complaint and written disclosure of substantially all material evidence and information the person possesses shall be served on the Government * * * The complaint shall be filed in camera, shall remain under seal for at least 60 days, and shall not be served on the defendant until the court so orders. The Government may elect to intervene and proceed with the action within 60 days after it receives both the complaint and the material evidence and information.

*   *   *

(4) Before the expiration of the 60–day period or any extensions obtained under paragraph (3), the Government shall—

(A) proceed with the action, in which case the action shall be conducted by the Government; or

(B) notify the court that it declines to take over the action, in which case the person bringing the action shall have the right to conduct the action.

*   *   *

(c) Rights of the parties to qui tam actions.—(1) If the Government proceeds with the action, it shall have the primary responsibility for prosecuting the action, and shall not be bound by an act of the person bringing the action. Such person shall have the right to continue as a party to the action, subject to the limitations set forth in paragraph (2).

*   *   *

(d) Award to qui tam plaintiff.—(1) If the Government proceeds with an action brought by a person under subsection (b), such person [shall receive between 15 and 25 percent of the proceeds of the action or settlement of the claim, depending on the extent to which the person contributed to the prosecution, plus attorneys' fees and costs. If the government does not proceed the person may receive between 25 and 30 percent plus attorneys' fees and costs. If the action was brought by a person who planned and initiated the violation of the statutes, the court may reduce the person's share of proceeds and if the person is convicted of a crime for his or her role that person may not share any proceeds.]

(e) Certain actions barred.

*   *   *

(3) In no event may a person bring an action under subsection (b) which is based upon allegations or transactions which are the subject of a civil suit or an administrative civil money penalty proceeding in which the Government is already a party.

(4)(A) The court shall dismiss an action or claim under this section, unless opposed by the Government, if substantially the same allegations or transactions as alleged in the action or claim were publicly disclosed— (i) in a Federal criminal, civil, or administrative hearing in which the Government or its agent is a party; (ii) in a congressional, Government Accountability Office, or other Federal report, hearing, audit, or investigation; or (iii) from the news media, unless the action is brought by the Attorney General or the person bringing the action is an original source of the information.

(B) For purposes of this paragraph, "original source" means an individual who either (i) prior to a public disclosure under subsection (e)(4)(a), has voluntarily disclosed to the Government the information on which allegations or transactions in a claim are based, or (2) who has knowledge that is independent of and materially adds to the publicly disclosed allegations or transactions, and who has voluntarily provided the information to the Government before filing an action under this section.

*   *   *

(h) Relief from retaliatory actions.—(1) In general.—Any employee, contractor, or agent shall be entitled to all relief necessary to make that employee, contractor, or agent whole, if that employee, contractor, or agent is discharged, demoted, suspended, threatened, harassed, or in any other manner discriminated against in the terms and conditions of employment because of lawful acts done by the employee, contractor, or agent on behalf of the employee, contractor, or agent or associated others in furtherance of other efforts to stop 1 or more violations of this subchapter. (2) Relief—Relief under paragraph (1) shall include reinstatement with the same seniority status that employee, contractor, or agent would have had but for the discrimination, 2 times the amount of back pay, interest on the back pay, and compensation for any special damages sustained as a result of the discrimination, including litigation costs and reasonable attorneys' fees. An action under this subsection may be brought in the appropriate district court of the United States for the relief provided in this subsection.

NOTES AND QUESTIONS

1. What advice would you have given to Mrs. Anderson, the assistant who helped prepare the claims submitted by Mrs. and Dr. Krizek in United States v. Krizek, *supra*, if she had approached you for legal advice before any investigation of her employer had begun? How would you have handled discussions with the U.S. Attorney's Office concerning her involvement in the matter? Could she continue to perform her job responsibilities for Dr. Krizek if she became a whistleblower or would it be necessary for her to quit? Before advising her, you may want to consult Luckey v. Baxter Healthcare Corp., 183 F.3d 730 (7th Cir. 1999) in which Judge Easterbrook rejected the relator's claim for whistleblower protection under § 3730(h). Baxter had fired Ms. Luckey before her qui tam suit was unsealed and the court concluded that Baxter was not aware of the pending action. The court rejected the claim that, because the employer knew of her strongly-held feelings about its testing practices, it should have been on notice of the possibility of her "assistance in" a suit. Likewise, despite Luckey's statements to co-workers that she planned to "shut down" the lab and "get rid" of her supervisors, the court concluded that Baxter was not prohibited from firing her: "Sabre-rattling is not protected conduct. Only investigation, testimony, and litigation are protected,

and none of these led to Luckey's firing." 183 F.3d at 733. Also, in giving your advice, take into account the specific requirements to obtain whistleblower protection under subsection (h) of the qui tam statute.

2.   A significant obstacle for qui tam relators is the statute's bar on actions in which there has been "public disclosure" of the allegations or transactions, which includes government hearings, investigations, or media reports. However, the law provides an exception (see § e(4)(B) *supra*) where the relator is an "original source" of the information, defined (after amendment by the ACA) as "knowledge that is independent of and materially adds to the publicly disclosed allegations or transactions." On the issue of whether a relator's information is "based upon" a public disclosure, courts have generally held the answer turns on whether the disclosure and the allegations are "substantially similar." However, recent case law holds that public disclosures that are highly general will not bar qui tam lawsuits raising particularized allegations containing genuinely new information. Reversing the dismissal of a qui tam claim brought by medical residents, the Seventh Circuit found their allegations were not "substantially similar" to disclosures made in PATH audits and a GAO report on a teaching hospital's alleged improper billing for unsupervised services rendered by residents. Goldberg and Beecham v. Rush University Medical Center, F. 3d. (7th Cir. 2012).

3.   Qui tam actions have become the principle means by which the government uncovers fraud as over 80 percent of all government false claims actions are initiated by whistleblowers. Although the Department of Justice intervenes in only 24 percent of qui tam actions and the large majority of those in which it does not intervene are unsuccessful, most of the largest health care fraud cases in recent years have been the result of qui tam actions. Over 60 percent of all qui tam actions and 80 percent of all settlements involved the health care industry, with the pharmaceutical industry drawing particular attention. For the view that "privatization" of public law enforcement through the qui tam statute creates incentives to over-enforce the False Claims Act, see Dana Bowen Matthew, The Moral Hazard Problem with Privatization of Public Enforcement: The Case of Pharmaceutical Fraud, 40 Mich. J.L. Ref. 281 (2007).

4.   What is the justification for qui tam actions? Do they advance legitimate law enforcement objectives? Might they create undesirable incentives that poison the employer-employee relationship?.

C. NEW ENFORCEMENT METHODS

RACs. An important—and controversial—enforcement innovation is the expanding role of Recovery Audit Contractors (RACs). RACs are private entities that contract with the federal government to audit payments made to providers and suppliers by the Medicare and Medicaid programs. RACs are paid for their auditing services on a contingency fee basis, receiving payments based on the amount of improper payments to providers they identify. Their mission is to identify both underpayments and overpayments and coordinate their efforts with other entities providing auditing services such as state and federal law enforcement officials. Providers have not been enthusiastic about this innovation, claiming the new levels of audits are burdensome and in some cases have proved to be arbitrary. On November 1, 2012, the American Hospital Association (AHA) and four hospitals, filed suit seeking to invalidate a RACs practice they called the CMS "Payment Denial Policy." The complaint challenges certain practices of Recovery Audit Contractors undertaken when they review Part A inpatient claims and decide that the inpatient should have been treated as an outpatient. When these claims are denied solely for site-of-service reasons, rather than due any purported lack of medical necessity, the CMS policy prohibits payment for more than a few, limited ancillary Part B services. The complaint also alleges that the CMS manual provisions that are relied upon by CMS are invalid for a failure to comport with notice and comment rulemaking requirements. American Hospital Ass'n v. Kathleen Sebelius (complaint filed Nov. 1, 2012, D.D.C.) Case No. 1:12–cv–1770.

Corporate Integrity Agreements. The government has increased its use of Corporate Integrity Agreements (CIAs) as part of settlements of healthcare fraud investigations where it is concerned about recurring compliance issues. These agreements impose continuing oversight and investigative and reporting obligations on providers, typically lasting at least five years and in some cases as long as ten years. David E. Matyas et al. Legal Issues in Healthcare Fraud and Abuse: Navigating the Uncertainties 431 (2012). CIAs with the Office of Inspector General (OIG) are usually accompanied by settlement agreements with the Department of Justice regarding civil and criminal actions within the scope of its enforcement responsibilities. Providers or other entities consent to these the obligations in exchange for the OIG's agreement not to exclude them from participation in Medicare, Medicaid, or other federal health care programs. The OIG states that CIAs address the specific facts at issue and "attempt to accommodate many of the elements of preexisting voluntary compliance programs" but typically include requirements to hire a compliance officer, implement employee training programs, adopt written standards and provide annual reports to OIG.

Critics question whether expansive CIAs go too far by intruding into matters of corporate governance, imposing excessive costs, and burdening boards with responsibilities they are not equipped to handle. CIAs are also controversial in situations in which the government seeks to encourage "best practices" in an industry by specifying that parties agree to conform to certain internal governance or monitoring requirements. Given that corporate counsel often advise clients to follow norms set out in CIAs adopted by other firms in their industry as a means of mitigating legal risks, CIAs may have widespread influence over corporate practices.

What response to these criticisms might you expect from the government? See Melissa Maleske, GSK Agrees to Unprecedented Settlement, Corporate Integrity Agreement, Inside Counsel (Sept. 2012); Kathleen Boozang & Simone Handler–Hutchinson, Monitoring Corporate Governance: DOJ's Use of Deferred Prosecution Agreements in Health Care, 35 Am. J. L. Med. 89 (2009).

Moving Away from "Pay and Chase." Because after-the-fact law enforcement ("pay and chase") has been unsuccessful in deterring fraud, the drafters of the Affordable Care Act adopted a number of measures designed to improve prevention. Recognizing that Medicare has had essentially an "open door" policy for providers which has enabled unscrupulous persons to freely enter and exploit the payment system, the ACA establishes controls designed to improve screening of providers. For example, HHS and OIG will conduct close screenings of certain providers depending on risk of fraud and other factors. These reviews include a criminal background check, fingerprinting, unscheduled and unannounced site visits, database checks, reviews of licensure status, and other screening as HHS deems appropriate. In addition, HHS may increase oversight of new providers and suppliers, installing prepayment reviews or placing caps on payments, for a period of up to one year as a condition of enrollment. It may also impose a temporary moratorium on enrollment of new providers or classes of providers if it concludes such action is necessary to combat fraud, waste, or abuse.

Transparency (The Sunshine Act). The ACA imposes significant new reporting requirements governing payments from device manufactures and pharmaceutical companies to physicians. Patient Protection and Affordable Care Act, Pub. L. 111–148, § 6002 (codified at 42 USCA § 1320a–7h (2010)). The Act requires drug, device, biological, and medical supply manufacturers to make detailed annual reports on payments or other transfers of value made to physicians and teaching hospitals. Certain manufacturers and group purchasing organizations must also disclose information concerning ownership or investment interests held by physicians, including the amount invested, the value, and terms of the ownership or investment interest. The Act provides exceptions for *de minimis* amounts (anything valued at less than $10 is exempted unless the total paid to a physician in one year exceeds $100), educational materials, in-kind items for charity use, product samples for patient use, and certain other items. The information reported will be publicly available on a searchable internet website.

II.   MEDICARE AND MEDICAID FRAUD AND ABUSE

A.   THE STATUTE: 42 U.S.C. § 1320A–7B

* * *

(b) Illegal remunerations

(1) Whoever knowingly and willfully solicits or receives any remuneration (including any kickback, bribe, or rebate) directly or indirectly, overtly or covertly, in cash or in kind—

(A) in return for referring an individual to a person for the furnishing or arranging for the furnishing of any item or service for which payment may be made in whole or in part under a Federal health care program, or

(B) in return for purchasing, leasing, ordering, or arranging for or recommending purchasing, leasing, or ordering any good, facility, service, or item for which payment may be made in whole or in part under a Federal health care program,

shall be guilty of a felony and upon conviction thereof, shall be fined not more than $25,000 or imprisoned for not more than five years, or both.

(2) Whoever knowingly and willfully offers or pays any remuneration (including any kickback, bribe or rebate) directly or indirectly, overtly or covertly, in cash or in kind to any person to induce such person—

(A) to refer an individual to a person for the furnishing or arranging for the furnishing of any item or service for which payment may be made in whole or in part under a Federal health care program, or

(B) to purchase, lease, order, or arrange for or recommend purchasing, leasing, or ordering any good, facility, service, or item for which payment may be made in whole or in part under a Federal health care program,

shall be guilty of a felony and upon conviction thereof shall be fined not more than $25,000 or imprisoned for not more than five years, or both.

* * *

[Subsection (c) prohibits knowing and willful false statements or representations of material facts with respect to the conditions or operation of any entity in order to qualify such an entity for Medicare or Medicaid certification. Subsection (d) prohibits knowingly and willfully charging patients for Medicaid services where such charges are not otherwise permitted.]

(f) "Federal health care program" defined

For purposes of this section, the term "Federal health care program" means—

(1) any plan or program that provides health benefits, whether directly, through insurance, or otherwise, which is funded directly, in whole or in part, by the United States Government [other than the federal employees health benefit program]; or

(2) any State health care program, as defined in section 1320a–7(h) of this title.

* * *

(h)With respect to violations of this section, a person need not have actual knowledge of this section or specific intent to commit a violation of this section.

B. PROBLEMS: ADVISING UNDER THE FRAUD AND ABUSE LAWS

Do any of the following transactions appear to violate the "anti-kickback" statute (AKS), as the foregoing law is sometimes called? Is there anything else wrong with them from a legal, ethical, or public policy perspective? As described in the *Greber* case *infra*, intent is a key element of the offense; consider whether intent can be inferred from the facts of each transaction. Note also that AKS "Safe Harbors," discussed *infra*, may protect some of these situations from legal challenge.

1. Starkville Community Hospital is located in a rural area in a distant corner of a large mid-western state. Recently, Dr. McPherson, the hospital's only obstetrician, announced his retirement. Few new physicians have settled in Starkville in recent years, and the community and hospital are very concerned about the loss of obstetric services. The hospital has decided, therefore, to implement a plan to attract a new obstetrician. It is offering to provide any board-certified obstetrician who will settle in Starkville and obtain privileges at Starkville Memorial the following for the first two years the physician is on staff at the hospital: (1) a guaranteed annual income of $110,000, (2) free malpractice insurance through the hospital's self-insurance plan, and (3) free rent in the hospital's medical practice building. The new obstetrician would not be required to refer patients to Starkville Community, though the closest alternative hospital is 60 miles away. The obstetrician would also be expected to assume some administrative duties in exchange for the compensation package Starkville is offering. Starkville Community is currently engaged in negotiations with a young doctor who has just finished her residency and appears likely to accept this offer. There is a potential problem, however. Dr. Waxman, who came to Starkville two years ago and is

the hospital's only cardiologist, has threatened that he will leave unless he gets the same terms.

2.   Dr. Ness, a successful ophthalmologist, advertises in the weekly suburban shopping newspaper, offering free cataract examinations for senior citizens. He in fact does not charge those who respond to the offer for the Medicare deductible or co-insurance amounts, but bills Medicare for the maximum charge allowable for the service.

3.   Managed care organizations are insisting that Samaritan Hospital offer wider geographic coverage in order to bid on contracts. A market study reveals that Samaritan is receiving few admissions from Arlington, a rapidly growing affluent suburb eight miles to the northwest. To remedy this problem, Samaritan has formed an MSO and has entered into negotiations to purchase the Arlington Family Practice Center, a successful group practice containing five board-certified family practitioners. The MSO has offered a generous price for the practice, which would be renamed Samaritan–Arlington Family Practice Center and its doctors would become salaried employees of the MSO entity. They would thereafter be required to admit patients only at Samaritan and to refer only to specialists who have privileges at Samaritan. The five doctors, who are weary of the administrative hassles of private practice, are eager to sell.

4.   MegaPharma, a leading pharmaceutical manufacturer, plans to roll out several new drugs next year. Once it receives approval from the FDA, it plans to market these drugs aggressively to physicians. Mega-Pharma's marketing director intends to have her "detailers"— representatives who visit doctors' offices to market pharmaceutical products and explain their benefits—upgrade the quality of lunches they supply to the doctors and staff when they visit, offer large amounts of free samples, and give each doctor a souvenir iPod inscribed with the Mega-Pharma logo and the names of the new drugs. In addition, MegaPharma will offer a $5000 honorarium and free travel to 50 physician "opinion leaders" from around the country to attend an annual educational seminar it sponsors. MegaPharma also hopes that many physicians will prescribe pezophine, one of its new drugs, for a use not approved by the FDA. (Such "off-label" prescribing is not in itself illegal, but FDA law forbids the manufacturer from marketing or advertising for that purpose). Mega-Pharma plans to offer honoraria to academics who have produced research about the off-label uses of pezophine and who themselves prescribe pezophine for off-label uses; it will offer honoraria for any talk or paper published regardless of whether other sources are also funding the academics' work.

5.   Twenty-three small rural hospitals in a mid-western state have entered into a contract with a group-purchasing agent to purchase medical equipment and supplies for them. The agent will take advantage of

volume discounts and of careful market research to significantly lower the cost of supplies and equipment purchased for the hospitals. The agent obtains, on average, a 5 percent rebate from suppliers for all goods it purchases.

6.   Intermodal Health System, an integrated delivery system, has suffered losses averaging $100,000 per year per doctor on the physician practices it acquired several years ago. It has developed a plan to terminate the contracts of half of the physicians it now employs. Pursuant to their employment contract, each physician will receive a severance fee of $50,000 even though some of the physicians are nearing the end of their employment contracts. Intermodal will also waive covenants not to compete contained in contracts with terminated physicians. In addition, Intermodal plans to offer to its "most valued" terminated physicians lease agreements to continue to occupy the medical office space owned by an Intermodal subsidiary.

C. PENALTIES FOR FRAUD AND ABUSE

As we have seen, false billing, illegal remuneration (bribes and kickbacks), misrepresentation of compliance with conditions of participation, and a variety of other abuses involving federal health care plans are federal crimes and in most instances felonies. Of equal concern to providers, however, are the civil penalty and exclusion powers of the Office of Inspector General (OIG) of the Department of Health and Human Services (HHS). For providers dependent on Medicare and Medicaid for a large share of their business, exclusion from these programs can be effectively a death warrant, at least as serious as a felony conviction. Civil sanction proceedings are administrative in nature, criminal intent need not be shown, and the standard of proof is a preponderance of the evidence rather than beyond a reasonable doubt.

The list of behaviors for which HHS can assess civil money penalties is long and grows with every annual budget reconciliation act. For example, civil penalties of up to $10,000 per item or service plus three times the amount claimed can be assessed for an item or service that a person "knows or should know" was "not provided as claimed." 42 U.S.C. § 1320a–7a(a). The array of additional sanctions includes: civil money penalties against any person who provides false or misleading information that could reasonably be expected to influence the decision of when to discharge a Medicare beneficiary from a hospital, 42 U.S.C. § 1320a–7a(a)(3); penalties against Medicare or Medicaid HMOs that fail substantially to provide medically necessary services with a substantial likelihood of adversely affecting beneficiaries, or that impose premiums in excess of permitted amounts, 42 U.S.C. § 1395mm(i)(6)(A)(i)–(iii); penalties against hospitals that make direct or indirect payments to physicians as incentives for reducing or limiting services provided to beneficiaries or against physicians who accept such payments, 42 U.S.C. § 1320a–7a(b); and penalties of up to $2000 per violation may be imposed on doctors who fail to provide diagnosis codes on non-assigned Medicare claims, 42 U.S.C. § 1395u(p)(3). Finally, the government may seek an injunction to enjoin any person from "concealing, removing, encumbering, or disposing" of its assets when seeking a civil monetary penalty. 42 U.S.C. § 1320a–7a(k).

As noted earlier, exclusion from participation in Federal health care programs is a potent and widely used weapon in the arsenal of those fight fraud. The law mandates exclusion for at least five years in four circumstances: conviction of a criminal offense related to the delivery of Medicare or state health care program services; conviction of a crime relating to neglect or abuse of patients; any federal or state felony conviction with respect to any act or omission in any health care program financed by any Federal, state or local government agency or involving fraud, theft, embezzlement, breach of fiduciary responsibility or other financial misconduct; and felony conviction for unlawful manufacture, distribution, prescription or dispensing of controlled substances. 42 U.S.C. § 1320a–7(a). See also Travers v. Sullivan, 791 F.Supp. 1471 (E.D. Wash. 1992) (no contest plea constitutes conviction of program-related crime and requires mandatory exclusion).

The OIG also has discretion to exclude providers for numerous other categories of offenses, including loss of professional license, submission of bills substantially in excess of usual charges or costs, substantial failure of an HMO to provide medically necessary services, substantial failure of a hospital to comply with a corrective plan for unnecessary admissions or other inappropriate practices to circumvent PPS, or default by health professionals on student loans. 42 U.S.C. § 1320a–7(b). An important amendment to the law allows for permissive exclusions of (1) persons who have direct or indirect ownership or control interests in a sanctioned entity and who know or should know of the violation; and (2) officers or managing employees, even if the individual did not participate in the wrongdoing. 42 U.S.C. § 1320a–7(b)(8). The law also fixes minimum periods of exclusion ranging from 1 to 3 years depending on the basis for exclusion. 42 U.S.C. § 1320a–7(b)(c)(3). However, in determining the length of permissive exclusions, the agency may consider other factors such as the availability of alternative sources of health care in the community. Exclusion or criminal conviction frequently results in disciplinary action by state professional licensure boards, and can thus end the professional career of even a professional who sees few Medicaid and Medicare patients.

D. PROHIBITIONS OF KICKBACKS AND OTHER REFERRALS UNDER THE FRAUD AND ABUSE LAWS

Sharing the profits of collective economic activity is common throughout the economy. Landlords rent commercial properties under percentage leases, agents sell goods and services produced by others on commission, merchants grant discounts to those who use their services or encourage others to do so. Such activity has, however, long been frowned upon as it relates to health care. It is widely believed that patients lack the knowledge and information (or even the legal right, in the case of prescription drugs) to make health care decisions for themselves. Therefore, providers have a fiduciary obligation to recommend goods and services for patients considering only the patient's medical needs and not the provider's own economic interest. With the advent of government financing of health care, this concern has been supplemented by another: that financial rewards to providers for patient referrals might drive up program costs by encouraging the provision of unnecessary or inordinately expensive medical care.

For these reasons, the fraud and abuse statutes reproduced above prohibit paying or receiving any remuneration (directly or indirectly, overtly or covertly) for referring, purchasing, or ordering goods, facilities, items or services paid for by Medicare or Medicaid. Thus the statutory provision set forth at the beginning of this section is often referred to as the "anti-kickback statute" (AKS). Interpreted broadly, however, these provisions seem to proscribe a wide variety of transactions that might encourage competition or efficient production of health care. Indeed, many of the arrangements undertaken in connection with forming or operating PHOs, ACOs, or integrated delivery systems discussed in Chapter 12 might, under a literal reading of the fraud and abuse statute, be felonies under the federal law. Considerable attention has been focused recently on the question of whether the statute and the judicial and administrative interpretations thereof successfully distinguish beneficial and detrimental conduct in the current market environment. Note that many of the behaviors prohibited by the AKS are also covered by the Stark Law and state laws discussed later in this chapter.

UNITED STATES V. GREBER

United States Court of Appeals, Third Circuit, 1985.
760 F.2d 68, cert. denied, 474 U.S. 988, 106 396, 88 L.Ed.2d 348.

WEIS, CIRCUIT JUDGE.

In this appeal, defendant argues that payments made to a physician for professional services in connection with tests performed by a laboratory cannot be the basis of Medicare fraud. We do not agree and hold that if one purpose of the payment was to induce future referrals, the Medicare statute has been violated. * * *

After a jury trial, defendant was convicted on 20 of 23 counts in an indictment charging violations of the mail fraud, Medicare fraud, and false statement statutes. Post-trial motions were denied, and defendant has appealed.

Defendant is an osteopathic physician who is board certified in cardiology. In addition to hospital staff and teaching positions, he was the president of Cardio–Med, Inc., an organization which he formed. The company provides physicians with diagnostic services, one of which uses a Holter-monitor. This device, worn for approximately 24 hours, records the patient's cardiac activity on a tape. A computer operated by a cardiac technician scans the tape, and the data is later correlated with an activity diary the patient maintains while wearing the monitor.

Cardio–Med billed Medicare for the monitor service and, when payment was received, forwarded a portion to the referring physician. The government charged that the referral fee was 40 percent of the Medicare payment, not to exceed $65 per patient.

Based on Cardio–Med's billing practices, counts 18–23 of the indictment charged defendant with having tendered remuneration or kickbacks to the referring physicians in violation of 42 U.S.C. § 1395nn(b)(2)(B) (1982).

*   *   *

The proof as to the Medicare fraud counts (18–23) was that defendant had paid a Dr. Avallone and other physicians "interpretation fees" for the doctors' initial consultation services, as well as for explaining the test results to the patients. There was evidence that physicians received "interpretation fees" even though defendant had actually evaluated the monitoring data. Moreover, the fixed percentage paid to the referring physician was more than Medicare allowed for such services.

The government also introduced testimony defendant had given in an earlier civil proceeding. In that case, he had testified that ". . . if the doctor didn't get his consulting fee, he wouldn't be using our service. So the doctor got a consulting fee." In addition, defendant told physicians at a hospital that the Board of Censors of the Philadelphia County Medical Society had said the referral fee was legitimate if the physician shared the responsibility for the report. Actually, the Society had stated that there should be separate bills because "for the monitor company to offer payment for the physicians . . . is not considered to be the method of choice."

The evidence as to mail fraud was that defendant repeatedly ordered monitors for his own patients even though use of the device was not medically indicated. As a prerequisite for payment, Medicare requires that the service be medically indicated.

The Department of Health and Human Services had promulgated a rule providing that it would pay for Holter-monitoring only if it was in operation for eight hours or more. Defendant routinely certified that the temporal condition had been met, although in fact it had not.

* * *

I. Medicare Fraud

The Medicare fraud statute was amended by P. L. 95–142, 91 Stat. 1183 (1977). Congress, concerned with the growing problem of fraud and abuse in the system, wished to strengthen the penalties to enhance the deterrent effect of the statute. To achieve this purpose, the crime was upgraded from a misdemeanor to a felony.

Another aim of the amendments was to address the complaints of the United States Attorneys who were responsible for prosecuting fraud cases. They informed Congress that the language of the predecessor statute was "unclear and needed clarification." H. Rep. No. 393, Part II, 95th Cong., 1st Sess. 53, *reprinted in* 1977 U.S. CODE CONG. & AD. NEWS 3039, 3055.

A particular concern was the practice of giving "kickbacks" to encourage the referral of work. Testimony before the Congressional committee was that "physicians often determine which laboratories would do the test work for their Medicaid patients by the amount of the kickbacks and rebates offered by the laboratory. . . . Kickbacks take a number of forms including cash, long-term credit arrangements, gifts, supplies and equipment, and the furnishing of business machines." Id. at 3048–3049.

To remedy the deficiencies in the statute and achieve more certainty, the present version of 42 U.S.C. § 1395nn(b)(2) was enacted. It provides:

"whoever knowingly and willfully offers or pays any remuneration (including any kickback, bribe or rebate) directly or indirectly, overtly or covertly in cash or in kind to induce such person—

(B) to purchase, lease, order, or arrange for or recommend purchasing . . . or ordering any . . . service or item for which payment may be made . . . under this title, shall be guilty of a felony."

The district judge instructed the jury that the government was required to prove that Cardio–Med paid to Dr. Avallone some part of the amount received from Medicare; that defendant caused Cardio–Med to make the payment; and did so knowingly and willfully as well as with the intent to induce Dr. Avallone to use Cardio–Med's services for patients covered by Medicare. The judge further charged that even if the physician interpreting the test did so as a consultant to Cardio–Med, that fact was immaterial if a purpose of the fee was to induce the ordering of services from Cardio–Med.

Defendant contends that the charge was erroneous. He insists that absent a showing that the only purpose behind the fee was to improperly induce future services, compensating a physician for services actually rendered could not be a violation of the statute.

The government argues that Congress intended to combat financial incentives to physicians for ordering particular services patients did not require.

The language and purpose of the statute support the government's view. Even if the physician performs some service for the money received, the potential for unnecessary drain on the Medicare system remains. The statute is aimed at the inducement factor.

The text refers to "any remuneration." That includes not only sums for which no actual service was performed but also those amounts for which some professional time was expended. "Remunerates" is defined as "to pay an equivalent for service." Webster Third New International Dictionary (1966). By including such items as kickbacks and bribes, the statute expands "remuneration" to cover situations where no service is performed. That a particular payment was a remuneration (which implies that a service was rendered) rather than a kickback, does not foreclose the possibility that a violation nevertheless could exist.

In United States v. Hancock, 604 F.2d 999 (7th Cir.1979), the court applied the term "kickback" found in the predecessor statute to payments made to chiropractors by laboratories which performed blood tests. The chiropractors contended that the amounts they received were legitimate handling fees for their services in obtaining, packaging, and delivering the specimens to the laboratories and then interpreting the results. The court rejected that contention and noted, "The potential for increased costs to the Medicare–Medicaid system and misapplication of federal funds is plain, where payments for the exercise of such judgments are added to the legitimate cost of the transaction. . . . [T]hese are among the evils Congress sought to prevent by enacting the kickback statutes. . . . " Id. at 1001.

Hancock strongly supports the government's position here, because the statute in that case did not contain the word "remuneration." The court nevertheless held that "kickback" sufficiently described the defendants' criminal activity. By adding "remuneration" to the statute in the 1977 amendment, Congress sought to make it clear that even if the transaction was not considered to be a "kickback" for which no service had been rendered, payment nevertheless violated the Act.

We are aware that in United States v. Porter, 591 F.2d 1048 (5th Cir.1979), the Court of Appeals for the Fifth Circuit took a more narrow view of "kickback" than did the court in *Hancock*. *Porter's* interpretation of the predecessor statute which did not include "remuneration" is neither binding nor persuasive. We agree with the Court of Appeals for the Sixth Circuit, which adopted the interpretation of "kickback" used in *Hancock* and rejected that of the *Porter* case. United States v. Tapert, 625 F.2d 111 (6th Cir. 1980).

We conclude that the more expansive reading is consistent with the impetus for the 1977 amendments and therefore hold that the district court correctly instructed the jury. If the payments were intended to induce the physician to use Cardio–Med's services, the statute was violated, even if the payments were also intended to compensate for professional services.

A review of the record also convinces us that there was sufficient evidence to sustain the jury's verdict.

* * *

Having carefully reviewed all of the defendant's allegations, we find no reversible error. Accordingly, the judgment of the district court will be affirmed.

NOTES AND QUESTIONS

1. What is controversial about the *Greber* decision? What kinds of salutary or benign practices might it affect?

2. What purposes does the anti-kickback legislation serve? Does it advance or impede the provision of quality medical services? What economic or efficiency arguments might be made in support of the law? Can it be argued that the law sweeps too broadly given the dynamics of today's market? At the time the legislation was passed, providers were almost uniformly paid on a cost-based, fee-for-service basis. With much of the private sector comprised of managed care or capitated provider payments, should a less restrictive rule be devised? See James Blumstein, The Fraud and Abuse Statute in an Evolving Health Care Marketplace: Life in the Health Care Speakeasy, 22 Am. J. L. & Med. 205 (1996). For the regulatory response to this problem, see the statutory exception applicable to risk-sharing arrangements, discussed *infra*.

4. *Greber* dealt with the issue of whether defendant's evidence of purpose satisfied the statutory standard that remuneration be given or received "in return for" an item or service reimbursable under Medicare or Medicaid. A second and distinct mens rea requirement concerns whether defendant knew that the transaction was unlawful. A few courts had held that the gov-

ernment must show not only that the defendant intentionally entered into a referral arrangement later determined to violate the statute, but also that when the defendant entered into the arrangement he or she knew the arrangement violated the dictates of the anti-kickback law. However, that approach was overruled by the ACA which amended the anti-kickback statute to provide that "a person need not have actual knowledge of this section or specific intent to commit a violation of this section." This change built upon the Supreme Court's decision in Bryan v. United States, 524 U.S. 184 (1998), which clarified the general principles of intent applicable in criminal cases, but did not fully resolve the issue with respect to the Medicare and Medicaid Fraud and Abuse statute. *Bryan* made it clear that the word "willfully" will be construed in the criminal context to require proof of knowledge of some law or legal standard: "As a general matter, when used in the criminal context, a 'willful' act is one undertaken with a 'bad purpose.' " Id. at 191. This standard, however, may be satisfied by showing that the defendant acted with "an evil-meaning mind," which the Court defined as acting "with knowledge that his conduct was unlawful." Id. at 193. At the same time, *Bryan* lowered the standard of proof necessary to satisfy its test by accepting an accused's knowledge of general illegality unless the relevant statute is "highly technical." See Sharon L. Davies, Willfulness Under the Anti–Kickback Rules—Lessons from Bryan v. United States, 10 Health Lawyer 14 (July 1998). See U.S. v. Starks, 157 F.3d833 (11th Cir. 1998)(pre-ACA case applying Bryan to Anti-Kickback law finding it not "highly technical").

PROBLEM: RECRUITING DR. RYAN

Anxious to develop its newly-enlarged surgical department, Community Hospital, located in Rocky Shoals, N.C. recruited Dr. Henry Ryan to relocate from Arizona and set up an independent practice in the area. Community's contract with Dr. Ryan recited the region's need for additional surgeons and specified it would provide a number of financial inducements for Dr. Ryan to relocate: a guarantee that the doctor's cash collections for professional services would not be less than an average of $40,000 per month; that Community would extend this commitment for an additional two additional one-year terms "should Physician and Hospital believe it to be necessary"; and that Community would lease medical office space on its campus to Dr. Ryan at a cost 50 percent below the market average and provide financial assistance in obtaining medical office furniture and equipment if desired. The contract goes on to provide as follows:

> You recognize that [Community] Hospital is a convenient acute care medical facility for the majority of patients likely to utilize your services for medical treatment and that the Hospital is duly accredited by the Joint Commission on Accreditation of Healthcare Organizations and is qualified for participation in the Medicare and Medicaid programs, and has excellent special facilities and treatment capabilities.

We, of course, hope that the quality and cost-effective nature of our Hospital's services will commend themselves to your patients. However, we clearly understand that the choice of services and the choice of service suppliers which you make on behalf of your patients must be, and will be, made ONLY with regard to the best interests of the patients themselves. Therefore, so there will be no misunderstanding, the compensation which you are to receive is not conditional on the use of any item or service offered by this Hospital.

Shortly after Dr. Ryan's arrival in Rocky Hills, Community Hospital was acquired by Nosh Hospital. After Nosh reneged on many of the commitments contained in the contract, Dr. Ryan sued claiming breach. Raising affirmative defenses including the unenforceability of the contract based on the federal anti-kickback law, the hospital has moved for summary judgment. In response, Dr. Ryan argues that the unambiguous language of the contract establishes that the parties did not have intent to induce referrals. How should the court rule?

E. STATUTORY EXCEPTIONS, SAFE HARBORS, AND FRAUD ALERTS

The fraud and abuse statute contains several common sense exceptions. For example, discounts or reductions in price obtained by providers of services, literally proscribed by the language of the statute, are permitted if properly disclosed and reflected in the claimed costs or charges of the provider. Likewise, amounts paid by employers to employees and rebates obtained by group purchasing organizations are exempted under specified circumstances. (The employment exception is discussed in Note 2 following U.S. v. Starks, *supra*.) The Health Insurance Portability and Accountability Act of 1996 added an exception for "risk-sharing" arrangements. As described below, this exception is designed to answer criticisms that the law unreasonably deters arrangements such as capitated payments that foster delivery of cost-effective care and pose no substantial risk of overutilization, the key concern of the anti-kickback rules.

In addition to these statutory exceptions, the Secretary of HHS, acting pursuant to Congressional directive, has promulgated so-called "Safe Harbor" regulations to describe conduct that is not criminal under the fraud and abuse laws. This is a somewhat unusual provision in that it permits an administrative agency to designate conduct otherwise illegal under federal law as not subject to prosecution by the Justice Department. 42 C.F.R. § 1001.952. The total number of safe harbors now stands at twenty-five. Among the more important of the safe harbors are the following:

Rental and Management Contracts

Three safe harbors for space and equipment rentals and management contracts have very similar standards. Leases for space or equipment must be in writing and signed by the parties; must identify the space or equipment covered; must specify when and for how long space or equipment will be used and the precise rental charge for each use if the lease is not for full time use; and must be for at least one year. The amount of rent must be set in advance, must not take into account the volume and value of any referrals or business generated, and, most importantly, must reflect the fair market value of the space or equipment. Fair market value is defined as the value of the property for "general commercial purposes," or "the value of the equipment when obtained from a manufacturer or professional distributor," and cannot take into account the proximity or convenience of the equipment or space to the referral course. The requirements for personal services or management contracts which are nearly identical to the rental provisions, excepts payments made by a principal to an agent as compensation for the agent's services for written agency agreements of at least one year, provided the agreement specifies and covers all the services that the agent provides during that period. The aggregate compensation for the services must be set in advance, consistent with fair market value in an arms-length transaction, and not take into account the volume or values of any referrals or business otherwise generated between the parties. An agent is defined as any person other than an employee of the principal who has an agreement to perform services for or on behalf of the principal.

Sale of Practice

A very limited safe harbor exists to protect sales of practices by retiring physicians. The sale must be completed within one year from the date of the agreement, after which the selling practitioner must no longer be in a professional position to refer Medicare or Medicaid patients or otherwise generate business for the purchasing practitioner. Sale options are not permitted unless they are completely performed within a year. This safe harbor does not protect arrangements in which a hospital-controlled entity such as a Management Service Organization purchases the practices of physicians who thereafter are retained on staff.

Practitioner Recruitment

A practitioner recruitment safe harbor protects recruitment efforts by hospitals and entities located in government-specified health professional shortage areas (HPSAs). It permits payments or other exchanges to induce practitioners relocating from a different geographic area or new practitioners (in practice within their current specialty for less than one year) provided nine conditions are met. Among those conditions are that the agreement be in writing; that at least 75 percent of the business of the relocated practice come from new patients; that at least 75 percent of the new practice revenue be generated from the HPSA or other defined underserved areas; that the practitioner not be barred from establishing staff privileges with or referring to other entities; and that benefits and amendments to the contract may not be based on the value or volume of practitioners' referrals.

Price Reductions Offered to Eligible Managed Care Organizations

After a lengthy negotiated rulemaking process, the OIG announced two interim final rules to implement the statutory exception governing certain Eligible Managed Care Organizations (EMCOs). The two safe harbors apply to (1) financial arrangements between managed care entities paid by a federal health care program on a capitated basis and individuals or entities agreeing to provide to the manage care entity items or services under a written agreement and (2) financial agreements that, through a risk sharing arrangement, place individuals or entities at "substantial financial risk" for the cost or utilization of the items or services which they are obligated to provide. Recognizing that EMCOs having risk contracts which operate on a capitated rather than fee-for-service basis present little risk of overutilization and increased health program costs, the safe harbor protects price reductions (and other exchanges or remunerations) between eligible MCOs and individuals and entities. The second part of the price reduction safe harbor regulation addresses financial arrangements (subcontracts) between first tier contractors and other individuals or entities, known as downstream contractors.

Referral Agreements for Specialty Services

This safe harbor is designed to reduce any untoward effects that the anti-kickback laws may have on continuity of care and patient access to specialists. It protects any exchange of value among individuals and entities if one provider agrees to refer a patient to another provider for the rendering of a specialty service in exchange for an agreement by the other party to refer that patient back at a later time, as long as neither party may pay the other for the referral, although members of the same group practice may share revenues of the group practice.

Ambulatory Surgery Centers

This safe harbor provides a detailed regulatory scheme that protects returns on an investment interest, such as dividend or interest income, in four kinds of Ambulatory Surgery Centers (ASCs): surgeon-owned ASCs, single-specialty ASCs, multi-specialty ASCs, and hospital/physician ASCs. It does not apply to an ASC located on a hospital's premises that shares operating or recovery room space with the hospital for treatment of the hospital's inpatients or outpatients. Advisory Opinion 03–05, set forth following this note, deals with this Safe Harbor.

Investment Interests

This complex safe harbor provides that there is no violation for returns on "investment interests" including both equity and debt interests in corporations, partnerships and other entities held directly or indirectly through family members or other indirect ownership vehicles. It covers, first, investments in large, publicly-traded entities registered with the SEC and having $50 million in net tangible assets. The investment must also be obtained on terms equally available to the public, the entity must market items and services in the same way to investors and non-investors, and must comply with other requirements. Second, certain investments in small entities are permitted provided no more than 40 percent of the value of the investment interests in each class of investment is held by persons who are in a position to make or influence referrals to, furnish items or services to, or otherwise generate business for the entity. Moreover, no more than 40 percent of the gross revenue of the entity may come from referrals, items or services from investors. A number of other requirements apply including several that are different for active investors and passive investors. Amendments to this safe harbor allow for higher investment percentages in medically underserved areas. The importance of this safe harbor is limited by the fact that it does not shelter arrangements covered by the Stark Law (discussed in the next section of this chapter) which applies different standards to investments. However, for services not covered by Stark, the safe harbor has continuing importance.

Group Practices

A safe harbor shelters payments (such as dividend or interest income) received in return for investment interests in group practices. 42 C.F.R. § 1001.952(p). It covers business arrangements having centralized decision-making, pooled expenses and revenues, and profit distribution systems "not based on satellite offices operating substantially as if they were separate enterprises or profit centers." Modeled on the Stark exception (see below), it adopts that statute's definition of "group practice" and provides that income from ancillary services must meet the Stark definition of "in-office ancillary services."

Electronic Health Records Arrangements
and Electronic Prescribing

Two safe harbors establish conditions under which hospitals and certain other entities may (1) donate to physicians interoperable electronic health records (EHR), software, information technology, and training services, and (2) provide physicians with hardware, software, or information technology and training services necessary and used solely for electronic prescribing. Substantially identical standards were adopted as exceptions to the Stark Law discussed in the next section.

The electronic prescribing safe harbor covers items and services that are necessary and used solely to transmit and receive electronic prescription information and requires that donated technology comply with standards adopted by the Secretary of HHS. Protected donors and recipients are: (1) hospitals to members of their medical staffs; (2) group practices to physician members; (3) Prescription Drug Plan sponsors and Medicare Advantage organizations to network pharmacist and pharmacies, and prescribing health care professionals. There is no limit on the value of donations but donors may not select recipients using any method that takes into account the volume or value of referrals from the recipient or other business generated between the parties.

The EHR safe harbor protects arrangements involving electronic health records software or information technology and training services necessary and used predominately to create, maintain, transmit, or receive electronic health records. While neither hardware nor software with a core functionality other than electronic health records is covered, software packages may include functions related to patient administration such as clinical support. Protected donors are individuals and entities that provide covered services to any Federal health care program and health plans. Donors may not select recipients using any method that takes into account directly the volume or value of referrals from the recipient or other business between the parties and while there is no limit on the aggregate value of technology that may qualify for safe harbor protection, recipients must pay 15 percent of the donor's cost for the donated technology.

A wide variety of other arrangements are covered by safe harbors, including subsidies for obstetrical malpractice insurance subsidies, and waivers of copayments and deductibles for inpatient hospital care and group purchasing organizations. Many of these safe harbors are narrowly drawn and afford only limited protection despite sometimes broader coverage sometimes implied by their titles. Moreover, safe harbor protection requires compliance with every requirement of all applicable safe harbors and the OIG has refused to adopt a standard of "substantial compliance" or to declaim intention to pursue "technical" or de minimis violations. See 56 Fed. Reg. 35,953, 35,957 (July 29, 1991). At the same time however, the safe harbors are not standards; conduct falling outside their boundaries may still pass muster under the intent-based statutory standard.

Another important source of guidance in this area are the fraud alerts issued by the Office of Inspector General of HHS. Dep't of Health & Human Services, Office of the Inspector General, Fraud Alerts. These alerts set forth the OIG's interpretation of the statute as applied in certain situations and are intended to encourage individuals to report suspected violations to the government. Among the most notable is the Special Fraud Alert on Joint Venture Arrangements issued in 1989. The alert identified "questionable features" of certain joint ventures such as where investors chosen are potential referral sources; the investment shares of physician investors are proportionate to the volume of referrals; physicians are encouraged to refer to the entity or to divest their interest if referrals fall below an acceptable level or if physicians become unable to refer; the joint venture is structured as a "shell;" or the amounts of the investment are disproportionately small and returns disproportionately large. Finally, an indicator of the government's enforcement policies is also found in the Advisory Opinions issued by the Office of the Inspector General at HHS. While these opinions disclaim having any binding effect, they often signal the agency's posture on controversial arrangements. See, e.g., Office of Inspector General, Dep't Health & Human Services, Advisory Opinion 03–5 (February 6, 2003).

NOTE: GAINSHARING, THE CMP LAW, AND THE ANTI–KICKBACK LAW

An area of continuing controversy involving fraud and abuse laws has been hospital "gainsharing" programs. Broadly defined, the term refers to "an arrangement in which a hospital gives physicians a share of any reduction in the hospital's costs attributable in part to the physicians' efforts." Hearing on Gainsharing Before the Subcomm. on Health of the H. Comm. on Ways and Means, 109th Cong. (2005) (testimony of Lewis Morris, Chief Counsel to the Inspector General, U.S. Dep't of Health and Human Services)[hereinafter Morris Testimony]. Some gainsharing practices are narrowly-targeted, such as those giving physicians a financial incentive to reduce the use of specific medical devices and supplies, to switch to specific products that are less expensive, or to adopt specific clinical practices or protocols that reduce costs. More comprehensive—and more legally problematic—arrangements include those that offer the physician payments to reduce total average costs per case below target amounts. Of special concern for the government have been "black box" gainsharing arrangements that give physicians money for overall cost savings without knowing what specific actions physicians are taking to generate those savings. See Office of Inspector General, Dep't Health & Human Services, Special Advisory Bulletin: Gainsharing Arrangements and CMPs for Hospital Payments to Physicians to Reduce or Limit Services to Beneficiaries (July 1999).

It can readily be seen that gainsharing arrangements may help align physician incentives with those of a hospital and thereby promote hospital cost reductions. Indeed, as discussed in Chapter 10, Medicare's inpatient prospective payment system provides a strong impetus for hospitals to encourage independent staff physicians to adopt practices that reduce costs. See Richard Saver, Squandering the Gain: Gainsharing and the Continuing Dilemma of Physician Financial Incentives, 98 Nw. U.L. Rev. 145, 146 (2003). At the same time, such payments may encourage physicians to use a particular provider, implicating concerns that underlie the anti-kickback law and the Stark Law (discussed in the next section of this chapter). Finally, gainsharing arrangements may serve as an inducement to deny services that are medically necessary. This risk is directly addressed by the Civil Monetary Penalty (CMP) law, 42 U.S.C. § 1320a–7a(b), which prohibits a hospital from "knowingly making a payment, directly or indirectly, to a physician as an inducement to reduce or limit items or services" furnished to Medicare or Medicaid beneficiaries under a physician's direct care.

The Office of Inspector General has been wary of gainsharing arrangements, but has issued a series of favorable advisory opinions in which it indicated it would not challenge certain carefully-tailored proposals. Office of Inspector General, Dep't Health & Human Services, Advisory Opinions 05–01 through 05–06 (2005). Notably, however, the OIG's General Counsel has cautioned that despite these rulings, "absent a change in law, it is not currently possible for gainsharing arrangements to be structured without implicating the fraud and abuse laws." Morris Testimony, *supra*. In each advisory opinion the OIG stressed the significance of safeguards and characteristics of the arrangement that alleviated its concerns. Three important factors guide the OIG's analysis: accountability, quality controls and safeguards against payments for referrals. To ensure accountability, OIG favors transparent arrangements that "clearly and separately identify the actions that will result in cost savings," thus permitting both objective reviews by the government (and by the malpractice system) and a more complete understanding by patients and their doctors. Morris Testimony, *supra*. To ensure that quality of care is not impaired, the OIG deems it important to have qualified, outside, independent parties "perform a medical expert review of each cost-savings measure to assess the potential impact on patient care" and to establish baseline thresholds based on historic data that set limits on reductions of service so they do not impair patient safety. Where product standardization incentives are involved, the OIG looks favorably on assurances that individual physicians will still have available the same selection of devices and can make a case-by-case determination of the most appropriate device for the patient.

Finally, the OIG's advisory opinions insist on certain safeguards to prevent gainsharing from being used to reward or induce patient referrals. These include limiting participation to physicians already on the hospital's medical staff; limiting the amount, duration, and scope of the payments; distributing the gainsharing profits on a per capita basis to all physicians in a single-specialty group practice; and basing cost sharing payments on all surgeries, regardless of payor, with procedures not being disproportionately performed on Medicare or Medicaid patients.

While many support steps to legalize gainsharing on a wider scale, there is still considerable uncertainty about the circumstances in which gainsharing should be permitted and what regulations are needed to assure quality and avoid the risks inherent in payment for referrals. Pursuant to Congressional directive HHS established a qualified gainsharing demonstration program to test and evaluate methodologies and arrangements between hospitals and physicians. Gainsharing issues can figure prominently in ACOs formed by joint ventures between hospitals and physicians; see discussion of ACOs *infra*.

III. THE STARK LAW: A TRANSACTIONAL APPROACH TO SELF–REFERRALS

An alternative approach to dealing with fraud and abuse is to list and describe exhaustively transactions that are alternatively legitimate or illegitimate under the law. The Ethics in Patient Referrals Act (commonly referred to as the Stark Law in recognition of the legislation's principal sponsor, former Rep. Fortney "Pete" Stark) does just that with respect to physician referrals for certain Medicare-financed services in which the physician (or immediate family member) has a financial interest. Besides making it illegal for physicians to make such referrals, Stark also prohibits any billings for services provided pursuant to illegal referrals. As originally enacted, the law only applied to referrals for clinical laboratory services. Its reach was significantly expanded by the 1993 Omnibus Budget Reconciliation Act which made Stark applicable to services paid for by Medicaid as well as by Medicare and expanded its scope to cover eleven "designated health services" (DHS): clinical laboratory services; physical therapy services; occupational therapy services; radiology, including MRI, CAT and ultrasound services; radiation therapy services and supplies; durable medical equipment and supplies; parenteral and enteral nutrients, equipment, and supplies; prosthetics, orthotics, and prosthetic devices; home health services and supplies; outpatient prescription drugs; and inpatient and outpatient hospital services. No payment can be made by Medicare or Medicaid for referrals for such services where the referring physician or member of his family has a financial interest. Any amounts billed in violation of the section must be refunded. Any person knowingly billing or failing to make a refund in violation of the prohibition is subject to a civil fine of $15,000 per item billed and to exclusion.

The Stark legislation responded to increasing evidence that "self-referrals" had become quite common, and quite costly. An OIG study issued in 1989 found that of 2690 physicians who responded to its study, 12 percent had ownership interests and 8 percent had compensation arrangements with businesses to which they referred patients. Office of Inspector General, Financial Arrangements Between Physicians and Health Care Businesses: Report to Congress (1989). It further determined that nationally 25 percent of independent clinical laboratories (ICLs), 27 percent of independent laboratories, and 8 percent of durable medical equipment suppliers were owned at least in part by referring physicians. Beneficiaries treated by physicians who owned or invested in ICLs received 45 percent more clinical laboratory services and 34 percent more services directly from ICLs than beneficiaries in general, resulting in $28 million in additional costs to the Medicare program. Do studies finding high rates of self-referral patterns establish that the additional services provided were unnecessary? Is strong and consistent empirical evidence of higher utilization among self-referring physicians sufficient to justify legislation that broadly proscribes the practice?

Note that, subject to the exceptions discussed below, Stark is said to adopt a "bright line" or strict liability standard. Unlike Medicare fraud and abuse laws, there is no requirement that the conduct involve the knowing and willful receipt of a kickback: if no exception applies, the law has been violated. However, as we will see, CMS has promulgated numerous exceptions and the Federal Register contains voluminous and detailed regulations and commentary purporting to clarify or simplify compliance with the law.

A. SCOPE OF THE PROHIBITION

The Stark law prohibits physicians who have (or whose immediate family member has) a "financial relationship" with a provider of designated health services from making "referrals" of Medicare or Medicaid patients to such providers for purposes of receiving any of the eleven "designated health services." The key terms are defined in 42 U.S.C. § 1395nn as follows:

(a) Prohibitions of certain referrals

*   *   *

(2) Financial relationship specified

For purposes of this section, a financial relationship of a physician (or an immediate family member of such physician) with an entity specified in this paragraph is—

(A) except as provided in subsections (c) and (d) of this section, an ownership or investment interest in the entity, or

(B) except as provided in subsection (e) of this section, a compensation arrangement (as defined in subsection (h)(1) of this section) between the physician (or an immediate family member of such physician) and the entity.

An ownership or investment interest described in subparagraph (A) may be through equity, debt, or other means and includes an interest in an entity that holds an ownership or investment interest in any entity providing the designated health service.

*   *   *

(h) Definitions and special rules

For purposes of this section:

(1) Compensation arrangement; remuneration

(A) The term "compensation arrangement" means any arrangement involving any remuneration between a physician (or an immediate family member of such physician) and an entity other than an arrangement involving only remuneration described in subparagraph (C).

(B) The term "remuneration" includes any remuneration, directly or indirectly, overtly or covertly, in cash or in kind.

* * *

(5) Referral; referring physician

(A) Physicians' services

Except as provided in subparagraph (C), in the case of an item or service for which payment may be made under part B of this subchapter, the request by a physician for the item or service, including the request by a physician for a consultation with another physician (and any test or procedure ordered by, or to be performed by (or under the supervision of) that other physician), constitutes a "referral" by a "referring physician."

* * *

(6) Designated health services

The term "designated health services" means any of the following items or services:

(A) Clinical laboratory services.

(B) Physical therapy services.

(C) Occupational therapy services.

(D) Radiology services, including magnetic resonance imaging, computerized axial tomography scans, and ultrasound services.

(E) Radiation therapy services and supplies.

(F) Durable medical equipment and supplies.

(G) Parenteral and enteral nutrients, equipment, and supplies.

(H) Prosthetics, orthotics, and prosthetic devices and supplies.

(I) Home health services.

(J) Outpatient prescription drugs.

(K) Inpatient and outpatient hospital services.

1.   Note several things about these provisions. First, recall that the principal problem identified by academic studies that led to the enactment of the original Stark law was excessive and perhaps inappropriate referrals by physicians to entities in which they had an ownership interest. Why did Congress extend the law's reach beyond "ownership and investment interests"? Was this a necessary or wise policy choice? Second, Stark reaches arrangements in which the flow of money is reversed from the normal self-referral pattern, i.e., the physician pays the entity for services provided. Why should such arrangements be outlawed? Third, consider the broad sweep of the term "referral" as used in the Act. Suppose Dr. Gillespe requests a consultation from Dr. Demento who in turn orders a lab test and physical therapy for the patient. For what referrals is Dr. Gillespe responsible?

2.   Strong criticisms have been lodged against Stark. Organized medicine argues that the law is too complex and needlessly duplicative of other laws affecting self-referrals. Moreover, opponents assert that the law goes far beyond prohibiting physician ownership of facilities and invites governmental "micromanagement" of evolving network structures. On the other side, the law has been defended as a pragmatic legislative choice that avoids the pitfalls of case-by-case litigation over issues of intent or reasonableness while unambiguously barring the most risk-prone referrals and permitting most efficiency-enhancing arrangements. One proposal, vetoed by President Clinton in 1995, would have eliminated the law's ban on "compensation arrangements." Would confining Stark Law's coverage to ownership and investment interests capture the most problematic relationships, or as Representative Stark has opined, would it create a "loophole you can drive an Armored Division through?" Despite the criticism the Stark Law has received, the ACA did not seek to undertake wholesale reform of the Stark law. Why do you think Congress failed to act? For a thoughtful and critical review of the law and its effects, see American Health Lawyers Association, Public Interest Committee, A Public Policy Discussion: Taking Stock of the Stark Law.

B. EXCEPTIONS

The Stark anti-referral law is an example of what is sometimes called an "exceptions bill." It sweepingly prohibits self-referrals but then legitimizes a large number of specific arrangements. Stark's exceptions are of three kinds: (1) those applicable to ownership or investment financial relationships; (2) those applicable to compensation arrangements; and (3) generic exceptions that apply to all financial arrangements.

Many of the exceptions cover self-referral arrangements that pose little risk of abuse. For example, the statute rules out liability where referring physicians' incentives are controlled in some way, as with prepaid health plans; or where other circumstances reduce the risk of excess utilization, such as where the physician is an employee of the entity to which the referral is made, has a personal services contract or a space or equipment rental that meets commercial reasonableness tests, or engages in isolated, one-time transactions with the entity. Perhaps the most important category involves situations in which a physician is part of a group practice that is directly involved in providing the service. Note that some exceptions, such as the very important ancillary services exception discussed later in this section, are not aimed at situations in which there is little risk of overutilization, but instead seem designed to foster other objectives, such as encouraging the integration of practice among physicians.

PROBLEM: SPACE AND EQUIPMENT RENTALS, PHYSICIAN RECRUITMENT

The Stark Law covers much of the same conduct as the bribe and kickback prohibition, but the legislation has its own exceptions that are worded somewhat differently. How does your analysis of problems 1 and 6 change under the exceptions reproduced below?

42 U.S.C. § 1395nn.

(e) Exceptions relating to other compensation arrangements

The following shall not be considered to be a compensation arrangement described in subsection (a)(2)(B) of this section:

(1) Rental of office space; rental of equipment

(A) Office space

Payments made by a lessee to a lessor for the use of premises if—

(i) the lease is set out in writing, signed by the parties, and specifies the premises covered by the lease,

(ii) the space rented or leased does not exceed that which is reasonable and necessary for the legitimate business purposes of the lease or rental and is used exclusively by the lessee when being used by the lessee, * * *

(iii) the lease provides for a term of rental or lease for at least 1 year,

(iv) the rental charges over the term of the lease are set in advance, are consistent with fair market value, and are not determined in a manner that takes into account the volume or value of any referrals or other business generated between the parties,

(v) the lease would be commercially reasonable even if no referrals were made between the parties, and

(vi) the lease meets such other requirements as the Secretary may impose by regulation as needed to protect against program or patient abuse.

(3) Personal service arrangements

[Certain personal service contracts are permitted if they meet certain conditions, including the condition that compensation not be related to the volume or value of referrals.]

(5) Physician recruitment

In the case of remuneration which is provided by a hospital to a physician to induce the physician to relocate to the geographic area served by the hospital in order to be a member of the medical staff of the hospital, if—

(A) the physician is not required to refer patients to the hospital,

(B) the amount of the remuneration under the arrangement is not determined in a manner that takes into account (directly or indirectly) the volume or value of any referrals by the referring physician, and

(C) the arrangement meets such other requirements as the Secretary may impose by regulation as needed to protect against program or patient abuse.

PROBLEM: GROUP PRACTICES

Drs. Chung, Snyder, Williams, Mendez, Patel, and Jones each operate independent solo practices. All have offices within a three square mile area, but none share offices with each other. Several years ago, they formed a joint venture to provide a variety of laboratory services to their patients. Their attorney has now informed them that their joint venture violates the prohibitions of the Stark legislation. He has suggested that they consider forming a group practice to operate the laboratory. What steps must they take to form a group practice that will permit them to operate a laboratory together under the relevant language of revised 42 U.S.C. § 1395nn?

42 U.S.C. § 1395nn:

(b) General exceptions to both ownership and compensation arrangement prohibitions

[The self-referral prohibitions] of this section shall not apply in the following cases:

(1) Physicians' services

In the case of physicians' services * * * provided personally by (or under the personal supervision of) another physician in the same group practice (as defined in subsection (h)(4) of this section) as the referring physician.

(2) In-office ancillary services

In the case of services (other than durable medical equipment (excluding infusion pumps) and parenteral and enteral nutrients, equipment, and supplies)—

(A) that are furnished—

(i) personally by the referring physician, personally by a physician who is a member of the same group practice as the referring physician, or personally by individuals who are directly supervised by the physician or by another physician in the group practice, and

(ii)(I) in a building in which the referring physician (or another physician who is a member of the same group practice) furnishes physicians' services unrelated to the furnishing of designated health services, or

(II) in the case of a referring physician who is a member of a group practice, in another building which is used by the group practice—

(aa) for the provision of some or all of the group's clinical laboratory services, or

(bb) for the centralized provision of the group's designated health services (other than clinical laboratory services), unless the Secretary determines other terms and conditions under which the provision of such services does not present a risk of program or patient abuse, and

(B) that are billed by the physician performing or supervising the services, by a group practice of which such physician is a member under a billing number assigned to the group practice, or by an entity that is wholly owned by such physician or such group practice, * * *

(h)(4)

(A) Definition of group practice

The term "group practice" means a group of 2 or more physicians legally organized as a partnership, professional corporation, foundation, not-for-profit corporation, faculty practice plan, or similar association—

(i) in which each physician who is a member of the group provides substantially the full range of services which the physician routinely provides, including medical care, consultation, diagnosis, or treatment, through the joint use of shared office space, facilities, equipment and personnel,

(ii) for which substantially all of the services of the physicians who are members of the group are provided through the group and are billed under a billing number assigned to the group and amounts so received are treated as receipts of the group,

(iii) in which the overhead expenses of and the income from the practice are distributed in accordance with methods previously determined,

(iv) except as provided in subparagraph (B)(i), in which no physician who is a member of the group directly or indirectly receives compensation based on the volume or value of referrals by the physician,

(v) in which members of the group personally conduct no less than 75 percent of the physician-patient encounters of the group practice, and

(vi) which meets such other standards as the Secretary may impose by regulation.

(B) Special rules

(i) Profits and productivity bonuses

A physician in a group practice may be paid a share of overall profits of the group, or a productivity bonus based on services personally performed or services incident to such personally performed services, so long as the share or bonus is not determined in any manner which is directly related to the volume or value of referrals by such physician.

NOTES AND QUESTIONS

1.   Is transparency an effective remedy to the problems associated with self-referrals? The ACA requires that physicians who bill for MRI, CT, or PET scans under the in-office ancillary exception to the Stark law must provide patients a list of other, nonaffiliated places they may go to get the same scans. The notice, which must be provided "at the time of referral" must include the name, address and telephone number of five other suppliers of the imaging test that are located within a 25–mile radius of the physician's office. How would you react if you received such a notice? How would your grandmother react?

2.   *U.S. ex rel. Drakeford v. Tuomey.* In a closely watched case, U.S. ex rel. Drakeford v. Tuomey Healthcare System, 395 F.3d 694 (4th Cir. 2012), the Fourth Circuit gave some noteworthy guidance about the reach of the Stark Law with respect to physicians employed by a hospital. Members of a gastroenterology specialty group informed Tuomey Hospital that they were considering performing outpatient surgical procedures in-office, rather than at Tuomey. To dissuade the group and other specialist physicians from performing their outpatient procedures elsewhere, Tuomey entered into exclusive dealing agreements with all specialist physicians on its medical staff. Except one. Dr. Drakeford, an orthopedic physician refused to enter into the proposed contract and eventually filed this qui tam case against Tuomey, alleging violations of the False Claims Act owing to the defendants' violation of the Stark law. The claim under Stark centered on the exclusive contracts pursuant to which the physicians agreed to perform outpatient surgeries at Tuomey Hospital rather than in their own offices or another facility. The physicians agreed to reassign all amounts paid by third party payers for professional services to Tuomey. Tuomey agreed to pay each physician a compensation package, which consisted of (1) an annual base salary that fluctuated based on Tuomey's net cash collections for the outpatient procedures; (2) a productivity bonus equal to 80 percent of the net collections; and (3) eligibility for a further incentive bonus for meeting certain quality measures. The government intervened, seeking relief under the FCA and asserting equitable claims grounded on the Stark law violations. The government contended that the arrangement did not satisfy the Stark employee exception because physicians' salaries exceeded the hospital's net collections for their services and the payments reflected the value or volume of referrals. A jury found that Tuomey did not violate the FCA, but did violate the Stark Law. As a result, the district court set aside this verdict and ordered a new trial but also

granted judgment on the equitable claims and ordered damages to be paid in the amount of $44,888,651.

After concluding that the district court's decision to award damages to the government violated Tuomey's Seventh Amendment right to a jury trial, the court proceeded to discuss in dicta "two threshold issues relating to liability under the Stark law . . . that are purely legal in nature and that the district court will be called upon to address upon retrial": (1) whether the facility components of the services would be considered a "referral" subject to the Stark law's referral prohibition even though the physicians were personally performing the services in the hospital pursuant to their contracts, and (2) whether the agreements between Tuomey and the physicians implicated the Stark law's "volume or value" standard. As to the first question, Medicare pays a separate payment for the technical or facility charges for inpatient or outpatient surgeries; physicians are paid separately for their professional services. Because the Stark law is only implicated if there is a "referral," the contracts would be outside the reach of the Stark law if the arrangement did not constitute a referral. The court gave strong deference to CMS's Stark regulations, which provide that in the context of inpatient and outpatient hospital services, there "would still be a referral of any hospital service, technical component, or facility fee billed by the hospital in connection with the personally performed service." U.S. v. Tuomey Healthcare System, 675 F.3d at 406)(citing 66 Fed. Reg. 856, 941 (Jan. 4, 2001)).

The court then addressed the second threshold question: whether the physicians contracts with Tuomey amounted to an "indirect compensation arrangement" which requires that the aggregate compensation received by the physician *"var[y] with, or take[ ] into account, the volume or value* of referrals or other business generated by the referring physician." 42 C.F.R. § 411.354(c)(2)(ii). The government contended that Tuomey's conduct fits within this definition because it included a portion of the value of the anticipated facility component referrals in the physicians' fixed compensation. While acknowledging that contractual arrangements may require a physician to refer patients to a hospital as a condition of compensation without running afoul of Stark, the court, again relying on Stark regulations, found that such arrangements do not implicate the Stark Law *only if* "certain conditions are met, one of which is that the physician's compensation must not take into account the volume or value of *anticipated* referrals." U.S. v. Tuomey Healthcare System, 675 F.3d at 409.

NOTE: STARK REGULATIONS

Complex as the statute might seem, it is only the beginning. Practitioners must master hundreds of pages of detailed regulations and commentary that interpret and explain the law. The first wave of regulations came in 1995, a full six years after the passage of Stark I, with the issuance of the final rule governing physician self-referrals under that Act. 60 Fed. Reg. 41,914 (Aug. 14, 1995) (codified at 42 C.F.R. § 411.350). In March 2004, CMS published its

Stark II "Phase II Regulations" which interpreted many statutory provisions, clarified some of the provisions of the "Phase I Regulations" issued in 2001, and added some new exceptions to the law. 69 Fed. Reg. 15,932 (Mar. 26, 2004). Among the more important provisions are those that define or explain a host of terms including the meaning of "fair market value," "referral," "indirect financial relationship," and, the most vexing of technical terms, "to." Critically important is what falls within the definition of certain designated health services, e.g., are PET scans within the statutory definition of "radiology services, including [MRI and CAT] scans and ultrasound services?" Can CMS include it by adopting a regulation?

Exceptions. The Phase I Regulations added six new exceptions governing compensation arrangements and five new all-purpose exceptions. Phase II added six more compensation exceptions and one all-purpose exception, while deleting one all-purpose exception and clarifying some of the 16 exceptions that preceded Phase I. Among the more important are exceptions for: non-monetary compensation to physicians up to a maximum of $300 per year; incidental benefits, such as free parking, for members of a hospital's medical staff; charitable donations by physicians; compliance training given by a hospital to its medical staff; hospital purchases of medical malpractice insurance for OB–GYNs practicing in a physician shortage area; DHS furnished by academic medical providers (subject to many requirements); risk sharing arrangements involving compensation between managed care organizations or IPAs and physicians furnishing services to enrollees in a plan; free or reduced fee services extended as professional courtesy to members of a physician's office staff; arrangements that have "unavoidably and temporarily fallen out of compliance" with an exception; physician recruitment payments permitted for physicians' "relocation" (defined in the regulations) and isolated transactions, defined now to permit certain installment payments. More recently exceptions have been added allowing entities furnishing DHSs to provide hardware or software used solely for electronic prescription systems and for interoperable electronic health records. These exceptions closely parallel the safe harbors established under the anti-kickback law described *supra*. Do these exceptions seem justified? Do they undermine the overarching purposes of the Stark law or are they pragmatic accommodations? In 2007, CMS posted the third phase of the final Stark II regulation (Phase III). Though lengthy and replete with detailed prescriptions, the Phase III regulations made relatively few major changes to Phase II and did not create any new exceptions.

The Stark Law Self-Referral Disclosure Protocol. Pursuant to a directive in the ACA, on September 23, 2010 CMS issued a "Self–Referral Disclosure Protocol" (SRDP) for providers of designated health services who wish to self-disclose actual or potential violations of the Stark Law. The agency indicated that although it has no obligation to reduce any fees or penalties, it is open to resolving violations for less than the maximum penalty through the SRDP. The Protocol states that the disclosing parties will have no appeal rights and must comply with strict disclosure obligations. In determining whether to reduce the amounts owed by the disclosing party, CMS will consider (1) the nature and extent of the improper or illegal practice; (2) the timeliness of the self-disclosure; (3) the cooperation in providing additional information related to the disclosure; (4) the litigation risk associated with the matter disclosed; and, (5) the financial position of the disclosing party. The SRDP states, however, that CMS has no obligation to reduce any amounts due and owing. Note, however, the implications of the SRDP for situation in which a provider has received and has "identified" his receipt of overpayments, discussed in the false claims section of this chapter. The SRDP suspends the sixty-day deadline for returning overpayments but also requires providers to comply with the overpayment provisions if CMS determines that an amount is owed. Providers are responsible for returning overpayments within 60 days until a settlement agreement is entered, the entity withdraws from the SRDP, or CMS removes the entity from the SRDP. Despite these benefits, the SRDP carries some risks: the Department of Justice and the Office of Inspector General may have access to the disclosure and may impose sanctions within their statutory authority; documentation requirements could lead to charges under false statement, obstruction of justice and other laws; and no appeals are available from the CMS resolution of the issue. For an analysis of the shortcomings of the SRDP and proposals for improving the process, see Jean Wright Veilleux, Catching Flies with Vinegar: A Critique of the Centers for Medicare and Medicaid Self–Disclosure Program, 22 Health Matrix 169 (2011).

PROBLEM: MEDICAL DIRECTORS

Facing declining admissions and rampant administrative inefficiency, Jeff Lewis, the CEO of Alta Bonita Central Hospital ("ABC") decided to create six new medical directorship positions effective January 1, 2007. Medical directors are typically independent staff physicians who enter into contracts with hospitals to perform certain administrative functions such as assisting in the development and implementation of standards of care, ensuring compliance with JCAHO standards and those of other regulatory bodies, providing consultations on high risk cases, and participating in the work of various hospital committees. The following chart indicates the specialty and number of referrals to ABC for each of its six medical directors for 2006, the year preceding their appointments, and for 2007.

Physician	Specialty	2007 Referrals	2006 Referrals
Dr. Singh	Orthopedics	80	68
Dr. Kaur	Nephrology/Dialysis	78	46
Dr. LaCombe	OB/GYN	40	38
Dr. Hicks	Cardiology	62	46

| Dr. Russell | Surgery | 45 | 45 |
| Dr. Anderson | Geriatrics | 50 | 27 |

These physicians were all among the top ten referring physicians at ABC, collectively accounting for 65% of the hospital's admissions before they became medical directors. The agreements delineated specific requirements that each medical director was to fulfill, including a requirement that he or she work 16 hours per month and document the number of "actual hours" worked, and specified a monthly stipend. Doctors LaCombe, Hicks and Russell were given stipends of $1500 per month and Doctors Singh, Kaur and Anderson were paid $2500 per month

Recently, the new outside counsel for ABC conducted a compliance audit and found the following in the reporting records of the doctors. Dr. Russell reported 4 hours in March 2007, 3 hours in April 2007, 0 hours in May 2007, and 0 hours in June 2007. Dr. Russell turned in these timesheets in December 2007. Dr. Hicks turned in her timesheets for April, May, June, July, and August 2007 in September 2007, reporting on each timesheet 8 hours of work. Regardless of when the timesheets were turned in or how they were filled out (hours worked, duties completed), all the medical directors were paid their full monthly stipend at the end of every month.

What issues are raised under the Stark Law by the way ABC established its medical directorships and the way it has implemented its agreements? Using the following exception and guidance, how should ABC have proceeded in contracting with its medical directors? What steps should it take now?

The Personal Services arrangements exception to compensation arrangements, 42 USC § 1395nn(e)(3)(A), provides:

Remuneration from an entity under an arrangement (including remuneration for specific physicians' services furnished to a nonprofit blood center), if—

(i) the arrangement is set out in writing, signed by the parties, and specifies the services covered by the arrangement,

(ii) the arrangement covers all of the services to be furnished by the physician (or an immediate family member of such physician) to the entity,

(iii) the aggregate services contracted for do not exceed those that are reasonable and necessary for the legitimate business purposes of the arrangement,

(iv) the term of the arrangement is for at least 1 year.

(v) the compensation to be paid over the term of each arrangement is set in advance, does not exceed fair market value, and except in the case of a physician incentive plan, is not determined in a manner that takes into account the volume or value of any referrals or other business generated between the parties,

(vi) the services to be performed under the arrangement do not involve the counseling or promotion or a business arrangement or other activity that violates any State or Federal law, and

(vii) the arrangement meets such other requirements as the Secretary may impose by regulation as needed to protect against program or patient abuse.

42 C.F.R. § 411.351 provides in pertinent part:

"Fair market value" means the value in arm's-length transactions, consistent with the general market value. "General market value" means the price that an asset would bring as the result of bona fide bargaining between well-informed buyers and sellers who are not otherwise in a position to generate business for the other party; or the compensation that would be included in a service agreement as the result of bona fide bargaining between well-informed parties to the agreement who are not otherwise in a position to generate business for the other party, on the date of acquisition of the asset or at the time of the service agreement. Usually, the fair market price is the price at which bona fide sales have been consummated for assets of like type, quality, and quantity in a particular market at the time of acquisition, or the compensation that has been included in bona fide service agreements with comparable terms at the time of the agreement, where the price or compensation has not been determined in any manner that takes into account the volume or value of anticipated or actual referrals.

The Phase III Regulations, *supra* state:

Nothing precludes parties from calculating fair market value using any commercially reasonable methodology that is appropriate under the circumstances and otherwise fits the definition [in the Act] and § 411.351. Ultimately, fair market value is determined based on facts and circumstances. The appropriate method will depend on the nature of the transaction, its location, and other factors. Because the statute covers a broad range of transactions, we cannot comment definitively on particular valuation methodologies.

NOTE: STATE APPROACHES TO KICKBACKS, REFERRALS AND FEE SPLITTING

Most states have enacted laws that prohibit kickbacks or deal in some way with the specific problem of referrals. These laws vary considerably in scope and detail. For example, most states prohibit Medicaid fraud, but some rely on more general statutes outlawing fraud or theft by deception or false statements to public officials; some impose both criminal and civil penalties for kickbacks; many apply regardless of whether government or private payment plans were involved; and a few have broadened federal anti-kickback laws, e.g., by prohibiting the provision of unnecessary care.

Among the states adopting self-referral legislation, most track with either the Medicare fraud and abuse or Stark legislation. However, some states have enacted disclosure statutes that do not prohibit physician ownership interests in facilities to which they refer, but require that the referring provider reveal such interests to her patients. Finally, a few states allow physician investment where there is a demonstrated "community need." Is mandating disclosure of providers' financial conflicts of interest a realistic solution? Are patients capable of evaluating the risks they face in accepting referrals from a doctor with a financial interest in the referred product or service? What kind of verbal disclosure can be expected from an interested physician? What effect would such disclosures have on the physician-patient relationship? What predictions would you make about the operation of a disclosure requirement based on your knowledge of informed consent? Finally, how valid are the premises of state community need laws? Are physicians likely to invest in facilities in areas where private investors are lacking? If so, why? Do these statutes create regulatory processes that may themselves be subject to abuse? This approach may be contrasted with the Stark law, which includes an exception for self-referrals of designated health services if provided in a rural area (using metropolitan statistical areas for delineating regions) and if substantially all the services are furnished to persons who reside in the rural area. 42 U.S.C. § 1395nn(d)(2). What are the pros and cons of the demonstrated community need approach as compared to the Stark exception?

Another source of law governing physician referral practices are the state medical practice acts. Such laws commonly provide that paying referral fees or "fee-splitting" constitutes grounds for revocation or suspension of a physician's license. See, e.g., Mass. Gen. L. Ch. 112 §§ 12AA, 23P (1991). These statutes have sometimes been construed to prohibit arrangements that go beyond simple sharing of fees in connection with referral arrangements. See, e.g., in Lieberman & Kraff v. Desnick, 614 N.E.2d 379 (1993). Florida's fee-splitting statute has called into question the legality of many physician practice management arrangements whereby a physician pays a large organization a percentage of profits in exchange for management, marketing, and networking services. See Gold, Vann & White, P.A. v. Friedenstab, 831 So.2d 692 (Fla. Dist. Ct. App. 2002) (service agreement between physicians and medical management company providing management company a percentage of revenue constituted an illegal fee splitting arrangement). See Richard O. Jacobs & Elizabeth Goodman, Splitting Fees or Splitting Hairs? Fee Splitting and Health Care—The Florida Experience, 8 Annals Health L. 239 (1999).

IV. FRAUD AND ABUSE LAWS AND PROVIDER INTEGRATION

As discussed in Chapter 12, providers are integrating rapidly under a wide variety of arrangements. Providers forming accountable care organizations through contractual arrangements and joint venture encounter obstacles under the laws discussed in this chapter. The ACA strongly encouraged these developments and sought to ease the legal burdens by empowering the Secretary of HHS to waive certain laws for Medicare ACOs.

ACOs and Fraud and Abuse Laws

Contemporaneously with the issuance of the notice of the Final Rule on Accountable Care Organizations (ACOs) discussed in Chapter 10, CMS and the Office of Inspector General (OIG) published an interim final rule establishing waivers of three federal fraud and abuse laws for ACOs participating in the Medicare Shared Savings Program (MSSP). 76 Fed. Reg. 67,992 (Nov. 2, 2011). Having waded through the material in this chapter, the need for such waivers should be fairly obvious. As one example: the ACO concept necessarily entails an exchange of payments among providers reflecting their contributions to the enterprise's goal of reducing costs. Although, in theory, distributions might come under existing exceptions requiring a showing of "fair market value," demonstrating the "costs" associated with physicians modifying their clinical practices and the value of physicians' work would be speculative and difficult to document. See Daniel H. Melvin & Webb Millsaps, The Proposed Waivers of the Fraud and Abuse Laws for ACOs: Have OIG and CMS Gone Far Enough? 15 Health Care Fraud Report (BNA) 422 (May 4, 2011).

Pursuant to the broad grant of authority to the Secretary of HHS to waive the anti-kickback statute (AKS), the Stark law (Stark), and the civil monetary penalties applicable to gainsharing (Gainsharing CMP), the interim final rule sets forth the following waivers for ACOs participating in the MSSP.

Pre–Participation Waiver. The intent of this waiver is to permit ACO participants to share resources in starting up ACOs. It waives the AKS, Stark, and Gainsharing CMP laws for start-up arrangements that meet various conditions, including acting in good faith with intent to develop an ACO that will participate in the MSSP; taking "diligent steps" to develop an ACO that is eligible to participate in the MSSP; and the ACO's governing board making a bona fide determination that the start-up arrangement is reasonably related to the purposes of the MSSP and contemporaneously documenting these steps.

Participation Waiver. This waiver of AKS, Stark, and Gainsharing CMP laws applies broadly to ACO-related arrangements during the term of the ACO's participation in the MSSP. Conditions include entering into and participating in the MSSP and meeting program requirements; having a duly authorized determination by the ACO's governing board that the arrangement is reasonably related to the purposes of the MSSP; and contemporaneously documenting and publicly disclosing the arrangement.

Shared Savings Distribution Waiver. This waiver, also applicable to AKS, Stark, and Gainsharing CMP laws, covers the actual distribution of savings to or among the ACO participants, ACO providers/suppliers, or individuals or entities that were its ACO participants or ACO providers/suppliers during the year that the shared savings were earned. The savings may also be "used" by the ACO for activities that are reasonably related to purposes of the MSSP such as paying parties outside the ACO. An additional requirement pertaining to the waiver of the Gainsharing CMP, provides that shared savings distributions that are made directly or indirectly from a hospital to a physician not be made knowingly to induce a physician to reduce or limit medically necessary items or services to patients under the direct care of the physician.

Compliance with the Stark Law Waiver. This waiver broadly waives the AKS and Gainsharing CMP with respect to any financial relationship between or among the ACO, its ACO participants, and its ACO providers/suppliers that implicates the Stark Law, provided that the financial relationship is reasonably related to the purposes of the MSSP and it fully complies with an exception to the Stark Law.

Waiver for Patient Incentives. This waiver waives the AKS and a CMP specifically applicable to beneficiary inducements. It applies to items or services provided by an ACO, its ACO participants, or its ACO providers/suppliers to beneficiaries for free or below fair-market value. The rule applies the following conditions: a reasonable connection between the items or services and medical care of the beneficiary; the items or services are in-kind and are preventive care, or advance one or more of the clinical goals of adherence to a treatment regime; adherence to a drug requirement; and, adherence to a follow-up care plan or management of a chronic disease or condition.

Note that these waivers are quite broad. For example, the participation and pre-participation waivers may allow donations by hospitals to physicians of electronic health records (EHRs) beyond current exceptions to the Stark law and also allow compensation by ACOs to physicians contingent upon reductions of length of stay, substitution of lower cost devices, and improvements in operating efficiency that would be prohibited under the Gainsharing CMP without a favorable advisory opinion from the OIG.

An important open question is the implications of the CMS/OIG waivers beyond the MSSP. CMS and OIG resisted appeals to make these waivers applicable to ACOs participating in arrangements with commercial insurers or employers. However, the interim final rule states "avenues exist to provide flexibility for ACOs participating in commercial

ACOs ... nothing precludes arrangements 'downstream' of commercial plans (for example, arrangements between hospitals and physician groups) from qualifying for the [MSSP] participation waiver." The interim final rule also solicited comments as to whether a specific waiver should apply to shared savings derived from commercial plans and "if so how we should define a comparable program with sufficient precision." On what basis should such a waiver be established? Does this imply a willingness by HHS to recognize that provider coordination serves the purposes of the MSSP even in the context of serving commercial payers?

REVIEW PROBLEM

Go back to the recommendations you made to enable Magna Hospital to partner with physicians in Chapter 12, page 528. What cautionary advice will you add in view of what you have learned in this chapter?

CHAPTER 14

ANTITRUST

■ ■ ■

I.   INTRODUCTION

Antitrust law has played a pivotal role in the development of institutional and professional arrangements in health care. Following the Supreme Court's decision in Goldfarb v. Virginia State Bar, 421 U.S. 773 (1975), which held that "learned professions" were not implicitly exempt from the antitrust laws and found the Sherman Act's interstate commerce requirement satisfied with regard to legal services, extensive antitrust litigation spurred significant changes in the health care industry. Most importantly, cases following *Goldfarb* helped remove a series of private restraints of trade that had long inhibited competition.

Antitrust enforcement has come to assume a somewhat different, albeit equally important, focus in today's market. The law has emerged as a powerful overseer of institutional and professional arrangements and ideally helps assure the evolution of market structures that will preserve the benefits of a competitive marketplace.

Many of the key elements of the Affordable Care Act discussed elsewhere in this casebook are designed to improve market competition. For example, health insurance exchanges are designed to facilitate comparison shopping by standardizing insurance products and encouraging competitive offerings. Some of the innovative programs created by the health reform law establish organizational structures more conducive to effective competition, most notably patient-centered medical homes and accountable care organizations. Changes to the mechanics of bidding for Medicare Advantage contracts, as well as expanded competitive bidding for medical devices, also reflect a greater reliance on competition. Consequently, antitrust enforcement will play a key role in effectuating the goals of the ACA. See generally, Thomas L. Greaney, The Affordable Care Act and Competition Policy: Antidote or Placebo? 89 Or. L. Rev. 811 (2011). However, antitrust law may not have an effective solution to the extensive concentration that has developed in many provider and health insurance markets which may undermine competition. See Robert A. Berenson et al., Unchecked Provider Clout In California Foreshadows Challenges To Health Reform, 29 Health Aff. 699 (2010).

Applying antitrust law to the health care industry entails some special problems. In particular, the peculiarities and distortions of health care markets often necessitate a sophisticated analysis in order to reach economically sound results. A host of questions arise: What place is there for defenses related to the quality of health care in a statutory regime designed to leave such issues to the market? Does the behavior of not-for-profit health care providers conform to traditional economic assumptions about competitors? If not, should they somehow be treated differently? What impact do the widespread interventions by state and federal government have on the application of federal antitrust law? Do "market failures" in health care, particularly imperfect information, suggest more restrained approaches to applying antitrust law? Perspectives on these and other questions underlying antitrust's role are found in a number of academic writings. See, e.g. Peter J. Hammer & William M. Sage, Antitrust, Health Care Quality, and the Courts, 102 Colum. L. Rev. 545 (2002); Thomas L. Greaney, Chicago's Procrustean Bed: Applying Antitrust Law in Health Care, 71 Antitrust L.J. 857 (2004) (courts' pervasive neglect of market failures in health care antitrust cases systematically biases outcomes); Thomas Rice, The Economics of Health Care Reconsidered (1998) (questioning whether market forces will produce efficient or socially desirable outcomes); Sara Rosenbaum, A Dose of Reality: Assessing the Federal Trade Commission/Department of Justice Report in an Uninsured, Underserved, and Vulnerable Population Context, 31 J. Health Pol. Pol'y & L. 657 (2006).

The Statutory Framework

The principal antitrust statutes are notable for their highly generalized proscriptions. Rather than specifying activities that it deemed harmful to competition, Congress vested the federal courts with the power to create a common law of antitrust.

This chapter will not deal with all of the antitrust laws applicable to the health care industry. The following introduction summarizes portions of the three principal federal statutes: the Sherman Act, the Federal Trade Commission Act, and the Clayton Act. It should be noted that most states have enacted antitrust statutes that are identical to or closely track these federal laws.

Sherman Act § 1: Restraints of Trade

Section One of the Sherman Act prohibits "every contract, combination . . . or conspiracy in restraint of trade." 15 U.S.C. § 1. This broad proscription establishes two substantive elements for finding a violation: an agreement and conduct that restrains trade. The concept of an agreement—the conventional shorthand for Section One's "contract, combination or conspiracy" language—limits the law's reach to concerted activities, i.e., those that are a result of a "meeting of the minds" of two or more independent persons or entities. The second requirement of Section One, that the agreement restrain trade, has generated extensive analysis by the courts. Recognizing that all commercial agreements restrain trade, the Supreme Court has narrowed the inquiry to condemn only "unreasonable restraints" and has developed presumptive ("*per se*") rules to simplify judicial inquiries in particular circumstances. Among the restraints of trade that are reached by Section One are: price fixing (the setting of prices or terms of sale cooperatively by two or more businesses that do not involve sharing substantial risk in a common business enterprise); market division (allocating product lines, customers, or territories between competitors); exclusive dealing (requiring that a person deal exclusively with an enterprise so that competitors are foreclosed or otherwise disadvantaged in the marketplace); group boycotts (competitors collectively refusing to deal, usually taking the form of denying a rival an input or something it needs to compete in the marketplace); and tying arrangements (a firm with market power selling one product on the condition that the buyer buy a second product from it).

Sherman Act § 2: Monopolization and Attempted Monopolization

Section Two of the Sherman Act prohibits monopolization, attempted monopolization, and conspiracies to monopolize. 15 U.S.C. § 2. Unlike Section One, it is primarily directed at unilateral conduct. Monopolization entails two elements: the possession of monopoly power, defined as the power to control market prices or exclude competition, and the willful acquisition or maintenance of that power as distinguished from growth or development as a consequence of a superior product, business acumen, or historic accident.

Clayton Act § 7: Mergers and Acquisitions

Section Seven of the Clayton Act prohibits mergers and acquisitions where the effect may be "substantially to lessen competition" or "to tend to create a monopoly." 15 U.S.C. § 18. To test the legality of a proposed merger or acquisition, courts emphasize market share and concentration data but also take other factors into consideration to determine whether a merger makes it more likely than not that the merged firm will exercise market power.

Defenses and Exemptions

There are numerous statutory and judicially-crafted defenses to antitrust liability, several of which are of particular importance to health care antitrust litigation. The state action doctrine exempts from antitrust liability actions taken pursuant to a clearly expressed state policy to restrict free competition, where the challenged conduct is under the active control and supervision of the state. The high degree of state regulation of health care has spawned state action defenses in staff privileges cases, for example, when state law authorizes public hospitals to undertake mergers that lessen competition and supervises their conduct. The McCarran–Ferguson Act generally exempts the "business of insurance" from antitrust enforcement to the extent that the particular insurance activities are regulated by state law. 15 U.S.C. § 1011. (This should not be taken to mean, however, that "insurance companies" are exempt from antitrust scrutiny). The Noerr–Pennington doctrine protects the exercise of the First Amendment right to petition the government, so long as the "petitioning" is not merely a "sham" to cover anti-competitive behavior. This defense is relevant to lobbying efforts on health care issues and to participation in administrative proceedings, such as certificate-of-need applications, each of which may lead to an outcome that lessens competition. The most recent statutory defense relevant to health care is the Health Care Quality Improvement Act, 42 U.S.C. §§ 11101–11152, enacted by Congress in 1986, which grants limited immunity for peer review activities.

Interpretive Principles

The Law's Exclusive Focus on Competitive Concerns

There has long been widespread agreement in the case law that antitrust inquiries should focus exclusively on competitive effects and should not take into account purported non-economic benefits of collective activities such as advancing social policies or even protecting public safety. See National Society of Professional Engineers v. United States, 435 U.S. 679 (1978) (rejecting as a matter of law a professional society's safety justifications for its ban on competitive bidding). This self-imposed boundary is based on the judiciary's skepticism about its competence to balance disparate social policies and the judgment that such concerns are more appropriately addressed to the legislature. Importantly, then, under Section One of the Sherman Act, courts will not consider justifications other than those asserting that a practice, on balance, promotes competition. As discussed *infra*, this constraint is in obvious tension with justifications by professionals that their collective activities have the purpose of advancing the quality of patient care.

Per Se Rules and the Rule of Reason

Traditionally, judicial analyses of conduct under Section One of the Sherman Act have employed two approaches to testing the "reasonableness" of restraints. Some activities, such as price fixing, market allocations, and certain group boycotts have been considered so likely to harm competition that they are deemed illegal *"per se."* That is, if a plaintiff can prove that the defendant's conduct fits within one of these categories, the inquiry ends; the agreement itself constitutes a violation of the statute. In effect, then, the per se categorization establishes a conclusive presumption of illegality.

Activities not falling within the *per se* rubric are subject to broader examination under the rule of reason. Under this form of analysis, defendants escape liability if they prove that the pro-competitive benefits of the challenged activity outweigh any anticompetitive effects so that competition, the singular policy concern of the statute, is strengthened rather than restrained. In theory, courts undertaking a full-blown rule of reason analysis will balance competitive harms against competitive benefits. For example, if a large number of hospitals collectively assembled and shared information about the utilization practices of physicians on their staffs, a court might balance the potential collusive harm resulting from lessened inter-hospital competition against the market-wide competitive benefits of dispensing such information—assuming the information was shared with payors.

In practice, however, such fact-specific balancing is rarely done. Courts usually truncate the process in one of several ways. For example, they may find that an alleged restraint has no possibility of harming competition where the colluding parties lack "market power." As a proxy for market power, which is defined as the ability profitably to raise price (or reduce quality or output), courts estimate the market shares of the colluding parties and examine other market conditions. Doing this, of course, requires that the fact finder define the dimensions of the geographic and product markets—determinations that require the exercise of considerable judgment. Even where a party has a high market share and there are relatively few competitors, however, market power still may be lacking. For example, the colluding parties may be unable to raise price because entry by others is easy or because buyers would quickly detect such an increase and cease dealing with the parties.

Indeed, in recent years, a series of Supreme Court decisions have shifted antitrust analyses away from a rigid per se/rule of reason dichotomy, treating the approaches instead as "complementary" and essentially establishing a continuum of levels of scrutiny. Thus, the modern approach allows courts to undertake threshold examinations of purported justifications and competitive effects before characterizing the conduct as governed by the per se rule. By the same token, courts may need only a "quick look" to condemn conduct under the rule of reason; they may dispense with prolonged factual inquiries when the truncated review reveals that purported efficiency benefits are lacking or an anticompetitive effect is obvious.

II.   CARTELS AND PROFESSIONALISM

A. CLASSIC CARTELS

IN RE MICHIGAN STATE MEDICAL SOCIETY
Federal Trade Commission, 1983.
101 F.T.C. 191.

Opinion of the Commission

BY CLANTON, COMMISSIONER:

I.   Introduction

This case involves allegations that direct competitors, acting through a professional association, conspired to restrain trade by organizing boycotts and tampering with the fees received from third party insurers of their services. Of particular antitrust significance is the fact that the competitors are medical doctors practicing in Michigan, the association is the Michigan State Medical Society ["MSMS"], and the insurers are Blue Cross and Blue Shield of Michigan ("BCBSM") and Michigan Medicaid.

More specifically, the complaint in this matter charges, and the administrative law judge found, that the medical society unlawfully conspired with its members to influence third-party reimbursement policies in the following ways: by seeking to negotiate collective agreements with insurers; by agreeing to use coercive measures like proxy solicitation and group boycotts; and by actually making coercive threats to third party payers. * * *

*   *   *

Becoming frustrated in its negotiations with BCBSM on [issues regarding reimbursement], MSMS authorized its first proxy solicitation. Reacting to what it perceived to be the recalcitrant attitude of Blue Shield on the subjects of regionalization of fees and physician profiles, coupled with what appears to be a total lack of willingness to cooperate with MSMS in the development of a uniform claim form or even consider the use of the CPT procedural code, [ ] the Negotiating Committee recommended that the House of Delegates urge MSMS members to write letters to BCBSM withdrawing from participation but mail them to the Negotiating Committee to be held as "proxies." The House of Delegates authorized the committee to collect the proxies, but to use them only at the discretion of the Council, with prior notice to the members who submitted them, "if a negotiating impasse develops with Michigan Blue Cross/Blue Shield." [ ]

*   *   *

Each member of MSMS was urged by letter to resist "so-called cost-containment programs that in effect reduce reimbursement to physicians or place the responsibility for the reduction of costs solely on the practicing physician." [ ] he letter, from the Council chairman, referred pointedly to the fact that a threshold percentage of physicians must formally participate in order for BCBSM to operate under its enabling legislation. It enclosed two blank "powers of attorney," one for BCBSM and one for Medicaid, empowering the Negotiating Committee to cancel the signer's participation in either program if such action was deemed warranted by the Council. These powers of attorney were revocable at any time. * * *

As a result of this response, [a] dispute over radiologists' and pathologists' reimbursement was resolved in MSMS' favor with the status quo being preserved and BCBSM withdrawing its proposal. [ ] As explained below, these proxies also played a role in MSMS' dealings with Medicaid.

[In response to additional efforts by BCBSM to reduce utilization of physician services, the leadership of MSMS advised members to react to new reimbursement policies by writing letters threatening departicipation or actually withdrawing from participation. In addition, MSMS representatives protested cuts of approximately 11% in physician reimbursement under the Medicaid program by "waving" the departicipation proxies during meetings with the Governor and Medicaid officials. Although evidence suggested that physician participants in the Medicaid program fell off markedly after the MSMS collective action, the Commission did not find that state officials had been coerced by these actions.]

* * *

Conspiracy Allegations

The threshold issue here is whether MSMS' importunings with BCBSM and the Medicaid program amounted to conspiratorial conduct of the kind alleged in the complaint or simply represented nonbinding expressions of views and policy, as argued by respondent. [ ] As discussed previously, the evidence quite clearly reveals that MSMS members, acting through their House of Delegates, agreed in 1976 to establish a Division of Negotiations for the purpose of working out differences with third party payers. The Division was specifically empowered, *inter alia*, to coordinate all negotiating activities of MSMS, collect "non-participation" proxies and obtain a negotiated participation agreement with third party payers that would obviate the need for physician non-participation. [ ] It also was specifically contemplated by MSMS that the Division of Negotiations would obtain authorization of all members to serve as their "exclusive bargaining agent." The debate in the House of Delegates clearly indicated that, although the Division would not negotiate specific fees, it would have authority to negotiate the manner by which fees or reimbursement levels would be established. [ ]

Thus, at the outset we find that the very creation of the Division of Negotiations reveals a collective purpose on the part of MSMS and its members to go beyond the point of giving advice to third party payers; in fact, it reveals a purpose to organize and empower a full-fledged representative to negotiate and resolve controversies surrounding physician profiles, screens and other similar matters. [ ] There is, in fact, considerable additional evidence that the Negotiating Division not only had the authority to reach understandings with third party payers but also utilized that authority (acting as agent for its members) in soliciting, collecting and threatening to exercise physician departicipation proxies, as well as in other negotiations with third party payers.

* * *

Turning to the boycott issue, the law is clear that the definition of that term is not limited to situations where the target of the concerted refusal to deal is another competitor or potential competitor. As the Supreme Court indicated, . . . a concerted refusal to deal may be characterized as an unlawful group boycott where the target is a customer or supplier of the combining parties. [ ] In the instant case, the alleged boycott involves concerted threats by MSMS and its members to refrain from participating in BCBSM and Medicaid unless the latter modified their reimbursement policies. Although BCBSM and Medicaid—the targets of the boycott—are not in competitive relationships with MSMS, that fact alone does not preclude a finding of a boycott.

Respondent, however, argues that the proxies were not exercised and, in the case of the departicipation letter campaign, that there was no adverse effect on BCBSM. As to the latter contention, MSMS points out that more physicians signed up to participate in BCBSM during the relevant period than withdrew from the program as a result of the campaign. The success [or] failure of a group boycott or price-fixing agreement, however, is irrelevant to the question of either its existence or its legality. Whether or not the action succeeds, "[i]t is the concerted activity for a common purpose that constitutes the violation." [ ] Furthermore, an agreement among competitors affecting price does not have to be successful in order to be condemned.

It is the "contract, combination. . . or conspiracy in restraint of trade or commerce" which § 1 of the [Sherman] Act strikes down, whether the concerted activity be wholly nascent or abortive on the one hand, or successful on the other. [ ]

Moreover, even if less than all members of an organization or association agree to participate, that fact does not negate the presence of a conspiracy or combination as to those who do participate. [ ]

As for the collection of proxies that were never exercised, the law does not require that a competitor actually refuse to deal before a boycott can be found or liability established. Rather, the threat to refuse to deal may suffice to constitute the offense. [ ] The evidence indicates that the threat implicit in the collection of departicipation proxies and the attendant publicity can be as effective as the actual execution of the threatened action. Indeed, it may be assumed that parties to a concerted refusal to deal hope that the announcement of the intended action will be sufficient to produce the desired response. That appears to be precisely what happened here, and there are contemporaneous testimonials by MSMS officials confirming the success of that strategy. For example, Dr. Crandall suggested that MSMS' "waving the proxies in the face of the legislature" persuaded the state attorney general that if he sued MSMS the state would have "orchestrated the demise of the entire Michigan Medicaid program." [ ] Also, as noted above, the Negotiations Division credited the members' response to the proxy solicitation with the favorable outcome of the dispute between the radiologists and BCBSM. [ ] And, as further evidence, there is the fact that MSMS reached a formal agreement with BCBSM which included the implementation of a statewide screen. [ ]

*   *   *

B. Legality of the Concerted Action

*   *   *

[I]t would appear that respondent's conduct approaches the kind of behavior that previously has been classified as per se illegal. Nevertheless, since this conduct does not involve direct fee setting, we are not prepared to declare it per se illegal at this juncture and close the door on all asserted pro-competitive justifications. * * *

To briefly recap, respondent has offered the following justifications for its behavior: (1) the practices had no effect on fee levels and, in any event, BCBSM and Medicaid took independent action to correct the perceived problems; (2) MSMS simply sought to insure that physicians were treated fairly especially in view of BCBSM's bargaining power; (3) the actions were, in part, an effort to counter BCBSM's violations of its charter and Michigan law in connection with its modified participation program; and (4) MSMS was striving to correct abuses of the Medicaid system and the poor perpetrated by "Medicaid mills."

With respect to respondent's first contention, MSMS claims that the conduct never led to uniform fees or prevented individual physicians from deciding whether to participate in BCBSM or Medicaid. We believe that these arguments miss the point with respect to the likely competitive effects of the restrictive practices. Where horizontal arrangements so closely relate to prices or fees as they do here, a less elaborate analysis of competitive effects is required. [ ] The collective actions under scrutiny clearly interfere with the rights of physicians to compete independently on the terms of insurance coverage offered by BCBSM and Medicaid. Moreover, the joint arrangements directly hamper the ability of third party payers to compete freely for the patronage of individual physicians and other physician business entities. * * *

* 　 * 　 *

On the question of whether the proposed policies of BCBSM and Medicaid were fair to physicians, respondent would apparently have us become enmeshed in weighing the comparative equities of the different parties to these transactions. In fact, considerable portions of the record are devoted to an assessment of the relative merits of MSMS' bargaining position. For us to consider whether the terms offered by the third party payers were fair or reasonable would lead us into the kind of regulatory posture that the courts have long rejected. [ ] It would be analogous to the Commission serving as a quasi-public utility agency concerned with balancing interests unrelated to antitrust concerns. We believe that it is undesirable and inappropriate for us to step in and attempt to determine which party had the better case in these dealings. [Ed. Note: The Commission found that the objective of correcting violations of law cannot justify a group boycott because alternative means of seeking redress were available.]

* 　 * 　 *

* * * Respondent also suggests that its activities were motivated by concern for the welfare of its members' patients, especially in the case of Medicaid where, it is alleged, reductions in reimbursement levels might lead to lower physician participation rates and force low-income patients to seek less reputable providers (the so-called Medicaid mills). [ ]

* * * We concluded there that the relationship between such reimbursement mechanisms and health care quality was simply too tenuous, from a competitive perspective, to justify the broad restrictions imposed.

While we are not addressing ethical standards in this case, many of the quality and patient welfare arguments asserted here have a ring similar to those advanced in *AMA* [Ed. Note: *In re AMA*, discussed *infra*, in which the FTC rejected a ban on advertising justified by defendants as protecting informed consumer choice and a prohibition on contract-based reimbursement which defendants claimed resulted in harm to the public and inferior quality of medical service]. Even in the case of Medicaid reductions, where an argument might be made that arbitrary cuts could be counter-productive by impairing physicians' economic incentives to treat the poor, it is difficult to see how concerted agreements and refusals to deal can be sanctioned as a means of fighting proposed payment cutbacks.

While granting MSMS' laudable concerns about the effects of physician withdrawal from Medicaid, we observe that respondent clearly had public forums [ ] available to it to correct perceived mistakes made by the state legislature or the administrators of Medicaid; it could have expressed its views in ways that fell well short of organized boycott threats.

Finally, we find no suggestion among MSMS' justifications that the concerted behavior here enhanced competition in any market by injecting new elements or forms of competition, reducing entry barriers, or facilitating or broadening consumer choice. The price-related practices in question here are not ancillary to some broader pro-competitive purpose, such as a joint venture, an integration of activities, or an offer of a new product or service. * * *

*   *   *

In fact, we believe there are less anti-competitive ways of providing such information to insurers. The order that we would impose upon respondent allows it to provide information and views to insurers on behalf of its members, so long as the Society does not attempt to extract agreements, through coercion or otherwise, from third party payers on reimbursement issues. [ ] In allowing respondent to engage in non-binding, non-coercive discussions with health insurers, we have attempted to strike a proper balance between the need for insurers to have efficient access to the views of large groups of providers and the need to prevent competitors from banding together in ways that involve the unreasonable exercise of collective market power. [ ]

*   *   *

NOTES AND QUESTIONS

1. Although the Commission does not invoke the per se label, note that its analysis does not require proof of an actual effect on prices. How does it treat the justifications proffered by the medical society? Do any meet the requirement discussed in the introduction to this chapter that justifications must concern pro-competitive benefits arising from the restraint? On the other hand, might there be situations in which collective negotiations could be viewed as a market-improving step if they corrected market imperfections? See Thomas L. Greaney, Quality of Care and Market Failure Defenses in Antitrust Health Care Litigation, 21 Conn. L. Rev. 605, 650–52 (1989). Boycotts traditionally have been subject to per se analysis, although the Supreme Court has cautioned in recent years that only certain collective refusals to deal will be summarily condemned. Northwest Wholesale Stationers, Inc. v. Pacific Stationery, 472 U.S. 284 (1985), While the exact boundaries of the per se rule applicable to boycotts remain murky, plausible pro-competitive justifications for collective refusals to deal will remove conduct from per se classification where, for example, providers were excluded from an IPA based on

valid cost containment objectives. See Hahn v. Oregon Physicians' Service, 868 F.2d 1022 (9th Cir. 1988). At the same time, the federal agencies have successfully challenged scores of provider cartels that engaged in a wide variety of practices designed to raise prices, thwart competition from other providers, or stymie cost containment efforts of managed care organizations. For example, the FTC challenged and settled by consent agreement the actions of Montana Associated Physicians, Inc., an organization of independent physician practices constituting 43% of all the physicians in Billings, Montana that had been formed to present a "united front" when dealing with managed care plans in order to resist competitive pressures to discount fees and forestall entry of HMOs and PPOs into the area. In re Montana Associated Physicians, Inc. and Billings Physician Hospital Alliance, Inc., FTC Docket No. C–3704, 62 Fed. Reg. 11,201 (1997). See also United (hospitals' joint refusal to extend discounts in bidding for contracts); American Medical Association, 94 F.T.C. 701 (1979) (final order and opinion), aff'd, 638 F.2d 443 (2d Cir. 1980), aff'd by an equally divided court, 455 U.S. 676 (1982) (ethical rules barring salaried employment, working for "inadequate compensation," and affiliating with non-physicians).

2.   In FTC v. Indiana Federation of Dentists, 476 U.S. 447 (1986), the FTC challenged an agreement among dentists to refuse to submit x-rays used for diagnosis and treatment of patients to insurers. Insurers required x-rays to carry out review of the necessity of treatment pursuant to dental insurance plans limiting payment to the "least expensive yet adequate treatment." While not employing the per se rule, the Court adopted the form of analysis described in CDA as a "quick look."

> Application of the Rule of Reason to these facts is not a matter of any great difficulty. The Federation's policy takes the form of a horizontal agreement among the participating dentists to withhold from their customers a particular service that they desire—the forwarding of x-rays to insurance companies along with claim forms. "While this is not price fixing as such, no elaborate industry analysis is required to demonstrate the anti-competitive character of such an agreement." ... A refusal to compete with respect to the package of services offered to customers, no less than a refusal to compete with respect to the price term of an agreement, impairs the ability of the market to advance social welfare by ensuring the provision of desired goods and services to consumers at a price approximating the marginal cost of providing them.

Id. at 459.

3.   Should courts consider defendant's potential to improve the quality of care as a defense or mitigating factor in a case involving professional restraints of trade? The Supreme Court addressed the defendants' quality of care justifications in Indiana Federation of Dentists, 476 U.S. at 462–463:

The gist of [defendant's] claim is that x-rays, standing alone, are not adequate bases for diagnosis of dental problems or for the formulation of an acceptable course of treatment. Accordingly, if insurance companies are permitted to determine whether they will pay a claim for dental treatment on the basis of x-rays as opposed to a full examination of all the diagnostic aids available to the examining dentist, there is a danger that they will erroneously decline to pay for treatment that is in fact in the interest of the patient, and that the patient will as a result be deprived of fully adequate care.

The Federation's argument is flawed both legally and factually. The premise of the argument is that, far from having no effect on the cost of dental services chosen by patients and their insurers, the provision of x-rays will have too great an impact: it will lead to the reduction of costs through the selection of inadequate treatment. . . . The argument is, in essence, that an unrestrained market in which consumers are given access to the information they believe to be relevant to their choices will lead them to make unwise and even dangerous choices. Such an argument amounts to "nothing less than a frontal assault on the basic policy of the Sherman Act." [ ]

Moreover, there is no particular reason to believe that the provision of information will be more harmful to consumers in the market for dental services than in other markets. Insurers deciding what level of care to pay for are not themselves the recipients of those services, but it is by no means clear that they lack incentives to consider the welfare of the patient as well as the minimization of costs. They are themselves in competition for the patronage of the patients—or, in most cases, the unions or businesses that contract on their behalf for group insurance coverage—and must satisfy their potential customers that they will not only provide coverage at a reasonable cost, but also that the coverage will be adequate to meet their customers' dental needs. . . .

See also National Society of Professional Engineers v. United States, 435 U.S. 679 (1978) (rejecting as a matter of law professional association's justification for banning competitive bidding based on claims that low bids would reduce quality and threaten public safety). See Thomas L. Greaney, Quality of Care and Market Failure Defenses in Antitrust Health Care Litigation, 21 Conn. L. Rev. 605 (1989).

PROBLEM: QUICK STOP CLINICS

Drug World, a pharmacy chain operating a large number of retail pharmacies in the upper Midwest, has announced plans to open 24–Hour "Quick Stop Clinics" at all its locations. The clinics will be staffed by RNs and PAs depending on state licensure and scope of practice laws. (Recall the "Retail Clinic" problem in Chapter 2). These providers will perform routine exams, take cultures, and prescribe medications within the scope of practice permitted under state law. Each clinic will enter into referral agreements with one or more local hospitals to assure direct access to physicians when the need presents. Good Samaritan Hospital (GSH) has entered into such an arrangement with a local Quick Stop Clinic. Under their partnership agreement, all doctors providing back up to Quick Stop RNs will have admitting privileges at GSH, and the clinics will be able to "streamline" a patient's journey to a specialist or through the emergency room at GSH, when medically appropriate.

A number of doctors holding staff privileges at GSH became quite upset when they got wind of this agreement. The group, though small (fewer than 5% of all doctors with privileges at the hospital), includes both primary care physicians who are concerned about losing current patients to the doctors to whom the clinic refers and several prominent specialists who feel they will lose established lines of referrals from primary care physicians. Some doctors believe that patients will come to them in worse shape, with missed diagnoses, and inadequate follow up. They have posted a notice at the hospital calling for an emergency meeting to discuss options to counter GSH's plan. The doctors propose three possible courses of action, asking colleagues to:

- Agree that no doctors will serve as a collaborating or supervisory physician to Quick Stop Clinic RNs or PAs or accept referrals from the Clinic;

- Sign a letter to GSH administrators announcing plans to change their admitting practices so as to reduce the number of patients they admit to GSH; or

- Send a letter to all GSH physicians supplying academic studies and historical evidence of potential risks to patients who receive care from nonphysicians under arrangements such as those proposed.

The CEO of GSH has approached you for advice on the legality of each action contemplated by the staff physicians. She says she wants to fight them vigorously and that she is willing to consider filing an antitrust lawsuit, complaining to the Department of Justice, terminating the staff privileges of the ringleaders of the group, or undertaking any other steps you recommend.

III.   HEALTH CARE ENTERPRISES, INTEGRATION AND FINANCING

As discussed in Chapter 12, *supra*, the integration and consolidation of the health care industry spawned a wide variety of provider networks, alliances, and new organizational arrangements. These entities and contractual relationships often entail cooperation or outright mergers between previously competing providers or health plans seeking to achieve efficiencies and improve quality of care. They also raise the full spectrum of antitrust issues. For health care attorneys counseling clients forming such organizations, antitrust law merits close attention because many entities are quite openly seeking to acquire the maximum leverage they can in the competitive fray.

A. PROVIDER–CONTROLLED NETWORKS AND HEALTH PLANS

ARIZONA V. MARICOPA COUNTY MEDICAL SOCIETY
Supreme Court of the United States, 1982.
457 U.S. 332, 102 S.Ct. 2466, 73 L.Ed.2d 48.

JUSTICE STEVENS delivered the opinion of the Court.

The question presented is whether § 1 of the Sherman Act [ ] has been violated by agreements among competing physicians setting, by majority vote, the maximum fees that they may claim in full payment for health services provided to policyholders of specified insurance plans. The United States Court of Appeals for the Ninth Circuit held that the question could not be answered without evaluating the actual purpose and effect of the agreements at a full trial. [ ] Because the undisputed facts disclose a violation of the statute, we granted certiorari, and now reverse.

* * *

II

[The Maricopa Foundation for Medical Care a nonprofit Arizona corporation composed of approximately 1,750 doctors, representing about 70% of the practitioners in Maricopa County. The Maricopa Foundation and another similarly structured foundation were organized for the purpose of promoting fee-for-service medicine and providing a competitive alternative to existing health insurance plans. [ ] The foundations establish a schedule of maximum fees that participating doctors agree to accept as payment in full for services performed for patients insured under plans approved by the foundation and review the medical necessity and appropriateness of treatment provided by its members to such insured persons. Foundation doctors are free to charge higher fees to uninsured patients, and they also may charge any patient less than the scheduled maxima].

* * *

III

The respondents recognize that our decisions establish that price-fixing agreements are unlawful on their face. But they argue that the *per se* rule does not govern this case because the agreements at issue are horizontal and fix maximum prices, are among members of a profession, are in an industry with which the judiciary has little antitrust experience, and are alleged to have pro-competitive justifications. * * *

* * *

B

Our decisions foreclose the argument that the agreements at issue escape *per se* condemnation because they are horizontal and fix maximum prices. [The cases] place horizontal agreements to fix maximum prices on the same legal—even if not economic—footing as agreements to fix minimum or uniform prices. [ ] The per se rule "is grounded on faith in price competition as a market force [and not] on a policy of low selling prices at the price of eliminating competition." [ ] In this case the rule is violated by a price restraint that tends to provide the same economic rewards to all practitioners regardless of their skill, their experience, their training, or their willingness to employ innovative and difficult procedures in individual cases. Such a restraint also may discourage entry into the market and may deter experimentation and new developments by individual entrepreneurs. It may be a masquerade for an agreement to fix uniform prices, or it may in the future take on that character.

* * *

We are equally unpersuaded by the argument that we should not apply the *per se* rule in this case because the judiciary has little antitrust experience in the health care industry. *****

The respondents' principal argument is that the *per se* rule is inapplicable because their agreements are alleged to have pro-competitive justifications. The argument indicates a misunderstanding of the *per se* concept. The anti-competitive potential inherent in all price-fixing agreements justifies their facial invalidation even if pro-competitive justifications are offered for some. [ ] Those claims of enhanced competition are so unlikely to prove significant in any particular case that we adhere to the rule of law that is justified in its general application. Even when the respondents are given every benefit of the doubt, the limited record in this case is not inconsistent with the presumption that the respondents' agreements will not significantly enhance competition.

It is true that a binding assurance of complete insurance coverage—as well as most of the respondents' potential for lower insurance premiums[25]—can be obtained only if the insurer and the doctor agree in ad-

---

[25] We do not perceive the respondents' claim of procompetitive justification for their fee schedules to rest on the premise that the fee schedules actually reduce medical fees and accordingly reduce insurance premiums, thereby enhancing competition in the health insurance industry. Such an argument would merely restate the long-rejected position that fixed prices are reasonable if they are lower than free competition would yield. It is arguable, however, that the existence of a fee schedule, whether fixed by the doctors or by the insurers, makes it easier—and

vance on the maximum fee that the doctor will accept as full payment for a particular service. Even if a fee schedule is therefore desirable, it is not necessary that the doctors do the price fixing. ***

* * *

IV

Having declined the respondents' invitation to cut back on the per se rule against price fixing, we are left with the respondents' argument that their fee schedules involve price fixing in only a literal sense. For this argument, the respondents rely upon Broadcast Music, Inc. v. Columbia Broadcasting System, Inc., 441 U.S. 1, 99 S.Ct. 1551, 60 L.Ed.2d 1 (1979).

In *Broadcast Music* we were confronted with an antitrust challenge to the marketing of the right to use copyrighted compositions derived from the entire membership of the American Society of Composers, Authors and Publishers (ASCAP). The so-called "blanket license" was entirely different from the product that any one composer was able to sell by himself. [ ] Although there was little competition among individual composers for their separate compositions, the blanket-license arrangement did not place any restraint on the right of any individual copyright owner to sell his own compositions separately to any buyer at any price. [ ] But a "necessary consequence" of the creation of the blanket license was that its price had to be established. [ ] We held that the delegation by the composers to ASCAP of the power to fix the price for the blanket license was not a species of the price-fixing agreements categorically forbidden by the Sherman Act. The record disclosed price fixing only in a "literal sense." [ ]

This case is fundamentally different. Each of the foundations is composed of individual practitioners who compete with one another for patients. Neither the foundations nor the doctors sell insurance, and they derive no profits from the sale of health insurance policies. The members of the foundations sell medical services. Their combination in the form of the foundation does not permit them to sell any different product. [ ] Their combination has merely permitted them to sell their services to certain customers at fixed prices and arguably to affect the prevailing market price of medical care.

The foundations are not analogous to partnerships or other joint arrangements in which persons who would otherwise be competitors pool their capital and share the risks of loss as well as the opportunities for profit. In such joint ventures, the partnership is regarded as a single firm competing with other sellers in the market. The agreement under attack is an agreement among hundreds of competing doctors concerning the price at which each will offer his own services to a substantial number of

to that extent less expensive—for insurers to calculate the risks that they underwrite and to arrive at the appropriate reimbursement on insured claims.

656 ANTITRUST CH. 14

consumers. It is true that some are surgeons, some anesthesiologists, and some psychiatrists, but the doctors do not sell a package of three kinds of services. If a clinic offered complete medical coverage for a flat fee, the cooperating doctors would have the type of partnership arrangement in which a price-fixing agreement among the doctors would be perfectly proper. But the fee agreements disclosed by the record in this case are among independent competing entrepreneurs. They fit squarely into the horizontal price-fixing mold.

The judgment of the Court of Appeals is reversed.

It is so ordered.

NOTES AND QUESTIONS

1. The plurality opinion in *Maricopa* has been criticized for its wooden application of the per se rule. Three dissenting Justices stressed that the foundations enabled the doctors to offer a "new product" that would be unavailable in the market and offered "otherwise unattainable efficiencies." Another notable feature was the fact that the foundations adopted maximum, rather than minimum, fee schedules. Commentators contend that the dangers of maximum price fixing are not sufficiently large to justify per se treatment. Is it possible that the foundation may have adopted its pricing policies with an eye to limiting the risk of entry by HMOs? In that case wouldn't the arrangement be objectionable for its propensity to preserve supracompetitive prices, albeit at a lower level than existed before the foundations were formed?

2. *Maricopa* left open many questions about when integration among providers would be permissible, especially those involving PPOs having little financial integration. The formation of networks or other joint ventures as part of accountable care organizations has focused considerable attention on degree of integration among participating physicians. The FTC/Department of Justice Policy Statements, which have been revised several times since their original promulgation in 1994, give guidance on several important issues. Compare the agencies' analysis in the following Policy Statement and Advisory Opinions with *Maricopa's* treatment of issues such as risk sharing, market power and efficiencies.

U.S. DEPARTMENT OF JUSTICE AND FEDERAL TRADE COMMISSION, STATEMENTS OF ANTITRUST ENFORCEMENT POLICY IN HEALTH CARE

4 Trade Reg. Rep. (CCH) para. 13,153.
(August 18, 1996).

8. Statement of Department of Justice and Federal Trade Commission Enforcement Policy on Physician Network Joint Ventures

* * *

A.   Antitrust Safety Zones

This section describes those physician network joint ventures that will fall within the antitrust safety zones designated by the Agencies. The antitrust safety zones differ for "exclusive" and "non-exclusive" physician network joint ventures. In an "exclusive" venture, the network's physician participants are restricted in their ability to, or do not in practice, individually contract or affiliate with other network joint ventures or health plans. In a "non-exclusive" venture, on the other hand, the physician participants in fact do, or are available to, affiliate with other networks or contract individually with health plans. * * *

1.   Exclusive Physician Network Joint Ventures That the Agencies Will Not Challenge, Absent Extraordinary Circumstances

The Agencies will not challenge, absent extraordinary circumstances, an exclusive physician network joint venture whose physician participants share substantial financial risk and constitute 20 percent or less of the physicians [ ] in each physician specialty with active hospital staff privileges who practice in the relevant geographic market. [ ] In relevant markets with fewer than five physicians in a particular specialty, an exclusive physician network joint venture otherwise qualifying for the antitrust safety zone may include one physician from that specialty, on a non-exclusive basis, even though the inclusion of that physician results in the venture consisting of more than 20 percent of the physicians in that specialty.

2.   Non–Exclusive Physician Network Joint Ventures That the Agencies Will Not Challenge, Absent Extraordinary Circumstances

The Agencies will not challenge, absent extraordinary circumstances, a non-exclusive physician network joint venture whose physician participants share substantial financial risk and constitute 30 percent or less of the physicians in each physician specialty with active hospital staff privileges who practice in the relevant geographic market. In relevant markets with fewer than four physicians in a particular specialty, a non-exclusive physician network joint venture otherwise qualifying for the antitrust safety zone may include one physician from that specialty, even though the inclusion of that physician results in the venture consisting of more than 30 percent of the physicians in that specialty.

3.   Indicia of Non–Exclusivity

* * * [T]he Agencies caution physician participants in a non-exclusive physician network joint venture to be sure that the network is non-exclusive in fact and not just in name. The Agencies will determine whether a physician network joint venture is exclusive or non-exclusive by its physician participants' activities, and not simply by the terms of the contractual relationship. * * *

4.   Sharing Of Substantial Financial Risk by Physicians in a Physician Network Joint Venture

To qualify for either antitrust safety zone, the participants in a physician network joint venture must share substantial financial risk in providing all the services that are jointly priced through the network. [ ] The safety zones are limited to networks involving substantial financial risk sharing not because such risk sharing is a desired end in itself, but because it normally is a clear and reliable indicator that a physician network involves sufficient integration by its physician participants to achieve significant efficiencies. [ ] Risk sharing provides incentives for the physicians to cooperate in controlling costs and improving quality by managing the provision of services by network physicians.

The following are examples of some types of arrangements through which participants in a physician network joint venture can share substantial financial risk: [ ]

(1) agreement by the venture to provide services to a health plan at a "capitated" rate; [ ]

(2) agreement by the venture to provide designated services or classes of services to a health plan for a predetermined percentage of premium or revenue from the plan;

(3) use by the venture of significant financial incentives for its physician participants, as a group, to achieve specified cost-containment goals. Two methods by which the venture can accomplish this are:

(a) withholding from all physician participants in the network a substantial amount of the compensation due to them, with distribution of that amount to the physician participants based on group performance in meeting the cost-containment goals of the network as a whole; or

(b) establishing overall cost or utilization targets for the network as a whole, with the network's physician participants subject to subsequent substantial financial rewards or penalties based on group performance in meeting the targets; and

(4) agreement by the venture to provide a complex or extended course of treatment that requires the substantial coordination of care by physicians in different specialties offering a complementary mix of services, for a fixed, predetermined payment, where the costs of that course of treatment for any individual patient can vary greatly due to the individual patient's condition, the choice, complexity, or length of treatment, or other factors. * * *

B.   The Agencies' Analysis Of Physician Network Joint Ventures That Fall Outside The Antitrust Safety Zones

Physician network joint ventures that fall outside the antitrust safety zones also may have the potential to create significant efficiencies, and do not necessarily raise substantial antitrust concerns.

*   *   *

1.   Determining When Agreements Among Physicians In A Physician Network Joint Venture Are Analyzed Under The Rule Of Reason

Antitrust law treats naked agreements among competitors that fix prices or allocate markets as *per se* illegal. Where competitors economically integrate in a joint venture, however, such agreements, if reasonably necessary to accomplish the pro-competitive benefits of the integration, are analyzed under the rule of reason. [ ] In accord with general antitrust principles, physician network joint ventures will be analyzed under the rule of reason, and will not be viewed as *per se* illegal, if the physicians' integration through the network is likely to produce significant efficiencies that benefit consumers, and any price agreements (or other agreements that would otherwise be *per se* illegal) by the network physicians are reasonably necessary to realize those efficiencies. [ ]

Where the participants in a physician network joint venture have agreed to share substantial financial risk as defined in Section A.4 of this policy statement, their risk-sharing arrangement generally establishes both an overall efficiency goal for the venture and the incentives for the physicians to meet that goal. The setting of price is integral to the venture's use of such an arrangement and therefore warrants evaluation under the rule of reason.

Physician network joint ventures that do not involve the sharing of substantial financial risk may also involve sufficient integration to demonstrate that the venture is likely to produce significant efficiencies. Such integration can be evidenced by the network implementing an active and ongoing program to evaluate and modify practice patterns by the network's physician participants and create a high degree of interdependence and cooperation among the physicians to control costs and ensure quality. This program may include: (1) establishing mechanisms to monitor and control utilization of health care services that are designed to control costs and assure quality of care; (2) selectively choosing network physicians who are likely to further these efficiency objectives; and (3) the significant investment of capital, both monetary and human, in the necessary infrastructure and capability to realize the claimed efficiencies.

*   *   *

Determining that an arrangement is merely a vehicle to fix prices or engage in naked anti-competitive conduct is a factual inquiry that must be done on a case-by-case basis to determine the arrangement's true nature and likely competitive effects. However, a variety of factors may tend to corroborate a network's anti-competitive nature, including: statements evidencing anti-competitive purpose; a recent history of anti-competitive behavior or collusion in the market, including efforts to obstruct or undermine the development of managed care; obvious anti-competitive structure of the network (e.g., a network comprising a very high percentage of local area physicians, whose participation in the network is exclusive, without any plausible business or efficiency justification); the absence of any mechanisms with the potential for generating significant efficiencies or otherwise increasing competition through the network; the presence of anti-competitive collateral agreements; and the absence of mechanisms to prevent the network's operation from having anti-competitive spillover effects outside the network.

*   *   *

[The Statement sets forth the methodology for balancing anticompetitive and procompetitive effects under the rule of reason: assessing the market power of the network in each physician services relevant market; evaluating effects by considering incentives for anticompetitive conduct and whether "there are many other networks or many physicians ... available to form competing networks;" evaluating the risks of "spillover" effects on contracts outside the networks; and weighing the offsetting efficiency benefits uniquely achievable through the networks.]

NOTES AND QUESTIONS

1.   The Statements repeatedly emphasize that merely because a physician network joint venture does not fall within a safety zone does not mean that it is unlawful under the antitrust laws. Many arrangements outside the safety zones have received favorable business review letters or advisory opinions from the agencies. See, e.g., Letter from Anne K. Bingaman, Assistant Attorney General, to John F. Fischer (Oklahoma Physicians Network, Inc.) (Jan. 17, 1996) (approving non-exclusive network with "substantially more" than 30% of several specialties, including more than 50% in one specialty).

2.   *Clinical Integration.* In a series of detailed advisory opinions and policy statements the FTC has provided a roadmap for physician-controlled networks to avoid per se treatment without undertaking the kind of financial integration stressed in *Maricopa* as the talisman of legitimate joint ventures. By integrating their services clinically, i.e. adopting an "active and ongoing program to evaluate and modify practice patterns" so as to create a "high degree of interdependence and cooperation among the physicians to control costs and ensure quality," PPOs and IPAs would be examined under the rule of reason, provided that collective price-setting was reasonably necessary to

accomplish those goals. Policy Statements supra, Statement 9. See FTC Advisory Opinion In Re MedSouth Inc. (Feb. 19,2002); FTC Staff Letter to Michael E. Joseph (Feb. 13, 2013)(advisory opinion finding PHO in Norman Oklahoma sufficiently clinically integrated); but see FTC Staff Letter to Clifton E. Johnson, Esq.(Mar. 28, 2006)(disapproving "super PHO," which would serve as the exclusive bargaining and agent for 192 primary care physicians employed at eight independent hospitals as lacking sufficient integration and not reasonably necessary to achieve efficiencies).

3. *Messenger Model Arrangements.* Another section of the 1996 Policy Statements established a way to avoid price fixing liability for physicians wanting to form networks but unwilling to undertake financial risk sharing or clinical integration. Under so-called "messenger model" networks agreements, physicians may use a common agent to convey information to and from payors about the prices and price-related terms they are willing to accept. Policy Statements, *supra*, Statement 9. However, the messenger must communicate individually with each network physician and not act as a conduit for information sharing or agreements among members. The permitted model is violated when:

> the agent coordinates the providers' responses to a particular proposal, disseminates to network providers the views or intentions of other network providers as to the proposal, expresses an opinion on the terms offered, collectively negotiates for the providers, or decides whether or not to convey an offer based on the agent's judgment about the attractiveness of the prices or price-related terms.

Id. In essence, the 1996 Policy Statements establish a presumption that physicians complying with the model's parameters have not collectively agreed upon prices, but instead have determined their prices individually. Central to the concept, of course, is the integrity of the messenger—he must function solely as a conduit for offers and exchanges between payors and individual providers

However, in an astounding number of cases, physician networks have engaged in blatant violations of the messenger model. The FTC has brought over 60 administrative actions challenging these, typically branding them as *per se* price fixing schemes. For the most part these cases involve noncompliance with obvious prohibitions of the model, such as polling members on desired prices and using those prices to negotiate on behalf of members. See Thomas L. Greaney, Thirty Years of Solicitude: Antitrust Law and Physician Cartels, 7 Hous. J. Health L. & Pol. 101 (2007).

4. Do recognized areas of specialization constitute a distinct market for analysis under the Policy Statements? Compare Letter from Anne K. Bingaman, Assistant Attorney General, Antitrust Division, to Steven J. Kern and Robert J. Conroy (March 1, 1996) (concluding that family practitioners and other primary care physicians who treat children were not widely accepted substitutes for pediatricians) with Letter from Anne K. Bingaman, Assis-

tant Attorney General, Antitrust Division to James M. Parker (Oct. 27, 1994) (board-certified pulmonologists are not exclusive providers of pulmonology-type services; merger of two pulmonology groups allowed to proceed because of significant competition from surgeons, family practitioners and other primary care physicians). What facts would you gather and what witnesses would you interview to decide whether a given specialty constitutes a relevant market?

B. ACCOUNTABLE CARE ORGANIZATIONS (ACOS)

Contemporaneously with CMS's Final Rule on ACOs (see Chapter 10 *supra*), the Federal Trade Commission and Department of Justice ("the Agencies") released a Final Statement of antitrust enforcement policy regarding Medicare Accountable Care Organizations which set forth a detailed exposition of the standards they will apply to review ACOs for potential antitrust violations. FTC & U.S. Dep't. of Justice Statement of Antitrust Enforcement Policy Regarding Accountable Care Organizations Participating in the Medicare Shared Savings Program, 76 Fed. Reg. 67, 026, (Oct. 28, 2011) (Final Statement). Unlike the fraud and abuse area, the ACA does not authorize the Secretary of HHS to waive the applicability of the antitrust laws to ACO formation and operation. Hence, clarification of the Agencies' approach to analyzing ACOs under the antitrust law was important to remove uncertainty for providers considering forming these entities. (Note, however, that state attorneys general and private parties may also bring actions under federal or state antitrust laws and are not bound by the standards contained in the Statement or by the decision of the Agencies not to pursue a case).

The overarching objective of the Statement is to prevent ACOs from enhancing or entrenching market power and to encourage, to the extent possible, the development of competitive ACOs in local markets around the country. See generally Thomas L. Greaney, Accountable Care Organizations—The Fork in the Road, 364 NEJM e1 (2011); Taylor Burke & Sara Rosenbaum, Accountable Care Organizations: Implications for Antitrust Policy (Robert Wood Johnson Foundation 2010). Although the Statement purports to deal primarily with procedural policies that will govern their review of ACOs, it also contains or hints at a number of important substantive determinations that will apply.

Clinical Integration. The Final Statement provides that ACOs meeting CMS's standards of participation in the MSSP will be deemed sufficiently integrated so that participants contracting with commercial payors will be judged under the rule of reason and not the per se standard of illegality. From the standpoint of removing uncertainty and clarifying the steps that ACOs must undertake to satisfy the Agencies' analysis of horizontal restraints this is an important concession. It was probably not a difficult one, however, as the ACA contains detailed prescriptions that go a long way in assuring that physicians and other providers are truly interdependent and invested in the success of the ACO. Somewhat more controversially, the Final Statement also indicates that if an ACO receives CMS approval, it will treat joint negotiations with private payors as reasonably necessary to realize the ACOs primary purpose of improving health care delivery.

Safety Zone. The Final Statement sets forth a "safety zone" stating that, absent extraordinary circumstances, the Agencies will not challenge an ACO comprised of independent ACO participants that provide a common service where the ACO's combined share of the common service is 30 percent or less in each ACO participant's primary service areas (PSAs). Note: a "common service" refers to services provided by two or more *previously independent* entities offering their services through the ACO; it does not cover services of a single entity. Several important restrictions and exceptions apply:

- *Hospitals and ASCs.* Any hospital or ambulatory surgery center participating in an ACO regardless of size must be non-exclusive to the ACO in order to qualify for the safety zone.

- *Rural provider exception.* ACOs may include one physician or one physician group practice per specialty from each rural area even if inclusion causes the ACO's share of any common service to exceed 30 percent, provided the physician or group participates on a non-exclusive basis. ACOs may also include rural hospitals, even if inclusion of a rural hospital causes the ACO's share of any common service to exceed 30 percent, again so long as the rural participant participates on a non-exclusive basis. For purposes of this exception, rural hospitals include "critical access hospitals" or a "sole community hospitals," as defined under Medicare regulations or any other hospital with fewer than 50 beds and located in a rural area not within 35 miles from any other acute care hospital.

- *Dominant Provider Limitation.* ACOs that include a dominant provider (a participant with greater than a 50 percent share in its primary service area for any service that no other ACO participant provides) must be non-exclusive to the ACO to qualify for the safety zone. In addition, an ACO with a dominant provider cannot require a payor to contract exclusively with the ACO or otherwise restrict the payor's ability to contract with other ACOs or provider networks.

The Statement goes on to identify specific categories of conduct which it counsels may, under certain circumstances, raise competitive concerns and should be avoided. The most obvious warning, applicable to all ACOs regardless of their market power, is directed at garden-variety horizontal collusion. It states that significant antitrust concerns arise when an

ACO's operation leads to price fixing or other collusion among ACO participants in their sale of competing services outside the ACO and suggests that participants avoid improper exchanges of price or other competitively sensitive information that may facilitate such collusion. The Statement goes on to identify four types of conduct that "may raise competitive concerns" for an ACO with high PSA shares or other indicia of market power:

1.   Discouraging private payers from directing or incentivizing patients to choose certain providers through contractual terms such as "anti-steering," "anti-tiering," "guaranteed inclusion," and "most favored nations" provisions.

2.   Tying sales of the ACO's services to the private payer's purchase of other services from providers outside the ACO, and vice versa.

3.   Contracting with ACO participants on an exclusive basis.

4.   Restricting a private payer's ability to make available cost, quality, efficiency and performance information to aid enrollees in evaluating and selecting providers in the health plan if it is similar to that used in the shared savings program.

Applying the Market Tests. Note that the above thresholds apply to each service provided by at least two *independent* ACO participants. Thus, an ACO combining an independent surgeon who has an 8 percent market share with a hospital that employs a surgery group with a 25 percent share would fall outside the safety zone of 30 percent. On the other hand, an ACO comprised of a single surgery group with 33 percent share would not fall outside the safety zone for that service. Thus, ACO applicants will need to calculate their shares for dozens of services. An ACO comprised solely of an integrated health system and its employed physicians would not have to submit an application to the Agencies even if the physicians or hospitals in the ACO hold a PSA share in excess of 50 percent.

The Statement proposes to employ primary service areas (PSAs) to calculate the foregoing shares and as a rough proxy for the markets served by ACO participants. For purposes of defining "services," a physician's "service" is the physician's primary specialty, as identified by the Medicare Specialty Code. A hospital's "services" consists of each major diagnostic category (MDC), a grouping of the diagnosis related groups (DRGs) used by Medicare for reimbursement purposes. ACOs must identify the PSA for each common service for each participant in the ACO. The Statement defines the PSA as "the lowest number of contiguous zip codes from which" the ACO participant "draws at least 75 percent" of its patients, which is a concept borrowed from the Stark Law. The ACO must calculate the ACO's PSA share for each common service in each PSA from which at least two ACO participants serve patients for that service.

NOTES AND QUESTIONS

1.   The ACO Statement attempts to balance the need for administrability, accuracy, and speed for antitrust reviews. Does it get the balance right? Consider some of the following criticisms.

- The Statement does not address the potential market power of ACOs formed through mergers and acquisitions.

- PSAs are an inadequate proxy to use for identifying antitrust markets (see FTC v. Tenet, *infra*).

- The emphasis on non-exclusivity in the Statement is inconsistent with ACOs' need to get providers to invest time and capital to efficiently integrate their delivery system.

2.   The primary reason for concern about the competitive effects of ACOs is that most entities will be offering their services in the private insurance market at the same time they are participating in the Medicare Shared Savings Program. Indeed, the ACA encourages such participation: Section 3022 provides that the Secretary of HHS "may give preference to ACOs who [sic] are participating in similar arrangements with other payers." At the same time, extensive scholarship has shown that hospital and many specialty physician markets are highly concentrated. What can the Agencies do about this? Do the four warnings contained in the Final Statement address the conduct that might harm competition by ACOs formed by dominant providers? How will they be used in the context of applying ACOs? For suggestions on this topic see, Clark C. Havighurst and Barak D. Richman, The Provider Monopoly Problem in Health Care, 89 Or. L. Rev. 847 (2011); Thomas L. Greaney, The Affordable Care Act and Competition Policy: Antidote or Placebo? 89 Or. L. Rev. 811 (2011); Joe Miller, The Proposed Accountable Care Organization Antitrust Guidance: A First Look, Health Aff. Blog (April 14, 2011).

PROBLEM: ORGANIZING AN ACO

Midsize Hospital is one of three hospitals in the town of Midlands. Three hundred independent physicians hold staff privileges at the hospital, with most belonging to groups of five or fewer doctors. There are two large multi-specialty groups (each consisting of 40 doctors) that practice at Midsize Hospital and also practice at Dominion, the largest hospital in town. The CEO of Midsize says he would like to "get the ball rolling on this ACO thing." He hopes he can be the first in town to organize his doctors and get them to agree to participate in a Medicare MSSP ACO which he also plans to market to private insurance companies. He wants to make sure his ACO is comprised of only the most capable doctors and those willing to abide by strict guidelines, protocols, and cost containment measures. He would like to get some, but not all, of the smaller practices on board. He is also thinking of enlisting only one of the two large multispecialty groups, but realizes that this may be "politically impossible." From past experience, it is likely that some physician groups will insist that others not be included.

The CEO is open to all possibilities, including "teaming up" with the other hospitals in town or acquiring physician practices. What general guidance can you give him about antitrust issues and practical problems that may arise as he starts discussions with potential participants in the ACO? What strategy should be adopted in lining up primary care physicians and specialists in connection with the Agencies' Policy Statement, *supra*? For example: should the hospital seek to come within the Safety Zone? What problems arise if the ACO results in a dominant provider for any common service?

WEST PENN ALLEGHENY HEALTH SYSTEM, INC. v. UPMC AND HIGHMARK, INC.

United States Court of Appeals, Third Circuit, 2010.
627 F.3d 85.

SMITH, CIRCUIT JUDGE.

The plaintiff in this antitrust case is Pittsburgh's second-largest hospital system. It sued Pittsburgh's dominant hospital system and health insurer under the Sherman Act and state law. The plaintiff asserts that the defendants violated Sections 1 and 2 of the Sherman Act by forming a conspiracy to protect one another from competition. The plaintiff says that pursuant to the conspiracy, the dominant hospital system used its power in the provider market to insulate the health insurer from competition, and in exchange the insurer used its power in the insurance market to strengthen the hospital system and to weaken the plaintiff. The plaintiff also asserts that the dominant hospital system violated Section 2 of the Sherman Act by attempting to monopolize the Pittsburgh-area market for specialized hospital services. * * * Because we conclude that the District Court erred in dismissing the Sherman Act claims, we will reverse in part, vacate in part, and remand for further proceedings.

I.   Facts

* * *

A.   Cast of Characters

This lawsuit involves three parties. The plaintiff, West Penn Allegheny Health System, Inc. ("West Penn"), is Pittsburgh's second-largest hospital system; it has a share of less than 23% of the market for hospital services in Allegheny County, which includes the City of Pittsburgh. The defendant University of Pittsburgh Medical Center ("UPMC") is Pittsburgh's dominant hospital system. It enjoys a 55% share of the Allegheny County market for hospital services, and its share of the market for tertiary and quaternary care services exceeds 50%.[ ] West Penn and UPMC are the two major competitors in the Allegheny County market for hospital services, and are the only competitors in the market for tertiary and quaternary care services. The defendant Highmark, Inc. is the dominant insurer in the Allegheny County market for health insurance. [ ] Highmark's market share has remained between 60% and 80% since 2000.

B.   Pre–Conspiracy Conduct

In 2000, The Western Pennsylvania Healthcare System merged with several financially distressed medical providers, including Allegheny General Hospital, to form West Penn. Highmark funded the merger with a $125 million loan. Highmark's largesse did not spring from a sense of altruism, but was intended to preserve competition in the market for hospital services. Had the financially distressed providers comprising West Penn failed, UPMC would have attained nearly unchecked dominance in the market. This would not have been good for Highmark: the more dominant UPMC becomes, the more leverage it gains to demand greater reimbursements from Highmark. * * *

After the merger, Highmark and West Penn continued to enjoy a good relationship, as Highmark recognized that preserving West Penn was in its interests. Thus, Highmark encouraged investors to purchase bonds from West Penn, touting its financial outlook and the quality of its medical services. And in early 2002, Highmark gave West Penn a $42 million grant to invest in its facilities.

In contrast to Highmark, UPMC has been hostile to West Penn since its inception. UPMC opposed the merger creating West Penn: it intervened in the merger proceedings, filed an unsuccessful lawsuit to prevent Highmark from funding the merger, and attempted (with some success) to dissuade investors from purchasing West Penn bonds. UPMC's hostility towards West Penn continued after the merger. Since West Penn's formation, UPMC executives have repeatedly said that they want to destroy West Penn, and they have taken action to further that goal on more than a few occasions. But more on that later. See Section I.E, *infra*.

Historically, UPMC has also had a bitter relationship with Highmark. For example, when UPMC demanded purportedly excessive reimbursement rates from Highmark, Highmark responded by forming Community Blue, a low-cost insurance plan. To participate in Community Blue, a hospital had to agree to accept reduced reimbursements, but would receive a higher volume of patients. West Penn participated in Community Blue, but UPMC did not, claiming that its reimbursement rates were too low. UPMC responded to Community Blue by forming its own health insurer, UPMC Health Plan. UPMC Health Plan has been Highmark's main competitor in the Allegheny County market for health insurance since its formation.

[Highmark also sued UPMC under the Lanham act over alleged false statements in an advertisement and challenged UPMC's acquisition of a children's hospital.]

C.   The Conspiracy Begins; the Dynamics Change

In 1998, UPMC offered a "truce" to Highmark. Under the terms of the truce, each entity would use its market power to protect the other from competition. Highmark initially rejected UPMC's offer, criticizing it as an illegal "attempt to form a 'super' monopoly for the provision of health care in Western Pennsylvania in which [UPMC], the leading provider of hospital services, and Highmark, the leading health insurer, would combine forces." [ ].

The complaint alleges, however, that in the summer of 2002, over the course of several meetings, Highmark reconsidered and decided to accept UPMC's offer of a truce. The complaint alleges that UPMC agreed to use its power in the provider market to prevent Highmark competitors from gaining a foothold in the Allegheny County market for health insurance, and in exchange Highmark agreed to take steps to strengthen UPMC and to weaken West Penn. The complaint offers the following factual allegations in support of the conspiracy claim.

UPMC engaged in conduct that effectively insulated Highmark from competition. First, it refused to enter into competitive provider agreements with Highmark's rivals. This prevented the rivals from entering the Allegheny County health insurance market because, given UPMC's dominance, an insurer cannot succeed in the market without being able to offer a competitively-priced plan that includes UPMC as an in-network provider.[3]

Second, UPMC shrunk UPMC Health Plan (Highmark's main competitor in the insurance market). It cut the Health Plan's advertising budget and increased its premiums, which led to a sharp drop in enrollment. It also refused to sell the Health Plan to insurers interested in buying it, which might have revived it as a Highmark competitor. UPMC acknowledged that it decided to shrink the Health Plan as a result of negotiations with Highmark, in which Highmark had agreed to take Community Blue off the market.

Meanwhile, Highmark took action that enhanced UPMC's dominance. Most significantly, it paid UPMC supracompetitive reimbursement rates. To afford UPMC's reimbursements, Highmark had to increase its insurance premiums (which, according to West Penn, it was able to do without losing business because UPMC had insulated it from competition). [Highmark also provided UPMC with a $70 million grant and $160

---

[3]   In fact, United Healthcare tried to enter the Allegheny County insurance market in 2005 and 2006, but it was effectively prevented from doing so because UPMC would not offer it a competitive contract.

million low interest loan to build a new facility and supported its acquisition of another facility.] In addition, Highmark vowed not to offer a health plan that did not include UPMC as an in-network provider. Thus, in 2004, Highmark eliminated its low-cost insurance plan, Community Blue, in which UPMC had declined to participate. With the elimination of a leading low-cost insurance plan, health insurance premiums in Allegheny County rose. Furthermore, in 2006, Highmark publicly supported UPMC's acquisition of Mercy Hospital, which, other than West Penn, was UPMC's only other competitor in the market for tertiary and quaternary care services. Finally, in 2006, Highmark leaked confidential financial information regarding West Penn to UPMC, "which in turn leaked a distorted version of the information to credit-rating agencies and to the business media in an attempt to destroy investor confidence in West Penn." [ ]

In addition, Highmark essentially cut West Penn off from its financial support, thus hampering its ability to compete with UPMC. Highmark, for instance, repeatedly rejected West Penn's requests to refinance the $125 million loan that was used to fund the 2000 merger. [ ] Although Highmark believed refinancing the loan made business sense, it declined to do so out of fear that UPMC would retaliate against it for violating their agreement—an agreement that Highmark candidly admitted was "probably illegal." Highmark said that it was under a "constant barrage" from UPMC and that UPMC was "obsessed" with driving West Penn out of business. Highmark explained that if it helped West Penn financially, UPMC would allow one of Highmark's competitors to enter the Allegheny County insurance market or would sell UPMC Health Plan to a Highmark competitor. Indeed, UPMC had sent Highmark a letter containing such a warning. [ ]

Moreover, Highmark maintained West Penn's reimbursement rates at artificially depressed levels and repeatedly refused to increase them. In 2005 and 2006, for example, West Penn asked Highmark for a general increase in its rates, which were originally set in 2002. Highmark initially acknowledged that West Penn's rates were too low and suggested that it would raise them, but it ultimately refused to follow through, explaining that it could not help West Penn because, if it did, UPMC would retaliate.

Finally, Highmark "discriminated against West Penn [ ] in the award of grants to improve the quality of medical care in" Allegheny County. * * *

D. The Effects of the Conspiracy

The conspiracy ended in 2007, when the Antitrust Division of the Department of Justice began investigating Highmark's and UPMC's relationship. During the years covered by the conspiracy, UPMC and Highmark reaped record profits. * * * On the other hand, West Penn struggled during the years covered by the conspiracy. It was forced to scale back its services, and to abandon projects to expand and improve its services and facilities. In essence, West Penn was unable to compete with UPMC as vigorously as it otherwise would have.

E. UPMC's Unilateral Conduct

Besides the conspiracy with Highmark, UPMC has taken a number of actions on its own to weaken West Penn. UPMC has systematically "raided" key physicians from West Penn . . . by paying them salaries that were well above market rates. Although UPMC incurred financial losses because of the hirings (that is, it paid the physicians more money than they generated), it admitted that it was willing to do so in order to injure the hospitals.

UPMC's physician "raiding" has "continued unabated" since West Penn's formation . . . As before, though, UPMC admitted that it was not trying to earn profits. It was trying to drive the hospital out of business. In the end, the anesthesiologists were lured away by UPMC's bloated salary offers. * * *

[The Court identifies other examples in the complaint of "so-called physician raiding"; pressuring community hospitals into entering joint ventures by threatening to build satellite facilities next to them; and making false statements about West Penn's financial health in order to discourage investors from purchasing West Penn bonds].

* * *

V.   The Conspiracy Claims

* * *

A. Agreement

* * *

West Penn's theory on the conspiracy claims is that in the summer of 2002, UPMC and Highmark formed an agreement to protect one another from competition. West Penn asserts that UPMC agreed to use its power in the provider market to exclude Highmark's rivals from the Allegheny County health insurance market, and that in exchange Highmark agreed to take steps to strengthen UPMC and to weaken its primary rival, West Penn. We conclude that the complaint contains non-conclusory allegations of direct evidence of such an agreement.

* * *

B. Unreasonable Restraint

The defendants make a half-hearted argument that even if the complaint alleges that they formed a conspiracy to shield one another from competition, the section 1 claim is still deficient because the complaint does not allege that the conspiracy unreasonably restrained trade. We disagree. At the pleading stage, a plaintiff may satisfy the unreasonable-restraint element by alleging that the conspiracy produced anticompetitive effects in the relevant markets. [ ]

* * * In . . . concluding [that plaintiff's allegations are sufficient to suggest that the conspiracy produced anticompetitive effects] we do not reach West Penn's argument that-given the horizontal aspect of the conspiracy, *i.e.*, UPMC's agreement to shrink UPMC Health Plan-the conspiracy is subject to *per se* condemnation. Even if the more demanding rule of reason applies, the complaint adequately alleges that the conspiracy stifled competition in the relevant markets.

C. Antitrust Injury

[T]he Supreme Court [has] held that an antitrust plaintiff must do more than show that it would have been better off absent the violation; the plaintiff must establish that it suffered an antitrust injury. An antitrust injury is an "injury of the type the antitrust laws were intended to prevent and that flows from that which makes [the] defendants' acts unlawful." * * *

[The Court rejected West Penn's claims that the conspiracy caused it antitrust injury based on Highmark's decision to take Community Blue off the market, noting that a supplier does not suffer an antitrust injury when competition is reduced in the downstream market in which it sells goods or services. The Court also rejected West Penn's allegation that it sustained an antitrust injury based on Highmark's refusals to refinance the $125 million loan noting that because Highmark was just one of many possible sources of financing, even if it acted with anticompetitive motives, Highmark's refinancing refusals could not have been competition-*reducing* aspects of the conspiracy.]

Finally, West Penn argues that it sustained an antitrust injury in the form of artificially depressed reimbursement rates. The complaint alleges that during the conspiracy, West Penn asked Highmark to renegotiate and raise its rates. The complaint suggests that Highmark acknowledged that the rates were too low and initially agreed to raise them, but that Highmark refused to follow through, citing its agreement with UPMC, under which it was not to do anything to benefit West Penn financially. West Penn asserts that the amount of the underpayments—*i.e.*, the difference between the reimbursements it would have received in a competitive market and those it actually received—constitutes an antitrust injury. For their part, the defendants do not take issue with West Penn's suggestion that its reimbursement rates would have been greater absent the conspiracy. They argue, instead, that paying West Penn depressed reimbursement rates was not an element of the conspiracy that posed antitrust problems. They reason that low reimbursement rates translate into low premiums for subscribers, and that it would therefore be contrary to a key purpose of the antitrust laws—promoting consumer welfare—to allow West Penn to recover the amount of the underpayments. West Penn has it right.

Admittedly, had Highmark been acting alone, West Penn would have little basis for challenging the reimbursement rates. A firm that has substantial power on the buy side of the market (*i.e.,* monopsony power) is generally free to bargain aggressively when negotiating the prices it will pay for goods and services. [ ] This reflects the general hesitance of courts to condemn unilateral behavior, lest vigorous competition be chilled. [ ]

But when a firm exercises monopsony power pursuant to a conspiracy, its conduct is subject to more rigorous scrutiny, [ ] and will be condemned if it imposes an unreasonable restraint of trade [ ] * * *

Here, the complaint suggests that Highmark has substantial monopsony power. It alleges that Highmark has a 60%–80% share of the Allegheny County market for health insurance, that there are significant entry barriers for insurers wishing to break into the market (including UPMC's unwillingness to deal competitively with non-Highmark insurers), and that medical providers have very few alternative purchasers for their services.[12] The complaint also alleges that Highmark paid West Penn depressed reimbursement rates, not as a result of independent decision making, but pursuant to a conspiracy with UPMC, under which UPMC insulated Highmark from competition in return for Highmark's taking steps to hobble West Penn. In these circumstances, it is certainly plausible that paying West Penn depressed reimbursement rates unreasonably restrained trade. Such shortchanging poses competitive threats similar to those posed by conspiracies among buyers to fix prices [ ], and other restraints that result in artificially depressed payments to suppliers—namely, suboptimal output, reduced quality, allocative inefficiencies, and (given the reductions in output) higher prices for consumers in the long run.

The defendants argue, though, that Highmark's paying West Penn depressed reimbursements did not pose antitrust problems because it enabled Highmark to set low insurance premiums, and thus benefited consumers. We disagree. First, even if it were true that paying West Penn depressed rates enabled Highmark to offer lower premiums, it is far from clear that this would have benefited consumers, because the premium reductions would have been achieved only by taking action that tends to diminish the quality and availability of hospital services. Second, the

---

[12] Indeed, the complaint alleges that the only other insurer with a significant market share is UPMC Health Plan, and that UPMC Health Plan has basically been unwilling to deal with West Penn.

complaint alleges that Highmark did *not* pass the savings on to consumers. It alleges, instead, that Highmark pocketed the savings, while repeatedly ratcheting up insurance premiums. *See also* Roger D. Blair & Jeffrey L. Harrison, Antitrust Policy and Monopsony, 76 Cornell L. Rev. 297, 339 (1991) (explaining that "lower input prices resulting from the exercise of monopsony power do not ultimately translate into lower prices to the monopsonist's customers").

But most importantly, the defendants' argument reflects a basic misunderstanding of the antitrust laws. The Ninth Circuit's discussion in Knevelbaard Dairies v. Kraft Foods, Inc., 232 F.3d 979 (9th Cir.2000), illustrates the point well. There, the plaintiff milk producers established that the defendant cheese makers had conspired to depress the price they paid for milk. The cheese makers argued that the plaintiffs' injuries were not antitrust injuries—*i.e.,* were not the kind of injuries "the antitrust laws were intended to prevent," [ ] because the conspiracy enabled them to purchase milk at lower costs and thus to sell cheese to consumers at lower prices. [ ] Ninth Circuit properly rejected this argument:

> The fallacy of [the defendants'] argument becomes clear when we recall that the central purpose of the antitrust laws . . . is to preserve competition. It is competition—not the collusive fixing of prices at levels either low or high—that these statutes recognize as vital to the public interest. The Supreme Court's references to the goals of achieving "the lowest prices, the highest quality and the greatest material progress," and of "assur[ing] customers the benefits of price competition," [ ], do not mean that conspiracies among buyers to depress acquisition prices are tolerated. Every precedent in the field makes clear that the interaction of competitive forces, not price-rigging, is what will benefit consumers. [ ]

Similar reasoning applies here. Highmark's improperly motivated exercise of monopsony power, like the collusive exercise of oligopsony power by the cheese makers in *Knevelbaard,* was anticompetitive and cannot be defended on the sole ground that it enabled Highmark to set lower premiums on its insurance plans.

Having concluded that paying West Penn artificially depressed reimbursement rates was an anticompetitive aspect of the alleged conspiracy, it follows that the underpayments constitute an antitrust injury. [ ]

*   *   *

VI. The Attempted Monopolization Claim

In addition to the conspiracy claims, West Penn alleges that UPMC violated section 2 of the Sherman Act by attempting to monopolize the Allegheny County market for specialized hospital services. The elements of attempted monopolization are (1) that the defendant has a specific intent to monopolize, and (2) that the defendant has engaged in anticompetitive conduct that, taken as a whole, creates (3) a dangerous probability of achieving monopoly power. [ ] The District Court dismissed the attempted monopolization claim on the ground that the complaint fails to allege anticompetitive conduct, and the parties have addressed only that issue here. We limit our review accordingly.

Broadly speaking, a firm engages in anticompetitive conduct when it attempts "to exclude rivals on some basis other than efficiency." [ ] * * *

For present purposes, it is sufficient to note that anticompetitive conduct can include a conspiracy to exclude a rival [ ] * * *

The complaint alleges the following anticompetitive conduct. First, the defendants engaged in a conspiracy, a purpose of which was to drive West Penn out of business. Second, UPMC hired employees away from West Penn by paying them bloated salaries. UPMC admitted to hiring some of the employees not because it needed them but in order to injure West Penn; UPMC could not absorb some of the employees and had to let them go; and UPMC incurred financial losses as a result of the hiring. These allegations are sufficient to suggest that at least some of the hirings were anticompetitive. [ ] Relatedly, UPMC tried unsuccessfully to lure a number of employees away from West Penn; UPMC could not have absorbed the additional employees, and although the employees remained with West Penn, they did so only after West Penn raised their salaries to supracompetitive levels. Third, UPMC approached community hospitals and threatened to build UPMC satellite facilities next to them unless they stopped referring oncology patients to West Penn and began referring all such patients to UPMC. Nearly all of the community hospitals caved in, which deprived West Penn of a key source of patients. Moreover, under pressure from UPMC, several of the community hospitals have stopped sending *any* of their tertiary and quaternary care referrals to West Penn and have begun sending them all to UPMC. Finally, on several occasions, UPMC made false statements about West Penn's financial health to potential investors, which caused West Penn to pay artificially inflated financing costs on its debt.

Viewed as a whole, these allegations plausibly suggest that UPMC has engaged in anticompetitive conduct, *i.e.*, that UPMC has competed with West Penn "on some basis other than the merits." [ ] The District Court erred in concluding otherwise.

* * *

For the reasons set forth above, the judgment of the District Court will be reversed in part and vacated in part, and the case will be remanded for further proceedings.

NOTES AND QUESTIONS

1.   Pittsburgh's health care *ménage a trois* did not end with the Third Circuit's decision. Following an unsuccessful petition for certiorari by UPMC, Highmark and West Penn announced plans to merge with Highmark promising to invest $475 million in West Penn. Not surprisingly, West Penn dismissed its complaint against Highmark (but not against UPMC). Following an investigation of the competitive implications of the merger, the Antitrust Division took the relatively unusual step of issuing a closing statement, explaining why it had decided not to oppose the transaction. The Division stressed that the affiliation was purely vertical and explained that it "holds the promise of bringing increased competition to western Pennsylvania's health care markets by providing [West Penn] with a significant infusion of capital" and by increasing the incentives for market participants to compete. U.S. Dept. of Justice, Press Release (April 10, 2012). The drama did not end there, however. West Penn attempted to walk away from the affiliation claiming Highmark breached the agreement by insisting that West Penn file for bankruptcy in anticipation of applying for approval from the Pennsylvania Insurance Department. Highmark responded by obtaining a preliminary injunction blocking West Penn from talking to other potential partners. Steve Twedt, Judge Grants Highmark Request to Block West Penn Allegheny's Affiliation Talks, Pitt. Post–Gazette (Nov. 9, 2012).

2.   Does the Third Circuit's opinion suggest that agreements between dominant hospitals and dominant insurers to achieve mutually beneficial terms will necessarily run afoul of Section 1 of the Sherman Act? What factors create an inference that the agreements will restrain trade? Note also that private litigants must prove that the alleged restraint of trade or acts of monopolization do more than harm them, but actually injure competition. Why is this showing problematic in the context of an insurer exercising its power *vis-a-vis* providers?

3.   Dominant hospitals flexing their muscle may run afoul of Section 2 of the Sherman Act as well. In February, 2011, the U.S. Department of Justice and Texas Attorney General's Office announced the simultaneous filing and settlement of monopolization claims under Section 2 of the Sherman Act against United Regional Health Care System of Wichita Falls, Texas. The complaint charged that United Regional, the dominant hospital in its market, coerced health insurers to refrain from contracting with other competing hospitals in the Wichita Falls area. U.S. Dept. of Justice, Press Release (Feb. 25, 2011). The alleged coercion took place by offering steep "discounts" to insurers ranging from 15 to 27 percent if the insurers refused to contract with other providers in the market. The government focused on the "exclusionary contracts" United Regional entered into with payors that it alleged "effectively prevent insurers from contracting with United Regional's competitors." For a critical examination of the underlying economics of the government's case, see David A. Argue and John M. Gale, Reexamining DOJ's Predation Analysis in United Regional (Jan. 2012).

C. MERGERS AND ACQUISITIONS

1. Hospital Mergers

IN THE MATTER OF HOSPITAL CORPORATION OF AMERICA
Federal Trade Commission, 1985.
106 F.T.C. 361.

CALVANI, COMM'R.

I.   Introduction to the Case

A.   The Acquisitions

In August 1981, Respondent Hospital Corporation of America ("HCA"), the largest proprietary hospital chain in the United States, acquired Hospital Affiliates International ("HAI") in a stock transaction valued at approximately $650 million. [ ] At the time of the acquisition, HAI owned or leased 57 hospitals and managed 78 hospitals nationwide. Prior to its acquisition by HCA, HAI owned or managed five acute care hospitals in the general area of Chattanooga, Tennessee, and HCA acquired ownership or management of these hospitals through the transaction. Some four months later HCA acquired yet another hospital corporation, Health Care Corporation ("HCC"), in a stock transaction valued at approximately $30 million. At the time of the acquisition, HCC owned a single acute care hospital in Chattanooga. These two transactions provide the genesis for the instant case.

As a result of the HCA–HAI acquisition, Respondent increased its hospital operations in Chattanooga and its suburbs from ownership of one acute care hospital to ownership or management of four of the area's eleven acute care hospitals. Within the six-county Chattanooga Metropolitan Statistical Area ("Chattanooga MSA"), HCA changed its position from owner of one hospital to owner or manager of six of fourteen acute care hospitals. With the acquisition of HCC, HCA obtained yet another acute care hospital in Chattanooga. Thus, HCA became owner or manager of five of the eleven acute care hospitals within the Chattanooga urban area and seven of the fourteen in the Chattanooga MSA.

* * * [Administrative Law Judge Parker] found that the acquisitions violated Section 7 of the Clayton Act and Section 5 of the Federal Trade Commission Act, and ordered HCA to divest two of the hospitals of which it had acquired ownership. Judge Parker also ordered that HCA provide prior notification to the Commission of certain of its future hospital acquisitions. HCA appeals the Initial Decision on several grounds; Complaint Counsel appeal certain of Judge Parker's findings as well.

* * * We affirm Judge Parker's finding of liability and modify his opinion only as stated below.

* * *

III. The Product Market

An acquisition violates Section 7 of the Clayton Act "where in any line of commerce in any section of the country, the effect of such acquisition may be substantially to lessen competition, or to tend to create a monopoly." [ ] Accordingly, we now turn to the definition of the relevant "line of commerce" or "product market" in which to measure the likely competitive effects of these acquisitions. In measuring likely competitive effects, we seek to define a product or group of products sufficiently distinct that buyers could not defeat an attempted exercise of market power on the part of sellers of those products by shifting purchases to still different products. Sellers might exercise market power by raising prices, limiting output or lowering quality. [ ]

Complaint Counsel argued below that the product market [ ] was properly defined as the provision of acute inpatient hospital services and emergency hospital services provided to the critically ill. [ ] This definition would exclude non-hospital providers of outpatient services, e.g., free standing emergency centers, as well as non-hospital providers of inpatient services, e.g., nursing homes, from the product market. It would also exclude the outpatient business of hospitals, except for that provided to the critically ill in the emergency room. The rationale for excluding outpatient care is that inpatient services are the reason for being of acute care hospitals; inpatient services are needed by and consumed by patients in combination and therefore can be offered only by acute care hospitals. Inpatients in almost all cases will purchase a range of services and not just one test or procedure; they will typically consume a "cluster" of services involving 24–hour nursing, the services of specialized laboratory and X-ray equipment, the services of equipment needed to monitor vital functions or intervene in crises, and so forth. An acutely ill patient must be in a setting in which all of these various services can be provided together. [ ] According to this reasoning, outpatient services are not an integral part of this "cluster of services" offered by acute care hospitals, and therefore must be excluded.

Respondent, on the other hand, urged that the market be defined to include outpatient care as well as inpatient care. Respondent's expert witness, Dr. Jeffrey E. Harris, testified that outpatient care is growing rapidly for hospitals, as well as for free-standing facilities such as emergency care and one-day surgery centers, which compete with hospitals for outpatients. Moreover, because of substantial changes in medical technology, there are a growing number of procedures that can be provided on an outpatient basis that previously could have been done on only an inpatient basis. [ ]

Judge Parker agreed that the market should include outpatient services provided by hospitals but excluded outpatient services provided by non-hospital providers, holding that only hospitals can provide the "unique combination" of services which the acute care patient needs. He defined the relevant product market to be the cluster of services offered by acute care hospitals, including outpatient as well as inpatient care, "since acute care hospitals compete with each other in offering both kinds of care and since . . . acute care outpatient facilities feed patients to the inpatient facilities." [ ]

Neither HCA nor Complaint Counsel appeal Judge Parker's product market definition.[ ] Accordingly, for purposes of this proceeding only, we accept Judge Parker's finding on this issue. [ ]

However, we do note that Judge Parker's definition does not necessarily provide a very happy medium between the two competing positions; the evidence in this case tended to show *both* that free-standing outpatient facilities compete with hospitals for many outpatients and that hospitals offer and inpatients consume a cluster of services that bears little relation to outpatient care. [ ] If so, it may be that defining the cluster of hospital inpatient services as a separate market better reflects competitive reality in this case. * * * Certainly, it is clear that anti-competitive behavior by hospital firms could significantly lessen competition for hospital inpatients that could not be defeated by competition from non-hospital outpatient providers. Our analysis will hence proceed with primary reference to the cluster of services provided to inpatients.

IV. The Geographic Market

* * * Because we are concerned only with an area in which competition could be harmed, the relevant geographic market must be broad enough that buyers would be unable to switch to alternative sellers in sufficient numbers to defeat an exercise of market power by firms in the area. * * * If an exercise of market power could be defeated by the entry of products produced in another area, both areas should be considered part of the same geographic market for Section 7 purposes, since competition could not be harmed in the smaller area. That is, the geographic market should determine not only the firms that constrain competitors' actions by currently selling to the same customers, but also those that would be a constraint because of their ability to sell to those customers should price or quality in the area change. [ ]

* * *

HCA would have us adopt Hamilton County, Tennessee, together with Walker, Dade and Catoosa counties in Georgia, the "Chattanooga urban area," as the relevant geographic market. HCA predicates its conclusion largely on an analysis of evidence concerning physician admitting patterns.

* * * With few exceptions, every physician who admitted to Chattanooga urban area hospitals admitted exclusively to other hospitals in the Chattanooga urban area. [ ] Conversely, physicians admitting and treating patients at hospitals outside the Chattanooga urban area rarely admitted and treated patients at hospitals in the Chattanooga urban area. [ ]

* * *

Additionally, the weight of the evidence concerning patient origin suggests that patients admitted to Chattanooga urban area hospitals who live outside of the Chattanooga urban area are, with few exceptions, in need of specialized care and treatment unavailable in their own communities. [ ] Hospitals in outlying communities do not always provide quite the same product that the urban area hospitals provide such patients, and therefore patient inflows are not necessarily indicative of the willingness of patients to leave their home areas for services that are available in those areas. Judge Parker agreed with HCA that the Chattanooga urban area is the relevant geographic market in this case. [ ]

* * *

V.   The Effect on Competition

A.   *The Effect of HCA–Managed Hospitals*

One of the major dimensions of HCA's purchase of HAI was the acquisition of some 75 to 80 hospital management contracts. [ ] Two of these were management contracts HAI had with two hospitals in the Chattanooga urban area—Downtown General Hospital and Red Bank Community Hospital. * * * HCA argues, and Judge Parker agreed, that Downtown General and Red Bank hospitals should be treated as entities completely separate from HCA, incapable of being significantly influenced by HCA in its role as administrator. * * *

We conclude that treating the two managed hospitals as entities completely independent of HCA is contrary to the overwhelming weight of the evidence in this case. As manager, HCA controls the competitive variables needed for successful coordination with the activities of HCA-owned hospitals in Chattanooga. Moreover, as manager it knows the competitive posture of managed hospitals so well that the likelihood of any anticompetitive behavior HCA wished to engage in is greatly increased.

* * *

B.   The Nature of Competition Among Chattanooga Hospitals

Traditionally, hospitals have competed for patients in three general ways: first, by competing for physicians to admit their patients; second, by competing directly for patients on the basis of amenities and comfort of surroundings; and third, by competing to a limited degree on the basis of price. The first two constitute "non-price" or "quality" competition, and by far have been in the past the most important of the three. [ ]

[The court explains that although nonprice competition has been the primary form of rivalry among hospitals, price competition is growing in the hospital industry and Chattanooga hospitals are now "far more likely to present themselves to insurers, employers and employee groups as less costly than their competitors as one method of attracting business."]

* * * We do not here conclude that price has been the prime arena in which hospitals in Chattanooga compete. However, we do think it clear that even though rates are not constantly adjusted due to a changing price structure, they have been periodically set with some reference to what the market will bear in face of the prices of other hospitals. [ ]

It is clear that Section 7 protects whatever price competition exists in a market, however limited. * * *

*   *   *

C.   Respondent's Market Share and Concentration in the Chattanooga Urban Area

[The Court concludes that HCA's market share increased significantly and that it considered "an increase in concentration in an already concentrated market to be of serious competitive concern, all other things being equal."]

. . . [A]ll other things being equal, an increase in market concentration through a reduction in the absolute number of competitive actors makes interdependent behavior more likely. [ ] These acquisitions decreased the number of independent firms in the market from 9 to 7. [ ] The costs of coordination or of policing any collusive agreement are less with fewer participants, and the elimination of competitive forces in this market facilitates joint anti-competitive behavior. [ ]

In sum, evidence of the increased concentration caused by these acquisitions points toward a finding of likely harm to competition, all other things being equal. [ ] HCA's acquisitions have made an already highly concentrated market more conducive to collusion by eliminating two of the healthiest sources of competition in the market and increasing concentration substantially. But all other things are not equal in this market, and statistical evidence is not the end of our inquiry. In the absence of barriers to entry, an exercise of market power can be defeated or deterred by the entry or potential entry of new firms regardless of the structure of the existing market. [ ] We now turn to the issue of entry barriers and conclude that they confirm and even magnify the inference to be drawn from the concentration evidence in this case.

D. Barriers to Entry

* * *

. . . [T]here is hardly free entry into the acute care hospital industry in either Tennessee or Georgia. Indeed, the CON [certificate of need] laws at issue here create a classic "barrier to entry" under every definition of that term. In *Echlin Manufacturing Co.*, we defined a "barrier to entry" to include "additional long-run costs that must be incurred by an entrant relative to the long-run costs faced by incumbent firms." [ ] We explained that "[t]he rationale underlying this definition is that low-cost incumbent firms can keep prices above the competitive level as long as those prices remain below the level that would provide an incentive to higher-cost potential entrants." [ ]

If a potential entrant desires to build a new hospital in Chattanooga, he must incur all the costs in time and money associated with obtaining a CON. The cost of starting a new hospital includes not only the start-up costs that any firm would incur to enter the market but also the costs of surviving the administrative process. Incumbents in this market, however, did not incur such costs during initial construction. They have only had to incur those costs for additions made to bed capacity since the enactment of the CON laws a decade ago. [ ] Incumbents thus have a long run cost advantage over potential entrants. The result is that market power could be exercised by incumbents without attracting attempts at entry as long as supracompetitive profits are not high enough for a potential entrant to justify incurring all the ordinary costs of starting a hospital *plus* the significant costs of obtaining a CON.

The evidence is clear that those costs are significant in this market. We agree with Judge Parker that because incumbent hospitals can oppose new entry, even an unsuccessful opposition to a CON application may delay its disposition by several years. * * *

* * *

In sum, it is not merely the costs of obtaining a CON that a potential entrant faces, but the significant risk of being denied entry once those costs have been incurred. This risk, which incumbents did not have to face when building their hospitals, in effect raises the costs of entry a significantly greater amount. As a result, many potential entrants may decide not to even attempt entry. Indeed, the evidence shows that CON regulation has had a deterrent effect in the Chattanooga market.

*   *   *

E.   *The Nature and Likelihood of Anti-competitive Behavior in*
     the Chattanooga Hospital Market

1.   *The Nature of Anti-competitive Behavior*

*   *   *

Some of the most likely forms of collusion between hospitals would involve collective resistance to emerging cost containment pressures from third-party payors and alternative providers. For example, joint refusals to deal with HMOs or PPOs may occur, or perhaps joint refusals to deal on the most favorable terms. Conspiracies to boycott certain insurance companies that are generating price competition may occur. Utilization review programs may also be resisted. Hospitals could concertedly refuse to provide the information desired by third-party payors—information that would otherwise be provided as hospitals vie to attract the business of those payors and their subscribers. The result of any such boycott would be to raise prices, reduce quality of services or both. [ ]

*   *   *

Quality competition itself might also be restricted. For example, the group of hospitals in a relevant market might agree to staff their wards with fewer nurses yet continue to maintain current rates for inpatient services. Patients would be harmed by the resulting drop in quality of services without any compensating reduction in price of services. Colluding hospitals in the market, however, would profit from their agreement by cutting costs without cutting revenues. Again, hospitals could accomplish anti-competitive ends not only by fixing staff-patient ratios but by agreeing on wages or benefits to be paid certain personnel—for example, laboratory technicians. Indeed, wage and salary surveys are common in this market. [ ] The result would be the same—to hold the cost of inputs down with probable harm to the quality of output of health care services. [ ] Hospitals could also agree not to compete for each other's personnel or medical staff. Indeed, some Chattanooga urban area hospital firms have already engaged in such behavior. [ ]

Moreover, under certificate of need legislation, the addition of new services and purchases of certain kinds of new equipment require a demonstration of need for the expenditure, and the existence of need is determined in part by the facilities already provided in the community. It would thus be to the advantage of competing hospitals to enter into agreements among themselves as to which competitor will apply for which service or for which piece of equipment. * * *

Anti-competitive pricing behavior could also take several forms. For example, hospitals could work out agreements with respect to pricing formulas. * * *

* * *

Hospitals could also successfully collude with respect to price by agreeing not to give discounts to businesses, insurers and other group purchasers such as HMOs and PPOs. * * *

In sum, we conclude that hospitals compete in a myriad of ways that could be restricted anti-competitively through collusion. [ ] Thus, it appears that a merger analysis in this case need be no different than in any other case; market share and concentration figures, evidence of entry barriers and other market evidence taken together appear to yield as accurate a picture of competitive conditions as they do in other settings. Nevertheless, although HCA concedes that many of the above described forms of collusion *could* occur, the heart of HCA's case is that collusion in this market is inherently unlikely, and to that contention we now turn.

2.   The Likelihood of Anti-competitive Behavior

Section 7 of the Clayton Act prohibits acquisitions that may have the effect of substantially lessening competition or tending to create a monopoly. Because Section 7 applies to "incipient" violations, actual anti-competitive effects need not be shown; an acquisition is unlawful if such an effect is reasonably probable. [ ]

The small absolute number of competitors in this market, the high concentration and the extremely high entry barriers indicate a market in which anti-competitive behavior is reasonably probable after the acquisitions. The fact that industry members recognize the enormity of entry barriers makes collusion even more probable. In addition, hospital markets have certain features that evidence a likelihood of collusion or other anti-competitive behavior when they become highly concentrated. [ ]

First, price elasticity of demand for hospital services is very low, [ ] which makes anti-competitive behavior extremely profitable and hence attractive. [ ] Second, because consumers of hospital services cannot arbitrage or resell them as is often possible with goods, discrimination among different groups of consumers is possible. That is, collusion may be directed at a certain group or certain groups of consumers, such as a particular insurance company, without the necessity of anti-competitive behavior toward other groups. [ ] Third, the traditions of limited price competition and disapproval of advertising [ ] provide an incentive for future anti-competitive restrictions of those activities. Fourth, and in the same vein, the advent of incentives to resist new cost containment pressures may create a substantial danger of hospital collusion to meet pressures. [ ] Fifth, the hospital industry has a tradition of cooperative problem solving which makes collusive conduct in the future more likely. Hospitals have historically participated in voluntary health planning in a coordinated manner, and along with other professional organizations, such as medical societies, have participated in developing joint solutions to industry problems. [ ]

* * * The most convincing evidence of the facility with which such collusion could occur is a blatant market allocation agreement executed in 1981 between Red Bank Community Hospital and HCC. [ ] The parties actually *signed a contract* under which Red Bank agreed that for a period of three years it would not "file any application for a Certificate of Need for psychiatric facilities or nursing home facilities." [ ] Moreover, the parties agreed that they would not compete for each other's personnel and medical staff during that time period, and that they would not oppose each other's CON applications in certain areas. Such an overt agreement to refrain from competition at the very least demonstrates the predisposition of some firms in the market to collude when it is in their interest; at worst it shows a callous disregard for the antitrust laws. [ ]

* * *

Furthermore, a basis for collusion is provided by the exchanges of rate, salary and other competitively sensitive information that occur in this market. * * *

* * *

* * * It is true that the undisputed evidence shows that more vigorous competition, including more direct price competition, is emerging in the health care industry, but it is a fallacy to conclude that growing competition in health care markets means that these acquisitions pose no threat to that competition. In fact, it is just that emerging competition that must be protected from mergers that facilitate the suppression of such competition. * * *

a. Non-profit Hospitals and the Likelihood of Collusion

HCA contends that the most fundamental difference between hospitals in Chattanooga is that several of the hospitals are "non-profit" institutions. Economic theory presumes that businesses in an industry are profit-maximizers and that output will be restricted in pursuit of profits. Non-profit hospitals, the argument goes, have no incentive to maximize profits, rather, they seek to maximize "output" or the number of patients treated. [ ] HCA contends that non-profit hospitals may have other goals as well, such as providing the most sophisticated and highest quality care possible, or pursuing religious or governmental goals. [ ] In short, HCA argues that collusion would not occur because the "for-profit" and "non-profit" competitors have no common goal. [ ]

We disagree that non-profit hospitals have no incentive to collude with each other or with proprietary hospitals to achieve anti-competitive ends. First, we note that non-profit status of market participants is no guarantee of competitive behavior. * * *

* * *

In addition, administrators of non-profit hospitals may seek to maximize their personal benefits and comfort through what would otherwise be known as profit-seeking activity. * * *

* * *

b.   *Purported Obstacles to Successful Coordination*

. . . HCA argues that even if hospitals in Chattanooga were inclined to collude, the administrators of those hospitals would find it difficult to reach anti-competitive agreements or understandings, or to sustain them if they ever were reached. This is so because the ideal market circumstances for collusion are not present, *i.e.* where manufacturers are selling "some simple, relatively homogeneous good, well characterized by a single price." [ ] HCA contends that hospital services are heterogeneous and influenced by a variety of complicating factors. Hospitals provide a large number of varied medical tests and treatments and each patient receives unpredictable personalized service the extent of which is determined by physicians. [ ] Moreover, HCA claims costs and demand vary between hospitals. And because the dominant avenues of competition relate to the quality of medical care and patient amenities, hospitals would have to agree on a whole host of things to eliminate competition in a manner sufficient to earn monopoly returns, it is alleged.

* * *

HCA's analysis of the likelihood of collusion distorts competitive reality. HCA would have us believe that the world of possible collusion is limited to complicated formulae concerning every aspect of hospital competition—that market power can only be exercised with respect to the entire cluster of services that constitutes the acute care hospital market through a conspiracy fixing the overall quantity or quality of treatment running to each patient in the market. Rather than focus on the likely avenues of collusion among hospitals, HCA assumes into existence a world in which collusion is infeasible.

* * *

HCA offers an additional reason why the acquisitions allegedly create no risk that Chattanooga hospitals will collude to eliminate price competition, arguing that price collusion is unlikely because of the role of Blue Cross in this market. * * *

We cannot accept HCA's claims that Blue Cross has both the omniscience and market power to halt successful collusion by Chattanooga hospitals. First, under the current Blue Cross charge approval system, collusion could be difficult to detect. [ ] If all the hospital firms in Chattanooga attempt to raise prices a similar amount in the review process, coordinated pricing could be overlooked; there is no *a priori* reason why Blue Cross would consider this to be the result of collusion rather than a rise in costs. * * *

Furthermore, even if detected, we do not think such collusion could be easily deterred by Blue Cross. HCA ignores the fact that Blue Cross has a contract not only with participating hospitals but also with its subscribers. Blue Cross must serve its subscribers in the Chattanooga area, and HCA does not explain how Blue Cross could reject a concerted effort by the hospitals there even if it wanted to; certainly, Blue Cross could not ask its subscribers to all go to Knoxville for hospital care if Chattanooga urban area hospitals colluded. * * *

                                   *   *   *

VII. Conclusion

We hold that HCA's acquisitions of HAI and HCC may substantially lessen competition in the Chattanooga urban area acute care hospital market in violation of Section 7 of the Clayton Act and Section 5 of the Federal Trade Commission Act.

                                   *   *   *

NOTES AND QUESTIONS

1.   The Seventh Circuit reviewed and upheld the decision of the Federal Trade Commission in Hospital Corporation of America v. FTC, 807 F.2d 1381 (7th Cir. 1986). Calling the FTC's decision a "model of lucidity," Judge Posner reviewed the Commission's analysis of the merger:

> When an economic approach is taken in a section 7 case, the ultimate issue is whether the challenged acquisition is likely to facilitate collusion. In this perspective the acquisition of a competitor has no economic significance in itself; the worry is that it may enable the acquiring firm to cooperate (or cooperate better) with other leading competitors on reducing or limiting output, thereby pushing up the market price. *Hospital Corporation* calls the issue whether an acquisition is likely to have such an effect "economic," which of course it is. But for purposes of judicial review, as we have said, it is a factual issue subject to the substantial evidence rule.

Judge Posner discussed HCA's arguments that collusion is unlikely because of the heterogeneity of hospital markets, the rapid technological and economic change experienced by the hospital industry, and the size of third party payers. He concluded: "Most of these facts do detract from a conclusion that collusion in this market is a serious danger, but it was for the Commission—it is not for us—to determine their weight." His analysis is directed at the risk of "coordinated effects" resulting from a merger—that is, an enhancement of the ability of the merged entity to exercise market power by acting in coordination with others competitors in a market. Compare this kind of harm with the "unilateral effects" analysis in the Evanston Hospital case *infra*.

2. Antitrust enforcement has reached mergers involving numerous other segments of the health care industry besides hospitals. For example, state and federal enforcers have challenged mergers of physician groups, rehabilitation hospitals; hospitals providing inpatient psychiatric care; skilled nursing facilities; retail pharmacies; and HMOs. Market definition poses difficult and fact-specific questions. For example, how would you go about determining the geographic market for skilled nursing home services? Who is the "buyer" of these services?

FEDERAL TRADE COMMISSION V. TENET HEALTH CARE CORPORATION

United States Court of Appeals Eighth Circuit, 1999.
186 F.3d 1045.

BEAM, CIRCUIT JUDGE.

Tenet Healthcare and Poplar Bluff Physicians Group, Inc., doing business as Doctors' Regional Medical Center (collectively, Tenet) appeal the district court's order enjoining the merger of two hospitals in Poplar Bluff, Missouri. After a five-day hearing, the district court granted a motion for a preliminary injunction filed by the Federal Trade Commission (FTC) and the State of Missouri. The district court found a substantial likelihood that the merger would substantially lessen competition between acute care hospitals in Poplar Bluff, Missouri, in violation of section 7 of the Clayton Act, 15 U.S.C. § 18. We reverse.

I.   Background

* * *

Tenet Healthcare Corporation owns Lucy Lee Hospital in Poplar Bluff, a general acute care hospital that provides primary and secondary care services 201 licensed beds ... [and] operates ten outpatient clinics in the surrounding counties. Doctors' Regional Medical Center in Poplar Bluff is presently owned by a group of physicians, ... has 230 licensed beds ... [and] also operates several rural health clinics in the area. Though profitable, both hospitals are underutilized and have had problems attracting specialists to the area.

Tenet recently entered into an agreement to purchase Doctors' Regional which it will operate as a long-term care facility, consolidating inpatient services of the two hospitals at Lucy Lee. It plans to employ more specialists at the merged facility and to offer higher quality care in a comprehensive, integrated delivery system that would include some tertiary care. * * *

The evidence adduced at the hearing shows that Lucy Lee and Doctors' Regional are the only two hospitals in Poplar Bluff, other than a Veteran's Hospital. The combined service area of these hospitals covers eight counties and an approximate fifty-mile radius from Poplar Bluff.[4] * * *

                    *   *   *

Market participants, specifically, employers, healthplans and network providers testified that they had negotiated substantial discounts and favorable per diem rates with either or both Lucy Lee and Doctors' Regional as a result of "playing the two hospitals off each other." These managed care organizations and employers testified that if the merged entity were to raise its prices by 10 percent, the health plans would have no choice but to simply pay the increased price. They testified that they perceive it is essential for the plans to include a Poplar Bluff hospital in their benefit packages because their enrollees would not travel to other towns for primary and secondary inpatient treatment. They stated that their employees and subscribers find it convenient to use a Poplar Bluff hospital; are loyal to their physicians in Poplar Bluff and would not be amenable to a health benefit plan that did not include a Poplar Bluff hospital.

The evidence shows that patient choice of hospitals is determined by many variables, including patient/physician loyalty, perceptions of quality, geographic proximity and, most importantly or determinatively, access to hospitals through an insurance plan. Managed care organizations have been able to influence or change patient behavior with financial incentives in other healthcare markets. This practice is known as "steering." Representatives of Poplar Bluff managed care entities testified, however, that they did not believe such efforts would be successful in the Poplar Bluff market. They testified it would be unlikely that they could steer their subscribers to another hospital, or could exclude the merged Poplar Bluff entity in the event of a price increase, in spite of the fact that such tactics had been successful in other markets. They did not regard the Cape Girardeau hospitals as an alternative to Poplar Bluff hospitals because the Cape Girardeau hospitals were more costly. Witnesses conceded, however, that employees had been successfully "steered" to other area

---

[4] A "service area" is generally defined as the area from which a hospital derives ninety percent of its inpatients.

hospitals in the past. Several employers testified that they could success-fully steer their employees to Missouri Delta Hospital in Sikeston, Missouri. The representative of one large employer testified that the large employers could prevent price increases through negotiation based on their market power and that the merged entity would provide better quality healthcare.

Lucy Lee and Doctors' Regional obtain ninety percent of their patients from zip codes within a fifty-mile radius of Poplar Bluff. In eleven of the top twelve zip codes, however, significant patient admissions-ranging from 22% to 70%-were to hospitals other than those in Poplar Bluff. There is no dispute that Poplar Bluff residents travel to St. Louis, Memphis, and Jonesboro for tertiary care. The evidence also shows, however, that significant numbers of patients in the Poplar Bluff service area travel to other towns for primary and secondary treatment that is also available in Poplar Bluff.

*   *   *

II.   Discussion

*   *   *

A geographic market is the area in which consumers can practically turn for alternative sources of the product and in which the antitrust defendants face competition. [ ] Market share must be established in a well-defined market. [ ] A properly defined geographic market includes potential suppliers who can readily offer consumers a suitable alternative to the defendant's services. [ ] Determination of the relevant geographic market is highly fact sensitive. [ ] The proper market definition can be determined only after a factual inquiry into the commercial realities faced by consumers. * * *

The government has the burden of proving the relevant geographic market. [ ] To meet this burden, the FTC must present evidence on the critical question of where consumers of hospital services could practicably turn for alternative services should the merger be consummated and prices become anticompetitive. [ ] This evidence must address where consumers could practicably go, not on where they actually go. [ ] *Bathke,* 64 F.3d at 346 (articulating the test as the distance "customers will travel in order to avoid doing business at [the entity that has raised prices]" rather than the distance customers would travel absent a price increase); [ ].

The FTC proposes a relevant geographic market that essentially matches its service area: a fifty-mile radius from downtown Poplar Bluff. It is from this service area that the two hospitals obtain ninety percent of their patients. A service area, however, is not necessarily a merging firm's geographic market for purposes of antitrust analysis. * * *

*   *   *

The question before us is whether the FTC provided sufficient evidence that the proposed merger will result in the merged entity possessing market power within the relevant geographic market. Because we conclude that the FTC produced insufficient evidence of a well-defined relevant geographic market, we find that it did not show that the merged entity will possess such market power. * * *

The district court found that statistical evidence did not establish either the geographic market proposed by the FTC or the market proposed by Tenet. [ ] It nonetheless found, relying on anecdotal evidence, that the merger would likely be anticompetitive. Our review of the record convinces us that the district court erred in several respects. The evidence in this case falls short of establishing a relevant geographic market that excludes the Sikeston or Cape Girardeau areas. The evidence shows that hospitals in either or both of these towns, as well as rural hospitals throughout the area, are practical alternatives for many Poplar Bluff consumers.

In adopting the FTC's position, the district court improperly discounted the fact that over twenty-two percent of people in the most important zip codes already use hospitals outside the FTC's proposed market for treatment that is offered at Poplar Bluff hospitals. [ ] The district court also failed to fully credit the significance of the consumers who live outside Poplar Bluff, particularly those patients within the FTC's proposed geographic market who actually live or work closer to a hospital outside that geographic market than to either of the Poplar Bluff hospitals. If patients use hospitals outside the service area, those hospitals can act as a check on the exercise of market power by the hospitals within the service area. [ ] The FTC's contention that the merged hospitals would have eighty-four percent of the market for inpatient primary and secondary services within a contrived market area that stops just short of including a regional hospital (Missouri Delta in Sikeston) that is closer to many patients than the Poplar Bluff hospitals, strikes us as absurd. The proximity of many patients to hospitals in other towns, coupled with the compelling and essentially unrefuted evidence that the switch to another provider by a small percentage of patients would constrain a price increase, shows that the FTC's proposed market is too narrow.

We question the district court's reliance on the testimony of managed care payers, in the face of contrary evidence, that these for-profit entities would unhesitatingly accept a price increase rather than steer their subscribers to hospitals in Sikeston or Cape Girardeau. Without necessarily being disingenuous or self-serving or both, the testimony is at least contrary to the payers' economic interests and thus is suspect.[14] In spite of

---

[14] We add that, in making this observation, we do not question the district court's assessment of the credibility of these witnesses. Although the witnesses may have testified truthfully

their testimony to the contrary, the evidence shows that large, sophisticated third-party buyers can do resist price increases, especially where consolidation results in cost savings to the merging entities. The testimony of the market participants spoke to current competitor perceptions and consumer habits and failed to show where consumers could practicably go for inpatient hospital services.

The district court rejected the Cape Girardeau hospitals as practicable alternatives because they were more costly. In so doing, it underestimated the impact of nonprice competitive factors, such as quality. The evidence shows that one reason for the significant amount of migration from the Poplar Bluff hospitals to either Sikeston, Cape Girardeau, or St. Louis is the actual or perceived difference in quality of care. The apparent willingness of Poplar Bluff residents to travel for better quality care must be considered. As the district court noted, healthcare decisions are based on factors other than price. It is for that reason that, although they are less expensive, HMOs are not always an employer's or individual's choice in healthcare services. *See* Blue Cross and Blue Shield United of Wisconsin v. Marshfield Clinic, 65 F.3d 1406, 1412, 1410 (7th Cir. 1995) (Posner, J.) (noting "[g]enerally you must pay more for higher quality" and "the HMO's incentive is to keep you healthy if it can but if you get very sick, and are unlikely to recover to a healthy state involving few medical expenses, to let you die as quickly and cheaply as possible."). Thus, the fact that Cape Girardeau hospitals are higher priced than Poplar Bluff hospitals does not necessarily mean they are not competitors. [ ] The district court placed an inordinate emphasis on price competition without considering the impact of a corresponding reduction in quality.

We further find that although Tenet's efficiencies defense may have been properly rejected by the district court, the district court should nonetheless have considered evidence of enhanced efficiency in the context of the competitive effects of the merger. The evidence shows that a hospital that is larger and more efficient than Lucy Lee or Doctors' Regional will provide better medical care than either of those hospitals could separately. The merged entity will be able to attract more highly qualified physicians and specialists and to offer integrated delivery and some tertiary care. * * *The evidence shows that the merged entity may well enhance competition in the greater Southeast Missouri area.

In assessing the "commercial realities" faced by consumers, the district court did not . . . consider the impact of the entry of managed care into the Cape Girardeau market. The evidence shows that managed care has reduced prices in Poplar Bluff and in other markets. A similar downward pressure on prices is now being felt in Cape Girardeau, with the re-

---

as to their present intentions, market participants are not always in the best opinion to assess the market long term. [ ]

692   ANTITRUST   CH. 14

cent entry of managed care into that market. The district court also relied on the seemingly outdated assumption of doctor-patient loyalty that is not supported by the record. The evidence shows, and the district court acknowledged, that the issue of access to a provider through an insurance plan is determinative of patient choice. Essentially, the evidence shows that patients will choose whatever doctors or hospitals are covered by their health plan. Undeniably, although many patients might prefer to be loyal to their doctors, it is, unfortunately, a luxury they can no longer afford. * * *As much as many patients long for the days of old-fashioned and local, if expensive and inefficient, healthcare, recent trends in healthcare management have made the old healthcare model obsolete.

The reality of the situation in our changing healthcare environment may be that Poplar Bluff cannot support two high-quality hospitals. Third-party payers have reaped the benefit of a price war in a small corner of the market for healthcare services in Southeastern Missouri, at the arguable cost of quality to their subscribers. Antitrust laws simply do not protect that benefit when the evidence shows that there are other practical alternatives for healthcare in the area. We are mindful that competition is the driving force behind our free enterprise system and that, unless barriers have been erected to constrain the normal operation of the market, "a court ought to exercise extreme caution because judicial intervention in a competitive situation can itself upset the balance of market forces, bringing about the very ills the antitrust laws were meant to prevent." [ ] This appears to have even more force in an industry, such as healthcare, experiencing significant and profound changes. Under the circumstances presented in this case, the FTC has not shown a likelihood of success on the merits of its section 7 complaint and we find the district court erred in granting injunctive relief.

NOTES AND QUESTIONS

1.   The geographic market determination turns on the question of where customers could practicably turn in the event that prices were increased as a result of enhanced market power (or in the terminology of the Merger Guidelines, there was a "small but significant increase in price"). In the context of hospital mergers, patient origin data (usually compiled using the zip code of the residence of each patient) has traditionally been used to calculate the inflow and outflow of patients to hospitals from a geographic region. This data, however, is at best a starting point for analysis, as the Eighth Circuit points out. Courts must ask where buyers (patients) or their health plans or employers would turn in the event of a price increase resulting from the merger. What evidence did the FTC and the State of Missouri rely on to answer this question? Do you agree with the reasons supplied by the court to dispute the government's analysis? Given the speculative nature of the question, what evidence would you regard as most reliable? Does the fact that some individuals are willing to travel some distance to receive hos-

pital services necessarily imply that others will also do so if prices are increased? For the view of economists branding these assumptions as fallacious because individuals have highly heterogeneous preferences regarding traveling for hospitals care based on the availability of family support, their place of employment, convenience, and because hospitals are highly differentiated in their services, of the Elzinga Hogarty Criteria: A Critique and New Approach to Analyzing Hospital Mergers. Nat'l Bureau of Econ. Research, Working Paper No. 8216, 2001; James Langenfeld & W. Li, Critical Loss Analysis in Evaluating Mergers, 46 Antitrust Bull. 299 (2001).

2.   The government lost seven consecutive hospital merger cases in the 1990s, most on the issue of whether the government had correctly defined the geographic market. See e.g., FTC v. Freeman Hospital, 69 F.3d 260 (8th Cir. 1995); California v. Sutter Health System, 84 F. Supp. 2d 1057 (N.D. Cal. 2000). Does the court's opinion in *Tenet* suggest hostility toward managed care or skepticism about the benefits of hospital competition in general? See id. (suggesting that the "managed care backlash" may have subtly influence courts in certain antitrust cases). Responding to their lack of success in court, the FTC and DOJ produced a lengthy report on competition policy in health care, and conducted retrospective studies of the impact of horizontal hospital mergers in selected markets around the country, including some that were the subject of unsuccessful litigation by the government. See FTC & Department of Justice, A Dose of Competition, *supra*. The FTC took the unusual step of challenging a consummated hospital merger in Evanston Illinois, asserting a very narrow geographic market consisting of the Evanston, Illinois but excluding other suburbs and the city of Chicago. In the matter of Evanston Northwetern Healthcare Corp. (FTC Docket No. 9315) (2007). In addition, the agency's analytic approach differed from prior litigation in several respects. First, it declaimed the usefulness of patient origin data in defining the relevant geographic market and instead, relied on the actual effects in the market place to prove the existence of a market. Second, it relied on a "unilateral effects" analysis to explain the competitive harm to competition resulting from the merger.   That is, the two merging hospitals were able to raise prices because each was the next best alternative of the other in the eyes of a significant number of patients. Hence they were able to raise prices after the merger without regard to the actions of other area hospitals. Although the majority of the Commission found it unnecessary to address the theory, FTC counsel alleged, and two commissioners agreed, that it would not be necessary to prove a geographic market in the case because anticompetitive effect was established independently.

3. With health reform has come a new "merger wave" of competing acute care hospitals. The FTC has responded challenging several mergers:

Phoebe Putney Health System/Palmyra Park Hospital. In a unanimous decision, the Supreme Court overturned a decision by the Eleventh Circuit that had found a hospital merger to monopoly in Albany Georgia was protected from federal antitrust challenge by the "state action" doctrine. FTC v.

Phoebe Putney Health System, Inc. __ U.S. __, 133 S.Ct. 1003 (2013). As noted in the introduction to this chapter, that doctrine immunizes private entities from antitrust law when their anticompetitive conduct is clearly contemplated and actively supervised by the State. The transaction at issue in *Phoebe Putney* involved a plan under which the county authority acquired Palmyra Park Hospital and subsequently leased it to a nonprofit corporation controlled by Phoebe. At issue was whether Georgia's grant of general corporate powers to hospital authorities was a "clear-articulation" of an intent to displace competition. The Court held that it was not, observing that a "substate governmental entity" such as a hospital authority, must "show that it has been delegated authority to act or regulate anticompetitively." 133 S.Ct. at 1009.

OSF/Rockford. In April 2012, a district court enjoined OSF Healthcare System's proposed acquisition of Rockford Health System pending an administrative trial. The parties abandoned their plans to merge soon thereafter. Agreeing with the market alleged by the FTC the court found that the merger would create a dominant health system controlling 64% of the market for general acute care inpatient services and would reduce the number of competitors from three to two. FTC v. OSF Healthcare System and Rockford Health System, 852 F.Supp.2d 1069 (N.D. Ill. 2012).

In the matter of ProMedica. In March 2012, the Federal Trade Commission blocked ProMedica Health System's acquisition of St. Luke's Hospital in Toledo. The FTC found the acquisition would likely result in higher health care costs for patients, employers, and employees, in violation of Section 7 of the Clayton Act. Notably, the case involved a consummated merger which closed at the end of August 2010, but in which the merging parties had agreed to refrain from renegotiating managed care contracts and or eliminating or reorganizing clinical services pending the FTC's investigation. The court rejected a number of proffered defenses including the claim that powerful insurance buyers would constrain defendants' ability to raise prices post-merger. ProMedica Health System, Inc., 2012–1 Trade Cas. (CCH) ¶ 77840, 2012 WL 1155392 (F.T.C. 2012).

4.   If the government establishes a *prima facie* case of illegality based on market share and market concentration data, defendants may overcome that presumption by showing that the merger is not likely to have anticompetitive effects. They may do this by proving that market conditions or special characteristics of the merging firms make it unlikely that they will exercise market power after the merger is consummated. A number of courts have refused to find that the not-for-profit status of the merging hospitals constitutes sufficient grounds to rebut the government's prima facie case. See, e.g., U.S. v. Rockford Memorial Corp., 898 F.2d 1278 (7th Cir. 1990). However, one district court has held that not-for-profit hospitals do not operate in the same manner as profit-maximizing businesses, especially when their boards of directors are comprised of community business leaders who have a direct stake in maintaining high quality, low cost hospitals. FTC v. Butterworth Health

Corporation and Blodgett Memorial Medical Center, 946 F.Supp. 1285 (W.D. Mich. 1996), aff'd 121 F.3d 708 (6th Cir. 1997).

5. *Efficiencies*. The law on efficiencies as a defense to an otherwise anticompetitive merger is somewhat unclear. Older Supreme Court case law and the legislative history of the Clayton Act does not seem to support an efficiencies defense, see Alan A. Fisher & Robert Lande, Efficiency Considerations in Merger Enforcement, 71 Cal. L. Rev. 1580 (1983). However, most lower courts have explicitly considered potential cost-savings and other efficiencies associated with mergers both as an absolute defense and as a factor to be considered in evaluating the merger's likely competitive effects. See, e.g., FTC v. University Health, Inc., 938 F.2d 1206 (11th Cir. 1991). The DOJ/FTC Merger Guidelines and most of the litigated cases require that the parties show that the claimed efficiencies cannot be realized by means short of a merger and that the efficiencies be "merger specific" (i.e., attributable to and causally related to the combination of the two firms). Merger Guidelines, § 4. Inability to clear these hurdles is often decisive in cases in which courts reject the efficiencies defense. The court in *Tenet* followed the approach of considering potential efficiencies resulting from the merger in the context of analyzing the merger's overall impact. Does this form of analysis permit a more speculative standard? Should the potential to enhance quality of care be folded into the competitive analysis of efficiencies? See Kristin Madison, Hospital Mergers in an Era of Quality Improvement, 7 Hous. J. Health L. & Pol. 265 (2007).

PROBLEM: EVALUATING A HOSPITAL MERGER IN YOUR COMMUNITY

Suppose the largest and third largest hospitals (or hospital systems) in your community proposed to merge. What will the key issues be? What facts would you gather in seeking to defend this transaction against antitrust challenge? What testimony from payors, employers, expert witnesses, or parties to the transaction would be helpful?

2. Managed Care Mergers

The health insurance industry has witnessed a rapid succession of major mergers. According to the AMA, there have been over 400 mergers involving health insurers over the past decade and the largest remaining companies, Aetna, Cigna, United Healthcare, Foundation Health Systems, and Wellpoint Health Networks, control a large share of the nation's private insurance business. See Edward Langston, "Statement of the American Medical Association to the Senate Committee on the Judiciary United States Senate: Examining Competition in Group Health Care," (study finding more than 95% of Metropolitan Statistical Areas (MSAs) had at least one insurer in the combined HMO/PPO market with a market share greater than 30% and more than 56% of MSAs had at least one insurer with market share greater than 50%). This data may overstate the risks of high concentration; however, as it does not include self-insurance by large corporations and the degree of actual concentration in well-defined insurance markets is disputed. See, A Dose of Competition, Ch. 6 at 7 (noting testimony that "health insurance markets in most geographic areas enjoy robust competition"). Although the Department of Justice has challenged several mergers involving large national organizations, these cases resulted in limited divestitures in a small fraction of the markets in which the firms did business. For example, Aetna's buyout of Prudential Health Care was settled by consent decree filed jointly by the U.S. Department of Justice and the Texas Attorney General's Office. U.S. and State of Texas v. Aetna Inc., No. 3–99 CV 1398–H (N.D. Tex.), 64 Fed. Reg. 44946–01 (1999). However, the government limited the market in one case to markets for small group insurance on the theory that these groups cannot self-insure and have fewer alternatives. U.S. v. United Health Group Incorporated and PacificCare Health Systems, No. 1:05–cv–02436 (D.D.C. filed Jan. 20, 2005).

3. Physician Practice Mergers

Antitrust attention has only occasionally focused on physician mergers. In the only case thus far decided by the courts, HTI Health Services, Inc. v. Quorum Health Group, Inc., 960 F.Supp. 1104 (S.D. Miss. 1997), the district court refused to enjoin a merger of the two largest physician clinics in Vicksburg, Mississippi with one of two hospitals in town. Notably, the court held that plaintiff had properly alleged four distinct physician service markets: primary care, general surgery, urology, and otolaryngology; in addition, it accepted a primary care sub-market for pediatrics. However, the court held that the absence of barriers to entry effectively obviated concerns about the defendant's potential exercise of market power, noting the plaintiff hospital had a highly successful record in recruiting new physicians into the market to serve its facility.

While state attorneys general have occasionally challenged physician mergers, the FTC and Department of Justice have rarely done so. Responding however to the wave of physician acquisitions by hospitals in the wake of health reform, the FTC challenged successive acquisitions of cardiology practices by Renown Health, the largest hospital system in Reno, Nevada. In the matter of Renown Health, FTC Docket No. c–4366, 2012 WL 6188550 (Nov. 12, 2012). The FTC agreed to a novel relief in the case in which Renown agreed to suspend noncompete provisions for at least 60 days, allowing as many as ten cardiologists to seek employment with other Reno hospitals or to practice independently. Because physician mergers fly under the radar screen for mandatory pre-merger reporting, the government typically must challenge an already-consummated transaction. What impediments exist in obtaining relief in such cases?

REVIEW PROBLEM: THE HEART SPECIALTY HOSPITAL

Heart-of-the-Midwest Orthopedic Surgical Hospital (HOTMOSH) has applied to its state health planning agency for a certificate of need (CON) to open a new acute care hospital in Bedrock, Kansas. It will offer facilities for inpatient and outpatient orthopedic surgery and related procedures and a variety of outpatient services including radiology and laboratory services. The hospital is owned by an LLC controlled by two groups of orthopedic surgeons each of which own 40 percent of the membership interest; the remaining ownership is held by other Bedrock physicians.

The three community hospitals in Bedrock are very concerned about the impact HOTMOSH will have on their revenues. Freda Fieldstone, CEO of Bedrock Community Hospital (BCH), has called a meeting with the other hospitals to discuss formulating a "joint response" to the CON application. Besides urging the other hospitals to ask the planning commission to reject the application, she hopes to enlist their support in a campaign to elicit help from managed care organizations. One idea is to have each hospital commit to contacting one managed care organization (MCO) (its "dancing partner") to urge that company not to contract with HOTMOSH and, if necessary, to "intimate" that the other hospitals in the market would probably be very unhappy if the MCO chose to include the specialty hospital in its network.

Because BCH is the largest orthopedic hospital in the area and other hospitals are not at risk for losing nearly as much business, Ms. Fieldstone believes she must come up with a strategy to ensure she will have the support of the other hospitals. Because St. Lucas Hospital has filed a CON application to add 20 new oncology beds to its campus, Ms. Fieldstone believes that if she "hints" that BCH might oppose this CON application unless St. Lucas supports her on the HOTMOSH issue, she will "get their attention." If that doesn't work, she plans to hint that BCH may also be thinking of opening a new oncology service.

Finally, Ms. Fieldstone has several "backup" plans:

- Terminate the staff privileges of every doctor at BCH who has an ownership interest or who refers more than five patients per year to HOTMOSH.

- Create a "super PHO" to bargain with MCOs on behalf of the other hospitals performing orthopedic services in town. If that is not possible, to "clinically integrate" the orthopedic surgeons on her staff who do not have an ownership in HOTMOSH so that they can negotiate as a unit with MCOs?

- If all else fails, negotiate a merger or joint venture with HOTMOSH once it establishes that it is successful in the market.

Recognizing that these ideas may raise some antitrust concerns, Ms. Feldstone has solicited your counsel. Advise on the possible antitrust risks you see for each strategic option and what might be done to reduce legal risk.

CHAPTER 15

CONTRACEPTION, ABORTION AND STERILIZATION

■ ■ ■

The law has been invoked regularly to order the relationships of private individuals and to constrain government to its appropriate role with regard to the limitation of reproduction. The law has also been engaged to regulate medical interventions designed to facilitate reproduction, such as artificial insemination, ovum and embryo transfer, in vitro fertilization, and surrogacy. While the propriety of legal intervention in these matters will undoubtedly remain a matter of dispute, the sexual nature of the issues, as well as their novelty and moral complexity, is likely to cause society to maintain a high interest in regulating them. The rest of this chapter is not intended to be a comprehensive analysis of all of these questions; many related issues are discussed elsewhere in this text or in other courses. It is the purpose of this chapter to provide structure to those issues surrounding contraception, abortion and sterilization that are likely to be of special concern to attorneys representing health care professionals, institutions, and their patients.

I.   CONTRACEPTION

The question of the Constitutionality of state statutes criminalizing the use of contraceptives reached the Supreme Court in Griswold v. Connecticut, 381 U.S. 479, 85 S.Ct. 1678, 14 L.Ed.2d 510 (1965). An official of the Planned Parenthood League of Connecticut and a Yale physician were charged with aiding and abetting "the use of a drug, medicinal article, or instrument for the purpose of preventing conception," a crime under Connecticut law, by providing contraceptives to a married couple. The Supreme Court reversed their conviction. Justice Douglas, writing for the Court, concluded:

> [S]pecific guarantees in the Bill of Rights have penumbras, formed by emanations from those guarantees that helped give them life and substance. Various guarantees create zones of privacy. The rights of association contained in the penumbra of the first amendment is one * * * the third amendment in its prohibition against the quartering of soldiers "in any house" in time of

peace without the consent of the owner is another facet of that privacy. The fourth amendment explicitly affirms the right of the people to be secure in their persons, houses, papers, and effects against unreasonable searches and seizures. The fifth amendment in its self-incrimination clause enables the citizen to create a zone of privacy which government may not force him to surrender to his detriment. The ninth amendment provides "the enumeration in the constitution of certain rights will not be construed to deny or disparage others retained by the people."

The present case * * * concerns a relationship lying within the zone of privacy created by several fundamental constitutional guarantees * * *.

We deal with a right of privacy older than the Bill of Rights— older than our political parties, older than our school system. Marriage is a coming together for better or worse, hopefully enduring, and intimate to the degree of being sacred. It is an association that promotes a way of life, not causes; a harmony in living, not political faith; a bilateral loyalty, not commercial or social projects. Yet it is an association for as noble a purpose as any involved in our prior decisions.

381 U.S. at 484, 85 S.Ct. at 1681. Although a majority concurred in Justice Douglas's opinion, Chief Justice Warren and Justices Brennan and Goldberg based their determination on the Ninth Amendment. Justice Harlan based his concurrence entirely on the due process clause of the Fourteenth Amendment. Separately, Justice White concurred in the judgment and based his determination on the Fourteenth Amendment. Justices Black and Stewart dissented. Justice Black wrote:

There is no single one of the graphic and eloquent strictures and criticisms fired at the policy of this Connecticut law either by the court's opinion or by those of my concurring brethren to which I cannot subscribe—except their conclusion that the evil qualities they see in the law make it unconstitutional. * * *

I like my privacy as well as the next one, but I am nevertheless compelled to admit the government has a right to invade it unless prohibited by some specific constitutional provision. For these reasons, I cannot agree with the court's judgment and the reasons it gives for holding this Connecticut law unconstitutional.

381 U.S. at 510, 85 S.Ct. at 1696. The *Griswold* case left open the question of whether this new right of privacy extended only to married couples or to single people as well. It also left open the question of whether it extended only to decisions related to procreation or whether it extended to all health care decisions. The first of these questions was answered in 1972 when the Court determined that a law that allowed married people,

but not unmarried people, to have access to contraceptives violated the equal protection clause of the Fourteenth Amendment because there could be no rational basis for distinguishing between married and unmarried people in permitting access to contraceptives. The Court suggested that "if the right of privacy means anything, it is the right of the individual, married or single, to be free from unwarranted government intrusion into matters so fundamentally affecting a person as a decision whether to bear a child." Eisenstadt v. Baird, 405 U.S. 438, 453, 92 S.Ct. 1029, 1038, 31 L.Ed.2d 349 (1972). In Carey v. Population Services International, 431 U.S. 678, 97 S.Ct. 2010, 52 L.Ed.2d 675 (1977), the Supreme Court confirmed that since *Griswold* declared it unconstitutional for a state to deny contraceptives to married couples, and *Eisenstadt* declared it unconstitutional for a state to distinguish between married couples and unmarried people in controlling access to contraceptives, a state was without authority to ban the distribution of contraceptives to any adult.

May a state still limit access to contraceptives for minors? Should different kinds of contraceptives be regulated in different ways? Could a state require that condoms be available only through a face-to-face encounter with a pharmacist? In the mid–2000s many state health and education officials became concerned over federally funded "abstinence only" programs that provided middle and high school students with sex education programs that did not even mention most forms of contraception. By early 2008 more than a dozen states had decided to turn down millions of dollars of federal money because of the apparent failure of these programs in limiting teen pregnancy, which was already far more common in the United States than in most of the developed world. Does government funding of these programs, which are strongly supported by religious groups, pose any legal issue? Does it make a difference that even those who advocate teaching about contraception agree that abstinence is the most healthy choice for individual teens? Should public entities be involved in encouraging or discouraging contraceptive use? Is there any legal limit on the ways in which they can be involved?

NOTE: THE BLURRY DISTINCTION BETWEEN CONTRACEPTION AND ABORTION—PLAN B AND ELLA (THE "MORNING AFTER" PILLS), AND MIFEPRISTONE (RU–486)

Are some "contraceptives" that work by making implantation difficult (like Plan B or ella, sometimes called "morning after pills") really contraceptives, subject to very limited government regulation, or are they agents of abortion, subject to far greater restriction and regulation (and, perhaps, prohibition)? In addition, there is some question about how to treat medications that are recognized as nonsurgical abortifacients, like the drug Mifepristone.

There are three medications approved in the United States for administration after intercourse to avoid pregnancy. Plan B (levonorgestrel) and ella (ulipristal acetate) are designed to avoid the development of pregnancy by inhibiting ovulation or follicle rupture, although in some cases they may alter the uterine lining and, possibly, make it less likely that a fertilized ovum will enter the uterus or implant (or remain implanted) in the uterine wall. Plan B became available in 2006 after a long and highly political history. In 1999 an FDA advisory panel had recommended that the drug be made available over the counter for all purchasers, but objections (arguably political and arguably medical) caused the FDA to delay approval until 2003 and then require a prescription for this medication. After a threat by some members of the Senate to withhold confirmation of a newly appointed FDA Commissioner in 2006, Plan B was finally made available over the counter for persons over 18, and that age was subsequently lowered to 17. Plan B is about 89% effective if taken immediately after intercourse, and its efficacy decreases over the 72 hours following intercourse when it can be administered. As a general matter, Plan B decreases the chance of pregnancy from about 1/20 (the base rate after sexual intercourse) to 1/40.

Ella, which was approved by the FDA in 2010 after its own long medical and political battle, works in largely the same way. While it may be slightly less effective than Plan B when used immediately after intercourse, it is effective for 120 hours, and it does not lose its efficacy during that five day period. As a general matter, it decreases the risk of pregnancy after unprotected sex to 1/50. Ella is available only by prescription in the United States.

Unlike either Plan B or ella, Mifepristone (RU–486) is designed to disrupt implantation of the fertilized embryo and to change the uterus to become less hospitable to the fertilized ovum, eventually expelling it. Mifepristone is available only through prescription, and it can be dispensed only by specially licensed physicians who are authorized to administer it. It is, thus, not available through pharmacies. Although the mechanism of operation is largely different, Mifepristone and ella are chemically closely related. For a general account of the pharmacology and medical use of these medications, see Robert Hatcher et al., Contraceptive Technology (20th rev. ed. 2011).

Addressing potential unintended pregnancies is an important issue. Half of all pregnancies are unintended, a million women who do not want to become pregnant have unprotected sex each day and 25,000 women become pregnant through sexual assault each year. See G. Harris, FDA Approves 5–Day Emergency Contraception, New York Times, August 14, 2010, A–1. Whether these unintended pregnancies are a problem, and whether intervention to avoid pregnancy after intercourse is ever appropriate, depends upon one's values.

If contraception refers to any process designed to prevent a pregnancy, and abortion refers to any process designed to end an established pregnancy, then the point at which the process of contraception becomes the process of abortion is at the commencement of the pregnancy. There is some ambiguity, however, about when the pregnancy begins, just as there is some ambiguity about when "conception" takes place. While standard medical texts equate conception with implantation of the fertilized ovum in the uterus, some state legislatures have provided that conception occurs at the moment of fertilization, some days before implantation. See Webster v. Reproductive Health Services, 492 U.S. at 561, (Stevens, J., concurring in part and dissenting in part).

When do you think the pregnancy begins? Does the fact that a large number of fertilized eggs—perhaps 50%—never implant, suggest that pregnancy does not begin until implantation? Is the fact that cells of the fertilized ovum are identical for about three days, and then begin to separate into differentiated cells that will become the placenta, on one hand, and cells that will become the embryo and fetus, on the other, relevant?

If there is to be a legal difference between contraception and abortion, the courts will have to determine when "conception" takes place and when a pregnancy begins. As Justice Stevens points out, some forms of what we now consider contraception are really devices designed to stop the fertilized egg from implanting in the uterus, not devices designed for avoiding fertilization of the egg in the first place.

> An intrauterine device, commonly called an IUD "works primarily by preventing a fertilized egg from implanting"; other contraceptive methods that may prevent implantation include "morning-after pills," high-dose estrogen pills taken after intercourse, particularly in cases of rape, and mifepristone (also known as RU 486), a pill that works "during the indeterminate period between contraception and abortion," low level estrogen "combined" pills—a version of the ordinary, daily ingested birth control pill—also may prevent the fertilized egg from reaching the uterine wall and implanting[ ].

Webster, 492 U.S. at 563, 109 S.Ct. at 3081 (Stevens, J., concurring in part and dissenting in part). If the law recognizes a distinction between contraception and abortion, should the law also be required to define that point at which contraception becomes abortion? Justice Stevens suggests that we must depend upon a medical definition of pregnancy, because any alternative would constitute the legal adoption of a theological position and thus be a violation of the establishment clause of the First Amendment. Do you agree? Can you develop a coherent legal argument that the state may regulate abortion in any way it sees fit, but *may not* prohibit a woman's choice to stop a fertilized ovum from reaching her uterus and implanting? Are we wrong to try to categorize the processes as contraception or abortion, and should we replace that dichotomy with a classification that recognizes contraception, interception (stopping a fertilized ovum from implanting), and abortion? Should the three processes be regulated differently? How? Of course, some churches and others hold that the only relevant question is whether there is an abortion. See Congregation for the Doctrine of the Faith, *Dignitas Personae*, par. 23 (2008).

PROBLEM: CONSCIENTIOUS REFUSAL TO DISPENSE EMERGENCY CONTRACEPTION

Carrie Snow is a pharmacist in the small town of Carver in the state of New Baxley. She has worked for many years in a DRUGCO pharmacy, where she is now the assistant pharmacy manager. The local DRUGCO pharmacy is owned by the DRUGCO Pharmacy Corporation, with headquarters in New York. Although the Carver DRUGCO employs several pharmacists, Snow frequently works alone because Carver is in a rural area of the state.

Unlike all of her fellow Carver DRUGCO pharmacists, Snow is concerned about the moral propriety of the emergency contraceptive Plan B and ella, which DRUGCO stocks at all of its pharmacies. Snow's moral problem with Plan B arises out of the several different ways in which these contraceptives work. Most worrisome to Snow is that, under some circumstances, these emergency contraceptives could dislodge an implanted fertilized ovum. Given the time at which they are used—before implantation would have occurred—dislodging a fertilized ovum would happen very rarely if at all, unless the woman were already pregnant before she engaged in the intercourse that caused her to seek emergency contraception. For that reason, some physicians will recommend or perform pregnancy tests before prescribing or recommending Plan B or ella. Snow has no idea whether such a test has been done on those coming into her pharmacy seeking these contraceptives. Snow's moral concern that there is a small chance Plan B or ella will result in an abortion is exacerbated by her religiously based doubt about the propriety of any artificial form of contraception and her politically based concern about the moral decay of a society that depends upon this form of medication. After a great deal of consideration, Snow has concluded that she should not dispense Plan B or ella under any circumstances because it would violate her own personal beliefs to do so.

Two years ago the State of New Baxley passed a statute entitled, "The Health Care Providers' Right of Conscience," which provides:

> Every individual possesses a fundamental right to exercise that person's religious belief and conscience. No individual health care provider or health care facility may be mandated to perform specific services if that provider or facility objects to doing so for reason of conscience or religion. Any person who chooses not to provide such treatment may not be discriminated against in employment or disadvantaged in terms of professional privileges, or in any other way, as a result of the choice. This provision shall not be construed so that any patient is denied timely access to any health service.

New Baxley Stat. Sec. 14–238. The New Baxley State Board of Pharmacy also regulates the conduct of pharmacists and has the authority to create rules for the dispensing, distribution, wholesaling, and manufacture of drugs and devices and the practice of pharmacy for the protection and promotion of the public health, safety and welfare. After reviewing the statute, they issued "duty to dispense" regulations that state the following:

(1) Pharmacies have a duty to deliver lawfully prescribed drugs or devices to patients and to distribute drugs and devices approved by the U.S. Food and Drug Administration for restricted distribution by pharmacies, or provide a therapeutically equivalent drug or device in a timely manner consistent with reasonable expectations for filling the prescription.

(2) A pharmacist may refuse to dispense a prescription because of his or her religious or moral views only if the pharmacist works simultaneously with another pharmacist who does dispense the medication in place of the pharmacist who has a conscientious objection to doing so.

(3) A pharmacist who refuses to dispense a prescription because of his or her religious or moral views is not in violation of this regulation if that pharmacist refers the patient to another pharmacist within a reasonable distance who has confirmed by telephone or through an electronic form of communication that the prescribed medication in stock and that it will be dispensed immediately upon the receipt of the prescription.

New Baxley Reg. Pharm–12.1632.

In a letter directed to the Pharmacy Board, the New Baxley State Human Rights Commission, which is authorized to enforce antidiscrimination laws in the state, offered its opinion on the subject of the right of conscience and access to Plan B and ella:

It is the position of the HRC that allowing pharmacists to refuse to dispense a lawful pharmaceutical that has been properly prescribed, based on their personal religious beliefs, would be discriminatory, unlawful, and against good public policy and the public interest. It is also HRC's position that allowing a practice of 'refuse and refer' as a means of addressing this issue merely perpetuates discriminatory behavior.

Jane Wishner, who also lives in Carver, is concerned that women in her community may not have access to Plan B or ella because Snow will not dispense them. She is concerned that because DRUGCO is the only pharmacy in Carver and Snow is sometimes the only pharmacist on duty for eight hour shifts, a woman seeking Plan B will not have the ability to get the medication quickly, thus reducing its effectiveness. If a woman in Carver had to travel four hours to the next closest pharmacy or wait until another pharmacist who will dispense the medication is on duty at the Carver DRUGCO, she might not get the treatment she needs in time for it to be effective if at all. Although

Wishner has not used Plan B or ella, she says that she may wish to do so in the future.

Wishner has aired her concerns on television news shows which have caught the attention of the CEO of DRUGCO in New York. He is concerned as to what possible legal effect Snow's refusal to dispense emergency contraceptives will have on the DRUGCO Corporation. He is not sure whether DRUGCO should support his assistant manager's decision not to dispense the medication, require his employee to dispense the medication, or attempt to schedule Snow only when there is some other pharmacist who will dispense Plan B or ella on duty. The last alternative will lead to extra expense for the corporation, and it is unacceptable to Snow because it will make it impossible for her to work the more lucrative graveyard shift, when only one pharmacist is on duty.

Because of your reputation as the leading health lawyer in New Baxley, all of the principals have sought to have you advise them. Your office assistant has phone messages from (1) Carrie Snow, who wants you to get "some kind of court order that says she doesn't have to dispense Plan B or ella," (2) Jane Wishner, who wants you to get "some kind of court order that will assure that women in Carver get Plan B and ella when they need it," and (3) the DRUGCO corporate office, which wants you to advise them on what limitations the law imposes on any policy they develop to apply in this case.

Whom will you choose to represent? Why? Are your own moral considerations relevant when you choose your client? Are those moral considerations any different for you, as a lawyer, choosing a client than they should be for a pharmacist or another health care provider choosing a patient?

Is Carrie Snow entitled to injuctive or other relief? Is Jane Wishner? Should DRUGCO be able to obtain a declaratory judgment, if that is permitted under state law? If the state were to sanction Carrie Snow for not dispensing the medication, would that violate her First Amendment free exercise rights? If a woman were to be denied the medication on religious or moral grounds, would she have been the subject of discrimination based on her religious beliefs? On her gender? If Carrie Snow diligently exercised a policy of "refuse and refer," described in section (3) of the regulation above, when it came to Plan B, would that meet all legal requirements? If Carrie Snow or Jane Wishner were to bring an action, should the other be able to intervene? Could DRUGCO intervene in this lawsuit in order to determine their legal responsibilities?

See Storman's, Inc. v. Selecky, 586 F. 3d 1109 (9th Cir.2009), and the subsequent District Court resolution of the matter, 844 F.Supp.2d 1172 (W.D. Wa. 2012), 854 F.Supp.2d 925 (W.D.Wa.2012). The Ninth Circuit in *Storman's* made it clear that the First Amendment (applied through the Fourteenth Amendment) provided for only rational basis review of a state's requirement that a pharmacist dispense emergency contraception. Is that the proper standard to be applied, or should the court have applied strict scrutiny to the state's requirement, which arguably burdened the pharmacist's religious freedom. See also Vandersand v. Wal–Mart Stores, 525 F.Supp.2d 1052 (C.D.Ill.2007) and Menges v. Blagojevich, 451 F.Supp.2d 992 (C.D.Ill.2006). For a more academic discussion, see Ryan Lawrence and Farr Curlin, Clash of Definitions: Controversies about Conscience in Medicine, 7 Am. J. Bioethics (12) 10 (2007). That issue of that journal also includes eleven commentaries focusing on this issue. See also Farr A. Curlin, et al., Religion, Conscience and Controversial Clinical Practice, 356 N.E.J.Med. 593 (2007), and R. Alta Charo, The Celestial Fire of Conscience–Refusing to Deliver Medical Care,352 N.E.J.Med. 2471 (2005).

The American College of Obstetrics and Gynecology ethics opinion on this issue provides:

1. In the provision of reproductive services, the patient's well-being must be paramount. Any conscientious refusal that conflicts with a patient's well-being should be accommodated only if the primary duty to the patient can be fulfilled.

2. Where conscience implores physicians to deviate from standard practices, including abortion, sterilization and provision of contraceptives, they must provide potential patients with accurate and prior notice of their personal moral commitments. * * *

4. Physicians and other health care professionals have the duty to refer patients in a timely manner to other providers if they do not feel that they can in conscience provide the standard reproductive services that their patients request.

* * *

6. In resource poor areas, access to safe and legal reproductive services should be maintained. * * *

American College of Obstetrics and Gynecology Committee on Ethics, The Limits of Conscientious Refusal in Reproductive Medicine, 110 Obstetrics Gynecology 1203 (2007). The College's Committee on Ethics reaffirmed this statement in 2010. Note the use of the passive voice in clause 6. Who should maintain those services?

NOTE: FEDERAL LAW AND CONSCIENCE CLAUSES

In 2010 the Obama administration reviewed regulations that the Bush administration had promulgated in 2008 to protect decisions made by health care workers based on conscience. Those regulations were based on decades-old statutes that protected providers who declined to participate in the provision of abortions and sterilizations; they had never been extended to contraception. The Bush administration rule was intended to expand the protection to all kinds of conscience-based decisions, including the provision of contraception and end of life care. The 2008 regulation provided:

45 CFR § 88.1, Purpose. (2008, later withdrawn)

The purpose of this Part is to provide for the implementation and enforcement of the Church Amendments * * * and the Weldon Amendment * * *. These statutory provisions protect the rights of health care entities/entities, both individuals and institutions, to refuse to perform health care services and research activities to which they may object for religious, moral, ethical, or other reasons. Consistent with this objective to protect the conscience rights of health care entities, the provisions [in those statutes] and the implementing regulations contained in this Part are to be interpreted and implemented broadly to effectuate their protective purposes.

In 2011 the Obama administration withdrew these regulations and replaced them with a very brief regulation that was limited to the reach of the authorizing statutes:

45 CFR § 88.1, Purpose. (2011, currently effective)

The purpose of this part is to provide for the enforcement of the Church Amendments * * * and the Weldon Amendment * * * referred to collectively as the "federal health care provider conscience protection statutes."

The Church and Weldon Amendments extended only to those who refuse to participate in abortion or sterilization procedures. Thus, this new regulation limited reach of the statutory conscience clauses to refusal to participate in the abortions and sterilizations. Doctors who refused to provide patients with contraceptives for reasons of conscience, most notably, are no longer protected by the new federal conscience clause.

After reviewing the 300,000 comments received on the proposed new regulations (two-thirds of which opposed any change in the 2008 protections, with most comments on both sides probably submitted by people who clicked on advocacy organizations' websites), the Obama administration decided to maintain enforcement of the conscience clause provisions in the Office of Civil Rights of the Department of Health and Human Services (as was the case under the Bush administration as well). Finally, a provision of the 2008 regulations that required written certification from each funding recipient (or subrecipient) that they were in compliance with the regulation as a condition of receiving federal funding—a provision that had never actually gone into effect—was withdrawn from the final rule. See 45 CFR § 88.1–2. For background on the rule change and a summary of the public comments, along with the DHHS responses, see 76 Fed. Reg. 9976 (Feb. 23, 2011).

Although this revision of the regulation, which took effect in early 2011, created a great deal of public controversy and press commentary, the actual change in policy was very slim indeed, given the fact that the statutes which authorized the regulations only apply to abortion and sterilization, not to contraception or any other medical care.

NOTE: COVERAGE OF CONTRACEPTION UNDER THE ACA

Under the Affordable Care Act, most group health plans and health insurance issuers must provide preventive services to their enrollees and insureds without requiring any copay, deductible, or other form of cost-sharing. In July of 2010 the Departments of Health and Human Services, Labor and Treasury (each of which had jurisdiction over some aspects of this requirement) issued an interim final rule that adopted the Health Resources and Services Administration guidelines, based on recommendations made by the independent Institute of Medicine, that such preventive services include all forms of contraception that are approved by the Food and Drug Administration (FDA). Thus, most health plans and health insurance policies would cover hormonal methods of contraception (i.e., birth control pills and post-intercourse emergency contraception like Plan B and ella), IUDs, sterilization, and patient education and counseling. Notably, neither condoms nor vasectomy must be covered because those do not require FDA approval. This interim final rule did not come as a surprise to anyone; 28 states already required some form of contraception coverage in at least some health insurance plans sold in their states.

On August 3, 2011 the three Departments issued an amended interim final rule (available at 76 Fed. Reg. 46621) which was influenced by comments the Departments had received suggesting that the requirement would be inconsistent with the beliefs of some religious groups that oppose the use of some of the approved forms of contraceptives. The 2011 amendments to the Rule exempted religious employers from this requirement. To qualify as a religious employer, though, an employer had to (1) have the purpose of inculcation of religious values, (2) employ primarily people who share its religious values, (3) primarily serve people who share its religious tenets, and (4) be a non-profit organization established to be a church, association of churches or a religious order. This exemption saved churches from the requirement of providing contraception coverage, and it also saved some religious primary and secondary schools that are organized to inculcate religious views and designed for attendance by coreligionists only. However, the exemption did not extend to most religious colleges and universities or social service organizations that have students of all faiths or serve the social services needs of people of all faiths; these still would have been required to provide contraception coverage. Because the rule was later extended to cover student health plans, the fact that religious colleges (and, in particular, Catholic universities open to students of all faiths) were not exempt proved to be very significant. The amended rule, which was to go into effect on August 1, 2012, would have applied to thousands of women who were employees of church-related schools or social service organizations and thousands of women who were students at religiously affiliated universities.

Responding to the strong and adverse response from religiously affiliated organizations (and the 200,000 comments received on the prior iteration of the rule), the Department of Health and Human Services issued a "Guidance on the Temporary Enforcement Safe Harbor * * * With Respect to the Requirement to Cover Contraceptive Services * * * ” on February 10, 2012. This guidance delayed for a year, until August 1, 2013, the requirement that non-church religiously affiliated institutions provide contraception coverage. The administration claimed that this would allow these complex organizations, many run by volunteer non-profit boards, time to work out appropriate ways to comply. Those who opposed the requirement argued that the delay was politically motivated and designed to put off the implementation of the new rule until after the 2012 election.

Many of those who opposed the requirement that the rule placed upon religiously affiliated organizations were not satisfied by the safe harbor. The opposition to the rule, led by the U.S. Conference of Catholic Bishops, evangelical Christians, and conservative politicians, believed the rule to be an unconscionable intrusion on religious liberty. They argued it was wrong for religious organizations to be required by government regulation to perform acts (like providing coverage for contraception) that are inconsistent with their religious beliefs. They committed to oppose the rule by any legal means at their disposal—including litigation, regulation and legislation.

While the political battle was brewing, the administration moved to find an approach that would assure that all women would receive coverage for the preventive services (including contraception) that they wanted while allowing religious employers (and, in the case of colleges and universities, those providing student health plans) to opt out of any participation in the provision of any services that they found to be morally objectionable. On March 21, 2012 the three Departments published an Advance Notice of Proposed Rulemaking (ANPRM) which provided, depending on your position on the underlying issue, a thoughtful compromise that would serve everyone's interests or a devious way of sidestepping the churches' religious concerns. The full text of the ANPRM is available at *Certain Preventive Services Under the Affordable Care Act,* 77 Fed. Reg. 16501 (March 21, 2012).

First, the ANPRM provided that if the religiously affiliated organization bought traditional health insurance for its employees (or students), the policy need not include the objectionable contraceptive services. Those services would have to be provided independently by the insurance provider, and they would be paid for by the insurer through actuarial savings realized by the insurer because it is cheaper to provide those contraceptive services than to provide the additional care necessitated by pregnancy and childbirth. Thus, the religiously affiliated organization would play no part in financing, administering or facilitating the morally objectionable contraceptive services. All of that would be done by the entity issuing the insurance policy.

Of course, as a result of ERISA and other market forces, large religious organizations are very likely to provide self-funded health coverage to their employees rather than traditional health insurance. How would a religious organization offering its employees self-funded health coverage allow for the coverage of contraception without being involved in the provision of or reimbursement for those services? Even when an employer's health coverage is self-funded, though, it is unusual for the employer not to contract with a third party administrator to administer the program. The ANPRM suggested that an employer offering self-funded coverage could decide to forgo compliance with the relevant part of the contraception rule and that the third party administrator would then be required to provide such coverage and administer claims made for contraceptive services independent of the employer. The proposed rule would require the employer to assure the Departments that it is contracting with a third party administrator, and that it has provided that administrator with written notice that (1) it is a religious organization, (2) it will not act as the plan administrator or the claims administrator with regard to contraceptive services, and (3) it will not contribute to the funding of such services.

While insurers may be able to fund contraceptive services through other savings, that financing avenue is not open to self-funded plan administrators who merely draft claims payments on the accounts of the employers. The ANPRM invited suggestions as to how contraception coverage could be funded under these circumstances. It suggested that among the alternatives are the use of special payments, like drug rebates, made available to the plan administrators, donations from non-profits committed to providing contraceptive services, and rebates available under the reinsurance program established by the Affordable Care Act. The ANPRM also raised the possibility that all third party administrators facing such circumstances could contract with a private insurance company designated by a federal agency to provide coverage for these contraceptive services under the Act.

Popular attention to this issue was eclipsed by the Supreme Court resolution of the ACA litigation in the summer of 2012, but the issue was hardly forgotten. In early 2013 the Departments of Treasury, Labor and Health and Human Services issued a new set of proposed regulations accommodating some of the concerns of those opposed to providing contraceptive coverage. The new regulations would extend the exemption from providing contraceptive coverage to more religiously affiliated organizations that employ and serve those who do not subscribe to the religious views of those organizations. In addition, they would impose the cost of providing this coverage on insurance companies, who would be able to recover the cost of doing so through credits they could apply against the fees imposed for participation in the exchanges established by the ACA. See Coverage of Certain Preventive Services Under the Affordable Care Act, 78 Fed. Reg. 8456 (February 6, 2013). See also Robert Pear, Birth Control Rule Altered to Allay Religious Objections, New York Times, February 2, 2013.

How do you think this issue should be resolved? Is the fact that the ACA requires coverage of preventive services dispositive of the legal question? Are contraceptive services "preventive" services? What, exactly, do contraceptive services prevent? Should the three Secretaries be bound by the Health Resources and Services Administration guidelines on this issue? By the Institute of Medicine report on this issue?

How strong are the First Amendment arguments raised by religious opponents of this rule? How strong is the free exercise clause argument? The establishment clause argument? Should for-profit and other non-religious employers who morally oppose the provision of contraceptive services also be protected by the First Amendment against the government imposition of the requirement that they provide their employees such services? This issue is currently subject to litigation in several districts across the country. See, e.g., Hobby Lobby Stores, inc. v. Sebelius, 870 F. Supp. 2d 1278 (W.D. Ok. 2012). Would it be a violation of the First Amendment to allow this exemption to churches and religious organizations, but not to others?

Is there an independent substantive due process or equal protection argument that opponents can raise in objecting to this rule? How sympathetic is the religious organizations' argument that they do not want their employees to have access to coverage for contraception that their employer believes is immoral when, as will now be the case, the employer will not be paying for that coverage or administering the claim?

Is there an argument that any government rule that affirmatively allows a woman's private employer to deny her contraceptive coverage violates her Constitutional rights? Under the establishment or free exercise clauses of the First Amendment? Under the substantive due process or equal protection clauses of the Fourteenth Amendment? What level of scrutiny would apply in such a challenge?

II.   ABORTION

The right to privacy discussed (and perhaps invented) in *Griswold* found its most significant articulation in Roe v. Wade, 410 U.S. 113, 93 S.Ct. 705, 35 L.Ed.2d 147 (1973), the original abortion case. Imagine Justice Blackmun writing this opinion, going through medicine and history texts hoping to find out just when a person protected by the Fourteenth Amendment really did come into existence. Justice Blackmun, who had been counsel to the Mayo Clinic earlier in his legal career, was keenly aware of the medical consequences of his determination. A comparison of Justice Blackmun's approach to this problem and Justice Douglas's approach, which is discussed in the note following *Roe*, suggests that Justice Blackmun viewed abortion as a medical problem, while Justice Douglas viewed it as a personal issue. In any case, Roe v. Wade clearly recognized a Constitutionally based right of privacy which extended to personal procreative decisions. Further, this right was based on the due process clause of the Fourteenth Amendment, not the penumbras and emanations that formed the unstable foundation for *Griswold*. While *Roe* was increasingly narrowed during the 1980s, and while its death was often predicted, in 1992 the Court concluded that "the essential holding of Roe v. Wade should be retained and once again reaffirmed." Planned Parenthood of Southeastern Pennsylvania v. Casey, 505 U.S. 833, 112 S.Ct. 2791, 120

L.Ed.2d 674 (1992). In 2007 the Supreme Court "assume[d] * * * the principles [of *Roe* and *Casey*] for the purpose of this opinion," although it was not clear that those principles continued to command the respect of the majority of the Court. Gonzales v. Carhart, 550 U.S. 124, 127 S.Ct. 1610, 167 L.Ed.2d 480 (2007). But what is the "essential holding" of *Roe* that was retained in *Casey* and "assumed" in *Carhart*?

ROE V. WADE

Supreme Court of the United States, 1973.
410 U.S. 113, 93 S.Ct. 705, 35 L.Ed.2d 147.

MR. JUSTICE BLACKMUN delivered the opinion of the Court.

* * *

We forthwith acknowledge our awareness of the sensitive and emotional nature of the abortion controversy, of the vigorous opposing views, even among physicians, and of the deep and seemingly absolute convictions that the subject inspires. One's philosophy, one's experiences, one's exposure to the raw edges of human existence, one's religious training, one's attitudes toward life and family and their values, and the moral standards one establishes and seeks to observe, are all likely to influence and to color one's thinking and conclusions about abortion.

In addition, population growth, pollution, poverty, and racial overtones tend to complicate and not to simplify the problem.

Our task, of course, is to resolve the issue by constitutional measurement, free of emotion and of predilection. We seek earnestly to do this, and, because we do, we have inquired into, and in this opinion place some emphasis upon, medical and medical-legal history and what that history reveals about man's attitudes toward the abortion procedure over the centuries. We bear in mind, too, Mr. Justice Holmes' admonition in his now-vindicated dissent in Lochner v. New York[ ]:

> [The Constitution] is made for people of fundamentally differing views, and the accident of our finding certain opinions natural and familiar or novel and even shocking ought not to conclude our judgment upon the question whether statutes embodying them conflict with the Constitution of the United States.

* * *

The principal thrust of appellant's attack on the Texas statutes is that they improperly invade a right, said to be possessed by the pregnant woman, to choose to terminate her pregnancy. Appellant would discover this right in the concept of personal "liberty" embodied in the Fourteenth Amendment's Due Process Clause; or in personal, marital, familial, and sexual privacy said to be protected by the Bill of Rights or its penumbras,[

]; or among those rights reserved to the people by the Ninth Amendment[ ]. Before addressing this claim, we feel it desirable briefly to survey, in several aspects, the history of abortion, for such insight as that history may afford us, and then to examine the state purposes and interests behind the criminal abortion laws.

VI

It perhaps is not generally appreciated that the restrictive criminal abortion laws in effect in a majority of States today are of relatively recent vintage. Those laws, generally proscribing abortion or its attempt at any time during pregnancy except when necessary to preserve the pregnant woman's life, are not of ancient or even of common-law origin. Instead, they derive from statutory changes effected, for the most part, in the latter half of the 19th century.

[The Court then reviewed, in great detail, ancient attitudes, the Hippocratic Oath, the common law, English statutory law, American Law, the position of the American Medical Association, the position of the American Public Health Association, and the position of the American Bar Association.]

VII

Three reasons have been advanced to explain historically the enactment of criminal abortion laws in the 19th century and to justify their continued existence.

[The first, Victorian sexual morality, is dismissed as an anachronism.]

A second reason is concerned with abortion as a medical procedure. When most criminal abortion laws were first enacted, the procedure was a hazardous one for the woman. * * * Thus, it has been argued that a State's real concern in enacting a criminal abortion law was to protect the pregnant woman, that is, to restrain her from submitting to a procedure that placed her life in serious jeopardy.

Modern medical techniques have altered this situation. Appellants and various amici refer to medical data indicating that abortion in early pregnancy, this is, prior to the end of the first trimester, although not without its risk, is now relatively safe. Mortality rates for women undergoing early abortions, where the procedure is legal, appear to be as low as or lower than the rates for normal childbirth. Consequently, any interest of the State in protecting the woman from an inherently hazardous procedure, except when it would be equally dangerous for her to forgo it, has largely disappeared. Of course, important state interests in the area of health and medical standards do remain. The State has a legitimate interest in seeing to it that abortion, like any other medical procedure, is performed under circumstances that assure maximum safety for the patient. * * *

The third reason is the State's interest—some phrase it in terms of duty—in protecting prenatal life.

*   *   *

It is with these interests, and the weight to be attached to them, that this case is concerned.

VIII

The Constitution does not explicitly mention any right of privacy. In a line of decisions, however, going back perhaps as far as[ ] 1891 the Court has recognized that a right of personal privacy, or a guarantee of certain areas or zones of privacy, does exist under the Constitution. In varying contexts, the Court or individual Justices have, indeed, found at least the roots of that right in the First Amendment,[ ] in the Fourth and Fifth Amendments,[ ] in the penumbras of the Bill of Rights, Griswold v. Connecticut,[ ] the Ninth Amendment,[ ] or in the concept of liberty guaranteed by the first section of the Fourteenth Amendment.[ ] These decisions make it clear that only personal rights that can be deemed "fundamental" or "implicit in the concept of ordered liberty,"[ ] are included in this guarantee of personal privacy. They also make it clear that the right has some extension to activities relating to marriage,[ ] family relationships,[ ] and child rearing and education[ ].

This right of privacy, whether it be founded in the Fourteenth Amendment's concept of personal liberty and restrictions upon state action, as we feel it is, or, as the District Court determined, in the Ninth Amendment's reservation of rights to the people, is broad enough to encompass a woman's decision whether or not to terminate her pregnancy. The detriment that the State would impose upon the pregnant woman by denying this choice altogether is apparent. Specific and direct harm medically diagnosable even in early pregnancy may be involved. Maternity, or additional offspring, may force upon the woman a distressful life and future. Psychological harm may be imminent. Mental and physical health may be taxed by child care. There is also the distress, for all concerned, associated with the unwanted child, and there is the problem of bringing a child into a family already unable, psychologically and otherwise, to care for it. In other cases, as in this one, the additional difficulties and continuing stigma of unwed motherhood may be involved. All these are factors the woman and her responsible physician necessarily will consider in consultation.

On the basis of elements such as these, appellant and some amici argue that the woman's right is absolute and that she is entitled to terminate her pregnancy at whatever time, in whatever way, and for whatever reason she alone chooses. With this we do not agree. * * * [A] State may properly assert important interests in safeguarding health, in maintaining medical standards, and in protecting potential life. At some point in pregnancy, these respective interests become sufficiently compelling to sustain regulation of the factors that govern the abortion decision.

* * *

X

* * *

With respect to the State's important and legitimate interest in the health of the mother, the "compelling" point, in the light of present medical knowledge, is at approximately the end of the first trimester. This is so because of the now-established medical fact * * * that until the end of the first trimester mortality in abortion may be less than mortality in normal childbirth. It follows that, from and after this point, a State may regulate the abortion procedure to the extent that the regulation reasonably relates to the preservation and protection of maternal health. * * *

This means, on the other hand, that, for the period of pregnancy prior to this "compelling" point, the attending physician, in consultation with his patient, is free to determine, without regulation by the State, that, in his medical judgment, the patient's pregnancy should be terminated. If that decision is reached, the judgment may be effectuated by an abortion free of interference by the State.

With respect to the State's important and legitimate interest in potential life, the "compelling" point is at viability. This is so because the fetus then presumably has the capability of meaningful life outside the mother's womb. State regulation protective of fetal life after viability thus has both logical and biological justifications. If the State is interested in protecting fetal life after viability, it may go so far as to proscribe abortion during that period, except when it is necessary to preserve the life or health of the mother.

* * *

XI

To summarize and to repeat:

1.   A state criminal abortion statute of the current Texas type, that excepts from criminality only a *lifesaving* procedure on behalf of the mother, without regard to pregnancy stage and without recognition of the other interests involved, is violative of the Due Process Clause of the Fourteenth Amendment.

(a) For the stage prior to approximately the end of the first trimester, the abortion decision and its effectuation must be left to the medical judgment of the pregnant woman's attending physician.

(b) For the stage subsequent to approximately the end of the first trimester, the State, in promoting its interest in the health of the mother, may, if it chooses, regulate the abortion procedure in ways that are reasonably related to maternal health.

(c) For the stage subsequent to viability, the State in promoting its interest in the potentiality of human life may, if it chooses, regulate, and even proscribe, abortion except where it is necessary, in appropriate medical judgment, for the preservation of the life or health of the mother.

* * *

NOTES AND QUESTIONS

1. Justice Blackmun's Fourteenth Amendment analysis is not the only way that the Court could have reached this result. Justice Douglas, concurring, would have depended on the Ninth Amendment, as did the District Court. His approach would have recognized a far broader right of privacy:

> The Ninth Amendment obviously does not create federally enforceable rights. It merely says, "The enumeration in the Constitution, of certain rights, shall not be construed to deny or disparage others retained by the people." But a catalogue of these rights includes customary, traditional, and time-honored rights, amenities, privileges, and immunities that come within the sweep of "the Blessings of Liberty" mentioned in the preamble to the Constitution. Many of them, in my view, come within the meaning of the term "liberty" as used in the Fourteenth Amendment.

> *First is the autonomous control over the development and expression of one's intellect, interests, tastes, and personality.*

> *Second is freedom of choice in the basic decisions of one's life respecting marriage, divorce, procreation, contraception, and the education and upbringing of children.*

> *Third is the freedom to care for one's health and person, freedom from bodily restraint or compulsion, freedom to walk, stroll, or loaf.*

Consider how the subsequent history of abortion legislation and litigation might have been different had this less medical, much broader, definition of the right been accepted by the Court in 1973.

2. The Court's opinion was vigorously criticized and stirred into action political forces opposed to abortion. They have encouraged state legislatures to seek creative ways to discourage abortions without directly running afoul of the requirements of the case. The Supreme Court at first resisted attempts

to limit the underlying rights recognized in 1973, although the number of justices supporting that decision declined over time. *Roe* was reaffirmed more than a dozen times in its first decade, but by 1986 the 7–2 majority was down to 5–4, Thornburgh v. American College of Obstetricians and Gynecologists, 476 U.S. 747, 106 S.Ct. 2169, 90 L.Ed.2d 779 (1986), and by 1989 the Court appeared to be evenly divided, with Justice O'Connor unwilling to confront the issue. Webster v. Reproductive Health Services, 492 U.S. 490, 109 S.Ct. 3040, 106 L.Ed.2d 410 (1989). The two most important cases reinterpreting *Roe*, Planned Parenthood of Southeastern Pennsylvania v. Casey, 505 U.S. 833, 112 S.Ct. 2791, 120 L.Ed.2d 674 (1992) and Gonzales v. Carhart, 550 U.S. 124, 127 S.Ct. 1610, 167 L.Ed.2d 480 (2007), are reprinted below.

3.   Government funding for abortions has been limited and the restrictions on the use of government funds for abortions have generally been upheld by the courts. In 1977, the Supreme Court upheld state statutes and Medicaid plans that refused to fund nontherapeutic abortions as well as a city's determination that its hospitals would not provide nontherapeutic abortions. Beal v. Doe, 432 U.S. 438, 97 S.Ct. 2366, 53 L.Ed.2d 464 (1977); Maher v. Roe, 432 U.S. 464, 97 S.Ct. 2376, 53 L.Ed.2d 484 (1977); Poelker v. Doe, 432 U.S. 519, 97 S.Ct. 2391, 53 L.Ed.2d 528 (1977).

4.   In Harris v. McRae, 448 U.S. 297, 100 S.Ct. 2671, 65 L.Ed.2d 784 (1980), the Supreme Court upheld the Hyde Amendment, which provided that federal funds could not be used for virtually any abortion. The Hyde Amendment was subsequently added to most federal legislation that funded any individual health care. Although the language was slightly modified over the past three decades, the most recent version of the Hyde Amendment, in its full text, reads this way:

SEC. 507 (a) None of the funds appropriated in this Act, and none of the funds in any trust fund to which funds are appropriated in this Act, shall be expended for any abortion.

(b) None of the funds appropriated in this Act, and none of the funds in any trust fund to which funds are appropriated in this Act, shall be expended for health benefits coverage that includes coverage of abortion.

(c) The term 'health benefits coverage' means the package of services covered by a managed care provider or organization pursuant to a contract or other arrangement.

SEC. 508. (a) The limitations established in the preceding section shall not apply to an abortion—

(1) if the pregnancy is the result of an act of rape or incest; or

(2) in the case where a woman suffers from a physical disorder, physical injury, or physical illness, including a life-

endangering physical condition caused by or arising from the pregnancy itself, that would, as certified by a physician, place the woman in danger of death unless an abortion is performed.

(b) Nothing in the preceding section shall be construed as prohibiting the expenditure by a State, locality, entity, or private person of State, local, or private funds (other than a State's or locality's contribution of Medicaid matching funds).

(c) Nothing in the preceding section shall be construed as restricting the ability of any managed care provider from offering abortion coverage or the ability of a State or locality to contract separately with such a provider for such coverage with State funds (other than a State's or locality's contribution of Medicaid matching funds).

About a third of the states have continued to provide entirely state-funded Medicaid abortions, as the Hyde Amendment explicitly permits. About two-thirds of the states prohibit the use of any state money on abortions that would be forbidden by the Hyde Amendment; in those states no government funded abortions are permitted (unless they fall into the rape, incest, or risk of death exceptions in the Hyde Amendment). One state, South Dakota, prohibits the use of state funding for the provision of abortion services even in circumstances in which the Hyde Amendment would permit it.

5. There were two legal lines of attack on the Supreme Court's decision in Roe v. Wade. The first argued that the Supreme Court had returned to the unhappy Lochnerian days of substantive due process, during which the Court acted as if it were free to make social policy without regard to legal or constitutional restrictions. Of course, the authors of the Fourteenth Amendment were not confronted with abortion as a political and social issue, and the intent of the framers with regard to this particular question is not likely to be helpful in resolving this issue. While the Fourteenth Amendment has been broadly interpreted, Roe v. Wade and the subsequent abortion cases are among the few examples of the application of a "right to privacy" that arise out of that amendment. The Supreme Court has refused to extend this right of privacy to other areas, even within the health care system. See, e.g., United States v. Rutherford, 442 U.S. 544, 99 S.Ct. 2470, 61 L.Ed.2d 68 (1979) (no privacy right to use an unproven cancer drug). In the first right to die case considered by the Court, none of the Justices even used the word "privacy" to describe the underlying constitutional right; instead they depended upon the apparently more limited "liberty interest" explicitly mentioned in the Fourteenth Amendment. Cruzan v. Director, Missouri Dept. of Health, 497 U.S. 261, 110 S.Ct. 2841, 111 L.Ed.2d 224 (1990). See Chapter 16. In 1986 the Supreme Court explicitly rejected the application of the right of privacy to protect those engaging in homosexual conduct in Bowers v. Hardwick, 478 U.S. 186, 106 S.Ct. 2841, 92 L.Ed.2d 140 (1986), and, in a strictly legal, conceptual sense, Roe v. Wade appeared to be a derelict on the waters of the law.

The vitality of the doctrine of substantive due process was suddenly revived when the Court overturned *Bowers* in 2003. In Lawrence v. Texas, 539 U.S. 558, 123 S.Ct. 2472, 156 L.Ed.2d 508 (2003) the Court announced that those who engaged in gay and lesbian sex are protected from criminal action by the state of Texas by the right of privacy, which itself is firmly rooted in the Due Process Clause of the Fifth and Fourteenth Amendments. Does the fact that the opinion was written by Justice Kennedy, who also wrote the 2007 opinion in Gonzales v. Carhart, below, suggest that the substantive due process right defined in Lawrence is not broad enough to encompass decisions relating to abortion?

The second line of attack on Roe v. Wade focused on the opinion's scientific foundation. Roe v. Wade made two kinds of distinctions. First, it identified that point at which it became more dangerous to abort than to bear the child; second, it identified that point at which the fetus was viable. The court identified those points as occurring at the end of the first and second trimesters. As the science of obstetrics improved and safer techniques of abortion developed, the first point moved back, closer to the time of delivery, and the second point moved forward, closer to the time of conception. It is now quite safe to have an abortion long after the end of the first trimester, and a fetus may be viable before the end of the second trimester. Should the Supreme Court stick to its scientifically justifiable points (the point of increased danger and the point of viability), which would create an ambiguity because it changes with the latest medical developments, or should it stick with the arbitrary first and second trimester timelines, which are easy to apply, even though they are no longer supported by science? The Court attempted to answer this question in City of Akron v. Akron Center for Reproductive Health, Inc., 462 U.S. 416, 103 S.Ct. 2481, 76 L.Ed.2d 687 (1983), and finally reconsidered the trimester division altogether in 1992.

PLANNED PARENTHOOD OF SOUTHEASTERN PENNSYLVANIA V. CASEY

Supreme Court of the United States, 1992.
505 U.S. 833, 112 S.Ct. 2791, 120 L.Ed.2d 674.

JUSTICE O'CONNOR, JUSTICE KENNEDY, and JUSTICE SOUTER announced the judgment of the Court and delivered the opinion of the Court with respect to Parts I, II, III, V–A, V–C, and VI, an opinion with respect to Part V–E, in which JUSTICE STEVENS joins, and an opinion with respect to Parts IV, V–B, and V–D.

I.

Liberty finds no refuge in a jurisprudence of doubt. Yet 19 years after our holding that the Constitution protects a woman's right to terminate her pregnancy in its early stages,[ ] that definition of liberty is still questioned. * * *

At issue in these cases are five provisions of the Pennsylvania Abortion Control Act of 1982. * * * The Act requires that a woman seeking an abortion give her informed consent prior to the abortion procedure, and specifies that she be provided with certain information at least 24 hours before the abortion is performed.[ ] For a minor to obtain an abortion, the Act requires the informed consent of one of her parents, but provides for a judicial bypass option if the minor does not wish to or cannot obtain a parent's consent.[ ] Another provision of the Act requires that, unless certain exceptions apply, a married woman seeking an abortion must sign a statement indicating that she has notified her husband of her intended abortion.[ ] The Act exempts compliance with these three requirements in the event of a "medical emergency," which is defined in the Act.[ ] In addition to the above provisions regulating the performance of abortions, the Act imposes certain reporting requirements on facilities that provide abortion services.[ ]

* * *

After considering the fundamental constitutional questions resolved by *Roe*, principles of institutional integrity, and the rule of stare decisis, we are led to conclude this: the essential holding of Roe v. Wade should be retained and once again reaffirmed.

It must be stated at the outset and with clarity that *Roe's* essential holding, the holding we reaffirm, has three parts. First is a recognition of the right of the woman to choose to have an abortion before viability and to obtain it without undue interference from the State. Before viability, the State's interests are not strong enough to support a prohibition of abortion or the imposition of a substantial obstacle to the woman's effective right to elect the procedure. Second is a confirmation of the State's power to restrict abortions after fetal viability, if the law contains exceptions for pregnancies which endanger a woman's life or health. And third is the principle that the State has legitimate interests from the outset of the pregnancy in protecting the health of the woman and the life of the fetus that may become a child. These principles do not contradict one another; and we adhere to each.

II.

* * *

Men and women of good conscience can disagree, and we suppose some always shall disagree, about the profound moral and spiritual implications of terminating a pregnancy, even in its earliest stage. Some of us as individuals find abortion offensive to our most basic principles of morality, but that cannot control our decision. Our obligation is to define the liberty of all, not to mandate our own moral code. The underlying constitutional issue is whether the State can resolve these philosophic questions in such a definitive way that a woman lacks all choice in the matter, except perhaps in those rare circumstances in which the pregnancy is itself a danger to her own life or health, or is the result of rape or incest. * * * Abortion is a unique act. It is an act fraught with consequences for others: for the woman who must live with the implications of her decision; for the persons who perform and assist in the procedure; for the spouse, family, and society which must confront the knowledge that these procedures exist, procedures some deem nothing short of an act of violence against innocent human life; and, depending on one's beliefs, for the life or potential life that is aborted. Though abortion is conduct, it does not follow that the State is entitled to proscribe it in all instances. That is because the liberty of the woman is at stake in a sense unique to the human condition and so unique to the law. The mother who carries a child to full term is subject to anxieties, to physical constraints, to pain that only she must bear. That these sacrifices have from the beginning of the human race been endured by woman with a pride that ennobles her in the eyes of others and gives to the infant a bond of love cannot alone be grounds for the State to insist she make the sacrifice. Her suffering is too intimate and personal for the State to insist, without more, upon its own vision of the woman's role, however dominant that vision has been in the course of our history and our culture. The destiny of the woman must be shaped to a large extent on her own conception of her spiritual imperatives and her place in society.

*   *   *

While we appreciate the weight of the arguments made on behalf of the State in the case before us, arguments which in their ultimate formulation conclude that *Roe* should be overruled, the reservations any of us may have in reaffirming the central holding of *Roe* are outweighed by the explication of individual liberty we have given combined with the force of stare decisis. We turn now to that doctrine.

III.

A.

[In this section, the court discussed the conditions under which it is appropriate for the Court to reverse its own precedent.]

So in this case we may inquire whether *Roe's* central rule has been found unworkable; whether the rule's limitation on state power could be removed without serious inequity to those who have relied upon it or significant damage to the stability of the society governed by the rule in question; whether the law's growth in the intervening years has left *Roe's* central rule a doctrinal anachronism discounted by society; and whether *Roe's* premises of fact have so far changed in the ensuing two decades as to render its central holding somehow irrelevant or unjustifiable in dealing with the issue it addressed.

* * *

The sum of the precedential inquiry to this point shows *Roe's* underpinnings unweakened in any way affecting its central holding. While it has engendered disapproval, it has not been unworkable. An entire generation has come of age free to assume *Roe's* concept of liberty in defining the capacity of women to act in society, and to make reproductive decisions; no erosion of principle going to liberty or personal autonomy has left *Roe's* central holding a doctrinal remnant; *Roe* portends no developments at odds with other precedent for the analysis of personal liberty; and no changes of fact have rendered viability more or less appropriate as the point at which the balance of interests tips. Within the bounds of normal stare decisis analysis, then, and subject to the considerations on which it customarily turns, the stronger argument is for affirming *Roe's* central holding, with whatever degree of personal reluctance any of us may have, not for overruling it.

B.

[The Court next distinguished the rule in the abortion cases from the rules in *Lochner* and the "separate but equal" cases, two areas in which the Supreme Court did reverse its well settled precedents this century. The Court also explained that it should not expend its political capital and put the public respect for the Court and its processes at risk by reversing *Roe*.]

IV.

From what we have said so far it follows that it is a constitutional liberty of the woman to have some freedom to terminate her pregnancy. We conclude that the basic decision in *Roe* was based on a constitutional analysis which we cannot now repudiate. The woman's liberty is not so unlimited, however, that from the outset the State cannot show its concern for the life of the unborn, and at a later point in fetal development the State's interest in life has sufficient force so that the right of the woman to terminate the pregnancy can be restricted.

* * *

We conclude the line should be drawn at viability, so that before that time the woman has a right to choose to terminate her pregnancy. We adhere to this principle for two reasons. First, as we have said, is the doctrine of stare decisis. * * *

The second reason is that the concept of viability, as we noted in *Roe*, is the time at which there is a realistic possibility of maintaining and nourishing a life outside the womb, so that the independent existence of the second life can in reason and all fairness be the object of state protection that now overrides the rights of the woman. * * *

The woman's right to terminate her pregnancy before viability is the most central principle of Roe v. Wade. It is a rule of law and a component of liberty we cannot renounce.

* * *

Yet it must be remembered that Roe v. Wade speaks with clarity in establishing not only the woman's liberty but also the State's "important and legitimate interest in potential life."[ ] That portion of the decision in *Roe* has been given too little acknowledgment and implementation by the Court in its subsequent cases. Those cases decided that any regulation touching upon the abortion decision must survive strict scrutiny, to be sustained only if drawn in narrow terms to further a compelling state interest.[ ] Not all of the cases decided under that formulation can be reconciled with the holding in *Roe* itself that the State has legitimate interests in the health of the woman and in protecting the potential life within her. In resolving this tension, we choose to rely upon *Roe,* as against the later cases.

* * *

We reject the trimester framework, which we do not consider to be part of the essential holding of *Roe.*[ ] Measures aimed at ensuring that a woman's choice contemplates the consequences for the fetus do not necessarily interfere with the right recognized in *Roe*, although those measures have been found to be inconsistent with the rigid trimester framework announced in that case. A logical reading of the central holding in *Roe* itself, and a necessary reconciliation of the liberty of the woman and the interest of the State in promoting prenatal life, require, in our view, that we abandon the trimester framework as a rigid prohibition on all previability regulation aimed at the protection of fetal life.

* * *

The fact that a law which serves a valid purpose, one not designed to strike at the right itself, has the incidental effect of making it more difficult or more expensive to procure an abortion cannot be enough to invalidate it. Only where state regulation imposes an undue burden on a woman's ability to make this decision does the power of the State reach into the heart of the liberty protected by the Due Process Clause.

* * *

Not all burdens on the right to decide whether to terminate a pregnancy will be undue. In our view, the undue burden standard is the appropriate means of reconciling the State's interest with the woman's constitutionally protected liberty.

*   *   *

A finding of an undue burden is a shorthand for the conclusion that a state regulation has the purpose or effect of placing a substantial obstacle in the path of a woman seeking an abortion of a nonviable fetus. A statute with this purpose is invalid because the means chosen by the State to further the interest in potential life must be calculated to inform the woman's free choice, not hinder it. And a statute which, while furthering the interest in potential life or some other valid state interest, has the effect of placing a substantial obstacle in the path of a woman's choice cannot be considered a permissible means of serving its legitimate ends. * * *

Some guiding principles should emerge. What is at stake is the woman's right to make the ultimate decision, not a right to be insulated from all others in doing so. Regulations which do no more than create a structural mechanism by which the State, or the parent or guardian of a minor, may express profound respect for the life of the unborn are permitted, if they are not a substantial obstacle to the woman's exercise of the right to choose.[ ]

[The Justices then summarized their new undue burden test:]

(a) To protect the central right recognized by Roe v. Wade while at the same time accommodating the State's profound interest in potential life, we will employ the undue burden analysis as explained in this opinion. An undue burden exists, and therefore a provision of law is invalid, if its purpose or effect is to place a substantial obstacle in the path of a woman seeking an abortion before the fetus attains viability.

(b) We reject the rigid trimester framework of Roe v. Wade. To promote the State's profound interest in potential life, throughout pregnancy the State may take measures to ensure that the woman's choice is informed, and measures designed to advance this interest will not be invalidated as long as their purpose is to persuade the woman to choose childbirth over abortion. These measures must not be an undue burden on the right.

(c) As with any medical procedure, the State may enact regulations to further the health or safety of a woman seeking an abortion. Unnecessary health regulations that have the purpose or effect of presenting a substantial obstacle to a woman seeking an abortion impose an undue burden on the right.

(d) Our adoption of the undue burden analysis does not disturb the central holding of Roe v. Wade, and we reaffirm that holding. Regardless of whether exceptions are made for particular circumstances, a State may not prohibit any woman from making the ultimate decision to terminate her pregnancy before viability.

(e) We also reaffirm *Roe's* holding that "subsequent to viability, the State in promoting its interest in the potentiality of human life may, if it chooses, regulate, and even proscribe, abortion except where it is necessary, in appropriate medical judgment, for the preservation of the life or health of the mother."[ ]

*   *   *

V.

*   *   *

A.

Because it is central to the operation of various other requirements, we begin with the statute's definition of medical emergency. Under the statute, a medical emergency is "that condition which, on the basis of the physician's good faith clinical judgment, so complicates the medical condition of a pregnant woman as to necessitate the immediate abortion of her pregnancy to avert her death or for which a delay will create serious risk of substantial and irreversible impairment of a major bodily function."[ ]

Petitioners argue that the definition is too narrow, contending that it forecloses the possibility of an immediate abortion despite some significant health risks.

[The Justices accepted the Court of Appeals interpretation of the statute, which assured that "abortion regulation would not in any way pose a significant threat to the life or health of a woman," and determined that the definition imposed no undue burden on a woman's right to an abortion.]

B.

We next consider the informed consent requirement.[ ] Except in a medical emergency, the statute requires that at least 24 hours before performing an abortion a physician inform the woman of the nature of the procedure, the health risks of the abortion and of childbirth, and the "probable gestational age of the unborn child." The physician or a qualified nonphysician must inform the woman of the availability of printed materials published by the State describing the fetus and providing information about medical assistance for childbirth, information about child support from the father, and a list of agencies which provide adoption and other services as alternatives to abortion. An abortion may not be performed unless the woman certifies in writing that she has been informed of the availability of these printed materials and has been provided them if she chooses to view them.

* * *

If the information the State requires to be made available to the woman is truthful and not misleading, the requirement may be permissible. [The Court then rejects the argument that the physician's first amendment speech rights trump the state-mandated obligation to provide patients with identified truthful information.]

* * *

The Pennsylvania statute also requires us to reconsider the holding[ ] that the State may not require that a physician, as opposed to a qualified assistant, provide information relevant to a woman's informed consent.[ ] * * * Our cases reflect the fact that the Constitution gives the States broad latitude to decide that particular functions may be performed only by licensed professionals, even if an objective assessment might suggest that those same tasks could be performed by others.[ ] Thus, we uphold the provision as a reasonable means to insure that the woman's consent is informed.

Our analysis of Pennsylvania's 24–hour waiting period between the provision of the information deemed necessary to informed consent and the performance of an abortion under the undue burden standard requires us to reconsider the premise behind the decision in *Akron I* invalidating a parallel requirement. In *Akron I* we said: "Nor are we convinced that the State's legitimate concern that the woman's decision be informed is reasonably served by requiring a 24–hour delay as a matter of course."[ ] We consider that conclusion to be wrong. The idea that important decisions will be more informed and deliberate if they follow some period of reflection does not strike us as unreasonable, particularly where the statute directs that important information become part of the background of the decision.

* * *

C.

Pennsylvania's abortion law provides, except in cases of medical emergency, that no physician shall perform an abortion on a married woman without receiving a signed statement from the woman that she has notified her spouse that she is about to undergo an abortion.

* * *

This information and the District Court's findings reinforce what common sense would suggest. In well-functioning marriages, spouses discuss important intimate decisions such as whether to bear a child. But there are millions of women in this country who are the victims of regular physical and psychological abuse at the hands of their husbands. Should these women become pregnant, they may have very good reasons for not wishing to inform their husbands of their decision to obtain an abortion. Many may have justifiable fears of physical abuse, but may be no less fearful of the consequences of reporting prior abuse to the Commonwealth of Pennsylvania. Many may have a reasonable fear that notifying their husbands will provoke further instances of child abuse; these women are not exempt from [the] notification requirement. Many may fear devastating forms of psychological abuse from their husbands, including verbal harassment, threats of future violence, the destruction of possessions, physical confinement to the home, the withdrawal of financial support, or the disclosure of the abortion to family and friends. * * *

The spousal notification requirement is thus likely to prevent a significant number of women from obtaining an abortion. It does not merely make abortions a little more difficult or expensive to obtain; for many women, it will impose a substantial obstacle. We must not blind ourselves to the fact that the significant number of women who fear for their safety and the safety of their children are likely to be deterred from procuring an abortion as surely as if the Commonwealth had outlawed abortion in all cases.

Respondents attempt to avoid the conclusion that [the spousal notification provision] is invalid by pointing out that it imposes almost no burden at all for the vast majority of women seeking abortions. * * * Respondents argue that since some of [the 20% of women who seek abortions who are married] will be able to notify their husbands without adverse consequences or will qualify for one of the exceptions, the statute affects fewer than one percent of women seeking abortions. For this reason, it is asserted, the statute cannot be invalid on its face.[ ] We disagree with respondents' basic method of analysis.

The analysis does not end with the one percent of women upon whom the statute operates; it begins there. Legislation is measured for consistency with the Constitution by its impact on those whose conduct it affects. * * * [A]s we have said, [the Act's] real target is narrower even than the class of women seeking abortions * * *: it is married women seeking abortions who do not wish to notify their husbands of their intentions and who do not qualify for one of the statutory exceptions to the notice requirement. The unfortunate yet persisting conditions * * * will mean that in a large fraction of the cases * * *, [the statute] will operate as a substantial obstacle to a woman's choice to undergo an abortion. It is an undue burden, and therefore invalid.

*　　*　　*

[The spousal notification provision] embodies a view of marriage consonant with the common-law status of married women but repugnant to our present understanding of marriage and of the nature of the rights se-

cured by the Constitution. Women do not lose their constitutionally protected liberty when they marry. * * *

D.

* * *

Our cases establish, and we reaffirm today, that a State may require
a minor seeking an abortion to obtain the consent of a parent or guardian,
provided that there is an adequate judicial bypass procedure.[ ] Under
these precedents, in our view, the [Pennsylvania] one-parent consent requirement and judicial bypass procedure are constitutional.

* * *

E.

[The Justices upheld all of the record keeping and reporting requirements
of the statute, except for that provision requiring the reporting of a married woman's reason for failure to give notice to her husband.]

VI.

Our Constitution is a covenant running from the first generation of
Americans to us and then to future generations. It is a coherent succession. Each generation must learn anew that the Constitution's written
terms embody ideas and aspirations that must survive more ages than
one. We accept our responsibility not to retreat from interpreting the full
meaning of the covenant in light of all of our precedents. We invoke it
once again to define the freedom guaranteed by the Constitution's own
promise, the promise of liberty.

* * *

[In addition to those parts of the statute found unconstitutional in the
three-justice opinion, Justice Stevens would find unconstitutional the requirement that the doctor deliver state-produced materials to a woman
seeking an abortion, the counseling requirements, and the 24-hour-
waiting requirement. His concurring and dissenting opinion is omitted.
Justice Blackman's opinion, concurring in the judgment in part and dissenting in part, is also omitted.]

CHIEF JUSTICE REHNQUIST, with whom JUSTICE WHITE, JUSTICE
SCALIA, and JUSTICE THOMAS join, concurring in the judgment in part
and dissenting in part.

The joint opinion, following its newly-minted variation on stare decisis, retains the outer shell of Roe v. Wade,[ ] but beats a wholesale retreat
from the substance of that case. We believe that *Roe* was wrongly decided,
and that it can and should be overruled consistently with our traditional
approach to stare decisis in constitutional cases.

*   *   *

The end result of the joint opinion's paeans of praise for legitimacy is the enunciation of a brand new standard for evaluating state regulation of a woman's right to abortion—the "undue burden" standard. As indicated above, Roe v. Wade adopted a "fundamental right" standard under which state regulations could survive only if they met the requirement of "strict scrutiny." While we disagree with that standard, it at least had a recognized basis in constitutional law at the time *Roe* was decided. The same cannot be said for the "undue burden" standard, which is created largely out of whole cloth by the authors of the joint opinion. It is a standard which even today does not command the support of a majority of this Court. And it will not, we believe, result in the sort of "simple limitation," easily applied, which the joint opinion anticipates.[ ] In sum, it is a standard which is not built to last.

In evaluating abortion regulations under that standard, judges will have to decide whether they place a "substantial obstacle" in the path of a woman seeking an abortion.[ ] In that this standard is based even more on a judge's subjective determinations than was the trimester framework, the standard will do nothing to prevent "judges from roaming at large in the constitutional field" guided only by their personal views.[ ]

*   *   *

The sum of the joint opinion's labors in the name of stare decisis and "legitimacy" is this: Roe v. Wade stands as a sort of judicial Potemkin Village, which may be pointed out to passers by as a monument to the importance of adhering to precedent. But behind the facade, an entirely new method of analysis, without any roots in constitutional law, is imported to decide the constitutionality of state laws regulating abortion. Neither stare decisis nor "legitimacy" are truly served by such an effort.

*   *   *

JUSTICE SCALIA, with whom the CHIEF JUSTICE, JUSTICE WHITE, and JUSTICE THOMAS join, concurring in the judgment in part and dissenting in part.

*   *   *

The States may, if they wish, permit abortion-on-demand, but the Constitution does not require them to do so. The permissibility of abortion, and the limitations upon it, are to be resolved like most important questions in our democracy: by citizens trying to persuade one another and then voting. As the Court acknowledges, "where reasonable people disagree the government can adopt one position or the other." [ ] The Court is correct in adding the qualification that this "assumes a state of affairs in which the choice does not intrude upon a protected liberty,"[ ]—

but the crucial part of that qualification is the penultimate word. A State's choice between two positions on which reasonable people can disagree is constitutional even when (as is often the case) it intrudes upon a "liberty" in the absolute sense. Laws against bigamy, for example—which entire societies of reasonable people disagree with—intrude upon men and women's liberty to marry and live with one another. But bigamy happens not to be a liberty specially "protected" by the Constitution.

That is, quite simply, the issue in this case: not whether the power of a woman to abort her unborn child is a "liberty" in the absolute sense; or even whether it is a liberty of great importance to many women. Of course it is both. The issue is whether it is a liberty protected by the Constitution of the United States. I am sure it is not. I reach that conclusion not because of anything so exalted as my views concerning the "concept of existence, of meaning, of the universe, and of the mystery of human life." [ ] I reach it for the same reason I reach the conclusion that bigamy is not constitutionally protected—because of two simple facts: (1) the Constitution says absolutely nothing about it, and (2) the longstanding traditions of American society have permitted it to be legally proscribed.

* * *

I am certainly not in a good position to dispute that the Court has saved the "central holding" of *Roe*, since to do that effectively I would have to know what the Court has saved, which in turn would require me to understand (as I do not) what the "undue burden" test means. * * * I thought I might note, however, that the following portions of *Roe* have not been saved:

— Under *Roe*, requiring that a woman seeking an abortion be provided truthful information about abortion before giving informed written consent is unconstitutional, if the information is designed to influence her choice[ ]. Under the joint opinion's "undue burden" regime (as applied today, at least) such a requirement is constitutional[ ].

— Under *Roe,* requiring that information be provided by a doctor, rather than by nonphysician counselors, is unconstitutional[ ]. Under the "undue burden" regime (as applied today, at least) it is not[ ].

— Under *Roe*, requiring a 24–hour waiting period between the time the woman gives her informed consent and the time of the abortion is unconstitutional. Under the "undue burden" regime (as applied today, at least) it is not[ ].

— Under *Roe*, requiring detailed reports that include demographic data about each woman who seeks an abortion and various information about each abortion is unconstitutional[ ]. Under the "undue burden" regime (as applied today, at least) it generally is not[ ].

* * *

GONZALES V. CARHART

Supreme Court of the United States, 2007.
500 U.S. 124 127 S.Ct. 1610, 167 L.Ed.2d 480.

JUSTICE KENNEDY delivered the opinion of the Court.

These cases require us to consider the validity of the Partial–Birth Abortion Ban Act of 2003 (Act),[ ] a federal statute regulating abortion procedures. * * * We conclude the Act should be sustained against the objections lodged by the broad, facial attack brought against it.

* * *

I

A

[The Medical Procedure]

The Act proscribes a particular manner of ending fetal life, so it is necessary here[ ] to discuss abortion procedures in some detail. * * *

Abortion methods vary depending to some extent on the preferences of the physician and, of course, on the term of the pregnancy and the resulting stage of the unborn child's development. Between 85 and 90 percent of the approximately 1.3 million abortions performed each year in the United States take place in the first three months of pregnancy, which is to say in the first trimester.[ ] The most common first-trimester abortion method is vacuum aspiration (otherwise known as suction curettage) in which the physician vacuums out the embryonic tissue. Early in this trimester an alternative is to use medication, such as mifepristone (commonly known as RU–486), to terminate the pregnancy.[ ] The Act does not regulate these procedures.

Of the remaining abortions that take place each year, most occur in the second trimester. The surgical procedure referred to as "dilation and evacuation" or "D & E" is the usual abortion method in this trimester.[ ] Although individual techniques for performing D & E differ, the general steps are the same.

A doctor must first dilate the cervix at least to the extent needed to insert surgical instruments into the uterus and to maneuver them to evacuate the fetus.[ ] The steps taken to cause dilation differ by physician and gestational age of the fetus. * * *

After sufficient dilation the surgical operation can commence. The woman is placed under general anesthesia or conscious sedation. The doctor, often guided by ultrasound, inserts grasping forceps through the woman's cervix and into the uterus to grab the fetus. The doctor grips a fetal part with the forceps and pulls it back through the cervix and vagina, continuing to pull even after meeting resistance from the cervix. The friction causes the fetus to tear apart. For example, a leg might be ripped off the fetus as it is pulled through the cervix and out of the woman. The process of evacuating the fetus piece by piece continues until it has been completely removed. A doctor may make 10 to 15 passes with the forceps to evacuate the fetus in its entirety, though sometimes removal is completed with fewer passes. Once the fetus has been evacuated, the placenta and any remaining fetal material are suctioned or scraped out of the uterus. The doctor examines the different parts to ensure the entire fetal body has been removed.[ ]

Some doctors, especially later in the second trimester, may kill the fetus a day or two before performing the surgical evacuation. They inject digoxin or potassium chloride into the fetus, the umbilical cord, or the amniotic fluid. Fetal demise may cause contractions and make greater dilation possible. Once dead, moreover, the fetus' body will soften, and its removal will be easier. * * *

The abortion procedure that was the impetus for the numerous bans on "partial-birth abortion," including the Act, is a variation of this standard D & E.[ ] The medical community has not reached unanimity on the appropriate name for this D & E variation. It has been referred to as "intact D & E," "dilation and extraction" (D & X), and "intact D & X."[ ] For discussion purposes this D & E variation will be referred to as intact D & E. The main difference between the two procedures is that in intact D & E a doctor extracts the fetus intact or largely intact with only a few passes. There are no comprehensive statistics indicating what percentage of all D & Es are performed in this manner.

Intact D & E, like regular D & E, begins with dilation of the cervix. Sufficient dilation is essential for the procedure. * * * In an intact D & E procedure the doctor extracts the fetus in a way conducive to pulling out its entire body, instead of ripping it apart. * * *

Intact D & E gained public notoriety when, in 1992, Dr. Martin Haskell gave a presentation describing his method of performing the operation.[ ] In the usual intact D & E the fetus' head lodges in the cervix, and dilation is insufficient to allow it to pass.[ ] Haskell explained the next step as follows:

" 'At this point, the right-handed surgeon slides the fingers of the left [hand] along the back of the fetus and "hooks" the shoulders of the fetus with the index and ring fingers (palm down).

" 'While maintaining this tension, lifting the cervix and applying traction to the shoulders with the fingers of the left hand, the surgeon takes a pair of blunt curved Metzenbaum scissors in the right hand. He carefully advances the tip, curved down, along the spine and under his middle finger until he feels it contact the base of the skull under the tip of his middle finger.

" 'The surgeon then forces the scissors into the base of the skull or into the foramen magnum. Having safely entered the skull, he spreads the scissors to enlarge the opening.

" 'The surgeon removes the scissors and introduces a suction catheter into this hole and evacuates the skull contents. With the catheter still in place, he applies traction to the fetus, removing it completely from the patient.' "[ ]

This is an abortion doctor's clinical description. Here is another description from a nurse who witnessed the same method performed on a 26–week fetus and who testified before the Senate Judiciary Committee:

" 'Dr. Haskell went in with forceps and grabbed the baby's legs and pulled them down into the birth canal. Then he delivered the baby's body and the arms—everything but the head. The doctor kept the head right inside the uterus. . . .

" 'The baby's little fingers were clasping and unclasping, and his little feet were kicking. Then the doctor stuck the scissors in the back of his head, and the baby's arms jerked out, like a startle reaction, like a flinch, like a baby does when he thinks he is going to fall.

" 'The doctor opened up the scissors, stuck a high-powered suction tube into the opening, and sucked the baby's brains out. Now the baby went completely limp. . . .

" 'He cut the umbilical cord and delivered the placenta. He threw the baby in a pan, along with the placenta and the instruments he had just used.' "[ ]

[JUSTICE KENNEDY next describes other varieties of this procedure in equally vivid terms.]

* * *

D & E and intact D & E are not the only second-trimester abortion methods. * * *

B

[The Statute]

After Dr. Haskell's procedure received public attention, with ensuing and increasing public concern, bans on " 'partial birth abortion' " proliferated. By the time of the *Stenberg* decision [finding Nebraska's statutory partial birth abortion ban to be unconstitutional in 2003], about 30 States had enacted bans designed to prohibit the procedure.[ ]. In 1996, Congress also acted to ban partial-birth abortion. President Clinton vetoed the congressional legislation, and the Senate failed to override the veto. Congress approved another bill banning the procedure in 1997, but President Clinton again vetoed it. In 2003, after this Court's decision in *Stenberg*, Congress passed the Act at issue here.[ ] President Bush signed the Act into law. It was to take effect the following day.[ ]

The Act responded to *Stenberg* in two ways. First, Congress made factual findings. Congress determined that this Court in *Stenberg* "was required to accept the very questionable findings issued by the district court judge,"[ ], but that Congress was "not bound to accept the same factual findings,"[ ]. Congress found, among other things, that "[a] moral, medical, and ethical consensus exists that the practice of performing a partial-birth abortion . . . is a gruesome and inhumane procedure that is never medically necessary and should be prohibited."[ ]

Second, and more relevant here, the Act's language differs from that of the Nebraska statute struck down in *Stenberg*.[ ] The operative provisions of the Act provide in relevant part:

"(a) Any physician who, in or affecting interstate or foreign commerce, knowingly performs a partial-birth abortion and thereby kills a human fetus shall be fined under this title or imprisoned not more than 2 years, or both. This subsection does not apply to a partial-birth abortion that is necessary to save the life of a mother whose life is endangered by a physical disorder, physical illness, or physical injury, including a life-endangering physical condition caused by or arising from the pregnancy itself. * * *

"(b) As used in this section—

"(1) the term 'partial-birth abortion' means an abortion in which the person performing the abortion—

"(A) deliberately and intentionally vaginally delivers a living fetus until, in the case of a head-first presentation, the entire fetal head is outside the body of the mother, or, in the case of breech presentation, any part of the fetal trunk past the navel is outside the body of the mother, for the purpose of performing an overt act that the person knows will kill the partially delivered living fetus; and

"(B) performs the overt act, other than completion of delivery, that kills the partially delivered living fetus;

*   *   *

"(e) A woman upon whom a partial-birth abortion is performed may not be prosecuted under this section, for a conspiracy to violate this section, * * *.

The Act also includes a provision authorizing civil actions [for damages following a "Partial Birth Abortion"] that is not of relevance here.[ ]

* * *

II

[The Holding in *Casey*]

The principles set forth in the joint opinion in *Casey*,[ ] did not find support from all those who join the instant opinion.[ ] Whatever one's views concerning the *Casey* joint opinion, it is evident a premise central to its conclusion—that the government has a legitimate and substantial interest in preserving and promoting fetal life—would be repudiated were the Court now to affirm the judgments of the Courts of Appeals. *Casey* involved a challenge to Roe v. Wade[ ]. [One of the three essential principles of *Roe* that was upheld in Casey was] the principle that the State has legitimate interests from the outset of the pregnancy in protecting the health of the woman and the life of the fetus that may become a child. * * * [W]e must determine whether the Act furthers the legitimate interest of the Government in protecting the life of the fetus that may become a child.

To implement its holding, *Casey* rejected both *Roe*'s rigid trimester framework and the interpretation of *Roe* that considered all previability regulations of abortion unwarranted. * * *

We assume the following principles for the purposes of this opinion. Before viability, a State "may not prohibit any woman from making the ultimate decision to terminate her pregnancy."[ ] It also may not impose upon this right an undue burden, which exists if a regulation's "purpose or effect is to place a substantial obstacle in the path of a woman seeking an abortion before the fetus attains viability."[ ] On the other hand, "regulations which do no more than create a structural mechanism by which the State, or the parent or guardian of a minor, may express profound respect for the life of the unborn are permitted, if they are not a substantial obstacle to the woman's exercise of the right to choose."[ ] *Casey*, in short, struck a balance. The balance was central to its holding. We now apply its standard to the cases at bar.

III

We begin with a determination of the Act's operation and effect. A straightforward reading of the Act's text demonstrates its purpose and the scope of its provisions: It regulates and proscribes, with exceptions or qualifications to be discussed, performing the intact D & E procedure.

Respondents agree the Act encompasses intact D & E, but they contend its additional reach is both unclear and excessive. Respondents assert that, at the least, the Act is void for vagueness because its scope is indefinite. In the alternative, respondents argue the Act's text proscribes all D & Es. Because D & E is the most common second-trimester abortion method, respondents suggest the Act imposes an undue burden. In this litigation the Attorney General does not dispute that the Act would impose an undue burden if it covered standard D & E.

We conclude that the Act is not void for vagueness, does not impose an undue burden from any overbreadth, and is not invalid on its face.

A
[Interpreting the Statute]

The Act punishes "knowingly performing" a "partial-birth abortion."[ ] It defines the unlawful abortion in explicit terms.[ ]

First, the person performing the abortion must "vaginally deliver a living fetus."[ ] The Act does not restrict an abortion procedure involving the delivery of an expired fetus. The Act, furthermore, is inapplicable to abortions that do not involve vaginal delivery (for instance, hysterotomy or hysterectomy). The Act does apply both previability and postviability because, by common understanding and scientific terminology, a fetus is a living organism while within the womb, whether or not it is viable outside the womb. * * *

Second, the Act's definition of partial-birth abortion requires the fetus to be delivered "until, in the case of a head-first presentation, the entire fetal head is outside the body of the mother, or, in the case of breech presentation, any part of the fetal trunk past the navel is outside the body of the mother." * * *

Third, to fall within the Act, a doctor must perform an "overt act, other than completion of delivery, that kills the partially delivered living fetus."[ ] For purposes of criminal liability, the overt act causing the fetus' death must be separate from delivery. And the overt act must occur after the delivery to an anatomical landmark. This is because the Act proscribes killing "the partially delivered" fetus, which, when read in context, refers to a fetus that has been delivered to an anatomical landmark.[ ]

Fourth, the Act contains scienter requirements concerning all the actions involved in the prohibited abortion. To begin with, the physician must have "deliberately and intentionally" delivered the fetus to one of the Act's anatomical landmarks. * * * In addition, the fetus must have been delivered "for the purpose of performing an overt act that the [doctor] knows will kill [it]." * * *

B
[Vagueness]

Respondents contend the language described above is indeterminate, and they thus argue the Act is unconstitutionally vague on its face. "As generally stated, the void-for-vagueness doctrine requires that a penal statute define the criminal offense with sufficient definiteness that ordinary people can understand what conduct is prohibited and in a manner that does not encourage arbitrary and discriminatory enforcement."[ ] The Act satisfies both requirements.

* * * Unlike the statutory language in *Stenberg* that prohibited the delivery of a " 'substantial portion' " of the fetus—where a doctor might question how much of the fetus is a substantial portion—the Act defines the line between potentially criminal conduct on the one hand and lawful abortion on the other.[ ]

* * *

C

[Undue Burden]

We next determine whether the Act imposes an undue burden, as a facial matter, because its restrictions on second-trimester abortions are too broad. A review of the statutory text discloses the limits of its reach. The Act prohibits intact D & E; and, notwithstanding respondents' arguments, it does not prohibit the D & E procedure in which the fetus is removed in parts.

* * *

A comparison of the Act with the Nebraska statute struck down in *Stenberg* confirms this point. The statute in *Stenberg* prohibited " 'deliberately and intentionally delivering into the vagina a living unborn child, or a substantial portion thereof, for the purpose of performing a procedure that the person performing such procedure knows will kill the unborn child and does kill the unborn child.' "[ ]. The Court concluded that this statute encompassed D & E because "D & E will often involve a physician pulling a 'substantial portion' of a still living fetus, say, an arm or leg, into the vagina prior to the death of the fetus." * * *

Congress, it is apparent, responded to these concerns because the Act departs in material ways from the statute in *Stenberg*. It adopts the phrase "delivers a living fetus,"[ ] instead of " 'delivering . . . a living unborn child, or a substantial portion thereof,' "[ ]. The Act's language, unlike the statute in *Stenberg*, expresses the usual meaning of "deliver" when used in connection with "fetus," namely, extraction of an entire fetus rather than removal of fetal pieces. * * *

The identification of specific anatomical landmarks to which the fetus must be partially delivered also differentiates the Act from the statute at issue in *Stenberg*. * * *

By adding an overt-act requirement Congress sought further to meet the Court's objections to the state statute considered in *Stenberg*. * * * The fatal overt act must occur after delivery to an anatomical landmark, and it must be something "other than [the] completion of delivery."[ ] This distinction matters because, unlike intact D & E, standard D & E does not involve a delivery followed by a fatal act.

The canon of constitutional avoidance, finally, extinguishes any lingering doubt as to whether the Act covers the prototypical D & E procedure. " 'The elementary rule is that every reasonable construction must be resorted to, in order to save a statute from unconstitutionality.' "[ ] It is true this longstanding maxim of statutory interpretation has, in the past, fallen by the wayside when the Court confronted a statute regulating abortion. * * * *Casey* put this novel statutory approach to rest. * * *

*   *   *

IV

[Substantial Obstacle]

Under the principles accepted as controlling here, the Act, as we have interpreted it, would be unconstitutional "if its purpose or effect is to place a substantial obstacle in the path of a woman seeking an abortion before the fetus attains viability." *Casey*,[ ] The abortions affected by the Act's regulations take place both previability and postviability; so the quoted language and the undue burden analysis it relies upon are applicable. The question is whether the Act, measured by its text in this facial attack, imposes a substantial obstacle to late-term, but previability, abortions. The Act does not on its face impose a substantial obstacle, and we reject this further facial challenge to its validity.

A

[Congressional Purpose]

The Act's purposes are set forth in recitals preceding its operative provisions. A description of the prohibited abortion procedure demonstrates the rationale for the congressional enactment. The Act proscribes a method of abortion in which a fetus is killed just inches before completion of the birth process. Congress stated as follows: "Implicitly approving such a brutal and inhumane procedure by choosing not to prohibit it will further coarsen society to the humanity of not only newborns, but all vulnerable and innocent human life, making it increasingly difficult to protect such life."[ ] The Act expresses respect for the dignity of human life. Congress was concerned, furthermore, with the effects on the medical community and on its reputation caused by the practice of partial-birth abortion. * * *

There can be no doubt the government "has an interest in protecting the integrity and ethics of the medical profession." Washington v. Glucksberg,[ ] [reprinted in Chapter 17, below]. Under our precedents, it is clear the State has a significant role to play in regulating the medical profession.

Casey reaffirmed these governmental objectives. The government may use its voice and its regulatory authority to show its profound respect for the life within the woman. * * * The three premises of *Casey* must coexist.[ ] The third premise, that the State, from the inception of the pregnancy, maintains its own regulatory interest in protecting the life of the fetus that may become a child, cannot be set at naught by interpreting *Casey*'s requirement of a health exception so it becomes tantamount to allowing a doctor to choose the abortion method he or she might prefer. Where it has a rational basis to act, and it does not impose an undue burden, the State may use its regulatory power to bar certain procedures and substitute others, all in furtherance of its legitimate interests in regulating the medical profession in order to promote respect for life, including life of the unborn.

* * * The Court has in the past confirmed the validity of drawing boundaries to prevent certain practices that extinguish life and are close to actions that are condemned. *Glucksberg* found reasonable the State's "fear that permitting assisted suicide will start it down the path to voluntary and perhaps even involuntary euthanasia."[ ]

Respect for human life finds an ultimate expression in the bond of love the mother has for her child. The Act recognizes this reality as well. Whether to have an abortion requires a difficult and painful moral decision.[ ] While we find no reliable data to measure the phenomenon, it seems unexceptionable to conclude some women come to regret their choice to abort the infant life they once created and sustained.[ ] Severe depression and loss of esteem can follow.[ ]

In a decision so fraught with emotional consequence some doctors may prefer not to disclose precise details of the means that will be used, confining themselves to the required statement of risks the procedure entails. From one standpoint this ought not to be surprising. Any number of patients facing imminent surgical procedures would prefer not to hear all details, lest the usual anxiety preceding invasive medical procedures become the more intense. This is likely the case with the abortion procedures here in issue.[ ]

It is, however, precisely this lack of information concerning the way in which the fetus will be killed that is of legitimate concern to the State.[ ] The State has an interest in ensuring so grave a choice is well informed. It is self-evident that a mother who comes to regret her choice to abort must struggle with grief more anguished and sorrow more profound when she learns, only after the event, what she once did not know: that she allowed a doctor to pierce the skull and vacuum the fast-developing brain of her unborn child, a child assuming the human form.

* * *

It is objected that the standard D & E is in some respects as brutal, if not more, than the intact D & E, so that the legislation accomplishes little. * * * It was reasonable for Congress to think that partial-birth abortion, more than standard D & E, "undermines the public's perception of the appropriate role of a physician during the delivery process, and perverts a process during which life is brought into the world." * * * In sum, we reject the contention that the congressional purpose of the Act was "to place a substantial obstacle in the path of a woman seeking an abortion." [ ]

B
[Protecting the Health of the Mother]

The Act's furtherance of legitimate government interests bears upon, but does not resolve, the next question: whether the Act has the effect of imposing an unconstitutional burden on the abortion right because it does not allow use of the barred procedure where " 'necessary, in appropriate medical judgment, for [the] preservation of the . . . health of the mother.' "[ ] The prohibition in the Act would be unconstitutional, under precedents we here assume to be controlling, if it "subjected [women] to significant health risks." * * * Here, by contrast, whether the Act creates significant health risks for women has been a contested factual question. The evidence presented in the trial courts and before Congress demonstrates both sides have medical support for their position.

*   *   *

The question becomes whether the Act can stand when this medical uncertainty persists. The Court's precedents instruct that the Act can survive this facial attack. The Court has given state and federal legislatures wide discretion to pass legislation in areas where there is medical and scientific uncertainty.

*   *   *

In reaching the conclusion the Act does not require a health exception we reject certain arguments made by the parties on both sides of these cases. On the one hand, the Attorney General urges us to uphold the Act on the basis of the congressional findings alone.[ ] Although we review congressional factfinding under a deferential standard, we do not in the circumstances here place dispositive weight on Congress' findings. The Court retains an independent constitutional duty to review factual findings where constitutional rights are at stake.[ ]

As respondents have noted, and the District Courts recognized, some recitations in the Act are factually incorrect. * * * Uncritical deference to Congress' factual findings in these cases is inappropriate.

On the other hand, relying on the Court's opinion in *Stenberg*, respondents contend that an abortion regulation must contain a health exception "if 'substantial medical authority supports the proposition that banning a particular procedure could endanger women's health.' " * * * *Stenberg* has been interpreted to leave no margin of error for legislatures to act in the face of medical uncertainty.[ ]

A zero tolerance policy would strike down legitimate abortion regulations, like the present one, if some part of the medical community were disinclined to follow the proscription. This is too exacting a standard to impose on the legislative power, exercised in this instance under the Commerce Clause, to regulate the medical profession. Considerations of marginal safety, including the balance of risks, are within the legislative competence when the regulation is rational and in pursuit of legitimate ends. * * * The Act is not invalid on its face where there is uncertainty over whether the barred procedure is ever necessary to preserve a woman's health, given the availability of other abortion procedures that are considered to be safe alternatives.

V

[Propriety of a Facial Attack on the Statute]

The considerations we have discussed support our further determination that these facial attacks should not have been entertained in the first instance. In these circumstances the proper means to consider exceptions is by as-applied challenge. * * * This is the proper manner to protect the health of the woman if it can be shown that in discrete and well-defined instances a particular condition has or is likely to occur in which the procedure prohibited by the Act must be used. In an as-applied challenge the nature of the medical risk can be better quantified and balanced than in a facial attack.

*   *   *

As the previous sections of this opinion explain, respondents have not demonstrated that the Act would be unconstitutional in a large fraction of relevant cases. * * *

The Act is open to a proper as-applied challenge in a discrete case. * * * No as-applied challenge need be brought if the prohibition in the Act threatens a woman's life because the Act already contains a life exception.[ ]

*   *   *

JUSTICE THOMAS, with whom JUSTICE SCALIA joins, concurring.

I join the Court's opinion because it accurately applies current jurisprudence, including *Casey*,[ ]. I write separately to reiterate my view that the Court's abortion jurisprudence, including *Casey* and *Roe*[ ] has no basis in the Constitution.[ ] I also note that whether the Act constitutes a permissible exercise of Congress' power under the Commerce Clause is not before the Court. The parties did not raise or brief that issue; it is outside the question presented; and the lower courts did not address it.[ ]

JUSTICE GINSBURG, with whom JUSTICE STEVENS, JUSTICE SOUTER, and JUSTICE BREYER join, dissenting.

* * *

In reaffirming *Roe*, the *Casey* Court described the centrality of "the decision whether to bear . . . a child,"[ ] to a woman's "dignity and autonomy," her "personhood" and "destiny," her "conception of . . . her place in society."[ ] Of signal importance here, the *Casey* Court stated with unmistakable clarity that state regulation of access to abortion procedures, even after viability, must protect "the health of the woman."[ ]

Seven years ago, in *Stenberg*,[ ] the Court invalidated a Nebraska statute criminalizing the performance of a medical procedure that, in the political arena, has been dubbed "partial-birth abortion." With fidelity to the *Roe–Casey* line of precedent, the Court held the Nebraska statute unconstitutional in part because it lacked the requisite protection for the preservation of a woman's health.[ ]

Today's decision is alarming. It refuses to take *Casey* and *Stenberg* seriously. It tolerates, indeed applauds, federal intervention to ban nationwide a procedure found necessary and proper in certain cases by the American College of Obstetricians and Gynecologists (ACOG). It blurs the line, firmly drawn in *Casey*, between previability and postviability abortions. And, for the first time since *Roe*, the Court blesses a prohibition with no exception safeguarding a woman's health.

I dissent from the Court's disposition. Retreating from prior rulings that abortion restrictions cannot be imposed absent an exception safeguarding a woman's health, the Court upholds an Act that surely would not survive under the close scrutiny that previously attended state-decreed limitations on a woman's reproductive choices.

I

A

As *Casey* comprehended, at stake in cases challenging abortion restrictions is a woman's "control over her [own] destiny." * * * Women, it is now acknowledged, have the talent, capacity, and right "to participate equally in the economic and social life of the Nation."[ ] Their ability to realize their full potential, the Court recognized, is intimately connected to "their ability to control their reproductive lives."[ ] Thus, legal challenges to undue restrictions on abortion procedures do not seek to vindicate some generalized notion of privacy; rather, they center on a woman's autonomy to determine her life's course, and thus to enjoy equal citizenship stature.[ ]

In keeping with this comprehension of the right to reproductive choice, the Court has consistently required that laws regulating abortion, at any stage of pregnancy and in all cases, safeguard a woman's health.[ ]

We have thus ruled that a State must avoid subjecting women to health risks not only where the pregnancy itself creates danger, but also where state regulation forces women to resort to less safe methods of abortion. * * *

In *Stenberg*, we expressly held that a statute banning intact D & E was unconstitutional in part because it lacked a health exception.[ ] We noted that there existed a "division of medical opinion" about the relative safety of intact D & E,[ ], but we made clear that as long as "substantial medical authority supports the proposition that banning a particular abortion procedure could endanger women's health," a health exception is required.[ ] We explained:

> "The word 'necessary' in *Casey*'s phrase 'necessary, in appropriate medical judgment, for the preservation of the life or health of the [pregnant woman],' cannot refer to an absolute necessity or to absolute proof. Medical treatments and procedures are often considered appropriate (or inappropriate) in light of estimated comparative health risks (and health benefits) in particular cases. Neither can that phrase require unanimity of medical opinion. Doctors often differ in their estimation of comparative health risks and appropriate treatment. And *Casey*'s words 'appropriate medical judgment' must embody the judicial need to tolerate responsible differences of medical opinion. . . . "[ ]

Thus, we reasoned, division in medical opinion "at most means uncertainty, a factor that signals the presence of risk, not its absence."[ ] "[A] statute that altogether forbids [intact D & E] . . . consequently must contain a health exception."[ ]

B

In 2003, a few years after our ruling in *Stenberg*, Congress passed the Partial–Birth Abortion Ban Act—without an exception for women's health.[ ] The congressional findings on which the Partial–Birth Abortion Ban Act rests do not withstand inspection, as the lower courts have determined and this Court is obliged to concede.

* * *

C

* * *

During the District Court trials, "numerous" "extraordinarily accomplished" and "very experienced" medical experts explained that, in certain circumstances and for certain women, intact D & E is safer than alternative procedures and necessary to protect women's health.[ ]

According to the expert testimony plaintiffs introduced, the safety advantages of intact D & E are marked for women with certain medical conditions, * * *. Further, plaintiffs' experts testified that intact D & E is significantly safer for women with certain pregnancy-related conditions, such as placenta previa and accreta, and for women carrying fetuses with certain abnormalities, such as severe hydrocephalus.[ ]

Intact D & E, plaintiffs' experts explained, provides safety benefits over D & E by dismemberment for several reasons [which Justice Ginsburg lists and describes]. * * *

*   *   *

Nevertheless, despite the District Courts' appraisal of the weight of the evidence, and in undisguised conflict with *Stenberg*, the Court asserts that the Partial–Birth Abortion Ban Act can survive "when . . . medical uncertainty persists."[ ] This assertion is bewildering.

*   *   *

II

A

The Court offers flimsy and transparent justifications for upholding a nationwide ban on intact D & E *sans* any exception to safeguard a women's health. Today's ruling, the Court declares, advances "a premise central to [*Casey*'s] conclusion"—i.e., the Government's "legitimate and substantial interest in preserving and promoting fetal life."[ ] But the Act scarcely furthers that interest: The law saves not a single fetus from destruction, for it targets only a *method* of performing abortion.[ ] And surely the statute was not designed to protect the lives or health of pregnant women.[ ]

*   *   *

Ultimately, the Court admits that "moral concerns" are at work, concerns that could yield prohibitions on any abortion.[ ] Notably, the concerns expressed are untethered to any ground genuinely serving the Government's interest in preserving life. By allowing such concerns to carry the day and case, overriding fundamental rights, the Court dishonors our precedent.[ ]

Revealing in this regard, the Court invokes an antiabortion shibboleth for which it concededly has no reliable evidence: Women who have abortions come to regret their choices, and consequently suffer from "severe depression and loss of esteem."[ ] Because of women's fragile emotional state and because of the "bond of love the mother has for her child," the Court worries, doctors may withhold information about the nature of the intact D & E procedure.[ ] The solution the Court approves, then, is *not* to require doctors to inform women, accurately and adequately, of the different procedures and their attendant risks.[ ] Instead, the Court deprives women of the right to make an autonomous choice, even at the expense of their safety.

This way of thinking reflects ancient notions about women's place in the family and under the Constitution—ideas that have long since been discredited. * * *

Though today's majority may regard women's feelings on the matter as "self-evident,"[ ] this Court has repeatedly confirmed that "the destiny of the woman must be shaped . . . on her own conception of her spiritual imperatives and her place in society." *Casey*[ ].

B

* * *

The Court's hostility to the right *Roe* and *Casey* secured is not concealed. Throughout, the opinion refers to obstetrician-gynecologists and surgeons who perform abortions not by the titles of their medical specialties, but by the pejorative label "abortion doctor."[ ] A fetus is described as an "unborn child," and as a "baby,"[ ]; second-trimester, previability abortions are referred to as "late-term,"[ ]; and the reasoned medical judgments of highly trained doctors are dismissed as "preferences" motivated by "mere convenience,"[ ]. Instead of the heightened scrutiny we have previously applied, the Court determines that a "rational" ground is enough to uphold the Act,[ ]. And, most troubling, *Casey*'s principles, confirming the continuing vitality of "the essential holding of *Roe*," are merely "assumed" for the moment,[ ], rather than "retained" or "reaffirmed," *Casey*[ ].

III

A

The Court further confuses our jurisprudence when it declares that "facial attacks" are not permissible in "these circumstances," i.e., where medical uncertainty exists. * * *

Without attempting to distinguish *Stenberg* and earlier decisions, the majority asserts that the Act survives review because respondents have not shown that the ban on intact D & E would be unconstitutional "in a large fraction of relevant cases."[ ] But *Casey* makes clear that, in determining whether any restriction poses an undue burden on a "large fraction" of women, the relevant class is *not* "all women," nor "all pregnant women," nor even all women "seeking abortions."[ ]. Rather, a provision restricting access to abortion, "must be judged by reference to those [women] for whom it is an actual rather than an irrelevant restriction,"[ ] Thus the absence of a health exception burdens *all* women for whom it is relevant—women who, in the judgment of their doctors, require an intact D & E because other procedures would place their health at risk.[ ] It makes no sense to conclude that this facial challenge fails because respondents have not shown that a health exception is necessary for a large fraction of second-trimester abortions, including those for which a health exception is unnecessary: The very purpose of a health *exception* is to protect women in *exceptional* cases.

B

If there is anything at all redemptive to be said of today's opinion, it is that the Court is not willing to foreclose entirely a constitutional challenge to the Act. "The Act is open," the Court states, "to a proper as-applied challenge in a discrete case."[ ] But the Court offers no clue on what a "proper" lawsuit might look like.[ ] Nor does the Court explain why the injunctions ordered by the District Courts should not remain in place, trimmed only to exclude instances in which another procedure would safeguard a woman's health at least equally well. Surely the Court cannot mean that no suit may be brought until a woman's health is immediately jeopardized by the ban on intact D & E. A woman "suffering from medical complications,"[ ] needs access to the medical procedure at once and cannot wait for the judicial process to unfold.[ ]

* * *

IV

As the Court wrote in *Casey,* "overruling *Roe's* central holding would not only reach an unjustifiable result under principles of *stare decisis,* but would seriously weaken the Court's capacity to exercise the judicial power and to function as the Supreme Court of a Nation dedicated to the rule of law." * * *

Though today's opinion does not go so far as to discard *Roe* or *Casey,* the Court, differently composed than it was when we last considered a restrictive abortion regulation, is hardly faithful to our earlier invocations of "the rule of law" and the "principles of *stare decisis.*" Congress imposed a ban despite our clear prior holdings that the State cannot proscribe an abortion procedure when its use is necessary to protect a woman's health.[ ] Although Congress' findings could not withstand the crucible of trial, the Court defers to the legislative override of our Constitution-based rulings.[ ] A decision so at odds with our jurisprudence should not have staying power.

In sum, the notion that the Partial–Birth Abortion Ban Act furthers any legitimate governmental interest is, quite simply, irrational. The Court's defense of the statute provides no saving explanation. In candor, the Act, and the Court's defense of it, cannot be understood as anything other than an effort to chip away at a right declared again and again by this Court—and with increasing comprehension of its centrality to women's lives.[ ] When "a statute burdens constitutional rights and all that can be said on its behalf is that it is the vehicle that legislators have chosen for expressing their hostility to those rights, the burden is undue."[ ]

For the reasons stated, I dissent from the Court's disposition and would affirm the judgments before us for review.

NOTES AND QUESTIONS

1.   At the beginning of 2013, *Casey* and Gonzales v. Carhart remain the governing United States Supreme Court cases with regard to abortion. Does *Casey* really affirm *Roe*? Did the holding of *Roe* survive *Casey*? Does Gonzales v. Carhart really affirm and apply *Casey*? Does the holding of *Casey* survive Gonzales v. Carhart? How would you articulate the current Constitutional standard with regard to what kinds of legislative restrictions on abortion are permissible?

2.   How, exactly, is a court to apply the Supreme Court's "undue burden" test? Does Gonzales v. Carhart provide any insight into what constitutes an "undue burden" or a "substantial obstacle" in the path of a woman seeking an abortion? In finding whether a state law "has the purpose or effect of placing a substantial obstacle in the path of a woman seeking an abortion of a nonviable fetus," is the Court really proposing a two-part (purpose and effect) analysis?

How is a court expected to divine the purpose of such an act? From the terms of the law? From formal legislative statements? Where did the Court look to determine the purpose of the Partial Birth Abortion Ban Act in Gonzales v. Carhart? Are you convinced by the Court's analysis? Is Congress (or any state legislature) likely to promulgate an enacting clause declaring that their purpose is to unduly burden those who seek to abort nonviable fetuses? Of course, we know that a state law has the effect of establishing an "undue burden" when it puts a "substantial obstacle" in the path of a woman seeking to abort a nonviable fetus, but how much does that advance the inquiry? Is an obstacle substantial because it imposes a serious limitation on any identifiable woman, or because it affects a large number of women, or because it affects a large percentage of the cases in which women would seek abortions? How does Does Gonzales v. Carhart answer these questions?

Unlike in Roe v. Wade, in which the Court dealt with virtually absolute bans on abortion, in *Casey* the Court faced several narrow regulations on abortion that had been promulgated by the Pennsylvania legislature, and it thus was required to apply its test to a series of articulated restrictions. These included the requirement that particular state-mandated information be provided to the pregnant woman before the abortion is performed, the requirement that the information be provided by a physician, a 24–hour waiting period between the receipt of the information and the pregnant woman's formal consent to the abortion (and thus a "two-step" procedure), the requirement that a minor get parental consent (with a judicial bypass procedure to avoid that requirement in some cases), and various state reporting requirements, none of which were found to constitute "undue burdens," at least in Pennsylvania on the evidence presented to the Court in 1992. On the other hand, the Court did find that a spousal notification requirement constituted an undue burden (as did any reporting requirement related to that notification requirement), and the Court struck that down.

3. Since 1973 many state legislatures have attempted to impose the most restrictive abortion laws that they can while recognizing that a complete ban would violate the Constitution. While the pace at which states were testing the Constitutional limits on statutes limiting abortion seemed to slow after the Casey decision in 1992, since *Gonzales* in 2007, the states' interest in imposing new and creative limits of abortion seems to have once again accelerated. Many of these limitations are discussed later in these notes.

Since *Casey* pro-choice advocates have also gone on the offensive in some state legislatures. Instead of merely opposing new restrictions on abortion, in some states advocates are supporting legislation that would make some procedures more easily available. For example, some state legislatures have passed legislation that requires hospital emergency rooms to have emergency contraception available for women who have been sexually assaulted.

4. What were the relevant differences between the partial birth abortion ban that was rejected in *Stenberg* and the one that was accepted in Gonzales v. Carhart? Was it the legislative findings that saved the federal statute? The more precise definition of the banned procedure? The scienter requirement? The fact that D & E abortions are still permitted? Some combination of these? Was the change in the Court's approach to partial birth abortion legislation the result of the form of the challenge, the language of the statute, or, perhaps, the replacement of Justice O'Connor by Justice Alito?

5. The Court did not formally address the question of whether Congress had authority to promulgate the Partial Birth Abortion Ban of 2003 because that issue was neither raised nor argued. Congress found its authority in its power to regulate commerce among the states. Is that an adequate basis? Is the argument that Congress had the authority to pass the Partial Birth Abortion Ban of 2003 strengthened or weakened by the Supreme Court's opinions in the Affordable Care Act litigation, National Federation of Independent Businesses v. Sebelius, 132 S.Ct 2566 (2012), reprinted below in Chapters 9 and 10? Is there any source of authority other than the commerce clause that could justify the Partial Birth Abortion Ban Act? As a matter of policy, is it more appropriate for abortion restrictions to be enacted on a state

by state basis (as had generally been the case before Congress passed this ban), or by Congress? Why?

6.   Although Gonzales v. Carhart rejected a facial attack on this federal statute, it left open the possibility that an "as applied" attack on the statute might be successful under the right circumstances. What are those circumstances? If you were to mount a judicial challenge to the Partial Birth Abortion Act of 2003 after Gonzales v. Carhart, who would be your ideal plaintiff? If you were defending such a challenge, whom would you like to see as the opposing party?

As a matter of Constitutional jurisprudence, should an issue like this be resolved in a facial challenge, or an "as applied" challenge, to the statute? Justice Kennedy pointed out that the Court had applied different standards with regard to facial Constitutional challenges to restrictions on abortions over the past few decades, and he indicated that there was no need for the Court to finally resolve the issue of when such a facial challenge would be appropriate. Justice Ginsburg was concerned about the difficulty that would be faced by anyone attempting the "as applied" challenge left open by the majority:

> The Court's allowance only of an "as-applied challenge in a discrete case,"[ ] jeopardizes women's health and places doctors in an untenable position. Even if courts were able to carve-out exceptions through piecemeal litigation for "discrete and well-defined instances,"[ ] women whose circumstances have not been anticipated by prior litigation could well be left unprotected. In treating those women, physicians would risk criminal prosecution, conviction, and imprisonment if they exercise their best judgment as to the safest medical procedure for their patients. The Court is thus gravely mistaken to conclude that narrow as-applied challenges are "the proper manner to protect the health of the woman."[ ]

7.   *Consent and Notification Requirements.* There remain, of course, other kinds of regulation with uncertain Constitutional status, too. It is now clear that it does not violate the United States Constitution for minors to be required to obtain the consent of a parent to an abortion, as long as the state permits a court (or, perhaps, an appropriate administrative agency) to dispense with that requirement under some circumstances. As of early 2013, thirty-seven states required some kind of parental involvement (either consent or notification, or, in four states, both) before a minor can be provided an abortion. The Supreme Court has never determined if a two-parent consent requirement (with a proper judicial bypass provision) would pass Constitutional muster, however. See Barnes v. Mississippi, 992 F.2d 1335 (5th Cir.1993), cert. denied, 510 U.S. 976, 114 S.Ct. 468, 126 L.Ed.2d 419 (1993) (upholding two-parent consent requirement because involvement of both parents will increase "reflection and deliberation" on the process, and if one parent denies consent the other will be able to go to court in support of the child) and S.H. v. D.H., 796 N.E.2d 1243 (Ind.App.2003) (family court judge cannot

require consent of both parents before an abortion is performed, even if the divorced parents have joint custody). The Supreme Court has suggested that a state requirement of mere parental notification (rather than consent) requires a judicial bypass, and lower courts have generally assumed that it does. Ohio v. Akron Ctr. for Reproductive Health, 497 U.S. 502, 110 S.Ct. 2972, 111 L.Ed.2d 405 (1990). One state supreme court has found that a parental notification requirement violates the state constitution's equal protection clause when it is imposed only on those who seek abortions, not on pregnant children making other, equally medically risky, reproductive decisions. Planned Parenthood of Central New Jersey v. Farmer, 165 N.J. 609, 762 A.2d 620 (2000).

It is not entirely clear what Constitutional standard a court must apply in a "bypass" case. Is the court required to waive consent or notification (1) if it finds that the minor is sufficiently mature that she should be able to make the decision herself, or (2) if it finds that if she seeks consent from (or notifies) her parents she will be subject to abuse, or (3) if it finds that it is in her best interest to have the abortion, or (4) if it finds that it is in her best interest not to be required to notify, or get consent from, her parent, or some combination of all of these? See Lambert v. Wicklund, 520 U.S. 292, 297, 117 S.Ct. 1169, 137 L.Ed.2d 464 (1997) (per curiam).

If the statute does include a substantively Constitutional bypass provision, what kind of procedural conditions may be placed on a bypass case? May the petitioner be required to prove her case by clear and convincing evidence? Is she entitled to counsel? Is she required to have a special guardian appointed for purposes of the litigation? Can the state require an expedited hearing? Can it allow the court to refuse an expedited hearing? Can it require the petition be filed within a very short time after the commencement of the pregnancy? Can it limit appeals by those who unsuccessfully seek judicial bypass?

The debate for and against consent and notification requirements reveals an even deeper debate about the current role of the family in contemporary life. While most agree that a teenager's abortion should be a decision made in consultation with her parents, that belief rests upon several assumptions. First, it assumes that the family dynamics are such that the daughter's disclosure will not trigger domestic violence or other forms of family abuse. Second, it assumes that the daughter lives within a traditional nuclear family, or can readily reach her biological parents. Finally, and most critically, it assumes that parents will act in the daughter's best interest. Some of these assumptions may, sadly, be based upon an idealized view of contemporary family life. While many children are brought up in healthy families, as Justice Kennard of the California Supreme Court has pointed out, "[n]ot every pregnant adolescent has parents out of the comforting and idyllic world of Norman Rockwell." American Academy of Pediatrics v. Lungren, 51 Cal.Rptr.2d 201, 224, 912 P.2d 1148, 1171 (1996) (Kennard, J., dissenting).

Those who support consent and notification statutes offer many stories of girls who had abortions secretly and now regret not discussing it with their parents. Indeed, those stories seem to have influenced Justice Kennedy's opinion in Gonzales v. Carhart. Those who oppose these statutes offer stories about girls who committed suicide rather than go through the notification procedures. Is this anecdotal evidence offered by both sides of much value? Could respectable research data on these issues be developed? Why do you think it has not been developed in any reliable way? Does it seem ironic that under a consent or notification statute a court could declare a pregnant minor to be too immature to proceed without parental consultation, with the result that she will become a mother?

Whatever may be the uncertain status of the details surrounding parental consent and notification, *Casey* established that spousal consent and spousal notification requirements are unconstitutional. See Jane L. v. Bangerter, 61 F.3d 1493 (10th Cir.1995) (rejecting notification done by someone other than the pregnant woman); Planned Parenthood of Southern Arizona, Inc. v. Woods, 982 F.Supp. 1369, 1380 (D.Ariz.1997) (rejecting statute that did not require spousal consent but provided for civil liability for physician providing abortion without that consent).

8.   *Regulation of Medical Procedures.* As a general matter, until Gonzales v. Carhart, courts had been reluctant to uphold statutory limitations on abortion procedures. Since 2007, it has been clear that such restrictions are Constitutional as long as they do not impose an undue burden on the woman seeking an abortion. In Gonzales v. Carhart, counsel for the government agreed that outlawing the classic D & E abortion would constitute an "undue burden," and thus would be unconstitutional. Should counsel have made that concession? After all, D & E abortions are very similar to the outlawed partial-birth abortions; some may even consider them more offensive because they require dismembering a fetus before removing it from the uterus. Might a future facial attack on a statute that bars all D & E abortions be successful?

One state supreme court has determined that a requirement that second trimester abortions be performed in a hospital violated the state constitution, which was read to be more protective of abortion rights than the United States Constitution. See Planned Parenthood of Middle Tennessee v. Sundquist, 38 S.W.3d 1 (Tenn.2000). But see Greenville Women's Clinic v. Bryant, 222 F.3d 157 (4th Cir.2000) (upholding rigid South Carolina licensing requirements for facilities where abortions are performed). Courts have had little trouble with the requirement (now in almost 40 states) that only licensed physicians, not physicians' assistants or others, perform abortions, because the authority granted with professional licenses is a matter of state law. Such licensing requirements are seen as ways of protecting the pregnant woman, not imposing a burden on her decision to have an abortion.

9.   *Two-trip Requirements and Waiting Periods.* When a state imposes a waiting period between the time the pregnant woman is provided the information that is to be the basis of her informed consent to an abortion and the medical procedure itself, it may, de facto, be requiring that the pregnant woman make two trips to the medical facility where the abortion is to be per-

formed. In *Casey* the Court announced that a 24–hour waiting period did not constitute an unconstitutional undue burden. For an interesting and controversial econometric argument that some kinds of waiting periods reduce the chance of suicide, and thus are valuable for women who are subject to them, see Jonathan Klick, Mandatory Waiting Periods for Abortions and Female Mental Health, 16 Health Matrix 183 (2006). The Tennessee Supreme Court determined that imposing what amounts to a three-day waiting period violated the state constitution's protected right of privacy. See Planned Parenthood of Middle Tennessee v. Sundquist, 38 S.W.3d 1 (Tenn.2000). As of early 2013, about half of the states imposed waiting periods of some sort.

10. *Other Informed Consent Requirements.* In *Casey* the Court upheld a statute that requires that a state-approved packet of material be given to the pregnant woman as a part of the informed consent process, and that the consent process be obtained by the physician, not by anyone else. The only requirement *Casey* appears to put on the distributed material is that it contain information that is true. In early 1996 a couple of epidemiological studies arguably suggested a very weak relationship between having an abortion and the subsequent risk of developing breast cancer and the severity of that cancer. Subsequent reports cast doubt on this relationship. See P.A. Newcomb, et al., Pregnancy Termination in Relation to Risk of Breast Cancer, 275 JAMA 283 (1996). May states require that physicians inform potential abortion patients that there is a correlation between abortion and the risk of breast cancer? May states require that patients be provided the information about this correlation even if they do not require that patients be told of the different, but significantly higher, risks of ordinary pregnancy? A handful of states do require by statute that a woman seeking an abortion be told of the purported breast cancer risk, and nearly a dozen require that the woman seeking the abortion be told of the possibility that the fetus can feel pain. Could the state require that a woman attend a short course on fetal development as a condition of having an abortion? See a graphic movie dealing with that same subject? Talk to other women who have had abortions? Speak with adoptive couples?

Over the last few years several states have added requirements that women seeking abortions be allowed or required to see ultrasounds of the fetus before they give formal consent to the abortion. A few states have debated requiring the highly intrusive transvaginal ultrasound, which may provide a clearer picture, before allowing a woman to choose to have an abortion. Abortion is the only procedure in current medical practice in which the state requires a patient to undergo and review a particular diagnostic test even if the patient does not wish to do so and her doctor believes the tests will not have any diagnostic or therapeutic value.

11. Could a state ban abortions for certain purposes? In 2013 North Dakota outlawed abortion because the mother wishes to engage in sex selection or because the mother does not want to bear a child with certain genetic conditions; can it legally prohibit abortion for either of these reasons? Could

the state outlaw abortion if it is used as a primary method of birth control? If it could do so legally, how would it do so as a practical matter?

12. Some believe that the ultimate disappearance of abortion practice will be the result of the fact that medical schools and residency programs are discontinuing training in abortion techniques because offering that training is not worth the political cost. Should all Obstetrics and Gynecology training programs include, at the very least, some exposure to the abortion process, or may a medical school decide that it will not provide that training because it finds the practice of abortion morally unacceptable? Should students who find such practice abhorrent be able to opt out of that training? Are there Constitutional implications to the removal of abortion from the medical school curriculum at a state university, or from the list of procedures done at a teaching hospital? See Barbara Gottlieb, Sounding Board, 332 JAMA 532 (1995).

13. Neighboring states often have very different laws regulating abortion, and women from one state may go to another state to take advantage of what they consider a favorable law. May a state prohibit a woman from crossing a state line to obtain an abortion that would be illegal in the first state? In 1996 a New York jury convicted a woman of "interfering with the custody of a minor," a felony, for taking a 13–year–old pregnant girl from Pennsylvania (which requires parental consent) to New York (which does not) to obtain an abortion. See David Stout, Guilty Verdict for Enabling Girl to Have An Abortion, *New York Times*, Oct. 31, 1996, A–8.

14. Although those in support of the Right to Choose movement are engaged in primarily defensive action to save what they can of *Casey* and assure that abortions are, in fact, truly available to those who choose them, they have also taken some legislative action. While most state legislatures are more disposed to Right to Life arguments than to Right to Choose arguments, that is not true of city councils and other local governing organizations. The Baltimore City Council, for example, promulgated a set of regulations for "Limited–Service Pregnancy Centers" that required those pregnancy centers to post signs saying that they do not provide abortions, referrals to abortion providers, or information about abortion services. The City Council acted after they received complaints that some limited-service pregnancy centers provided misleading information to clients about the availability of abortion services. Just as Right to Choice groups responded to Right to Life legislation with litigation (mostly grounded in the substantive due process clause of the Fourteenth Amendment), Right to Life groups (and the Catholic limited-service pregnancy information center itself) responded to this city ordinance with litigation based in the speech and religion clauses of the First Amendment. On June 27, 2012, the Fourth Circuit, over a strong dissent, found the Baltimore ordinance to violate the Center's First Amendment free speech rights by requiring it to communicate to its clients a message it did not want to convey. The majority found no compelling state interest to justify the intrusion on free speech. See Greater Baltimore Center for Pregnancy Concerns, Inc. v. Mayor and City Council of Baltimore, 683 F.3d 539 (4th Cir. 2012).

15. There may be some basic value issues upon which the pro-choice and pro-life partisans agree. While pro-choice supporters argue that an abortion should be among the choices of a pregnant woman, no one views an abortion as a happy event. Both sides would be pleased if society reached a point where there were no need for abortions. Similarly, while some pro-life supporters believe that every fetus is entitled to be born alive, many recognize that there are some times when the mother's interest does trump that of the fetus—when the mother's life is at stake, for example, and, perhaps, when the pregnancy is a result of rape or incest—and many recognize that the medical condition of the fetus is a relevant consideration. Very few people oppose early abortions of anencephalic fetuses, for example, or early abortions of other fetuses who are certain to be stillborn or to die within the first few minutes of birth. Both sides may also support expanded state funding for prenatal care and post-natal care, each of which may make abortion a less attractive alternative to pregnant women. Is there a common ground that could give rise to some kind of generally acceptable state policy on abortion, at least in some states? If pro-choice partisans and pro-life partisans were to sit with you and enumerate their common concerns, would there be some basic issues and basic principles upon which they would agree?

16. There has been a great deal of writing about abortion law and not all of it is polemical. Some recent and particularly thoughtful articles include C. Sanger, About Abortion: The Complications of the Category, 54 Ariz. L. Rev. 849 (2012), Nadia N. Sawicki, The Abortion Informed Consent Debate: More Light, Less Heat, 21 Cornell J. L. & Pub. Pol'y 1 (2011), and J. Robertson, Abortion and Technology: Sonograms, Fetal Pain, Viability, and Early Prenatal Diagnosis, 14 U. Pa. J. Const. L. 327. For a more thorough analysis of the relationship between the role of women in society and reproductive rights, see Reva Siegel, Sex Equality Arguments for Reproductive Rights: Their Critical Basis and Evolving Constitutional Expression, 56 Emory L.J. 815 (2007). For a broad ranging symposium on this issue, see Symposium—If Roe Were Overruled: Abortion and the Constitution in a Post–Roe World, 51 St. Louis U. L. J. 611 (2007). For a comparative approach, see Timothy Stoltzfus Jost, Rights of Embryos and Foetuses in Private Law, 50 Am. J. Comp. L. 633 (2002).

NOTE: THE ABORTION COMPROMISE THAT GAVE US THE AFFORDABLE CARE ACT

Given the role of abortion in every political issue from the selection of the judiciary to foreign aid to the funding of local libraries and school curricula, it is not surprising that it was a high profile issue in the debate over the restructuring of health care in the United States. While some Right to Life organizations opposed the Affordable Care Act because, they argued, it did not go far enough in limiting the possibility that sometime in the future federal funding might be used inappropriately to provide abortion services, the outcome must be counted as a substantial victory for the Right to Life movement. Ironically, because many who support Right to Life organizations also opposed the ACA for other reasons (conservatives are more likely to oppose both abortion and an increased role for government in the health care system), Right to Life advocates are reluctant to claim this victory (on abortion) amidst their defeat (with regard to restructuring American health care). In addition, Right to Life organizations were not successful in their effort to kill the exceptions in the Hyde Amendment that have long allowed abortions to be performed where the life of the mother is at risk or the pregnancy is the result of rape or incest.

The ACA itself does much to limit abortion. It generally applies principles derived from the Hyde Amendment, described above, which has been attached to all relevant DHHS appropriations since the 1970s. The ACA requires each health insurance exchange to offer at least one plan that does not include abortion coverage (although there is no requirement that there be one that does offer such coverage), and it allows the states to promulgate statutes that forbid coverage sold through the exchange from including abortion coverage (again, except in cases of rape or incest, or where the life of the mother is at risk). In addition, any plan that offers abortion coverage must charge a separate, actuarially segregated and accurate premium for that service, and this premium must be paid separately by each insured who desires that coverage (and each insured's employer, if the employer contributes to the employee's health coverage). In determining the actuarial value of the abortion coverage, the plan or insurer may not count any savings that might arise from the performance of an abortion. In addition, plans may not advertise the price of their abortion related services, and they may not discriminate against providers who refuse to provide abortions (or refuse to refer patients to doctors who will perform them). The cost of providing the bookkeeping services for those plans that offer abortion services will probably exceed the actual cost of all abortions that are subsequently provided, and it is hard to imagine—from a financial and administrative perspective—just why any commercially driven plan would offer an abortion rider.

Those who opposed the ACA because it didn't go far enough to limit abortion argued that the statute would provide billions of dollars of appropriations to community health centers, which were not forbidden by language in the statute from spending that money on abortions. While school-based health clinics, which were also expanded by the ACA, were explicitly forbidden from using any funding for non-Hyde-permitted abortions, the ban on community health center use of these resources depended on the Hyde amendment language that was already in all relevant federal appropriations. In fact, at the time of the ACA debate, all community health center appropriations were covered by the Hyde amendment (as they still are), and none offered any abortions, except in cases of rape or incest or where there was a risk to the life of the mother. Still, in order to head off any worry that federal funds intended for community health centers would ever be used for abortions, the President promised to (and then did) issue an executive order clarifying his position immediately upon the enactment of the ACA:

**EXECUTIVE ORDER 13535 OF MARCH 24, 2010
ENSURING ENFORCEMENT AND IMPLEMENTATION OF
ABORTION RESTRICTIONS IN THE PATIENT PROTECTION
AND AFFORDABLE CARE ACT**

* * *

Sec. 1. Policy. Following the recent enactment of the Patient Protection and Affordable Care Act (the "Act"), it is necessary to establish an adequate enforcement mechanism to ensure that Federal funds are not used for abortion services (except in cases of rape or incest, or when the life of the woman would be endangered), consistent with a longstanding Federal statutory restriction that is commonly known as the Hyde Amendment. * * *

The Act maintains current Hyde Amendment restrictions governing abortion policy and extends those restrictions to the newly created health insurance exchanges. * * *

Sec. 2. Strict Compliance with Prohibitions on Abortion Funding in Health Insurance Exchanges. The Act specifically prohibits the use of tax credits and cost-sharing reduction payments to pay for abortion services (except in cases of rape or incest, or when the life of the woman would be endangered) in the health insurance exchanges that will be operational in 2014. The Act also imposes strict payment and accounting requirements to ensure that Federal funds are not used for abortion services in exchange plans (except in cases of rape or incest, or when the life of the woman would be endangered) and requires State health insurance commissioners to ensure that exchange plan funds are segregated by insurance companies * * *.

I hereby direct the Director of the OMB and the Secretary of HHS to develop, within 180 days of the date of this order, a model set of segregation guidelines for State health insurance commissioners * * *.

Sec. 3. Community Health Center Program. The Act establishes a new Community Health Center (CHC) Fund within HHS, which provides additional Federal funds for the community health center program. Existing law prohibits these centers from using Federal funds to provide abortion services (except in cases of rape or incest, or when the life of the woman would be endangered), as a result of both the Hyde Amendment and longstanding regulations containing the Hyde language. Under the Act, the Hyde language shall apply to the authorization and appropriations of funds for Community Health Centers * * *.

This executive order did not satisfy those who opposed health care reform in any case, who argued that it could be withdrawn by the President later, overturned by Congress or found to be beyond the authority of the President acting through the mechanism of an executive order. It was all the supporters could offer, though, because any actual amendment of the bill would have required that it be sent back to the Senate to concur in the amendment, and the Democrats had just lost their 60 senator (and, thus, filibuster-proof) majority, with the election of Senator Brown in Massachusetts. While other problems with the ACA could be solved through the subsequent reconciliation process (which required only 50 votes in the Senate), this section would not have been eligible for such treatment.

In any case, the House Democrats who supported health care reform but opposed abortion were sufficiently satisfied by the executive order, and, armed with the President's promise to remain true to this executive order, they supported the ACA, which consequently passed. The promulgation of the ACA has given rise to some state legislation forbidding policies that cover abortion services from being offered through the state's exchanges (indeed, some state legislatures began considering such proposals even before ACA was signed), and there remains a national legislative efforts to get a general, permanent Hyde Amendment to cover all federal funding. In fact, though, that is mostly a matter of political posturing and symbolism; ACA makes the growth of abortion services within the newly restructured American health care system very unlikely. Abortion services are likely to remain available, if at all, through sources outside of federal (or state) programs and outside of insurance policies administered through exchanges

PROBLEM: THE CONSTITUTION AND NEW STATE LAWS ON ABORTION

The Supreme Court has provided no guidance on the Constitutional limits on state laws restricting abortion since Gonzales v. Carhart was decided in 2007. State legislatures (and the rest of us) thus remain uncertain about just how much of Casey actually survived Gonzales v. Carhart. Increasingly over the last few years state legislators have been willing to push the envelope, perhaps believing that the Court is ready to further cut back on the right first described in *Roe*, or, perhaps believing that there is no political cost to passing a law that is later found to be unconstitutional in any case. How do you think the Supreme Court should (and would) rule today on state laws (some passed, some still only proposed) that:

<u>General Limitations on Abortion</u>

1.   Prohibit all abortions under all circumstances, unless an abortion is necessary to save the life of the mother (or unless it is necessary to save

the life or physical health of the mother, or unless the pregnancy is a result of rape or incest),

2.   Prohibit all abortions after a fetal heartbeat is detectible,

3.   Prohibit all abortions after 20 weeks gestation because, according to legislative findings, the fetus can feel pain at that point,

Regulation of Abortion Processes

4.   Require all abortions to be performed in licensed hospitals (even in states where no current abortion providers have privileges at any licensed hospital, and both religious principles and politics dictate that no hospital in the state will ever grant privileges to any provider to perform an abortion),

5.   Require the presence of a second physician at the abortion if the fetus is viable (or if the fetus is 20 weeks gestation, or 24 weeks),

6.   Require a woman seeking an abortion to be screened by an independent psychologist (or some other health care provider) to confirm that she was not pressured into seeking the abortion,

7.   Require a woman to undergo ultrasound examination before choosing to have an abortion in order to accurately establish the fetal age (and, in addition, require the examination be done through vaginal ultrasound, which requires inserting the ultrasound probe into the vagina, if that is necessary to accurately determine gestational age, even where there is no medical doubt that the fetus is in the first trimester),

Regulation of Health Plans and Insurance

9.   Prohibit health plans offered to state employees (or employees of private firms that contract with the state) from including coverage for any abortion (or for any abortion not necessary to save the life or physical health of the pregnant woman),

10.   Prohibit the sale of any insurance policy that includes coverage of any abortion services through the exchange set up by the ACA,

11.   Prohibit any private health plan offered for sale in the state from including coverage for any abortion (or for any abortion not necessary to save the life or physical health of the pregnant woman),

Regulation of the Informed Consent Process

12.   Require women to be told of the link (supported by some older studies but now denied by most researchers) between abortion and breast cancer, or between abortion and later miscarriages, or between abortion and depression and other mental illnesses,

13. Require women to be told that a fetus over 20 weeks gestation will feel pain during an abortion (even though most researchers believe that is not true),

14. Require a woman to view an ultrasound of the fetus before she chooses to have an abortion,

15. Require a physician to allow the pregnant woman to hear the fetal heartbeat before choosing to have an abortion,

16. Require a woman seeking an abortion to be told of any adverse physical, psychosocial or emotional reaction that has been reported (at the time the information is provided) in any peer-reviewed journal to be statistically related to abortion,

Regulation of Tort Litigation

17. Provide that for purposes of informed consent actions, a provider's failure to provide all data associated with risk factors (which are factors statistically related to complications of abortion) creates a rebuttable presumption of the lack of properly informed consent by the person who receives an abortion,

18. Provide for attorneys' fees, relaxed rules on damages for emotional distress, and punitive damages against an abortion provider when they would not be available in other malpractice and informed consent cases,

19. Provide that advertising or offering abortion services in a state constitutes the transaction of business in the state and makes the one offering abortion services subject to the civil and criminal jurisdiction of the state (even if all of the medical services are provided outside of the state by a provider licensed where the services are provided).

These are merely a sample of the various limitations that the Supreme Court may (or may not) address in the next few years. Are there any that are clearly Constitutional? Are there any that are clearly unconstitutional? Does the "death by a thousand cuts" approach to abortion services taken by those who support the Right to Life movement suggest the need for the Supreme Court to reconsider the more general issue, or is it a reason for the Supreme Court not to take up abortion yet again?

III.   STERILIZATION

The sterilization of the mentally retarded has given rise to considerable discussion beginning with the development of the eugenics movement in the late 19th century. While there is no significant evidence that most forms of mental retardation are genetic and inheritable, there remains a residue of social support for the notion that this society can purify its gene pool by sterilizing those who would pollute it, such as the mentally retarded and criminals. The aim of the eugenics movement was confirmed by Justice Holmes in Buck v. Bell, 274 U.S. 200, 47 S.Ct. 584, 71 L.Ed. 1000 (1927), which dealt with an attempt by the State of Virginia to sterilize Carrie Buck, who had been committed to the State Colony for Epileptics and the Feeble Minded. The State was opposed on the grounds that the statute authorizing sterilization violated the Fourteenth Amendment by denying Ms. Buck due process of law and the equal protection of the law. Justice Holmes responded:

> Carrie Buck is a feeble minded white woman who was committed to the State Colony above mentioned in due form. She is the daughter of a feeble minded mother in the same institution and the mother of an illegitimate feeble minded child * * *.

> [The lower court found] "that Carrie Buck is the probable potential parent of socially inadequate offspring, likewise afflicted, that she may be sterilized without detriment to her general health and that her welfare and that of society will be promoted by her sterilization." * * * We have seen more than once that the public welfare may call upon the best citizens for their lives. It would be strange if it could not call upon those who already sapped the strength of the state for these lesser sacrifices, often not felt to be such by those concerned, in order to prevent our being swamped with incompetence. It is better for all the world if instead of waiting to execute degenerate offspring for crime, or to let them starve for their imbecility, society can prevent those who are manifestly unfit from continuing their kind. The principle that sustains compulsory vaccination is broad enough to cover cutting the fallopian tubes.[ ] Three generations of imbeciles are enough.

* * *

The Supreme Court has never overturned the decision in Buck v. Bell, although it is of questionable precedential value today. Society's perception of the mentally incompetent has changed and, especially after the Nazi experience, for which Buck v. Bell was cited as precedent, arguments based upon eugenics are held in low regard. In fact, when Carrie Buck was discovered in the Appalachian hills in 1980, she was found to be mentally competent and extremely disappointed that throughout her life she was unable to bear another child. Subsequent research determined that Carrie Buck's illegitimate daughter Vivian, who was conceived as the result of a rape by a relative of Carrie Buck's foster parents, was an honor role student. At the trial that, on appeal, gave rise to Justice Holmes' regrettable opinion, Carrie Buck was poorly represented by a lawyer who did not develop the evidence or the legal arguments necessary to overcome the statute or its application to his client. For an engaging account of this case by a scholar who met Ms. Buck in the 1980s, and for pictures of Ms. Buck and her daughter, see Paul Lombardo, Facing Carrie Buck, 33 Hastings Ctr. Rep. (March–April) 14 (2003).

The Supreme Court addressed eugenic sterilizations once more, in Skinner v. Oklahoma, 316 U.S. 535, 62 S.Ct. 1110, 86 L.Ed. 1655 (1942). The Court determined that the equal protection clause prohibited Oklahoma from enforcing its statute which required sterilizing persons convicted of repeated criminal acts, but only if the crimes were within special categories. White collar crimes were exempted from these categories, and the Supreme Court's determination was based on the state's irrational distinction between blue collar (sterilizable) and white collar (unsterilizable) crimes. The Court was asked to, but did not, overrule Buck v. Bell. The Governor of Virginia apologized for the sterilization of Carrie Buck on the seventy-fifth anniversary of the Supreme Court decision in 2002.

More recent programs to sterilize individual mentally retarded people have been based on the convenience of sterilization for the patient and her (the one for whom sterilization is sought is virtually always a woman) family. Some who have sought sterilization for the mentally retarded have been worried about the consequences of sexual exposure upon people who can barely cope with the minimal requirements of daily life; some have suggested that it would be much easier to care for patients, especially menstruating women, if they were sterilized; and others have suggested that sterilization might make it practical for mentally retarded people who would otherwise be institutionalized to live at home. Generally, courts have acted to restrict sterilization for the mentally retarded if there is any less restrictive alternative that would serve the same interests.

In California, the Probate Code was amended to prohibit the sterilization of mentally retarded persons. This statute was challenged by the conservator of an incompetent mentally retarded woman who argued that the legislature had denied her a procreative choice that was extended to all other women in the community. She argued that to deny her the opportunity for a sterilization when there would be no other safe and effective method of contraception available to her would be to deny her important Constitutionally protected rights. While a mentally retarded person may have a right not to be unfairly sterilized, she argued, she has a correlative right not to be unfairly and arbitrarily denied a sterilization (and thus an opportunity to engage is sexual activity).

In Conservatorship of Valerie N., 40 Cal.3d 143, 219 Cal.Rptr. 387, 707 P.2d 760 (1985), the California Supreme Court upheld the challenge and threw out the statute as a violation of the state constitutional.

One justice wrote a particularly strong dissent:

Today's holding will permit the state, through the legal fiction of substituted consent, to deprive many women permanently of the right to conceive and bear children. The majority run roughshod over this fundamental constitutional right in a misguided attempt to guarantee a procreative choice for one they assume has never been capable of choice and never will be. * * *

The majority opinion opens the door to abusive sterilization practices which will serve the convenience of conservators, parents, and service providers rather than incompetent conservatees. The ugly history of sterilization abuse against developmentally disabled persons in the name of seemingly enlightened social policies counsels a different choice.

Rather than place an absolute prohibition upon the sterilization of the developmentally disabled as the California legislature attempted to do, most courts attempt to safeguard those who may be subject to sterilization by applying very strict procedural requirements to any proposed sterilization. For example, the standard that has been most often emulated is that provided in In re Guardianship of Hayes, 93 Wash.2d 228, 608 P.2d 635 (1980), where the court set out the procedural requirements simply and explicitly:

> The decision can only be made in a superior court proceeding in which (1) the incompetent individual is represented by a disinterested guardian ad litem, (2) the court has received independent advice based upon a comprehensive medical, psychological, and social evaluation of the individual, and (3) to the greatest extent possible, the court has elicited and taken into account the view of the incompetent individual.

> Within this framework, the judge must first find by clear, cogent and convincing evidence that the individual is (1) incapable of making his or her own decision about sterilization, and (2) unlikely to develop sufficiently to make an informed judgment about sterilization in the foreseeable future.

> Next it must be proved by clear, cogent and convincing evidence that there is a need for contraception. The judge must find that the individual is (1) physically capable of procreation, and (2) likely to engage in sexual activity at the present or in the near future under circumstances likely to result in pregnancy, and must find in addition that (3) the nature and extent of the individual's disability, as determined by empirical evidence and not solely on the basis of standardized tests, renders him or her permanently incapable of caring for a child, even with reasonable assistance.

Finally, there must be no alternatives to sterilization. The judge must find that by clear, cogent and convincing evidence (1) all less drastic contraceptive methods, including supervision, education and training, have been proved unworkable or inapplicable, and (2) the proposed method of sterilization entails the least invasion of the body of the individual. In addition, it must be shown by clear, cogent and convincing evidence that (3) the current state of scientific and medical knowledge does not suggest either (a) that a reversible sterilization procedure or other less drastic contraceptive method will shortly be available or (b) that science is on the threshold of an advance in the treatment of the individual's disability.

Some have read the procedural requirements of *Hayes* as effectively removing the possibility of the sterilization of the developmentally disabled. Can you imagine a case that would meet the stiff "procedural" requirements of *Hayes*?

Courts and legislatures have considered interventions that are designed to provide sterilization or some form of castration as criminal punishments (or "treatment" for those disposed to criminal conduct). In State v. Kline, 155 Or.App. 96, 963 P.2d 697 (1998) the Oregon Court of Appeals found that a criminal defendant's right to procreate was not unconstitutionally abridged when he was ordered not to have children upon his conviction for mistreatment of children. In State v. Oakley, 245 Wis.2d 447, 629 N.W.2d 200 (2001), the Wisconsin Supreme Court upheld an order that a defendant not father additional children as a condition of his probation after conviction for intentional failure to pay child support, a felony. A similar "no procreation" order was found to be overbroad by the Ohio Supreme Court in 2004 in a father's appeal from a conviction for failing to pay child support for three of his children. State v. Talty, 103 Ohio St.3d 177, 814 N.E.2d 1201 (2004). For an analysis of this line of cases, see A. Felecia Epps, Unacceptable Collateral Damage: The Danger of Probation Conditions Restricting the Right to Have Children, 38 Creighton L.Rev. 611 (2005).

One group, Project Prevention, has offered a cash payment of $300 to any drug addict who can prove that he or she has been sterilized or put on some long-term contraceptive. The group was started by a woman who adopted children who had been affected by prenatal drug abuse, and the bounty is paid upon proof of both addiction (an arrest record or doctor's note will do) and sterilization. The organization does not pay for the sterilization or long-term contraception itself. As of 2012, the group had paid the sterilization incentive to over 4000 people. For a description of the program see the organization's website, http://www.projectprevention.org (visited January 15, 2013). See also C.M. Vega, Sterilization Offer to Addicts Reopens Ethics Issue, New York Times, January 6, 2003, at A–1. Is there any ethical problem with this program? What is it? Who is being more paternalistic, those who want to encourage drug addicted people not to have children, or those who want to save these same poor, drug addicted people from considering this offer? Are there people our society should discourage from reproducing, or is that always improper? If so, are the drug addicted among those people? Are issues of race, ethnicity and gender relevant to your consideration of this issue? How?

For thoughtful discussion of sexuality in the developmentally disabled, see S.F. Haavik and K. Menninger, Sexuality, Law and the Developmentally Disabled Person (1981). For a discussion of "chemical castration" provisions that apply to convicted sex offenders, see William Winslade et al., Castrating Pedophiles Convicted of Sex Offenses Against Children: New Treatment or Old Punishment?, 51 S.M.U L.Rev. 349 (1998). Finally, for an interesting argument that the "new eugenics" will be accomplished through genetic screening and manipulation, which will pose many of the problems formerly posed by eugenic sterilization, see Sonia Suter, A Brave New World of Designer Babies, 22 Berkeley Tech. L.J. 897 (2007)

CHAPTER 16

LIFE AND DEATH DECISIONS

. . .

I. MAKING HEALTH CARE DECISIONS ABOUT DEATH AND DYING: THE CONSTITUTIONAL FOUNDATION

CRUZAN V. DIRECTOR, MISSOURI DEPARTMENT OF HEALTH

Supreme Court of the United States, 1990.
497 U.S. 261, 110 S.Ct. 2841, 111 L.Ed.2d 224.

CHIEF JUSTICE REHNQUIST delivered the opinion of the Court.

Petitioner Nancy Beth Cruzan was rendered incompetent as a result of severe injuries sustained during an automobile accident. Co-petitioners Lester and Joyce Cruzan, Nancy's parents and co-guardians, sought a court order directing the withdrawal of their daughter's artificial feeding and hydration equipment after it became apparent that she had virtually no chance of recovering her cognitive faculties. The Supreme Court of Missouri held that because there was no clear and convincing evidence of Nancy's desire to have life-sustaining treatment withdrawn under such circumstances, her parents lacked authority to effectuate such a request. We granted certiorari and now affirm.

On the night of January 11, 1983, Nancy Cruzan lost control of her car as she traveled down Elm Road in Jasper County, Missouri. The vehicle overturned, and Cruzan was discovered lying face down in a ditch without detectable respiratory or cardiac function. Paramedics were able to restore her breathing and heartbeat at the accident site, and she was transported to a hospital in an unconscious state. An attending neurosurgeon diagnosed her as having sustained probable cerebral contusions compounded by significant anoxia (lack of oxygen). The Missouri trial court in this case found that permanent brain damage generally results after 6 minutes in an anoxic state; it was estimated that Cruzan was deprived of oxygen from 12 to 14 minutes. She remained in a coma for approximately three weeks and then progressed to an unconscious state in which she was able to orally ingest some nutrition. In order to ease feeding and further the recovery, surgeons implanted a gastrostomy feeding and hydration tube in Cruzan with the consent of her then husband. Subsequent rehabilitative efforts proved unavailing. She now lies in a Missouri state hospital in what is commonly referred to as a persistent vegetative state: generally, a condition in which a person exhibits motor reflexes but evinces no indications of significant cognitive function. The State of Missouri is bearing the cost of her care.

After it had become apparent that Nancy Cruzan had virtually no chance of regaining her mental faculties her parents asked hospital employees to terminate the artificial nutrition and hydration procedures. All agree that such a removal would cause her death. The employees refused to honor the request without court approval. The parents then sought and received authorization from the state trial court for termination. The court found that a person in Nancy's condition had a fundamental right under the State and Federal Constitutions to refuse or direct the withdrawal of "death prolonging procedures." The court also found that Nancy's "expressed thoughts at age twenty-five in somewhat serious conversation with a housemate friend that if sick or injured she would not wish to continue her life unless she could live at least halfway normally suggests that given her present condition she would not wish to continue on with her nutrition and hydration."

The Supreme Court of Missouri reversed by a divided vote. * * *

We granted certiorari to consider the question of whether Cruzan has a right under the United States Constitution which would require the hospital to withdraw life-sustaining treatment from her under these circumstances.

*   *   *

State courts have available to them for decision a number of sources—state constitutions, statutes, and common law—which are not available to us. In this Court, the question is simply and starkly whether the United States Constitution prohibits Missouri from choosing the rule of decision which it did. This is the first case in which we have been squarely presented with the issue of whether the United States Constitution grants what is in common parlance referred to as a "right to die."

*   *   *

The Fourteenth Amendment provides that no State shall "deprive any person of life, liberty, or property, without due process of law." The principle that a competent person has a constitutionally protected liberty interest in refusing unwanted medical treatment may be inferred from our prior decisions. * * *

But determining that a person has a "liberty interest" under the Due Process Clause does not end the inquiry;[7] "whether respondent's constitutional rights have been violated must be determined by balancing his liberty interests against the relevant state interests." [ ]

Petitioners insist that under the general holdings of our cases, the forced administration of life-sustaining medical treatment, and even of artificially-delivered food and water essential to life, would implicate a competent person's liberty interest. Although we think the logic of the cases discussed above would embrace such a liberty interest, the dramatic consequences involved in refusal of such treatment would inform the inquiry as to whether the deprivation of that interest is constitutionally permissible. But for purposes of this case, we assume that the United States Constitution would grant a competent person a constitutionally protected right to refuse lifesaving hydration and nutrition.

Petitioners go on to assert that an incompetent person should possess the same right in this respect as is possessed by a competent person. * * *

The difficulty with petitioners' claim is that in a sense it begs the question: an incompetent person is not able to make an informed and voluntary choice to exercise a hypothetical right to refuse treatment or any other right. Such a "right" must be exercised for her, if at all, by some sort of surrogate. Here, Missouri has in effect recognized that under certain circumstances a surrogate may act for the patient in electing to have hydration and nutrition withdrawn in such a way as to cause death, but it has established a procedural safeguard to assure that the action of the surrogate conforms as best it may to the wishes expressed by the patient while competent. Missouri requires that evidence of the incompetent's wishes as to the withdrawal of treatment be proved by clear and convincing evidence. The question, then, is whether the United States Constitution forbids the establishment of this procedural requirement by the State. We hold that it does not.

Whether or not Missouri's clear and convincing evidence requirement comports with the United States Constitution depends in part on what interests the State may properly seek to protect in this situation. Missouri relies on its interest in the protection and preservation of human life, and there can be no gainsaying this interest. As a general matter, the States—indeed, all civilized nations—demonstrate their commitment to life by treating homicide as serious crime. Moreover, the majority of States in this country have laws imposing criminal penalties on one who assists another to commit suicide. We do not think a State is required to

---

7   Although many state courts have held that a right to refuse treatment is encompassed by a generalized constitutional right of privacy, we have never so held. We believe this issue is more properly analyzed in terms of a Fourteenth Amendment liberty interest. See *Bowers v. Hardwick,* 478 U.S. 186, 194–195 (1986).

remain neutral in the face of an informed and voluntary decision by a physically-able adult to starve to death.

But in the context presented here, a State has more particular interests at stake. The choice between life and death is a deeply personal decision of obvious and overwhelming finality. We believe Missouri may legitimately seek to safeguard the personal element of this choice through the imposition of heightened evidentiary requirements. It cannot be disputed that the Due Process Clause protects an interest in life as well as an interest in refusing life-sustaining medical treatment. Not all incompetent patients will have loved ones available to serve as surrogate decisionmakers. * * * A State is entitled to guard against potential abuses in such situations. Similarly, a State is entitled to consider that a judicial proceeding to make a determination regarding an incompetent's wishes may very well not be an adversarial one, with the added guarantee of accurate factfinding that the adversary process brings with it. [ ] Finally, we think a State may properly decline to make judgments about the "quality" of life that a particular individual may enjoy, and simply assert an unqualified interest in the preservation of human life to be weighed against the constitutionally protected interests of the individual.

In our view, Missouri has permissibly sought to advance these interests through the adoption of a "clear and convincing" standard of proof to govern such proceedings.

* * *

We think it self-evident that the interests at stake in the instant proceedings are more substantial, both on an individual and societal level, than those involved in a run-of-the-mine civil dispute. But not only does the standard of proof reflect the importance of a particular adjudication, it also serves as "a societal judgment about how the risk of error should be distributed between the litigants." [ ] The more stringent the burden of proof a party must bear, the more that party bears the risk of an erroneous decision. We believe that Missouri may permissibly place an increased risk of an erroneous decision on those seeking to terminate an incompetent individual's life-sustaining treatment. An erroneous decision not to terminate results in a maintenance of the status quo; the possibility of subsequent developments such as advancements in medical science, the discovery of new evidence regarding the patient's intent, changes in the law, or simply the unexpected death of the patient despite the administration of life-sustaining treatment, at least create the potential that a wrong decision will eventually be corrected or its impact mitigated. An erroneous decision to withdraw life-sustaining treatment, however, is not susceptible of correction.

* * *

In sum, we conclude that a State may apply a clear and convincing evidence standard in proceedings where a guardian seeks to discontinue nutrition and hydration of a person diagnosed to be in a persistent vegetative state. * * *

The Supreme Court of Missouri held that in this case the testimony adduced at trial did not amount to clear and convincing proof of the patient's desire to have hydration and nutrition withdrawn. * * * The testimony adduced at trial consisted primarily of Nancy Cruzan's statements made to a housemate about a year before her accident that she would not want to live should she face life as a "vegetable," and other observations to the same effect. The observations did not deal in terms with withdrawal of medical treatment or of hydration and nutrition. We cannot say that the Supreme Court of Missouri committed constitutional error in reaching the conclusion that it did.

* * *

JUSTICE O'CONNOR, concurring.

I agree that a protected liberty interest in refusing unwanted medical treatment may be inferred from our prior decisions, and that the refusal of artificially delivered food and water is encompassed within that liberty interest. I write separately to clarify why I believe this to be so.

As the Court notes, the liberty interest in refusing medical treatment flows from decisions involving the State's invasions into the body. Because our notions of liberty are inextricably entwined with our idea of physical freedom and self-determination, the Court has often deemed state incursions into the body repugnant to the interests protected by the Due Process Clause. [ ] The State's imposition of medical treatment on an unwilling competent adult necessarily involves some form of restraint and intrusion. A seriously ill or dying patient whose wishes are not honored may feel a captive of the machinery required for life-sustaining measures or other medical interventions. Such forced treatment may burden that individual's liberty interests as much as any state coercion. [ ]

The State's artificial provision of nutrition and hydration implicates identical concerns. Artificial feeding cannot readily be distinguished from other forms of medical treatment. * * * Whether or not the techniques used to pass food and water into the patient's alimentary tract are termed "medical treatment," it is clear they all involve some degree of intrusion and restraint. Feeding a patient by means of a nasogastric tube requires a physician to pass a long flexible tube through the patient's nose, throat and esophagus and into the stomach. Because of the discomfort such a tube causes, "[m]any patients need to be restrained forcibly and their hands put into large mittens to prevent them from removing the tube." * * * A gastrostomy tube (as was used to provide food and water to Nancy

Cruzan), or jejunostomy tube must be surgically implanted into the stomach or small intestine. * * * Requiring a competent adult to endure such procedures against her will burdens the patient's liberty, dignity, and freedom to determine the course of her own treatment. Accordingly, the liberty guaranteed by the Due Process Clause must protect, if it protects anything, an individual's deeply personal decision to reject medical treatment, including the artificial delivery of food and water.

I also write separately to emphasize that the Court does not today decide the issue whether a State must also give effect to the decisions of a surrogate decisionmaker. In my view, such a duty may well be constitutionally required to protect the patient's liberty interest in refusing medical treatment. Few individuals provide explicit oral or written instructions regarding their intent to refuse medical treatment should they become incompetent. States which decline to consider any evidence other than such instructions may frequently fail to honor a patient's intent. Such failures might be avoided if the State considered an equally probative source of evidence: the patient's appointment of a proxy to make health care decisions on her behalf.

* * *

Today's decision, holding only that the Constitution permits a State to require clear and convincing evidence of Nancy Cruzan's desire to have artificial hydration and nutrition withdrawn, does not preclude a future determination that the Constitution requires the States to implement the decisions of a patient's duly appointed surrogate. Nor does it prevent States from developing other approaches for protecting an incompetent individual's liberty interest in refusing medical treatment. * * * Today we decide only that one State's practice does not violate the Constitution; the more challenging task of crafting appropriate procedures for safeguarding incompetents' liberty interests is entrusted to the "laboratory" of the States, in the first instance.

JUSTICE SCALIA, concurring.

* * *

While I agree with the Court's analysis today, and therefore join in its opinion, I would have preferred that we announce, clearly and promptly, that the federal courts have no business in this field; that American law has always accorded the State the power to prevent, by force if necessary, suicide—including suicide by refusing to take appropriate measures necessary to preserve one's life; that the point at which life becomes "worthless," and the point at which the means necessary to preserve it become "extraordinary" or "inappropriate," are neither set forth in the Constitution nor known to the nine Justices of this Court any better than they are known to nine people picked at random from the Kansas City telephone directory; and hence, that even when it *is* demonstrated by clear and convincing evidence that a patient no longer wishes certain measures to be taken to preserve her life, it is up to the citizens of Missouri to decide, through their elected representatives, whether that wish will be honored. It is quite impossible (because the Constitution says nothing about the matter) that those citizens will decide upon a line less lawful than the one we would choose; and it is unlikely (because we know no more about "life-and-death" than they do) that they will decide upon a line less reasonable.

The text of the Due Process Clause does not protect individuals against deprivations of liberty *simpliciter*. It protects them against deprivations of liberty "without due process of law." To determine that such a deprivation would not occur if Nancy Cruzan were forced to take nourishment against her will, it is unnecessary to reopen the historically recurrent debate over whether "due process" includes substantive restrictions. [ ] It is at least true that no "substantive due process" claim can be maintained unless the claimant demonstrates that the State has deprived him of a right historically and traditionally protected against State interference. [ ] That cannot possibly be established here.

* * * "[T]here is no significant support for the claim that a right to suicide is so rooted in our tradition that it may be deemed 'fundamental' or 'implicit in the concept of ordered liberty.' "[ ]

Petitioners rely on three distinctions to separate Nancy Cruzan's case from ordinary suicide: (1) that she is permanently incapacitated and in pain; (2) that she would bring on her death not by any affirmative act but by merely declining treatment that provides nourishment; and (3) that preventing her from effectuating her presumed wish to die requires violation of her bodily integrity. None of these suffices.

[Scalia points out (1) that pain and incapacity have never constituted legal defenses to a charge of suicide, (2) that the distinction between "action" and "inaction" is logically and legally meaningless, and (3) that preventing suicide often (or always) requires the violation of bodily integrity, and it begs the question of whether the refusal of treatment is itself suicide.]

* * *

Are there, then, no reasonable and humane limits that ought not to be exceeded in requiring an individual to preserve his own life? There obviously are, but they are not set forth in the Due Process Clause. What assures us that those limits will not be exceeded is the same constitutional guarantee that is the source of most of our protection—what protects us, for example, from being assessed a tax of 100% of our income above the subsistence level, from being forbidden to drive cars, or from being required to send our children to school for 10 hours a day, none of which horribles is categorically prohibited by the Constitution. Our salvation is the Equal Protection Clause, which requires the democratic majority to accept for themselves and their loved ones what they impose on you and me. This Court need not, and has no authority to, inject itself into every field of human activity where irrationality and oppression may theoretically occur, and if it tries to do so it will destroy itself.

JUSTICE BRENNAN, with whom JUSTICE MARSHALL and JUSTICE BLACKMUN join, dissenting.

*   *   *

Today the Court, while tentatively accepting that there is some degree of constitutionally protected liberty interest in avoiding unwanted medical treatment, including life-sustaining medical treatment such as artificial nutrition and hydration, affirms the decision of the Missouri Supreme Court. The majority opinion, as I read it, would affirm that decision on the ground that a State may require "clear and convincing" evidence of Nancy Cruzan's prior decision to forgo life-sustaining treatment under circumstances such as hers in order to ensure that her actual wishes are honored. Because I believe that Nancy Cruzan has a fundamental right to be free of unwanted artificial nutrition and hydration, which right is not outweighed by any interests of the State, and because I find that the improperly biased procedural obstacles imposed by the Missouri Supreme Court impermissibly burden that right, I respectfully dissent. Nancy Cruzan is entitled to choose to die with dignity.

*   *   *

The right to be free from unwanted medical attention is a right to evaluate the potential benefit of treatment and its possible consequences according to one's own values and to make a personal decision whether to subject oneself to the intrusion. For a patient like Nancy Cruzan, the sole benefit of medical treatment is being kept metabolically alive. Neither artificial nutrition nor any other form of medical treatment available today can cure or in any way ameliorate her condition. Irreversibly vegetative patients are devoid of thought, emotion and sensation; they are permanently and completely unconscious. As the President's Commission concluded in approving the withdrawal of life support equipment from irreversibly vegetative patients:

> "[T]reatment ordinarily aims to benefit a patient through preserving life, relieving pain and suffering, protecting against disability, and returning maximally effective functioning. If a prognosis of permanent unconsciousness is correct, however, continued treatment cannot confer such benefits. Pain and suffering are absent, as are joy, satisfaction, and pleasure. Disability is to-

tal and no return to an even minimal level of social or human functioning is possible." [ ]

There are also affirmative reasons why someone like Nancy might choose to forgo artificial nutrition and hydration under these circumstances. Dying is personal. And it is profound. For many, the thought of an ignoble end, steeped in decay, is abhorrent. A quiet, proud death, bodily integrity intact, is a matter of extreme consequence. "In certain, thankfully rare, circumstances the burden of maintaining the corporeal existence degrades the very humanity it was meant to serve." * * *

Such conditions are, for many, humiliating to contemplate, as is visiting a prolonged and anguished vigil on one's parents, spouse, and children. A long, drawn-out death can have a debilitating effect on family members. [ ] For some, the idea of being remembered in their persistent vegetative states rather than as they were before their illness or accident may be very disturbing.

*   *   *

The only state interest asserted here is a general interest in the preservation of life. But the State has no legitimate general interest in someone's life, completely abstracted from the interest of the person living that life, that could outweigh the person's choice to avoid medical treatment. * * * [T]he State's general interest in life must accede to Nancy Cruzan's particularized and intense interest in self-determination in her choice of medical treatment. There is simply nothing legitimately within the State's purview to be gained by superseding her decision.

*   *   *

As the majority recognizes Missouri has a *parens patriae* interest in providing Nancy Cruzan, now incompetent, with as accurate as possible a determination of how she would exercise her rights under these circumstances. * * *

Accuracy, therefore, must be our touchstone. Missouri may constitutionally impose only those procedural requirements that serve to enhance the accuracy of a determination of Nancy Cruzan's wishes or are at least consistent with an accurate determination. The Missouri "safeguard" that the Court upholds today does not meet that standard. The determination needed in this context is whether the incompetent person would choose to live in a persistent vegetative state on life-support or to avoid this medical treatment. Missouri's rule of decision imposes a markedly asymmetrical evidentiary burden. Only evidence of specific statements of treatment choice made by the patient when competent is admissible to support a finding that the patient, now in a persistent vegetative state, would wish to avoid further medical treatment. Moreover, this evidence must be clear and convincing. No proof is required to support a finding that the incompetent person would wish to continue treatment.

Even more than its heightened evidentiary standard, the Missouri court's categorical exclusion of relevant evidence dispenses with any semblance of accurate factfinding. The court adverted to no evidence supporting its decision, but held that no clear and convincing, inherently reliable evidence had been presented to show that Nancy would want to avoid further treatment. * * * The court did not specifically define what kind of evidence it would consider clear and convincing, but its general discussion suggests that only a living will or equivalently formal directive from the patient when competent would meet this standard.

*   *   *

Finally, I cannot agree with the majority that where it is not possible to determine what choice an incompetent patient would make, a State's role as *parens patriae* permits the State automatically to make that choice itself. [ ] Under fair rules of evidence, it is improbable that a court could not determine what the patient's choice would be. Under the rule of decision adopted by Missouri and upheld today by this Court, such occasions might be numerous. But in neither case does it follow that it is constitutionally acceptable for the State invariably to assume the role of deciding for the patient. A State's legitimate interest in safeguarding a patient's choice cannot be furthered by simply appropriating it.

*   *   *

JUSTICE STEVENS, dissenting.

*   *   *

Choices about death touch the core of liberty. Our duty, and the concomitant freedom, to come to terms with the conditions of our own mortality are undoubtedly "so rooted in the traditions and conscience of our people as to be ranked as fundamental," [ ] and indeed are essential incidents of the unalienable rights to life and liberty endowed us by our Creator. [ ]

The more precise constitutional significance of death is difficult to describe; not much may be said with confidence about death unless it is said from faith, and that alone is reason enough to protect the freedom to conform choices about death to individual conscience. We may also, however, justly assume that death is not life's simple opposite, or its necessary terminus, but rather its completion. Our ethical tradition has long regarded an appreciation of mortality as essential to understanding life's significance. It may, in fact, be impossible to live for anything without being prepared to die for something. * * *

These considerations cast into stark relief the injustice, and unconstitutionality, of Missouri's treatment of Nancy Beth Cruzan. Nancy Cruzan's death, when it comes, cannot be an historic act of heroism; it will inevitably be the consequence of her tragic accident. But Nancy Cruzan's interest in life, no less than that of any other person, includes an interest in how she will be thought of after her death by those whose opinions mattered to her. There can be no doubt that her life made her dear to her family, and to others. How she dies will affect how that life is remembered. The trial court's order authorizing Nancy's parents to cease their daughter's treatment would have permitted the family that cares for Nancy to bring to a close her tragedy and her death. Missouri's objection to that order subordinates Nancy's body, her family, and the lasting significance of her life to the State's own interests. The decision we review thereby interferes with constitutional interests of the highest order.

To be constitutionally permissible, Missouri's intrusion upon these fundamental liberties must, at a minimum, bear a reasonable relationship to a legitimate state end. [ ] Missouri asserts that its policy is related to a state interest in the protection of life. In my view, however, it is an effort to define life, rather than to protect it, that is the heart of Missouri's policy.

*   *   *

Life, particularly human life, is not commonly thought of as a merely physiological condition or function. Its sanctity is often thought to derive from the impossibility of any such reduction. When people speak of life, they often mean to describe the experiences that comprise a person's history, as when it is said that somebody "led a good life."[20] They may also mean to refer to the practical manifestation of the human spirit, a meaning captured by the familiar observation that somebody "added life" to an assembly. If there is a shared thread among the various opinions on this subject, it may be that life is an activity which is at once the matrix for and an integration of a person's interests. In any event, absent some theological abstraction, the idea of life is not conceived separately from the idea of a living person. Yet, it is by precisely such a separation that Missouri asserts an interest in Nancy Cruzan's life in opposition to Nancy Cruzan's own interests.

*   *   *

Only because Missouri has arrogated to itself the power to define life, and only because the Court permits this usurpation, are Nancy Cruzan's life and liberty put into disquieting conflict. If Nancy Cruzan's life were defined by reference to her own interests, so that her life expired when her biological existence ceased serving *any* of her own interests, then her

---

[20] It is this sense of the word that explains its use to describe a biography: for example, Boswell's Life of Johnson or Beveridge's The Life of John Marshall. The reader of a book so titled would be surprised to find that it contained a compilation of biological data.

constitutionally protected interest in freedom from unwanted treatment would not come into conflict with her constitutionally protected interest in life. Conversely, if there were *any* evidence that Nancy Cruzan herself defined life to encompass every form of biological persistence by a human being, so that the continuation of treatment would serve Nancy's own liberty, then once again there would be no conflict between life and liberty. The opposition of life and liberty in this case are thus not the result of Nancy Cruzan's tragic accident, but are instead the artificial consequence of Missouri's effort, and this Court's willingness, to abstract Nancy Cruzan's life from Nancy Cruzan's person.

* .* *

The Cruzan family's continuing concern provides a concrete reminder that Nancy Cruzan's interests did not disappear with her vitality or her consciousness. However commendable may be the State's interest in human life, it cannot pursue that interest by appropriating Nancy Cruzan's life as a symbol for its own purposes. Lives do not exist in abstraction from persons, and to pretend otherwise is not to honor but to desecrate the State's responsibility for protecting life. A State that seeks to demonstrate its commitment to life may do so by aiding those who are actively struggling for life and health. In this endeavor, unfortunately, no State can lack for opportunities: there can be no need to make an example of tragic cases like that of Nancy Cruzan.

NOTES AND QUESTIONS

1. Subsequent to this judgment the Missouri trial court heard additional evidence, provided by Nancy Cruzan's friends and colleagues, that she had made explicit and unambiguous statements that demonstrated, clearly and convincingly, that she would not want continued the treatment that she was receiving. Without opposition from the Attorney General of Missouri, the trial court authorized Ms. Cruzan's guardians to terminate her nutrition and hydration.

2. There are many ethical approaches to health care decision-making. The approach that has most influenced judicial decision-making is one that relies on the identification and application of particular principles, often called the "principlist approach." Tom Beauchamp and James Childress, Principles of Biomedical Ethics (7th ed. 2012). There are three primary substantive principles that operate here: autonomy, beneficence, and social justice. Autonomy and beneficence have been the principles most often relied upon in caselaw, which has largely ignored questions of cost (and allocation and rationing) and health disparities that implicate social justice. The principle of autonomy declares that each person is in control of his own person, including his body and mind. This principle, in its purest form, presumes that no other person or social institution ought to overrule a person's choice, whether or not that choice is "right" from an external perspective. Essential-

ly, it is a libertarian principle. The principle of beneficence declares that what is best for each person should be done. The principle incorporates both the negative obligation of nonmaleficence ("primum non nocere"—"first of all, do no harm"—the foundation of the Hippocratic Oath) and the positive obligation to do that which is good. Thus, a physician is obliged to provide the highest quality of medical care for her patients. Similarly, a physician ought to treat a seriously ill newborn, or incapacitated adult child, in a way that best serves that patient, whatever she may think her patient "wants" and whatever the parents of the patient may desire.

When a person does not desire what others determine to be in her best interests, the principles of autonomy and beneficence conflict. For example, if we consider the continued life of a healthy person to be in that person's interest, the values of autonomy and beneficence conflict when a healthy competent adult decides to take his own life. You can see that there can be serious conflict over what is in any individual's self interest and that values other than autonomy and beneficence will come into play in some of these cases. Did the *Cruzan* opinions address autonomy and beneficence? Did they imply any other values?

3.   Does the Opinion of the Court recognize a Constitutional right to die? Many authoritative sources presumed that the opinion did recognize a Constitutionally protected liberty interest in a competent person to refuse unwanted medical treatment. Indeed, the syllabus prepared for the Court says just that, and the case was hailed by the New York Times as the first to recognize a right to die. On the other hand, the Chief Justice's language does not support such a conclusion. While the majority agrees that "[t]he principle that a competent person has a Constitutionally protected liberty interest in refusing unwanted medical treatment *may* be inferred from our prior decisions," (emphasis added) the Court never makes the inference itself. In fact, the opinion says explicitly that "*for purposes of this case,* we assume that the United States Constitution would grant a competent person a Constitutionally protected right to refuse life saving nutrition and hydration." (emphasis added)

Why is this assumption limited to the "purposes of this case"? Does the Court question (1) whether there is a Constitutionally protected liberty interest in refusing unwanted medical treatment, (2) whether the right extends to life-sustaining treatment, or (3) whether it covers hydration and nutrition?

It must have been difficult for the Chief Justice to craft an opinion that would be joined by a majority of the court. Justice Scalia clearly does not believe that there is any Constitutional right implicated. If the Chief Justice were to formally recognize a Constitutional right, he might have lost Justice Scalia's signature—and thus lost an opportunity for there to be any majority opinion.

The dissents filed in this case are long and obviously heartfelt. Do the dissenters, all of whom would recognize a Constitutionally protected right to refuse life-sustaining treatment, and Justice O'Connor, who would also do so, create a majority in support of this Constitutional position?

4.   The majority opinion permits a state to limit its consideration to those wishes previously expressed by the patient and to ignore the decisions of another person acting on behalf of the patient. In fact, the Court explicitly does not address the question of whether a state must defer to an appropriately nominated surrogate acting on behalf of the patient. On the other hand, the dissenting justices would recognize the decisions of a surrogate under appropriate circumstances, and Justice O'Connor suggests that the duty to give effect to those decisions "may well be constitutionally required." What is the Constitutional status of surrogate decision-making after *Cruzan*?

5.   Note that none of the opinions refers to the "right of privacy," a term which had caused the Court such tremendous grief in the abortion context. The Chief Justice analyzes this issue in the more general terms of a Fourteenth Amendment liberty interest, and none of the counsel argued the case in terms of the right to privacy. Apparently the Court just did not wish to entangle itself any further with the "P" word.

6.   Seven years after *Cruzan* was decided, the Supreme Court again considered end-of-life medical decision-making in Washington v. Glucksberg, in Chapter 17, below, which addressed the Constitutional status of medically assisted dying. Chief Justice Rehnquist, writing for the Court, announced in *Glucksberg* that "We have * * * assumed, and strongly suggested, that the Due Process Clause protects the traditional right to refuse unwanted lifesaving medical treatment." Is that an accurate description of the holding in *Cruzan*? A few pages later, in the same opinion, Chief Justice Rehnquist describes the *Cruzan* case slightly differently: "[A]lthough Cruzan is often described as a 'right to die' case [ ], we were, in fact, more precise: we assumed that the Constitution granted competent persons a 'constitutionally protected right to refuse lifesaving hydration and nutrition.' " Is that a more accurate account of what the Court decided in *Cruzan*?

Justice O'Connor, concurring in *Glucksberg*, says that "there is no need to address the question whether suffering patients have a constitutionally cognizable interest in obtaining relief from the suffering that they may experience in the last days of their lives." This issue, according to Justice O'Connor, was decided by *Cruzan*. Is she right? Justice Stevens also commented on the *Cruzan* case in the course of his concurring opinion in *Glucksberg*. He explained that "Cruzan did give recognition * * * to the more specific interest in making decisions about how to confront an imminent death. * * * Cruzan makes it clear that some individuals who no longer have the option of deciding whether to live or to die because they are already on the threshold of death have a constitutionally protected interest [in deciding how they will die] that may outweigh the State's interest in preserving life at all costs." Is this an accurate description of *Cruzan*? If the Justices who participated in both the *Cruzan* and *Glucksberg* cases cannot agree on just what the case really means, how can your health law teacher expect you to do so?

7.   Constitutional arguments are not limited to those who want to forgo treatment; they can be asserted by seriously ill patients who want access to treatment, too. In Abigail Alliance v. von Eschenbach, 495 F.3d 695 (D.C. Cir. 2007), the D.C. Circuit, *en banc*, addressed the argument that a terminally ill patient had a Constitutional right to access drugs that had not yet been approved by the FDA. The Abigail Alliance, named for a 21–year–old student who died of cancer after being denied drugs in the earliest stages of testing, argued that *Cruzan* and *Glucksberg* paved the way for the recognition of a Constitutional right to access these not-yet-approved treatments, at least when those treatments provided the only hope of survival for the patient. The Court found, 8–2, that there was no such right, reversing the decision of the original three judge panel, Abigail Alliance v. von Eschenbach, 445 F.3d 470 (D.C. Cir. 2006), in part because of the longstanding tradition of governmental drug safety efforts in our legal system. The majority and the spirited dissenters disagreed about the way to articulate the right that Abigail Alliance sought to have recognized in this case. Was the right asserted the right "to access experimental and unproven drugs," as the majority suggested, or the right to "try to save one's life," as the dissent argued? As you have seen in *Cruzan*, and as you will recognize in *Glucksberg*, below, the due process arguments often depend upon the precise articulation of the right sought to be protected. Do you think the *Cruzan* case provides support for the position that an otherwise terminally ill cancer patient has access to drugs that have not yet been found to be safe or effective through the government's required administrative process? From a Constitutional perspective, is the argument that a patient is entitled to forgo treatment any different from the argument that a patient is entitled to have access to treatment? Similar issues were at stake in the litigation over access to marijuana for medical purposes.

8.   Except for a glancing reference by Justice Stevens in his dissent, the opinions do not consider the cost of providing care to Nancy Cruzan. Should the cost be relevant? Should the Constitutional right (to liberty or to life) vary depending on who bears the cost? Would your analysis of this case be any different if the costs were being paid by an insurance company, by Ms. Cruzan's parents, or by community fund raising in Nancy Cruzan's neighborhood, rather than by the state of Missouri? Should the one who pays the bills get to do the health care decision-making?

Judge Blackmar's dissent to the Missouri Supreme Court's opinion in *Cruzan* addresses the inconsistency of requiring some patients to be kept alive, at great expense, while the state is unable (or unwilling) to provide adequate care to others who actually want that care. He points out:

The absolutist position is also infirm because the state does not stand prepared to finance the preservation of life, without regard to the cost, in very many cases. In this particular case the state has Nancy in its possession, and is litigating its right to keep her. Yet, several years ago, a respected judge needed extraordinary treatment which the hospital in which he was a patient was not willing to furnish without a huge advance deposit and the state apparently had no desire to help out. Many people die because of the unavailability of heroic medical treatment. It simply cannot be said that the state's interest in preserving and prolonging life is absolute.

760 S.W.2d at 429. Judge Blackmar also points out, in a footnote, that "an absolutist would undoubtedly be offended by an inquiry as to whether the state, by prolonging Nancy's life at its own expense, is disabling itself from [providing] needed treatment to others who do not have such dire prognosis." 760 S.W.2d at 429 n. 4.

9.   The result of the *Cruzan* case is that most law regarding health care decision-making has continued to be established on a state-by-state basis; there seems to be very little, if any, United States Constitutional limit on what states may do. *Cruzan* may have deflected the "right to die" debate to the political decision-making process in the same way that several abortion decisions have done. See Chapter 15, above.

10.   The decision of the United States Supreme Court to opt out of providing much Constitutional guidance to the states may allow a crazy quilt of state laws to persist such that a patient who would have a right to forgo life-sustaining treatment that could be exercised by his family in California or New Jersey would not have that right (or would not have a right that could be exercised by his family) in Missouri or Michigan. Indeed, the conditions and extent of, and the restrictions and exceptions to, any right to forgo life-sustaining treatment might be different in each state. State policies will thus require different results in factually identical cases. Is there anything wrong with this?

What would happen if Nancy Cruzan's family had decided to move her to the Yale Medical Center "because of the more favorable medical facilities" there? Could they have moved her from Missouri to Connecticut, where removal of the gastrostomy tube clearly would be legally permitted, just for the purpose of removing the gastrostomy tube? If they could not, then Nancy Cruzan could have become a prisoner of a state that rejects her family's values—values that have been incorporated into official state policies in other jurisdictions. If they could move her, however, Missouri would have allowed the family to undercut the important policy objectives of the state law and imperil the very life the law was designed to protect. Would it violate any criminal statute to move someone across state lines for the purpose of avoiding the laws governing termination of life support in the first state? Could a state make such an action a crime?

In early 1991 the father and guardian of Christine Busalacchi sought to have his daughter moved from Missouri to Minnesota for medical consultation with a nationally known neurologist who had consulted on several leading cases that resulted in the withdrawal of life-sustaining treatment. Ms. Busalacchi, who had been living in the same nursing home that had housed Nancy Cruzan, was arguably in a persistent vegetative state. The state of

Missouri sought (and obtained) an order forbidding the move because of the fear that her father wanted only to find some place where his daughter could die. A divided Missouri Court of Appeals determined that the trial court was required to commence a new hearing on whether the move could be justified by other medical objectives. In deciding the case, the majority made it clear that " * * * we will not permit [the] guardian to forum shop in an effort to control whether Christine lives or dies." The dissent argued that "Minnesota is not a medical or ethical wasteland * * *. There is a parochial arrogance in suggesting, as the state does, that only in Missouri can Christine's medical, physical, and legal well being be protected and only here will her best interests be considered." Matter of Busalacchi, 1991 WL 26851 (Mo.App.1991). Ultimately, the State decided not to pursue the case, and Busalacchi died in Missouri. See also Mack v. Mack, 329 Md. 188, 618 A.2d 744 (1993) (Maryland Court denies full faith and credit to Florida judgment appointing the Florida-resident wife of a Maryland patient in persistent vegetative state as guardian so that patient could be moved to Florida, where life-sustaining treatment could be withdrawn.)

NOTE: STATE LAW BASES FOR A "RIGHT TO DIE"

Although some courts have found the right to forgo life-sustaining treatment in the United States Constitution, *Cruzan*'s interpretation of the Fourteenth Amendment has encouraged state courts to look for other bases for this right, too. State courts find this right in state common law, state statutes, or state constitutions.

The vast majority of state courts recognizing a right to refuse life-sustaining treatment have found that right in state common law, usually in the law of informed consent, often applied even after the patient has lost the capacity to make decisions. As the Chief Justice recognized in *Cruzan*, the informed consent doctrine has become firmly entrenched in American tort law * * * the logical corollary of the doctrine of informed consent is that the patient generally possesses the right not to consent, that is, to refuse treatment. * * *"

Once a court finds a common law right, it is not necessary to determine whether the right is also conferred by statute or by the United States or a state Constitution. See, e.g., In re Storar, 52 N.Y.2d 363, 438 N.Y.S.2d 266, 420 N.E.2d 64 (1981).

Some courts, however, bolster their common law basis for a "right to die" with references to the state and federal Constitutions. See In the Matter of Tavel, 661 A.2d 1061 (Del.1995). While the New Jersey court initially recognized a Constitutional "right to die" in In re Quinlan, 70 N.J. 10, 355 A.2d 647, 664 (1976), it later recognized that the Constitutional determination was unnecessary and retrenched:

While the right of privacy might apply in a case such as this, we need not decide that since the right to decline medical treatment is, in any event, embraced within the common law right to self deter-mination. In re Conroy, 98 N.J. 321, 486 A.2d 1209, 1223 (1985).

Some courts have found the right to refuse life-sustaining treatment in state statutes. Generally, courts that rely on a statutory "right to die" also find a consistent common law right. See, e.g., McConnell v. Beverly Enter-prises–Connecticut, 209 Conn. 692, 553 A.2d 596, 601–602 (1989). The Illi-nois Supreme Court, for example, explicitly rejected state and federal consti-tutional justifications for a "right to die" because of the existence of both state common law and state statutory remedies. In re Estate of Longeway, 133 Ill.2d 33, 139 Ill.Dec. 780, 549 N.E.2d 292, 297 (1989).

Several state courts have found the "right to die" in their state constitu-tions. A decision based on the state constitution may be the strongest kind of support such a right can ever find, because it is not subject to review by the United States Supreme Court (absent an improbable argument that a state created right would itself violate the United States Constitution) and it is not subject to change by the state legislature (except through the generally cum-bersome state constitutional amendment process). Relevant state constitu-tional provisions take different forms. For example, the Florida Constitution provides that "[e]very natural person has the right to be let alone and free from governmental intrusion into his private life except as otherwise provid-ed herein. * * * " Fla. Const., art. 1, section 23. The Arizona Constitution pro-vides that "[n]o person shall be disturbed in his private affairs or his home invaded, without authority of law." Arizona Const., art. 2, section 8. Both of these constitutional provisions have given rise to state court recognized rights to forgo life-sustaining treatment. See In re Guardianship of Barry, 445 So.2d 365 (Fla.App.1984) and Rasmussen v. Fleming, 154 Ariz. 207, 741 P.2d 674 (1987). See also DeGrella v. Elston, 858 S.W.2d 698 (Ky.1993) and Lenz v. L.E. Phillips Career Dev. Ctr., 167 Wis.2d 53, 482 N.W.2d 60 (Wis. 1992). The California Court of Appeal also found that such a right for compe-tent patients could be found in the California Constitution. See Bouvia v. Su-perior Court, 179 Cal. App. 3d 1127, 225 Cal. Rptr. 297 (1986), reprinted be-low following the next problem. In 2009 the Montana Supreme Court hinted that the Montana Constitution's "dignity" clause might be interpreted to give competent terminally ill individuals a right to seek and receive a prescription for a lethal dose in some circumstances. It seems likely that the same sub-stantive constitutional source of law would guarantee the right to remove life-sustaining medical care. See Baxter v. Montana, 354 Mont. 234, 224 P.3d 1211 (2009), reprinted in Chapter 17.

II. HEALTH CARE DECISION–MAKING BY ADULTS WITH DECISIONAL CAPACITY

PROBLEM: THE CHRISTIAN SCIENTIST IN THE EMERGENCY ROOM

Shortly after Ms. Elizabeth Boroff was hit by a drunk driver who went through a red light and directly into her Volkswagen bus, she found herself being attended by paramedics and loaded into an ambulance for a trip to the Big County General Hospital emergency room. Although she was briefly unconscious at the scene of the accident, and although she suffered a very substantial blood loss, several broken bones and a partially crushed skull, she had regained consciousness by her arrival at the hospital. The doctors explained to her that her life was at risk and that she needed a blood transfusion and brain surgery immediately. She explained that she was a Christian Scientist, that she believed in the healing power of prayer, that she rejected medical care, and that she wished to be discharged immediately so that she could consult a Christian Science healer.

A quick conference of emergency room staff revealed a consensus that failure to relieve the pressure caused by her intracranial bleed would result in loss of consciousness within a few hours, and, possibly, her death. When this information was provided to her she remained unmoved. The hospital staff asked her to identify her next of kin, and she explained that she was a widow with no living relatives except for her seven minor children, ages 1 through 9. Further inquiries revealed that she was the sole support for these children, that she had no life insurance, that she had an elementary school education, and that she had been employed as a clerk since her husband, a self-employed maintenance man, was himself killed in an automobile accident a year ago. Uncertain of what to do, the emergency room staff called you, the hospital legal counsel, for advice. What advice should you give? Should they discharge Ms. Boroff, as she requests? Should you commence a legal action to keep her in the hospital and institute treatment? If you were to file a legal action, what relief would you seek, and what would be the substantive basis of your claim?

BOUVIA v. SUPERIOR COURT

California Court of Appeal, Second District, 1986.
179 Cal.App.3d 1127, 225 Cal.Rptr. 297.

BEACH, ASSOCIATE JUSTICE.

Petitioner, Elizabeth Bouvia, a patient in a public hospital, seeks the removal from her body of a nasogastric tube inserted and maintained against her will and without her consent by physicians who so placed it for the purpose of keeping her alive through involuntary forced feeding.

* * *

Petitioner is a 28–year–old woman. Since birth she has been afflicted with and suffered from severe cerebral palsy. She is quadriplegic. She is now a patient at a public hospital maintained by one of the real parties in interest, the County of Los Angeles. Other parties are physicians, nurses and the medical and support staff employed by the County of Los Angeles. Petitioner's physical handicaps of palsy and quadriplegia have progressed to the point where she is completely bedridden. Except for a few fingers of one hand and some slight head and facial movements, she is immobile. She is physically helpless and wholly unable to care for herself. * * * She suffers also from degenerative and severely crippling arthritis. She is in continual pain. * * *

She is intelligent, very mentally competent. She earned a college degree. She was married but her husband has left her. She suffered a miscarriage. She lived with her parents until her father told her that they could no longer care for her. She has stayed intermittently with friends and at public facilities. A search for a permanent place to live where she might receive the constant care which she needs has been unsuccessful. She is without financial means to support herself and, therefore, must accept public assistance for medical and other care.

She has on several occasions expressed the desire to die. In 1983 she sought the right to be cared for in a public hospital in Riverside County while she intentionally "starved herself to death." A court in that county denied her judicial assistance to accomplish that goal. * * * Thereafter, friends took her to several different facilities, both public and private, arriving finally at her present location. Efforts by * * * social workers to find her an apartment of her own with publicly paid live-in help or regular visiting nurses to care for her, or some other suitable facility have proved fruitless.

Petitioner must be spoon fed in order to eat. Her present medical and dietary staff have determined that she is not consuming a sufficient amount of nutrients. Petitioner stops eating when she feels she cannot orally swallow more, without nausea and vomiting. As she cannot now retain solids, she is fed soft liquid-like food. Because of her previously announced resolve to starve herself, the medical staff feared her weight loss might reach a life-threatening level. Her weight since admission to real parties' facility seems to hover between 65 and 70 pounds. Accordingly, they inserted the subject tube against her will and contrary to her express written instructions.[2]

Petitioner's counsel argue that her weight loss was not such as to be life threatening and therefore the tube is unnecessary. However, the trial court found to the contrary as a matter of fact, a finding which we must

---

[2]   Her instructions were dictated to her lawyers, written by them and signed by her by means of her making a feeble "x" on the paper with a pen which she held in her mouth.

accept. Nonetheless, the point is immaterial, for, as we will explain, a patient has the right to refuse any medical treatment or medical service, even when such treatment is labeled "furnishing nourishment and hydration." This right exists even if its exercise creates a "life threatening condition."

The Right to Refuse Medical Treatment

"[A] person of adult years and in sound mind has the right, in the exercise of control over his own body, to determine whether or not to submit to lawful medical treatment." [ ] It follows that such a patient has the right to refuse *any* medical treatment, even that which may save or prolong her life. [ ]

* * *

A recent Presidential Commission for the Study of Ethical Problems in Medicine and Biomedical and Behavioral Research concluded in part: "The voluntary choice of a competent and informed patient should determine whether or not life-sustaining therapy will be undertaken, just as such choices provide the basis for other decisions about medical treatment. Health care institutions and professionals should try to enhance patients' abilities to make decisions on their own behalf and to promote understanding of the available treatment options * * *. Health care professionals serve patients best by maintaining a presumption in favor of sustaining life, while recognizing that competent patients are entitled to choose to forgo any treatments, including those that sustain life."

* * *

The American Hospital Association Policy and Statement of Patients' Choices of Treatment Options, approved by the American Hospital Association in February of 1985 discusses the value of a collaborative relationship between the patient and the physician and states in pertinent part: "Whenever possible, however, the authority to determine the course of treatment, if any, should rest with the patient" and "the right to choose treatment includes the right to refuse a specific treatment *or all treatment* * * *."

* * *

Significant also is the statement adopted on March 15, 1986, by the Council on Ethical and Judicial Affairs of the American Medical Association. It is entitled "Withholding or Withdrawing Life Prolonging Medical Treatment." In pertinent part, it declares: "The social commitment of the physician is to sustain life and relieve suffering. Where the performance of one duty conflicts with the other, the choice of the patient, or his family or legal representative if the patient is incompetent to act in his own behalf, should prevail."

* * *

It is indisputable that petitioner is mentally competent. She is not comatose. She is quite intelligent, alert and understands the risks involved.

The Claimed Exceptions to the Patient's Right to Choose Are Inapplicable

* * * The real parties in interest, a county hospital, its physicians and administrators, urge that the interests of the State should prevail over the rights of Elizabeth Bouvia to refuse treatment. Advanced by real parties under this argument are the State's interests in (1) preserving life, (2) preventing suicide, (3) protecting innocent third parties, and (4) maintaining the ethical standards of the medical profession, including the right of physicians to effectively render necessary and appropriate medical service and to refuse treatment to an uncooperative and disruptive patient. Included, whether as part of the above or as separate and additional arguments, are what real parties assert as distinctive facts not present in other cases, i.e., (1) petitioner is a patient in a public facility, thereby making the State a party to the result of her conduct, (2) she is not comatose, nor incurably, nor terminally ill, nor in a vegetative state, all conditions which have justified the termination of life-support system in other instances, (3) she has asked for medical treatment, therefore, she cannot accept a part of it while cutting off the part that would be effective, and (4) she is, in truth, trying to starve herself to death and the State will not be a party to a suicide.

* * *

At bench the trial court concluded that with sufficient feeding petitioner could live an additional 15 to 20 years; therefore, the preservation of petitioner's life for that period outweighed her right to decide. In so holding the trial court mistakenly attached undue importance to the *amount of time* possibly available to petitioner, and failed to give equal weight and consideration for the *quality* of that life; an equal, if not more significant, consideration.

All decisions permitting cessation of medical treatment or life-support procedures to some degree hastened the arrival of death. In part, at least, this was permitted because the quality of life during the time remaining in those cases had been terribly diminished. In Elizabeth Bouvia's view, the quality of her life has been diminished to the point of hopelessness, uselessness, unenjoyability and frustration. She, as the patient, lying helplessly in bed, unable to care for herself, may consider her existence meaningless. She cannot be faulted for so concluding. If her right to choose may not be exercised because there remains to her, in the opinion of a court, a physician or some committee, a certain arbitrary number of years, months, or days, her right will have lost its value and meaning.

Who shall say what the minimum amount of available life must be? Does it matter if it be 15 to 20 years, 15 to 20 months, or 15 to 20 days, if such life has been physically destroyed and its quality, dignity and purpose gone? As in all matters lines must be drawn at some point, somewhere, but that decision must ultimately belong to the one whose life is in issue.

Here Elizabeth Bouvia's decision to forgo medical treatment or life-support through a mechanical means belongs to her. It is not a medical decision for her physicians to make. Neither is it a legal question whose soundness is to be resolved by lawyers or judges. It is not a conditional right subject to approval by ethics committees or courts of law. It is a moral and philosophical decision that, being a competent adult, is hers alone.

* * *

Here, if force fed, petitioner faces 15 to 20 years of a painful existence, endurable only by the constant administrations of morphine. Her condition is irreversible. There is no cure for her palsy or arthritis. Petitioner would have to be fed, cleaned, turned, bedded, toileted by others for 15 to 20 years! Although alert, bright, sensitive, perhaps even brave and feisty, she must lie immobile, unable to exist except through physical acts of others. Her mind and spirit may be free to take great flights but she herself is imprisoned and must lie physically helpless subject to the ignominy, embarrassment, humiliation and dehumanizing aspects created by her helplessness. We do not believe it is the policy of this State that all and every life must be preserved against the will of the sufferer. It is incongruous, if not monstrous, for medical practitioners to assert their right to preserve a life that someone else must live, or, more accurately, endure, for "15 to 20 years." We cannot conceive it to be the policy of this State to inflict such an ordeal upon anyone.

* * * Being competent she has the right to live out the remainder of her natural life in dignity and peace. It is precisely the aim and purpose of the many decisions upholding the withdrawal of life-support systems to accord and provide as large a measure of dignity, respect and comfort as possible to every patient for the remainder of his days, whatever be their number. This goal is not to hasten death, though its earlier arrival may be an expected and understood likelihood.

* * *

Moreover, the trial court seriously erred by basing its decision on the "motives" behind Elizabeth Bouvia's decision to exercise her rights. If a right exists, it matters not what "motivates" its exercise. We find nothing in the law to suggest the right to refuse medical treatment may be exercised only if the patient's *motives* meet someone else's approval. It certainly is not illegal or immoral to prefer a natural, albeit sooner, death than a drugged life attached to a mechanical device.

* * *

We do not purport to establish what will constitute proper medical practice in all other cases or even other aspects of the care to be provided petitioner. We hold only that her right to refuse medical treatment even of the life-sustaining variety, entitles her to the immediate removal of the nasogastric tube that has been involuntarily inserted into her body. The hospital and medical staff are still free to perform a substantial, if not the greater part of their duty, i.e., that of trying to alleviate Bouvia's pain and suffering.

Petitioner is without means to go to a private hospital and, apparently, real parties' hospital as a public facility was required to accept her. Having done so it may not deny her relief from pain and suffering merely because she has chosen to exercise her fundamental right to protect what little privacy remains to her.

Personal dignity is a part of one's right of privacy. * * *

NOTES AND QUESTIONS

1.   The *Bouvia* court depended, in large part, upon Bartling v. Superior Court, 163 Cal.App.3d 186, 209 Cal.Rptr. 220 (1984), the first case to confirm a competent patient's right to make decisions to forgo life-sustaining treatment. Mr. Bartling was a competent adult suffering from depression (the original reason for his hospitalization), a tumor on his lung, and emphysema. He had a living will, a separate declaration asking that treatment be discontinued, and a durable power of attorney appointing his wife to make his health care decisions. He and his wife continuously asked that the ventilator that was preserving his life be removed, and he, his wife, and his daughter all executed documents releasing the hospital from any liability claims arising out of honoring Mr. Bartling's request. Still, the hospital, which was a Christian hospital established and operated on pro-life principles, opposed discontinuation of Mr. Bartling's ventilator on ethical grounds. The California Court of Appeal found that the trial court should have granted Mr. Bartling's request for an injunction against the hospital, concluding that, "if the right to patient self-determination as to his own medical treatment means anything at all, it must be paramount to the interests of the patient's hospital and doctors. The right of a competent adult to refuse medical treatment is a constitutionally guaranteed right which must not be abridged."

2.   Do you agree that the hospital had an obligation to accept Ms. Bouvia and provide her with medical relief from her pain and suffering, even

though the physicians and hospital found her conduct immoral and her request an abuse of the medical profession? Is the obligation anything more than to provide adequate end-of-life care, even when the patient refuses a particular course of treatment? Cf. Brophy v. New England Sinai Hospital, Inc., 398 Mass. 417, 497 N.E.2d 626 (1986), where the Massachusetts Supreme Judicial Court found that a patient in a persistent vegetative state could, through his family, deny consent to feeding through a gastric tube, but that the hospital need not remove or clamp the tube if it found it to be contrary to the ethical dictates of the medical profession. The *Brophy* decision required that the family move the patient to another medical institution more receptive to his apparent desires for his feeding tube to be removed. The New Jersey Supreme Court took a middle ground in In re Jobes, 108 N.J. 394, 529 A.2d 434, 450 (1987):

> The trial court held that the nursing home could refuse to participate in the withdrawal of the j-tube by keeping Mrs. Jobes connected to it until she is transferred out of that facility. Under the circumstances of this case, we disagree, and we reverse that portion of the trial court's order.
>
> Mrs. Jobes' family had no reason to believe that they were surrendering the right to choose among medical alternatives when they placed her in the nursing home. [ ] The nursing home apparently did not inform Mrs. Jobes' family about its policy toward artificial feeding until May of 1985 when they requested that the j-tube be withdrawn. In fact there is no indication that this policy has ever been formalized. Under these circumstances Mrs. Jobes and her family were entitled to rely on the nursing home's willingness to defer to their choice among courses of medical treatment. * * *
>
> We do not decide the case in which a nursing home gave notice of its policy not to participate in the withdrawal or withholding of artificial feeding at the time of a patient's admission. Thus, we do not hold that such a policy is never enforceable. But we are confident in this case that it would be wrong to allow the nursing home to discharge Mrs. Jobes. The evidence indicates that at this point it would be extremely difficult, perhaps impossible, to find another facility that would accept Mrs. Jobes as a patient. Therefore, to allow the nursing home to discharge Mrs. Jobes if her family does not consent to continued artificial feeding would essentially frustrate Mrs. Jobes' right of self-determination.

Some state statutes governing end-of-life decision-making include specific provisions for situations in which health care professionals or facilities object to the decisions of patients (or their surrogates). See, e.g., Uniform Health–Care Decisions Act, below. The option to inform patients in advance of particular policies and then seek transfer is the most common compromise. See generally George Annas, Transferring the Ethical Hot Potato, 17 Hastings Ctr. Rep. 20 (1987) (explaining how patients' rights are threatened by legal decisions that allow medical institutions to discharge "patients who do not accept everything they offer"). Many states also have enacted statutes allowing such conscience-based actions by health care professionals in particular contexts, such as abortion and medically assisted dying. For a thorough discussion of this issue in the context of the pharmacist's obligation to dispense some controversial kinds of contraceptive medication, see Chapter 15. For a discussion of the employment issues that could arise out of a decision by a health care professional to refrain from providing legal but morally objectionable care, see Chapter 11. Might such a decision also constitute abandonment? See Chapters 3, 4 and 8.

3.   If we take seriously the *Bouvia* suggestion that hospitals have an obligation to provide comfort to patients who choose to forgo treatment and thus die, do physicians have an obligation to inform patients of the various ways of dying that are available to them, and the consequences of choosing any one of them?

Consider Margaret Battin, The Least Worst Death, 13 Hastings Ctr. Rep. 13–16 (April 1983):

> In the face of irreversible, terminal illness, a patient may wish to die sooner but "naturally," without artificial prolongation of any kind. By doing so, the patient may believe he is choosing a death that is, as a contributor to the *New England Journal of Medicine* has put it, "comfortable, decent, and peaceful". "[N]atural death," the patient may assume, means a death that is easier than a medically prolonged one.

> [H]e may assume that it will allow time for reviewing life and saying farewell to family and loved ones, for last rites or final words, for passing on hopes, wisdom, confessions, and blessings to the next generation. These ideas are of course heavily stereotyped * * *: Even the very term "natural" may have stereotyped connotations for the patient: something close to nature, uncontrived, and appropriate. As a result of these notions, the patient often takes "natural death" to be a painless, conscious, dignified, culminative slipping-away.

> Now consider what sorts of death actually occur under the rubric of "natural death." A patient suffers a cardiac arrest and is not resuscitated. Result: sudden unconsciousness, without pain, and death within a number of seconds. Or a patient has an infection that is not treated. Result: * * * fever, delirium, rigor or shaking, and light-headedness; death usually takes one or two days, depending on the organism involved.

> *   *   *

> What the patient who rejects active euthanasia or assisted suicide may realistically hope for is this: the least worst death among those

that could naturally occur. Not all unavoidable surrenders need involve rout: in the face of inevitable death, the physician becomes strategist, the deviser of plans for how to meet death most favorably.

* * *

To recognize the patient's right to autonomous choice in matters concerning the treatment of his own body, the physician must provide information about all the legal options open to him, not just information sufficient to choose between accepting or rejecting a single proposed procedure.

In the current enthusiasm for "natural death" it is not patient autonomy that dismays physicians. What does dismay them is the way in which respect for patient autonomy can lead to cruel results. The cure for that dismay lies in the realization that the physician can contribute to the *genuine* honoring of the patient's autonomy and rights, assuring him of "natural death" in the way in which the patient understands it, and still remain within the confines of good medical practice and the law.

4.   Growing concerns that patients are provided more treatment at the end of life than they really want gave rise to the promulgation of the Right to Know End of Life Options Act in California in 2009 and the stronger Palliative Care Information Act in New York in 2010. Both statutes are designed to assure that patients are given all of the information they request (in California) or need (in New York) once they have been diagnosed as terminally ill. In California the Right to Know End of Life Options Act was opposed by Right to Life organizations and medical professional groups, which generally object to all statutory intrusion on the doctor-patient relationship. The stronger New York statute was opposed only by medical professional organizations, and it passed by large margins in both houses of the legislature. The New York statute is a simple statement of principle, more hortatory than enforceable:

Palliative Care Patient Information
New York Pub. Health Law § 2997–c

1.   Definitions. * * *

(a) "Appropriate" means consistent with applicable legal, health and professional standards; the patient's clinical and other circumstances; and the patient's reasonably known wishes and beliefs.

* * *

(c) "Palliative care" means health care treatment, including interdisciplinary end-of-life care, and consultation with patients and family members, to prevent or relieve pain and suffering and to enhance the patient's quality of life, including hospice care * * *.

(d) "Terminal illness or condition" means an illness or condition which can reasonably be expected to cause death within six months whether or not treatment is provided.

2.   If a patient is diagnosed with a terminal illness or condition, the patient's attending health care practitioner shall offer to provide the patient with information and counseling regarding palliative care and end-of-life options appropriate to the patient, including but not limited to: the range of options appropriate to the patient; the prognosis, risks and benefits of the various options; and the patient's legal rights to comprehensive pain and symptom management at the end of life. The information and counseling may be provided orally or in writing. Where the patient lacks capacity to reasonably understand and make informed choices relating to palliative care, the attending health care practitioner shall provide information and counseling under this section to a person with authority to make health care decisions for the patient. The attending health care practitioner may arrange for information and counseling under this section to be provided by another professionally qualified individual.

Is this kind of a statute a good idea? Should other states follow the lead of California and New York? Writing in The New England Journal of Medicine just three months after the statute became effective, two New York physicians argue that legislation is the wrong way to address problems with care at the end of life:

> What is needed in such cases is not simply information, but an appreciation for the profound anxiety everyone feels at the border between life and death. In asserting power over the way in which deep and troubling human questions should be addressed—and showing so little interest in or understanding of the physician's experience— the New York legislature seems likely only to generate cynicism at the times when critically ill patients and their families are most in need of honesty, kindness, and engagement.

Alan Astrow and Beth Propp, Perspective: The Palliative Care Information Act in Real Life, (Topics: Public Health, N.Eng.J.Med, May 18, 2011). Are they right? Should the underlying question be one about patients' and families' experiences, physicians' experiences, or both? The original Right to Know End of Life Options bill introduced in California explicitly mentioned some alternatives about which patients should be informed in appropriate circumstances—for example, palliative sedation (described in the *Cruzan* case) and the voluntary stopping of eating and drinking. Political compromise required that mention of those specific alternatives be deleted from the bill. Would general language, like that in the New York statute, require that a patient be told of those end-of-life alternatives? Under what circumstances?

5.   After the California Supreme Court confirmed Ms. Bouvia's right to choose to die, she decided to accept the medical care necessary to treat her pain and to keep her alive. She appeared on television (on "60 Minutes") in 1998, where she expressed the hope that she would die soon. Why would someone seek judicial confirmation of a "right to die" and then not act upon it? Does it indicate that people waver on this issue? Does it suggest that knowing that one has the choice—when it becomes necessary—contributes to that person's well being? Are those who seek a judicially confirmed "right to die" really seeking control over their destiny, not their death? Ironically, the existence of a right to die may be the reason that some people choose to live, just as the existence of medically assisted dying may be a reason that many people choose not to ingest the lethal dose of medication they have been legally prescribed. See chapter 17, below. For a discussion of related issues, see L.M. Cohen, M.J. Germain and D.M. Poppel, Practical Considerations in Dialysis Withdrawal: "To Have That Option is a Blessing," 289 JAMA 2113 (2002).

6.   The court describes the quality of Elizabeth Bouvia's life in startling terms. Are they also offensive terms? Does the court describe her life as useless, meaningless, and embarrassing solely because that was her view of her own life, or does the court agree that this must be the case? *Bouvia* is viewed by disabilities rights advocates as a case which denigrated the value of the lives of persons who were dependent and disabled and in which a disabled person was driven to desperate measures for lack of the support she needed to live to her fullest capacity. See, e.g., Paul K. Longmore, Elizabeth Bouvia, Assisted Suicide and Social Prejudice, 3 Issues L. & Med. 141 (1987). For a wonderful attempt to reconcile the principles of bioethics (and especially the principle of autonomy) with the principles of protection (and beneficence) that underlie the disabilities rights movement, see Alicia Ouellette, Bioethics and Disability: Toward a Disability–Conscious Bioethics (2011). The disabilities rights movement has become a key player in controversies over end-of-life decision-making, generally seeking to assure that those who seek to justify ending life by terminating life-sustaining treatment or by medically assisted dying have not equated the worth or dignity of an individual with the absence of any disability or abnormality.

7.   Is it surprising that the fundamental principle that competent adults can make all of their own health care decisions has made it into the statutes of only a very few states? For an exception to this general rule, see N.M. Stat. Ann. Section 24–7A–2. Especially after the concern shown for this issue in *Bouvia*, one might expect more legislatures to have confirmed this right. Have they failed to do so because the law is so clear that legislative confirmation is unnecessary, or because there is a real dispute about the substance of the principle?

8.   The right to choose to die is usually based upon the premise that a person rationally may decide that death is preferable to the pain, expense, and inconvenience of receiving the proposded treatment that is necessary to maintain life. Given that the process of weighing the value of life and death is necessarily based in personal history, religious and moral values, and individual sensitivity to a number of different factors, and given that it finds its philosophical basis in the principle of autonomy, is there any justification for independent second-party evaluation of whether the balancing was properly, or even rationally, performed by the patient when it is based on religious principles? In fact, the most difficult cases have arisen over decisions based upon the dictates of religious principles. For example, Christian Scientists generally accept the healing power of prayer to the exclusion of medical assistance—most Christian Scientists refuse most traditional medical care. Jehovah's Witnesses, on the other hand, accept most medical care, but they do not accept blood transfusions, which they perceive to be a violation of the biblical prohibition on the ingestion of blood. Should a court treat a Christian Scientist or Jehovah's Witness who chooses for religious reasons to forgo necessary care any differently than it treats Elizabeth Bouvia? Is it relevant that others consider the religious ban on the ingestion of blood or the rejection of all medical treatment to be irrational?

Because courts were less able to empathize with patients who had unusual religious beliefs than with others, for many years courts were less willing to entertain the right to forgo life-sustaining treatment on religious grounds than on other grounds. Over the past several years, this has changed and today most courts allow competent adults to choose to live (or die) in a way that is consistent with whatever religious views they possess. Are the arguments used to justify judicial intervention to require blood transfusions for Jehovah's Witnesses when such transfusions are necessary to preserve life persuasive examples of the social value of law and medicine, or are they unconvincing examples of the paternalistic heritage of both professions?

9.   It is not always easy to determine the wishes of a competent patient. In order to express a wish, the patient must be fully informed, but the very information that is most useful to a patient in deciding whether to forgo life-sustaining medical treatment may not be available, or the health care providers may not realize that it is relevant to the patient making the decision. One recent study set out to determine what kind of information is significant to patients making decisions about the removal of life-sustaining medical care:

> The provision of care at the end of life should honor patients' preferences. If these preferences are to be honored, they must first be understood. Our results suggest than an understanding of patients' preferences depends on an assessment of [1] how they view the burden of treatment [2] in relation to their possible outcomes and [3] their likelihood. The possibility of functional or cognitive impairment has a particularly important role in patients' preferences and thus merits explicit consideration in advance care planning.

Terri R. Fried et al., Understanding the Treatment Preferences of Seriously Ill Patients, 346 N. Eng. J. Med. 1061 (2002). What information would be relevant to you in making decisions about end-of-life care? Do you think that this study was correct in determining the significance of possible functional or cognitive impairments? For an interesting approach to this issue, see D.E. Meier & R.S. Morrison, Autonomy Reconsidered, 346 NEJM 1087 (2002). For evaluations of these issues within particular medical specialties, A.K. Simonds, Ethics and Decision-making in End Stage Lung Disease, 58 Thorax 272 (2003) and C.O. Granai, What Matters Matter?, 102 Obstetrics & Gynecology 393 (2003).

NOTE: COUNTERVAILING STATE INTERESTS USED TO JUSTIFY THE STATE'S DETERMINATION THAT PATIENTS MAY NOT REJECT LIFE–SUSTAINING TREATMENT

The right to choose to forgo life-sustaining treatment is not absolute, even for competent adults. In Superintendent of Belchertown State School v. Saikewicz, 373 Mass. 728, 370 N.E.2d 417 (1977), the Massachusetts Supreme Judicial Court first identified the four "countervailing State interests" that could overcome a patient's choice: (1) preservation of life; (2) protection of the interests of innocent third parties; (3) prevention of suicide; and (4) maintenance of the ethical integrity of the medical profession.

Although Saikewicz involved an incompetent, mentally retarded patient, the mantra of those four interests has also been applied in later cases involving competent patients—including Bouvia—but they have never been found to be sufficient to overcome the choice of a competent patient. You will see the state's interests discussed in almost every case in this chapter.

In Saikewicz the Massachusetts Supreme Judicial Court explored the significance of these four state interests and their limitations:

It is clear that the most significant of the asserted State interests is that of the preservation of human life. Recognition of such an interest, however, does not necessarily resolve the problem where the affliction or disease clearly indicates that life will end soon, and inevitably be extinguished. The interest of the State in prolonging a life must be reconciled with the interest of an individual to reject the traumatic cost of that prolongation. There is a substantial distinction in the State's insistence that human life be saved where the affliction is curable, as opposed to the State interest where, as here, the issue is not whether but when, for how long, and at what cost to the individual that life may be briefly extended. Even if we assume that the State has an additional interest in seeing to it that individual decisions on the prolongation of life do not in any way tend to "cheapen" the value which is placed on the concept of living, we believe it is not inconsistent to recognize a right to decline medical treatment in a situation of incurable illness. The constitutional right to privacy, as we conceive it, is an expression of the sanctity of

individual free choice and self-determination as fundamental con-
stituents of life. The value of life as so perceived is lessened not by a
decision to refuse treatment, but by the failure to allow a competent
human being the right of a choice.

A second interest of considerable magnitude, which the State may
have some interest in asserting, is that of protecting third parties,
particularly minor children, from the emotional and financial damage which may occur as a result of the decision of a competent adult
to refuse life-saving or life-prolonging treatment. Thus, even when
the State's interest in preserving an individual's life was not sufficient, by itself, to outweigh the individual's interest in the exercise
of free choice, the possible impact on minor children would be a factor which might have a critical effect on the outcome of the balancing process.

* * *

The last State interest requiring discussion[11] is that of the maintenance of the ethical integrity of the medical profession as well as allowing hospitals the full opportunity to care for people under their
control. The force and impact of this interest is lessened by the prevailing medical ethical standards. Prevailing medical ethical practice does not, without exception, demand that all efforts toward life
prolongation be made in all circumstances. Rather, the prevailing
ethical practice seems to be to recognize that the dying are more often in need of comfort than treatment. Recognition of the right to refuse necessary treatment in appropriate circumstances is consistent
with existing medical mores; such a doctrine does not threaten either the integrity of the medical profession, the proper role of hospitals in caring for such patients or the State's interest in protecting
the same. It is not necessary to deny a right of self-determination to
a patient in order to recognize the interest of doctors, hospitals, and
medical personnel in attendance on the patient. Also, if the doctrines of informed consent and right of privacy have as their foundations in the right to bodily integrity, and control of one's own fate,
then those rights are superior to the institutional considerations.
370 N.E.2d at 425–427.

In fact, these four interests raise issues beyond those discussed in
Saikewicz:

---

[11] The interest in protecting against suicide seems to require little if any discussion. In the
case of the competent adult's refusing medical treatment such an act does not necessarily constitute suicide since (1) in refusing treatment the patient may not have the specific intent to die,
and (2) even if he did, to the extent that the cause of death was from natural causes, the patient
did not set the death producing agent in motion with the intent of causing his own death. Furthermore, the underlying State interest in this area lies in the prevention of irrational self-
destruction. What we consider here is a competent, rational decision to refuse treatment when
death is inevitable, and the treatment offers no hope of cure or preservation of life. There is no
connection between the conduct here in issue and any State concern to prevent suicide.

(1) *Preservation of life.* If the value of the preservation of life is the very question faced by the court in right-to-die cases, does it make sense to define it, *a priori,* as a value that is countervailing to the patient's desire to discontinue treatment?

The nature of the state's interest in the preservation of life was discussed in the *Cruzan* case, in which it was the only interest advanced by the state of Missouri. The Chief Justice said that

> a state may properly decline to make judgments about the 'quality' of life that a particular individual may enjoy, and simply assert an unqualified interest in the preservation of human life to be weighed against the constitutionally protected interests of the individual.

Not surprisingly, the dissenters viewed the state's interest in the preservation of life very differently. Justice Stevens objected to Missouri's policy of "equating [Cruzan's] life with the biological persistence of her bodily functions." He pointed out that,

> [l]ife, particularly human life, is not commonly thought of as a merely physiological condition or function. Its sanctity is often thought to derive from the impossibility of any such reduction. When people speak of life, they often mean to describe the experiences that comprise a person's history. * * *

Justice Brennan was especially offended by the notion that the generalized state interest in life could overcome the liberty interest to forgo life-sustaining treatment. One's rights, he argued, may not be sacrificed just to make society feel good:

> If Missouri were correct that its interests outweigh Nancy's interests in avoiding medical procedures as long as she is free of pain and physical discomfort, [ ] it is not apparent why a state could not choose to remove one of her kidneys without consent on the ground that society would be better off if the recipient of that kidney were saved from renal poisoning * * *, patches of her skin could also be removed to provide grafts for burn victims, and scrapings of bone marrow to provide grafts for someone with leukemia. * * * *. Indeed, why could the state not perform medical experiments on her body, experiments that might save countless lives, and would cause her no greater burden than she already bears by being fed through her gastrostomy tube? This would be too brave a new world for me and, I submit, for our constitution.

497 U.S. 261, 312–14 n. 13, 110 S.Ct. 2841, 2869–70 n. 13, 111 L.Ed.2d 224. Chief Justice Rehnquist states in *Glucksberg,* Chapter 17 below, that *Cruzan* had decided that states may choose to act to protect the sanctity of all life, independent of any inquiry into quality of life, and independent of the value of that life to the one living it.

(2) *Protection of innocent third parties.* Does the protection of the interests of innocent third parties have any meaning if courts are not willing to force people to stop pursuing their own interests and to serve some undefined communal goal? Is it merely a make-weight argument in a society as individualistic as ours? On the other hand, might children, for example, have a claim on the lives of their parents? Under what circumstances would such a claim be strongest?

(3) *Prevention of suicide.* Although *Glucksberg* confirmed that a state could make assisting suicide a crime, committing suicide is no longer a crime in any state. Is there still a consensus behind Justice Nolan's position, dissenting in Brophy v. New England Sinai Hosp., 398 Mass. 417, 497 N.E.2d 626, 640 (1986), that "suicide is direct self-destruction and is intrinsically evil. No set of circumstances can make it moral * * *."

(4) *Protecting the ethical integrity of the medical profession.* Finally, there is no longer any reason to believe that the ethics of the medical profession do not permit discontinuation of medical treatment to a competent patient who refuses it. See AMA Ethical Opinion 2.20, Withholding or Withdrawing a Life–Prolonging Medical Treatment. Even if there were, though, should the protection of the "ethical integrity of the medical profession" overcome an otherwise proper decision to forgo some form of treatment? If all other analyses point to allowing a patient to deny consent to some form of treatment, in what cases, if any, should the medical profession be able to require the treatment in the interest of its own self-defined integrity?

Are there special circumstances in which the interest of the patient ought not to be recognized or the interest of the state is especially important? Can the state require a criminal defendant to submit to medical treatment to make him competent to stand trial? See Sell v. U.S., 539 U.S. 166, 123 S.Ct. 2174, 156 L.Ed.2d 197 (2003), holding that forced medication may violate Due Process rights. Does the national interest allow the military to require its soldiers to undergo life saving (or other) medical care so that they can be returned to the front? Can a prisoner refuse kidney dialysis that is necessary to save his life unless the prison administration moves him from a medium to minimum security prison? See Commissioner of Correction v. Myers, 379 Mass. 255, 399 N.E.2d 452 (1979) (interest in "orderly prison administration" outweighs any privacy right of the prisoner to refuse dialysis unless he were moved to another site); People ex rel. Illinois Department of Corrections v. Millard, 335 Ill.App.3d 1066, 270 Ill.Dec. 407, 782 N.E.2d 966 (2003) (force feeding of prisoner allowed). For a general discussion of several courts' approaches to balancing a patient's right to refuse treatment with these countervailing state interests, see Alan Meisel & Kathy L. Cerminara, The Right to Die, 3rd ed. (2004).

III. HEALTH CARE DECISIONS FOR ADULTS WITHOUT DECISION–MAKING CAPACITY

A. ADVANCE DIRECTIVES

It is very difficult to serve the underlying goal of autonomy, if that goal is defined as personal choice, in patients without decisional capacity. One way to serve this principle is through the application of the doctrine of substituted judgment. Under this doctrine, a person, committee, institution or other substitute decision maker attempts to determine what the patient would do if the patient had decisional capacity. It may be possible to review the values of a formerly competent patient to determine whether that patient would choose to undergo or forgo proposed medical care. This can be done through a thoughtful analysis of the patient's values during life or through review of formal statements made by the patient when the patient had capacity. The most relevant considerations may be statements made by the patient about the proposed treatment itself. Indeed, such statements may provide the only *Constitutionally* relevant information about an incompetent patient's wishes with regard to life-sustaining medical treatment after *Cruzan*.

Of course, there is no way to know with certainty what the now-incompetent patient would do under the precise circumstances at the time the decision must be made. Some have argued that the doctrine of substituted judgment is too speculative to be applied reliably and that there is simply no way to protect the autonomy of a patient without decisional capacity. Where there is no possible method for establishing what the autonomous patient would do, bioethicists (and increasingly, courts) move to the second principle of bioethical decision-making, beneficence. In these circumstances, the alternative to serving autonomy is serving beneficence, and the alternative to the doctrine of substituted judgment is the doctrine of the "best interest" of the patient. As we shall see, the more difficult it becomes to decide what the patient would do if that patient had decisional capacity, the more likely it is that the court will apply the principle of beneficence rather than the principle of autonomy.

Although there are several kinds of statutes that allow competent individual patients to control some element of their health care when they lose decisional capacity, here are examples of two very different statutory approaches to what the law has come to call advance directives—directives about health care provided in advance of when they will actually be needed and applied. The Uniform Health–Care Decisions Act was promulgated by the Uniform Law Commissioners in the early 1990s. Although it hasn't been fully adopted by many states, it forms the basis of several states' laws with regard to advance directives. The relatively new New York Family Health Care Decisions Act, which was first urged upon the New York legislature by a bioethics commission twenty years ago, finally became law in 2010. Which provides the better approach to advance directives? Why do you think so? The research clearly establishes that the way that end-of-life choices are presented has a very substantial impact on the choices that patients actually make. See Scott Halpern et al., Default Options in Advance Directives Influence How Patients Set Goals for End of Life Care, 32 Health Affairs 408 (2013).

UNIFORM HEALTH–CARE DECISIONS ACT
Uniform Law Commissioners, 1993.

SECTION 1.   DEFINITIONS. In this [Act]:

(1) "Advance health-care directive" means an individual instruction or a power of attorney for health care.

(2) "Agent" means an individual designated in a power of attorney for health care to make a health-care decision for the individual granting the power.

(3) "Capacity" means an individual's ability to understand the significant benefits, risks, and alternatives to proposed health care and to make and communicate a health-care decision.

(4) "Guardian" means a judicially appointed guardian or conservator having authority to make a health-care decision for an individual.

(5) "Health care" means any care, treatment, service, or procedure to maintain, diagnose, or otherwise affect an individual's physical or mental condition.

(6) "Health-care decision" means a decision made by an individual or the individual's agent, guardian, or surrogate, regarding the individual's health care, including:

   (i) selection and discharge of health-care providers and institutions;

   (ii) approval or disapproval of diagnostic tests, surgical procedures, programs of medication, and orders not to resuscitate; and

   (iii) directions to provide, withhold, or withdraw artificial nutrition and hydration and all other forms of health care.

*   *   *

(9) "Individual instruction" means an individual's direction concerning a health-care decision for the individual.

*   *   *

(12) "Power of attorney for health care" means the designation of an agent to make health-care decisions for the individual granting the power.

*   *   *

(16) "Supervising health-care provider" means the primary physician or, if there is no primary physician or the primary physician is not reasonably available, the health-care provider who has undertaken primary responsibility for an individual's health care.

(17) "Surrogate" means an individual, other than a patient's agent or guardian, authorized under this [Act] to make a health-care decision for the patient.

SECTION 2.   ADVANCE HEALTH–CARE DIRECTIVES.

(a) An adult or emancipated minor may give an individual instruction. The instruction may be oral or written. The instruction may be limited to take effect only if a specified condition arises.

(b) An adult or emancipated minor may execute a power of attorney for health care, which may authorize the agent to make any health-care decision the principal could have made while having capacity. The power must be in writing and signed by the principal. The power remains in effect notwithstanding the principal's later incapacity and may include individual instructions. * * *

(c) Unless otherwise specified in a power of attorney for health care, the authority of an agent becomes effective only upon a determination that the principal lacks capacity, and ceases to be effective upon a determination that the principal has recovered capacity.

(d) Unless otherwise specified in a written advance health-care directive, a determination that an individual lacks or has recovered capacity, or that another condition exists that affects an individual instruction or the authority of an agent, must be made by the primary physician.

(e) An agent shall make a health-care decision in accordance with the principal's individual instructions, if any, and other wishes to the extent known to the agent. Otherwise, the agent shall make the decision in accordance with the agent's determination of the principal's best interest. In determining the principal's best interest, the agent shall consider the principal's personal values to the extent known to the agent.

(f) A health-care decision made by an agent for a principal is effective without judicial approval.

(g) A written advance health-care directive may include the individual's nomination of a guardian of the person.

(h) An advance health-care directive is valid for purposes of this [Act] if it complies with this [Act], regardless of when or where executed or communicated.

*   *   *

SECTION 4.   OPTIONAL FORM. The [form included in this Act] may, but need not, be used to create an advance health-care directive.

*   *   *

SECTION 5.   DECISIONS BY SURROGATE.

(a) A surrogate may make a health-care decision for a patient who is an adult or emancipated minor if the patient has been determined by the primary physician to lack capacity and no agent or guardian has been appointed or the agent or guardian is not reasonably available.

(b) An adult or emancipated minor may designate any individual to act as surrogate by personally informing the supervising health-care provider. In the absence of a designation, or if the designee is not reasonably available, any member of the following classes of the patient's family who is reasonably available, in descending order of priority, may act as surrogate:

> (1) the spouse, unless legally separated;
>
> (2) an adult child;
>
> (3) a parent; or
>
> (4) an adult brother or sister.

(c) If none of the individuals eligible to act as surrogate under subsection (b) is reasonably available, an adult who has exhibited special care and concern for the patient, who is familiar with the patient's personal values, and who is reasonably available may act as surrogate.

(d) A surrogate shall communicate his or her assumption of authority as promptly as practicable to the members of the patient's family specified in subsection (b) who can be readily contacted.

(e) If more than one member of a class assumes authority to act as surrogate, and they do not agree on a health-care decision and the supervising health-care provider is so informed, the supervising health-care provider shall comply with the decision of a majority of the members of that class who have communicated their views to the provider. If the class is evenly divided concerning the health-care decision and the supervising health-care provider is so informed, that class and all individuals having lower priority are disqualified from making the decision.

(f) A surrogate shall make a health-care decision in accordance with the patient's individual instructions, if any, and other wishes to the extent known to the surrogate. Otherwise, the surrogate shall make the decision in accordance with the surrogate's determination of the patient's best interest. In determining the patient's best interest, the surrogate shall consider the patient's personal values to the extent known to the surrogate.

(g) A health-care decision made by a surrogate for a patient is effective without judicial approval.

*   *   *

SECTION 7.   OBLIGATIONS OF HEALTH–CARE PROVIDER.

(a) Before implementing a health-care decision made for a patient, a supervising health-care provider, if possible, shall promptly communicate to the patient the decision made and the identity of the person making the decision.

(b) A supervising health-care provider who knows of the existence of an advance health-care directive, a revocation of an advance health-care directive, or a designation or disqualification of a surrogate, shall promptly record its existence in the patient's health-care record and, if it is in writing, shall request a copy and if one is furnished shall arrange for its maintenance in the health-care record.

(c) A primary physician who makes or is informed of a determination that a patient lacks or has recovered capacity, or that another condition exists which affects an individual instruction or the authority of an agent, guardian, or surrogate, shall promptly record the determination in the patient's health-care record and communicate the determination to the patient, if possible, and to any person then authorized to make health-care decisions for the patient.

(d) Except as provided in subsections (e) and (f), a health-care provider or institution providing care to a patient shall:

> (1) comply with an individual instruction of the patient and with a reasonable interpretation of that instruction made by a person then authorized to make health-care decisions for the patient; and

> (2) comply with a health-care decision for the patient made by a person then authorized to make health-care decisions for the patient to the same extent as if the decision had been made by the patient while having capacity.

(e) A health-care provider may decline to comply with an individual instruction or health-care decision for reasons of conscience. A health-care institution may decline to comply with an individual instruction or health-care decision if the instruction or decision is contrary to a policy of the institution which is expressly based on reasons of conscience and if the policy was timely communicated to the patient or to a person then authorized to make health-care decisions for the patient.

(f) A health-care provider or institution may decline to comply with an individual instruction or health-care decision that requires medically ineffective health care or health care contrary to generally accepted health-care standards applicable to the health-care provider or institution.

(g) A health-care provider or institution that declines to comply with an individual instruction or health-care decision shall:

> (1) promptly so inform the patient, if possible, and any person then authorized to make health-care decisions for the patient;

> (2) provide continuing care to the patient until a transfer can be effected; and

> (3) unless the patient or person then authorized to make health-care decisions for the patient refuses assistance, immediately make all reasonable efforts to assist in the transfer of the patient to another health-care provider or institution that is willing to comply with the instruction or decision.

(h) A health-care provider or institution may not require or prohibit the execution or revocation of an advance health-care directive as a condition for providing health care.

* * *

SECTION 11. CAPACITY.

(a) This [Act] does not affect the right of an individual to make health-care decisions while having capacity to do so.

(b) An individual is presumed to have capacity to make a health-care decision, to give or revoke an advance health-care directive, and to designate or disqualify a surrogate.

* * *

SECTION 14. JUDICIAL RELIEF. On petition of a patient, the patient's agent, guardian, or surrogate, a health-care provider or institution involved with the patient's care, or an individual described in Section 5(b) or (c), the [appropriate] court may enjoin or direct a health-care decision or order other equitable relief. A proceeding under this section is governed by [here insert appropriate reference to the rules of procedure or statutory provisions governing expedited proceedings and proceedings affecting incapacitated persons].

* * *

FAMILY HEALTH CARE DECISIONS ACT
NY PUB HEALTH § 2994–d.

1. *Identifying the surrogate.* One person from the following list from the class highest in priority when persons in prior classes are not reasonably available, willing, and competent to act, shall be the surrogate for an adult patient who lacks decision-making capacity. However, such person may designate any other person on the list to be surrogate, provided no one in a class higher in priority than the person designated objects:

(a) A guardian authorized to decide about health care pursuant to article eighty-one of the mental hygiene law;

(b) The spouse, if not legally separated from the patient, or the domestic partner;

(c) A son or daughter eighteen years of age or older;

(d) A parent;

(e) A brother or sister eighteen years of age or older;

(f) A close friend.

* * *

3. *Authority and duties of surrogate.*

(a) Scope of surrogate's authority.

> (i) Subject to the standards and limitations of this article, the surrogate shall have the authority to make any and all health care decisions on the adult patient's behalf that the patient could make.

* * *

(c) Right and duty to be informed. Notwithstanding any law to the contrary, the surrogate shall have the right to receive medical information and medical records necessary to make informed decisions about the patient's health care. Health care providers shall provide and the surrogate shall seek information necessary to make an informed decision, including information about the patient's diagnosis, prognosis, the nature and consequences of proposed health care, and the benefits and risks of and alternative to proposed health care.

4. *Decision-making standards.*

(a) The surrogate shall make health care decisions:

> (i) in accordance with the patient's wishes, including the patient's religious and moral beliefs; or

(ii) if the patient's wishes are not reasonably known and cannot with reasonable diligence be ascertained, in accordance with the patient's best interests. An assessment of the patient's best interests shall include: consideration of the dignity and uniqueness of every person; the possibility and extent of preserving the patient's life; the preservation, improvement or restoration of the patient's health or functioning; the relief of the patient's suffering; and any medical condition and such other concerns and values as a reasonable person in the patient's circumstances would wish to consider.

(b) In all cases, the surrogate's assessment of the patient's wishes and best interests shall be patient-centered; health care decisions shall be made on an individualized basis for each patient, and shall be consistent with the values of the patient, including the patient's religious and moral beliefs, to the extent reasonably possible.

5.   *Decisions to withhold or withdraw life-sustaining treatment.*

In addition to the standards set forth in subdivision four of this section, decisions by surrogates to withhold or withdraw life-sustaining treatment shall be authorized only if the following conditions are satisfied, as applicable:

(a)

(i) Treatment would be an extraordinary burden to the patient and an attending physician determines, with the independent concurrence of another physician, that, to a reasonable degree of medical certainty and in accord with accepted medical standards,

(A) the patient has an illness or injury which can be expected to cause death within six months, whether or not treatment is provided; or

(B) the patient is permanently unconscious; or

(ii) The provision of treatment would involve such pain, suffering or other burden that it would reasonably be deemed inhumane or extraordinarily burdensome under the circumstances and the patient has an irreversible or incurable condition, as determined by an attending physician with the independent concurrence of another physician to a reasonable degree of medical certainty and in accord with accepted medical standards.

(b) In a residential health care facility, a surrogate shall have the authority to refuse life-sustaining treatment * * * only if the ethics review committee, including at least one physician who is not directly responsible for the patient's care, or a court of competent jurisdiction, reviews the decision and determines that it meets the standards set forth in this article. * * *

(c) In a general hospital, if the attending physician objects to a surrogate's decision * * * to withdraw or withhold nutrition and hydration provided by means of medical treatment, the decision shall not be implemented until the ethics review committee, including at least one physician who is not directly responsible for the patient's care, or a court of competent jurisdiction, reviews the decision and determines that it meets the standards [of this statute].

(d) Providing nutrition and hydration orally, without reliance on medical treatment, is not health care under this article and is not subject to this article.

NOTES AND QUESTIONS

1. How does the decision-making process provided by the New York statute differ from the process provided by the Uniform Health Care Decisions Act? Are the decision-making standards (subsection 4 of section 2994–d of the New York law, and section 5(f) of the Uniform Health Care Decisions Act) different? How do they vary? Which is better? Why?

2. Should decisions to terminate life-sustaining medical treatment be treated differently from other kinds of health care decisions? Why do you think the New York legislature took this path, while the Uniform Law Commissioners did not?

3. Does it make sense to defer to an "ethics review committee," as the New York statute does, at least in the most serious of cases? Might the fact that these committees now have formal statutory authority enhance the status of hospital and nursing home ethics committees? Does it make sense to look to the courts as an alternative to a determination of institutional ethics committees? Since they now have formal legal authority, should these committees be required to provide due process?

4. The first reported case to address the New York statute, written by a trial court judge with clear antipathy to the statute, suggested that it changed the foundation of health care decision-making, at least under some circumstances, in New York:

> The FHCDA statute reflects a major change from the prior "presumption of life." [ ] Previously, absent indication from the principal to the contrary, a "presumption of life" applied. Here, absent such indication, a "presumption of termination" applies, especially by deprivation of artificially administered food and water. [ ] Ironically, now when a principal selects a person whom he or she trusts in a health care proxy to make decisions on his or her behalf, the law of that proxy is that, absent an indication to the contrary, that person must provide food and water [ ], while someone designated

by statute in whom the patient may have no trust whatsoever, can terminate his or her life earlier than his or her natural death by such deprivation of food and water, despite the principal never having indicated a desire for such earlier termination. Under the statute, the "quality of life ethic" has become the automatic main ethic while the "sanctity of life ethic" is given the affirmative burden to "opt out." Further, the grant of immunity to those implementing the decision for ordinary tort liability and accountability reinforces that shift in ethic.

Matter of Zornow, 919 N.Y.S.2d 273 (S. Ct. 2010). Do you think that the trial court justice is right in his analysis? He went on to do a lengthy and detailed analysis of the Catholic position on the treatments there in question after determining that Ms. Zornow, a 93–year–old woman with advanced Alzheimer's, was a Catholic and had been a daily communicant at Mass. Is that an appropriate analysis for a court to undertake? Is it relevant to deciding what the Ms. Zornow would have wanted? The court was addressing issues about which there is some dispute among Catholic theologians. Should the court hear evidence on the "real" Catholic position or use its own understanding?

NOTE ON ADVANCE DIRECTIVES AND SURROGATE CONSENT LAWS

The History of Advance Directives: The Rise of Living Wills. Nearly two decades before the Uniform Health–Care Decisions Act was proposed, many people first became concerned about the potential abuses of powerful new forms of life-sustaining medical treatment. Frightened by the "treatment" provided to Karen Quinlan, whose life was thought to be sustained by a ventilator but who was given no chance of regaining consciousness, people began to search for a way to avoid a similar fate. Within two years of the first press reports of the *Quinlan* case, several states had adopted statutes that formally recognized certain forms of written statements requesting that some kinds of medical care be discontinued. These statutes, generally referred to as "living will" statutes, "right to die" legislation, or "natural death" acts, provided a political outlet for the frustration that accompanied the empathy for Ms. Quinlan.

The statutes, which still provide the only statutory advance directive in some jurisdictions, vary among the states in several respects. In some states living wills may be executed by any person, at any time (and in some states they may be executed on behalf of minors), while in other states they require a waiting period, and may not be executed during a terminal illness. In most states they are of indefinite duration, although in some states they expire after a determined number of years.

Some statutes address only the terminally ill, others include those in "irreversible coma" or persistent vegetative state, and still others provide for different conditions to trigger the substantive provisions of the document. In many states, living wills are not effective while the patient is pregnant. Some states require the formalities of a will for the living will to be recognized by statute, while other states require different formalities. Living will statutes that do not apply to those in persistent vegetative state, irreversible coma, or any other medical condition that may not be considered "terminal" are of no assistance to people in the position of Nancy Cruzan. Is there a reason to limit legislation to terminal conditions, or should such statutes be extended to other conditions where there is broad social consensus that patients should have the right to forgo life-sustaining treatment?

The statutes generally relieve physicians and other health care providers of any civil or criminal liability for withdrawal of treatment if they properly follow the requirements of the statute. A living will is always relevant as evidence of a patient's intent, although immunity doesn't apply unless the statute is followed.

Some of the statutes require that any physician who cannot, in good conscience, carry out those provisions, transfer the patient to a physician who can. The statutes also provide that carrying out the provisions of a properly executed living will does not constitute homicide or suicide for any legal purposes. It is hard to know whether the absence of litigation over the terms of living wills means that these documents are working well or that they are not working at all. Because health care providers were not used to seeing these documents and were used to making these decisions on their own, many were reluctant to accept and follow the instructions in living wills. Many health care professionals are still reluctant to carry out advance directives, even when they are clearly legally authorized.

Many living will statutes specifically exclude "the performance of any procedure to provide nutrition or hydration" from the definition of death-prolonging or life-sustaining procedures, and thus do not extend any statutory protection to those who remove nutrition or hydration from a patient. For the most famous example, see Vernon's Ann.Mo.Stat. § 459.010(3). After the United States Supreme Court decision in *Cruzan,* are such exceptions legally meaningful? Are they Constitutional? For a fuller discussion of the legal position of the withdrawal of nutrition and hydration, see subsection C, below. For an example of judicial avoidance of the unwelcome consequences of a nutrition and hydration exception to a living will statute, see McConnell v. Beverly Enterprises–Connecticut, 209 Conn. 692, 553 A.2d 596 (1989). See also In re Guardianship of Browning, 568 So.2d 4 (Fla.1990).

The Next Step: Durable Powers of Attorney for Health Care. Another means of identifying who should speak for the patient when the patient is incompetent is to allow the competent individuals to designate a spokesperson or agent to act if the patient becomes incompetent. This may be accomplished through the patient's execution of a durable power of attorney, the most common form of advance directive available today.

Powers of attorney have been available over the past several centuries to allow for financial transactions to be consummated by agents of a principal. A power of attorney may be executed by any competent person. It provides that the agent designated shall have the right to act on behalf of the principal for purposes that are described and limited in the document itself. Thus, a principal may give an agent a power of attorney to enter into a particular contract, a particular kind of contract, or all contracts. The power may be limited by time, by geographic area, or in any other way. It may be granted to any person, who, upon appointment, becomes the agent and "attorney-in-fact" for the principal. At common law, a power of attorney expired upon the "incapacity" of the principal. This was necessary to assure that the principal could maintain adequate authority over his agent. As long as a power of attorney expired upon the incapacity of the principal, the power of attorney had no value in making medical decisions. After all, a competent patient could decide for himself; there was no reason for him to delegate authority to an agent.

In the mid–1970s it became clear that the value of the power of attorney could be increased if it could extend beyond the incapacity of the principal. For example, as an increasing number of very elderly people depended upon their children and others to handle their financial affairs, it became important that there be some device by which they could delegate their authority to these agents. For such principals it was most important that the authority remain with their agents when they did become incapacitated. The Uniform Probate Code was amended to provide for a durable power of attorney; that is, a power of attorney that would remain in effect (or even become effective) upon the incapacity of the principal if the document clearly stated that. There is no reported judicial opinion formally holding that the authority of a durable power of attorney executed under the Uniform Probate Code extends to health care decision-making. The President's Commission assumed, without any discussion, that it could be used for this purpose. See President's Commission, Deciding to Forego Life–Sustaining Treatment, 145–149 (1983). The vast majority of states have now adopted statutes that formally authorize the execution of durable powers of attorney for health care decisions.

Health care providers, who were uncertain about how to deal with living wills that were often ambiguous and rarely written with knowledge of the patient's eventual diagnosis and prognosis, were more accepting of the durable power of attorney for health care, at least in theory. Providers need a sure decision by a clear decision maker when they cannot get informed consent from a patient, and the durable powers allowed clearly identified decision makers to make exactly the decision that confronted the patient at any given moment. Durable powers, then, protected patients, who could appoint trusted family members and friends to make decisions, and physicians, who needed someone they could rely upon to be present and actually make the decisions.

Some state statutes now allow an agent authorized by a durable power of attorney to make health care decisions for a principal even if the principal has capacity—as long as that is the explicit desire of the principal. Why should an agent make a decision for a principal *with* capacity? Doesn't that undermine the principle of autonomy? Such a provision gives health care providers a surrogate decision maker to turn to in the case of a patient with capacity that is highly variable. Some argue that, in such cases, health care providers ought to be able to depend upon the consent of a patient-designated surrogate without doing a full competency analysis each time a health care decision is to be made. Of course, the decision of the surrogate can always be overruled by the patient herself if she has capacity.

The legal significance of a durable power of attorney for health care is defined by each state's durable power statute. In her concurring opinion in *Cruzan*, though, Justice O'Connor suggested that there may also be Constitutional significance to a properly executed durable power of attorney:

> I also write separately to emphasize that the Court does not today decide the issue whether a state must also give effect to the decisions of a surrogate decision-maker. In my view, such a duty may well be Constitutionally required to protect the patient's liberty interest in refusing medical treatment.

497 U.S. at 289, 110 S.Ct. at 2857. She commends those several states that have recognized "the practical wisdom of such a procedure by enacting durable power of attorney statutes;" and she suggests that a written appointment of a proxy "may be a valuable additional safeguard of the patient's interest in directing his medical care." In the final paragraph of her opinion she points out that "[t]oday's decision * * * does not preclude a future determination that the Constitution requires the states to implement the decisions of a patient's duly appointed surrogate."

The Development of the Uniform Health–Care Decisions Act. The Uniform Health–Care Decisions Act (UHCDA), excerpted above, takes a comprehensive approach to the issue by combining the living will (which is retitled the "individual instruction"), the durable power of attorney (now called the "power of attorney for health care"), a family consent law, and some provisions concerning organ donation together in one statute. Further, the statute integrates the current living will and durable power (and statement of desire to donate organs) into a single document. The UHCDA provides a statutory form, but it also explicitly declares that the form is not a mandatory one, and that individuals may draft their own form that includes only some of the kinds of instructions permitted in the unified form.

The new "individual instruction" can apply to virtually any health care decision, not just the end of life decisions to which living wills are typically applicable. Further, "health care decision" is defined very broadly.

The uniform act also makes the execution of the unified document very easy. It has no witness requirement, and it does not require that the document be notarized. The drafters of the proposed act concluded that the formalities often associated with living wills and durable powers served to discourage their execution more than to deter fraud. Despite this approach of the uniform act, most adopting states have added some execution formalities. Do you think that executing these documents ought to require witnesses, an oath, a seal, a notary, or some other formalizing act?

The residual decision-making portion of the Act is very much like the family consent statutes that have now been adopted in a majority of states and this section of the act applies only if there is no applicable individual instruction or appointed agent. While it provides for a common family hierarchy of decisionmakers for decisionally incapacitated patients, it also provides that the family can be trumped by an "orally designated surrogate," who may be appointed by a patient informing her "supervising physician" that the surrogate is entitled to make health care decisions on her behalf. Thus, patients can effectively orally appoint decision-making agents who previously could only be appointed in a writing signed pursuant to a rigorous process. Thus, in essence, any health care decision will be made by the first available in this hierarchy:

(1) the patient, if the patient has decisional capacity,

(2) the patient, through an individual instruction,

(3) an agent appointed by the patient in a written power of attorney for health care, unless a court has given this authority explicitly to a guardian,

(4) a guardian appointed by the court,

(5) a surrogate appointed orally by the patient,

(6) a surrogate selected from the list of family members and others who can make health care decisions on behalf of the patient.

The drafters of the UHCDA make it clear in their comments that one purpose of the statute is to assure that these intimate health care decisions remain within the realm of the patient, the patient's family and close friends, and the health care providers, and that others not be permitted to disrupt that process. The court would very rarely have a role in any decision-making under this statute, and outsiders (including outside organizations) who do not think a patient is adequately protected have no standing to seek judicial intervention. See Protection and Advocacy System, Inc. v. Presbyterian Healthcare Services, 128 N.M. 73, 989 P.2d 890 (1999).

The UHCDA explicitly provides that the decision maker (whether an agent, guardian or surrogate) should make a decision based on the principle of substituted judgment rather than the best interest principle. If it is impossible to apply the substituted judgment principle, the statute would allow the substitute decision maker to apply the best interests principle.

The UHCDA includes the normal raft of recordkeeping provisions, limitations on the reach of the criminal law, assurances regarding the insurance rights of those who execute the documents, and restrictions on the liability of those who act under the statute in good faith. A provision for $500 in liquidated damages in actions for breach of the act may not encourage litigation when the statute is ignored, but the provision for attorney's fees in those cases might provide an incentive for lawyers to bring those cases. The act applies only to adults.

Family Consent Laws. Over the past century, it became standard medical practice to seek consent to any medical procedure from close family members of an incompetent patient. There is no common law authority for this practice; it is an example of medical practice (and good common sense) being subtly absorbed by the law. The President's Commission suggests five reasons for this deference to family members:

(1) The family is generally most concerned about the good of the patient.

(2) The family will also usually be most knowledgeable about the patient's goals, preferences, and values.

(3) The family deserves recognition as an important social unit that ought to be treated, within limits, as a responsible decision maker in matters that intimately affect its members.

(4) Especially in a society in which many other traditional forms of community have eroded, participation in a family is often an important dimension of personal fulfillment.

(5) Since a protected sphere of privacy and autonomy is required for the flourishing of this interpersonal union, institutions and the state should be reluctant to intrude, particularly regarding matters that are personal and on which there is a wide range of opinion in society.

President's Commission, Deciding to Forego Life–Sustaining Treatment, 127 (1983). It is difficult to determine whether the resort to close relatives to give consent is merely a procedural device to discover what the patient, if competent, would choose, or whether it is based in an independent substantive doctrine. Although it seems essentially procedural—the family is most likely to know what the patient would choose—many courts are willing to accept most decisions of family members even when there is little support for the position that these family members are actually choosing what the patient would choose. Of course, the assumptions about family relationships are quite optimistic. Consulting with family members also neutralizes potential malpractice plaintiffs; this factor partially accounts for part of the longstanding popularity of this decision-making process among health care providers.

Over the past two decades most states have enacted family consent laws that authorize statutorily designated family members to make health care decisions for their relatives in circumscribed situations. These statutes often apply to a wide range of health care decisions (including, in most cases, decisions to forgo life-sustaining treatment), although sometimes they apply only when there has been a physician's certification of the patient's inability to make the health care decision. Sometimes they are limited to particular kinds of treatment (e.g., cardiopulmonary resuscitation) or excluded from deciding about particular treatments (like discontinuing nutrition and hydration). In addition, "family consent laws" often provide immunity from liability for family members and physicians acting in good faith, and judicial authority to resolve disputes about the authority of the family members under the statutes. The definition of "family member" and the position of each family member in the hierarchy vary from state to state, although you should note that the Uniform Health Care Decisions Act and the New York Family Health Care Decisions Act have the same family hierarchy: spouse, adult child, parents, sibling, close friend. Are there other classes of decision makers you would add to that hierarchy? In some states those in a long term spouse-like relationship with the patient are included in the list of family members who can make decisions for the incompetent patient; in some states they are not. Some lists include a residuary class of anyone who knows the values, interest, and wishes of the patient; some states list the physician as the residuary decision maker; some provide for no residuary decision maker. Some states give a general guardian top priority; some states place surrogates actually appointed by the patient (whether family members or not) ahead of the general guardian.

Physicians' orders regarding end-of-life care. Health care providers remain inconsistent in their recognition and implementation of advance directives, even when there is no doubt about the authenticity or legality of the advance directive under local law. By custom, health care institutions and health care workers caring for patients rely on orders given by the health care professional responsible for the patient's treatment, not on documents signed outside of the health care system. Recognizing the strength of this custom, some patient advocates argue that the best way to protect a patient's interests at the end of life is to incorporate the patient's health care decisions into a physician's order. One particularly effective way of doing this is to incorporate those decisions into a Physician Order for Life Sustaining Treatment (POLST). A POLST (which goes by a variety of other names with other acronyms in other states—MOST, MOLST, SMOST, TPOP, or, in the Veteran's Administration hospitals, SAPO) may include information about a patient's decisions with regard to resuscitation orders, the extent of appropriate medical intervention, the use of antibiotics and other pharmaceuticals, the provision of nutrition and hydration, the desired place of treatment (home, hospital or nursing home), the identity of the authorized health care decision maker, and other relevant issues likely to arise in each case. Modeled on emergency medical services' DNR or DNAR ("do not resuscitate," or, more recently, "do not attempt resuscitation") orders, the POLST is a real medical order, signed by a health care provider—in some states it must be a physician, but not in most—with authority to issue that order. As a result, it is more likely to be implemented across health care settings: in the emergency room, at the rehabilitation hospital, in the nursing home, and in the field. It is designed to travel with the patient as the patient moves among these health care settings.

POLST forms are generally entered in the patient's medical record after the provider has discussed all of the relevant issues with the patient, the patient's family, the agent or surrogate authorized to make health care decisions, and others. The POLST form may include a summary of the values and goals of the patient that form the basis of the order, and the nature of the discussions that gave rise to the order. The patient or the patient's decision maker is often asked to countersign the order, so it is clear that it represents the agreed view of the patient and the provider. Sometimes the patient's (or the patient's representative's) signature is required; sometimes it is not. In some jurisdictions there is no place for the countersignature at all. In order to assure that these forms are not lost in the patient's chart, they are often printed on distinctively colored (usually bright pink or bright green) paper. Such orders can be recognized by state law (as they are in a many states), or by institutional or community policy.

The process of entering a POLST requires discussion among all of the relevant parties, and it provides a way of integrating a patient's advance directive and the physician's order. It does not trump a legally authorized advance directive, but it may make it easier for succeeding health care providers to be aware of advance directives made earlier by the patient; and it eliminates a provider's concern over the obligation to carry out an advance directive that appears to be inconsistent with an order of a physician. The POLST is usually filled out when the need for end-of-life care is imminent by those familiar with the current medical needs of the patient, and those factors may also account for the very high level of implementation of these documents.

Some people are concerned that the development of the POLST paradigm marks a return to the days of paternalistic medicine when it was the physician, not the patient, who decided the treatment to be applied in each case. Here, the provider's signature on the POLST effectively supplants the patient's signature on an advance directive, although the effect is ameliorated by the fact that the entry of a POLST requires a discussion with the patient or the substitute decision maker, and, often, that person's signature as well. Does the POLST require a patient to give up some level of autonomy that the patient might have had when making decisions through other forms of advance directives? Is the fact that the POLST really will be honored enough to get in return to justify giving up that autonomy? For a full account of the current state of POLSTs in the United States (and Canada, and Australia, where similar concepts have developed) see Thaddeus Mason Pope and Melinda Hexum, Legal Briefing: POLST: Physicians Order for Life–Sustaining Treatment, 36 J. Clinical Ethics 353 (2012). See also, Keith Sonderling, POLST: A Cure for the Common Advance Directive—It's Just What the Doctor Ordered, 33 Nova L. Rev. 451 (2009) and Susan Hickman et al., Hope for the Future: Achieving the Original Intent of Advance Directives, 35 Hastings Ctr. Rep. (6) Supp. 26–30 (2005).

Religious objections to some provisions of advance directives.
Some religious denominations have principled objections to facilitating certain decisions that might be made in advance directives. These objections are reflected in a range of state statutes because those statutes are products of political compromise. For example, as this note suggests, many states limit the applicability of advance directives when the patient is pregnant or when the patient wishes to reject some forms of nutrition or hydration. These limitations are consistent with the tenets of particular religious groups (although there are secular arguments to support them as well). Advance directive laws without these explicit limitations often include other "conscience" provisions which serve to relieve health care institutions and individual providers from taking actions which violate their own values. See section 7(e) of the Uniform Health–Care Decisions Act, above.

What should happen when a patient with particular values makes a decision that is protected by law in that jurisdiction but inconsistent with the religious values of a health care institution? What if the legally authorized decision maker (through a durable power of attorney) or the patient (through an individual instruction) requests that all artificial nutrition and hydration be terminated if the patient is in persistent vegetative state, but the patient finds himself in a religious hospital that refuses to honor that decision? What if a patient seeking palliative sedation finds himself at a religious hospital that, as a matter of religious and ethical principle, will not provide that form of treatment? What if the family of a religious person seeks the continuation of nutrition and hydration as long as the patient remains in persistent vegetative state, treatment arguably required by the patient's faith, in an institution that considers it to be a medically useless and futile form of treatment? Several advocacy groups now provide sample language that individuals can include in their advance directives to request that, if the patient must be hospitalized, the hospitalization take place—for example—in a Catholic hospital bound by the Ethical and Religious Directives of the Catholic Church, or alternatively, that the patient *not* be hospitalized in a Catholic hospital bound by the ERDs. Should providers be bound by that kind of request, on either side? Under the California Right to Know End of Life Options Act and the New York Palliative Care Information Act, must hospitalized patients be told of legal alternatives that might not be available at the hospital because they are not permitted by religious doctrine? Is it a violation of the First Amendment to require that those institutions provide care (or information about care) to which they have strong moral objection?

The Patient Self–Determination Act and Advance Directives. The federal Patient Self–Determination Act applies to hospitals, skilled nursing facilities, home health agencies, hospice programs, and HMOs that receive Medicaid or Medicare funding. It requires each of those covered by the Act to provide each patient with written information concerning:

(i) an individual's rights under State law (whether statutory or as recognized by the courts of the State) to make decisions concerning * * * medical care, including the right to accept or refuse medical or

surgical treatment and the right to formulate advance directives
* * * and

(ii) the written policies of the provider or organization respecting
the implementation of such rights.

42 U.S.C.A. § 1395cc(a)(1)(f)(1)(A). In addition, those covered must document
in each patient's record whether that patient has signed an advance directive,
assure that the state law is followed in the institution, and provide for education of both the staff and the public concerning living wills and durable powers of attorney.

A few states have also taken action to increase the utility of advance directives. For example, some states have central registries of advance directives, and a handful of states provide for drivers' licenses to show if a patient
has an advance directive. At least one statute requires managed health care
providers to discuss advance directives with their patients/enrollees. There
has also been some attention given to how to make advance directives of various stripes enforced across state and provincial borders.

B. DECISION–MAKING IN THE ABSENCE OF ADVANCE DIRECTIVES OR STATUTORILY DESIGNATED SURROGATES

IN RE EICHNER

New York Court of Appeals, 1981.
52 N.Y.2d 363, 438 N.Y.S.2d 266, 420 N.E.2d 64.

WACHTLER, JUDGE.

For over 66 years Brother Joseph Fox was a member of the Society of
Mary, a Catholic religious order which, among other things, operates
Chaminade High School in Mineola. * * *

While [an] operation was being performed * * * he suffered cardiac
arrest, with resulting loss of oxygen to the brain and substantial brain
damage. He lost the ability to breathe spontaneously and was placed on a
respirator which maintained him in a vegetative state. The attending
physicians informed Father Philip Eichner, who was the president of
Chaminade and the director of the society at the school, that there was no
reasonable chance of recovery and that Brother Fox would die in that
state.

After retaining two neurosurgeons who confirmed the diagnosis, Father Eichner requested the hospital to remove the respirator. The hospital, however, refused to do so without court authorization. Father Eichner
then applied * * * to be appointed committee of the person and property of
Brother Fox, with authority to direct removal of the respirator. The appli-

cation was supported by the patient's 10 nieces and nephews, his only surviving relatives. The court appointed a guardian ad litem and directed that notice be served on various parties, including the District Attorney.

At the hearing the District Attorney opposed the application and called medical experts to show that there might be some improvement in the patient's condition. All the experts agreed, however, that there was no reasonable likelihood that Brother Fox would ever emerge from the vegetative coma or recover his cognitive powers.

There was also evidence, submitted by the petitioner, that before the operation rendered him incompetent the patient had made it known that under these circumstances he would want a respirator removed. Brother Fox had first expressed this view in 1976 when the Chaminade community discussed the moral implications of the celebrated *Karen Ann Quinlan* case, in which the parents of a 19–year–old New Jersey girl who was in a vegetative coma requested the hospital to remove the respirator [ ]. These were formal discussions prompted by Chaminade's mission to teach and promulgate Catholic moral principles. At that time it was noted that the Pope had stated that Catholic principles permitted the termination of extraordinary life support systems when there is no reasonable hope for the patient's recovery and that church officials in New Jersey had concluded that use of the respirator in the *Quinlan* case constituted an extraordinary measure under the circumstances. Brother Fox expressed agreement with those views and stated that he would not want any of this "extraordinary business" done for him under those circumstances. Several years later, and only a couple of months before his final hospitalization, Brother Fox again stated that he would not want his life prolonged by such measures if his condition were hopeless.

* * *

In this case the proof was compelling. There was no suggestion that the witnesses who testified for the petitioner had any motive other than to see that Brother Fox' stated wishes were respected. The finding that he carefully reflected on the subject, expressed his views and concluded not to have his life prolonged by medical means if there were no hope of recovery is supported by his religious beliefs and is not inconsistent with his life of unselfish religious devotion. These were obviously solemn pronouncements and not casual remarks made at some social gathering, nor can it be said that he was too young to realize or feel the consequences of his statements [ ]. That this was a persistent commitment is evidenced by the fact that he reiterated the decision but two months before his final hospitalization. There was, of course, no need to speculate as to whether he would want this particular medical procedure to be discontinued under these circumstances. What occurred to him was identical to what happened in the *Karen Ann Quinlan* case, which had originally prompted his decision. In sum, the evidence clearly and convincingly shows that Brother Fox did not want to be maintained in a vegetative coma by use of a respirator.

* * *

NOTES AND QUESTIONS

1.   The Illinois Supreme Court described the principle of substituted judgment clearly and simply:

> Under substituted judgment, a surrogate decisionmaker attempts to establish, with as much accuracy as possible, what decision the patient would make if he were competent to do so. Employing this theory, the surrogate first tries to determine if the patient had expressed explicit intent regarding this type of medical treatment prior to becoming incompetent. [ ] Where no clear intent exists, the patient's personal value system must guide the surrogate. * * *

In re Estate of Longeway, 133 Ill.2d 33, 139 Ill.Dec. 780, 549 N.E.2d 292, 299 (1989).

2.   In applying the principle of substituted judgment, most courts look wherever they can to determine the patient's wishes. In Brophy v. New England Sinai Hosp., Inc., 398 Mass. 417, 497 N.E.2d 626 (1986), the Massachusetts Supreme Court based its conclusion that food and hydration could be withheld from a comatose adult on the substituted judgment analysis done by the lower court.

> [After full hearing] the judge found on the basis of ample evidence which no one disputes, that Brophy's judgment would be to decline the provision of food and water and to terminate his life. In reaching that conclusion, the judge considered various factors including the following: (1) Brophy's expressed preferences; (2) his religious convictions and their relation to refusal of treatment; (3) the impact on his family; (4) the probability of adverse side effects; and (5) the prognosis, both with and without treatment. The judge also considered present and future incompetency as an element which Brophy would consider in his decision-making process. The judge relied on several statements made by Brophy prior to the onset of his illness. Although he never had discussed specifically whether a G-tube or feeding tube should be withdrawn in the event that he was diagnosed as being in a persistent vegetative state following his surgery, the judge inferred that, if presently competent, Brophy would choose to forgo artificial nutrition and hydration by means of a G-tube. The judge found that Brophy would not likely view his own religion as a barrier to that choice.

3.   Other factors that have been considered include the patient's diagnosis, life history, ability to knowingly participate in treatment, potential quality of life, and, more generally, the patient's values and attitude toward health care. See, e.g., Mack v. Mack, 329 Md. 188, 618 A.2d 744 (1993) (focusing on the "moral views, life goals, and values" of the patient, and her "attitudes toward sickness, medical procedures, suffering and death"), and De-Grella v. Elston, 858 S.W.2d 698 (Ky.1993). For a thorough and well annotated list of relevant factors that have been considered by the courts see Alan Meisel & Kathy L. Cerminara, The Right to Die, 3rd ed. (2004).

4.   How difficult is it for a surrogate decision maker to distinguish what the patient would really want from what that decision maker would want if she were in the position of that patient? Is it really possible to clearly distinguish the subjective "substituted judgment" standard from an objective standard that asks what a reasonable person would do under the circumstances? Courts do struggle to distinguish the "substituted judgment" and "best interest" principles, and even those who appear to adopt the "best interest" approach may qualify it by requiring that the best interest of the patient be defined in terms of the wishes, values and desires of the patient. Some state courts appear to adopt the best interest test while they actually take the "substituted judgment" approach. See Conservatorship of Drabick, 200 Cal.App.3d 185, 245 Cal.Rptr. 840 (1988) (discussed in *Wendland*, below) and In re Gordy, 658 A.2d 613 (Del.Ch.1994).

IN RE CONROY

Supreme Court of New Jersey, 1985.
98 N.J. 321, 486 A.2d 1209.

SCHREIBER, JUSTICE.

* * * [W]e hold that life-sustaining treatment may be withheld or withdrawn from an incompetent patient when it is clear that the particular patient would have refused the treatment under the circumstances involved. The standard we are enunciating is a subjective one, consistent with the notion that the right that we are seeking to effectuate is a very personal right to control one's own life. The question is not what a reasonable or average person would have chosen to do under the circumstances but what the particular patient would have done if able to choose for himself.

* * *

We * * * hold that life-sustaining treatment may also be withheld or withdrawn from a patient in Claire Conroy's situation [i.e., a patient who was competent but is now incompetent] if either of two "best interests" tests—a limited-objective or a pure-objective test—is satisfied.

Under the limited-objective test, life-sustaining treatment may be withheld or withdrawn from a patient in Claire Conroy's situation when there is some trustworthy evidence that the patient would have refused the treatment, and the decision maker is satisfied that it is clear that the burdens of the patient's continued life with the treatment outweigh the benefits of that life for him. By this we mean that the patient is suffering, and will continue to suffer throughout the expected duration of his life, unavoidable pain, and that the net burdens of his prolonged life (the pain and suffering of his life with the treatment less the amount and duration of pain that the patient would likely experience if the treatment were withdrawn) markedly outweigh any physical pleasure, emotional enjoyment, or intellectual satisfaction that the patient may still be able to derive from life. This limited-objective standard permits the termination of treatment for a patient who had not unequivocally expressed his desires before becoming incompetent, when it is clear that the treatment in question would merely prolong the patient's suffering.

* * *

This limited-objective test also requires some trustworthy evidence that the patient would have wanted the treatment terminated. This evidence could take any one or more of the various forms appropriate to prove the patient's intent under the subjective test. Evidence that, taken as a whole, would be too vague, casual, or remote to constitute the clear proof of the patient's subjective intent that is necessary to satisfy the subjective test—for example, informally expressed reactions to other people's medical conditions and treatment—might be sufficient to satisfy this prong of the limited-objective test.

In the absence of trustworthy evidence, or indeed any evidence at all, that the patient would have declined the treatment, life-sustaining treatment may still be withheld or withdrawn from a formerly competent person like Claire Conroy if a third, pure-objective test is satisfied. Under that test, as under the limited-objective test, the net burdens of the patient's life with the treatment should clearly and markedly outweigh the benefits that the patient derives from life. Further, the recurring, unavoidable and severe pain of the patient's life with the treatment should be such that the effect of administering life-sustaining treatment would be inhumane. Subjective evidence that the patient would not have wanted the treatment is not necessary under this pure-objective standard. Nevertheless, even in the context of severe pain, life-sustaining treatment should not be withdrawn from an incompetent patient who had previously expressed a wish to be kept alive in spite of any pain that he might experience.

* * * [W]e expressly decline to authorize decision-making based on assessments of the personal worth or social utility of another's life, or the value of that life to others.

*   *   *

We are aware that it will frequently be difficult to conclude that the evidence is sufficient to justify termination of treatment under either of the "best interests" tests that we have described. Often, it is unclear whether and to what extent a patient such as Claire Conroy is capable of, or is in fact, experiencing pain. Similarly, medical experts are often unable to determine with any degree of certainty the extent of a nonverbal person's intellectual functioning or the depth of his emotional life. When the evidence is insufficient to satisfy either the limited-objective or pure-objective standard, however, we cannot justify the termination of life-sustaining treatment as clearly furthering the best interests of a patient like Ms. Conroy.

* * * When evidence of a person's wishes or physical or mental condition is equivocal, it is best to err, if at all, in favor of preserving life. * * *

NOTES AND QUESTIONS

1.   The most substantial criticism of the "subjective", "limited-objective" and "pure objective" classifications is provided in In re Martin, 450 Mich. 204, 538 N.W.2d 399 (1995):

> Rather than choose between the best interest standard and the substituted judgment standard, the New Jersey Supreme Court attempted to synthesize these two standards by creating an hierarchical decision-making continuum. [ ]. The starting point on the continuum is anchored by a purely subjective analysis, an approach that requires more definitive evidence of what the patient would choose than the substituted judgment standard. The other end of the continuum is anchored by a purely objective analysis, which is, in essence, a best interest standard.

> We find that a purely subjective analysis is the most appropriate standard to apply under the circumstances of this case. The pure subjective standard allows the surrogate to withhold life-sustaining treatment from an incompetent patient "when it is clear that the particular patient would have refused the treatment under the circumstances involved." [ ]. Given that the right the surrogate is seeking to effectuate is the incompetent patient's right to control his own life, "the question is not what a reasonable or average person would have chosen to do under the circumstances but what the particular patient would have done if able to chose for himself."

> The subjective and objective standards involve conceptually different bases for allowing he surrogate to make treatment decisions. The subjective standard is based on a patient's right to self-determination, while the objective standard is grounded in the state's parens patriae power. [ ]. An objective, best interest, stand-

ard cannot be grounded in the common-law right of informed consent because the right and the decision-making standard inherently conflict.

*   *   *

Any move from a purely subjective standard to an analysis that encompasses objective criteria is grounded in the state's parens patriae power, not in the common-law right of informed consent or self-determination. Thus, while the clearly expressed wishes of a patient, while competent, should be honored regardless of the patient's condition, we find nothing that prevents the state from grounding any objective analysis on a threshold requirement of pain, terminal illness, foreseeable death, a persistent vegetative state, or affliction of a similar genre.

Martin, 538 N.W.2d at 407–408. Do you agree that only the decision to apply the subjective standard (and not the decision to apply the two objective standards) can be justified by the principles behind the doctrine of informed consent? Is the application of any form of objective test (whether it be termed "substituted judgment" or "best interest") a *per se* violation of the principle of autonomy, as *Martin* suggests? If this is true, what is the justification for the application of the theory of substituted judgment? See Rebecca Dresser & John Robertson, Quality of Life and Non–Treatment Decisions for Incompetent Patients, a Critique of the Orthodox Approach, 17 L. Med. & Health Care 234 (1989).

2.   Despite its rejection in the *Martin* case, the *Conroy* case and its tests have been extremely influential. Even the New Jersey courts, however, have been reluctant to apply it when the patient is in persistent vegetative state. Persistent vegetative state describes a condition where a patient is physically alive but "functioning entirely in terms of [the body's] internal controls;" where "there is no behavioral evidence of either self-awareness or awareness of the surroundings * * *." In re Jobes, 108 N.J. 394, 529 A.2d 434, 438 (1987). See also *Cruzan*, above. As the New Jersey Supreme Court pointed out in a companion case,

> While a benefits-burdens analysis is difficult with marginally cognitive patients like Claire Conroy, it is essentially impossible with patients in a persistent vegetative state. By definition such patients, like Ms. Peter, do not experience any of the benefits or burdens that the *Conroy* balancing tests are intended or able to appraise. Therefore, we hold that these tests should not be applied to patients in the persistent vegetative state.

In re Peter, 108 N.J. 365, 529 A.2d 419, 424–425 (1987). Essentially, the court found that there were no measurable benefits or burdens of continuing life in the case of a patient with persistent vegetative state. There could be no pain, happiness, sadness, sense of dignity, sense of hope, or, really, any meaningful sense of the current experience of a patient who is in persistent vegetative state, and thus no way to balance any such burdens and benefits.

Does it make any sense to treat a patient in a persistent vegetative state any differently from another incompetent patient? Should it be easier or harder to remove life-sustaining medical care from a patient in a persistent vegetative state? What position does the Uniform Health–Care Decisions Act take with respect to patients in a persistent vegetative state? Are they treated any differently from patients who are not in that condition?

NOTE ON DISTINCTIONS AS TO TREATMENT: "ACTIVE" AND "PASSIVE" CONDUCT, "WITHHOLDING" AND "WITHDRAWING" TREATMENT, AND "ORDINARY" AND "EXTRAORDINARY" TREATMENT

Distinctions between "active" and "passive" conduct and between "withholding" and "withdrawing" treatment are anachronistic distinctions which have not found a safe harbor in the law, just as they have been increasingly recognized as meaningless in ethics. The *Conroy* opinion considered each of these distinctions, and summarized the ethical and legal literature and the reasons for rejecting the distinctions. As to the distinction between active and passive conduct, the *Conroy* court announced:

> We emphasize that in making decisions whether to administer life-sustaining treatment to patients such as Claire Conroy, the primary focus should be the patient's desires and experience of pain and enjoyment—not the type of treatment involved. Thus, we reject the distinction that some have made between actively hastening death by terminating treatment and passively allowing a person to die of a disease as one of limited use in a legal analysis of such a decision-making situation.

> Characterizing conduct as active or passive is often an elusive notion, even outside the context of medical decision-making * * *. The distinction is particularly nebulous, however, in the context of decisions whether to withhold or withdraw life-sustaining treatment. In a case like that of Claire Conroy, for example, would a physician who discontinued nasogastric feeding be actively causing her death by removing her primary source of nutrients; or would he merely be omitting to continue the artificial form of treatment, thus passively allowing her medical condition, which includes her inability to swallow, to take its natural course? [ ] The ambiguity inherent in this distinction is further heightened when one performs an act within an over-all plan of non-intervention, such as when a doctor writes an order not to resuscitate a patient. * * *

> For a similar reason, we also reject any distinction between withholding and withdrawing life-sustaining treatment. Some commentators have suggested that discontinuing life-sustaining treatment

once it has been commenced is morally more problematic than merely failing to begin the treatment. Discontinuing life-sustaining treatment, to some, is an "active" taking of life, as opposed to the more "passive" act of omitting the treatment in the first instance.

This distinction is more psychologically compelling than logically sound. As mentioned above, the line between active and passive conduct in the context of medical decisions is far too nebulous to constitute a principled basis for decision-making. Whether necessary treatment is withheld at the outset or withdrawn later on, the consequence—the patient's death—is the same. Moreover, from a policy standpoint, it might well be unwise to forbid persons from discontinuing a treatment under circumstances in which the treatment could permissibly be withheld. Such a rule could discourage families and doctors from even attempting certain types of care and could thereby force them into hasty and premature decisions to allow a patient to die. [ ]

486 A.2d at 1233–1234.

As to the distinction between "ordinary" and "extraordinary" treatment, *Conroy* pointed out:

We also find unpersuasive the distinction relied upon by some courts, commentators, and theologians between "ordinary" treatment, which they would always require, and "extraordinary" treatment, which they deem optional. * * * The terms "ordinary" and "extraordinary" have assumed too many conflicting meanings to remain useful. To draw a line on this basis for determining whether treatment should be given leads to a semantical milieu that does not advance the analysis.

The distinction between ordinary and extraordinary treatment is frequently phrased as one between common and unusual, or simple and complex, treatment [ ]; "extraordinary" treatment also has been equated with elaborate, artificial, heroic, aggressive, expensive, or highly involved or invasive forms of medical intervention [ ]. Depending on the definitions applied, a particular treatment for a given patient may be considered both ordinary and extraordinary. [ ] Further, since the common/unusual and simple/complex distinctions among medical treatments "exist on continuums with no precise dividing line," [ ] and the continuum is constantly shifting due to progress in medical care, disagreement will often exist about whether a particular treatment is ordinary or extraordinary. In addition, the competent patient generally could refuse even ordinary treatment; therefore, an incompetent patient theoretically should also be able to make such a choice when the surrogate decision-making is effectuating the patient's subjective intent. In such cases, the ordinary/extraordinary distinction is irrelevant except insofar as the particular patient would have made the distinction.

The ordinary/extraordinary distinction has also been discussed in terms of the benefits and burdens of treatment for the patient. If the benefits of the treatment outweigh the burdens it imposes on the patient, it is characterized as ordinary and therefore ethically required; if not, it is characterized as extraordinary and therefore optional. [ ] This formulation is extremely fact-sensitive and would lead to different classifications of the same treatment in different situations.

* * * Moreover, while the analysis may be useful in weighing the implications of the specific treatment for the patient, essentially it merely restates the question: whether the burdens of a treatment so clearly outweigh its benefits to the patient that continued treatment would be inhumane.

468 A.2d at 1234–1235. See also Brophy v. New England Sinai Hosp., Inc., 398 Mass. 417, 497 N.E.2d 626 (1986) ("while we believe that the distinction between extraordinary and ordinary care is a factor to be considered, the use of such a distinction as the sole, or major, factor of decision tends * * * to create a distinction without meaning.")

NOTE: THE SPECIAL STATUS OF NUTRITION AND HYDRATION

The issue of withdrawing nutrition and hydration has become an especially contentious one. Medical sources generally recognize the irrelevancy of distinguishing between nutrition and hydration and other forms of medical treatment. The Council on Ethical and Judicial Affairs of the American Medical Association has determined that "[l]ife-sustaining treatment may include, but is not limited to, * * * artificial nutrition or hydration." Opinion 2.20 (2006–2007 ed.). Generally, courts also have concluded that the termination of nutrition and hydration is no different from the termination of other forms of mechanical support. For example, Conroy suggested:

Some commentators, * * * have made yet [another] distinction, between the termination of artificial feedings and the termination of other forms of life-sustaining medical treatment. * * * According to the Appellate Division:

If, as here, the patient is not comatose and does not face imminent and inevitable death, nourishment accomplishes the substantial benefit of sustaining life until the illness takes its natural course. Under such circumstances nourishment always will be an essential element of ordinary care which physicians are ethically obligated to provide. [ ]

Certainly, feeding has an emotional significance. As infants we could breathe without assistance, but we were dependent on others for our lifeline of nourishment. Even more, feeding is an expression of nurturing and caring, certainly for infants and children, and in many cases for adults as well.

Once one enters the realm of complex, high-technology medical care, it is hard to shed the emotional symbolism of food. * * * Analytically, artificial feeding by means of a nasogastric tube or intravenous infusion can be seen as equivalent to artificial breathing by means of a respirator. Both prolong life through mechanical means when the body is no longer able to perform a vital bodily function on its own.

Furthermore, while nasogastric feeding and other medical procedures to ensure nutrition and hydration are usually well tolerated, they are not free from risks or burdens; they have complications that are sometimes serious and distressing to the patient.

Finally, dehydration may well not be distressing or painful to a dying patient. For patients who are unable to sense hunger and thirst, withholding of feeding devices such as nasogastric tubes may not result in more pain than the termination of any other medical treatment. * * * Thus, it cannot be assumed that it will always be beneficial for an incompetent patient to receive artificial feeding or harmful for him not to receive it. * * *

Under the analysis articulated above, withdrawal or withholding of artificial feeding, like any other medical treatment, would be permissible if there is sufficient proof to satisfy the subjective, limited-objective, or pure-objective test. A competent patient has the right to decline any medical treatment, including artificial feeding, and should retain that right when and if he becomes incompetent. In addition, in the case of an incompetent patient who has given little or no trustworthy indication of an intent to decline treatment and for whom it becomes necessary to engage in balancing under the limited-objective or pure-objective test, the pain and invasiveness of an artificial feeding device, and the pain of withdrawing that device, should be treated just like the results of administering or withholding any other medical treatment.

98 N.J. 321, 486 A.2d 1209, 1235–1237.

See also Gray v. Romeo, 697 F.Supp. 580 (D.R.I.1988) ("Although an emotional symbolism attaches itself to artificial feeding, there is no legal difference between a mechanical device that allows a person to breathe artificially and a mechanical device that allows a person nourishment. If a person has right to decline a respirator, then a person has the equal right to decline a gastrostomy tube."); Brophy v. New England Sinai Hosp., Inc., 398 Mass. 417, 497 N.E.2d 626 (1986); Corbett v. D'Alessandro, 487 So.2d 368 (Fla.App.1986) ("we see no reason to differentiate between the multitude of artificial devices that may be available to prolong the moment of death."); Bouvia v. Superior Court, 179 Cal.App.3d 1127, 225 Cal.Rptr. 297 (1986).

In McConnell v. Beverly Enterprises–Connecticut, 209 Conn. 692, 553 A.2d 596 (1989), the court authorized the withdrawal of feeding by a gastrostomy tube despite a statute that appeared to say that under such circumstances "nutrition and hydration must be provided." The court reasoned that the nutrition and hydration that was implicated in the statute was that provided by "a spoon or a straw," and that feeding by gastrostomy tube was no different than any other mechanical or electronic medical intervention.

In 1990, at least, a majority of the Supreme Court (the four dissenters and concurring Justice O'Connor in *Cruzan*) viewed nutrition and hydration as another form of medical care. As Justice O'Connor pointed out, "artificial feeding cannot readily be distinguished from other forms of medical treatment. Whether or not the techniques used to pass food and water into the patient's alimentary tract are termed 'medical treatment,' it is clear they all involve some degree of intrusion and restraint." She concluded that "the liberty guaranteed by the due process clause must protect, if it protects anything, an individual's deeply personal decision to reject medical treatment, including the artificial delivery of food and water."

In his dissent, Justice Brennan reached the same conclusion, vividly describing the medical processes involved:

> The artificial delivery of nutrition and hydration is undoubtedly medical treatment. The technique to which Nancy Cruzan is subject—artificial feeding through a gastrostomy tube—involves a tube implanted surgically into her stomach through incisions in her abdominal wall. It may obstruct the intestinal tract, erode and pierce the stomach wall, or cause leakage of the stomach's contents into the abdominal cavity. [ ] The tube can cause pneumonia from reflux of the stomach's contents into the lung. [ ] Typically, and in this case, commercially prepared formulas are used, rather than fresh food. [ ] The type of formula and method of administration must be experimented with to avoid gastrointestinal problems. [ ] The patient must be monitored daily by medical personnel as to weight, fluid intake and fluid output; blood tests must be done weekly.

> Artificial delivery of food and water is regarded as medical treatment by the medical profession and the federal government. * * * The federal government permits the cost of the medical devices and formulas used in enteral feeding to be reimbursed under Medicare. [ ] The formulas are regulated by the Federal Drug Administration as "medical foods," [ ] and the feeding tubes are regulated as medical devices [ ].

497 U.S. at 306–308, 110 S.Ct. at 2866–67.

To many, nutrition and hydration remain symbols of the bonds between human beings; the care we provide to the ones we love includes, at the very least, food and water. For others, the provision of artificial nutrition and hydration has religious and moral significance.

C. THE ROLE OF THE COURTS WHERE THERE IS DISAGREEMENT AMONG POTENTIAL DECISION– MAKERS

There is a near consensus that where a patient has not left a formal prior directive, the goal of medicine should be to do what that patient, if competent, would want done. When, if ever, is it necessary for a court to be involved in making that decision—and when should the decision be left to the family, health care providers, or others? If the court is involved, what procedures should it employ? The procedural issues which have caused the greatest difficulty for state courts are the nature of evidence that would be relevant in determining a patient's wishes and the burden of proof to be applied to decisions to authorize the removal of life-sustaining treatment. As you read the next case, which formally address these issues, ask what kind of evidence should be (1) relevant and (2) sufficient for a determination of this issue.

CONSERVATORSHIP OF WENDLAND
Supreme Court of California, 2001.
26 Cal.4th 519, 28 P.3d 151, 110 Cal.Rptr.2d 412.

WERDEGAR, J.

In this case we consider whether a conservator of the person may withhold artificial nutrition and hydration from a conscious conservatee who is not terminally ill, comatose, or in a persistent vegetative state, and who has not left formal instructions for health care or appointed an agent or surrogate for health care decisions. Interpreting the Probate Code in light of the relevant provisions of the California Constitution, we conclude a conservator may not withhold artificial nutrition and hydration from such a person absent clear and convincing evidence the conservator's decision is in accordance with either the conservatee's own wishes or best interest.

The trial court in the case before us, applying the clear and convincing evidence standard, found the evidence on both points insufficient and, thus, denied the conservator's request for authority to withhold artificial nutrition and hydration. The Court of Appeal, which believed the trial court was required to defer to the conservator's good faith decision, reversed. We reverse the decision of the Court of Appeal.

I. FACTS AND PROCEDURAL HISTORY

On September 29, 1993, Robert Wendland rolled his truck at high speed in a solo accident while driving under the influence of alcohol. The accident injured Robert's brain, leaving him conscious yet severely disabled, both mentally and physically, and dependent on artificial nutrition and hydration. Two years later Rose Wendland, Robert's wife and conservator, proposed to direct his physician to remove his feeding tube and allow him to die . . . Robert's mother and sister . . . objected to the conservator's decision. This proceeding arose under the provisions of the Probate Code authorizing courts to settle such disputes.

Following the accident, Robert remained in a coma, totally unresponsive, for several months. During this period Rose visited him daily, often with their children, and authorized treatment as necessary to maintain his health.

Robert eventually regained consciousness. * * * At his highest level of function * * * Robert was able to do such things as throw and catch a ball, operate an electric wheelchair with assistance, turn pages, draw circles, draw an "R" and perform two-step commands. For example, "[h]e was able to respond appropriately to the command 'close your eyes and open them when I say the number 3.' . . . He could choose a requested color block out of four color blocks. He could set the right peg in a pegboard. He remained unable to vocalize. Eye blinking was successfully used as a communication mode for a while, however no consistent method of communication was developed."

Despite improvements made in therapy, Robert remained severely disabled, both mentally and physically. [One] medical report summarized his continuing impairments as follows: "severe cognitive impairment that is not possible to fully appreciate due to the concurrent motor and communication impairments . . . "; "maladaptive behavior characterized by agitation, aggressiveness and non-compliance"; "severe paralysis on the right and moderate paralysis on the left"; "severely impaired communication, without compensatory augmentative communication system"; "severe swallowing dysfunction, dependent upon non-oral enteric tube feeding for nutrition and hydration"; "incontinence of bowel and bladder"; "moderate spasticity"; "mild to moderate contractures"; "general dysphoria"; "recurrent medical illnesses, including pneumonia, bladder infections, sinusitis"; and "dental issues."

After Robert regained consciousness and while he was undergoing therapy, Rose authorized surgery three times to replace dislodged feeding tubes. When physicians sought her permission a fourth time, she declined. She discussed the decision with her daughters and with Robert's brother Michael, all of whom believed that Robert would not have approved the procedure even if necessary to sustain his life. Rose also discussed the decision with Robert's treating physician, Dr. Kass, other physicians, and the hospital's ombudsman, all of whom apparently supported her decision. Dr. Kass, however, inserted a nasogastric feeding tube to keep Robert alive pending input from the hospital's ethics committee.

Eventually, the 20–member ethics committee unanimously approved Rose's decision. In the course of their deliberations, however, the committee did not speak with Robert's mother or sister. [They] learned, apparently through an anonymous telephone call, that Dr. Kass planned to remove Robert's feeding tube [and] applied for a temporary restraining order to bar him from so doing, and the court granted the motion ex parte.

Rose immediately thereafter petitioned for appointment as Robert's conservator. In the petition, she asked the court to determine that Robert lacked the capacity to give informed consent for medical treatment and to confirm her authority "to withdraw and/or withhold medical treatment and/or life-sustaining treatment, including, but not limited to, withholding nutrition and hydration." [Robert's mother and sister] (hereafter sometimes objectors) opposed the petition. After a hearing, the court appointed Rose as conservator but reserved judgment on her request for authority to remove Robert's feeding tube. * * *

After [a 60 day observation period] elapsed without significant improvement in Robert's condition, the conservator renewed her request for authority to remove his feeding tube. The objectors asked the trial court to appoint independent counsel for the conservatee. * * * Appointed counsel, exercising his independent judgment [ ], decided to support the conservator's decision.

* * *

The [consequent] trial generated the evidence set out above. The testifying physicians agreed that Robert would not likely experience further cognitive recovery. Dr. Kass, Robert's treating physician, testified that, to the highest degree of medical certainty, Robert would never be able to make medical treatment decisions, walk, talk, feed himself, eat, drink, or control his bowel and bladder functions.

* * *

Robert's wife, brother and daughter recounted preaccident statements Robert had made about his attitude towards life-sustaining health care. Robert's wife recounted specific statements on two occasions. The first occasion was Rose's decision whether to turn off a respirator sustaining the life of her father, who was near death from gangrene. Rose recalls Robert saying: "I would never want to live like that, and I wouldn't want my children to see me like that and look at the hurt you're going through as an adult seeing your father like that." On cross-examination, Rose acknowledged Robert said on this occasion that Rose's father "wouldn't want to live like a vegetable" and "wouldn't want to live in a comatose state."

After his father-in-law's death, Robert developed a serious drinking problem. After a particular incident, Rose asked Michael, Robert's brother, to talk to him. When Robert arrived home the next day he was angry to see Michael there, interfering in what he considered a private family matter. Rose remembers Michael telling Robert: "I'm going to get a call from Rosie one day, and you're going to be in a terrible accident." Robert replied: "If that ever happened to me, you know what my feelings are. Don't let that happen to me. Just let me go. Leave me alone." . . . Robert's daughter Katie remembers him saying on this occasion that "if he could not be a provider for his family, if he could not do all the things that he enjoyed doing, just enjoying the outdoors, just basic things, feeding himself, talking, communicating, if he could not do those things, he would not want to live."

[The trial] court found the conservator "ha[d] not met her duty and burden to show by clear and convincing evidence that conservatee Robert Wendland, who is not in a persistent vegetative state nor suffering from a terminal illness would, under the circumstances, want to die. Conservator has likewise not met her burden of establishing that the withdrawal of artificially delivered nutrition and hydration is commensurate with conservatee's best interests. * * * " Based on these findings, the court granted the objectors' motion for judgment [ ], thus denying the conservator's request for confirmation of her proposal to withdraw treatment. The court also found the conservator had acted in good faith and would be permitted to remain in that office. Nevertheless, the court limited her powers by ordering that she would "have no authority to direct . . . [any] health care provider to remove the conservatee's life sustaining medical treatment in the form of withholding nutrition and hydration." [ ]

The conservator appealed this decision. The Court of Appeal reversed. In the Court of Appeal's view, "[t]he trial court properly placed the burden of producing evidence on [the conservator] and properly applied a clear and convincing evidence standard. However, the court erred in requiring [the conservator] to prove that [the conservatee], while competent, expressed a desire to die in the circumstances and in substituting its own judgment concerning [the conservatee's] best interests * * *." Instead, the trial court's role was "merely to satisfy itself that the conservator had considered the conservatee's best interests in good faith * * *." * * * We granted review of this decision.

II. DISCUSSION

A. *The Relevant Legal Principles*

*   *   *

1. *Constitutional and common law principles*

One relatively certain principle is that a competent adult has the right to refuse medical treatment, even treatment necessary to sustain life.

*   *   *

The same right survives incapacity, in a practical sense, if exercised while competent pursuant to a law giving that act lasting validity. For some time, California law has given competent adults the power to leave formal directions for health care in the event they later become incompetent.

*   *   *

[The] laws just mentioned merely give effect to the decision of a competent person, in the form either of instructions for health care or the designation of an agent or surrogate for health care decisions. Such laws may accurately be described, as the Legislature has described them, as a means to respect personal autonomy by giving effect to competent decisions: * * *

In contrast, decisions made by conservators typically derive their authority from a different basis—the *parens patriae* power of the state to protect incompetent persons. Unlike an agent or a surrogate for health care, who is voluntarily appointed by a competent person, a conservator is appointed by the court because the conservatee "has been adjudicated to lack the capacity to make health care decisions."

*   *   *

2. *[The Probate Code]*

[The court then analyzed the history of the relevant Probate Code provision.]

B. *The Present Case*

This background illuminates the parties' arguments, which reduce in essence to this: The conservator has claimed the power under [the Probate Code] to direct the conservatee's health care providers to cease providing artificial nutrition and hydration. In opposition, the objectors have contended the statute violates the conservatee's rights to privacy and life under the facts of this case if the conservator's interpretation of the statute is correct.

*   *   *

1.   The primary standard: a decision in accordance with the conservatee's wishes

The conservator asserts she offered sufficient evidence at trial to satisfy the primary statutory standard, which contemplates a decision "in accordance with the conservatee's * * * wishes * * *." [ ] The trial court, however, determined the evidence on this point was insufficient. The conservator did "not [meet] her duty and burden," the court expressly found, "to show by clear and convincing evidence that [the] conservatee . . . , who is not in a persistent vegetative state nor suffering from a terminal illness would, under the circumstances, want to die." * * *

The conservator argues the Legislature understood and intended that the low preponderance of the evidence standard would apply. Certainly this was the Law Revision Commission's understanding [in drafting the statute]. * * *

The objectors, in opposition, argue that [the relevant section] would be unconstitutional if construed to permit a conservator to end the life of a conscious conservatee based on a finding by the low preponderance of the evidence standard that the latter would not want to live. We see no basis for holding the statute unconstitutional on its face. We do, however, find merit in the objectors' argument. We therefore construe the statute to minimize the possibility of its unconstitutional application by requiring clear and convincing evidence of a conscious conservatee's wish to refuse life-sustaining treatment when the conservator relies on that asserted wish to justify withholding life-sustaining treatment * * *. [W]e see no constitutional reason to apply the higher evidentiary standard to the majority of health care decisions made by conservators not contemplating a conscious conservatee's death.

*   *   *

Notwithstanding the foregoing, one must acknowledge that the primary standard for decision-making set out in [the Probate Code] does articulate what will in some cases form a constitutional basis for a conservator's decision to end the life of a conscious patient: deference to the patient's own wishes. * * *. Because a competent adult may refuse life-sustaining treatment [ ], it follows that an agent properly and voluntarily designated by the principal may refuse treatment on the principal's behalf * * *.

The only apparent purpose of requiring conservators to make decisions in accordance with the conservatee's wishes, when those wishes are known, is to enforce the fundamental principle of personal autonomy. The same requirement, as applied to agents and surrogates freely designated by competent persons, enforces the principles of agency. A reasonable person presumably will designate for such purposes only a person in whom the former reposes the highest degree of confidence. A conservator, in contrast, is *not* an agent of the conservatee, and unlike a freely designated agent cannot be presumed to have special knowledge of the conservatee's health care wishes.* * * While it may be constitutionally permissible to assume that an agent freely designated by a formerly competent person to make all health care decisions, including life-ending ones, will resolve such questions "in accordance with the principal's . . . wishes" [ ] one cannot apply the same assumption to conservators and conservatees. [ ] For this reason, when the legal premise of a conservator's decision to end a conservatee's life by withholding medical care is that the conservatee would refuse such care, to apply a high standard of proof will help to ensure the reliability of the decision.

The function of a standard of proof is to instruct the fact finder concerning the degree of confidence our society deems necessary in the correctness of factual conclusions for a particular type of adjudication, to allocate the risk of error between the litigants, and to indicate the relative importance attached to the ultimate decision. [ ] Thus, "the standard of proof may depend upon the 'gravity of the consequences that would result from an erroneous determination of the issue involved.' "[ ] The default standard of proof in civil cases is the preponderance of the evidence. [ ] Nevertheless, courts have applied the clear and convincing evidence standard when necessary to protect important rights.

*   *   *

In this case, the importance of the ultimate decision and the risk of error are manifest. So too should be the degree of confidence required in the necessary findings of fact. The ultimate decision is whether a conservatee lives or dies, and the risk is that a conservator, claiming statutory authority to end a conscious conservatee's life "in accordance with the conservatee's . . . wishes" [ ] by withdrawing artificial nutrition and hydration, will make a decision with which the conservatee subjectively disagrees and which subjects the conservatee to starvation, dehydration and death. This would represent the gravest possible affront to a conservatee's state constitutional right to privacy, in the sense of freedom from unwanted bodily intrusions, and to life. * * * Certainly it is possible, as the conservator here urges, that an incompetent and uncommunicative but conscious conservatee might perceive the efforts to keep him alive as unwanted intrusion and the withdrawal of those efforts as welcome release. But the decision to treat is reversible. The decision to withdraw treatment is not. The role of a high evidentiary standard in such a case is to adjust the risk of error to favor the less perilous result. * * *

In conclusion, to interpret [the Probate Code] to permit a conservator to withdraw artificial nutrition and hydration from a conscious conservatee based on a finding, by a mere preponderance of the evidence, that the conservatee would refuse treatment creates a serious risk that the law will be unconstitutionally applied in some cases, with grave injury to fundamental rights. Under these circumstances, we may properly ask whether the statute may be construed in a way that mitigates the risk. * * * Here, where the risk to conservatees' rights is grave and the proposed construction is consistent with the language of the statute, to construe the statute to avoid the constitutional risk is an appropriate exercise of judicial power.

*   *   *

One amicus curiae argues that "[i]mposing so high an evidentiary burden [i.e., clear and convincing evidence] would . . . frustrate many genuine treatment desires—particularly the choices of young people, who are less likely than older people to envision the need for advanced directives, or poor people, who are less likely than affluent people to have the resources to obtain formal legal documents." But the Legislature has already accommodated this concern in large part by permitting patients to nominate surrogate decision makers by orally informing a supervising physician [ ] and by giving effect to specific oral health care instructions [ ]. To go still farther, by giving conclusive effect to wishes inferred from informal, oral statements proved only by a preponderance of the evidence, may serve the interests of incompetent persons whose wishes are correctly determined, but to do so also poses an unacceptable risk of violating other incompetent patients' rights to privacy and life, as already explained. To the argument that applying a high standard of proof in such cases impermissibly burdens the right to determine one's own medical treatment, one need only repeat the United States Supreme Court's response to the same assertion: "The differences between the choice made *by* a competent person to refuse medical treatment, and the choice made *for* an incompetent person by someone else to refuse medical treatment, are so obviously different that the State is warranted in establishing rigorous procedures for the latter class of cases which do not apply to the former class." *Cruzan [ ]*

*   *   *

In the case before us, the trial court found that the conservator failed to show "by clear and convincing evidence that conservatee Robert Wendland, who is not in a persistent vegetative state nor suffering from a terminal illness would, under the circumstances, want to die."

*   *   *

2.   *The best interest standard*

Having rejected the conservator's argument that withdrawing artificial hydration and nutrition would have been "in accordance with the conservatee's * * * wishes" [ ], we must next consider her contention that the same action would have been proper under the fallback best interest standard.

* * *

In the exceptional case where a conservator proposes to end the life of a conscious but incompetent conservatee, we believe the same factor that principally justifies applying the clear and convincing evidence standard to a determination of the conservatee's wishes also justifies applying that standard to a determination of the conservatee's best interest: The decision threatens the conservatee's fundamental rights to privacy and life. * * *

We need not in this case attempt to define the extreme factual predicates that, if proved by clear and convincing evidence, might support a conservator's decision that withdrawing life support would be in the best interest of a conscious conservatee. Here, the conservator offered no basis for such a finding other than her own subjective judgment that the conservatee did not enjoy a satisfactory quality of life and legally insufficient evidence to the effect that he would have wished to die. On this record, the trial court's decision was correct.

III. CONCLUSION

For the reasons set out above, we conclude the superior court correctly required the conservator to prove, by clear and convincing evidence, either that the conservatee wished to refuse life-sustaining treatment or that to withhold such treatment would have been in his best interest; lacking such evidence, the superior court correctly denied the conservator's request for permission to withdraw artificial hydration and nutrition. We emphasize, however, that the clear and convincing evidence standard does not apply to the vast majority of health care decisions made by conservators under [the Probate Code]. Only the decision to withdraw life-sustaining treatment, because of its effect on a conscious conservatee's fundamental rights, justifies imposing that high standard of proof. Therefore, our decision today affects only a narrow class of persons: conscious conservatees who have not left formal directions for health care and whose conservators propose to withhold life-sustaining treatment for the purpose of causing their conservatees' deaths. Our conclusion does not affect permanently unconscious patients, including those who are comatose or in a persistent vegetative state [ ], persons who have left legally cognizable instructions for health care [ ], persons who have designated agents or other surrogates for health care [ ], or conservatees for whom conservators have made medical decisions other than those intended to bring about the death of a conscious conservatee.

NOTES AND QUESTIONS

1.   The *Wendland* court applies the "clear and convincing evidence" standard to two separate substantive issues—to the determination of Robert's wishes (when the court applies a substituted judgment standard) and, separately, to the determination of what is in Robert's best interest (when the court decides that it cannot make a determination based on substituted judgment). More than ten years before, in a seminal New York case, In re Westchester County Medical Ctr. (O'Connor), 72 N.Y.2d 517, 534 N.Y.S.2d 886, 531 N.E.2d 607 (1988), the Court of Appeals applied the "clear and convincing evidence" standard to determine if a family member could make a substituted judgment to remove life-sustaining medical treatment. The Court articulated the standard it was applying in deciding that this high level of proof was absent in the case before the court:

> Neither of the doctors had known Mrs. O'Connor before she became incompetent and thus knew nothing of her attitudes toward the use of life-sustaining measures. The respondents' first witness on this point was * * * a former co-worker and longtime friend of Mrs. O'Connor. * * * He testified that his first discussion with Mrs. O'Connor concerning artificial means of prolonging life occurred about 1969. At that time his father, who was dying of cancer, informed him that he would not want to continue life by any artificial method if he had lost his dignity because he could no longer control his normal bodily functions. The witness said that when he told Mrs. O'Connor of this she agreed wholeheartedly and said: "I would never want to be a burden on anyone and I would never want to lose my dignity before I passed away." He noted that she was a "very religious woman" who "felt that nature should take its course and not use further artificial means." They had similar conversations on two or three occasions between 1969 and 1973. During these discussions Mrs. O'Connor variously stated that it is "monstrous" to keep someone alive by using "machinery, things like that" when they are "not going to get better"; that she would never want to be in the same situation as her husband * * * and that people who are "suffering very badly" should be allowed to die.

> Mrs. O'Connor's daughter Helen testified that her mother informed her on several occasions that if she became ill and was unable to care for herself she would not want her life to be sustained artificially. * * * Mrs. O'Connor's other daughter, Joan, essentially adopted her sister's testimony. She described her mother's statements on this subject as less solemn pronouncements: "it was brought up when we were together, at times when in conversations you start something, you know, maybe the news was on and maybe that was the topic that was brought up and that's how it came about."

However, all three of these witnesses also agreed that Mrs. O'Connor had never discussed providing food or water with medical assistance, nor had she ever said that she would adhere to her view and decline medical treatment "by artificial means" if that would produce a painful death. When Helen was asked what choice her mother would make under those circumstances she admitted that she did not know. Her sister Joan agreed, noting that this had never been discussed, "unfortunately, no."

*   *   *

It has long been the common-law rule in this State that a person has the right to decline medical treatment, even life-saving treatment, absent an overriding State interest [ ]. In 1981, we held, in two companion cases, that a hospital or medical facility must respect this right even when a patient becomes incompetent, if while competent, the patient stated that he or she did not want certain procedures to be employed under specified circumstances. [*Eichner*]

* * * *Eichner* had been competent and capable of expressing his will before he was silenced by illness. In those circumstances, we concluded that it would be appropriate for the court to intervene and direct the termination of artificial life supports, in accordance with the patient's wishes, because it was established by "clear and convincing evidence" that the patient would have so directed if he were competent and able to communicate. We selected the "clear and convincing evidence" standard in *Eichner* because it " 'impress[es] the factfinder with the importance of the decision' * * * and it 'forbids relief whenever the evidence is loose, equivocal or contradictory' "[ ] Nothing less than unequivocal proof will suffice when the decision to terminate life supports is at issue.

Dissenting Judge Simons responded:

The majority refuses to recognize Mrs. O'Connor's expressed wishes because they were not solemn pronouncements made after reflection and because they were too indefinite.

Respondents have established the reliability of the statements under any standard. * * * These were not "casual remarks," but rather expressions evidencing the long-held beliefs of a mature woman who had been exposed to sickness and death in her employment and her personal life. Mrs. O'Connor had spent 20 years working in the emergency room and pathology laboratory of Jacobi Hospital, confronting the problems of life and death daily. She suffered through long illnesses of her husband, stepmother, father and two brothers who had died before her. She herself has been hospitalized for congestive heart failure and she understood the consequences of serious illnesses.

Because of these experiences, Mrs. O'Connor expressed her wishes in conversations with her daughters, both trained nurses, and a co-employee from the hospital who shared her hospital experience. There can be no doubt she was aware of the gravity of the problem she was addressing and the significance of her statements, or that those hearing her understood her intentions. She clearly stated the values important to her, a life that does not burden others and its termination with dignity, and what she believed her best interests required in the case of severe, debilitating illness. * * *

Notwithstanding this, the majority finds the statements entitled to little weight because Mrs. O'Connor's exposure was mostly to terminally ill cancer patients, or because her desire to remain independent and avoid burdening her children constituted little more than statements of self-pity by an elderly woman. There is no evidence to support those inferences and no justification for trivializing Mrs. O'Connor's statements. She is entitled to have them accepted without reservation. * * *

* * *

The [majority's] rule is unworkable because it requires humans to exercise foresight they do not possess. It requires that before life-sustaining treatment may be withdrawn, there must be proof that the patient anticipated his or her present condition, the means available to sustain life under the circumstances, and then decided that the alternative of death without mechanical assistance, by starvation in this case, is preferable to continued life [ ].

* * *

Even if a patient possessed the remarkable foresight to anticipate some future illness or condition, however, it is unrealistic to expect or require a lay person to be familiar with the support systems available for treatment—to say nothing of requiring a determination of which is preferable or the consequences that may result from using or foregoing them. Indeed, the conditions and consequences may change from day to day. * * *

In short, Mary O'Connor expressed her wishes in the only terms familiar to her, and she expressed them as clearly as a lay person should be asked to express them. To require more is unrealistic, and for all practical purposes, it precludes the right of patients to forego life-sustaining treatment.

Would the *Wendland* court agree with the majority in *O'Connor*, or with Judge Simons? Who do you think has the better argument about the propriety of applying the "clear and convincing evidence" standard?

2.   The propriety of the "clear and convincing evidence" standard applied by the Missouri Supreme Court was the primary issue before the United States Supreme Court in *Cruzan.* The Court concluded that

> a state may apply a clear and convincing evidence standard in proceedings where a guardian seeks to discontinue nutrition and hydration of a person diagnosed to be in a persistent vegetative state.

This holding, which, the Chief Justice assures us, describes only the outer limit of what the Constitution permits, is supported by a lengthy description of civil cases in which the "clear and convincing evidence" standard is applied. See *Cruzan, supra* in this chapter.

3.   The choice of the appropriate burden of proof is not always between "clear and convincing evidence" and the normal civil "preponderance" standard. In *Eichner,* in which this issue was first raised before the New York Court of Appeals, the district attorney seeking the continuation of treatment for Brother Fox argued that "proof beyond a reasonable doubt" was the appropriate burden. The Court of Appeals explained why it chose the clear and convincing evidence standard:

> Although this is a civil case in which a preponderance of the evidence is generally deemed sufficient, the District Attorney urges that the highest burden of proof, beyond a reasonable doubt, should be required when granting the relief may result in the patient's death. But that burden, traditionally reserved for criminal cases where involuntary loss of liberty and possible stigmatization are at issue [ ] is inappropriate in cases where the purpose of granting the relief is to give effect to an individual's right by carrying out his stated intentions. However, we agree with the courts below that the highest standard applicable to civil cases should be required. There is more involved here than a typical dispute between private litigants over a sum of money. Where particularly important personal interests are at stake, clear and convincing evidence should be required. It is constitutionally required in cases of involuntary civil commitments and we have recognized the need for the higher standard in exceptional civil matters. Clear and convincing proof should also be required in cases where it is claimed that a person, now incompetent, left instructions to terminate life sustaining procedures when there is no hope of recovery. This standard serves to "impress the factfinder with the importance of the decision" and it " 'forbids relief whenever the evidence is loose, equivocal or contradictory' "[ ].

In re Eichner, 420 N.E.2d at 72.

4.   Of course, the "clear and convincing evidence" standard is not a symmetrical one; it applies to one seeking to *terminate* life-sustaining treatment, but not to one seeking to *maintain* it. Really, the application of the

"clear and convincing evidence" standard to these cases serves only to recognize a policy that it is better to err on the side of maintaining life. Many courts have repeated this principle of direction-of-error almost as a mantra, but does it make sense to establish the maintenance of life-sustaining treatment as the default position in all cases? As the *Martin* court points out,

> To err either way has incalculable ramifications. To end the life of a patient who still derives meaning and enjoyment from life or to condemn persons to lives from which they cry out for release is nothing short of barbaric.

Martin at 401. Despite this, the court goes on to say that "[i]f we are to err, however, we must err in preserving life." But should the default position—the presumed desire of the patient—be the *continuation* of treatment for every subgroup of cases? Should it be the default position where the patient is in excruciating and intractable pain, or where the patient is in persistent vegetative state? How many people do you know who wish to be kept alive under those circumstances? Should the default position be determined by empirical data on majority preferences?

5.   The question of what burden of proof is appropriate is different from the issue of what kinds of evidence ought to be admissible to meet the burden. While most courts agree on the appropriate burden of proof in these cases, there is little agreement about the admissibility or weight to be given to different kinds of potential evidence.

What evidence is relevant will depend upon what facts are material to the resolution of the case under state substantive law. Assume that the wishes of the patient are material to the outcome of the case. How should the court consider previous statements of a currently incompetent patient? Should it make any difference that the statements were in writing? Made to relatives? In response to news events (like the *Schiavo* case)? In response to a family emergency or a death in the family? Would your prior statements about this issue be considered serious or off-hand by a court if tomorrow you were in a persistent vegetative state? Obviously, the characterization a court puts upon the nature of the evidence will determine the weight it is to be accorded. That, in turn, is likely to determine whether a petitioner can meet the generally accepted "clear and convincing evidence" standard. The Michigan Supreme Court has determined that, "Statements made in response to seeing or hearing about another's prolonged death do not fulfill the clear and convincing standard." In re Martin, 450 Mich. 204, 538 N.W.2d 399, 410–411 (1995). Do you agree? The dissenting judge in *Martin* argued that "[t]his bright line rule ignores that many persons only consider their own mortality seriously upon hearing about the end of other people's lives. Admittedly the emotional content of such statements must be carefully considered in weighing their probative value. But the majority's categorical exclusion of [this] relevant evidence dispenses with any semblance of accurate factfinding." Martin, at 399 (Levin, J., dissenting).

6. Whether the courts have any role at all in these matters has been the subject of some debate. On the one hand, there is a fear that the absence of judicial oversight will lead to arbitrary decisions and, thus, arbitrary deaths. On the other hand, any attempt to bring all of these cases to the courts would yield an intolerable caseload and delay the deaths of many patients who desperately seek that relief. In addition, as the *Wendland* case suggested, there is little reason to believe that courts have any wisdom that will make them better than a patient's family at making these decisions. The Massachusetts Supreme Judicial Court changed its view of the necessity of judicial confirmation of a guardian's decision that a patient should forgo life-sustaining treatment. See In re Spring, 380 Mass. 629, 405 N.E.2d 115 (1980) (no review required in most circumstances; reversing prior position requiring judicial review). Should judicial review of all decisions to terminate life-sustaining treatment be required? Should such judicial review be required in some cases? In cases in which there is no written advance directive? In which there is no agreement among family members? In which the patients disagree with the health care providers? In which the health care providers disagree among themselves? In which the decision maker is self interested? In which there is an ambiguity in the previous statements of the patient? Is there any way to adequately categorize those cases in which judicial review ought to be required? If judicial review is not required, should some other form of review—by an ethics committee, for example—be required in its stead? Is the choice of the Uniform Health–Care Decisions Act, above in subsection A, which would rarely countenance judicial involvement in any health care decision, the best choice? Why?

7. In *Wendland*, the California Supreme Court would have supported the decision of the conservator, and allowed for the termination of life-sustaining medical care, if Robert had been unconscious. Of course, Robert Wendland *was* unconscious for some time before he emerged from the coma. Could Rose have decided to terminate life-sustaining medical treatment if she had acted quickly, before he regained consciousness? Might the *Wendland* case encourage families to act quickly to discontinue life-sustaining treatment to protect the patient from the harsh rule—virtually forbidding termination of treatment—that would apply if the patient should regain the tiniest amount of consciousness? Perhaps the California Supreme Court meant to exempt only the "permanently unconscious" from the *Wendland* rule, not any "unconscious" patient. Can we ever be sure that a patient is "permanently unconscious"? What tests should physicians apply to make this diagnosis? Some medical and ethics literature refers to patients in a "minimally conscious state" as distinguished from the persistent vegetative state. See, e.g., J.T. Giacino, et al., The Minimally Conscious State: Definition and Diagnostic Criteria, 58 Neurology 349 (2002). See also Stacey A. Tovino & William J. Winslade, A Primer on the Law and Ethics of Treatment, Research, and Public Policy In the Context of Severe Traumatic Brain Injury, 14 Annals Health L. 1, 12 (2005).

8.   If there is to be a judicial process, should it be an adversary process? While the Chief Justice appears to think that the adversary process is helpful in these cases (see *Cruzan*, in Section II, above), that part of the opinion gave Justice Stevens pause:

> The Court recognizes that "the state has been involved as an adversary from the beginning" in this case only because Nancy Cruzan "was a patient at a state hospital when this litigation commenced." * * * It seems to me, however, that the Court draws precisely the wrong conclusion from this insight. The Court apparently believes that the absence of the state from the litigation would have created a problem, because agreement among the family and the independent guardian *ad litem* as to Nancy Cruzan's best interests might have prevented her treatment from becoming the focus of a "truly adversarial" proceeding. [ ] It may reasonably be debated whether some judicial process should be required before life-sustaining treatment is discontinued; this issue has divided the state courts. [ ] * * * I tend, however, to agree * * * that the intervention of the state in these proceedings as an *adversary* is not so much a cure as it is part of the disease.

Cruzan v. Director, Missouri Dept. of Health, 497 U.S. 261, 341, n.13, 110 S.Ct. 2841, 2884, n.13, 111 L.Ed.2d 224 (1990) (Stevens, J., dissenting). A decade earlier the Florida Supreme Court had expressed the same reservations:

> Because the issue with its ramifications is fraught with complexity and encompasses the interests of the law, both civil and criminal, medical ethics and social morality, it is not one which is well suited for a solution in an adversary judicial proceeding.

Satz v. Perlmutter, 379 So.2d 359, 360 (Fla.1980). See also *Protection and Avocacy System*, *supra* note 4. Are the "advantages" of an adversary proceeding truly advantageous in these agonizing cases? See Nancy Dubler, Conflict and Consensus at the End of Life, Hastings Ctr. Spec. Rep. on Improving End of Life Care (Jennings, et al., eds. 2005); Alan Meisel, The Role of Litigation in End of Life Care: A Reappraisal, Hastings Ctr. Spec. Rep. on Improving End of Life Care (Jennings, et al., eds. 2005).

PROBLEM: NOT QUITE PERSISTENT VEGETATIVE STATE

When unhelmeted 57–year–old Tad Gonzales ran his motorcycle into a bridge support post on an interstate highway, he was revived at the scene and rushed to Big Central Hospital. There he underwent several hours of emergency surgery designed to preserve his life and repair the very substantial head injuries he sustained. A few days after the surgery, he began to regain consciousness, and a week later he was able to be removed from the ventilator which was supporting his breathing, although he still needs ventilator assistance from time to time. During his first two weeks in the hospital, Tad showed little improvement. He was not in a coma, but he was only occasionally responsive, and he demonstrated no awareness of Ralph, his partner of twenty-two years, or his two brothers and his parents, even though Tad had always shared a close relationship with all of them.

After two weeks, Big City Hospital transferred Tad to Commercial Affiliated Nursing Home, where he began receiving physical and occupational therapy. After a year of care there, he has shown little improvement. He still does not seem to recognize Ralph, who visits daily, or anyone else. He is able to sit up and his eyes sometimes seem to be following images on a screen. He grunts when he is hungry or uncomfortable. He cannot eat or drink, and he is fed through a feeding tube in his abdomen. He cannot control his bowels or bladder. He has regularly suffered from urinary tract infections and asthma during his nursing home stay, although his need for the ventilator is becoming rarer. On a few, increasingly rare, occasions, his heart stopped beating, but he was resuscitated immediately. Doctors believe that there is little chance of substantial improvement in his condition (although, in the words of one doctor, "Who knows? Anything can happen.") Tad's doctors estimate that his life expectancy could be another twenty years or more.

Tad's doctor and Ralph have developed a good working relationship, and the doctor has called upon Ralph to approve any change in Tad's treatment regimen even though Tad never signed any kind of advance directive. Ralph has now informed the doctor that he believes that Tad would want the use of the feeding tube (and the occasional use of the ventilator) discontinued, and that he would not want to be resuscitated (i.e., if his heart were to stop beating, he would not want health care providers to try to start it again). When the doctor challenged him on this, Ralph respectfully ordered the doctor to terminate feeding, and to note that Tad was not to be mechanically ventilated or resuscitated. Ralph explained that he had spoken with Tad often about "this kind of thing," and that Tad had said that the indignity of being fed, or wearing diapers, or being bed-bound, was not worth the value of life to him. In particular, Ralph remembers Tad describing one of their friends, another motorcyclist who became a quadriplegic and suffered some intellectual impairment after an accident, as "better off dead." Tad and Ralph promised each other that neither would ever let that happen to the other. Tad's parents and one of his brothers agree that there is no doubt that Tad would want all treatment terminated under these circumstances. Tad's other brother disagrees. As he has articulated it, "How can we know what he would want? He could never have imagined himself in this situation, and we shouldn't read anything in to what he said about other people. Maybe he thought those other people could feel more pain than he can."

Tad's doctor has approached you, the hospital counsel, to ask you what she should do. Should she discontinue feeding? The use of the ventilator? Should the hospital pursue an action in court? What position should the hospital take if Ralph, or Tad's dissenting brother, pursues an action in court? How should that action be resolved?

D. MAKING DECISIONS FOR ADULTS WHO HAVE NEVER BEEN COMPETENT

Where the patient has never been competent—where the patient has been severely developmentally disabled from birth, for example—the courts still make an attempt to determine what the patient's choice would be. Of course, it is exceptionally difficult to imagine what an incompetent person, who has never been competent, would want to do if that person were suddenly competent. Compare the next two cases and the statute that follows. The first case, *Superintendent of Belchertown State School v. Saikewicz,* involves a 67–year–old profoundly retarded adult suffering from leukemia without any family willing to aid in decision-making. The court, applying the substituted judgment standard, addresses the question of whether the chemotherapy that would be likely to be provided to other patients with this condition should be withheld from this patient. The second case, *Matter of Storar,* which is the companion case to *Matter of Eichner,* above, concerns the propriety of a blood transfusion for a profoundly retarded 52–year–old cancer patient. Here the court felt obliged to apply the best interest standard rather than the substituted judgment standard..

SUPERINTENDENT OF BELCHERTOWN STATE SCHOOL V. SAIKEWICZ

Supreme Judicial Court of Massachusetts, 1977.
373 Mass. 728, 370 N.E.2d 417.

LIACOS, JUSTICE.

*   *   *

The question of what legal standards govern the decision whether to administer potentially life-prolonging treatment to an incompetent person encompasses two distinct and important subissues. First, does a choice exist? That is, is it the unvarying responsibility of the State to order medical treatment in all circumstances involving the care of an incompetent person? Second, if a choice does exist under certain conditions, what considerations enter into the decision-making process?

We think that principles of equality and respect for all individuals require the conclusion that a choice exists * * *. We recognize a general right in all persons to refuse medical treatment in appropriate circumstances. The recognition of that right must extend to the case of an incompetent, as well as a competent, patient because the value of human dignity extends to both.

This is not to deny that the State has a traditional power and responsibility, under the doctrine of *parens patriae,* to care for and protect the "best interests" of the incompetent person.

The "best interests" of an incompetent person are not necessarily served by imposing on such persons results not mandated as to competent persons similarly situated. It does not advance the interest of the State or the ward to treat the ward as a person of lesser status or dignity than others. To protect the incompetent person within its power, the State must recognize the dignity and worth of such a person and afford to that person the same panoply of rights and choices it recognizes in competent persons. If a competent person faced with death may choose to decline treatment which not only will not cure the person but which substantially may increase suffering in exchange for a possible yet brief prolongation of life, then it cannot be said that it is always in the "best interests" of the ward to require submission to such treatment. Nor do statistical factors indicating that a majority of competent persons similarly situated choose treatment resolve the issue. The significant decisions of life are more complex than statistical determinations. Individual choice is determined not by the vote of the majority but by the complexities of the singular situation viewed from the unique perspective of the person called on to make the decision. To presume that the incompetent person must always be subjected to what many rational and intelligent persons may decline is to downgrade the status of the incompetent person by placing a lesser value on his intrinsic human worth and vitality.

* * * This leads us to the question of how the right of an incompetent person to decline treatment might best be exercised so as to give the fullest possible expression to the character and circumstances of that individual.

*   *   *

To put the above discussion in proper perspective, we realize that an inquiry into what a majority of people would do in circumstances that truly were similar assumes an objective viewpoint not far removed from a "reasonable person" inquiry. While we recognize the value of this kind of indirect evidence, we should make it plain that the primary test is subjective in nature—that is, the goal is to determine with as much accuracy as possible the wants and needs of the individual involved. This may or may not conform to what is thought wise or prudent by most people. The problems of arriving at an accurate substituted judgment in matters of life and death vary greatly in degree, if not in kind, in different circumstances. * * * Joseph Saikewicz was profoundly retarded and noncommunicative his entire life, which was spent largely in the highly restrictive atmosphere of an institution. While it may thus be necessary to rely to a greater degree on objective criteria, such as the supposed inability of pro foundly retarded persons to conceptualize or fear death, the effort to bring the substituted judgment into step with the values and desires of the affected individual must not, and need not, be abandoned.

The "substituted judgment" standard which we have described commends itself simply because of its straightforward respect for the integrity and autonomy of the individual. * * *

* * * [W]e now reiterate the substituted judgment doctrine as we apply it in the instant case. We believe that both the guardian *ad litem* in his recommendation and the judge in his decision should have attempted (as they did) to ascertain the incompetent person's actual interests and preferences. In short, the decision in cases such as this should be that which would be made by the incompetent person, if that person were competent, but taking into account the present and future incompetency of the individual as one of the factors which would necessarily enter into the decision-making process of the competent person. Having recognized the right of a competent person to make for himself the same decision as the court made in this case, the question is, do the facts on the record support the proposition that Saikewicz himself would have [declined treatment]. We believe they do.

* * *

IN RE STORAR
New York Court of Appeals, 1981.
52 N.Y.2d 363, 438 N.Y.S.2d 266, 420 N.E.2d 64.

WACHTLER, JUDGE.

* * *

John Storar was profoundly retarded with a mental age of about 18 months. At the time of this proceeding he was 52 years old and a resident of the Newark Development Center, a State facility, which had been his home since the age of 5. His closest relative was his mother * * *.

In 1979 physicians at the center noticed blood in his urine and asked his mother for permission to conduct diagnostic tests. She * * * gave her consent. The tests, completed in July, 1979, revealed that he had cancer of the bladder. It was recommended that he receive radiation therapy at a hospital in Rochester. When the hospital refused to administer the treatment without the consent of a legal guardian, Mrs. Storar applied to the court and was appointed guardian of her son's person and property in August, 1979. With her consent he received radiation therapy for six weeks after which the disease was found to be in remission.

However in March, 1980, blood was again observed in his urine. The lesions in his bladder were cauterized in an unsuccessful effort to stop the bleeding. At that point his physician diagnosed the cancer as terminal, concluding that after using all medical and surgical means then available, the patient would nevertheless die from the disease.

In May the physicians at the center asked his mother for permission to administer blood transfusions. She initially refused but the following day withdrew her objection. For several weeks John Storar received blood transfusions when needed. However, on June 19 his mother requested that the transfusions be discontinued.

The director of the center then brought this proceeding, pursuant to [ ] the Mental Hygiene Law, seeking authorization to continue the transfusions, claiming that without them "death would occur within weeks." Mrs. Storar cross-petitioned for an order prohibiting the transfusions, and named the District Attorney as a party. The court appointed a guardian ad litem and signed an order temporarily permitting the transfusions to continue, pending the determination of the proceeding.

At the hearing in September the court heard testimony from various witnesses including Mrs. Storar, several employees at the center, and seven medical experts. All the experts concurred that John Storar had irreversible cancer of the bladder, * * * with a very limited life span, generally estimated to be between 3 and 6 months. They also agreed that he had an infant's mentality and was unable to comprehend his predicament or to make a reasoned choice of treatment. In addition, there was no dispute over the fact that he was continuously losing blood.

* * *

It was conceded that John Storar found the transfusions disagreeable. He was also distressed by the blood and blood clots in his urine which apparently increased immediately after a transfusion. He could not comprehend the purpose of the transfusions and on one or two occasions had displayed some initial resistance. To eliminate his apprehension he was given a sedative approximately one hour before a transfusion. He also received regular doses of narcotics to alleviate the pain associated with the disease.

On the other hand several experts testified that there was support in the medical community for the view that, at this stage, transfusions may only prolong suffering and that treatment could properly be limited to administering pain killers. Mrs. Storar testified that she wanted the transfusions discontinued because she only wanted her son to be comfortable. She admitted that no one had ever explained to her what might happen to him if the transfusions were stopped. She also stated that she was not "sure" whether he might die sooner if the blood was not replaced and was unable to determine whether he wanted to live. However, in view of the fact that he obviously disliked the transfusions and tried to avoid them, she believed that he would want them discontinued.

* * *

John Storar was never competent at any time in his life. * * * Thus it is unrealistic to attempt to determine whether he would want to continue potentially life prolonging treatment if he were competent. * * * Mentally, John Storar was an infant and that is the only realistic way to assess his rights in this litigation. Thus this case bears only superficial similarities to *Eichner* and the determination must proceed from different principles.

A parent or guardian has a right to consent to medical treatment on behalf of an infant. [ ] The parent, however, may not deprive a child of life saving treatment, however well intentioned. * * *

In the *Storar* case there is the additional complication of two threats to his life. There was cancer of the bladder which was incurable and would in all probability claim his life. There was also the related loss of blood which posed the risk of an earlier death, but which, at least at the time of the hearing, could be replaced by transfusions. Thus, as one of the experts noted, the transfusions were analogous to food—they would not cure the cancer, but they could eliminate the risk of death from another treatable cause. Of course, John Storar did not like them, as might be expected of one with an infant's mentality. But the evidence convincingly shows that the transfusions did not involve excessive pain and that without them his mental and physical abilities would not be maintained at the usual level. With the transfusions on the other hand, he was essentially the same as he was before except of course he had a fatal illness which would ultimately claim his life. Thus, on the record, we have concluded that the application for permission to continue the transfusions should have been granted. Although we understand and respect his mother's despair, as we respect the beliefs of those who oppose transfusions on religious grounds, a court should not in the circumstances of this case allow an incompetent patient to bleed to death because someone, even someone as close as a parent or sibling, feels that this is best for one with an incurable disease.

* * *

NOTES AND QUESTIONS

1.   How would the Supreme Judicial Court of Massachusetts have decided *Storar?* How would the New York Court of Appeals have decided *Saikewicz?* How would either of these cases be decided under the Uniform Health–Care Decisions Act? Which is preferable? Why?

2.   The approach of the Massachusetts court in *Saikewicz* has been criticized on the grounds that it makes no sense to apply the doctrine of substi-

tuted judgment to the case of a patient who has never been competent. Do you agree with this criticism? Not all justices on the Massachusetts court agree with the approach of the majority. One justice strongly disagrees for reasons he expressed briefly in dissent from an opinion in which the court applied the doctrine of substituted judgment to allow for the removal of life-sustaining treatment for an infant who had been in an irreversible coma since an auto accident in her first year of life:

> [T]he court again has approved application of the doctrine of substituted judgment where there is not a soupçon of evidence to support it. The trial judge did not have a smidgen of evidence on which to conclude that if this child who is now about five and one half years old were competent to decide, she would elect certain death to a life with no cognitive ability. The route by which the court arrived at its conclusion is a cruel charade which is being perpetuated whenever we are faced with a life and death decision of an incompetent person.

Care and Protection of Beth, 412 Mass. 188, 587 N.E.2d 1377, 1383 (1992) (Nolan, J., dissenting.) Is the debate between those who would apply the best interest standard and those who would apply the substituted judgment standard in the case of a patient who had never been competent really just a debate between those who presume that life-sustaining treatment must be continued in virtually every case and those who believe that it is sometimes inappropriate treatment? For two examples of judicial decisions that equate maintaining life-sustaining medical treatment with an incompetent patient's best interest, at least in cases involving children, see In re D.H., 15 Misc.3d 565, 834 N.Y.S.2d 623 (Sup. 2007) and J.N. v. Superior Court, 156 Cal.App.3d 384, 67 Cal.Rptr.3d 384 (2007).

IV.   "FUTILE" TREATMENT

TEX. HEALTH & SAFETY CODE § 166.046 § 166.052; § 166.053
[THE "TEXAS FUTILITY STATUTE," A PART OF THE TEXAS ADVANCE DIRECTIVES ACT]

* * *

§ 166.046—Procedure if Not Effectuating a Directive or Treatment Decision

(a) If an attending physician refuses to honor a patient's advance directive or a health care or treatment decision made by or on behalf of a patient, the physician's refusal shall be reviewed by an ethics or medical committee. The attending physician may not be a member of that committee. The patient shall be given life-sustaining treatment during the review.

(b) The patient or the person responsible for the health care decisions of the individual who has made the decision regarding the directive or treatment decision:

    (1) may be given a written description of the ethics or medical committee review process and any other policies and procedures related to this section adopted by the health care facility;

    (2) shall be informed of the committee review process not less than 48 hours before the meeting called to discuss the patient's directive, unless the time period is waived by mutual agreement;

    (3) at the time of being so informed, shall be provided:

        (A) a copy of the appropriate statement [describing this process]; and

        (B) a copy of the registry list of health care providers and referral groups that have volunteered their readiness to consider accepting transfer or to assist in locating a provider willing to accept transfer * * *; and

    (4) is entitled to:

        (A) attend the meeting; and

        (B) receive a written explanation of the decision reached during the review process.

(c) The written explanation * * * must be included in the patient's medical record.

(d) If the attending physician, the patient, or the person responsible for the health care decisions of the individual does not agree with the decision reached during the review process under Subsection (b), the physician shall make a reasonable effort to transfer the patient to a physician who is willing to comply with the directive. If the patient is a patient in a health care facility, the facility's personnel shall assist the physician in arranging the patient's transfer to:

    (1) another physician;

    (2) an alternative care setting within that facility; or

    (3) another facility.

(e) If the patient or the person responsible for the health care decisions of the patient is requesting life-sustaining treatment that the attending physician has decided and the review process has affirmed is inappropriate treatment, the patient shall be given available life-sustaining treatment pending transfer * * *. The patient is responsible for any costs incurred in transferring the patient to another facility. The physician and the health care facility are not obligated to provide life-sustaining treatment after the 10th day after the written decision required under Subsection (b) is provided to the patient or the person responsible for the health care decisions of the patient unless ordered to do so under Subsection (g).

(e–1) If during a previous admission to a facility a patient's attending physician and the review process * * * have determined that life-sustaining treatment is inappropriate, and the patient is readmitted to the same facility within six months from the date of the decision reached during the review process conducted upon the previous admission, Subsections (b) through (e) need not be followed if the patient's attending physician and a consulting physician who is a member of the ethics or medical committee of the facility document on the patient's readmission that the patient's condition either has not improved or has deteriorated since the review process was conducted.

(f) Life-sustaining treatment under this section may not be entered in the patient's medical record as medically unnecessary treatment until the time period provided under Subsection (e) has expired.

(g) At the request of the patient or the person responsible for the health care decisions of the patient, the appropriate district or county court shall extend the time period provided under Subsection (e) only if the court finds, by a preponderance of the evidence, that there is a reasonable expectation that a physician or health care facility that will honor the patient's directive will be found if the time extension is granted.

(h) * * * This section does not apply to hospice services provided by a home and community support services agency * * *.

*   *   *

§ 166.052—Statements Explaining Patient's Right to Transfer

(a) In cases in which the attending physician refuses to honor an advance directive or treatment decision requesting the provision of life-sustaining treatment, the statement required * * * shall be in substantially the following form:

> You have been given this information because you have requested life-sustaining treatment,* which the attending physician believes is not appropriate. This information is being provided to help you understand state law, your rights, and the resources

---

    *   "Life-sustaining treatment" means treatment that, based on reasonable medical judgment, sustains the life of a patient and without which the patient will die. The term includes both life-sustaining medications and artificial life support, such as mechanical breathing machines, kidney dialysis treatment, and artificial nutrition and hydration. The term does not include the administration of pain management medication or the performance of a medical procedure considered to be necessary to provide comfort care, or any other medical care provided to alleviate a patient's pain.

available to you in such circumstances. It outlines the process for resolving disagreements about treatment among patients, families, and physicians. It is based upon [this section].

When There Is A Disagreement About Medical Treatment: The Physician Recommends Against Life–Sustaining Treatment That You Wish To Continue

When an attending physician refuses to comply with an advance directive or other request for life-sustaining treatment because of the physician's judgment that the treatment would be inappropriate, the case will be reviewed by an ethics or medical committee. Life-sustaining treatment will be provided through the review.

You will receive notification of this review at least 48 hours before a meeting of the committee related to your case. You are entitled to attend the meeting. With your agreement, the meeting may be held sooner than 48 hours, if possible.

You are entitled to receive a written explanation of the decision reached during the review process.

If after this review process both the attending physician and the ethics or medical committee conclude that life-sustaining treatment is inappropriate and yet you continue to request such treatment, then the following procedure will occur:

1.   The physician, with the help of the health care facility, will assist you in trying to find a physician and facility willing to provide the requested treatment.

2.   You are being given a list of health care providers and referral groups that have volunteered their readiness to consider accepting transfer, or to assist in locating a provider willing to accept transfer* * *. You may wish to contact providers or referral groups on the list or others of your choice to get help in arranging a transfer.

3.   The patient will continue to be given life-sustaining treatment until he or she can be transferred to a willing provider for up to 10 days from the time you were given the committee's written decision that life-sustaining treatment is not appropriate.

4.   If a transfer can be arranged, the patient will be responsible for the costs of the transfer.

5.   If a provider cannot be found willing to give the requested treatment within 10 days, life-sustaining treatment may be withdrawn unless a court of law has granted an extension.

6.   You may ask the appropriate district or county court to extend the 10–day period if the court finds that there is a reasonable expectation that a physician or health care facility willing to provide life-sustaining treatment will be found if the extension is granted.

*   *   *

(c) An attending physician or health care facility may, if it chooses, include any additional information concerning the physician's or facility's policy, perspective, experience, or review procedure.

§ 166.053—Registry to Assist Transfers

(a) The Texas Health Care Information Council shall maintain a registry listing the identity of and contact information for health care providers and referral groups * * * that have voluntarily notified the council they may consider accepting or may assist in locating a provider willing to accept transfer of a patient under [this statute].

(b) The listing of a provider or referral group in the registry described in this section does not obligate the provider or group to accept transfer of or provide services to any particular patient.

*   *   *

CHRISTUS ST. VINCENT HOPITAL POLICY
MEDICAL "FUTILITY": COMMUNICATING TREATMENT OBJECTIVES AND POTENTIAL OUTCOMES; DETERMINING MEDICAL INEFFECTIVENESS; RESOLVING CONFLICTS
(APPROVED 2005).

Purpose: To inform health care professionals of their legal and moral obligations when they are asked to provide treatments that they believe have no benefit for a patient. To describe processes available to address conflicts over treatments that may be medically ineffective.

Policy: Health care professionals are not morally or legally required to provide ineffective treatments, or to participate in aspects of care or treatment that conflict with their deeply held moral or religious beliefs. Providers should communicate to patients and/or their families or surrogate decision-makers why they believe particular treatment measures are inappropriate, and should endeavor to understand the patient's values and goals that may lead to a different conclusion. Communication should be honest and respectful, and the language used should be understandable to people who are not medical professionals. Health care professionals are never justified in abandoning their patients. If necessary, the provider must arrange for orderly transfer of the patient to another health care giver. Treatments already in process are to be continued until the conflict is resolved or care is transferred.

Discussion: Concerns over what is often called "medical futility" may give rise to conflicts among health care providers, patients and families. The terms "futile" and "futility" are unclear and should be avoided. In particular, the term "futile" should never be used to refer to a patient.

Instead, health care providers should speak clearly about specific proposed treatments and why the provider believes they are likely to be ineffective. Resolution of disagreements regarding choice and effectiveness of treatment depends on good communication among the involved parties.

"Medically ineffective health care" is defined in New Mexico law as "treatment that would not offer the patient any significant benefit, as determined by a physician". (NM Uniform Health Care Decisions Act of 1995, as amended, § 24–7A–7(F) NMSA 1978) Legal definitions do not end the inquiry, however; moral considerations and obligations are also relevant to health care decision-making.

Providers often use the term "futile" as shorthand for a number of different concepts. For example, the provider may mean that:

- the treatment has no chance of achieving the desired physiological effect,
- the treatment is statistically extremely unlikely to achieve its immediate goals,
- the treatment may be able to achieve immediate physiological goals but would fail to achieve long-term goals or would cause the patient to undergo continual or repeated interventions over a very short time prior to death,
- the harm caused by the treatment will most likely outweigh its benefit,
- the provider believes the patient's quality of life following treatment would be unacceptable, or
- the overall costs of treatment are grossly disproportionate to the expected benefit. However, cost-effectiveness should never be the primary or determining factor in deciding on treatments.

Providers bring to the discussion of treatment decisions biomedical expertise and experience in caring for patients. However, providers have no special expertise in making moral, religious or quality of life judgments regarding individual patients. Providers should respect choices made by patients and families, even if those choices vary from those of the provider. While a provider is not required to provide any particular treatment measure simply because a patient requests it, it is the patient's values and goals that should guide treatment decision-making.

Procedure:

When disagreements over treatment arise, the following procedure must be followed

    1.   There must be a reasonable degree of medical certainty that the proposed medical intervention meets the legal definition of medically ineffective care.

    2.   There must be documentation in the patient's medical record, by the attending physician, of discussion with the patient, surrogate decision-maker, and/or family about the patient's values and goals of care and the basis for the physician's opinion as to whether a proposed intervention is appropriate.

    3.   In the case of disagreement concerning the choice and effectiveness of treatment a process of <u>conflict avoidance</u> may be invoked. In this event, the case manager:

- is notified of the disagreement or potential disagreement.
- confers separately with the patient (or surrogate decision makers) to identify their main concerns, fears and goals.
- confers separately with the physician(s) and/or other members of the treatment team to identify the healthcare providers' goals and treatment plans.
- provides the patient and family with opportunities to talk things through
- notifies the patient's primary care physician (if s/he is not already involved) of the pending conflict.
- advises the physician(s) and/or other members of the team as to the nature of the differences.
- advises the patient/surrogate of the availability of the Bioethics Committee to help clarify goals and options regarding treatments.
- monitors the progress of communication and compromise.

    4.   If a satisfactory resolution is not forthcoming, the case manager will invoke a process of <u>conflict resolution</u>:

- The healthcare team recommends an independent medical opinion be obtained. The case manager should facilitate the independent medical consultation.
- The patient/surrogate is offered the opportunity to transfer treatment to another physician or institution; the case manager should facilitate such a transfer.

- A meeting is arranged with members of the Bioethics Committee. The meeting may include patient/surrogate, family and friends, the physician(s), any other members of the treatment team and/or representatives from [Christus] St. Vincent Hospital administration. The aim of this meeting is to:
- clarify the concerns and goals of both parties; and,
- help identify possible solutions and compromises

5.   If a satisfactory plan of action is not determined at that meeting a follow-up meeting with members of the Bioethics Committee and other parties may be scheduled in a reasonably short period of time. If not already done, the case manager at this point informs the [Christus] St. Vincent Hospital Risk Manager and/or in-house counsel of the ongoing conflict.

6.   At the follow-up meeting another attempt is made to achieve resolution through compromise. If the parties continue to disagree, the meeting facilitator should openly acknowledge the failure of the process up to this point. Further meetings with the Bioethics Committee are offered on an as-desired basis.

7.   The patient/surrogate should be informed of his/her legal rights and given guidance as to how to invoke advocacy through the legal system. The patient/surrogate is informed of the hospital's corresponding legal rights and its intent, if that is the case, to seek remedy through the courts.

8.   At any time, the physician has the right to recuse him/herself from this case and must identify an alternate physician to assume the patient's treatment unless the patient/surrogate refuses and chooses to assume this responsibility on their own. At any time, the patient/surrogate has the right to attempt to identify an alternate physician and/or facility willing and available to assume the patient's treatment. The attending physician will continue to treat until an alternate has accepted the responsibilities of treatment.

FROEDTERT HOSPITAL—MEDICAL COLLEGE OF WISCONSIN, FUTILITY POLICY
(revised 2007).

*   *   *

If, in the well-grounded judgment of the attending physician and a staff physician consultant, life-sustaining medical treatment would be futile, the attending physician may write an order withholding or withdrawing the treatment after notifying the patient (or other responsible individual if the patient lacks decision-making capacity). Appropriate palliative care measures should be instituted. A life-sustaining medical intervention should be considered "futile" if it cannot be expected to restore or maintain vital organ function or to achieve the expressed goals of the patient when decisional.

Life-sustaining medical treatment includes cardiopulmonary resuscitation, mechanical ventilation, artificial nutrition and hydration, blood products, renal dialysis, vasopressors, or any other treatment that prolongs dying.

Consultation with Palliative Medicine, Social Services, and Chaplaincy, as appropriate, is strongly encouraged. If there are remaining questions, the physician should consult the Ethics Committee. If the patient (or surrogate) disagrees, the attending physician should consider whether transfer to another attending physician, or another health care facility willing to accept the patient, is feasible. If transfer to a physician or facility willing to accept the patient is not feasible, further life-sustaining medical treatment may be withdrawn.

The attending physician must inform the Office of the Senior Vice President for Medical Affairs verbally when this policy is invoked and document the notice in the patient's medical record.

NOTES AND QUESTIONS

1. Who has the final authority to make that decision under the Texas statute and the two hospital policies? Who would you allow to be the final arbiter of whether a proposed treatment is futile? For a review of existing hospital policies, see Sandra H. Johnson, et al., Legal and Institutional Policy Responses to Medical Futility, 30 J. Health & Hosp. L. 1 (1997).

2. When is requested care truly "futile"? Under the Froedtert Hospital Policy, how is futility defined? Who has the authority to make that decision? How is it defined for purposes of the St. Vincent policy? Under the Texas statute, how is futility defined? Which definition makes the most sense, given the purposes of futility laws and policies? How would you define futility? Meir Katz, When Is Medical Care Futile? The Institutional Competence of the Medical Profession Regarding the Provision of Life–Sustaining Medical Care, 90 Neb.L.Rev.1 (2011).

3. The term futility, is subject to a variety of interpretations, as the language of the St. Vincent policy suggests. Treatment is *scientifically futile* (or *medically futile*) when it cannot achieve the medical result that is expected by the patient (or by the family) making the request. As a general matter, scientifically futile treatment need not be offered or provided to a patient. A seriously ill cancer patient need not be provided with laetrile, a useless drug that has been popularized by those who would prey upon desperate patients and their families, even if that treatment is requested. A child with a viral illness need not be prescribed an antibiotic, even if the child's parents

request one, because, as a matter of science, the antibiotic will not be effective in treating that illness. Doctors need not do a CAT scan on a patient with a cold, even if that is what the patient wants, because there is no reason to believe that there will be any connection between what can be discovered on the scan and the appropriate treatment of the cold. As a general matter healthcare providers, who are trained in the science of medicine, are entitled to determine which treatments are scientifically futile.

A harder question arises when a patient requests treatment that is not scientifically futile, but that is, in the opinion of the health care provider, *ethically futile*. Treatment is ethically futile if it will not serve the underlying interests of the patient. For example, some providers believe that it is ethically futile to keep a patient's body aerated and nourished when that patient is in persistent vegetative state. These healthcare providers believe that it is beyond the scope of medicine to sustain mere corporeal existence. Some healthcare providers believe that it would be ethically futile to engage in CPR under circumstances in which the most that can be accomplished through that intervention would be to prolong the patient's life by a few hours. Families may disagree with physicians over what constitutes ethically futile treatment. Is there any reason to adopt the provider's perspective, rather than the family's, as the ethically "correct" one?

The Council on Ethical and Judicial Affairs of the AMA has determined that:

> [p]hysicians are not ethically obliged to deliver care that, in their best professional judgment, will not have a reasonable chance of benefiting their patients. Patients should not be given treatments simply because they demand them. Denials of treatment should be justified by reliance on openly stated ethical principles and acceptable standards of care, * * * not on the concept of "futility," which cannot be meaningfully defined.

Council on Ethical and Judicial Affairs, American Medical Association, Current Opinion 2.035, *Futility,* Code of Medical Ethics. Is the Council's position a convincing one, or is it merely a device to transfer the authority to make ethically charged decisions from patients to physicians? See Patrick Moore, An End-of-Life Quandry in Need of a Statutory Response: When Patients Demand Life–Sustaining Treatment That Physicians Are Unwilling to Provide, 48 B.C.L.Rev. 433 (2007).

4.   Under the Texas statute, what process must be followed before a patient seeking futile care is discharged from the hospital? You might prepare a flow chart including all of the steps required by the statute. Do these requirements seem reasonable? Is ten days enough to find an alternative placement for one who is about to have futile treatment removed? While the statute requires the creation of a registry of those who are willing to assist in the transfer of patients whose treatment has been found to be futile, as of

early 2013 there were only two health care providers—one doctor and one home health care company—on the list. Why are there so few physicians willing to assist patients under these circumstances?

5. The Texas statute has given rise to litigation. In one celebrated case the mother of Sun Hudson, an infant, sought judicial intervention to avoid the discontinuation of treatment that physicians believed to be futile. In another case involving an adult, Spiro Nikolouzos, had been transferred once after ventilator support was found to be futile. When the receiving institution reached the same conclusion and began to prepare for his discharge, his family sought more time to arrange for yet a second transfer. Both cases were decided on procedural grounds largely unrelated to the substantive provisions of the statute, but each ultimately recognized the authority of the health care provider to make futility determinations. See Hudson v. Texas Children's Hosp., 177 S.W.3d 232 (Tex. Ct. App. 2005) and Nikolouzos v. St. Luke's Episcopal Hosp., 162 S.W.3d 678 (Tex. Ct. App. 2005). Several other litigated cases have resulted in a great deal of press coverage but no reported opinions.

6. Some states with statutes modeled on the Uniform Health–Care Decisions Act provide that physicians need not give futile care. Recall that section 7(f) of that UHCDA provides that "A health-care provider or institution may decline to comply with an individual instruction or health-care decision that requires medically ineffective health care or health care contrary to generally accepted health-care standards applicable to the health-care provider or institution." See also Md. Code Ann., Health–Gen. section 5–611 and Va. Code Ann. section 54.1–2990. The Texas statute differs from these earlier statutes by providing an authoritative and conclusive endpoint for disputes.

7. Robert Truog, a thoughtful physician and bioethicist, writes that medical futility issues are based in "power, trust, hope, money, and suffering." Robert Truog, Medical Futility, 25 Ga. St. U.L. Rev. 985, 986 (2009). Is he right? If he is right, is this fact helpful in figuring out how to resolve disputes over medical futility? Mediation is often employed to help resolve these disputes in health care institutions. How helpful is mediation in dealing with conflict based in power, trust, hope, money and suffering?

8. There is a great deal of good writing on the proper legal approach to arguably futile treatment. The Summer, 2008 issue of Health Matrix has an excellent symposium on futility in health care and the legal response. For a good account of the fundamental issues at stake, see Lawrence Schneiderman & Nancy Jecker, Wrong Medicine (1995). See also Robert Truog, Medical Futility, 25 Ga. St. U.L. Rev. 985 (2009)(focus on the Sun Hudson case), Jerry Menikoff, Demanded Medical Care, 30 Ariz. St. L. J. 1091 (1998), and Judith Daar, Medical Futility and Implications for Physician Autonomy, 21 Am. J. L. & Med. 221 (1995). For a useful account of issues related to physicians' willingness to accept decisions to continue futile care, see M. Fetters et al., Conflict Resolution at the End of Life, 29 Critical Care Med. 921 (2001).

CHAPTER 17

MEDICALLY ASSISTED DYING

■ ■ ■

I. INTRODUCTION

There has been a significant debate in the United States and else-where over the past two decades over the propriety of medically assisted death; that is, medical care designed to help a patient die how and when the patient wants to die. As the last chapter established, every state allows a physician to assist a patient who wishes to discontinue life-sustaining medical care, at least under most circumstances. May a health care provider also provide affirmative intervention that will hasten the patient's death? Under what circumstances?

The language we use to discuss these questions has become especially divisive over the past few years, and we must be careful how we use words that have become laden with political and philosophical meaning. "Euthanasia," for example, generally refers to an affirmative act that directly and immediately causes the death of a patient for the benefit of that patient. "Involuntary euthanasia" is sometimes used to describe euthanasia against the will of the patient, although sometimes it means euthanasia without the formal and expressed consent of the patient. "Voluntary euthanasia" is sometimes used to refer to euthanasia upon request of the patient, although most careful thinkers avoid using that term altogether. "Active euthanasia" sometimes refers to some affirmative act of euthanasia, while "passive euthanasia" generally refers, technically incorrectly, to withholding or withdrawing life-sustaining treatment.

"Suicide" can refer to any act taken by a person to intentionally end his life (including the act of a patient taking a prescribed lethal dose of medication), but sometimes it refers only to an act taken by someone acting irrationally, or under the influence of extraordinary emotional distress or mental disease (and not, for example, to the act of a terminally ill, competent patient who knowingly takes a prescribed lethal dose to end his suffering). Both "euthanasia" and "suicide" have highly negative connotations, and the people who use those terms generally oppose the propriety of the act. The words "death" and "killing" in this context also have strong negative connotations, and those terms are used to describe medically assisted dying primarily by those who oppose its legality.

On the other hand, "Death with Dignity," which often refers to these same acts, has a positive connotation. Is anyone opposed to death with dignity? That is why advocates of the practice now made legal in Oregon and Washington placed the "Death with Dignity" title on the initiatives that were ultimately approved by the voters in each of those states. Similarly, "Right to Die" is generally a popular concept, and that term is used almost exclusively by those who approve of the use of this practice. For years, however, the phrase was used to describe the withdrawal of life-sustaining treatment. Using the same phrase in this context implicitly argues that there is no difference between the two. Although earlier editions of this casebook used the term, "physician assisted suicide" or "physician assisted death," both are abandoned in this edition because these terms are now used primarily by those who oppose this role for physicians. The authors were tempted by the term, "Aid in Dying," which has been adopted by many medical organizations to describe the practice, but that term is used primarily by those who support this role for physicians.

As you read the materials that follow, make sure that you identify with specificity exactly what practice is being considered. While there are a few countries that permit euthanasia under certain limited circumstances, that has never really been an option available in the United States and it is rarely part of the legal debate. In this country, the debate has centered on the propriety (and legality) of a medically prescribed lethal dose designed to be ingested by a competent, fully informed patient who originally requested a prescription for it from a physician. It is that practice that forms the core of the discussion in this chapter, and that the authors have chosen to call "Medically Assisted Dying."

II.   THE CONSTITUTIONAL FRAMEWORK

WASHINGTON V. GLUCKSBERG

Supreme Court of the United States, 1997.
521 U.S. 702, 117 S.Ct. 2258, 138 L.Ed.2d 772.

REHNQUIST, C. J., delivered the opinion of the Court, in which O'CONNOR, SCALIA, KENNEDY, and THOMAS, JJ., joined. O'CONNOR, J., filed a concurring opinion, in which GINSBURG and BREYER, JJ., joined in part. STEVENS, J., SOUTER, J., GINSBURG, J., and BREYER, J., filed opinions concurring in the judgment.

CHIEF JUSTICE REHNQUIST delivered the opinion of the Court.

The question presented in this case is whether Washington's prohibition against "causing" or "aiding" a suicide offends the Fourteenth Amendment to the United States Constitution. We hold that it does not.

*   *   *

The plaintiffs assert [ ] "the existence of a liberty interest protected by the Fourteenth Amendment which extends to a personal choice by a mentally competent, terminally ill adult to commit physician-assisted suicide." [ ] Relying primarily on Planned Parenthood v. Casey, [ ] and Cruzan v. Director, Missouri Dept. of Health, [ ] the District Court agreed, [ ] and concluded that Washington's assisted-suicide ban is unconstitutional because it "places an undue burden on the exercise of [that] constitutionally protected liberty interest." [ ] The District Court also decided that the Washington statute violated the Equal Protection Clause's requirement that " 'all persons similarly situated . . . be treated alike.' "[ ]

A panel of the Court of Appeals for the Ninth Circuit reversed, emphasizing that "in the two hundred and five years of our existence no constitutional right to aid in killing oneself has ever been asserted and upheld by a court of final jurisdiction." [ ] The Ninth Circuit reheard the case en banc, reversed the panel's decision, and affirmed the District Court. [ ] Like the District Court, the en banc Court of Appeals emphasized our Casey and Cruzan decisions. [ ] The court also discussed what it described as "historical" and "current societal attitudes" toward suicide and assisted suicide, [ ] and concluded that "the Constitution encompasses a due process liberty interest in controlling the time and manner of one's death—that there is, in short, a constitutionally-recognized 'right to die.' "[ ] After "weighing and then balancing" this interest against Washington's various interests, the court held that the State's assisted-suicide ban was unconstitutional "as applied to terminally ill competent [ ] adults who wish to hasten their deaths with medication prescribed by their physicians." [ ] We granted certiorari [ ] and now reverse.

I

We begin, as we do in all due-process cases, by examining our Nation's history, legal traditions, and practices. [ ] In almost every State—indeed, in almost every western democracy—it is a crime to assist a suicide. The States' assisted-suicide bans are not innovations. Rather, they are longstanding expressions of the States' commitment to the protection and preservation of all human life. [ ] Indeed, opposition to and condemnation of suicide—and, therefore, of assisting suicide—are consistent and enduring themes of our philosophical, legal, and cultural heritages. [ ]

More specifically, for over 700 years, the Anglo—American common-law tradition has punished or otherwise disapproved of both suicide and assisting suicide. * * * [The Chief Justice then reviews the common law of England and the American colonies and states with regards to suicide, from the 13th century to the present.]

*　　*　　*

Attitudes toward suicide itself have changed since [the 13th Century prohibitions on suicide] * * * but our laws have consistently condemned, and continue to prohibit, assisting suicide. Despite changes in medical technology and notwithstanding an increased emphasis on the importance of end-of-life decisionmaking, we have not retreated from this prohibition. Against this backdrop of history, tradition, and practice, we now turn to respondents' constitutional claim.

II

The Due Process Clause guarantees more than fair process, and the "liberty" it protects includes more than the absence of physical restraint. [ ] The Clause also provides heightened protection against government interference with certain fundamental rights and liberty interests. [ ] In a long line of cases, we have held that, in addition to the specific freedoms protected by the Bill of Rights, the "liberty" specially protected by the Due Process Clause includes the rights to marry, [ ]; to have children, [ ]; to direct the education and upbringing of one's children, [ ]; to marital privacy, [ ]; to use contraception, [ ]; to bodily integrity, [ ] and to abortion, [ ]. We have also assumed, and strongly suggested, that the Due Process Clause protects the traditional right to refuse unwanted lifesaving medical treatment. [ ]

But we "have always been reluctant to expand the concept of substantive due process because guideposts for responsible decisionmaking in this unchartered area are scarce and open-ended." [ ] By extending constitutional protection to an asserted right or liberty interest, we, to a great extent, place the matter outside the arena of public debate and legislative action. We must therefore "exercise the utmost care whenever we are asked to break new ground in this field" [ ] lest the liberty protected by the Due Process Clause be subtly transformed into the policy preferences of the members of this Court [ ].

Our established method of substantive-due-process analysis has two primary features: First, we have regularly observed that the Due Process Clause specially protects those fundamental rights and liberties which are, objectively, "deeply rooted in this Nation's history and tradition" [ ] and "implicit in the concept of ordered liberty," such that "neither liberty nor justice would exist if they were sacrificed" [ ]. Second, we have required in substantive-due-process cases a "careful description" of the asserted fundamental liberty interest. [ ] Cruzan, supra, at 277–278. Our Nation's history, legal traditions, and practices thus provide the crucial "guideposts for responsible decisionmaking" [ ] that direct and restrain our exposition of the Due Process Clause. As we stated recently in Flores, the Fourteenth Amendment "forbids the government to infringe . . . 'fundamental' liberty interests at all, no matter what process is provided, unless the infringement is narrowly tailored to serve a compelling state interest." [ ]

*   *   *

Turning to the claim at issue here, the Court of Appeals stated that "properly analyzed, the first issue to be resolved is whether there is a liberty interest in determining the time and manner of one's death" [ ] or, in other words, "is there a right to die?" [ ]. Similarly, respondents assert a "liberty to choose how to die" and a right to "control of one's final days," [ ] and describe the asserted liberty as "the right to choose a humane, dignified death" [ ] and "the liberty to shape death" [ ]. As noted above, we have a tradition of carefully formulating the interest at stake in substantive-due-process cases. For example, although Cruzan is often described as a "right to die" case [ ] we were, in fact, more precise: we assumed that the Constitution granted competent persons a "constitutionally protected right to refuse lifesaving hydration and nutrition." [ ] The Washington statute at issue in this case prohibits "aiding another person to attempt suicide," [ ] and, thus, the question before us is whether the "liberty" specially protected by the Due Process Clause includes a right to commit suicide which itself includes a right to assistance in doing so.

* * * With this "careful description" of respondents' claim in mind, we turn to Casey and Cruzan.

[The Chief Justice next discusses the Cruzan case, where, he says,] "we assumed that the United States Constitution would grant a competent person a constitutionally protected right to refuse lifesaving hydration and nutrition."

*   *   *

The right assumed in Cruzan, however, was not simply deduced from abstract concepts of personal autonomy. Given the common-law rule that forced medication was a battery, and the long legal tradition protecting the decision to refuse unwanted medical treatment, our assumption was entirely consistent with this Nation's history and constitutional traditions. The decision to commit suicide with the assistance of another may be just as personal and profound as the decision to refuse unwanted medical treatment, but it has never enjoyed similar legal protection. Indeed, the two acts are widely and reasonably regarded as quite distinct. [ ] In Cruzan itself, we recognized that most States outlawed assisted suicide— and even more do today—and we certainly gave no intimation that the right to refuse unwanted medical treatment could be somehow transmuted into a right to assistance in committing suicide. [ ]

Respondents also rely on Casey. There, the Court's opinion concluded that "the essential holding of Roe v. Wade should be retained and once again reaffirmed." [ ] We held, first, that a woman has a right, before her fetus is viable, to an abortion "without undue interference from the State"; second, that States may restrict post-viability abortions, so long as exceptions are made to protect a woman's life and health; and third, that the State has legitimate interests throughout a pregnancy in protecting the health of the woman and the life of the unborn child. [ ] In reaching this conclusion, the opinion discussed in some detail this Court's substantive-due-process tradition of interpreting the Due Process Clause to protect certain fundamental rights and "personal decisions relating to marriage, procreation, contraception, family relationships, child rearing, and education," and noted that many of those rights and liberties "involve the most intimate and personal choices a person may make in a lifetime." [ ]

* * *

That many of the rights and liberties protected by the Due Process Clause sound in personal autonomy does not warrant the sweeping conclusion that any and all important, intimate, and personal decisions are so protected, [ ] and Casey did not suggest otherwise.

The history of the law's treatment of assisted suicide in this country has been and continues to be one of the rejection of nearly all efforts to permit it. That being the case, our decisions lead us to conclude that the asserted "right" to assistance in committing suicide is not a fundamental liberty interest protected by the Due Process Clause. The Constitution also requires, however, that Washington's assisted-suicide ban be rationally related to legitimate government interests. [ ] This requirement is unquestionably met here. As the court below recognized, [ ] Washington's assisted-suicide ban implicates a number of state interests. [ ]

First, Washington has an "unqualified interest in the preservation of human life."

* * *

Relatedly, all admit that suicide is a serious public-health problem, especially among persons in otherwise vulnerable groups. [ ] The State has an interest in preventing suicide, and in studying, identifying, and treating its causes. [ ]

* * *

The State also has an interest in protecting the integrity and ethics of the medical profession. * * * [T]he American Medical Association, like many other medical and physicians' groups, has concluded that "physician-assisted suicide is fundamentally incompatible with the physician's role as healer." [ ] And physician-assisted suicide could, it is argued, undermine the trust that is essential to the doctor-patient relationship by blurring the time-honored line between healing and harming. [ ]

Next, the State has an interest in protecting vulnerable groups—including the poor, the elderly, and disabled persons—from abuse, neglect, and mistakes. * * * [One respected state task force] warned that "legalizing physician-assisted suicide would pose profound risks to many individuals who are ill and vulnerable. . . . The risk of harm is greatest for the many individuals in our society whose autonomy and well-being are already compromised by poverty, lack of access to good medical care, advanced age, or membership in a stigmatized social group." [ ] If physician-assisted suicide were permitted, many might resort to it to spare their families the substantial financial burden of end-of-life health-care costs.

* * * The State's assisted-suicide ban reflects and reinforces its policy that the lives of terminally ill, disabled, and elderly people must be no less valued than the lives of the young and healthy, and that a seriously disabled person's suicidal impulses should be interpreted and treated the same way as anyone else's. [ ]

Finally, the State may fear that permitting assisted suicide will start it down the path to voluntary and perhaps even involuntary euthanasia. * * * [Justice Rehnquist then discussed how this fear could arise out of the practice in the Netherlands.]

We need not weigh exactingly the relative strengths of these various interests. They are unquestionably important and legitimate, and Washington's ban on assisted suicide is at least reasonably related to their promotion and protection. We therefore hold that [ ] [the Washington ban on assisting suicide] does not violate the Fourteenth Amendment, either on its face or "as applied to competent, terminally ill adults who wish to hasten their deaths by obtaining medication prescribed by their doctors."[24] [ ]

*   *   *

Throughout the Nation, Americans are engaged in an earnest and profound debate about the morality, legality, and practicality of physician-assisted suicide. Our holding permits this debate to continue, as it should in a democratic society. The decision of the en banc Court of Ap-

---

[24] Justice Stevens states that "the Court does conceive of respondents' claim as a facial challenge—addressing not the application of the statute to a particular set of plaintiffs before it, but the constitutionality of the statute's categorical prohibition. . . . "[ ] We emphasize that we today reject the Court of Appeals' specific holding that the statute is unconstitutional "as applied" to a particular class. [ ] Justice Stevens agrees with this holding, [ ] but would not "foreclose the possibility that an individual plaintiff seeking to hasten her death, or a doctor whose assistance was sought, could prevail in a more particularized challenge," ibid. Our opinion does not absolutely foreclose such a claim. However, given our holding that the Due Process Clause of the Fourteenth Amendment does not provide heightened protection to the asserted liberty interest in ending one's life with a physician's assistance, such a claim would have to be quite different from the ones advanced by respondents here.

peals is reversed, and the case is remanded for further proceedings consistent with this opinion.

It is so ordered.

JUSTICE O'CONNOR, concurring [in both Glucksberg and Vacco].*

Death will be different for each of us. For many, the last days will be spent in physical pain and perhaps the despair that accompanies physical deterioration and a loss of control of basic bodily and mental functions. Some will seek medication to alleviate that pain and other symptoms.

The Court frames the issue in this case as whether the Due Process Clause of the Constitution protects a "right to commit suicide which itself includes a right to assistance in doing so," [ ] and concludes that our Nation's history, legal traditions, and practices do not support the existence of such a right. I join the Court's opinions because I agree that there is no generalized right to "commit suicide." But respondents urge us to address the narrower question whether a mentally competent person who is experiencing great suffering has a constitutionally cognizable interest in controlling the circumstances of his or her imminent death. I see no need to reach that question in the context of the facial challenges to the New York and Washington laws at issue here. [ ] The parties and amici agree that in these States a patient who is suffering from a terminal illness and who is experiencing great pain has no legal barriers to obtaining medication, from qualified physicians, to alleviate that suffering, even to the point of causing unconsciousness and hastening death. [ ] In this light, even assuming that we would recognize such an interest, I agree that the State's interests in protecting those who are not truly competent or facing imminent death, or those whose decisions to hasten death would not truly be voluntary, are sufficiently weighty to justify a prohibition against physician-assisted suicide. [ ]

Every one of us at some point may be affected by our own or a family member's terminal illness. There is no reason to think the democratic process will not strike the proper balance between the interests of terminally ill, mentally competent individuals who would seek to end their suffering and the State's interests in protecting those who might seek to end life mistakenly or under pressure. As the Court recognizes, States are presently undertaking extensive and serious evaluation of physician-assisted suicide and other related issues. [ ] In such circumstances, "the . . . challenging task of crafting appropriate procedures for safeguarding . . . liberty interests is entrusted to the 'laboratory' of the States . . . in the first instance." [ ]

---

* Justice Ginsburg concurs in the Court's judgments substantially for the reasons stated in this opinion. Justice Breyer joins this opinion except insofar as it joins the opinions of the Court.

In sum, there is no need to address the question whether suffering patients have a constitutionally cognizable interest in obtaining relief from the suffering that they may experience in the last days of their lives. There is no dispute that dying patients in Washington and New York can obtain palliative care, even when doing so would hasten their deaths. The difficulty in defining terminal illness and the risk that a dying patient's request for assistance in ending his or her life might not be truly voluntary justifies the prohibitions on assisted suicide we uphold here.

JUSTICE STEVENS, concurring in the judgments [in both Glucksberg and Vacco].

The Court ends its opinion with the important observation that our holding today is fully consistent with a continuation of the vigorous debate about the "morality, legality, and practicality of physician-assisted suicide" in a democratic society. [ ] I write separately to make it clear that there is also room for further debate about the limits that the Constitution places on the power of the States to punish the practice.

I

The morality, legality, and practicality of capital punishment have been the subject of debate for many years. In 1976, this Court upheld the constitutionality of the practice in cases coming to us from Georgia, Florida, and Texas. In those cases we concluded that a State does have the power to place a lesser value on some lives than on others; there is no absolute requirement that a State treat all human life as having an equal right to preservation. Because the state legislatures had sufficiently narrowed the category of lives that the State could terminate, and had enacted special procedures to ensure that the defendant belonged in that limited category, we concluded that the statutes were not unconstitutional on their face. In later cases coming to us from each of those States, however, we found that some applications of the statutes were unconstitutional.

Today, the Court decides that Washington's statute prohibiting assisted suicide is not invalid "on its face," that is to say, in all or most cases in which it might be applied. That holding, however, does not foreclose the possibility that some applications of the statute might well be invalid.

* * *

History and tradition provide ample support for refusing to recognize an open-ended constitutional right to commit suicide. Much more than the State's paternalistic interest in protecting the individual from the irrevocable consequences of an ill-advised decision motivated by temporary concerns is at stake. There is truth in John Donne's observation that "No man is an island." The State has an interest in preserving and fostering the benefits that every human being may provide to the community—a community that thrives on the exchange of ideas, expressions of affection, shared memories and humorous incidents as well as on the material contributions that its members create and support. The value to others of a person's life is far too precious to allow the individual to claim a constitutional entitlement to complete autonomy in making a decision to end that life. Thus, I fully agree with the Court that the "liberty" protected by the Due Process Clause does not include a categorical "right to commit suicide which itself includes a right to assistance in doing so." [ ]

But just as our conclusion that capital punishment is not always unconstitutional did not preclude later decisions holding that it is sometimes impermissibly cruel, so is it equally clear that a decision upholding a general statutory prohibition of assisted suicide does not mean that every possible application of the statute would be valid. A State, like Washington, that has authorized the death penalty and thereby has concluded that the sanctity of human life does not require that it always be preserved, must acknowledge that there are situations in which an interest in hastening death is legitimate. Indeed, not only is that interest sometimes legitimate, I am also convinced that there are times when it is entitled to constitutional protection.

II

In Cruzan [ ] the Court assumed that the interest in liberty protected by the Fourteenth Amendment encompassed the right of a terminally ill patient to direct the withdrawal of life-sustaining treatment. As the Court correctly observes today, that assumption "was not simply deduced from abstract concepts of personal autonomy." [ ] Instead, it was supported by the common-law tradition protecting the individual's general right to refuse unwanted medical treatment. [ ] We have recognized, however, that this common-law right to refuse treatment is neither absolute nor always sufficiently weighty to overcome valid countervailing state interests. * * *

Cruzan, however, was not the normal case. Given the irreversible nature of her illness and the progressive character of her suffering, Nancy Cruzan's interest in refusing medical care was incidental to her more basic interest in controlling the manner and timing of her death. In finding that her best interests would be served by cutting off the nourishment that kept her alive, the trial court did more than simply vindicate Cruzan's interest in refusing medical treatment; the court, in essence, authorized affirmative conduct that would hasten her death. When this Court reviewed the case and upheld Missouri's requirement that there be clear and convincing evidence establishing Nancy Cruzan's intent to have life-sustaining nourishment withdrawn, it made two important assumptions: (1) that there was a "liberty interest" in refusing unwanted treatment protected by the Due Process Clause; and (2) that this liberty interest did not "end the inquiry" because it might be outweighed by relevant state interests. [ ] I agree with both of those assumptions, but I insist that the source of Nancy Cruzan's right to refuse treatment was not just a common-law rule. Rather, this right is an aspect of a far broader and more basic concept of freedom that is even older than the common law. This freedom embraces, not merely a person's right to refuse a particular kind of unwanted treatment, but also her interest in dignity, and in determining the character of the memories that will survive long after her death. In recognizing that the State's interests did not outweigh Nancy Cruzan's liberty interest in refusing medical treatment, Cruzan rested not simply on the common-law right to refuse medical treatment, but—at least implicitly—on the even more fundamental right to make this "deeply personal decision," [ ].

*   *   *

While I agree with the Court that Cruzan does not decide the issue presented by these cases, Cruzan did give recognition, not just to vague, unbridled notions of autonomy, but to the more specific interest in making decisions about how to confront an imminent death. Although there is no absolute right to physician-assisted suicide, Cruzan makes it clear that some individuals who no longer have the option of deciding whether to live or to die because they are already on the threshold of death have a constitutionally protected interest that may outweigh the State's interest in preserving life at all costs. The liberty interest at stake in a case like this differs from, and is stronger than, both the common-law right to refuse medical treatment and the unbridled interest in deciding whether to live or die. It is an interest in deciding how, rather than whether, a critical threshold shall be crossed.

III

The state interests supporting a general rule banning the practice of physician-assisted suicide do not have the same force in all cases. First and foremost of these interests is the " 'unqualified interest in the preservation of human life' "[ ].

* * *. Although as a general matter the State's interest in the contributions each person may make to society outweighs the person's interest in ending her life, this interest does not have the same force for a terminally ill patient faced not with the choice of whether to live, only of how to die. * * *

Similarly, the State's legitimate interests in preventing suicide, protecting the vulnerable from coercion and abuse, and preventing euthanasia are less significant in this context. I agree that the State has a compelling interest in preventing persons from committing suicide because of depression, or coercion by third parties. But the State's legitimate interest in preventing abuse does not apply to an individual who is not victimized by abuse, who is not suffering from depression, and who makes a rational and voluntary decision to seek assistance in dying.

* * *

The final major interest asserted by the State is its interest in preserving the traditional integrity of the medical profession. The fear is that a rule permitting physicians to assist in suicide is inconsistent with the perception that they serve their patients solely as healers. But for some patients, it would be a physician's refusal to dispense medication to ease their suffering and make their death tolerable and dignified that would be inconsistent with the healing role * * *.

* * * I do not * * * foreclose the possibility that an individual plaintiff seeking to hasten her death, or a doctor whose assistance was sought, could prevail in a more particularized challenge. Future cases will determine whether such a challenge may succeed.

IV

* * *

There may be little distinction between the intent of a terminally-ill patient who decides to remove her life-support and one who seeks the assistance of a doctor in ending her life; in both situations, the patient is seeking to hasten a certain, impending death. The doctor's intent might also be the same in prescribing lethal medication as it is in terminating life support. * * *

Thus, although the differences the majority notes in causation and intent between terminating life-support and assisting in suicide support the Court's rejection of the respondents' facial challenge, these distinctions may be inapplicable to particular terminally ill patients and their doctors. Our holding today in Vacco v. Quill that the Equal Protection Clause is not violated by New York's classification, just like our holding in Washington v. Glucksberg that the Washington statute is not invalid on its face, does not foreclose the possibility that some applications of the New York statute may impose an intolerable intrusion on the patient's freedom.

There remains room for vigorous debate about the outcome of particular cases that are not necessarily resolved by the opinions announced today. How such cases may be decided will depend on their specific facts. In my judgment, however, it is clear that the so-called "unqualified interest in the preservation of human life," [ ] is not itself sufficient to outweigh the interest in liberty that may justify the only possible means of preserving a dying patient's dignity and alleviating her intolerable suffering.

JUSTICE SOUTER, concurring in the judgment.

*   *   *

When the physicians claim that the Washington law deprives them of a right falling within the scope of liberty that the Fourteenth Amendment guarantees against denial without due process of law, they are not claiming some sort of procedural defect in the process through which the statute has been enacted or is administered. Their claim, rather, is that the State has no substantively adequate justification for barring the assistance sought by the patient and sought to be offered by the physician. Thus, we are dealing with a claim to one of those rights sometimes described as rights of substantive due process and sometimes as unenumerated rights, in view of the breadth and indeterminacy of the "due process" serving as the claim's textual basis. The doctors accordingly arouse the skepticism of those who find the Due Process Clause an unduly vague or oxymoronic warrant for judicial review of substantive state law, just as they also invoke two centuries of American constitutional practice in recognizing unenumerated, substantive limits on governmental action. * * *

*   *   *

[Justice Souter explained that he was adopting Justice Harlan's approach to the Constitutional evaluation and protection of unenumerated rights under the Due Process Clause, as articulated in his dissent in Poe v. Ullman.] My understanding of unenumerated rights in the wake of the Poe dissent and subsequent cases avoids the absolutist failing of many older cases without embracing the opposite pole of equating reasonableness with past practice described at a very specific level. [ ] That understanding begins with a concept of "ordered liberty," [ ] comprising a continuum of rights to be free from "arbitrary impositions and purposeless restraints" [ ].

*   *   *

This approach calls for a court to assess the relative "weights" or dignities of the contending interests, and to this extent the judicial method is familiar to the common law. Common law method is subject, however, to two important constraints in the hands of a court engaged in substantive due process review. First, such a court is bound to confine the values that it recognizes to those truly deserving constitutional stature, either to those expressed in constitutional text, or those exemplified by "the traditions from which [the Nation] developed," or revealed by contrast with "the traditions from which it broke." [ ]

The second constraint, again, simply reflects the fact that constitutional review, not judicial lawmaking, is a court's business here. The weighing or valuing of contending interests in this sphere is only the first step, forming the basis for determining whether the statute in question falls inside or outside the zone of what is reasonable in the way it resolves the conflict between the interests of state and individual.

* * *

The State has put forward several interests to justify the Washington law as applied to physicians treating terminally ill patients, even those competent to make responsible choices: protecting life generally [ ], discouraging suicide even if knowing and voluntary [ ], and protecting terminally ill patients from involuntary suicide and euthanasia, both voluntary and nonvoluntary [ ].

It is not necessary to discuss the exact strengths of the first two claims of justification in the present circumstances, for the third is dispositive for me. * * * [Justice Souter then explained why the Washington state legislature, on the basis of information now available, could have reasonably decided that a statute forbidding assisting suicide might protect terminally ill patients.]

* * *

The Court should accordingly stay its hand to allow reasonable legislative consideration. While I do not decide for all time that respondents' claim should not be recognized, I acknowledge the legislative institutional competence as the better one to deal with that claim at this time.

JUSTICE BREYER, concurring in the judgments [in both Glucksberg and Vacco].

I believe that Justice O'Connor's views, which I share, have greater legal significance than the Court's opinion suggests. I join her separate opinion, except insofar as it joins the majority. * * *

I agree with the Court in Vacco v. Quill [ ] that the articulated state interests justify the distinction drawn between physician assisted suicide and withdrawal of life-support. I also agree with the Court that the critical question in both of the cases before us is whether "the 'liberty' specially protected by the Due Process Clause includes a right" of the sort that the respondents assert. [ ] I do not agree, however, with the Court's formulation of that claimed "liberty" interest. The Court describes it as a "right to commit suicide with another's assistance." [ ] But I would not reject the respondents' claim without considering a different formulation, for which our legal tradition may provide greater support. That formulation would use words roughly like a "right to die with dignity." But irrespective of the exact words used, at its core would lie personal control over the manner of death, professional medical assistance, and the avoidance of unnecessary and severe physical suffering—combined.

* * *

I do not believe, however, that this Court need or now should decide whether or a not * * * [a right to die with dignity] is "fundamental." That is because, in my view, the avoidance of severe physical pain (connected with death) would have to comprise an essential part of any successful claim and because * * * the laws before us do not force a dying person to undergo that kind of pain. [ ] Rather, the laws of New York and of Washington do not prohibit doctors from providing patients with drugs sufficient to control pain despite the risk that those drugs themselves will kill. [ ] And under these circumstances the laws of New York and Washington would overcome any remaining significant interests and would be justified, regardless.

*　　*　　*

Were the legal circumstances different—for example, were state law to prevent the provision of palliative care, including the administration of drugs as needed to avoid pain at the end of life—then the law's impact upon serious and otherwise unavoidable physical pain (and accompanying death) would be more directly at issue. And as JUSTICE O'CONNOR suggests, the Court might have to revisit its conclusions in these cases.

*　　*　　*

VACCO V. QUILL

Supreme Court of the United States, 1997.
521 U.S. 793, 117 S.Ct. 2293, 138 L.Ed.2d 834.

CHIEF JUSTICE REHNQUIST delivered the opinion of the Court.

In New York, as in most States, it is a crime to aid another to commit or attempt suicide, but patients may refuse even lifesaving medical treatment. The question presented by this case is whether New York's prohibition on assisting suicide therefore violates the Equal Protection Clause of the Fourteenth Amendment. We hold that it does not.

* * * Respondents, and three gravely ill patients who have since died, sued the State's Attorney General in the United States District Court. They urged that because New York permits a competent person to refuse life-sustaining medical treatment, and because the refusal of such treatment is "essentially the same thing" as physician-assisted suicide, New York's assisted-suicide ban violates the Equal Protection Clause. [ ]

The District Court disagreed * * *.

The Court of Appeals for the Second Circuit reversed. [ ] The court determined that, despite the assisted-suicide ban's apparent general applicability, "New York law does not treat equally all competent persons who are in the final stages of fatal illness and wish to hasten their deaths," because "those in the final stages of terminal illness who are on life-support systems are allowed to hasten their deaths by directing the removal of such systems; but those who are similarly situated, except for the previous attachment of life-sustaining equipment, are not allowed to hasten death by self-administering prescribed drugs." [ ] The Court of Appeals then examined whether this supposed unequal treatment was rationally related to any legitimate state interests, and concluded that "to the extent that [New York's statutes] prohibit a physician from prescribing medications to be self-administered by a mentally competent, terminally-ill person in the final stages of his terminal illness, they are not rationally related to any legitimate state interest." [ ] We granted certiorari [ ] and now reverse.

The Equal Protection Clause commands that no State shall "deny to any person within its jurisdiction the equal protection of the laws." This provision creates no substantive rights. [ ] Instead, it embodies a general rule that States must treat like cases alike but may treat unlike cases accordingly. [ ] If a legislative classification or distinction "neither burdens a fundamental right nor targets a suspect class, we will uphold [it] so long as it bears a rational relation to some legitimate end." [ ]

New York's statutes outlawing assisting suicide affect and address matters of profound significance to all New Yorkers alike. They neither infringe fundamental rights nor involve suspect classifications. [ ] These laws are therefore entitled to a "strong presumption of validity." [ ]

On their faces, neither New York's ban on assisting suicide nor its statutes permitting patients to refuse medical treatment treat anyone differently than anyone else or draw any distinctions between persons. Everyone, regardless of physical condition, is entitled, if competent, to refuse unwanted lifesaving medical treatment; no one is permitted to assist a suicide. Generally speaking, laws that apply evenhandedly to all "unquestionably comply" with the Equal Protection Clause. [ ]

The Court of Appeals, however, concluded that some terminally ill people—those who are on life-support systems—are treated differently than those who are not, in that the former may "hasten death" by ending treatment, but the latter may not "hasten death" through physician-assisted suicide. [ ] This conclusion depends on the submission that ending or refusing lifesaving medical treatment "is nothing more nor less than assisted suicide." [ ] Unlike the Court of Appeals, we think the distinction between assisting suicide and withdrawing life-sustaining treatment, a distinction widely recognized and endorsed in the medical profession and in our legal traditions, is both important and logical; it is certainly rational. [ ]

The distinction comports with fundamental legal principles of causation and intent. First, when a patient refuses life-sustaining medical treatment, he dies from an underlying fatal disease or pathology; but if a patient ingests lethal medication prescribed by a physician, he is killed by that medication. [ ]

Furthermore, a physician who withdraws, or honors a patient's refusal to begin, life-sustaining medical treatment purposefully intends, or may so intend, only to respect his patient's wishes and "to cease doing useless and futile or degrading things to the patient when [the patient] no longer stands to benefit from them." [ ] The same is true when a doctor provides aggressive palliative care; in some cases, painkilling drugs may hasten a patient's death, but the physician's purpose and intent is, or may be, only to ease his patient's pain. A doctor who assists a suicide, however, "must, necessarily and indubitably, intend primarily that the patient be made dead." [ ] Similarly, a patient who commits suicide with a doctor's aid necessarily has the specific intent to end his or her own life, while a patient who refuses or discontinues treatment might not. [ ]

The law has long used actors' intent or purpose to distinguish between two acts that may have the same result. [ ] Put differently, the law distinguishes actions taken "because of" a given end from actions taken "in spite of" their unintended but foreseen consequences. [ ]

Given these general principles, it is not surprising that many courts, including New York courts, have carefully distinguished refusing life-sustaining treatment from suicide. * * *

Similarly, the overwhelming majority of state legislatures have drawn a clear line between assisting suicide and withdrawing or permitting the refusal of unwanted lifesaving medical treatment by prohibiting the former and permitting the latter. [ ] And "nearly all states expressly disapprove of suicide and assisted suicide either in statutes dealing with durable powers of attorney in health-care situations, or in 'living will' statutes." [ ] Thus, even as the States move to protect and promote patients' dignity at the end of life, they remain opposed to physician-assisted suicide.

*   *   *

This Court has also recognized, at least implicitly, the distinction between letting a patient die and making that patient die. In Cruzan [ ] we concluded that "the principle that a competent person has a constitutionally protected liberty interest in refusing unwanted medical treatment may be inferred from our prior decisions," and we assumed the existence of such a right for purposes of that case [ ]. But our assumption of a right to refuse treatment was grounded not, as the Court of Appeals supposed, on the proposition that patients have a general and abstract "right to hasten death," [ ] but on well established, traditional rights to bodily integrity and freedom from unwanted touching [ ]. In fact, we observed that "the majority of States in this country have laws imposing criminal penalties on one who assists another to commit suicide." [ ] Cruzan therefore provides no support for the notion that refusing life-sustaining medical treatment is "nothing more nor less than suicide."

For all these reasons, we disagree with respondents' claim that the distinction between refusing lifesaving medical treatment and assisted suicide is "arbitrary" and "irrational.[11] Granted, in some cases, the line between the two may not be clear, but certainty is not required, even were it possible. Logic and contemporary practice support New York's judgment that the two acts are different, and New York may therefore, consistent with the Constitution, treat them differently. By permitting everyone to refuse unwanted medical treatment while prohibiting anyone from assisting a suicide, New York law follows a longstanding and rational distinction.

New York's reasons for recognizing and acting on this distinction—including prohibiting intentional killing and preserving life; preventing suicide; maintaining physicians' role as their patients' healers; protecting vulnerable people from indifference, prejudice, and psychological and financial pressure to end their lives; and avoiding a possible slide towards euthanasia—are discussed in greater detail in our opinion in Glucksberg, ante. These valid and important public interests easily satisfy the constitutional requirement that a legislative classification bear a rational relation to some legitimate end.

The judgment of the Court of Appeals is reversed.

*   *   *

JUSTICE SOUTER, concurring in the judgment.

Even though I do not conclude that assisted suicide is a fundamental right entitled to recognition at this time, I accord the claims raised by the patients and physicians in this case and Washington v. Glucksberg a high degree of importance, requiring a commensurate justification. [ ] The reasons that lead me to conclude in Glucksberg that the prohibition on assisted suicide is not arbitrary under the due process standard also support the distinction between assistance to suicide, which is banned, and practices such as termination of artificial life support and death-hastening pain medication, which are permitted. I accordingly concur in the judgment of the Court.

---

[11] Respondents also argue that the State irrationally distinguishes between physician-assisted suicide and "terminal sedation," a process respondents characterize as "inducing barbiturate coma and then starving the person to death." [ ] Petitioners insist, however, that " 'although proponents of physician-assisted suicide and euthanasia contend that terminal sedation is covert physician-assisted suicide or euthanasia, the concept of sedating pharmacotherapy is based on informed consent and the principle of double effect.' "[ ] Just as a State may prohibit assisting suicide while permitting patients to refuse unwanted lifesaving treatment, it may permit palliative care related to that refusal, which may have the foreseen but unintended "double effect" of hastening the patient's death. [ ]

*   *   *

NOTES AND QUESTIONS

1.   The Ninth Circuit's en banc decision and an extraordinarily diverse and thoughtful set of opinions in Glucksberg can be found at Compassion in Dying v. Washington, 79 F.3d 790 (9th Cir.1996). The en banc court reversed a 2–1 decision of the original panel, which also included an impassioned opinion on each side of the issue. See 49 F.3d 586 (9th Cir.1995). The meticulously organized district court opinion in the Compassion in Dying case is reported at 850 F.Supp. 1454 (W.D.Wash.1994). The Second Circuit's opinion in Quill v. Vacco can be found at 80 F.3d 716 (2d Cir.1996).

2.   These cases generated many highly emotional responses. Although the Supreme Court's unanimous decision brought a semblance of propriety back to the discussion of these issues, supporters and opponents of medically assisted dying continue to attack the arguments of their opponents—and, as in the case of the abortion debate—they continue to attack their opponents, too. Some of the commentary on the Ninth Circuit opinions was especially personal. Judge Reinhardt (who wrote the primary decision finding the Washington law to be unconstitutional) was roundly criticized for his ACLU connections, which, some said, made it impossible for him to fairly decide the case. On the other hand, Judge Noonan (who would have upheld the statute for the first panel) had been criticized for his Right to Life connections and his Catholic faith which, others argued, made it impossible for him to be impartial. Should judges recuse themselves from cases involving these difficult and controversial bioethics issues if they have deeply held personal beliefs about the underlying practice—here medically assisted dying? Does it make a difference if they were members (or officers, or high ranking employees) of organizations which have taken explicit positions on the underlying issues? On the particular case in litigation? Should they recuse themselves if the issue is one on which the religion to which they subscribe has taken a formal position? Should Catholic judges recuse themselves from abortion and medically assisted dying cases? Should judges who belong to the United Church of Christ (which has been strongly pro-choice for decades) recuse themselves from abortion cases? Should the member of a congregation whose rabbi helped organize a voting rights march recuse himself from all voting rights cases? Is their obligation any different from the obligation of a judge who is a dedicated ACLU (or American Family Association or Republican Party) member and who confronts a case upon which the ACLU (or the American Family Association, or the Republican Party) has taken a firm position?

3.   Judge Calabresi concurred in the Second Circuit decision in the Quill case, but on entirely different grounds. Depending on the theory of statutory construction that he had explained fifteen years earlier in his text, A Common Law for the Age of Statutes (1982), he concluded that the history of the New York manslaughter statute suggested that there was no reason to believe that its framers ever intended it to apply to cases of competent terminally ill patients seeking aid in dying from physicians. Still, as he pointed

out, "neither Cruzan, nor Casey, nor the language of our Constitution, nor our constitutional tradition clearly makes these laws invalid."

So, what should the court do with a "highly suspect" but "not clearly invalid" statute that may no longer serve the purposes for which it was originally promulgated? The answer, according to Judge Calabresi, is the "constitutional remand."

I contend that when a law is neither plainly unconstitutional * * * nor plainly constitutional, the courts ought not to decide the ultimate validity of that law without current and clearly expressed statements by the people or their elected officials of the state involved. It is my further contention, that, absent such statements, the courts have frequently struck down such laws, while leaving open the possibility of reconsideration if appropriate statements were subsequently made.

Thus, Judge Calabresi finds the New York statute unconstitutional, but he "takes no position" on whether verbatim identical statutes would be constitutional "were New York to reenact them while articulating the reasons for the distinctions it makes. . . . " Is this a reasonable way to deal with ancient statutes effectively criminalizing medically assisted dying? Is this argument still available to those challenging state statutes that forbid assisting suicide?

4.   Why has medically assisted dying engendered such passion over the last several decades? Daniel Callahan has a suggestion:

The power of medicine to extend life under poor circumstances is now widely and increasingly feared. The combined powers of a quasi-religious tradition of respect for individual life and a secular tradition of relentless medical progress creates a bias toward aggressive, often unremitting treatment that appears unstoppable.

How is control to be gained? For many the answer seems obvious and unavoidable: active euthanasia and assisted suicide.

19 Hastings Ctr. Rep., Special Supplement, 4 (1989). Dr. Callahan goes on to suggest that those who strongly oppose euthanasia, as he does, ought to focus on "dampening . . . the push for medical progress, a return to older traditions of caring as an alternative to curing, and a willingness to accept decline and death as part of the human condition (not a notable feature of American medicine)." Is he right? It used to be that people were afraid that if they went to the hospital they would die there. Now people are afraid that if they go to the hospital they will be kept alive there. Is it this fear that gives rise to our current interest in euthanasia?

5.   Medically assisted dying may constitute murder, manslaughter, some other form of homicide, or no crime at all, depending on the language of the state statute and the nature of the physician's act. While most states

criminalize assisting suicide, it is not always easy to determine what conduct is prohibited by those statutes. Consider one representative statute:

> Every person who deliberately aids, or advises, or encourages another to commit suicide, is guilty of a felony. Cal. Pen. Code § 401.

Would this statute apply to a physician who clamps a feeding tube? To a physician who withholds antibiotics? To a physician who prescribes morphine to a patient in persistent pain, and provides enough tablets to take a lethal dose? To a physician who prescribes that same morphine and tells the patient what would constitute a lethal dose? To those who publish instructions on how to commit suicide for the use of those who are terminally ill or in excruciating pain? To those who make generally available information about how to commit suicide at home? See McCollum v. CBS, Inc., 202 Cal.App.3d 989, 249 Cal.Rptr. 187 (1988), rejecting application of the statute to those who play rock music with lyrics that suggest that suicide is acceptable on free speech grounds.

6.   Might women, specifically, be put at risk in a society that permits medically assisted dying? That argument is made by Susan Wolf, who regularly has argued that women's requests should be better respected by the health care system and that requests to remove life-sustaining treatment should be heeded.

> As I have argued, there is a strong right to be free of unwanted bodily invasion. Indeed, for women, a long history of being harmed specifically through unwanted bodily invasion such as rape presents particularly compelling reasons for honoring a woman's refusal of invasion and effort to maintain bodily intactness. When it comes to the question of whether women's suicides should be aided, however, or whether women should be actively killed, there is no right to command physician assistance, the dangers of permitting assistance are immense, and the history of women's subordination cuts the other way. Women have historically been seen as fit objects for bodily invasion, self-sacrifice, and death at the hands of others. The task before us is to challenge all three.

> Certainly some women, including some feminists, will see this problem differently. That may be especially true of women who feel in control of their lives, are less subject to subordination by age or race or wealth, and seek yet another option to add to their many. I am not arguing that women should lose control of their lives and selves. Instead, I am arguing that when women request to be put to death or ask help in taking their own lives, they become part of a broader social dynamic of which we have properly learned to be extremely wary. These are fatal practices. We can no longer ignore questions of gender or insights of feminist argument.

Susan Wolf, Gender, Feminism and Death: Physician Assisted Suicide and Euthanasia, in S. Wolf, Feminism and Bioethics: Beyond Reproduction 308 (1996). For an account of Professor Wolf's thoughtful approach to death and dying, see Daniel Bergner, Death in the Family, New York Times Magazine (December 2, 2007), reporting that 72% of the 75 individuals assisted by Kervorkian were women. But see data on Oregon's experience, below.

Susan Wolf also wrote a moving account of her own father's death, including her own response when he inquired whether it could be "accelerated" beyond withdrawing treatment. Her answer to her father was no, and she explains why in her essay; but she doesn't romanticize his dying and the great difficulties he and his family faced in getting the end-of-life care he needed. Confronting Physician–Assisted Suicide and Euthanasia: My Father's Death, 38 Hastings Ctr. Rept. 23 (2008).

7.   Organized medical groups generally oppose any medical participation in euthanasia or assisted death. As to euthanasia, the AMA Council on Ethical and Judicial Affairs provides:

Opinion 2.21, Euthanasia

> Euthanasia is the administration of a lethal agent by another person to a patient for the purpose of relieving the patient's intolerable and incurable suffering.

> It is understandable, though tragic, that some patients in extreme duress—such as those suffering from a terminal, painful, debilitating illness—may come to decide that death is preferable to life. However, permitting physicians to engage in euthanasia would ultimately cause more harm than good. Euthanasia is fundamentally incompatible with the physician's role as healer, would be difficult or impossible to control, and would pose serious societal risks.

> The involvement of physicians in euthanasia heightens the significance of its ethical prohibition. The physician who performs euthanasia assumes unique responsibility for the act of ending the patient's life. Euthanasia could also readily be extended to incompetent patients and other vulnerable populations.

> Instead of engaging in euthanasia, physicians must aggressively respond to the needs of patients at the end of life. Patients should not be abandoned once it is determined that cure is impossible. Patients near the end of life must continue to receive emotional support, comfort care, adequate pain control, respect for patient autonomy, and good communication. (issued 1994)

The Council has adopted a parallel position on Physician Assisted Suicide. See Opinion 2.211, Physician Assisted Suicide

Does the AMA oppose both of these kinds of medically assisted dying because it is morally reprehensible, or because it is too morally complicated?

A strict proscription against aiding in death may betray a limited conceptual framework that seeks the safety of ironclad rules and principles to protect the physician from the true complexity of individual cases. Patients seeking comfort in their dying should not be held hostage to our inability or unwillingness to be responsible for knowing right from wrong in each specific situation. Christine Cassel and Diane Meier, Morals and Moralism in the Debate Over Euthanasia and Assisted Suicide, 323 NEJM 750, 751 (1990).

8.   In a footnote in Vacco, Justice Rehnquist raises the issue of the legal status of "terminal sedation," which is sometimes described as "palliative sedation" because it is employed to provide palliation both in patients who are quickly approaching death and in those who are suffering but not yet otherwise terminal. Patients whose suffering cannot be ameliorated in any other way can be sedated with enough medication so that they are put into a medication-induced coma. This sedation may be accompanied by the withdrawal of other forms of treatment, including artificial nutrition and hydration. This withdrawal may (and, with the withdrawal of nutrition and hydration, will) lead to the patient's death. Justice Rehnquist suggests that terminal sedation, which has not given rise to the ethical objections that have come with medically assisted dying, is distinguishable from an affirmative act intended to bring about death, applying the principle of "double effect." Do you agree? Under Vacco, whether terminal sedation is treated like the withdrawal of life-sustaining treatment or like an affirmative act causing death makes all the legal difference. As an ethical and legal matter, should terminal sedation be treated like the withdrawal of treatment or like medically assisted dying? See J.A. Rietjens et al., Terminal Sedation and Euthanasia: A Comparison of Clinical Practices, 166 Archives Internal Med. 749 (2006). T. Morita et al., Terminal Sedation for Existential Distress, 17 Am. J. Hospital Palliation 189 (2000).

In 2008, over a decade after Glucksberg was decided, the AMA adopted a policy providing that it was the ethical obligation of physicians to offer palliative sedation, at least to some terminally ill patients:

Opinion 2.201, Sedation to Unconsciousness in End-of-Life Care

The duty to relieve pain and suffering is central to the physician's role as healer and is an obligation physicians have to their patients. Palliative sedation to unconsciousness is the administration of sedative medication to the point of unconsciousness in a terminally ill patient. It is an intervention of last resort to reduce severe, refractory pain or other distressing clinical symptoms that do not respond to aggressive symptom-specific palliation. It is an accepted and appropriate component of end-of-life care under specific, relatively rare circumstances. When symptoms cannot be diminished through all other means of palliation, including symptom-specific treatments, it is the ethical obligation of a physician to offer palliative sedation to unconsciousness as an option for the relief of intractable symptoms.

When considering the use of palliative sedation, the following ethical guidelines are recommended:

(1) Patients may be offered palliative sedation to unconsciousness when they are in the final stages of terminal illness. The rationale for all palliative care measures should be documented in the medical record.

(2) Palliative sedation to unconsciousness may be considered for those terminally ill patients whose clinical symptoms have been unresponsive to aggressive, symptom-specific treatments.

(3) Physicians should ensure that the patient and/or the patient's surrogate have given informed consent for palliative sedation to unconsciousness.

(4) Physicians should consult with a multidisciplinary team, if available, including an expert in the field of palliative care, to ensure that symptom-specific treatments have been sufficiently employed and that palliative sedation to unconsciousness is now the most appropriate course of treatment.

(5) Physicians should discuss with their patients considering palliative sedation the care plan relative to degree and length (intermittent or constant) of sedation, and the specific expectations for continuing, withdrawing, or withholding future life-sustaining treatments.

(6) Once palliative sedation is begun, a process must be implemented to monitor for appropriate care.

(7) Palliative sedation is not an appropriate response to suffering that is primarily existential, defined as the experience of agony and distress that may arise from such issues as death anxiety, isolation and loss of control. Existential suffering is better addressed by other interventions. For example, palliative sedation is not the way to address suffering created by social isolation and loneliness; such suffering should be addressed by providing the patient with needed social support.

(8) Palliative sedation must never be used to intentionally cause a patient's death.

Council on Ethical and Judicial Affairs (2008)

Why did the AMA conclude that palliative sedation was inappropriate for "existential" suffering, i.e., agony and loss of control? What if no other treatments are available to deal with the existential suffering? Can all suffering (except physical pain) be treated through the provision of social support?

Should palliative sedation be reserved for those with physical, not psychic, pain? See A. de Graeff and M. Dean,. Palliative Sedation Therapy in the Last Weeks of Life: A Literature Review and Recommendations for Standards, 10 J. Palliat Med. 67 (2007). At least one study suggests that palliative sedation does not actually shorten the lives of cancer patients. M. Maltoni et al., Palliative Sedation in End-of-Life Care and Survival: a Systematic Review, 30 J. Clin.Oncology 1378 (2012).

III.   LEGISLATION TO SUPPORT MEDICALLY ASSISTED DYING—"DEATH WITH DIGNITY" INITIATIVES

The debate over the proper role of physicians in assisting their patients in death has been carried on through the legislative and citizen initiative processes as well as through litigation. "Death with Dignity" initiatives were narrowly defeated in California in 1991 and in Washington in 1992. However, Oregon's "Death with Dignity" initiative was approved by voters in the November 1994 election, and it thus became part of the statute law of Oregon.

DEATH WITH DIGNITY ACT
Or.Rev.Stat. §§ 127.800–.897.

127.800. Definitions.

The following words and phrases, whenever used in ORS 127.800 to 127.897, have the following meanings:

(1) "Adult" means an individual who is 18 years of age or older.

(2) "Attending physician" means the physician who has primary responsibility for the care of the patient and treatment of the patient's terminal disease.

(3) "Capable" means that in the opinion of a court or in the opinion of the patient's attending physician or consulting physician, psychiatrist or psychologist, a patient has the ability to make and communicate health care decisions to health care providers, including communication through persons familiar with the patient's manner of communicating if those persons are available.

(4) "Consulting physician" means a physician who is qualified by specialty or experience to make a professional diagnosis and prognosis regarding the patient's disease.

(5) "Counseling" means one or more consultations as necessary between a state licensed psychiatrist or psychologist and a patient for the purpose of determining that the patient is capable and not suffering from

a psychiatric or psychological disorder or depression causing impaired judgment.

(6) "Health care provider" means a person licensed, certified or otherwise authorized or permitted by the law of this state to administer health care or dispense medication in the ordinary course of business or practice of a profession, and includes a health care facility.

(7) "Informed decision" means a decision by a qualified patient, to request and obtain a prescription to end his or her life in a humane and dignified manner, that is based on an appreciation of the relevant facts and after being fully informed by the attending physician of:

(a) His or her medical diagnosis;

(b) His or her prognosis;

(c) The potential risks associated with taking the medication to be prescribed;

(d) The probable result of taking the medication to be prescribed; and

(e) The feasible alternatives, including, but not limited to, comfort care, hospice care and pain control.

(8) "Medically confirmed" means the medical opinion of the attending physician has been confirmed by a consulting physician who has examined the patient and the patient's relevant medical records.

(9) "Patient" means a person who is under the care of a physician.

(10) "Physician" means a doctor of medicine or osteopathy licensed to practice medicine by the Board of Medical Examiners for the State of Oregon.

(11) "Qualified patient" means a capable adult who is a resident of Oregon and has satisfied the requirements of ORS 127.800 to 127.897 in order to obtain a prescription for medication to end his or her life in a humane and dignified manner.

(12) "Terminal disease" means an incurable and irreversible disease that has been medically confirmed and will, within reasonable medical judgment, produce death within six months.

127.805.Who may initiate a written request for medication.

(1) An adult who is capable, is a resident of Oregon, and has been determined by the attending physician and consulting physician to be suffering from a terminal disease, and who has voluntarily expressed his or her wish to die, may make a written request for medication for the purpose of ending his or her life in a humane and dignified manner in accordance with ORS 127.800 to 127.897.

(2) No person shall qualify under the provisions of ORS 127.800 to 127.897 solely because of age or disability.

127.810. Form of the written request.

(1) A valid request for medication under ORS 127.800 to 127.897 shall be in substantially the form described in ORS 127.897, signed and dated by the patient and witnessed by at least two individuals who, in the presence of the patient, attest that to the best of their knowledge and belief the patient is capable, acting voluntarily, and is not being coerced to sign the request.

(2) One of the witnesses shall be a person who is not:

(a) A relative of the patient by blood, marriage or adoption;

(b) A person who at the time the request is signed would be entitled to any portion of the estate of the qualified patient upon death under any will or by operation of law; or

(c) An owner, operator or employee of a health care facility where the qualified patient is receiving medical treatment or is a resident.

(3) The patient's attending physician at the time the request is signed shall not be a witness.

(4) If the patient is a patient in a long term care facility at the time the written request is made, one of the witnesses shall be an individual designated by the facility and having the qualifications specified by the Department of Human Services by rule.

127.815. Attending physician responsibilities.

(1) The attending physician shall:

(a) Make the initial determination of whether a patient has a terminal disease, is capable, and has made the request voluntarily;

(b) Request that the patient demonstrate Oregon residency pursuant to ORS 127.860;

(c) To ensure that the patient is making an informed decision, inform the patient of:

(A) His or her medical diagnosis;

(B) His or her prognosis;

(C) The potential risks associated with taking the medication to be prescribed;

(D) The probable result of taking the medication to be prescribed; and

(E) The feasible alternatives, including, but not limited to, comfort care, hospice care and pain control;

(d) Refer the patient to a consulting physician for medical confirmation of the diagnosis, and for a determination that the patient is capable and acting voluntarily;

(e) Refer the patient for counseling if appropriate pursuant to ORS 127.825;

(f) Recommend that the patient notify next of kin;

(g) Counsel the patient about the importance of having another person present when the patient takes the medication prescribed pursuant to ORS 127.800 to 127.897 and of not taking the medication in a public place;

(h) Inform the patient that he or she has an opportunity to rescind the request at any time and in any manner, and offer the patient an opportunity to rescind at the end of the 15 day waiting period pursuant to ORS 127.840;

(i) Verify, immediately prior to writing the prescription for medication under ORS 127.800 to 127.897, that the patient is making an informed decision;

(j) Fulfill the medical record documentation requirements of ORS 127.855;

(k) Ensure that all appropriate steps are carried out in accordance with ORS 127.800 to 127.897 prior to writing a prescription for medication to enable a qualified patient to end his or her life in a humane and dignified manner; and

(A) Dispense medications directly* * *or [(B) through a pharmacist].

(2) Notwithstanding any other provision of law, the attending physician may sign the patient's death certificate.

127.820. Consulting physician confirmation.

Before a patient is qualified under ORS 127.800 to 127.897, a consulting physician shall examine the patient and his or her relevant medical records and confirm, in writing, the attending physician's diagnosis that the patient is suffering from a terminal disease, and verify that the patient is capable, is acting voluntarily and has made an informed decision.

127.825. Counseling referral.

If in the opinion of the attending physician or the consulting physician a patient may be suffering from a psychiatric or psychological disorder or depression causing impaired judgment, either physician shall refer the patient for counseling. No medication to end a patient's life in a humane and dignified manner shall be prescribed until the person performing the counseling determines that the patient is not suffering from a psychiatric or psychological disorder or depression causing impaired judgment.

127.830. Informed decision.

No person shall receive a prescription for medication to end his or her life in a humane and dignified manner unless he or she has made an informed decision as defined in ORS 127.800 (7). Immediately prior to writing a prescription for medication under ORS 127.800 to 127.897, the attending physician shall verify that the patient is making an informed decision.

127.835. Family notification.

The attending physician shall recommend that the patient notify the next of kin of his or her request for medication pursuant to ORS 127.800 to 127.897. A patient who declines or is unable to notify next of kin shall not have his or her request denied for that reason.

127.840. Written and oral requests.

In order to receive a prescription for medication to end his or her life in a humane and dignified manner, a qualified patient shall have made an oral request and a written request, and reiterate the oral request to his or her attending physician no less than fifteen (15) days after making the initial oral request. At the time the qualified patient makes his or her second oral request, the attending physician shall offer the patient an opportunity to rescind the request.

127.845. Right to rescind request.

A patient may rescind his or her request at any time and in any manner without regard to his or her mental state. No prescription for medication under ORS 127.800 to 127.897 may be written without the attending physician offering the qualified patient an opportunity to rescind the request.

127.850. Waiting periods.

No less than fifteen (15) days shall elapse between the patient's initial oral request and the writing of a prescription under ORS 127.800 to 127.897. No less than 48 hours shall elapse between the patient's written request and the writing of a prescription under ORS 127.800 to 127.897.

* * *

127.860. Residency requirement.

Only requests made by Oregon residents under ORS 127.800 to 127.897 shall be granted. Factors demonstrating Oregon residency include but are not limited to [being licensed to drive, registering to vote, owning property, and paying taxes in Oregon.]

*   *   *

127.880. Construction of Act.

Nothing in ORS 127.800 to 127.897 shall be construed to authorize a physician or any other person to end a patient's life by lethal injection, mercy killing or active euthanasia. Actions taken in accordance with ORS 127.800 to 127.897 shall not, for any purpose, constitute suicide, assisted suicide, mercy killing or homicide, under the law.

*   *   *

127.897. Form of the request.

A request for a medication as authorized by ORS 127.800 to 127.897 shall be in substantially the following form:

REQUEST FOR MEDICATION TO END MY LIFE IN A HUMANE AND DIGNIFIED MANNER

I, _____, am an adult of sound mind.

I am suffering from _____, which my attending physician has determined is a terminal disease and which has been medically confirmed by a consulting physician.

I have been fully informed of my diagnosis, prognosis, the nature of medication to be prescribed and potential associated risks, the expected result, and the feasible alternatives, including comfort care, hospice care and pain control.

I request that my attending physician prescribe medication that will end my life in a humane and dignified manner.

INITIAL ONE:

_____ I have informed my family of my decision and taken their opinions into consideration.

_____ I have decided not to inform my family of my decision.

_____ I have no family to inform of my decision.

I understand that I have the right to rescind this request at any time.

I understand the full import of this request and I expect to die when I take the medication to be prescribed. I further understand that although most deaths occur within three hours, my death may take longer and my physician has counseled me about this possibility.

I make this request voluntarily and without reservation, and I accept full moral responsibility for my actions.

[SIGNATURE LINE; WITNESS LINES]

*   *   *

Early in 1999 the Oregon Department of Health issued its first annual report, which collected data on those who received lethal prescriptions under the Act during its first year of operation. Each year for eight years the Oregon Department of Health issued a comprehensive annual report describing activity under the Death with Dignity Act. Starting with the report for the ninth year of the operation of the statute, reflecting activity in 2006 and released in 2007, the Department of Health made available a brief summary of activity under the statute and other charts and tables. All of the annual reports, and the summaries (starting in 2007), are available at the Oregon Department of Health website. The Summary released in 2013 provides detailed information on the first fifteen years of operation under the statute, with a focus on activity over the most recent year.

OREGON DEPARTMENT OF HUMAN SERVICES, OREGON'S DEATH WITH DIGNITY ACT—2012
(released January, 2013).

Under Oregon's Death with Dignity Act (DWDA), terminally-ill adult Oregonians are allowed to obtain and use prescriptions from their physicians for self-administered, lethal medications. The Oregon Public Health Division is required by the Act to collect information on compliance and to issue an annual report. The key findings from 2012 are listed below. * * *

- Since the law was passed in 1997, a total of 1,050 people have had DWDA prescriptions written and 673 patients have died from ingesting medications prescribed under the DWDA.

- Of the 115 patients for whom DWDA prescriptions were written during 2012, 67 (58.3%) ingested the medication; 66 died from ingesting the medication, and one patient ingested the medication but regained consciousness before dying of underlying illness and is therefore not counted as a DWDA death. The patient regained consciousness two days following ingestion, but remained minimally responsive and died six days following ingestion.

- Eleven (11) patients with prescriptions written during the previous year (2011) died after ingesting the medication during 2012.

- Twenty-three (23) of the 115 patients who received DWDA prescriptions during 2012 did not take the medications and subsequently died of other causes.

- Ingestion status is unknown for 25 patients who were prescribed DWDA medications in 2012. Fourteen (14) of these patients died, but follow-up questionnaires indicating ingestion status have not yet been received. For the remaining 11 patients, both death and ingestion status are pending (Figure 2).

- Of the 77 DWDA deaths during 2012, most (67.5%) were aged 65 years or older; the median age was 69 years. As in previous years, most were white (97.4%), well-educated (42.9% had a least a baccalaureate degree), and had cancer (75.3%).

- Most (97.4%) patients died at home; and most (97.0%) were enrolled in hospice care either at the time the DWDA prescription was written or at the time of death. Excluding unknown cases, all (100.0%) had some form of health care insurance, although the number of patients who had private insurance (51.4%) was lower in 2012 than in previous years (66.2%), and the number of patients who had only Medicare or Medicaid insurance was higher than in previous years (48.6% compared to 32.1%).

- As in previous years, the three most frequently mentioned end-of-life concerns were: loss of autonomy (93.5%), decreasing ability to participate in activities that made life enjoyable (92.2%), and loss of dignity (77.9%).

- Two of the 77 DWDA patients who died during 2012 were referred for formal psychiatric or psychological evaluation. Prescribing physicians were present at the time of death for seven patients (9.1%) during 2012 compared to 17.3% in previous years.

- A procedure revision was made mid-year in 2010 to standardize reporting on the follow-up questionnaire. The new procedure accepts information about the time of death and circumstances surrounding death only when the physician or another health care provider was present at the time of death. Due to this change, data on time from ingestion to death is available for 11 of the 77 DWDA deaths during 2012. Among those 11 patients, time from ingestion until death ranged from 10 minutes to 3.5 hours.

- Sixty-one (61) physicians wrote the 115 prescriptions provided during 2012 (range 1–10 prescriptions per physician).

- During 2012, no referrals were made to the Oregon Medical Board for failure to comply with DWDA requirements.

NOTES AND QUESTIONS

1.   The Oregon Death with Dignity Act provides that no contract or statute can affect a person's request for physician assisted suicide, and that no insurance policy can be conditioned upon, or affected by, a patient's decision to choose (or reject) physician assisted suicide. The measure includes a section providing immunity for those who follow the requirements of the statute, and imposing liability on those who violate it.

2.   Does the report address whether the requirements of Section 127.815 were followed? How would the Department determine the answer to that question? Those who are skeptical about whether the annual report accurately presents the impact of the Act point out that the report can describe only those cases that are reported to the state. They argue that cases that do not comply with the specific requirements of the statute will not be reported. It is in this potential body of unreported cases that evidence for concerns over the effectiveness of the statute's boundaries would be found.

3.   As the Summary published in 2013 indicates, most Oregonians who have sought medically assisted dying have done so because of their fear of losing control of their lives (and the concomitant suffering that would follow), not because of physical pain. In 2013, more than three times as many patients listed loss of autonomy as a reason for seeking medically assisted dying as listed inadequate pain control. An excerpt from Oregon's Second Annual Report, published in 2000, explains this:

> Responses from both physician and family interviews indicate that patient's decisions to request PAS were motivated by multiple interrelated concerns. Physical suffering was discussed by several families as a cause of loss of autonomy, inability to participate in activities that made life enjoyable, or a "non-existent" quality of life. For example, "She would have stuck it out through the pain if she thought she'd get better . . . [but she believed that] when quality of life has no meaning, it's no use hanging around." For another participant, a feeling of being trapped because of ALS contributed to concern about loss of autonomy. Family members frequently commented on loss of control of bodily functions when discussing loss of autonomy. Those reporting patient concern about being a burden on friends and family also reported concern about loss of autonomy and control of bodily functions. Reasons for requesting a prescription were sometimes so interrelated they were difficult to categorize. According to one family member being asked to distinguish reasons for the patient's decision, "It was everything; it was nothing; [he was suffering terribly]."

Difficulty categorizing and differences in interpreting the nature of the concerns made physician and family member responses hard to compare quantitatively. Nonetheless, family interviews corroborate physician reports from both years that patients are greatly concerned about issues of autonomy and control. In addition, responses of both physicians and family consistently pointed to patient concerns about quality of life and the wish to have a means of controlling the end of life should it become unbearable. As one family member said, "She always thought that if something was terminal, she would [want to] control the end . . . It was not the dying that she dreaded, it was getting to that death."

* * *

Oregonians choosing physician-assisted suicide appeared to want control over how they died. One woman had purchased poison over a decade before her participation, when her cancer was first diagnosed, so that she would never be without the means of controlling the end of her life should it become unbearable. Like many others who participated, she was described as "determined" to have this control. Another woman was described as a "gutsy woman" who was ". . . determined in her lifetime, and determined about [physician-assisted suicide]." Family members expressed profound grief at losing a loved one. However, mixed with this grief was great respect for the patient's determination and choice to use physician-assisted suicide. As one husband said about his wife of almost 50 years, "She was my only girl; I didn't want to lose her . . . but she wanted to do this."

Could the expressed concerns have been relieved by better medical and nursing care? Should these individuals have toughed it out, or did they choose the better course for themselves? For their families? Are those who do take advantage of the statute brave? Cowardly?

4.   The Oregon initiative was immediately challenged for a wide range of reasons. Some argued that it discriminated against the disabled, for example, by coercing them into choosing medically assisted dying, and others argued it discriminated against the disabled because those with physical disabilities that made it impossible to take oral medications would not be able to use the statute. The United States District Court in Oregon issued a preliminary injunction against enforcing the initiative shortly after its passage and issued a permanent injunction several months later. Ultimately, the Ninth Circuit reversed the District Court, finding that those challenging the Oregon initiative had no standing to raise the issue in federal court. Lee v. Oregon, 107 F.3d 1382 (9th Cir.1997).

5.   The federal government has not ignored medically assisted dying, either. Even before the Oregon statute became effective, Congress passed the

Assisted Suicide Prevention Restriction Act of 1997, which outlawed the use of federal money to aid medically assisted dying, directly or indirectly.

Shortly after the Oregon Death with Dignity Act became effective, some suggested that any physician who prescribed a lethal drug under that statute would be prescribing that drug without a "legitimate medical purpose," and thus would be acting inconsistently with the federal Controlled Substances Act (CSA). A physician's violation of the Act could lead to both the loss of prescribing authority and criminal indictment. In 1998, after the matter had been pending for some time, the United States Department of Justice published a report concluding that use of controlled substances under the Oregon statute would satisfy the "legitimate medical purpose" requirement of the federal Act..

Members of the House and Senate then introduced the Lethal Drug Abuse Prevention Act of 1998, which would have expanded the authority of the Drug Enforcement Agency to investigate lethal use of controlled substances, which could not be used with the intent of causing death. Supporters of medically assisted dying joined many of their staunchest opponents and mainstream medical organizations (including the AMA) to oppose the bill because, they said, it would be likely to chill physicians from providing adequate pain relief at the end of life. Although the bill failed, it was resurrected in slightly milder form in 2000 as the Pain Relief Promotion Act (PRPA), which included a well publicized section announcing that the provision of medication with the intent to manage pain (and not the intent to cause death) was protected. The 2000 version of the bill also provided for the education of health-care professionals on issues related to pain management, and it was supported by the AMA (but opposed by the ABA, the American Cancer Society and most groups advocating for improved pain management). Although the stated purpose of PRPA was to promote adequate pain relief practices, its effect would be (and, some say, its real purpose was) to render it impossible for physicians in Oregon to carry out the provisions of the Death With Dignity Act. The PRPA died when Congress adjourned in late 2000, and there have not been serious attempts to undermine the Oregon statute through federal legislation since that time.

In 2001, however, the Attorney General, John Ashcroft, issued an interpretive rule that reversed the 1998 Department of Justice position on the issue of the application of the CSA and implemented an enforcement action. Within a day of the announcement of this change in the federal position, Oregon sought relief from the Attorney General's decision in the federal court. A private action seeking an injunction against the Ashcroft position was filed shortly thereafter on behalf of an Oregon oncologist. The District Court immediately restrained the United States from enforcing the new interpretation of the CSA, and in 2006 the Supreme Court determined that the Attorney General's interpretive rule was beyond the scope of his authority and was improperly promulgated. Gonzales v. Oregon, 546 U.S. 243, 126 S.Ct. 904, 163 L.Ed.2d 748 (2006). The Court left open the possibility that the Attorney

General could properly promulgate a substantive rule that would bar the operation of the Oregon Death with Dignity Act, and that Congress could amend the Controlled Substances Act to achieve this end.

6. The Oregon statute has been amended, but the changes are not substantial. The legislature added the definition of "capable," added some new language designed to encourage patients to discuss the matter with their families, and provided some factors to be considered in determining residency. The amendments also made clear the broad extent of the institutional conscience exception to the statute, which permits health-care institutions to limit physicians from engaging in assisted death on their premises or in their organizations, and it changed the written consent form to assure that patients recognize that death will probably, but not always, take place about three hours after taking the medication.

7. Emboldened by the success in Oregon, many groups have sought state statutes that would accomplish what Oregon's Measure 16 did. A measure similar to the Oregon statute was very narrowly defeated at the polls in Maine in 2000. In part as a result of the narrow defeat of the Maine measure, during the next legislative session both supporters and opponents of medically assisted dying joined to support a number of bills improving the quality of end-of-life care in that state. In 2002 the Hawai'i House of Representatives passed an Oregon-like bill that came within a couple of votes of passing the Senate. More recently, the California legislature has given serious consideration to a bill that would have provided for medically assisted dying, and advocates in that state expect the issue to arise again over the next few years.

8. Advocates for medically assisted dying in Washington made that state the second to use the initiative process to provide for medically assisted dying. Former Washington Governor Booth Gardner, who had Parkinson's disease, became the leading advocate for an Oregon-like statute. For the story of Governor Gardner's "last campaign" from the perspective of someone who opposes medically assisted dying, see Daniel Bergner, Death in the Family, New York Times Magazine (December 2, 2007). The Washington Death with Dignity statute, R.C.W. section 70.245, became effective in 2009. Like Oregon, Washington has published annual reports with substantial detail about the use of the statute within the state. Overall, the Washington data looks very much like that from Oregon. In 2011, 103 Washington patients received prescriptions under the statute, and 90 died from ingesting the medication. Almost all were from west of the Cascades, 94% were White Non–Hispanics, about half were married, and three fourths had at least some college education. Washington State Department of Health, 2011 Death with Dignity Report. After a very hard-fought and expensive initiative battle over an almost identical statute in 2012, the voters of Massachusetts soundly rejected any change in the law. For an account of the meaning of euthanasia and suicide in our society and others, and a description of how these arguments are likely to be discussed in the future, see Margaret Battin, Ending Life: Ethics and the Way We Die (2005).

9.   Is there some common ground available to those, on the one hand, who believe that permitting medically assisted dying is necessary for patients to be properly treated at the end of life, and those, on the other hand, who believe that medically assisted dying must be outlawed for patients to be properly treated? Both groups agree that pain is often inadequately treated at the end of life, in part because physicians fear legal action for homicide (if pain relief results in the death of the patient) or distribution of drugs (if the condition of a patient requires a larger dose of narcotic medication than is standard).

In some states advocates on both sides of the medically assisted dying issue have joined together to support intractable pain relief statutes, which are designed to protect health-care providers who deliver adequate pain relief from adverse licensing and criminal actions. These statutes generally provide that a health-care provider will not be liable in a state disciplinary proceeding or a criminal action for the aggressive prescription of pain medication as long as the use of that medication is in accord with accepted guidelines for pain management. Several states have promulgated intractable pain relief acts, and several more are considering them. For a model pain relief act," see 24 J.L., Med. Ethics 317 (1996). See also, Ann Alpers, Criminal Act or Palliative Care? Prosecutions Involving the Care of the Dying, 26 J. L. Med. Ethics 308 (1998), identifying factors that create a risk of prosecution. For a series of articles on the relationship between pain relief and medically assisted dying, with the conclusion that we ought to create a system that provides excellent palliative care in every case and allows for medically assisted dying in the rare cases in which it is necessary, see Timothy Quill and Margaret Battin, eds., Physician–Assisted Dying: the Right to Excellent End-of-Life Care and Patient Choice (2004). See also, Kathleen Foley, The Case Against Assisted Suicide: For the Right to End of Life Care (2002), written by a leading palliative care physician.

10.   Federal and state policy may conflict on one kind of palliative care— the use of marijuana. Some cancer patients, patients with glaucoma, AIDS patients, patients with multiple sclerosis, those with migraine headaches and others find that they can obtain relief from some of the symptoms of the disease—or from some of the side effects of the treatments for the disease— through the use of marijuana. In particular, some cancer patients find that marijuana helps them overcome the nausea that follows the use of many chemotherapeutic agents. While several states have now legalized the use of marijuana under such circumstances, the manufacture and distribution of marijuana is still a felony under the Federal Controlled Substances Act (CSA). In 2001, the Supreme Court determined that there was no medical necessity defense available to those who manufactured or distributed marijuana to patients in violation of the federal law. U.S. v. Oakland Cannabis Buyers' Cooperative, 532 U.S. 483, 121 S.Ct. 1711, 149 L.Ed.2d 722 (2001). Four years later the Supreme Court confirmed that the CSA marijuana prohibition fell within Congress's commerce power. Gonzales v. Raich, 545 U.S. 1, 125 S.Ct. 2195, 162 L.Ed.2d 1 (2005). Several states now have institution-

alized formal programs for distributing marijuana to those who are found to be in medical need (under highly varying state standards). In 2012 the federal government indicated that it would not seek legal redress against those who acted strictly within their state legal limitations in providing patients with medical marijuana through non-commercial enterprises. Despite this, though, the United States has sought to close down several large and otherwise legal medical dispensaries in California and elsewhere. In 2012 the voters in Colorado and Washington approved new regulatory schemes that would allow (and tax) the use of marijuana, even for non-medical purposes, and that has added a measure of additional confusion to the resolution of problems caused by the apparent conflict between federal and state laws. On the same day, voters in California, where medical marijuana is easily available, rejected the same approach. In Colorado, which has allowed and regulated medical marijuana for over a decade, the provisions with regard to recreational use go into effect in 2014.

11. The public interest in this issue is not limited to the United States. Medically assisted dying has been tolerated in the Netherlands, as a legal matter, since 1969, and it was formally legalized by the parliament in 2001 in cases of intractable suffering (not just pain), where the patient has been informed of all of the alternative treatments available, has consulted two physicians, and has followed other requirements established by the national medical association. Belgium recently joined the Netherlands in legalizing medically assisted dying through the legislative process, and the practice is now officially tolerated under some circumstances in Switzerland. The Constitutional Court of Colombia has approved legislation that provides for medically assisted dying, and there has been an active debate over the propriety of permitting medically assisted dying in France, Venezuela and Australia. Australia's Northern Territory's Parliament passed The Rights of the Terminally Ill Act (1995), which permitted what some have called "voluntary euthanasia" under some circumstances; however, the national parliament effectively overturned that territorial statute. For a brief description of the current state of the law in other countries, see Alan Meisel and Kathy Cerminara, The Right to Die (3d ed. 2005).

The European Court of Human Rights considered a challenge to the laws of the United Kingdom that outlawed medically assisted dying in Pretty v. United Kingdom, 35 Eur. H. R. Rep. 1 (2002). Applying analysis similar, in many respects, to that in Glucksberg and Vacco, the Court found that the United Kingdom had the authority to enforce its law. An English court again confirmed the legal prohibition against medically assisted dying in 2012.

During that same year a trial court in British Columbia reached a different conclusion, announcing that a terminally ill, competent patient had a right to medically assisted dying under conditions more or less equivalent to those in the laws of neighboring Washington and Oregon, where there was unbearable physical or psychic suffering. Finally, in 2012 the Dying with Dignity Committee, made up of Quebec National Assembly members, recommended that medically assisted dying be permitted in the Province despite the fact that Canada criminalizes assisting suicide. A legal commission report in 2013 backed up the original Committee report, and the Quebec parliament is expected to undertake the issue in late 2013. Representatives of the Parti Quebecois, which included the legislation as a part of their election platform, explained that medically assisted dying was not any kind of "suicide," and that, in any case, it was an issue of health, which is within the jurisdiction of the provinces, not the national government. The Canadian Medical Association has encouraged a national debate on the issue and expressed the view that changes to the law of "therapeutic homicide" should come through the legislative process, not the judicial process. Several years before the Glucksberg case was decided on this side of the border, the Canadian Supreme Court reached essentially the same conclusion in Rodriguez v. British Columbia (Attorney General), [1993] 3 S.C.R. 519, which remains good law.

IV.   LITIGATION UNDER STATE LAW

BAXTER V. MONTANA
Supreme Court of Montana, 2009.
2009 MT 449, 354 Mont. 234, 224 P.3d 1211.

JUSTICE LEAPHART delivered the Opinion of the Court.

* * *

We rephrase the following issue[ ] on appeal:

Whether the District Court erred in its decision that competent, terminally ill patients have a constitutional right to die with dignity, which protects physicians who provide aid in dying from prosecution under the homicide statutes.

* * *

BACKGROUND

This appeal originated with Robert Baxter, a retired truck driver from Billings who was terminally ill with lymphocytic leukemia with diffuse lymphadenopathy. * * *. Mr. Baxter wanted the option of ingesting a lethal dose of medication prescribed by his physician and self-administered at the time of Mr. Baxter's own choosing.

* * *

DISCUSSION

The parties in this appeal focus their arguments on the question of whether a right to die with dignity—including physician aid in dying—exists under the privacy and dignity provisions of the Montana Constitution. The District Court held that a competent, terminally ill patient has a right to die with dignity under Article II, Sections 4 and 10 of the Montana Constitution. Sections 4 and 10 address individual dignity and the right to privacy, respectively. The District Court further held that the right to die with dignity includes protecting the patient's physician from prosecution under Montana homicide statutes. The District Court concluded that Montana homicide laws are unconstitutional as applied to a physician who aids a competent, terminally ill patient in dying.

[T]his Court is guided by the judicial principle that we should decline to rule on the constitutionality of a legislative act if we are able to decide the case without reaching constitutional questions. [ ] Since both parties have recognized the possibility of a consent defense to a homicide charge

[ ] we focus our analysis on whether the issues presented can be resolved at the statutory, rather than the constitutional, level.

We start with the proposition that suicide is not a crime under Montana law. In the aid in dying situation, the only person who might conceivably be prosecuted for criminal behavior is the physician who prescribes a lethal dose of medication. In that the claims of the plaintiff physicians are premised in significant part upon concerns that they could be prosecuted for extending aid in dying, we deem it appropriate to analyze their possible culpability for homicide by examining whether the consent of the patient to his physician's aid in dying could constitute a statutory defense to a homicide charge against the physician.

The consent statute would shield physicians from homicide liability if, with the patients' consent, the physicians provide aid in dying to terminally ill, mentally competent adult patients. We first determine whether a statutory consent defense applies to physicians who provide aid in dying and, second, whether patient consent is rendered ineffective [ ] because permitting the conduct or resulting harm "is against public policy."

Section 45–5–102(1), MCA, states that a person commits the offense of deliberate homicide if "the person purposely or knowingly causes the death of another human being. . . . " Section 45–2–211(1), MCA, establishes consent as a defense, stating that the "consent of the victim to conduct charged to constitute an offense or to the result thereof is a defense." Thus, if the State prosecutes a physician for providing aid in dying to a mentally competent, terminally ill adult patient who consented to such aid, the physician may be shielded from liability pursuant to the consent statute. This consent defense, however, is only effective if none of the statutory exceptions to consent applies. Section 45–2–211(2), MCA, codifies the four exceptions:

Consent is ineffective if: * * *(d) it is against public policy to permit the conduct or the resulting harm, even though consented to.

* * * [W]e find no indication in Montana law that physician aid in dying provided to terminally ill, mentally competent adult patients is against public policy.

Section 45–2–211(2)(d), MCA, renders consent ineffective if "it is against public policy to permit the conduct or the resulting harm, even though consented to." [The Court discussed Montana precedent, which had considered the application of the "public policy" exception to the consent provision in the case of mutual violence of combatants.] This "against public policy" exception to consent applies to conduct that disrupts public peace and physically endangers others. Clearly [ ] unruly, physical and public aggression between individuals falls within the parameters of the "against public policy" exception. * * *

A survey of courts that have considered this issue yields unanimous understanding that consent is rendered ineffective as "against public policy" in assault cases characterized by aggressive and combative acts that breach public peace and physically endanger others.

*   *   *

[S]heer physical aggression that breaches public peace and endangers others is against public policy. In contrast, the act of a physician handing medicine to a terminally ill patient, and the patient's subsequent peaceful and private act of taking the medicine, are not comparable to the violent, peace-breaching conduct that this Court and others have found to violate public policy.

*   *   *

[A] physician who aids a terminally ill patient in dying is not directly involved in the final decision or the final act. He or she only provides a means by which a terminally ill patient himself can give effect to his life-ending decision, or not, as the case may be. Each stage of the physician-patient interaction is private, civil, and compassionate. The physician and terminally ill patient work together to create a means by which the patient can be in control of his own mortality. The patient's subsequent private decision whether to take the medicine does not breach public peace or endanger others.

*   *   *

Under § 45–5–102, MCA, a "person commits the offense of deliberate homicide if: (a) the person purposely or knowingly causes the death of another human being. . . . " In physician aid in dying, the physician makes medication available for a terminally ill patient who requests it, and the patient would then choose whether to cause his own death by self-administering the medicine. The terminally ill patient's act of ingesting the medicine is not criminal. There is no language in the homicide statute indicating that killing "oneself," as opposed to "another," is a punishable offense, and there is no separate statute in Montana criminalizing suicide. There is thus no indication in the homicide statutes that physician aid in dying—in which a terminally ill patient elects and consents to taking possession of a quantity of medicine from a physician that, if he chooses to take it, will cause his own death—is against public policy.

There is similarly no indication in the Terminally Ill Act that physician aid in dying is against public policy.

*   *   *

The Rights of the Terminally Ill Act very clearly provides that terminally ill patients are entitled to autonomous end-of-life decisions, even if enforcement of those decisions involves direct acts by a physician.

*   *   *

The Terminally Ill Act, in short, confers on terminally ill patients a right to have their end-of-life wishes followed, even if it requires direct participation by a physician through withdrawing or withholding treatment. [ ] Nothing in the statute indicates it is against public policy to honor those same wishes when the patient is conscious and able to vocalize and carry out the decision himself with self-administered medicine and no immediate or direct physician assistance.

*   *   *

The Dissent * * * cites § 45–5–105, MCA, stating that a person may be prosecuted for aiding or soliciting suicide only if the individual does not die. [ ] The statute's plain meaning is clear. It is also inapplicable. The narrow scenario we have been asked to consider on appeal involves the situation in which a terminally ill patient affirmatively seeks a lethal dose of medicine and subsequently self-administers it, causing his own death. Section 45–5–105, MCA, unambiguously applies only when the suicide does not occur.

* * * Here, the legislature could not have provided clearer, more unambiguous language. If the person does not die, the statute is triggered. If they do die, the statute is not triggered. * * *.

*   *   *

Even if this Court were to extend consideration to § 45–5–105, MCA, as a generalized reflection of the legislature's views on third party involvement in suicides, there remains no indication that the statute was ever intended to apply to the very narrow set of circumstances in which a terminally ill patient himself seeks out a physician and asks the physician to provide him the means to end his own life. As the Dissent states, the original enactment addressed situations of a third party "encouraging" a suicide. [ ] The present version reflects the same focus in the "soliciting" language. The statute's plain language addresses the situation in which a third party unilaterally solicits or aids another person. In physician aid in dying, the solicitation comes from the patient himself, not a third party physician.

There is no indication that the 1973 Montana legislators contemplated the statute would apply to this specific situation in which a terminally ill patient seeks a means by which he can end his own incurable suffering.

* * *

In conclusion, we find nothing in Montana Supreme Court precedent or Montana statutes indicating that physician aid in dying is against public policy. The "against public policy" exception to consent has been interpreted by this Court as applicable to violent breaches of the public peace. Physician aid in dying does not satisfy that definition. We also find nothing in the plain language of Montana statutes indicating that physician aid in dying is against public policy. In physician aid in dying, the patient—not the physician—commits the final death-causing act by self-administering a lethal dose of medicine.

Furthermore, the Montana Rights of the Terminally Ill Act indicates legislative respect for a patient's autonomous right to decide if and how he will receive medical treatment at the end of his life.

* * *

[The concurring opinion of **JUSTICE WARNER**, who agreed that there was no need to address the Constitutional issue, is omitted.]

JUSTICE NELSON, specially concurring.

* * *

* * * For the reasons which follow, I agree with the Court's analysis under the consent statute (§ 45–2–211, MCA), and I further conclude that physician aid in dying is protected by the Montana Constitution as a matter of privacy [ ] and as a matter of individual dignity [ ].

* * *

CONSTITUTIONAL ANALYSIS

* * * [P]hysician aid in dying is also firmly protected by Montana's Constitution. [B]ecause I so passionately believe that individual dignity is, in all likelihood, the most important—and yet, in our times, the most fragile—of all human rights protected by Montana's Constitution, I proceed to explain what I believe the right of dignity means within the context of this case—one of the most important cases the courts of this state have ever considered.

* * *

A. Terminology and Language

First, let me be clear about one thing: This case is not about the "right to die." Indeed, the notion that there is such a "right" is patently absurd, if not downright silly. No constitution, no statute, no legislature, and no court can grant an individual the "right to die." Nor can they take such a right away. "Death is the destiny of everything that lives. Nothing ever escapes it." [ ] Within the context of this case, the only control that a person has over death is that if he expects its coming within a relatively short period of time due to an incurable disease, he can simply accept his fate and seek drug-induced comfort; or he can seek further treatment and fight to prolong death's advance; or, at some point in his illness, and with his physician's assistance, he can embrace his destiny at a time and place of his choosing. The only "right" guaranteed to him in any of these decisions is the right to preserve his personal autonomy and his individual dignity, as he sees fit, in the face of an ultimate destiny that no power on earth can prevent.

Thus noted, the Patients and the class of individuals they represent are persons who suffer from an illness or disease, who cannot be cured of their illness or disease by any reasonably available medical treatment, who therefore expect death within a relatively short period of time, and who demand the right to preserve their personal autonomy and their individual dignity in facing this destiny.

In choosing this language, I purposely eschew bright-line tests or rigid timeframes. What is "relatively short" varies from person to person. I take this approach [ ] for the following nonexclusive reasons. **First,** the amount of physical, emotional, spiritual, and mental suffering that one is willing or able to endure is uniquely and solely a matter of individual constitution, conscience, and personal autonomy. **Second,** "suffering" in this more expansive sense may implicate a person's uniquely personal perception of his "quality of life." This perception may be informed by, among other things, one's level of suffering, one's loss of personal autonomy, one's ability to make choices about his situation, one's ability to communicate, one's perceived loss of value to self or to others, one's ability to care for his personal needs and hygiene, one's loss of dignity, one's financial situation and concern over the economic burdens of prolonged illness, and one's level of tolerance for the invasion of personal privacy and individual dignity that palliative treatment necessarily involves. Suffering may diminish the quality of life; on the other hand, the lack of suffering does not guarantee a life of quality. There is a difference between living and suffering; and the sufferer is uniquely positioned and, therefore, uniquely entitled to define the tipping point that makes suffering unbearable. **Third**, while most incurable illnesses and diseases follow a fairly predictable symptomatology and course, every illness and disease is a unique and very personal experience for the afflicted person. Thus, the afflicted individual's illness or disease informs his end-of-life choices and decisions in ways unique and personal to that individual's life, values, and circumstances. **Fourth**, advancements in medical treatment may become available during the period between the time when he is diagnosed as being incurably ill and the predicted (estimated) time of death. With those advancements, a person initially given three months to live may well expect to live two more months or two more years with a new medicine or treatment. **Fifth**, individual access to medical care may vary. A person living in proximity to a medical research facility may have access to medicines and treatments as part of a clinical trial, while another person living in a sparsely populated rural area may not have that opportunity. One individual may have access to hospice care; another may not. Sadly, an insured individual may have access to medicine and treatment that an uninsured individual does not. **Sixth**, each individual's family situation is different. One individual may not have close family relationships; another may have a strongly involved and supportive family. One person's family may live within a short distance, while another person's family may be spread across the country or around the globe. The ability to say final goodbyes and the ability to die, at a predetermined time and place, perhaps in the company of one's partner or friends and loved ones, is important to many individuals and to their families. **Seventh**, and lastly, to many who are incurably ill and dying, the prospect of putting their partner or family through their prolonged and agonizing death is a source of deep emotional and spiritual distress.

Additionally, in my choice of language, I have intentionally chosen not to use emotionally charged and value-laden terms such as "terminal" and "suicide." "Terminal" conjures up the notion that the individual is on some sort of inevitable slide or countdown to death. This term trivializes the fact that many individuals, with what appear to be medically incurable diseases, nevertheless retain steadfast hope and faith that their condition will be reversed, along with a personal resolve to fight for life until the very end. Labeling an individual as "terminal" may not only discourage the individual from seeking treatment but may also discourage further treatment efforts by healthcare providers. A "terminal" diagnosis fails to acknowledge that medicine usually cannot predict the time of death with the sort of exactitude that the use of the term connotes.

Similarly, the term "suicide" suggests an act of self-destruction that historically has been condemned as sinful, immoral, or damning by many religions. Moreover, in modern parlance, "suicide" may be linked with terrorist conduct. Importantly, and as reflected in the briefing in this case, society judges and typically, but selectively, deprecates individuals who commit "suicide." On one hand, the individual who throws his body over a hand grenade to save his fellow soldiers is judged a hero, not a person who committed "suicide." Yet, on the other hand, the individual who shoots herself because she faces a protracted illness and agonizing death commits "suicide" and, as such, is judged a coward in the face of her illness and selfish in her lack of consideration for the pain and loss her act causes to loved ones and friends. Assisting this person to end her life is likewise denounced as typifying " 'a very low regard for human life.' [ ] To the contrary, however, the Patients and their amici argue that a physician who provides aid in dying demonstrates compassionate regard for the patient's suffering, recognition of the patient's autonomy and dignity, and acknowledgement of death's inevitability.

"Suicide" is a pejorative term in our society. Unfortunately, it is also a term used liberally by the State and its amici (as well as the Dissent) in this case. The term denigrates the complex individual circumstances that drive persons generally—and, in particular, those who are incurably ill and face prolonged illness and agonizing death—to take their own lives. The term is used to generate antipathy, and it does. * * * The Patients and the class of people they represent do not seek to commit "suicide." Rather, they acknowledge that death within a relatively short time is inescapable because of their illness or disease. And with that fact in mind, they seek the ability to self-administer, at a time and place of their choosing, a physician-prescribed medication that will assist them in preserving their own human dignity during the inevitable process of dying. Having come to grips with the inexorability of their death, they simply ask the government not to force them to suffer and die in an agonizing, degrading, humiliating, and undignified manner. * * *

Finally, I neither use the terms nor address "euthanasia" or "mercy killing." Aside from the negative implications of these terms and the criminality of such conduct, the Patients clearly do not argue that incompetent, nonconsenting individuals or "vulnerable" people may be, under any circumstances, "euthanized" or "murdered." * * * The only reason that "homicide" is implicated at all in this case is because (a) the State contends that a licensed physician who provides a mentally competent, incurably ill patient with the prescription for a life-ending substance, to be self-administered by the patient if she so chooses, is guilty of deliberate homicide and (b) our decision holds that it is not against public policy under the consent statute to permit the physician to do so.

With that prefatory explanation, I now turn to Article II, Section 4 and the right of individual dignity.

Construction of Article II, Section 4

Article II, Section 4 of Montana's 1972 Constitution provides:

Individual dignity. The dignity of the human being is inviolable. No person shall be denied the equal protection of the laws. Neither the state nor any person, firm, corporation, or institution shall discriminate against any person in the exercise of his civil or political rights on account of race, color, sex, culture, social origin or condition, or political or religious ideas.

[I]t is my view that the first clause of Article II, Section 4 (the Dignity Clause) is a stand-alone, fundamental constitutional right. [ ]

* * *

The Right of Human Dignity

Human dignity is, perhaps, the most fundamental right in the Declaration of Rights. This right is "inviolable," * * *. Significantly, the right of human dignity is the only right in Montana's Constitution that is "inviolable." [ ] No individual may be stripped of her human dignity under the plain language of the Dignity Clause. No private or governmental entity has the right or the power to do so. Human dignity simply cannot be violated—no exceptions. * * *

But what exactly is "dignity"? It would be impractical here to attempt to provide an exhaustive definition. Rather, the meaning of this term must be fleshed out on a case-by-case basis (in the same way that the parameters of substantive due process have been determined on a case-by-case basis). * * * [I]n our Western ethical tradition, especially after the Religious Reformation of the 16th and 17th centuries, dignity has typically been associated with the normative ideal of individual persons as intrinsically valuable, as having inherent worth as individuals, at least in part because of their capacity for independent, autonomous, rational, and responsible action.

* * *

Given its intrinsic nature, it is entirely proper, in my view, that the right of dignity under Article II, Section 4 is absolute. Indeed, human dignity transcends the Constitution and the law. Dignity is a fundamental component of humanness. It is inherent in human self-consciousness. * * * While the government may impinge on privacy rights, liberty interests, and other Article II rights in proper circumstances (e.g., when one becomes a prisoner), the individual always retains his right of human dignity. So too with persons suffering from mental illness or disability and involuntary commitment: Each retains the right to demand of the State that his dignity as a human being be respected despite the government's sometimes necessary interference in his life.

I am convinced that each of us recognizes this intrinsic, elemental nature of human dignity. Indeed, that recognition explains why we collectively recoil from the pyramid of naked enemy soldiers prodded by troops with guns and dogs at Abu Ghraib; why disgust fills most of us at the descriptions and depictions of water boarding and torture; and why we revolt from ethnic cleansing and genocide. It is why we should collectively rebel, as well, when we see our fellow human beings in need from lack of food, clothing, shelter, medical care, and education.

* * *

I believe this is why we also collectively recoil from accounts of our fellow human beings forced to endure the humiliation and degradation of an agonizing death from an incurable illness. Pain may, in theory, be alleviated to the point of rendering the person unconscious. But in those circumstances, we still cannot deny that the individual's human dignity has been dealt a grievous blow long before death claims her body.

* * *

The State asserts that it has compelling interests in preserving life and protecting vulnerable groups from potential abuses. This broad assertion, however, is entirely inadequate to sustain the State's position in opposition to physician aid in dying. We are dealing here with persons who are mentally competent, who are incurably ill, and who expect death within a relatively short period of time. The State has failed to explain what interest the government has in forcing a competent, incurably ill person who is going through prolonged suffering and slow, excruciating physical deterioration to hang on to the last possible moment. Moreover, the State has not come close to showing that it has any interest, much less a "compelling" one, in usurping a competent, incurably ill individual's autonomous decision to obtain a licensed physician's assistance in dying so that she might die with the same human dignity with which she was born. * * *

* * *

CONCLUSION

* * *

This right to physician aid in dying quintessentially involves the inviolable right to human dignity—our most fragile fundamental right. Montana's Dignity Clause does not permit a person or entity to force an agonizing, dehumanizing, demeaning, and often protracted death upon a mentally competent, incurably ill individual for the sake of political ideology, religious belief, or a paternalistic sense of ethics. * * *

JUSTICE RICE, dissenting.

The prohibition against homicide—intentionally causing the death of another—protects and preserves human life, is the ultimate recognition of human dignity, and is a foundation for modern society, as it has been for millennia past. Based upon this foundation, Anglo–American law, encompassing the law of Montana, has prohibited the enabling of suicide for over 700 years. [ ]. However, in contradiction to these fundamental principles, the Court concludes that physician-assisted suicide does not violate Montana's public policy. In doing so, the Court has badly misinterpreted our public policy: assisting suicide has been explicitly and expressly prohibited by Montana law for the past 114 years. More than merely setting aside the District Court's order herein, I would reverse the judgment entirely.

A flaw that underlies the Court's analysis is its failure to distinguish between the physician's basic intention in the assisted-suicide case from the physician's intention while rendering treatment in other cases. As developed further herein, the intentions in these two cases are diametrically opposed, and create the very difference between a criminal and non-criminal act. Physician-assisted suicide occurs when a physician provides a lethal drug with the intent to cause, when the drug is taken by the patient, the patient's death. With palliative care, the physician does not intend his or her actions to cause the patient's death, but rather intends to relieve the patient's pain and suffering. For this reason a physician providing palliative care, even in cases where the treatment arguably contributes to the patient's death, lacks the requisite mental state to be charged under homicide statutes. [ ] A similar distinction arises in the withholding or withdrawal of medical treatment that merely prolongs the dying process, pursuant to the Montana Rights of the Terminally Ill Act. Under the Act, a patient may refuse treatment and allow death to occur naturally, and physicians incur no liability, having not administered any death-causing treatment. [ ]

* * *

The Statutory Prohibition on the Aiding or Soliciting of Suicide

* * *

In 1973, the Legislature revised the [aiding or soliciting suicide] statute to read:

(1) A person who purposely aids or solicits another to commit suicide, but such suicide does not occur commits the offense of aiding or soliciting suicide.

(2) A person convicted of the offense of aiding or soliciting a suicide shall be imprisoned in the state prison for any term not to exceed ten (10) years.

Section 94–5–106, RCM (1973). The Legislature codified this provision within the homicide statutes. The current version of the statute is the same as the 1973 version, except that the Legislature has increased the potential punishment for the crime by authorizing a $50,000 penalty. [ ]

Under the wording of the current version of the statute, a person may be prosecuted for aiding or soliciting another to commit suicide only if the victim survives. The purpose of this change of the statutory language from the pre–1973 version was explained by the Criminal Code Commission that proposed it. When the victim dies, the act is to be prosecuted as a homicide. * * *

Thus, under Montana law, physicians who assist in a suicide are subject to criminal prosecution irrespective of whether the patient survives or dies. If the patient survives, the physician may be prosecuted under aiding or soliciting suicide. [ ]. If the patient dies, the physician may be prosecuted under the homicide statutes. [ ]

Importantly, it is also very clear that a patient's consent to the physician's efforts is of no consequence whatsoever under these statutes. The Commission Comments explain that a physician acting as the agency of death may not raise "consent or even the solicitations of the victim" as a defense to criminal culpability.

* * *

The Montana Rights of the Terminally Ill Act

* * *

The operative words in the Montana Act are those permitting a patient to "withhold" and "withdraw" life-sustaining treatment. [ ] Largely self-evident, to "withhold" means "to desist or refrain from granting, giving, or allowing." [ ] Similarly, "withdraw" is defined as "to take back or away (something bestowed or possessed)." [ ] Neither word incorporates the concept of affirmatively issuing a life-ending drug to a patient. Rather, the plain language permits only the taking away of, or refraining from giving, certain medical treatment—that which merely prolongs the dying process. [ ]

[I]t is incongruous to conclude there is no legal distinction between the withdrawal of life-prolonging medical treatment and the provision of life-ending treatment. This distinction is clearly recognized by the wording of our statutes, discussed above, and by the courts. * * *

* * *

The 1972 Montana Constitution

* * *

The Constitutional Convention adopted the Individual Dignity Section for the express purpose of providing equal protection and prohibiting discrimination. * * * Nothing within [the Montana Constitutional Convention's] discussions or explanations suggests even a thought that the dignity clause contained vague, lurking rights that might someday manifest themselves beyond what the delegates or the citizens of Montana who approved the Constitution believed, and overturn long-established law, here, the policy against assisted suicide. The reference to dignity therefore provides an aspirational introduction to the already well-established substantive legal principles providing the operative vehicles to achieve dignity: equal protection and the prohibition upon discrimination. [ ] Likewise, the right to privacy did not alter the State's policy against assisted suicide. There is nothing within either the language of the provision or the convention proceedings which would reflect any such intention. [ ] For such reasons, not one court of last resort has interpreted a constitutional right of privacy to include physician-assisted suicide. [ ] * * *

Because we live in a democracy, this policy may someday change. Controlling their own destiny, Montanans may decide to change the State's public policy after what would be, no doubt, a spirited public debate. In fact, efforts in that regard have already started. [ ] This Court should allow the public debate to continue, and allow the citizens of this State to control their own destiny on the issue.

Until the public policy is changed by the democratic process, it should be recognized and enforced by the courts. It is a public policy which regards the aiding of suicide as typifying "a very low regard for human life," [ ], and which expressly prohibits it. Instead, the Court rejects the State's longstanding policy. It ignores expressed intent, parses statutes, and churns reasons to avoid the clear policy of the State and reach an untenable conclusion: that it is against public policy for a physician to assist in a suicide if the patient happens to live after taking the medication; but that the very same act, with the very same intent, is not against public policy if the patient dies. In my view, the Court's conclusion is without support, without clear reason, and without moral force.

I would reverse.

NOTES AND QUESTIONS

1. What difference does it make that the opinion of the court rests upon statutory and common law analysis, and not on state constitutional law? In what ways is the opinion of Justice Leaphart stronger than the opinion of Justice Nelson, and in what ways would Justice Nelson's approach provide a stronger basis for the right to medically assisted dying? Note that Justice Leaphart's opinion sets the statutory and common law default position—the state of law without any specific state legislation—as one that permits medically assisted dying. As a legal matter, which approach is stronger? As a political matter, which approach is stronger?

2.   What kind of statutory changes in Montana would lead to a change in the law of medically assisted dying in that state? At the next plenary legislative session following Baxter, in 2011, the legislature was squarely confronted with bills that would outlaw medically assisted dying, and with a bill that would formally legalize it and impose the same kinds of restrictions that are imposed in Washington and Oregon. The bills were carefully followed by the press, and there was a good deal of advocacy activity by partisans on both sides of the issue. Ultimately, the legislature rejected all of the bills on both sides of the issue, and left the law as it stood the day after Baxter was decided. Under these circumstances, what, exactly, is the law of medically assisted dying in Montana?

In 2013 the Montana state legislature again faced bills to both institutionalize and prohibit aid in dying. As this book went to press, one bill that would criminalize aid in dying under some circumstances had passed one house and was awaiting action in the other.

3.   Those opposed to aid in dying also sought to use the administrative process to reinstate the ban. An attempt to have the Montana Board of Medical Examiners declare that they would impose professional sanctions against any Montana physician who provided medically assisted dying in accord with the Baxter opinion was met with this response in 2012:

Physician Aid in Dying

As a result of [Baxter], the Montana Board of Medical Examiners has been asked if it will discipline physicians for participating in such aid-in-dying. This statement reflects the Board's position on this controversial question.

The Board recognizes that its mission is to protect the citizens of Montana against the unprofessional, improper, unauthorized and unqualified practice of medicine by ensuring that its licensees are competent professionals. [ ] In all matters of medical practice, including end-of-life matters, physicians are held to professional standards. If the Board receives a complaint related to physician aid-in-dying, it will evaluate the complaint on its individual merits and will consider, as it would any other medical procedure or intervention, whether the physician engaged in unprofessional conduct as defined by the laws and rules pertinent to the Board.

Mont. Bd. Of Med. Examiners, Position Statement No. 20 (2012). This statement was applauded by those who support aid-in-dying and who believe that it should be treated like any other medical procedure. Montanans Against Assisted Suicide and for Living with Dignity, an advocacy group opposed to aid-in-dying, asked the Board to withdraw the statement, which, those advocates said, was issued without proper notice, without statutory authority, and in violation of the principle of separation of powers. They argued that the Position Statement put doctors and the public at risk.

4. Are you convinced by Justice Leaphart's analysis of the consent defense in a homicide case? His argument has two steps. First, consent is a defense to homicide unless that would be contrary to public policy (for example, where it would lead to a breach of the peace). Second, the Montana statute criminalizing aiding suicide does not apply to this case because it only applies when the victim does not die. Does it make sense to read the Montana law on aiding suicide as criminalizing such conduct only if the subject of the suicide actually dies? Suppose that, in an effort to cause a lovelorn teenager to kill himself, a person purchases a handgun and gives it to that person while taunting him. If the suicide victim shoots himself and dies, the person providing the handgun appears to have committed the crime of aiding suicide. But what if the victim has bad aim and only maims himself? Has anyone committed a crime? What is the logical justification for this?

5. Although litigation to establish the kind of right recognized in Baxter has been rejected by appellate courts as a matter of state law in Florida, California, Alaska, and, on procedural grounds, in Connecticut, several years have passed since the substantive cases were litigated. Would you expect to see more litigation modeled on the Montana approach? Litigation seeking a right to medically assisted dying under state constitutional law has failed in the few states where it has been tried. In Krischer v. McIver, 697 So.2d 97 (Fla.1997), a terminally ill AIDS patient and his physician sought an injunction against the prosecution of the physician for assisting in his patient's suicide. The Florida Supreme Court rejected a claim that the privacy provision of the Florida Constitution included the right to have a physician assist in one's suicide. The Court announced that a properly drawn statute authorizing physician-assisted suicide would be constitutionally permissible, but that principles of separation of powers left the decision about whether it should be made legal to the legislature. The Chief Justice filed a vigorous dissent, arguing that, " * * *the right of privacy attaches with unusual force at the death bed. * * * What possible interest does society have in saving life when there is nothing of life to save but a final convulsion of agony? The state has no business in this arena." 697 So.2d at 111. See also Sampson v. State, 31 P.3d 88 (Alaska 2001).

6. Oregon and Washington have changed their statutes by initiative to allow for some form of medically assisted dying, and Montana has done so through litigation that has also enjoyed substantial public support in the state. Is there some reason that this phenomenon is centered in the Northwest? Demographically and politically, how is that part of the country different from the rest of the country? Might matters of race and ethnicity, religion, cultural values, and a deep libertarian streak distinguish this part of the country?

7. Montana is the only state with a "human dignity" provision in its constitution (although Puerto Rico also has such a provision, also taken from the German constitution). Why do you think no other state has adopted such a provision? Could other state constitutional guarantees ("privacy" or "right

to pursue happiness" provisions, for example) serve the same purpose and lead to the same result?

8.   Baxter allows for physicians to participate in medically assisted dying, at least to the extent of providing a prescription for a lethal dose of medication under limited circumstances. How far does this right go? Does the logic of the opinion also support extending the right to more affirmative acts of a physician—administering the lethal dose, for example? Also, is the protection that extends to those who engage in aid in dying limited to physicians? Could nurses and other health-care workers engage in this same conduct, at least if they are otherwise authorized to do so under Montana scope of practice limitations? Does this opinion also permit family members and friends to participate and assist a patient? By being present when the patient takes a lethal dose that has been prescribed by a physician? By providing a patient a glass of water? By encouraging the patient to take the dose? In other ways?

9.   The Affordable Care Act forbids the federal and state governments, and all health-care providers and health plans that receive funding through the ACA (i.e., virtually all providers and health plans) from discriminating against institutional or individual providers who do not provide goods or services for purposes of "assisted suicide, euthanasia or mercy killing." Under this section, a religious hospital that refuses to permit "assisted suicide, euthanasia or mercy killing" at its facilities, for example, even when such conduct is legal under state law, must be treated just like a hospital that will permit those procedures. Does "assisted suicide, euthanasia or mercy killing," for purpose of ACA, include the kind of medically assisted dying permitted in Montana under Baxter? In any case, the ACA explicitly provides that this assisted suicide non-discrimination provision does not affect the physician's legal obligations with regard to withholding or withdrawing medical treatment, including nutrition and hydration, and that it does not affect treatment provided with the purpose of alleviating pain or discomfort, even if that palliative care increases the risk of death, as long as the treatment is not furnished with the purpose of causing the death of the patient.

PROBLEM: MEDICALLY ASSISTED DYING, A LEGAL ISSUE OR A MEDICAL ISSUE?

Our conflict over medically assisted dying has been fought in the arena of law. Is there a right to engage in medically assisted dying? Do homicide and suicide statutes prohibit the practice of medically assisted dying? Those with more libertarian views tend to support finding such a right; those with strongly developed religious views or a more expansive view of criminal law are less likely to find such a right. The battles over legislation and most of the reported litigation reflect this rights-oriented legal battle over this issue.

Instead, should we be asking whether medically assisted dying is within the medical standard of care? If we were to take this approach, we would treat medically assisted dying as one of many end-of-life care possibilities, and we would let providers determine if it is appropriate on a case by case basis. Instead of arguing about the issue to courts, we would leave it to health-care professionals, who could offer to their patients whatever came within the standard of care.

Do you think the issue is best analyzed as one of legal rights and obligations, ultimately to be decided by courts, or is it best analyzed as one of good medicine, ultimately to be determined by the physician and her patient in each case?

For an account of an early effort by phyicians to establish a standard of care in this area, see T.E. Quill, C.K. Cassel and D.E. Meier, Care of the Hopelessly Ill: Proposed Clinical Criteria for Physician-Assisted Suicide, 327 N.Eng.J.Med. 1380 (1992). For a more recent legal suggestion that physicians should be developing standards of practice in this area, written by an advocate for medically assisted death, see Kathryn Tucker, Aid in Dying:Guidance for an Emerging End-of-Life Practice, 142 Chest 218 (2012).

CHAPTER 18

POPULATION HEALTH AND PUBLIC HEALTH

∎ ∎ ∎

I.   INTRODUCTION TO POPULATION HEALTH AND PUBLIC HEALTH LAW

Between 1900 and 2000, life expectancy in the United States increased by thirty years. Five of those thirty years are attributable to the individualized health care that is the subject of most of this casebook and the basis of most of our healthcare industry. Twenty-five of those additional years of life, though, are a result of more general public health interventions where the goal is less to protect individual patients (although that is often part of it), and more to protect the health of the public as a whole. Public health, then, is what a community, generally through its government, does to establish the conditions that allow members of that community to lead long and healthy lives. As the Institute of Medicine has pointed out, public health generally involves collective action. Because the principle of autonomy and the value of individualism are so important in the United States, and because we tend to be suspect of government and collective action, we are called upon to weigh the benefit of public health interventions with the cost of government-imposed requirements more often than is the case in similar countries. While we do not often think about the way public health interventions protect us, we do when we need public health resources and help—when an epidemic spreads through our schools, for example.

Because public health generally requires collective and sometimes coercive action, law is implicated in most public health interventions. The law may set standards for purity of food and water, for example, or at least designate those with appropriate expertise who will. The law may encourage or require immunization, as we will see, and it may require medical testing for diseases or conditions—either among the general population or subgroups like teachers, students, pilots, food workers, or prisoners. Public health law may also protect the public by placing exceptions on limitations imposed by other laws—in allowing for needle exchanges or opiate replacement therapy to avoid communicable diseases among addicts, for example, when drug laws may otherwise prohibit those actions. The law may also require the reporting of medical status to government agencies to allow those agencies to determine if there is a public health problem, and then to protect the public health. The application of public health law sometimes breaches some notions of individual privacy. Indeed, the collection of huge amounts of health information, some of it identifiable and some not, is one of the most important tools, and one of the greatest risks, of public health operations. When individually identifiable data is collected, particular follow-up measures—including, for example, tracing the contacts of those who could be transmitting communicable diseases—heighten privacy concerns. In rare circumstances, the law can require patients to receive treatment (or be placed in isolation or quarantine).

What makes an issue a "public health" issue? Is the quality of the gene pool a public health issue? The widespread use of alternative medicines? Tobacco? Gun violence? The availability and use of video games (or just violent video games)? Domestic violence? Restrictive licensure for midwives? What difference does it make whether an issue is characterized as a public health issue? Are we more likely to defer to governmental decisions, and more likely to accept governmental intrusions on individual liberties, where the public health is involved? Article 25 of the Universal Declaration of Human Rights says:

> Everyone has a right to a standard of living adequate for the health and well-being of [oneself] and [one's] family, including food, clothing, housing and medical care and necessary social services, and the right to security in the event of unemployment, sickness, disability, widowhood, old age or other lack of livelihood in circumstances beyond one's control.

Is this a principle of public health?

Public health can endeavor to encourage healthy individual behavior just as it can act to prohibit or discourage risky behavior. For example, while the Affordable Care Act was designed to support a private health care system, it also recognizes the value of public health approaches to many issues. The Act provides subsidies for small employers who wish to establish employee wellness programs and it allows employers of all sizes to give premium discounts to those employees who participate in some kinds of wellness programs. Participation can result in up to a 30% discount in premium costs (up to 50% with approval of the Secretary of DHHS). In addition, the ACA eliminates copays, deductibles, and other payments for some preventive care provided by private health plans, Medicare or Medicaid, and it also uses public relations strategies to increase national rates of immunization and other forms of preventive care. The ACA also requires the collection of data, including health disparity data, which will make the creation of public health approaches easier in the future.

In addition to supporting these traditional public health strategies, the ACA moves the health care system toward a greater concern for population health. The ACA, for example, encourages the formation of accountable care organizations as a system for delivering care. ACOs' performance will be measured against their impact on outcomes relating to population health and wellness. Susan DeVore and R. Wesley Champion, Driving Population Health through Accountable Care Organizations, 30 Health Affs. 41 (2011).

The ACA also institutes some more focused public health changes. It requires chain restaurants (those with more than 20 outlets serving essentially standardized products) to provide nutritional information on those products by posting calorie information on the menu or menu board and making additional nutritional information available to customers. It imposes the same obligations on those who sell products through vending machines, at least where customers cannot read the nutritional information already on the packaged food. The ACA also requires that employers with more than 50 employees (and others where it would not cause hardship) allow employees to express milk whenever that is necessary during the year following the birth of their children; employers must provide a clean and private space for this and allow adequate break time, although it may be unpaid time. The law also provides for public education on a host of lifestyle and preventive care issues. As we move toward government programs that encourage wellness, is public health entering a new era in the United States—one that depends more on incentives and price regulation rather than statutory mandates? Are these new efforts—encouraging Americans to exercise, eat healthy food, stop smoking, and breast feed their children—appropriately within the realm of government?

For a discussion of the ACA and public health, see Elizabeth Weeks Leonard (ed.), Public Health Reform: Patient Protection and Affordable Care Act Implications for the Public's Health (Symposium), 39 J. L. Med. & Ethics 312, et seq. For a very thoughtful summary of the overlap of law and public health, see Barry Levy, Twenty–First Century Challenges for Law and Public Health, 32 Ind. L. Rev. 1149 (1999). For a comprehensive account of the law of public health, see Lawrence Gostin, Public Health Law: Power, Duty Restraint (2d ed. 2008). See also Lawrence Gostin, et al., The Law and the Public's Health: A Study of Infectious Disease Law in the United States, 99 Colum. L. Rev. 59 (1999). For an interesting historical and constitutional approach to these issues, see Wendy Parmet, From Slaughter–House to Lochner: The Rise and Fall of the Cosnstitutionalization of Public Health, 40 Am. J. Leg. Hist. 476 (1996). For a good account of the international public health issues, see Roger Detels, et al., eds., Oxford Textbook of Public Health (4th ed. 2004).

PROBLEM: OBESITY AS A PUBLIC HEALTH PROBLEM

As a legislator in your state, you have become very concerned about obesity in the population, and you are worried about the long range consequences of this condition on the vitality of the public. In particular, you have become concerned about the proliferation of fast food sites that offer primarily economical but very high fat foods. You are concerned about "food deserts" in your state—areas where there are no supermarkets and limited public transportation. You are also disturbed by the relatively unhealthy foods available at the public schools throughout the state, many of which have contracts with beverage companies to run their vending machines and snack bars, and by the disappearance of mandatory physical education requirements at the high school level. There is also an indication that a comparatively sedentary lifestyle that includes watching television and playing video games contributes to what some have called the "epidemic" of obesity. Furthermore, studies have repeatedly shown that obesity alone is not a predictor for shortened lifespans or significantly greater health risks. Rather, a lack of exercise or fitness is more closely associated with health risks than is obesity. A person can be obese and healthy.

Is the problem of obesity a "public health" problem, or simply a problem for some individuals? What qualifies as "obese" for public health purposes? Is it a matter of personal responsibility that should be unrelated to the obligations of the law? Would it make any difference if you classified obesity as a "public health" problem? What legal responses might be available to the state legislature to address this problem? Are there ways to use school law, tax law, criminal law, tort law, food and drug law, insurance rate-setting, public program eligibility standards or general public health regulatory law to address this problem? What are the legal, political and social consequences of doing so? Are there civil liberty interests of persons who are obese (or others) that are at stake in using the law in this way?

Do you feel the same way about tobacco, gun violence, bullying, or "extreme sports" as public health problems?

II.   THE CONSTITUTIONAL FOUNDATION OF PUBLIC HEALTH LAW

JACOBSON V. MASSACHUSETTS
Supreme Court of the United States, 1905.
197 U.S. 11, 25 S. Ct. 358, 49 L. Ed. 643.

[The Revised Laws of that Commonwealth, c. 75, § 137, provide that "the board of health of a city or town if, in its opinion, it is necessary for the public health or safety shall require and enforce the vaccination and revaccination of all the inhabitants thereof and shall provide them with the means of free vaccination. Whoever, being over twenty-one years of age and not under guardianship, refuses or neglects to comply with such requirement shall forfeit five dollars."

* * *

Proceeding under the above statutes, the Board of Health of the city of Cambridge, Massachusetts, on the twenty-seventh day of February, 1902, adopted the following regulation: "Whereas, smallpox has been prevalent to some extent in the city of Cambridge and still continues to increase; and whereas, it is necessary for the speedy extermination of the disease, that all persons not protected by vaccination should be vaccinated; and whereas, in the opinion of the board, the public health and safety require the vaccination or revaccination of all the inhabitants of Cambridge; be it ordered, that all the inhabitants of the city who have not been successfully vaccinated since March, 1, 1897, be vaccinated or revaccinated."] [Ed. Note: This description is reprinted from the syllabus of the Court.]

MR. JUSTICE HARLAN, after making the foregoing statement, delivered the opinion of the court.

We pass without extended discussion the suggestion that the particular section of the statute of Massachusetts now in question [ ] is in derogation of rights secured by the Preamble of the Constitution of the United States. Although that Preamble indicates the general purposes for which the people ordained and established the Constitution, it has never been regarded as the source of any substantive power conferred on the Government of the United States or on any of its Departments. Such powers embrace only those expressly granted in the body of the Constitution and such as may be implied from those so granted. Although, therefore, one of the declared objects of the Constitution was to secure the blessings of liberty to all under the sovereign jurisdiction and authority of the United States, no power can be exerted to that end by the United States unless, apart from the Preamble, it be found in some express delegation of power or in some power to be properly implied therefrom. [ ]

We also pass without discussion the suggestion that the above section of the statute is opposed to the spirit of the Constitution. * * * We have no need in this case to go beyond the plain, obvious meaning of the words in those provisions of the Constitution which, it is contended, must control our decision.

What, according to the judgment of the state court, is the scope and effect of the statute? What results were intended to be accomplished by it? These questions must be answered.

* * *

The authority of the State to enact this statute is to be referred to what is commonly called the police power—a power which the State did not surrender when becoming a member of the Union under the Constitution. Although this court has refrained from any attempt to define the limits of that power, yet it has distinctly recognized the authority of a State to enact quarantine laws and "health laws of every description;" indeed, all laws that relate to matters completely within its territory and which do not by their necessary operation affect the people of other States. According to settled principles the police power of a State must be held to embrace, at least, such reasonable regulations established directly by legislative enactment as will protect the public health and the public safety. [ ]. It is equally true that the State may invest local bodies called into existence for purposes of local administration with authority in some appropriate way to safeguard the public health and the public safety. The mode or manner in which those results are to be accomplished is within the discretion of the State, subject, of course, so far as Federal power is concerned, only to the condition that no rule prescribed by a State, nor any regulation adopted by a local governmental agency acting under the sanction of state legislation, shall contravene the Constitution of the United States or infringe any right granted or secured by that instrument. * * *

We come, then, to inquire whether any right given, or secured by the Constitution, is invaded by the statute as interpreted by the state court. The defendant insists that his liberty is invaded when the State subjects him to fine or imprisonment for neglecting or refusing to submit to vaccination; that a compulsory vaccination law is unreasonable, arbitrary and oppressive, and, therefore, hostile to the inherent right of every freeman to care for his own body and health in such way as to him seems best; and that the execution of such a law against one who objects to vaccination, no matter for what reason, is nothing short of an assault upon his person. But the liberty secured by the Constitution of the United States to every person within its jurisdiction does not import an absolute right in each person to be, at all times and in all circumstances, wholly freed from restraint. There are manifold restraints to which every person is necessarily subject for the common good. On any other basis organized society could not exist with safety to its members. Society based on the rule that each one is a law unto himself would soon be confronted with disorder and anarchy. Real liberty for all could not exist under the operation of a principle which recognizes the right of each individual person to use his own, whether in respect of his person or his property, regardless of the injury that may be done to others. * * * The good and welfare of the Commonwealth, of which the legislature is primarily the judge, is the basis on which the police power rests in Massachusetts[ ]

Applying these principles to the present case, it is to be observed that the legislature of Massachusetts required the inhabitants of a city or town to be vaccinated only when, in the opinion of the Board of Health, that was necessary for the public health or the public safety. The authority to determine for all what ought to be done in such an emergency must have been lodged somewhere or in some body; and surely it was appropriate for the legislature to refer that question, in the first instance, to a Board of Health, composed of persons residing in the locality affected and appointed, presumably, because of their fitness to determine such questions. To invest such a body with authority over such matters was not an unusual nor an unreasonable or arbitrary requirement. Upon the principle of self-defense, of paramount necessity, a community has the right to protect itself against an epidemic of disease which threatens the safety of its members. * * * Smallpox being prevalent and increasing at Cambridge, the court would usurp the functions of another branch of government if it adjudged, as matter of law, that the mode adopted under the sanction of the State, to protect the people at large, was arbitrary and not justified by the necessities of the case. We say necessities of the case, because it might be that an acknowledged power of a local community to protect itself against an epidemic threatening the safety of all, might be exercised in particular circumstances and in reference to particular persons in such an arbitrary, unreasonable manner, or might go so far beyond what was reasonably required for the safety of the public, as to authorize or compel the courts to interfere for the protection of such persons. * * * There is, of course, a sphere within which the individual may assert the supremacy of his own will and rightfully dispute the authority of any human government, especially of any free government existing under a written constitution, to interfere with the exercise of that will. But it is equally true that in every well-ordered society charged with the duty of conserving the safety of its members the rights of the individual in respect of his liberty may at times, under the pressure of great dangers, be subjected to such restraint, to be enforced by reasonable regulations, as the safety of the general public may demand.

* * *

Looking at the propositions embodied in the defendant's rejected offers of proof it is clear that they are more formidable by their number than by their inherent value. Those offers in the main seem to have had no purpose except to state the general theory of those of the medical profession who attach little or no value to vaccination as a means of preventing the spread of smallpox or who think that vaccination causes other diseases of the body. What everybody knows the court must know, and therefore the state court judicially knew, as this court knows, that an opposite theory accords with the common belief and is maintained by high medical authority. We must assume that when the statute in question was passed, the legislature of Massachusetts was not unaware of these opposing theories, and was compelled, of necessity, to choose between them. It was not compelled to commit a matter involving the public health and safety to the final decision of a court or jury. It is no part of the function of a court or a jury to determine which one of two modes was likely to be the most effective for the protection of the public against disease. That was for the legislative department to determine in the light of all the information it had or could obtain. * * * Upon what sound principles as to the relations existing between the different departments of government can the court review this action of the legislature? If there is any such power in the judiciary to review legislative action in respect of a matter affecting the general welfare, it can only be when that which the legislature has done comes within the rule that if a statute purporting to have been enacted to protect the public health, the public morals or the public safety, has no real or substantial relation to those objects, or is, beyond all question, a plain, palpable invasion of rights secured by the fundamental law, it is the duty of the courts to so adjudge, and thereby give effect to the Constitution." [ ]

Whatever may be thought of the expediency of this statute, it cannot be affirmed to be, beyond question, in palpable conflict with the Constitution. Nor, in view of the methods employed to stamp out the disease of smallpox, can anyone confidently assert that the means prescribed by the State to that end has no real or substantial relation to the protection of the public health and the public safety. Such an assertion would not be consistent with the experience of this and other countries whose authorities have dealt with the disease of smallpox. [The Court then summarizes the history of vaccination in Europe and America.]

* * *

Since then vaccination, as a means of protecting a community against smallpox, finds strong support in the experience of this and other countries, no court, much less a jury, is justified in disregarding the action of the legislature simply because in its or their opinion that particular method was—perhaps or possibly—not the best either for children or adults.

* * *

We are not prepared to hold that a minority, residing or remaining in any city or town where smallpox is prevalent, and enjoying the general protection afforded by an organized local government, may thus defy the will of its constituted authorities, acting in good faith for all, under the legislative sanction of the State [by refusing to be vaccinated]. If such be the privilege of a minority then a like privilege would belong to each individual of the community, and the spectacle would be presented of the welfare and safety of an entire population being subordinated to the notions of a single individual who chooses to remain a part of that population. * * * The safety and the health of the people of Massachusetts are, in the first instance, for that Commonwealth to guard and protect. They are matters that do not ordinarily concern the National Government. So far as they can be reached by any government, they depend, primarily, upon such action as the State in its wisdom may take; and we do not perceive that this legislation has invaded by right secured by the Federal Constitution.

Before closing this opinion we deem it appropriate, in order to prevent misapprehension as to our views, to observe * * * that the police power of a State * * * may be exerted in such circumstances or by regulations so arbitrary and oppressive in particular cases as to justify the interference of the courts to prevent wrong and oppression. Extreme cases can be readily suggested. Ordinarily such cases are not safe guides in the administration of the law. It is easy, for instance, to suppose the case of an adult who is embraced by the mere words of the act, but yet to subject whom to vaccination in a particular condition of his health or body, would be cruel and inhuman in the last degree. We are not to be understood as holding that the statute was intended to be applied to such a case, or, if it was so intended, that the judiciary would not be competent to interfere and protect the health and life of the individual concerned.

MR. JUSTICE BREWER and MR. JUSTICE PECKHAM dissent [without opinion].

NOTES AND QUESTIONS

1.   This oft-cited case established the foundation for public health regulation that came during the ensuing century. While it plainly recognizes the authority of the state to exercise its police powers by imposing public health restrictions on willing and unwilling citizens (and others), it does leave some questions open. It provides that the legislature (or others, with powers properly delegated from the legislature) may make judgments on scientific questions relating to public health. However, the state may not act "by regulations so arbitrary and oppressive in particular cases as to justify the interference of the courts to prevent wrong and oppression." When will the state cross this line? The Court says that, "Extreme Cases can readily be suggested," but it doesn't actually suggest them. Can you identify these cases? In 1922 the Supreme Court upheld a Texas school immunization law requiring smallpox immunization even though the community had not faced a case of smallpox for a decade. Zucht v. King, 260 U.S. 174 (1922) (Brandeis, J.).

2.   *Jacobson* was not the first vaccination case to be litigated in the federal courts. In Wong Wai v. Williamson, 103 F. 1 (N.D.Cal.1900) the Circuit Court faced an action by Wong Wai, "a subject of the emperor of China, residing in the city and county of San Francisco," seeking to enjoin the city from enforcing a resolution of the board of health that prohibited Chinese

residents from traveling outside of the city without proof that they had been inoculated with the "Haffkine Prophylactic," which was thought to provide immunization against bubonic plague. The resolution applied only to those of Chinese extraction, although there was no evidence that they were any more likely than other to be subject to the plague. The Circuit Court recognized the public health authority of the city, but also recognized that there were limits to the exercise of this police power.

> The conditions of a great city frequently present unexpected emergencies affecting the public health, comfort, and convenience. Under such circumstances, officers charged with the duties pertaining to this department of the municipal government should be clothed with sufficient authority to deal with the conditions in a prompt and effective manner. Measures of this character, having a uniform operation, and reasonably adapted to the purpose of protecting the health and preserving the welfare of the inhabitants of a city, are constantly upheld by the courts as valid acts of legislation, however inconvenient they may prove to be, and a wide discretion has also been sanctioned in their execution. But when the municipal authority has neglected to provide suitable rules and regulations upon the subject, and the officers are left to adopt such methods as they may deem proper for the occasion, their acts are open to judicial review, and may be examined in every detail to determine whether individual rights have been respected in accordance with constitutional requirements.

> * * *

> In the light of these well-established principles [that provide that public health measures must have an appropriate relationship with the ends they seek to serve], the action of the defendants as described in the bill of complaint cannot be justified. They are not based upon any established distinction in the conditions that are supposed to attend this plague, or the persons exposed to its contagion, but they are boldly directed against the Asiatic or Mongolian race as a class, without regard to the previous condition, habits, exposure to disease, or residence of the individual; and the only justification offered for this discrimination was a suggestion made by counsel for the defendants in the course of the argument, that this particular race is more liable to the plague than any other. No evidence has, however, been offered to support this claim, and it is not known to be a fact. This explanation must therefore be dismissed as unsatisfactory.

103 F. at 12–15. The Court went on to find that the actions of the board of health violated not only "the express provisions of the constitution of the United States, in several particulars, but also of the express provisions of our several treaties with China and of the statutes of the United States." 13 F. at 23.

3.   The Court suggests that it may be improper to apply the Massachusetts statute and the Cambridge order to an adult whose health would be
placed at risk by vaccination, even though the only exception in the statute is
for children whose health would be at risk. Could an adult with some legitimate health concerns about vaccination forgo it? Would this be a matter to be
determined by the Board of Health, or by the courts?

4.   In a long historical footnote, the Court traces the history of vaccination from the "first compulsory act" in England in 1853. In fact, as early as
1827 the city of Boston required vaccination for school attendance, and in
1855 Massachusetts became the first state with required childhood vaccination laws associated with school attendance. The laws were fairly common by
the end of the nineteenth century, but, for political and other reasons, they
were not regularly enforced. Some were limited to application when there
was a public health threat in the community, and some courts recognized religious defenses to the obligation to be vaccinated. See Rhea v. Board of Education, 171 N.W. 103 (N.D. 1919). Today all states provide for exemptions
when the vaccination would threaten the health of the child; almost all allow
for religious exemption (although the nature of those exemptions varies from
state to state); and many states allow for an exemption on "moral" or other
grounds. Are states Constitutionally required to have religious exemptions? If
a state has a religious exemption, should that legislation also permit a "moral" exemption? Is it Constitutionally required to do so under the establishment clause of the First Amendment or the equal protection clause of the
Fourteenth Amendment?

5.   The immunizations children must have to be enrolled in school is a
matter of state law, but, as a general matter, states adopt the Centers for
Disease Control (CDC) list of recommended immunization by the Advisory
Committee on Immunization Practices. In order to keep some kinds of federal
funding, the states now must make an effort to enforce their own immunization laws. This issue is not entirely a scientific one, though, and vaccine
manufacturers do lobby state legislatures to have their own products included on the mandatory list. See the Note: HPV Vaccine and Public Health Law,
below.

6.   While the health value of continued required immunization is now
well established, those who fear government conspiracies have often had special concerns about vaccinations. It is unclear just why this has become a political issue as well as a public health issue, but it is not hard to find those
who oppose vaccination with missionary zeal. The CDC, the World Health
Organization, and other organizations have joined together to refute several
myths about vaccination that sometimes scare parents into seeking exemptions. For a full list of the most common arguments against vaccination and
the refutation of each, see the World health Organization's publication, 6
Common Misconceptions about Vaccinations and How to Respond to Them
(2010). For an excellent account of this issue, and the basis for much of these
notes, see James Hodge Jr., School Vaccination Requirements: Legal and So-

cial Perspectives, 27 NCSL State Legislative Report, No. 14 (August 2002). See also S. Omer et al., Nonmedical Exemptions to School Immunization Requirements, 296 JAMA 1757 (2006) and S. Omer, Correspondence: Vaccination Polices and Rates of Exemption from Immunization, 2005–2011, 367 N.Eng.J.Med. 1170 (2012). For a an excellent overview of the issue and a clever proposal to finesse the opposition to immunization while respecting individuals' liberties, see Ross Silverman, No More Kidding Around: Restructuring Childhood Immunization Exceptions in Insure Public Health Protection, 12 Ann. Health L. 277 (2003).

7. Of course, there are side effects to vaccination, and some are very serious, although a recent comprehensive study review found "no evidence of major safety concerns" associated with childhood vaccination, including current scheduling which requires delivery of multiple vaccines at one time. Institute of Medicine, Childhood Immunization Schedule and Safety: Stakeholder Concerns, Scientific Evidence, and Future Studies (2013). While we are all safer if everyone is vaccinated, the safest possible course of action for your child is to assure that everyone else's child is vaccinated, and yet not have your own child vaccinated. If everyone else is immunized, there is almost no chance you will be subject to the disease, whether or not you have been vaccinated. Is it an altruistic decision to decide against seeking an exemption from a required immunization law? Is there any way to avoid this version of the prisoner's dilemma without eliminating all exemptions?

8. Compensation for injuries that arise out of immunization is specifically addressed in the National Vaccine Injury Compensation Program, 42 U.S.C. § 300aa–10, et seq. This statute provides scheduled (and thus limited) compensation for those who can prove that their injury has been caused by a covered vaccine. It does not require proof of negligence or products liability for compensation. The payment is made by a government agency and the compensation payments and administration of the program are financed by an excise tax on the vaccines. Thus, the manufacturers pay the cost of the program, but they can pass that cost on and spread it out among those who are vaccinated—virtually everyone. This statute may be unique in providing that attorneys must inform potential plaintiffs in vaccine injury cases of the existence of the law and the remedy it provides:

> It shall be the ethical obligation of any attorney who is consulted by an individual with respect to a vaccine-related injury or death to advise such individual that compensation may be available under the program for such injury or death.

42 U.S.C. § 300aa–10(b). For an excellent history of the liability litigation-induced vaccine shortages that gave rise to this no-fault compensation scheme and its predecessors, see Elizabeth Scott, The National Childhood Vaccine Injury Act Turns Fifteen, 56 Food & Drug L.J. 351 (2001). See also L. Rutkow et al., Balancing Consumer and Industry Interests in Public Health: The National Vaccine Injury Compensation Program and Its Influence During the Last Two Decades, 111 Penn St. L. Rev. 681 (2007).

9.   How does the Jacobson case affect other kinds of public health regulation? Does it place limits on the efforts of states to limit pollution? Maintain vital statistics? Do involuntary disease testing? Engage in contact tracing? Impose mandatory treatment, quarantine, or isolation? Do genetic screening? Attack problems like obesity and bullying?

PROBLEM: EXEMPTIONS FROM IMMUNIZATION REQUIREMENTS

You are the legal counsel to the school district in Gadsden, Alabama. The Code of Alabama, § 16–30–1, et seq., requires certain immunizations as a condition of school attendance. Exemptions to this provision are found in § 16–30–3:

The provisions of this chapter shall not apply if:

(1) In the absence of an epidemic or immediate threat thereof, the parent or guardian of the child shall object thereto in writing on grounds that such immunization or testing conflicts with his religious tenets and practices; or

(2) Certification by a competent medical authority providing individual exemption from the required immunization or testing is presented the admissions officer of the school.

First grader Miranda Black's parents, who resent the heavy burden of government, have decided that they will not submit to any immunization requirement. They reason that Miranda should not have to shoulder the public health value of immunization by risking the side effects of the immunizations. Her doctor will not provide the "certification" that the school authorities want because there is no medical reason for her to avoid immunization, and thus her parents have submitted to the school authorities a statement that "compulsory immunization violates our Christian view that the government cannot make us do anything." School health officials are concerned because there were four cases of whooping cough in Gadsden during the last year—up from two the year before, and one the year before that. They attribute the increase to the increasing number of people who have obtained exemptions. The school officials have asked you how they should react to the request that Miranda be exempt.

NOTE: THE HPV VACCINE AND PUBLIC HEALTH LAW

The Human Papillomavirus (HPV), which is the most common sexually transmitted disease, is the major cause of cervical cancer and an important cause of genital warts. It is implicated in over 99% of cervical cancer cases in the United States. One in four women have evidence of the HPV, and the rate is considerably higher for African–American, Hispanic and poor women. The virus is transmitted primarily through sexual intercourse, although it might be communicated through other forms of sexual conduct, like oral sex, as well. There are dozens of strains of the virus, and many (but not all) carry the risk of disease. HPV usually does not manifest itself in identifiable symptoms early on; the resulting cancer and genital warts may not manifest themselves until years after the original infection.

There are two vaccines now available for HPV. Gardasil, first approved in 2006, is available to immunize both men and women, while Cervarix, approved in 2009, is only available to immunize women. While the two vaccines are effective against only some of the strains of HPV, they are effective against the strains most likely to cause cervical cancer or genital warts. Gardasil protects against some strains that Cervarix does not. For either immunization to be effective, there must be three injections at appropriate time intervals during a six month period. These vaccines are effective only against subsequent exposure to HPV; they do not provide any benefit for those who already are infected with HPV. The three-immunization regimen is effective for at least six years, although whether it will provide life long protection, or whether a booster will be necessary, has yet to be determined (because it has only been the subject of clinical testing over that six year period). Each immunization costs about $130, and thus the series costs $390.

The CDC's Advisory Committee on Immunization Practices recommends vaccination of boys and girls at age 11 or 12, before they are likely to be sexually active and when they are very likely to be HPV-free. It also recommends that men and women up to age 26 be vaccinated if they have not been before. Most insurance companies cover HPV immunization, and virtually all will be required to do so when the relevant ACA provision goes into effect in 2014. Children (and adults in about half the states) are also covered by Medicaid, and the Vaccines for Children program provides coverage for most children who are uninsured or underinsured. A few states have promulgated insurance mandates requiring this immunization be covered, and in some states public health agencies will provide the immunizations to those who request them. The manufacturers of the drug have assistance programs for those not covered by any other source.

Some school districts have considered adding HPV to the list of conditions for which enrolled students must be immunized, primarily as a result of the Advisory Committee's recommendation. Only the District of Columbia and Virginia require immunization before a girl enters the sixth grade, and the statutes in those states have broadly defined opt-out provisions. The issue became particularly politicized in Texas, where Merck, which manufactures Gardasil, lobbied in 2006 and 2007 to have the state require the immunization. In 2007 Governor Perry issued an executive order requiring the immunization for school enrollment and providing state funds, through other established programs, to pay for the immunization of girls and women under 21. There was a strong and angry public reaction to the promulgation of the executive order, and a backlash to the immunization developed out of what some claimed was Merck's profit-driven decision to lobby on behalf of requiring the immunization. Ultimately, Merck stopped its lobbying on this issue, the legislature overturned the Governor's executive order by statute, and the Governor allowed it to become law without his signature.

The arguments in favor of some kind of mandatory immunization for HPV are very powerful. A vaccination with few and relatively insignificant side effects will utterly eliminate cervical cancer (and eliminate most cases of genital warts) if it is administered before girls become sexually active. The development of a vaccine against a form of cancer is a truly remarkable scientific achievement. While the benefit may not be as direct and immediate for boys, their immunization will lower their risk of other cancers, and, most significantly, it will stop the disease from being communicated to women.

Some parent groups and some religious organizations oppose any HPV immunization mandate. First, they argue that long term health risks of the vaccine are unknown and that it is too expensive to mandate without more information. Some believe that in creating the immunization requirement the government would be doing nothing more than conspiring with the drug companies to increase their profits. Perhaps the most significant opposition comes from those who are concerned that Gardasil and Cervarix remove one of the costs of sexual intercourse and thus increase the possibility that young girls would participate in such immoral activity, or that the vaccination communicates an expectation that sexual activity will occur at a young age. Many who oppose an immunization requirement believe that the issue should be left to the parents of the girls and boys to be immunized. This essentially libertarian objection to any immunization requirement is based on the notion that we are freer and better off with less government control of our lives. Finally, at least one commentator has argued that any mandate would violate the sexual privacy interests of adolescents.

What is the appropriate policy for local school districts? For state government? For the federal government? Should HPV immunization be a requirement for attending school? Should it otherwise be required by law? Should the government fund these immunizations? For everyone, or just for those who cannot otherwise afford it? What opt-out provisions should be available to those parents (or children) who do not want their sons or daughters to be immunized? Was it appropriate to extend the requirement of immunization to boys as well as girls?

See Kaiser Family Foundation, The HPV Vaccine: Access and Use in the U.S. (2011). For a complete account of all state legislative proposals dealing with HPV, see National Council of State Legislatures, HPV (2013). For an interesting argument that a right to sexual privacy is at stake, see Martha Presley, The Constitutionality of an HPV mandate and Its Implication for the Minor Patient, 25(2) The Health Lawyer 1 (2012). An excellent survey of the arguments is available in Pauline Self, The HPV Vaccination: Necessary or Evil, 19 Hastings Women's L.J. 149 (2008). See also R. Skov, Examining Mandatory HPV Vaccination for All School–Aged Children, 62 Food Drug L.J. 805 (2007).

INDEX

References are to Pages